THE PUBLICATIONS

OF THE

𝔖𝔢𝔩𝔡𝔢𝔫 𝔖𝔬𝔠𝔦𝔢𝔱𝔶

περὶ παντὸς τὴν ἐλευθερίαν

VOLUME CXXXVI

FOR THE YEAR 2019

Selden Society

FOUNDED 1887
To Encourage the Study and Advance the Knowledge of the History of English Law

2019

PATRON

HIS ROYAL HIGHNESS THE PRINCE PHILIP, DUKE OF EDINBURGH, K.G.

PRESIDENT

NICHOLAS LE POIDEVIN, Q.C.

VICE-PRESIDENTS

Professor PAUL BRAND, F.B.A.
The Honourable SUSAN KIEFEL C.J.

COUNCIL

Mr David Ainger
The Hon. Morris S. Arnold
Mr Richard Bagley
Sir John Baker, Q.C., F.B.A.
Dr Susanne Brand
His Hon. Donald Cryan
Professor W. R. Cornish, Q.C., F.B.A.
Dr David Crook
Dr Sean Cunningham
Professor Charles Donahue, Jr.
Professor George Garnett
Professor Joshua Getzler
Dr Elizabeth Goldring
Professor Richard H. Helmholz, F.B.A.
Mr John Howell, Q.C.
Professor J. G. H. Hudson, F.B.A.

Professor D. J. Ibbetson, F.B.A.
The Right Hon. Lord Judge
The Revd Professor A. D. E. Lewis
Professor Janet Loengard
Professor Catharine MacMillan
Dr Michael Macnair
Dr John Maddicott, F.B.A.
Professor Wilfrid Prest
Professor Rebecca Probert
Professor Chantal Stebbings
Professor Joshua Tate
Mr A. C. Taussig
Mr P. W. E. Taylor, Q.C.
The Revd Professor T. G. Watkin, Q.C.
Dr Ian Williams
Mr D. E. C. Yale, Q.C., F.B.A.

LITERARY DIRECTOR

DR N. G. JONES, Magdalene College, Cambridge CB3 0AG

TREASURER

PROFESSOR CATHARINE MACMILLAN, King's College, London WC2R 2LS

SECRETARY

PROFESSOR MICHAEL LOBBAN, F.B.A., Department of Law, London School of Economics, Houghton Street, London WC2A 2AE

TRUSTEES

MR DAVID AINGER   MR ANTHONY TAUSSIG
PROFESSOR CATHARINE MACMILLAN

HONORARY SECRETARIES AND TREASURERS OVERSEAS

Australia: Mr DAVID BRATCHFORD (Supreme Court Library, Brisbane, Queensland 4000)
Canada: Professor MARGARET MCGLYNN (University of Western Ontario, London N6A 5C2)
New Zealand: Professor WARREN SWAIN (Faculty of Law, University of Auckland, Private Bag 92019, Auckland 1142)
United States: Professor JOSHUA TATE (Treasurer), Mr GREGORY IVY (Secretary) (Southern Methodist University School of Law, Dallas, Texas, 75205)

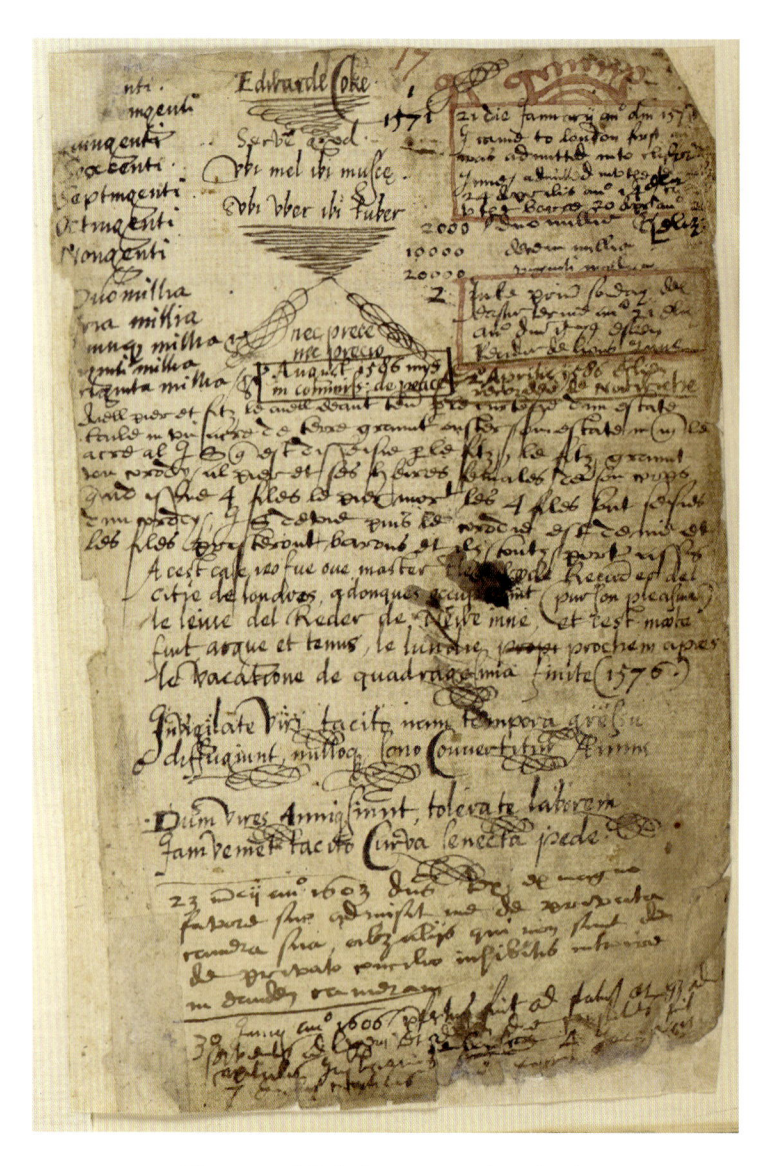

The start of Coke's commonplace book

Coke's signature is dated 1571, and is followed by 'Serve god' and the verses, 'Ubi mel ibi musce, Ubi uber ibi tuber'. In the panel boxed in red at the top right are contemporary memoranda of his admission to Clifford's Inn (1571) and to the Inner Temple (1572), and of his call to the bar (1578). In the second box outlined in red is a note of his election as reader of Lyons Inn (1579), and below that of his election as recorder of Norwich and appointment as justice of the peace in 1586. Beneath these notes is a case (in French) argued with William Fleetwood at New Inn in 1576. At the foot of the page are notes of Coke's admission into the king's privy chamber in 1603, and of his creation as a serjeant at law and appointment as chief justice of the Common Pleas in 1606.

BL MS. Harley 6687A, fo. 17

© The British Library Board

REPORTS FROM THE NOTEBOOKS OF EDWARD COKE

VOLUME I
1572–1579

EDITED FOR
THE SELDEN SOCIETY
BY
SIR JOHN BAKER Q.C., LL.D., F.B.A.
*Emeritus Downing Professor of the Laws of England, Cambridge;
barrister and honorary bencher of the Inner Temple and Gray's Inn*

LONDON
SELDEN SOCIETY
2022

© Selden Society 2022

Printed on acid-free paper

ISBN 978-0-85423-232-1

Typeset by Waveney Typesetters, Wymondham, Norfolk
Printed and bound by CPI Group (UK) Ltd, Croydon, CR0 4YY

CONTENTS OF VOLUME I

Preface	vii
List of Manuscripts and Sigla	x
Abbreviations	xiv
List of Illustrations	xix
Table of Cases reported and cited in Volume I	xx
Table of Cases reported in Volumes I–IV	xl
Table of Statutes cited in Volumes I–IV	lxiii
Introduction	lxxiii
Coke's legal education	lxxiii
The learning of Westminster Hall	lxxix
The Rylands manuscript, 1572–77	lxxxv
Coke's autograph notebooks	xcii
Cases in the commonplace-books, mostly 1572–79	xciii
Cases in marginalia at Holkham, 1572–87	xcvii
Coke's earliest chronological reports, 1579–88	xcviii
Shelley's Case	cii
The circulation of Coke's early reports	cvii
The missing Notebook *B*, 1588–91	cxiii
Notebook *C*, 1591–1606	cxiii
Coke's interest in history	cxx
Treason and matters of state	cxviii
Royal revenue and the law	cxxxv
The Chancery jurisdiction	cxlii
Judicial review	cxlvi
Statutory interpretation	clii
Chudleigh's Case	clv
Perpetuity clauses	clix
The later reports	clxviii
This Edition	clxix
Appendix I: Reports of Michaelmas Term 1572 on two Fly-Leaves at Holkham	clxxiv
Appendix II: Contents of the Rylands Manuscript, 1572–77	cxciv

Appendix III: References to the Notebooks in Coke's Copy of Dyer . ccv
Appendix IV: Cases Copied by Others from Coke's First Notebook . ccxviii
Appendix V: Coke's Charge to the Admiral Sessions at Norwich, 1583 ccviii
Appendix VI: Cases in which Coke Argued, 1587–88 . . . ccxxii
Appendix VII: Coke's Manuscript of Spelman's Reports . . . ccxxxi
Appendix VIII: Peryam's Manuscript of Dyer's Reports . . . ccxxxiii

Cases from Coke's Commonplace-Books and Marginalia, mostly
   1572–79 1
   Chronological Table of the Named Cases Reported in Volume I . 1
   Cases from the Commonplace-Books 3
   Cases from Marginalia at Holkham Hall 154

PREFACE

The most exciting manuscript discovery of my career was made fifty years ago, when I identified Coke's earliest autograph notebooks of cases in what was then the British Museum library, followed soon afterwards by finding another of the notebooks in Cambridge University Library. My first thought was that a desirable future project would be to produce a Fourteenth Part of Coke's reports, containing those cases in the notebooks which were never printed. The project was deferred, chiefly in the hope (still unrealised) of finding the remaining notebooks, but partly because of uncertainty as to how best to do it. The main advantage of a Fourteenth Part would be that it might see the light of day more speedily than a complete edition. But there were strong arguments against selection. Problems would arise over the inclusion and treatment of cases which were substantially altered in the printed editions, or incorporated into reports of other cases. And any decision as to what cases might seem most interesting or accessible to today's reader would impose today's passing predispositions upon a extremely varied store of legal material. A full edition, on the other hand, would show us what was of interest to Coke himself, and what he thought fit to preserve for future reference. Moreover, given the criticisms of Coke for embroidering his reports, it is of value to know the form in which they originated, how far they were non-contemporary or second-hand, and how far they were altered for the press. There are no comparable precedents for guidance. Plowden's notebooks have long since disappeared. Dyer's reports were printed posthumously, presumably verbatim but not completely, or entirely accurately, and the unprinted residue (so far as it can be reconstructed from manuscript copies) has now been published by the Society (in volumes 109–110). The autograph manuscript of George Croke's reports survives in the Hertfordshire Record Office, but it is uncertain whether it contains much of substance not to be found in the posthumous English edition, which was translated directly from it. Coke's printed *Reports* are far more complex than any of these, since they were not printed directly from his notes but were edited and rewritten by Coke himself. They were not published in the same order as the autograph notebooks, and there were many omissions, alterations and enlargements, including the addition of some cases decided earlier but not found in the contemporary notebooks. The manuscript notebooks are therefore very different from the *Reports* which the profession has known for four hundred years. The omitted material is obviously of interest, especially in cases where it was kept private because it was too sensitive for the press at the time; but even notes which formed the basis of printed reports are useful, since they reveal the contemporary antecedents of the better known printed texts.

For the work of a lesser reporter it might be justifiable for an editor to cut corners. But such is Coke's position in the history of English law that it came to seem preferable to embark upon the present more ambitious project, whether or not the present editor would ever be able to complete it himself. The third and later volumes

in this edition contain cases from what Coke called his 'Liber Primus', beginning in 1591 and covering the first half of Coke's time as attorney-general. But Coke had begun reporting earlier than this, as he acknowledged in his citations, and these earlier reports are printed in the first two volumes. The second volume contains the whole of Coke's first two chronological notebooks (1579–88), commenced soon after his call to the bar and ending two years before he became a bencher of the Inner Temple. He was rapidly achieving success at the Bar, and becoming familiar with the foremost leaders of the profession. These notes record his earliest forensic successes and, occasionally, the evolution of his legal ideas. They contain much that did not find its way into the printed *Reports*. Together with a third notebook of shorter length (now lost), they all preceded the massive 'Liber Primus'. They were nevertheless much resorted to by Coke himself, whose constant use has caused some loss of text at the edges and corners. He also permitted copies to be made from the notebooks by others during the 1580s ad 1590s, and the transcripts have occasionally proved useful in supplying some of the wording lost through wear.

The chronological series printed in the second volume was still not the beginning. Well before his call to the bar in 1578, indeed as soon as he entered the Inner Temple as a student in 1572, and perhaps even as a student of Clifford's Inn in 1571, Coke was writing notes of cases in his commonplace-books. These early notes from the 1570s form the main content of this first volume. (Apart from a few additions from the early 1580s, the entries end in 1579, the year in which volume II of this edition begins.) They were not perceived by Coke as a discrete series of reports, but rather as useful snippets distributed under headings for future reference. Nevertheless, he acknowledged them as his own, referring to some of them in later citations as 'my reports', or as cases which he 'heard and noted' himself. Whatever their origin, it is valuable to have Coke's own summaries of some of the leading cases which he saw argued, or learned about in discussion, during his formative years. The first volume, naturally, contains a good deal of technical doctrine concerning real property and points of procedure, sometimes digested with an abridger's economy of language and therefore not altogether accessible or immediately interesting to the modern reader. It was inspired more by the year books with which Coke's notes were intermingled than by the more sophisticated model provided by Plowden in 1571, which did not lend itself so readily to abridgment. And yet, although the reports from the 1570s and 1580s are not generally as noteworthy as those from the 1590s, which were written when Coke was at the centre of public life, already in them we see the extent of Coke's immense learning, and his delight in the intricacies which could win or lose cases, in the years when he was establishing himself – with remarkable speed – as the paragon of the Bar. In any case, his summaries of the leading property cases of the 1570s, some of which are not so clearly reported in print, are useful to have.

This edition is not intended to supplant the printed *Reports*, which contain much that is not in the notebooks, but to supplement them. The reports here are printed in the form in which they were first set down in Coke's own hand, complete with the autograph corrections, emendations and additions. They have not been collated with the printed *Reports*, which were often changed so heavily that they cannot be regarded as the same text, though references have been provided to the places in Coke's

writings where they may be found edited, abridged, incorporated or cited. The minute handwriting used in the notebooks is in places difficult to read, especially in the badly lit Manuscripts Reading Room of the present British Library, and the contents of the first volume were painfully transcribed in pencil with the aid of a magnifying glass. Work on the remainder was greatly eased by the welcome decision to allow readers to use digital cameras. However, even when the pages were captured electronically and enlarged on screen, a few passages proved problematic, mainly because of the tangle of interlineations, but occasionally because words (or even whole sentences) have completely worn away at the edges. It is not altogether surprising that so little attention has been paid to them. But I have taken heart from Coke's own example. In the preface to his *Fourth Institute* he remarked that it had been

> a labour of as great pain as difficulty; for, as in a high and large building, he that beholds the same after it is finished seeth not the carriages, scaffolding and other invisible works of labour ... so he that looketh on a book full of variety and important matter, especially concerning sacred laws, after it is printed and fairly bound and polished, cannot see therein the carriage of the materials, the searching, finding out, perusing and digesting of authorities in law.

So it must be for anyone with the temerity to edit the notes which Coke himself has left us, and I hope that the quiet struggles involved in turning his hieroglyphs into a printed edition, with the 'authorities in law' identified, will not be too apparent on the surface of the finished books when they appear in their fairly bound Selden Society livery.

The introduction printed in this volume serves for the whole of the present edition, and the excuse for its length is that it is intended to show what can be learned from the notebooks about Coke's legal thought and career before he was appointed to the bench in 1606. It seems unlikely that a definitive biography of Coke will ever be produced, but there is much in his notebooks which has in the past been neglected on account of its inaccessibility. Since it may be a long time before volume VI appears, the introduction has taken some account of entries between 1600, when the present edition ends, and mid–1606, when the principal manuscript notebook ends. Indexes to all the volumes in this edition will appear in volume V.

The main texts in this edition were transcribed and translated from the autograph notebooks in the British Library. I am grateful to Edward Coke's descendant, the eighth Earl of Leicester, for permission also to examine and copy the annotations in Coke's printed law books preserved at Holkham Hall, for his kind hospitality at Holkham, and for the assistance given by his librarian, Dr Mac Graham.

The Stenton Fund of the British Academy made a generous subvention towards this edition, which is gratefully acknowledged.

J.H.B.

LIST OF MANUSCRIPTS AND SIGLA

A BL MS. Harley 6687, which was divided in 1804 or 1805 into four volumes lettered A to D (cited here as *AA*, *AB*, *AC* and *AD*), all the folios being interleaved with blank paper of larger dimensions. The original pages measure about 89 × 145 mm. The numbering in magenta ink, which runs throughout all four volumes from 1 to 922, dates from soon after the rebinding. A note at the beginning, in the same ink, acknowledges that it was imperfectly done: some leaves were numbered twice, in which case the duplicate number has been distinguished with an asterisk; some irregular leaves were not numbered at all; and some numbers were accidentally omitted (e.g. fos. 52–57). The manuscript was collated some decades later by the British Museum and the leaves renumbered in pencil, each volume separately; the total number of leaves so numbered is 956. There is also an earlier pencil numbering, in the bottom right-hand corners. To avoid confusion, neither of the pencil numberings has been used in this edition. Coke's own folio-numbers were written in black ink, in the top right-hand corner of the rectos, though many figures have been lost through wear and rebinding. In this edition folios are referred to as far as possible by Coke's numbering, to facilitate the identification of his cross-references, followed in parentheses by the magenta numbering. References in the introduction, however, are to the magenta numbers unless otherwise stated.

AA BL MS. Harley 6687A (fos. 1–243 in magenta; fos. 1–244 in pencil). This contains the first of Coke's commonplace-books (numbered by him fos. 1–120) and the beginning of his annotated copy of the 1572 edition of Littleton's *Tenures*. The commonplace-book may have begun as an interleaving of the Littleton, but the original numbering of the folios was independent of those of the printed book (which Coke did not include in his numbering); and there are so many of these additional leaves that it is difficult to imagine how the volumes expanded to such proportions. It begins with some biographical memoranda, which were published in the nineteenth century, followed by commonplaced material under non-alphabetical headings. The legal material begins at fo. 18 in magenta (with a stray leaf of the same nature at fo. 9). Coke's numbering begins a new sequence (fos. 1–47) at the beginning of Littleton, with notes under the heading 'Estates' (fo. 189 in magenta).

AB BL MS. Harley 6687B (fos. 244–496 in magenta; fos. 1–261 in pencil). This section begins with a continuation of the annotated

copy of Littleton (beginning at fo. 8 of the printed book = fo. 247 in magenta) interleaved with a continuation of the first commonplace-book (fos. 48–76 in Coke's numbering). A new notebook begins on fo. 292 in magenta (Coke's fo. 1); Coke's fos. 1–12 in this notebook are mostly cases from Bendlowes' reports (fos. 292–299 in magenta) and the second part of Plowd. (1579); fos. 12v–54/55 (fos. 304v–338 in magenta) contain the First Notebook of Coke's autograph reports (1579–84), as printed in volume ii, with an alphabetical table of subjects (fos. 338–339 in magenta). Seven or eight leaves are missing near the end (fos. 45–51/52) of the reports; these were gone before the numbering in magenta (between fos. 336 and 337; fo. 337 is Coke's fo. 52/53). After fo. 339 in magenta there is more of the commonplace-book (resumed from fo. 292 in magenta), numbered fos. 77–176 by Coke. On fo. 278v in magenta is an alphabetical table of the named cases between fos. 64 and 85 (in Coke's numbering), including the cases from Plowd.

AC   BL MS. Harley 6687C (fos. 498–706 in magenta; fos. 1–222 in pencil). This is a continuation of the commonplace-book, containing fos. 177–284 in Coke's numbering, interleaved with the remainder of Littleton (from fo. 72 to the end).

AD   BL MS. Harley 6687D (fos. 707–922 in magenta; fos. 1–229 in pencil). Fos. 708–755 are the 'Second Notebook' of Coke's autograph reports, from Easter term 1585 to Michaelmas term 1588, as printed in vol. ii. These are continued from those in *AB* but in a separate booklet with the leaves numbered by Coke as fos. 1–48. This is followed by a new commonplace-book, under non-alphabetical titles, numbered by Coke as fos. 1–145. At the end are some notes on leaves unnumbered by Coke. The alphabetical collections of maxims on fos. 907–914 (magenta) seem to date from the early seventeenth century. On fo. 915 (magenta) is an index of 'les titles queux sont mixt inter les tenures de Littleton', and on fo. 916 a table of regnal years from 1066 to 1603.

B   The missing notebook, formerly belonging to Robert Harley, with reports from Michaelmas term 1588 to Trinity term 1591, in approximately 55 leaves. For what is known of it see below, p. cxiii; vol. ii, pp. 405–407.

C   BL MS. Harley 6686. Coke's autograph reports from Michaelmas term 1591 to Trinity term 1606. He called this his 'Liber primus'. The volume is of 700 leaves (fos. 1–713 in Coke's numbering, with chasms and irregularities) and is now bound in two parts (6686A and 6686B), the second beginning at fo. 306 in Coke's numbering. Coke's numbering omits 190–199, 378–387, 471–479 and 481–489; and numbers 145, 225–227, 249, 519–528 are duplicated.

	Citations in this edition, which comprises the contents of fos. 1–433, are to Coke's numbering.
D	'Liber secundus' (now missing) with Coke's autograph reports from Easter term 1606 to Michaelmas term 1608, in 81 folios.
E	CUL MS. Ii.5.21. Coke's autograph reports ('Liber tercius') from Michaelmas term 1608 to Easter term 1610, in 111 folios.[1]
F	Missing notebook with Coke's autograph reports from Trinity term 1610 to Easter term 1616, in 222 folios.
Ff	CUL MS. Ff.5.4. Fos. 156–210 contain cases selected from *AB* as far as Pas. 1584; there is nothing in the whole volume later than the 1580s. Fos. 156–157 are headed 'Copyholdes	Reportes Cook'; fos. 157v–164v are blank; fo. 165 has cases of 1584, apparently not from Coke; fos. 165v–170v and 178 contain cases from the first commonplace-book, confined to the portion in *AB* (1558–84); on fo. 170v is a single case from *AA* (no. 1 in this edition); fos. 172–173 are blank; fos. 174–184, 200v–210 are from the first notebook of cases in *AB* (1581–84). Interpolated at fos. 184v–199v are cases also found in JRL MS. Fr. 118, and probably derived from that manuscript; the selection is different from that in *Gg*.
G	Missing notebook with Coke's autograph reports from Hilary term 1615 to Hilary term 1616, supplementary to those in *F*, in 26 folios.
Gg	CUL MS. Gg.5.4, fos. 22–35v, 37–50 (headed 'Cases escrie ex libro Cooke que il mesme collect 22 et 23 Eliz. in Bancke le Roy'), 62v–68v, 71–72. This is an early seventeenth-century transcript of cases from another volume (not *Ff*), the folio numbers of which are preserved in the margin, with cases selected from *AB* (including the commonplace-book) as far as Pas. 1584. The selection is closely similar to that in *Ff*, though it omits some cases which are in *Ff* and contains a few cases not in *Ff*. The cases from Coke are interspersed with cases from Thomas Durdent's reports and other sources, some of which are also in *Ff*, though some are as late as the 1620s. In *CELMC*, p. 287, it was suggested that there might be further cases from Coke after fo. 68v, but this is true only of fo. 71. On fos. 53–61 are some cases also found in JRL MS. Fr. 118, and probably derived from that manuscript; but the selection is different from that in *Ff*.
H	CUL MS. Ff.5.16, fo. 46. Slightly abridged version of a case of 1582 from *AB*.
I	IT MS. Barrington 17, fos. 216v–218, 237v, contain seven cases

---

[1] In Baker, *Collected Papers*, ii. 729, the volume is wrongly said to end in 1611, reproducing an error made in 1972.

from Coke's notebooks, 1581–82; and on fos. 7, 247, there are two others from 1584.

L   BL MS. Lansd. 1084, fos. 37–38: 'Cases collect ex auter reportes [*erasure*]'; the erased word does not seem to have been Coke. Fifteen cases abridged from *AB*, from 1582 to 1584, copied in reverse order. These are immediately followed (fos. 38–42v) by a group of Common Pleas cases from 1585 attributed to 'Wrai', probably Christopher Wray of Lincoln's Inn (called 1587). There are three slightly earlier cases (1581–82) at the foot of fo. 42v, also in reverse order, two of them identified as 'report per Cooke'. All the cases from Coke are also in *Ff*. The volume is mostly in the hand of Henry Calthorpe of the Middle Temple (called 1614).

La   BL MS. Lansd. 1068, fos. 103–108. Twenty-one cases slightly abridged from *AB*, from 1581 to 1584, interspersed with a few other reports. On fo. 130v is the *Countess of Lennox's Case* (1580), also abridged from *AB*.

Lb   BL MS. Lansd. 1095, fo. 6. Twenty-one cases abridged from *AB*.

Lc   BL MS. Lansd. 1076, fos. 119v–120. Three cases abridged from *AB*.

Rylands MS.   JRL MS. Fr. 118, fos. 15–19v Reports of Common Pleas cases, Michaelmas term 1572 to Michaelmas term 1577, in Coke's autograph. The first fourteen folios of the original manuscript have long been missing. See below, pp. lxxxv–xcii, and Appendix II.

Twysden-Finch MS.   BL MSS. Add. 24281–24283. A interleaved copy of J. Cowell, *The Interpreter* (1637), with annotations by Sir Roger Twysden (d. 1672), including notes extracted from a transcript (now lost) of Coke's notebooks made by his uncle Sir Heneage Finch (d. 1631): see below, pp. cviii–cix. Purchased for the British Museum at Puttick & Co., 12 July 1861, lot 758.

V   Hertfordshire Record Office, Verulam MS. XII.A.6A. Autograph notebook of George Croke of the Inner Temple (admitted 1574, called 1584), with extracts from manuscript reports by Serjeant Bendlowes, Sir James Dyer, Edward Coke, William Lewis, Thomas Chamberlain, Lawrence Tanfield, John Fountayn, William Clayton and John Jackson: see 109 Selden Soc., introduction, pp. xcviii–xcix. Most of the notebook was probably written after Dyer's death (1582) but before the publication of his printed reports (1586), to which references are added in the margins; there is also a selection of 'Cases ex le printed liver de Seignior Diers reports' at the end (fos. 102–134v). Croke's next notebook (MS. XII.A.6B) begins in 1583 with reports of his own authorship, mixed with a few others, one of which (on fo. 18v) is also from Coke.

ABBREVIATIONS

accord.	accordant, in accordance (with a proposition or authority). Following professional usage, and to avoid circumlocution, this is kept as an abbreviation.
adm.	admitted.
B. & M.	*Baker and Milsom: Sources of English Legal History. Private Law to 1750*, 2nd edition by Sir John Baker (Oxford, 2010).
Baker, *Collected Papers*	Sir John Baker, *Collected Papers on English Legal History* (Cambridge, 2013), three volumes.
Baker, *Magna Carta*	Sir John Baker, *The Reinvention of Magna Carta 1216–1616* (Cambridge, 2017).
Baker, *English Law under two Elizabeths*	Sir John Baker, *English Law under two Elizabeths: The Late Tudor Legal World and the Present* (Cambridge, 2021).
BL	British Library, London.
Bodl. Lib.	Bodleian Library, Oxford.
Boyer, *Coke and the Elizabethan Age*	A. D. Boyer, *Sir Edward Coke and the Elizabethan Age* (Stanford, CA, 2003).
Bracton	*Bracton on the Laws and Customs of England*, ed. G. E. Woodbine, tr. S. E. Thorne (1968–77), four volumes.
Bro. Abr.	Sir Robert Brooke, *La Graunde Abridgement* (1573), two volumes.
C 2, C 3, C 8	PRO: Court of Chancery, bills and pleadings.
C 21–22	PRO: Court of Chancery, depositions.
C 33	PRO: Court of Chancery, decree and order books.
C 78	PRO: Court of Chancery, decree rolls.
C 142	PRO: Chancery inquisitions *post mortem*.
called	called to the bar.
c.a.v.	*curia advisari vult* ('the court will be advised'), indicating an adjournment for further consideration.
Cecil Papers	*Catalogue of the Manuscripts of the Most Honourable the Marquess of Salisbury preserved at Hatfield House* (1880–1976), twenty-four volumes.
CELMC	J. H. Baker, *Catalogue of English Legal Manuscripts in Cambridge University Library* (Woodbridge, 1996).
cit.	cited, citing.
cit. record	citing the record, i.e. the same roll as given in Coke's report or in the identifying footnote in this edition.
Co. Copyh.	*The Complete Copyholder ... by Sir Edward Coke*, ed. W. C., in *Three Law Tracts ... by Sir Edward Coke*

	(1764). This contains a number of copyhold cases not found in the printed reports. But the attribution to Coke is no longer considered safe: below, p. cvii.
Co. Ent.	Sir Edward Coke, *A Booke of Entries* (1614) (the 1671 edition was used).
Co. Inst.	Sir Edward Coke, *Institutes of the Laws of England* (1628–44), four volumes. The first part is cited as Co. Litt.
Co. Litt.	Sir Edward Coke, *First Part of the Institutes of the Laws of England* (1628), a commentary on Litt. (q.v.).
Co. Rep.	*The Reports of Sir Edward Coke*, first published in French, in eleven parts with various titles (1600–15), supplemented by two posthumous parts (1658, 1659). The first English translation was published in 1658.
Co. Uses	Sir Edward Coke, reading in the Inner Temple on the Statute of Uses (1592) BL MS. Harg. 33, fos.134–159v.
Coke's Dyer	Coke's manuscript annotations to J. Dyer, *Ascuns Novel Cases* (1585) Holkham Hall, BN 8014.
Coke's Sta. P.C.	Coke's manuscript annotations to W. Staundeforde, *Les Plees del Coron* (1567 edition) Holkham Hall, BN 7171.
Coke's *Statuta*	Coke's manuscript annotations to *Magna Charta cum Statutis* (1576 edition), Holkham Hall, BN 7834. This is the volume covered with red velvet mentioned in *Library of Sir Edward Coke*, p. 30, no. 372. Coke himself cited it as his 'Magna Carta'. The second copy of this edition at Holkham (BN 8085) does not contain notes.
Coke's *Statuta*, 2	Coke's manuscript annotations to *Magna Charta cum Statutis* (1556 edition): Holkham Hall, BN 7831. This is the volume, formerly covered with blue velvet, mentioned in *Library of Sir Edward Coke*, p. 30, no. 370 ('havinge printinge and wrightinge intermixed'). Although this is an earlier edition than the previous item, the annotations are later and mostly relate to Parliament, taxation, monopolies and other constitutional matters.
Coventry	Reports by Thomas Coventry of the Inner Temple. Unless otherwise indicated, references are to the text in BL MS. Add. 25203.
CP 40	PRO: Common Pleas, plea rolls.
CPR	*Calendar of Patent Rolls*.
CSPD	*Calendar of State Papers (Domestic)*.
CUL	Cambridge University Library. The manuscript law reports are all available on microfiche from Brill (originally published by Inter Documentation Company), 'English Legal Manuscripts Project'.
d.	(Before a date:) died. (In a case-name:) on the demise of.

Dean, *Law-Making and Society*	D. Dean, *Law-Making and Society in Late Elizabethan England: The Parliament of England, 1584-1601* (Cambridge, 1996).
decd	deceased.
D'Ewes, *Journals*	S. D'Ewes, *The Journals of all the Parliaments during the Reign of Queen Elizabeth* (1684).
DKR	*Reports of the Deputy Keeper of Public Records.*
DL	PRO: Duchy Chamber, pleadings and depositions.
Dyer	Sir James Dyer, *Ascuns Novel Cases* ('1585', issued in 1586, new style) (the 1688 edition was used). (*See also* Coke's Dyer.)
E 133, E134	PRO: Court of Exchequer, depositions.
E 150	PRO: Exchequer inquisitions *post mortem*.
E 159	PRO: Exchequer, memoranda rolls of the queen's remembrancer.
E 368	PRO: Exchequer, memoranda rolls of the lord treasurer's remembrancer.
Eliz.	Queen Elizabeth I.
Exch.	Exchequer.
Exch. Ch.	Exchequer Chamber.
Fitz. Abr.	Sir Anthony Fitzherbert, *La Graunde Abridgement* [1514–16] (the 1577 edition was used).
Fitz. N.B.	Sir Anthony Fitzherbert, *La Novel Natura Brevium* (1538) (the 1635 edition was used).
Gray, *Copyhold*	C. M. Gray, *Copyhold, Equity and the Common Law* (Cambridge, Mass., 1963).
Harg.	BL: Hargrave collection.
Hawarde	J. Hawarde, *Les Reportes del Cases in Camera Stellata 1593–1609*, ed. W. P. Baildon (1894). The original manuscript is now in the Carl H. Pforzheimer Library, University of Texas at Austin, MS. 36.
HEHL	Henry E. Huntington Library, San Marino, California.
HLS	Harvard Law School Library, Cambridge, Massachusetts. Many of the manuscripts are being renumbered, though some of the old numbers have been retained. This may cause confusion with respect to citations during the past forty years using the old numbers. Citations here are by the new number (if known) followed by the old number in parentheses. The law reports are available on microfiche (cf. CUL) and some have been digitised.
Holkham	Books and manuscripts in the library of Thomas Coke, eighth earl of Leicester, Holkham Hall, Norfolk. Four-figure numbers refer to printed books, which at Holkham are cited with the prefix BN (for Book Number). Manuscripts have a separate numbering.

Holkham 7831(2)	A small notebook of 7 folios, in Coke's hand, bound into his copy of *Magna Charta cum Statutis* (1556 edition), Holkham Hall, BN 7831, following the printed pages. It seems to have been written around the time of his dismissal from office in 1616.
IT	Inner Temple Library, London. The law reports have been published on microfilm by World Microfilms.
JRL	University of Manchester, John Rylands Library.
JUST 1	PRO: Justices Itinerant.
KB 8	PRO: King's Bench, *Baga de Secretis*.
KB 27	PRO: King's Bench, plea rolls.
Lansd.	BL: Lansdowne collection.
Letters & Papers	*Letters and Papers of the Reign of Henry VIII*, ed. J. S. Brewer and others (1862–1932), 21 volumes in 33.
LI	Lincoln's Inn Library, London.
Lib. Ass.	*Liber Assisarum*, printed together with YB (q.v.)
Liber Bowyer	A volume of historical collections, cited by Coke as 'Lib. Boier', attributable to William Bowyer (d. 1569/70), keeper of records in the Tower of London. See below, p. cxxi.
Library of Sir Edward Coke	*A Catalogue of the Library of Sir Edward Coke*, ed. W. O. Hassall ([New Haven], 1950). This is an annotated edition of the parchment inventory roll, now at Holkham Hall, which was compiled under Coke's direction shortly before his death in 1634.
Litt.	[Sir Thomas Littleton], *Les Tenures du Monsieur Littelton* (1572 edition). This was the edition used by Coke. It does not have numbered sections and was therefore cited by folio. The numbering of sections was introduced in the 1585 edition and retained thereafter. The folio references are retained here in the translation, but the sections are cited in the footnotes.
m.	membrane.
Mar.	Queen Mary I.
Men of Court	Sir John Baker, *The Men of Court 1440–1550* (18 Selden Soc. Supplementary Series, 2012), two volumes.
OHLE	Sir John Baker, *Oxford History of the Laws of England*, vol. vi (Oxford, 2003).
PCC	Prerogative Court of Canterbury will registers (PROB 11 in the PRO).
Plowd.	E. Plowden, *Les Comentaries* (1571, 1579), two parts, with continuous folio numbering (the 1613 edition was used).
PRO	Public Record Office, Kew, Surrey.
Proc. Parl.	*Proceedings in the Parliaments of Elizabeth I*, ed. T. E. Hartley (1981, 1995), three volumes.

Registrum Omnium Brevium	*Registrum Omnium Brevium* (1531) (the 1634 edition was used).
Rot. Parl.	*Rotuli Parliamentorum ut et Petitiones et Placita in Parliamento* [1767–77].
RS	Rolls Series, i.e. 'Chronicles and Memorials of Great Britain and Ireland during the Middle Ages. Published … under the Direction of the Master of the Rolls'.
sjt	serjeant at law.
Smith, *Sir Edward Coke*	D. C. Smith, *Sir Edward Coke and the Reformation of the Laws: Religion, Politics, and Jurisprudence 1578–1616* (Cambridge, 2014).
SP 12	PRO: State Papers (Domestic), Elizabeth I.
SP 13	PRO: State Papers (Domestic), Elizabeth I to Charles I, large documents.
SP 46	PRO: State Papers (Domestic), supplementary.
Sta. P.C.	W. Staundeforde, *Les Plees del Coron* [1557] (the 1574 edition was used). (*See also* Coke's Sta. P.C.)
Sta. Prerog.	W. Stanford, *An Exposicion of the Kinges Prerogative* (1567).
STAC 3, 5, 7	PRO: Court of Star Chamber proceedings.
Star Ch.	Court of Star Chamber.
Statuta	*See* Coke's *Statuta*.
tr.	translated.
vol. i, ii, iii, iv, v	The five volumes of this edition.
WARD 7	PRO: Court of Wards, inquisitions *post mortem*.
YB	Year books, cited by term, regnal year, folio, and *placitum* (case-number). The 'vulgate' edition of 1679–80 has been used unless otherwise stated.
YLS	Yale Law School library, New Haven, Connecticut. The collection of Elizabethan manuscript reports came from the library of Sir Matthew Hale (d. 1676), chief justice of the King's Bench. The law reports are available on microfiche (cf. CUL).

Editorial markings:

[a]	Added in the spaces around the text.
[d]	Deleted.
[i]	Interlined in the text.
[m]	Written in the margin.
[s]	Superscribed above the text or in a headline.
[…]	Words missing or illegible.
[*blank*]	Blank space in the manuscript.
[ ]	Words supplied by the editor.
< >	Words to which a footnote, or one of the above markings, refers.
{ }	Later addition (translation side only). On the text side, used to distinguish selected words within angle brackets.

LIST OF ILLUSTRATIONS IN VOLUME I

The pages from MS. Harley 6687 are shown in approximately the actual size

Frontispiece

The start of Coke's first commonplace-book
BL MS. Harley 6687A, fo. 17

Between pp. xcvi and xcvii

1. Autobiographical memoranda
   BL MS. Harley 6687A, fo. 13

2. Heavy annotation in the commonplace-books
   BL MS. Harley 6687D, fo. 818v

3. Marginal annotations to Littleton
   BL MS. Harley 6687C, fo. 499

4. First page of the Rylands manuscript (1572)
   JRL MS. Fr. 118, fo. 15

5. Conversation with Mr Justice Gawdy (1577)
   (a) JRL MS. Fr. 118, fo. 81v
   (b) BL MS. Harley 6687B, fo. 288v

6. Marginal annotations to the 1576 statute-book
   Holkham Hall BN 7834, fo. 3

7. Beginning of the second notebook of reports (1585)
   BL MS. Harley 6687D, fo. 708

8. Report of *Cheyny* v. *Frankwell* (1587)
   BL MS. Harley 6687D, fo. 730

TABLE OF CASES REPORTED AND CITED IN VOLUME I

Cases printed in this volume are in capitals and small capitals.
Anonymous Tudor cases are not included unless in the year books or abridgments.

1: Named Cases

Abraham v. Twigge (1596)	clxiv
Aburgavenny (Lord) v. Waller (1577)	88
Acton v. Hore (1596)	clxii
Agard v. Candish (1599)	lxxxiv
Aldworth's Case (1605)	cxli
Allen's Case (1587)	xcix
Alton Woods, Case of (1600)	cvi, cxxxvii, clv, clxix
ANDROWES V. BLUNT (1573)	lxxxvii, cxcix, 39, 52, 90, 108
Androwes v. Cromwell (Lord) (1579)	6, 52
Androwes v. Nedeham (1598)	6
APOT'S CASE (1572)	159
APPULTON'S CASE (1577)	29
Archdale v. Beston (1409)	59, 112
ARCHER'S CASE (1578)	10, 161
Archer's Case (1597)	123
Arnold v. Wynter (1572)	43
Arundel (Earl of) v. Bradstocks (1575)	38
ARUNDEL (EARL OF) V. LANGAR (1576)	ccii, 32, 37, 70, 80, 94
Arundell's Case (1587)	cxviii
Ashpole v. Hundred of Evingar (1585)	88
Astwick's Case (1567)	cxliii
Atkyns v. Atkyns (1592)	cxiv
Att.-Gen. v. Carie and Dodington (1596)	cxxxv
ATT.-GEN. V. CONSTABLE (1578)	151
Att.-Gen. v. Joiners' Co. (1582)	cxlvii
Att.-Gen. v. Nix (Bishop of Norwich) (1534)	ccxxxii
Att.-Gen. v. Perrot (c. 1595)	clxi
Att.-Gen. v. Smyth (1596)	cxxxv
Att.-Gen. v. Twyne (1602)	cxxxiv
Att.-Gen. v. Walsingham (1573-79)	89, 131
Atwill v. Tailor (1481)	91, 140
AUDLEY (LORD) HIS CASE (1573)	122
Austin v. Baker (1554)	96

CASES REPORTED AND CITED IN VOLUME I

Babb v. Clarke (1595)	cxlviii
Baker v. Johnson (1493)	clxxxix
BAKER V. RAYMOND (1577)	47, 149
BAKER V. SMITH (1581)	163
Baldwyn v. Smith (1597)	123
BARBOUR V. LONG (1578)	158
BAREWELL V. LUCAS (Bracebridge's case) (1572/73)	73, 104, 105, 106, 107
Barham v. Denys (1599)	cxlviii
BARKER V. LONG (1578), *see* Barbour v. Long	
Basset v. Prior of St John's (1423)	11
Bataille v. Cooke (1512)	60
Bateman v. Allen (1595)	clxi
Bate's Case (1601)	cxlix
Baynton's Case, *see* Sharington v. Strotton	
BEAUMONT'S CASE (1575)	157
Beaupré v. Bishop of Norwich (1563)	100
Beche's Case (1567/71)	37
BEDINGFIELD V. PICKERING (1570)	134
Bence's Case (1588)	ccxxi
Benjamen v. Hundred of Buxton (1564)	88
Bermingham's Case (1443)	9
BESBETCH V. SCOTT (1572)	clxxiv
BETTISFORD V. FOORD (1574)	61
Beverley (Provost of) his Case (1367)	clxxxvii, cxc
Bevil's Case (1579)	128
Bildistone v. Reyne (1388)	124
BLACKALLER V. MARTIN (1575)	82
Bonham v. Broughton (1455)	63
Bonham's Case (1610)	clv
Borough v. Taylor (1596)	clxix
Bracebridge v. Cooke (1572)	4, 73
BRACEBRIDGE'S CASE (1573), *see* Barewell v. Lucas	
BRADSTOCK'S CASE (1575)	38
BRENT'S CASE (1574/75)	xc, clviii, clx, cxcvii, cxcix, 9, 85, 107, 109, 115
Brentford (Fraternity of the Nine Orders of Angels) v. Pokit (1482)	16
BROADBRIDGE'S CASE (1576)	101, 130
BRODERERS' COMPANY (THE), CASE OF (temp. Eliz.)	77
BROWNE V. SAKEVYLE (*c.* 1560)	79
Browne's Case (1581)	35
Browne (Sir George) his Case (1594)	155
Buckbeard's Case (1589/90)	cxiii
Buckhurst (Lord) his Case (1576)	cxcix
BULLOCK V. BURDETT (1570)	110, 111
BURGH V. HOLCROFT (1579)	52, 162
BURRE'S CASE (1577)	47

Burton Lazars (Master of) v. Prior of Sempringham (1469).	16
Bury (Abbot of) v. Bokenham (1536)	36
Butler v. Baker (1591)	clvi, 48
BUTTELL V. WYLFORD (Dean of St Paul's Case) (1577)	lxxxix, cci, cciv, 11, 68, 162, 163
Callard v. Callard (1596)	lxxxiii, clxi
CALTHROP'S CASE (1586)	163
CALVERLEY (SIR GEORGE) HIS CASE (1577)	cciii, 147
Camoys (Lord) v. Regem (1410)	79
Capel's Case (1592)	clxii
Carell's Case (1565)	44
Carter v. Ringstead (1590)	clx
Castleacre (Prior of) v. Dean of St Stephen's (1503)	68
Cavendish's Case (1587)	cxxix
Cawdrye v. Atton (1594)	cxlix
Chapman v. Dalton (1564)	xcv, 36
Chapman's Case (1574)	78
Chiseldon (Margaret) her Case (1371)	64
Cholmeley v. Humble (1593)	clxv
Cholmley's Case (1597)	41
Cholmondeley v. Hanmer (1597)	cxxxvii, clxii
Chudleigh v. Dyer (1586)	clv
Chudleigh's Case (1594), see Dillon v. Freine	
CHYCKE'S CASE (1576/77), see Baker v. Raymond	
CLACHES'S CASE (1574), see Glover v. Berye	
Clarke v. Gape (1595)	cxlvii, cxlviii
Clayton's Case (1585)	3
Clere (Sir Edward) his Case (1595)	43
Clifton v. Southcote (1593)	138
Coke (Sir Edward) v. Baxter (1585)	c
Coke v. Old (1601)	cxli
Cokkys v. Playfote (1536)	142
Colchester (Abbot of) his Case (1442)	16
Colchester (Abbot of), Case of the (c. 1570), see Beche's Case	
Coleworth v. Waltham (1343)	9
Colthirst v. Bejushin (1550)	46, 120
COMPTON (LORD) V. EGERTON (temp. Eliz.)	23
Constable v. Gamble (Sir Henry Constable's Case) (1601)	ccxxi, 151
Cooke v. Brombill (1597)	clxv
COOKS' CASE (THE) (1578), see Croft v. Howel	
COPLESTON V. STOWELL (1573)	12
Copley's Case (temp. Eliz.)	lxxxviii, cciv
Copping's Case (undated)	148
COPWOOD V. CLARKE (1571-72)	58, 103, 108, 110, 133
Corbet (Sir Andrew) his Case (1599)	clxv

CASES REPORTED AND CITED IN VOLUME I   xxiii

Corbet (Arthur) (fictitious) his Case (1599-1600)	clxv-clxvi
Corbett v. Corbett (1600)	clxv
Corbyn v. Corbyn (1598)	clvii, clix
Cordal's Case (temp. Eliz.)	xcvii
Cornwall (Earl of) v. Bishop of Rochester (1322)	64
Coveney v. Hundred of Denton (1521)	88
COVENTRY'S CASE (1577)	156
Cowper v. Lane (1575)	40
CRANE V. BROXHOLE (1572/73)	cxcvii, 29
CRANMER'S CASE (1572), see Kyrke d. Cranmer v. Bales	
Crewte's Case (1576)	109
CROFT V. HOWELL (1578)	15
Cromwell (Lady) her Case (1553)	8
CROMWELL (LORD) V. ANDROWES (1577)	4, 39, 82
CROMWELL (LORD) V. DENNYE (1577-81)	27, 103
Cromwell (Lord) v. Taverner (1573)	cxcvi
Cuppledyke's Case (1602)	133
Curson (Sir George) his Case (1607)	147
Dacre of the South, Re (1535)	131
Dacres (Lord) v. Lassells (1561)	17, 18
Darcy v. Allen (1602)	cxxix, cxxxix, cxl
Davenant v. Hurdys (1599)	cxl
Davye v. Pepys (1573)	63
Dawson v. Pickworth (1605)	cxxxvii
Degore v. Rowe (1592)	clvi
Delamere v. Barnard (1568)	xcv, clvii
DELAPRÉ'S CASE (1575)	44, 144
DELAWARE'S CASE (1575)	lxxxix, 25
Denby v. Heathcott (1585)	cliv
DENHAM V. DORMAN (temp. Eliz.)	122
Denys (Lady) her Case (1566)	76
Derebought v. Taillour (1330)	113
Digges v. Palmer (1600)	clxi
Dillon v. Freine (Chudleigh's Case) (1594)	cliv, clv-clix, 123
DIMES' CASE (1574)	28
DINELEY V. ASSHETON (1581)	61, 128, 162
Dorchester (Prioress of) her Case (1364)	16
DORRELL V. COLYNS (1577)	51, 97
Dowce v. Sutton (1583)	103
Downing v. Franklyn (1593)	cxxxviii
Draper (Matthew) his Case (1580)	147
DRURY V. LEVENTHORPE (1582)	158, 163
Dudley v. Mallery (1576)	140
DUKE'S CASE (1573), see Ryngrose d. Leson v. Prest	
Dumpor's Case (1603)	43

Dyngle v. Hamely (1588)	clxi
Dynham (Sir John) v. Bishop of Exeter (1443)	60, 63, 112
Dynham (Sir Thomas) his Case (1459)	60, 63
EARE V. SNOWE (1578)	133
ECCLESTON AND IRELAND V. TUCHETT (1576)	cciv, 8
Eden v. Downing (1590)	cxxxviii
EDEN V. HARRIS (1576)	86, 87
Edington (Rector of) his Case (1441)	16
Edrich's Case (1603)	cliv, 161
Elliott v. Nutcombe (1559)	92
ELLIS V. VAVASOUR (1573)	136, 137
Englefield's Case (1591)	lxxxv, cxxxvii, cliv
ESSEX (COUNTESS OF) HER CASE (1577)	106
Essex (Earl of) his Case (1600)	cxli, cxxxiv
EYSTON V. STUDDE (Latton's Case) (1575)	lxxxix, cliii, cxcviii, 25, 30, 155, 157
Farington v. Darell (1431)	74, 122, 146
Farley v. Holder (1604)	cl
FARRAND d. OWEN V. RAMSEY (1579)	147
Fauconberg v. Courtney (1328)	clxxxv, cxciii
Fermor v. Savage (1583)	cxxxix
Finch v. Finch (1597)	clvi
Finch v. Throckmorton (1589-94)	cix, cxliii, 55
Fitzherbert's Case (1593)	cxvii
FITZWILLIAM V. COPLEY (1571)	159
Fleming (Sir Francis) his Case (1574)	110
Floyer's Case (1611)	159
Fontevraud (Abbot of) his Case (1334)	15
Foster (Sir William) his Case (1608)	161
Fountains (Abbot of) his Case (1431)	106, 135
FOX V. COLLIER (*c*. 1579)	143
Frampton v. Frampton (1604)	clvi, clxvii
Franklyn v. Cantrell (1573)	cxcvii
FRANKLYN V. DAVISON (1571)	93
Friske v. Peche (1411)	47
Fulmerston v. Steward (1554)	clv
Gaunte v. Hundred of Cheveley (1513)	88
Gawen's Case (1598)	cxviii
Germyn v. Arscott (1595)	clxi-clxvi, clxix
Gibbons v. Maltywarde (1592)	clxiv
GILES V. COLSHILL (1576), *see* Gyles v. Colshill	
Giles v. John (1535)	56
Gilford (Sir Henry) his Case (*c*. 1578)	
Gloucester (Dean and Chapter of) their Case (1573)	92
Glover and Brown v. Forden (1459)	146
GLOVER V. BERYE (Clache's Case) (1574)	22, 131, 145

CASES REPORTED AND CITED IN VOLUME I   xxv

Gold v. Abbot of Abingdon (1355) 111
Good (Dr) his Case (1577) cciii
Goring's Case (1600) cliv
Gravenor v. Tedd (1593) cliv
Gray's Case (1572) 147
GRENDON V. DEAN OF WORCESTER (1577) . . . . cciv, 3, 64, 77
Gresham (Sir Thomas) his case (1588) clvi
Gresley's Case (1538) 131
Grimsby (Prior of) his Case (1343) . . . . cxci, cxciii, 116, 123, 132
GYLES V. COLSHILL (1576) . lxxxix, cci, 35, 63, 112, 134, 135, 150, 157, 164
HADDON'S CASE (1576), see Mannyng v. Androwes . . .
Hamond v. Griffites (1598) cxxxvii
HARE V. BYCKLEY (1578) 32, 59, 112
Harvey v. Facey (1594) clvii
HAWLES'S CASE (temp. Eliz.) 86
Heydon's Case (1584) clii
Hill (Sir Rowland) his Case (temp. Eliz.) 148
HILL'S CASE (1577) 49
Hill v. Grange (1556) 80
HINDE V. LYONS (1578) 149
HODY d. BRENT V. GILBERT (1575) see Brent's Case . . .
Hody d. Brent v. Paulet (1576) 115
HOLCROFT'S CASE (1578) 162
Hollingworth's Case (1597) cxix
Holme v. Taylor (1581) 35
Holt's Case (1611) 64
Holygrave v. Knightsbridge (1535) 152
Hothersall v. Mildmay (1605) . . . . clxvii-clxviii
Humfreys' Case (1572) cxliii
HUMPHRESTON'S CASE ('seniori puero') . . 24, 35, 40, 101, 107, 108, 110,
    (1575) 114, 122, 123, 129, 137
Hungerford (Lady) her Case (1464) 80
Huntingfield's Case (1329) 68
Hynde's Case (1576) cxviii
Ilderton's Case (1581) xcv
Ireland's Case (temp. Eliz.) lxxxix
JACKSON V. DARCY (1575) 13, 21, 61
Joan (Queen) her Case (1430) 97
Jordan's Case (1375) 146
JULIO (DR) HIS CASE (1578) 86
Kayser's Case (1465) cxviii
Kedwelly's Case (1475) 16*bis*
Kent (Earl of) his Case (1405) 95
Kent (Earl of) v. Onley (1586) 124
Killio v. Taverner (1595) cxlvi

King's College, Cambridge v. Hekker (1522)	16
KIRKEBY v. THORNBOROUGH (1579-80)	3, 157
KYRKE d. CRANMER V. BALES (Cranmer's Case) (1572)	lxxvii, xci, clx, clxxxi, cxcvi, 21, 58, 78, 85, 123, 129, 131, 144
Lamme's Case (1572)	cxcv
LANCASTELL V. ALLER (1577)	84, 109
LANE v. COWPER (1575), see Humphreston's Case	
LATTON'S CASE (1575), see Eyston v. Studde	
Leathersellers' Co. v. Darcy (1595)	cxxix
Lee's Case (1368)	cxlvii
Lee's Case (1568)	clviii
Leicester (Abbot of) his Case (1414)	134
Leicester (Abbot of) his Case (1465)	60, 64, 95
LEICESTER (EARL OF) HIS CASE (temp. Eliz.)	7
Lennard's Case (1586)	82
LENNOX (COUNTESS OF) HER CASE (c. 1576)	62
Lewes (Prior of) his Case (1406)	139
Lilley v. Whitney (1568)	84
LINCOLN (EARL OF) HIS CASE (1577)	lxxxvi, xcvi, cciii, 50
Littleton's Case (1602)	clvi
LODGE'S CASE (1573)	28
Lombard (The) his Case (1460)	27
London (City of) (Chamberlain of) his Case (1468)	16
London Apprentices, Case of (1595)	cxxx
Lovelace v. Lovelace (1584)	clxiii
LOVELACE'S CASE (1579)	160
LOVELL (LORD) HIS CASE (1574), see Nichols v. Nichols	
Magdalen College, Oxford, Case of (1491)	66, 67
MANNYNG V. ANDROWES (Haddon's Case) (1576)	21, 58, 78, 110, 118
MANSER V. ANNESLEY (1575)	lxxxix, cxcviii, cciv, 17, 25
Markham v. Markham (1410)	clxxxv
Markyate (Prioress of) her Case (1375)	63
Merton College, Oxford v. Wodelark (1463)	91
Merton (Prior of) v. Mayor of Windsor (1440)	15
Mildmay v. Mildmay (1601)	clxiv, clxvi-clxvii
Mildmay v. Standish (1584)	cvii
Mildmay's Case (1605)	clxv
Minors' Case (1539)	44
Morgan's Case (undated)	117
Morris v. Francklen (1584)	38
Mower v. Carvanell (1543)	142
MULTON V. COVENEY (Wyatt's Case) (1576)	cc, ccii, 49, 79, 89, 93, 94, 95, 96, 101, 139
MYNNE V. GREY (1572)	clxxvii, 64
Needham v. Price (1605)	cxlix

Nevile v. De la Pole (1355)	17, 19
Nevill (Sir Henry) his Case (1570)	95
Newdegate's Case (1566)	44
Newys v. Larke, *see* Scholastica's Case	
NICHOLS v. NICHOLS (Lovell's Case) (1574)	lxxxix, cxcviii, cciv, 22, 45, 94, 130, 132, 138
Nokes's Case (1599)	113
Norfolk (Duke of) his Case (1518/19)	ccxxxi, 97
Norfolk (Duke of) his Case (1557)	79, 90
Northumberland (Earl of) his Case (1463)	80
Norwich (Bishop of) his Case (1347)	cxvii
Norwich (Bishop of) his Case (1356)	73
Norwich (Bishop of) his Case (1534), *see* R. v. Nix	
NORWICH (BISHOP OF) HIS CASE (1576)	38
Norwich (Dean and Chapter), Case of (1597)	cxxxviii
Norwich (Hospital of St Giles), Case of (1597)	cxxxviii
Norwich Corporation, Case of (1481)	16
Odingsells v. Prior of Maxstoke (1455)	60
OGNEL v. UNDERHILL (1587)	106, 161
ONLEY v. EARL OF KENT (1577)	lxxxvii, cciii, 20, 118, 124, 127, 152
Onley v. Earl of Kent (No. 2) (1588)	124
Ormond (Lord) his Case (1489)	72, 80
Oxford Corporation, Case of (1498)	16
Paget (Lord) his Case (1591)	clvii
Paine's Case (1587)	22
Parker v. Gravenor (1557)	clxxxiii
PARR (LORD) HIS CASE (1576)	126
PASTON v. DREWRY (1582)	104
PAYNE'S CASE (temp. Eliz.)	161
PECKSALL'S CASE (1572)	49
Peddington v. Otteworth (1406)	cxlvii
PERROT'S CASE (1584)	cxxxvii, 164
Peter v. Knoll (1584)	107
PICKERING'S CASE (1569/70)	lxxvii, xcv
Pilkington's Case (1441)	72
Plat v. Sheriffs of London (1550)	cliii, 17, 18
Pledall v. Annesley (1570)	17, 19
Plesington's Case (1382)	120
Pontefract College, Case of (1428)	16
Portington v. Rogers (1613)	clix
POWELL v. MONOUX (1572), *see* Winter's Case	
Powes (Lord) his Case (1489)	57
Price v. Jones (1593)	clvi
Prideaux's Case (1409)	cxciii
Prohibitions del Roy, Case of (1608)	cxlvii

Purre v. Grene (1491)	66, 67
PUTTENHAM v. DUNCOMBE (1558)	39, 55
RADCLIFFE'S CASE (temp. Eliz.)	39
RAMSEY'S CASE (1579), see Farrand d. Owen v. Ramsey	
Rayner v. Rayner (1552)	131
Reade v Rochforth (1556)	52
Repps' Case (1550s)	22
R. v. Atmere (1599)	cxlix
R. v. Audley (Lord) (1631)	cx
R. v. Bec Hellouin (Abbot of) (1344)	64
R. v. Clervaux (Abbot of) (1343)	67
R. v. Cobham (Lord) (1604)	cxxx
R. v. Dacre (Lord) (1534)	ccxxxii
R. v. Digby (1606)	cxxxi
R. v. Douglas (1605)	cxxxi
R. v. Essex (Earl of) (1601)	cxxxi
R. v. Fawkes (Guy) (1605)	cx, cxxxi
R. v. Foxe (1558)	18
R. v. Lacy (1583)	cxxxiii, ccxxi
R. v. London (Sheriffs of), ex parte Harryson (1566)	17
R. v. Maninge (1590)	cxix
R. v. Nix, bishop of Norwich (1534)	lxxxii
R. v. PASTON (EDMUND) (1584)	25
R. v. Philpot and Young (1595)	cxxxiii
R. v. Ralegh (1603)	lxxiii, cxxx-cxxxii
R. v. Rice ap Griffith (1531)	ccxxxii
R. v. Rufford (Abbot of) (1343)	66, 67
R. v. Salisbury (Bishop of) (1410)	135
R. v. Somerset (Duchess of) (1554)	76
R. v. St John's (Prior of) (1335)	164
R. v. St Oswald's (Abbot of) (1350)	38
R. v. Stafford (1606)	cxxxiv
R. v. Syon (Abbess of) (1460)	63, 84
R. v. Throgmorton (John) (1570)	lxxiii
R. v. TRUGEON (1578)	51, 97
R. v. Vaux (1591)	cxxxiii
R. v. Watson (1603)	cli
R. v. WOOD (1579)	55
R. v. Wynter and Faux (1605)	cxxxi
R. v. York (Archbishop of) (1343)	134
Richardson v. Yardley (1595)	xcvii
ROLFE'S CASE (undated)	117
Roofe v. Light (1578)	93
Rooke v. Withers, see Wythers v. Rookes	
Rudde v. Topfield (1600)	134

Rudhall v. Myller (1584).	clxiv
Russel's Case (1482)	cxviii, cxlvi
Rutland (Countess of) v. Earl of Rutland (1604)	clvi
RUTLAND (EARL OF) HIS CASE (1577)	12
RUTLAND (EARL OF) v. MARKHAM (c. 1579)	7
RYNGROSE d. LESON v. PREST (Duke's Case) (1573)	57
St Bartholomew's (Prior of) v. Prior of Blythburgh (1411)	42
St John's (Prior of) his Case (1433)	15, 16
St John's (Prior of), *see also* R. v. St John's (Prior of)	
St Mary's, York (Abbot of) v. Abbot of Selby (1334)	16
ST PAUL'S (DEAN OF) HIS CASE (1577), *see* Buttle v. Wilford	
Saltpetre, Case of (1606)	cxli. cxlii
SAVAGE v. CHESTER (1576)	100
SAVERY'S CASE (1575), *see* Blackaller v. Martin	
Say's Case (1573)	47
Saye v. Smith (1562)	xcv
Scholastica's Case (1571)	xcv, clx-clxiii, clxvi
Scott v. Mayne (1596)	clxix
Scroggs's Case (1560)	cxviii
Sengedon v. Lancastell (1389).	101
SENIORI PUERO, CASE OF (1575), *see* Humphreston's Case	
SERJEANTS' CASE (THE) (1579)	128, 156, 159, 162
Seymour's Case (1601)	cxxxviii
Sharington v. Strotton (1565)	42
Shaw v. Harries (1606)	cxli
Sheen (Prior of) v. Swillington (1532)	ccxxxi
SHELDON v. GILBERT (1574)	78
Shelley's Case (1581)	cii-cvii, 58, 145
Sherborne (Abbot of) his Case (1410)	93
Sherington v. Mynors (1596-99)	clxii, clxiii
Shrewsbury (Earl of) his Case (1597)	clvi, clxiv
Skipwith's Case (1591)	lxxx
Skrene's Case (1475)	40
Slade's Case (1602)	cvi
Slowlye's Case (1565)	72
Smith (John) his Case (1600)	cxlix
Smith v. Lane (1586)	8
Smith v. Thorpe (or Aslam) (1597)	clix, cxii
Snowe v. Beverley (1603)	cxlix
SOME'S CASE (temp. Eliz.)	155
Soulle v. Garrard (1595)	clxiv
Southampton Corporation, Case of (1484)	16
SPELL d. CROMWELL v. ANDROWES (1577)	4, 99
SPELL d. CROMWELL v. NEDEHAM (1579)	4, 5
Spencer v. Burton (1583)	lxxxii

Spencer v. Cleydon (1519)	29
Stafford (Lord) his Case (temp. Eliz.)	ccvi
Steere's Case (1563)	72
Stephens v. Wall (1569)	164
Stepneth v. Lloyd (1598)	cxlviii
Stockbridge's Case (1575)	cxcix, 26
Stoneley v. Bracebridge (1580-86)	73
Stourton (Lord) v. Chaffyn (1553)	88
Stowell v. Lord Zouche (1562-69)	cxxv, cliii, 14
Stratford (Abbot of) his Case (1406)	152
Stringfellow v. Brownesoppe (1549)	63
Stroud's Case (1584)	clv
Suffolk (Duchess of) her Case (1551)	lxxvii
Tailour v. Morice (1573)	cxcvii
Tarrant's Case (1597)	clxiii
Tewkesbury (Abbot of) his Case (1493)	84
Themilthorpe's Case (1605)	cxlvi
Thomas v. Popham (1562)	3, 157
Thornhill v. Wilford (1580)	68
Thornton's Case (1575)	147
Thoroughgood v. Cole (1584)	lxxxii
Throckmorton v. Finch (1597)	cxliii, cxlvii, clxix
Throckmorton v. Tracy (1555)	102
Tisur's Case (1583)	159
Toppe v. Eden (1575)	145
Torre (Abbot of) v. Toning (1443)	clxxxi
Tresham's Case (1576)	138
Trinity Priory, London v. Abbess of Stratford (1355)	100
Trott v. Taylor (1605)	cli
Trudgin's Case (1578), *see* R. v. Trugeon; and Trugeon's Case	
Trugeon's Case (1579)	52, 96
Tucke v. Frencham (1558)	131, 148
Turner d. Fleming v. Gray (1574)	110
Turner's Case (1585)	5
Underwood's Case (1562)	156
Vampage's Case (temp. Edw. IV)	122
Vaudrey v. Pannel (1615)	cxlv
Vaux v. Brooke (1586)	cxxxiii
Vele v. Darcy (1351)	79
Vernon v. Madder (1571)	141, 160
Vernon v. Stanley and Manners (1572)	cxcvi, 13, 36, 128, 141, 159
Vernon v. Vernon (1573)	lxxxix, cliv, cxcvii, 75, 98, 130, 157, 160
Villers v. Beamont (1557)	155
Walpole v. Corbett (1580)	64
Walsh v. Edmonds (1577)	ccii

Walsingham's Case (1573)	clv, 79
Waltham v. Austen (1599)	cxlviii
Ward's Case (1586)	lxxix
WARING'S CASE (1574)	159
Warnecombe v. Carell (1564)	9
Webster's Case (1572)	78
Weekes' Case (1580)	52
Wellocke v. Hamonte (1590)	clxii
WELTDEN V. ELKINGTON (1578)	56, 96, 150
WEST V. STOWELL (1577)	20
Whetherley v. Whetherley (1605)	cl
White-Tawyers (Guild of) their Case (1375)	16
WHOPER V. HAREWOOD (1574)	27
Wilkes v. Leuson (1559)	77, 130
Willion v. Lord Berkeley (1561)	cxli
Willoughby v. Egerton (1604)	lxxviii
WILSHIRE'S CASE (temp. Eliz.)	104
Wimbish v. Tailbois (1550)	160
Winchester (Bishop of) v. Jonys (1510)	88
Windsor (Dean and Canons of) their Case (1440)	15
Winsmore v. Hubbert (1586)	103
WINTER'S CASE (1572)	lxxvii, cxcvi, 26, 43, 81, 99, 114, 125, 126, 136, 160
Wiseman's Case (1583)	cliv
Wodeward v. Kyp (1490)	139
Woodland v. Mantell (1553)	107
Woodley v. James (1570)	156
WOODWARD V. LORD DARCY (1557)	150
Worcester (Dean of) his Case (1577)	lxxxix
Worcester (Earl of) v. Finch (1600)	cxliv
Worlay v. Harrison (1566)	17
WOTTON V. COOKE (1572)	24, 127, 129
Wrote v. Wigges (1591)	cxxxiii
WYATT (SIR THOMAS) HIS CASE (1576), see Multon v. Coveney	
Wyrlay v. Harryson (1566)	17
Wythers v. Rookes (1598)	cxlviii
Yelverton v. Yelverton (1593)	clvii
Yelverton's Case (temp. Eliz.)	clxvi
York (Abbot of) his Case (1370)	91

2: Cases cited by Year

27 Edw. I, Eyre of Ely (unprinted)	clxxxvii
Pas. 3 Edw. II, Fitz. Abr., *Dower*, pl. 126	77
Mich. 11 Edw. II, Fitz. Abr., *Garrantie*, pl. 83	76
Mich. 18 Edw. II, Fitz. Abr., *Feffements et faits*, pl. 109	58

19 Edw. II, Fitz. Abr., *Covenant*, pl. 25	clxxxviii, cxciii
1 Edw. III, Lib. Ass., pl. 11	clxxxiii, cxci, 116
Hil. 2 Edw. III, fo. 1, pl. 1-2	clxxxv, cxciii
Pas. 3 Edw. III, fo. 7, pl. 1	68
Mich. 3 Edw. III, Fitz. Abr., *Corone*, pl. 284	
Hil. 4 Edw. III, fo. 8, pl. 14	20
Pas. 4 Edw. III, fo. 18, pl. 12	137
Hil. 4 Edw. III, Eyre of Northampton, 98 Selden Soc.	680
4 Edw. III, Eyre of Derby (unprinted)	clxxxv
5 Edw. III, Lib. Ass., pl. 6	100, 126
Mich. 6 Edw. III, fo. 56, pl. 65	64
Hil. 7 Edw. III, Fitz. Abr., *Quare impedit*, pl. 19	66
Mich. 7 Edw. III, Fitz. Abr., *Assise*, pl. 132	100
7 Edw. III, Lib. Ass., pl. 1	100, 126
Pas. 8 Edw. III, fo. 20, pl. 8	15
Mich. 8 Edw. III, fo. 59, pl. 16	84, 103
8 Edw. III, Lib. Ass., pl. 24	16
Hil. 9 Edw. III, fo. 9, pl. 20	100
Pas. 9 Edw. III, fo. 15, pl. 26	113
Trin. 9 Edw. III, fo. 25, pl. 24	164
Mich. 9 Edw. III, fo. 35, pl. 37.	126
9 Edw. III, Lib. Ass., pl. 24	125, 126
Pas. 10 Edw. III, fo. 26, pl. 52; Fitz. Abr., *Avowrie*, pl. 159	41, 101
Mich. 10 Edw. III, fo. 45, pl. 8; Fitz. Abr., *Resceit*, pl. 40	123
Trin. 11 Edw. III, Fitz. Abr., *Quare impedit*, pl. 157	134
Hil. 12 Edw. III, Fitz. Abr., *Condicion*, pl. 8	47
12 Edw. III, Lib. Ass., pl. 41	36
Trin. 13 Edw. III, Fitz. Abr., *Briefe*, pl. 264	60
Mich. 13 Edw. III, Fitz. Abr., *Estoppell*, pl. 231	9
Pas. 14 Edw. III, Fitz. Abr., *Dett*, pl. 138	91
Trin. 14 Edw. III, Fitz. Abr., *Execucion*, pl. 73	62
15 Edw. III, Lib. Ass., pl. 11	100, 126
Mich. 15 Edw. III, Fitz. Abr., *Execution*, pl. 63	100
Hil. 16 Edw. III, Fitz. Abr., *Continuall claime*, pl. 10	14
Pas. 16 Edw. III, Fitz. Abr., *Graunt*, pl. 56	68
Pas. 16 Edw. III, Fitz. Abr., *Quid juris clamat*, pl. 22	clxxxix
Hil. 17 Edw. III, fo. 75, pl. 112	66
Pas. 17 Edw. III, fo. 29, pl. 28	9
Pas. 17 Edw. III, fo. 29, pl. 30	cxci, cxciii, 116, 123, 132
Trin. 17 Edw. III, fo. 40, pl. 17	134
Mich. 17 Edw. III, fo. 51, pl. 24	125
Mich. 17 Edw. III, fo. 51, pl. 25	67
Mich. 17 Edw. III, fo. 52, pl. 29	100
Mich. 17 Edw. III, fo. 68, pl. 92	137
Hil. 17 Edw. III, fo. 75, pl. 112	66, 67

Mich. 17 Edw. III, fo. 78, pl. 116	125
17 Edw. III, Lib. Ass., pl. 10	100
Trin. 18 Edw. III, fo. 29, pl. 38	62
Mich. 18 Edw. III, fo. 32, pl. 7	126
Mich. 18 Edw. III, fo. 57, pl. 87	64
Mich. 18 Edw. III, fo. 59, pl. 91	clxxxiii, 123, 132
Hil. 19 Edw. III, Fitz. Abr., *Judgement*, pl. 124	67
Hil. 19 Edw. III, Fitz. Abr., *Resceit*, pl. 113	36
Pas. 19 Edw. III, Fitz. Abr., *Graunt*, pl. 58	67
Mich. 20 Edw. III, Fitz. Abr., *Annuitie*, pl. 34	60
Mich. 20 Edw. III, Fitz. Abr., *Quid juris clamat*, pl. 31	clxxxiii
Mich. 21 Edw. III, fo. 60, pl. 7	cxvii
Hil. 22 Edw. III, fo. 2, pl. 11	67, 68
Mich. 22 Edw. III, fo. 16, pl. 63	151
22 Edw. III, Lib. Ass., pl. 13	36
22 Edw. III, Lib. Ass., pl. 34	35
22 Edw. III, Lib. Ass., pl. 37	clxxxiii, 41
22 Edw. III, Lib. Ass., pl. 52	89
22 Edw. III, Lib. Ass., pl. 93	ccxxxi
23 Edw. III, Lib. Ass., pl. 18	108
Mich. 24 Edw. III, fo. 33, pl. 29	38
Mich. 24 Edw. III, fo. 72, pl. 84	38
Mich. 25 Edw. III, fo. 91 (48), pl. 1	79
Hil. 26 Edw. III, fo. 1 (55), pl. 1	139
Hil. 26 Edw. III, fo. 3 (56), pl. 10	106
26 Edw. III, Lib. Ass., pl. 24	cxxiv
Trin. 27 Edw. III, fo. 5, pl. 19	11
Mich. 27 Edw. III, fo. 11, pl. 40; Fitz. Abr., *Age*, pl. 108	
27 Edw. III, Lib. Ass., pl. 31	144
27 Edw. III, Lib. Ass., pl. 60	clxxxvii, 146
Hil. 28 Edw. III, fo. 3	60
Hil. 29 Edw. III, fo. 13, pl. 31	17, 19, 67
Trin. 29 Edw. III, fo. 39; Fitz. Abr., *Grauntes*, pl. 101	100
Trin. 29 Edw. III, fo. 40, pl. [24]	57
Mich. 29 Edw. III, fo. 44, pl. [3]	135
29 Edw. III, Lib. Ass., pl. 34	41
29 Edw. III, Lib. Ass., pl. 55	111
Hil. 30 Edw. III, fo. 5	73
Hil. 31 Edw. III, Fitz. Abr., *Briefe*, pl. 331	99
Hil. 31 Edw. III, Fitz. Abr., *Briefe*, pl. 335	152
Pas. 31 Edw. III, Fitz. Abr., *Garde*, pl. 116	139
Mich. 31 Edw. III, Fitz. Abr., *Saver de defaut*, pl. 37	62
Pas. 32 Edw. III, Fitz. Abr., *Voucher*, pl. 94	63
Hil. 33 Edw. III, Fitz. Abr., *Verdit*, pl. 47	29
34 Edw. III, Lib. Ass., pl. 1	29

34 Edw. III, Lib. Ass., pl. 7	36
37 Edw. III, Lib. Ass., pl. 5	13
Hil. 38 Edw. III, fo. 3	63
Hil. 38 Edw. III, fo. 4	60
Pas. 38 Edw. III, fo. 9	133
Trin. 38 Edw. III, fo. 14	16
Mich. 38 Edw. III, fo. 26	116
Mich. 38 Edw. III, fo. 28	16
Pas. 39 Edw. III, fo. 7	cliv
Mich. 39 Edw. III, fo. 20	88
Mich. 39 Edw. III, fo. 35	151
39 Edw. III, Lib. Ass., pl. 20	21
Hil. 40 Edw. III, fo. 9, pl. 18	clxxxvii, cxc
Trin. 40 Edw. III, fo. 27, pl. 5	66
Mich. 40 Edw. III, fo. 42, pl. 26	76
40 Edw. III, Lib. Ass., pl. 25	cxx
Mich. 41 Edw. III, fo. 17, pl. 2	146
Mich. 41 Edw. III, fo. 21, pl. 7	138
41 Edw. III, Lib. Ass., pl. 19	67
42 Edw. III, Fitz. Abr., *Corone*, pl. 226	12
42 Edw. III, Lib. Ass., pl. 5	cxlvii
42 Edw. III, Lib. Ass., pl. 6	91
42 Edw. III, Lib. Ass., pl. 11	17
42 Edw. III, Lib. Ass., pl. 31	12
Mich. 43 Edw. III, fo. 27, pl. 11, Fitz. Abr., *Audita querela*, pl. 16	62
Mich. 43 Edw. III, fo. 35, pl. 52	138
Hil. 44 Edw. III, fo. 3, pl. 14	63
Pas. 44 Edw. III, fo. 8, pl. 10	91
Mich. 44 Edw. III, fo. 27, pl. 4	93
Pas. 45 Edw. III, fo. 9, pl. 13	11
Mich. 45 Edw. III, Fitz. Abr., *Exchaunge*, pl. 1	60, 64
Mich. 45 Edw. III, Fitz. Abr., *Exchaunge*, pl. 10	112
45 Edw. III, Lib. Ass., pl. 6	64
Hil. 46 Edw. III, Fitz. Abr., *Forfeiture*, pl. 18	155
Trin. 46 Edw. III, fo. 17, pl. 14	124
Trin. 46 Edw. III, fo. 18, pl. 17	clxxxv
Mich. 46 Edw. III, fo. 31, pl. 32	clxxxvi
46 Edw. III, Lib. Ass., pl. 4	66
Hil. 49 Edw. III, fo. 3, pl. 7	146
Hil. 49 Edw. III, fo. 5, pl. 8	63
Pas. 49 Edw. III, fo. 16, pl. 10	121
49 Edw. III, Lib. Ass., pl. 5	92
49 Edw. III, Lib. Ass., pl. 8	16
Mich. 50 Edw. III, fo. 26, pl. 8	66
50 Edw. III, Lib. Ass., pl. 1	clxxxvi, 122

Trin. 2 Ric. II, Fitz. Abr., *Attournement*, pl. 8 106
Mich. 6 Ric. II, Fitz. Abr., *Quid juris clamat*, pl. 20 120
Pas. 11 Ric. II, Fitz. Abr., *Detinue*, pl. 46 123
Pas. 12 Ric. II, Fitz. Abr., *Dower*, pl. 54 clxxix
Trin. 12 Ric. II, Fitz. Abr., *Barre*, pl. 243 124
Mich. 13 Ric. II, Fitz. Abr., *Avowrie*, pl. 89 101
Trin. 19 Ric. II, Fitz. Abr., *Estoppell*, pl. 281 62
Pas. 21 Ric. II, Fitz. Abr., *Devise*, pl. 27 146
Mich. 2 Hen. IV, fo. 8, pl. 38 38
Mich. 2 Hen. IV, fo. 10, pl. 47 67
Pas. 2 Hen. IV, fo. 19, pl. 15 80
Pas. 3 Hen. IV, fo. 15, pl. 8 38
Hil. 5 Hen. IV, fo. 3, pl. 11 clxxxv
Mich. 7 Hen. IV, fo. 4, pl. 26 18
Hil. 7 Hen. IV, fo. 6, pl. 2 123
Hil. 7 Hen. IV, fo. 8, pl. 10 152
Trin. 7 Hen. IV, fo. 16, pl. 9 125
Mich. 7 Hen. IV, fo. 23, pl. 2 clxxxv
Mich. 7 Hen. IV, fo. 32, pl. 19 95
Hil. 8 Hen. IV, fo. 11, pl. 5 clxxxv
Mich. 8 Hen. IV, fo. 15, pl. 17 116
Mich. 11 Hen. IV, fo. 14, pl. 31 cxciii
Mich. 11 Hen. IV, fo. 17, pl. 40 . . . . . . 59, 112
Mich. 11 Hen. IV, fo. 17, pl. 41 12
Mich. 11 Hen. IV, fo. 34, pl. 65 clxxxvii
Hil. 11 Hen. IV, fo. 45, pl. 20 cliii
Hil. 11 Hen. IV, fo. 52, pl. 30 79
Pas. 11 Hen. IV, fo. 55, pl. 1 clxxxv
Trin. 11 Hen. IV, fo. 76, pl. 18 135
Mich. 12 Hen. IV, fo. 1, pl. 3 clxxxv
Mich. 12 Hen. IV, fo. 5, pl. 11 93
Mich. 12 Hen. IV, fo. 11, pl. 21 60
Hil. 12 Hen. IV, fo. 12, pl. 1 42
Hil. 12 Hen. IV, fo. 16, pl. 11 9
Mich. 13 Hen. IV, fo. 6, pl. 13 47
Hil. 13 Hen. IV, fo. 17, pl. 14 11
Hil. 14 Hen. IV, fo. 17, pl. 20 66
Hil. 14 Hen. IV, fo. 19, pl. 21 124
Hil. 14 Hen. IV, fo. 31, pl. 43 clxxxvii
Hil. 1 Hen. V, fo. 1, pl. 2 . . . . 60, 64, 134
Pas. 2 Hen. V, fo. 4, pl. 19 106
Hil. 5 Hen. V, fo. 12, pl. 30 . . . . 11, 106
Hil. 8 Hen. V, fo. 1, pl. 1 106
Mich. 2 Hen. VI, fo. 1, pl. 9 11
Trin. 2 Hen. VI, fo. 15, pl. 16 139

Mich, 3 Hen. VI, fo. 16, pl. 22	93
Hil. 3 Hen. VI, fo. 28, pl. 10	16
Hil. 3 Hen. VI, fo. 33, pl. 26	152
Trin. 3 Hen. VI, fo. 48, pl. 9	77
Trin. 4 Hen. VI, fo. 25, pl. 3	106
Mich. 7 Hen. VI, fo. 1, pl. 6	87
Mich. 7 Hen. VI, fo. 5, pl. 9	17*bis*
Mich. 7 Hen. VI, fo. 7, pl. 10	82, 152
Mich. 7 Hen. VI, fo. 10, pl. '36' [16]	clxxvii, 35
Mich. 7 Hen. VI, fo. 13, pl. 18	16
Pas. 7 Hen. VI, fo. 26, pl. 14	11
Pas. 7 Hen. VI, fo. 35, pl. 39	cliv
Mich. 8 Hen. VI, fo. 6, pl. 15	139
Pas. 9 Hen. VI, fos. 9-10, pl. 26	6
Trin. 9 Hen. VI, fo. 16, pl. 8	66
Trin. 9 Hen. VI, fo. 19, pl. 12	6
Trin. 9 Hen. VI, fo. 23, pl. 19	74, 122, 146
Trin. 9 Hen. VI, fo. 25, pl. 21	106
Trin. 9 Hen. VI, fo. 30, pl. 35	6
Mich. 9 Hen. VI, fo. 32, pl. 2	6
Mich. 9 Hen. VI, fo. 32, pl. 3	135
Trin. 9 Hen. VI, fo. 35, pl. 6	90
Mich. 9 Hen. VI, fo. 53, pl. 36	97
Mich. 10 Hen. VI, fo. 24, pl. 83	81, 127
Mich. 11 Hen. VI, fo. 2, pl. 5	52
Mich. 11 Hen. VI, fo. 3, pl. 8	cliii
Mich. 11 Hen. VI, fo. 12, pl. 28	146
Hil. 11 Hen. VI, fo. 18, pl. 11	67
Pas. 11 Hen. VI, fo. 32, pl. 19	15
Trin. 11 Hen. VI, fo. 51, pl. 13	16
Mich. 16 Hen. VI, Fitz. Abr., *Accion sur le case*, pl. 44	152
Trin. 18 Hen. VI, fo. 12, pl. 1	15
Trin. 18 Hen. VI, fo. 16, pl. 4	15
Mich. 19 Hen. VI, fo. 6, pl. 12	140
Trin. 19 Hen. VI, fo. 22, pl. 17	6
Mich. 19 Hen. VI, fo. 35, pl. 76	12
Mich. 19 Hen. VI, fo. 47, pl. 101	103
Pas. 19 Hen. VI, fo. 62, pl. 1	16
Mich. 20 Hen. VI, fo. 8, pl. 17	72
Pas. 20 Hen. VI, fo. 27, pl. 17	16
Mich. 21 Hen. VI, fo. 4, pl. 8	16
Mich. 21 Hen. VI, fo. 10, pl. 24	125
Hil. 21 Hen. VI, fo. 33, pl. 21	clxi
Pas. 21 Hen. VI, fo. 36, pl. 4	32
Pas. 21 Hen. VI, fo. 46, pl. 23	clxxxi

Mich. 22 Hen. VI, fo. 13, pl. 17	9
Mich. 22 Hen. VI, fo. 24, pl. 45	88
Mich. 22 Hen. VI, fo. 25, pl. 46, Bro. Abr., *Quare impedit*, pl. 83	60, 63, 112
Trin. 22 Hen. VI, fo. 57, pl. 7	11
Hil. 27 Hen. VI, fo. 7, pl. 3	133
Trin. 30 Hen. VI, fo. 6, pl. 5	18
Trin. 30 Hen. VI, Statham Abr., *Devise*	130
Mich. 32 Hen. VI, fo. 14, pl. 21	139
Hil. 32 Hen. VI, fo. 25, pl. 13	cxl
Hil. 33 Hen. VI, fo. 5, pl. 16	clxxxvii
Pas. 33 Hen. VI, fo. 12, pl. 3	63
Trin. 33 Hen. VI, fo. 24, pl. 3	60
Mich. 34 Hen. VI, fo. 14, pl. 27	67
Trin. 37 Hen. VI, fo. 30, pl. 11	146
Mich. 38 Hen. VI, fo. 14, pl. [32] ('14')	60, 63
Hil. 38 Hen. VI, fo. 19, pl. 1	67
Pas. 38 Hen. VI, fo. 29, pl. 12	27
Trin. 38 Hen. VI, fo. 33, pl. 2	63, 84
Mich. 1 Edw. IV, fo. 5, pl. 13	28
Trin. 3 Edw. IV, fo. 1, pl. 1	91
Mich. 3 Edw. IV, fo. 24, pl. 19	80
Mich. 4 Edw. IV, fo. 21, pl. 1	80
Pas. 5 Edw. IV, fo. 2, pl. 10	100
Pas. 5 Edw. IV, fo. 2, pl. 23	cxci
Trin. 5 Edw. IV, fo. 5, pl. 18	27, 103
Pas. 5 Edw. IV, *Long Quinto*, fo. 9	6
Mich. 5 Edw. IV, fo. 7, pl. 16	clxxxix
Mich. 5 Edw. IV, *Long Quinto*, fo. 118, Bro. Abr., *Petition*, pl. 26	95
Mich. 5 Edw. IV, *Long Quinto*, fo. 136, Bro. Abr., *Travers per sans ceo*, pl. 201	6
Pas. 7 Edw. IV, fo. 5, pl. 13	62
Mich. 7 Edw. IV, fo. 19, pl. 17	6
Mich. 8 Edw. IV, fo. 18, pl. 29	16
Trin. 9 Edw. IV, fo. 22, pl. 24	91
Mich. 9 Edw. IV, fo. 43, pl. 30	153
Pas. 10 Edw. IV, fo. 3, pl. 6	122
Trin. 10 Edw. IV, fo. 10, pl. 1	63
Mich. 14 Edw. IV, fo. 1, pl. 1	cliii, cliv
Pas. 14 Edw. IV, fo. 3, pl. 1	17
Mich. 15 Edw. IV, fo. 1, pl. 2	16*bis*
Mich. 15 Edw. IV, fo. 10, pl. 16	40
Mich. 16 Edw. IV, fo. 8, pl. 5	124
Pas. 17 Edw. IV, fo. 1, pl. 2	100
Hil. 18 Edw. IV, fo. 26, pl. 20	6
Mich. 19 Edw. IV, fo. 1, pl. 1	139
Trin. 19 Edw. IV, fo. 11, pl. 19	16

Trin. 20 Edw. IV, fo. 6, pl. 7	67
Mich. 20 Edw. IV, fo. 12, pl. 15	16
Hil. 20 Edw. IV, fo. 18, pl. 8	72
Trin. 20 Edw. IV, fo. 19, pl. 22	28
Pas. 21 Edw. IV, fo. 7, pl. 22	60
Trin. 21 Edw. IV, fo. 37, pl. 3	67
Mich. 21 Edw. IV, fo. 38, pl. 4	91, 140
Mich. 21 Edw. IV, fo. 44, pl. 5	clxxxv
Mich. 21 Edw. IV, fo. 50, pl. 10	101
Mich. 21 Edw. IV, fo. 52, pl. 16	93
Mich. 21 Edw. IV, fo. 53, pl. 20	20
Mich. 21 Edw. IV, fo. 55, pl. 28	16
Mich. 21 Edw. IV, fo. 66, pl. 46	103
Mich. 22 Edw. IV, fo. 34, pl. 13	16
Mich. 2 Ric. III, fo. 7, pl. 13	16
Hil. 2 Ric. III, Fitz. Abr., *Quare impedit*, pl. 102	134
Hil. 1 Hen. VII, Fitz. Abr., *Feffements et faits*, pl. 30	123
Pas. 1 Hen. VII, fo. 17, pl. 3	101
Trin. 1 Hen. VII, fo. 28, pl. 6	123
Hil. 2 Hen. VII, fo. 13, pl. 16	cxciii, 123
Pas. 4 Hen. VII, fo. 7, pl. 6	72
Trin. 4 Hen. VII, fo. 10, pl. 6	142
Mich. 5 Hen. VII, fo. 1, pl. 1	57
Trin. 6 Hen. VII, fo. 4, pl. 3	139
Mich. 6 Hen. VII, fo. 6, pl. 1	139
Mich. 6 Hen. VII, fo. 10, pl. 18	139
Hil. 6 Hen. VII, fo. 13, pl. 2	66
Mich. 7 Hen. VII, fo. 4, pl. 3	139
Trin. 8 Hen. VII, fo. 1, pl. 1	84
Pas. 9 Hen. VII, fo. 25, pl. 11	cxciii
Pas. 9 Hen. VII, fo. 25, pl. 12	101
Mich. 11 Hen. VII, fo. 8, pl. 30	67
Trin. 11 Hen. VII, fo. 25, pl. 5	11
Trin. 12 Hen. VII, fo. 27, pl. 7	clxxxix
Mich. 13 Hen. VII, fo. 9, pl. 5	clxxxix
Hil. 13 Hen. VII, fo. 14, pl. 6	16
Hil. 13 Hen. VII, fo. 17, pl. 22	146
Mich. 14 Hen. VII, fo. 1, pl. 1	19
Mich. 14 Hen. VII, fo. 1, pl. 2	16
Hil. 14 Hen. VII, fo. 17, pl. 7	cliii
Pas. 14 Hen. VII, fo. 21, pl. 4	63
Mich. 15 Hen. VII, fo. 2, pl. 4	127
Trin. 15 Hen. VII, fo. 10, pl. 13	32
Trin. 15 Hen. VII, fo. 10, pl. 16	46
Trin. 15 Hen. VII, fo. 11, pl. 22	146

Mich. 15 Hen. VII, fo. 13, pl. 2	122
Mich. 15 Hen. VII, fo. 14, pl. 5	125
Trin. 16 Hen. VII, fo. 13, pl. 7	147
Hil. 21 Hen. VII, fo. 1, pl. 1	68
Mich. 21 Hen. VII, fo. 30, pl. 9	11
Trin. 22 Hen. VII, Keil. 93, pl. 8	115
Mich, 14 Hen. VIII, fo. 2, pl. 2	16
Mich. 18 Hen. VIII, fo. 5, pl. 18	153
Trin. 19 Hen. VIII, fo. 9, pl. 4	146
24 Hen. VIII, Bro. Abr., *Feffements al uses*, pl. 40	131
Pas. 27 Hen. VIII, fo. 5, pl. 15	56
Pas. 27 Hen. VIII, fo. 9, pl. 22	131
Trin. 27 Hen. VIII, fo. 20, pl. 9	108
Mich. 27 Hen. VIII, fo. 23, pl. 1	30
Mich. 27 Hen. VIII, fo. 24, pl. 3	152
29 Hen. VIII, Bro. Abr., *Faits enrol*, pl. 14	62
29 Hen. VIII, Bro. Abr., *Testament et volunt*, pl. 18	146
30 Hen. VIII, Bro. Abr., *Devise*, pl. 29	78
30 Hen. VIII, Bro. Abr., *Feffements al uses*, pl. 47	115
30 Hen. VIII, Bro. Abr., *Feffements al uses*, pl. 48	108, 131
30 Hen. VIII, Bro. Abr., *Feffements al uses*, pl. 50	107, 119, 121
36 Hen. VIII, Bro. Abr., *Feffements al uses*, pl. 54	118
2 Edw. VI, Bro. Abr., *Testament*, pl. 24	146
Mich. 4 Edw. VI, Bro. Abr., *Estates*, pl. 78	146
5 Edw. VI, Bro. Abr., *Feffements al uses*, pl. 57	121
7 Edw. VI, Bro. Abr., *Devise*, pl. 39	146
3 Mar., Bro. Abr., *Feffements al uses*, pl. 59	121

TABLE OF CASES REPORTED IN VOLUMES I–V

This table does not include anonymous cases or cases which are cited but not reported. Each volume will contain a table of cases cited as well as reported in that volume. This table also includes cases which were in the missing third notebook. References are to the pages where the cases are reported; cross-references and citations to the same cases may be found in the tables of cases in each volume.

Acton v. Hore (1596)	682
Agard qui tam etc. v. Cavendish (1594-99)	579, 1035
Ailmer v. Geale (1588)	385
Albany v. Strelley (1587)	359
Aldham v. Bohun (1596)	731
Alexander's Case (1597)	771
Alford v. Reade (1584)	265
Allen's Case (1587)	346
Alton Woods, Case of (1600)	1061
Ameredith's Case (1598)	862
Amner d. Fulshurst v. Luddington (1584)	167
Anderson v. Sibthorpe (1599)	985
Androwes v. Blunt (1573)	39, 52, 90, 108
Ap Harry v. Morgan (1587)	328
Ap Richard v. Evans (1586)	310
Ap Richard v. Penryn (1597)	830
Ap Thomas v. Hanmer, *see* Thomas v. Hanmer	
Apot's Case (1572)	159
Appulton's Case (1577)	129
Archer's Case (1578)	10, 161
Archer's Case (1597)	818
Armiger v. Holland (1598)	849
Armstrong's Case (1597)	771
Arundel (Earl of) his Case (1581)	175
Arundel (Earl of) his Case (1586)	290
Arundel (Earl of) v. Langar (1576)	32, 37, 70, 80, 94
Arundel (Earl of) v. Lumley (1582)	195
Arundel's Case (1594)	604, 614
Arundell v. Short (1589)	413
Arundell's Case (1587)	324
Arundell's Case, *see also* R. v. Arundell	
Ascough v. Hollingworth (1596)	978
Aston v. Byron (1553/58)	180

Aston v. Whithall (1587)	355
Atmere's Case (1599)	1045
Att.-Gen. v. Brache (1582)	206, 212
Att.-Gen. v. Bushopp (1600)	1061
Att.-Gen. v. Carie and Dodington (1597)	787
Att.-Gen. v. Constable (1578)	151
Att.-Gen. v. Darcy (Lord) (1596, 1598)	616, 722, 897
Att.-Gen. v. Delves (1585)	279
Att.-Gen. v. Dowty (1584)	259
Att.-Gen. v. Englefield (1591)	441
Att.-Gen. v. Framingham (1597)	803
Att.-Gen. v. Heydon (1584)	253
Att.-Gen. v. London (City of) (1596)	671
Att.-Gen. v. Page (1587)	358
Att.-Gen. v. Payne (1593)	550
Att.-Gen. v. Porter (1592)	486
Att.-Gen. v. Smyth (1598)	873, 1043
Att.-Gen. v. Vaughan (Hugh) (1591, 1596)	452
Att.-Gen. v. Vaughan (John Owen) (1597)	699
Att.-Gen. v. Wood (1587)	330
Audley (Lord) his Case (1573)	122
Audley (Lord) v. Audley (1596)	712
Austin d. Austin v. Twyne (1597)	809, 817
Austin v. Baker (1561)	719
Avery d. Kipping v. Bunning (1588)	386
Ayer v. Jenour (1599)	1027
Ayleworth's Case, *see* Harris v. Winge	
Ayscough v. Fulshawe (1592)	470
Ayscough v. Lincoln (Earl of) (1595)	621
Babington v. Warner (1600)	1088
Bacon v. Hill (1596)	712
Bagnold v. Stokes (1588)	360
Baker (Sir John) his Case (1583, 1586)	214, 303
Baker d. Ludlam v. Raymond (1576)	47, 149
Baker v. Smith (1581)	163
Baker's Case (1600)	1085
Baldwyn v. Morton (1598)	909
Baldwyn v. Smith (1597)	818
Baldwyn v. Wyseman (1595)	821
Banastre v. Banastre (1583)	226, 405
Bankrupts, Case of (1589)	405
Baptiste v. Michelborne (1596)	972
Barbour v. Long (1578)	158
Barewell v. Lucas (Bracebridge's Case) (1572/73)	73, 104, 105, 106, 107
Barker v. Long, *see* Barbour v. Long	

Barnard v. Smithe (1594)	590
Barro v. Gray (1597)	979
Barthelett v. Baxter (1583)	243
Barton v. Gellybrond (1583)	227
Barton v. Leigh (1600)	286, 1046
Barton v. Lever (1595)	648
Barwick's Case (1597)	770
Bassett v. Corporation of Torrington (1568)	586
Bassett's Case (1594)	613
Bastard v. Lady Heydon (1595)	625
Bateman d. Hill v. Allen (1595)	959
Baxter v. Barthelett, *see* Barthelett v. Baxter	
Bayne v. Moone (1593)	540
Baynham v. Brooke (1587)	370
Beale v. Carter (1592)	484
Beaumont's Case (1575)	157
Beckwith v. Slingsby (1587)	339
Beckwith's Case, *see* Colgate v. Blyth	
Bedell v. Moore (1588)	394
Bedingfield v. Bedingfield (1586)	300, 302
Bedingfield v. Jakes (1596)	679
Bedingfield v. Leder (1585)	216, 273
Bedingfield v. Pickering (1570)	134
Bedingfield's Case (1592)	481
Bence's Case (1587)	300
Bennet v. Bishop of Norwich (1596)	970
Bereblock v. Reade (1600)	1056
Besbetch v. Scott (1572)	clxxiv
Bettisford v. Ford (1574)	61
Bettisford v. Ford (1596)	678
Beverley v. Cornwall (1586)	309
Bibithe's Case (1597)	753
Biggin's Case (1599)	1005
Birchley's Case (1585)	284
Bird v. Robertes (1582)	184
Birde v. Adams (1589)	911
Birde v. Wilford (1596)	969
Bishop v. Harecourt, *see* Harecourt v. Bysshopp	
Blackaller v. Martin (1575)	82
Bland v. Moseley (1587)	347
Blincoe v. Barkesdale (1597)	925
Blitheman's Case (1591)	406
Blodwell v. Edwardes (1596)	741
Blofield d. Earl of Kent v. Havers (1592)	495
Blomfeild v. Wythe (1598)	944

Bloure v. Willyams (1584)	234
Blumfield's Case (1598)	944
Blytheman v. Blytheman (1593)	513
Boddye v. Hargrave (1599)	1018
Bonyfant v. Greynvyle (1587)	325
Boraston's Case, *see* Hynde d. Brand v. Ambry	
Borough d. Dodington v. Dickes (1582)	193
Boroughe d. Doddington v. Taylor (1596)	685
Boulston v. Hardie (1597)	816
Bouth v. Skevyngton (1595)	633
Bowes v. Leisley (1581)	181
Boyton v. Andrewes and Simpson (1592)	501
Bracebridge's Case, *see* Barewell v. Lucas	
Brache's Case (1582-83)	206, 212
Bradstock's Case (1575)	38
Brandon v. Morist (1590)	1013
Bredon's Case (1597)	819
Brent's Case (1574/75)	9, 85, 107, 109, 115
Brereton v. Evans (1600)	1110
Brett v. Acland, *see* Harvye d. Brett v. Facye	
Bright v. Fort (1595)	964
Broadbridge's Case (1576)	101, 130
Broderers' Company (The), Case of (temp. Eliz.)	77
Brome v Hore (1598)	936
Brooke's Case (1588)	370
Broughton v. Pretty (1600)	1112
Browne (Sir George) his Case (1597)	701, 831
Browne v. Eyre (1598)	941
Browne v. Terry (1596)	815
Browne's Case (1581)	176
Brownloe v. Farre and Mawe (1592)	506
Brudenell's Case, *see* Skydmore v. Brudenell	
Brunker v. Robotoham (1580)	308
Buckbeard's Case (1589)	405, 407
Buckhurst (Lord) v. Fenner (1598)	876
Buckler v. Hardye (1597)	829
Bucknam v. Prymount (1597)	948
Bulkeley v. Wood (1591)	454
Buller v. Sylver (1584)	252
Bullock v. Burdett (1570)	110, 111
Bullock v. Dibley (1594)	565
Bulwer v. Smythe (1583)	238
Bunting v. Leppingwell (1585)	277
Burgh v. Holcroft (1579)	52, 162
Burre's Case (1577)	47

Burton v. Hobart (1591)	450
Bury Grammar School (Governors) v. Cratchroode (1597)	772
Butler v. Baker and Delves (1591)	424
Butler v. Paynter (1593)	561
Butler v. Wallys (1596)	970
Buttell d. Thornhyll v. Wylford (1577)	11, 68, 162, 163
Button v. Dowman (1598)	935
Byrom v. Byrom (1595)	652
Bysshopp v. Harecourt (1592, 1596)	734
Caesar v. Corsini (1593)	560
Caesar v. Dent (1599)	989
Callard d. Callard v. Callard (1594, 1596)	604, 742
Calthorpe's Case (1574)	408
Calthrop's Case (1586)	163
Calverley (Sir George) his Case (1577)	147
Caly's Case (1584)	249
Canterbury (Archbishop of) his Case, *see* Greene v. Balser	
Capell's Case, *see* Hunt v. Gateley	
Carpenter v. Death (1583)	217
Carre (John), Re (1587)	335
Carrington's Case (1589)	405
Carter d. All Souls College v. Lord Cromwell (1591)	592
Carter v. Ringstead (1590)	535
Cater's Case (1582)	205
Cavendish v. Agard (1599)	1035
Cawdrye v. Atton (1595)	617
Cecil (Sir Thomas) his Case (1597)	784
Chaloner v. Cooke (1599)	1000
Chamberlain v. Nichols (1595)	963
Chamberlaine v. Lincoln College, Oxford (1596)	834
Chedington (Rector of) his Case (1598)	951
Chester (County Palatine of), Case of (1595)	631
Cheyne (Lord) his Case (1582)	187
Cheyne (Lord) his Case, *see* Perrot (Sir Thomas) his Case	
Cheyny v. Cheyny and Oxenbridge (1585)	275
Cheyny v. Frankwell (1587)	333
Cheyny's Case (1588)	405
Cholmeley v. Humble (1595)	654, 806
Cholmondley v. Hanmer and Barne (Cholmley's Case) (1597)	758
Chybnale d. Wytton v. Wytton (1588)	375
Chycke's Case, *see* Baker v. Raymond	
Claches's Case, *see* Glover v. Berye	
Clampe d. Clampe v. Clampe (1587)	369
Clarke v. Gape and Babb (1596)	1014
Clarke v. Penyfather (1584)	258, 330

Claypoole v. Carter (1594)	592
Clayton v. Presenham (1585)	286
Clement v. Peers (1582)	183
Clere (Sir Edward) his Case (1599)	1015
Clerke v. Penruddocke (1598)	902
Clifton v. Molyneux (1585)	282
Clifton's Case, *see* Southcote v. Clifton	
Clun v. Pease (1596)	682
Cobb v. Nore (1465)	776
Codwell v. Parker (1593)	544
Colgate v. Blythe (Beckwith's Case) (1585-87)	352, 868
Colier v. Norington (1595)	646
Collard v. Collard, *see* Callard d. Callard v. Callard	
Collett v. Marshe (1594)	577
Collins v. Willis (1600)	1111
Collyer v. Walker (1595)	821
Compton (Lord) v. Egerton (temp. Eliz.)	23
Cooke v. Brombill and Blakewey (1597)	810
Cooke v. Hewke (1582)	281
Cooks' Case (The), *see* Croft v. Howel	
Copleston v. Stowell (1573)	12
Copwood v. Clarke (1572)	58, 103, 108, 110, 133
Corbet's Case, *see* Cooke v. Brombill	
Corbin v. Brown (1599)	967
Corington v. Cadbury (1583)	238
Cornwallis v. Reginam (1583)	209
Costerd v. Wyndeat (1600)	109
Cottington v. Hulett (1587)	341
Cotton v. Venables (1587)	317
Coulter v. Ireland (1598)	937
Coventry's Case (1577)	156
Cowper v. Ashfield (1583)	236
Coxe v. Colson (1595)	1000
Crane v. Broxhole (1572/73)	29
Cranmer v. Cromer (1566)	207, 226
Cranmer's Case, *see* Kyrke d. Cranmer v. Bales	
Creswell v. Holmes (1598)	949
Croft (Sir James) his Case (before 1590)	924
Croft v. Howell (the Cooks' case) (1578)	15
Croker (Elizabeth) her Case (1587)	336
Cromwell (Lord) v. Androwes (1577, 1581)	4, 39, 82, 180
Cromwell (Lord) v. Dennye (1577-82)	27, 103, 191
Croppe v. Hambledon (1586)	298
Crosby v. Willett, *see* Willett v. Crosby	
Crossman and Gyll v. Rede (1588)	398

Crowche's Case (1573)	670
Cullamore's Case (1589)	405
Cutter v. Dixon (1585)	283
Dacre (Lord) his Settlement (1594)	599
Dale (Peter de) his Case (1372)	882
Dalton d. Hubbard v. Hamond (1600)	1106
Damport v. Simpson, *see* Davenport v. Sympson	
Darcy (Francis) his Case (1596)	731
Darcy (Lord) his Case, *see* Att.-Gen v. Darcy (Lord)	
Davenant v. Hurdys (1600)	1057
Davenport v. Sympson (1596)	704
Daver v. Chambers (1584)	251
Davis v. Gardiner (1593)	558
Davyes v. Shurtington (1586)	300
Dawbney v. Gore and Gore (1581)	172, 405
Dawes v. Molyns (1584)	256, 262
Degore v. Rowe (1592)	483
Delapré's Case (1575)	44, 144
Delaware's Case (1575)	25
Dell d. Fanche v. Hygden (1596)	681
Denby v. Heathcott (1585)	275
Denham v. Dorman (temp. Eliz.)	122
Denny v. Turnour (1587)	356
Derby (Countess of) her Case (1595)	964
Derby (Earl of) his Case (1598)	886
Devon (Earl of) his Case (1596)	692
Dicons v. Marshe (1593)	875
Digby (Lady) her Case (1594)	574
Digby's Case (1599)	960
Digges v. Palmer (1600)	1082
Dimes' Case (1574)	28
Dineley v. Assheton (1581)	61, 128, 162, 895
Dixie v. Spencer (1587)	319
Docton v. Prust (1588)	390
Dodge v. Cooke (1582)	196
Dormer v. Yorke (1593)	533
Dorrell v. Colyns (1577)	51, 97
Doughty v. Drake (1582)	185, 243
Dove v. Chambers (1584)	251
Dowce v. Sutton (1583)	244
Downe v. Hopkins (1594)	585
Downhale v. Catesby (1598)	943
Downing v. Franklyn and Eden (1593)	621
Doyle v. Manning (1583)	232
Drake (Sir Francis) his Case, *see* Doughty v. Drake	

Draper's Case (1586)	303
Drewe and Williams v. Williams, *see* Williams v. Williams	
Drury v. Cordra (1585)	271
Drury v. Leventhorpe (1582)	158, 163
Drywood v. Appleton (1600)	1059
Duke's Case, *see* Ryngrose d. Leson v. Prest	
Dun d. Sleford v. Lawe (1593)	541
Dunstable Corporation, Case of (1598)	927
Dyer (Chief Justice) his Lease (1581)	171
Dyott v. Shepperde (1582)	201
Eare v. Snowe (1578)	133
East and Skydmore v. Vanden Steene (1587)	331
Eaton and Monoxe v. Lawghter (1595)	626
Eaton v. Allen, *see* Eyton v. Allen	
Eccleston and Ireland v. Tuchett (1576)	8
Ede v. Knottisford (1598)	940
Eden and Franklyn v. Browne (1594)	602
Eden v. Harris (1576)	86, 87
Edolfe's Case (1579)	167
Edwardes v. Holmeden (1592)	595
Ellis v. Vavasour (1573)	136, 137
Elmer v. Geale, *see* Ailmer v. Geale	
Elmer v. Thatcher (1591)	457
Ely (Bishop of) his Case (1596)	670
Englebert v. Jones (1588)	387
Essex (Countess of) her Case (1577)	106
Essex (Earl) his Case (1600)	1097
Eve and Finch v. Tracy (1587)	341
Ewer v. Heydon (1596)	180
Exeter (Marquess of) his Case (1593)	552, 692
Eyston d. Latton v. Studde (Latton's Case) (1575)	25, 30, 155, 157
Eyton v. Allen (1599)	1002
Farmer v. Brookes (1590)	406
Farmor v. Savage (1583)	216
Farrand d. Owen v. Ramsey (1579)	147
Fenner v. Fysher (1592)	500
Fenwycke v. Mytfourth (1590)	527
Ferrers v. Arden (1599)	1029
Ferrers v. Oughton (1596)	663
Fettiplace's Case (1597)	755
Finch d. Heneage v. Throckmorton (1590-94)	406, 598
Finch v. Finch (1598)	923
Finch v. Risley, *see* Finch d. Heneage v. Throckmorton	
Fineux v. Hovenden (1599)	1011
Fisher v. Boys (1587)	365

Fisher v. Truslove (1596)	823
Fitch v. Hockley (1595)	999
Fitzherbert's Case (1596)	718
Fitzwilliam v. Copley (1571)	159
Fitzwilliam's Case (1593)	509
Fleming (Sir Francis) his Case (1574)	110
Floud v. Perrot, see Lloyd v. Perrot	
Foiston v. Crachrood (1587)	354
Ford v. Gardiner (1582)	194
Fortescue's Case, see Knyght d. Fortescue v. Breche	
Foster and Milles v. Sponer and Ford (1586)	311
Foster and Pecock v. Lennard (1584)	262
Fox v. Collier (c. 1579)	143
Foxley v. Ansley (1599)	1022
Frampton v. Stiles (1596)	675
Franklyn v. Davison (1571)	93
Freeman v. Drewe (1588)	463
Freeman's Case (1599)	979
French v. Burrell (1582)	201
Friendship v. Cole (1584)	258
Frost v. Sheriffs of London (1599)	1008
Fuller v. Fuller (1595)	827
Fulwood v. Ward (1593)	519
Futter v. Clements and Whiskard (1593)	531
Fyton v. Hall (1596)	832
Gage v. Tawyer (1599)	1006
Gallys v. Burbry (1587)	350
Gardiner v. Bredon (1597)	819
Garforde v. Graye (1594)	586
Garnon's Case (1599)	1017
Garnons v. Hereford (1600)	1082
Gawdy (Thomas) his Case (1583)	242
Germyn v. Arscott (1595)	652
Gervois's Case (1589)	405
Gibbons d. Peacock v. Maltywarde and Martyn (1592)	492
Gibson v. Thorpnell (1580)	170
Giles v. Colshill, see Gyles v. Colshill	
Giles v. Wescot (1596)	965
Gloucester (Bishop of) and Savacre v. Reginam (1588, 1592)	391, 482
Gloucester (Dean and Chapter of) their Case (1573)	92
Glover v. Berye (Clache's Case) (1574)	22, 131, 145
Goddard v. Denton (1584)	918
Gomersall v. Gomersall (1586)	311
Gooch's Case (1590)	406
Goodale v. Butler (1598)	879

Goodall d. Goodall v. Wyat (1595)	781
Goodwyn v. Franklyn (1585)	274
Goodwyn v. Wolnaughe and Owles (1592)	505
Gorge (Ambrosia) her Case (1598, 1600)	938, 1058
Goring (Sir George) his Case (1600)	1087
Gosling v. Harrison (1583)	209
Goughe v. Bybeth (1597)	753
Gravenor v. Tedd (1593)	546
Gray v. Fletcher (1595)	630
Gray v. Pawlet (1594)	609
Green's Case (c. 1568)	231
Greene v. Balser (1596)	693
Greene v. Buffkyn (1596)	697
Greene v. Harrison (1598)	907
Gregorie v. Oldburie (1598)	948
Gregory v. Blashfield (1596)	976
Grendon v. Dean of Worcester (1577)	3, 64, 77
Grene v. Hunne (1599)	1029
Gresham (Lady) her Case (1589)	405
Gresham (Lady) v. Markham and Booth (1595)	647
Gresham (Lady) v. Vaughan (1582)	189
Gresham v. Digby (1586)	289
Gresley's Case (before 1596)	705
Grevill v. Trott (1596)	690
Grey's Case (1596)	697
Grilles v. Rydgway (1594)	588
Grimsby v. Eyre (1456)	883
Grisman v Lewes (1595)	963
Grute v. Locrofte (1592)	615
Gurney d. Gurney v. Seare (1583)	240
Gurney v. Seare, see also Seare v. Gurney	
Gyles v. Colshill (1576)	35, 63, 112, 134, 135, 150, 157, 164
Haddon v. Arrowsmith (1596)	685
Haddon's Case, see Mannyng v. Androwes	
Hall d. Dodyngton v. Pearte (1594)	609
Hall v. Digby (c. 1582)	289
Hall v. Jones (1600)	1107
Hall v. Mather (1600)	1113
Hall v. Vaughan (1595)	828
Hall v. Wingate (1587)	348
Hallings v. Connard (1596)	734
Halswell v. Borough of Bridgwater (1583)	636
Hamond v. Griffites (1598)	876
Hamond's Case (1590)	405
Hanmer v. Thomas (1596)	981

Harbert's Case (1585)	276
Hare v. Byckley (1578)	32, 59, 112
Harecourt v Bysshopp (1592)	470, 734
Hargrave's Case (1599)	1018
Harris d. Doddington v. Winge (1591)	405, 420
Harris v. Jaye (1599)	1010
Harris v. Venables (1587)	322
Hartupp's Case (1591)	406
Harvy d. Pennant v. Owsolde (1597)	766
Harvy v. Wrote (1599)	991
Harvye d. Brett v. Facye (1594)	725
Hasilrig v. Grey (1580)	174
Hatton (Sir Christopher) his Case (1597)	754
Hatton (Sir William) his Case (1593)	703
Hawes v. Smith (1588)	370
Hawkins v. Franke (1576)	622
Hawkins' Case (1587)	317
Hawles's Case (temp. Eliz.)	86
Hayward (Sir Rowland) his Case (1595)	624
Hayward v. Bettysworth (1598)	907
Heddy v. Wheelowes (1597)	804
Hegge v. Crosse, see Hogge v. Crosse	
Heigham v. Best (1594)	969
Hemsley d. Armstronge v. Brice (1598)	944
Henstead's Case (1594)	998
Herbert v. Reginam (1585)	276
Herbert v. Walkeley (1593)	990
Herlakenden's Case (1589)	405
Herlizoun (William) his Case (1340)	886
Hext v. Yeomans (1585)	622
Heydon v. Heydon (1597)	768
Heydon's Case, see Att.-Gen. v. Heydon	
Higges d. Lord Windsor v. Burre (1580)	958
Higham d. Buttery v. Harewood (1586)	294
Highgate v. Jefferson (1595)	626
Hill v. Castle (1582)	198
Hill v. Upcher (1587)	327
Hill's Case (1577)	49
Hinde v. Lyons (1578)	149
Hitchcock v. Skynner and Catcher (1594)	578
Hobart v. Hammond (1600)	1106
Hobbes v. Clerke (1591)	406
Hoddes v. Stone (1585)	281
Hodges v. Newcomin (1588)	392
Hody d. Brent v. Gilbert, see Brent's Case	

Hoe v. Boulton (1600)	1089
Hoe's Case, *see* Hoo v. Marshall	
Hogge d. Ryce v. Crosse (1591)	411
Holcroft's Case (1578)	162
Holcroft's Case (1590)	406
Holland's Case (1598)	849
Holme v. Taylor ('Facie') (1581)	176
Holt v. Hill (1586)	305
Hone v. May (1599)	994
Hoo v. Marshall (1597)	805
Hoo v. Tayler (1596)	825
Houghton v. Marwood (1583)	231
Huddye v. Fisher (1586)	285
Hughes v. Robothome (1593)	236, 524
Hume v. Ogle (1590)	406
Humphreston's Case ('seniori puero') (1575)	24, 35, 40, 101, 107, 108, 110, 114, 122, 123, 129, 137
Hunt v. Bushey (1586)	310
Hunt v. Gateley (1583, 1592)	246, 485
Hunt v. Michellot (1597)	747
Hunt v. Singleton (1597)	1001
Huntingdon (Earl of) v. Lord Mountjoy (1583, 1586)	214, 303
Hurdeman v. Cadwallader (1584)	256
Hurleston v. Reginam (1587)	320
Hyde v. Corriet and Baillie (1594)	607
Hyde v. Windsor (Dean and Canons of) (1599)	980
Hynde d. Brand v. Ambry (1593)	525
Hysson v. Masterson (1596)	978
Isod (Nicholas) his Case (1591)	254, 478
Ive v. Awbrey (1595)	620
Ive v. Sammes (1597)	833
Ive v. Tracy, *see* Eve and Finch v. Tracy	
Ive's Case (1591)	452
Ivy v. Herlakenden (1589)	405
Jackson d. Mosier v. Neale (1595)	809
Jackson v. Darcy (1575)	13, 21, 61
James v. Rutleeche (1599)	1016
Jeffrey v. Kenshley and Foster (1591)	422
Jenninges v. Bragge (1595)	973
Johnson v. Aubrey (1599)	982
Julio (Dr) his Case (1578)	86
Junynge v. Love (1587)	327
Kendall v. Helyer (1583)	237
Kettle v. Mason and Esterley (1594)	580
King v. Robinson, *see* Kynge v. Robinson	

Kirkeby v. Thornorough (1579-80) 3, 157
Knevitt v. Poole (1596) 686
Knight v. Breche, *see* Knyght d. Fortescue v. Breche
Knight v. Winscombe (1584) 261
Knightley v. Spencer (1592) 690
Knyght d. Fortescue v. Breche (1584, 1588) . . 269, 353, 870
Knyvet v. Poole, *see* Knevitt v. Poole
Kynge v. Robinson (1587) 355
Kyrke d. Cranmer v. Bales (Cranmer's Case) (1572) . . 21, 58, 78, 85, 123, 129, 131, 144
Lacy's Case, *see* R. v. Lacy and Lacy
Lambe v. Brownwent (1599) 1028
Lancastell v. Aller (1577) 84, 109
Lane v. Cowper, *see* Humphreston's Case
Latton's Case (1582) 194
Latton's Case, *see* Eyston d. Latton v. Studde
Laughton's Case (1595) 617
Launceston (Mayor etc.) v. Barne (1587) 357
Launde d. Dennys v. Tooker (1591) 412
Leake v. Randall (1596) 705
Leat v. Jenning, *see* Junynge v. Love
Leche v. Cole (1599) 988
Lee (Humphrey) his Case (1597) 810
Lee v. Colshill (1597) 796
Leicester (Earl of) his Case (temp. Eliz.) 7
Leighton v. Garnons (1599) 1017
Lennox (Countess of) her Case (*c.* 1576) 62
Lepur v. Wroth (1586) 389
Lewis's Case (1581) 174
Lichfield and Coventry (Bishop of) his Case (1590) . . . 405
Lincoln (Earl of) his Case (1577) 50
Lincoln (Earl of) v. Countess of Lincoln (1586) . . . 291
Littleton v. Lord Dudley (1596) 662
Lloyd d. Roberts v. Wilkinson (1598) 951
Lloyd v. Perrot (1585) 273
Lodge's Case (1573) 28
London (Chamberlain) his Case (1590) 1013
London (City of) v. Tyler (1596) 675
London's Case (*c.* 1590) 462
Longford v. Barnard (1596) 687
Loveday's Case (1582) 195
Lovelace v. Lovelace (1584) 920
Lovelace v. Ranoldes (1597) 630
Lovelace's Case (1579) 160
Lovell (Lord) his Case, *see* Nichols v. Nichols

Lowen v. Cockes (1599)	1021
Lucrofte v. Grute, *see* Grute v. Locrofte	
Luddington v. Amner (1584)	167, 319
Lybb v. Hynde (1592)	602
Lynch d. Browne v. Spencer (1596, 1597)	701, 831
Mallorie v. Jennynges (1600)	1103
Man (Isle of), Case of (1596, 1598)	667, 880, 886
Mannyng v. Androwes (Haddon's Case) (1576)	21, 58, 78, 110, 118
Manser v. Annesley (1575)	17, 25
Manser's Case (1584)	916
Mariott v. Smith (1598)	853
Marke v. Mathewe (1583)	226
Marowe v. Turpyn (1599)	1018
Marshall v. Lord Dacre (1593)	540
Marshe v. Archbishop of Canterbury (1581)	176
Marshe v. Collett (1594)	577
Marshe v. Dicons (1593)	875
Marshe's Case (1591)	456
Maryott d. Fanshawe v. Pascall (1588)	391
Mathewe d. Robotham v. Curle (1586)	308
Mathewson v. Lidyate (1597)	816
Matthew v. Straunsham (1585)	285
Mayne v. Scott (1596)	704
Maynye v. Maynye (1586)	302
Mayowe's Case, *see* Kettle v. Mason and Esterley	
Meares v. St John (1595)	648
Melwiche d. Melwiche v. Luter (1588)	374
Menville (Ninian) his Case (1585)	266
Mere v. Knyght (1578)	623
Meredith's Case (1587)	338
Meredith's Case (1595)	616
Mervin v. Maynard (1595)	958
Michelborne v. Baptiste (1596)	972
Middlemore v. Warlowe (1588)	388
Middleton d. Rogers v. Baker (1600)	1085
Mildmay (Anthony) his Case (1585)	912
Mildmay (Sir Walter) his Case (1597)	787
Mildmay's Case (1589)	405
Mitton's Case (1584)	252
Moleyns (Sir John) his Case (1598)	860
Monday v. Martin (1599)	1009
Moore v. Bedell, *see* Bedell v. Moore	
Moore v. Rowsewell (1593)	521
Mordaunt (Lord) v. Bridges (1594)	586
Mordaunt (Lord) v. Vaux (1593)	516

More v. Farrand (1584)	255
Morgan v. Griffith (1575)	482
Morrice v. Maule (1588)	405
Morrice's Case (1585)	975
Morris v. Eaton (1588)	405
Mounson (Serjeant), Re (1584)	266
Moyse d. Gilbert v. Grigg (1600)	1092
Multon v. Coveney (Wyatt's Case) (1576)	49, 79, 89, 93, 94, 95, 96, 101, 139
Muncke v. Phillipps (1582)	185
Muriell d. Lane v. Smithe (1591)	412
Muschampe v. Reade (1593)	515
Mynne v. Grey (1572)	64
Nayler v. Partheriche (1597)	837
Nedham v. Beaumont (1590)	469
Nelson and Bugge v. Woodward (1593)	520
Nevill v. Barrington, *see* Sale d. Nevill v. Barrington	
Nichols v. Chamberlain (Nchols's Case) (1595)	963
Nichols v. Nichols (Lovell's Case) (1574)	22, 45, 94, 130, 132, 138
Nichols' Case (*c.* 1567)	702
Nokes v. James (1599)	1007
Norreys (Lord) v. Barret (1597)	1034
Northumberland (Countess) her Case (1597)	832
Norton v. Rowland (1592)	464
Norwich (Bishop of) his Case (1576)	38
Norwich (Dean and Chapter of) their Case (1594)	572
Norwich (Dean and Chapter) their Case (1597, 1598)	843, 928
Norwich, St Giles Hospital in, Case of (1597)	842
Offley and Saltingstall v. Paine (1591)	456
Ogle's Case (1590)	406
Ognel v. Underhill (1587)	106, 161
Oland v. Burdwicke (1596)	973
Onley v. Earl of Kent (1577)	20, 118, 124, 127, 152, 408
Osborne's Case (1592)	506
Owen (Mr Justice) his Case (1587)	769
Owen v. Morgan (1587)	371
Oxford v. Crosse (1599)	1011
Page v. Griffin (1590)	405
Paget (Lord) his Case (1579)	884
Paget (Lord) his Case (1583)	660
Paget (Lord) his Case (1591, 1592, 1595)	406, 408, 468, 616
Paget v. Cary (1593)	562
Palmer d. Hanger v. Humfrey (1597)	778
Pancefoote v. Blount (1593)	563
Parker v. Clere (1599)	1015
Parker v. Harward (1598)	879

Parlet v. Gray (1594)	609
Parr (Lord) his Case (1576)	126
Parrot (Sir John) his Case, *see* Lloyd v. Perrot	
Partheriche v. Nayler (1597)	837
Partridge v. Poole (1584)	255
Paston v. Drewry (1582)	104, 190
Pawle v. Major (1587)	342
Pawlet (Sir Thomas) his Case, *see* Brent's Case	
Payne's Case (temp. Eliz.)	161
Payne's Case, *see also* Att.-Gen. v. Payne	
Paynter v. Manser (1584)	916
Pecksall's Case (1572)	49
Peers v. Clement (1582)	183
Pelham (Sir William) his Case (1590)	405
Pelham v. Bowes (1583)	229
Pembroke (Earl of) v. Berkeley (1593-1596)	544, 664, 959
Pembroke (Earl of) v. Symes (1600)	1101
Pennant's Case (1597)	766
Penruddock v. Clerke (1598)	902
Penryn's Case (1597)	830
Percy v. Bridges (1582)	203
Perkyn v. Comberford (1599)	1026
Perman v. Bower (1599)	996
Perrot (John) his Case (1584)	164, 266
Perrot (Sir Thomas) his Case (1591)	450
Perrot v. Mathew (1588)	372
Perryman's Case (1599)	996
Pettywade v. Cooke (1587)	317
Phelipps v. Badby (1582)	193
Pickering's Case, *see* Bedingfield v. Pickering	
Pigot v. Garnishe (1599)	1003
Pigot v. Gascoigne and Furthoe (1598)	844
Pigott v. Sympson (1600)	1091
Pilkington v. Winnington, *see* Pylkyngton v. Wynnyngton	
Playter v. Warne (1583)	230
Porter's Case, *see* Att.-Gen. v. Porter	
Portman v. Montgomery (1598)	943
Portman v. Willes (1596)	734
Powell v. Monoux, *see* Winter's Case	
Powis (Lord) his Case, *see* Vernon's Case (1581)	
Pratt v. Russell (1588)	401
Preston v. Tooley (1587)	353
Prichard v. Evans, *see* Ap Richard v. Evans	
Prince's Case (1599)	1020
Prouse v. Cave (1588)	390

Prynce v. Sympson (1599)	1020
Purseglove d. Molineux v. Parker (1600)	1052
Purslowe's Case (1581)	177
Puttenham v. Duncombe (1558)	39, 55
Pygott v. Russell (1588)	529
Pylkington v. Wynnyngton (1598)	933
Radcliffe's Case (temp. Eliz.)	39
Radford (Thomas) his Case (1569)	631
Ramsey (Abbot) his Case (1369)	881
Ramsey's Case, see Farrand d. Owen v. Ramsey	
Randall v. Browne (1581)	177
Randes d. Artys v. Warden and Eade (1588)	382
Rasyn v. Ruddocke (1599)	982
Ratcliffe's Case (1592)	464
Rawlyns and Rawlyns v. Somerford (1587)	344, 373
Rawlyns v. Swynnerton (1585)	272
Raynolde v. Kingman (1588)	399
Reade v. Armiger (1599)	1031
R. v. Archer (1587)	367
R. v. Arundell (John) (1594)	596
R. v. Atmere (1599)	1045
R. v. Blanchell (1587)	338
R. v. Bradshaw, Burton and Bompas (1597)	756
R. v. Coventry (Bishop of) (1583)	235
R. v. Da Gama (1594)	571
R. v. Dacre (1593)	557
R. v. Flower (1597)	951
R. v. Heydon (James) (1586)	305, 306
R. v. King (1588)	362
R. v. Lacy and Lacy (1582, 1583)	218
R. v. Lassington (1600)	1061
R. v. Lincoln (Bishop) and Hussey (1599)	968
R. v. Lopez (1594)	569
R. v. Mary, Queen of Scots (1571)	566
R. v. Menvile (1584)	264
R. v. Moore (1593)	536
R. v. Morgan (1588)	381
R. v. O'Cullen (1594)	569
R. v. O'Rourke (1591)	566, 1113
R. v. Paston (Edmund) (1584)	25
R. v. Penry (1593)	535
R. v. Perrot (1592)	566
R. v. Plowden (1594)	597
R. v. Smith (1588)	361
R. v. Tinoco (1594)	571

R. v. Trugeon (1578)	51, 97
R. v. Vaux (1591)	406
R. v. Walker (1599)	1004
R. v. Wall (1598)	906
R. v. Winchester (Marquess of) (1583)	221
R. v. Wirrall and Bosvyle (1599)	965
R. v. Wood (1579)	55
R. v. Wurrall (1593)	536
R. v. Young and Sanger (1592)	475
R. v. Young, Garland and others (1586)	290, 300, 304
Reynold's Case (1585)	361
Reynolds v. Clayton (1596)	687
Reynolds v. Kingman (1588)	399
Reynolds, *see also* Raynolde	
Richard v. Evans, *see* Ap Richard v. Evans	
Richardson d. Fanne v. Yeardley (1595)	959
Richmond v. Butcher (1591)	908
Ridyare's Case (before 1596)	705
Robyns d. Wickham v. Gerrard and Prynce (1599)	960
Rolfe v. Rolfe (1582)	198
Rolfe's Case (undated)	117
Rookes v. Withers (1598)	844
Roos v. Aldwick (1596)	698, 1028
Rosewel's Case, *see* Moore v. Rosewell	
Rosse v. Serle (1596)	671
Rosse's Case, *see* Roos v. Aldwick	
Rous v. Artys (1587)	329
Rous v. Gooch (1590)	406
Rowe v. White (1596)	981
Rowland v. James and Sherive (1593)	545
Rudde v. Topfield (1600)	1108
Ruddocke v. Rasyn (1599)	982
Rudhall v. Myller (1584)	866, 922
Rush v. Heighgate (1588)	405
Russell v. Handford (1583)	233
Russell v. Pratt (1584, 1588)	250
Rutland (Countess of) her Case (1592, King's Bench)	504
Rutland (Countess of) her Case (1592, Wards)	507
Rutland (Earl of) his Case (1577, 1579)	12, 166
Rutland (Earl of) v. Markham (*c.* 1579)	7
Ryngrose d. Leson v. Prest (Duke's Case) (1573)	57
St Giles Hospital, Norwich (Case of) (1597)	842
St Paul's (Dean of) his Case, *see* Buttell v. Wylford	
Sale d. Nevill v. Barrington (1596)	698
Sale v. Bishop of Lichfield and Coventry (1590)	495

Samon v. Pytt (1595)	658
Sampson v Worthington (1600)	1061
Sandes v. Wingate (1582)	203
Saunders v. Knight (1599)	1002
Saunders v. Lord Lumley (1597)	748
Saunders v. Marwood (1599)	995
Saunton v. Merewether (1599)	990
Savacre v. Reginam, *see* Gloucester (Bishop of) and Savacre v. Reginam	
Savage (Sir John) his Case (1600)	1045
Savage v. Chester (1576)	100
Savery's Case, *see* Blackaller v. Martin	
Savile v. Reginam (1584, 1585)	268, 285
Savill v. Wood (1587)	365
Sawyer d. Sawyer v. Hardye (1597)	826
Scott v. Mayne (1596)	704
Scott v. Scott (1584)	263
Scovell d. Payne v. Cabell (1588)	400
Seare v. Gurney (1584)	247
Seniori Puero, Case de, *see* Humphreston's Case	
Serjeants' Case (The) (1579)	128, 156, 159, 162
Serjeants' Case (The) (1582), *see* Muncke v. Phillipps	
Serle v. Rosse (1596)	671
Shane's Case (1596)	668
Sharington's Case (1585)	912
Sharpe v. Purslowe (1588)	393
Sharpe v. Sharpe and Swanne (1600)	1060
Shawe v. Tompson (1595)	831
Shawe v. Whorewood (1599)	1024
Sheldon v. Gilbert (1574)	78
Shelley (Mrs) her Case (1593)	513
Shelton's Case (1583)	229
Sherington v. Fletewood (1596)	699, 968
Sherly v. Clifton (1600)	1106
Sherpe v. Purslowe, *see* Sharpe v. Purslowe	
Sherwood v. Winchcombe (1593)	515
Shirland v. White (1584)	354
Short v. Arundell (1589)	413
Shrewsbury (Countess) v. Crompton (1600)	1100
Shrewsbury (Earl of) his Case (1597)	754
Shrewsbury (Earl) his Case (1598)	945
Shuckburgh v. Byggyn (1599)	1005
Simpson d. Bendlowes v. Titterell (1592)	472
Skalehorne v. Harrison (1599)	1032
Skydmore v. Brudenell (1592)	480
Slanning v. Fitz (1600)	1111

Slifield's Case (1600)	1111
Slingsby v. Beckwith (1587)	339
Smith (John, attorney) his Case (1600)	1048
Smith (Thomas, customer) his Case (1598, 1599), *see* Att.-Gen. v. Smyth	
Smith v. Howe and Redman (1587)	338
Smith v. Morris (Morrice's Case) (1585)	975
Smith, Cullamor and others v. Mills (1589)	405
Smith's Case (1593)	550
Smithe v. Barnard (1594)	590
Smyth v. Clarke (1592)	467
Smythe v. Bonsall (1597)	814
Smythe v. Freeman (1599)	979
Smythe v. Shepperde (1599)	1023
Snagge v. Gee (1597)	963
Snelling v. Norton (1595)	824
Some's Case (1583)	155, 232
Somerford v. Rawlyns (1588)	344, 373
Soulle v. Garrard (1596)	835
Southcote v. Clifton (1593)	561
Southwell College, Case of (1587)	337
Southwell v. Warde (1595)	688
Sparke v. Sparke (1599)	986
Spell d. Cromwell v. Androwes (1577)	4, 99
Spell d. Cromwell v. Nedeham (1579)	4, 5
Spencer v. Clarke (1583)	210
Sprake d. Sprake v. Sprake (1599)	981
Stafford v. Higginbothome (1593)	530
Standen v. Bullocke (1597, 1600)	754, 1093
Standyshe v. Mildmay (1585)	912
Stanhope v. Blithe (1585)	622
Staunton d. Staunton v. Barnes (1594)	613
Stepneth v. Lloyd (1598)	950
Stone v. Withipole (1588)	403
Strata Marcella (Abbey of), Case of (1597)	743
Strelley v. Albany (1587)	359
Stubbe v. Rightwise (1588)	377
Style v. Butt (1595)	962
Swans, Case of, *see* R. v. Young and Sanger	
Symes's Case (1596)	670
Symons d. Fitzherbert v. Hawksworth and Bamford (1595)	718
Taverner v. Cromwell (1584)	257
Tayler v. Moore (1586)	287
Taylor v. Sawyer (1600)	1051
Tayre v. Pepyat (1584)	367
Thetford v. Thetford (1590)	405

Thirkettle v. Reve and Tye (1588) 399
Thomas v. Hanmer (1596) 981
Thornhill v. Atmer (1600) 1090
Thoroughgood's Case, *see* Throughgood v. Cole
Throckmorton v. Finch (Chancery, 1597) 797
Throckmorton v. Finch (Exch. Ch., 1594) 598
Throughgood v. Cole (1583) 915
Tomlinson v. De Vale (1594) 595
Tooley v. Preston (1587) 353
Toppe v. Eden (1575) 145
Townshend d. Howes v. Wales (1595) 595
Tregeon's Case, *see* R. v. Trugeon; Trugeon's Case
Treport's Case (1594) 600
Tresham's Case (1576) 138
Tresham's Case (1591) 406
Trevilian d. Trevilian v. Leyne (1587) 326
Trott's Case (1590, 1592) 406, 467
Trudgin's Case, *see* R. v. Trugeon; Trugeon's Case
Trugeon's Case (1579) 52, 96
Turner's Case (1585) 272
Turnor v. Andrews (1579) 797
Unwell v. Lodge (1580) 168
Vaughan's Case (1593) 562
Vaughan's Case (1595) 828
Vaux v. Brooke (1586) 287
Veale v. Reade (1599) 997
Vere v. Jeffrey (1580) 169
Vernon v. Stanley and Manners (1572) 13, 36, 128, 141, 159
Vernon v. Vernon (1573) 75, 98, 130, 157, 160
Vernon's Case (1581) 173
Vincent v. Ashby (1582) 192
Vincent v. Lece (1584) 249
Vines v. Dinham (1581) 171
Vowe d. Vowe v. Smythe (1580) 643, 705
Walcott v. Apowell (1588) 389
Walker v. Collyer (1595) 821
Walker v. Harris (1587) 316
Waltham v. Austen (1599) 1007
Warde v. Lambard (1597) 808
Waring's Case (1574) 159
Warner v. Fletewood (1599) 1021
Watkins v. Astwick (1586) 288
Wattes v. Braynes (1600) 1085
Weaver v. Cariden (1595) 622
Webber d. Bury v. Bury (1598) 942

TABLE OF CASES REPORTED IN VOLUMES I–IV

Welden v. Bridgewater (1595)	826
Wellock v. Hammond (1590)	405
Weltden v. Elkington (1578)	56, 96, 150
Wentworth (Lord) his Case (1586)	313
Wentworth v. Bishop of Lincoln and Wright (1597)	836
Wentworth v. Tailour (1600)	1092
West v. Stowell (1577)	20
Westbie v. Skynner and Catcher (1595)	822
Westby's Case (1597)	822
Westmoreland (Earl) his Case (1598)	864
Westwick v. Wyer (1591)	453
Wetherell v. Darby (1593)	521
Wharton v. Morley (*c.* 1565)	233
Whitby Haven, Re (1584)	248
White v. West (1599)	1025
Whitestones v. Hickford (1594)	583
Whithall v. Aston (1587)	355
Whoper v. Harewood (1574)	27
Widdowson v. Clerke (1587)	357
Wigley v. Blackwall (1600)	1115
Wikes v. Fermor (1599)	984
Wikes v. Martyn (1585)	279
Wikes v. Tillerd (1597)	777
Wilcockes v. Watson (1595)	624
Wilde's Case, *see* Richardson v. Yeardley	
Wilford v. Birde (1596)	969
Wilkins' Case (1582)	188
Willett v. Crosby (1583)	246
Williams v. Blower (15830	234
Williams v. Drewe (*c.* 1590)	538
Williams v. Jones (1592)	498
Williams v. Williams (1593, 1599)	538, 992
Wilmot v. Cottle (1587)	362
Wilshire's Case (temp. Eliz.)	104
Wilson v. Lady Gresham (1588)	398
Wilson v. Packnam (1596)	977
Winchester (Bishop of) his Case, *see* Wright v. Wright	
Winchester (Marquess) v. Powlett (1599)	1012
Windsor v. Archbishop of Canterbury and Fletcher (1599)	
Windsor (Dean and Canons) v. Hyde (1599)	980
Wingate v. Hall (1587)	348
Winnington's Case, *see* Pylkington v. Wynnyngton	
Winter's Case (1572)	26, 43, 81, 99, 114, 125, 126, 136, 160
Wirrall's Case, *see* R. v. Wirral	
Wiscot's Case, *see* Giles v. Wescot	

Wiseman v. Barnard (1585)	919
Wiseman v. Crowe (1597)	748
Wiseman v. Jennings, *see* Wyseman v. Gennynges	
Wiseman's Case (1583)	227, 231
Witham v. Waterhouse, *see* Wytham v. Waterhowse	
Withers v. Drewe (1599)	1006
Withers' Case (1584)	262
Woodhouse v. Paston (1597)	825
Woodleffe v. Curteis (1596)	975
Woodward v. Lord Darcy (1558)	150
Woolley v. Bradwell (1595)	625
Worcester (Earl of) v. Finch (1600)	1094
Worseley v. Charnock (1588)	397
Wortley v. Herpingham (1600)	1092
Wotton v. Cooke (1572)	24, 127, 129
Wright v. Wright (1596)	738
Wrote v. Harvye (1599)	991
Wrote v. Wigges (1591, 1592)	413, 461
Wyat v. Goodall (1597)	781
Wyatt (Sir Thomas) his Case, *see* Multon v. Coveney	
Wybarde v. Reynoldes (1583)	242
Wydeston v. Clerke, *see* Widdowson v. Clerke	
Wylde's Case, *see* Richardson v. Yeardley	
Wymark's Case, *see* Dun d. Sleford v. Lawe	
Wynsmore d. Longe v. Hulbert (1586)	314
Wyrral's Case, *see* Wirrall's Case	
Wyseman v. Gennynges (1591)	715
Wyseman, *see also* Wiseman	
Wytham v. Waterhowse (1596)	661
Wythers v. Rookes and Smythe (1598)	844
Yate v. Wyrdnam (1587)	368
Yealdinge v. Faye (1597)	768
Yeardley v. Pescodde (1583)	208
Yelverton v. Yelverton (1594)	578
Yolland v. Yolland (1593)	671
Zouche (Lord) v. Bampfield (1587)	318, 343

TABLE OF STATUTES CITED IN VOLUMES I–IV

9 Hen. III, Magna Carta, c. 3, wardship	40
9 Hen. III, Magna Carta, c. 4, waste by a guardian	330
9 Hen. III, Magna Carta, c. 8, debts owed to the king	184
9 Hen. III, Magna Carta, c. 9, customs of London	825
9 Hen. III, Magna Carta, c. 11, common pleas	1036
9 Hen. III, Magna Carta, c. 29, liberty of the subject	cxviii, cxix, cxliv, cxlvii-cli, 799, 1014
9 Hen. III, Magna Carta, c. 30, merchants	873, 874
9 Edw. III, Carta de Foresta, c. 10, hunting	48
9 Hen. III, Carta de Foresta, c. 16, pleas of the forest	666
20 Hen. III, Provisions of Merton c. 11, malefactors in parks	27
51 Hen. III, Statutum de Scaccario	861
52 Hen. III, Statute of Marlborough, c. 3, unlawful distress	852
52 Hen. III, Statute of Marlborough, c. 6, wardships	77
52 Hen. III, Statute of Marlborough, c. 12, distress	88
52 Hen. III, Statute of Marlborough, c. 21, replevin	191, 756
52 Hen. III, Statute of Marlborough, c. 28, trespass	402
3 Edw. I, Statute of Westminster I, c. 9, pursuit of felons	756
3 Edw. I, Statute of Westminster I, c. 17, distresses	756
3 Edw. I, Statute of Westminster I, c. 34, false news	604
3 Edw. I, Statute of Westminster I, c. 46, age	1053
4 Edw. I, De Bigamis, c. 3, dower	301
4 Edw. I, De Bigamis, c. 6, warranty	114, 128, 1008
6 Edw. I, Statute of Gloucester, c. 3, aiel, besaiel and cosinage	76
6 Edw. I, Statute of Gloucester, c. 5, waste by a guardian	330, 443, 458, 459, 562, 979
7 Edw. I, Statute of Mortmain	490
11 Edw. I, stat. 1, Statute of Acton Burnell	24, 979
12 Edw. I, Statute of Rhuddlan	830
13 Edw. I, Statute of Westminster II, c. 1, conditional gifts	31, 56, 76, 95, 191, 224, 253, 254, 328, 547, 548, 637, 1067, 1068
13 Edw. I, Statute of Westminster II, c. 3, receipt	114, 254, 459, 716
13 Edw. I, Statute of Westminster II, c. 4, quod ei deforceat	458
13 Edw. I, Statute of Westminster II, c. 5, advowsons	534, 800
13 Edw. I, Statute of Westminster II, c. 5, s. 2, judgments in the king's courts	
13 Edw. I, Statute of Westminster II, c. 11, actions of account	17, 18
13 Edw. I, Statute of Westminster II, c. 12, appeals of felony	435
13 Edw. I, Statute of Westminster II, c. 14, waste	460
13 Edw. I, Statute of Westminster II, c. 18, elegit	254

13 Edw. I, Statute of Westminster II, c. 19, intestates' debts . . 191
13 Edw. I, Statute of Westminster II, c. 23, executors 402
13 Edw. I, Statute of Westminster II, c. 24, s. 2, churches . . . 933
13 Edw. I, Statute of Westminster II, c. 30, special verdicts . . . 213
13 Edw. I, Statute of Westminster II, c. 40, property of married women 637
13 Edw. I, Statute of Westminster II, c. 41, religious houses . . 694, 721
13 Edw. I, Statute of Westminster II, c. 43, Hospitallers and Templars . 861
13 Edw. I, stat. 2, Statute of Winchester 88
13 Edw. I, Circumspecte Agatis 423
13 Edw. I, stat. 3, merchants 24, 470
18 Edw. I, Quia Emptores Terrarum 126, 937
25 Edw. I, stat. 1, Confirmatio Cartarum 1043
28 Edw. I, stat. 3, Articuli super Cartas, c. 3, marshalsea . 414, 415, 417, 418, 462
28 Edw. I, stat. 3, Articuli super Cartas, c. 4, common pleas . . 803, 1036
28 Edw. I, Articuli super Cartas, c. 5, marshalsea . . . 972
28 Edw. I, stat. 3, Articuli super Cartas, c. 6, petit seals . . . 793
30 Edw. I (unprinted), London 972
31 Edw. I, De Forstallariis 777
31 Edw. I, De Ponderibus et Mensuris 674
33 Edw. I, stat. 5, Ordinatio Forestae, c. 5 959
33 Edw. I, stat. 6, De Terris Mensurandis 180
34 Edw. I, De Tallagio non Concedendo 873, 874, 1043
9 Edw. II, Articuli Cleri 541
17 Edw. II, stat. 3, De Terris Templariorum 444, 445
17 Edw. II (so printed), Prerogativa Regis, c. 1, wardship . . 697
17 Edw. II (so printed), Prerogativa Regis, c. 6, wardship . . 697
17 Edw. II (so printed), Prerogativa Regis, c. 15, advowsons . . 381, 1077
Incerti temporis, Modus Calumpniandi Essonia 300
1 Edw. III, stat. 2, c. 4, stalling of debts to the king . . . 861
2 Edw III, c. 3, going armed 756
2 Edw. III, c. 12, hundreds 274
4 Edw. III, c. 7, executors 402
5 Edw. III, c. 2, marshalsea 972
5 Edw. III, c. 9, proceeding contrary to the great charter . . 799
5 Edw. III, c. 12, pardons for outlawry 1009
9 Edw. III, stat. 1, c. 1, merchant strangers . . . . ccxix, 874
10 Edw. III stat. 2, c. 3, marshalsea 414, 972
14 Edw. III, stat. 1, c. 1, liberties of the Church 933
14 Edw. III, stat. 1, c. 6, mistakes by clerks 734
14 Edw. III, stat. 1, c. 9, hundreds 274
14 Edw. III, stat. 1, c. 10, keeping of gaols 816
14 Edw. III, stat. 1, c. 12, weights and measures . . . 539
14 Edw. III, stat. 1, c. 17, juris utrum 933
14 Edw. III, stat. 1, c. 21, subsidy 873, 874*ter*
14 Edw. III, stat. 2, c. 1, subsidy 874

14 Edw. III, stat. 2, c. 2, merchant strangers	ccxix
14 Edw. III, stat. 4, Pro Clero, c. 1, purveyance	899
15 Edw. III, stat. 3, c. 5, subsidy	874
18 Edw. III, stat. 2, c. 3, sea open to merchants	ccxix
18 Edw. III, stat. 3, c. 7, tithes	541
23 Edw. III, Statute of Labourers, c. 2, departure from service	239
23 Edw. III, Statute of Labourers, c. 6, victuals	539, 674, 775
25 Edw. III, stat. 4, c. 2, merchant strangers	ccxix
25 Edw. III, stat. 5, c. 2, Statute of Treasons	cxxx, 522-523, 535, 620, 639-640, 693, 757, 838-842
25 Edw. III, stat. 5, c. 4, due process	239, 799
25 Edw. III, stat. 5, c. 5, executors	402
25 Edw. III, stat. 5, c. 21, butlerage	751
25 Edw. III, stat. 6, c. 1, provisors	931
27 Edw. III, stat. 1, c. 1, praemunire	620, 800
27 Edw. III, stat. 1, c. 4, subsidy	874
27 Edw. III, stat. 1, cc. 5-8, importing of wines	751
27 Edw. III, stat. 2, c. 1, customs	874
27 Edw. III, stat. 2, c. 2, merchants' goods	874
28 Edw. III, c. 3, due process of law	372, 799
31 Edw. III, stat. 1, c. 5, gauging wines	751, 775
31 Edw. III, stat. 1, c. 10, victuallers in London	674
31 Edw. III, stat. 1, c. 11, administrators	178, 825, 987
31 Edw. III, stat. 1, c. 12, error from the Exchequer	207, 1040, 1041
34 Edw. III, c. 14, offices before escheators	507
34 Edw. III, c. 17, trade in Ireland	ccxix
36 Edw. III, stat. 1, c. 13, escheators	507
36 Edw. III, stat. 1, c. 15, form of declarations	1113
37 Edw. III, c. 16, wines	751
38 Edw. III, stat. 1, c. 2, exporting gold and silver	874
38 Edw. III, stat. 1, c. 11, wines	751
42 Edw. III, c. 3, due process of law	372, 799
42 Edw. III, c. 8, wines	751
43 Edw. III, c. 2, wines	751
43 Edw. III, c. 3, butlerage	751
45 Edw. III, c. 3, tithes of wood	262, 1061
45 Edw. III, c. 4, impositions	873
1 Ric. II, c. 12, bail and mainprise	17
1 Ric. II (unprinted), marshalsea	972
2 Ric. II, stat. 1, c. 1, merchants	ccxix
2 Ric. II, stat. 1, c. 5, scandalum magnatum	88, 103, 191, 604
3 Ric. II (unprinted), murder of Janus Imperial	641
5 Ric. II, stat. 1, c. 7, forcible entry	835
5 Ric. II, stat. 1, c. 9, pleas in the Exchequer	1040
5 Ric. II, stat. 2, c. 3, safeguard of the sea	ccxix

5 Ric. II, stat. 2, c. 4, summons to parliament 511
6 Ric. II, stat. 1, c. 6, ravishment by consent 466
6 Ric. II, stat. 1, c. 12, fishmongers 674
7 Ric. II, c. 11, victuallers in London 673
8 Ric. II, Statute of Salisbury (apocryphal) 257
9 Ric. II, c. 3, reversioners 225, 716
11 Ric. II, cc. 1-6, attainders of treason 639
11 Ric. II, c. 7, merchants ccxix
11 Ric. II, c. 9, impositions 873
12 Ric. II, c. 11, scandalum magnatum 604
13 Ric. II, stat. 1, c. 2, constable and marshal 186
13 Ric. II, stat. 1, c. 3, marshalsea of the household . . . 416
13 Ric. II, stat. 1, c. 4, clerk of the market 539, 774, 775
13 Ric. II, stat. 1, c. 5, admiralty jurisdiction 222, 948
13 Ric. II, stat. 1, c. 8, victuallers 674
13 Ric. II, stat. 2, c. 1, pardons 906
13 Ric. II, stat. 2, c. 8, gauging wine 775
14 Ric. II, c. 8, gauging wine 751
14 Ric. II, c. 9, merchant strangers ccxix
15 Ric. II, c. 3, admiralty 222
15 Ric. II, c. 5, mortmain 116, 488-489
15 Ric. II, c. 6, appropriations 66
16 Ric. II, Statute of Winchester, c. 5, provisors . . . 96, 164, 620, 800
17 Ric. II, c. 5, alnagers and customers 711
17 Ric. II, c. 8, suppression of riots 756
21 Ric. II, cc. 3, 4, 12-13, 20, treasons 639, 640
1 Hen. IV, c. 3 and c. 10, repeals 639
1 Hen. IV, c. 14, constable and marshal . . . 185, 220, 221, 243
2 Hen. IV, c. 11, admiralty jurisdiction 948
4 Hen. IV, c. 11, weirs ccxix
4 Hen. IV, c. 12, appropriations 66
4 Hen. IV, c. 20, butlerage 751
4 Hen. IV, c. 23, judgments in the king's courts . . . cxlii, cxliv, 799, 800
4 Hen. IV, c. 24, alnage 711
5 Hen. IV, c. 14, notes of fines 9
7 Hen. IV, c. 4, gaolers 17
7 Hen. IV, c. 5, estates of the earl of Northumberland . . . 890
7 Hen. IV, c. 6, tithes 515
7 Hen. IV, c. 13, attorneys 747
13 Hen. IV, c. 7, suppression of riots 756
1 Hen. V, c. 2, weirs ccxix
1 Hen. V, c. 5, Statute of Additions 77, 205
1 Hen. V, c. 1, parliamentary elections 510
2 Hen. V, stat. 1, c. 6, treaty-breaking 639, 840
2 Hen. V, stat. 2, c. 3, qualifications of jurors 561

TABLE OF STATUTES CITED IN VOLUMES I–IV　　　　lxvii

3 Hen. V, c. 6, clipping coin	522, 640
3 Hen. V, c. 7, counterfeiting money	640
6 Hen. VI, c. 1, process upon indictments	614, 615
6 Hen. VI, c. 5, commissions of sewers	845
8 Hen. VI, c. 4, Statute of Liveries	435
8 Hen. VI, c. 6, burning houses	639
8 Hen. VI, c. 7, parliamentary elections	510
8 Hen. VI, c. 9, Statute of Forcible Entry	15, 154, 367, 568
8 Hen. VI, c. 10, process upon indictments	264, 614-615
8 Hen. VI, c. 12, misprision by clerks	196, 734
8 Hen. VI, c. 15, faults in records	734
8 Hen. VI, c. 16, escheators	692, 710, 711
8 Hen. VI, c. 29, juries de medietate linguae	561
11 Hen. VI, c. 5, waste	611, 633
15 Hen. VI, c. 4, subpoena	799
18 Hen. VI, c. 1, letters patent	669
18 Hen. VI, c. 6, inquisitions	692, 711, 925
20 Hen. VI, c. 11, treason	ccxix
23 Hen. VI, c. 7, sheriffs	593
23 Hen. VI, c. 9, sheriffs	203, 275, 950, 976
23 Hen. VI, c. 10, knights of the shire	510
23 Hen. VI, c. 14, parliamentary elections	510, 781
27 Hen. VI, c. 5, fairs	1108
28 Hen. VI (unprinted), Act of Resumption	616, 661, 724, 884
29 Hen. VI, c. 1, war levied by John Cade	640
31 Hen. VI, c. 5, alnagers and customers	711
31 Hen. VI, c. 7, effect of the resumption	616, 661
33 Hen. VI, c. 7, attorneys in Norfolk and Suffolk	636
1 Edw. IV, c. 1, acts done by Lancastrian kings	616, 661
1 Edw. IV, c. 2, sheriffs' tourns	435
3 Edw. IV (unprinted), Act of Resumption	616, 661
8 Edw. IV, c. 2, Statute of Liveries	579, 1035-1036, 1038, 1039
12 Edw. IV, c. 7, weirs	ccxix
12 Edw. IV, c. 8, victuals	674, 675, 775
17 Edw. IV, c. 2, courts of piepowder	1108
17 Edw. IV, c. 5, farm of subsidy and alnage	711
22 Edw. IV, c. 6, games and marks of swans	477, 478
1 Ric. III, c. 1, uses	108, 118, 127, 205, 205, 410, 582, 638, 807, 812, 813, 837-838
1 Ric. III, c. 6, courts of piepowder	1108
1 Ric. III, c. 9, Italian merchants	ccxix
1 Hen. VII, c. 7, hunting in the night	48
1 Hen. VII, c. 8, shipping	ccxix
1 Hen. VII, c. iii (private), attainder of Lord Lovell	45, 132
3 Hen. VII, c. 1, misdemeanours; coroners	417, 418, 608

3 Hen. VII, c. 4, gifts to defraud creditors 563
3 Hen. VII, c. 14, compassing the king's death 640
4 Hen. VII, c. 13, benefit of clergy 1005
4 Hen. VII, c. 17, wardship of cestui que use . . . 116, 267, 410
4 Hen. VII, c. 18, counterfeiting foreign coin 639, 841
4 Hen. VII, c. 24, final concords . 12, 30, 155, 318, 343, 730, 851, 865, 866
7 Hen. VII, c. 4, weights and measures 539, 774
11 Hen. VII, c. 3, summary trial 334
11 Hen. VII, c. 4, weights and measures 539, 774
11 Hen. VII, c. 20, property of married women . . 25, 155*bis*, 254, 593, 701, 831, 834-835
19 Hen. VII, c. 15, execution against lands of cestui que use . . 116, 410
19 Hen. VII, c. 21, import of silks 595
19 Hen. VII, c. 34, attainder of the earl of Warwick 1062
1 Hen. VIII, c. 5, butlerage 751
1 Hen. VIII, c. 8, due process of law 325
3 Hen. VIII, c. 14, Tallow Chandlers 674, 775
4 Hen. VIII, c. 1, bulwarks for sea-coasts ccxix
4 Hen. VIII, c. i, restitution of the earl of Devon 554
6 Hen. VIII, c. 4, proclamation of outlawries 129, 264, 615
6 Hen. VIII, c. 15, letters patent 420
7 Hen. VIII, c. 2, shipping ccxix
21 Hen. VIII, c. 4, executors 325
21 Hen. VIII, c. 11, restitution of stolen goods 206, 795
21 Hen. VIII, c. 13, benefices   156*ter*, 245, 583-584, 593, 810, 850-851, 879, 960-962
21 Hen. VIII, c. 15, falsification of common recoveries . . . 128, 160
23 Hen. VIII, c. 1, benefit of clergy 449
23 Hen. VIII, c. 4, ale and beer 775
23 Hen. VIII, c. 5, commissions of sewers 845
23 Hen. VIII, c. 7, shipping ccxix
23 Hen. VIII, c. 10, uses in the nature of mortmain . . 487-490, 493-494, 753
24 Hen. VIII, c. 2, dyers 1112
25 Hen. VIII, c. 2, price of victuals 775
25 Hen. VIII, c. 3, benefit of clergy 461
25 Hen. VIII, c. 12, treason of Elizabeth Barton 839
25 Hen. VIII, c. 19, ecclesiastical jurisdiction 489, 620, 929
26 Hen. VIII, c. 1, supreme headship of the Church . . . 65, 489
26 Hen. VIII, c. 13, treason . 49, 70, 94, 95, 97, 260, 535, 553, 640, 650, 693, 721, 839, 1064, 1114
27 Hen. VIII, c. 2, treason 841
27 Hen. VIII, c. 10, Statute of Uses . cxvi, clvi-clxviii, cxciii, 10, 21, 58, 75-76, 80, 85, 115, 117, 118-121, 122, 128, 204, 215, 276, 297, 409, 410, 425, 426, 428, 432, 433, 446, 479, 514, 528, 606, 607, 649, 743, 785, 807, 851, 866, 867, 869, 887, 922, 1072-1073, 1104-1105
27 Hen. VIII, c. 11, warrants under the signet 576

TABLE OF STATUTES CITED IN VOLUMES I–IV lxix

27 Hen. VIII, c. 16, Statute of Enrolments   3, 157, 177, 189, 190, 432, 450, 542, 603, 606, 607, 624, 777, 851, 1104-1105
27 Hen. VIII, c. 20, tithes 330
27 Hen. VIII, c. 24, recontinuing liberties 617, 722-724, 899-901
27 Hen. VIII, c. 26, laws in Wales 828, 1038
27 Hen. VIII, c. 28, lesser monasteries . . . 187, 489, 743-744, 746
28 Hen. VIII, c. 7, attainder of Henry Norreis 224
28 Hen. VIII, c. 10, bishop of Rome 489
28 Hen. VIII, c. 15, admiralty and piracy . . . ccxix, ccxxi, 204, 218, 219
28 Hen. VIII, c. 16, dispensations 620
28 Hen. VIII, c. v (private), lands of the earl of Warwick . 1063, 1066, 1073-1074, 1078, 1080-1082
31 Hen. VIII, c. 2, stealing fish in ponds and moats 609
31 Hen. VIII, c. 13, monasteries . 68, 187, 208, 253, 261, 669, 691, 694-697, 699, 870, 871, 929, 1034, 1072
31 Hen. VIII, c. i (private), attainder of the marquess of Exeter . . 552
32 Hen. VIII, c. 1, Statute of Wills . . clvi-clxviii, 44, 147, 149, 158, 159, 163, 175, 214, 228, 231, 296, 325, 341, 425, 429-439, 481, 491, 494, 657, 836, 851, 879, 887, 990-991, 1015-1016
32 Hen. VIII, c. 2, Statute of Limitations . 159*bis*, 160, 253, 254, 549, 664, 990
32 Hen. VIII, c. 4, treason in Wales 1114
32 Hen. VIII, c. 7, tithes 330, 515, 593, 739, 740
32 Hen. VIII, c. 9, embracery and maintenance 608
32 Hen. VIII, c. 16, aliens 924
32 Hen. VIII, c. 20, monastic franchises . 187, 452, 539, 744, 745-746, 775, 1034
32 Hen. VIII, c. 28, lessees . . 39, 57, 108, 128, 160, 326, 363, 421, 422, 638, 653
32 Hen. VIII, c. 30, Statute of Jeofails . . 160, 312, 389, 828, 967
32 Hen. VIII, c. 31, common recoveries 37, 103, 716, 989
32 Hen. VIII, c. 32, partition 975
32 Hen. VIII, c. 33, disseisin 48, 160
32 Hen. VIII, c. 34, grantees of reversions . . . 26, 44, 114, 178, 867
32 Hen. VIII, c. 36, final concords . . 10, 13*bis*, 61, 161, 177, 318, 343, 727, 729-730, 832, 851, 865, 866, 920
32 Hen. VIII, c. 37, recovery of rents by executors 161
32 Hen. VIII, c. 46, Court of Wards 925
33 Hen. VIII, c. 20, s. 1, trial by peers 640
33 Hen. VIII, c. 20, s. 2, attainders of treason . . 47, 49, 70-72, 80, 94, 260, 443-445, 553, 871, 1064, 1074
33 Hen. VIII, c. 21, royal assent by commission 779, 781
33 Hen. VIII, c. 23, trials for treason 558
33 Hen. VIII, c. 27, corporations 774
33 Hen. VIII, c. 29, religious persons 929
33 Hen. VIII, c. 39, Court of Surveyors . . 184, 209, 277, 286, 622, 702, 784-786, 786-787, 965, 985

34 & 35 Hen. VIII, c. 5, explanation of the Statute of Wills . 161, 335, 425, 426, 428-439, 481, 491, 494, 836, 851, 879, 887, 990-991
34 & 35 Hen. VIII, c. 20, recoveries when the king is in reversion . 13, 61, 128, 162, 192, 762, 865, 895-896, 919-920
34 & 35 Hen. VIII, c. 21, confirmation of letters patent . . 610, 611, 968
34 & 35 Hen. VIII, c. 26, laws in Wales 482, 633, 1038
34 & 35 Hen. VIII, c. 45, Southwell College 337
35 Hen. VIII, c. 1, the king's succession 593
35 Hen. VIII, c. 2, treasons committed overseas . 557, 558, 566, 569, 614, 1113-1114
35 Hen. VIII, c. 6, jurors 560
37 Hen. VIII, c. 4, colleges and chantries 69, 337, 489, 696
37 Hen. VIII, c. 9, usury 162
37 Hen. VIII, c. 21, union of churches 810
37 Hen. VIII, c. 23, s. 2, prices of wines 775
1 Edw. VI, c. 2, election of bishops, ecclesiastical process . . . 334, 565
1 Edw. VI, c. 8, confirmation of letters patent . . . 506, 626, 932
1 Edw. VI, c. 10, proclamation of outlawries 632
1 Edw. VI, c. 12, repeals of statutes concerning treason . . . 839
1 Edw. VI, c. 14, Statute of Chantries . 69, 162, 163, 337, 376, 694-697, 1072
2 & 3 Edw. VI, c. 8, officers before escheators 452
2 & 3 Edw. VI, c. 13, tithes 330, 740, 1092
2 & 3 Edw. VI, c. 18, attainder of Lord Sudeley 218
2 & 3 Edw. VI, c. 37, exporting gun-metal 747
3 & 4 Edw. VI, c. 4, letters patent 680
5 & 6 Edw. VI, c. 5, prices of wines 775
5 & 6 Edw. VI, c. 7, sale of wools 281
5 & 6 Edw. VI, c. 9, benefit of clergy 449, 460, 461
5 & 6 Edw. VI, c. 10, benefit of clergy 52
5 & 6 Edw. VI, c. 11, treason . . . 94, 553, 640, 721, 839, 1114
5 & 6 Edw. VI, c. 14, engrossing 516, 777
5 & 6 Edw. VI, c. 16, buying and selling offices . . 166, 490, 796 1094
5 & 6 Edw. VI, c. 18, foreign ships . . . . . ccxix, 751
1 Mar., sess. 1, c. 1, treason 94, 523, 757
1 Mar., sess. 2, c. 2, repeals 565, 639, 641
1 Mar., sess. 2, c. 6, counterfeiting foreign coin 841
1 Mar., sess. 2, c. 7, proclamations upon fines 498
1 Mar., sess. 2, c. xiii (private), attainder of the duke of Norfolk . . 95
1 & 2 Phil. & Mar., c. 5, navy ccxix
1 & 2 Phil. & Mar., c. 9, praying for the queen's death . . . 639
1 & 2 Phil. & Mar., c. 10, treason 558, 614, 1114
1 & 2 Phil. & Mar., c. 12, severing distresses 837
1 & 2 Phil. & Mar., c. iii (private), attainder of Thomas Wyatt . . 95
2 & 3 Phil. & Mar., c. 7, sale of horses 205
4 & 5 Phil. & Mar., c. 1, letters patent 555

TABLE OF STATUTES CITED IN VOLUMES I–IV   lxxi

4 & 5 Phil. & Mar., c. 5, weavers	976
4 & 5 Phil. & Mar., c. 8, taking away heiresses	465-466
1 Eliz., c. 1, ecclesiastical jurisdiction	333, 617-620, 818, 1048-1051
1 Eliz., c. 2, uniformity of common prayer	508, 509, 618
1 Eliz., c. 4, restitution of the first fruits	421, 593
1 Eliz., c. 6, speaking false news of the queen	523, 640, 758, 839
1 Eliz., c. 13, imports	ccxviii
1 Eliz., c. 19, temporalities of bishops	143, 176, 385, 1001
1 Eliz., c. 24, monasteries and chantries	752
5 Eliz., c. 1, bishop of Rome	618
5 Eliz., c. 4, artificers and labourers	976
5 Eliz., c. 5, shipping	ccxix
5 Eliz., c. 5, s. 29, sowing of hemp and flax	180
5 Eliz., c. 9, Statute of Perjury	356, 951, 1092
5 Eliz., c. 11, clipping coin	841
5 Eliz., c. 14, forgery	361, 622, 647
5 Eliz., c. 23, de excommunicato capiendo	1050
8 Eliz., c. 1, consecration of bishops	843
13 Eliz., c. 1, treason	cxxx, cxxxi, 277, 523, 628, 629, 640, 757-758, 1114
13 Eliz., c. 2, bulls and superstitious things	51, 513, 618, 839
13 Eliz., c. 3, fugitives	181, 563
13 Eliz., c. 4, the queen's accountants and receivers	576, 622, 703, 946-947, 1087-1088
13 Eliz., c. 5, fraudulent conveyances	163, 303, 949, 977
13 Eliz., c. 6, exemplification of letters patent	358, 680
13 Eliz., c. 7, bankrupts	274, 845
13 Eliz., c. 8, Statute of Usury	52, 77, 450, 650, 687, 935
13 Eliz., c. 10, dilapidations	26, 37, 142, 722
13 Eliz., c. 12, articles of religion	184, 245, 467, 993
13 Eliz., c. 16, attainders of treason confirmed	449, 865
13 Eliz., c. 20, leases of benefices	392, 506, 1001, 1099
14 Eliz., c. 1, treason	840
14 Eliz., c. 8, common recoveries	133, 143, 229, 715-717, 748, 989
14 Eliz., c. 11, continuation of statutes	506, 1001
18 Eliz., c. 1, impairing coin	841
18 Eliz., c. 2, letters patent	cxxxvii, 289, 421, 556, 562, 563, 636
18 Eliz., c. 3, parents of bastards	559, 620
18 Eliz., c. 5, common informers	357, 976
18 Eliz., c. 6, college leases	593
18 Eliz., c. 7, benefit of clergy	978, 1005
18 Eliz., c. 11, ecclesiastical leases	506
18 Eliz., c. 14, jeofails	160, 230, 234, 332, 471, 542, 545, 828
18 Eliz., c. 24, general pardon	638
23 Eliz., c. 1, recusancy	217, 508, 509, 537, 570, 647, 839, 840
23 Eliz., c. 2, false news	629, 640

23 Eliz., c. 9, s. 1, logwood	1007, 1112-1113
23 Eliz., c. 16, general pardon	322
27 Eliz., c. 3, lands of the queen's accountants	576-577, 703, 946
27 Eliz., c. 4, fraudulent conveyances	303, 469, 760, 1093
27 Eliz., c. 5, demurrers	329
27 Eliz., c. 6, qualifications of jurors	560
27 Eliz., c. 8, error from the King's Bench	299, 340, 373, 375, 388, 395, 396, 399, 402, 543, 586, 587
27 Eliz., c. 14, malt	804
28 Eliz., c. 1, attainder of Sir Francis Englefield	441
28 Eliz., c. 3, lands of attainted traitors	441, 442, 448
28 Eliz., c. 6, recusancy	509, 563, 570, 647, 786-787, 852
31 Eliz., c. 3, proclamations upon outlawries	577
31 Eliz., c. 5, informers	874, 949
31 Eliz., c. 12, stealing horses	205
35 Eliz., c. 1, recusants	cxxxiii, 509, 537
35 Eliz., c. 2, recusants	564
35 Eliz., c. 3, confirmation of letters patent	572, 930
35 Eliz., c. 5, estates of Sir Francis Englefield	441
35 Eliz., cc. 12-13, subsidies	529
35 Eliz., c. 14, s. 8, general pardon	621, 647, 662, 828
39 Eliz., c. 4, rogues	893
39 Eliz., c. 7, lands of the queen's accountants	946-947, 1087-1088
39 Eliz., c. 8, deprivation of bishops and deans	843, 855
39 Eliz., c. 16, malt	804
39 Eliz., c. 22, bishopric of Norwich	cxxxviii, 928
1 Jac. I, c. 9, selling ale	675
1 Jac. I, c. 19, searchers of colours and painting	675
21 Jac. I, c. 15, expulsion of lessees	15

INTRODUCTION

Coke's legal education

In January 1571, at the age of eighteen, Edward Coke was admitted to Clifford's Inn from Trinity College, Cambridge, having previously attended Norwich Grammar School.[1] It is just possible that when he went down to London he had some undergraduate knowledge of the assizes at Norwich, since in 1582 he was able to recount a case which had occurred in the summer vacation of 1570 following the rebellion there.[2] But his legal education began in London. Although he would have become well versed in the art of logic at Cambridge,[3] he could not have read Law, which was then a postgraduate subject limited to Roman law. Like most laymen, including even the philosophically minded Francis Bacon, he did not remain in residence long enough to take a first degree, let alone progress to the law faculty. His only likely encounter with the law at that stage would have been to make some acquaintance with the elements of Roman law, as a private diversion, and perhaps one law book he already possessed on leaving Cambridge was a copy of Justinian's *Institutes*.[4] There was no law library at home in Mileham.[5] Although his father was a

---

[1] According to his autobiographical memoranda in *AA*, fos. 13, 17 (see plate 1), he was admitted to Trinity College in Sept. 1567 and stayed for three years; he was then admitted to Clifford's Inn on 21 Jan. 1571. His arms were placed in Clifford's Inn hall in the seventeenth century, and some remains of the jumbled panel are now in the Judge's Room of the Mayor's Court, London, with an inscription taken from the companion panel for Sir Robert Heath: see J. Baker, *The Inns of Chancery 1340–1640* (2017), pp. 249–250, and plate 13B.

[2] CUL MS. Gg.3.26, fo. 118 (an inaccurate transcript in court-hand of a report 'ex relaxatione [*recte* relatione] Cooke'). The recollection was that John Throgmorton stood mute of malice in order to avoid the forfeiture of his property, but it was held that this was not permitted in case of treason and so he was tried and convicted by a jury. No date is there given, but the incident occurred before Catlyn C.J. at the summer assizes 1570: F. Blomefield, *An Essay towards a Topographical History of the County of Norfolk*, iii (City of Norwich) (1806), p. 284; D. Jardine, *Criminal Trials* (1832), i. 405, n. †. Forty years later, Coke held the law to be clear that in such a case the defendant was to be condemned without trial, as if he had confessed, making no mention of the Norwich decision: 2 Co. Inst. 177; 3 Co. Inst. 217 (citing Dyer 205). But he cited the same case in the trial of Sir Walter Ralegh (1603) for the proposition that the two-witness rule no longer applied in treason cases: E. Edwards, *The Life of Sir Walter Ralegh* (1868), i. 389–390.

[3] Co. Litt. 235b.

[4] His copy of the *Institutes* (Lyons, 1559/57) (Holkham Hall, BN 8090) has the signature 'Edw. Coke' (not adding the Inner Temple) and contains some notes in an italic hand which he probably wrote as an undergraduate. It had also belonged to one 'Underwood' (cf. p. 156, below), who may have been responsible for some of the annotations. Most of Coke's Roman law books (*Library of Sir Edward Coke*, pp. 38–41) were acquired later.

[5] Coke lived in the vacations at his ancestral home of Mileham Hall, Norf., until his marriage in 1582. Upon the old gate of the hall were the arms of Coke (modern) impaling Knightley, for Edward's parents: E. Blomefield, *History of Norfolk*, x (1809), p. 22. The same arms are on the monument of Coke's mother (1569) at Tittleshall, Norf. But these arms (*Per pale azure and gules, three eagles displayed argent*) were almost certainly obtained by Edward and not used in his father's lifetime. His father's arms as displayed on his monument in St Andrew's, Holborn, were completely different: *Men of Court*, i. 494. Mileham Hall was rebuilt in the eighteenth century and demolished in the 1950s.

bencher of Lincoln's Inn, he had practised as an attorney and did not achieve any distinction in the law. He had in any case died in 1561, when Edward was only nine years old, and such law books as he possessed had been dispersed.[6]

After one year at Clifford's Inn learning the rudiments of legal language, writs and pleading, Coke proceeded to the Inner Temple on 24 April 1572. Within the latter he would remain 'Coke, junior'[7] until his rise to fame in the 1580s,[8] to distinguish him from the unrelated and distinctly less significant William Coke.[9] He started to collect his own library, and over the course of his long life he would become an ardent bibliophile.[10] The collection had to begin, of course, with the essentials. Like every new law student, he acquired a copy of Littleton's *Tenures* – his was the 1572 edition – and, in accordance with common practice, he had it interleaved so that he could annotate it. The annotations, written in a miniscule hand,[11] with frequent additions and extra pages added over many years, would grow into a massive apparatus which still survives.[12] Coke referred to them simply as 'my notes'.[13] These notes doubtless inspired, but were in no sense a draft of, the celebrated commentary on Littleton which he completed in old age. Their description in 1804 as the 'original manuscript' of Coke upon Littleton was seriously misinformed.[14] The anonymous writer of 1804 was critical of Francis Hargrave and Charles Butler for not using the manuscript in their edition of Coke upon Littleton, saying that they had confessed to him their

---

[6] *The Men of Court*, i. 494. Coke said they had been sold to a Mr Crowe, from whom he recovered at least two of them: a volume of printed statutes which he inscribed, 'Iste liber fuit patris mei Edw. Coke'; and a *Glanvill* (Holkham Hall, BN 7821) which he inscribed, 'Iste liber fuit Roberti Coke de Mileham patris Edwardi Coke capitalis justiciarii de Banco'. See *Library of Sir Edward Coke*, pp. 31, 36; *The Men of Court*, i. 494.

[7] He had also been 'Coke, junior' in Trinity College: Boyer, *Coke and the Elizabethan Age*, p. 19, n. 22.

[8] See *V*, fos. 24, 32 ('ex libro Cooke junioris'), and fo. 27 ('collect per Edward Cooke le puisne'); this probably dates from soon after 1580.

[9] William Coke, adm. 1562, called 1571. He gave a reading in chancery but made no progress in the law, reaching the law reports only as the unsuccessful plaintiff in *Coke* v. *(Robert) Bacon* (1590) Cro. Eliz. 182; KB 27/1318, m. 684. In 1602 the Inn granted him an allowance of commons because he had 'fallen into decay': *Calendar of Inner Temple Records*, ed. F. A. Inderwick, vol. i (1896), p. 447.

[10] By the time of his death his library was one of the most important in the country, and the legal section alone was more extensive than those of all the inns of court together. Much of it is still preserved at Holkham Hall, where his descendants settled. It is thought Coke and Selden were the largest collectors of their time: A. G. Watson, *The Library of Sir Simonds D'Ewes* (1966), p. 40.

[11] For specimen pages see plates 2–3. It was the fashion to use small writing in commonplace-books, in order to compress as much material as possible into a portable volume; but Coke's was smaller than most and in places almost illegible without a glass, especially in the meagre lighting of the British Library. Notoriously very short-sighted, Coke is said to have disdained the use of spectacles: *'Brief Lives', Chiefly of Contemporaries, set down by John Aubrey*, ed. A. Clark (Oxford, 1898), p. 178.

[12] BL MS. Harley 6687A-D. For its division into four volumes in 1804/05 see below, p. lxxviii.

[13] E.g. below, p. 29, no. 60 ('mes notes demesne'); p. 51, no. 98; p. 91, no. 149; p. 129, no. 227; p. 131, n. 2 (all sim.); *C*, fo. 133; vol. iii, p. 668 ('Vide in mes notes tit. County Palatine'); Coke's Dyer, fos. 326v ('Vide tit. Prerogative in mes notes, 47), 329 ('Vide in mes notes tit. Condition, 180b'), 331v ('mes notes tit. Patent, 61b'); Coke's *Statuta*, fos. 117 (below, p. 154, no. 288) and 191 ('Vide in mes notes, 91'); Coke's Sta. Prerog., fo. 62v ('Vide in mes notes tit. Fauxer de recovery, plusors cases').

[14] Anon., 'Account of Sir Edward Coke's original Manuscript of his Commentary upon Littleton' (1804) 1 *Law Journal* 112–120, 134–145. The writer's interest in the text of Co. Litt. suggests that he was a lawyer, though his article was confined to the autobiographical section in MS. Harley 6687A. Cf. *The Christian Observer*, iii. 440 (July 1804): 'The original MS. of Sir Edward Coke's *Commentaries upon the Tenures of* Littleton has been lately discovered in the British Museum ... Some account of this curious MS. will shortly be given, we understand, to the public.'

inability to decipher it, and that Butler had even doubted its authenticity. He proposed to collate it with the printed edition. But evidently he had not attempted to do so, or he would soon have discovered his mistake. Probably he found the decryption more difficult than he had foreseen. At any rate, he never saw fit to retract his initial conclusion. The new description was fortunately omitted in what is still the only printed catalogue of the Harleian manuscripts. The compiler, Robert Nares F.R.S., keeper of manuscripts at the British Museum, was a clergyman with no knowledge of legal manuscripts and he more or less reproduced the entry in the 1759 catalogue by Humphrey Wanley and others.[15] More seriously, he failed to notice that the adjacent manuscript (MS. Harley 6686) was also in Coke's handwriting. As a consequence of this cataloguing failure, still not rectified,[16] Plucknett was unaware of it when he speculated in the 1940s about the origins of Coke's reports.[17] Plucknett's unfortunate conclusion was, 'The first glance at Coke is enough to show that the set of reports as a whole does not come from a chronologically arranged register like Plowden's.'[18] This serves as a warning never to rely on printed sources alone.[19] As will be shown, Coke did keep reports chronologically from 1580 until 1616, though he chose not to publish them in their original order, or in the same words.

The autograph draft of Coke upon Littleton has not, in fact, been seen since it was seized with other manuscripts from Coke's study in 1634,[20] though the other three parts of the *Institutes* were returned to Coke's family in 1641 and published.[21] None of these manuscripts has been heard of since. But they all belonged to a different

---

[15] R. Nares, *Catalogue of the Harleian Manuscripts*, iii (1808), p. 384 ('... an extremely scarce printed edition of Littelton's Tenures ... interleaved ... containing the original Observations & Enlargements of the L. C. Justice Coke in his own hand-writing ...'). Cf. *A Catalogue of the Harleian Collection of Manuscripts* (1759), ii, sig. 7O[2] ('A thick Octavo, containing in Print Les Tenures de Monsieur Littleton Anno 1572. With the original Observations and Enlargements of the L. C. Justice Coke in his own handwritng.')

[16] It is a national disgrace that there is still no proper catalogue of the Harleian collection. Another of Coke's autograph notebooks, now at Cambridge (CUL MS. Ii.5.21), was likewise missed by a nineteenth-century cataloguer.

[17] 'The Genesis of Coke's Reports' (1942) 27 *Cornell Law Quarterly* 190–213.

[18] Ibid. 200. Plucknett's study of the printed reports did, however, help to elucidate the thinking behind the choice of cases for publication in the early seventeenth century. There is an account of the unique nature of the *Reports* in his *Concise History of the Common Law* (5th ed., 1956), pp. 280–281.

[19] Plucknett made a similar mistake in attributing Fleetwood's treatise on statutes to Egerton: Baker, *Magna Carta*, p. 234. But both his essays were written during the Second World War, when access to manuscripts in England was impossible.

[20] An account of the books confiscated by Secretary Windebank in 1634 listed 'Sir Edward Coke's Comment upon Littleton, and the History of his Life before it': Roger Coke, *A Detection of the Court and State of England* (1697), p. 253. The 'History of his Life' probably referred to Littleton's life, not Coke's, in which case it was indeed the manuscript of Co. Litt., which is preceded by a biography of Littleton. This was the opinion of A. Kippis, *Biographia Britannica* (1748), ii. 1398, and it is corroborated by the fact that Roger Coke listed it together with the drafts of the other parts of the *Institutes*. The author of 'Sir Edward Coke's Original Manuscript' (above, n. 14), having just discovered MS. Harley 6687, said that Kippis's opinion was 'plainly a mistake' and that 'his Life' referred to Coke's autobiographical notes at the front of what he wrongly supposed to be the draft of Co. Litt. This false conclusion was followed by the present writer in 1972: Baker, *Collected Papers*, ii. 745 ('obviously MS A').

[21] *Journals of the House of Commons*, ii. 45, 80, 470, 554. In the interim they seem to have been in the possession of Sir John Finch, chief justice of the Common Pleas (1634–40), and his successor, Sir Edward Littleton (1640–41): ibid. 69; Baker, *Collected Papers*, ii. 745–746. On 20 March 1640 part II was delivered to Sir John Bankes, Att.-Gen.: receipt in IT MS. Petyt 538.17, fo. 352. In the same year Elias Ashmole made a transcript of part IV, while it was in Finch C.J.'s possession: Bodl. Lib., MS. Ashmole 1159.

stage in Coke's life, since they were probably written half a century later, in the 1620s.[22] Most of the interleaved matter in Coke's 1572 edition of Littleton bears no relation to the text of Littleton itself or to Coke upon Littleton, and it was continued in the same manner in other notebooks which came to be bound up with it.[23] It begins (like Littleton) with 'Estates', and some of it was loosely connected with Littleton's subject-matter, especially where written in the margins of the printed book. But most of it constituted a general commonplace-book or abridgment, under somewhat random headings: not the result of a coherent plan but the fruit of industrious reading through the printed year books, filling up blank spaces with continuations and new headings. It was also full of Latin maxims, which Coke was fond of collecting;[24] since he seldom cited a source for them, he has been credited with wholesale invention, though this is a question yet to be explored.

Coke acquired a set of year books in the 1570s.[25] They were bound up in nine composite volumes,[26] which cost him around 12 shillings each.[27] These early acquisitions are heavily annotated with reading-notes and cross-references to legal authorities, written in his hand, though he did not use them for the kind of original memoranda found in the commonplace-books (where many of them were digested), and they contain no cross-references to those books. Coke also owned the printed abridgments, but he was no mere 'abridgment man'.[28] Abridgments might be of value to those who compiled them, he wrote, 'but as they are used have brought no small prejudice to others':[29] serious lawyers should trust only 'the books at large' (the full editions).[30] Coke's commonplace-books, and the year books on which they were largely based, are evidence that Coke read, marked and digested all the old reports,

---

[22] They were completed by 1630: 3 Co. Inst. 147.

[23] There is an index to the titles in *AD*, fo. 915, which is located more than 200 folios after the ending of the interleaved portion.

[24] Many of them were assembled in *AD*, fos. 906–913, 916*v ('Regule'), 918, 921v, sometimes with references to the folios in the commonplace-books where they are mentioned. Note also the propositions which he called axioms ('αχιωματα') ibid., fo. 914.

[25] Like most early printed year books in contemporary bindings, Coke's volumes were sammelbände made up from single years or small groups of years, and in his case nearly all of them were printed by Tottell in the 1550s and 1560s. Coke had presumably obtained his full set well before Tottell's reprints of the 1580s.

[26] They are all now at Holkham Hall: *1–10 Edward III* (BN 8099), *17–39 Edward III* (BN 7935), *40–50 Edward III* (BN 8106: 'Wenefred Cokes boke wedow'), *Liber Assisarum* (BN 7937), *Henry IV and V* (BN 7852), *1–20 Henry VI* (BN 8098), *21–39 Henry VI* (BN 7938), *Edward IV* (BN 7839) and *Richard III to Henry VII* (BN 8104). Coke acquired a number of different editions later, but they were not much annotated by him, if at all: e.g. *Henry IV*, 'ex libris Johannis Maunsell' (BN 7934), apparently acquired when he was chief justice; *Edward IV*, with the Hatton arms stamped in gold (BN 7853); and *Henry VII*, 'ex dono Johannis Stanley' (BN 8102).

[27] The volumes containing the years *17–39 Edward III* (Holkham 7935) and *1–20 Henry VI* (Holkham 8098) are marked in his hand with this price.

[28] In 1606, as chief justice of the Common Pleas, he spoke contemptuously of 'abridgment men that never read the books at large': J. Hawarde, *Les Reportes del Cases in Camera Stellata 1593–1609*, ed. W. Baildon (1894), p. 301. He was aiming this dart particularly at 'Mr Richardson', who was later himself to be chief justice of the Common Pleas.

[29] *Le Quart Part des Reportes* (1604), sig. B3.

[30] Ibid.: 'the advised and orderly reading of the books at large ... I absolutely determine to be the right way to enduring and perfect knowledge, and to use abridgments as tables and to trust only to the books at large'. This was probably an indirect attack on Francis Bacon's proposal to codify the common law, which would have involved abridging it (see Baker, *Magna Carta*, pp. 344–345). Cf. 10 Co. Rep. 41.

INTRODUCTION   lxxvii

including the abridged cases which were not to be found in the printed year books.[31] The year books were the chief repositories of the 'common learning' of the profession,[32] inherited from later medieval times, a corpus not only of the common law but of the true understanding of the old statutes, as expounded by the judges.[33] However perplexing they sometimes were, it was necessary for a law student to 'dive into the depth' until they made sense.[34] There is little doubt that Coke himself followed the course which he later laid down as a precept for others: the student should 'set upon the year books' as soon as he was able, 'that he be furnished with the whole course of the law', and should look up every case he heard cited, in order to 'fasten it in his memory'.[35] It was not light work. The student was advised that six hours' sleep a night should be sufficient.[36]

Besides constituting a personal digest of the year books, the commonplace-books contained Coke's first efforts at reporting current cases, starting as early as 1572,[37] when he started inserting notes of current cases under the appropriate headings;[38] these early reports will be discussed below. The book was a treasured possession, and was later given 'a cover of crimson sattine curiouslie imbrodred with gold, silver and silke, and over that a cover of crimson damaske'.[39] The 922 octavo leaves of thin paper had evidently by that time been combined into a single *vade mecum*,[40] which

---

[31] There are numerous citations throughout to Fitz. Abr., normally by section-title and *placitum*, without the author's name, though occasionally adding 'F'. Bro. Abr. (first printed in 1573) was distinguished with a 'B'. In *AB*, fo. 415, is an unattributed report of the *Duchess of Suffolk's Case* (1551), in which it was held that the duchess was not the next of kin to her own son; this is in fact from Bro. Abr., *Administration*, pl. 47. Coke also owned a copy of Statham (Holkham Hall, BN 8107), which was already considered archaic and cost only 2 shillings; there are no notes in his hand, though he cited it (e.g. vol. ii, pp. 311, 379).

[32] Coke referred in 1597 to the 'common erudition in nostre livers': vol. iv, p. 832; 5 Co. Rep. 98. For the expression 'common erudition', which became current in fifteenth century, see 94 Selden Soc., introduction, p. *161*; J. H. Baker, *The Law's Two Bodies* (Oxford, 2001), pp. 67–70; *OHLE*, vi. 467–472; Baker, *Collected Papers*, i. 164, 353; iii. 1560–66.

[33] Coke's glosses on the statutes, which culminated in 2 Co. Inst., were heavily based on case-law.

[34] Co. Litt. 71: '... albeit the beginnings of this study seem difficult, yet when the professor of law can dive into the depth it is delightful easy, and without any heavy burden, so long as he keep himself in his own proper element.'   [35] Ibid. 70.

[36] Ibid. 64v, citing the 'ancient verses' beginning *Sex horas somno*.

[37] There are three cases from Michaelmas term 1572, all digested in several places: *Cranmer's Case* occurs six times, and *Winter's Case* seven times. That was probably the true beginning. There is one report of Trin. 1571 (below, p. 93, no. 154), and also a full report of *Pickeringe's Case* (1570) in the Common Pleas (*AD*, fo. 842), which are difficult to account for; but all the other Elizabethan cases before 1572 seem to be taken either from the first part of Plowd. (printed in 1571) or from a manuscript of Bendlowes. References to Dyer were inserted after its publication in 1586 (new style).

[38] He was not the first to do this, since the same technique was used by John Spelman at the beginning of the century, and by Christopher Yelverton of Gray's Inn (perhaps emulating Spelman) in the 1560s: below, p. xciii, n. 54.

[39] *Library of Sir Edward Coke*, p. 29, no. 369 ('Littleton mixed not onely with booke cases and many titles of the lawe intermixed therewith, but with many reports of cases in the raigne of Queene Eliz: before the 32. yeare of the same Q: with a cover ...'). The embroidery was said to be the work of Coke's daughter: *Catalogue of the Harleian Collection of Manuscripts* (1759), sig. 7O[2]v ('... covered with a rich Embroidery wrought by his own Daughter ...'). The 1808 catalogue added the word 'formerly'.

[40] It was presumably the book which he himself so styled. See T. Fuller, *History of the Worthies of England* [1662], ed. P. A. Nuttall (1840), ii. 452; repeated in D. Lloyd, *State-Worthies* (1670), p. 824 ('... most pleasing himself with a manual, which he called his "Vade Mecum", from whence, at one view, he took a prospect of his life passed, having noted therein most remarkables'). BL MS. Harley 6687A, fos. 10v–15v, is a series of personal memoranda, kept up throughout his life and ending with an accident when his horse fell on him in 1632, 'being above 80 years old'. These were identified as the *vade mecum* in *The*

must have had the same thickness as its height. The three sequences in Coke's numbering of the leaves (1–120, 1–76 and 1–284) show that originally there were three parts,[41] besides the two notebooks of reports from 1579 to 1588 (each numbered 1–48), and the printed Littleton (171 folios), all of which became combined into one. By 1805 the whole was so badly decayed, with the leaves becoming detached, that the cover had to be discarded and the book divided into four parts, with protective interleaving.[42] This massive work included almost all the texts in the first two volumes of the present edition, and much more besides.[43]

Coke was a year younger than the average student when he entered the Inner Temple, but he was already deeply immersed in the intricacies of the law. He would have attended moots and readings in the Inner Temple and inns of chancery in the 1570s, though there are no known reports of Inner Temple moots in this period through which his participation might be observed. He did not report any of them himself, as far as is known, though he did copy prominently on the fly-leaf of his first commonplace-book the case which he argued with William Fleetwood at New Inn in 1576[44] and in 1604 he referred in court to the form of pleading at moots in the Temple.[45] The first surviving records of his participation in learning exercises derive from his precocious readings at Lyons Inn in 1579–80, a duty undertaken only a year after his call to the bar.[46] The lectures were on the 1299 statute *De Finibus Levatis*, and as a reader in chancery he also had the duty of presiding over all the exercises of

---

Penny Cyclopaedia of the Society for the Diffusion of Useful Knowledge, ed. G. Long (1837), ii. 332, note; followed by J. B[ruce], 'Sir Edward Coke's Vade Mecum' (1840) 6 *Collectanea Topographica et Genealogica* 108 at p. 109; and in *The Cambridge Portfolio*, ed. J. T. Smith (1840), i. 217. But the personal memoranda were only a very small part of the whole. Coke also referred to his third notebook (MS. *B*) as his *vade mecum*: below, p. cxiii. Timothy Tourner used the same expression for Coke's later notebooks: UCL MS. Ogden 29(6), fo. 59.

[41] Coke's numbering did not include the pages of the printed Littleton with which the leaves are interspersed. The first 120 folios of commonplaced material are bound before Littleton, and the second sequence of numbers begins on the inserted leaves.

[42] R. Nares, *Catalogue of the Harleian Manuscripts*, iii (1808), p. 384 ('As it was much decayed, & in great danger of being mutilated & misplaced, it has been lately re-bound, in four convenient volumes, 1805. R. N.'). The author of 'Coke's Original Manuscript' (next note) wrote in 1804 that 'little now remains' of the cover, and that the leaves were damaged and loose.

[43] The principal omissions from this edition are (i) notes derived from printed books, chiefly the year books; (ii) undatable notes and expositions for which no authority is cited; and (iii) the autobiographical memoranda at the beginning. The last were printed in Anon., 'Account of Sir Edward Coke's Original Manuscript of his Commentary upon Littleton' (1804) 1 *Law Journal* 112–120, 134–145; and in J. B[ruce], 'Sir Edward Coke's Vade Mecum' (1840) 6 *Collectanea Topographica et Genealogica* 108–122. (Bruce seems to have been unaware of the more complete 1804 edition.) The only additions to MS. Harley 6687 in the main text of this volume are the autograph marginalia from books at Holkham: see below, pp. xcvii–xcviii, 154–164.

[44] *AA*, fo. 17 (see the frontispiece to this volume); Baker, *Readers and Readings*, pp. 210, 300. Fleetwood was at this time a bencher of the Middle Temple and (most unusually in someone of his seniority) occupying the place of reader at New Inn 'pur son pleasure'.

[45] *Willoughby* v. *Egerton* (1604) CUL MS. Gg.4.9, fo. 95 ('... Cooke attorney generall al contra, et il cyte le forme des mootes in le Temple, et dit que ceo fuit construction de pleadinge, et que al primer jour del moote le plaintife comence "Vous aves cy etc." et count, et sur ceo imparlance, et al prochein jour commence "Vous aves bien intend", issint que le second nest forsque recytall, come Tanfeild ad dit'). The reporter added, 'nest issint in Lincolns Inne.'

[46] He was elected reader in Easter term 1579: *AA*, fos. 13, 17. There is some evidence that he may have served as a deputy reader there before his call, but the reading proper lasted one calendar year: Baker, *Readers and Readings*, p. 207. For the prefatory lecture see below, p. cxxiv.

learning in the inn during his year of office.[47] Coke knew the value of readings and moots. He owned a massive book of 802 folio leaves containing manuscript readings, beginning with one on Magna Carta and ending with his own Inner Temple reading of 1592.[48] It has not been found, and the catalogue description does not indicate how much of the content was Elizabethan. But Coke, like his contemporaries, did not regard readings as a regular source of authority and seldom cited them in his notebooks[49] or in court.[50] They contained unofficial law, and some history, necessary to a student's formation but not part of a lawyer's forensic stock-in-trade.[51] Some, in fact, were more concerned with showing off the reader's dexterity, or stirring the students out of their natural state of inattention, than with authoritative legal restatement.[52] Coke was scathing about the decline in the quality of readings,[53] though he cited some of the better known modern texts in his commonplace-books.[54]

The learning of Westminster Hall

In term-time Coke went regularly to Westminster Hall to listen to the arguments in court, a practice which he began in 1571 while at Clifford's Inn, aged nineteen.[55] The

---

[47] Two disputed cases survive in BL MS. Add. 16169, fos. 191v–194 ('Lions In, per Cook lector, 26 Februarii 1579 [1580], 22 Eliz.'), 252v–253v ('L. Yn. Cooke lector', early 1581). George Wilde of the Inner Temple was his deputy in 1581: ibid., fo. 253v.

[48] *Library of Sir Edward Coke*, pp. 24–25, no. 318. Only one (partial) text of Coke's own reading, on the Statute of Uses, is known to survive: below, p. clv.

[49] Examples of old readings being cited are *AA*, fo. 221v ('ex lectura Wood'); *AB*, fos. 167 (on Winchester), 275v ('launcient reading' on castle-guard); *AC*, fo. 515v ('Nota per Carell et Wood reder ...'); *AD*, fos. 766 ('Nota ex quadam lectura sur lestatut de 1 R. 3'), 770 (Westminster II, c. 13), 777 (Gloucester); Coke's *Statuta*, fo. 8 ('Nota Herle [*recte* Hesketh] dit in son lecture sur cest statute [Carta de Foresta] ...'). He twice referred to Dyer C.J.'s citation of Thomas Frowyk's reading (1495): below, pp. 46, 132. In 1586 he explained the origin of ancient demesne with reference to 'un aunciect readinge': CUL MS. Dd.11.64, fo. 31; cf. BL MS. Harley 443, fo. 126 ('un larned lecture' on the same point). Coke's *Statuta* contains eight marginal references to 'launcient reading' on Merton, Westminster I and Westminster II: fos. 10v, 11, 28, 33, 35, 74, 79, 80v. Cf. Co. Litt. 32b ('an ancient and learned reading' on Merton). There are several references in the commonplace-books to Thomas Marow's reading of 1503 on justices of the peace; and see Coke's *Statuta*, fo. 115 ('Marowe in son reading fo. 17').

[50] E.g. *Ward's Case* (1586) BL MS. Harley 443, fo. 126 ('Coke dit que ad vieue un larned lectur que dit que le reason daunciert demesne fuit pur ceo que le Roy Edward le Confessor et Roy William teignont lour terre ove garisons ...'); differently reported in BL MS. Add. 25195, fo. 73 (tr. in 132 Selden Soc. 98, n. 6).

[51] See also Baker, *Reinvention of Magna Carta*, pp. 237–238.

[52] This was not a new phenomenon in the Elizabethan period: ibid. 82–85.

[53] In Co. Litt. 280 he lamented that they had become 'liker rather to riddles than lectures ... and the readers are like to lapwings, who seem to be nearest their nests when they are farthest from them, and all their study is to find nice evasions out of the statute'. The lapwing figure was taken from his own reading of 1592 (Co. Uses, fo. 136v): 'I have not followed the nature of a lapwing who to deceive the seeker flieth farthest from her nest and yet seemeth to be alwayes next it, for in this readinge by plaine and expresse wordes I bringe you to the closett of myne owne conceipt ...'. It was a well-known contemporary simile: see J. E. Harting, *The Ornithology of Shakespeare* (1871), p. 220.

[54] Examples are *AA*, fos. 220 ('per Mr Bromley en son lecture sur ceux estatutes); *AC*, fos. 501v ('le lecture de Segnior Dier sur le statut de willes'), 659 ('Nota per Manwood in son reding ...'); *AD*, fo. 882* ('lectura Gilbert').

[55] Below, p. 86, no. 140 ('Nota que jeo oy in le common banke Weston in 13 Eliz. adire que ...'). For cases of 1571 which he may have reported see above, p. lxxvii, n. 37; below, pp. 93, 103. See also Co. Litt. 148 ('Hill. 14 Eliz. which I myselfe heard and observed'), probably referring to *Winter's Case* (1572) below, p. 81, no. 128.

court of greatest interest to the serious student was still the Common Pleas, where complex property cases were argued with deep learning by the serjeants at law, and Coke's earliest reports concentrated on that court. There he could see at first hand how the common learning of the year books was pressed into service in real life. After he was called to the bar in 1578, he usually attended the King's Bench,[56] where he was to establish a substantial practice in the 1580s.[57] On the way home from Westminster, perhaps on the ferry to Temple Stairs, he could engage in conversations with judges and serjeants,[58] and other senior members of the Bar.[59] Ambulatory instruction is first mentioned in the year books by a fifteenth-century reporter who frequently returned in the company of Sir Thomas Littleton (d. 1481),[60] though the practice may have come to an end in the Elizabethan period.[61] It was a valuable opportunity for personal contact between young men and their elders. Coke, of course, was hardly typical of the former. Indeed, he made such an impression on everyone that within three years of call he was engaging professionally with senior counsel at the highest level.[62]

For the period after 1535, the last year printed in the year-book canon,[63] access to reports of cases was largely a matter of self-help. However, the beginning of Coke's legal education coincided by chance with the publication of the first part of Plowden's *Comentaries* (1571), an important and influential volume which inaugurated a new phase in law reporting.[64] Coke owned two copies, and commonplaced much of the

---

[56] Coke consistently so referred to the court in the time of Elizabeth I, and his usage is followed here. He took the view that, as with a King's or Queen's College (vol. ii, p. 349), it did not change its name with the sovereign. But the formal name did change in the Latin of the records.

[57] Coke was called to the bar on 20 April 1578. Barristers had no right of audience in the Common Pleas. But Coke was occasionally retained of counsel in Common Pleas cases, presumably to assist serjeants: e.g. *Skipwith's Case* (1591) BL MS. Harley 4552, fo. 125 (cited by Coke in 1597).

[58] See below, p. 23, no. 45 (Manwood J., 1577); p. 50, no. 97 (Thomas Gawdy J., 1577); vol. ii, p. 203 (Francis Gawdy sjt, 1583); p. 283 (Wray C.J., 1585).

[59] See BL MS. Harg. 322, fo. 130v ('come Serjeant Barrham a moy [*Christopher Yelverton*] dit veignant del Westm.', 1567/77); MS. Add. 36080, fo. 103v ('Mr Humphrey Bridges dit a moy veniendo de Westm.', 1586); MS. Add. 35949, fo. 132, and CUL MS. Ll.3.9, fo. 141 ('veniendo de Westm. ove Lawrence Tanfield, il cite judgement 28 Eliz. in Banck le Roy', 1590).

[60] YB Mich. 7 Edw. IV, fo. 20, pl. 22 (1467); Mich. 49 Hen. VI, fo. 14, pl. 8 (1470); Pas. 12 Edw. IV, fo. 2, pl. 5, and fo. 24, pl. 10 (1472). Cf. YB Hil. 6 Hen. VII, fo. 15, pl. 8 (Townshend J., 1491); Pas. 10 Hen. VII, fo. 23, pl. 27 (Kebell sjt); Mich. 20 Hen. VII, fo. 9, pl. 18 (Fyneux C.J., 1504); *Anon.* (1526) 120 Selden Soc. 58, pl. 44 (Fitzherbert J., 1526); Mich. 27 Hen. VIII, fo. 26, pl. 5 (Fitzherbert J., 1535).

[61] Other examples, though from different routes, are in Richard Baker's reports, All Souls College, Oxford, MS. 156, fo. 70v ('Jovis 22 Maii 1589, veniendo de Saint Johns ove Egerton, sollicitor la Roigne, jeo demaund de luy cest question ...'); Bodl. Lib. MS. Rawlinson C. 85, fo. 203 ('Manwood chief baron mist cest case en le voye chivauchant a London al Mich. tearme anno 32 Eliz.', which evidently refers to his journey up from home in Kent in 1590).

[62] In 1581 Coke was more than once retained as junior to the attorney-general (Popham): below, p. ciii (*Shelley's Case*); vol. ii, p. 182 (*Bowes* v. *Leisley*). The following year he held his own in argument against Plowden, 'an ancient apprentice': *Borough* v. *Dickes* (1582) vol. ii, p. 193. The next year he was arguing against the solicitor-general (Egerton): *R.* v. *Marquess of Winchester* (1583) vol. ii, p. 223. And against Popham: *Wiseman's Case* (1583) ibid. 228. In the same year he was engaged by the lord chancellor to move a question to the two chief justices: *Pelham* v. *Bowes* (1583) ibid. 229.

[63] It was printed in the 1540s, and there is no significance in the date 1535.

[64] Baker, *Collected Papers*, ii. 565–568; *OHLE*, vi. 474–475. For Plowden's influence on the criminal law, which occupied only eight folios in his reports (fos. 97–100v, 473–476v), see J. Baker, '*R v Saunders and Archer* (1573)' in *Landmark Cases in Criminal Law*, ed. P. Handler, H. Mares and I. Williams (Oxford, 2017), pp. 29–57.

content in his notebooks,⁶⁵ often citing it by the name of the case rather than that of the reporter: every case in Plowden was engrained in the student's memory. Two far less polished series of Common Pleas reports covering the same extensive period, and circulating widely in manuscript, were those of Mr Justice Harper (for the period 1546 to 1573) and Mr Serjeant Bendlowes (1534 to 1578); but it is doubtful whether the former was available before 1577, when Harper died, or the latter before 1578, where most copies end.⁶⁶ Coke never cited Harper,⁶⁷ though he did make regular use of Bendlowes and at some point possessed a manuscript copy which he claimed to be the autograph.⁶⁸ Chief Justice Dyer's reports were not at large before they were printed in 1585/86, but after their publication Coke added numerous references to them throughout his commonplace-books,⁶⁹ and at some time he gained access to a copy of the autograph notebooks⁷⁰ – containing many cases not in print – through Sir William Peryam (d. 1604), chief baron of the Exchequer, who had been a puisne justice of the Common Pleas at the time of Dyer's death and had reportedly been Dyer's favourite to succeed him.⁷¹ Coke made extensive use of the Peryam

---

⁶⁵ His prime copy is Holkham Hall, BN 8017, which has a table written in his early, italic hand, presumably compiled by himself. The book is in pristine condition and is annotated only with sparse reading-notes. The other copy (BN 7943) bears his signature, but the marginal notes are in another hand, probably that of William Heydon, whose signature is also present, or William's father Sir Christopher Heydon (d. 1579) of Baconsthorpe, Norf., whose initials are stamped on the cover. Christopher was overseer of Coke's father's will. For William see below, p. ccxix.

⁶⁶ In *AB*, fos. 292–299 there is a selection of cases 'Ex libro Bendlowes servientis ad legem 1578', preceding some abridgments from the second part of Plowden (1579), which shows that Coke had access to a manuscript by 1578 or 1579. Bendlowes died in 1584.

⁶⁷ The reports are difficult to isolate since few manuscripts bear his name and they seem often to be mixed with other cases or continued with later reports. Moreover, they typically begin in Mich. 1546 with reports which have also been attributed (less solidly) to Dalison: see 124 Selden Soc., pp. xix-xx. There is a citation of the true Dalison in *AA*, fo. 100 (petit treason). But the citation in *AC*, fo. 641v ('Dalison, 8 Eliz., fol. 5') refers to a date after Dalison's death in 1559.

⁶⁸ BL MS. Harley 1331, fo. 52; quoted below, p. 56, n. 2. Cf. *Library of Sir Edward Coke*, p. 28, no. 349 ('Bendloes reports in fol:'). He nearly always cited the reports without folio: see e.g. *AD*, fo. 120v (below, p. 148, no. 272: 'Bendlowes, 9 H. 8.'); *C*, fos. 32 (vol. iii, p. 479: 'report per Mr Bendlowes'), 145 (vol. iii, p. 690: 'Bendlowes serjaunt report que …'), 149 (vol. iii, p. 696: 'report per Serjaunt Bendlowes'), 171 (vol. iii, p. 729: 'come Bendlowes report'), 323 (vol. v, p. 960: 'Vide Bendlowes case vide Tr. 4 Eliz. in Bendlowes report'), 347v (vol. ibid. 1006: 'Et issint fuit adjudge in autiel case report per Bendlowes in case dun Broughton'), 556v ('Nota lecture [*sic*] un case report per Serjant Bendlowes M. 3 H. 8, rott. 349'), 674 ('le report de Serjant Bendlowes'). But cf. *AA*, fo. 145 ('Vide fo. 9, Bendlowes, Tr. 4 Eliz.'); *C*, fo. 67v (vol. iii, p. 548: 'Bendl. 240'). A citation in *C*, fo. 341 ('Vide Bendl. 4 E. 6, 110b, Periam') suggests he had the copy of Bendlowes as well as Dyer from Peryam, but it is a solitary reference in that form and more likely a slip. The references in *AB*, fo. 274 ('in mes notes escries hors del livre de Serjaunt Bendeloes'), and *AC*, fo. 505v ('Bendlowes in mes notes, fol. 5b') are to Coke's own selection from Bendlowes in *AB*, fos. 292–299. George Croke copied some 'Cases hors del liver Serjant Benlowes collect per Edward Cooke le puisne' (*V*, fos. 27–29v; for Coke's juniority see above, p. lxxiv).

⁶⁹ Sir James Dyer, *Ascun Novel Cases* (1585, old style). Conversely, Coke's copy of this (Holkham Hall, BN 8014, cited below as Coke's Dyer) contains many marginal cross-references to his own reports of the same cases: see Appendix III, below. The book cost him 13s. 4d.

⁷⁰ There is a citation in *Arundell's Case* (1587) vol. ii, p. 325, in what does not seem to be an addition, though the whole report is possibly in a later hand. The compiler of BL MS. Add. 48186 (section P to Q of an important abridgment) also had access to a manuscript copy of Dyer, possibly the autograph, but it is not there cited by folio: e.g. fo. 201v ('H. 7 Eliz. Dyer's MS.': *habeas corpus* to the Fleet); fo. 323 ('M. 4 & 5 Eliz. Dyer's manuscript': *Warner's Case*); fo. 435 ('T. 7 Eliz., Dyer's MS.': *Wilkes's Case* of a protection).

⁷¹ 109 Selden Soc., introduction, p. xxxiii. There were only two other justices of the court in 1582, Thomas Mead and Francis Wyndham.

manuscript, and may have acquired it himself after Peryam's death;[72] by 1610 he had acquired two volumes of the autograph manuscript as well.[73] Also occurring as later additions to the commonplace-books, and likewise in the form of bare citations rather than abridged extracts, are citations to the manuscript reports by Sir John Spelman (d. 1546),[74] Mr Serjeant Caryll (d. 1523),[75] the younger John Caryll (d. 1566),[76] and 'Wyndam'.[77] The last was presumably an autograph manuscript which Coke acquired in his capacity as one of the supervisors of Mr Justice Wyndham's will after his death in 1592.[78] Although Wyndham had served as a judge since 1579, there seems to have been only one surviving volume running from 1581 to 1589.[79] Coke did not copy

[72] The citations in MSS. *A* and *C* are mostly in the form 'Dier Periam': see the table of citations in Appendix VIII, below, p. cxxxiii. That this was not the autograph is shown by a citation in *AA*, fo. 42, as 'Dier fol. 95 nient imprint', to which Coke later added 'manu propria 110': the passage is identifiable in 109 Selden Soc. 17, and fo. 95 is in sequence with other Peryam citations, while fo. 110 is in sequence with what we know of the autograph. The Peryam MS. is that referred to in the edition of Dyer's notebooks (109–110 Selden Soc.) as the 'volumes in secretary hand'. Since they were later owned together with the autograph volumes which Coke owned, it seems likely that he owned these as well: 109 Selden Soc. xli.

[73] Baker, *Collected Papers*, ii. 734. He showed one in the King's Bench in 1615: Timothy Tourneur's reports, BL MS. Add. 35957, fo. 8. For references to his ownership in and after 1614 see also 10 Co. Rep., preface (1614); 11 Co. Rep. 77 (1615); 3 Buls. 49–50 (1615); 2 Co. Inst. 61; *Library of Sir Edward Coke*, p. 23, no. 302. Sir George Treby said, when he produced the autograph manuscript in court in 1682, that it was annotated in Coke's hand: *R.* v. *City of London* (1682) 8 St. Tr. at col. 1112. It has not been heard of since.

[74] See Appendix VII, below. For further references to Spelman in Coke's printed works see Baker, *Collected Papers*, ii. 734, n. 55.

[75] *AC*, fos. 521v ('8 H. 8 ... come Carrell report'), 635 ('5 H. 8 report Carell'); *AD*, fo. 846v (same); *C*, fo. 635 (same). These reports were printed in 1602, anonymously, from a manuscript of Robert Keilwey which had passed to John Croke. Coke cited the printed book as Keilwey: *AA*, fo. 76v ('Keil. Rep.'); *AB*, fo. 420v ('Vide 8 H. 8, Keylwey 190'); *C*, fo. 579 ('21 H. 7, Kelwey 82').

[76] E.g. *AA*, fo. 49v ('Nota que il fuit loppinion de Carell, si market soit grant per le roy, et puis reveigne a maynes le roy, que le market nest exteinte'); *AB*, fo. 341v ('28 H. 8, Carell'); *AD*, fo. 35 (vol. ii, p. 363: 'Carell, un famous apprentice del ley, ad note in son livre ...'). In 1586 Coke cited a case of 1553 'hors de report Carrell': BL MS. Lansd. 1095, fo. 35v. This John Caryll, the serjeant's son, was a bencher of the Inner Temple and attorney of the Duchy. For his reports see 120 Selden Soc., introduction, pp. xl-xli. They seem to have been in circulation in the Inner Temple by the 1580s: CUL MS. Dd.11.64, fo. 22, *per* Hele ('Carell report que fuit tenus en 1 M. 1 ...'). They were also sometimes cited as Keilwey's, presumably because Keilwey owned them: e.g. Richard Baker's reports, All Souls College, Oxford, MS. 156, fo. 74 ('In un report del Mr Kellaway fuit demande des justices 20 H. 8 ...').

[77] In *Davenant* v. *Hurdis* (1599) BL MS. Harg. 5, fo. 73v, and CUL MS. Dd.8.48, p. 105, Coke cited the case of *Spencer* v. *Burton*, Trin. 25 Eliz., rot. 606, from Wyndham's reports (abridged on fo. 82 as 'report per J. W.'). The reports were also known to others: see e.g. Moo. 371, *per* Popham Att.-Gen. (1594), citing *Lovelace* v. *Lovelace* (1585) 'report per Justice Windham'; IT MS. Misc. 46, fos. 129, 178v ('Mich. 26 & 27 Eliz. in communi banco del report de Justice Windham'); HLS MS. 1193 (2070), fo. 44 ('Harris monstre un case, et le maine de Justice Windam escry a ceo', concerning robbery). There is no mention of the manuscript in Coke's library catalogue.

[78] Coke was one of the judge's two testamentary supervisors, the other being Sir Francis Gawdy. He cited the reports in court in 1595: Moo. 371 ('il vouch un case report per Justice Windham en le Common Bank en 26 & 27 Eliz. Reginae rot. 343 ou 323 et adjudge Trin. 27 Eliz. en accion de wast per Leonard Lovelace vers Thomas Lovelace ...').

[79] The earliest seems to be *AD*, fo. 765 ('Wyndam 23 El. fol. 3'), and the latest ibid. 711v, 753v ('Tr. 31 El. Wyndam 63'), which seems out of sequence with a reference in *AA*, fo. 198v ('Notleys case, P. 31 Eliz. Wyndam fol. 70b'); cf. *AB*, fo. 387 ('Wyndam 31 Eliz. 57'). On fo. 6v of the Wyndham MS. (cit. in *AA*, fo. 212v) there was a report of 26 Eliz. identifiable as *Thoroughgood* v. *Cole* (1584) (which Coke noted from the record in 1598: *C*, fo. 297v; 2 Co. Rep. 9). The case of 1587 cit. in *AD*, fo. 868v ('Vide 29 Eliz. pl. 32, Wynd[ham], inter Beverley et Cor[n]ewall') was also reported by Coke: vol. ii, p. 309. In *AC*, fo. 569, Coke cited the case of *praemunire* against Richard Nix, bishop of Norwich, 'in les reportes de Justice

excerpts from it, or provide much information about it beyond the bare citations, and the manuscript has not come to light. The Spelman citations seem also to refer to a copy which he owned himself, though it was not the autograph.[80] There is no evidence that he owned a copy of Caryll, though he said in his Lyons Inn reading of 1580 that 'il ad viewe le written report de le famous Carrell de le Inner Temple'.[81] Since he referred to it, prior to publication, as 'liber Keylwey',[82] it was almost certainly the copy made by or for Robert Keilwey and used as the text for John Croke's edition of 1602; no doubt it was made available to Coke somewhere in the Inner Temple.[83] Bendlowes and Harper, and perhaps Caryll, were 'published', in the sense that (though unprinted) they were often copied and generally known to the more learned members of the profession, as opposed to the more or less 'private reports'[84] which circulated within closer circles. Printing, of course, immediately placed 'private reports' in the public domain. But the distinction may still have been of value in assessing their content. Coke understood that Dyer's reports – most of which were printed posthumously, against the author's wishes – were written 'only for his private remembrance' and were not always accurate.[85] Plowden, on the other hand, was carefully edited for publication. And the year books, for all their deficiencies, were believed to have been of official origin.[86]

How far Coke made unacknowledged use of 'private' manuscript reports in the 1570s is unclear.[87] There had been a tradition in earlier generations of circulating notes of cases within the inns of court,[88] and – since there is evidence that the tradition

---

Wyndam'. But this was a case of 1534, and it seems probable that Wyndam here was a slip for Spelman, or that Wyndham had copied Spelman's report of the case: as to which see 93 Selden Soc. 192; 94 Selden Soc. 69, n. 5; 102 Selden Soc. 75.

[80] This was mentioned in *Library of Sir Edward Coke*, p. 26, no. 328 ('One great booke of Judiciall records intitled liber j^{us} precedentium et recordorum etc. cont. 514 leaves, wherein fol. 111 are parte of Justice Spilmans reports ...'). The part containing Spelman is not to be found at Holkham Hall, where only fos. 488–512 (concerning Mary, queen of Scots) appear to have survived. A table in Coke's hand to an unidentified volume of his own collections includes 'Spilmans reports 1': YLS MS. G.R24.1, fo. 177.

[81] BL MS. Add. 16169, fo. 192; quoted more fully in 115 Selden Soc. xvii, n. 67. He was referring to the elder Caryll, who was a bencher of the Inner Temple prior to taking the coif in 1510.

[82] E.g. *AC*, fos. 138 ('extra librum Keylwey'), 245v (ex libro Kelywaye'); vol. iii, p. 567 ('je ay vieu un report in le livre de Keylwey', 1594); vol. iv, p. 837 ('Nota ex libro Kelywaye fuit adjudge in 19 H. 7 ...', cit. in 1597). On the title-page of his copy of the 1602 edition (Holkham Hall, BN 7932), Coke wrote that 'Caril fuit le reporter de cest livre', and on fo. 82, in the margin, he identified 'moy' in the report as 'Carill'.

[83] Keilwey and Croke were both Inner Templars. See below, p. cx.

[84] For this phrase see BL MS. Add. 35941, fo. 240v (1586/87): 'Fenner vouch cest case hors del private report in 18 Eliz.' It was also used merely for reports which were not printed. E.g. in *Shelley's Case* Coke cited a case of 28 Hen. VIII 'privately reported by Mr Serjant Bendlows, which was begun in 26 H. 8 in the book at large' (i.e. the printed year book): BL MS. Add. 24845, fo. 220v. The printed version of Coke's report (1 Co. Rep. at fo. 96) omits the word 'privately', but retains 'at large' for the year book.

[85] In *R.* v. *O'Rourke* (1591) vol. iii, p. 566, 'they all resolved that the case in the lord Dyer's book, Mich. 19 & 20 Eliz., pl. 6, is not law, and Wray C.J. denied that he ever gave any such opinion as is there reported'. See also *Callard* v. *Callard* (1594) vol. iii, p. 606, referring to *Page* v. *Multon* (1571) Dyer 296, which Coke said did not agree with the record; and vol. v, p. 1075, where it is said that *Basset* v. *Corporation of Torrington* (1568) Dyer 276 was 'not fully reported'.

[86] This was Plowden's speculation, based on hearsay ('as I have of credit heard'), but Coke absorbed it as fact and led posterity astray by turning it into firm history: *Le Tierce Part des Reportes* (1602), sig. Cij. See Baker, *Collected Papers*, ii. 544–545.

[87] This is discussed further below, pp. xc–xcii.

[88] *OHLE*, vi. 475–486.

continued in the Inner Temple in the 1580s,[89] 1590s and 1600s[90] – it seems more than likely that it was also the current practice in Coke's student days. It was not an activity limited to students. Several more senior lawyers who became judges in the Elizabethan period are known to have kept reports in the 1570s which were, at least to some extent, made available to others.[91] But there is little overt evidence in Coke's earlier notebooks that he made use of such material.[92] There are more indications of borrowing, albeit without attribution, towards the end of the century.[93]

Another medium of transmission was oral reporting, or relation by word of mouth, in the sense of talking with others about cases one had watched or knew something about. Senior members of an inn of court could be particularly valuable teachers in this regard. In the Middle Temple, for instance, the venerable Edmund Plowden and the solicitor-general, John Popham, each assisted the students by telling them about current cases which might otherwise have been beyond their knowledge.[94] In Gray's

---

[89] In the period 1583–89 Richard Baker obtained reports from Edward Littleton (fos. 14, 15), Ralph Tilston (fos. 63, 70v, 74) and John Walter (fos. 73, 75, 79, 89): All Souls College, Oxford, MS. 156. These were all Inner Templars: Baker (from Monmouthshire), adm. 1579, called 1587; Littleton (from Shropshire), adm. 1574, called 1584; Tilston (from Cheshire), adm. 1582, called 1590; Walter (from Shropshire), adm. 1583, called 1590. Other reports by Inner Templars (1582–88) are noted in IT MS. Barrington 17, fos. 12–14 (Edmund Prideaux, adm. 1574, called 1584), 15 ([William] Cleyton, adm. 1578, called 1587), 98v ([John] Hatch, adm. 1576, called 1587) and 97v (John Walter). This manuscript also includes cases occurring verbatim in Coke's notebooks (below, p. cvii) and in the reports of George Croke (adm. 1575, called 1584). Croke's printed reports (Cro. Eliz.) include cases related in the 1580s by John Fountaine (adm. 1578, called 1587) (p. 15), Thomas Coventry (next note) (p. 48), John Walter (pp. 56, 58) and Edward Coke (pp. 28, 58). In CUL MS. Ll.3.8, fo. 357v, there is a case of 1576 'per le report de Dyett del Inner Temple' (Anthony Dyot, adm. 1576, called 1586).

[90] D. Ibbetson, 'Law Reporting in the 1590s' in *Law Reporting in Britain*, ed. C. Stebbings (1995), pp. 73–88; 'Coventry's Reports' (1995) 16 *Legal History* 281–303. Professor Ibbetson found no less than eighteen surviving copies of parts of Thomas Coventry's reports, with cases from 1598 to 1604. One of them (BL MS. Add. 25203) includes two quires of 160 folios each, in different hands, indicating commercial copying (fos. 213–372, 395–554, each numbered 1–160). Coventry, an Inner Templar, had access to Coke's manuscripts: below, pp. cviii–cix.

[91] Besides Richard Harper (whose reports continue to 1573) may be noticed Christopher Wray [C.J.K.B. 1574–92] (BL MS. Lansd. 1084, fo. 81: 'ante 27 Eliz. en Wrais reportes'); Robert Mounson [J.C.P. 1572–80] (BL MS. Add. 35953, fo. 29: *Vernon* v. *Vernon*, 1573, from 'Le report de Justice Mounson come fuit escrye desouth sa mayne'); John Clench [J.K.B. 1584–1602] (BL MS. Harley 4556: cases from 1571 to 1592, seemingly in his own hand); Francis Rodes [J.C.P. 1585–89] (BL MS. Harg. 374, fos. 81v, 167–175: cases from 1571 and 1572 'libro Magistri Rodes'; Cro. Eliz. 399: a case from 1576 in 'Justice Rhodes' reports; Golds. 52, where he refers to his own book of reports); Thomas Fleming [C.B. 1604–07, C.J.K.B. 1607–13] (CUL MS. Hh.2.9, fo. 65v; LI MS. Maynard 87, fo. 142v: 'le report de Mr Fleming' of a case of Mich. 1571); Lawrence Tanfield [C.B. 1607–25] (Dyer, ed. Treby, fo. 196a, n. 41: a case of 1577 in 'Tanfield's Rep. 51'). Some brief reports from 1591 to 1600 which may be Tanfield's are in BL MS. Add. 25201; at fo. 165v the writer says 'jeo fui accouncell cum Mr Candishe' in *Agard* v. *Candish* (1599), and Candish's counsel is identified in Cro. Eliz. 327 and Moo. 564 as Tanfield.

[92] There is a solitary reference to Bullock's reports: below, p. 143, no. 262. This is probably the Inner Temple bencher, John Bullock.

[93] Below, pp. xci–xcii.

[94] E.g. BL MS. Harley 5030, fos. 22 ('Nota que Popham le sollicitor [general] report cest case le 18 jour de November anno 1579, que il fuit decree in le Chauncery …'), 27 ('Nota bene que reporte fuit per le sollicitor [Popham] destre rule per le opinion de toutes les justices …'), 27v ('Popham, sollicitor et speaker de le Parliament report ceo destre rule …'), 33v ('Nota que come report fuit per Nedwolp [Plowden] et Popham, attorney le roy, lez justices avoient diverse foites done lour opinion in cest case ..'), 71 ('Un case rule in bank le roy per le reporte del Popham, attorney le roigne …'). (It is a matter for speculation why the unidentified reporter habitually wrote Plowden's name backwards as Nedwolp.) Note also MS. Harley 1699, fo. 53v ('Quere entre les studentes dun case que fuit in Banke', 1578).

Inn a regular informant was Gilbert Gerrard, attorney-general for the first half of Elizabeth's reign.[95] To judge from some indications in Coke's notes,[96] a like service may have been performed in the Inner Temple by Edmund Anderson, and it was to be continued later by Coke himself.[97] As Coke's notebooks bear witness, a further source of information about relatively recent case-law was the oral citation of remembered earlier cases by senior counsel arguing at the bar. Oral reports were, however, always more open to challenge than those in written versions of known authenticity. In 1586 Coke said of some manuscript reports cited by Tanfield that they were as easy to deny as to affirm.[98] And in *R.* v. *Englefield* (1591)[99] Serjeant Drew objected to three cases vouched by Popham, saying he had vouched only the parts which made for him and omitted what was against him, and that since the cases were not put into writing 'to the view and consideration of students', he would not answer them, but counter them with reason and as many authorities as he could.[1] Popham later brought along the records of two of the cases, only one of which was adjudged. Coke then sought to distinguish the adjudged case, dismissing the other as still *sub judice* and suggesting that if it was ever decided it would certainly be ruled the other way. These were the natural moves of advocates. But without doubt such exchanges were of considerable educational value for the students, and a source of case-law both for the students and their seniors. So, too, were private conversations with reliable informants.[2] No doubt a good deal of legal education also consisted in the oral transmission of doctrine without reference to cases.[3]

The Rylands manuscript, 1572–77

The only manuscript reports explicitly cited by Coke in the 1570s were those of Bendlowes, but he may have had access to others. His library catalogue mentions 'Thurston's three books of reports in folio' and 'two other manuscripts of reports in

---

[95] He is mentioned throughout Christopher Yelverton's commonplace-book, BL MS. Harg. 322: e.g. fos. 23, 38v, 50, 68, 73, 73v, 83, 89, 99, 101, 104 *ter*, 104v, 113, 115, 115v, 116v, 117, 120v, 130, 130v, 131, 134. Gerrard was attorney-general 1559–81, then master of the rolls. Yelverton occasionally acknowledged other benchers, such as Thomas Colby (fo. 131), Thomas Seckford (fo. 130) and Robert Shirburne (fos. 74, 82). Cf. fo. 104v ('Greys Inn apud le fyer').

[96] E.g. below, p. 39, no. 85; p. 102, no. 175. The first of these was cited by Coke in *R.* v. *Englefield* (1591) Moo. 303, at p. 324, as 'per un report que il ad del segnior Anderson'. Coke also noted information received from Anderson after he became a serjeant in 1577: below, p. 37, no. 80; p. 48, no. 92; p. 122, no. 213.

[97] E.g. BL MS. Harg. 8, fo. 260 ('Cooke dit a moy ...', referring to an *assumpsit* case of 1584); MS. Harg. 363, fo. 213v ('E. Cooke dit a moy ...', referring to *Lady Gresham's Case*).

[98] Godb. 84 ('As to the reports which are not printed, vouched by Tanfield, *eâdem facilitate negantur quâ affirmantur*').

[99] *R.* v. *Englefield* (1591) Moo. 303, at pp. 331–332.

[1] Moo. 331: '... al queux cases, n'esteant mise en escript al view et consideration des students, il ne voit faire responce, mes voiloit eux encounter ove reason et tant d'authorities come il poit.'

[2] Coke rarely made this explicit. But note, e.g., below, p. 85, no. 136 ('Quere de auters persons ...'); p. 155, no. 290 ('Plowden dit a moy'); vol. ii, p. 255 ('loppinion del segnior Aunderson, ut audivi'). Note also the 'I have heard' passages cited below, p. xciv, n. 62.

[3] This is the inference from *AB*, fo 466v ('Et nota que jeo ay oye le ley clerement prise que ...'). It is also implicit in references beginning 'Il est dit que ...' or 'Est communement prise que ...'. No doubt many of the notes in the commonplace-books which do not refer to authorities represent what Coke had 'heard'.

folio'.[4] The named reporter must be John Thurston, barrister of the Inner Temple, who was elected to read in 1560 but excused on grounds of illness; his date of death has not been ascertained, and it is not known when or how Coke acquired his reports or exactly what they contained,[5] though a solitary citation shows that they started before the beginning of Mary I's reign.[6] The identity of the other two is almost beyond speculation. But there is a puzzling manuscript in the John Rylands Library, University of Manchester, which may be one of them.[7] By the time it was bound up in its present form, in a collection of unrelated quires of law reports in different hands extending up to 1651,[8] it had lost any outward indicia of association with Coke. It has in consequence been overlooked. But it is entirely written in Coke's hand, and contains fifty-three cases between Michaelmas term 1572 and Trinity term 1577, nearly all from the Common Pleas.[9] This chronological series covers much the same period as the scattered cases in the commonplace-books, and it includes reports of several of the prominent cases which occur in the latter.

Given the same commencement date and the same handwriting, it would be easy to jump to the conclusion that these were Coke's own reports from his student days. What is more, one of the cases near the end – a note of something said to the reporter in 1577 by Mr Justice Gawdy on the way back from Westminster ('Nota Justice Gawdy dit a moy veniendo de Westminster …') – is duplicated in closely similar words in the commonplace-book.[10] The telling word 'moy' suggests that the author of the note in the Rylands manuscript was the same person as the 'moy', written in the same hand, in the Harleian manuscript. It seems unlikely that Coke would have copied it into his private commonplace-book without altering the pronoun if it meant someone else.[11] Gawdy was Coke's maternal uncle,[12] and is mentioned as an informant elsewhere in the notebooks.[13] In 1588 Coke cited this note, from the

---

[4] *Library of Sir Edward Coke*, p. 28, nos. 347–348. This inventory was compiled shortly before Coke's death.

[5] *The Men of Court*, ii. 1532 (adm. in or before 1547, called by 1553). His reports would be of considerable interest, but they have not been found. If he was John Thurston J.P. of Hoxne, Suff., he is likely to have been adm. around 1540; his brass at Hoxne says he was aged 89 when he died in 1606.

[6] Coke's Dyer, fo. 338, citing '1 Mar. Thurst. 107'. Thurston is almost certainly the source of the serjeants' case of 1555 'reported by an ancient and learned bencher of the Inner Temple': 10 Co. Rep. 128. The paucity of references, compared with the manuscript reports of Dyer and Wyndham (both judges), shows that Coke did not esteem them highly.

[7] JRL MS. Fr. 118, fos. 15–90v. The first remaining page (fo. 15r) is illustrated in plate 4. It is tatty, with some loss in the top right-hand corner, showing that this item (already without fos. 1–14) spent some of its life without a cover. The contents are listed in Appendix II.

[8] Baker, *Collected Papers*, ii. 753.

[9] The first eleven were numbered by Coke, and the numbering is extended in Appendix II from 12 to 57. Four of the entries are continuations of cases reported earlier in the manuscript.

[10] JRL MS. Fr. 118, fo. 81v; below, p. 50, no. 97 (Trin. 1577); abridged (by another hand) in *V*, fo. 33. The first two texts, both in Coke's hand, are illustrated in plate 5.

[11] It is to be observed, however, that George Croke retained the 'moy' when he abridged the same case in his own notebook: *V*, fo. 33.

[12] He was the husband of Coke's aunt Audrey (née Knightley).

[13] Below, p. 71, no. 116 (reporting a private judicial discussion in 1576); p. 158, no. 301 (Gawdy J.); cf. 4 Co. Inst. 37. Likewise Serjeant (Francis) Gawdy: vol. ii, p. 203 (1583). In 1586 Coke lent Thomas Gawdy money, and in 1588 purchased from him a share of Bevis Marks (a house in Aldgate, London): Coke's Dyer, endpaper. Coke helped to prepare the judge's will, which contained annotations in his hand: Boyer, *Coke and the Elizabethan Age*, p. 44.

commonplace-book, as a case 'reported by me'.[14] And when he cited it again, in 1591, he said it was a case 'which I had from the report of Sir Thomas Gawdy ... see in my reports'.[15] These citations seem naturally to mean that he was the author of the report. When the two texts of this note are compared, however, they are found to differ in several respects. In the commonplaced version some further explanation for the decision was added, with an illustrative example, a reference to actions on the case was dropped, and the dissent by Wray C.J. was edited out. It is thus evident that the Rylands version was reworked as it went into the commonplace-book.

These few lines of text raise the problematic question whether the whole of the Rylands text was Coke's own composition. The Gawdy note, and the case which follows it,[16] are written at the top of the page and, unlike all the other cases in the manuscript, are written full out into the margin. Although they are in a very similar style of neat handwriting, they have the appearance of having been inserted into a blank space. But the Gawdy item was not the only text to find its way, in edited form, into Coke's commonplace-books. There are other passages in both texts which are close enough in wording to indicate that Coke occasionally copied or paraphrased parts of the Rylands text into his *vade mecum*. For instance, the anonymous copyhold case in *AB* (no. 59) is clearly a thoughtful précis of the report in the Rylands manuscript, omitting the names of counsel and some other details. Although the revised version is only about half the length, little of legal significance was omitted. The report in *AD* (no. 231) of Manwood J.'s argument in *Onley* v. *Earl of Kent* has some distinctive phrases[17] which suggest that it, too, was based on the Rylands text. On the other hand, most of the snippets from that case in the notebooks (nos. 29, 173, 178, 230 and 231) – three of which mention Dyer C.J. – are evidently not based on the Rylands manuscript, in which Dyer C.J.'s speech is omitted altogether.[18] Moreover, the Manwood passage in *AD* appears to have been added at the end of what Coke had originally written, as if he were using the Rylands text to add missing detail. *Androwes* v. *Blunt* presents a different peculiarity. The Rylands version lacks the arguments, but has a statement of the case in almost exactly the same words as *AB* (no. 86), apart from a passage at the end. The Rylands text mistook the defendant's name, which is correctly given in *AB*, and yet it followed the pleadings more closely.[19]

A further complexity in this connection arises from the discovery of two leaves of reports from Michaelmas term 1572 on the front endpapers of Coke's year books of *21–39 Henry VI* at Holkham Hall (BN 7938). There are six cases, very neatly and closely written in Coke's hand, and three of them – occupying the last three of the four pages – occur in variant form in the Rylands manuscript.[20] The first three cases,

---

[14] Vol. ii, p. 396 ('le case del segnior admirall 19 Eliz. report per moy, fol. 73b').

[15] *C*, fo. 21v; vol. iii, p. 455 ('quod habui ex relatione Thome Gawdy militis unius justiciariorum banci regii, et vide in mes reportes fol. [*blank*]').

[16] This second case is not matched by anything found in the commonplace-books.

[17] E.g. 'weight and substance of the action', 'if he has spent much he will recover much'.

[18] This is not attributable to the loss of leaves at the end, because the report ends with the speech of Manwood J. at the top of the last page, the remainder of the page being blank.

[19] Unlike the version in *AB*, it mentioned an earlier presentation to the benefice in dispute by the queen. But this may have been edited out as legally irrelevant.

[20] The fourth case is pl. 5 in the Rylands MS., the fifth is pl. 6, and the sixth is pl. 13 (*Cranmer's Case*).

however, cannot be found there.[21] And the last item, a report of *Cranmer's Case*, stops short of giving the opinions of the judges, which are present in the Rylands manuscript. Comparison of the three cases which occur in both manuscripts shows that the Rylands manuscript contains a number of improvements which are the result of active thought.[22] This might point to the fly-leaves being a draft for the more extensive text. It would not be at all surprising if reports began life as drafts on odd sheets of paper,[23] and it seems likely that Coke prepared some of his later reports in draft.[24] A fly-leaf might serve just as well as a sheet of paper.[25] On the other hand, the Holkham fragment has none of the appearance of a draft. As with the longer manuscript, it is not strewn with authorial corrections or additions of the kind which typify Coke's own reports, but only a few corrections of slips made in the course of writing, some of which appear to be haplographies. It is not an attempt to frame the report of a single case, but part of a chronological series belonging to a single term, and it is in the conventional year-book format which Coke did not follow in his known reports. It is clearly a transcript of something else. But it is extremely difficult to explain why Coke copied out the two versions so carefully. The little series of six cases at Holkham has no connection with the printed year books to which it is prefixed. And its relationship with the Rylands text is far from clear. It contains some material which is not in the longer manuscript: not just the three initial cases, but matter within the overlapping reports. Moreover, the last two cases, though found in both manuscripts, are separated from each other in the Rylands manuscript by several other cases. This is not, therefore, simply a piece of the same text in an earlier form. A plausible explanation for the existence of the two texts in Coke's hand may be connected with 1572 being the very year in which Coke joined the Inner Temple. Copying reports had long been part of a student's induction process. It seems possible that Coke borrowed some contemporary reports to copy out, to help him understand the cases he was listening to in Westminster Hall, and that after copying some of them out on the fly-leaves of his year book he found a better text to copy out in full as a separate book. But this is speculation.

Yet another puzzle in the Rylands manuscript is the endorsement in Coke's hand on the last page. This mentions seven cases to be found in three books, the *Liber primus*, the *Liber secundus* and the *Liber longus*. The first, Book One, cannot be the surviving *Liber primus* (in this edition designated *C*) which bears that title in Coke's hand. All we are told of it is that it contained *Copley's Case*, concerning a joint

[21] The whole text is printed in Appendix I, below, pp. clxxiii–cxciii.

[22] The first of them is collated with the Rylands MS. (pl. 5) in Appendix II, below, p. cxciv. The second is collated with the Rylands MS. (pl. 6) below, p. 50, following no. 96. The third is printed in Appendix I, p. clxxvii, collated with the Rylands MS.

[23] For an explicit reference to this practice in 1572 see BL MS. Harg. 374, fo. 152 ('Plus de termino Michaelis anno 14 et 15 que jeo escrye en papers primes'). An example of a rough note, probably made in court, is BL MS. Add. 42855, fos. 45–51 (originally separate sheets), with jottings of arguments by 'Mr Atturney' and 'Mr Ed. Coke' on 26 April and 14 May 1591.

[24] In *Wynsmore* v. *Hulbert* (1586) vol. ii, p. 314, at p. 315, a note referring to the following Trinity term (1587) is apparently written in the same hand, without disturbing the layout. Cf., likewise, the note at the end of *Amner* v. *Lodington* (1587) ibid. 319. *Owen* v. *Morgan* (Pas. 1588) ibid. 371, is entered as 'circa hunc terminum'. A number of the verbal slips which Coke himself corrected in the first and second notebooks are suggestive of rapidly detected haplographies, though others indicate deliberate rewording.

[25] There are, however, no comparable manuscript reports on the other fly-leaves in Coke's library.

tenancy by fine; but this cannot be identified in any of Coke's notebooks. From the *Liber secundus* are cited *The Dean of St Paul's Case* and *The Dean of Worcester's Case* (which was to be found at 'le commencement'). These cases are noted by Coke, in *AA* and *AB*, but the latter case is on Coke's folio 79, not at the beginning. And there is no evidence that there was an earlier autograph notebook which could have been an anterior *Liber primus*. From the third book mentioned, the so-called *Liber longus*, are cited *Manser's Case*, *Lord Lovell's Case* (presumably *Nichols* v. *Nichols*) and *Ireland's Case*. But these cases are in the same Harleian manuscript. *Lord Lovell's Case* is in the second sequence of folio numberings in *AA*, which was once a separate notebook (continued in *AB*), but the other two are in the same notebook as the cases assigned to the *Liber secundus*. Since the first notebook bound up in *AA* is in fact longer (at 120 folios) than the second one, which is now divided between *AA* and *AB* (76 folios), and they are of the same height, the latter could not have qualified for the appellation *longus*. It is therefore impossible to square these citations with Coke's autograph notebooks.[26] But this is a diversion from the main one.

If all the parallel texts exhibited the same kinds of interconnection as those mentioned in the penultimate paragraph, a case might be built up for saying that the Rylands manuscript contained a series of original reports by Coke from which he edited extracts for insertion in his *vade mecum*. It would not be inconsistent with that to suppose that Coke's editing, for the purpose of inclusion in a commonplace-book, included the addition or omission of detail and the correction of errors.[27] This is a superficially attractive hypothesis, and yet there are major difficulties with it. The Rylands text is traditional in form, giving the arguments of counsel and judges in order of seniority, as they spoke, following their own subdivisions of the points to be argued, whereas Coke's style in his earlier known reports was to analyse the points of law first, and arrange the judges' views within that scheme, generally ignoring counsel. Although the Rylands reports are on the whole fuller, they are sometimes incomplete, omitting judicial remarks which are nevertheless noticed in Coke's commonplace-books. The report of *Manser* v. *Annesley* is completely different, and clearly not the source of the version in *AA* (printed below, no. 30). Likewise, *Gyles* v. *Colshill* (below, no. 113 is reported quite differently in the two manuscripts. Then again, the full report of *Winter's Case* in the Rylands text contains only the arguments of counsel, whereas the shorter version in *AB* (no. 88) abridges the opinions of the judges by name. The report of *Vernon* v. *Vernon* in *AB* (no. 118) has something in common with the Rylands manuscript, but it is differently arranged and has arguments by Dyer C.J., whereas the Rylands text is incomplete and lacks Dyer C.J.'s contribution. Sometimes, conversely, it is the Rylands manuscript which has more information than the commonplaced version. For instance, the report of *Latton's Case* (*Eyston* v. *Studde*) in the former contains significant legal arguments which are not in *AA* (no. 51), and reports *Delaware's Case* (an addendum to *Latton's Case* in both

---

[26] Cf. Baker, *Collected Papers*, ii. 753, endnote, which rested on too hasty a presumption.
[27] E.g. the report of *Vernon* v. *Vernon* (1573) in JRL MS. Fr. 118, fo. 27, begins 'Un Mary [*altered to* Margery] Vernham port brefe de dower envers John Vernham …', whereas the version in *AB*, fo. 84 (below, p. 75, no. 118) begins 'M. Vernon port brefe de dower del terce parte del mannour de Sudbury in Darb. vers J. Vernon'. Mary was in fact correct, whereas Vernham was wrong.

manuscripts[28]) with an opposite conclusion to that in *AA*. The report of *Brent's Case* in the Rylands text is much fuller than that in *AD* (below, no. 209) and includes a long disquisition by Mounson J. on the origin of uses;[29] but it omits the speech of Dyer C.J., which is nevertheless noticed in the commonplace-book. The report of *Lord Lovell's Case* (*Nichols* v. *Nichols*) also omits all mention of Dyer C.J., whose remarks in that case are prominent in *AB* (below, nos. 90, 236, 237, 250).

It is thus perfectly clear that each manuscript contains significant material which is not matched in the other. The omission in the Rylands text of three important arguments by Dyer C.J. is particularly telling,[30] since Dyer was greatly admired by Coke[31] and his name occurs frequently in Coke's known reports. But there are even more telling mismatches. Most of the 200 or so cases in Coke's commonplace-books do not occur in the Rylands manuscript at all, and thirty-one of the fifty-three cases in the Rylands manuscript do not occur in the commonplace-books. Of the twenty-two cases which occur in both, only nine show signs of possible textual influence, and then to a varying degree.

Given all these textual puzzles, what conclusion should be drawn about the authorship of the Rylands manuscript, and of the two fly-leaves at Holkham? The arguments in favour of Coke's authorship are that they are written in his own hand; that there are indications of deliberate improvement in the text between the Holkham version and the Rylands version; and that the Gawdy dictum addressed 'a moy' must have been addressed to Coke. But there are equally strong arguments, if not stronger, on the other side. The style is different from Coke's known reports and closer to the conventional year-book format. The appearance is also very different, in that the pages are not covered with corrections and annotations as in his known reports (where there was much less room for them), but neatly written out in folio format. The reports therefore have the appearance, even at first glance, of being a copy of something else. Only a small number of them were abridged in Coke's commonplace-books – notably *Cranmer's Case*, which attracted his attention as a new student in 1572[32] – and those that were abridged differ considerably from the Rylands text in wording. It is inherently unlikely that Coke would have written two very different series of reports simultaneously, with thirty cases occurring differently in both. Even if that is conceivable, it is virtually impossible that he would have done so without inserting any cross-references between the two, given the large number of manuscript citations to his early reports. The Rylands manuscript is not specifically listed in his library catalogue, though MSS. *A* to *G* are all described there in detail, and there is not a single cross-reference to it in any of Coke's writings. He evidently did not treat is as his own work, though he did allow others to copy from it, and George Croke

---

[28] This is paralleled by the report in B. & M. 158, but the Rylands version is more detailed.

[29] According to the Rylands MS. both were decided on the same day, but *AA* says only that they were the same term.

[30] It is difficult to explain, especially since Dyer C.J. is reported in several other cases in the Rylands MS.

[31] See the encomium in the preface to 9 Co. Rep. (1613), printed in 109 Selden Soc., introduction, p. xxxiv.

[32] He nevertheless only commonplaced some of the arguments as found in the Rylands MS. Even more surprisingly, he did not in *Shelley's Case* refer to the string of cases cited there concerning remainders to heirs.

apparently cited one of the cases as being 'ex relatione Edwardi Coke'.[33] As already suggested, the most likely explanation for its existence is that Coke borrowed the reports for copying during his student days, and made use of them as an *aide memoire* when compiling his commonplace-books, occasionally even using pieces of the same wording, but disdained to claim anything as his own which did not bear out what he had himself 'seen and heard'.

This hypothesis is seemingly corroborated by the fact that three of the 1572 reports which occur in the Rylands manuscript[34] may be found, in more or less the same words, in a Lincoln's Inn manuscript.[35] Assuming that the Lincoln's Inn versions were not themselves derived from Coke's volume, which possibly they were,[36] they are evidence that at least some of the cases in the Rylands manuscript were in circulation. Since they are reports of the individual cases, not embedded in a continuous chronological series but surrounded by material of later date, it could be that they were passed around 'at large'[37] as reports of single cases. Coke's own first published case, his manuscript report of *Shelley's Case*, was circulated in that way in 1582.[38] A limited publication, in manuscript, of reports of individual cases could explain the variations between the Rylands manuscript and the Holkham fly-leaves. It is true that no further versions have as yet been found, other than some which demonstrably *are* derived from Coke's manuscript and which show that Coke wrote it out in the 1570s.[39] But law reporting was no monopoly, and there is evidence that leading cases such as Cranmer's attracted much notice and circulated in numerous different texts,[40] some

---

[33] Cro Eliz. 27; below, p. cvii, n. 57, cciii. The attribution is at the end of a report of *Tanfield* v. *Finch*, which is not in Coke's notebooks.

[34] The report of *Cranmer's Case* here is akin to the Rylands version rather than the Holkham version.

[35] LI MS. Misc. 361, fos. 29–31v, *Vernon* v. *Vernon* (as in the Rylands MS., pl. *19*); fos. 32–34, *Cranmer's Case* (ibid., pl. *13*); fos. 74–79v, *Powell* v. *Monoux* (ibid., pl. *14*). Before the first case, and between the second and third cases, are reports dated from 1583 to 1586, though not in chronological order. The volume begins with Coke's widely circulated report of *Shelley's Case* (1581), and then some cases abridged from Bendlowes.

[36] The volume is a collection assembled from different sources in the 1580s or 1590s, rather than the 1570s, and it is therefore a possibility that the three cases mentioned in the previous note were copied from the Rylands MS. rather than from an independent text. In J. H. Baker, *English Legal Manuscripts*, vol. ii (Zug, 1978), p. 106, it was suggested that some of the later reports in LI MS. Misc. 361 'seem to be from the unpublished collections of Sir Edward Coke'. Subsequent more careful comparison has failed to confirm this suggestion, which was prompted solely by the three cases mentioned. Besides those cases, only the brief note of *Copwood's Case* (1572) on fo. 80 is similar to one in Coke's notebook (below, p. 58, no. 107), but it ends differently and is not obviously derived from it.

[37] Note George Croke's citation of *Wisley's Case* (1590) 'per le reporte del case alarge': BL MS. Lansd. 1071, fo. 166v (1596).

[38] Below, p. cii.

[39] *Ff*, fos. 184v–199v; *Gg*, fos. 53–61; *V*, fos. 32–33 (this last abridged by George Croke 'ex libro Cooke junioris'). For the cases found both in the Rylands MS. and in these selections, see the notes in Appendix II. The same three manuscripts also include copies from Coke's notebooks, as detailed in Appendix IV. For Edward Coke's description as 'junior' see above, p. lxxiv.

[40] Seven manuscript reports of *Cranmer's Case* are known to the writer: BL MS. Harg. 373, fos. 48–50; MS. Harg. 374, fos. 77v–81 (in a chronological series); MS. Lansd. 1060, fos. 91v–100 (between *Vernon* v. *Vernon* and *Winter's Case*, but this trio from 1572 is interpolated between later cases); CUL MS. Gg.5.2, fos. 103v–104v (in a chronological series, probably of Middle Temple origin); Bodl. Lib. MS. Rawlinson C.112, pp. 411–435; IT MS. Petyt 511.12, fos. 203v–204v (in a chronological series); HLS MS. 1202 (2079), fos. 3–23 (a single case, followed by a case of 1560). There are three further reports of the case in print: below, p. 56, n. 1. Brief reports of *Winter's Case* and *Vernon's Case* are interpolated among reports of the 1580s and 1590s in BL MS. Harley 1693, fos. 71v–73 (and cf. the next note).

of which begin in similar words to those in Coke's manuscript but are considerably shorter.[41] There is still much to learn about Elizabethan reporting, and only meticulous editorial attention could reveal the interconnections between the many surviving manuscripts.

The relationship between Coke and the reports in the Rylands manuscript is evidently not free from doubt. In the absence, however, of any clear evidence that the reports are of Coke's own composition, or of any evidence whatsoever that he himself treated them as such, and without prejudice to a future separate edition if it should be thought requisite, it has not been thought proper to include them in this edition of cases from Coke's notebooks.[42] The cases in the commonplace notebooks are another matter, and must be considered in more detail.

Coke's autograph notebooks

The cases in this first volume are all culled from Coke's commonplace-books and the interleaved Littleton, which were bound up together in Coke's lifetime and since divided into four volumes in the Harleian collection (BL MS. Harley 6687A-D). They are here designated *A*.[43] Together with the volumes here designated *B* (now missing) and *C* (MS. Harley 6686A-B),[44] they were all acquired by Robert Harley in 1715 from 'Madam Thynne'.[45] She is identifiable as Grace Thynne (d. 1725), daughter and heir of Sir George Strode (d. 1701), serjeant at law, and widow of Henry Thynne (d. 1708), son of Viscount Weymouth.[46] The serjeant's father, John Strode (d. 1642), was a bencher of the Middle Temple in Coke's lifetime. And the serjeant's mother, Anne Wyndham, was the niece of Francis Wyndham, the judge; her brothers Hugh and Wadham (both later judges) were members of Lincoln's Inn in Coke's lifetime. A full-length portrait of Coke belonged at some point to the Wyndhams.[47] How the Strodes or the Wyndhams might have acquired the books is obscure, and the obscurity begins with the dispersal of Coke's books and papers after his death in 1634. The manuscripts in question were doubtless among those in Coke's chambers in the Inner Temple, some of which were seized on ministerial instructions for fear that they contained material dangerous to the

---

[41] BL MS. Harg. 373, fos. 48–50 (immediately following *Winter's Case*); MS. Harg. 10, fos. 38–39 (the same report, but ending 'Vide contra en mon reporte fo. 7 et 55b'). The 1572 reports in MS. Harg. 373 are interpolated in reports of the 1590s (cf. the previous note).

[42] Those texts which seem to have been used by Coke in his commonplace-books have here been printed, in smaller type, as appendices to the cases in question. An edition of the remainder would require another volume.

[43] Cited here by the sigla *AA, AB, AC* and *AD*. The division was arbitrary in terms of the contents, the only object being to create four volumes of roughly equal size. The result is that some of the original books are split between the present volumes.

[44] For *B* see below, p. cxiii. For *C* see below, pp. cxiii–cxv, clxviii–clxix.

[45] *The Diary of Humphrey Wanley*, ed. C. E. and R. C. Wright (1966), i. 13–14. This says she was the daughter of 'Sir William Stroud'.

[46] H. W. Woolrych, *Lives of Eminent Serjeants-at-Law* (1869), i. 437–440.

[47] See the frontispiece to vol. ii, and the note there. A list of books in Sir Wadham Wyndham's chambers in Serjeants' Inn (*c.* 1668) includes numerous folio manuscripts, undescribed, but the numbers of the folios do not match those of Coke's notebooks (copy in the Somerset Record Office, DD/WY).

crown as it strove to rule without Parliament. The immediate successor to the chambers seems to have been Sir Edward Littleton,[48] who obtained possession of the draft third and fourth *Institutes*, and perhaps of the second, soon after they had been confiscated.[49] The unpublished *Institutes* were returned to Coke's family early in the 1640s[50] but are not now at Holkham. There is no evidence, however, that the autograph notebooks were among the materials seized in 1634, or that they were ever returned to the family; probably they did not look very important. One of the other autograph volumes of reports (MS. *E*, now in Cambridge University Library) was in the hands of a bookseller in the Temple in 1658,[51] but the remaining three (MSS *D*, *F* and *G*) have not been heard of since the time of Charles I, when several incomplete and confused copies were in circulation.[52] It is probable, therefore, that they were sold. The question of their immediate fate must for the time being remain unanswered. But there is no doubt that the Harleian notebooks were written and annotated by Coke himself throughout his working life at the Bar.

Cases in the commonplace-books, mostly 1572–79

Together with a far greater quantity of notes from the year books, in which they are embedded, the notes in MS. *A* are closely written on small leaves of very fine paper in Coke's tiny handwriting, and in many places buried under layers of later interlineation, annotation and correction which are crammed into the small spaces between cases and spill into the margins, sometimes overlapping with the lines originally written, and occasionally written between the lines of Littleton's printed text. The resulting appearance is of extreme disorder; but it is rather, of course, a consequence of Coke's meticulous attention to accuracy and constant updating. It is easy to forget, in an age of electronic word-processing, the inevitable untidiness of heavy editing with pen on page. But the tangled nature of these accretions, together with the wear caused by constant use,[53] has rendered some words illegible, especially along the lower edges and corners.

---

[48] *Calendar of Inner Temple Records*, ii. 217. Part of the chambers was privately owned, and their exact devolution is not recorded: below, p. cx.

[49] He cited them in CUL MS. Ee.4.7, fos. 9 ('Coke MS jurisdn of courtes'), 13–15 ('Coke MS pl. cor.').

[50] See above, p. lxxiv.

[51] *Certain Select Cases in Law, reported by Sir Edward Coke ... Translated out of a Manuscript written with his own Hand* (1659) (13 Co. Rep.), sig. A2v ('If any should doubt of the truth of these reports of Sir Edward Coke, they may see the originall Manuscript in French, written with his own hand, at Henry Twyford's shop in Vine-Court Middle Temple'). See J. H. Baker, *Catalogue of English Legal Manuscripts in Cambridge University Library* (1996), p. 386. It is possible that it came from the library of Robert Nicholas (d. 1667), justice of the Upper Bench in 1659.

[52] It seems from these copies that MSS *D*, *E* and *F* were originally kept together. Sir John Bramston had a manuscript with cases transcribed from all three, which he lent to Pheasant J. in 1649: BL MS. Lansd. 1079, fo. 123 ('hors de un copy que Sir John Brampstone, jades cheife justice d'Bank le Roy, lende a moy, Anno 1649, Peter Phesaunt'). Sir Matthew Hale also had a volume with cases from all three (now MS. Lansd. 601).

[53] Coke was still adding material in the seventeenth century: below, p. xciii, n. 58. For an example of a particularly crowded page see plate 2.

Not only is the year-book learning in the commonplace-books unusually copious, but also, and to a greater extent than in other contemporary books of a similar nature,[54] there are frequent references to current law. The contemporary cases, which range in date between 1572 and 1579 (with four later additions from the early 1580s), number around 160.[55] The bulk of them date from before 1578, when Coke was still preparing for the Bar but perhaps already practising.[56] References to the second part of Plowden (1579) and to Dyer (issued in 1586) occur as interlined citations rather than as commonplaced sources.[57] There are also added references to Dyer's unprinted reports, to Coke's own 'Liber Primus' (1591–1604) (MS. C), and very occasionally to his later printed and manuscript reports (1600–15). But there is hardly any original material after about 1580.[58]

Since Coke recalled in 1600 that he began reporting in 1579/80,[59] it would be easy to jump to the conclusion that the pre–1580 cases, though incorporated in the body of his notes, were not of Coke's own taking. Several date from 1572, the very year in which Coke was admitted to the Inner Temple, and are written in a mature style for a student aged 20, after only one year's legal study, even such a precocious student as Edward Coke. In a few instances Coke gives only an approximate date, or merely says that a case was heard recently ('ore tard'[60]) or 'in the time of the present queen',[61] a vagueness which presumably indicates hearsay. These few nevertheless stand out

---

[54] The closest comparison is with Christopher Yelverton's commonplace-book, BL MS. Harg. 322, which digests a large number of modern cases from Dyer and from his own experience between 1560 and 1599, but does not contain year-book cases. Much of it is similarly written in a tiny hand, but it is heavily abridged, omitting factual details and arguments. Another of Yelverton's commonplace-books (MS. Harg. 430) includes abridged Elizabethan cases. He also noted cases chronologically from 1556 to 1562 (MS. Harg. 388, fos. 243v–255v), and there are some notes of his own arguments from 1590 to 1612 (MS. Harg. 17). He entered Gray's Inn in 1552, at an unusually early age, and became a Queen's Bench judge in 1602; he was around 75 when he died in 1612.

[55] Some of the cases recur several times, with different points (and occasionally the same points) digested in different places. See the alphabetical table of the named cases, below, pp. 1–2.

[56] In BL MS. Add. 35941, fo. 218v (below, p. c, n. 14), he is said to have appeared with Plowden and other apprentices in a case of 1575. There was a legend that 'the first occasion of his rise' was his 'stating of the Cooks Case of the Temple so exactly that all the House [the Inner Temple], who were puzzled with it, admired him': D. Lloyd, *State Worthies* (1670), p. 820 (punctuation adjusted). This statement has itself caused puzzlement (see Smith, *Sir Edward Coke*, p. 21, n. 15), since it seems unlikely that a complaint about food would have involved any legal perplexity. It might conceivably have referred to *The Cooks' Case* (1578), concerning the Corporation of Cooks of London, below, p. 15, no. 29 (which he may have stated to fellow students). Alternatively, it may be that someone unlearned had misinterpreted a reference to 'Cooke del Temple'. It seems that Coke's first motion in Westminster Hall was in 1580 or 1581: below, pp. ciii–civ.

[57] There is a small separate section of abridged cases from Plowden in *AB*, fos. 301v–304v; below, p. c.

[58] The latest noticed, in a distinctly later hand, is a brief report of a rape case at Bedford assizes in 1611: *AA*, fo. 87. Note also *AA*, fo. 77v, a reference to his own case in the Exchequer in 1626 ('Trin. 2 Caroli in Exchequer adjudge in mon case demesne'); and *AB*, fo. 288v (printed below, p. 51, no. 98), a reference to another case of his own in 1619 ('ceo fuit mon case demesne pur le manour de Stoke etc. in leschequer 17 Jac.'). His chronological notebooks of reports ended in 1616.

[59] *Les Reports de Edward Coke* (1600), sig. iii verso ('sithence the xxij year of her majesty's reign'); below, p. xcvii.

[60] See e.g. below, p. 81, no. 127 ('come jeo ay oye destre adjudge ore tard ...'); vol. ii, p. 181 ('fuit dit ... que fuit adjudge ore tard ...', 1581), 205 ('Egerton ... dit a moy que cest case fuit ore tard adjudge ...', 1583), 249 ('Periam, justice, dit que fuit adjudge ore tard ...').

[61] E.g. *AB*, fo. 348 ('Nota in temps le roigne que ore est fuit adjudge ...' and 'Nota fuit tenus circa annum 10 mesme le roigne ...'). No source is stated.

because of the way they are referred to, for in other cases he took the trouble to state when a report was not first-hand.[62] The post-1571 texts which have no acknowledged authorship do not seem to be based on Plowden, Dyer or Bendlowes,[63] even though many of the cases – unsurprisingly, since they were among the leading cases of the age – were also reported there. When Coke used Plowden,[64] Dyer,[65] or manuscript reports such as Bendlowes and Wyndham, he was usually careful to say so.[66] The lack of such acknowledgments in the cases printed below strongly suggests that they are Coke's own. Moreover, the occasional record of a conversation with a judge or serjeant clearly involved Coke personally.[67]

There is no need to rely on inference alone, because Coke's authorship is corroborated by cross-references to the same cases throughout Coke's notes and writings. In some of these he says only that he had 'heard' or 'observed' the cases himself,[68] though one was 'heard and noted'.[69] Others he cited as 'mes notes demesne'.[70] Noting

[62] E.g. p. 7, no. 8 ('Nota que jeo ay oye que …'); p. 39, no. 83 ('come jeo oye'); p. 79, no. 124 ('jeo ay oye que …'); *AD*, fo. 11 ('Nota que jeo ay oye que est common experience a cest jour que …'); p. 130, no. 232 ('come jeo oye'); vol. ii, pp. 174, 155, 298, 299, 315 ('ut audivi').

[63] As to the few examples found in the Rylands MS. see above, pp. lxxxvii, lxxxix–xc.

[64] Cases from Plowden are often cited by simply by name, without date or citation, e.g. *Chapman* v. *Dalton* [1565] in *AB*, fo. 280v; *Saye* v. *Smith and Fuller* [1562] in *AD*, fo. 847v; *Delamere's Case* [1568] in *AD*, fos. 763 and 830v; *Scholastica's Case* (1571) ibid., fo. 882*. The statement in Baker, *Collected Papers*, ii. 734, that Coke had a manuscript of Plowden is mistaken; the citation mentioned there may be found in Plowd. 560.

[65] References to Dyer's printed reports usually mention 'Dier' but are sometimes in year-book format, e.g. 17 Eliz. 340. The latter formula was tacitly understood to mean Dyer, for cases before 1586. In *AD*, fo. 761v, he cited Keil. in the same way ('22 H. 7, 93'). Coke followed the same practice for his own manuscript reports after 1585, as if they continued from Dyer: E.g. *AA*, fo. 72 ('Vide P. 36 Eliz. 87, le case de Torrington'), fo. 73 ('Vide le case de Man, 42 El. 276'); *AB*, fo. 77 ('13 Jac. fo. 15', a reference to Coke's final notebook, which is lost); *AD*, fo. 806 ('40 Eliz. 284'); *AD*, fo. 859v ('39 Eliz. 880').

[66] Not always: e.g. a case of 1575 in *AB*, fo. 299, is copied from Bendlowes (Benl. 263, pl. 273). In *AD*, fo. 842, is a full report of *Pickeringe's Case* in the Common Pleas, 12 Eliz., without citation. *Bullocke's Case*, which is included below (p. 110, nos. 198–199) because it is dated 15 & 16 Eliz. (1573), seems actually to date from Pas. 1570.

[67] See below, p. 48, no. 92 ('Serjaunt Anderson dit a moy …'); p. 50, no. 97 ('Justice Gawdy dit a moy …'); p. 55, no. 103 ('Serjaunt Fenner dit a moy …'), which is rendered by the copyist in *Ff*, fo. 168, as 'Sergeant Fenner dit a Ed. C.'. There is one case in which he said he was of counsel: *Paston* v. *Drewry* (1582) below, p. 104, no. 180; this is also reported in his first series of chronological reports, vol. ii, p. 190.

[68] E.g. cases 'which I myself heard and observed': below, p. 25, n. 3 (Co. Litt. 365b–366); p. 29, no. 8 (Co. Litt. 31b); p. 52, n. 10 (11 Co. Rep. 48; Co. Litt. 222b); p. 63, n. 6 (Co. Litt. 249); p. 29, n. 8 (Co. Litt. 59b); p. 89, n. 2 (Co. Litt. 221b, 269); p. 113, n. 2 (4 Co. Rep. 80; Co. Litt. 384); p. 155, n. 7 (3 Co. Rep. 51); next note. He used similar language when citing cases in the first notebook: e.g. vol. ii, p. 169 (Co. Litt. 211); ibid. 177 (Co. Litt. 210: 'which I observed'). In 11 Co. Rep. 60 he cited something he heard Dyer C.J. say in 1572: below, p. 154, no. 288. And in Co. Litt. 317 he mentions something he heard Dyer C.J. say in *Bracebridge's Case* (1573), which is perhaps based on the note of that case below, p. 106, no. 186. Cf. Co. Litt. 148 ('Hill. 14 Eliz. which I myselfe heard and observed'), probably referring to *Winter's Case* (1572) below, p. 81, no. 128, though it is not the point which he commonplaced. See also *Gyles* v. *Colshill* (1576) ibid. 164, no. 324 ('I heard the argument of this case').

[69] Co. Litt. 77 (*Wyat's Case*, 'which my self heard and noted'); cf. the same case noted at Co. Litt. 221b and 269a, and 2 Co. Inst. 502 ('which I heard and observed'). However, he also cited a case which he had 'seen and observed' which is not found in the commonplace-books: Co. Litt. 31b (Common Pleas, 17 Eliz.; dower of a castle); despite the date given there, this must be *Ilderton's Case* (1581), which he cited elsewhere from Peryam's manuscript of Dyer (see Appendix VIII, below, p. ccxxxviii). Another example is Co. Litt. 49b (Common Pleas, Pas. 1576 or Pas. 1577, 'which I myselfe heard and observed').

[70] E.g. below, pp. 14 (n. 4), 29, 51, 75 (n. 1), 129. This could refer generally to the commonplace-books: e.g. *AA*, fo. 95; *AD*, fo. 776v ('Mes vide pur ceo in mes notes demesne devant … fol. 9 in medio'); below, pp. 91, 133 (n. 4).

does not unambiguously import authorship,[71] but there are six instances in which he referred to different cases in his notes from the mid–1570s as being from 'mes reportes'.[72] Even that expression could refer to cases which he had collected from elsewhere.[73] Less ambiguously, however, in his manuscript reports for 1588 he refers to a case of 1577 (communicated to him by Gawdy J.) as 'reported by me'.[74] All these citations may be identified from the folio numbers as referring to Coke's autograph commonplace-books. Moreover, Coke later incorporated at least three of the texts in his printed reports.[75] There is further corroboration from contemporaries, who cited cases from the commonplace-books as deriving from Coke.[76]

For all these reasons, it seems certain that these notes are Coke's personal observations, or at least contemporary information as interpreted by him and in an intellectual sense owned by him. They were, to that extent, 'his' reports. No doubt the reason why he did not always account them as belonging properly to his reporting career[77] was that they were mostly brief snippets or dicta, not entered up in a chronological series but distributed in appropriate places for ease of reference, sometimes duplicating the content. They were also the work of a young man still in his twenties. That is why Coke more often characterised them as his 'notes' than as reports. But it is enough for present purposes that he considered them as 'his'. Whatever their origin, or their relative brevity (for the most part) when compared with Coke's later reports, it is of interest to have his versions of cases from the 1570s in his own words.

---

[71] See *AB*, fo. 274 ('Vide Buckenhams case in mes notes escries hors del livre de Serjaunt Bendeloes'); *AC*, fo. 505v ('Bendlowes in mes notes, fol. 5b'). There are numerous citations to the commonplace-books as 'mes notes'. But he also used 'mes notes' for the chronological series of reports: e.g. *Brache's Case* (1583) vol. ii, p. 212, n. 1; *Sir John Baker's Case* (1583) ibid. 214, n. 1; *Russell v. Pratt* (1584) ibid. 250, n. 12; *Tailor v. Moore* (1586) ibid. 287, n. 6.

[72] See *Manser v. Annesley* (1575) below, p. 15, no. 30, n. 1; *Humphreston's Case* (1575) p. 40, no. 87, n. 5; *Gyles v. Coleshill* (1576) p. 63, no. 113, n. 8; *Buttell v. Wylford* (1577) p. 68, no. 115, n. 9; *Earl of Arundel v. Langar* (1576) p. 70, no. 116, n. 1; *Vernon v. Vernon* (1573) p. 75, no. 118, n. 1; *Trudgin's Case* (1579) p. 96, n. 4. See also below, pp. ccv–ccix.

[73] As with 'mes notes', it occasionally denoted his commonplace-books: e.g. *AA*, fo. 69 ('Vide in mes reportes tit. seales'). An explicit example is *AB*, fo. 465 ('Vide 14 E. 3 in mes reportes …'). However, in *Brent's Case* (1575) below, p. 115, no. 209, n. 1, he altered 'mes reportes' (meaning the commonplace-books) to 'mes notes'.

[74] *Bedell v. Moore* (1588) vol. ii, p. 396, referring to the *Earl of Lincoln's Case* (1577) below, p. 50, no. 97. The 'report' here cited is the problematic note which also occurs in JRL MS. Fr. 118, fo. 81v; above, p. lxxxv. Note also Coke's *Statuta*, fo. 202v ('Vide le serjeauntes case anno 21 Eliz. report per moy, ou lun point fuit [upon the statute 34 Hen. VIII, c. 20] …'); the report has not been identified, though there is a brief note on the case below, p. 128, no. 224.

[75] *Repps' Case* (cited in 1574), as noted below, p. 22, no. 41, incorporated in 8 Co. Rep. 35; *Winter's Case* (1572) p. 43, no. 88, incorporated in 4 Co. Rep. 120; and *Calverley's Case* (1577) p. 147, no. 271, incorporated in 6 Co. Rep. 76.

[76] E.g. *Humphreston's Case* (1575) below, p. 40, no. 87, copied by George Croke 'ex libro Cooke junioris' (*V*, fo. 24); *Countess of Lennox's Case* (1580) below, p. 62, no. 111, as abridged in BL MS. Harley 1693, fo. 101v ('Ex libro Coke'), and in BL MS. Lansd. 1068, fo. 130v ('… ex libro Cooke reportes come jeo escrye ex libro Crewe'). These references do not explicitly indicate authorship. But the 'moy' in p. 55, below, no. 103, is rendered in *Ff*, fo. 168, as 'Ed. C.' and in *Gg*, fo. 26 as 'E. C.'

[77] This is the implication of his entitling MS. *C* his 'Liber Primus'. But cf. the reference to his reports as beginning in 20 Eliz. (twelve years before the reports in *C*): below, p. xcviii.

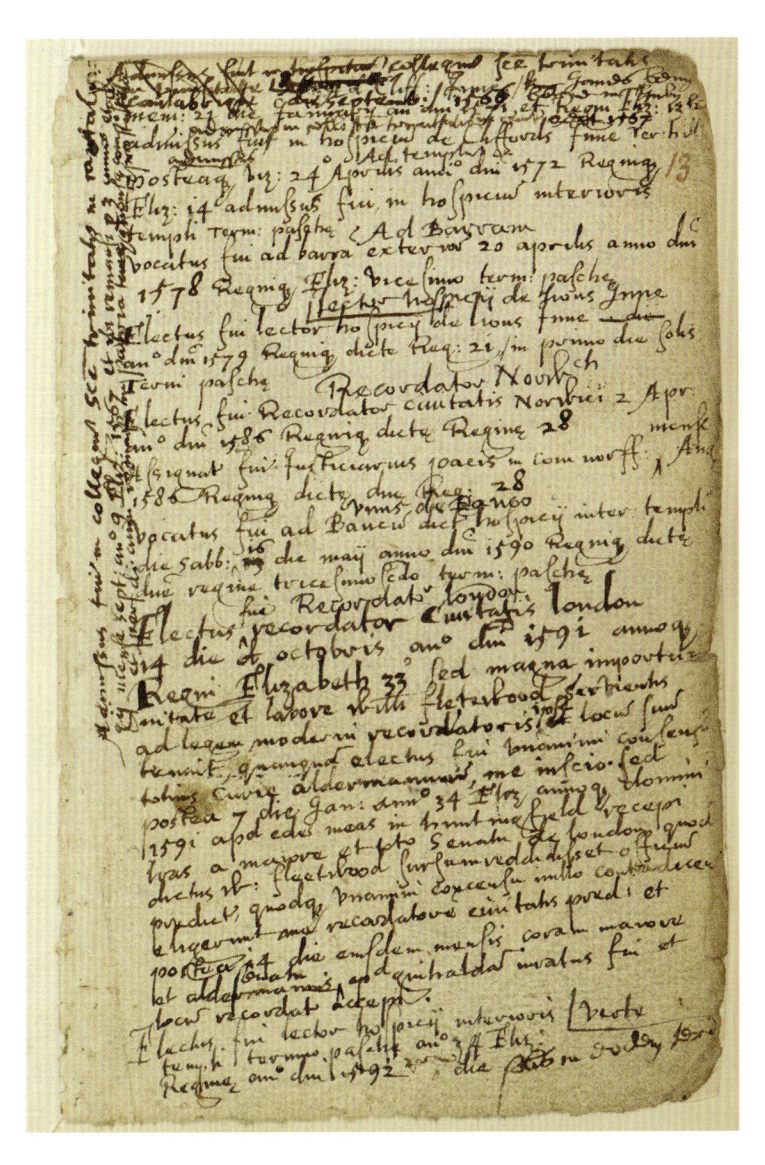

Plate 1   Autobiographical memoranda

Here Coke again notes his admissions to Clifford's Inn and the Inner Temple, and his other advancements (as in the frontispiece), continuing with his call to the bench of the Inner Temple in 1590, the details of his election as recorder of London in 1592, and his election as reader of the Inner Temple in 1592. He added in the margins a note on his membership of Trinity College, Cambridge. The memoranda continue with notes of his family and further advancements.

BL MS. Harley 6687A, fo. 13

© The British Library Board

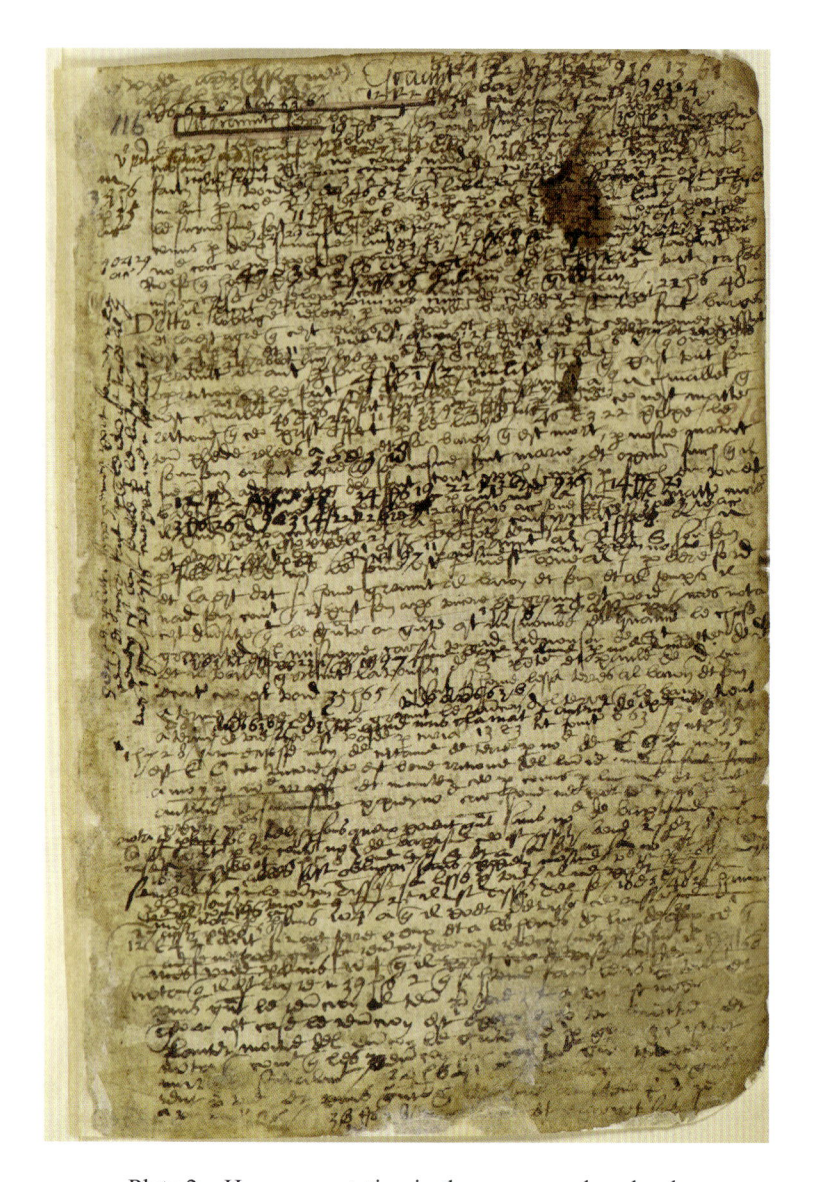

Plate 2   Heavy annotation in the commonplace book

This page, headed 'Grauntz', shows how heavy encrustations of notes, together with wear and tear, can make Coke's commonplace difficult to unravel. With the exception of some cross-references to other pages in the commonplace (including 'tit. Estoppell, 257, in mes notes demesne'), and citations to Dyer and Perkins, all the notes here are based on printed year books.

BL MS. Harley 6687D, fo. 818v

© The British Library Board

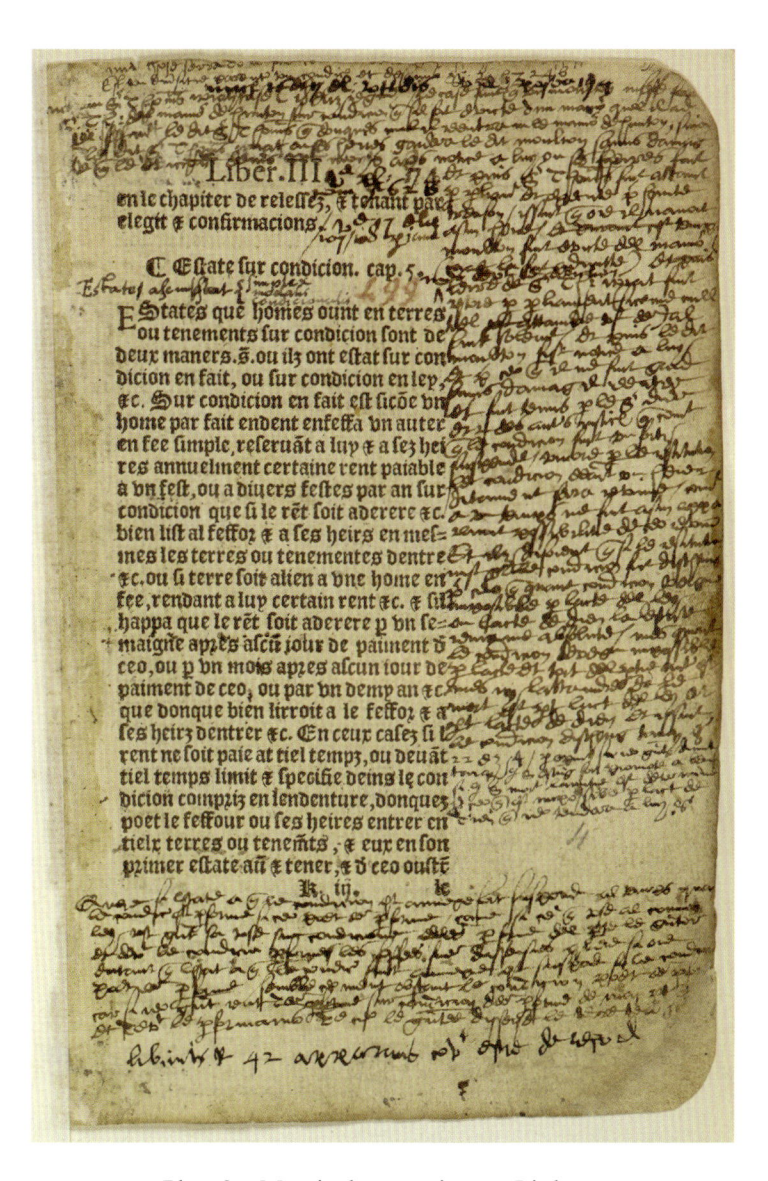

Plate 3   Marginal annotations to Littleton

This page shows annotations to fo. 74r of Littleton, including two notes relating to the text; two notes from year books; a longer note of Sir Thomas Wyat's case, *Multon* v. *Coveney* (1576) (printed in this volume at pp. 79-80), to which he later added a reference to the record, to Dyer's manuscript report of the case ('17 Eliz. 107, 108 Periam'), and to the 1579 edition of Plowden; and, at the foot, a later reference to Lib. Intr. R. 42, meaning Rastell's *Entrees*.

BL MS. Harley 6687C, fo. 499

© The British Library Board

Plate 4

First page of the Rylands manuscript (1572)

It is evident from the case-numbers in the left margin, in Coke's hand, that this is the first page of the series of reports, entirely copied in his hand, beginning in Michaelmas term 1572 and continuing to 1577. It is written in an early form of his hand, with elaborate capital letters, but with no revisions or annotations by Coke. The notes in the margin, apart from the marginal titles, are in a different, somewhat later hand. The page here is reduced from the original folio size. The first case is printed in this volume, at pp. 33-34.

JRL MS. Fr. 118, fo. 15

© The University of Manchester

Plate 5   Conversation with Mr Justice Gawdy (1577)

Two variants of the same text, both written in Coke's hand. They are printed in this volume, at pp. 50-51.

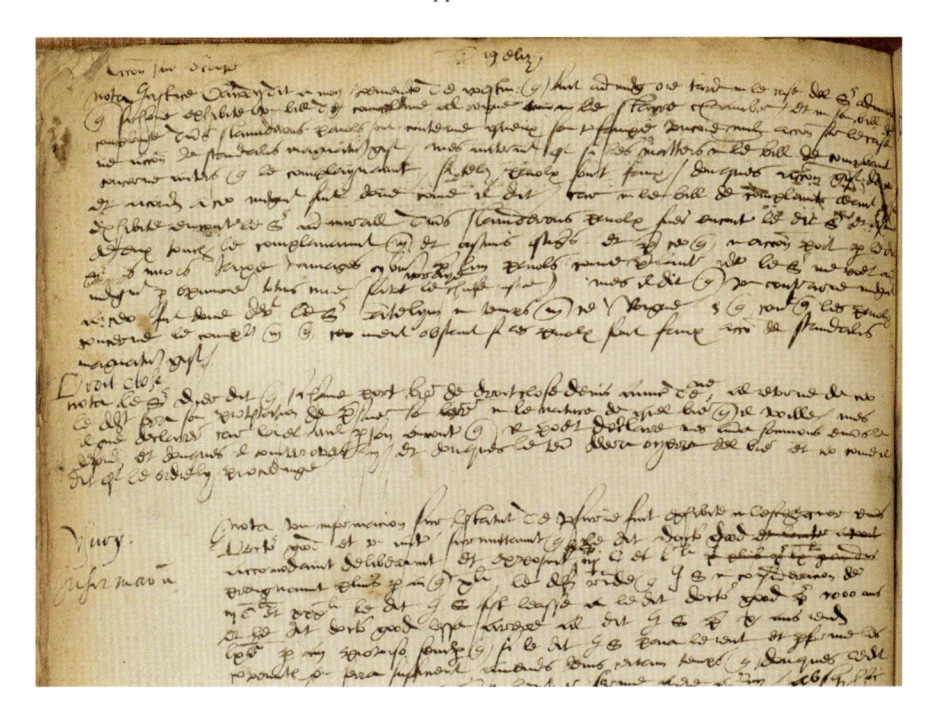

(a) JRL MS. Fr. 118, fo. 81v

© The University of Manchester

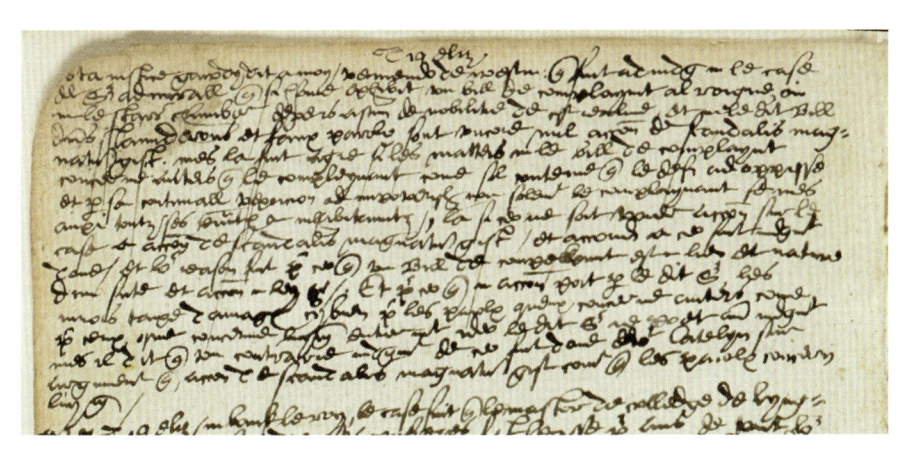

(b) BL MS. Harley 6687B, fo. 288v

© The British Library Board

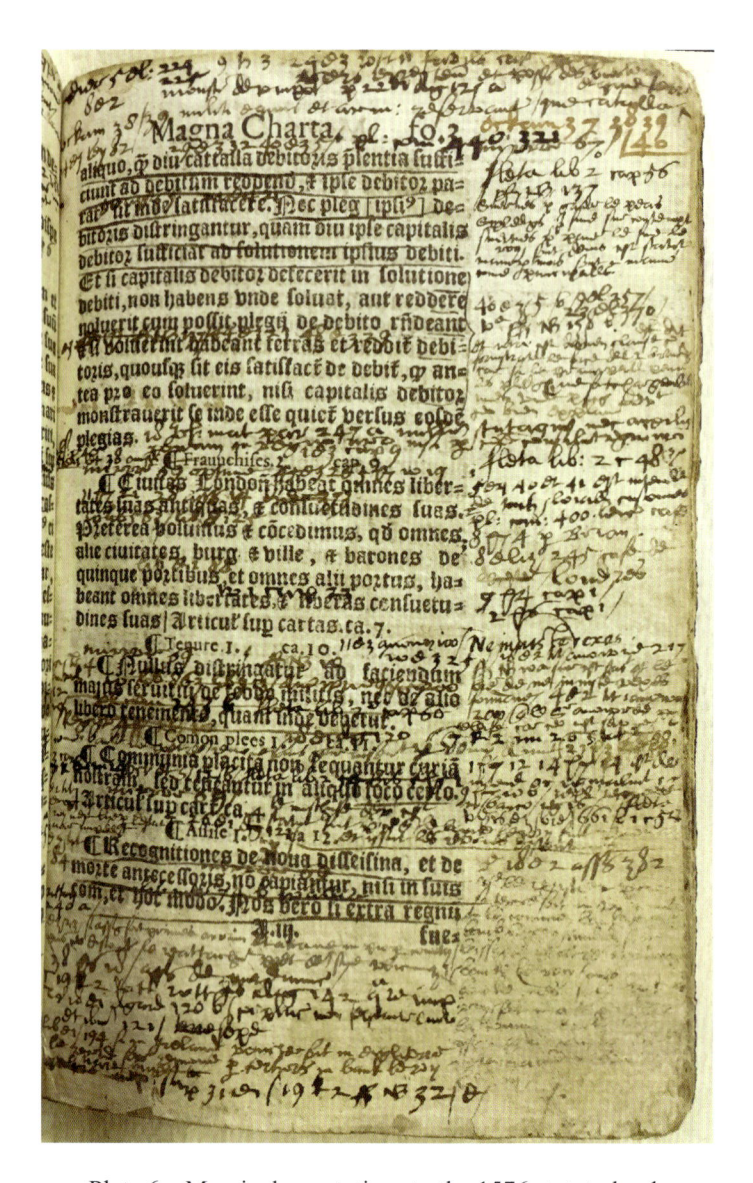

Plate 6   Marginal annotations to the 1576 statute-book

This page from Coke's annotated *Magna Carta cum Statutis* (1576 edition) at Holkham, on Magna Carta, cc. 8-12, shows the range of his citations, including Matthew Paris, Fleta, the *Mirror of Justices*, Agard's *Repertory*, the *Registrum Brevium*, year-books (including 'Lib. E. 1'), other statutes, a plea roll of Richard II, Fitz. Abr., Fitz. N.B., Plowd. and Dyer.

Holkham Hall BN 7834, fo. 3

© By kind permission of the Earl of Leicester and the Trustees of the Holkham Estate

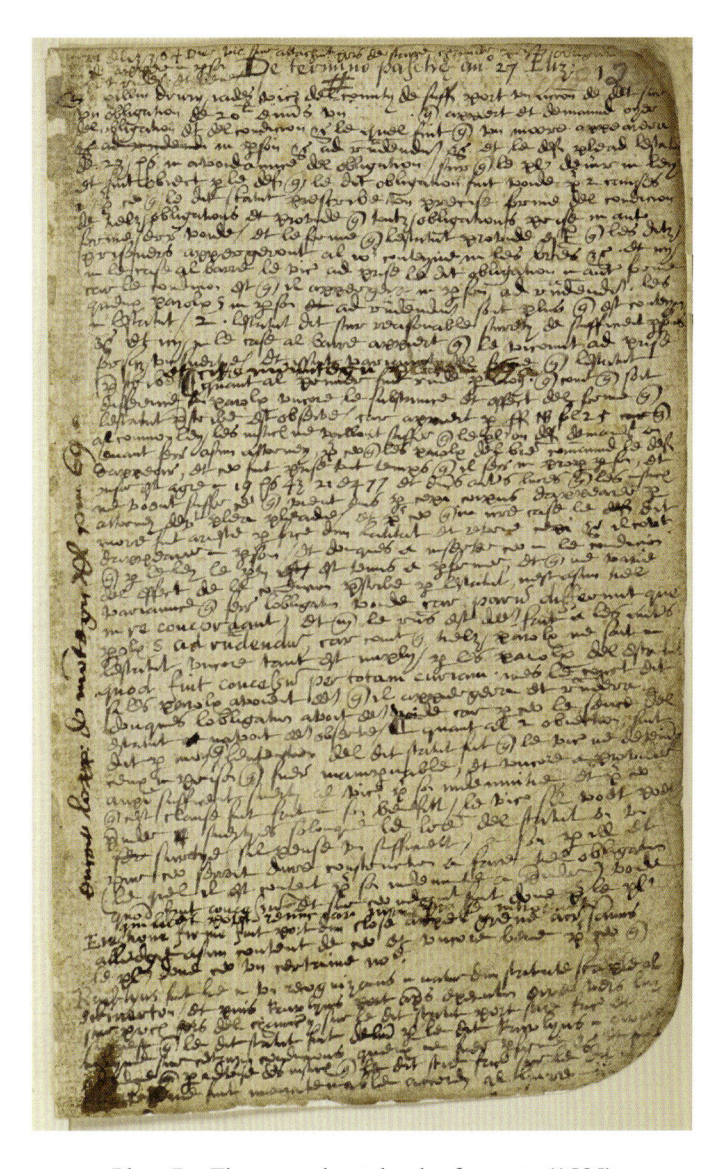

Plate 7   The second notebook of reports (1585)

The second notebook begins with this report of Sir William Drury's case, identifiable as *Drury v. Cordra* (1585), printed in vol. ii, at pp. 271–272. The page is relatively free from annotation, apart from citations to Dyer (top margin) and to Plowd. (interlineation and left margin). Two further cases follow at the foot of the page.

BL MS. Harley 6687D, fo. 708

© The British Library Board

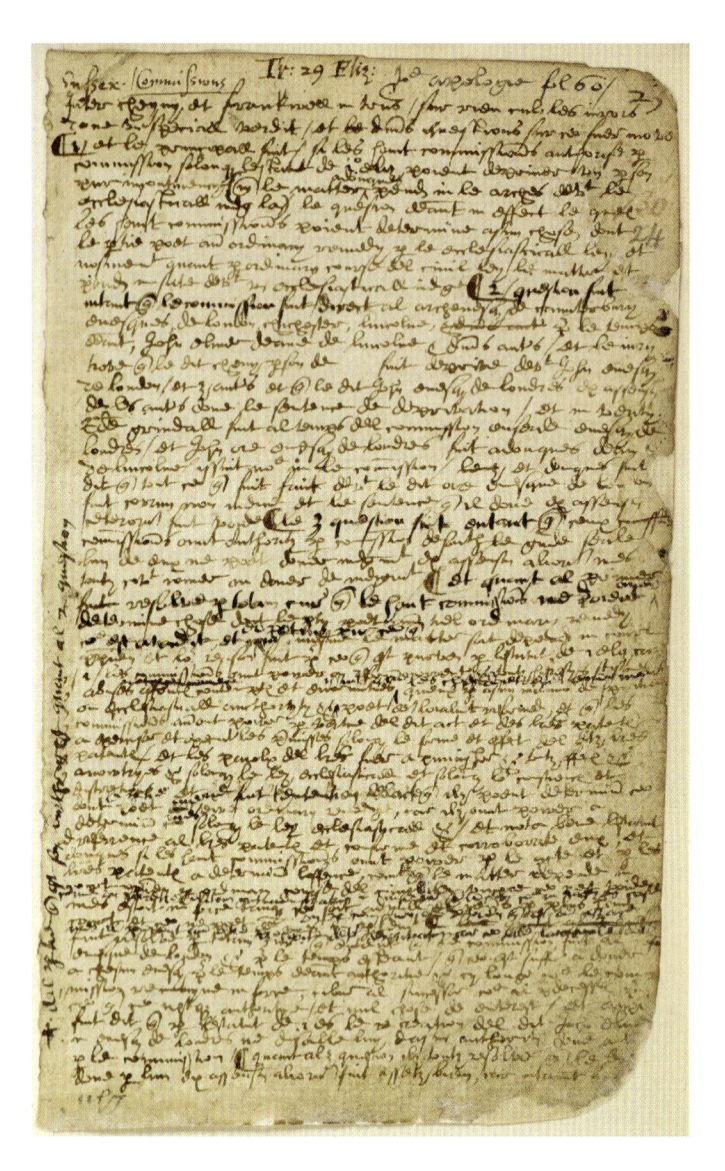

Plate 8 Report of *Cheyny* v. *Frankwell* (1587)

This report of an important case concerning the High Commission (never published) contains significant later interlineations, which are not wholly decipherable. Their gist was to qualify the decision that a judgment of deprivation given by the commissioners was valid until reversed in Parliament. The insertion indicated that this problem could be overcome by means of a prohibition before the event, because that would prevent the commissioners giving judgment. It also indicated an alternative means of appeal by a commission of review. In the top margin is an added reference to Dr Cosin's *Apologie* (1591). The case is printed in vol. ii, pp. 333-334.

BL MS. Harley 6687D, fo. 730

© The British Library Board

INTRODUCTION   xcvii

Cases in marginalia at Holkham, 1572–87

Around forty additional notes of cases, in the same style as those in the commonplace-books, occur in the margins of some of Coke's printed law books now at Holkham Hall,[78] and these have been added at the end of this volume. Nearly all of them are in his interleaved copy of *Magna Charta cum Statutis* (1576) (Holkham, BN 7834).[79] This was one of three small statute-books which he filled with manuscript additions. The second, a copy of the 1556 edition (Holkham, BN 7831), contains for the most part marginalia and insertions relating to Parliament, taxation, monopolies, habeas corpus and other constitutional issues, and these clearly belong to a later stage in his career. Coke also owned Berthelet's edition of the statutes (1531), which is said to have contained copious notes, but this was stolen in 1948 and has not been recovered.[80] Another heavily annotated volume was a copy of Fitzherbert's *Natura Brevium*, covered in green velvet, the fate of which is unknown.[81]

The 1576 edition of *Magna Charta cum Statutis* at Holkham seems to have been Coke's companion more or less from the time of publication, though it is not interleaved and is not annotated as heavily as his 1572 Littleton. One problematic feature of the notes is that nine of them refer to cases decided before 1576, when the printed book was published. Two of these begin 'See (*Vide*) ...', reinforcing the obvious conclusion that these are based on earlier reports or notes, albeit without indicating where one was supposed to look for them.[82] A few of these pre–1576 cases are noted in the commonplace-books as well, but that cannot be the source, because the information is in some cases different. None are derived from the Rylands manuscript. They seem, nevertheless, to be Coke's own. There is a similarity of style, and in a case from Michaelmas term 1572 Coke explicitly wrote that he had himself 'heard' what Chief Justice Dyer said.[83] Coke may simply have been relying on the sharp memory of a young man. Alternatively, he may have been using other notes which no longer exist.[84] He certainly did keep other notes. When his study in the Temple was ransacked in 1634, one of the items removed was a 'A booke in folio intitled with Sir Edward Coke's owne hand "a booke of notes of my arguments at the

---

[78] When the present writer first studied them in 1990 they were on loan to the Inner Temple with a view to possible purchase. But they have long since returned to Holkham.

[79] For a specimen page see plate 6.

[80] *Library of Sir Edward Coke*, p. 30, no. 371. In 1840, however, the librarian at Holkham reported that the two editions of 1556 and 1576 were the only books to contain annotations by Coke: *The Cambridge Portfolio*, ed. J. T. Smith (1840), i. 217 at p. 218.

[81] *Library of Sir Edward Coke*, p. 30, no. 373. Dr Hassall confused this with the autograph notebooks bound in velvet and said it was one of the books given to Harley in 1715; but there is no evidence that it ever belonged to Harley, or indeed the Strodes.

[82] One of them (below, p. 162, no. 316) is explicit: 'See the serjeants' case in the year 21 Eliz., reported by me ...'. The other is on p. 155, no. 291, referring to *Latton's Case* (1575). The 'See ...' formula is also used, however, for post–1575 cases: see p. 158, no. 303 (1582); p. 161, no. 314 (1587).

[83] Below, p. 154, no. 288 ('I heard the lord Dyer say in Michaelmas term 14 Eliz.). Cf. p. 164, no. 324 ('I heard the argument of this case', in Easter term 1576). Cf. the previous note ('reported by me', 1579).

[84] There are examples in MSS. *A* and *C* of cases which were not written down in the term in which they were decided. Coke also cited cases not found in his notebooks: e.g. *Cordal's Case* (before 1594) Cro. Eliz. 315 ('Nota: Coke shewed me a resolution of Gawdy and Anderson in a case referred to them by the Queens commandment ...'; but this seems to mean a written opinion). The report of *Richardson* v. *Yardley* (1595–96) in BL MS. Add. 3594, fos. 18, 71, has 'report per Coke' added, but it is not in *C*

barre when I was solicitour, attournie *and before*".[85] This was obviously an important book, but it was never heard of again. There may well have been other ephemeral notes which have not survived. That can only be a matter of conjecture; but, whatever the ultimate source of the marginalia in the 1576 statute-book, their similarity to the notes in the commonplace-books is a sufficient justification for their inclusion in this edition.

Coke's earliest chronological reports, 1579–88

A change occurred in Coke's reporting practices a year after his call to the bar in 1578. He recollected this himself in 1600, when he reminisced about his compilation of reports over the previous twenty years:[86]

> I have, sithence the xxij year of her majesty's reign, which is now xx years complete, observed the true reasons as near as I could of such matters in law (wherein I was counsel, and acquainted with the state of the question) as have been adjudged upon great and mature deliberation. And, as I never meant (as many have found) to keep them secret for mine own private use, as to deny the request of any friend to have either view or copy of any of them, so till of late I never could be persuaded (as many can witness) to make them so public as by any entreaty to commit them to print ...

The twenty-second year of the reign began on 17 November 1579, which (leaving aside the three additions) is later than the scattered reports just described. Coke was evidently referring in this passage to the chronological series which he started in 1579, and which is referred to in this introduction as the first notebook.[87] The series started, in fact, with one case from Hilary term 1579, apparently written down later in the year, but it reached 1580 on the next folio and continued until the Lent vacation of 1585, when the original notebook was filled. The notebook comprises fifty-six leaves, the first twelve of which contain earlier cases from the 1570s, some of them abridged from Plowden, but his own reports occupy the remaining forty-eight leaves.[88] Seven or eight of the leaves are now missing near the end, with parts of Michaelmas 1584 and Hilary term 1585; these had evidently disappeared before the volumes were rebound in the nineteenth century.[89] The reports were continued from

---

[85] 'A note of the bookes and papers brought out of Sir Edward Cokes study from the Temple remayning in the box', PRO, SP 16/278, fo. 73, no. 35 (emphasis added). Since no. 35 was a single volume, and a folio, it cannot be identified with the Harleian notebooks.

[86] *Les Reports de Edward Coke* (1600), sig. iii verso.

[87] *AB*, fos. 304v–338. A specimen page (fo. 305r) is illustrated in plate 7.

[88] Coke's folio numbering shows that the notebook began on fo. 293 (his fo. 1), with some extracts from a Bendlowes manuscript, and that his chronological series of reports began on the verso of twelfth leaf (fo. 304v), following some abridgments from the second part of Plowd., published in July 1579. Another case of Hil. 1579, on fo. 301, is printed here as from the commonplace-books (below, p. 62, no. 112) since it is not contiguous with the reports beginning on fo. 304v. *The Countess of Lennox's Case*, which immediately precedes it (no. 111), seems actually to date from 1580. It is not obvious how the material in fos. 1–12 came to be compiled, though it is evident that it was not all written down contemporaneously with the cases.

[89] There is no hiatus in the later foliation. The leaves may still have been present in 1668, when Sir Heneage Finch cited a case which was probably on one of them: vol. ii, p. 266. Some of the contents can be reconstructed: ibid. pp. 405–407.

Easter term 1585 to Michaelmas term 1588 in a second notebook,[90] which contains another forty-eight leaves. Both of these notebooks will be printed in the second volume of this edition.

By the time Coke reached the end of this second notebook of chronological reports, he had become the busiest advocate in Westminster Hall other than a law officer, reported as speaking in legal arguments in about a hundred cases a year – a different one more or less every day in term-time[91] – and such was his reputation that he was described by a reporter in 1588 as 'the famous utter-barrister of the Inner Temple',[92] a unique mark of distinction. Though still an utter-barrister rather than a bencher,[93] which was the import of the description, he was frequently matched against the law officers Thomas Egerton and John Popham, and his arguments often prevailed. He may not necessarily have been retained in all the cases in which he spoke, since (following medieval tradition) he was apt to join in any discussion at which he was present:[94] when he spoke, in whatever capacity, everyone listened intently, and his very dicta were already thought to be worth reporting.[95] It was also still possible for counsel to move questions to the court which arose from their professional work and were not depending in suit,[96] or even for the sake of learning.[97] Yet it is clear that his

---

[90] Now bound as *AD*, fos. 708–755.

[91] In 1587 and 1588 together, a total of 190 cases have so far been noted in which Coke was reported as speaking, chiefly in the King's Bench: see Appendix VI, below, pp. ccxxii–ccxxx. There must have been others, especially in the Chancery and revenue courts. The courts at Westminster were open for little more than 100 days a year. There is no record of his conduct of trials at the assizes in vacations, though he reckoned to have made £80 from the Lent assizes in 1587: Coke's Dyer, rear endpaper. He must also have been busy giving oral and written opinions.

[92] Goulds. 89 (1588). The reporter was William Brocke of the Inner Temple, who used the expression again in HLS MS. 1041 (1057), fos. 187, 188v (abridged in Goulds. 93, 95); and cf. fo. 191v ('le famous utterbarrister', rendered in Goulds. 99 as 'the famous Coke'). Note also BL MS. Harg. 26, fo. 131 ('le famous utter barrester Coke').

[93] He did not become a bencher until 1590, two years before his reading in 1592. The serjeants at law were still nominally the leaders of the Bar, but it was not a rank which Coke needed to seek; he only took the coif on becoming a judge in 1606.

[94] Suggestive of this are *Vaux* v. *Brooke* (1586) vol. ii, p. 287 ('… ceo jeo monstre al court come amicus curie'); BL MS. Harley 1331, fo. 40 ('… mes Cooke et multes al barre disont que …'); ibid., fo. 53 ('Nota que Cooke dit al court …'); *Downe* v. *Hopkins* (1594) MS. Harley 6745, fo. 48 ('Coke attorny le roigne ut amicus curiae, car ne fuit a counsell de ascun parte …'); *Gibbons* v. *Warner* (1594) ibid., fo. 42v ('Coke attorny general le roigne argue *se improviso* …'); Coventry, fo. 416 ('Coke Att.-Gen. esteant present dit …'). It was not unknown for the court to put questions to all the counsel present: e.g. *Anon.* (1572) CUL MS. Hh.2.9, fo. 58v ('In Banke le Roy le chief justice demand de toutes les counsellors al barre, et auxi des clarkes …'). Cf. also vol. ii, p. 291 ('ceo [Cooke] dit per voy de parlance, et auters counselors al barr ceo luy oiant valde praise luy').

[95] Besides the examples in the previous note, see e.g. BL MS. Lansd. 1121, fos. 90, 91 (dicta 'per Cooke', 1588).

[96] E.g. *Note* (1582) vol. ii, p. 291 (question raised as steward of a Norfolk manor); *Allen's Case* (1587) ibid. 346 (question raised as an arbitrator). Both were moved by Coke in the King's Bench. In the 1587 case Popham Att.-Gen. was present at the bar and added his own opinion. Less explicably, Coke sometimes moved cases which were not argued: e.g. BL MS. Harley 6745, fos. 37 ('Coke solicester le roigne move un case [concerning superstitious uses] … quere car riens fuit parle'), 107v ('Coke le attorny le roy mit le case mes il ne argue').

[97] E.g. Dyer 174, pl. 20, where a case depending in the Court of Wards for thirty years without resolution was discussed in 1559. Coke (*AB*, fo. 273v) said the case was moved 'for lerning'. Cf. BL MS. Harley 4552, fo. 38v ('Coke attorney mitt ceo case al court de scavoir lour opinion'); *Callard* v. *Callard* (1594) vol. iii, p. 607, n. 2 ('… nul reasons fueront done appertment coment que le atturney [*Coke*] ceo request pur son learninge …'). See also Ibbetson. 'Law Reporting in the 1590s', at p. 78.

well-earned reputation had brought him a vast practice and the foundations of a considerable fortune.[98] When he sued a Norfolk gentleman for defamation in 1585, his assertion that for several years past he had received 'exceedingly great gains, profits and fees' from his many clients, though perfectly true, was merely common form in such cases. His further assertion that as a result of the slander he had fallen into discredit and was deserted by clients, though also common form, was very far from the reality.[99] A more telling indication of his success was that the damages for his supposed loss of fee income were laid as £1,000.[1] There is some direct evidence of his material good fortune in a note of 1587 written on an endpaper in his copy of Dyer. He then reckoned his liquid assets ('redy money') as amounting to £869, including £500 in gold.[2] He was already investing heavily in land purchases, especially around his birthplace at Mileham.[3] As he wrote on the title-page of the same book:[4]

> By learning he which else hath nought
> from low estate to high is brought ...

His learning had indeed begun to earn him great treasure, but it is obvious from his notes and writings that he revelled in learning for its own sake and enjoyed the discovery of subtle distinctions, forensic insights and potentially useful historical information.[5] Later in his career he would apply his massive learning to more altruistic ends, at some personal cost. But those purposes were not within his reach, and were therefore not his concern, as a junior member of the Bar in the 1580s.[6] The significant but relatively few notes on public law in his commonplace-books were

---

[98] He had already received a dowry valued at £3,000 and a country house (Huntingfield Hall, Suff.) on marrying Bridget Paston in 1582: C. W. James, *Chief Justice Coke: His Family and his Descendants at Holkham* (1929), pp. 10–12. For Bridget and her mother Anne Bedingfield see vol. ii, p. 300, n. 6.

[99] *Coke v. Baxter* (1585) KB 27/1293, m. 322; printed with translation in *Select Cases on Defamation to 1600*, ed. R. H. Helmholz (101 Selden Soc., 1985), pp. 66–67. The defendant, Thomas Baxter, was alleged to have said that Coke had taken fees from both sides in a case at Norfolk assizes in July 1584. Baxter pleaded Not Guilty, but there is no record of any trial, and the action was presumably settled.

[1] The same sum was laid in *Boughton v. Bishop of Coventry* (1583) 101 Selden Soc. 64, 1 And. 119, for an alleged libel on Edward Boughton M.P. in a letter sent to his patron, the earl of Leicester. They were, no doubt, ambitious claims. In 1592 Sir Julius Caesar recovered only £200 for an allegation of corruption as judge of the Admiralty: 101 Selden Soc. xcviii.

[2] Coke's Dyer, rear endpaper, referring to Easter term 1587. The cash represented at least £250,000 in today's money.

[3] See Boyer, *Coke and the Elizabethan Age*, pp. 193–196. He was eventually to amass over sixty manors. The trouble he took in maximising and securing his property interests in Mileham, Tittleshall and Godwick is evident from two deeds which he had enrolled in the King's Bench: KB 27/1316, m. 39 (purchase from William Yelverton, for £560, of all the manors and lands which he had there by his father's will, 29 Jan. 1591); KB 27/1324, m. 20 (purchase from Francis Warde, for a 'certain sum', of lands and tithes in Tittleshall formerly belonging to Coxall priory, 6 Feb. 1593). Note also C 2/Eliz/C1/59 (suit against Yelverton for the title-deeds); C 2/Eliz/Y1/47 (suit by Charles Yelverton against Coke concerning the title to lands in Tittleshall).

[4] Coke's Dyer, title-page (spelling modernised).

[5] For his interest in history see below, pp. cxx–cxxviii.

[6] He first entered the House of Commons in 1589, and became solicitor-general three years later (*AA*, fo. 13; *C*, fo. 34; below, p. cxv).

probably inserted after he became a law officer,[7] though there are a few reports towards the end of his second notebook which show an awakening interest in the protection of individual liberty.[8]

The reports printed in the second volume of this edition were still sometimes referred to by Coke as 'mes notes',[9] the same expression that he used for his commonplace-books. But they were more often cited as 'mes reportes',[10] and they were now continuous, more orderly, and on the whole more neatly written. One reason for this new departure may have been the appearance of the second part of Plowden's *Comentaries* in June of that year.[11] Coke's new series of reports was immediately preceded in the notebook by some abridged material taken from that volume, and he perhaps saw his own efforts as a continuation of Plowden's enterprise, even though they were considerably more concise.[12] Another factor, however, is revealed by Coke's words quoted above, '... wherein I was counsel, and acquainted with the state of the question'. He gave the same reason in the preface to his *Fourth Institute*, where he said he had made use of judicial resolutions 'in many cases never published before, wherewith I was well acquainted, and which I observed and set down in writing while it was fresh in memory.'[13] The commencement of his new reports more or less coincided with his beginning at the Bar, starting the year after his call – by which time he was already being retained as counsel[14] – and just before he made his first motion at the King's Bench bar in 1581.[15] Many of the cases reported in the earlier 1580s came from Suffolk or Norfolk, and it is a fair conjecture that much of his early practice was generated in his home region. To a considerable extent

---

[7] E.g. *AA*, fo. 2 (on the royal arms, and how England came to be quartered after France); *AA*, fo. 42 (on torture); *AA*, fos. 84, 101–102 (on the royal prerogative), 107v–110, 128; *AA*, fo. 88v (on the king's dispensing power, citing, inter alia, a case of 1615 from his MS. *G*) and *AD*, fo. 805 (on the same subject); *AA*, fo. 123 (on the Star Chamber); *AA*, fo. 181 (on the descent of the crown to siblings of the half-blood); *AA*, fo. 238 (on *habeas corpus*); *AB*, fo. 429 (on war); *AB*, fos. 492, 493, 495 ('Roy'); *AB*, fos. 492, 494v (on Parliament). See also below, pp. cxlvi–clii.

[8] Below, pp. cxviii–cxix.

[9] E.g. *AD*, fo. 920, referring to *Farmor* v. *Savage* (1583) vol. ii, p. 216; Coke's Dyer, fo. 135, referring to *Brache's Case* (1583) vol. ii, p. 212; Coke's Dyer, fo. 357, referring to *Lepur* v. *Wroth* (1588) vol. ii, p. 389; Coke's Dyer, fo. 371v, referring to *Russell* v. *Pratt* (1584) vol. ii, p. 401; Coke's Dyer, fo. 373v, referring to *Tayler* v. *Moore* (1586) vol. ii, p. 287.

[10] See the examples in Appendix III.

[11] *Short-Title Catalogue of Books printed in England ... 1475–1640*, 2nd ed. by K. Pantzer (1976), ii. 241, no. 20046.3; *OHLE*, vi. 884. The first edition of the *Short-Title Catalogue* had listed the first edition of the second part as that of 1584.

[12] *AB*, fos. 301v–304v. Plowden's reports were not arranged chronologically in print. He lived until 1585 but did not produce any more published reports.

[13] 4 Co. Inst., proeme.

[14] *Edolfe's Case* (1579) vol. ii, p. 167. This was not in the King's Bench and it is not clear whether Coke made oral submissions himself. In 1594 he cited an Exchequer case of 1573 concerning Lord Cromwell 'en que il mesme fuit de counsell': BL MS. Harley 4505, fo. 46v. He was then aged 21. But the case dragged on until the end of the century, and he was probably alluding to his involvement as counsel at a later stage. Note also *Sir William Waller's Case* (1575) BL MS. Add. 35941, fo. 218v: '17 Eliz. Nota que Cooke fuit ove Plowden, Farmer et Atkynson apprentises sur cest case'.

[15] Coke himself said that this was in *Lord Cromwell* v. *Dennye* (1578–82) 4 Co. Rep. 12, at fo. 14; cf. below, p. 103, no. 178 (1578); vol. ii, p. 191 (noted belatedly under Pas. 1582). In 4 Co. Rep. 12 he says the case was moved in Trin. 1581; he must have been referring to the second action brought in 1580 and settled in the summer of 1581. He was of counsel in two other King's Bench cases the same term: *Vines* v. *Dinham* (Trin. 1581) vol. ii, p. 171, *Shelley's Case* (Trin. 1581) below, p. ciii. See also *Purslowe's Case* (Mich. 1581) vol. ii, p. 177, in which he was led by Serjeant Anderson.

the reports thereafter were a record of his own involvement in cases,[16] and it is noticeable that he did not often refer to other counsel by name.

It was not unique or entirely new for a reporter to identify himself as one of the counsel in the cases reported, but it is unusual to find so many such references. There is much self-satisfaction, perhaps calculated to become self-advertisement, even as early as the 1580s. Coke delighted in setting out a number of seemingly convincing arguments on one side until his own turn came to argue, whereupon 'I, being of counsel with the other party' proceeded to demolish the previous arguments one by one. He frequently boasted of being counsel for the winning party. Once he said he was brought in too late and would have pursued a different course,[17] or that after being brought in he found some new point which saved the day.[18] Even when his own main argument failed, he might deftly produce a technical point to stave off defeat.[19] And he was not above pointing out, when his own arguments prevailed, what the other side should have argued.[20] He did not often admit to losing a case, or (at any rate) choose to report such a failure.

(a) Shelley's Case

The reason for the emphasis on his own career may simply be, as he wrote in 1600, that he knew most about the cases in which he was personally engaged. This inside knowledge gave his reports the status so obviously possessed by those of Plowden and Dyer, even though he had not yet reached their standing in the profession. And they were no longer merely kept for his 'own private use'. The tone – and perhaps the manner of emendation[21] – suggest that he may already have had publication in mind,[22] as he later indicated in saying that he 'never meant to keep them secret'. His first publishing venture was, in fact, as early as 1582, when he put into circulation (in manuscript form) one of his most famous reports, that of *Shelley's Case*, which

---

[16] There is still some hearsay: e.g. vol. ii, pp. 196, 268 ('come jeo oye'); p. 341 ('ex relatione aliorum'); p. 343 (sim.); p. 372 ('ex relatione Magistri Wisemanne').

[17] *Rolfe* v. *Rolfe* (1582) vol. ii, p. 199 ('I never argued upon any good advisement, for I was not of counsel with the joining of the demurrer').

[18] *Gallys* v. *Burbry* (1587) ibid. 351 ('But I, being newly retained with the defendant ... asked the court to give a further day to show other matter in arrest of judgment ... In the mean time, I considered the replication, and I found the replication wholly insufficient ...'); *Hawes* v. *Smith* (1588) ibid. 371 ('But I, being newly retained with the defendant, utterly misliked the course of argument which had been taken before ... However, I moved another point ...').

[19] *Avery* v. *Bunning* (1588) vol. ii, p. 387 ('perceiving the opinion of the court to be against me, I moved an incurable fault in the replication ...').

[20] *Randes* v. *Warden* (1588) vol. ii, p. 384 ('But it seems to me that, if I had been of Artys's counsel, I could have avoided the said estoppel ...').

[21] The alterations in the commonplace-books were mostly intended to add information, whereas in the chronological reports there seems to be a greater concern with improving the wording. E.g. in C, fo. 213*bis* (vol. iv, p. 779, he studiously (and repeatedly) amended 'segnior keper' to 'segnior gardein del graund seale', and on the same page, more incongruously, altered 'upper house' to 'upper meason'.

[22] The first 'Nota lecteur' occurs in an added marginal note to a case of 1583: vol. ii, p. 221. But Coke did not generally address the reader in that way until the 1590s. There is a clear indication of intention to publish in 1598: vol. v, p. 932 ('quel resolution jeo ay pense necessarie (come petit temps voet moy permit a reporter) pur le benefit del dit cathedrall eglise et de toutes lour fearmours ...'). See further below, p. clxviii.

INTRODUCTION   ciii

commenced in 1579.²³ Following a trial at bar in Westminster Hall in 1580, the case was argued in Hilary and Easter terms 1581. Coke, though still very junior, was retained with the attorney-general (Popham) as counsel for the defendant Henry Shelley, with whom he was acquainted.²⁴ Although judgment was given for the defendant, the judges did not give detailed reasons in public.²⁵ Coke therefore took the opportunity to write a long report explaining the decision, setting out successful arguments which were modestly attributed to an unnamed barrister of the Inner Temple. The case is nowhere to be found in his extant notebooks, though George Croke abridged a short report of it 'ex libro Cooke' not long after it was decided.²⁶ This book was presumably the long report, written separately and widely disseminated, with a preface dedicated to Lord Buckhurst and signed by Coke on 2 January 1581/82. Coke's own text of this report is preserved at Holkham Hall,²⁷ and more than a dozen copies still survive, indicating a wide publication.²⁸ It was clearly a piece of self-promotion, since the signed preface effectively lifted the veil and by strong implication identified the anonymous barrister of the Inner Temple whose ingenuity seemed to have won the case.²⁹

Coke's involvement as counsel for Shelley in Easter term 1581 seems to be at odds with his statement that the first motion he made in the King's Bench was in Trinity term that year. But there may be an explanation. Although Shelley's suit was in the King's Bench, the queen had intervened to request an expeditious resolution,³⁰ and

---

²³ KB 27/1269, m. 58 (Pas. 1579, continued from Hil. 1579); printed in 1 Co. Rep. 88; B. & M. 163; also reported in 1 And. 69; Dyer 373; Moo. 136; and the manuscripts cited below. The special verdict was delivered at bar in Pas. 1580, and judgment was entered in Trin. 1581. For the background, and the parallel Chancery and Star Chamber suits, see A. W. B. Simpson, *Leading Cases in the Common Law* (1995), pp. 13–44. (*Pace* Simpson, ibid. 27, there are Chancery pleadings in C 8/3/103, and orders in C 33/57, fos. 8v, 285, 309; C 33/60, fos. 6, 31, 76v.) See also D. A. Smith, 'Was there a Rule in Shelley's Case?' (2009) 30 *Journal of Legal History* 53–70. For an attempt to overturn the family settlement see *Shelley* v. *Cowper* (1576) KB 27/1256, m. 432.

²⁴ Shelley was a member of the Inner Temple, though there is no record that he was called to the bar. Coke referred to him, in the preface to his manuscript report, as a 'friend': below, p. cvi.

²⁵ 1 And. 71. The judges did not speak seriatim, but Wray C.J. announced the decision on their behalf, with brief reasons: BL MS. Lansd. 1084, fo. 24v; Moo. 140–141.

²⁶ *V*, fo. 30: 'Shelleys case argue in banck le roygne Hill. 23 Eliz. ex libro Cooke.' This term is wholly missing from Coke's first notebook, without any gap in the pagination. There are reports in the notebook from Trinity term 1581, when the judgment was given, but there are no missing leaves. George Croke's report was written long before 1 Co. Rep. was published in 1600, and so it is likely that the 'book' refers to the circulated manuscript pamphlet.

²⁷ Holkham Hall MS. 251, headed in Coke's hand, 'A reporte of the judgment and part of the arguments of Shelleys case'. The dedication is signed in Coke's autograph and there are a few corrections in his hand. The corrections did not find their way into the copies and must have been made later.

²⁸ BL MS. Harley 443, fos. 1–9; MS. Harg. 373, fos. 56–73; MS. Lansd. 1072, fos. 107–120; MS. Add. 24845, fos. 218v–227v; MS. Add. 25233, fos. 56–75; MS. Add. 35953, fos. 13v–21; CUL MS. Dd.13.24, fos. 52v–58; Bodl. Lib. MS. Rawlinson C.85, fos. 180–191; All Souls College, Oxford, MS. 156, fos. 1–5; LI MS. Maynard 29, fos. 267v–275v; MS. Misc. 361, fos. 1–11; Marsh's Library, Dublin, MS. Z4.2.8(4); East Sussex Record Office, MS. QCP/5, fos. 115–127v; Suffolk Record Office, Ipswich, MS. HA 93/8/111, fos. 42–51v; Longleat House MS. 240; Yale Univ., Osborn fa 59.

²⁹ He may have had second thoughts about the appropriateness of this, because in the Holkham MS. the signature is struck through and 'E. C.' put in its place. But most of the copies have a facsimile of the whole signature.

³⁰ BL MS. Lansd. 1084, fo. 24v: 'Pur avoider del tedious suites en le dit case le roigne mande a le segnior chancelor de Angliter que il assemblera les justices et barons del escheker pur aver toutes lour opinions et resolutions en le case, que fist accordant, et tandem toutes forsque Justice Mead agreont en

Coke had reargued the case – apparently as the defendant's only counsel on this occasion – at York House (the lord chancellor's residence), before all the justices of England.[31] In the earlier hearings in Westminster Hall his role had been subsidiary to Popham's, and perhaps his statement referred only to motions in which he was the leading or only counsel, and not to mere appearances alongside a leader.[32]

Coke's prefatory address to Lord Buckhurst is so stilted, and its sentences so long and convoluted, that it reads as if it had been composed originally in Latin. Several of the copyists evidently had such difficulty with it that they adjusted the wording, usually making it ungrammatical in the process. The main reason for writing it was clear enough. No one of Coke's junior standing at the Bar[33] had ever before presumed to publish reports under his own name, and this was an essay justifying his presumption. The excuse was that he had been pressed by others to do it, and that it was in the interests of his client to oblige. But it is of greater interest as incidentally affording an early insight into Coke's thinking about the importance of law reporting. The profession had (in his view) all but abandoned the tradition represented by his sacred year books,[34] and was in danger of losing for ever the oral wisdom released daily into the air of Westminster Hall:[35]

> Nothing is so fixed in mind or fastened in memory (right honourable my very good lord) but in short time is loosened out of the one and little by little quite gone out of the other. It is necessary, therefore, that memorable things should be committed to writing (the witness of times, the light and the life of truth) and not wholly betaken to slippery memory, that seldom yieldeth any certain reckoning. And herein our present age is, of all that ever was, to future posterity the most ungrateful; for those of former (though not of such flourishing) time, to the great benefit of themselves, of us, and our posterity, have faithfully and carefully registered in books as well the sayings as the doings that were in their time worthy of

---

tiel maner que Wray, chief justice, deliverast en court ove le judgment …'. Cf. 1 Co. Rep. at fo. 105v: 'Puis que le dit case avoit estre overtment et a large argue … le roigne, oiant de ceo (car tiel fuit le rareness et difficulty de le case, esteant de importance, que il fuit generalment conus) et de son gracious disposition, a preventer que longe et, tedious et chargeable suites enter parties cy prochein de sanke, que serroit le undoing del ambideux, esteant gentlehomes de un bone et ancient family, direct ses gracious letters a Sir Thomas Bromley …'. In fact there were strong religious divisions underlying the dispute, the plaintiff being a well-known obstinate papist: Simpson, *Leading Cases*, pp. 29–33.

[31] This is indicated by Coke's report: 1 Co. Rep. 93, at fo. 105 (referring to himself anonymously as 'un de le parte de le defendant', though his name slipped out on fo. 94v).

[32] Coke nevertheless says he argued on the earlier (undated) occasion: 1 Co. Rep. at fo. 94v. Some reports of his argument are dated as early as Mich. 1580: BL MS. Harley 1699, fos. 164–168; MS. Harg. 37, fos. 11–12; MS. Lansd. 1078, fos. 8–9. Anderson seems to date the decision to that term (1 And. 71), but it was probably the date of his own opening argument for the plaintiff. The reports of the case in BL MS. Add. 16169, fo. 204, and CUL MS. Gg.2.5, fos. 298–300 (Hil., Pas. 1582), name Popham, Cowper and 'Cooke puisne' for Henry, and Anderson, Gawdy and Fenner for Richard. That in BL MS. Lansd. 1057, fos. 30v–32 (undated), names the counsel only as Anderson, Popham and Fenner. Cf. BL MS. Harley 6882, fos. 20v–26: 'Largument de Shelleys case per Cooke del Inner Temple' (undated).

[33] He was only of three years' call, and was still 'Coke puisne': see the report in the previous note.

[34] Cf. Coke's *Statuta*, 2, fo. 6, where he did criticise the year books. They were 'darke, for that the reporter reported the case without seing the record'. At the time of writing this, he thought reporting had begun in the time of Edward II, or even Edward III, after the plea rolls stopped giving the arguments and the reasons for judgments. He seems not then to have been acquainted with the earliest year books, or with the generality of early plea rolls. For his belief that there were official reports see above, p. lxxxiii, n. 86.

[35] Holkham Hall MS. 251 (spelling modernised). This text contains a few alterations in Coke's hand, made after the text was circulated. He amended it further when he incorporated parts of it in the preface to his first volume of *Reports* (1600). A few slight corrections are here introduced from that preface.

memory, for omitting others and taking one example for all, how carefully have those of our profession in former times reported to posterity the opinions, censures and judgments of the reverend judges and sages of the common laws: which, if they had silenced and not set forth in writing, certainly, as their bodies in the bowels of the earth are long ago consumed, so had their grave opinions, censures and judgments been with them buried in their graves and long 'ere this time worn away and wasted with the worm of oblivion. But we, as justly to be blamed as the thing itself to be bewailed, having greater cause are less careful, having better opportunity are less occasioned, and being in greatest necessity are of all others the most negligent, whom neither the excellency and perfection of knowledge (a thing most pleasant) nor the practice thereof in furtherance of justice (a thing most profitable), albeit one learned and grave man hath made an entrance, can among so many in this flourishing time[36] move another to register and report the cases that upon great deliberation and study, as well of the court as of the counsel, receive resolution.

The 'one learned and grave man' was Plowden, whose book had deeply influenced the students of Coke's generation. Coke would not have known that the aged Dyer, who died three months later, was about to leave to posterity another important series of reports extending over the previous half century. But they, unlike Plowden's reports, would have to be printed in their unedited state, since Dyer himself had evidently taken no steps towards preparing them for the press. The fact is that in 1582 no one was known to be writing reports with a view to publication. Although there were plenty of reports in circulation, as mentioned above, they were of variable quality and often anonymous. Yet the neglect of good reporting was, Coke argued, positively dangerous. It led to error and confusion, and could be damaging even to a party who prevailed, if his case was misreported:

... first, for want of a true and certain report, the case that is adjudged, standing upon the rack of many running reports, is so diversely drawn out that each part of the case is disordered and disjointed, and the right reason and rule of the case utterly mistaken and falsified. Hereout there spring many absurd and strange opinions, which, being carried about in a common charm, and fathered on grave and reverend judges, many times with the multitude (and sometimes with the learned) receive allowance, and either beguile or bedazzle their judgments. Therefore, as the student that maketh memory his storehouse shall at his greatest need want of his store, so he that stuffeth his storehouse with wandering and masterless reports may retain them for his pleasure without finding any profit. Dangerous it is also for the client, whose case, being once doubtful and drawn into such question as each party justly suspecteth the sequel, when the reason and the cause of judgment (which a short time will bring to pass) is slipped out of memory, may be eftsoons called into question and receive (or be in danger of) a contrary judgment.

Memory was a recurrent theme of Coke's. His own must have been better than most, but even so it depended on support from his growing library.[37] The danger of relying on memory was given as the principal justification for producing the present report. Coke claimed to have composed it at the instance of Henry Shelley himself, his client and friend, who was apparently also a protégé of the dedicatee, Lord Buckhurst:

---

[36] spring time of knowledge *1 Co. Rep.*

[37] See his letter to Burghley on 7 March 1596 (BL MS. Lansd. 83, fo. 83, spelling modernised) concerning a different case: '... At my coming to my study I found that case, which (though it concerned mine own profession) I retained not so well in memory as I remembered the party's name. But it was admirable to me that your lordship, amongst so many infinite other matters of greater moment, should so perfectly remember the same ...'.

The consideration thereof (right honourable), being also importuned by my good friend and client whom the matter so much imported, hath moved me to make report of his case that lately received judgment. Wherein I have not taken upon me to set forth at large the arguments of the counsel of either party, save only of one with whose argument I was best acquainted. I have as near as I could faithfully and truly collected and set down the effect of those three learned arguments of the three serjeants which argued for the plaintiff, for to have enterprised to make report of their arguments in such method and so largely as they were delivered, lest I should bewrong them, I durst not; lest I should offend your lordship with too large a volume, I would not; <for straitness of time, I could not. If leisure had served, I minded not, seeing that for any necessity of matter, the substance being set down, I needed not>.[38] I have of purpose wholly omitted two other arguments on the part of the defendant, <both>' because <I heard them not myself and for that>'[39] I am in good hope my friend[40] shall obtain the same of themselves that argued.

The report of *Shelley's Case* revealed a trait which is more than hinted at in this passage, and has been noticed in respect of later cases reported by Coke.[41] Judges did not always give full reasons for their decisions in public, and Coke was ready to fill the void in such cases by making the assumption that they must have adopted the reasoning of counsel on the winning side, especially when that was himself. Although this may have been a broadly correct inference, it is open to the objection that, where several lines of argument were pursued, the judges may not have agreed with every one of them.[42] Coke was also accustomed to prune and refine arguments, which in some cases had been delivered at great length, and which some other reporters liked to record in every remembered detail. Coke aimed to produce a more compact and coherent report. That is what he meant by reports being 'so diversely drawn out that each part of the case is disordered and disjointed', and it was the reason for his setting down the 'effect' of the serjeants' arguments rather than following their method or reproducing them 'so largely as they were delivered'. In 1600 he would note with pleasure Popham C.J.'s remark that 'reporters do wisely to omit opinions which are spoken obiter (*accidentalment*) and which do not deal with the point in question'; ironically, though, he wrote it down in the longest drawn-out of all the reports in his notebook.[43]

In his report of *Shelley's Case*, Coke seems to have been more concerned with supplying omissions than making them. Although the ultimate decision was the outcome of meetings between all the justices of England in Serjeants' Inn, little by way of explanation had been given in public. When Coke's report was printed in

---

[38] These words have been struck through, presumably by Coke.
[39] This interlined addition, in Coke's hand, is not found in the copies.
[40] I.e. Henry Shelley.
[41] E.g. *Slade's Case* (1602) *C*, fos. 547–550v; 4 Co. Rep. 91. See J. H. Baker, 'New Light on *Slade's Case*' (1972), reprinted in *Collected Papers*, iii. 1129–1175, especially at p. 1172. Because of irreconcilable differences between the King's Bench and Common Pleas, the judges in this case were not permitted to give reasons seriatim and only a brief announcement was made of the outcome.
[42] In *Shelley's Case* itself the judges expressly declined to express an opinion on one of the four points argued: BL MS. Lansd. 1084, fo. 24v.
[43] *Case of Alton Woods* (Trin. 1600) *C*, fos. 398–414, at fo. 409; 1 Co. Rep. at fo. 50 ('reporters font sagement a omitter opinions queux sont parle accidentalment et queux ne conclude al point in question'). The point was taken up by Egerton L.K. in *C*, fo. 412v; 1 Co. Rep. at fo. 52 ('en les reports et arguments de matters in ley le point adjudge est principalment destre observe, et nemy matters de discourse que ne tend al point adjudge'). As to *obiter dicta* see also *R.* v. *Englefield* (1591) Moo. 303 at p. 321, *per* Popham C.J., referring to a case in Statham, 'Le dit livre nest prise pur ley, ne adjudge la, mes est solement un collateral opinion que ne doit receiver credit encounter reason et les rules del ley'.

1600, Sir Edmund Anderson – who in 1581 had been one of the serjeants on the losing side – remarked that 'Mr Attorney Coke has now made a report in print of this case, with the arguments and agreements of the chancellor and other judges, but nothing of that was spoken in court or shown there'.[44] The manuscript collector Edward Umfreville went further and opined that a comparison of the contemporary manuscript report with the printed version of 1600 showed that Coke 'would take liberties in his reports to the public not strictly justifiable or warranted by his private notes', and that this 'proves in a great measure the just censure of his contemporaries Ellesmere and Bacon, vizt. too much *de proprio*'.[45] Beneath this note, however, the more learned Francis Hargrave wrote: 'How the following report of Shelley's case by lord Coke justifies the preceding censure of him, I am at a loss to see. F. H. 12 July 1796.' In this instance, the version which circulated in manuscript was already fully worked up and needed minimal editing when it came to be printed, unlike the reports in Coke's notebooks, which sometimes underwent substantial augmentation for the press.[46] Apart from one significant change,[47] the text is so similar that it has not seemed necessary to include it in this edition.[48]

Whatever its shortcomings as a record of the case, rather than an essay on it, it was Coke's report which posterity received without question. And it may be supposed that it did little harm to the furtherance of his career. He may have intended to repeat the exercise with a full report of *Mildmay* v. *Standish* (1585),[49] though (unlike *Shelley's Case*) there is a relatively compact version in his contemporary notebook as well.[50] A separate manuscript report was mentioned in his library catalogue,[51] though no copy has been certainly identified as Coke's.[52] *Shelley's Case* was therefore the only report by Coke which was generally made public before the appearance of the first part of his printed reports in 1600.

(b) The circulation of Coke's early reports

In the interim, the principal means of making Coke's reports available to others was by lending them to be copied. This was merely a continuation of the professional

---

[44] 1 And. 71: 'Nota le Atturney Master Cooke ad ore fait report en print de cest case ove arguments et les agreements del chanceler et auters juges, mes rien de ceo fuit parle en le court ne la monstre'. Cf. BL MS. Harley 6882, fo. 26 (postscript): 'Les points argue in le case et le resolutions de eux collect per Cooke in effect accordant al son argument (mes que un point est omitted supra) et mist a Seignior Buckhurst: vide subscript[ion]. Les argued pointes fueront 4 …'.

[45] BL MS. Harg. 373, fo. 55v. For Lord Ellesmere's criticisms see below, p. clii, n. 83.

[46] The amount of alteration varied greatly. The report of *Slade's Case* (1602), for instance, was substantially the same as that in the notebook.

[47] See Smith, 'Was there a Rule in Shelley's Case?', at p. 64.

[48] It even retains (1 Co. Rep. 98) a reference to the first volume of Plowd. as 'Mr Plowden's new reports'.

[49] CP 40/1423, m. 1745 (printed in Co. Ent. 30); KB 27/1291, m. 35; 1 Co. Rep. 175.

[50] *C*, fos. 295–297 (vol. iv, p. 912): 'Le graunde case de Sir Henry Sharington, Hill. 26 Eliz. in le court de gardes, et Trin. 26 Eliz. in le common banke inter Mildmay, pleintife, et Standishe, defendant, in action sur le case pur slaundering del title etc.'

[51] *Library of Sir Edward Coke*, p. 29, no. 365: 'A report 26 Eliza: in le case de Mildmaye et Standish in fol:'. This was presumably the basis of the report printed in 1 Co. Rep. 175.

[52] There is a long report in *Ff*, fos. 111–122v, a manuscript containing a good deal of Coke material. There are shorter reports in BL MS. Harley 1693, fo. 57; MS. Harg. 15, fos. 102v–103.

custom mentioned earlier. Transcripts from Coke's first notebook have so far been found in thirteen different volumes of reports by others. Six of these are substantial selections,[53] the others single cases;[54] and there are several dubiously attributed collections of copyhold cases.[55] At least one reporter also took a few cases from Coke's earlier, non-chronological, commonplace-books,[56] and another borrowed several cases from what is now the Rylands manuscript when it was in Coke's possession.[57] All the known copies were made at an early stage in the life of the notebooks, in some cases before Coke had made amendments to the text,[58] and they usually omitted the encrustations of interlineations and marginalia. None of the transcripts yet discovered extends as far as the second notebook.[59] There is no ready explanation for this, because access was certainly given to his third notebook (*B*), missing since the eighteenth century.[60]

At a later period, Coke gave leave to Heneage Finch, a barrister of the Inner Temple,[61] to copy all his notebooks, but his transcript – which might have been invaluable in supplying lost portions of text[62] – was destroyed in the seventeenth

---

[53] CUL MS. Ff.5.4, fos. 156–209v (here designated *Ff*); CUL MS. Gg.5.4, fos. 22–35v, 37–50, 62v–68v, 71r-v (here designated *Gg*); fo. 37 is headed 'Cases escrie ex libro Cooke que il mesme collect 22 et 23 Eliz. in Bancke le Roy'; BL MS. Lansd. 1068 (here designated *La*; twenty-one cases, 1581–84); MS. Lansd. 1095, fos. 4–6v (here designated *Lb*; twenty-one different cases, 1576–83); MS. Lansd. 1084, fos. 37–38 (here designated *L*; thirteen cases, 1581-4, in reverse order), 42v; IT MS. Barrington 17 (here designated *I*), fos. 7 (1584), 216v–218 (six cases, 1581–92), 237v (1582) and 247 (1584).

[54] BL MS. Lansd. 1076, fos. 119v–120 (below, nos. 81, 123); BL MS. Add. 35941, fo. 222 (no. 94); CUL MS. Hh.2.9, fo. 233 (no. 67); LI MS. Maynard 29, fo. 1v (no. 58); Longleat MS. 240 (no. 97). Two contain *The Countess of Lennox's Case* (1580), which is included here with the non-chronological reports (no. 111) because it precedes and is separated from the chronological series, though it is physically in the first notebook: BL MS. Harley 1693, fo. 100v; MS. Lansd. 1068, fo. 130v.

[55] BL MS. Harley 4552, fos. 5–9v, is a series of copyhold cases headed (in red ink) 'Cookes Reports'; but some of the cases are as early as 1560 and they do not seem to be Coke's. There is a similar group in CUL MS. Ii.5.38, fos. 1–4v. Cf. CUL MS. Ff.5.4, fos. 156–157v: 'Copyholdes. Reportes Cook'. Coke himself published a group of copyhold cases, mostly gathered from the notebooks, in 4 Co. Rep. 21–32. The association between Coke and these reports of copyhold cases may explain the attribution of Co. Copyh., which is no longer accepted: see Smith, *Sir Edward Coke*, p. 29, n. 62.

[56] BL MS. Lansd. 1095, fo. 4.

[57] *Ff*, fos. 184v–199v; see Appendix II. Since these extracts are embedded in the transcripts from MS. *A* (above, n. 53), it may be assumed they were all copied from Coke's manuscripts. Cf. Cro. Eliz. 27–28, a citation of *Dr Good's case* (1577) 'ex relatione Edwardi Coke': Appendix II, p. cciii.

[58] A case in *AB*, fo. 331v (vol. ii, p. 248) has 'chief justice Wraye', whereas the same passage has 'recorder de London' in *Ff*, *Gg* and *La*, which suggests that all three copies came from a common source. That source seems to have been Coke's manuscript itself, before emendation, since in the original notebook 'chief justice Wraye' is written in darker ink over an illegible erasure.

[59] A collated list of known transcripts is provided in Appendix IV. Since this edition is based on the autograph manuscript, it has not been necessary to construct a *stemma*. But it is clear that *Gg* is not derived from *Ff*: above, p. xii.

[60] Below, p. cxiii. In HLS MS. 105, fo. 54v, among a series of Elizabethan cases copied by Arthur Turnour *c.* 1620 'hors del liver Magistri Roberti Browne' (of the Middle Temple, called 1612), there is a report of *Att.-Gen.* v. *Carie and Doddington* (1597) 'ex relatione Coke attorney generall'; but it is very much shorter than the lengthy report in vol. iv, pp. 787–796, and is more likely to have been based on an oral relation than an abridgment from *C*.

[61] Adm. to the Inner Temple 1598, called 1606, created serjeant at law 1623; died 1631.

[62] See above, p. xcviii, n. 89. Since it was all said to be contained in one volume, albeit a thick one, it seems unlikely that it was a complete copy of everything in the notebooks. Unless the material was copied out of order, however, there was more than one sequence in the folio numbering. The case of *Turnor* v. *Andrews* (1597) was on fo. 341: n. 64, opposite. But the *Case of Proclamations* (here dated Hil. 1611) was on fos. 5–7 and 10: BL MS. Add. 24283, fo. 17.

century in a fire. Sir Roger Twysden (d. 1672) made use of Finch's transcript while it was in the possession of his brother Sir Thomas Twisden (d. 1683), justice of the King's Bench,[63] and inserted about thirty extracts or paraphrases from it in his interleaved copy of Cowell's *Interpreter* (1637). Most, if not all, of the cases so extracted concerned questions of public law and correspond with texts later printed in the twelfth and thirteenth parts of Coke's *Reports* (1657–58);[64] none of them relate to the period covered by the present volumes. Sir Thomas made even less use of it, though there are a few references in his abridgment.[65] In 1668 Serjeant Finch's son, another Heneage Finch (later Lord Nottingham), cited a case of 1585 from MS. *A*, probably relying on the same transcript.[66]

Another early-seventeenth-century copy is in the library of the duke of Northumberland at Alnwick Castle.[67] It is a complete transcript, in 1,111 folios, of MS. *C* as far as the end of Elizabeth I's reign. Since it ends exactly at the end of the reign, it seems probable that there was a second volume continuing with the reign of James I. It is unfortunate that the second volume seems not to have survived, since a volume of similar length would have contained cases from the manuscripts now lost.[68] The provenance is unknown, though in the 1660s the book was still in the hands of a lawyer, who added a few marginal references to law reports of that period.[69]

Mention should also be made of a manuscript in the Bodleian Library which is entitled on the front endpaper 'Liver de abridgement dez casez de Tho. Co. queux il abridge luy mesme'.[70] Tho. Co. is doubtless Thomas Coventry, though this is not an abridgment of his reports,[71] and it seems not to be his autograph original but a copy

---

[63] He described it as follows on the fly-leaf of his copy of Cowell's *Interpreter* (1637), now BL MS. Add. 24281, fo. 1: 'Sir Edward Coke's reports MSS. – it is a great thick booke in fol. having on the leaves C.C.C. It is now in my brother Thom's, and was my uncle Heneage's. Sir Edward Cooke, when my uncle had once argued for hym passing well, and saved hym from beeing fyned, in requitall of his paynes, permitted him to write all the reports that he, a long practiser and a judge, had collected, of which some were published, but, in my slender judgment, the best remayned only in writing. These, I say, hee suffer'd my uncle to copy out. <This book is since burnt *added*.>' Sir Roger and Sir Thomas, who chose to spell their surname differently, were both sons of Sir William Twysden Bt and his wife Anne, sister of Sir Heneage Finch (d. 1631), serjeant at law. Sir Thomas Twisden's other manuscripts have been widely dispersed: see J. H. Baker, *English Legal Manuscripts in the U.S.A.*, ii (Selden Soc., 1990), p. 140.

[64] Nearly all the citations give folio references, which would have been helpful in reconstructing the composition of the later notebooks if the numbering had been Coke's; but they refer to Finch's numbering, not that of the original notebooks. The earliest identified reference is from 1597. BL MS. Add. 24281, fo. 36v, s.v. Altaragium, cites 'M. 30 [*recte* 39] & 40 Eliz. fol. 341a'; this is *Turnor* v. *Andrews* (1597) in *C*, fo. 226v. A passage on ancient measures of land, which Coke copied in 1598 from a book belonging to Thomas Fanshawe, was printed from the same manuscript, s.v. Knights-fee, in 2 *Archaeologia Cantiana* (1859), p. 313. Twysden said this was on fo. 361v of Finch's copy; in *C* it is on fo. 256v.

[65] E.g. HLS MS. 531 (5016) (the portion from F to W), fos. 151 (cit. 'Coke MSS 241', identifiable in *C*, fo. 69) and 291v (cit. 'Coke MSS 204, 205, 261, 341', i.e. *Finch* v. *Throckmorton*, identifiable as *B*, fo. 34; *C*, fos. 93, 226v). There are thus references to two different cases on *C*, fo. 226v (cf. the previous note), both on fo. 341 of the transcript.

[66] 2 Keb. 427; quoted in vol. ii, p. 266.

[67] Alnwick Castle MS. 516.

[68] On fo. 70 the text copies Coke's own added marginal reference (*C*, fo. 40) to a case of 6 Jac., indicating that the copy cannot have been made before 1608.

[69] There are references to Owen (1656), Cro. Eliz. (1661) and Moore (1663).

[70] Bodl. Lib., MS. Rawlinson C. 756.

[71] As to which see p. lxxxiv, n. 90, above.

or further abridgment of some cases abridged by him.[72] The cases are in a number of more or less chronological sequences, sometimes wrongly dated, and very briefly summarised. But they are virtually all derived from Coke's MS. *C*, concentrating on material not in print.[73] There are also some notes on patents for monopoly which were declared void in the Exchequer in 1597, when informations in the nature of *quo warranto* were brought by Coke as attorney-general. These notes are not from *C* but are based on two leaves found in Coke's annotated *Magna Carta cum Statutis* (1556), now at Holkham.[74] These inserted leaves have been cut down and folded at the top and bottom, as if taken from a larger volume, and it is possible that they became detached at some stage from *C*, which has an irregular foliation at this point. The only other contents of the Rawlinson manuscript are a few Jacobean cases, ending with a small group from 1620–22, and a note of *Lord Audley's Case* in 1631.[75] These later items suggest that the abridgment may have been made after 1631, perhaps after Coke's death in 1634. On the other hand, if the two leaves relating to monopolies were formerly part of MS. *C*, it may be more likely that they were abridged before then, when still in situ. At any rate, it seems that the abridger expected to have continued recourse to the original.[76] All of this would be consistent with 'Tho. Co.' being Coventry, who was close to Coke in his lifetime. Bacon famously opposed his appointment to the recordership of London in 1616 on the grounds that he was 'bred by my lord Coke and seasoned in his ways'.[77] One of the latest entries in the abridgment concerns Coke's committal to the Tower in December 1621, noting a private remark of Cranfield's that he expected him to be out within a fortnight because he was 'the right hand of the lower house of Parliament'.[78] Coventry was at that time attorney-general. And it was Coventry who, as lord keeper of the great seal, presided at the trial of Lord Audley in 1631; he was still lord keeper at the time of Coke's death in 1634. The manuscript is of no textual value in editing Coke's reports, but it is of interest as being possibly the last known sighting of MS. *C* before the eighteenth century.

The large number of extracts copied from Coke's notebooks in the late-Elizabethan period does not necessarily indicate that he gave completely free access to them. The repetition of errors, interpolations and omissions in different manuscripts shows that

---

[72] There may have been more than one exemplar. On fo. 31 a new series begins 'Lib. BB'. The endpaper has a monogrammatic siglum which appears to read 'HhE'.

[73] The earliest, on fo. 40v, is *Lord Paget's Case* (Mich. 1591) (from *C*, fo. 7), and the latest, on fo. 36v, are the cases of Guy Fawkes and Henry Garnett (wrongly dated 'Mich. 5 Ja.', *recte* Mich. 3 Jac., 1605) (from *C*, fo. 695). There are a few cases dated before Mich. 1591, but they are all from *C*, where the earlier dates are given.

[74] MS. Rawlinson C. 756, fo. 49 (interpolated between a note on the clerk of the market, from *C*, fo. 212, and a note on the judges' resolutions concerning Parliament, from *C*, fo. 213*bis*). The source is identifiable as Coke's *Statuta*, 2, part II, endpapers, fos. [iii]-[iv].

[75] MS. Rawlinson C. 756, fo. 38. The other late cases are *Leighton's Case* (Pas. 18 Jac. I) on fo. 31, *Keppin's Case* (Hil. 19 Jac. I) on fo. 37v, and *John Browne's Case* (undated) on fo. 38.

[76] This is suggested by the casual reference on fo. 60v to Coke's tract of 1604 on chapter 29 of Magna Carta: 'Vide bon comment sur lestatut Magna Charta, c. 29.' For the tract (in *C*, fos. 600–604v) see 132 Selden Soc. 394–402; Baker, *Magna Carta*, pp. 346–347, 500–520; below, p. cl.

[77] *Letters and Life of Francis Bacon*, ed. J. Spedding and others, vol. vi (1857), p. 97.

[78] MS. Rawlinson C. 756, fo. 37; the remark was made to 'le clerke'. Cf. Coke's *Statuta*, front free endpaper: a different note (in Coke's hand) concerning his imprisonment in the Tower in Trinity term 1622.

some of the copies were copies of copies,[79] and so it seems possible that favoured students were allowed to transcribe some of the cases and then put them into circulation.[80] The Inner Temple records reveal the names of only three members of the inn who shared Coke's chambers,[81] and that is probably because the chambers, or at least the portion which he acquired in 1588, were in the gift of the earl of Leicester rather than the inn.[82] But one of the three was George Croke, who took up reporting himself at the beginning of 1582.[83] He was, as it happens, one of the known Coke copyists,[84] though he probably did the copying before he was admitted to the chambers in 1588; the admission seems therefore to reflect an earlier association. Another of the known copyists was Thomas Gawen, an exact contemporary of Coke's in the Inner Temple.[85] He was better known as a litigant than as a practitioner, and as a plaintiff he was represented on different occasions in 1596 both by Coke and by Croke.[86] Although he is not known to have moved into Coke's chambers – indeed, he built some of his own in the late 1570s – Gawen had been a co-tenant with George Croke in his previous set in Fig Tree Court.[87] The chambers in Fig Tree Court had a prior association with law reporting in that they had once belonged to Robert Keilwey (d. 1581), whose manuscript copy of Caryll's reports was known to Coke and would be edited for publication by George Croke's brother John in 1602;[88] and they were also shared for a time with George's brother-in-law Edward Bulstrode, whose son Edward was to be a prominent reporter in the next century.

Two other partial copyists whose names are known were, however, from Gray's Inn. Three cases from the first notebook were collected by Edward Henden, admitted

---

[79] See, e.g., vol. ii, p. 252, no. 4, where 'a son office' in the autograph manuscript is explained as 'al office de vicount' in *Ff*, *Gg* and *La*. At the end of the same case, where Coke said he was of counsel with one Silver, the copyist added the quip 'pur son silver', an addition which is found in all three copies and also in *I*, fo. 247. See also below, p. 57, n. 4.

[80] See also above, p. xci, n. 39.

[81] John Scott was in occupation before Coke: *Calendar of Inner Temple Records*, ii, ed. F. A. Inderwick (1898), p. 345. In Jan. 1595 'Mr Holte' was granted an admittance to the attorney-general's chamber at the instance of the countess of Leicester: *Calendar of Inner Temple Records*, i, ed. F. A. Inderwick (1896), p. 402. This is presumably Francis Holte of Dudston, Warw., adm. 1595.

[82] He came to occupy a group of chambers in the Elizabethan brick buildings at the top of King's Bench Walk. One of them, known as Dudley's Building, was put up by Robert Dudley, earl of Leicester, in 1576: *Calendar of Inner Temple Records*, i. 286–287, 402; J. Baker, *An Inner Temple Miscellany* (2004), pp. 136–139.

[83] *Calendar of Inner Temple Records*, ii. 345. His notebooks are now in the Herts. Record Office. Their contents were printed in English translation under the editorship of Sir Harbottle Grimstone in the middle of the next century.

[84] Above, pp. xc, ciii. George Croke entered the Inner Temple in 1574 and was called to the bar in 1584. His transcripts from Coke's notebooks are in *V*, fos. 24–26, 30, 32–33. He also noted two cases 'ex relatione Edward[i] Coke' in Cro. Eliz. 28, 58.

[85] He was adm. 18 April 1572, six days before Coke; for the reference to him see below, p. cxiii. Popham C.J. said he had a bad reputation: below, p. cxviii, n. 45.

[86] BL MS. Harley 1697, fo. 99 (Coke, Pas. 1596); MS. Harley 4552, fo. 44 (Coke, Hil. 1596); MS. Harley 4998, fo. 54v (Hil. 1596); MS. Harley 6745, fo. 205 (George Croke, Trin. 1596). See also below, p. cxviii, n. 45. There is a letter from Gawen to Coke, dated 16 Sept. 1599, in the John Rylands Library, RYCH/3269.

[87] *Calendar of Inner Temple Records*, i. 274, 349. Gawen was admitted to the chambers in 1574, together with Edward Bulstrode; John Croke had been admitted earlier. The second reference shows that George Croke shared the chambers with his elder brother John. Bulstrode was their brother-in-law.

[88] See above, p. lxxxii.

to Gray's Inn in 1586 and called to the bar in 1591.[89] And another case abridged from the first notebook is said to have been taken 'ex libro Cooke reportes come jeo escrye ex libro Crewe'.[90] The 'jeo' who abridged it is not identified, but Crewe is presumably Thomas Crewe (d. 1634), admitted to Gray's Inn in 1585 and called to the bar in 1590, with a distinguished career ahead of him. It is not obvious how Crewe might have become acquainted with Coke in his student days, though his brother Randall (later chief justice) was one of Coke's executors. There is no obvious connection with Henden.

The thinking behind Coke's selection of cases to include in his notebooks is difficult to fathom. Some were relatively minor cases which have not been found in other reports. Their presence may simply be a consequence of Coke's personal involvement. Others were obvious choices, cases well known at the time in learned circles and reported in different words by several contemporaries. The extent to which the more prominent cases were reported by various hands is indicated in the footnotes to this edition, where references to comparable reports are collected.[91] Many of these independent reports are considerably longer than Coke's, and supply details which he did not record, though his versions seem generally accurate as to the legal issues[92] and always to contain the essence of the arguments and outcomes. But the reports by Coke's contemporaries include many cases which he did not choose to report himself, even though he was of counsel, and even though his own arguments were victorious or at least noteworthy. It is less than clear why he omitted these. It may simply have been a matter of time. Had he tried to record all the cases in which he spoke, he would hardly have had time to prepare and argue them as well.[93] All that can be said with confidence is that the notes we have are such as Coke thought would be useful to him later. Whether or not he always envisaged usefulness to others as well, by lending and eventual publication, he certainly had occasion to use them for his own purposes. He cited them at the bar in later cases, and in 1599 he may have produced the second notebook in the King's Bench and shown it to the court.[94] His own notes contain many references to them. At first he usually cited them with the folio number, though it is observable that in his later reports the folio references are usually omitted even when he was clearly making use of the notebooks. The reason for this change is doubtless that the reports were coming to be aimed at the public: his private folio references were of no value to the larger readership.

---

[89] LI MS. Misc. 791, fo. 111: 'Cases collect per Henden ex lib. Coke'. They are *Earl of Arundel's Case* (1576) below, p. 70, *Hasilrig* v. *Grey* (1580) vol. ii, p. 174, *Dineley* v. *Assheton* (1581) ibid. 192.

[90] BL MS. Lansd. 1068, fo. 130v. This is *The Countess of Lennox's Case* (1580) above, p. cviii, n. 54.

[91] It has not been possible to collate them, and many of them will doubtless be found to contain different versions of the same report.

[92] Sometimes the factual information is less accurate, by comparison with the record.

[93] For the extent of his engagements in the 1580s see above, p. c.

[94] Vol. v, p. 964 ('Et le case de Melwiche, que fuit adjudge in banke le roy Tr. 30 Eliz., fol. 37, fuit vouche et monstre al court ...'). This may, of course, mean only that he showed a copy of the case to the court. (The case was *Melwich* v. *Luter* (1588) vol. ii, p. 374.) Coke had such a fund of case-law to call upon that at times some suspected the credibility of his citations: see CUL MS. Ll.3.9, fo. 337 (1593), *per* Gawdy J. ('Jeo marvell de vostre president Mr Sollicitour ...').

INTRODUCTION

The missing Notebook B, 1588–91

Coke continued his reports in another notebook (in this edition designated *B*), which contained the remainder of Michaelmas term 1588 and proceeded until Trinity term 1591, in approximately 55 leaves. Coke called it his 'little book of reports'.[95] The rest of the book, at any rate as bound up in its final form, contained an index to his reports, and also a repertory of records and statutes. It was thus described in the library catalogue of 1634:[96]

> A little booke covered with blewe velvett containing reports of 31, 32 and 33 Eliza: containing also a table to the reports of the Cheife Justice, and lastlie a table or repertorie of records and acts of parliament, which the Cheife Justice called his Vade Mecum. in 8°.

It was presumably the third of the three volumes in Coke's hand, all bound in velvet, which Robert Harley acquired in 1715;[97] but it can no longer be found in the Harleian collection and there is no likelihood of its being found anywhere else. An outline of its contents may, nevertheless, be reconstructed from cross-references in Coke's notebooks.[98] The text of only one case has been found verbatim, a copy of *Buckbeard's Case* (1589/90) made in Hilary term 1596 and surviving in at least four manuscripts.[99] It is headed: 'Le report del Buckbeards case fuit deliver a moy per Gawyn, quel il copie hors del reportes de Mr Attorney (come il dit), come ensuist …'. The copyist was the Thomas Gawen mentioned above,[1] who was admitted to the Inner Temple a week before Coke (on 18 April 1572). It thus seems that Coke was still giving access to his notes in the 1590s, though the circumstances were special inasmuch as the report was relevant to a case in which Gawen was his client. Copies from the reports written after 1590 are far fewer.[2] This, again, may reflect a decision to prepare edited versions for the press rather than to keep the material to himself.

Notebook C, 1591–1606

In Michaelmas term 1591 Coke's law reporting took a new turn. Having filled the 'little book' (*B*), now missing, he began what was to become the largest of all his volumes. Whether it started out as a large album of blank leaves is less than clear,

---

[95] *C*, fo. 680v (1605): 'Vide fort bone case in mes reportes Mich. 30 et 31 Eliz. regine fol. 1 in le petit livre de reportes.'

[96] *Library of Sir Edward Coke*, p. 27, no. 36.

[97] The three volumes were received on 6 Aug. 1715: *The Diary of Humfrey Wanley*, ed. C. E. and R. C. Wright (1966), pp. 13–14 ('The Secretary brought in 4 thick octavo books … Those three which are in Covers of Velvet, &c. are supposed to be of the Hand of the Lord Chief Justice Sir Edward Coke'). The other two bound in velvet were MSS. Harley 6686 and 6687.

[98] See vol. ii, pp. 405–407.

[99] BL MS. Harley 4998, fos. 154v–155v; MS. Harg. 7A, fo. 161v; MS. Harg. 14, fo. 116v; MS. Add. 25211, fo. 131; printed with translation in vol. ii, p. 407. The Harg. MSS. show that it was produced for citation in *Gawen* v. *Ludlow*, in which Thomas Gawen was the plaintiff and Coke appeared of counsel; in other reports of that case (see above, p. cxi, n. 86) it is cited without mention of its source.

[1] Gawen formerly shared chambers with George Croke, another copyist from Coke's notebooks: above, pp. xc, ciii.

[2] See p. cviii, above. Although there are several surviving copies of MSS. *D* to *G*, or parts of them, it is probable that they were made after Coke's death.

since it has been rebound twice, though it is all written on similar thin paper of high quality. The occasional lapses in strict chronology may point to it having been written originally on loose quires;[3] but it is equally possible that Coke wrote drafts on loose sheets and copied them into the book later.[4] By the later 1590s, there is a substantial proportion of cases inserted retrospectively. These must either be from rough notes no longer in existence or (more probably) from borrowed reports:[5] for instance, the numerous Common Pleas cases noted in the 1590s – often a few years after their date – are unlikely to taken from Coke's own observation.[6] There is, however, a continuous contemporary numbering of the leaves, with occasional alterations, duplications and chasms. It is clear that Coke perceived the book as a new departure, for at some point he wrote at the top of the first page 'Liber primus'. By the time he ended it, in Trinity 1606,[7] it was a thick volume of 700 folios, and when his library was catalogued in 1634 it was covered with black velvet.[8] It was acquired in 1715 by Robert Harley, together with MS. *A*, and is still in the Harleian collection. The velvet covers were abandoned around 1804, and later in the century it was rebound in two more manageable volumes (MS. Harley 6686A-B).

Although Coke treated this volume as his 'Liber primus', we have already noticed that he often referred to the cases in the older notebooks as his own reports. There is no obvious change in style, and the new reports are to all appearances (as the chronology alone indicates) a continuation of the earlier reports. This is made explicit on the first leaf, which has a continuation of *Lord Paget's Case* from an earlier report in the missing notebook *B*, to which there is a cross-reference ('Principium devant …'). The most plausible explanation for making a new start is that Coke's nomination to the recordership of London in October 1591[9] brought home to him that he was now an acknowledged leader of the Bar and would soon be a candidate for further positions of eminence on the profession,[10] as indeed came to pass very rapidly. The effect of his promotions in 1592–94 on the contents of the notebook will be addressed

---

[3] A clear example of this is the report of Coke's appointment as solicitor-general on the last day of Trinity term 1592 (vol. iii, p. 473), which is followed by further reports from that term.

[4] Note e.g. *Arundel's Case* (1594) vol. iii, p. 604, which Coke began to copy a second time (p. 614) and then stopped.

[5] An explicit example is *Eve and Finch* v. *Tracy* (1584), a copy of which was delivered to Coke in 1587: vol. ii, p. 341. A copy of the record in *Tayre* v. *Pepyat* (1583) was delivered to Coke in 1588: ibid. 367.

[6] Not being a serjeant, Coke had no right of audience in most cases there, and by 1591 he would have been too busy to attend when not retained. As attorney-general he had the right to argue within the bar of the Common Pleas, but only in cases where the queen had an interest: e.g. *Worsley's Case* (1597) BL MS. Harley 1575, fo. 37 ('Cooke attorney le roigne argue pur le defendant deins le barre'); *Arderne* v. *Darcy* (1598) BL MS. Harg. 7B, fo.125.

[7] There is some doubt about the correctness of the date in the headline: below, p. cxxxiv.

[8] *Library of Sir Edward Coke*, p. 22, no. 293: 'One booke of reports covered with black velvett in 8°. beginning with Pasche 33 Eliz: and ending Tr: 4 Jac: regis and cont' 713. leaves.' Coke's numbering indeed runs from 1 to 713, but there are chasms and duplications, and according to a later numbering there are actually 700 folios. The reference to 'Pasche' is to the report of *Elmer* v. *Thacker* written on the preliminary leaves, before the original fo. 1.

[9] He was elected on 14 Oct. 1591, but his predecessor William Fleetwood held on to the office 'magna importunitate et labore' until the election was confirmed by the court of aldermen on 7 Jan. 1592: *AA*, fo. 13.

[10] Coke was elected recorder of Norwich on 2 April 1586 (*AA*, fo. 13), but the London position was one of considerably greater eminence. In *Atkyns* v. *Atkyns* (Hil. 1592) BL MS. Add. 25201, fo. 15v, Coke argued in a case of error from Norwich, brought to reverse one of his own judgments there.

below. Little of his involvement in state affairs reached printed form in the *Reports* published in his own lifetime,[11] but it nevertheless seems probable that Coke was beginning to contemplate publication of the more significant private-law cases for the benefit of the profession.[12] By the time the notebook was filled, five volumes of his edited *Reports* had already been published.

Coke was sworn in as recorder of London on 14 January 1592,[13] and he was passingly noticed by that title in other law reports.[14] But his sitting at the Old Bailey occasioned only one report in the notebook – the first case he tried there, on 20 January 1592, in company with Chief Baron Manwood.[15] It was an intriguing case, from which Coke concluded that in some cases it was safer for a defendant to plead Guilty than Not Guilty, since it widened the scope of benefit of clergy. He was to report more criminal cases later in the 1590s, but as prosecutor rather than as judge. The reason why Newgate disappears so rapidly from view is that Coke was destined to serve the City for less than five months.[16] On 16 June 1592 he was sworn solicitor-general, in succession to Egerton, and the following day he surrendered the recordership.[17]

Coke gives a detailed account of his meeting with the queen at Greenwich on 14 June 1592,[18] a stressful interview apparently spent on his knees. The queen first reduced him to tears by questioning his role in giving counsel to persons who had claimed title to the property of attainted traitors,[19] a suspicion of disloyalty which so 'appalled and dismayed' him that, for once in his life, he was utterly lost for words.[20] She seems in fact to have been teasing him, but in a manner calculated to bring home his dependence on her good will. As soon as he had recovered some composure, she reduced him to further tears, this time of relief, by telling him she had chosen him to be her solicitor-general. Coke recorded in his autobiographical memoranda that

---

[11] It is another matter with parts 12 and 13, printed in the 1650s from MSS. *D* and *E*. The corresponding material in MS. *C* remained in obscurity.

[12] He chose to publish them in law French, since they were not for general consumption. In 1604 he wrote to Sir Robert Cecil, 'I have published three books of law … I would the cases themselves could be as well understood as the prefaces': *Cecil Papers*, xvi. 236.

[13] *AA*, fo. 13. A painting attributed to Gilbert Jackson in the Guildhall Art Gallery, London, which was formerly reputed to be of Coke as recorder, is certainly not of Coke; it seems to be a later recorder of London *c*. 1630, probably Robert Mason.

[14] E.g. BL MS. Harg. 26, fo. 34 ('Stevins demande de Cooke adonques recorder de Lond. in son chamber le maner de conveiance dun manor …') and fo. 37 (several similar questions put to him); LI MS. Hale 134, fo. 183v. Both are from Hil. 1592. Coke mentioned in his reports a custom which he certified as recorder: vol. iv, p. 662, 5 Co. Rep. 83.

[15] Vol. iii, p. 460.

[16] Another Newgate case, which Coke attended as Att.-Gen., is *The Case of Market Overt* (1596) vol. iv, p. 662; 5 Co. Rep. 83.

[17] *AA*, fo. 13v.   [18] Vol. iii, p. 473.

[19] She referred specifically to *Lord Paget's Case* (1591–92) vol. iii, pp. 408, 468; and *R.* v. *Englefield* (1591) ibid. 441. See also *Att.-Gen.* v. *Dowty* (1584) vol. ii, p. 259. In 1587 the Commons had debated trusts devised by 'crafty counsel' to avoid forfeitures for treason, referring in particular to Paget and Englefield: Dean, *Law-Making and Society*, p. 219.

[20] His defence, when he had recovered himself, was that he 'had been of counsel with her highness's subjects that had acquired and purchased lands or had leases of such offenders before their offences were known, and … (being a professor of her highness's laws) … was of counsel in divers of those cases, and that the rather for that most of those cases were of great difficulty and imported in them great understanding and learning, and being handled by her highness's counsel learned, being most excellent learned men, I knew the knowledge of those cases should the better enable me to discharge the duty of my profession'.

Burghley had written to him on 11 June with notice of the impending appointment,[21] and he had presumably received the message before meeting the queen. He cannot, therefore, have been stunned by surprise. The incident affords evidence of Coke's sometimes fragile emotions, but it is also a reminder of the tremendous distance between queen and commoner, a distance which could completely overawe anyone brought into her presence.[22]

The appointment as solicitor-general was the beginning of a new stage in Coke's life. Already the most prominent utter barrister in England when the Inner Temple elected him to the bench in 1590, he was now one of the queen's counsel[23] and at the centre of public affairs. The year 1592 proved to be a busy one for Coke. In addition to his new public duties, he was elected by the Inner Temple to be their Autumn reader, and had to prepare an original series of lectures on the Statute of Uses.[24] Coke said in his opening lecture that, although he was aware that others had read on the statute, he had never come across a copy of such a reading; in fact, the only known previous Inner Temple reading on the subject was given before he was born, by James Smith in 1550. The lectures began on 2 August, but the reading was curtailed after the fifth day when a member of the Middle Temple died of the plague and the Temple was promptly vacated. Coke noted with evident gratification that nine benchers and forty barristers of the Inn escorted him as far as Romford on his journey home to Huntingfield.[25]

These promotions were not all. On 28 January 1593, doubtless because of his perceived reliability as solicitor-general, Coke was nominated by the queen and Privy Council to be Speaker of the Parliament which it was proposed to hold in February. He was duly elected a knight of the shire[26] for Norfolk on 5 February, proudly noting that he was chosen by over 7,000 electors with no dissent, and he was formally elected Speaker by the Commons when Parliament commenced on 19 February.[27] The notebook contains some brief observations on the procedure at the state opening of Parliament, which Coke deduced from Lambarde's account to date from the time of Edward III. He noted how he had 'disabled' himself in the accustomed manner, standing in his place, before taking the chair. The report does not mention that he then made a second speech in the Lords, formally to request liberty of speech for the Commons in the usual manner, but also relating the history of the royal supremacy since the time of Henry III.[28] Coke's notes set out in detail the appointment of

---

[21] Vol. iii, p. 475, n. 2. Burghley was doubtless responsible for the appointment.

[22] Coke himself acknowledged this: Boyer, *Coke and the Elizabethan Age*, p. 224. Cf. the dismay and confusion caused by the queen's unannounced appearance in the Middle Temple Hall in the course of a reading on 13 March 1578: J. Baker, 'A Royal Visit to the Temple in 1578' (2017) 133 LQR 535.

[23] I.e. the queen's counsel in ordinary. The position of queen's counsel extraordinary (precursor of the present rank) was created for Francis Bacon in 1594: below, p. clvii.

[24] Only one copy is known, BL MS. Harg. 33, fos. 134–159v. Apart from the preface (below, p. cxxv) nothing survives but the illustrative cases. Coke's autograph text of the cases is Holkham Hall MS. 725.

[25] *AA*, fo. 13v.

[26] Coke did not receive an actual knighthood until 22 May 1603: *AA*, fo. 14v ('apud Grenewich in privata camera ... ex magno favore'). He had written to Cecil on 4 May citing precedents for attorneys general to be knighted: *Cecil Papers*, xv. 72.

[27] *AA*, fos. 13v–14; vol. iii, pp. 509–513. He was not new to Parliament, having previously served as member for Aldeburgh. He owned a volume of speeches from that Parliament, perhaps his own, bound in black velvet: *Library of Sir Edward Coke*, p. 58, no. 703.

[28] Proc. Parl., iii. 66.

receivers and triers of bills, which was done in antiquated French, and still provided formally for bills from France and Scotland. He observed that the mention of bills from Ireland showed that originally the English Parliament had extended its authority there.[29] But the old formulae were not wholly ceremonial, since the triers of English and Welsh bills had the power in theory to reject any bill considered unsuitable. Whether or not the power was actively used, Coke took the trouble to note the queen's remark that the veto was 'the old and true usage of the Parliament', and that this was confirmed by Burghley.[30] He also noted that the Speaker's presence was indispensable to proceedings in the Commons, because when he succumbed to illness on 24 February the House had to adjourn. There were a number of legal questions to be determined in consultation with the judges: in particular, whether an outlaw could be received a member.[31] It is evident that Coke enjoyed pursuing the historical research which these questions required. The little collection in his commonplace-books headed 'Pur lantiquitie de parliament' relied mainly on Lambarde, but there are later added references to the thirteenth-century *Mirror of Justices* and *Fleta*.[32] He did not there mention the *Modus tenendi Parliamentum*, which was wrongly believed to be Anglo-Saxon,[33] though he referred to it in Parliament the same year.[34] He had also discovered in a year book of 1347 a direct assertion that a parliament was held by William the Conqueror.[35] That was enough for Coke. The year books were unimpeachable authorities on history as well as law.[36]

The speakership was a delicate role, since Coke was the mouthpiece of the Commons but also the government's nominee and a law officer of the crown. The queen had made it quite clear, through Lord Keeper Egerton, when Coke had made his traditional request for liberty of speech, that it did not extend to urging reforms in Church or commonwealth; nor was it a licence for everyone to speak 'whatsoever cometh into his brain'. It was, according to Egerton, no more than a liberty to say 'aye' or 'no'.[37] This was a matter of serious practical importance. The 'Puritan' lawyer

---

[29] Cf. *AC*, fo. 673v (similar observation as to Wales and Ireland). Note also *AB*, fo. 490v ('Et vide que al chescun parlement la sont appoint triers de petitions et billes').

[30] Cf. Lord Keeper Egerton's remark, in replying to Coke's speech, that he should not receive bills proposing changes in the Church or commonwealth 'until they be viewed and considered by those whom it is fitter should consider of such things and can better judge them': Proc. Parl., iii. 68.

[31] *Thomas Fitzherbert's Case* (1593) vol. iii, p. 509; Boyer, *Coke and the Elizabethan Age*, pp. 234–236. Coke's ruling is noted in BL MS. Add. 25197, fo. 38. Another legal question in which Coke was involved was the validity of the election of Richard Hutton, bailiff of Southwark: Proc. Parl., iii. 103, 118. For some of his procedural rulings see Proc. Parl., iii. 4–5 (from BL MS. Harley 6265).

[32] *AD*, fo. 805v. This is difficult to date. The interlineation 'Vide le Mirror des Justices et Fleta 2. cap. 2' must be one of the earliest citations of either text. There are numerous citations to *Fleta* throughout the commonplace-books. The only contemporary manuscript belonged to Sir Robert Cotton, though a few transcripts were made in the early seventeenth century.

[33] In *AB*, fo. 274v, he cited it as dating from the time of King Edmund, son of King Ethelred (i.e. 1016).

[34] Proc. Parl., iii. 160. He said he had been shown a copy, but did not mention its date. (At some stage he acquired a sixteenth-century copy, now in the Isabella Stewart Gardner Museum, New York.) In the previous sentence he said he had a precedent of a Parliament held in the time of Edward, son of Ethelred. Cf. ibid. 170, where he claimed that there was a Parliament in the time of the Heptarchy.

[35] *The Bishop of Norwich's Case* (1347) YB Mich. 21 Edw. III, fo. 60, pl. 7. For a later discovery of what he took to be a grant made in 1021 by King Canute in Parliament, see below, p. cxxv.

[36] See further below, pp. cxxiv–cxxviii.

[37] Proc. Parl., iii. 68. Four members were sent to prison days afterwards for daring to propose that the crown be entailed.

members, with whom Coke felt much political sympathy, were beginning to challenge the prerogative powers of imprisonment and deprivation exercised by the ecclesiastical High Commission, and had rediscovered Magna Carta as a potentially powerful weapon. When one of their number, James Morice, a bencher of the Middle Temple, promoted a bill to explain Magna Carta in the context of prerogative imprisonment, he was 'sharply chidden' at the queen's behest for his effrontery and placed under house arrest. Coke was immediately summoned before the queen and firmly told that there should be no dealing in the House of Commons with matters of state. She had not summoned Parliament to make new laws, let alone innovations in government, and since she had the power to dissolve it whenever she chose, she could direct what was proper to be discussed.[38] It was not the only tense moment in the session. But Coke's ordeal was relatively brief and ended with the dissolution on 10 April 1593. He was not to serve in the Commons again until 1621, though as attorney-general he would be called upon for parliamentary advice.[39]

Even before his appointment to the speakership, Coke had begun to assemble the armoury which would be deployed over the coming decades in protecting the rule of law and the liberties of the individual. In 1587 he noted the utility and ubiquity of the writ of *habeas corpus*, which the King's Bench 'cannot in justice deny' to anyone in custody.[40] The report shows that he had already come across the record of *Kayser's Case* (1465) in the King's Bench plea rolls, which then or later he copied into his own book of precedents. It was the earliest example of *habeas corpus* to release a prisoner of the Church, and its usefulness had been recognised by Dyer, Catlyn and Wray C.JJ. in their turn. He also knew of *Lee's Case* (1568) in Dyer's unpublished reports,[41] where the writ was used to release a prisoner of the High Commission.[42] And he was aware of the many precedents of *habeas corpus* in the rolls of the clerk of the crown (now KB 29), which were shown him by the secondary of the crown Office. Later annotations to the report, which cannot easily be dated, added *Russel's Case* (1482), *Scrogges's Case* (1560), *Hynde's Case* (1576), and chapter 29 of Magna Carta.[43] All these authorities would be cited again and again in challenging the prerogative courts, the Chancery, and ministerial powers of imprisonment.[44] In two prohibition cases shortly afterwards, Coke lent his weight to the campaign against compulsory self-incrimination by the oath *ex officio*, as administered by the High Commission.[45]

---

[38] Baker, *Magna Carta*, p. 273, citing James Morice's account.

[39] E.g. in 1597 he assisted the judges in advising Parliament on what could be done in the queen's absence, and on the distinction between prorogation and continuance: vol. iv, p. 779. He also promoted a number of bills.

[40] *Arundell's Case* (1587) vol. ii, p. 324.

[41] For these see above, p. lxxxi.

[42] Baker, *Magna Carta*, pp. 160, 265. It was a Common Pleas case, and the *habeas corpus* in question was a writ of privilege for an attorney. Litigants also were entitled to writs of privilege. Coke noted in *Arundell's Case* that in the King's Bench there was no need to rely on privilege, since the writ was available in that court to everyone. He made the same point forty years later in 4 Co. Inst. 71.

[43] The same authorities, and others, are collected on a leaf devoted to *habeas corpus* in *AD*, fo. 238; and in another such collection in Coke's *Statuta*, 2, fo. 6.

[44] The following year Coke himself cited c. 29 in court: *Jerom v. Neal* (Pas. 1588) 1 Leon. 105 (battery).

[45] *Anon.* (1589) MS. Harley 1633, fo. 68v; *Collier v. Collier* (1590) CUL MS. Ff.5.20, fo. 39; Cro. Eliz. 201. See also *Gawen's Case* (1598) CUL MS. Dd.8.48, p. 35 (*habeas corpus* for Thomas Gawen of the Inner Temple, whom Popham C.J. said was a person of ill repute).

Prohibition was the most effective weapon against the commissioners and other ecclesiastical courts,[46] being pre-emptive. Once a decree was made it could not be treated as void by a common-law court even if it was wrong. Coke accepted that principle himself, and persuaded the King's Bench to follow it in a series of cases which he reported.[47] The regular remedy was to appeal to a higher ecclesiastical court, but in the case of the High Commission this was not in practice an option, and Coke claimed that this defect was 'dangerous'.[48] The common lawyers held that the High Commission, like the Delegates, could in theory be challenged by *supplicavit* and a commission of review, since the queen was supreme ordinary.[49] But the law reports contain no evidence that this ever happened.

In 1588 Coke reported a decision by 'all the judges' that there was no prerogative power to erect new courts of equity or to confer equitable jurisdiction on existing courts.[50] Here there is another later annotation, to the effect that erecting a 'court of discretion' was against chapter 29 of Magna Carta and the statutes of due process,[51] since they amounted to a guarantee that everyone should be adjudged according to the common law. Doing justice was a prerogative of the crown, but it was one of the ordinary royal prerogatives which were subsidiary to Magna Carta and could be reviewed by the judges.[52] This report affords early evidence of Coke's constitutionalism in that, as early as 1588, he saw the precedential value of an important case which traditional reporters ignored. The guiding principle, however, had recently become commonplace outside the law reports through the influence of a disparate group of Middle Temple members of Parliament: William Fleetwood, John Popham, James Morice and Robert Snagge. It was not Coke's inn but it was not far away, and their voices had been heard throughout the legal community. In 1599 Snagge, who was something of a 'Puritan' firebrand, mentioned Coke in his will among the 'friends that I ever found kind and constant'.[53]

---

[46] *Habeas corpus* was used only to challenge the High Commission, because other ecclesiastical courts did not claim the power of imprisonment.

[47] *Cheyny* v. *Frankwell* (1587) vol. ii, p. 333; *Bunting* v. *Leppingwell* (1588) ibid, p. 277; *Cawdrye* v. *Atton* (1595) vol. iii, p. 617; BL MS. Lansd. 108, fo. 109; *Webber* v. *Bury* (1598) vol. v, p. 942. He attributed it to a more general principle that experts should be trusted in their own field. As to that see also *AB*, fo. 451 ('Authoritates philosophorum, medicorum et in quavis arte peritorum sunt in causis allegande et tenende ... Cawdryes case et Buntings case in mes reports').

[48] *R.* v. *Maninge* (1590) CUL MS. Ll.3.9, fo. 62v (Exch.). Here a party was allegedly fined £200 by the High Commission though no witnesses had been examined, and Coke remarked, '(tr.) it is dangerous that their censure should be without controlment of any court by error or traverse, and a great inconvenience'.

[49] *Anon.* (1584/85) BL MS. Lansd. 1078, fo. 57; *Cheyny* v. *Frankwell* (1587) vol. ii, p. 333. This was confirmed by Popham C.J. in *Maunsell's Case* (1607) Baker, *Magna Carta*, p. 523. The availability of a commission of review after a final decree of the Delegates was demonstrated by Coke Att.-Gen. in *Hollingworth's Case* (1597) HLS MS. 110, fos. 274, 279v; 4 Co. Inst. 341; also reported in Cro. Eliz. 571, sub nom. *Gervis* v. *Hallewel*; Moo. 462, sub nom. *Halliwell* v. *Jervoise*.

[50] *Perrot* v. *Mathew* (Pas. 1588) vol. ii, p. 372.

[51] Cf. CUL MS. Ii.5.25, fo. 100 (tr. 'Note, by the report of Coke C.J., upon the statutes of [28 and 42 Edw. III concerning] due process of law, namely by ordinary course of the law, it was held by all the justices in the time of Queen Elizabeth, when George Gerrard was attorney-general, that since the making of these statutes a Chancery court cannot be erected by letters patent').

[52] See below, p. cxli.

[53] Baker, *Magna Carta*, pp. 249–261, 276, 468. For Popham see below, p. cxlvii, n. 47. The other three all served in the Commons when Coke was Speaker.

(a) Coke's interest in history

A noticeable trend in MS. *C* is an increasing interest in historical records. It was once supposed that Coke acquired his interest in legal history in the time of James I and Charles I, for political reasons. It is true that he was to find important uses for ancient precedents as antidotes to Stuart notions of absolutism. But it is also a fact that Coke had always been fond of history.[54] This interest came, in the first place, from profound legal scholarship.[55] The common law, though constantly developing, was unquestionably old, and for everyday purposes the year books back to the fourteenth century were essential reading. Lip-service had long been paid to history in explaining statutes in the inns of court readings, although (as Fleetwood noted) the history often amounted to no more than an assumption that the common law must have been the opposite of what a statute enacted.[56] Coke noted that even in the time of Edward III 'judges took cognizance of history',[57] and that the most learned in the profession had made use of 'chronicles'.[58] It was, on the whole, an old-fashioned kind of history such as one might hear across the dinner-table, a blend of myth and garbled tradition. It could hardly be in advance of the books of the day, though lawyers were generally more careful with historical evidence than schoolmen. Coke's fascination with the past nevertheless went well beyond the necessary accomplishments of a competent barrister. Most lawyers did not find the need to explore beyond Edward III's reign, which was two centuries back in time, and the printers had not thought it worthwhile to print the year books of Edward I or Edward II, though manuscripts were plentiful. Coke, however, always wanted to delve back as far as he could. His commonplace-books are full of citations to *Bracton*[59] and to early cases. The latter were mostly culled from Fitzherbert's abridgment, but at some stage he himself acquired manuscript year

---

[54] See I. Williams, 'The Tudor Genesis of Edward Coke's Immemorial Common Law' (2012) 43 *Sixteenth Century Journal* 103–123; G. Garnett, '"The Ould Fields": Law and History in the Prefaces to Sir Edward Coke's Reports' (2013) 34 *Journal of Legal History* 245–284; Smith, *Sir Edward Coke*, pp. 115–138; Baker, *Magna Carta*, pp. 442–451; Boyer, *Coke and the Elizabethan Age*, pp. 135–155.

[55] Cf. Coke's interest in the history of words, which recurs constantly in his writings. An early example is the note of 1582 on *decanus* and related ecclesiastical titles: *AB*, fo. 24v (vol. ii, p. 200). In *AA*, fos. 166–175, there is an alphabetical glossary of unusual words, with some etymology, followed (fos. 177–186v) by extensive collections on 'Exposition de parols'; and see *AB*, fos. 403v ('Apothegmata' and 'Equivoca' gathered from the year books), 450 ('Equipollences in sentences et parolz'); *AC*, fo. 579v ('Etimologie'). Philology was also an interest of Fleetwood's.

[56] Baker, *Magna Carta*, pp. 85, 222–223.

[57] *AB*, fo. 451, citing 40 Edw. III, Lib. Ass., pl. 25. The conclusion was inferential. The court had held that a Norman master of a pirate ship did not owe allegiance and so could not be convicted of treason. Coke said this must have been based on judicial knowledge that the Normans had 'revolted' (seceded) in the time of King John, and the judges must have learned this from 'histories'. Cf. *AA*, fo. 1v, where he noted that 'le roy John perde Normandy, car les Normans revolt de luy al roy de France, que fuit treason in eux come appiert per lestatut de Prerogativa Regis, cap. 12'.

[58] *AD*, fos. 908 ('Cronicles vouch per Stanf. Pr. 39b, Pl. Com., Broke, *Corone*, 180'), 909v ('Judges conferr ove learned in chescun arte, et ove historians et cronciles …'). Some 20 volumes of chronicles are among the books noticed as belonging to members of the inns in *The Men of Court*. John Skewys (d. 1544), a bencher of Lincoln's Inn, actually wrote a history of Britain up to the death of Edward III (BL MS. Harley 2258), and Sir Thomas More (d. 1535), a fellow bencher, wrote a history of the reign of Henry VII.

[59] For Coke's later promotion of *Bracton* as a useful authority see D. E. C. Yale, 'Some Later Uses of Bracton' in M. S. Arnold and others (ed.), *On the Laws and Customs of England: Essays in Honor of Samuel E. Thorne* (Chapel Hill, 1981), pp. 383–396, at pp. 388, 390–391.

INTRODUCTION   cxxi

books of Edward I, Edward II and Edward III.⁶⁰ He may also have owned a volume
of year books of Edward I attributed to 'Hingham' (Ralph de Hengham), which
he produced in court in 1608 'written in parchment in an ancient hand of that time'.⁶¹
He was primarily interested in the forensic uses of these ancient materials, and he has
been uncomprehendingly criticised for interpreting them with the mind of a lawyer
rather than that of a modern history professor; yet he did, undoubtedly, enjoy history
for its own sake. He read chronicles and cartularies,⁶² and at some point in his life he
became a collector of non-legal medieval manuscripts.⁶³ He was well read in histories,
and cited Holinshed, Camden and Lambarde throughout his commonplace-books.
Chronicles were not in his view reliable as sources of law,⁶⁴ but he noted that they had
occasionally been vouched by respected judicial writers such as Brooke and
Staunford.⁶⁵ They provided valuable historical background to the legal records, which
(by contrast) were almost sacrosanct. This was as much a legal as a historical doctrine:
records were the highest form of evidence, superior for legal purposes to private
writings. Coke was familiar with most of the classes of public records in the Tower,⁶⁶
and possessed many transcripts, such as those in his 'Great Book' of records (the
Liber Precedentium et Recordorum),⁶⁷ his 'Great Book' of parliamentary records,⁶⁸ a
'book of records out of the Tower',⁶⁹ a 'book of records and pleas of Edward I and
Edward II, all in parchment and bound in old parchment board' (which remains at

---

⁶⁰ *Library of Sir Edward Coke*, p. 24, no. 313 (YB 1–18 Edw. II); ibid. 25, no. 321 (YB 31–32, 39 Edw. III); ibid. 27, no. 343 ('Reports tempore E: 2. E: 3. and H. 6'). There are occasional citations in his notes: e.g. *AA*, fo. 190v ('H. 16 E. 2. fol. 8b'); *AC*, fo. 587 ('Vide 14 E. 3, mon livre de reportes'). In 1603 Coke cited a case of 16 Edw. II 'ex relatione John Doderidge': *C*, fo. 580v. For Edw. I see the next note and n. 66. The references to these reigns overleaf are to plea rolls.

⁶¹ *Calvin's Case* (1608) 7 Co. Rep., pt 1, at fo. 9. The volume has not been traced.

⁶² In *AA*, fo. 1 are some apparently early notes 'ex veteri chronographo' concerning the laws of the early British, Saxon and Danish kings, and the 'six manners of people that have inhabited this land', i.e. British, Picts, Scots, Saxons ('which Saxons and Angles came out of Germany), Danes and Normans. Here he wrote that St Edward 'made one common law' from the earlier British, Saxon and Danish laws. The reference to Molmutius Dunvallo in *AA*, fo. 185 (on highways), is taken from Fabyan's chronicle. In 1596 he cited the chronicle of Battle Abbey for the origin of *inspeximus* patents: vol. iv, p. 680. (Perhaps this is the 'Lib. Hastinges' cited in *AB*, fos. 446v, 447v.)

⁶³ Besides those listed in his library catalogue, some of them very ancient, mention should be made of the finely illuminated genealogical history of the kings of England (*c.* 1467), with parallel historical commentary, which he acquired from Henry Warner (d. 1617). This came to light at Sotheby's, 11 July 2018, lot 53, and is now in the Cloisters Collection, Metropolitan Museum of Art, New York (2018.631). A chronicle from 1066 to 1447, part of a fifteenth-century miscellany given to him by Sir William Dethick (d. 1612), was sold at Sotheby's, 28 Nov. 1967, lot 107 (Phillipps MS. 12086); it is now in the Yale Center for British Art.

⁶⁴ See *Le Tierce Part des Reportes* (1602), sig. Ciij ('I pray thee beware of chronicle law reported in our annals, for that will undoubtedly lead thee to error …').

⁶⁵ *AD*, fo. 908, cit. Sta. Prerog. 116v–117 (Polydore Vergil); Bro. Abr., *Corone,* pl. 180 ('un chronicle tempore Henrici sexti').

⁶⁶ E.g. in his notes on papal authority in *AC*, fo. 671, he cited (all on one page) Parliament rolls, patent rolls, close rolls, Gascon rolls, Brevia Regis, and a year book of Edward I. The rolls of Parliament are frequently cited throughout his commonplace-books, usually just by regnal year and number.

⁶⁷ *Library of Sir Edward Coke*, p. 26, nos. 328–329 (where the catalogue gives the incorrect impression that it survives). This is cited throughout his notebooks as 'Lib. Presid.'

⁶⁸ Ibid. 23, no. 306. This contained 676 fos. It is cited e.g. in *AC*, fo. 674: 'Vide Mag. Lib. Parl. 130b benevolences 6 E. 2.'

⁶⁹ *AC*, fo. 181v (pencil numbering) ('Vide mon livre de recordes hors del tower, pag. 45').

Holkham Hall),[70] a volume containing four monastic registers bound together,[71] a 'book of antiquities',[72] and various record collections made by Arthur Agard,[73] William Bowyer,[74] William Hakewill[75] and Peter Proby.[76] It is impossible to date the citations of these long-lost manuscripts, since they are either in the commonplace-books, which were added to over forty years, or inserted in the margins and between the lines of the dated reports. Many of them probably date from the early seventeenth

---

[70] *Library of Sir Edward Coke*, p. 24, no. 312. This may be the source of the citations in *AA*, fo. 88v ('P. 16 E. 1 in banco, 10'); *AB*, fos. 492v ('Hill. 18 E. 1, fol. 8'), 494v ('Hill. 18 E. 1, fol. 1 ... fol. 6'); *AC*, fo. 660 ('32 E. 1, Lib. E. 1 et E. 2, fol. [*blank*]') and fo. 671v ('Hill. 18 E. 1, fol. 1'). There are notes from a Yorkshire eyre roll in *AA*, fos. 223–224 (pencil numbering, following fo. 225).

[71] *Library of Sir Edward Coke*, p. 24, no. 311 ('Four books annexed together, viz: liber prioratus de Coventrey, Abbathie de Missenden, Prioratus de Dunstable, and certaine yeares of E: I, wherein are many notable cases in lawe'). The 'Liber Dunstable' is cit. in *AA*, fos. 46 ('Lib. Dunstab.'), 77 ('in libro de Dunstaple'). The 'Liber Missenden' is cited in *AA*, fos. 45v, 231; *AB*, fo. 490v (*bis*). There are numerous citations to 'Lib. Cov.': e.g. Coke's *Statuta*, fos. 10v, 15, 41, 43v, 47, 50v, 109v; below, vol. ii, p. 180; *AA*, fos. 28 ('Itinere Huntingdon temp. E. 1, Lib. Cov. 224'), 46 ('Lib. Cov. 165v, lettres patentes a faire parke'), 178 ('Vide Lib. Cov. 152, expos. antiq. vocab.') and 199 ('Lib. Cov. 14 E. 1, 222'); *AB*, fo. 406 ('Lib. Cov. 203, 204, in itinere Huntingdon temp. E. 1'); *C*, fo. 502 ('Lib. Cov. temps E. 1, Barsets case').

[72] *AB*, fo. 479v ('Vide 14 E. 3 in mon livre de antiquities ... et ibidem 41 E. 3 ...'); *AC*, fo. 674 ('Lib. Antiquitat. 9 E. 1, fo. 347'). Cf. *AB*, fo. 350 ('Vide le authoritie et credit des brefes in mon livre de presidentes et antiquities in treatise de ecclesiasticall causes').

[73] Listed as a 'book entitled liber Agard, of records and judgments in the raignes of E: I. E: 2. E: 3. R: 2. H: 4. H: 5. cont' 145 leaves': *Library of Sir Edward Coke*, p. 24, no. 316. It apparently remains at Holkham Hall; but cf. *Catalogue of the Legal Manuscripts of Sir Thomas Phillipps*, ed. J. Baker (2008), p. 148. For some citations in the notebooks see vol. ii, pp. 243, 249; vol. iii, p. 498; *AA*, fos. 108v ('3 H. 4, Agard 143, Sperhauke pro verbis ... Lib. Agard, treason, 142, 143, 144, 145'), 114 ('Pasche 39 E. 3, Lib. Agard 339'), 118v ('3 R. 2, Lib. Ag. 140'), 138v ('Lib. Agard Trin. 35 E. 1 ... fol. 123'), 230 ('Agard 19 E. 1, 121') and 465 ('Pasch. 39 E. 3, Ag. 139 [*altered from* 339]', '29 E. 1, Agard 122'); *AB*, fos. 384v ('Libr. Agard, 8 E. 1, fol. 17'), 485 ('35 E. 3, Ag. 138, nul del clargy serra contribute al lay charges', '2 E. 3, Ag. 12, nulla expeditatio canis abbatis') and 492 ('Vide Agard, 12 E. 1, le case de Margerie Weyland'); *AC*, fos. 514 ('Lib. Agard 17 E. 2 ... fol. 70'), 573 ('Hill. 13 E. 2, Ag. 129, roy recover 2000 li. damages', '29 E. 3, Ag. 138, non attempt. etc. in prejudicium regis'); *AD*, fo. 920v ('P. 29 E. 3, Ag. 138'); Coke's *Statuta*, fos. 5, 6v, 9. Agard, a notable antiquary, was deputy chamberlain of the Receipt 1570–1615, and compiled a number of collections from the plea rolls.

[74] There are several references in the notebooks to 'Lib. Boier': e.g. *AB*, fo. 493 ('Deceits al roy', a table of 16 citations from 'Libro Boier', fos. 125–150); *AC*, fo. 541 ('Lib. Boier 129b, 130b, Lord Latimers case'); *C*, fos. 110v and 117; vol. iii, pp. 629, 640 (treason cases, 21 Ric. II to 28 Hen. VI, from Lib. Boier, fos. 137–151). Cf. *AB*, fo. 171 ('Lib. Boyer 136, evesque depart de parlement quant attaindre serra 10 E. 4'). This was almost certainly one of the historical collections of William Bowyer (d. 1569/70), keeper of records in the Tower of London, some of which – not including the one used by Coke – are now in the College of Arms (B.1–5, 11, 12, 15): see L. Campbell and F. Steer, *A Catalogue of Manuscripts in the College of Arms: Collections*, i (1988), pp. 197–199. No such manuscript is listed in the *Library of Sir Edward Coke*.

[75] Cited as 'Lib. Hack.': e.g. vol. ii, p. 249; *AA*, fos. 29 ('Lib. Hackw. 124'), 69 ('16 R. 2, nu. 29, Hackw. 69'), 77v ('Lib. Hack. 39 E. 3, fol. 56, 57'), 109 ('Lib. Hack. 124, 6 E. 2, counterfetter del grand seale'); *AB*, fo. 169 (245 in pencil) ('50 E. 3, Lib. Hack. 66 pur defence del mere vers Scarburgh'); *AC*, fo. 674 ('Vide Lib. Hackw. per totum', as to impositions). William Hakewill of Lincoln's Inn (adm. 1598, called 1606) made a celebrated speech on impositions in Parliament in 1610: Baker, *Magna Carta*, p. 331. One of Charles Fairfax's manuscripts, MS. Phillipps 11126 (now belonging to the present writer), contains on fos. 26–27v an account of Edward I's submission to the king of France, with opinions of doctors of law on the French law of succession, 'In manuscripto de Hackwell'.

[76] *Library of Sir Edward Coke*, p. 24, no. 315 ('A Boke entitled Probe'). Coke cited it as Liber Proby: *AA*, fos. 109v, 139v ('Vide Lib. Proby in tab.'); *AB*, fos. 145v (pencil) ('Proby 88, 12 R. 2 create esquire'), 465 ('Vide in libro de Prob. mult de guerre'); ibid., fo. 484v ('Vide lib. Prob. 42, 43, etc.'); *AC*, fo. 674 ('Vide libr. Proby, Lambart, mult bone matter pur les 5 portes'); *AD*, fo. 908 ('Proby 44, 27 E. 3'); *C*, fo. 602 ('Vide Lib. Prob. 110, Michael de la Pole pur selling des leys'). Peter Proby was keeper of records in the Tower with Lambarde 1601–04.

century. But the present edition shows that Coke was copying record material himself, or having it copied, soon after he became attorney-general in the 1590s.[77] Some of his research was occasioned by current litigation.[78] At other times it had no obvious forensic utility, as when he made a list of serjeants from the time of Edward I,[79] or procured a copy of the writ of 1292 'concerning attorneys and apprentices',[80] or when in transcribing charters he described the seals.[81] He also liked to collect documentary precedents which raised interesting questions: for instance, an assignment of a supposedly hereditary swan-mark to an heir apparent,[82] which raised an implicit question about the ownership of personal signs, to be contrasted with the more orthodox ruling by a fifteenth-century earl marshal that a coat of arms could not be assigned.[83] He was told about the latter by Lord Burghley, who was himself fond of history and a patron of historians.

The legal profession was already associated with new research into historical topics, and of course the history of English law in particular. William Fleetwood, Coke's predecessor as recorder of London, had been promoting legal history since the beginning of the reign,[84] and was probably still circulating drafts of his historical essays as late as the 1580s.[85] In 1568 Richard Gynes of the Inner Temple had shown the importance of contemporary evidence in establishing the antiquity of the administrative royal supremacy over the Church in

[77] An earlier example, partly attributed to Wray C.J. and with a later addition citing Agard and Hakewill, is in vol. ii, p. 248 (concerning ports). There are several examples from 1595–96 (copied by an amanuensis) in vol. iii, pp. 634, 635, 641–643; vol. iv, pp. 846, 875, 881–883, 886. Note also *AA*, fo. 43: 'Le notable case de alnage de worsteades et canvas ... Inter recorda term. Mich. anno 13 E. 3 ex rem. thesaur.'

[78] E.g. vol. iv, pp. 676, 682 (concerning grand serjeanty); ibid. 880–881, 886–893 (concerning the Isle of Man).

[79] *AD*, fo. 918v: 'Les nosmes queux jeo trove in nostre livers queux ont professe le ley'. On the same page he collected the names of attorneys-general from himself back to the time of Henry V.

[80] Vol. iii, p. 635 (1595). The text had been brought to light by Arthur Agard in a paper given to the legal antiquaries in 1591: Baker, *Collected Papers*, i. 148–150.

[81] Vol. iii, pp. 642, 643.

[82] Vol. iii, p. 642 (1595), citing a deed poll of 1436. In commenting on the case later, Coke said that a swan-mark could only be claimed by royal grant or prescription but that it could be assigned: 7 Co. Rep. 17. He did not discuss whether, or how, it could in law be hereditary. In the 1436 case it was based on the family arms and may have been thought to descend as a heraldic badge. The game of swans was not itself hereditary, unless it was considered as a kind of fungible heirloom.

[83] BL MS. Add. 25201, fo. 61 (1597): '(tr.) Lord Hoo's case, who had arms and because he had no children wanted to give his arms to a friend. But the lord marshal of England would not allow it, because it is a thing in respect of himself, which cannot be given or departed withal. 22 E. 4. Reported by Edward Cook, attorney-general, and he said that the lord treasurer reported it to him. 39 Eliz.' This case has not been found in the notebooks, but cf. *AB*, fo. 485v, tit. 'Notabilia': 'Fuit adjudge in le case del Segnior Hoo que il ne poet graunter ses armes ... Vide in mes reportes.' (Lord Hoo died in 1455, so the date of the ruling is uncertain.)

[84] Baker, *Magna Carta*, pp. 216–248. Coke seems (from the absence of citations) to have ignored most of Fleetwood's writings, though he did own a copy of his treatise on forest law: *Library of Sir Edward Coke*, p. 26, no. 334; cit. in vol. ii, p. 248.

[85] He was possibly the author of *De Legibus Angliae* (1587) BL MS. Harley 5265, fos. 176–198, which includes (fos. 176–177v) a discerning account of early legal history, including a criticism of Coke (below, p. cxxvi, n. 7). It is dated by the allusion to 'this year 1587' on fo. 177v. The author was familiar not only with historical sources but with basic principles of Roman law as well as common law, and there is an emphasis on statutes and their interpretation (fos. 188–198), all features which point to Fleetwood. But the same volume contains (fos. 201–216v) a text of Fleetwood's discourse on the exposition of statutes, which is considerably different from that in the *De Legibus Angliae*.

England.[86] And by the 1590s a circle of younger lawyers was meeting to discuss topics of legal history in an informal society of antiquaries.[87] Antiquity was revered by the Elizabethans.[88] Since it was taken for granted that the fundamental features of the common-law system were ancient, the legal antiquaries were chiefly concerned with origins: the origins of Parliament, of courts, of sheriffs, of the inns of court, of tenures, and so forth. Coke did not present papers to the society, but he shared the same interests and took the research as seriously as any of them.

The early stages of Coke's enthusiasm for historical questions can be traced from several disquisitions on the antiquity of the common law.[89] What is probably an early note, written on the second leaf of his Littleton (1572), shows that his desire to settle the matter began with his earliest legal studies; but it also reveals his limitations (and those of his contemporaries) in attempting to do so. He was particularly intrigued by the effect of the Norman conquest, since he could not accept that the common law was Norman:[90]

> Note that although some say that our law, namely the common law of this land, was invented by the Normans when William the Conqueror obtained the crown, this may be proved to be a lie (*fauxine*), and utterly contrary to the truth, by many authorities in our law. For it appears by a book in 26 Ass., pl. 24, that the abbot of Bury demanded cognizance in an assize and showed how his predecessors had used to have cognizance of all pleas and to have original [writs[91]] out of the [king's[92]] court in the time of Kings Edmund and St Edward, as appears more fully in the said book: by which book it appears that our law was long before the reigns of Kings Edmund and Edward,[93] for the abbot's predecessors had it by prescription in the time of all reigns, and every period of prescription is at least 80 or 100 years in common presumption, but no one knows the commencement of it.

English lawyers had long believed that the common law was anterior to the Normans,[94] and Coke deserves credit for trying to find explicit proof of it rather than

---

[86] Prefatory lecture from his reading on tithes (Inner Temple, 1568): Baker, *Magna Carta*, p. 220. (Coke had a copy, bound with Liber Proby: *Library of Sir Edward Coke*, p. 24, no. 315.) This little-known work was a lawyer's reaction to the recent controversy represented by R. Horne, *An Answere ... touchinge the Othe of Supremacy* (1566), and T. Stapleton, *A Counterblast to Mr Horne's Vain Blast* (1567). On these two tracts and their impact see A. Gajda, 'The Elizabethan Church and the Antiquity of Parliament' in *Writing the History of Parliament in Tudor and Early Stuart England*, ed. P. Cavill and A. Gajda (Cambridge, 2018), pp. 77–105.

[87] M. Stuckey, 'Antiquarianism and Legal History' in *Making Legal History: Approaches and Methodologies*, ed. A. Musson and C. Stebbings (Cambridge, 2012), pp. 215–243. See also C. W. Brooks, *Law, Politics and Society in Early Modern England* (Cambridge, 2008), pp. 83–84; *Writing the History of Parliament*, ed. Cavill and Gajda (previous note), pp. 45–46.

[88] See Williams, 'Coke's Immemorial Common Law', at pp. 109–110, n. 39. To the examples there given could be added the desire, especially among newly risen families, to establish pedigrees reaching back to the Norman Conquest: see J. Baker, 'Tudor Pedigree Rolls and their Uses' in *Heralds and Heraldry in Shakespeare's England*, ed. N. Ramsay (2014), pp. 125–165.

[89] This was pointed out by Williams, 'Coke's Immemorial Common Law', p. 107. See also above, p. cxx, n. 54.

[90] *AA*, fo. 187v (on the verso of the table). The quotation is tr. from French.

[91] The missing word is supplied from the Lyons Inn reading (n. 99, opposite): BL MS. Harley 244, fo. 57; MS. Harley 5265, fo. 165.

[92] Ibid.

[93] Coke was here abandoning his original assumption that the common law was attributable to Edward the Confessor: above, p. lxxix, n. 50.

[94] See Baker, *Magna Carta*, pp. 76, 85, 223.

relying on mere tradition. But the first sentence of the note exposes a fundamental flaw in Coke's history, if read as history rather than as law. The question was answered conclusively, as he asserted, by 'authorities in our law'. But the assertion was deduced from the false premise that the abbot of Bury's prescriptive claim was literally true, and would have been understood to be historically true in 1352. In Coke's approach, the year book of 1352 was not simply hearsay evidence of fact, to be weighed in context, but an 'authority' closer to 1066 than his own age, and therefore to be accepted in the absence of countervailing authority. Yet, if Coke thought of legal history as part of the law, he knew the value of factual evidence. At a later date he discovered a grant (now believed to be an early forgery) made to the abbey of Bury St Edmunds in 1021 by King Canute in a kind of parliament, with assembled bishops, lords, abbots, knights and a great number of people.[95] This was not 'authority' in the same sense, but it was contemporary evidence and – on the generous assumption that the *concilium* mentioned in the charter was the same as Parliament – it was useful enough. A more convincing case could have been based on the forged letter from Pope Eleutherius to King Lucius, which according to Fleetwood showed that Parliament, the central courts, and the common law itself, dated back to the second century.[96] Coke was certainly aware of it in 1576,[97] and he was to acquire a thirteenth-century copy of it when he was chief justice.[98]

The theme of antiquity was taken up publicly in the introductory lecture before Coke's reading at Lyons Inn in 1579.[99] After repeating the conclusion drawn from the 1352 case, he added three new arguments. The first was drawn from an observation by Catlyn C.J. that there were many final concords concerning the abbot of Crowland which dated from before the Conquest.[1] Coke deduced from this that there must have been original writs (upon which the fines could be levied) before the Conquest, and that if there were original writs there must have been a Chancery and sheriffs. No doubt Coke can be excused, together with Catlyn, for not knowing that the Crowland muniments – like the Bury charter of Canute – had been forged

---

[95] YLS MS. G.R24.1, fo. 120 ('ex libro monasterii de Bury Sancti Edmundi'). This is written in Coke's hand on a scrap of paper; date uncertain.

[96] Baker, *Magna Carta*, pp. 223–224; F. Heal, 'What can King Lucius do for You?' (2005) 120 *English Historical Review* 593–614. Richard Gynes relied on the letter in his 1568 lecture in the Inner Temple: BL MS. Harley 813, fo. 112 (here dated 200 B.C., but since Lucius is described as the first Christian king this is evidently a slip for A.D.).

[97] It was cited by Manwood J. in *Grendon* v. *Dean of Worcester* (1576) below, p. 65, no. 114.

[98] BL MS. Add. 49366, fo. 123 (Holkham MS. XVI). This collection of Anglo-Saxon laws, which had belonged to Matthew Parker, has the ownership inscription (on fo. 1), 'Edw: Coke cap. justiciarius de banco'. It is identifiable in *Library of Sir Edward Coke*, p. 27, no. 337. The British Library catalogue mistakenly identifies it as no. 377 in Coke's list, which was a printed copy of Lambarde.

[99] *Le Reading del mon Seignior Coke sur Lestatute de 27. E. 1. appelle Lestatute de Finibus Levatis* (1662), at pp. 2–4. For the date see above, p. lxxviii. There are manuscript versions, with the English preface, in Bodl. Lib., MS. Rawlinson C. 85, fos. 69–80v; BL MS. Harley 244, fo. 57 (preamble only); MS. Harley 3209, fos. 9–16v (lacks beginning of preface); MS. Harley 5265, fos. 165–175v; MS. Harley 6853, fo. 251 (dated 1577); MS. Lansd. 1121, fos. 1–20v; MS. Add. 25195, fos. 7–9v; LI MS. Misc. 486(4), fos. 217–226v; Nottingham Univ., MS. Mellish L. 4, fos. 1–12; East Sussex Record Office, QCP/5, fos. 128–137v; and see J. H. Baker ed, *Readers and Readings in the Inns of Court and Chancery* (13 Selden Soc. Suppl. Series, 2000), p. 207.

[1] *Stowell* v. *Lord Zouche* (1562) Plowd. 353, at fos. 368v–369 ('Et il cite multes fines de antiquitie, s. ascuns devant le Conquest, touchant les possessions del Abbe de Crowland ...').

by the monks. Coke knew well enough that monks could not be trusted, but the full extent of their deceit was yet to be uncovered.[2] That apart, we see here another of Coke's weaknesses, an assumption of essential continuity: if an institution existed by its present name in the distant past, it must have existed in the same form as in the present.[3] His next argument suffered from a similar failure to distinguish between times. It was intended to refute the 'apparently false' statement by Polydore Vergil that jury trial was invented by William the Conqueror.[4] Tenants in ancient demesne were tenants of the manors recorded in Domesday Book as belonging to King Edward the Confessor before the Conquest; it was a privilege of tenants in ancient demesne to be discharged from jury service and from contributing to the fees of knights of the Parliament: ergo, both Parliament and jury trial must have been before the Conquest.[5] Coke's two premises were true in isolation, but the fallacy lay in assuming that the tenants must have had exactly the same privileges in the time of Edward the Confessor as they did in the year-book period. It was unimaginable to Coke that such important attributes of tenure could have been invented or redefined later, since the law required them to be immemorial. His third argument was directed against the common fallacy that the law must be Norman because the legal language was French.[6] This, thought Coke, was of no weight: it was surely more likely that the Normans put the English laws into the Norman tongue so that they could be introduced into Normandy, where there was nothing as excellent.[7] In any case, the common laws were not written in any tongue at all but were unwritten, 'divinely infused into the heart of man and builded upon the irremovable rock of reason'.[8] One might as well maintain that hunting was invented by the Normans because its terms of art were French.[9]

---

[2] For the dawning of scepticism about them see W. Dugdale, *Origines Juridiciales* (1666), p. 92; T. Madox, *Formulare Anglicanum* (1702), p. xiii.

[3] Cf. Williams, 'Coke's Immemorial Common Law', pp. 114, 117; Baker, *Magna Carta*, p. 348. Note also his assumption about the 'parliament' convened by William I: above, p. cxvii.

[4] Vergil was particularly disliked by English lawyers, e.g. Fleetwood and Morice: Baker, *Magna Carta*, p. 224. See further P. Cavill in *Writing the History of Parliament*, ed. Cavill and Gajda, pp. 37–59.

[5] Coke did not make the mistake of attributing jury trial to Magna Carta, though he allowed that c. 29 might have confirmed it: 2 Co. Inst. 46; Baker, *Magna Carta*, p. 38.

[6] For the assumption, which was supported by the authority of Sir John Fortescue, see J. H. Baker, *A Manual of Law French* (2nd ed., 1999), p. 1; Smith, *Sir Edward Coke*, p. 120.

[7] In 1598 he reported Popham C.J. as saying that William I took an oath to observe the laws of St Edward the Confessor 'but added to them so many of the laws and customs of Normandy as he pleased' (vol. iv, p. 880, n. 2); however, he later deleted these words and added that 'he was so opposed to changing any of the laws of England than he transferred many of them to Normandy' (ibid., tr.). And in *Le Tierce Part des Reportes* (1602), sig. Ei verso, Coke prayed in aid 'William de Rouell' (Guillaume de Rouillé, d. c. 1550), a jurist of Alençon, who had shown that 'most of the customs of Normandy were derived out of the laws of England, in or before the time of the said King Edward the Confessor'. The argument was challenged in the anonymous treatise *De Legibus Angliae* (1587) in BL MS. Harley 5265, fo. 176 (modernised): 'But me thinketh all this is not probable. For besides that our law savoureth somewhat of a conqueror, how is it like that a vanquisher desired rather to learn laws of the vanquished than to prescribe laws unto them? We may be sure he was able to change laws here, being a king, but was he able to induce new or antiquate old laws in Normandy, where he was but a vassal?'

[8] BL MS. Harley 244, fo. 57v (modernised); MS. Lansd. 1121, fo. 2; slightly different in MS. Harley 5265, fo. 165v ('but divinely engrafted into …').

[9] Reading on Uses (1592), next note, at fo. 136v.

Coke chose to begin his Inner Temple reading on 2 August 1592 with another preliminary discourse on legal history.[10] He noted that it was becoming a controversial subject as more historical works were being printed, the worst culprits being ignorant non-lawyers. The history of English law, he observed, was now a matter of great danger and still greater difficulty: 'Of danger, in respect of so many mighty and malicious adversaries, both domestical and foreign, furiously bent against one ... Of difficulty, forasmuch as the antiquities of this realm ... by reason of the several and sundry conquests of this land, be either worn out and forgotten or are become subject to so many and so divers conjectures':

> I can but wonder with what face our chronographers of England dare so constantly affirm many things, especially concerning our laws, which either be conjectures upon conjectures or so apparently contrary to truth as they have almost reaped the reward of those that, though they could or would tell the truth, should not be believed. A writer of histories ought to be so careful in setting down the truth as though he should adventure his whole credit upon the truth of every particular matter he publisheth to the world.

Among the 'adversaries' were the foreign jurists whom he suspected of having ulterior motives for decrying English law. He had come to learn of François Hotman's diatribe against Littleton, joined in 'malicious ignorance' by the Italian historian Polydore Vergil.[11] Hotman, who failed to grasp that *feodum* in England meant something different from the feud as understood by civilian feudists, had castigated Littleton's pellucid definition as 'confused, absurd and awkward'.[12] Coke was incensed by this display of intellectual arrogance.[13] He concluded that it was necessary to defend the 'excellent government of this realm' against the 'reproachful slanders proclaimed and imprinted against our laws'.

First and foremost of these 'slanders' was the myth of a Norman origin, which had bothered Coke since his student days. Beginning the history this time with Brutus and the ancient Britons, he repeated the arguments based on the case of 1352 and on tenants in ancient demesne. But he had now found a better historical argument.[14] There was a record in Domesday Book that St Mary's church, Worcester, owned the hundred of Oswaldshaw, where (as it stated) the bishop had since ancient times enjoyed all *redditiones socharum*, *regis servicium* and exemption from the sheriff's

---

[10] The autograph manuscript cannot be traced, but there is a copy in BL MS. Harg. 33, fos. 134–159v; above, p. cxvi. Only the prefatory lecture (fos. 134–138) is set out verbatim, in English. Quotations here are rendered in modern spelling. For the date of the first lecture see *AA*, fo. 13v.

[11] Hotman purported to rely on Vergil, but the passage cannot be found in his printed history. The actual source of Hotman's error was suggested by F. W. Maitland, *English Law and the Renaissance* (1901), p. 59. In his lecture, Coke referred to Hotman (d. 1590) anonymously as 'a foreign civilian'. His irritation with the passage is best known from the prefaces to 10 Co. Rep. (1614) and Co. Litt. (1629). In the former he observed that 'It is a desperate and dangerous matter for civilians and canonists ... to write either of the common laws of England which they profess not, or against them which they know not ... their pages are so full of palpable errors and gross mistakings, as these new authors are out of charity pitied ... I will not sharpen the nib of my pen against them, for that I pity the persons, and wish they had more discretion ...'.

[12] He said the exposition of *feoda Anglicana* was 'incondite, absurde et inconinne scriptum': F. Hotman, *De Feudis Commentatio* (Cologne, 1573), p. 661, s.v. *feodum*.

[13] Hotman's arrogance annoyed some Continental jurists as well. For a modern assessment of his work see G. Garnett, 'Scholastic Thought in Humanist Guise: François Hotman's ancient French constitution' in *The Medieval World*, 2nd ed. by P. Linehan, J. L. Nelson and M. Costambeys (2018), pp. 789–810.

[14] Cf. *Le Tierce Part des Reportes* (1602), sig. Ciiij.

jurisdiction. Given that 'ancient times' must have meant before the Conquest, Coke took this as showing that socage tenure and knight-service were pre-Conquest, and that the sheriff had a court before the Conquest. He had also discovered from 'a learned man, and a late writer' (probably William Lambarde[15]) that the bishop of Worcester's privileges had been granted by King Edgar, which furnished a satisfactory *terminus ad quem*. He did not have time, he said, to set out the 'many other notable proofs to this purpose'; but he had said enough, in his submission, to make it manifestly apparent that 'the courts, the writs, the trials, the proceedings, the judges, the officers, and the ministers of the common laws now used were time out of mind of man before the Conquest'. This proposition would become of practical importance in the following reign, perhaps of more importance than Coke could yet have foreseen. But the research was mostly done before Coke became attorney-general, let alone chief justice. In purely historiographical terms, it would obviously not pass muster by the standards of professional historians today, and yet – especially given the limitations of the available evidence – it was an advance on what had passed for history in the earlier Tudor period. Moreover, it did not mean that Coke was unable to countenance change. He did not, it is true, approve of unnecessary innovation.[16] But his study of history had taught him that laws did change, and his commonplace-book contained a collection of cases where the received common law had been changed on the strength of better reasoning.[17] It was the system as a whole which was timeless, not the details.[18]

(b) Treason and matters of state

Only two years after Coke's appointment as solicitor-general he was promoted to be attorney-general, when Egerton became master of the rolls. This occasioned another emotional crisis, this time in the queen's privy chamber at Whitehall, when Coke was reduced to silence by his unrestrained tears.[19] Elizabeth's speech to him, remembered verbatim in MS. *C*, set out her understanding of his constitutional role. He was expected to defend her lawful rights, but with due regard to those of her subjects also:[20]

---

[15] Assuming 'late' to mean recent rather than deceased.

[16] *Le Quart Part des Reportes* (1604), sig. B2v ('... that which hath been refined and perfected by the wisest men in former succession of ages, and proved and approved by continual experience to be good and profitable for the common wealth, cannot without great hazard and danger be altered or changed'). He made a collection of cases where judges had repressed innovations: *AB*, fo 464.

[17] *AC*, fo. 688; indexed at *AD*, fo. 909v, as 'Ley, et in queux cases les judges ount chaunge le former received opinion.'

[18] See Baker, *English Law under two Elizabeths*, p. 443–444.

[19] Vol. iii, p. 572. Coke's original patent as Att.-Gen., dated 10 April 1594, is on display at Holkham Hall. William West of the Inner Temple lost no time in dedicating to him, in May 1594 under his new title, a new edition of his *Symbolaeographia* ('Viro jurisprudentiae et pietatis laude illustrissimo Edwardo Coke armigero, serensissimae Reginae Majestatis procuratori summo').

[20] Cf. Coke's recollection in 1615 (3 Buls. 44): 'When I was the queen's attorney, she said unto me, "I understand that my counsel will strongly urge *praerogativa reginae*, but my will is that they stand *pro domina veritate* rather than *pro domina regina*, unless that *domina regina* hath *veritatem* on her side"; and she also used to give this in charge many times, when anyone was called to any office by her, that they should ever stand *pro veritate* rather than *pro regina*.' Cf. a different version in 3 Co. Inst. 79. She gave a similar charge to Egerton: Baker, *Magna Carta*, pp. 149–150.

INTRODUCTION   cxxix

> I charge thee that my subjects receive at thy hands that which to them appertaineth, according to law and justice; for a better prince hereafter you may have when I have gone, but never any that have a more fervent desire to execute justice and to do right to all, and see that my subjects have justice with expedition, and with as small charge as conveniently may be.

On the strength of these words, Coke felt authorised to play an active role as attorney-general in seeking to uphold the rule of law by curbing abuses of authority in the queen's name, including the excesses of prerogative jurisdictions which operated outside the common law.[21]

Immediately after the appointment, Coke faced a challenge from the monopolist Edward Darcy, a groom of the chamber, who had sought to appoint his nominee Wiseman – a man 'utterly unmeet and insufficient' – as clerk of the outlawries. He received a letter written in the queen's name asking him to give way, and thereupon (on 16 April 1594) wrote to Sir Robert Cecil:[22]

> The place is so incident to my office ... as both her majesty may be infinitely prejudiced, the subjects divers ways injured and a-wronged, and myself – for all must be done in my name – utterly discredited and undone. I perceive there is gain, and extreme gain, sought by it, which would turn both to her majesty's and her subjects' losses, for the giver must get it up again by oppression to the subject or deceit to her majesty in her lawful forfeitures, or both. And besides, I shall be in no small danger. I assure your honour I can neither, with my duty to her majesty, rent this place nor take any fine, but to see everything duly done, and to recompense my clerk his travail according to his desert ... But it is given out, and some men believe it, that this chaffering and merchandising of this place of trust and confidence proceeded from me, which I protest I am free of, and never intend to take any rent or fine, but to have my clerk accountable to me, as Sir Thomas Egerton did before me.

Coke prevailed on this occasion, though the matter was to raise its head again under James I.[23] The unsavoury experience almost certainly reinforced what was to become a lifelong aversion to court favourites and monopolists such as Darcy.[24]

Coke's long tenure as a law officer,[25] unlike his brief service as a member of Parliament, had a pervasive effect on his reports. He was not allowed to set down state secrets, since they might then reach other eyes,[26] but he did record many of the cases in which he was involved, including meetings to which none but the judges and law officers could have been privy. It was an exhausting role, which involved

---

[21] See Baker, *Magna Carta*, pp. 276–339; below, pp. cxlvi–clii.

[22] *Calendar of the MSS. of the Marquis of Salisbury, preserved at Hatfield House*, iv. 511, no. 1179 (spelling modernised).

[23] Ibid., xv. 368. Cf. the analogous attempt to create a monopoly for a clerk of the *supersedeas*: *Cavendish's Case* (1587) 1 And. 152; Baker, *Magna Carta*, p. 266; *Brownlow v. Michell and Cox* (1615) ibid. 422–424.

[24] On monopolies see *Farmor v. Savage* (1583) vol. ii, p. 216. For Darcy, a favoured courtier, and his notoriously contentious monopolies, see Baker, *Magna Carta*, pp. 183, 196, 319–323; *Leathersellers Co. v. Darcy* (1595) BL MS. Harg. 26, fos. 51v–52; *Darcy v. Allen* (1602) C, fos. 571v–574; 11 Co. Rep. 84; B. & M. 678; 2 Co. Inst. 47; below, p. cxxxix.

[25] He was to remain in post for fifteen years, the longest tenure but one since the fifteenth century.

[26] See vol. iii, p. 474. after his meeting with the queen at Greenwich in 1592, 'Her highness most graciously vouchsafed to speak with me privately, and imparted to me some matters of such moment and secrecy as are not meet to be here set down'.

him in such a vast range of business that it is a wonder how he found time to write reports at all.[27] The most heavily worked notes were those concerning the law of treason and its intricate history of repeals and modifications.[28] It was clearly the most exacting of Coke's concerns. In an age of plots and intrigue, with the queen's life and throne constantly under threat by persons trained to deceive, the strain placed on the queen's principal law officer was immense. Coke regarded it as constitutionally imperative not to enlarge the law of treason,[29] since the judges had no power to do so without consulting Parliament.[30] On the other hand, he was not squeamish about relying on constructive treason in dealing with major uprisings, as a preferable alternative to martial law,[31] by treating them as a constructive levying of war against the queen; and the judges, led by Popham C.J., took the same position.[32]

Treason by compassing or 'imagining' (plotting) the sovereign's death raised the question of how to prove a state of mind, and this caused some anxiety in connection with the prosecutions of Lord Cobham and Sir Walter Ralegh in 1603–04.[33] Compassing[34] was a species of treason committed merely by a mental resolve, without the need for an attempt to bring it to fruition, but the Treason Act 1351 required proof by some open act or deed (*overt fait*) in all treason cases. This raised the question whether words alone could constitute an overt act. On the face of it, a man's words revealed more clearly than anything else the inward imagination of his heart, and the Treason Act 1571 had treated 'speech, words or sayings' as sufficient forms of proof. Although the 1571 statute lapsed on the queen's death, some of the judges thought these words were a declaration of the common law, and in reporting their discussion Coke originally wrote that an oral confession under examination was 'the surest proof that can be, for the judge may say *ex ore tuo te judico*'. This, he wrote, had been resolved by the judges.[35] However, at some point he decided this was wrong and altered the passage to read that a confession was not such an overt act as the Act of 1350 required. Although it is uncertain when the revision was made, Coke's final

---

[27] In 1601 he admitted to Sir Robert Cecil being 'overwhelmed with business': *Cecil Papers*, xi. 65. Note also vol. v, p. 932 ('though little time permits me').

[28] There is more of the like in *AA*, fos. 99, 106v, 102v (pencil number), 109–110, 114. Some of these notes were written around the same time as those in *C*, or even later.

[29] See e.g. *R.* v. *Penry* (1593) vol. iii, p. 535.

[30] See vol. iii, pp. 521–523, 535; vol. iv, p. 756.

[31] The queen was ever ready to sanction martial law, but Coke eschewed it as a threat to the common law: Baker, *Magna Carta*, pp. 430–431, n. 114.

[32] Coke wrote notes on this in 1593, citing Fyneux C.J.'s decision of 1517 following the Evil May Day rising in London: vol. iii, p. 567. The matter came to the fore in the *Case of the London Apprentices* (1595) ibid. 628–629 (and the associated notes on p. 639); 2 And. 5; J. Stow, *Annales* (1631), fos. 769, 770. And it arose again two years later after the Oxfordshire rising against enclosures: *R.* v. *Bradshawe and Burton* (1597) vol. iv, pp. 756–758; J. Bellamy, *The Tudor Law of Treason* (1979), pp. 78–79; C. W. Brooks, *Law, Politics and Society in Early Modern England* (2008), pp. 342–343.

[33] *C*, fos. 581v–587v (Hil. 1604); 3 Co. Inst. 14; Smith, *Sir Edward Coke*, pp. 85–86. Some of the passages which Coke reported in connection with Cobham are closely paralleled in his language at Ralegh's trial a few months earlier.

[34] Under the Treason Act 1351, compassing was only treason in relation to plotting the queen's death, not to levying war. But between 1571 and 1603 compassing to levy war (without actually levying war) was also treason by virtue of the statute 13 Eliz., c. 1: see vol. iv, p. 757. The 1571 Act was applied in *R.* v. *Campion* (1581) vol. iii, p. 629 (conspiracy to levy war for alteration of religion). But it referred only to treasons against Queen Elizabeth, by name, and it was taken not to extend to her successors.

[35] *C*, fo. 587v (tr.). The quotation is from Luke 19:22 ('Out of thine own mouth will I judge thee').

report accepted the position that 'sayings are not deeds'.[36] Other questions requiring careful analysis, in the context of plots by Jesuits and their foreign agents, and Roman Catholic exiles, concerned the trial of treasons planned overseas,[37] and the nature of the allegiance owed by foreigners coming into the realm.[38] The memoranda in MS. C on the trials of Essex, Ralegh and Guy Fawkes are not about the factual evidence – law reports were about law – but about technical matters such as the use of commissions and the choice of venue, both for the indictment by the grand jury and for the trial.[39] Another troublesome issue which arose following the expiry of the 1571 Act was whether two witnesses were still required in a treason trial.[40]

These passages in the notebooks demonstrate Coke's anxiety to observe the law punctiliously in treason cases. Their thoroughness, and the many layers of revision, offset the more familiar picture of the unscrupulous prosecutor, out to secure convictions at all costs. Indelible damage to Coke's reputation resulted from his intemperate language in the trials of the earl of Essex in 1601 and Sir Walter Ralegh in 1603.[41] As his tearful encounters with the queen demonstrated, he was unable to contain his emotions in highly charged situations. And his quick-wittedness as a lawyer, second to none in technical argument, was not matched by a measured temperament when confronted with an intelligent and spirited defendant in a public arena. The best that can be said is that, whilst his emotional speech was extreme and earned him lasting obloquy, it is possible that some contemporaries saw it as appropriately forceful and necessary.[42] If he became too heated, it was 'out of the zeal

---

[36] *C*, fo. 587v, margin ('Dicta non sunt acta').

[37] See *R. v. Sir Brian O'Rourke* (1591) and *R. v. Sir John Perrot* (1592) vol. iii, p. 566 (noted in 1594); *R. v. Francis Dacre* (1593) vol. iii, p. 557; *R. v. Richard Hesketh* (1593) ibid. 558; *R. v. Patrick O'Cullen* (1594) ibid. 569. Sir Francis Englefield had been outlawed in 1584 for treason committed at Namur in Wallonia: ibid. 441. The matter had been clarified by the statute of 35 Hen. VIII, c. 2.

[38] *R. v. Dr Lopez* (1594) vol. iii, p. 569; *R. v. Stephano Ferrera da Gama and Emanuel Luys Tinoco* (1594) ibid. 571; *R. v. Douglas* (1605) *Cecil Papers*, xvii. 272. It was doubtless in this connection that Coke took a retrospective interest in the trial of Mary, queen of Scots, ibid. 566; there are notes on her status in *AA*, fos. 3v–4. See also his note on the visit by Harald, king of Man, in 1249: vol. iv, p. 880.

[39] See vol. iii, pp. 566–571 (Hil. 1594) and 614 (Mich. 1594); *R. v. Lopez* (1594) ibid. 569; *R. v. Arden and Somervile* (1583) *C*, fo. 581v; *R. v. Sir Walter Ralegh* (1603) and *R. v. Lord Cobham* (1604) ibid.; 3 Co. Inst. 12, 27; *R. v. Thomas Wynter, Guy Faux and others* (1605) *C*, fo. 695; *R. v. Sir Everard Digby* (1606) ibid.; *R. v. Abbingdon* (1606) *C*, fo. 699 (for receiving Garnet in Worcs.); 3 Co. Inst. 138.

[40] When the question was raised by Ralegh at his trial in Nov. 1603, it was ruled that the statutes on which he relied had been repealed and that there was no such rule in being: Edwards, *Life of Ralegh* (next note), i. 411. But it was only in Hilary term 1604 that the matter was fully considered by the assembled judges: *C*, fos. 503–504v (some of which was later crossed out). The judges confirmed that the rule did not apply to common-law treason (as confirmed by the 1350 Act), that 'accusers' did not in any case have to be witnesses, and that an accusation by someone who confessed treason was as strong as a verdict of twelve (an assertion made by both Coke and Popham C.J. in Ralegh's trial, where the conviction depended on Cobham's confession).

[41] The various reports of Ralegh's trial are collated in E. Edwards, *The Life of Sir Walter Ralegh* (1868), i. 381–439. See also M. Nicholls, 'Sir Walter Ralegh's Treason: A Prosecution Document' (1995) 38 *Historical Journal* 821–842 (where it is concluded that Ralegh was rightly, if not fairly, convicted).

[42] This was the opinion of T. G. Barnes, *Shaping the Common Law*, ed. A. D. Boyer (2008), p. 121 ('Coke's vigorousness and harshness in prosecution were remarked upon by his contemporaries only as manifestations of remarkable patriotism and loyalty to his sovereign. Victorian Englishmen, largely unfamiliar with war or treason, enjoyed the luxury of roundly condemning Coke for his choleric severity. Our age ought to be better disposed to understanding him'). On the other hand, there is some evidence that Coke's conduct in Ralegh's trial was disapproved of at the time.

of his duty, for the service of the king'.[43] More problematic in terms of fairness was the reliance on unsigned confessions by alleged co-conspirators to prove the overt acts, in spite of Ralegh's plea for the deponents to be brought to court so that he could question them face to face. The judges present at the trial declared that confrontation was not allowed 'in cases of this nature',[44] a decision which earned them their own share of condemnation from posterity. Coke was following a procedure supported by precedent, if not by general assent, in glossing and contextualising the confessions rhetorically, without calling viva voce evidence, and this naturally led him into the deplorable altercation with the defendant: a defendant who was unable by law to give evidence, and could only contradict the attorney-general's coloured interpretation of the documents. Whether Coke was pleased with his fraught day's work we shall never know; but the layers of alteration in his notebook, which lie outside the reach of this edition and merit further study, may be an indication of subsequent misgivings about the law. What is clear is that, in gathering the evidence for such prosecutions, Coke was more than equal in industriousness to any law officer before him. The Elizabethan state papers, though piecemeal, show how much paper was amassed in preparation for a state trial, some of it by interrogation in person.[45] There might even be detective work, sometimes in conjunction with Popham C.J.[46] The survival of so much pre-trial material has no doubt been fortuitous; but nothing on the same scale remains from any previous generation.

The prosecution of Roman Catholic recusants, relentless but less severe than the prosecution of traitors, also fell under the aegis of the law officers, though much of the work could be left to local magistrates and the assize judges.[47] It was Coke's belief that before Pope Pius's bull *Regnans in excelsis* of 1570 there had been no recusants,[48] but the drastic effect of that ill-judged declaration of papal enmity, which required otherwise law-abiding Roman Catholics to be disloyal, had been the introduction of harsh legislation requiring (inter alia) attendance at church on pain of cumulative penalties. Coke's notes show his concern to obtain authoritative clarification of all matters of principle arising from this legislation. He was present at no less than six judicial assemblies to discuss it, some of them convened on his own motion.[49] The

---

[43] 2 St. Tr. 10 (Edwards, *Life of Ralegh*, i. 395), *per* Popham C.J., who acknowledged that Ralegh was entitled to a similar latitude in speaking for his life, but told both of them to calm down.

[44] Folger Shakespeare Library, Washington, MS. V.b.142, fos. 78–83, at fo. 81. Cf. 2 St. Tr. 18 (Edwards, *Life of Ralegh*, i. 417), *per* Popham C.J. ('This thing cannot be granted, for then a number of treasons should flourish'). The principal evidence was contained in the written confession of Lord Cobham, which he was thought to have retracted.

[45] Like other law officers (including Francis Bacon), Coke was named in a number torture warrants from the Privy Council, in order to extract information or confessions: that for Guy Fawkes is a notorious example. In later life he held torture to be contrary to common law and to Magna Carta: Baker, *Magna Carta*, p. 172. His earlier but undated notes on torture in *AA*, fo. 42, cite Fortescue's statement that it was against the common law ('et vide la un horrible example').

[46] E.g. *Cecil Papers*, xi. 28, 37; xii. 513.

[47] Magistrates were recommended to prosecute at the assizes rather than the quarter sessions, to avoid the need to remove the indictments into the King's Bench: vol. iii, p. 598.

[48] *Att.-Gen.* v. *Pounde* (1603) Hawarde 182, at p. 183; *Cawdrye's Case* (1594) 5 Co. Rep. (1605), part 1, at fo. 34v, Boyer, *Coke and the Elizabethan Age*, p. 157; Baker, *Magna Carta*, p. 127, n. 89.

[49] See vol. iii, pp. 508, 537 (Hil. 1593), 564 (Hil 1594) and 597 (Mich. 1594); vol. iv, pp. 786 (1597) and 852 (1598). There are also notes on the calculation of fines due after a submission in vol. iii, p. 570 (Hil. 1594). See further Baker, *Magna Carta*, pp. 127–129.

statutes were on the whole construed literally, whether for or against recusants. But there was room for beneficial equity: for instance, if a recusant was ordered to be confined to a specified locality, he was not liable to a fine if he was imprisoned elsewhere against his will or forcibly removed by wrongdoers.[50] Coke was nevertheless committed to making the legislation effective. The first of the cases, which he argued before all the justices of England in 1593, resulted in a ruling that married women were liable to fines and imprisonment for recusancy, for otherwise (in Coke's words) it would be 'mischievous and against the intention of the Act to have married women outside the Act, being a great part of the realm, and dangerous through the education of the offspring and family'. On the other hand, their husbands could not be punished for their offences, not being parties to the indictments, and therefore the fine could not be levied against the husband's property.[51] This was a serious shortcoming, since mixed marriages were evidently not uncommon, and so a bill was passed shortly afterwards to enable a husband to be joined in the same indictment as his wife.[52] Two years later Coke persuaded the King's Bench that husbands could be imprisoned until they put in bail for wives accused of recusancy, though Popham C.J. said the course of the King's Bench differed from that of the Common Pleas.[53]

The prosecution of murder and felony was not normally a matter for the attorney-general, and he may not have been involved even in the reserved criminal cases discussed by the judges in Serjeants' Inn. Coke had represented defendants in several murder cases before entering the queen's service in 1592,[54] but the number of reports thereafter does not increase. The questions in such cases, usually either appeals of murder[55] or indictments challenged by *certiorari* – both being situations in which counsel were allowed – did not require much analysis of the substantive criminal law, and Coke generally contented himself with the basic learning in Marow's reading (1503) and Staunford's *Plees del Coron* (1557).[56] The one piece of substantive learning which did receive attention, no doubt because it was too unusual to be found in the standard legal sources, was the definition of buggery. This arose from a

---

[50] Vol. iii, p. 564 (Hil. 1593).

[51] Vol. iii, p. 508. Coke had noted a previous decision of all the judges to the same effect in 1583: vol. ii, p. 217.

[52] Vol. iii, p. 509; 35 Eliz., c. 1. This, as Coke pointed out, was during his Speakership.

[53] *R.* v. *Philpot and Young* (1595) (not in *C*) BL MS. Harley 4998, fos. 86v–87; MS. Harg. 7A, fo. 66v; MS. Harg. 26, f. 49v ('femes recusants in Hampshire'); MS. Add. 25200, fo. 116v; MS. Add. 25222, fos. 119v–120 ('Les femes del Philpot et Younge et divers auters'); CUL MS. Ff.5.16, fo. 105v (sim.); MS. Ii.5.24, fo. 83; *Acts of the Privy Council*, xxiii. 182, 193. Cf. *Dr Foster's Case* (1614) 11 Co. Rep. 56, at fo. 61.

[54] Coke represented the defendants in *R.* v. *Lacy* (1583) vol. ii, p. 218 (murder on Scarborough Sands); and in cases concerning indictments, ibid. 304, 306. He appeared several times for the defendant in the poisoning case of *R.* v. *Vaux* (1591), which fell within the period of the missing notebook *B* but was noted by several other reporters: J. Baker in *Landmark Cases in Criminal Law*, ed. P. Handler, H. Mares and I. Williams (2017), pp. 37–41. He appeared for the appellor in *Wrote* v. *Wigges* (1591) vol. iii, p. 413 (appeal of murder).

[55] See *Wetherell* v. *Darby* (1593) vol. iii, p. 521; *Gough* v. *Bybeth* (1597) vol. iv, p. 753; *R.* v. *Wall* (1598) ibid. 906 (appeal following an indictment); *Wattes* v. *Braynes* (1600) ibid. vol. v, p. 1085.

[56] See e.g. *AA*, fos. 113–115 (homicide), 116 (larceny) and 117 (burglary). In 1596 he reported a point concerning burglary related to him by Popham C.J.: vol. iv, p. 663. But, for forensic purposes, it was just as important to know the correct Latin for burglary: *Vaux* v. *Brooke* (1586) vol. ii, p. 287.

notorious prosecution in the King's Bench in 1606 or 1607, the very last case which Coke reported in MS. C.[57]

A range of prosecutions in which Coke was regularly involved were those in the Star Chamber, an ancient forum[58] in which the attorney-general had the privilege of presenting criminal informations orally (*ore tenus*). Although most of the Star Chamber cases which Coke reported were essentially civil,[59] many prosecutions were brought in his name as attorney-general either on behalf of the crown or on the relation of interested parties.[60] The court had a flexible criminal jurisdiction 'by the absolute power of the said court and not by the ordinary course of the law',[61] but it was limited to misdemeanours and was not yet an instrument of governmental oppression. On the contrary, its jurisdiction in the public sphere was more typically directed against misconduct and overbearing by officials acting in the queen's name. Coke's record in this connection was exemplary, bringing to heel errant sheriffs, justices of the peace, deputy lieutenants and constables in order to uphold the rule of law and prevent the abuse of ordinary people.[62]

The last matter of state in this edition was the investigation of the earl of Essex in 1600 for his irresponsible mishandling of the military campaign in Ireland.[63] This was conducted by a 'select council' at York House, the lord keeper's home. Essex relied for his defence on the immensely broad language of his written commission, which gave him plenipotentiary power; but he had disobeyed the queen's express commands. The council decided that the queen could by letter or word of mouth override or qualify the terms of a military commission under the great seal, because the conduct of war was a matter of absolute prerogative. The immediate outcome was the relatively light penalty of a censure, house arrest and disqualification from military positions. But the earl's trial for treason the following year was noted later in MS. C.[64] At the end of the report, Coke recorded that Essex was executed on a new

---

[57] *R.* v. *Humphrey Stafford* (1606/07) *C*, fos. 712–713; KB 27/1402, Rex, m. 3 (printed in Co. Ent. 351); 12 Co. Rep. 36; 3 Co. Inst. 59; earlier notes in *AA*, fo 115v. See Anon., *The Arraignement, Judgement, Confession and Execution of Humfrey Stafford* (1607). Coke's report is dated Trin. 4 Jac. (1606), though it says Stafford had already been indicted and ends with a note of the conviction and execution. Since the indictment was found on 5 May 1607, alleging the fact on 12 May 'ultimo preterito' (1606), and the trial was on 8 June 1607, the report must be misdated; but there is a forward reference 'Vide 5 Jac. 56b', referring to a report of 1607 in the lost MS. *D* (presumably that translated in 12 Co. Rep. 36). Coke was appointed C.J.C.P. on 30 June 1606, so if he was involved as Att.-Gen. it must have been very soon after the fact.

[58] Coke was never taken in by the erroneous tradition (long accepted by Bacon) that it owed its origin to a statute of 1487: *AA*, fo. 128 (partly based on precedents shown him by [William] Mill, clerk of the Star Chamber). See Baker, *Magma Carta*, pp. 201, 306, 404.

[59] Technically, however, 'all suits in the Star Chamber are but informations for the queen, even though the suit is exhibited by the party': *Shukburgh* v. *Byggyn* (1598) vol. v, p. 1005, *per* Popham C.J. (tr.). Cf. *Drywood* v. *Appleton* (1600) ibid. 1059 (tr. 'every suit in the Star Chamber is for the queen').

[60] For informations by relation see E. Kadens, 'New Light on *Twyne's Case*' (2020) 94 *American Bankruptcy Law Journal* 1–84, at pp. 53–59. Coke's lengthy report of *Att.-Gen.* v. *Twyne* (1602) is in *C*, fos. 520v–526. The Att. Gen. could take over a prosecution if a party died or abandoned it: *Drywood* v. *Appleton* (1600) previous note.

[61] *Eaton* v. *Allen* (1598) vol. v, p. 1002.

[62] See e.g. Smith, *Sir Edward Coke*, pp. 63–66; Baker, *English Law under Two Elizabeths*, pp. 52–53, 75–76. For Coke's prosecution of economic offences see vol. iv, p. 776. For his prosecution of purveyors see Baker, *Magna Carta*, pp. 324–326; below, p. cxlii.   [63] Vol. v, p. 1097.

[64] *C*, fos. 452v–455v. Cf. 3 Co. Inst. 12.

scaffold erected on the green within the Tower, at the earl's special request not to be beheaded in public on Tower Hill. 'Note', added Coke, 'that the reward of treason is always death and destruction, as by woeful examples may be remembered within the memory of some now living', namely, under Henry VIII, the dukes of Buckingham and Norfolk, the marquess of Exeter, five earls, four lords and a great number of knights and gentlemen of good families; under Edward VI, Admiral Seymour, the duke of Somerset, and a great multitude of commoners; in the time of Mary, the dukes of Suffolk and Northumberland, three other peers, and a multitude of knights, gentlemen and commons in Wyatt's rebellion; and in the present queen's time the duke of Norfolk and five earls: 'so that six dukes, two marquesses, ten earls and ten lords have been attainted of treason within our memory. *Foelix quem faciunt aliena pericula cautum.*'[65] The work of prosecuting for treason was not for the faint-hearted.

(c) Royal revenue and the law

The attorney-general was much concerned with the revenue of the crown, and there are more Exchequer cases and precedents in Coke's notebooks than in any other contemporary reports. Two are particularly worthy of note. In 1595 Coke preferred an information against the executors of Sir Walter Mildmay, chancellor of the Exchequer, to render an account of £1,525 received from the queen's treasure for his expenses ('diet and attendance').[66] The report provides much information about the chains of authority for the disbursement of money by treasurer's warrants. Coke's successful argument, beginning with *Glanvill*, disputed the proposition that the treasurer could dispose of any of the queen's treasure ex officio: 'his office is to keep and not to spend'. No officer could spend money from the treasury without a special warrant. Moreover, although one penny could not be known from another, the queen's money could in law be traced into anyone's hands. Tracing was only possible in the case of a common person if the money was in a bag, but 'the law preserves and protects the queen's money and treasure in more safety than a bag, and that is the reason why the king shall have an action of account for his treasure against the executors of an accountant.' Even the debtor's lands were chargeable, and indeed 'all the lands that he had, into whosesoever hands they come, are liable for payment of the queen's money which came to his hands.' The other case of note was a similar information in the nature of an action of account, brought against the executor of Customer Smyth.[67] This was commenced in 1596, and sought an account of £1,613. 18s. 4d. received from an imposition levied on alum imported from the dominions of the bishop of Rome. The queen had in 1580 granted a lease to Thomas

---

[65] *C*, fo. 455v (tr.). The epithet, meaning 'Happy is he who learns from other men's perils', is found in Sebastian Brandt's *Ship of Fools*. By 'our memory', Coke meant the memory of people still living.

[66] *Att.-Gen.* v. *Carie and Dodington* (1596) vol. iv, p. 787; cf. 11 Co. Rep. 89 at fos. 90–93. In 1598 Coke noted that the king's jewels could be recovered from someone who had acquired them innocently: *Grimsby* v. *Eyre* (1456) vol. iv, p. 883.

[67] *Att.-Gen.* v. *Smyth* (1596–1600) vol. iv, p. 873; vol. v, p. 1043 (noted in 1598); cf. 12 Co. Rep. 34. This was discussed in G. D. G. Hall, 'Impositions and the Courts' (1953) 69 L.Q.R. 200, at pp. 213–214, cit. Bodl. Lib. MS. Rawlinson C. 756, fo. 52, a tantalisingly brief report which is in fact an abridgment of Coke's text, probably by Thomas Coventry (see above, pp. cix–cx).

Smyth, collector of customs in the port of London, of all impositions to be received over the next four years.[68] The alum duty was imposed in 1581. This raised two constitutional questions. The first was whether the imposition was valid, or whether it infringed the statutes for the protection of merchants, since it was not warranted by any act of Parliament. And the second was whether receipts from future taxation could be granted or leased to a subject in advance. As to the first, the court held that the queen had a prerogative power as 'parent of the public weal' to lay impositions on imported goods for the advancement of trade and traffic, and an imposition would be presumed valid unless a party could show that it hindered trade and traffic. As to the second, although Tanfield argued that the queen could grant future income, because by her prerogative she could assign a future chose in action,[69] the court held that it was not necessary to decide that point because future impositions did not come within the wording of Smyth's grant. In a second report, which Coke later struck out, a different reason was given. The queen could not grant future impositions because it would take away her power to reduce or remove an imposition when the public good so required. The answer to this, as Coke must have foreseen when he took his pen across it, was that a grant of impositions naturally meant only such impositions as were in fact exacted from time to time.

The exploitation of royal resources was effected through the machinery of inquisitions of office, to identify property to which the crown was entitled; particulars, to value and define the crown's property which it was intended to grant out;[70] and letters patent, whereby the property was granted or leased to those willing to pay for it. Usurpations of the crown's real property were frequently challenged by informations for intrusion,[71] usually in the Exchequer, or (less frequently) by informations in the nature of *quo warranto* in the Exchequer or King's Bench.[72] Both forms of procedure were initiated by the attorney-general, and Coke's reports show that he regularly argued them in person.[73] Informations might be brought on the relation of an interested party,[74] but relator proceedings were distinct from criminal informations brought by common informers under statutory provisions. The attorney-general had less involvement with the latter.[75] He could not intervene to confess a

---

[68] There is a letter on the subject from Smyth to Lord Burghley, 10 Oct. 1585, in BL MS. Lansd. 44, fo. 169.

[69] BL MS. Harg. 5, fo. 91 (tr. 'the queen may grant a future profit before it is imposed, for the queen is not sparing to her subjects and may grant a right and thing in action, for she has a more liberal power than another common subject'). Choses in action were not generally assignable.

[70] See *Hall* v. *Pearte* (1595) vol. iii, p. 609, in which it was held that no regard should be had to a particular in construing letters patent.

[71] The corresponding procedure for a money claim was an information in the nature of an action of account, as brought against the executors of Sir Walter Mildmay and Customer Smyth, above, p. cxxxv.

[72] Here the procedure by information had been devised because writs of *quo warranto* were returnable only before justices in eyre. Coke described *quo warranto* as the king's writ of right: *AD*, fo. 769.

[73] For *quo warranto* see *Att.-Gen.* v. *Payne* (1593) vol. iii, p. 550; *Att.-Gen.* v. *City of London* (1596) vol. iv, p. 671; *Att.-Gen.* v. *Lord Darcy of Chiche* (1596, 1598) ibid. 722, 897; *Att.-Gen.* v. *Owen Vaughan* (1597) ibid. 743; below, p. cxxxix (used against monopolists, 1597).

[74] This is alluded to in the London case (previous note).

[75] Coke had outlined the different roles of the attorney-general in both types of proceeding in the Exchequer in *AA*, fo. 122v.

plea, because the informer had a financial interest as well as the queen,[76] but he could continue proceedings for the benefit of the crown if the informer died.[77]

The crown owned a great deal of real property, much of it through the dissolution of the monasteries, and a large number of patents were issued, some under the great seal, but many under the seals of the Exchequer, the Court of Augmentations (before 1554) or the duchy of Lancaster. The attorney-general had some responsibility for grants and commissions under the great seal, and he was expected to peruse and settle important patents and charters in person.[78] For instance, Coke is said to have drawn three ecclesiastical high commissions,[79] and at least two commissions for the Council in the North.[80] Some of this work must have been distasteful to him, especially in connection with monopolies, which he disliked.[81] It is hardly surprising that questions on the construction of letters patent occur again and again in the notebook.[82] Most of them concerned the doctrine that a patent was void if the queen was deceived in her grant, and the countervailing doctrine that a patent granted 'of our certain knowledge and mere motion' could not be impugned on the grounds of factual misinformation.[83]

The complexities and uncertainties of the law concerning patents gave rise to the pernicious concept of concealment. If there was a flaw in an earlier patent, because of some technical non-disclosure or misdescription, there was nothing to prevent the crown from granting the same property again; and time did not run against the crown. Despite a number of legislative interventions to confirm defective patents,[84] many loopholes remained. Racketeers made a profitable business of exploiting the loopholes by obtaining patents which granted them the right to take concealed lands, especially in ill-prepared grants of monastic property. The device had been invented

---

[76] This was decided by all the justices of England in the time of Wray C.J. and Popham Att.-Gen. (i.e. between 1581 and 1592); Warburton's reports, BL MS. Harley 4817, fos. 214v–215, and HLS MS. 1036 (1051), p. 338, *per* Tanfield C.B. But cf. *Perrot's Case* (1584) below, p. 164, no. 325.

[77] *Hamond* v. *Griffites* (1598) vol. iv, p. 876. See also vol. v, p. 976.

[78] There are numerous references in the *Cecil Papers* to his preparation of patents, commissions, bills, proclamations, and even particulars and leases of crown property. Presumably much of the work was delegated to his clerks, and his role was to perfect the drafts: see e.g. *Cecil Papers*, ix. 73 ('I have taken pains to perfect these four commissions' for Ireland, 1599); xvi. 126 (where he 'caused his man' to draw a warrant). His supposed role in the preparation of the Virginia charter of 1606 is not supported by direct evidence: M. S. Bilder, 'Charter Constitutionalism: The Myth of Edward Coke and the Virginia Charter' (2016) 94 *North Carolina Law Review* 1545–1598.

[79] Baker, *Magna Carta*, p. 337.

[80] *Cecil Papers*, ix. 258; xv. 113.

[81] See below, pp. cxxxviii–cxli. He introduced the practice of inserting a proviso for revocation in the event of abuse: Baker, *Magna Carta*, p. 337, n. 10.

[82] His predecessor, Thomas Egerton, gave a reading in Lincoln's Inn in 1582, when he was Sol.-Gen., on the statute 18 Eliz., c. 2, concerning letters patent. But the subject was of general importance to practitioners, and Coke probably began in the 1570s or 1580s to make the extensive collection of medieval cases on patents in *AA*, fos. 70–83v.

[83] See e.g. *Ayleworth's Case* (1591) vol. iii, p. 419; *Englefield's Case* (1591) ibid. 441; *Brownloe* v. *Farre* (1592) ibid. 506; *Marquess of Exeter's Case* (1593) ibid. 552; *Vaughan's Case* (1593) ibid. 562; *Hall* v. *Pearte* (1595) ibid. 609; *Lord Darcy's Case* (1595) ibid. 616; *Earl of Devon's Case* (1596) vol. iv, p. 692; *Att.-Gen.* v. *Owen Vaughan* (1597) ibid. 743; *Saunders* v. *Lord Lumley* (1597) ibid. 748; *Sir Christopher Hatton's Case* (1597) ibid. 754; *Cholmondley* v. *Hanmer* (1597) ibid. 758; *Lord Norreys* v. *Barret* (1597) vol. v, p. 1034; *Ameredith's Case* (1598) vol. iv, p. 862; *Wikes* v. *Fermor* (1599) vol. v, p. 984; *Case of Alton Woods* (1600) ibid. 1061; *Dawson* v. *Pickworth* (1605) C, fos. 656v–658v; CP 40/1725, m. 3010.

[84] 18 Eliz., c. 2; 35 Eliz., c. 3; 43 Eliz., c. 1.

under Mary I, but over a hundred such patents were granted in the first thirty years of Elizabeth.[85] Coke singled out patents of concealment for bitter condemnation after they threatened the cathedral church of his native Norwich. Some 'greedy and indigent persons', armed with a patent of 1585, 'endeavoured to repair their declining estates' by taking over the possessions of the dean and chapter, merely on the grounds of a supposed historical mistake in the name used when the cathedral was refounded by Edward VI from the earlier priory. This skulduggery attracted the queen's attention and in 1597 she ordered the lord keeper to look into it. Coke reported the conference at Egerton's house with the three chief justices, when he argued successfully against the concealers.[86] This resolution, he said, 'I have thought necessary to report ... (though little time permits me) for the benefit of the said cathedral church and of all their farmers and others who derive any estate or interest from them'.[87] Coke's outrage against these 'graceless and wicked men'[88] is evident. He had a special name for concealers, *helluones*,[89] and when he published a revised version of the report he made public the name of the principal *helluo* in the Norwich case, William Downing.[90] What he did not mention was that Downing's associates were Peter Osborne and Thomas Fanshawe, the two remembrancers of the Exchequer.[91] The immediate outcome of the proceedings was a statute of 1598, probably drafted by Coke himself, which confirmed the title of the dean and chapter.[92]

Another of Coke's bugbears was the patent of monopoly. While there was no objection to the private exploitation of bona fide discoveries and inventions, which rather deserved encouragement, the granting of monopolies over existing English trades or manufactures was not only damaging to the private livelihoods of those directly affected but also against the public interest. It was akin to the common-law offence of engrossing, or hoarding commodities in order to drive up prices.[93] There

---

[85] Coke reported two cases in 1596: *Att.-Gen.* v. *Hugh Vaughan* (1596) vol. iv, p. 699; *Shane's Case* (1596) ibid. 668. See also *Alexander's Case* (1597) ibid. 771; *Edward Seymour's Case* (1601) *Cecil Papers*, xi. 206.

[86] *Case of the Dean and Chapter of Norwich* (1597) vol. iv, p. 843; revised in 3 Co. Rep. 73; cf. *Case of St Giles Hospital, Norwich* (1597) vol. iv, p. 842. See further A. Hassall Smith, *County and Court: Government and Politics in Norfolk 1558-1603* (1974), pp. 265-275; Boyer, *Coke and the Elizabethan Age*, pp. 75–78; Baker, *Magna Carta*, pp. 200–201.

[87] Vol. v, p. 932. He did not find the time until Mich. 1598. But the discussion which he reported must have preceded the statute (below), passed in Feb. 1598. Anderson's date of Mich. 1597 (2 And. 120) is more likely to be correct.   [88] 4 Co. Inst. 257.

[89] Vol. v, p. 933; 4 Co. Inst. 76, 257. Cf. 10 Co. Rep. 109 ('thievish concealers').

[90] There are hints of Downing's enterprise in *Eden* v. *Downing* (1590) 1 And. 268; *Downing* v. *Franklyn* (1593) vol. iii, p. 621; these suits concerned the rectory of Downham, formerly belonging to Norwich priory. Downing was an attorney of the Common Pleas and served as M.P. for Orford in 1586.

[91] Fanshawe, the queen's remembrancer, supplied Coke with precedents and their dealings were evidently amicable: vol. iv, pp. 846, 854.

[92] 39 Eliz., c. 22; 4 Co. Inst. 257; D'Ewes, *Journals*, p. 582; Dean, *Law-Making and Society*, pp. 129–130. The statute shows that the concealment in question was limited to the possessions of the monastery of St Benet Hulme, annexed to the see of Norwich in 1535. It expressly excluded St Giles's hospital. The same question was revisited in the Common Pleas in 1599 in connection with leases previously granted: 2 And. 165 (1599–1601). Note also the conference between Popham C.J. and Coke Att.-Gen. concerning concealments in *C*, fo. 601 (1604).

[93] This was the subject of a judicial conference of 1597: vol. iv, p. 776 (and see also p. 926); 3 Co. Inst. 196. It was also, but less closely, akin to the prerogative of purveyance, which was being abused for private profit. Purveyance was worrying Coke in the 1590s (Baker, *Magna Carta*, p. 324) and became a dominant concern in 1605: below, p. cxlii.

was already a strong body of opinion that patents granting monopolies of the objectionable kind were illegal and void,[94] and there are two passages to that effect in MS. *C*, one of which followed a conference of all the judges to consider engrossing in 1597.[95] There was little or nothing to be found in the year books on the subject, and so Coke was driven to search for ancient and foreign sources to show how universally it was condemned. But the governing principle was clear enough, and Coke summarised it in an autograph note preserved among the state papers.[96]

> If any bring in any new invention that hath not been put in ure before within this realm and is profitable to the commonwealth, her majesty may grant him a privilege for a convenient time, that he may recover his charge and reap some convenient reward for his service. Upon like reason, if any at their own charges will undertake a new voyage for trade of merchandise, that never was found out nor undertaken before, her majesty may grant him the like privilege as before.

Without such a justification, a monopoly was necessarily against the public interest and arguably invalid as an unlawful restraint of trade.

The abuse of monopolies was a constant source of complaint in the House of Commons, and in 1598 the anger reached such a pitch that the queen vouchsafed to promise that all patents would be examined, 'to abide the trial and touchstone of the law'.[97] Coke had already taken the initiative by preferring informations of *quo warranto* against some of the monopolists in the Exchequer. A note of eight such informations laid in Michaelmas term 1597, written in his own hand and probably detached from MS. *C*,[98] is to be found on two pages folded into his copy of *Magna Carta cum Statutis* (1556) at Holkham Hall.[99] All eight monopolies were held to be illegal, as contrary to the liberty of the subject, and the patents were declared void.[1]

---

[94] E.g. *Farmor* v. *Savage* (1583) vol. ii, p. 216; Baker, *Magna Carta*, pp. 190–192. The monopoly of baking in Towcester which Sir George Farmor claimed was based on prescription rather than a grant, but the arguments against it were the same.

[95] Note 93, opposite.

[96] 'Notes of prerogative', SP 12/276/81 (dated *c*. 1600 by the State Paper Office); this may have been written in preparation for *Darcy* v. *Allen* (below). He also considered that the queen could by letters patent '*pro bono publico* charge her subjects, as for repairing a highway', and could 'for the advancement of trade and traffic ... prescribe an order or manner of trade, so always it be good for the weal public', and also prohibit anything 'hurtful or prejudicial to the commonwealth or the state, albeit the same be not prohibited by law'.

[97] Proc. Parl., iii. 242 (9 Feb. 1598), following debates in 1597. This was communicated to the Commons by Egerton L.K. Coke compiled a 'great collection' concerning monopolies at the request of Lord Buckhurst prior to the Parliament of 1601: *Cecil Papers*, xi. 324.

[98] See above, p. cx. For Coke's response see also Proc. Parl., iii. 372, 380.

[99] Coke's *Statuta*, 2, endpapers (Holkham 7831). Coke also noted four *quo warranto* proceedings which he brought in 1600 to seize franchises claimed in London by Lord Rich (St Bartholomew's), William Moore (Blackfriars), Lord De la Warr (Whitefriars) and the earl of Pembroke (Barnard's Castle). He brought a similar *quo warranto* against the countess of Shrewsbury for the liberty of Coldharbour, London: HLS MS. 531 (5016), fo. 207.

[1] They may be identified from the rolls of the queen's remembrancer, E 159/413, Mich. recorda, mm. 432 (Elizabeth Mathews: buying and selling fish blubbers to make train oil), 433 (Edward Darcy: searching leather), 434 (Sir Thomas Wilkes: making and selling white salt in Kings Lynn and Boston), 435 (William Sympson: buying imported stoneware and earthenware pots and bottles), 436 (Sir John Pakington: importing and making starch), 437 (William Harbourne: making and selling white salt in Yarmouth), 438 (Robert Alexander and Richard Mompesson: importing aniseed and sumac) and 439 (John Collyns and others: making cloth called 'myldering and powledavies'). Coke noted that Popham C.J. agreed with the decisions by the Court of Exchequer.

Moreover, as Coke observed, Sir John Pakington's patent for starch was struck down even though it did not concern a 'thing of necessity'. In 1599 Coke had an opportunity to argue against a different kind of monopoly in *Davenant* v. *Hurdys*, which is reported briefly in *C*.[2] This was an attack on an ordinance of the Merchant Taylors' Company which operated in restraint of trade. Coke argued that it was against the liberty of the subject as guaranteed by chapter 29 of Magna Carta, and that monopolies were abhorred by both the common law and the Civil law. The argument succeeded: 'it was adjudged that this ordinance was against law, because it was against the liberty of the subject ... and amounted to a monopoly'.

In 1602 Coke reported the leading case of *Darcy* v. *Allen*, which he called *The Case of Monopolies*.[3] Edward Darcy, the courtier who had already crossed swords with Coke over patronage and over his leather monopoly,[4] brought an action on the case to obtain damages for infringement of his patent for the sole manufacture and selling of playing-cards. Coke was obliged to argue in support of the patent, possibly at the queen's insistence, and his main argument was that since playing-cards were luxuries which led to idleness their supply needed regulation. Judgment was nevertheless given against Darcy in 1603. The judges had delayed the final judgment temporarily at Coke's earnest request,[5] a request probably made to avoid upsetting a dying queen.[6] Yet it is obvious from Coke's report that he did not disapprove of the outcome. According to his report, the whole court of King's Bench under Popham C.J. ruled that the patent was 'utterly void'. This was consistent with Popham C.J.'s approval of the Exchequer decisions in 1597, and there is a marginal annotation to Coke's note on Sir John Pakington's case, putting *Darcy's Case* in the same category: the patent was objectionable even though the commodity concerned was not 'a thing of necessity'. All such monopolies were against the law because they increased prices and were in restraint of trade. In his manuscript report, though not in the printed version of 1615, Coke explained that the power of granting monopolies was not an absolute prerogative but one of the ordinary prerogatives 'determinable by the ordinary course of the law in any court of justice'; and it was a maxim that the king could not by his prerogative do wrong to a subject.[7] These were hardly the words of a subservient law officer smarting from a countercheck. Coke accepted that there

---

[2] *Davenant* v. *Hurdys* (1599) vol. v, p. 1057; Baker, *Magna Carta*, pp. 315–317.

[3] *C*, fos. 590v–593; printed as an appendix to J. I. Corré, 'The Argument, Decision and Reports of *Darcy* v. *Allen*' (1996) 45 *Emory Law Journal* 1261–1327; amended version in 11 Co. Rep. 84; record in KB 27/1373, m. 435 (B. & M. 678). See also Baker, *Magna Carta*, pp. 319–323.

[4] Above, p. cxxix, and p. cxxxix, n. 1.

[5] LI MS. Maynard 82, fo. 52v (tr. 'nevertheless at the importunate motion of Coke, the king's attorney, the judgment was respited until another day, at which day judgment was given against the patentee'). The report is dated Pas. 1603, which presumably refers to the judgment.

[6] The queen died on 24 March, after a mortal illness lasting several months. For all her conciliatory speeches in Parliament, she had considered monopolies to be the 'principal pearl in her crown': Baker, *Magna Carta*, p. 197.

[7] Coke traced this idea to *Bracton*, fos. 368–369 (iv. 159), cited in *AA*, fos. 102 (magenta ink) ('Le prerogative le roy ferra tort a nulluy') and 102 (pencil) ('Le roy per son prerogative ne poet faire tort'). Note also *AD*, fo. 845 ('Le roy sauns parlement ne poet toller le droit del subjecte', cit. YB Hil. 32 Hen. VI, fo. 25, pl. 13, *per* Fortescue C.J. Cf. 3 Co. Inst. 84 ('these monopolies being *malum in se*, and against the common laws, are consequently against the prerogative of the king, for the prerogative of the king is given to him by the common law and is part of the laws of the realm').

were certain absolute prerogatives which could not be disputed;[8] but he was also much taken with Plowden's phrase, that the common law 'admeasured' the prerogative.[9] He had done his duty as counsel, presenting the case as best he could; but the common law had triumphed.

Closely related to the prerogative of conferring monopolies in new trades and manufactures was the power to dispense with penal statutes. This was an application both of the principle that the crown was not bound by a statute unless specifically mentioned,[10] and of a more general principle that the queen could dispense with law on grounds of necessity.[11] But a dispensation gave the beneficiary a monopolistic authority to do what the statute prohibited everyone else from doing, and was open to objection for that reason.[12] In a note on monopolies, now in the state papers, Coke expressed the view that the queen could dispense with any penal statute by means of a licence '*non obstante* the statute', and could even grant a licence *non obstante* a statutory provision that there should be no dispensations *non obstante*.[13] However, he reported without dissent the significant qualification in *Sir Walter Ralegh's Case* (1604) that the king could not grant the power to dispense with a statute which was beneficial to the public,[14] and another decision later the same year that the prerogative power of dispensation could not be delegated.[15]

---

[8] See the note on absolute and ordinary prerogatives (1594) in vol. iii, p. 589; and *The Earl of Essex's Case* (1600) vol. v, at p. 1098. Coke held that the absolute prerogatives were beyond review: *AA*, fo. 128 (tr. 'The absolute prerogatives are such that no subject ought to dispute ... And although in truth this absolute prerogative *non est inclusa sub legibus*, and no one has nor could write upon it, yet this absolute [*sic*] may appear, as the sun through the mist (*sol per nubem*), by various statutes and cases in law, for the king may dispense with law in case of necessity'). He listed nine of them in *AA*, fo. 101 (printed in vol. iii, p. 589, n. 5). In *Coke* v. *Old* (1601) BL MS. Add. 25215, fos. 2v–3, he argued as Att.-Gen. that the prerogative power to quash an inquisition by *supersedeas* was beyond the law ('ultra legem'). See also Smith, *Sir Edward Coke*, pp. 255–259.

[9] *Willion* v. *Lord Berkeley* (1561) Plowd. 227, at fo. 236. Coke cited this at least four times in the commonplace-books: tit. 'Prerogative', *AA*, fos. 101v, 107v (*bis*); *AD*, fo. 98 (pencil). It is also alluded to in 3 Co. Inst. 84 (below, p. cxlii).

[10] *AD*, fo. 804v. Coke added the qualification (fo. 805, tr.) that 'all statutes which are made in preventing of fraud and in remedying of a wrong shall bind the king, for the king is the head of justice and equity and therefore does all he can (*tout son devoir*) to suppress the contrary'. And, of course, the king could take the benefit of a statute without being named.

[11] *AC*, fo. 641v (tr. 'Note that the king may in case of necessity dispense with the law for the benefit of the subject, as by granting him [power] to make an attorney where he cannot do so by law'). He attributed the absolute prerogatives to the same principle: above, n. 8.

[12] In 1571 Robert Bell of the Middle Temple had complained in Parliament of dispensations by licence, whereby 'a few were enriched and the multitude impoverished', and this drew a conciliatory promise from the queen: Proc. Parl., i. 202, 207, 238.

[13] 'Notes of prerogative', SP 12/276/81. Coke had argued in *Darcy* v. *Allen* that Darcy's patent could be seen as an implied dispensation from a statute of 1463 which prohibited the importation of playing-cards: Baker, *Magna Carta*, pp. 320–321. There is a dense body of notes on dispensations *non obstante* in *AA*, fo. 82v, continued on fo. 88v. The papers found in Coke's study after his death included 'A manuscript in folio intitled on the backside "Licences and Monopolies in Q. Eliz. time"': PRO, SP 16/278, fo. 73, no. 35.

[14] *C*, fo. 643v. For licences *non obstante* see Baker, *Magna Carta*, pp. 187–190. Note also Coke's advice on the grant of a dispensation in 1604: *Cecil Papers*, xvi. 226.

[15] 'Le certificat de touts les justices d'Angleterre concernant grants de penall leys et statutes' (8 Nov. 1604) *C*, fo. 602; 7 Co. Rep. 36. In *Shaw* v. *Harries* (1606) BL MS. Add. 35954, fos. 441–442v, Coke Att.-Gen. persuaded the King's Bench that the grantee of a licence *non obstante* could not assign his interest to anyone else. Cf. *Aldworth's Case* (1605) BL MS. Add. 35954, fos. 369–370; Baker, *Magna Carta*, pp. 325–326, where he argued that the prerogative right of purveyance could not be delegated or demised; this was confirmed in *Case of Saltpetre* (1606) 12 Co. Rep. 12, at p. 13; 3 Co. Inst. 83.

Yet another kind of monopoly was that arising from the prerogative of purveyance. In the 1580s the queen had authorised the law officers to deal with abuses, and they were the subject of one of Coke's last campaigns as attorney-general in 1604–06.[16] He persuaded the assembled judges that it was against Magna Carta and other statutes for purveyors to take any part of a man's inheritance, such as timber or parts of a house, or to imprison anyone who proved disobedient; and he actively enforced the decision.[17] Coke asserted that by taking remedial action 'his majesty's true and just prerogative was confirmed, for *confirmat usum qui tollit abusum.*'[18] An exception would have to be made for saltpetre, since it was needed to make gunpowder for the defence of the realm. Even so, while approving it on that ground, Coke was at pains to explain that the common law 'hath so admeasured the king's prerogatives that they should neither take away nor prejudice the inheritance of any'.[19] The prerogative did not extend to demolishing or weakening the foundations of dwelling houses or barns; the ground had to be made good afterwards; and landowners could not be restrained from digging for saltpetre in their own land.[20]

(d) The Chancery jurisdiction

An issue which had been rumbling before Coke entered the queen's service was the claim by courts of equity to grant relief to parties who had fought and lost cases at common law. This jurisdiction was justified by its defenders on the footing that courts of equity were concerned solely with the conscience of the party, not with challenging the legal position as embodied in the judgment. The objection to it was that it appeared to undermine the authority of the courts of common law. The finality of judgments given in the king's courts had been guaranteed by a statute of 1402 which provided that, after judgment given in the king's courts, the parties should be 'in peace thereof' unless the judgment was annulled by attaint or writ of error.[21] The objection was not to equity itself, as a corrective to law,[22] but to procedural impropriety: those who sought equity ought to take the first step before losing their case at common law, for otherwise there would be no certainty in

---

[16] The prerogative itself was beyond question. Indeed, Coke wrote that it was 'a higher point of prerogative than wardship': vol. iv, p. 274. But he linked it with unlawful monopolies in 3 Co. Inst. 83.

[17] *C*, fos. 623v–626, 662v–664v, 695v–699; 2 Co. Inst. 35; 3 Co. Inst. 82; Smith, *Sir Edward Coke*, pp. 69–74; Baker, *Magna Carta*, pp. 324–326.

[18] *Cecil Papers*, xvii. 145–146 (tr. 'one confirms the use by taking away the abuse').

[19] 3 Co. Inst. 84. Cf. above, p. cxli, n. 9.

[20] *Case of Saltpetre* (1606) 12 Co. Rep. 12; 3 Co. Inst. 83; Warburton's reports, BL MS. Harley 4817, fo. 213v; Folger Shakespeare Library Washington, MS. V.b.173, fos. 179–188; Baker, *Magna Carta*, pp. 327–328; Smith, *Sir Edward Coke*, p. 112. This was referred to all the judges, after a complaint in Parliament, just after Coke became chief justice; it was presumably reported in MS. *D*. But as Att.-Gen. in 1597 Coke had complained to Burghley of exactions by the saltpetre patentees as well as by ordinary purveyors: BL MS. Lansd. 84(63). A previous patent had been held unlawful in 1604, and Coke was required to prepare a new one: *Cecil Papers*, xvi. 277.

[21] 4 Hen. IV, c. 23. St German considered this binding on the Chancery, as did Richard Crompton in his treatise of 1594 on the queen's courts: Baker, *Magna Carta*, p. 213.

[22] Coke had written in his notebook that 'le absolut power del chauncellour est above et pluis haut que le banke le roy': *AA*, fo. 232.

judgments.[23] This was a controversy which affected the jurisdiction of all the English-bill courts,[24] but the logic extended above all to the Court of Chancery.[25] In 1597 Coke – perhaps with the implicit support of Popham and Anderson C.JJ. – was willing to take on the Chancery directly in the leading case of *Thomas Throckmorton* v. *Sir Moyle Finch*, concerning a crown lease of the manors of Ravenstone and Stoke Goldington in Buckinghamshire.[26] As with the cases leading to his downfall in 1616, the merits were distinctly against him. He admitted himself that there was a strong case in equity, and Throckmorton had almost succeeded on the same merits even in the action at law.[27] But he had not resorted to the Chancery until judgment had been given against him following a majority vote of all the judges of England.[28]

The report of the case in MS. *C* was copied by an amanuensis from a separate 'book' written by Coke, and then heavily annotated in Coke's hand. It is clear from what Coke originally wrote, and confirmed by the Chancery record,[29] that he himself argued the case for Finch, though – perhaps with a view to possible publication – he later emended 'the attorney-general' to 'the solicitor-general'. He objected to Throckmorton's suit on the ground that judgment had been given at law and affirmed on a writ of error. Lord Keeper Egerton denied that this was a valid defence in equity, reasserting that in cases such as this the court of equity did not seek to impugn the judgment but rather to 'correct the corrupt conscience of the party'. However, 'because the case was of great consequence and likely to be a precedent for many others', he was commanded by the queen to refer the case to all the justices of England for their consideration.[30]

Against Egerton's position, Coke argued that 'all the effect and fruit of the judgment would be taken away' by a decree in equity:

> And it would be perilous to permit men after judgment and trials in law to surmise matter in equity and thereby put the person who recovered to excessive charges. Suits by this means would be infinite, and no one could be in peace for anything which the law by judgment had given him, but a contentious and able person who has an unquiet spirit might continually surmise matter in equity and thus continually vex the person who recovered,

---

[23] The principle that equity would not assist a party who slept on his rights was affirmed by the Chancery in *Lord Compton* v. *Egerton* (1570s) below, p. 23, no. 43.

[24] The wider aspects are absent from the notebooks. In 1604 Coke wrote, with reference to the claim made by the Council in the Marches to an equitable jurisdiction, that 'nothing is more repugnant to law': *Cecil Papers*, xvi. 412. See further Baker, *Magna Carta*, pp. 162–163, 213–214, 303, 384, 388.

[25] The point had arisen before: *Astwick's Case* (1567) ibid. 162, n. 103 (King's Bench); *Humfreys' Case* (1572) ibid., n. 108 (Common Pleas); *Anon.* (1596) ibid. 303, n. 148 (Common Pleas).

[26] Vol. iv, pp. 797–803. The intricacies of the case and its background, drawing on the Throckmorton muniments, will be explored in an essay to be published elsewhere.

[27] A majority had decided in the time of Wray C.J. to reverse the judgment, but the case was adjourned, and following some judicial changes there was a slender majority to affirm it. One reporter observed, '*Sic transit gloria mundi*. The law in these days altered and changed as the justices did alter and change': BL MS. Lansd. 1060, fo. 141v.

[28] The original ejectment action in the Exchequer in 1589 had been reported by Coke in the lost MS. *B*. The argument in the Exchequer Chamber was summarised in *Throckmorton* v. *Finch* (1594) vol. iii, p. 598.

[29] Below, n. 32.

[30] Finch brought the original ejectment as lessee of Thomas Heneage (d. 1595), vice-chamberlain of the queen's household, and the freehold title was claimed by Heneage's widow, the dowager countess of Southampton. Throckmorton's claim was to the residue of a 70-year lease granted by the crown in 1557.

which would be a great inconvenience. And it is absurd that a court which (as to equity) is not of record should control judgments which are of record

That, explained Coke, was the reasoning behind the 1402 statute, which referred specifically to petitions to the king and Council. There might even be severe sanctions. 'It seemed to some', he hinted warily, that such proceedings might incur the danger of a *praemunire*. At any rate, they were against chapter 29 of Magna Carta. According to Coke's report, all the judges of England except Walmsley J. accepted his argument, and Popham C.J. conveyed their collective opinion to the lord keeper. Coke added a note on the possible next step if the Chancery persisted, setting out authorities to prove that a writ of prohibition would lie.

Some mystery has surrounded this case, since it does not seem to have been reported by anyone other than Coke and is printed for the first time in this edition. The meeting of all the judges must have been in private. But the true reason for its obscurity seems to be that the decision did not have any effect.[31] Having formally referred the case to the judges, as instructed by the queen, the Court of Chancery – that is, Egerton – edged away from a definite conclusion. The final order on 12 November 1597 was evasive:[32]

> Upon the opening of the matter this present day by her majesty's attorney-general, being of the defendant's counsel and praying the resolution of this court touching the defendant's demurrer, wherein this court meant to have the opinion of the judges, forasmuch as the counsel were not now present, and the lord chief justice of England hath by word only and not by writing shewed the resolution of the judges touching this matter to the lord keeper, it is ordered that the counsel on both parts shall be present in court on Tuesday morning next, at which time his lordship mindeth to declare what opinion was signified to him from the judges, and will be pleased to shew his lordship's own opinion also and give such order in the cause as shall be thought meet.

No further order can be found. The explanation is that the matter was taken over by the House of Commons. Throckmorton, evidently fearing that Egerton would find a way to side-step the judges' opinion, which was not binding on him, asked Sir Walter Ralegh MP and other friends in Parliament to insert into a bill currently before the Commons an *ad hominem* proviso which would have settled the case. This 'special proviso for Mr Throckmorton' reached a second reading, and counsel for both parties were heard at the bar. The case was then referred to arbitrators and a compromise solution adopted.[33]

That was the end of the dispute for the time being. But it was still not the end of the Ravenstone business, or of Coke's involvement with it. While Throckmorton's case was pending, Sir Moyle Finch and his wife were made defendants in a second suit in Chancery in respect of a settlement in trust of part of the same property.[34] The

---

[31] Cf. *Darcy* v. *Allen* (1603), above, p. cxl, which is thought to have been ignored until Coke published a report of it in 1615.
[32] C 33/93, fo. 361; C 33/94, fo. 351v.
[33] See S. D'Ewes, *The Journals of All the Parliaments During the Reign of Queen Elizabeth*, ed. P. Bowes (1682), p. 575; P. W. Hasler, *The House of Commons 1558–1603* (1981), ii. 118, 265. iii. 500.
[34] *Earl of Worcester* v. *Finch* (1600) vol. v, p. 1094. After a false start, the filed bill was received on 18 April 1597: C 2/Eliz/W11/62/2. John Hele's briefs in the case are in Egerton's papers, HEHL MS. EL 5913–5914.

questions in this case were whether Stoke Goldington was a distinct manor or part of Ravenstone, and whether Lady Finch as a married woman could be charged with a trust.[35] The former point raised a question of law, and so, after another intervention by the queen in person, this case too was referred to all the judges.[36] Coke's report tells us a great deal more than the Chancery record, though he omitted to mention one detail in the record, that he was on this occasion retained as counsel against Finch.[37] The judges certified their resolution to the Chancery that Egerton's decree could not stand because the question concerned freehold and was therefore not determinable in Chancery.[38] According to Popham C.J., the Chancery could not determine anything except in cases of fraud, breach of trust, or accident.[39] Even if a suit was brought for discovery of title-deeds, the chancellor could not proceed if title came in issue. This resolution was sufficient for the purposes of the suit, and the ensuing decree of 24 January 1601 merely recited that the judges had confirmed the decree concerning the factual status of Stoke Goldington but had advised that the issues relating to the freehold ought to be tried at common law.

Thus, on two occasions within three years, Egerton had managed to avert a major open collision with the judges. But Coke, and perhaps the judges, saw things more broadly. Coke wrote an addendum to his contemporary report of the 1600 case to the effect that if the chancellor made a decree contrary to right, the queen (who had committed her conscience to the chancellor) could refer it to the judges to decide whether to affirm or reverse it, implying that the present case was an example of this procedure. He later crossed this out in his notebook, though he continued to maintain that the decree had been 'reversed' upon the judges' certificate.[40] Moreover, according to Coke's representation of the case, the judges had incidentally resolved several questions of equity. For one thing, they held that since Lady Finch had acquired the freehold by inheritance, and was a married woman, she could not be bound by a trust. Secondly, even if there was a trust, the beneficial interest could not have been assigned to the plaintiffs because a trust was analogous to a chose in action, which could not be granted over. A trust, they said, was 'not like a use, for that by general allowance was esteemed as a hereditament and of greater estimation than a bare confidence and trust'.[41] They foresaw 'great inconvenience' if trusts could be assigned, because 'they might be assigned to great men and thereby justice would be subverted'. Thirdly, it was held by a majority, including the three chiefs, that if a feoffment was made expressly to the use of the feoffee and his heirs, the feoffor could not allege that the conveyance was upon trust unless this was supported by written or other independent

---

[35] Demurrer in C 2/Eliz/W11/62/3; cf. the answer in C 2/Eliz/W11/62/3.
[36] 4 Co. Inst. 85.
[37] C 33/99, fo. 240 (names the Att.-Gen. as counsel for the plaintiffs).
[38] In Nov. 1600: C 33/99, fo. 422, 743v; C 33/100, fos. 701–702; 2 And. 163–164 (verbatim copy of the certificate); C33/99, fo. 240.
[39] Coke said this was an 'ancient rule': 4 Co. Inst. 84. He had noted it as a couplet in *AA*, fo. 208 (tr.): 'Three things are to be helped in court of conscience, | Covin, accident and breach of confidence.' Rolle said he had heard Coke attribute these verses to Sir Thomas More: Rolle Abr., i. 174, line 10.
[40] *Vaudry* v. *Pannel* (1615) 3 Buls. 116, at p. 118, *per* Coke C.J.; 4 Co. Inst. 85. This is not borne out by the Chancery's own record.
[41] Cf. Coke's argument in 1594 that a use had been neither *jus in re* nor *jus in rem*, and was of no account in law, but rather a viper in the bosom of the law: below, p. clvii.

evidence. If evidence of oral declarations of trust was allowed, contrary to uses expressed in writing, 'all the inheritances of England might by such bare averments be drawn in question'. These were important resolutions, but they were not in the judges' signed certificate and the Chancery was not bound by them.[42] To Coke's way of thinking, no doubt, the case showed that the common-law judges could reverse Chancery decrees on equitable as well as legal grounds. In reality, the only influence that the common-law judges had on the Chancery was by consultation rather than judicial review, as when in 1602 Popham and Anderson C.JJ. persuaded Egerton not to follow the law as to curtesy in relation to a trust for the benefit of a married woman.[43]

In a third case, reported by Coke in 1605, he argued that the lord chancellor had no power to impose a fine for not performing a decree. A fine had been imposed by Egerton (now Lord Ellesmere L.C.) and estreated into the Exchequer, whereupon Coke as attorney-general intervened to confess the party's demurrer and thereby stop the fine from being enforced. Coke's contention was that, if the chancellor had such a power, 'the interest of the land would indirectly be bound, whereas he has power only upon the person'.[44] The court agreed. At the end of his short note of the case, Coke added the citation '22 E. 4'. This was a decision by Hussey C.J. in 1482 that the only coercive power possessed by the Chancery was imprisonment in the Fleet, and that if the power was misused the King's Bench could release the party by *habeas corpus*.[45] The precedent was already a favourite.[46]

These decisions did not bear the fruit which Coke desired. None of them found their way into his printed reports. They do not seem to have affected Ellesmere's approach in practice, and the question in Throckmorton's case was to be reopened in 1616 and decisively determined the other way by James I in person shortly before Coke's downfall. But that was the end of the story, as far as Coke was concerned, not the beginning. The beginning was the expansive concept, developed by Coke while Elizabeth's attorney-general, of a rule of law which kept all courts within their proper bounds.

(e) Judicial review

As a servant of the crown, Coke was obviously not free to challenge government decisions at the highest level. He held office during the sovereign's pleasure, and his

---

[42] They may have been made public. The last point, about oral declarations of trust, was reported (and attributed to the two chief justices) in 117 Selden Soc. 166, no. 104. Cf. *Killio v. Taverner* (1595) Powle's reports, ibid. 203, no. 183.

[43] BL MS. Lansd. 1058, fo. 45. The question was whether a lease held in trust for a married woman went on her death to her husband or her administrators. Egerton was at first of opinion that it went to the husband, but he changed his mind on receiving the advice and also on finding a Chancery precedent exactly in point. Note also UCL MS. Add. 205, p. 241 (trust for recusants).

[44] *Themilthorpe's Case* (1605) C, fo. 658v. It seems that the land was potentially bound because it might be subject to execution if the fine was unpaid: *pace* Baker, *Magna Carta*, p. 339, the decree itself did not concern title to land. The controversy over whether the Star Chamber could award damages raised the same issue: ibid. 403–406.

[45] *Russel's Case* (1482) YB Mich. 22 Edw. IV, fo. 37, pl. 21.

[46] It had been cited in *AA*, fo. 207 (tit. 'Conscience'), in the note on *Arundell's Case* (1587) above, p. cxviii, and in *Throckmorton v. Finch* (1597) vol. iv, at p. 800.

role was to give legal advice and representation in the courts, not to thwart the queen's ministers. But, as his predecessor John Popham had shown,[47] and as he had learned from the lips of the queen herself, it was not inconsistent with the role of attorney-general to protect the interests of the queen's subjects against those claiming to act under the queen's authority. Long before his contretemps with James I in 1608,[48] Coke was inspired by Bracton's teaching that the king was under God and the law, since it was the law which made him king.[49] In 1594 he noted that, 'as someone said', the prince ought not only to rule through laws but to conform himself to laws.[50] If the queen ruled only through law, and could not do wrong to her subjects,[51] it followed that all authority exercised under the queen was subject to review by her judges, on her behalf, to ensure that no legal wrong was done in her name.[52] The term 'judicial review' had not yet been invented, but the concept was in place. And it extended beyond administrative acts to the exercise of prerogative jurisdiction and to the validity of commissions and letters patent which granted authority over, or infringed the property interests of, subjects. This had all become common learning in the 1580s, with the revived interest in Magna Carta,[53] though it was traced back to medieval times.[54] What may strike us as remarkable, however, is that the queen's attorney-general was so frequently the supporter and promoter of judicial review rather than the ex officio defender of its targets.

During the 1590s, Coke's notes on such matters focused on the Common Pleas. This may seem anomalous, since the King's Bench under Popham C.J. was wholly in tune with the new learning, and writs of *habeas corpus*, *quo warranto* and prohibition were already in common use there. But the Common Pleas, though

---

[47] See e.g. Popham's argument in *Att.-Gen.* v. *Joiners' Company* (1582) in Baker, *Magna Carta*, p. 468 (tr. 'Every subject born and begotten in the realm has two privileges, one to inherit the inheritance of his father or other ancestor, and the other to inherit the laws of the realm, from which no subject ought to be barred: in confirmation whereof is the statute of Magna Carta, c. 29 ...'). For Popham as Coke's role-model see Smith, *Sir Edward Coke*, p. 21.

[48] *Prohibitions del Roy* (1608) 12 Co. Rep. 63.

[49] The passage is quoted in vol. iii, p. 589 (1594), and also at least twice in the commonplace-books, *AA*, fo. 84v, and *AB*, fo. 495. In *AD*, fo. 801*bis* (98 in pencil), there is a note that the king could not alter a 'rule del ley' without Parliament, because 'le rule del ley overrule toutes ceux et semblable pointes [of the prerogative]'. Note also *AA*, fo. 107v ('Nihil tam proprium est imperii quam legibus vivere'); cit. in 2 Co. Inst. 63.

[50] Vol. iii, p. 590.

[51] *AA*, fo. 78v ('Nota le roy esteant teste de justice ne poet estre fait instrument a faire tort al ascun ou ascun chose encounter ley').

[52] Coke had found this idea also in *Bracton*, fos. 368–369 (iv. 159), cited in *AA*, fos. 102 (pencil), 108 ('Si factum regis fuerit injustum perinde non erit factum regis et disputari potest'); *AB*, fo. 492v. Bracton added a qualification, that the offending deed could only be amended or revoked by the king; but that could perhaps have been reinterpreted as meaning in the court *coram rege* (see the quotation on p. cli, below).

[53] Above, p. cxviii. Coke's continuing interest in Magna Carta, c. 29, is shown by its citation in *Throckmorton* v. *Finch* (1597) vol. iv, p. 799; by his report of *Clarke* v. *Gape* (written in 1599) vol. v, p. 1014; and by his copy (also made in 1599) of a 1340 case in which it was cited: ibid. 1041. For other cases in which he cited c. 29 while Att.-Gen. see Baker, *Magna Carta*, p. 338. In his notes (*AA*, fo. 84) he attributed to c. 29 the presumption that the king will do right to everyone ('Nota le ley intende que le roy ferra droit a toutz ...').

[54] The prime authority was *Sir John atte Lee's Case* (1368) 42 Edw. III, Lib. Ass., pl. 5. At some point Coke also learned of the record in *Peddington* v. *Otteworth* (1406), where the King's Bench disallowed the jurisdiction of Oxford University, granted by royal charter, to decide cases according to the Civil law. In an autograph note on the case (YLS MS. G.R24.1, fo. 190) Coke noted, 'Le graunt le roy fuit voide car il ne poet alter le ley d'Engliterre per chartre ...'.

characteristically conservative in the field of private law, and theoretically restrained in public law by its lack of jurisdiction to award prerogative writs except in cases of privilege,[55] had shown an active interest in personal liberty since the time of Dyer C.J. (1559–1582). The libertarian propensity continued under Anderson C.J. (1582–1605)[56] and his outspokenly conservative colleague Walmsley J. Coke noted several landmark Common Pleas cases in the 1590s, presumably by the report of others. In *Clarke* v. *Gape* (1595) a town bye-law permitting imprisonment by the mayor, though made under the authority of a royal charter, was struck down as contrary to Magna Carta.[57] In *Stepneth* v. *Lloyd* (1598) the court declared, with more conviction than real effect, that the Court of Requests had no legal foundation and no power of arrest.[58] The important case of *Wythers* v. *Rookes* (1598), decided the same year, has resounded down to the present day – thanks to Coke's printed report – as authority for the proposition that a discretionary decision, even when made under statutory authority, is reviewable by the courts. Discretion, wrote Coke (paraphrasing Anderson C.J.), is a science, 'limited and bounded by the rule of law and reason'.[59] And in *Waltham* v. *Austen* (1599) it was held that the king could not grant to a livery company the right to seize defective goods from outsiders.[60] These were not cases of judicial review in the later sense, since they did not involve prerogative writs: the points arose in civil actions of false imprisonment, debt, replevin and trespass respectively. But the jurisdictional restriction did not prevent the Common Pleas from making significant pronouncements in such cases, and it was in effect embarking on judicial review. In 1599, when the court turned its guns on the High Commission, Walmsley J. said it was against Magna Carta for the commissioners to arrest anyone. The court in that case had qualms about granting *habeas corpus*,[61] and in 1601 (as Coke reported) an action of false imprisonment in respect of the same arrest failed because the action was brought by the imprisoned party's father.[62] But in 1600 the

---

[55] Coke set this aside this after he became chief justice: Baker, *Magna Carta*, pp. 354, 384.

[56] Anderson C.J. seems to have been the prime mover behind the judges' memorandum to the queen in 1592 concerning *habeas corpus* and the abuse of imprisonment by councillors: Baker, *Magna Carta*, pp. 167, 496. As a serjeant, he had made the first known connection between *habeas corpus* and Magna Carta, c. 29: ibid. 250.

[57] Vol. v, p. 1014, noted in 1599, when it probably surfaced as a precedent cited in *Davenant* v. *Hurdys* (cf. 5 Co. Rep. 64). Coke says it was a Common Pleas case, but exactly the same point was decided in the King's Bench *against* the same Clarke: *Babb* v. *Clarke* (1595) KB 27/1334, m. 916; Baker, *Magna Carta*, pp. 488–489 (where the two cases are conflated). Magna Carta was cited in both cases. Cf. the report of *Babb* v. *Clarke* in HLS MS 110, fo. 163v (tr. 'Everyone is born a free man and is to have his liberty, and therefore without an offence to the queen … no one may be imprisoned by any private act or bye-law').

[58] Vol. v, p. 950. The following year the Common Pleas relied on Magna Carta, c. 29, in a similar case: Baker, *Magna Carta*, pp. 279–280.

[59] Vol. iv, p. 844; Baker, *English Law under Two Elizabeths*, pp. 110–111. Here the court effectively overturned a decision by commissioners of sewers, acting under a statute.

[60] Vol. v, p. 1007.

[61] *Barham* v. *Denys* (1599) in Baker, *Magna Carta*, p. 290. See especially BL MS. Lansd. 1074, fo. 304 ('Walmsley. What authority have the high commissioners to imprison the body of any man? It is directly against the Magna Charta, *nullus homo etc.*'). This stage of the case was not reported by Coke.

[62] *Barham* v. *Denys* (1601) *C*, fo. 452; CP 40/1632, m. 515 (action by Thomas Barham alleging an imprisonment of his daughter Mary on 12 Feb. 1599, and still continuing on 16 April); there was a verdict for the plaintiff, but a successful motion in arrest of judgment. Mary Barham had been excommunicated for contumacy in a matrimonial cause. In HEHL MS. EL 5898 there is a bond for her appearance, dated 30 Aug. 1599.

authority of the commissioners arose again on a motion for prohibition.[63] Their pursuivant had broken into a house at night, and the plaintiff – an attorney with privilege in the Common Pleas – had been cited for helping constables to rescue the woman they arrested. Although the outcome was again ambivalent, Coke's report is more assertive.[64] According to Coke, the whole court held the woman's imprisonment unlawful, but the report ends with an unexplained annotation that a consultation was later granted. Whatever the reason for that, it was accepted by the court that any new power of imprisonment had to be derived from statute:

> This imprisonment of the subject is not only an injury to the queen but to the subject also ... If such imprisonments as in the case at the bar, by letters missive of the commissioners, were to be lawful, then the subject might be in perpetual prison at the pleasure of the commissioners and would have no ordinary remedy for his deliverance, which would be unacceptable and greatly against the liberty of the subject ...The queen by her letters patent alone cannot alter the course either of the ecclesiastical law or of the common law, for every subject has an inheritance and interest in the laws by which he is governed, and this may not be abrogated, altered or changed except by act of Parliament.

In asserting that the wrongful imprisonment of a subject by a prerogative tribunal was an injury to the queen herself, the court was identifying the essence of the prerogative writs and the key to their success. In another case of 1601, not reported by Coke, Walmsley J. was even prepared to release a prisoner of the Privy Council by *habeas corpus*, saying that chapter 29 of Magna Carta protected the subject even against the king; but his brethren were less bold and found a technical way out.[65]

Coke played no part in those cases, since he was not a serjeant at law. His own involvement in similar cases in the 1590s, though more extensive than his notes suggest, is indicated in MS. *C* only in respect of the *quo warranto* cases which he initiated, and his decision in 1599 to enter a *nolle prosequi* to prevent the enforcement of a fine imposed by the High Commission.[66] In the next reign, however, he began to report cases which emphasised the role of the King's Bench in protecting the subject.[67] The interest reached a new pitch in 1604, when he became involved in a major clash between the King's Bench and Lord Zouche, the autocratic president of the Council in the Marches of Wales.[68]

---

[63] *John Smith's Case* (1600) vol. v, p. 1048.

[64] Cf. Robert Cawdrye's case, to which Coke was to devote a lengthy discourse in 1605: *Cawdrye v. Atton* (1595) KB 27/1316, m. 340; vol. iii, p. 617; 5 Co. Rep., part 1; Smith, *Sir Edward Coke*, pp. 190–193; Baker, *Magna Carta*, pp. 141–143, 295–296. This was an action of trespass.

[65] *Bate's Case* (1601) LI MS. Maynard 66, fo. 143; BL MS. Lansd. 1058, fo. 13v; Baker, *English Law under Two Elizabeths*, pp. 49–50. Bate had claimed privilege as a Common Pleas litigant, but the court found that he had made himself a litigant collusively. The judges had agreed collectively in 1591 that they would not release someone imprisoned by order of the queen or the Privy Council: 1 And. 297; Baker, *Magna Carta*, pp. 166–8, 495–9. The original memorial of 1591, signed in autograph by all the judges (including Walmsley J.), is in the Burghley papers, BL MS. Lansd. 68(87).

[66] *R. v. Atmere* (1599) vol. v, p. 1045.

[67] E.g. in *Snowe v. Beverley* (1603) *C*, fos. 537v–544 (4 Co. Rep. 123) he moved for a prohibition to the Court of Requests on the ground that no relief could be given in equity contrary to an express rule of law (in this case concerning the defence of insanity); and in *Needham v. Price* (1605) Baker, *Magna Carta*, p. 296, he moved successfully for *habeas corpus* and a prohibition against the High Commission.

[68] For more detail see Baker, *Magna Carta*, pp. 303–311.

The initial issue was the geographical extent of the Council's jurisdiction, and this was brought before the Privy Council at Westminster in 1604. Francis Bacon K.C. argued in favour of Zouche's pretensions to exercise jurisdiction in the nearest English counties, saying that it was based on the royal prerogative, and if that were to be shaken the repercussions would affect all other conciliar courts and courts of equity. But Coke Att.-Gen. responded, with success, that the Council's encroachment into the English counties was contrary to Magna Carta and the common law, and could if necessary be restrained by prohibition.[69] This setback did not immediately curb Lord Zouche, who had ordered the arrest of one of the parties and ignored a writ of *habeas corpus* from the King's Bench. There ensued what Coke called the 'great case between the King's Bench and the Lord Zouche'.[70] In the course of it, Coke wrote a treatise on chapter 29 of Magna Carta, which settled the principles in his own mind but was not published until 2015. The heavily annotated text in MS. *C*, under Michaelmas term 1604,[71] began with an eloquent encomium of the statute:

> Everything that anyone has in this world, or that concerns the freedom of his body or his freehold, or the benefit of the law to which he is inheritable, or his native country in which he was born, or the preservation of his reputation or goods, or his life, blood and posterity: to all these things this Act extends. Now, suppose someone is taken (by whatever person) and sent to prison without lawful warrant, or detained contrary to law, what remedy shall the aggrieved party have? [The principal remedy] is to move the judges of the King's Bench and inform them of the truth of the cause, and thereupon obtain a *habeas corpus cum causa*, and if he was imprisoned contrary to the statute of Magna Carta and the other statutes, then the judges must discharge him from his unlawful imprisonment. The court of King's Bench may do this even though the aggrieved party has no privilege there,[72] by virtue of the said Acts.

The treatise then descended into recondite detail, full of manuscript precedents gathered from the plea rolls and the controlment rolls of the clerk of the crown.[73] It is an early example of the marshalling of record material to support a constitutional argument, a technique which was to become familiar over the next two decades. In Easter term 1605, when the matter came before the King's Bench on a second *habeas corpus*, Coke, 'being present in court when this cause was moved, prayed the justices to give him their patience to hear him speak a little for the king's prerogative, the jurisdiction of the court, and the benefit of all the king's subjects. The judges attended to him seriously, and he began':[74]

> Some men learned in the laws of this land today have privately delivered their opinion that when a subject is committed to prison by a member of the king's Privy Council, or by the

---

[69] *C*, fo. 634 (617 in pencil) (Mich. 1604); tr. in Baker, *Magna Carta*, p. 307; abridged in 4 Co. Inst. 242. The matter began with the writ of prohibition in *Farley* v. *Holder* (Trin. 1604) BL MS. Lansd. 1113, fo. 38v; MS. Add. 25244, fos. 5–33, 74–83v. See also *Cecil Papers*, xvi. 412.

[70] *C*, fo. 621 ('un graund case inter le banke le roy et le Segnior Zouch, president del councel de Gales'). Cf. *C*, fo. 634 ('le grand case del Segnior Souche, president de Gales').

[71] *C*, fos. 617–621v (600–604v in pencil) (quotation tr. with some silent omissions); printed in 132 Selden Soc. 394–402 (French and English); annotated translation in Baker, *Magna Carta*, pp. 500–510. Coke cited it in *AD*, f. 238 ('Vide 2 Jac. 617, bone matter sur lestatut de Magna Carta').

[72] Cf. above, p. cxviii.

[73] It may be recalled that he had been furnished with some of these in the 1580s: ibid.

[74] *Whetherley* v. *Whetherley* (1605) BL MS. Lansd. 1075, fos. 101v–103v, tr. in Baker, *Magna Carta*, at p. 512. On this case see also P. Halliday, *Habeas Corpus: From England to Empire* (Cambridge, Mass., 2010), pp. 11–14, 338. It was not reported in *C*.

Council in the Marches of Wales, the Council of York, or the like, this court of King's Bench has no power to send a *habeas corpus* for the person who is thus committed; and they allege that there is no book, or law in writing, which proves such a jurisdiction to exist in this court. But he said that this was a great error, and that there *is* a written law which proves it. This is the statute of Magna Charta, chapter 29, which is a positive law in force at this day ... All courts of justice within the king's dominions are subordinate, this court alone excepted, in which the king is always presumed by law to be present and which is restrained to no place but extends to all his dominions; and therefore this court alone shall have the examination of all the other courts of justice.[75] Even if the king gives authority by his commission to some person to execute justice, or the law does so by act of Parliament, nevertheless the examination thereof, as to what may be done by such authority, must remain in the absolute and supreme power of the king, that is, in his bench, which is the proper seat of justice. And although there are no law reports to be found to prove this, yet he said that he had by search found infinite precedents to prove the continual use of it.

Popham C.J. responded that the court strongly approved of everything he had said, and eventually Lord Zouche and his minions were forced to obey the *habeas corpus*. The Council's commission was subsequently reformed, and in 1607 Zouche resigned. Although none of these reports was printed, the case must count as a landmark in the history of the rule of law. And the unpublished reports show that the decisive groundwork was done by Coke, not as chief justice (though more was to follow) but as the king's attorney-general. As he was at pains to emphasise in the 1605 case, the learning was not new;[76] but he was appropriating it for the king. He had addressed the court '*for* the king's prerogative', not against it, and shown that the judicial surveillance of powers and authorities within the realm was not an assault on the prerogative – as Francis Bacon had represented it – but an exercise of the royal prerogative through the king's own bench. Once again, this was an exposition of the philosophical basis for judicial review, calculated to satisfy even King James's concept of monarchy. Indeed, the final determination, confirming the jurisdiction of the King's Bench, was reputedly made by King James himself.[77]

There are various lesser matters of public law to be found in MS. *C*. For instance, the ownership and status of the Isle of Man raised questions about the effect of annexing territory to the crown by conquest.[78] The queen's death in 1603 occasioned reflections on the demise of the crown, and the principle that the king never dies.[79] The union of the crowns of England and Scotland raised some vexed legal questions

---

[75] Cf. *Trott* v. *Taylor* (Hil. 1605) CUL MS. Ii.5.26, fo. 227v, *per* Coke Att.-Gen. (tr. 'The Court of King's Bench has power to control any court which proceeds out of course or which meddles with things which do not belong to them, as if the Court of Common Bench would proceed contrary to Magna Carta; and likewise of the Exchequer, the Cinque Ports, or another court of equity'). A prohibition was there awarded, on Coke's motion, against the Court of Requests.

[76] Much the same argument for the supremacy of the King's Bench had been made by Catlyn C.J. (d. 1574), though we have only a brief report of what he said: Baker, *Magna Carta*, p. 159.

[77] 2 Rolle Abr. 69, line 23 ('sur grand controversie'). Rolle did not enter the Inner Temple until 1609, and so must have gathered this by hearsay.

[78] Vol. iv, p. 667 (1596); vol. iv, pp. 880, 886 (1598).

[79] *C*, fo. 570v. See also 'Souldiers' (1601) *C*, fo. 501 ('cest parol roy include tout son succession, car le roy ne morust in respect de son politique capacitie'); *R.* v. *Watson and Clark* (1604) 7 Co. Rep. 10–11; 3 Co. Inst. 7. William Watson and William Clark, Jesuit conspirators in the Bye Plot, had argued that James was not king until he had been crowned, and that there was no law until forty days thereafter: JHB MS. 2496, fos. 45v–47 (memorandum book of Anthony Kynnersley JP Staffs.). This was a wide rumour in 1603: *Cecil Papers*, xvi. 38 (concerning Carr, a lawyer in prison at Norwich).

with which Coke was actively concerned, though they left only brief traces in his reports. Within a year, the status of *post-nati* was under consideration,[80] and a judicial decision as to the name of King James's conjoined kingdom was noted by Coke in a detached autograph note:[81]

> Note, in Trinity term [1603] in the first year of King James, the question concerning the point of law was referred to the judges, and they resolved that the name could not be changed to Great Britain in legal proceedings ... This was the resolution of all the judges, *nullo contradicente*, and thereupon see the proclamation ('except judicial proceedings'): Egerton *in contraria (et absurda) opinione*.

This brief report shows that Coke, who had followed in Egerton's footsteps as solicitor-general and attorney-general, was already in 1603 beginning to find some of his constitutional positions 'absurd'.[82]

These were significant and troublesome cases, but Coke did not think it politic to publish them. He stirred up enough trouble with those that he did print.[83] They naturally catch our interest today; and yet matters of state do not dominate the later reports in MS. *C*. A law officer was not expected to give up his private practice, and Coke maintained his until he became a judge in 1606. That aspect of his work is amply reflected in the range of cases he reported on all manner of topics in which he was involved or which caught his attention. Before considering the most important of those cases, which concerned the Statutes of Uses and Wills, some attention should be paid to the topic of statute-law in general.

(f) Statutory interpretation

Over a third of the cases in this edition turned on the interpretation of statutes, and one of them contains the original version of what was to become the best-known formulation of the 'mischief rule'.[84] It was a topic of increasing practical importance as statutes grew in number and complexity, and in 1602 Coke went so far as to write that the greatest questions in law arose not upon the rules of the common law but on the interpretation of acts of Parliament 'overladen with provisos and additions, and many times on a sudden penned or corrected by men of none or very little judgment in law.'[85]

---

[80] *C*, fo. 589 (1604). It was to be fully debated, after Coke's appointment to the bench, in *Calvin's Case* (1607) 7 Co. Rep., part 1; Moo. 790.

[81] YLS MS. G.R24.1, fo. 149v, margin (tr.). When he drew the patent for Prince Charles to be duke of York in 1605, Coke took exception to his being described as 'Charles of Scotland': *Cecil Papers*, xvii. 4.

[82] Cf. the list of Ellesmere's absurd opinions which he began to compile a few years later: below, p. clxix, n. 97.

[83] See Ellesmere's 'Observations upon the Lord Coke's Reports' (1616) in *Law and Politics in Jacobean England: The Tracts of Lord Chancellor Ellesmere*, ed. L. A. Knafla (1977), pp. 297–318; Baker, *Magna Carta*, pp. 90, 314, 397–398, 435.

[84] *Heydon's Case* (1584) vol. ii, p. 253, at p. 254, *per* Manwood C.B.

[85] *Le Second Part des Reportes* (1602), sig. v verso. The remedy, he said, was that 'if Acts of Parliament were after the old fashion penned, and by such only as perfectly knew what the common law was ... then should very few questions in law arise, and the learned should not so often and so much perplex their heads to make atonement and peace by construction of law between insensible and disagreeing words, sentences and provisos, as they now do.' In *C*, fos. 585v–586, he noted in 1604 that bills in Parliament were often preferred by men unlearned in the law and sometimes passed without being seen by the judges.

It was as much a case-law subject as the common law. The statute-books contained the letter of the text, but (in cases of difficulty) only the law reports contained 'the true and genuine sense and construction of such statutes and Acts of Parliament as were from time to time made and enacted'.[86] The subject had been a particular interest of Plowden's, whose *Commentaries* contained several influential pronouncements on the general principles, apparently culled from the arguments of judges and counsel. Partly inspired by Plowden, at least four treatises were written on statutes in the later Elizabeth period, and the densely filled title 'Statutes' in Coke's commonplace-book – written before the 1579 edition of Plowden, but updated with references to it – had the makings of a fifth.[87] Coke liked the metaphor in Plowden that every statute consisted of two parts, the words and the sense; the former was the body, whereas the latter was the life and the soul.[88] Finding the sense was a matter of 'equity', in the Aristotelian meaning of the word which had been current among lawyers long before it was appropriated by the Chancery. But the writers all concluded that it is not in the nature of equity to be reducible to rules and precepts, especially since the equitable interpretation of a statute – that is, the true sense, or the supposed legislative intention[89] – might sometimes be at odds with the words.[90] It could only be illustrated, with strings of examples from the reports. Most of the examples concerned broadly worded medieval statutes, which had traditionally been expounded in a generous way if they were considered generally beneficial.[91] This was justified by an expansive application of the mischief rule, which enabled cases falling within the same mischief as that addressed, though not mentioned in the words, to be treated as if they were within the statute.[92] A classical example was that of the statute which made the warden of the Fleet prison liable to creditors for the escape of debtors from his custody; this had been interpreted to extend to all gaolers, for the benefit of creditors in general.[93] That was an extreme case, but the principle was still current in a weaker form. For instance, a

---

[86] *Le Tierce Part des Reportes* (1602), sig. C.ij.

[87] *AD*, fos. 804v–813v (including 'Equitie'). For the other four treatises, none of which was published in the Tudor period, see Baker, *English Law under two Elizabeths*, p. 98–99. Fleetwood, a fellow bencher of Plowden's in the Middle Temple, had composed the first draft of his treatise before the publication of the *Commentaries*.

[88] *AD*, fo. 810, derived from *Eyston* v. *Studde* (1574) Plowd. 463, at pp. 465–467. Cf. *AD*, fo. 807v, where another reference to the case is signalled as 'optime'. (He noted the case himself, sub nom. *Latton's Case*, but without reference to the principles of interpretation: no. 51, below). He also cited *Stowell* v. *Lord Zouche* (1574) Plowd. 353, which contains much discussion of statutory interpretation.

[89] For the interrelationship of the three concepts of equity, legislative intention, and the 'mischief rule', see Baker, *English Law under two Elizabeths*, pp. 96–105.

[90] See *AD*, fos. 808v ('Equities contra as parols …'), 809v ('Lentent des fesors destre prise ascun foitz encounter les parolx …'), 811v ('Entent prise encounter les parolx …').

[91] *AD*, fo. 807v, citing YB Mich. 14 Edw. IV, fo. 1, pl. 1, *per* Billing C.J. (tr. 'when an Act is made for the common profit of the realm it shall be interpreted broadly (*largement*)').

[92] E.g. *AD*, fo. 808v, abridging YB Mich. 11 Hen, VI, fo. 3, pl. 8, at fo. 4 (tr. 'inasmuch as the lesser mischief is remedied by the statute, the greater shall always be included in the same remedy'); ibid. 810, abridging YB Hil. 11 Hen. IV, fo. 45, pl. 20, at fo. 47 (tr. 'it is to be considered in the construction of statutes what mischief was at common law before the making of the statute, and such a case as is in like mischief shall be within the same remedy even though it is not expressed in the statute').

[93] *AD*, fo. 813v; *Platt's Case* (1550) Plowd. 35; Bro. Abr., *Escape*, pl. 9; Baker, *English Law under Two Elizabeths*, pp. 106–108. Another example cited by Coke (*AD*, fo. 806) was YB Hil. 14 Hen. VII, fo. 17, pl. 7, where a statute referring to actions of formedon in remainder was held to extend to a *scire facias* to execute a remainder in tail created by fine, since it fell within the same mischief.

remainder in use was held to be within the equity of the jointure provisions of the Statute of Uses, though not explicitly mentioned, on the footing that the instances given in the statute were intended as examples rather than as an exhaustive definition.[94] And in 1585 a fifteenth-century statute concerning bonds taken by sheriffs was held to extend to oral promises, because a statute extending to a greater mischief would necessarily apply also to a lesser.[95] But the scope of equity was seriously curtailed by the elaborate draftsmanship of modern statutes, with preambles setting out the legislative intention and specific provisions for different eventualities. There are very few cases in Coke's Elizabethan reports which refer explicitly to the equity of a statute. The general principle was to stick to the letter: *A verbis legis non est recedendum*.[96] Although statutes could in theory be extended by equity even when they restricted the common law,[97] a statute which undid someone's inheritance was supposed to be taken strictly,[98] and so, perhaps, was any 'particular' statute.[99] Statutes could not readily be set aside or restricted on grounds of equity. Parliament could in law do anything,[1] because it represented the body of the whole kingdom,[2] and therefore in the absence of ambiguity its every word was law. The one limitation was that it could not alter facts, and therefore it could not bring about the impossible.[3] For the same reason, it could not enact two inconsistent things at the same time, and so an inconsistent minor part could be rejected as repugnant to the whole. Another useful principle of interpretation was that Parliament could not be supposed to have intended its words to have absurd consequences, since that could only be true if the members of Parliament were stupid.[4]

---

[94] *Vernon* v. *Vernon* (1573) below, p. 75, *per* Mounson J. Here there was an analogy with the Statute *De Donis*, which gave illustrations of different kinds of entail but was not treated as excluding others: Litt., s. 21; Plowd. 251; *AD*, fo. 806. See also *Gravenor* v. *Tedd* (1593) vol. iii, p. 546, where Coke argued that 'great absurdity would follow' if copyholds were not held to be within *De Donis*.

[95] *Denby* v. *Heathcott* (1585) vol. ii, p. 275, *per* Wray C.J.

[96] *Edrich's Case* (1603) 5 Co. Rep. 118 (tr. 'One must not depart from the words of the statute'). Coke was here reversing the maxim of Roman law, that departure from the words is permissible when equity so requires.

[97] *AD*, fo. 809. But cf. the next note.

[98] *AD*, fo. 810. This was applied in *Wiseman's Case* (1583) vol. ii, p. 228, where it was held that the Statute of Wills 1540 could not be extended by equity, because it was a revenue statute which 'goes in abridgment of the common law and imposes a charge on the inheritance'. See also Baker, *English Law under two Elizabeths*, pp. 102–103.

[99] *AD*, fo. 807v, citing YB Mich. 14 Edw. IV, fo. 1, pl. 1, *per* Billing C.J. By 'particular', Billing C.J. was not referring to the level of detail in a statute but to its scope, since he was drawing a contrast with statutes made 'for the common profit of the realm'.

[1] *Englefield's Case* (1591) vol. iii, p. 445, *per* Manwood CB ('Parliamentum omnia potest'). The Latin maxim echoed the canonists' *Papa omnia potest*.

[2] *AD*, fo. 805, abridging YB Pas. 39 Edw. III, fo. 7. This meant that a statute bound everyone even if it was not publicly proclaimed, because the law would presume that everyone was party to it. It also meant that a statute arguably did not bind tenants in ancient demesne, because they were not represented in Parliament: *AD*, fo. 805, abridging YB Pas. 7 Hen. VI, fo. 35, pl. 39.

[3] *AD*, fos. 806 ('Un act covient estre expound que poet estre possible'), 807v ('Lex non cogit ad impossibilia'). Coke said in 1597 that Parliament could not make a man a woman: Proc. Parl., iii. 236.

[4] See e.g. *Goring's Case* (1600) vol. v, p. 1087, *per* Coke Att.-Gen. (tr.: '… that would be absurd and inconvenient, and therefore it was never intended by the makers of the Act'). The principle was turned against an equitable interpretation in *Dillon* v. *Freine* (1594) 1 And. 309, at fo. 336 (tr. 'It is inappropriate in expounding a statute by equity to maintain that which no wise or honest Parliament man could have said, for that is nothing other than saying that those of the Parliament at the time of making the Act were out of their minds').

This explained how a statute could be expounded contrary to the words when the text was 'contrary to all reason',[5] and how a saving in a statute could be void for absurdity or repugnancy.[6] These principles of impossibility, repugnancy and absurdity, as noted by Coke in the Elizabethan period, would be drawn together in his famous declaration in 1610 that the common law would control acts of Parliament 'and sometimes adjudge them utterly void'.[7]

(g) *Chudleigh's Case*

Some notice should next be taken of a leading case involving Coke which, strangely, is not in MS. *C*. The absence of *Shelley's Case* from the notebooks has already been considered.[8] An even more remarkable omission is *Dillon* v. *Freine*, better known as *Chudleigh's Case*,[9] which was one of the great cases on uses chosen (with *Shelley's Case*) for inclusion in the first printed volume of the *Reports* in 1600. The case arose from the same family settlement as *Chudleigh* v. *Dyer*,[10] which Coke had argued in 1586 but did not report – presumably because the parties settled. The circumstances behind the settlement are revealed in a manuscript in the Bodleian Library:[11]

> Afterwards, in Trinity term [1586], her majesty being apprised by divers of the Privy Council that she stood to lose many privileges and prerogatives, and that many purchasers' titles depended on the same difficulty, she thought it best to let the sleeping dog lie (*de ne muer le chien dormant*) and sent to Sir Christopher Hatton, chancellor, and Sir Francis Walsingham, secretary, to effect an agreement between the parties.

The parties duly agreed to the award made by Hatton and Walsingham; but the dog was not allowed to sleep for long. John Chudleigh, the real plaintiff in the ejectment, died in 1589, and a new action was commenced that year by a feoffee of other lands held by the same title.[12] The 'difficulty' which worried the queen and her councillors

---

[5] *Fulmerston* v. *Steward* (1554) Plowd. 102, at fo. 110; cited in *AD*, fo. 807v.

[6] *Stroud's Case* (1574) Dyer 313 (saving clause disregarded 'propter absurditatem'); cited in *AD*, fo. 808v ('void'). The four other reports of this case now in print make no mention of absurdity or of being 'void': 1 And. 45; 3 Leon. 58; 4 Leon. 40; Benl. 237. Cf. Plowden's argument in *Walsingham's Case* (1573) Plowd. 552, at fo. 565 (tr. 'which proviso and saving served to please many of the ignorant patentees who were members of that Parliament, but in fact it was utterly void ... and he said it was a flattering proviso, which served to make fools merry [i.e. content]'). Coke cited this in his argument in *The Case of Alton Woods* (1600) vol. v, at p. 1072.

[7] *Bonham's Case* (1610) *E*, fo. 93v; 8 Co. Rep. 114. For commentary on this case see Baker, *Magna Carta*, p. 90, and the citations there.

[8] See above, p. cii.

[9] The name Chudleigh was frequently spelt Chidley, and presumably so pronounced.

[10] *Chudleigh* v. *Dyer* (1584–86) KB 27/1292, m. 714; BL MS. Lansd. 1067, fos. 136–140v (Hil. 1586; arguments by Egerton and Coke); MS. Lansd. 1072, fos. 201–207, 211–225; MS. Harg. 37, fos. 149–153; CUL MS. Dd.11.64, fo. 1; MS. Hh.2.1, fos. 83–87v (arguments by Tanfield and Coke); B. & M. 170, n. 30. The record shows that the suit was commenced in Mich. 1584 and tried before Peryam J. in Lent 1585; the jury found a special verdict, and there are continuances for advisement to Pas. 1586.

[11] Bodl. Lib. MS. Rawlinson C.85, fo. 180 (tr.).

[12] *Dillon* v. *Freine*, or *Chudleigh's Case* (1594) 1 Co. Rep. 113; KB 27/1308, m. 65; B. & M. 169. Coke referred to it in 1597 as 'le graund case inter Dillon et Freine': *C*, fo. 203v; vol. iv, p. 763. The reports in 1 And. 309 and Poph. 70, and some of the manuscripts, are confined to the judges' speeches in the Exchequer Chamber. The case concerned land in Tawstock, Devon, whereas the 1584 case had concerned land in Pelynt, Corn.

was the vexed question of the validity of perpetuities created by means of contingent uses.[13] It was a difficulty which could not be suppressed by private settlements. The new case was tried at Exeter assizes in 1589 and argued by Coke on at least five occasions in 1591, 1593 and 1594.[14] Coke's initial argument fell within the period of the missing third notebook, but it seems unlikely that it was reported in any substantial way there; if it had been, there would surely have been cross-references to it. The omission from the notebooks calls for some explanation, given its importance and Coke's keen commitment to the eradication of perpetuities. The most likely reason is that – as with *Shelley's Case*, and *Mildmay* v. *Standish* (1585) – Coke kept substantial notes of his arguments in the case elsewhere.[15]

Coke's involvement as counsel in *Chudleigh's Case* no doubt explains his choice of the Statute of Uses for the Inner Temple reading of 1592, when the case was pending.[16] At the beginning of the reading he said he had chosen the statute because:[17]

> no one thing tended so much to the subversion of the ancient common laws of this realm as feoffments and other estates made to secret and subtle uses[18] ... A matter so necessary for every professor of the law (such and so many difficulties and questions falling out upon perpetuities and conveyances to uses) as the knowledge of many others is not comparable to the right understanding of this one. Infinite inconveniences shall follow and increase in the commonwealth if this statute be not rightly expounded and construed.

He began his argument in court in a similar way, and gave an account of the peculiar nature of uses:[19]

---

[13] Coke referred to 'those conveyances called perpetuities' in *Degore* v. *Rowe* (1592) vol. iii, p. 484. A devise which tended to a perpetuity had been challenged in *Price* v. *Jones* (Hil. 1593) CUL MS. Ii.5.16, fo. 214v. Rather oddly, 'Wynter opened le case mes ne argue, car il dit que il ne conust coment de comencer de arguer'. Popham C.J. stepped in to help him, but the case was adjourned. Wynter did not proceed far in the profession. For perpetuity clauses see below, pp. clix–clxviii.

[14] CUL MS. Ii.5.12, fos. 81–85 (Wyatt and Coke, Hil, Pas. 1591 and Hil. 1594); MS. Ii.5.16, fos. 44 (Fleming, Glanville and Wyatt, Mich. 1590), 61 (Wyatt, Fleming and Coke, Hil. 1591) and 282–289 (Wyatt and Coke, Hil. 1594); BL MS. Harley 6745, fos. 23–26 (sim.); HLS MS. 110, fos. 71v–74v (Wyatt and Coke, Trin. 1593); MS. 1060 (1080), fos. 31v–32v (Exch. Cha., 4 May 1594). These reports corroborate Coke's statement that his opponent in 1594 was Hugh Wyatt. Cf. BL MS. Harley 1059, fo. 121v, with 'mon argument' (unidentified) for the plaintiff, seemingly in Hil. 1593. The judges' arguments are in LI MS. Maynard 63(1), p. 36. The report in Lancs. Record Office, DDSH15/17, is reputed to have been Popham's own. There is also a brief report by Clench in BL MS. Harley 4556, fo. 44 (Trin. 1591).

[15] See above, p. cvii. *Throckmorton* v. *Finch* (1597) was copied into MS. *C* from a separate 'book': above, p. cxliii. For a lost volume of Coke's arguments at the bar see above, pp. xcvii–xcviii.

[16] He also had experience of the debate in Parliament. A bill was presented in 1593, during Coke's speakership, to restrain perpetuities, though it did not become law: Proc. Parl., iii. 117; Smith, *Sir Edward Coke*, p. 33. Another was introduced in 1597: W. S. Holdsworth, 'An Elizabethan Bill Against Perpetuities' (1919) 35 LQR 258.

[17] Co. Uses, fo. 136v. Note also *Finch* v. *Finch* (1597) BL MS. Harg. 51, fo. 139v, *per* Glanville sjt (tr.: 'Mr Savill, a grave and learned man, was wont to say that if the judges did not well heed the constructions of this statute, a thousand more mischiefs would follow from its making than there were at common law').

[18] It was for this reason that Coke disliked powers of revocation and variation in settlements, which he described as 'new inventions and fooleries': *Earl of Shrewsbury's Case* (1597) vol. iv, p. 755. See also *Sir Thomas Gresham's Case* (1588) CUL MS. Gg.2.5, fo. 302; *Littleton's Case* (1602) *C*, fo. 529v; *Countess of Rutland* v. *Earl of Rutland* (1604) ibid., fos. 603–604v; *Frampton* v. *Frampton* (1604) ibid., fos. 605v–607; Moo. 1020; cit. 10 Co. Rep. 144. An anonymous writer of 1602 complained that 'you may by this doctrine alter the freehold of the land every hour in a corner': BL MS. Lansd. 216, fo. 61. The parol revocation of wills raised similar problems: *Butler* v. *Baker* (1591) 3 Co. Rep. 25, at fo. 36.

[19] BL MS. Harley 6745, fo. 24 (tr.); HLS MS. 110, fo. 72v (same report). For this reading see also above, pp. cxvi, cxxvii. Coke had collected much material on uses in *AD*, fos. 761–766, 829–832.

He said he would not put any case but cases of uses, because in the law a use has no fellow.[20] First, it is to be seen what thing a use is at common law. And, as appears in the case of Dalamere and Barnard,[21] it is a trust and confidence reposed in the terre-tenant to the use of the feoffor, for he does not have *jus in re* or *ad rem*, nor is there any remedy at common law except a subpoena in the Chancery.[22] He also said that there are various kinds of uses: uses *in esse* and uses in contingency. Uses *in esse* are of three kinds, in possession, reversion and remainder. A use in contingency is a thing in expectancy, and *in futuro*. And he said that uses in contingency could have been discontinued before the statute ...

He ended with a characteristically surly attack on uses and perpetuities in general:[23]

As to what has been said that the common law magnifies and conserves uses in the bosom of the law (*in gremio legis*), the law does not do that; for a use is a viper, and a destruction of the common law, and if it were so the common law would keep a viper in its bosom. But before the present time statutes were always construed strongly against uses ... He also said that perpetuities have always been confuted by the law ...

The following term, the case was argued on the same side by Francis Bacon in the Exchequer Chamber. Coke was not there to hear the argument. It was just as well, because it was a tour-de-force and clearly outshone his own. Indeed, it made Bacon's name.[24] Bacon had been called to the bar in 1582, four years after Coke, and although he had been made a bencher and a reader before Coke, out of deference to his father, he had not been in evidence in Westminster Hall before 1593.[25] But the mark he made in *Chudleigh's Case* was directly responsible for the introduction of the rank of queen's counsel for his benefit – or, rather, to prevent him from using his talents against the crown – later in the year.[26]

---

[20] This figure was quoted by Bacon in his reading (1600): *The Learning Reading of Francis Bacon ... upon the Statute of Uses* (1642), p. 9 ('Coke, solicitor, entering into his argument of *Chudleigh's Case*, said sharply and fitly, "I will put never a case but shall be of a use, for a use in law hath no fellow", meaning that the learning of uses is not to be matched with other learnings').

[21] *Delamere* v. *Bernard* (1567) Plowd. 346.

[22] Cf. *Lord Paget's Case* (1591) vol. iii, p. 410, where it is said that, before the statute, uses were only 'a charge upon the land in conscience', whereas the statute had made cestui que use a 'complete owner'.

[23] BL MS. Harley 6745, fo. 26 (tr.). In another version he is reported as saying: 'A use is nothing in law but a trust (*confidence*) reposed in the feoffee, for cestui que use does not have *jus in re* or *ad rem* ... a use is not something which the law respects but is abhorred in law, for uses were made by fear or fraud to deceive others ...': BL MS. Harg. 7A, fo. 42 (tr.). Cf. *The Learned Reading of Francis Bacon*, p. 17 (modernised): 'Coke, in his reading, doth say well that they were produced sometimes for fear and many times for fraud; but I hold that neither of these cases were so much the reasons of uses as another reason in the beginning, which was that lands by the common law of England were not testamentary ...'. In 1598 Coke argued that it was because uses were of no account in law that they could pass without writing: *Corbyn* v. *Corbyn* (1598) BL MS. Lansd. 1084, fo. 139 ('per common ley de antiquo uses fueront solement choses restant en confidence enter homes et de nul estimation ou accompt in lei quant as estates ... et issint ne besoyn daver escripture de eux passer').

[24] See D. R. Coquillette, *Francis Bacon* (1992), pp. 128–136; L. Jardine and A. Stewart, *Hostage to Fortune* (1998), pp. 156–158; Boyer, *Coke and the Elizabethan Age*, pp. 120–124; *The Oxford Francis Bacon*, i: *Early Writings 1584–1596*, ed. A. Stewart (2012), pp. 452–455.

[25] He argued against Coke in *Harvey* d. *Brett* v. *Facey* (Hil. 1594) BL MS. Harley 6745, fos. 29–30; CUL MS. Ll.3.9, fo. 389v (where Bacon is misspelt as 'Baker'); vol. iv, p. 725. This must be the 'most famous Checker Chamber case', on which Anthony Bacon wrote to his mother in Feb. 1594: Jardine and Stewart, *Hostage to Fortune*, p. 157. Bacon's unsuccessful argument in 1593 in *Yelverton* v. *Yelverton* is noted in MS. Harley 6745, fo. 132v (cf. vol. iii, p. 578). Coke reported both cases but did not mention Bacon.

[26] Bacon was not promoted when Coke became Att.-Gen. in April, having had such a slender practice. But the queen agreed to him being one of her 'learned counsel extraordinary, without patent or fee': *Letters and Life of Francis Bacon*, ed. J. Spedding and others, vol. vii (1874), p. 168. He was admitted to move

Bacon's speech began with some praise of his leader, more faint than real, in which he contrived to hint that the previous arguments had strayed from the point:[27]

> The cause, being of great importance touching her majesty in prerogative and the subject in assurance, was of this side argued notably and declared by Mr Attorney-General, who, foreseeing the downfall and destruction of these uses that have so long reigned, made an history of their lives and ripped them up from their cradle in shewing that they were engendered, nursed and ripened[28] in fraud and deceit, and in manifesting the note and discredit that divers good laws from time to time have inflicted upon them. Which course I do not intend to pursue, but the matter thereof is good and pertinent, but that seconding such a man should make the same worse. Neither will I in confutation bind myself to Mr Atkinson's order,[29] but pursue my own course, which is the order that the matter itself doth induce, as best for the resolution and decision. It shall suffice that nothing material is objected but shall be answered, and that which is ponderous shall be expressly refuted, the other of less importance I will shake off in the course of my argument … then, having made the statute clear, or at least favourably ambiguous for me, I will then capitulate the multitude of inconveniences which those springing uses daily set afoot in the state of the government. For as no expediency ought to cause the judges to swerve from the truth of the law when it is express and direct, so *in ambiguis eam sequamur interpretationem quae vitio caret*.

Later on, he became more directly critical of Coke's argument:[30]

> And I confess when I heard Mr Attorney argue so strongly out of the preamble, I objected in myself that it was but a *fallax*, and that it was the equivocation of the word 'use'. For the word 'use' against which this statute and others inveigh signifieth a thing which stands by itself divided and severed from the possession, which was the cause of the mischief and fraud; but now since this statute is no such matter, it resteth only in easy conveyance, but the use severed is merely extinct. And for that this objection is colourable, that these statutes and others more ancient intended only severed uses, it behoveth to examine and review if all the mischiefs that this statute recites of uses cannot be extended and verified of contingent uses …

> I am not of Mr Attorney's mind that upon a feoffment to use at this day all strangers' rights are gone, but I conceive he said that *in terrorem* to be more vehement against uses …

> And [as] to that which hath been objected that the use is in preservation of law, and that nothing is in the feoffees, it is true that the use is preserved by the law, but [it is] not executed by the statute before the time, and then it appears by evident demonstration that an interest abides in the feoffees …[31]

---

within the bar in Nov. 1594: BL MS. Harley 1697, fo. 43 ('Bacon de Greys Inne, esteant admitted de mover deins le barre …'); MS. Harg. 50, fo. 97v ('le darreigne jour del terme Mr Bacon de Grayes Inne vient deins le barre et demaund le opinion del court …').

[27] BL MS. Harley 6745, fos. 59–67 (English text, here modernised). There is a less complete law French version in BL MS. Lansd. 1121, fos. 112–120v; printed (tr. only) in *Letters and Life of Francis Bacon*, ed. J. Spedding, vii. 617–636; and with parallel texts in *The Oxford Francis Bacon*, i: *Early Writings 1584–1596*, ed. A. Stewart (2012), pp. 460–497 ('the only known text'). The English version is generally superior to the French text behind the Oxford edition.

[28] The manuscript reads 'rightened', but this is probably a slip for 'ripened': cf. *Romans* 8:32. The words 'nursed and rightened' are not in the French version.

[29] Robert Atkinson had argued for the plaintiff in the Exchequer Chamber.

[30] BL MS. Harley 6745, fos. 63, 64v, 65. Cf. *The Oxford Francis Bacon*, i. 474, 480, 484.

[31] I.e. what Dyer C.J. had termed the *scintilla juris*: *Brent's Case* (1575) Dyer 340; B. & M. 162. Coke noted with amusement Peryam C.B.'s remark in *Chudleigh's Case* that the *scintilla juris* was 'like Sir Thomas More's *Utopia*', i.e. a figment of the imagination: 1 Co. Rep. 120 at fo. 132 ('semblable a Sir Thomas Moores Eutopia'); B. & M. 171.

Between them the arguments succeeded, and judgment was given for the defendant in Hilary term 1595. It was the beginning of the end for perpetuity clauses, and Bacon hailed it in 1600 as the first true exposition of the Statute of Uses.[32] But it must have been galling for Coke to be so eclipsed by someone with so little forensic experience, an upstart who had had the discourtesy to slight his own leader.[33] As a fellow member of Gray's Inn quipped after the hearing, 'all is as well as words can make it, and if it please Her Majesty to add deeds, the bacon may be too hard for the cook'.[34] That was not to be, since Bacon had to wait for the solicitor-generalship until 1607. But the wound never healed, and Bacon was to be the bane of Coke's future existence. Coke's report of the case, as printed in 1600 (the year of Bacon's reading on uses), could be read as a justification of his own argument in 1594.

(h) Perpetuity clauses

Chudleigh's Case was only the beginning of the end for the perpetuity clause because there were other issues still to be resolved. The problem of the Statute of Uses was not wholly removed by the decision in that case, and there were parallel problems arising from the Statute of Wills. The controversies surrounding their exposition account for some of Coke's longest reports. However, he did not report all the relevant cases in which he was involved. No doubt this was partly because they traversed the same ground. Indeed, another reporter omitted one of the same cases for the express reason that only Coke had argued and that his arguments could be found in other cases.[35] But the principal reason for not putting all the cases into MS. *C* was that, being inconclusive, they tended only to perpetuate the uncertainty. Coke's involvement in the struggle has therefore to be collected largely from other sources. It was to be a prolonged campaign, and success was not finally achieved until 1613.[36] The first part of the story can only be related here in outline.

---

[32] *The Learned Reading of Francis Bacon*, p. 2: '... in 37 Reginae, by the notable judgment, upon solemn arguments, of all the judges assembled in the Exchequer Chamber in the famous case between *Dillon* and *Frayne*, concerning an assurance by Chudley, this law began to be reduced to a true and sound exposition, and the false and the perverted exposition which had continued for so many years ... grew to be controlled.' Coke and Bacon also argued in the Exchequer Chamber three years later in a case concerning parol uses: *Corbyn* v. *Corbyn* (1598) KB 27/1328, m. 465; Coventry, fos. 5–6v; BL MS. Harg. 7B, fos. 137v–139, 158v–160; MS. Lansd. 1084, fo. 139; MS. Add. 25198, fos. 170v–172, sub nom. *Corbyn* v. *Corbett*; MS. Add. 25201, fos. 136v, 149; HLS MS. 110, fos. 215–216; MS. 200.1 (1180.1), fos. 142v–143; MS. 206 (5066), fos. 128v–129v (same report); MS. 1042 (1058), fos. 49v–50.

[33] Boyer, *Coke and the Elizabethan Age*, p. 123, suggests that 'the judges found Coke more persuasive than Bacon'. But his account of Coke's argument is based on Coke's own retrospective version, which is counterbalanced by the contemporary reports.

[34] Letter from Henry Gosnold to Anthony Bacon, quoted in *The Oxford Francis Bacon*, i. 453.

[35] *Smith* v. *Thorpe* (1597) BL MS. Harley 1697, fo. 138v ('... fuit solement argue per Coke, attorney le roigne, mes les justices ne parleront a ceo, et pur ceo jeo moy mesme referre a les auters cases de perpetuityes en queux veyes bones argumentes faits per mr attorney le roigne de cest matter'). At the end of the volume, however, on fos. 145v–147, the reporter did add Coke's argument, sub nom. *Smyth* v. *Aslam*, below, p. clxii.

[36] *Mary Portington's Case*, *Portington* v. *Rogers* (1613) 10 Co. Rep. 37.

In one of the cases which Coke omitted, he 'proffered himself to argue the case gratis *pro bono publico*',[37] in the hope that *Scholastica's Case* (1571)[38] – the leading case on the subject – might be overruled. The 1571 case arose from the will made in 1557 by Henry Clerke, pewterer of London.[39] Clerke had two sons and one daughter, Scholastica Newes (or Newys). He left his property in South Mimms to the elder son in tail male, remainder to the younger son in tail male, remainder to Scholastica in tail male, with various other remainders in tail male to other relations and a final remainder in fee simple to the Pewterers' Company. Then followed a complex perpetuity clause, which the testator spelt out in detail in order (as he said) to make it clear even to those 'not well digesting the whole meaning of this present testament and last will'. The purpose of it, he said, was that the land should 'as long as might be continue and be amongst the name of the Clerkes, to the further memorial of mine own name', and that he would not have any of the 'entailees' (tenants in tail) make any conveyance which would interfere with the succession he had specified. To that end, he declared his mind that if any of the persons to whom the land was entailed should mortgage, sell, incumber or waste it, then such person should forthwith be excluded from the entail and the land should pass to the person next in tail 'as effectually as if such disorderous person or persons had never been minded of in this my present testament and last will'. After his death, disregarding this clause, both sons joined in a fine and recovery to Larke. When the elder son died without issue, Scholastica entered upon Larke, claiming that the estates of both her brothers had been forfeited. Larke's counsel relied on the common-law learning that such a condition was ineffective, because a condition could only be enforced by re-entry by the donor or his heirs, and such a re-entry would destroy the entire settlement. However, the judges of the Common Pleas decided unanimously in favour of Scholastica, because the common-law rule did not apply to wills. Wills were favoured in law, and conditions in wills were to be given effect in accordance with the testator's intention as limitations of the estate rather than as conditions. The case had become standard reading for law students since the publication of the second part of Plowden's *Commentaries* in 1578. Even before then, in 1575, the Common Pleas had affirmed that the same principle applied to uses: 'although uses are of such antiquity, yet they are not directed by the rules of the common law but by the will of the owner of the lands; for the use is in his hands as clay is in the hands of the potter, which he in whose hands it is may put into whatever form he pleaseth.'[40] Clerke's will was declared void by the Prerogative Court of Canterbury in 1577, at the instance of his widow, Elizabeth;[41] but that did not affect the Common Pleas decision. It remained axiomatic

---

[37] CUL MS. Dd.8.48, p. 5 (James Whitelocke's report, tr.); below, p. clxii, n. 49.

[38] *Scholastica's Case*, i.e. *Newys v. Larke* (1571) Plowd. 403; Benl. 196; Dyer's notebooks, 109 Selden Soc. 198; 110 Selden Soc. 235; CUL MS. Gg.2.5, fo. 99v. It was commonplaced by Coke from Benl. in *AB*, fo. 293, and from Plowd. in *AD*, fo. 880*. Note also, to the same effect, *Cranmer's Case* (1572) below, Appendix I, p. clxxxi.

[39] The will was registered by the Prerogative Court: PROB 11/39/372 (PCC 32 Wrastley).

[40] *Brent's Case* (1575) 2 Leon. 14, at fo. 16, *per* Manwood J. Cf. Coke's report, below, at p. 116 ('uses are not subject to the rules and maxims of the common law ... they are directed and ruled by the words of the parties according to their wishes'). See also *Carter v. Rinsgtead* (1590) vol. iii, pp. 535, 536.

[41] Definitive sentence in PROB 11/59/333 (PCC 25 Daughtry). Elizabeth was appointed administratrix. Scholastica Newes, in her widowhood, also faced a Chancery suit brought by the heirs of her sister Anne: *Hill v. Newes*, C 2/Eliz/H15/64.

that wills, and uses, were governed and guided by the intentions of the parties who created them. But those intentions might not accord with the common law, and it was less easy to accept that uses and wills enabled parties to create interests in land which were outside the legal rules, merely because they wished it.[42] *Scholastica's Case* gave an affirmative answer to that question.

By the 1590s, however, opinion on the question was shifting the other way. Bacon had argued in *Chudleigh's Case* (1594) that if the perpetuity clause there was overturned it would effectively overturn *Scholastica's Case* as well, for 'to say that the will shall be as an act of Parliament, to do a thing which is impossible to be done in substance and intent by any form of conveying, carries no sense'.[43] The same point was made in argument in *Germyn* v. *Arscott* (1595), and apparently then accepted by the Common Pleas.[44] And, around the same time, Coke took an opportunity to attack perpetuities in the Exchequer:[45]

> These perpetuities have always by the providence of God been defeated and prevented by the act of the law, as in the cases of Thirning and Rikhill, being two of the justices of this realm.[46] And in later times uses and perpetual freeholds, intended to make perpetuities, have been weakened (*enfeable*) by the opinion of the justices in the case of *Dillon* v. *Freine*, commonly called *Chudleigh's Case*, argued recently by all the justices of England and thereupon adjudged in the King's Bench against perpetuities.

The King's Bench, nevertheless, passed by an opportunity to reconsider the 1571 case that same year, when another title was claimed through Scholastica, and Clerke's will was set out in a special verdict. Popham C.J. indicated that he was against the 1571 decision,[47] but the puisnes were seemingly of another mind and the court declined to hear any argument of the point in law, choosing to decide the case on a technical point. This evasive decision was noted briefly by Coke, but not until 1599.[48]

---

[42] *Callard* v. *Callard* (1594) vol. iii, p. 604. Here Coke persuaded the court to adopt a benign interpretation, but the judgment was reversed on the grounds that the interpretation ran counter to the 'rule of the law'. Cf. his citation of *Digges* v. *Palmer* (1600) 6 Co. Rep. 34 (tr. 'It was agreed in that case that the best construction of the Statute of Uses, 27 Hen. VIII, is to make them subject to the rules of the common law, which are certain and well known to the professors of the law, and not to make them so extravagant that no-one shall know any rule to determine the questions which arise upon them, which will produce uncertainty, the cause of infinite troubles, controversies and suits'). This passage is not in the contemporary report, vol. v, p. 1082; 1 Co. Rep. 173.

[43] *The Works of Francis Bacon*, ed. J. Spedding and others, xv. 186.

[44] *Germyn* v. *Arscott* (1595) vol. iii, p. 652; below, p. clxiii.

[45] *Att.-Gen.* v. *Perrot* (*c.* 1595) Moo. 369, at p. 372 (tr.). This was an information for intrusion brought by Coke against Lady Perrot and James Perrot following the attainder of Sir John Perrot for treason.

[46] Litt., ss. 720–723; YB Hil. 21 Hen. VI, fo. 33v, pl. 21. They are perhaps the same case, the name being misremembered in the year book: B. & M. 77, 79. Coke later commented on them that 'it is not safe for any man (be he never so learned) to be of counsel with himself in his own case', and that it was 'an excellent point of learning that when any innovation or new invention starts up to try it with the rules of the common law ... for these be the true touchstones to sever the pure gold from the dross and sophistications of novelties and new inventions': Co. Litt. 377b, 379b.

[47] BL MS. Add. 25198, fo. 72, margin ('quere pur le matter en ley, car Popham fuit contra liver'). An even earlier opportunity, in *Dyngle* v. *Hamely* (1588) BL MS. Harley 4556, fos. 201v–202 (Clench's reports), was passed over when the court learned that the suit had only been brought to test the court's opinion how the land could be sold, notwithstanding the limitation; the case concerned a recovery by Sir Walter Ralegh.

[48] *Bateman* v. *Allen* (1595) KB 27/1330, m. 339d; vol. v, p. 959; cit. in *Mary Portington's Case* (1613) 10 Co. Rep. 35 at fo. 42.

The case in which Coke appeared gratis in 1597 was *Sherington* v. *Mynors* in the same court, and once again it arose from the same will. It was an action of ejectment against a servant of Thomas Forster, to whom Scholastica (with her husband Robert) had levied a fine of the land in suit. The special verdict again set out Clerke's will, and the effect of the perpetuity clause was this time revisited in earnest. Although Coke chose not to report the case, it attracted the interest of several other reporters.[49] George Croke, endeavouring to uphold the perpetuity clause, cited 'Wenlock v. Halley', identifiable as *Wellocke* v. *Hamonte* (1590),[50] where a proviso in a will for successive remaindermen to pay sums of money to their siblings was construed as a limitation and not a condition. But Coke countered that it was a 'golden rule' that one could not leave by will something which one could not grant in one's lifetime; and since one could not create a perpetuity by deed, it could not be done by will. As usual with difficult cases, it was adjourned.

While that case was depending, Coke argued in three other King's Bench cases against perpetuity clauses which purported to exclude any tenant in tail who attempted to bar the entail. The first, *Acton* v. *Hore*, was straightforward.[51] The conveyancer had limited the remainder after an estate tail to take effect only after an attempt to bar the entail, and the tenant in tail had died without issue but without having made any such attempt; the remainder was therefore void. In *Smith* v. *Aslam (or Thorpe)*[52] Coke argued that a perpetuity clause was void for three reasons. It was uncertain, because 'no learned man, or anyone else, can judge what will be called an "attempt"'. It was against law, because by the rules of the law a freehold or inheritance could not cease without an entry. And it was repugnant, because a common recovery with voucher could not be restrained by a condition, it being the birthright of every tenant in tail to convey the inheritance in fee simple.[53] The common recovery was not an alienation within the meaning of *De Donis*, but a judgment in a real action.[54] In the present case, the tenant in tail had suffered a recovery which barred all the remainders; but this, according to Coke, did not prejudice the remaindermen because in contemplation of law the estate tail could have lasted for ever, and in any case there was recompense in value. That had been decided by all the judges in *Capel's Case* (1592).[55] Coke asserted that 'there is no book in all our law nor any judgment whatever against me, and this is but a fantastical imagination of some of this age to perpetuate their names and family, whereas in truth it is the ready way to ruin them'.[56]

---

[49] *Sherington* v. *Mynors* (1596–99) KB 27/1336, m. 602; Moo. 543, cit. record; Coventry, fos. 3v–5; BL MS. Harley 4552, fos. 153v–154v; LI MS. Hill 121, fos. 136v–137 (same report); BL MS. Add. 25201, fo. 130v; MS. Add. 25203, fos. 3v–5, 14; MS. Add. 35947, fos. 103v–104, 118v–119; CUL MS. Dd.8.48, pp. 5, 34 (Whitelocke's reports); MS. Ff.5.26, fos. 166v–167v; MS. Gg.2.5, fo. 291; MS. Ii.5.26, fo. 210 (1599); MS. Ll.3.10, fos. 5, 37v–39; HLS MS. 200.1 (1180.1), fo. 140v.

[50] KB 27/1310, m. 481 (judgment for the plaintiff, Mich. 1590); cit. in BL MS. Add. 25201, fo.130v, *per* Croke.

[51] *Acton* v. *Hore* (1596) vol. iv, p. 682; KB 27/1329, m. 348.

[52] *Smyth* v. *Aslam* (Mich. 1597) BL MS. Harley 1697, fo. 145v; CUL MS. Ff.2.14, fos. 33–35v, sub nom. *Smith* v. *Thorpe*.

[53] Cf. *Cholmondeley* v. *Hanmer* (1597) vol. iv, p. 758; 2 Co. Rep. 50 at fo. 54

[54] CUL MS. Ff.2.14, at fo. 35.

[55] Vol. iii, p. 485; cf. vol. ii, p. 246.

[56] BL MS. Harley 1697, at fo. 145v (tr.).

The next case was *Tarrant's Case* (1597–98),[57] first heard the same term, in which Coke advanced essentially the same argument. Neither of the last two cases seems to have resulted in a judgment. Probably the court regarded both of them as depending on *Sherington's Case*, which was still awaiting judgment, since the point was exactly the same as in *Scholastica's Case*. Popham C.J. remained throughout in favour of reversing the 1571 decision, referring to the Common Pleas decision in *Germyn v. Arscott* (1595), to be considered presently. But his three brethren could not be persuaded to agree, and so in *Sherington's Case* judgment was finally given for the plaintiff, in accordance with the majority view, in Easter term 1599.[58] Coke's repeated arguments had failed to win over the puisnes, and he did not deign to report the decision. Indeed, it was the occasion for his reporting the inconclusive earlier case instead.[59] This, then, was a major obstacle to be overcome in the struggle against the perpetuity clause.

For the time being, the battle was fought with more success in the Common Pleas. Coke had no right of audience there except on the queen's business, but he tried to keep abreast of its most useful decisions. He composed a report of *Germyn v. Arscott* (1595), presumably relying on others.[60] It was seen as a major case at the time, and was indeed selected – probably by Anderson C.J. – to be the 'serjeants' case' argued by all the new serjeants called in 1594.[61] It concerned a more elaborate kind of perpetuity clause than in the previous cases, contained in a will made in 1583. In addition to providing that any offender's estate should cease as if he were dead and pass to the person next entitled, it went on to provide that on the offender's death the estate should remain, descend or come to the person who would have been entitled if there had been no attempt at alienation. It is evident from Coke's report that the judges greeted this extraordinary concept with some colourful rhetoric, which it is unnecessary to repeat here. Coke's version may be supplemented from some of the many other reports. Serjeant Fleetwood, arguing in the first action between the parties, said he had understood it to be a maxim that 'if a devise is repugnant to the law, the devisor's will shall not take effect as expressed in the will but according to the intent of the law'.[62] He thought the peculiar wording of the clause in the present case enabled it to be distinguished from that in *Scholastica's Case*:[63]

> It seems to me that he who was of counsel in the penning of this will had great regard to Scholastica's case; but there, by the cesser of the estate, it was determined for ever, whereas in our case it is not so, for after the death of the offender the estate shall be recontinued as if no such deed had been done.

---

[57] Moo. 470; CUL MS. Ff.2.14, fos. 39v–43v, sub nom. *Torrand v. Torrand* (1598); MS. Ii.5.26, fos. 193–194, sub nom. *Torrant v. Torrant* (1598).

[58] KB 27/1336, m. 602 (judgment for 12d. damages and £15. 2s. 4d. costs).

[59] He noted it in Hil. 1599, the term before judgment was entered in *Sherington v. Mynors*.

[60] Vol. iii, p. 652; cit. in 1 Co. Rep. 85; CP 40/1543, m. 1758. There had been an earlier action between the parties, raising the same question, in 1587–90.

[61] LI MS. Maynard 66, fo. 150v (1601), *per* Williams sjt (who had been one of the new serjeants); BL MS. Harg. 26, fo. 55.

[62] BL MS. Harg. 4, fo. 326 (tr.). Cf. *Lovelace v. Lovelace* (1584) vol. iv, p. 920.

[63] Ibid., fo. 327 (tr.).

Walmsley J. thought it also differed from *Scholastica's Case* in that here there was a condition and not a limitation.[64] There are some very full reports of the judges' opinions, fully matching the oratory captured by Coke.[65] Anderson C.J. began by indicating his low opinion of the draftsmanship:[66]

> Before I enter into consideration of the parts, I will say generally that every part is absurd, repugnant, contrariant, impossible and against the law, and (as I think) all the absurdities, contrarieties, repugnancies and inconveniences which could be devised or imagined to be in a will are brought together in this will.

It was right, he said, to show some indulgence to a layman making a will without counsel. He was not bound to follow the strict forms of law, and if his intent was clear it would be respected. But if his intent was to do something not permitted by law, such as creating new kinds of estate and limitation, this could not be given effect. It would be equally ineffective if drawn up in a formal conveyance by counsel.[67] Indeed, it would be ineffective even if sanctioned by an act of Parliament, since Parliament could not breathe sense into an absurdity:

> As to what has been said that an act of Parliament has done all that this proviso has limited, it seems to me that if there was such an Act it would be a vain Act[68] ... In this will many things are limited which, even if they were in an act of Parliament, the law ought to adjudge them utterly vain and void, for indeed (as it seems to me) an act of Parliament cannot make an estate tail cease and yet after the cesser he will still retain it so that it will descend to his issue.

He went on to set out the inconveniences which had been enumerated in *Chudleigh's Case*, and concluded:

> If this devise should be allowed, then by the same reasons all the land in England might be tied up with these perpetuities. If that should happen, no termor or occupier would be sure of his term or interest, and from thence it would follow that there would be no bargaining or contracting between man and man for land. And the mischief would not stop there, but by these means the land itself would in a short time lie fresh and untilled for want of occupiers ... Therefore, the mischiefs being so great, the law ought to have providence and foresight to prevent such things before they come about.

It is true that Warburton J. a few years later would reject this apocalyptic argument as frivolous.[69] But the perpetuity clause was struck down by the unanimous agreement of Anderson C.J., Walmsley, Beaumont and Owen JJ. They foresaw that if entails could never be broken, then every time an estate was entailed it would be removed

---

[64] Bodl. Lib. MS. Rawlinson C.85, fo. 193. The turning point here may have been *Rudhall* v. *Myller* (1584) vol. iv, p. 866, though there the clause was explicitly called a condition. As to conditions and limitations, see also *Gibbons* v. *Maltywarde* (1592) vol. iii, p. 492; *The Earl of Shrewsbury's Case* (1597–98) vol. iv, p. 754; vol. v, p. 945.

[65] The following account is based on LI MS. Misc. 491, fos. 88v–100v.

[66] Ibid., fo. 98v (tr.). Anderson CJ's judgment continues on fos. 99–100v.

[67] See the remarks to the same effect in *Soulle* v. *Garrard* (1595) vol. iv, p. 835 ('An ignorant man who is *inops consilii* cannot by his will ... create such an estate as a man could not by the common law create in his lifetime by an act executed by advice of counsel, for then the will of an ignorant man would be like an act of Parliament. ... Although the statutes of 32 and 34 Hen. VIII say that everyone may devise "at his will and pleasure", nevertheless this will and pleasure must be referred to the rules of the law, for otherwise a devise to a monk would be good.'); and in *Abraham* v. *Twigge* (1596) Cro. Eliz. 478; Moo. 424; as reported in HLS MS. 206 (5066), fo. 118v.

[68] Cf. 1 Co. Rep. 87v.

[69] *Mildmay* v. *Mildmay* (1601) LI MS. Maynard 66, fo. 165; quoted below, p. clxvii.

from the world of alienability, so that more and more land would become locked up in tail as time passed. This was hard enough on would-be purchasers, as the land market steadily diminished, but it was even worse for tenants in tail themselves. If landowners were tenants in tail they were unable to sell land in order to consolidate their estates, to assist their daughters and younger children, or to raise money by mortgage. And they might even find it difficult to obtain a proper income from what they had. Tenant farmers did not like to take leases from tenants in tail, who were unable to grant them for more than twenty-one years, and then only subject to various qualifications.[70]

In addition to *Germyn* v. *Arscott*, Coke later came by a report of the slightly earlier Common Pleas case of *Cholmeley* v. *Humble* (1593–95), decided in the term in which *Germyn* v. *Arscott* commenced, though it was not entered in his notebooks until 1597.[71] It was a stronger case than the other, because the clause (created in a deed of 1579) was less eccentric and closer to that in *Scholastica's Case*. The court nevertheless struck the clause down, albeit with some hesitation on the part of Owen J. Presumably *Germyn* v. *Arscott* attracted more attention than this earlier decision because it concerned a will rather than a settlement by deed, and also because it was confirmed by all the judges of England.[72]

When he prepared the first volume of the *Reports* for publication in 1600, Coke incorporated abridgments of both cases into an extended report of a third Common Pleas case which – like *Shelley's Case* and *Chudleigh's Case* – is not in the notebook.[73] *Corbet's Case* was commenced in Hilary term 1599 and adjudged in Hilary term 1600. It was actually a case between feigned parties, designed to test the water.[74] Possibly the name was chosen because there were several other cases of the same name around the same time.[75] The true plaintiff was Anthony Mildmay, and when Anderson C.J. was first told of this 'he flung out the Hall, saying he came not thither to argue any counterfeit cases'.[76] However, not wishing to miss another opportunity to rule against perpetuities, he calmed down and the case proceeded. The case arose from a settlement of the manor of Stokefaston, Leicestershire, made in 1588 by Sir Walter Mildmay (d. 1589). The deed contained an inordinately long perpetuity clause – Coke counted over a thousand words – to the effect that the estate

---

[70] 32 Hen. VIII, c. 28. Lessees of entailed land were always at risk of being evicted by the issue in tail.

[71] Vol. iv, p. 806; CP 40/1516, m. 2018; cit. in 1 Co. Rep. 86. There had been an earlier King's Bench case between the same parties: KB 27/1318, m. 522 (1591).

[72] Popham C.J. said it had been affirmed on a writ of error: BL MS. Harley 4552, fo. 154v. No trace of this has been found in the record. Moo. 364 says that the Common Pleas judges conferred with all the judges of England in Serjeants' Inn, which may be a more accurate recollection.

[73] *Corbett* v. *Corbett* (1600) CP 40/1021, m. 1049; 1 Co. Rep. 77; 2 And. 134; Moo. 601; BL MS. Lansd. 1074, fos. 311v–312 (Trin. 1599); CUL MS. Gg.2.5, fo. 306; cit. in *The Learned Reading of Francis Bacon*, pp. 9–10.

[74] See *Mildmay's Case* (No. 3) (1605) HLS MS. 1192 (2069), fo. 49 ('Le case de Corbett adjudge. Cooke, attorney, vient al barre in Banc le Roy de argue per le nosme de Mildmayes case, car semble que le primer fuit solement pur conuster le opinion des judges, et ore le very cas vient sans vizard et fuit argue per Brooke del Inner Temple pur les perpetuities …').

[75] Three were noted by Coke: *Cooke* v. *Brombill* (Common Pleas, 1597) vol. iv, p. 810; cit. by Coke in 1600 as *Corbet's Case* (vol. v, p. 1084); *Sir Andrew Corbet's Case* (Wards, 1599) 4 Co. Rep. 81; and *Richard Corbet's Case* (Wards, 1600) C, fos. 552–554.

[76] W. Burton, *The Description of Leicester Shire* (1622), p. 271. Burton was a barrister of the Inner Temple, and witnessed the scene when he was 'standing by, being a reporter in the same court'.

of anyone 'going about' or even making a mental resolution to bar the entail would cease as if he were naturally dead. The point was no different from that in the other cases, and the judges held unanimously, or at least *nemine contradicente*,[77] that the clause was ineffective to undo the effect of a common recovery of 1594. Anderson C.J. observed that *Germyn* v. *Arscott* was a stronger case than the present, 'being in the case of a will, which receives a benign interpretation according to the testator's intent'.[78] Although the record notes that a writ of error was obtained, it seems that it was not pursued. The only reason the case caused difficulty was that it raised some tangential issues on which the judges were not agreed.[79]

Despite all these decisions, the Mildmay clause was litigated again in 1601, with the parties 'unmasked',[80] as *Mildmay* v. *Mildmay*.[81] Serjeant Williams attacked the perpetuity clause as illegal, and also argued that 'go about, resolve and determine' was too subjective a concept to be tried, while 'as if he were dead' was repugnant if he was still alive.[82] He relied on *Germyn* v. *Arscott*, *Cholmley* v. *Humble*, *Corbet's Case* 'in Mr Coke's reports', and *Yelverton's Case*, 'ruled in the very point'.[83] Against this tide of authority, Serjeant Daniel attempted a brave defence. He started by defining a use as 'nihil aliud quam le putting del mynde de un home en le mynde dun auter', and called it 'a Chancery inheritance':

> Before 27 Hen. VIII there were two commanders over the land, the feoffees and cestui que use, but this was mischievous; and therefore came 27 [the Statute of Uses] and buried the use, for it is quasi its grave and sepulchre. As for contingent and future uses, if the necks thereof are not broken before their raising they may arise well enough. And it is plain that a use may cease.

He urged the court to follow *Scholastica's Case* (1571), and pointed out that the author of the conveyance was Sir Walter Mildmay, chancellor of the Exchequer, who 'without doubt did it with great advice and counsel'. (Perhaps everyone knew who the culprit was.[84]) The words 'as if he were dead' were not repugnant but merely 'words of comparison and similitude'. Warburton J. was sympathetic to this argument. The phrase was mere surplusage, and the obvious meaning of the simile was that the estate should cease during the offender's lifetime. That was not repugnant to law. He also dismissed the policy argument:

---

[77] 1 Co. Rep. 88. If this wording means there was a dissentient, it was not on this occasion Walmsley J., though he repented of it later: see opposite.

[78] Ibid. 86.

[79] Ibid. 84. Cf. BL MS. Lansd. 1061, fo. 33v (1600): 'Cook atturney vouch le case de Corbet ... agree per touts les justices. Mes il dit que ascun des justices teignont que coment que use de enheritance ne poit cesser sans entre, nient pluis quam estate de enheritance, uses ne sont extinguish, eins possession ensue le use. Uncore quant party mesme que est daver le benefit per le cesser est en le possession, la il ne besoigne denter ... Et ceo il vouche en case enter Sir Moyle Finch et Henry Finch son frere ...'.

[80] Above, p. clxv, n. 74 ('sans vizard').

[81] *Mildmay* v. *Mildmay* (1601) CP 40/1661, m. 829; Moo. 632; LI MS. Maynard 66, fos. 149v–151, 165–168v (from which the quotations below are tr.).

[82] It could also be seen as a draconian penalty. In the same year Lady Russell complained that, under the earl of Bedford's settlement, anyone who went about to alienate the premises 'should be presently dead in law': *Cecil Papers*, xi. 562.

[83] This does not refer to *Yelverton* v. *Yelverton* (1594) vol. iii, p. 578.

[84] Popham C.J. said that the clause in the form 'until the tenant in tail goes about to alienate, and then to the use of another' had been invented by 'un que fuit un graund judge': *Frampton* v. *Frampton* (1604) C, fo. 605v, at fo. 606.

As to the objection that, if these perpetuities should be permitted, no one could buy land,[85] he said that it was frivolous; for without question everyone who has enough money may buy as much land as he wants ... Were there not perpetuities for many ages by reason of the Statute of Westminster II concerning estates tail? No one was discontented with them, but they were well allowed.

As for *Corbet* v. *Corbet*, it was 'a feigned case and none in truth, and therefore he believed that no judge's conscience was bound by such a judgment'. *Cholmley's Case* and *Germyn* v. *Arscott* were distinguishable.[86] Walmsley and Warburton JJ. agreed. But Anderson C.J. spoke against the clause 'totis viribus':

And he began to inveigh against uses, and said that such toys and trifles should not govern England, but the common law; and the old usages ought to be maintained. And he said that the common law is reason, and something which is alienated from reason is against law.

While he did not approve of the deceit in *Corbet's Case*, 'a judgment given with great advice ought to be reverenced and not so easily repealed'. A will which was contrary to law and reason should not to be allowed, 'and this rule he would have kept in all acts of Parliament, deeds and writings whatsoever'. He explained this as an application of the mischief rule, reading out the preamble to the Statute of Uses to show that 'the intent of this statute was utterly to extinguish all uses, for uses were found to be wholly mischievous and perilous at common law'. The present uses were 'lewd practices and devices', and it was necessary to strike them down because their fate was of widespread importance:

He said it was not the case of Sir Anthony and Humphrey Mildmay alone, but the case of the whole land, and therefore such confusion and absurdity, contrariety and repugnancies are not to be permitted. For lawyers must always consider *quid bonum, quid malum, quid conveniens, quid inconveniens, quid possibile, quid impossibile*. It is, therefore, very reasonable to avoid all such mischiefs and faults in conveyances of estates which are so bad and inconvenient to the commonwealth, and so pernicious to the state, and so absurd and ridiculous in consideration of the law.

Kingsmill J. agreed, but the action was discontinued in Easter term 1602 with the court still evenly divided. Walmsley J. conceded that he had been of a different opinion in *Corbet's Case*, but it had been a doubtful opinion, and now 'upon better advice and deliberation' he agreed with Warburton J. that the clause was not repugnant to the law. Any emerging clarity seemed to be fast evaporating; but at least there was no final decision reaffirming *Scholastica's Case*.

In the King's Bench, Popham C.J. continued with his attack. An opportunity arose to restate his position obiter in 1604, and Coke wrote it down,[87] though the passage did not find its way into the printed *Reports*:[88]

---

[85] This refers to Anderson C.J.'s argument, above, p. clxiv.

[86] The report does not indicate what the distinction was.

[87] *Frampton* v. *Frampton* (1604) C, fos. 605v–607, at fo. 606 (tr. and turned into direct speech). The case concerned a power to revoke uses by parol (by a signed writing), even though the uses were declared by deed. This raised the general question of the extent to which uses enabled the rules of law to be undermined. According to Moo. 735, the case was also argued by Coke in the Exchequer Chamber.

[88] It was overtaken by *Hothersall* v. *Mildmay* (1605), which he published in 1607: n. 90, overleaf.

Great controversies and mischiefs arise in these days upon last wills and new limitations and contingencies of uses. Upon the first, because they are drawn by persons ignorant in the law; upon the latter, because these new limitations are not devised by men learned in the law (for those who are of greater knowledge and judgment refuse to meddle with them) but by scriveners and some ignorant practitioners (*professors del ley*) according to former precedents.

He set out the four stages by which perpetuity clauses had been developed since the Statute of Uses, and held all the inventions to be uncertain, against the law and ineffective:

He who well observes the preamble and the body of the Act of 27 Hen. VIII will find that these provisos are against the intent and letter of the said law, for it intended to consolidate the use to the estate of the land, and thus to restore the ancient common law of the land and to subject estates in uses to the rules of the common law. If such provisos should be adjudged good in law, such a construction would be not only against the intention and letter of the law but would also introduce greater mischiefs than were before the Act ... The true construction of the Act of 27 was to make limitations of uses within the compass and rules of the common law. He said, moreover, that by the rule of the common law no future contingency can be annexed to another contingency ...

When the Mildmay clause was fought over for a third time in 1605, the chosen forum was the King's Bench, giving Coke the chance to argue the case at the bar. The new action was brought by a lessee of Humphrey Mildmay against Sir Anthony Mildmay, as he now was, for a trespass in a different county, but the point was exactly the same as in the previous cases. The puisnes who had previously outnumbered Popham C.J. had by now been replaced[89] and the court was at last able to accept Coke's arguments and adjudge the troublesome clause void. Coke inserted a full report in his notebooks, and published to the world in 1607 that the decision to condemn perpetuity clauses had been made by both benches.[90]

(i) The later reports

By the late 1590s there are clear internal signs in MS. *C* that Coke was thinking of publication, as in remarks addressed to the 'reader' or in the rendering of Coke himself as 'lattorney le roigne' in the third person, rather than as 'jeo'.[91] And there was a more subtle change in the presentation. Coke was becoming more inclined to condense the successful arguments into a statement of what the court decided, arranged as numbered resolutions, and to relegate the losing arguments to an aside, or omit them altogether. The forensic skirmishing had become of less concern than the clarification of what had been resolved. There is also a higher proportion of Common Pleas cases, presumably collected from other reporters, or in some cases

---

[89] Clench J. retired in 1602 and was replaced by Yelverton J. In 1604 an additional puisne, Williams J., was added. And in Aug. 1605 Gawdy J. became C.J.C.P.

[90] *Hothersall* d. *Mildmay* v. *Mildmay* (Mich. 1605) KB 27/1365, m. 439 (issue only); Co. Ent. 678v–684v; *C*, fos. 685–689; 6 Co. Rep. 40.

[91] Note the consequential emendation from 'jeo cite' to 'il cite' at *C*, fo. 374 (vol. v, p. 1039). See also above, pp. cii, cxii, cxv, cxliii.

directly from the plea rolls, because of their precedential value. Some of the King's Bench reports also were entered in the book several years after their date, strongly suggesting that they too had come to Coke's notice after the event as useful precedents. All this points towards intended publication. Even so, the reports should not be seen merely as drafts for the printed books. For one thing, Coke did not print his reports in chronological order. The *Reports* were successive selections from his store of material. Only a minority were printed as he first wrote them, with very few changes. The longest of these, such as *The Case of Alton Woods* (1600),[92] were evidently crafted with care even before they were written into the notebook and required little change. There is internal evidence that the report of *Throckmorton* v. *Finch* (1597), which was not printed, was copied into MS. *C* by an amanuensis from a draft 'book'.[93] But some cases were considerably extended when they went into print, and the expanded versions sometimes give details of what was argued, or what judges said, which are not in the notebook.[94] Here again Coke may have been making use of reports by others, unless he had retained the details in his memory. Other cases, such as *Germyn* v. *Arscott* and *Cholmley's Case*, were abridged or summarised and worked into reports of other cases. And the residue, including those with a politically controversial element, such as *Throckmorton* v. *Finch*, surfaced only much later as citations in the *Institutes* or were never mentioned in print at all.

MS. *C* ends with Coke's last term as attorney-general, Trinity term 1606. He was then appointed chief justice of the Common Pleas, and during the ten increasingly turbulent years of his judicial career he continued the reports in four more volumes.[95] These volumes were considerably shorter than MS. *C*,[96] but full of important matter. Only one of the four seems to have survived, in Cambridge University Library (MS. Ii.5.21), which Coke inscribed as 'Liber tercius', covering the period from Michaelmas term 1608 to Easter term 1610. Most of its content was incorporated in the *Reports*. The remainder was published in translation in the 1650s, in the twelfth and thirteenth parts of the *Reports*. An edition of the French texts from 1606 to 1616 would still be desirable, to correct errors in the printed translations, but it would require a collation of the many manuscript copies which circulated in the first half of the seventeenth century.[97]

This edition

This edition is, principally, a transcription and translation of all the cases reported by Coke before 1601, which are found in MS. *A* and folios 1–433 of MS. *C*. It does not

---

[92] Vol. v, pp. 1061–1082.

[93] Vol. iv, pp. 797–803, at p. 799.

[94] E.g. *Borough* v. *Taylor* (1596) vol. iv, p. 685; 4 Co. Rep. 72; *Scott* v. *Mayne* (1596) vol. iv, p. 704; 5 Co. Rep. 20.

[95] *Library of Sir Edward Coke*, p. 22, nos. 294–297.

[96] The longest (MS. *F*) was the volume from Trin. 1610 to Pas. 1616, which contained 222 folios. The last volume (MS. *G*), containing some additional cases from 1615–16, filled only 26 folios.

[97] For an example showing how these copies can correct errors in the printed translation see Baker, *Magna Carta*, p. 367, emending *Prohibitions del Roy* (1608) 12 Co. Rep. 63. A major omission from the printed editions was Coke's list of 'Dangerous and absurd opinions affirmed before the king' by Lord Ellesmere (CUL MS. Ii.5.21, fos. 47v–48), although it occurs in more than one of the copies.

include the cases from the same period found in his later notebooks and printed reports. To have interpolated them in their chronological place would not only have been an artificial alteration of the text but would have given the false impression that they were composed en suite by Coke, whereas their source is not always known.[98]

The cases of the 1570s from the commonplace-books, printed in the present volume, are for the like reason reproduced in the order in which they occur in the manuscript, with indications (where appropriate) of the headings under which they were entered. There was a temptation to rearrange them chronologically, to match the later reports and carry them back in sequence to 1572, bringing together disjointed references to the same case, but this would have created the false impression of a regular chronicle. The contemporary cases were embedded in a mass of surrounding material, far too voluminous to include here, and did not seem justifiable to disturb the text further by rearranging them artificially. It would also have posed editorial problems, in that Coke did not write all the cases down at the time they were decided, and some are not exactly dated. There is a chronological table on pp. 1–2, below, of the nominate cases in this part.

The second volume contains cases from 1579 to 1588 in chronological order, as written in the first two notebooks of reports bound into MS. *A*, and the remaining volumes contain cases from 1591 to 1600 as continued in MS. *C*. The same editorial conventions have been applied throughout, and there is a continuous pagination.

The various layers of autograph correction have been indicated on the left-hand side, but for ease of reading the translation generally represents the text as corrected. All the annotations by Coke have been included, save in the very few cases where they have become completely illegible through wear and tear. There is no obvious hierarchical distinction between the annotations added above the reports and those below, since their location was governed by the space available at the time of writing. Such additions have therefore been gathered at the end of each report, marked where appropriate with a superscript [a]. Marginal notes are interpolated close to the text to which they refer, in angle brackets, with a superscript [m]. Additions in the form of interlineations have likewise been interpolated as closely as possible to the text where they are written, marked with a superscript [i]. Although it is not always easy to distinguish a more-or-less contemporary adjustment from a later addition, obvious later additions – such as citations of later material – have been distinguished on the translation side with { }.

In writing Latin, Coke sometimes adopted a slightly more formal hand. Occasionally he used an e with a hook (ę) to indicate æ, but more usually just a plain e (as in writs and records); in the transcription a simple e is used throughout, but where Latin is quoted on the translation side 'ae' is used in accordance with modern usage. As in previous Selden Society volumes, the awkward abbreviation 'trns' has been rendered as 'trespas' rather than 'transgressio'. The abbreviation 'v^e' has been rendered as *vide*, though Coke usually extended it as *vies* in law French. For greater clarity 'fo.' and 'p.' have been inserted in the translation before folio and page references, and likewise 'pl.' for *placita* or case numbers. In accordance with the

---

[98] Some were derived solely from the plea-roll entries, which Coke explained with his own commentary.

usage of his day, Coke distinguished the rectos and versos of folios with the suffixes a and b, and his references are shown thus in the text; but these have been adjusted in the translation to accord with modern usage, so that f. 100a becomes fo. 100, and f. 100b becomes fo. 100v. In the notes, however, in deference to professional tradition, Co. Litt. is cited in the old manner.

It will hardly need pointing out that Coke's French is atrocious. There is a pervasive (but irregular) disregard for tense, mood, gender, and even number, though of course Coke knew grammar well enough from his schooling and was fully capable of declining and conjugating French when he chose to do so. But he was not addressing French readers – at the outset, he may have been writing for nobody but himself – and he naturally used what may be regarded as common lawyers' shorthand.[99] It should also be remembered that he was reporting what he had heard spoken in English, and for that purpose it sometimes made better sense to leave an English word untranslated. In no place do the linguistic shortcomings obscure the obvious meaning, though it would be absurd to translate the words literally and grammatically. The use of parallel texts entitles an editor to deal with such matters silently, and to mediate in other ways between the original notes and the modern reader, by assuming some latitude in translation. Although nearly all the words in the French text have been accounted for in the English, occasionally words have been omitted where they are unnecessary, particularly conjunctions used as punctuation. Coke used etceteras freely; these have sometimes been extended into what was obviously intended, sometimes (in quotations from statutes or documents) replaced with ellipses, and sometimes omitted as having no clear meaning. The present historic, often used by reporters, has usually been rendered into the past tense; and the future tense has occasionally (where the sense so requires) been rendered as 'may' rather than 'shall'. Double emphasis has been removed in phrases such as 'tout ousterment' (rendered as 'utterly') and 'forsque tantsolement' (rendered as 'only'). Punctuation, including the use of capital and lower-case letters, has been lightly adjusted or introduced on the text side in conformity with the usual Selden Society practice. The translation is more heavily punctuated than the text, since Coke tended to write long and convoluted sentences, with conditional clauses, and sometimes conditional sub-clauses within conditional clauses, usually involving a superfluous 'that'. Coke's long sentences also sometimes result in duplicated verbs, as in 'It was adjudged that where x ... it was agreed that y'. It has seemed better usually to leave these in place, but in especially awkward cases they have been rewritten. On the translation side, place-names have been modernised, and personal names have been adjusted according to the spelling in the record.

No attempt has been made to reconstruct Elizabethan English usage, which would have required 'doth', 'meseemeth' and the like, and yet it has in general seemed appropriate to preserve Coke's modes of expression, which by and large can be translated directly into English. A few words have been changed to help the sense.

---

[99] It may be noted, however, that he did not trouble to improve the French substantially in his printed *Reports*. The retention of French in those volumes defined the readership, and that readership was concerned with the sense rather than with the purity of the language. (Cf. p. cxv, n. 12, above.) Latin was another matter altogether; as the language of record, it required (and was generally given) precise treatment, though contractions sometimes obscure the intended endings of inflected words.

For instance, 'cause' – in such phrases as 'the cause of the judgment', 'the plea was bad for three causes', or 'per cause de' – has usually been rendered as 'reason'. Coke was fond of drawing a distinction, which he usually called a 'differens'[1] or a 'diversitie' (using year-book French) or, after 1596, a 'variousitie'; these words have been rendered as 'distinction'. The principal changes in the translation have been adjustments to the word-order and the tenses, and the insertion of punctuation, in order to facilitate understanding. One other convention ought to be mentioned. Following contemporary usage, Coke consistently gave both chief justices and the chief baron the courtesy title 'segnior', though none of them were peers; it is the same courtesy which was later bestowed on Coke himself as chief justice, and which survives in the vocative 'my lord' with which male superior judges are still addressed in English courts. To avoid confusion with peers, this has been rendered here as 'the lord Dyer' (or whoever), with 'lord' in lower case.

A brief observation is required concerning dates. Dates using regnal years have usually been standardised in the form 10 Hen. VI or 35 Eliz., with the calendar year inserted in brackets on the translation side where appropriate. The dating of Michaelmas terms under Queen Elizabeth involves some potential ambiguity. The date of the queen's accession, 17 November 1558, fell in the middle of the Michaelmas term. A whole Michaelmas term therefore had to be given two regnal years. For instance, Mich. 1577 is Mich. 19 & 20 Eliz. In some places, however, only one regnal year is given in the manuscript. Mich. 19 Eliz., for example, could be 1576 or 1577, depending on whether it relates to the part of the term before or after 17 November. It can be shown in one instance that when Coke wrote Mich. 16 Eliz. he meant Mich. 16 & 17 Eliz. (1574),[2] and in another that by Mich. 19 Eliz. he meant Mich. 19 & 20 Eliz. (1577).[3] Even though he may not always have been consistent,[4] these examples have been taken as indicating his usual practice. It has therefore been assumed in such cases, subject to evidence in rebuttal, that he intended the later of the two possible years.

On the text side, the headings and headnotes (printed in smaller type) are Coke's, apart from the line containing the manuscript reference, and all editorial annotations to the text are in the footnotes. On the translation side, Coke's headings and headnotes are translated, but above them is a line inserted by the editor, in the same smaller type, with the name of the court and (in this volume only) the date. The names assigned to cases in the headings follow modern conventions, so that, for instance, a plaintiff in error is named first even when he was defendant in the court below.[5] In ejectment cases, the name of the plaintiff's lessor is given in the later form (with d., for 'on the demise of), since he is often the real plaintiff.

---

[1] Eg. *AC*, fos. 611 633, 643 ('un bone differens'). It is not clear whether the abbreviation 'dr̄e' represents *difference* or *diversite*.

[2] Cf. below, p. 89, no. 147, and p. 95, no. 158 (the plea-roll citation).

[3] The anonymous case below, p. 48, no. 93, is dated Mich. 19 Eliz. in the commonplace-book but Mich. 19 & 20 Eliz. in 3 Co. Inst. 77.

[4] See below, p. 147, no. 271, where a case cited as of Mich. 18 Eliz. is reported in Dyer under Mich. 17 & 18 Eliz.

[5] This convention was followed by Coke himself, though not consistently. He did not use the *versus* form, but 'between ... and ...'. It was also a convenient contemporary practice to cite cases by the name of the foremost real party, who was not necessarily a party on the record, e.g. *Ayleworth's Case* (*Harris* v. *Winge*) and *Beckwith's Case* (*Colgate* v. *Blythe*). These alternative names are noted in the apparatus.

The footnotes are mainly devoted to identifying the sources cited by Coke, and most of them are free from doubt. The principal difficulties have arisen from year-book references which either lack a folio number or which cite a folio on which there is nothing obviously relevant.[6] Some of these have been conjecturally identified, where they are cited as authority for a specific proposition. But the strings of cases which Coke was fond of inserting in his reports, and of adding from time to time above, below and in between the lines of his reports, should not necessarily be understood as authorities in that sense. Often they were; but sometimes the analogy with the case in hand is so difficult to discern that it can only be supposed that the cases were merely those which Coke might wish to find later in connection with related arguments.[7] In case of doubt, the footnote will indicate that the source is unidentified.

Some departures have had to be made from the conventions established for the Year Book Series and used also for early Tudor reports. Records corresponding to the reports have been identified where possible – usually where roll-references are given in the reports[8] – but no attempt has been made to read through the gargantuan bundles of plea rolls from 1572 to 1600, many of which are in any case in a fragile state and unfit for production.[9] Although many of the plea-roll entries have been found, the texts have not been inserted. As may be gauged from the first volume of Coke's own printed *Reports*, their bulk would be excessive. Coke had started out by following Plowden's example of printing the record in full, but he soon gave up the practice and (where known to him) provided a roll-reference instead. Today, there is even less cause to print the records in full, since they are mostly available online. Moreover, Coke usually summarised the pleadings sufficiently for each report to be properly understood without them. For the same reasons, there are no full 'Notes from the record' as in previous editions of year books and reports. Some details from the record have instead been given in footnotes, chiefly in order to identify the parties and the subject-matter, and to show how the legal question was determined.

The large quantity of surviving law reports from this period has enabled numerous references to be given to parallel reports by other hands, many of them still unpublished. Here too, for purely practical reasons, no attempt has been made to list every one of them, or to compare them,[10] let alone to print any of them here. It is noteworthy that a number of different dates are commonly given in various reports of the same case, sometimes years apart. Although this may occasionally result from error, the usual explanation is that difficult cases were reargued on several occasions, sometimes over several years. Since many of the parallel reports are more detailed than Coke's notes of the same cases, and may refer to arguments which Coke did not hear, they should be consulted, together with the record, by anyone interested in a particular case.

[6] It should be noted that Coke used the 1567 edition of YB 22–28 Edw. III, the continuous folio numbering of which is different from the annual numbering in the vulgate edition (which is derived from the composite volume of 1619).

[7] Cf. *Le Tierce Part des Reportes* (1602), sig. iij verso ('mine advice is that whensoever a man is enforced to yield a reason of his opinion or judgment, that then he set down all authorities, precedents, reasons, arguments and inferences whatsoever that may be probably applied to the case in question …').

[8] Coke gave them accurately, but other reports frequently garbled them.

[9] King's Bench cases whose names are known can often be traced via the chief clerk's docket rolls (now PRO, IND 1/1341–1354, for this period). But the docket rolls are imperfect, with several years missing.

[10] It is expected that a good number of the manuscript reports will be found to duplicate each other.

APPENDIX I

REPORTS OF MICHAELMAS TERM 1572
ON TWO FLY-LEAVES AT HOLKHAM

This text is collated with the related text in the Rylands manuscript to show the principal differences between the two versions. Both are written in Coke's hand. Minor changes which do not affect the sense are not noted.

Holkham 7938, fos. i(v)-ii(v) (H); collated with JRL MS. Fr. 118, fos. 2v–3v (J).

[1]

14 Eliz. cest case fuit move in le common banke devant Sir James Dier et Justice Harper. Un port ejectione firme et pendant le brefe il entra: si cest entre abatera le brefe, cest fuit le question.

Et loppinion del Harper fuit que le brefe abatera pur ceo que un recover in brefe de ejectione firme son terme que est a vener et auxi damages, et quant il ad recover il avera habere facias possessionem de mitter luy mesme en possession, et pur ceo que il ad entre il ad determine ceo per son act quel le ley voille aver done a luy. Et issint nota que il ne poet estre mise in possession per habere facias possessionem que est in possession [et] pur cest cause il semble que le brefe abatera.

Le segnior Dier al contrarie. Et il prist cest ground, que in toutz cases ou nontenure est plea, la si le demandant entre pendant le brefe le brefe abatera. Mes icy in cest ejectione firme clerement nontenure nest plea, per que etc. Auxi il dit que si jeo soy ouste de mon terme et deins un heure entre, jeo avera ejectione firme pur le damages solement. Issint si jeo soy possesse dun terme et soy ouste et jeo reentra, et apres le terme finie, ou jeo reentra devant le terme finie, il dit que il avera ejectione firme apres le terme finie et recovera damages.

Harper demand de luy, si ne fuit bon plea en un ejectione firme adire que le pleintife mesme est in possession. Et Dier respond que non, car ceo amount a un especial nontenure.

[2]

A mesme le temps in attaint le petit jury demande oyer del record, et habuit.

APPENDIX I

REPORTS OF MICHAELMAS TERM 1572 ON TWO FLY-LEAVES AT HOLKHAM

In the translation of cases 3–6, passages which occur only in the Holkham manuscript are printed in italics; angle-brackets are also placed around such of those passages as are differently rendered in the Holkham manuscript. Passages which occur only in the Rylands manuscript are in sans-serif type in square brackets.

1. BESBETCH v. SCOTT[1]

In 14 Eliz. this case was moved in the Common Bench before Sir James DYER and HARPER J. Someone brought *ejectione firmae*, and while the writ was pending he entered: does this entry abate the writ? That was the question.

The opinion of HARPER was that the writ should abate, because in a writ of *ejectione firmae* one recovers his term which is to come, and also damages, and when he has recovered he shall have a *habere facias possessionem* to put him in possession; but because he has entered, he has by his own act determined what the law would have given him. Thus note that someone who is in possession cannot be put in possession by *habere facias possessionem*. And, for that reason, he thought the writ should abate.

The lord DYER to the contrary. And he took it to be a maxim (*ground*) that [only] in cases where nontenure is a plea, the writ will abate if the demandant enters while the writ is pending. But here, in this *ejectione firmae*, nontenure is clearly not a plea, and so [the writ will not abate]. He also said that if I am ousted from my term, and within an hour I re-enter, I may have an *ejectione firmae* for the damages alone. Likewise if I am possessed of a term and am ousted, and I re-enter before the term ended, he said that – if I enter before the term ended – [I] shall have *ejectione firmae* after the term is ended and recover damages.

HARPER asked him whether it was a plea in an *ejectione firmae* to say that the plaintiff is himself in possession. And DYER answered that it was not, for that amounts to special nontenure.

2. ANON.

At the same time, in an attaint, the petit jury demanded oyer of the record, and had it.

---

[1] So identified from the report in BL MS. Lansdowne 1060, fo. 57v; HLS MS. 2079, fo. 134 (same). According to that reporter, 'Broxalme [Broxholme] de Grais Inn dit a moy que il mesme mynister cest ple deins les termes precedent in banck le roigne et que fuit receave et le pleint per ceo abate.'

[3]

In mesme le terme le case fuit tiell. Un enfaunt dage de x ans <fuit seisie de terres en fe et>^i prist fem al age de xvj ans, et morust. Le fem port brefe de dower. Cesti que fuit heire plede Ne unques accouple en loiall matrimonie, le demandant dit Accouple en loiall matrimonie, et sur ceo brefe fuit agard al evesque de Norwich pur certifier le quel ceo fuit un loiall matrimonie ou nemi. Levesque, recitant en son certificat coment le baron fuit del age de x ans, infra annos nubiles, et le fem de xvj ans, et ouster que fuerunt immunes ab omnibus precontractibus et omni alio impedimento, et puis conclude 'et issint loiallment accouple in matrimonie'.

Manwood argue que le tenant doit judgment aver, car luy semble clerement que si levesque ad certifie que ilz ne fueront loialment accouples adonques le tenant averoit son judgment, et come luy semble cest certificat taunt amount, car primerment il recite que lun fuit infra annos nubiles et pur cest cause il est clere per le ley civile que ilz ne fueront loialment espouse, car consensus facit legittimum matrimonium [et] consentire non potuit quia fuit infra annos 14, le quel est lage de consente. Mes jeo voille agre que cest matrimonium inchoatum et inceptum mes nemi perfectum et consummatum. Et pur ceo que icy nous sumus a issue sur le loialtie del mariage, pur ceo que nest forsque inchoatum et nemi legittimum moy semble que tenant judgment doit aver. Et coment que icy <que>^d levesque conclude 'et issint loialment accouple' moy semble que cest 'issint' est voide pur ceo que est mere contrariaunt et repugnaunt a le matter precedent. Et jeo toutz foitz ay prise cest diversitie pur bone leye, que quaunt le 'issint' est sur le point del brefe adonques le 'issint' waivera le matter precedent. Come en det sur un leas pur ans, le defendant plede Levie per distres, ou autermen plede releas le pleintife, et conclude 'et issint rien luy <doit>^i', ore in cest case lissint waivera le matter precedent. Mes quant lissue est hors del point del brefe sur un collaterall matter, adonques lissint ne waivera le matter precedent. Come en debt sur un obligation le defendant plede que il fuit lay home et nient lettred etc. 'et issint nient son fait', pur ceo que lissint est sur un collaterall matter etc. le matter precedent nest waive.

Gawdy al contrarie. Et luy semble que le matter precedent estoit bien ove le sequel del mariage, pur ceo que nient obstaunt que un soit infra 14 annos uncore luy semble que ceo fuit un loial mariage. Car mariage est bon tanque il soit avoided, scilicet per un disagrement. Car si ambideux ont vive tanque al age de disrcetion <et nad>^d et

APPENDIX I   clxxvii

3. MYNNE v. GREY[1]

In the same term there was this case. An infant aged 10,[2] who was seised of lands in fee, married a woman aged 16,[3] and died. The woman brought a writ of dower; the person who was heir pleaded 'Never joined in lawful matrimony'; and the demandant said 'Joined in lawful matrimony'. Thereupon a writ was awarded to the bishop of Norwich to certify whether this was lawful matrimony or not. The bishop, reciting in his certificate that the husband was 10 years old, under the age of marriage (*infra annos nubiles*), and the woman 16, and further that they were free from all precontracts and any other impediments, concluded 'and thus lawfully joined in matrimony'.

Manwood[4] argued that the tenant ought to have judgment, for it seemed to him clearly that if the bishop had certified that they were not lawfully joined then the tenant would have had his judgment, and (as it seemed to him) this certificate is tantamount to that, for he first recited that one of them was *infra annos nubiles* and for that reason it is clear by the Civil law that they were not lawfully espoused, for 'consent makes lawful matrimony' (*consensus facit legittimum matrimonium*) and he could not consent because he was under the age of 14, which is the age of consent. I would agree that it was an inchoate and begun marriage (*matrimonium inchoatum et inceptum*), but it was not perfected and consummated (*perfectum et consummatum*).[5] Because we are here at issue upon the lawfulness of the marriage, and because it is only *inchoatum* and not *legittimum*, it seems to me that the tenant ought to have judgment. Even though the bishop concluded 'and thus lawfully joined', it seems to me that this word 'thus' is void, because it is absolutely contrariant and repugnant to the preceding matter. I have always taken this distinction to be good law: when the word 'thus' is upon the point of the writ, 'thus' waives the preceding matter. For instance, in debt on a lease for years, if the defendant pleads 'Levied by distress', or pleads a release from the plaintiff, and concludes 'and thus he owes him nothing', in this case 'thus' waives the preceding matter. But when the issue is outside the point of the writ, upon a collateral matter, then the 'thus' does not waive the preceding matter. As, in debt on a bond, if the defendant pleads that he was a layman and illiterate etc., 'and thus it was not his deed', the preceding matter is not waived, because the word 'thus' here is upon a collateral matter.

Gawdy to the contrary. It seemed to him that the preceding matter stands well with the sequel of the marriage, because even if one of them is under the age of 14 it still seemed to him that it was a lawful marriage. For a marriage is good until it is avoided, namely by a disagreement. If both of them had lived until the age of discretion and

---

[1] CP 40/1289, m. 1716. Differently reported in Dyer 305, 313, 368; 110 Selden Soc. 379; Dal. 79. Most reports are from the much later hearing in 1580, when judgment was finally given: BL MS. Lansd. 1086, fos. 5–6 (arguments by Rodes and Anderson); LI MS. Misc. 487, fos. 6v–8 (sim.); CUL MS. Mm.4.31, fo. 4. For the tortuous proceedings, involving four successive writs to the bishop, see J. Baker, 'Some Elizabethan Marriage Cases' in *Studies in Canon and Common Law in Honor of R. H. Helmholz*, ed. T. L. Harris (Berkeley, 2015), pp. 181–211, at pp. 189–194. An opinion written by doctors of law this term is copied in BL MS. Harley 443, fo. 57v.
[2] Thomas Grey (1555–66), only son and heir of Thomas Grey (d. 1562) of Merton, Norfolk.
[3] Elizabeth, daughter of Robert Drury of Hawstead, subsequently married to Nicholas Mynne, the plaintiff.
[4] Still a serjeant. For his appointment as J.C.P. a few days later see below, p. clxxxi.
[5] Cf. YB Mich. 7 Hen. VI, fo. 11, pl. '36' [16], *per* Cokayn J.

adonques ne disagreont il est clere que donques cest fuit un loiall mariage. Et a prover que cest un mariage, si un garden in chivalrie marie son gard deins lage de discretion, il est clere [quil] ne unques avera le mariage apres, quel prove que est un mariage, car le ley done luy le mariage un foitz. Auxi sil fuit marie en le vie son auncestre deins lage de discretion le segnior (come le ley dit) ne poet luy marie que est marie. Et pur direct authoritie in cest case le livre est adjudge in 11 E. 2 que coment que le baron fuit forsque al age de 10 al temps del morant uncore la fem ad judgment daver sa dower.

Harper, justice, al contrarie etc. Et luy semble come Manwood adevant que lissint fuit voide et le matter precedent est voier etc. Et al livre que est vouche in 11 E.[1] 2, jeo voille agre le dit livre destre bon ley, car come appiert per le common ley del terre la fem fuit endowable coment [que] son baron morust deins lage de discretion. Et issint in nostre case si ceo ust estre trie per le common ley, le fem sauns doubt serroit endowe. Mes icy le matter est referre al trial de la ley civille, que dit clerment que le mariage nest pas loiall. Et pur ceo si home soit nee devant espousells et apres les parties intermariont, ore per le ley civile il est <bastard per n>[d] <mes>[d] mulier, mes per nostre <ley>[i] bastard. [Si en] cest case in un action les parties sont a issue sur <generall>[d] <especiall>[i] bastardie les jurores covient trover que il est bastarde solonque le common ley, mes si lissue soit sur <especiall>[d] <generall>[i] bastardie et nous escriomus al evesque, il covient ceo certifie solonque le ley civile que il est mulier. Issint que le triall fait le diversitie: ad quod Dier concessit, et argue mult in effect come Harper.

Et nota que solonque loppinion de le court per cest voy si le baron <ou la fem>[d] soit deins lage de consent et morust, la [fem] ne unques avera sa dower, car ilz agreont que si le tenant plede Ne unques accouple in loiall mariage le demandant per voy de replication ne poet disclose lespecial matter mes luy besoigne de joindre issue ove le tenant sur le loialtie del mariage, et donques cest matter covient ex necessitate estre trie per le certificat le bishope, que est oblige de certifier solonque le ley civile, que dit que le mariage nest pas loiall. [fo. i, verso]

[4][2]

[Replegiare.[3]] Loppinion del segnior Dier et Harper fuit que si le tenauncie soit in un countie <et le>[4] <ten>[d] segnior distreine les avers le tenant et eux enchase (come il bien poet) en le countie ou son mannour est et la eux empound, le tenant covient suer son replegiare in le countie ou ilz sont empounde, et luy covient disclose tout lespeciall matter <per no>[d] en son declaration, et issint le lieu ne serra traversable ou le prisell fuit.

---

[1] *Seemingly altered from* R *(which was correct).*
[2] *Also in JRL MS. Fr.118 (L), fo. 15v.*
[3] *L.*
[4] mannour in que le tenement est tenus en auter countie, et le *L.*

had not then disagreed, it is clear that it would then have been a lawful marriage. And, to prove that it is a marriage: if a guardian in chivalry marries off his ward below the age of discretion, it is clear that he shall never have the right of marriage again, which proves that it is a marriage; for the law gives him the marriage only once. Also, if the ward was married in the lifetime of the lord's ancestor, while under the age of discretion, the law says that the lord may not marry him off, as he is already married. For a direct authority in this case, there is a book adjudged in 11 [Ric.] II,[1] that even though the husband was only 10 years of age at the time of his death, the wife nevertheless had judgment to have her dower.

HARPER J. to the contrary. It seemed to him, as Manwood said before, that the word 'thus' is void and the preceding matter true. As to the book which is vouched in 11 [Ric.] II, I would agree the said book to be good law, for as it appears by the common law of the land the woman was endowable even though her husband died below the age of discretion. And here, in our case, if it had been tried by the common law, the woman would without doubt have been endowed. But here the matter has been referred to the trial of the Civil law, which says clearly that the marriage is not lawful. In the same way, if someone is born before espousals, and afterwards the parents marry each other, now by the Civil law he is legitimate (*mulier*), but by our law a bastard. And in that case, if the parties in an action are at issue upon special bastardy, the jurors must find that he is a bastard, according to the common law; but if the issue is upon general bastardy, and we write to the bishop, he must certify according to the Civil law that he is legitimate. Thus the trial makes the difference: which DYER granted, and he argued to much the same effect as Harper.

Note that, according to the opinion of the court, if the husband dies below the age of consent, the woman shall never have her dower in this way; for, as they agreed, if the tenant pleads 'Never joined in lawful marriage', the demandant may not by way of replication disclose the special facts but must needs join issue with the tenant upon the lawfulness of the marriage, and then the facts must of necessity be tried by the bishop's certificate, and he is obliged to certify according to the Civil law, which says that the marriage is not lawful.

4. ANON.[2]

[Replevin.] The opinion of the lord DYER and HARPER was that if the tenancy is in one county, and the [manor in which the tenement is held is in another county, and the] lord distrains the tenant's cattle and drives them (as well he may) into the county where his manor is, and impounds them there, the tenant must sue his *replegiare* in the county where they are impounded, and must disclose all the special facts in his declaration. Thus the place where the taking occurred is not traversable.

---

[1] Probably Pas. 12 Ric. II, Fitz. Abr., *Dower*, pl. 54.
[2] See this text collated with the Rylands MS. below, Appendix II, p. cxciv.

[5]

[Conditions.[1]] Home seisie des terres en fe fist leas pur ans reservant un rent <en le leas>[2] et le lessour covenant [in mesme le fait][3] que le lesse avera sufficient fuell <pur>[d] de toutz ces arbres, purveu toutz foitz et le lessee covenant que il ne prendera[4] timber <pur son fuell>.[5] Et apres le lesse succide certen [grosse][6] arbres <que fueront>[7] timbre. Le question fuit le quel cest proviso ferra [tantsolement][8] le covenant precedent conditionell ou que tout le leas serra conditionell et issint lentre le lessor[9] congeable en tout pur le condition enfreint.

Dier dit que le lesse <pur ans>[10] al common ley avera trois botes, scilicet houseboot, heibot et plougheboot, coment que le leas soit per paroll, come est agre in 21 H. 6. Et le lessor icy nad done ascun chose per cest covenant al lesse mes ceo que le ley <sauns ascun covenaunt>[11] voille aver done a luy. Et luy semble que cest proviso ferra[12] le covenant conditionell et serra come un limitation <de>[d] queux arbres il [ne][13] prendera pur son fuell.

Manwood, <en mesme le jour fait>[14] justice, prist cest diversitie, si nul sentence soit parenter le covenant et le proviso donques le proviso trenchera solement al covenant, [coment que le covenant et le proviso soient in divers sentences],[15] <mes>[d] <car>[i][16] si nul[17] sentence soit enterlace <coment que ne soit tout in mesme sentence mes in divers uncore ex necessitate serra prise un limitation del covenant precedent mes si ascun sentence soit enterlace>[18] donques est tout auterment: quod Harper concessit.

[6][19]

[Demurrer en ley parenter [...][20] et Kircke.][21] Cranmer larchevesque fist feffment in fe al use de luy mesme pur terme de son vie sauns impechment de wast, le remainder [apres son decesse][22] a ses executores pur terme de xxj ans, et apres les xxj ans <complete et>[23] ended a remainer a son fitz en taile, le remainder [a luy et][24] a ces droit heires. Et apres en temps le Roy Philipp et Mary Cranmer fuit attaint de treason <per acte de parliament>[25] et apres combust pur heresye. Et puis le Roy Philippe et Marie grant cest terme <de xxj ans>[26] a divers homes <per lour lettres patentes>[27] [que grant mesme le terme ouster a un Bath sur que cesti en le remainder en taile entre et fist leas pur ans a un Kirke, le quel fuit oust per Bath, et Kirke port un ejectione firme][28] <sur queux cesti in le remainder en taille entre et fist leas pur ans, et les patentes ouste le lesse hors de son terme, et il port ejectione firme>[29]. Et sur

---

[1] *L.* [2] *L.* [3] *Cf. below, p. 4.* [4] succidera ascun *L.* [5] etc. *L.* [6] *L.*
[7] esteant *L.* [8] *L.* [9] lesse *L.* [10] *Om. L.* [11] *Om. L.* [12] *Reads* serra.
[13] *L.* [14] *Om. L.* [15] *L.* [16] mes *L.* [17] un. *L.* [18] *Om. L.*
[19] *There is another version of the same text in LI MS. Misc. 361, fos. 32–34.*
[20] *Word lost, presumably* Bales. [21] *J.* [22] *J.* [23] *Om. J.* [24] *J.*
[25] *Om. J.* [26] *Om. J.* [27] *Om. J.* [28] *J.* [29] *Om. J.*

APPENDIX I   clxxxi

5. ANON.[1]

[Conditions.] Someone seised of lands in fee made a lease for years, reserving a rent *in the lease* [by deed indented], and the lessor covenanted [in the same deed] that the lessee should have sufficient fuel from all his trees, provided always (and the lessee covenanted) that he should not *take* [fell any] timber *for his fuel* [etc.]. Afterwards the lessee felled certain [large] trees which were timber. The question was, whether this proviso will [only] make the preceding covenant conditional, or whether the whole lease shall be conditional and therefore the lessor's entry in the whole congeable for breach of the condition.

DYER said that the lessee *for years* at common law shall have three kinds of bote, *namely* housebote, haybote and ploughbote, even if the lease is by parol, as is agreed *in* 21 Hen. VI.[2] And the lessor here has not given anything to the lessee by this covenant but that which the law would have given him *without any covenant*. It seemed to him that this proviso makes the covenant conditional and limits what trees he can take for his fuel.

MANWOOD, *on the same day made* justice,[3] drew this distinction: if there is no sentence between the covenant and the proviso, then the proviso will trench solely to the covenant, [even though the covenant and the proviso are in distinct sentences], for [but] if no [a] sentence is interposed, *even if it is not in the same sentence but in various sentences, nevertheless of necessity it shall be taken as a limitation of the preceding covenant, whereas if any sentence is interposed* it is altogether otherwise: which HARPER granted.

6. KYRKE d. CRANMER v. BALES [4]

[Demurrer in law between Bales and Kirk.] Cranmer, the archbishop, made a feoffment in fee to the use of himself for term of his life, without impeachment of waste, the remainder [after his decease] to his executors for term of twenty-one years, and, after the twenty-one years *completed and* ended, remainder to his son in tail, the remainder [to him and] to his right heirs. Afterwards, in the time of King Philip and [Queen] Mary, Cranmer was attainted of treason *by act of Parliament* and afterwards burned for heresy. Then King Philip and [Queen] Mary granted this term *of twenty-one years* to various people <*by their letters patent, upon whom the remainderman in tail entered and made the lease for years, and the patentees ousted the lessee from his term, and he brought ejectment*> [who granted the same term over to one {Bales},[5] upon whom the

---

[1] Cf. below, p. 50. Differently reported in CUL MS. Gg.5.2, fo. 102.
[2] *Abbot of Torre v. Toning* (1443) YB Pas. 21 Hen. VI, fo. 46, pl. 23.
[3] Manwood's patent as J.C.P. was dated 14 Oct. 1572: *CPR 1569–72*, p. 393. His appointment on that day is noted in BL MS. Lansd. 1060, fo. 111 (which records that Burghley was sworn lord treasurer on the same day); HLS MS. 2079, fo. 135 (same report). Cf. Dyer 310, where it is said that the first case Manwood argued after becoming a justice was *Cranmer's Case* (no. 6, below), and that it was on the feast of the Apostles Simon and Jude (28 Oct.).
[4] See below, p. 58, no. 106, and the note there.
[5] So spelt in LI MS. Misc. 361

cest matter le parties ont[1] demurre etc. [Et][2] le principall et sole point in cest case fuit le quel <cest estate pur xxj ans fuit vest in Cranmer, car si ne fuit vest en luy adonques il ne poet forfeit>[3] [cest terme fuit in le lesse pur vie ou nemi, car si ceo fuit en luy adonques le roy ad ceo per forfeiture per son atteindre et donques les patentes ont bon title et droit et issint le ejectione nient maintenable, al auter side si riens fuit in luy adonques il forfeit riens et issint laction bien maintenable].[4]

Benloes primerment argue. Et luy semble que cest use[5] <ne>[i] fuit <vest en le segnior Cranmer etc.>[6] [in le lesse pur ans et issint le roy prist riens per son atteindre].[7] <Et pur ceo primerment luy semble que executores ne sont bone nosme de purchase. Et pur ceo il resemble eux al case de churchwardens. Et il cite un case hors de 1 Lib. Ass. p. [*blank*] que un feffment fuit fait a un et a luy que serroit son primer fem, et adjudge que la fem prist riens. Mes autrement fuit si ceo ust estre per voy de remainder, come le case est in 18 E. 3, terres fueront dones a un home, le remainder primogenito filio suo, la le remainder tenus bon et son primer fitz prist per ceo. Mes come moy semble cest use nunques fuit in le segnior Cranmer <dit>[d] >[8] car [il dit que][9] Bracton dit quod feodum et terminus possunt simul [incipere][10] sed non possunt simul stare. <Et pur ceo si jeo face un leas pur vie, le remainder a <luy>[d] <ces executors>[i] pur xx ans pur ceo que cest terme non incipit cum feodo pur ceo simul stare non potest.>[11] [Et icy cest terme et franktenement commence a un temps et pur ceo luy semble quod simul stare non possunt.][12] <Et a cest purpose il cite le livre in 22 E. 3, [*blank*]. En un quid juris clamat vers tenant pur terme de vie il dit que il voile attorne {que}[d] si le terme que il ad apres son vie soit a luy save, et pur ceo que le terme ad son commencement ove lestate pur vie le livre est adjudge que son terme serra save a luy {mes}[d] apres son mort, scilicet a ces executores. Mes ceo ne fuit in luy mesme, pur ceo que feodum et terminus ne possunt simul instare. Et a cest intent il vouche auxi le livre in 22 Lib. Ass. p. {*blank*}, in un latten case. {et appiert per un estatut fait in 33 H. 8}[d] >[13] Et il dit que in T. 5 Philippi et Marie cest case fuit in experiens. <Un leas fuit fait per le prior de Canterbury>[14] a un pur terme de son vie, et le lessor granta que si le lesse devie deins lx ans que adonques les <lesses>[d] executors <et assignes>[i] le lesse <averoit ceo en droit le lesse>[15] <et>[d] jesque al <fine del>[16] lx ans [complete et ended][17]. Le lesse morust deins les ans, et sur cest case duex[18] matters fueront moves: un, si les executores ceo averoit come un novell leas, auter <si enuera>[19] per voy de remainder. Et [le][20] segnior Brooke, <adonques chief justice, perswade>[21] les parties a accorder, car il dit que les executores ne <poet prender ascun chose>[22] per force de cest leas.

---

[1] *Om. J.*   [2] *J.*   [3] *Om. J.*   [4] *J.*   [5] terme *J.*
[6] *Om. J.*   [7] *J.*   [8] *Om. J.*   [9] *J.*
[10] *J.* percipere *H.*
[11] *Om. J.*   [12] *J.*   [13] *Om. J.*
[14] Le prior de Canterbury fist leas *J.*
[15] come en droit et title lour testator averont ceo *J.*
[16] *Om. J.*   [17] *J.*   [18] *Sic.*
[19] sils ceo averont *J.*
[20] *J.*
[21] counsaile *J.*
[22] prendront riens *J.*

APPENDIX I clxxxiii

remainderman in tail entered and made a lease for years to one Kirk, who was ousted by {Bales}, and Kirk brought an ejectment]. And upon this matter the parties demurred. And the principal and sole point in this case was whether <*this estate for twenty-one years was vested in Cranmer, for if it was not vested in him he cannot forfeit it*> [this term was in the lessee for life or not; for, if it was in him, the king has it by forfeiture, through his attainder, and the patentees have a good title and right, and so the ejectment is not maintainable; but, on the other side, if nothing was in him, then he forfeited nothing, and so the action is well maintainable].

Bendlowes argued first. And it seemed to him that this <*use*> [term] was not <*vested in the lord Cranmer etc.*> [in the lessee for years, and so the king took nothing by his attainder]. <*As to this, it seemed to him, firstly, that 'executors' is not a good name of purchase. And he likened them to the case of churchwardens. And he cited a case out of 1 Lib. Ass., pl. [11],*>[1] *where a feoffment was made to someone and to whomever should be his first wife, and it was adjudged that the wife took nothing. But it would have been otherwise by way of remainder, as the case is in 18 Edw. III,*[2] *where lands were given to someone, remainder to his firstborn son (*primogenito filio suo*), and there the remainder was held good and his first son took by it. But, as it seems to me, this use was never in the lord Cranmer*> for [he said that] Bracton says that a fee and a term may begin together but cannot stand together ('quod feodum et terminus possunt simul incipere sed non possunt simul stare').[3] <*Therefore if I make a lease for life, remainder to his executors for twenty years, because this term does not begin with the fee it cannot stand together with it.*> [And here this term and freehold commence at one time, and therefore it seems that they cannot stand together.] <*To this purpose he cited the book in 22 Edw. III, [*blank*],*[4] *where in a* quid juris clamat *against tenant for term of life he said that he would attorn if the term which he has after his life could be saved to him, and because the term had its commencement with the estate for life the book is adjudged that his term should be saved to him after his death, namely, to his executors. But it was not in himself, because the fee and the term cannot stand together. To this purpose he also vouched the book in 22 Lib. Ass., pl. [*blank*], in a Latin case.*[5]> And he said that in Trin. 5 Phil. & Mar. this case was in experience:[6] a lease was made by the prior of Canterbury to someone for term of his life, and the lessor granted that if the lessee died within sixty years then the lessee's executors and assigns should have it <in right of the lessee> [*as in right and title of their testator*] until the end of the sixty years; and the lessee died within the years. Upon this case two matters were moved: (1) whether the executors should have it as a new lease, (2) <whether it should enure> [*whether they should have it*] by way of remainder. And the lord Brooke, <then chief justice, persuaded> [*counselled*] the parties to settle, for he said that the executors could not take anything by virtue of this lease.

[1] 1 Edw. III, Lib. Ass., pl. 11.
[2] YB Mich. 18 Edw. III, fo. 59, pl. 91, continued from Pas. 17 Edw. III, fo. 29, pl. 30.
[3] Paraphrase of a passage in *Bracton*, ii. 73–74; cf. ibid., p. 138.
[4] Perhaps meaning Mich. 20 Edw. III, Fitz. Abr., *Quid juris clamat*, pl. 31: see Dyer 309.
[5] 22 Edw. III, Lib. Ass., pl. 37 (special verdict in Latin).
[6] *Parker* v. *Gravenor* (1557) CP 40/1170, m. 1189; cited in 2 Leon. 7, *per* Dyer C.J.; Dyer 150. This is dated Trin. 3 & 4 Phil. & Mar. in Dyer. But Dyer's report (not printed until 1585) does not mention Brooke C.J.

Lovelace al contrarie. <Et luy semble que in multes cases un person que nest nosme en le graunt prendra bien per le graunt. Et primerment {luy semble}[d] luy semble que les executores ont lour interest in et per lour testatour et pur ceo il cite le livre in 21 E. 4 {*blank*}, home fuit tenus que il et ses assignes ferront tiel chose , et pur ceo que les assignes conveiont lour authoritie de luy, le livre est que il poet ceo faire solement. Issint icy in nostre case pur ceo que les executores claimont eins per le testatour moy semble que cest use est vest en le testatour. Et come jeo ay dit adevant moy semble que en multes case[s] un chose passera [sa][d] implicative et sauns ascun nosme expresse en le graunt. Et pur ceo le livre est in 8 H. 4, un graunt que J. S. distrenera pur xx s. de rent en son mannour de D. et tenus bon graunt de rent, et uncore ne sont ascun parolx de graunt. 46 E. 3 [*blank*] un graunt rent a un auter ad distringendum per ballivum domini regis, coment que nul parlauns fuit del graunte, uncore le livre est que il mesme distrenera pur ceo. Issint in nostre case, coment que cest limitation soit solement as executores, uncore ceo taunt amount come sil ust dit a luy et a ces executores, et donques le case ad estre assetz clere. Et, sir, moy semble que jeo poy>[1] [Et il][2] resemble cest <remainder al>[3] remainder as droit heires, car come pier et heire sont correlativa en mesme le manner sont testatour et executour. Mes il est clere <come jeo provera per divers>[4] authorities que si les soit fait al pier, le remainder a ses heires, que en cest case [le] lease est vest in le pier. In mesme le mannour in nostre case icy quant leas est fait al testatour pur vie, le remainder pur ans a ces executores, cest remainder est vest in le testatour. <Et pur ceo le livre est>[5] agre in 7 et 10 H. 4 [*blank*], que si jeo face [lease] pur vie a J. S., le remainder as droit heires J. N., J. N. morust, et puis <J. S. esteant>[6] lesse pur vie morust, et tenus [(coment durement)][7] que <in cest case>[8] les heires <J. N.>[i] esteant implied ont[9] lour age. Et a cest intent est Maundeviles case in 2 E. 3, terres fueront dones a un [Robert][10] et al fem del Maundevile, esteant mort, et <a les heires>[11] de sa corps per Maundevile engendres, et tenus clerement que la fem ad estate in especialle taile, et que cest parol heire ne fuit nosme de purchase mes nosme de limitation. Mesme le case in 5 H. 4, [*blank*], 12 H. 4, [*blank*], 4 E. 3, fol. [*blank*], itinere <North>[d] Darby, terres done a 2, le remainder as heires de lun de eux, cesty que ad le inheritauns morust, lauter survive [*fo. ii*] et ad tout per le survivor, et puis morust, et le fitz lauter <jointenant a queux heires le remainder fuit limite>[12] maintein un assize de mordauncestre, quel prove que il vient a ceo come heire et nemi come un purchaser. 11 H. 4, [*blank*], terres dones al pier, le remainder a ses droit heires, et le livre agre que le fe fuit execute en le piere. Si le ley soit tiel in le case del pier et fitz, verament le ley ne

---

[1] *Om. J.*
[2] *J.*
[3] case al case de *J.*
[4] per multes *J.*
[5] Et quant al case de droit heires le livres sont *J.*
[6] le *J.*
[7] *J.*
[8] *Om. J.*
[9] averont *J.*
[10] *J.* Robettz *H.*
[11] al heire *J.*
[12] jointenant que ad le inheritauns *J.*

APPENDIX I   clxxxv

Lovelace to the contrary. <*And it seemed to him that in many cases a person who is not named in a grant may well take by the grant. Firstly, it seemed to him that the executors have their interest in and through their testator, and for this he cited the book in 21 Edw. IV,*[1] *where a man was bound that he and his assigns should do a certain thing, and because the assigns traced their authority from him, the book is that he could do it alone. Likewise in our case, because the executors claim to be in through the testator, it seems to me that this use is vested in the testator. And, as I have said before, it seems to me that in many cases a thing may pass by implication, without any name expressed in the grant. For this there is a book in 8 Hen. IV,*[2] *where someone granted that John Style could distrain for 20 shillings of rent in his manor of Dale, and it was held a good grant of rent even though there are no words granting the rent. In 46 Edw. III*[3] *someone granted a rent to another to be distrained for by the lord king's bailiff, and, although there was no mention of it in the grant, the book nevertheless says that he could himself distrain for it. Likewise in our case, although this limitation is solely to the executors, nevertheless it amounts to as much as if he had said 'him and his executors', and then the case would have been clear enough. Sir, it seems to me that I may liken*> [And he likened] this <*remainder to the*> [case to the case of a] remainder to right heirs, for just as father and heir are correlatives, so likewise are testator and executor. But it is clear, <*as I will prove*> by several authorities, that if a lease is made to the father, remainder to his heirs, the lease in this case is vested in the father. Similarly in our case here, when a lease is made to the testator for life, remainder for years to his executors, this remainder is vested in the testator. <*For this, the book is* > [As to the case of the right heirs, the books are] agreed in 7 and 10 Hen. IV[4] that if I make a lease for life to John Style, remainder to the right heirs of John Noke, and John Noke dies, and then <*John Style being*> the lessee for life dies, it was held [(however harshly)] that <*in this case*> the heirs of John Noke, being implied, [should] have their age. To the same effect is Mandevile's case in 2 Edw. III,[5] where lands were given to one Robert and the wife of Mandevile,[6] he being dead, and to the <*heirs*> [heir] of her body begotten by Mandevile, and it was held clearly that the woman had an estate in special tail, and that this word 'heir' was not a name of purchase but a name of limitation. The same case is in 5 Hen. IV,[7] 12 Hen. IV,[8] and 4 Edw. III (in the eyre of Derby),[9] where lands were given [to two], remainder to the heirs [of one] of them, and the one who had the inheritance died, the other survived and had the whole by survivorship, and then died, and the son of the other <*joint tenant to whose heirs the remainder was limited*> [joint tenant who had the inheritance] maintained an assize of mort d'ancestor, which proves that he came to it as heir and not as a purchaser. In 11 Hen. IV,[10] lands were given to the father, remainder to his right heirs, and the book is

[1] YB Mich. 21 Edw. IV, fo. 44, pl. 5.   [2] YB Hil. 8 Hen. IV, fo. 11, pl. 5.
[3] YB Trin. 46 Edw. III, fo. 18, pl. 17.
[4] YB Mich. 7 Hen. IV, fo. 23, pl. 2.
[5] *Fauconberg* v. *Courtney* (1328) YB Hil. 2 Edw. III, fo. 1, pl. 1–2. For this case see M. Nathan, *The Annals of West Coker* (1957), p. 82.
[6] Roberga, widow of John de Mandevile.
[7] Perhaps YB Hil. 5 Hen. IV, fo. 3, pl. 11.
[8] Perhaps *Markham* v. *Markham* (1410) YB Mich. 12 Hen. IV, fos. 1–3, pl. 3.
[9] Cited in Co. Litt. 184, margin.
[10] Probably YB Pas. 11 Hen. IV, fo. 55, pl. 1.

clxxxvi

poet estre auter in le testatour et ses executores, car ilz [come jay dit]¹ sont correlativa. <Item, Eli>² 27 E. 1, terres dones a un home et a sa fem et a les heires issauntes hors <de son corps>³, coment cest parol issuaunt nest apt <in cest ple, mes>⁴ engendres ou tiel semble, uncore tenus bon estate taile. 40 E. 3, [*blank*], provost of Beverlyes case, terres fueront dones a un pur vie, le remainder en taile, le remainder as droit heires le lesse pur vie, et tenus que les parolz heires in cest cas <case>ᵈ ne fueront nosmes de purchase mes un limitation et que le fe fuit vest en le pier. 14 H. 4, [*blank*], terres done en taile, le remainder a ces droit heires, tenant en taile fist feffment in fe [et morust]⁵, leire recontinuera lestate taile mes le fe remaine en le feffe. 27 Lib. Ass. p. [*blank*], a mesme lentent.⁶ 33 H. 6, <Yelverton a mesme lentent>.⁷ Et ore tard cest case fuit adjudge in banke le roy, terres fueront devise per testament a un home pur terme de son vie, le remainder as droit heires, et adjudge que le fe fuit vest in luy coment que fuit in un devise. <Ore, south correction, si le ley soit tiel come jeo ay prove in case del pier et ses droit heires, a fortiori icy in nostre case de executores, car ilz representont le testatour et son person demesne.>⁸ 11 H. 4, [*blank*], un annuitie fuit graunt pur vie a J. S., le remainder a luy pur 3 ans, [et agre que apres son mort]⁹ ses executores navera scire facias etc.¹⁰ Et la Hankford dit que in cest cas un terme et un estate pur vie sunt simul et semel in un mesme person, ergo <it taketh>¹¹ effect in him et ses executores per luy. 46 E. 3, 47, leas fuit fait a un home pur son vie, le remainder a luy pur un [demi]¹² an, et puis il morust, et ces executores fieront wast, et [le] lessor port <brefe de>ⁱ wast <in le tenuit>ⁱ suppose que le lesse pur terme de vie tenuit, quel prove fortment que le terme fuit in le testatour. 39 E. 3, 33, leas fuit fait pur vie, le remainder a luy pur ans, in un quid juris clamat vers luy supposant estre tenant pur vie <gen>ᵈ sil ad attorne generalment le livre est que il perdroit¹³ son terme, et pur ceo il prist ceo per protestation. Mes icy poet estre dit que ceux cases differont mult a le cas al barre pur ceo que in ceux case[s] le remainder est limitt a luy [et a ces executores],¹⁴ et en le cas al barre nest limitte a luy eyns a les executores [solement].¹⁵ Jeo voille mitter ascuns cases in queux le terme est limitte a ces executores et uncore vest en luy. Et pur ceo le livre est adjudge in 50 Lib. Ass. p. 1, terres fueront done a un pur vie, le remainder a ses executores, et <tenus que en quid juris clamat sil ust attorne generalment il perdroit son terme, coment que ceo fuit limitte a ces executores.>¹⁶ Mes icy poet estre dit [que]¹⁷ cest cas auxi differ <al>ᵈ del case al barre, car le case al barre est dun use, le quel poet estre in abeiauns <et le case in 50 Lib. Ass. {est}ⁱ des terres in possession, les queux ne sont pas semblables.>¹⁸ Mes, south correction, moy

---

¹ *J*.   ² Auxi in itinere Elye *H*.   ³ del corps le baron *J*.
⁴ paroll sicome *J*.   ⁵ *J*.   ⁶ le purpose *J*.
⁷ Yelvertonnes opinion *J*.
⁸ Mes sont cases agrees en nostre livres que touche mesme le point de nostre case *J*.
⁹ *J*.   ¹⁰ pur executer ceo *J*.
¹¹ il prist *J*.   ¹² *J*.
¹³ ust perde *J*.   ¹⁴ *J*.   ¹⁵ *J*.
¹⁶ per largument del livre est pleinment prove que le terme fuit in le lesse pur vie *J*.
¹⁷ *J*.   ¹⁸ Om. *J*.

---

⁷ YB Mich. 46 Edw. III, fo. 31, pl. 32, in the vulgate edition.
⁸ Cited in Dyer 310 and 3 Leon. 21 as YB 39 Edw. III, fo. 25.
⁹ 50 Edw. III, Lib. Ass., pl. 1.

agreed that the fee was executed in the father. If the law is thus in the case of the father and son, then truly the law cannot be otherwise in the case of the testator and his executors, for [*as I have said*] they are correlative. <*Item, Ely*> [Also, in the eyre of Ely] in 27 Edw. I, lands were given to a man and his wife and the heirs issuing from <*his body*> [the husband's body], even though this word 'issuing' is not apt in this plea, but [it should be] 'begotten' or such like, nevertheless it was held a good estate tail. In 40 Edw. III,[1] in the provost of Beverley's case, lands were given to someone for life, remainder in tail, remainder to the right heirs of the lessee for life, and it was held that the word 'heirs' in this case was not a name of purchase but a limitation, and that the fee was vested in the father. In 14 Hen. IV[2] lands were given in tail, remainder to his right heirs, the tenant in tail made a feoffment in fee [and died]: the heir may recontinue the estate tail, but the fee remains in the feoffee. 27 Lib. Ass., pl. [*blank*],[3] is to the same purpose; and Yelverton['s opinion] in 33 Hen. VI,[4] to the same effect. And recently this case was adjudged in the King's Bench: lands were devised by testament to a man for term of his life, remainder to the right heirs, and it was adjudged that the fee was vested in him, even though it was in a devise.[5] <Now, subject to correction, if the law is as I have proved it to be in the case of the father and his right heirs, a fortiori it is so here in our case of executors, for they represent the testator and his own person.> [But there are cases agreed in our books which touch the same point as our case.] In 11 Hen. IV[6] an annuity was granted for life to John Style, remainder to him for three years, [and it was agreed that after his death] his executors could not have *scire facias* [to execute it]. And Hankford there said that in this case a term and an estate for life are simultaneously in one same person, ergo it takes effect in him, and in his executors through him. In 46 Edw. III, fo. 47,[7] a lease was made to someone for his life, remainder to him for a [half] year, and then he died, and his executors committed waste, and the lessor brought a writ of waste in the *tenuit*, alleging that the lessee for term of life held (*tenuit*): which proves strongly that the term was in the testator. In 39 Edw. III, fo. 33,[8] a lease was made for life, remainder to him for years, and in a *quid juris clamat* against him, supposing him to be tenant for life, the book says that had he attorned generally he would <*lose*> [have lost] his term, and therefore he took this point by protestation. But it might be said here that those cases differ much from the case at bar, because in those cases the remainder was limited to him [and his executors], and in the case at bar it is not limited to him but to his executors [*alone*]. But I will put some cases in which the term is limited to his executors and is nevertheless vested in him. As to this, the book is adjudged in 50 Lib. Ass., pl. 1,[9] where lands were given to someone for life, remainder to his executors, and <*it was held that in a* quid juris clamat, *if he had attorned generally, he would have lost his term, even though it was limited to his executors*> [by the argument of the book it is fully proved that the term was in the lessee for life]. But here it might be said that this case also differs from the case at bar in that the case at bar is of a use, which may be in abeyance, *and the case in 50 Lib. Ass. is of lands in possession, and these are not alike*. But, subject to correction, it seems to

---

[1] *Provost of Beverley's Case* (1367) YB Hil. 40 Edw. III, fo. 9, pl. 18; B. & M. 76.
[2] YB Hil. 14 Hen. IV, fo. 31, pl. 43.   [3] 27 Edw. III, Lib. Ass., pl. 60.
[4] YB Hil. 33 Hen. VI, fo. 5, pl. 16.   [5] For this passage cf. below, p. 78, no. 123, and p. 85, no. 137.
[6] YB Mich. 11 Hen. IV, fo. 34, pl. 65, *per* Hankford C.J.

semble que tout est un dun use et des terres in possession, car usus sequitur naturam terre, et pur ceo [le]¹ livre est agre in 5 E. 4, 7, si tenant en brough englise enfeffe un al use de luy et ces heires, son puisne fuitz avera² ceo solonque le custome. 12 H. 7, [blank], feffment in fe al use de [parrochiauns est]³ voide sicome il ust estre des terres in <demesne et>⁴ possession. 31 E. 1, tit. Graunt [a cest purpose, vide librum.]⁵ ⁶<Et cest case fuit devant le segnior Mountague, chief justice. Un parson que nad forsque estate pur vie fist leas pur ans a commencer apres son mort, et le patron et ordinarie ceo confirme, et le segnior Mountague tient que ceo fuit un bon graunt coment que le parson nad forsque estate pur vie issint que il ne poet graunt un chose apres son mort, son estate esteant determine.>⁷ Et ore jeo voille move un chose et mitte ceo al consideration del court <que pur ceo que>⁸ les parolx sont post terminum viginti annorum finitum <post mortem etc.>⁹ adonques remanebit filio suo in taillio, et pur ceo coment que cest terme ne fuit in le roy uncore occupanti conceditur pur ceo que son temps nest uncore venus.

Barrham al contrarie. Les cases in 46 E. 3 et 39 E. 3 et 50 Lib. Ass. etc. ne sont [pas]¹⁰ semblables a <nostre case icy>,¹¹ car la le limitation fuit fait a luy, <car un leas fuit fait a {luy}ᵈ tenant pur vie, le remainder a luy pur ans>,¹² et donques ex necessitate <acordant as parolx le terme est en luy>,¹³ <mes icy le terme nest limitte a luy eins a ses executores>.¹⁴ Et quant al case de 16 E. 3 del quid juris camat, lou le case fuit que un leas fuit fait a luy <et post>ᵈ pur vie et post mortem ejus a ses executores, <sil ust attorne generalment il ne perdroit ascun terme car nul interest fuit in luy mes il perderoit un libertie de nosmer tielx executores queux poient ceo prender et {ew}ᵈ enjoier, issint que il fuit pur saver son libertie et election et nemi de saver son terme.>¹⁵ <Et issint>¹⁶ jeo responde le case in 20 E. 3, [blank], que il <save le nomination et libertie de electer executores et nemi de saver son terme, que ne unques fuit in luy>.¹⁷ Car le case in effect nest forsque tiel, si jeo face un feffment al segnior Dier a enfeffer eux queux jeo voille nosmer et assigner, les assignes ne prendront ascun chose per moy, et <ne>ᵈ jeo ne poet forfeite les terres, car jeo nad <que un libertie et assignment, mes jeo poy forfeit un nomination etc.>¹⁸ Et il cite le case in 19 E. 2, [blank], <lou un fuit seisie des terres tenus per service de chivaller [...]¹⁹ [*fo. ii verso*] et cest nest pas semble al case lou jeo face leas pur vie, le

---

¹ *J.* que *H.*   ² inheritera *J.*
³ *J. Unclear in H.*   ⁴ *Om. J.*   ⁵ *J.*
⁶ *Following a line space, the latter half of the previous line being blank.*
⁷ *Om. J.*   ⁸ *Om. J.*   ⁹ *Om. J.*
¹⁰ *J.*   ¹¹ cest case *J.*
¹² ou a luy et a ces executores *J.*
¹³ est in luy accordant a le limitatione. *J.*   ¹⁴ *Om. J.*
¹⁵ pur ans, la pur saver son libertie et nomination de tielx executores que poient ceo prender il ne attorne generalment mes il ne save ascun terme car null fuit limitte a luy mes solement come jay dit il save son libertie et nomination etc. *J.*
¹⁶ In mesme le manner *J.*
¹⁷ ne attorne generalment nemy pur saver son terme mes pur saver son election et nomination etc. *J.*
¹⁸ forsque le nude nomination *J.*
¹⁹ *Remaining half of line blank.*

---

⁷ Presumably 19 Edw. II, Fitz. Abr., *Covenant*, pl. 25; below, p. cxciii.
⁸ The remaining half of the line is blank.

me that a use and lands in possession are to be treated as one, for a use follows the nature of the land (*usus sequitur naturam terrae*); and for this reason the book is agreed in 5 Edw. IV, fo. 7,[1] that if a tenant in borough English enfeoffs someone to the use of him and his heirs, his younger son shall <have> [inherit] it in accordance with the custom. In 12 Hen. VI,[2] a feoffment in fee to the use of parishioners is void, just as it would have been of lands in <demesne and> possession. 31 Edw. I, tit. Graunt,[3] [is to this purpose: see the book.] <*And this case was before the lord Mountague, chief justice: a parson (who has only an estate for life) made a lease for years to begin after his death, and the patron and ordinary confirmed it, and the lord Mountague held that it was a good grant, even though the parson has only an estate for life and so cannot grant something after his death, his estate being determined.*[4]> Now I will move something and submit it to the consideration of the court, *which is that* the words are 'after the term of twenty years ended after his death etc. it should then remain to his son in tail': therefore, even though this term was not in the king, nevertheless it shall be allowed to the occupant (*occupanti conceditur*) because his time is not yet come.[5]

Barham to the contrary. The cases in 46 Edw. III, 39 Edw. III, and 50 Lib. Ass. etc. are not like our case here, for there the limitation was made to him, <*for a lease was made to tenant for life, remainder him for years*> [or to him and his executors], and then necessarily <*according to the words the term is in him*> [it is in him according to the limitation], *but here the term is not limited to him but to his executors.* As for the case of 16 Edw. III of the *quid juris clamat*,[6] where the case was that a lease was made to him for life, and after his death to his executors: <*if he had attorned generally he would not have lost any term, for there was no interest in him, but he would lose the liberty of naming the executors who might take and enjoy it, and so it was done to save his liberty and election and not to save his term*> [for years, and there in order to save his liberty and nomination of such executors who could take it he did not attorn generally, but he did not save any term, for none was limited to him, but he only (as I have said) saved his liberty and nomination etc.] I can answer in the same way the case in 20 Edw. III, that he <*saved the nomination and liberty of choosing executors and not his term, which was never in him*> [did not attorn generally, not to save his term but to save his election and nomination {of executors}.] For the case in effect is but this, if I make a feoffment to the lord Dyer, in order to enfeoff those whom I should name and assign, the assigns will not take anything through me, and I cannot forfeit the lands, for I have <*only a liberty and assignment; but I may forfeit a nomination.*> [only the bare nomination]. And he cited the case in 19 Edw. II,[7] <*where someone was seised of lands held by knight-service [...]*,[8] *and that is not like the case where I make a lease for life, remainder to*

---

[1] YB Mich. 5 Edw. IV, fo. 7, pl. 16.
[2] Probably a slip for YB Trin. 12 Hen. VII, fo. 27, pl. 7, continued in Mich. 13 Hen. VII, fo. 9, pl. 5; identifiable as *Baker* v. *Johnson*, KB 27/945, m. 34d; Caryll's reports, 115 Selden Soc. 361.
[3] There are three cases from this year in Fitz. Abr., *Graunte* (pl. 85, 86 and 90), but they are unrelated to this point.
[4] Also reported as *Anon.* (1551) Dyer 69, pl. 30. The citation cannot be to Dyer, which was not yet in print.
[5] Cf. below, p. 144, no. 265.
[6] Probably Pas. 16 Edw. III, Fitz. Abr., *Quid juris clamat*, pl. 22.

remainder as droit heires etc., la jeo voille agre que le fe est execute pur ceo que est forsque un estate, mes icy sont severall estates, lun pur vie, lauter pur ans>¹ [le quel Manwood apres pluis pleinment remember al contrarie side].² Et, sir, come moy semble un use [nesq]ᵈ nest forsque un trust et confidence parenter les parties et hors del groundes del common ley, et lentent le partie in uses serra prise et le common ley ne <serra observe>³ [controllera ceo].⁴ Et pur ceo si jeo soy seisi des terres en fe et face feffment in fe a J. S. sur condition que sil morust sauns heire de son corps que donques il remaindra a J. N. et a ses heire[s], <ceo est void al common ley,>⁵ mes si jeo soy seisie des terres en fe et face feffment in fe al use de J. S. et a ses heires et sil morust sauns heires que donques ceo remaindra a J. N. et a ses heires, ceo est <bon clerment>,⁶ car lentent le partie in uses serra observe. Al common ley cesti que use ad nul remedie a vener a le terre, car nest forsque un trust et confidens. <Al common ley cesti que use ne puit distreine.>⁷ Al common ley il navera assise ne trespas pur trespas fait sur le soile de quel il ad le use, et al common ley il ne puissoit compell ses feffes pur punisher ceo. Et il cite le case in 1 E. 3, Lib. Ass., p. [*blank*], lou terres fueront dones a un home et a [luy que serroit]⁸ sa fem, <et al temps il nad fem>,⁹ si apres il prist fem le fem prendra riens. 17 E. 3, lou terres fueront dones a un home et a son 2 fitz, lou il nad nul fitz as temps forsque un, si apres il ad auter fitz son 2 fitz prendra riens. Mes icy cest cas fuit adjudge, que un fuit seisie in fe et fist feffment in fe al use de luy et de sa fem, lou il nad fem al temps, puis il prist fem, et adjudge que la fem prendra per ceo, issint que il est un graund differens parenter uses et terres en possession. Et al darrein conceit que le fitz in le remainder <ne>ᵈ poet prender riens devant le terme finy, moy semble que le terme esteant voide, come jeo entende le ley destre, cesti en le remainder poet bien entre. Et pur ceo si jeo face un leas pur vie, le remainder a un moigne, et que apres son decesse a remainder a J. N., si le lesse pur vie morust, lentre del J. N. est congeable et nul occupauns en cest case pur ceo que le primer remainder est void.¹⁰ Issint in nostre case etc.

Jeffries al contrarie. Et il prist cest diversitie, que in toutz grauntes lou un estate est fait a un home et apres mention est fait de ces heires, ceux parolx heires sont forsque un limitation et ne sont ascun nosme de purchase. Et issint des executores, car tout est un. Mes auterment est lou launcestre nest pas nosme, mes le heire ou executor solement, la¹¹ sont nosmes de purchase. Et a prover le primer braunche de cest diversitie le livre est agre in 5 E. 4, 2, si jeo face leas pur terme de vie, le remainder <pur vie>ᵈ en taile, le remainder as droit heires le lesse, in cest cas pur ceo que launcestre fuit nosme devant ceux parolx heires sont forsque un limitation del estate et le <fuit>ᵈ fe en le lesse pur charger ou doner ou forfeiter etc. Issint le case in 40 E. 3 devant reherse. [Et auxi]¹² 11 H. 4, [*blank*], mesme le case. Mes de lauter part, si launcestre ne soit nosme, donques est bon nosme de purchase. Et pur ceo le

---

¹ *Om. J.*   ² *J.*   ³ *Om. J.*   ⁴ *J.*
⁵ si ceo soit in possession le common ley dit que ceo fuit void *J.*
⁶ assetz bon *J.*   ⁷ *Om. J.*
⁸ *J.*   ⁹ *Om. J.*   ¹⁰ fait *J.*
¹¹ adonques *J.*   ¹² *J.*

⁴ *Provost of Beverley's Case* (1367) YB Hil. 40 Edw. III, fo. 9, pl. 18; B. & M. 76.
⁵ Cited above, p. clxxxvii.

the right heirs [of the lessee], for there I will agree that the fee is executed, because it is but one estate; but here there are several estates, one for life and the other for years> [which MANWOOD afterwards remembered more fully on the contrary side]. Sir, it seems to me that a use is only a trust and confidence between the parties and outside the grounds of the common law; and in uses the intention of the party shall be followed, and the common law shall not *<be observed>* [control it]. Thus, if I am seised of lands in fee, and make a feoffment in fee to John Style upon condition that if he should die without heir of his body it should remain to John Noke and his heirs, *<this is void at common law>* [if this is in possession, the common law said that it was void], whereas if I am seised of lands in fee and make a feoffment in fee to the use of John Style and his heirs, and should he die without heirs then it should remain to John Noke and his heirs, this is *<clearly good>* [good enough], for in uses the intention of the party shall be observed. At common law, cestui que use had no remedy to come by the land, for it is but a trust and confidence. *<At common law cestui que use could not distrain.>* At common law he could not have an assize or trespass for a trespass committed upon the soil whereof he had the use, and at common law he could not compel his feoffees to punish it. And he cited the case in 1 Edw. III, Lib. Ass., pl. [11],[1] where lands were given to a man and [to the person who should become] his wife, *and at the time he had no wife*: if he marries a wife afterwards, the wife will take nothing. In 17 Edw. III,[2] where lands were given to a man and his second son, whereas he has only one son at the time, if afterwards he has another son the second son shall take nothing. But this case was adjudged here: someone was seised in fee and made a feoffment in fee to the use of him and his wife, whereas he had no wife at the time; then he married a wife, and it was adjudged that the wife should thereby take. Thus there is a great difference between uses and lands in possession. As to the last point, that the son in the remainder may take nothing before the term is ended, it seems to me that, the term being void (as I presume the law to be), the remainderman may well enter. Therefore if I make a lease for life, remainder to a monk, and (after his decease) remainder to John Noke, and the lessee for life dies, the entry of John Noke is congeable, and there shall be no occupancy in this case because the first remainder is void. Likewise in our case.

Jeffrey to the contrary. And he drew this distinction: in all grants where an estate is made to someone, and afterwards mention is made of his heirs, the word 'heirs' is only a limitation and not a name of purchase. Likewise of executors, for it is all one. But it is otherwise where the ancestor is not named, but only the heir or executor, for then they are names of purchase. To prove the first branch of this distinction, the book is agreed in 5 Edw. IV, fo. 2,[3] that if I make a lease for term of life, remainder in tail, remainder to the right heirs of the lessee, in this case, because the ancestor was named before, the word 'heirs' is only a limitation of the estate, and the fee is in the lessee for the purpose of charging, or giving, or forfeiting. So is the case in 40 Edw. III recited earlier.[4] [And also] 11 Hen. IV,[5] the same case. On the other side, however, if the ancestor is not named, then it is a good name of purchase. For this, the book in 2

---

[1] 1 Edw. III, Lib. Ass., pl. 11.
[2] *Prior of Grimsby's Case* (1343) YB Pas. 17 Edw. III, fo. 29, pl. 30.
[3] YB Pas. 5 Edw. IV, fo. 2, pl. 23.

livre est in 2 H. 7, si jeo face leas pur vie a J. S., le remainder as droit heires J. N., icy ilz sont purchasores. Et auxi le case in 9 H. 7, 25a, si jeo face leas pur vie a J. S., le remainder as droit heires J. N., et il ad issue file al temps <que le remainder vest, si apres il ad fitz il navera ceo>,¹ quel prove que il ad ceo per purchase [car el ne poet aver per discent].² <Et le case de Maundevile devant reherce prove ceo auxi. 11 H. 4, [blank], lease fuit fait per fine pur vie, le remainder al doit heir un W. W., et tenus que il^d les heires <averont lour>^d naveront lour age, mes aid de eux fueront graunt. Issint 22 E. 3, [blank], mesme le case.>³ <Mesme le differens est destre prise in executores, lou lour testatour est nosme ilz sont forsque limitation, mes lou eux son[t] nosmes solement, bon nosme de purchase. 17 E. 3, fo. 29, leas fuit fait pur vie, le remainder a ces executores pur 8 ans [two lines blank] le quel case prove que tout est un lou le limitation est fait <al>^d a luy et a ses executores et lou a ses executores solement. 19 E. 3, [blank], leas fuit fait pur vie, et sil devie duraunt xij ans que ces executores averoit ceo per xij ans, in un brefe de covenant [two lines blank].>⁴ Et [al darrein]⁵ il prist cest diversitie [sur lestatute de uses],⁶ si jeo face leas pur ans et le lesse graunt son terme al use dun auter, icy lestatut ne transfer cest use in possession mes est sicome devant lestatute de 27 H. 8, pur ceo que lestatute parle⁷ si ascun soit seised des terres et tenementes, et icy il nest seised [mes possessed].⁸ Mes si home soit seisie des terres in fe, et fist feffment al use de luy pur ans, la lestatut execute le possession pur ceo que il fuit seisie al temps del feffment et issint deins lestatute.

¹ el avera ceo coment que il ad fitz apres. *J.*
² *J.*
³ Maundeviles case 11 H. 4, et 22 E. 3, [*bank*], mesme le case prove directment *J.*
⁴ Mesme le diversitie est destre prise lou le testatour est nosme, ses executores sont forsque un limitatione, autermen lou ilz sont nosmes solement. Et il cite le case 17 E. 3, [*blank*], a prover que coment que le remainder soit limite a ces executores, uncore ceo fuit vest en luy mesme etc. Et a mesme lentent il cite le case in 19 E. 3 in case del covenant. *J.*
⁵ *J.*
⁶ *J.*
⁷ *Om. J.*
⁸ *J.*

APPENDIX I cxciii

Hen. VII[1] is that if I make a lease for life to John Style, remainder to the right heirs of John Noke, here they are purchasers. Also the case in 9 Hen. VII, fo. 25:[2] if I make a lease for life to John Style, remainder to the right heirs of John Noke, and he has issue a daughter at the time <*when the remainder vests, if he afterwards has a son he shall not have it*> [she shall have it, even if he has a son afterwards], which proves that he has it by purchase [for she could not have it by descent]. <*And the case of Mandevile recited earlier also proves it.*[3] *In 11 Hen. IV,*[4] *a lease was made by fine for life, remainder to the right heirs of one W. W., and it was held that the heirs should not have their age, but aid of them was granted. Likewise in 22 Edw. III, the same case.*[5]> [Mandeville's case, 11 Hen. IV, and 22 Edw. III,[6] the same case, proves it directly.] And the same distinction is to be taken as to 'executors': where their testator is named, it is only a limitation, but where they alone are named it is a good name of purchase. <*In 17 Edw. III, fo. 29,*[7] *a lease was made for life, remainder to his executors for eight years* …[8] *which case proves that it is all one where the limitation is made to him and his executors and where to his executors alone. In 19 Edw. III,*[9] *in a writ of covenant, a lease was made for life, and should he die within twelve years his executors should have it for twelve years* ….[10]> [And he cited the case of 17 Edw. III[11] to prove that, even if the remainder is limited to his executors, it was still vested in himself. To the same effect he cited the case in 19 Edw. III,[12] in a case of covenant.] And [finally] he drew this distinction [upon the Statute of Uses]: if I make a lease for years, and the lessee grants his term to the use of another, the statute does not here transfer this use into possession, but it is as it was before the statute of 27 Hen. VIII,[13] because the statute says 'if anyone is seised of lands and tenements', and here he is not 'seised' [but possessed]. If, however, a man is seised of lands in fee, and makes a feoffment to the use of himself for years, there the statute executes the possession, because he was seised at the time of the feoffment and so within the statute.

The Holkham text ends here, but the Rylands text continues with the arguments of the justices.

---

[1] Perhaps YB Hil. 2 Hen. VII, fo. 13, pl. 16.
[2] YB Pas. 9 Hen. VII, fo. 25, pl. 11.
[3] *Fauconberg* v. *Courtney* (1328) YB Hil. 2 Edw. III, fo. 1, pl. 1–2; above, p. clxxxv.
[4] *Prideaux's Case* (1409) YB Mich. 11 Hen. IV, fo. 14, pl. 31.
[5] See above, pp. clxxxiii, clxxxv, n. 4.
[6] See above, pp. clxxxiii, clxxxv.
[7] *Prior of Grimsby's Case* (1343) YB Pas. 17 Edw. III, fo. 29, pl. 30; Co. Litt. 54b.
[8] Two lines blank.
[9] A slip for 19 Edw. II, Fitz. Abr., *Covenant*, pl. 25: see 3 Leon. 21. Cf. Dyer 310, when Manwood J. in this case cites both 19 Edw. II and 19 Edw. III (unidentified by the editors).
[10] Two lines blank.
[11] See n. 7, above.
[12] Presumably 19 Edw. II: see n. 9, above.
[13] Statute of Uses, 27 Hen. VIII, c. 10.

APPENDIX II

CONTENTS OF THE RYLANDS MANUSCRIPT, 1572–77

JRL MS. Fr. 118, fos. 15–90

The leaves are numbered 1–82 in Coke's hand (and there is another unnumbered leaf, perhaps part of a cover sheet), but some are misbound as indicated below. The folio references here (full out left) are to the modern numbering, which duplicates fo. 15, with Coke's numbering is added in parentheses. The first eleven cases are numbered by Coke, and the numbering has here been carried on in square brackets, all in italic arabic. The keywords at the beginning of each report are mostly written in the margin.

Fo. 15 (1)   'M. 14 Ely: Regine'

    1.   'Copiholde. Le roygne est seisie dun manour a quel mannour certaine copiholders ysont …'.

    Printed below, pp. 33–34, after no. 73. Continued as pl. *4*, below. Copied in *Ff*, fos. 184v–185.

    2.   'Ejectione firme. Meade vient al barre et move cest case. Un esteant possesse dun terme fuit ouste de ceo et port ejectione firme …'.

    Copied in *Ff*, fo. 186.

    3.   'Residuum fol. 2. Home fist feffment in fee per ceux parolles dedi et concessi, habendum a luy et a ses heires et assignes a toutz joures …' (continues on fo. 1v).

    Continued as pl. *8*, below. Copied in *Ff*, fos. 185v–186. Briefly noted below, p. 128, no. 225 (dated 15 Eliz.).

Fo. 15v (1v)   'M. 14 Ely: Regine'

    4.   'Principium pagina superiora 1. Le case de copihold fuit ore reherce al Dier. Et luy semble …'.

    Continued from pl. *1*, above.

    5.   'Replegiare. Loppinion del Segnior Dier et Harper fuit que si le tenauncie soit in un countie et le <mannour in que le tenement est tenus>[1] en

---

[1] seignorie *Holkham MS*.

cxciv

auter countie, et le segnior distreine les avers le tenant et eux enchase (come il poet bien) en le countie ou son mannour est et la eux empound, le tenant covient suer son replegiare en le countie ou ilz sont impound et luy covient a disclose tout lespecial matter en son declaratione, et issint le lieu <ou le prisel fuit ne serra traverse>[1].'

Also in Holkham 7938, with the minor variations noted here: see Appendix I, p. clxxviii. Copied in *Ff*, fo. 186.

6. 'Conditions. Home seisie de terres en fe fist leas pur ans reservant rent per fait indent et le lessor covenant in mesme le fait que le lessee avera sufficient fuell de toutz ces arbres …'.

Also in Holkham 7938, with some variations: see Appendix I, p. clxxx. Printed below, p. 50, after no. 96. Copied in *Gg*, fo. 53 (immediately after pl. 7, below).

7. 'Devises. Benloes mova, home seisie des terres en fe fist feffment anno 25 H. 8 al use …' (continued on fo. 15v).

Copied in *Ff*, fos. 186v–187; *Gg*, fo. 53.

Fo. 15*bis* (2)   'M. 14 Ely: Regine'

8. 'Principium supra fo. 1. A auter jour le case del garrantie per force de cest paroll dedi fuit auterfoitz rehers …'.

Continued from pl. *3*, above.

9. 'Feffments. Home fist feffment a J. S. apres le mort dun tiel que fuit son copiholder …'.

Printed below, p. 84, after no. 134. Copied in *Ff*, fo. 186.

10. 'Charge. Le Segnior Dier dit, si lesse pur vie grant rent charge et apres surrender a luy …'.

11. 'Un formedone fuit port vers un Lamme, esteant deins age, et il fuit admitt per gardianum.'

This is the whole note. There is a report of the case in BL MS. Harg. 8, fo. 161v.

Fo 15*bis*v (2v)   'M. 14 Ely: Reg.'

[*12*]   'In un formedon le tenant vouche J. S., vers que un sommons est agard, le vicont retorne que il mesme est vicont et issint il ne poet sommon luy mesme …'.

---

[1] ne serra traversable ou le prisell fuit *Holkham MS*.

[13]   'Demurrer en ley parenter [Bales] et Kircke. Cranmer larchevesque fist feffment in fe al use de luy mesme pur terme de sa vie sauns impechment de wast …' (continued to fo. 17v).

A variant text, omitting the arguments of the judges, is in Holkham 7938: see Appendix I, pp. clxxxi–cxciii. Abridged below, p. 58, no. 106.

Fo. 18 (4)   'M. 14 Ely: Regine'

[14]   'Demurrer in le common banke parenter <George Winter et auter et Sir Nicholas Arnold chivaller>^d Powell et Moneux. Sir Nicholas Leae chivaller, esteant seisie des mannours de Newell, Pentlo et Dimmocke, lessa mesme ceux mannours ove les parsonages de Newell, Pentlo et Dimmock impropriate a un Sir Nicholas Arnold …' (continued to fo. 19v).

Continued below, pl. *19*. Also reported below, p. 43, no. 88. The report here is confined to the arguments of counsel.

Fo. 19v (6v)   'M. 14 Ely: Regine'

[15]   'Demurrer en ley parenter Vernham et Stanley ove auters. Un formedon fuit port per un Vernham vers Sir H. Stanley …' (continued to fo. 21).

Briefly noted below, p. 36, no. 78; p. 141, p. 258.

Fo. 21v (8v)

[16]   'Un fist lease pur terme de vie et puis grant le revercion a J. S. habendum mesme le revercion post mortem <de le lesse pur vie>ⁱ. Et loppinion del court fuit que a cest grant ne besoigne ascun attornment car le tenant apres son mort per null voy poet atturner.'

This is the whole note.

[17]   '14 Eliz. rott. 1015. A auter jour le demurrer parenter Powell et Moneux fuit argue per les justices …' (continued to fo. 25v, where the end of the report has centred lines tapering to a point, and below it 'Τελοσ').

Continued from pl. *14*, above.

Fo. 26 (13)   'Anno 15'

[18]   'Toutz les justices dengliterre fueront assembles in Serjauntes Inne et le case fuit tiell. James Taverner de Northelmam …' (continued to fo. 26v, most of which is blank save for the word 'jovis').

Copied in *Ff*, fo. 187. See vol. ii, p. 257, n. 4.

APPENDIX II

Fo. 27 (14)   '15 Elyz. Regine termino Pasche'

[*19*]   'Demurrer parenter Margaret Vernham et John Vernham tenant in dower. Un <Mary>ᵈ Margery Vernham port brefe de dower envers John Vernham …' (continued to fo. 28v, where it ends abruptly; fos. 29–31 blank).

The report contains the argument of Mounson J. and part of that of Manwood J., but is incomplete at the end and lacks the argument of Dyer C.J. Differently reported below, p. 75, no. 118, sub nom. *Vernon* v. *Vernon*.

Fo. 32 (22)   'T. 15 Elyz.'

[*20*]   'Dower. Un Crane et sa fem port brefe de dower envers J. Broxhole, le tenant plead un fine levie per son baron …'.

Copied in *Ff*, fos. 187v–188. More briefly noted below, p. 29, no. 63.

[*21*]   'Dette. Barre. Un Tailour port brefe de dette vers un Morice sur un obligation endorce ove tiell condition que si un J. Morice le puisne serra bone et loiall servant a le dit Tailour et auxi son factor ouster le mere …'.

Copied in *Ff*, fo. 188; *Gg*, fos. 53v–54.

[*22*]   'En quare impedit port per le roygne fuit agree per tout le court que si le roygne present un per ses lettres patentes et apres present un auter per ses lettres patentes …'.

Copied in *Ff*, fo. 188v.

Fo. 32v (22v)   'M. Anno 15 Eliz.'

[*23*]   'Replegiare port per un R. Franklyn envers un Cantrell, que fist conusauns come baillie a le Segnior Cromwell …'.

Copied in *Ff*, fos. 188v–189v (followed by three short cases not in the Rylands MS., which were presumably on Coke's missing fo. 23); *Gg*, fos. 54v–56 (followed by the first of the three additional cases in *Ff*, concerning the lease of an inn with the 'household stuff').

[Fo. 23 in Coke's numbering is missing.]

Fo. 33 (24)   'Anno 17 Eliz. Reg.'

[*24*]   (After a blank space for a third of the page) 'Mounson justice, moy semble que le pleintife recovera …' (continued on fos. 33v, 44).

Brent's Case, differently reported below, p. 115, no. 209.

Fo. 33v (24v) 'H. 17 Eliz.'

[*24, continued*] '... uncore cest power et authoritie nest pas done included' (ends abruptly).

This breaks off in the course of Mounson J.'s argument, which resumes on fo. 44. The explanation is that the leaves have become misbound; fo. 44 is the next leaf (fo. 25) in Coke's numbering.

[For fo. 25 in Coke's numbering see fo. 44.]

Fo. 34 (26) is blank.

Fo. 35 (27) 'P. 15 Eliz.'

[*25*] 'Lattons case. In un ejectione firme trove fuit per verdit ...' (continued to fo. 35v, the lower half of which is blank).

Differently reported below, p. 25, no. 51.

Fo. 36 (28) 'Trinitatis 17 Eliz.'

[*26*] 'Le case. Un bill de det fuit port envers le garden del Fleete per un Manser' (a blank space then follows for about a third of the page) 'Le argument. Mounson semble que le pleintife recovera ...' (continued on fo. 36v, the lower half of which is blank).

The argument of Mounson J. only. Differently reported below, p. 17, no. 30.

Fo. 37 (29) is blank.

Fo. 38 (31, fo. 30 being misplaced after it) 'Anno 17 Eliz.'

[*27*] 'Fraunces, Segnior Lovell, esteant seisie del fearme vocat. Bowels in fe, anno 18 E. 4 ceo lesse per fait indent a un Thomas Wright ...' (continued on fos. 38v, 40–42, the intervening leaf being misplaced).

Differently reported below, p. 45, no. 90.

Fo. 39 (30) is blank but should have preceded fo. 38

Fos. 40–42 (32–34) contain the rest of Lord Lovell's case.

Fos. 42v and 43 (35) are blank.

APPENDIX II

[Coke's fo. 36 is missing; his fo. 37 is fo. 46 below.]

The missing leaf may have contained *Stockbridge's Case*, noted by George Croke as 'Pasch. 17 Eliz. ex libro Cooke junioris' in *V*, fo. 32, where it is immediately followed by pl. *29*, below, and two pages of further extracts from this volume. For *Stockbridge's Case* see below, p. 26, n. 1.

Fo. 44 (25, bound out of order)

[*24*, continued] 'mes le primer feffees poient enter et faire vendition …' (ends at fo. 44v, the rest of the page being blank).

A continuation of *Brent's Case*, with the speeches of Mounson and Manwood JJ.

Fo. 45 (26, bound out of order)   'M. 15 & 16 Eliz.'

[*28*] 'Loffice Lone.[1] J. Blunt seisie de mannour de Alaxon in Lecestershire, a que ladvowson de mesme le ville est appendant, in special taile …'.

A statement of the case only, the same as that printed below, p. 52, no. 101, but with a different ending (printed on p. 53, n. 3).

Fos. 45v–46 (26v, 37) are blank.

Fo. 47 (38)   'Pasch. 18 Eliz. Regine'

[*29*] 'Capias sur recognisans. Nota il fuit agre in le common bank per le segnior Dier et les auters justices que capias ad satisfaciendum ne gist sur un recognisans …'.

Abridged in *V*, fo. 32.

[*30*] 'Challendge. Un brefe de dower fuit port vers le Segnior Buckhurst … le Segnior Dier dit que chescun baron del realme covient daver un chivaler al meins retorne in le panel …'.

[*31*] 'Leas per un person devant induction. Jeffries serjeant mova, si <un>[i] parson apres admission et institution et devant induction fist leas …'.

This may have been the source of the second part of p. 112, below, no. 201; if so, it was heavily abridged. Abridged in *V*, fo. 32.

[*32*] 'Damages in dower. In brefe de dower al primer jour le tenant viens eins et render dower al demandant …'.

Abridged in *V*, fo. 32.

---

[1] Richard Lone was third prothonotary, and presumably the entry was on his rolls.

[*33*] 'Priviledge. Nota le Segnior Dier dit clerement, et nient denie, si home soit impled in le common banke et puis est condemne in Londres …'.

Abridged in *V*, fo. 32.

Fo. 47v (38v)   'P. 18 Eliz. Regine'

[*34*] 'Detinue. Nota le Segnior Dier dit clerement que si le oblige baille le obligation al obligor il ne poet in cest case declare sur un baillement …'.

Abridged in *V*, fo. 32.

[*35*] 'Lease de 3 partes. Nota in un ejectione firme port per un Jenour fuit agre …'.

Abridged in *V*, fo. 32.

[*36*] 'Triall per proves. Nota si in un brefe de dower le tenant pleade que le baron le demandant est in pleine vie etc. et lauter mainteine que il est mort, ceo serra trie per proves, come la il fuit. Nota cest mannour de triall.'

This is the whole note.

[*37*] '5 portes. In un action de wast le defendant vient eins al grand distres et plede que le terre est deins les 5 portes …'.

Abridged in *V*, fo. 32.

Fo. 48 (39)   'P. 18 Eliz. Regine'

[*38*] 'Common recoverie barre formedon in reverter. Lovelace mova que un ad port formedon in le reverter …'.

Abridged in *V*, fo. 32.

[*39*] 'Un copiholder surrender al opes de ses executors al purpose que ilz venderont ceo al paiment de ces detz …'.

[*40*] 'Nota que il fuit enacte per un estatut fait in anno 35 H. 8 a tiel effect, That all leasses made et hereafter to be made by the Lord Dacre (que fuit le marques de Northampton) …' (continued on fo. 48v, the bottom half of which is blank).

Fo. 49 (40)   'Pasch. 18 Eliz. Regine'

[*41*] 'In trespas le case fuit tiel. Sir Thomas Wiat esteant seasie del mannour de <Hunton>[d] Peccham[i] in le countie de [*blank*] …' (continued to fo. 50, where there are only seven lines of text, the remainder being blank).

Continued below, pl. *45*. Also reported below, p. 89, no. 147.

APPENDIX II

Fo. 51 (42) is blank.

Fo. 52 (43) 'M. 18 Eliz.'

[*42*] 'Lease pur vie et puis auter lease pur vie grant de mesme le terre … Meade vient al barre et move cest case. Home fist lease a 3 pur lour vies et puis per son fait grant le revercion habendum a 3 auters …' (half a page, the remainder blank).

Fos. 52v–54v (43v–44v) are blank.

Fo. 55 (46) 'P. 18 Eliz. Regine'

[*43*] 'Un formedone fuit port envers un enfant deins age que appiert et confesse laction …' (two-thirds of a page, the remainder blank).

Abridged in *V*, fo. 32.

Fo. 55v (46v) 'P. 18 Eliz.'

[*44*] 'Un quare impedit fuit port envers levesque de Excestre et un [*blank*] Collsile de esglise de Asperington in Devonshire …' (continued to fo. 59, on which there are four lines of text and the remainder is blank).[1]

Differently and more shortly reported below, p. 63, no. 113, sub nom. *Gyles* v. *Colshill*.

Fos. 59v–60v (50v–51v) are blank.

Fo. 61 (52) [no headline]

[*45*] 'Le case' (for which a blank space is left, and then about a third of the way down the page) 'Pointz move deins le case. 1. Si le volunt de Guilford done le terre a les executors ou solement authoritie, et coment le dean et chapter prendra …' (continued to fo. 64, where, after a blank space, 'Bromeley sollicitor le roygne argue a auter jour …').[2]

This is *Thornhill's Case* in the King's Bench (named on fo. 63v) concerning the dean and chapter of St Paul's, London. It is partly in note form. Also reported below, p. 68, no. 115, sub nom. *Buttell* v. *Wylford*.

---

[1] On fo. 58v is a remark in the first person, 'Harper argue mult come Manwood dit et agrea a luy in toutz pointz, et pur ceo jeo ne voille reporter son argument a large.'
[2] On fo. 60 is a parenthetical note, 'Et nota que jeo ay oye cest diversitie …'. In the margin of fo. 63 are some notes in Coke's hand questioning the authorities cited: 'Fitz. fol. 180 mes le case nest issint la … 39 E. 3, 37, mes jeo ne poy trove ceo la, mes il est in 9 H. 7, fol. 1.'

Fos. 64v–66v (55v–57v) are blank.

Fo. 67 (58)   'Trinit. 18 Eliz. cest case fuit argue per le justices del common banke.'

[*46*] 'Sir Thomas Wiatz case. Le case briefment fuit reherse in tiel mannour. Un Moulton port brefe de trespas envers Colvenly …' (continued to fo. 70v).

Also reported below, p. 89, no. 147, sub nom. *Multon* v. *Coveney*.

Fos. 71–72 (62–63) are blank.

Fo. 73 (64)   'M. 19 Eliz.'

[*47*] 'Le counte de Arundell port brefe de trespas envers un David Langor de son close debruse …'.

This is the source of part of p. 70, below, no. 116. . The statement of the case is almost verbatim the same, but the only sequel here is the argument of Fettiplace. Coke mentions Fettiplace's argument below, p. 37, no. 80, but what he says of it there is not based on anything here.

Fos. 74–75 (65–66) are blank.

Fo 76 (67)   'H. 19 Eliz.'

[*48*] 'Det sur judgment. Home conust un recognisauns et puis suist scire facias et avoit judgment sur ceo …'.

[*49*] 'Assumpsit. Home port action sur le case envers administrator et le consideration sur que laction fuit conceive fuit que le administrator promise et assume que in consideration que il avoit implye sur luy ladministration de toutz les biens …'.

Abridged in *V*, fo. 33.

[*50*] 'Ejectione firme. In ejectione firme le defendant plede que J. S. son pier fuit seisie et morust seisie …'.

Fo. 76v (67v)   'P. 19. The case in the Duchy Chamber between John Walsh and other complainant[s], against Thomas Edmonds, defendant.'

[*51*] 'Le roy H. 8, seisie del mannour de Dedington in le counte de Oxford …' (continued to fo. 77v, most of which page is blank).

Copied in *Ff*, fos. 193–195; *Gg*, fos. 56–59.

APPENDIX II

Fo. 78 (69)   'P. 19 Eliz.'

[*52*] 'Le darren jour del terme apres maunger cest case fuit argue in le court de gardes devant le segnior tresourer et les 2 chiefe justices in le open courte, et le case fuit come jeo conceive: Sir George Calverley et sa fem, seisie de certen terre in droit sa feme …' (continued to fo. 79v, where there are eleven lines and the remainder is blank).

Differently reported below, p. 147, no. 271. Copied in *Ff*, fos. 195–197v.

Fos. 80–81 (71–72) are blank.

Fo. 81v (72v)   'T. 19 Eliz.'

[*53*] 'Action sur le case. Nota Justice Gawdy dit a moy veniendo de Westm. …'.

Printed below, p. 50, after no. 97, which is closely similar in wording (see above, pp. lxxxvi–lxxxvii). Slightly abridged in *V*, fo. 33.

[*54*] 'Droit close. Nota le Segnior Dier dit que si home port brefe de droit close deins ancient demesne …'.

[*55*] 'Usury. Nota un information sur lestatut de usurie fuit exhibite in lexchequer envers Doctor Good et un auter …'.

Copied in *Ff*, fos. 197v–199v; *V*, fo. 33. This is 'Doctor Goads Case, Trin. 19 Eliz. in the Exchequer', cited in 1584 'ex relatione Edward[i] Coke': Cro. Eliz. 27.

Fo. 82 (73)   'T. 19 Eliz.'

[*56*] 'Dismes. Le case pur matter in ley fuit breifement tiel. Un abbot seisie dun mannour deins le precincte dun parsonage et puis mesme le parsonage fuit approprie a mesme le abbathie, et puis labbey vient in les mayns le roy per le dissolution … Et fuit argue per Yson, utterbarrester de Grayes Inne …' (continued on fo. 82v, where Plowden argues the contrary, and the lower half of the page is blank).

Copied in *Gg*, fos. 59–61.

Fo. 83 (75) is blank.

Fo. 84 (76)   '19 Eliz.'

[*57*] 'Tr. 18 Eliz. Regine Dccccxxxiiij, Northt. Henricus comes Cantie et Maria uxor ejus summoniti fuerunt ad respondendum Edwardo Onley armigero …' (continued to fo. 86, most of which is blank).

The arguments of Mounson and Manwood JJ. only. The latter is the source of the passage below, pp. 153–154, no. 286, where this is printed. Copied in *Ff*, fos. 189v–193; abridged in *V*, fo. 32v.

Fo. 86v contains notes, in another hand, of cases in Michaelmas term 1598.

Fos. 87–90 (79–82 and another unnumbered leaf) are blank.

Fo. 90v is blank apart from this endorsement in Coke's hand:

'Deane of Powles case vide in le liver intitle Liber secundus.[1]

Deane de Worcestres case vide in mesme le liver, le commencement.[2]

Copleys Case, jointenancy per fine, in le liver entitle Liber primus.[3]

Mansuers case[4]
Segnior Lovels case[5] } in libro longo
Irelandes case[6]

Bromley sollicitors case.'[7]

---

[1] Below, p. 11, no. 17 (from *AA*).
[2] Below, p. 64, no. 114 (from *AB*).
[3] Unidentified.
[4] Cf. *Manser* v. *Annesley*, below, p. 17, no. 30 (from *AA*), and in the Rylands MS., pl. 26.
[5] Cf. *Nichols* v. *Nichols*, below, p. 22, no. 39 (from *AA*, fo. 2v in the second foliation), and p. 45, no. 90 (from *AB*), and in the Rylands MS., pl. 27.
[6] Cf. *Eccleston* v. *Tuchett*, below, p. 8, no. 13 (from *AA*).
[7] Cf. the dictum by Bromley as solicitor-general, below, p. 142, no. 259.

APPENDIX III

REFERENCES TO THE NOTEBOOKS IN COKE'S COPY OF DYER[1]

A Concordance with the Notebooks and with this Edition

Where cited *Form of citation*

Fo. 116, para. 70 'Vide 29 Eliz. in mes reportes, fol. 24.'
  Unidentified on that folio.

Fo. 120v, para. 12 'Vide Trin. 34 Eliz. in mes reportes.'
  Unidentified in *C*.

Fo. 135, para. 12 'Vide Braches case P. 25 Eliz. in mes notes.'
  Brache's Case (1583) in vol. ii, p. 212.

Fo. 138, para. 27 'Vide Bendlowes P. 4 Eliz. in mes notes fol. 2.'
  AB, fo. 293.

Fo. 140v, para. 43 'Vide Wing et Harris case in mes reportes.'
  Harris v. *Winge* (1591) in *C*, fo. 5; vol. iii, p. 419.

Fo. 162v, para. 51 'Vide Bendlowes in mes notes fol. 6.'
  AB, fo. 297.

Fo. 229, para. 49: 'Vide P. 32 Eliz. in mes reportes fol. 23.'
  Lost MS. *B*.

Fo. 251, para. 89 'Vide Pasche 26 Eliz. 40 in mes reportes.'
  Dove v. *Chambers* (1584) in vol. ii, p. 251.

Fo. 269, para. 19 'Hil. 38 Eliz. 134.'
  Shane's Case (1596) in vol. iv, p. 668.

Fo. 270v, para. 23 'Vide 26 Eliz. 40 in mes reportes.'
  Dove v. *Chambers* (1584) in vol. ii, p. 251.

---

[1] Marginalia in Coke's hand in his copy of J. Dyer, *Ascuns Novel Cases* (1585), at Holkham Hall (BN 8014).

Fo. 280, para. 13   'Vide Winge et Harris case in mes reportes.'

     Harris v. *Winge* (1591) in vol. iii, p. 419.

Fo. 282v, para. 26   'Vide P. 33 Eliz. 44b in mes reportes.'

     Lost MS. *B*.

Fo. 289, para. 57   'Vide Doubtyes case in mes reportes Tr. 26 Eliz.'

     Att.-Gen v. *Dowty* (1578) in vol. ii, p. 259.

Fo. 296v, para. 24   'Vide 17 Eliz. in mes notes tit. Eschape. Tr. 16 Eliz. rott. 1343.'

     Manser v. *Annesley* (1575) below, p. 17, no. 30.

Fo. 297, para. 24   'Vide in mes reportes tit. Eschape 108.'

     Manser v. *Annesley* (1575) below, p. 17, no. 30.

Fo. 306v, para. 64   'Vide M. 33 et 34 Eliz. in mes reportes fol. 20.'

     Anon. (1591) in *C*, where there is a cross-reference to Dyer 306; cf. 2 Co. Inst. 292

Fo. 307, para. 67   'Vide Mich. 27 et 28 in mes reportes.'

     Clayton v. *Pesenham* (1585) in vol. ii, p. 286.

Fo. 308, para. 74   'Vide in case de seniori puero in mes reportes fol. 69. Pasch. 17 Eliz.'

     Humphreston's Case (1575) below, p. 40, no. 87.

Fo. 315, para. 98   'Vide Segnior Staffords case adjudge encontre in mes reportes.'

     Unidentified, presumably in a missing portion. To judge from the text in Dyer, this concerned the attachment of a peer.

Fo. 316, para. 2   'Vide Allens case M. 29 et 30 in mes reportes fo. 27.'

     Allen's Case (1587) in vol. ii, p. 346.

Fo. 317, para. 5   'Vide M. 32 et 33 fol. 28 in mes reportes, Hamondes case.'

     Lost MS. *B*.

Fo. 317, para. 6   'Vernons case. Vide in mes reportes fol. 84 cest case report.'

     Vernon v. *Vernon* (1573) below, p. 75, no. 118.

APPENDIX III   ccvii

Fo. 319v, para. 16   'Vide in mes reportes M. 33 et 34 fol. 10.'
    Butler v. *Baker* (1591) in *C*, fo. 10; vol. iii, p. 424.

Fo. 320, para. 17   'Vide Rolfes case in mes reportes M. 24 et 25 fol. 24.'
    Rolfe v. *Rolfe* (1582) in vol. ii, p. 198.

Fo. 326v, para. 2   'Lacyes case Tr. 25 fol. 30 in mes reportes.'
    R v. *Lacy and Lacy* (1583) in vol. ii, p. 218.

Ibid.   'Vide tit. Prerogative in mes notes 47.'
    AA, fo. 243.

Fo. 328, para. 8   'Vide Hill. 33 fo. 40 in mes reportes.'
    Lost MS. *B*.

Fo. 329, para. 12   'Vide in mes notes tit. Condition, 180b … Vide in report de Bendlowes in mes notes fo. 1.'
    AB, fo. 292.

Fo. 329, para. 13   'Averment, vide in mes reportes Tr. 33, fol. 54.'
    Lost MS. *B*.

Fo. 331v, para. 22   'Vide in mes notes tit. Patent, 61b.'
    AB, fo. 61v.

Fo. 337v, para. 39   'Vide in mes reportes, Slingesbyes case, M. 29 et 30 Eliz. fol. 25.'
    Beckwith v. *Slingsby* (1587) in vol. ii, p. 339.

Fo. 339v, para. 48   'Vide in mes <reportes>[d] notes, tit. Uses, fol. 7, et ceo fuit Brentes case.'
    Brent's Case (1575) below, p. 115, no. 209.

Fo. 341, para. 51   'Vernons case … Vide in mon report de cest case.'
    Vernon v. *Madder* (1572) below, p. 141, no. 258.

Fo. 342v, para. 55   'Vide mon report de cest case inter mes reportes fol. 82.'
    Earl of Arundel v. *Langar* (1576) below, p. 70, no. 116.

Fo. 344, para. 59   'Vide in mes reportes de cest case fol. 82 in fine, bone diversitye.'

Earl of Arundel v. *Langar* (1576) below, p. 70, no. 116.

Fo. 347, para. 11   'Vide in mon report de cest case que jeo mesme oia.'

Gyles v. *Colshill* (1576) below, p. 63, no. 113.

Fo. 349, para. 15   'Vide Cheynyes case in mes reportes.'

Cheyny v. *Cheyny and Oxenbridge* (1585) in vol. ii, p. 275.

Fo. 351, para. 22   'Vide in mes reportes Pasch. 25, fol. 27.'

Yeardley v. *Pescodde* (1583) in vol. ii, p. 208.

Fo. 352, para. 26   'Vide in mes reportes M. 33 et 34 inter Harrys et Winge, et vide la Owen Woodes case. Et vide inter Gresham et Digby Hill. 28 in mes reportes fol. 7b.'

Harris v. *Winge* (1591) in vol. iii, p. 419, *Gresham* v. *Digby* (1586) in vol. ii, p. 289.

Fo. 354, para. 32   'Vide in mes reportes M. 22 et 23 Eliz. fol. 13b.'

Anon. (1580) in vol. ii, p. 168.

Fo. 355, para. 37   'Vide Hartupps case in mes reportes Tr. 33 fol. 49 et 50.'

Lost MS. *B*.

Fo. 356, para. 40   'Vide Stones case M. 30 Eliz. in mes reportes, 48b.'

Stone v. *Withipole* (1588) in vol. ii, p. 403.

Fo. 357, para. 43   'Vide in mes notes Tr. 30 Eliz. 43b.'

Lepur v. *Wroth* (1588) in vol. ii, p. 389.

Fo. 358v, para. 50   'Vide Edolfes case 22 Eliz. in mes reportes 13, et vide Amner et Loddingtons case 25 Eliz.'

Edolfe's Case (1580) in vol. ii, p. 167.

Fo. 360v, para. 7   'Vide in mes reportes, 78b.'

Gyles v. *Colshill* (1576) below, p. 63, no. 113.

Fo. 361, para. 8   'Vide M. 28 et 29 Eliz. in mes reportes, fol. 17.'

Probably *Wynsmore* v. *Hulbert* (1586) in vol. ii, p. 314, though that is on fo. 18v.

APPENDIX III

Fo. 363, para. 24   'Vide in mes reportes 22 Eliz. fol. 13.'
     Edolfe's Case (1580) in vol. ii, p. 167.

Fo. 364, para. 39   'P. 27 in mes reportes fol. 1.'
     Sir William Drury's Case (1585) in vol. ii, p. 271.

Fo. 365v, para. 33   'Vide le record del Morrice et Maule in mes reportes M. 30 et 31 Eliz. fol. 1.'
     Lost MS. *B*.

Fo. 366, para. 35   'P. 29 Eliz. in mes reportes 21b.'
     Unidentified on that page.

Fo. 367, para. 40   'Tr. 27 Eliz. contra in banco regis in mes reportes fol. 2.'
     Goodwyn v. *Franklyn* (1585) in vol. ii, p. 274.

Fo. 368, para. 45   'Vide Mich. 29 et 30 in mes reportes fol. 28.'
     Unidentified on that folio.

Fo. 368, para. 46   'Vide in mes reportes in medio fol. 9.'
     Anon. (1579) below, p. 62, no. 112.

Fo. 368, para. 47   'Vide in mes reportes fo. 80b, M. 19 Eliz. inter Burton et Wilford, ceo fuit le deane de Powles case.'
     Buttell v. *Wylford* (1577) below, p. 68, no. 115.

Fo. 369v, para. 54   'Vide 18 Eliz. mes reportes, Giles case, 78.'
     Gyles v. *Colshill* (1576) below, p. 63, no. 113.

Fo. 370, para. 56   'Vide in mes reportes M. 30 et 31 Eliz. fol. 46.'
     Moore v. *Bedell* (1588) in vol. ii, p. 394.

Fo. 371v, para. 3   'Vide P. 26 Eliz. 39b in mes notes.'
     Russell v. *Pratt* (1584) in vol. ii, p. 401.

Ibid.   'Vide M. 32 et 33 fol. [*blank*] in mes reportes.'
     Lost MS. *B*.

Fo. 373, para. 13   'Vide 29 Eliz. fol. 21 in mes reportes.'
     Probably *Hurleston* v. *Reginam* (1587) in vol. ii, p. 320.

Fo. 373v, para. 13   'Vide M. 27 et 28 Eliz. fol. 3 in mes reportes.'
   Wikes v. *Martyn* (1585) in vol. ii, p. 279.

Ibid.   'Vide Hill. 28 fol. 7 in mes notes.'
   Tayler v. *Moore* (1586) in vol. ii, p. 387.

APPENDIX IV

CASES COPIED BY OTHERS FROM COKE'S FIRST NOTEBOOK

case number	folio in AB[1]	other versions
{1	[*AA*, fo. 9]	*Ff*, fo. 170v; *Lb*, fo. 4}
79	281v	*Ff*, fo. 165v; *Gg*, fo. 22v
80	282v	*Ff*, fo. 166; *Gg*, fo. 23v; *Lb*, fo. 5v
81	282v	*Lb*, fo. 5v
82	282v	*Ff*, fo. 166; *Gg*, fos. 23v–24
83	283	*Ff*, fo. 166; *Gg*, fo. 24; *Lb*, fo. 5v
85	284	*Ff*, fo. 166; *Gg*, fo. 24
87	286	*Ff*, fo. 166v–167v; *Gg*, fos. 24–26; *V*, fos. 25–26
89	287v	*Ff*, fo. 167v; *Gg*, fo. 26; *V*, fo. 26
91	287v	*Ff*, fo. 167v; *Gg*, fo. 26; *Lb*, fo. 4
98	288v	*Ff*, fo. 168
99	288v	*Ff*, fo. 168
100	288v	*Ff*, fo. 168; *Gg*, fo. 27
102	290v	*Ff*, fo. 168v; *Gg*, fo. 27
103	290v	*Ff*, fo. 168; *Gg*, fo. 26v; *Lb*, fo. 4
105	291	*Ff*, fo. 168v; *Gg*, fo. 27v
107	291v	*Ff*, fo. 168v; *Gg*, fo. 27v
111	301	*Ff*, fo. 178; *Gg*, fos. 33v–34; *La*, fo. 130v; BL MS. Harley 1693, fo. 101v
112	301	*Ff*, fo. 178
116	345	*Ff*, fo. 169v–170v; *Gg*, fos. 28–30

[1] Numbers in magenta ink.

21 Eliz.

1	304v	
2	305	*Ff*, fo. 178v; *Gg*, fo. 37
3	305	*Gg*, fo. 38v

Mich 1580

1	305v	*Ff*, fo. 178v; *Gg*, fo. 37
2	305v	*Ff*, fo. 178v; *Gg*, fo. 37
3	305v	*Ff*, fo. 179; *Gg*, fo. 37v; *Lb*, fo. 4
4	305v	*Ff*, fo. 179
5	306	*Ff*, fo. 179; *Gg*, fo. 37v
6	306	*Ff*, fo. 179; *Gg*, fo. 37v; *Lb*, fo. 4

Trin 1581

1	306	*Ff*, fo. 179; *Gg*, fo. 37v
2	306	*Ff*, fo. 179; *Gg*, fo. 38
3	306	*Ff*, fo. 179; *Lb*, fo. 4
4	306	*Ff*, fo. 179v; *Gg*, fo. 38; *La*, fo. 103
5	306v	*Ff*, fo. 179v; *Gg*, fo. 34; *I*, fo. 217v; *Lb*, fo. 4
6	307	*Ff*, fo. 180; *Gg*, fo. 35
7	307	*Ff*, fo. 180
8	307	

Mich. 1581

1	307v	*Gg*, fo. 38v
2	307v	*Ff*, fo. 174; *Gg*, fo. 38v
3	308	*Ff*, fo. 180v; *Gg*, fo. 39v
4	308	*Ff*, fo. 180v; *Gg*, fo. 39; *L*, fo. 42v
5	308	*Ff*, fo. 180v; *Gg*, fo. 39v; *La*, fo. 103
6	308v	*Ff*, fo. 174; *La*, fo. 103
7	309v	*Ff*, fo. 181; *Lb*, fo. 6
8	309v	*Ff*, fo. 181; *Gg*, fos. 35v, 40

9	310	*f*, fo. 181v; *Gg*, fo. 40v
Hil. 1582		
1	311	*Ff*, fo. 182; *Gg*, fo. 41v
2	311	*Ff*, fo. 182; *Gg*, fo. 42
3	311	*Ff*, fo. 182
4	311	*Ff*, fo. 182
5	311v	*Ff*, fo. 182; *Gg*, fo. 42; *La*, fo. 103
6–7	311v	
Lent 1582		
1	312	*Ff*, fo. 182v; *Gg*, fo. 42; *I*, fo. 217; *La*, fo. 103; *Lb*, fo. 6
Pas. 1582		
1	312v	*Ff*, fo. 183; *Gg*, fo. 43; *I*, fo. 217; *La*, fo. 103
2	312v	*Ff*, fo. 182v
3	312v	*Ff*, fo. 182v
4	313	*Ff*, fo. 183; *Gg*, fo. 43v
5	313	*Ff*, fo. 183v; *Gg*, fo. 44
6–7	313	
8	313v	*Ff*, fo. 183v
9	313v	
10	314	*Gg*, fo. 44; *Lb*, fo. 6
11	314	*Ff*, fo. 184; *Gg*, fo. 44v
12	314v	*Gg*, fo. 45
13	314v	*Ff*, fo. 183v; *Gg*, fo. 45
14	314v	*Gg*, fo. 45v; *I*, fo. 27v.
Trin. 1582		
1	315	
Long Vacation 1582		
1	315v	*Ff*, fo. 184

2	315v	*Gg*, fo. 46
3	315v	*Gg*, fo. 46

Mich. 1582 (at Hertford)

1	315v	*Ff*, fo. 184; *Gg*, fo. 46; *I*, fo. 216v; CUL MS. Hh.2.9, fo. 233
2	316	*Ff*, fo. 200v; *I*, fo. 217; *L*, fo. 38
3	316v	*Ff*, fo. 201; *Gg*, fo. 71; *H* fo. 46; *La*, fo. 105; *Lb*, fo. 6
4	316v	*Ff*, fo. 201
5	316v	*Ff*, fo. 201; *L*, fo. 38
6	316v	*Ff*, fo. 201v; *Lb*, fo. 6
7	317	*Gg*, fo. 49
8	317	

Hil. 1583

1	317v	*Ff*, fo. 201v
2	317v	*Ff*, fo. 201v; *La*, fo. 105
3	317v	*Ff*, fo. 201v
4	317v	*Ff*, fo. 202; *Gg*, fo. 48v
5	317v	*Ff*, fo. 202
6	317v	*Ff*, fo. 202; *Gg*, fo. 48v
7	318	*Ff*, fo. 202; *Gg*, fo. 48v; *La*, fo. 105; *Lb*, fo. 6
8	318	*Ff*, fo. 202; *Gg*, fo. 48v; *La*, fo. 105
9	318	*Gg*, fo. 48v; *Lc*, fo. 119v
10	318	*Ff*, fo. 202; *Gg*, fo. 49
11	318v	
12	318v	*Ff*, fo. 203; *Lb*, fo. 6

Pas. 1583

1	319	
2	319	*Ff*, fo. 203
3	319	

4	319v	*Ff*, fo. 202v; *Gg*, fo. 71v; *L*, fo. 38; *La*, fo. 105v
5	319v	*Ff*, fo. 202v; *Gg*, fo. 62v; *L*, fo. 38
6	320	*Ff*, fo. 203v; *Gg*, fo. 63; *L*, fo. 37v
7	321	*Ff*, fo. 175, 204v; *L*, fo. 37v; *La*, fo. 105; BL MS. Add. 35941, fo. 222
8	321v	

Trin. 1583

1	322	*Ff*, fo. 204v; *La*, fo. 106v; *Lb*, fo. 6; *Lc*, fo. 120
2–4	322–324	
5	325v	*Ff*, fo. 205v; *Gg*, fo. 64v; *L*, fo. 37; *Lb*, fo. 6
6	325v	*Ff*, fo. 205v
7	325v	*Ff*, fo. 205v; *Gg*, fo. 65
8	325v	*Ff*, fo. 205v; *L*, fo. 37
9	326	*Ff*, fo. 206v
10	326	*Ff*, fo. 206v; *Gg*, fo. 65; *Lb*, fo. 6

Long Vacation 1583

1	326	*Ff*, fo. 206v; *Gg*, fo. 65v
2	326v	*Ff*, fo. 207; *Gg*, fo. 65v

Mich. 1583

1	326v	*Ff*, fo. 207
2	326v	*Ff*, fo. 206
3	327	*Ff*, fo. 207; *Gg*, fo. 65v
4	327	*Ff*, fo. 207
5	327	*Ff*, fo. 207v
6	327v	*Ff*, fo. 207v; *La*, fo. 106v
7	327v	*Ff*, fo. 207v; *Gg*, fo. 66; *La*, fo. 104v
8	327v	*Ff*, fo. 207v; *L*, fo. 37

9	327v	*Ff*, fo. 208
10	327v	*Ff*, fo. 208
11–12	327v–328	
13	328v	*Ff*, fo. 208
14	328v	
15	328v	*Ff*, fo. 208
16–22	329–330v	
23	331	*Ff*, fo. 208; *Gg*, fo. 66v
24	331	*Ff*, fo. 208; *Gg*, fo. 66v; *L*, fo. 37
25	331	*Ff*, fo. 208v; *Gg*, fo. 66v

Hil. 1584

1	331	
2	331	*Ff*, fo. 208v; *Gg*, fo. 67
3	331v	*Ff*, fo. 208v; *Gg*, fo. 67; *L*, fo. 37
4	331v	*La*, fo. 107
5	331v	*Ff*, fo. 208v; *Gg*, fo. 67; *La*, fo. 107

Lent 1584

1	331v	*Ff*, fo. 208v; *Gg*, fo. 67v; *Lc*, fo. 119v

Pas. 1584

1	331v	*Ff*, fo. 209
2	331v	*Ff*, fo. 208v; *Gg*, fo. 67v; *L*, fo. 37, *La*; fo. 107
3	332	*Ff*, fo. 209v; *La*, fo. 108
4	332	*Ff*, fo. 209v; *Gg*, fo. 68; *I*, fo. 247; *La*, fo. 108
5	332v	*Ff*, fo. 177; *Gg*, fo. 32; *La*, fo. 107
6–7	333v	

Trin. 1584

1–6	333v–334v	

Mich. 1584

1–6	335v–336v	

[missing leaves]

Hil. 1585

    1–5   337–338

APPENDIX V

COKE'S CHARGE TO THE ADMIRAL SESSIONS IN NORWICH, 1583

AA, fo. 5.

Leffect del charge que jeo done a les admirall cessions at castle de Norwich le 2 de July anno regni Eliz. 25°, la esteant present Sir Roger Woodhouse, Serjaunt Flowerdewe, William Heydon, esquier, vice-admirall, Doctor Masters, chancellour de Norwich, William Rugg, esquier, Christofer Heydon, esquier, John Stubbes, et auters.

Primerment, le commoditie et necessitie de navigation.

2, coment les progenitors le roygne avoient provide pur le maintenaunce des merchauntes et des mariners. Magna Carta: omnes mercatores habeant salvum et securum conductum etc. E. 1, anno 13, fait estatut de mercatoribus pur speedy remedy de lour detes. E. 3, anno 9, cap. 1; 14, cap. 2; 28, cap. 11; 34, cap. 17; 18 E. 3, tit. Sea, 1. R. 2: 2 R. 2, cap. 11; 5 R. 2, cap. 3, pur increaser le navy dengleterre. 12 R. 2, cap. 7; 14 R. 2, cap. 9. 4 H. 4 et 3 H. 5, pur weres etc. 20 H. 6, piracy fait treason. 12 E. 4, pur destruction de weares, fishgarthes etc. 1 R. 3, que nul Italien vendera wares in grosse. 1 H. 7, act pur maintenance del navy. 4 H. 8, bulwerkes pur les costes del mere. 7 H. 8, speciall act pur le maintenance del navy. Et issint in 23 H. 8 et 34 et 35 H. 8, et principalment in 28 H. 8. E. 6 et le Roigne Mary prohibite divers chose[s] destre transport pur le meliour maintenance del navy. Le roigne que ore est fist un notable act pur le preservation del navy, anno 5°. Et issint anno 1° et anno 13°.

---

[13] Perhaps 28 Hen. VIII, c. 15, concerning piracy, discussed below.
[14] 1 & 2 Phil. & Mar., c. 5. Cf. 5 & 6 Edw. VI, c. 18, which removed restrictions on importing wines in foreign ships; but see 1 Eliz., c. 13.
[15] An Act touching Politic Constitutions for the Maintenance of the Navy, 5 Eliz., c. 5
[16] 1 Eliz., c. 13; 5 Eliz., c. 5.

APPENDIX V

COKE'S CHARGE TO THE ADMIRAL SESSIONS IN NORWICH, 1583[1]

The effect of the charge which I gave to the admiral sessions at Norwich castle on 2 July [1583], 25 Eliz., there being present Sir Roger Woodhouse,[2] Serjeant Flowerdew,[3] William Heydon, esquire,[4] vice-admiral, Dr Masters,[5] chancellor of Norwich, William Rugg, esquire,[6] Christopher Heydon, esquire,[7] John Stubbes,[8] and others.

[1] First, of the commodity and necessity of navigation.

2. How the queen's forebears have provided for the maintenance of merchants and mariners. Magna Carta, [c. 30]: 'all merchants shall have safe and secure passage' (*omnes mercatores habeant salvum et securum conductum* ...). Edward I, in the thirteenth year, made the Statute *De Mercatoribus*,[9] for a speedy remedy for their debts. Edward III: 9 Edw. III, [stat. 1], c. 1; 14 Edw. III, [stat. 2], c. 2; 28 Edw. III, c. 11.[10] 34 Edw. III, c. 17; 18 Edw. III, tit. *Sea*, 1.[11] Richard II: 2 Ric. II, [stat. 1], c. [1]; 5 Ric. II, [stat. 2], c. 3, for increasing the shipping of England; [11] Ric. II, c. 7; 14 Ric. II, c. 9. 4 Hen. IV, [c. 11], and [1] Hen. V, [c. 2], for weirs etc. 20 Hen. VI, [c. 11], piracy made treason. 12 Edw. IV, [c. 7], for destruction of weirs, fishgarths and so forth. 1 Ric. III, [c. 9], that no Italian should sell wares in gross. 1 Hen. VII, [c. 8], an Act for maintenance of shipping. 4 Hen. VIII, [c. 1], bulwarks for the sea-coasts. 7 Hen. VIII, [c. 2], a special Act for maintenance of shipping. Likewise in 23 Hen. VIII, [c. 7], 34 & 35 Hen. VIII,[12] and principally in 28 Hen. VIII.[13] Edward VI and Queen Mary prohibited various things from being transported, for the better maintenance of shipping.[14] The present queen passed an Act in the fifth year for the preservation of shipping.[15] Likewise in the first and thirteenth years.[16]

---

[1] This was before he became recorder. In *AA*, fo. 8v, there is an outline charge to quarter sessions ('Leffect dun charge'), but it is not attributed to Coke or dated.
[2] Sir Roger Woodhouse JP (d. 1588) of Kimberley, Norfolk.
[3] Edward Flowerdew (d. 1586) of Hethersett, Norfolk; created serjeant at law 1580; baron of the Exchequer 1584–6.
[4] William Heydon (d. 1594) of Baconsthorpe, Norfolk; vice-admiral of the Norfolk coasts from 1579; knighted 3 Nov. 1583; sheriff of Norfolk 1583–84. It was Sir William Heydon who suggested to Coke that he write his treatise on bail and mainprise: BL MS. Lansdowne 577, fo. 39. His grandson of the same name (son of Christopher, below) was admitted to the Inner Temple in 1578. See also above, p. lxxxi, n. 65.
[5] William Maister (d. 1590), LL.D. (Cantab.); advocate of the Arches since 1570.
[6] Of Felmingham, Norfolk.
[7] William's son (d. 1623); later knighted.
[8] John Stubbs (d. 1590) of Thelveton, Norfolk, and Lincoln's Inn, whose hand was struck off in 1579 for daring to write against the queen's proposed marriage to the duc d'Alençon: Baker, *Reinvention of Magna Carta*, p. 174.
[9] 13 Edw. I, stat. 3.
[10] *Sic*, but probably a slip for 25 Edw. III, stat. 4, c. 2.
[11] 18 Edw. III, stat. 2, c. 3; W. Rastell, *A Collection of all the Statutes* (1574 edn), fo. 491v, *Sea*, no. 1.
[12] It is uncertain to what this refers.

3, que le roigne que ore est ad direct cest commission etc. a nous, le quel coment que ceo fuit apell le admirall cession uncore le admirall ne proceade in ceo solonque son admirall authoritie, mes solonque le course del common ley, car devant lestatut de 28 H. 8 le admirall procede solonque le ley civill, in quel ley un graunde defect fuit trove, car come appert per le preamble del dit statut de 28 H. 8 per le civill ley piracy et robbery sur le mere ne puit <de>[d] aver estre puny sinon per tesmoignes ou per le confession del party etc., et pur ceo fuit purveu per mesme lestatut que tiels offences sur le mere serra trie solonque le course del common ley etc., issint que cest commission est equivalent in jurisdiction et authoritie al commission del corps del county.

4, intant que Cicero dit quod sapientis est cogitare tantum sibi esse permissum quantum sit commissum et creditum. Et pur ceo toutz offences ne sont enquirable per force de cest commission, ne tielz offences que sont enquirable [fo. 5v] sont inquirable in chescun lieu. Pur ceo primerment jeo monstre in quel lieu le admirall ad jurisdiction, 2, queux offences fueront inquirable.

Le admirall ad jurisdiction per le dit statute in toutz lieus ou il ad ou lou il pretende daver jurisdiction. Il ad jurisdiction per le common ley sur le mere, et cy farre come le mere flowe et reflowe, come appert per 22 E. 3, Lib. Ass., quo vide tit. Nusans, Br. Bracton dit, littera maris sicut mare sunt communia quasi maris accessoria.

Le admirall pretende daver jurisdiction (come moy semble) lou le ley civill (per que procede devant) done a luy jurisdiction, et ceo est a quibuscumque primis pontibus usque ad mare. Car ouster les primer bridges les niefes ne poient passer, et per consequens ne fuit reason que ladmirall averoit jurisdiction plus ouster.

Des offences queux sont inquirable, ascuns sont enconter le commen ley, ascuns enconter divers estatutes.

Les offences inquirable al common ley sont treason, pyracy, murder, homicide, robbery, felony, wrecke de mere, petit larceny, chaunce medley, touts accessories. Nota quod pirata dicitur a peirao, scilicet πειραο, quod est transire, quia pirate per mare transeunt, vel dicitur a pirausta, le quel signifie un worme ou flye que destroy honey, per metaphor. Wrecke de mere: 1, flotzson, 2, jectsam, 3, lagan, 4, wreck. Treasor trove. Roiall pishons etc. Biens wayve sive derelict.

Offences enconter estatutes …

3. The present queen has directed this commission to us; but, although it is called the admiral session, the admiral does not proceed therein according to his admiral authority but according to the course of the common law. Before the statute of 28 Hen. VIII, [c. 15], the admiral proceeded according to the Civil law, in which law a great defect was found; for, as appears from the preamble of the said statute of 28 Hen. VIII, by the Civil law piracy and robbery upon the sea could not be punished except [upon proof by two] witnesses, or by the party's confession. Therefore it was provided by the same statute that such offences upon the sea should be tried according to the course of the common law. So this commission is equivalent in jurisdiction and authority to the commission for the body of the county.

4. Inasmuch as Cicero said, 'quod sapientis [judicis] est cogitare tantum sibi esse permissum quantum sit commissum et creditum',[1] therefore not all offences are inquirable by force of this commission, nor are all inquirable offences inquirable in every place. Therefore I will show, firstly, in what place the admiral has jurisdiction, and, secondly, what offences are inquirable.

The admiral has jurisdiction by the said statute in all places where he has, or pretends to have, jurisdiction. He has jurisdiction, by the common law, upon the sea, and as far as the sea flows and reflows, as appears by 22 Edw. III, Lib. Ass., which you may see in tit. *Nusans*, B.[2] Bracton says, 'littera maris sicut mare sunt communia quasi maris accessoria'.[3]

The admiral 'pretends' to have jurisdiction, as it seems to me,[4] where the Civil law – by which he proceeded previously – gave him jurisdiction, and that is 'from the first bridges to the sea' ('a quibuscumque primis pontibus usque ad mare').[5] Ships cannot pass beyond the first bridges, and in consequence it was not reason that the admiral should have jurisdiction any further.

Of the offences which are inquirable, some are against the common law and some against various statutes.

The offences inquirable at the common law are treason, piracy, murder, homicide, robbery, felony, wreck of sea, petit larceny, chance medley, and all accessories. Note that a pirate (*pirata*) is so called *a peirao*, that is, πειραο, which means to pass over (*transire*), because pirates pass over the sea; or else he is so called metaphorically from *pirausta*, which signifies a worm or fly which destroys honey. Wreck of sea [is of four kinds]: 1, flotsam; 2, jetsam; 3, lagan; 4, wreck.[6] Treasure trove. Royal fish etc. Goods waived or abandoned.

Offences against statutes ...[7]

---

[1] 'It is the part of a wise judge to reflect that he is only allowed to do what has been committed and entrusted to him.' From Cicero, *Pro Cluentio*, s. 159.
[2] 22 Edw. III, Lib. Ass., pl. 93; Bro. Abr., *Nusans*, pl. 22.
[3] 'Sea-shores are as common as the sea itself, being as it were accessories of the sea': *Bracton*, ii. 39–40.
[4] Cf. Coke's argument in *Lacy's Case* (Trin. 1583) vol. ii, p. 218, at p. 219.
[5] Cf. the report of *Bence's Case* (1588) translated in vol. ii, p. 323, n. 5.
[6] Cf. *Constable's Case* (1601) 5 Co. Rep. 106, 107–108.
[7] Here follows a long list of statutory provisions, from 13 Edw. I to 23 Eliz.

APPENDIX VI

CASES IN WHICH COKE ARGUED, 1587–88

This table shows the extent and diversity of Coke's arguments in court in the later 1580s. The cases are arranged alphabetically by term. All were in the King's Bench unless otherwise stated. Coke may not necessarily have been retained in all of them, since (following medieval tradition) he was apt to join in discussions when he was present.[1] The table is confined to cases reported in print (including this edition), and in twelve selected manuscripts, and is therefore far from being a complete record of all the cases in which Coke was engaged.

Cases in the present edition are cited as 'Coke', with the case-number. The representative manuscript reports are cited by siglum and folio:

A. = BL MS. Add. 25196
B. = BL MS. Add. 35943
C. = BL MS. Add. 35945
D. = CUL MS. Dd.11.64
E. = BL MS. Harley 4562
F. = BL MS. Harley 1331
H. = CUL MS. Hh.2.9
I. = CUL MS. Ii.5.38
L. = BL MS. Add. 35949
M. = BL MS. Harley 1633
N. = BL MS. Add. 25208
Y. = YLS MS. G.R29.8 (Mich. 1588 only)

Hilary Term 1587

Anon. (from the Chancery)	Coke, no. 6.
Baynton v. Barrowe	D. 40v.
Bence's Case	Coke, no. 10.
Brookes' Case	2 Leon. 83.
Coney's Case	Godb. 122.
Delve's Case	D. 44v.
Hurleston v. Reginam	Coke, no. 8.
Morgan v. Kiffe	Cro. Eliz. 52.

---

[1] See above, p. xcix, n. 94.

APPENDIX VI

Pettywade v. Cooke	Coke, no. 2; Cro. Eliz. 53 (sub nom. Pettywood v. Cooke); 2 Leon. 193 (sub nom. Pretiman); A. 43 (name garbled); I. 227v (sim.).
Scott v. Scott	D. 41v; I. 224v. [Cf. Coke, Mich. 1584, no. 3.]
Trevilian v. Leyne	Coke, no. 13; Cro. Eliz. 56 (sub nom. Lane, Pas. 1587); D. 55 (sim.); H. 345.

EASTER TERM 1587

Apharry v. Morgan	Coke, no. 4.
Att.-Gen. v. Wood	Coke, no. 6; E. 78.
Cambridge University, Re (assize of bread and ale)	B. 133v (20 May 1587); E. 78 (same).
Eastes v. Jose	I. 238.
Essex v. Vandanstern	D. 63; I. 239v (sub nom. Eastes). [Cf. Trin. 1587, sub nom. Skidmore.]
Hill v. Upcher	Coke, no. 3.
Lane v. Fermour	D. 59v.
Rous v. Artys (Serjeants' Inn)	Coke, no. 5; Moo. 236; B. 28 (sub nom. Rames v. Artois, Hil. 1587); E. 78; D. 52 (under Hil. 1587). [Cf. Trin. 1588.]
Skynner v. Coppinger	D. 54; I. 233 (sub nom. Popinger).
Storke v. Laurence	I. 234.
Upton v. Didsbury	D. 63; I. 237.
Windsmore v. Hubbard	Cro. Eliz. 58; H. 359 (sub nom. Winsemore v. Hulborne). [Cf. Coke, Mich. 1586, no. 152, sub nom. Winsmore v. Hulbert.]

TRINITY TERM 1587

Anon. (fraudulent conveyances)	D. 83v; I. 247v.
Anon. (assumpsit for return of marriage money)	D. 84.
Bunny v. Stafford	E. 80; B. 135 (Mich. 1587).
Carre, Re	Coke, no. 3.
Cheyny v. Frankwell	Coke, no. 2. [Cf. Trin. 1588.]
Croker's Case	Coke, no. 4.

Dingley d. Raleigh v. Hamden	I. 242 (Coke for Sir Walter Raleigh).
Doune's Case	Cro. Eliz. 62.
Glasier v. Hurston	I. 240.
Lincoln (Bishop) and Savacre v. Reginam	D. 82; I. 247v. [Cf. Trin. 1588.]
Marsh v. Rainsford	Cro. Eliz. 59; D. 79; I. 246.
Parrot's Case	Cro. Eliz. 63.
Skydmore v. Vanden Steene	Coke, no. 1; Cro. Eliz. 56 (sub nom. Skidmore v. Vaudstevan, Pas. 1587). [Cf. Pas. 1587, sub nom. Essex.]
Southwell College, Case of	Coke, no. 5.

Michaelmas Term 1587

Anon. (assumpsit against executors)	D. 92v; I. 249v*bis*.
Anon. (case for nuisance)	D. 93.
Anon. (covenant to save harmless)	B. 134v.
Anon. (killing coneys in pasture)	2 Leon. 201.
Anon. (payment in Kilmerston) (Exch. Cha.)	3 Leon. 193.
Allen's Case	Coke, no. 7; Cro. Eliz. 61 (related by Coke); D. 85; I. 248v.
Arundel (Earl) v. Dacre	1 Leon. 91.
Allen v. Andrewes	I. 258v.
Bacon (Nathaniel) his Case	3 Leon. 192; D. 111.
Barns v. Smith (Exch.)	3 Leon. 171; 2 Leon. 21 (no term).
Beckwith v. Slingsby	Coke, no. 1.
Bland v. Maddox	Cro. Eliz. 79; H. 389 (sub nom. Madock).
Bland v. Moseley	Coke, no. 8; D. 93v; H. 389v; I. 250.
Cadee v. Oliver	3 Leon. 157.
Carfar v. Goodard	H. 389.
Cottington v. Hulett	Coke, no. 3; H. 359 (sub nom. Cottinge v. Hullet); C. 46v (sub nom. Plotting v. Hulett, Trin. 1588).
Devenly v. Welbore	Cro. Eliz. 85; H. 392v (sub nom. Devenley v. Welburne, Hil. 1588).
Farrer v. Scarlett	D. 98v (anon.); H. 383; I. 255.
Foiston v. Crachrood	Coke, no. 14; D. 118v (sub nom. Cracherwood v. Phison).
Foskew's Case (Exch.)	2 Leon. 91 ('And afterwards (as Coke reported) …').
Gabriel v. Clerke	Cro. Eliz. 77.
Gallys v. Burbry	Coke, no. 10; D. 88v; H. 376v; I. 249v; Cro. Eliz. 62 (sub nom. Gallies v. Budbery, Trin. 1587).

Giggens's Case	I. 258v. [Identifiable as Simpson v. Ardes, H. 354v.]
Golding's Case	1 Leon. 71.
Glover v. Pipe	I. 252.
Gomersall v. Bishop	H. 375v. [Cf. Gomersall v. Gomersall, Mich. 1586, Coke, no. 50.]
Gresham (Sir Thomas) his Case	1 Leon. 90.
Hall v. Wingate	Coke, no. 9; D. 46 (sub nom. Wyngate v. Hall, Hil. 1587); M. 2v (sub nom. Hill v. Wingate, Pas. 1588).
Harris v. Baker	3 Leon. 193.
Hawkins's Case	2 Leon. 129.
Kynge v. Robinson	Coke, no. 16; D. 110v; H. 389; I. 254v.
Pawle v. Major	Coke, no. 4.
Payne's Case (Exch. Cha.)	2 Leon. 207.
Putnam v. Cook	3 Leon. 180.
Rawlyns v. Somerford	Coke, no. 6; D. 68 ('cest le verie case come il fuit escrye per le mayne de Cooke mesme'); Goulds. 89 (Pas. 1588). [Cf. Mich. 1588.]
Robsert v. Andrews	Cro. Eliz. 84; D. 130 (Hil. 1588); H. 392 (sim.).
Savel v. Wood	Cro. Eliz. 71; H. 384; 1 Leon. 94 (Hil. 1588); I. 253 (sub nom. Saull). [Cf. Hil. 1588.]
Scott v. Scott	2 Leon. 128; 4 Leon. 71. [Cf. Pas. 1587.]
Strelley v. Albany	Coke, no. 21. [Also in Cro. Eliz. 67, sub nom. Sturlyn]; I. 251 (sub nom. Shirley).
Venable's Case	3 Leon. 190.
Wentworth (Lord) his Case	Moo. 244.
Widdowson v. Clerke	Coke, no. 19; I. 257.
Wolley v. Mayor of Norwich	I. 256v.

Hilary Term 1588

Anon. (ejectment)	A. 25v.
Anon. (error – alien party)	D. 143v.
Anon. (indictment for forcible entry)	Coke, no. 9.
Anon. (indictment of a minister)	F. 40.
Anon. (jeofails)	A. 25v.
Boulton v. Lyllye	D. 136.

Fisher v. Boys	Coke, no. 7; L. 69; cf. Moo. 266 (Trin. 1588, mentions Coke).
Gosnal v. Kindlemarsh	Cro. Eliz. 88; D. 134v (sub nom. Cordell v. Kindlemarshe); H. 394v (sub nom. Gesnol v. Kindlemersh).
Howell v. Trevanian	1 Leon. 93; Cro. Eliz. 91 (sub nom. Trewinian v. Howell); H. 397 (sub nom. Trevanian v. Howell).
Jerome v. Phear	Cro. Eliz. 93. [Cf. Pas. 1588.]
King's Case	Cro. Eliz. 86.
Nicholson v. Lyne	Cro. Eliz. 94; A. 21; H. 416v (Pas. 1588).
Norris's Case	D. 144.
R. v. King	Coke, no. 4; A. 6; D. 125 (anon., Mich. 1587).
R. v. Knaresborowe	D. 140.
Savill v. Wood	Coke, no. 6. [Cf. Mich. 1587.]
Stransham's Case	Cro. Eliz. 98.
Trafford v. Bishop	H. 395.
Wilmot v. Cottle	Coke, no. 5; A. 14v; H. 398.
Yate v. Wyrdnam	Coke, no. 10; Cro. Eliz. 65 (sub nom. Yate v. Windnam). H. 378 (sub nom. Brooke v. Windman).

Easter Term 1588

Anon. (articles of religion)	B. 138.
Anon. (venue; St Martin's, Oxford)	L. 70v.
Allen v. Palmer	1 Leon. 101.
Baynham v. Brooke (Exch.)	Coke, no. 1.
Brooke's Case (Exch. Cha.)	Coke, no. 2.
Coney v. Chomley	BL MS. Lansdowne 1095, fo. 48.
Dellaby v. Hassal	1 Leon. 123.
Erith v. Nevell	B. 141.
Gresham (Lady) her Case	Moo. 262.
Hawes v. Smith	Coke, no. 3; Cro. Eliz. 96; A. 25 (Hil. 1587); H. 420v (sub nom. Smyth v. Hawes); I. 198v; M. 4v.
Jerom v. Knight	1 Leon. 107; M. 1; H. 383 (sub nom. Knight v. German, Mich. 1587).
Jerom v. Neale	1 Leon. 106; H. 416 (sub nom. Hierom v. Phear). [Cf. Hil. 1588.]
Partridge's Case	2 Leon. 212.

Pearle v. Edwards	1 Leon. 102.
Pigott's Case	B. 140v.
Rosse v. Morrice	2 Leon. 24.
Sheparde v. Blackaller	BL MS. Harley 1624, fo. 133.
Walcott v. Powell	3 Leon. 206; L.70v (anon.). [Cf. Trin. 1588.]

Trinity Term 1588

Avery d. Kipping v. Bunning	Coke, no. 8; A. 37v; H. 427; M. 11; cf. A. 134 (sub nom. Alverie v. Rippinge); F. 52.
Bunny v. Wright	I. 204; 1 Leon. 59 (sub nom. Buny, Pas. 1587).
Cheyny v. Frankwell	2 Leon. 176; C. 47. [Cf. Coke, Trin. 1587, no. 74.]
Chybnale v. Wytton	Coke, no. 3; H. 427; M. 20v (sub nom. Witton v. Shepnall, Mich. 1588).
Clavery v. Selby	M. 12v.
Colbourne v. Mixstone	1 Leon. 129.
Day v. Elred	I. 203.
Elred v. Wass	Cro. Eliz. 104; A. 42v; H. 428v (sub nom. Eldred v. Wase); M. 11 (sub nom. Wase v. Elred).
English v. Pellitary	1 Leon. 124.
Estrigge v. Owle	3 Leon. 200.
Farman v. Bowen	F. 42v.
Fordingbridge (Inhabitants) v. Berman	C. 51 ('Fadingberge'); H. 399 (sub nom. Fodringberge, Hil. 1588).
Freeman v. Drew	2 Leon. 182.
Garberie v. Browne	A. 139 ('Coke le famous utterbarrester'); same report, but without the epithet, in Goulds. 94.
Gloucester (Bishop) and Savacre v. Reginam	Cro. Eliz. 65. [= Coke, no. 15.]
Harris (of Middle Temple) his Case	4 Leon. 112.
Harris v. Caverley	4 Leon. 98 ('103').
Henbeck's Case (Exch.)	2 Leon. 39.
Juell's Case	F. 52v.
Kipping's Case	Goulds. 95 ('Cooke the famous utterbarrister').
Marriott v. Pascall (Exch.)	H. 431; B. 205v (sub nom. Merriot, Mich, 1588). [= Coke, no. 16].
Melwiche v. Luter	Coke, no. 2; A. 134; D. 203v.

Morryce v. Eaton	M. 8v; CUL MS. Mm.6.58, fo. 116 (sub nom. Eton v. Morris, Mich. 1588). [= Maurice v. Eaton, cited in 6 Co. Rep. 29.]
Palmer v. Smalbrooke	1 Leon. 132.
Paramour v. Robinson	3 Leon. 209.
Piers v. Hoe	1 Leon. 125.
Piers v. Leversuch	1 Leon. 121.
Randes d. Artys v. Warden	Coke, no. 6. [Cf. Pas. 1587.]
Raus v. Rouse	M. 6v.
R. v. Cripson and others	I. 209v; cf. M. 26v (R. v. Gipson, Mich. 1588).
R. v. Grey	F. 53 (Coke assigned to be of counsel).
R. v. Lewis	1 Leon. 119.
R. v. Morgan	Cro. Eliz. 101; A. 33; H. 425.
R. v. Partridge	2 Leon. 28.
R. v. Wallwin	F. 50.
Roper's Case	2 Leon. 108; 4 Leon. 48.
Stafford (Lord) v. Thomas	I. 200.
Stafford (Lord) v. Thyn	M. 7v (perhaps the same as the foregoing).
Strantham v. Medcalf	1 Leon. 130.
Stubbe v. Rightwise	Coke, no. 4; Cro. Eliz. 102; A. 110v; B. 155; F. 47; D. 141 (Hil. 1588).
Toft v. Tomplins	1 Leon. 127.
Walcott v. Apowell	Coke, no. 11; H. 423 (sub nom. Walcot v. Floide).
Winsmore v. Holborne	C. 45v. Doubtless *Wynsmore* v. *Hulbert*.
Wolley's Case	BL MS. Hargrave 15, fo. 111v.
Woodward v. Buggs	2 Leon. 29.

Michaelmas Term 1588

Anon. (error to reverse a fine)	A. 150v.
Anon. (lease to executors until Michaelmas after death)	3 Leon. 211.
Austen and Selde v. Courtney	A. 144v; M. 23.
Bagnam v. Throgmorton	Y. 14v.
Barnistone [Barnardiston] v. Selwine	M. 27.
Bedell v. Moore	Coke, no. 2; Gouls. 91 (Trin. 1588); A. 138 (Trin. 1588: 'Coke le famous utterbarrester').
Berry v. Goodman	2 Leon. 147.
Braunche (Sir John) his Case	1 Leon. 104.

Bucher v. Samford	Goulds. 99 ('The famous Cook'); Cro. Eliz. 113 (sub nom. Boocher); A. 150v (sub nom. Boutcher); M. 28 (sub nom. Butcher).
Fisher v. Sadler	A. 141, 150.
Gregorye v. Milles	M. 25.
Hodson v. Lee	A. 144 [4 Co. Rep. 43]; M. 24v (sub nom. Hodston); Y. 2 (sub nom. Lye).
Howes v. Coovey	A. 145v.
Ive v. Harlakenden	C. 77. [Cf. Coke, Trin. 1589, in the missing MS. *B*; vol. ii, p. 405.]
Launceston Corporation, Case of	N. 2. [= Coke, Mich. 1587, no. 18, sub nom. Mayor of Launceston v. Barne.]
More v. Pyne	Y. 9v.
Mornington v. Try	Cro. Eliz. 112; Y. 9.
Perry v. Some	2 Leon. 28.
Pigott v. Russel	Cro. Eliz. 115; C. 80. [Reported under 1593 in vol. iii, p. 529.]
Pratt v. Russell	Coke, no. 9; A. 121v (Pas. 1588: 'Coke le famous utterbarrester de Inner Temple'); C. 71v; H. 418v (Exch. Chamber, Pas. 1588); anon. translation in Goulds. 90.
Rawlins v. Somerford	4 Leon. 116. [Cf. Mich. 1587.]
R. v. Marsh (Exch.)	N. 3.
Revenell v. Young	A. 143v; M. 19v.
Rivet v. Rivet	A. 145v; L. 79; M. 26v.
Ross v. Morris	Cro. Eliz. 109; C. 58v; M. 21 (sub nom. Rosset v. Morice); Y. 8.
Scovell v. Cabell	Coke, no. 8; Cro. Eliz. 107 (sub nom. Scovel); A. 133 (sub nom. Covin, Trin. 1588); M. 20 (sub nom. Cabell v. Covin); Y. 1 (Scovell v. Cavell).
Sharpe v. Purslowe	Coke, no. 1; A. 133 (Trin. 1588); H. 429 (Trin. 1588); M. 25v; P. 44v (Trin. 1588).
Sheparde v. Blakenell	A. 148v. [=5 Co. Rep. 4.]
Smith v. Hardcastle	Y. 9v.
Stone v. Withipole	Coke, no. 10; 1 Leon. 114 (Trin. 1588); A. 146; L. 80; Y. 13.
Tay v. Drury	A. 141; M. 17v.
Thirkettle v. Reve	Coke, no. 6.
Trussel v. Aston	Cro. Eliz. 108; C.70; Y. 9.
Waltham's Case (Requests)	Y. 16.
Wilson v. Lady Gresham	Coke, no. 5.

Worseley v. Charnock — Coke, no. 3; 1 Leon. 115 (sub nom. Charnock v. Worsley, Trin. 1588).

Anno 1588

Rushe v. Heighgate — 3 Leon. 204.

APPENDIX VII

COKE'S MANUSCRIPT OF SPELMAN'S REPORTS

This table shows the citations of Spelman which have been noticed in Coke's annotations. (For references to Spelman in Coke's printed works see Baker, *Collected Papers*, ii. 734 n. 55.) They presumably all refer to the lost manuscript mentioned in Coke's library catalogue. Coke seldom cited this manuscript by folio, and so it is impracticable to try to reassemble the references in order. The folio references which he did give cannot be reconciled either with an alphabetical arrangement (as in 93 Selden Soc.) or with a chronological rearrangement (as in BL MS. Hargrave 388).

Where cited	*Form of citation and identification (where known)*
AA, fo. 38	'Nota bene fuit tenus in 24 H. 8, come Justice Spilman report, que si jurors apres que ilz depart del barre et devant ou apres lour agrement maunge ou boier de lour costes demesne ou dascun de lour amyes ceo ne avoidera lour verdit, mes si ceo fuit del cost ou del pleintife ou del defendant, ou dascun auter per lour procurement, devant agrement, ceo avoidera lour verdit, autermẽt est si soit apres lour agremẽt.' (Cf. 93 Selden Soc. 222, pl. 5, which deals with the same principles but is differently dated and seems not to be the same.)
AA, fo. 48	'20 H. 8, Spilman 11. Roy recite lease et grant revercion, le rent ne passera, car le roy nest bien informe, car le rent est tout son profitt.' (Untraced in 93 Selden Soc., unless it is *The Duke of Norfolk's Case* (1518/19), mistaking 10 for 20: cf. the next citation, which also refers to fo. 11. In one text the case is dated 10 Hen. VIII: 93 Selden Soc. 149.)
AB, fo. 427v	'Spilman fol. 11b, le pardon le roy ne barrera le partie a porter premunire …'. (Tit. *Provision*, 93 Selden Soc. 191, pl. 2: *Prior of Sheen* v. *Swillington* (1532).)
AC, fo. 540	'Spilman, 11 H. 8, fol. 11.' (See below, p. 97, no. 163; Co. Litt. 146. Possibly *The Duke of Norfolk's Case* (1518/19) in tit. *Grauntes*, 93 Selden Soc. 149, pl. 10.)
AC, fo. 569	'Vide in les reportes de Justice Wyndam[1] coment un bill de premunire fuit mys eins vers Nick [Nix] evesque de Norwich in custodia marescalli sauns estre somon per 2

---

[1] Evidently a slip: above, p. lxxxii, n. 79.

	moys …'. (Tit. *Provision*, 93 Selden Soc. 192: *Att.-Gen.* v. *Bishop of Norwich*, Hil. 1534.)
AD, fo. 859	'Spilman 17, 18' (concerning tenures).
AD, fo. 920	'Spilman fol. 11b. (Under the heading 'Precedents et lour authoritie'.)
C, fo. 587	'Hen. 8, Spilman, Rices case, treason sur prophecy.' (Tit. *Corone*, 93 Selden Soc. 47: *R.* v. *Rice ap Griffith*, Mich. 1531.)
C, fo. 648	'Vide report Spilman, 25 H. 8, fol. 3.' (Tit. *Prohibition*, 93 Selden Soc. 188, pl. 8).
Coke's *Statuta*, fo. 101	'Mich. 31 H. 8, Spilman, infreinder del prison levesque est felony.' (Tit. *Corone*, 93 Selden Soc. 66, pl. 57: undated there.)
Coke's *Statuta*, fo. 106	'Spilman rep. 111, 24 H. 8, pri[e]st execute pur treason.' (Tit. *Corone*, 93 Selden Soc. 49, pl. 15.)
Coke's *Statuta*, fo. 173	'Temps H. 8, Spilman, lib. preced. 130. Covient monstre season des services auterment nad remedy pur gard ne reliefe. Inter Grey et Wrenne.' (Untraced in 93 Selden Soc.)
Coke's Sta. P.C., fo. 152	'Nota Spilman 4, le steward ne demandera opinion des judges mes in le presence del prisoner. Apres evidence done et departe nul novell evidence.' (Tit. *Corone*, 93 Selden Soc. 54–55: the trial of Lord Dacre and Greystock by his peers, Pas. 1534.)

APPENDIX VIII

PERYAM'S MANUSCRIPT OF DYER'S REPORTS

See above, pp. lxxxi–lxxxii. References in the centre column from *AB-AD* are to the numbering in magenta ink; those from *C* are to Coke's numbering.

Form of citation	Where cited	Identification (if known)
6 E. 6, Dier Periam 28	*AC*, fo. 33v (pencil)	[outlawry in appeal]; not in 109 Selden Soc. (1552).
Dier man: 45, 1° Mar.	*AC*, fo. 569	'... per acceptans de provision del pape per assent ...'; not identified in 109 Selden Soc. (1553).
Dier 48 script.[1]	*AA*, fo. 100	'Scrops case', 109 Selden Soc. 7, pl. 10[2] (said to be on fo. 46 of the autograph) Cited in *Lord Dacre's Case* (1553).
Dier 1 Mar. in script. 48a	*AC*, fo. 559v	[descent]; not in 109 Selden Soc. 8, between pl. 11 and pl. 12 (1553).
Dier script. 48 Dier 1 Mar. script. 48 Dier 1 Mar. script. 48 Dier script. 48	*AA*, fo. 99v *AA*, fo. 100 *AA*, fo. 194 *AB*, fo. 477	Dyer 99. *R.* v. *Thomas* (1554).
Dier 1 Mar. script. 50b	*AA*, fo. 100 (*bis*)	Dyer 10, pl. 16. *R.* v. *Duke of Suffolk* (1554).
Dier in script. 50b	*C*, fo. 213	109 Selden Soc. 11, pl. 17. *Adjournment of Parliament* (1554).
Dier fol. 95 nient imprint <fol. 110 manu propria> Dier man: 110, 2 & 3 Ph. & Mar.	*AA*, fo. 42 *AA*, fo. 100	109 Selden Soc. 16, pl. 29, at p. 17. *Trials for Treason* (1556) and *R* v. *Somervile* (1584).
3 Mar. 96,[3] Periam	*C*, fo. 584	109 Selden Soc. 16, pl. 29. *Trials for Treason* (1556).

[1] I.e. fo. 48 of Dyer's first autograph volume: cf. 109 Selden Soc. 8 for fos. 46 and 49. Coke identified it also as '1 Mar. 99b', i.e. *R.* v. *Thomas* (Pas. 1554) Dyer 99b.
[2] *Scrope's Case* (1415) was also cited in *Lord Lumley's Case* (1572) 110 Selden Soc. 251, but that was on fo. 77 of the Dyer-Peryam manuscript.
[3] The report began at fo. 95: 109 Selden Soc. 16, left (where it is said to be the first volume in secretary-hand, though it seems from the sequence to have been the autograph volume).

Dier 4 Mar. fol. 114	*C*, fo. 249v *C*, fo. 583v	[resolutions concerning treason]; not identified in 109 Selden Soc.
Dier man. 117b,[1] 4 & 5 Ph. & Mar.	*AA*, fo. 115v	[trial of murder]; not identified in 109 Selden Soc. (1558).
Mich. 5 et 6 Ph. et Mar. Dier man. 143	*AD*, fo. 882	[devise]; not in 109 Selden Soc. 25, between pl. 41 and pl. 42 (1558).
Dier 145[2] man. 1 Eliz	*AC*, fo. 671v	109 Selden Soc. 28, pl. 47. *Bishops* (1559).
Dier man. 1 Eliz. 149	*AB*, fo. 355	109 Selden Soc. 30. *Bunye* v. *Stubley*, *The Case of the Duchy of Lancaster* (1560).
Dier Periam fol. 20	*AC*, fo. 544v	[forfeiture of franchise]; not identified in 109 Selden Soc.
Dier 3 Eliz. Periam 21b	*AA*, fo. 102v	109 Selden Soc. 43–44, pl. 71. *Anon.* (1560).
Dier 22b 3 Eliz. Periam	*AB*, fo. 267	'per toutes les justices que Scot nest alien'; not identified in 109 Selden Soc.
Dier Periam Tr. 7 Eliz. fol. 38, 39	*AD*, fo. 907	'appeales ecclesiasticall'; not identified in 109 Selden Soc.
Periam 41b	*Dyer*, fo. 251	[copyhold]; not identified in 109 Selden Soc. (*c.* 1565).
Dier Tr. 8 Eliz. Dier Periam 45	*Statuta*, fo. 120	'nul proclamation quant lengrossing est in temps le heire'; not identified in 109 Selden Soc.
Trin. 9 Eliz. Dier manuscr. fol. 49b	*AC*, fo. 159 (pencil)	[return of writ]; not in 109 Selden Soc. *Morgan* v. *Wikes* (1567).
Dier 9 Eliz. 49 Periam	*AC*, fo, 255	[process]: not identified in 109 Selden Soc.[3]
Dier man. Mich. 8 Eliz. 119	*AB*, fo. 256v *AB*, fo. 491v	109 Selden Soc. 123, pl. 174. *Election of Speaker* (1566).
ibm 121b	ibid.	109 Selden Soc. 125, pl. 177. *Freedom of Speech in Parliament* (1566).

---

[1] This is out of sequence and, though clearly written, is probably a mistake for fo. 137. There was a case of Trin. 4 & 5 Phil. & Mar. on fo. 140: 109 Selden Soc. 21.

[2] Or fo. 147: see vol. iv, p. 924. Powle said the case of the bishopric of Chichester began on fo. 146 of the autograph, so this may refer to some general notes on bishops ('renomination des evesques temps E. 1 et E. 2 des bulls') preceding that case.

[3] The point is not stated, but this seems not to be *Stucley* v. *Thynne* (1567) 109 Selden Soc. 127.

ibm [1]23	ibid.	109 Selden Soc. 126, pl. 179. *The same, continued* (1566).
Dier Periam 11 Eliz. 57	*AA*, fo. 96 [no. 18]	'irreplevisable'; not identified in 109 Selden Soc. (1569).
[11] Eliz. Dier Periam 57	*AB*, fo. 383v	'sur forein plea in assise in pays le record est remove in banke …'; not identified in 109 Selden Soc. (1569).
Dier Periam 11 Eliz. 57	*AB*, fo. 415*bis* (178 in pencil)	109 Selden Soc. 160, pl. 218. *Molton* v. *Ilcombe* (1569).
11 Eliz. 61b Periam	*AB*, fo. 421v	109 Selden Soc. 171, pl. 233. *Clarke* v. *Gawdy* (1569).
Livre Periam de Dier fol. 61[1]	*AA*, fo. 101v, 102	109 Selden Soc. 173, pl. 236. *Hampton and Whitacre's Case* (1569).
11 Eliz. 62 Periam	*AD*, fo. 807	109 Selden Soc. 172, pl. 235. *Trials in South Wales* (1569).
Periam 63	Dyer, fos. 286v, 287 Sta. P.C., fo. 89	109 Selden Soc. 175, pl. 240. *Case of the Northern Rebels* (1569).
Periam 65, 66	Dyer, fo. 287, pl. 49	Perhaps 109 Selden Soc. 182, pl. 249. *Cranwell* v. *Malin* (1570).
13 Eliz. 67 Periam	*AB*, fo. 451v	109 Selden Soc. 193. *Lynche* v. *Osfeld* (1570).
13 Eliz Dier 67 Periam	*AA*, fo. 100	109 Selden Soc. 207, pl. 283 (anon.). *Mary, Queen of Scots* (1571).
Dier Periam 13 Eliz. fol. 68	*AA*, fo. 88v *AB*, fo. 490v *Statuta*, fo. 4	109 Selden Soc. 207, pl. 285. *Sir Lewis Mordant's Case* (1571).
Dier Periam 13 Eliz. 68	*AB*, fo. 385 *C*, fo. 249 *Statuta*, fo. 5	'le case del roigne descoce'. 110 Selden Soc. 240, pl. 327 (which in the only known manuscript text follows pl. 289, below). *Mary, Queen of Scots* (1571).
13 Eliz. Periam 68	*AB*, fo. 267 *C*, fo. 79v	[status of Scots]; related to the previous case.
Dier Periam 13 Eliz. 68	*AB*, fo. 490v	'baron [peer] poet estre testmoigne'; probably related to the previous case, but not in 109–110 Selden Soc.

---

[1] Also cited on *AA*, fo. 102, as 11 Eliz.

Dier Periam 13 Eliz. 68	*AD*, fo. 903	'perjurie in chauncerie'; not identified in 109 Selden Soc. (1571).
Periam 13 Eliz. 69	*AB*, fo. 490v	109 Selden Soc. 210, pl. 289.
Dier Periam 69	*AB*, fo. 490v *AD*, fo. 769	109 Selden Soc. 209, pl. 289. *Case of the Earldom of Kent* (1571).
Dier P[er]i[am] 13 Eliz. 71b	*C*, fo. 634v	109 Selden Soc. 217, pl. 300. *Execution of Process* (1571).
Dier P[er]i[am] 13 Eliz. 72[1]	*AB*, fo. 380v	Cf. 109 Selden Soc. 185, pl. 258; 110 Selden Soc. 310, pl. 404 (not the same report). *Office found in Chester* (1571).
14 Eliz. 76 Periam	*AB*, fo. 385	110 Selden Soc. 247, pl. 333. *Taverner* v. *Lord Cromwell* (1572).
Dier man: 110[2]	*AA*, fo. 100	110 Selden Soc. 241, pl. 327. *R.* v. *Rolston* (1571).
Periam Dier 13 Eliz. 13 Eliz. 75 Periam 13 Eliz. Dier Periam 75 13 & 14 Eliz. 75b Periam 13 Eliz. 75 Periam	*AA*, fo. 100 *AD*, fo. 920 *C*, fo. 454v *C*, fo. 582 *C*, fo. 699v	110 Selden Soc. 243, pl. 328. *R.* v. *Duke of Norfolk* (1571).
M. 13 & 14 Eliz. Periam 75b	Co. Sta. P.C. 167v	[challenge]; probably the same case.
14 Eliz. 77 Dier Periam 14 Eliz. 77 P[er]i[am]	*AA*, fo. 100 *C*, fos. 583v, 584 Sta. P.C., fos. 37v, 153	110 Selden Soc. 250, pl. 336. *Lord Lumley's Case* (1572).[3]
14 Eliz. 85 Periam	*AB*, fo. 83	110 Selden Soc. 261, pl. 350. *Bracebridge's Case* (1572).
Dier Periam 102, 103, 16 Eliz.	*Statuta*, fo. 34v *AA*, fo. 128	110 Selden Soc. 337–346, pl. 424. *Precedents of Criminal Slander*.
Dier Periam Hill. 17 Eliz. 105	*Statuta*, fo. 230	[inquest of office]; not identified in 110 Selden Soc. (1575).

[1] *Seemingly* 172.
[2] This is out of sequence and the reference seems to indicate more than one case: 'Rolstons treason. Dier man: 110. 2 & 3 Ph. et Mar. in fine casus.'
[3] Cf. 3 Co. Inst. 24: 'Lord Lumley's case, Hil. 14 Eliz., reported by the Lord Dier under his own hand, which we have seen, but left out of the print.'

17 Eliz. 108 Periam	*AC*, fo. 534	110 Selden Soc. 329, pl. 417. *Multon* v. *Coveney* (1575).
P. 17 Eliz. Periam Dier 110b	*AA*, fos. 44v, 48	110 Selden Soc. 334, pl. 423. *Att.-Gen.* v. *Mildmay* (1575).
17 Eliz. 112 Periam	*AA*, fo. 160	110 Selden Soc. 349, pl. 429. *Manser* v. *Annesley* (1575).
Mich 17 & 18 El. Dier 113 Periam	*AA*, fo. 74	[old patent granting fines]; not identified in 110 Selden Soc. (1575).
Dier man. 118b	*AB*, fo. 173v	110 Selden Soc. 344, pl. 424.19. 'Chief justice of England' in 1537.
Dier Periam 19 Eliz. 126	*AC*, fo. 556	110 Selden Soc. 358, pl. 440. *Anon.* (1577).
Periam 19 Eliz. 131b	*AB*, fo. 314v	110 Selden Soc. 358, pl. 441. *Anon.* (1577).
Periam 129	*C*, fo. 240	110 Selden Soc. 359, pl. 443. *Hynde* v. *Lyon* (1578).
Dier Periam 20 Eliz. 136	*AB*, fo. 288v	Cf. 110 Selden Soc. 380, pl. 482. *Weekes' Case* (1580).[1]
Dier Periam 136b	*Statuta*, fo. 158v	'Fletw. case'; not identified in 110 Selden Soc. (1578).
20 Eliz. Dier Periam 137	*AD*, fo. 806v	[conveyance by married woman]; not identified in 110 Selden Soc.
20 Eliz. 137 Dier Periam	*Statuta*, fo. 169	'baron et fem levy fine del inheritance la fem al use del baron in fee de terre tenus in capite, [la] fem morust, et per opinion del court in curia wardorum le roygne navera le terre …'; not identified in 110 Selden Soc.
Dier Periam 20 Eliz. 138	*AC*, fo. 529 *AD*, fo. 826v	110 Selden Soc. 359, pl. 444. *Roofe* v. *Light* (1578).
Dier Periam 21 Eliz. 140	*AC*, fo. 321v *AD*, fo. 835v	110 Selden Soc. 373, pl. 460. *Farrand* d. *Owen* v. *Ramsey* (1579).
Dier 21 Eliz. 140b Periam	*C*, fo. 396	110 Selden Soc. 371, pl. 457. *Freston* v. *Huggon* (1579).
Periam 142	Dyer, fo. 364v	[bond to answer for contempt of the Council: 'Vide Periam 142 que le ley ad sovent foitz estre adjudge contra']; not identified in 110 Selden Soc. (1579).

---

[1] See the citation by Coke below, p. 52, no. 100.

Dier 21 Eliz. 143, Periam	*AC*, fo. 539v *AD*, fo. 811v	110 Selden Soc. 368, pl. 455. *Trudgin's Case* (1579).
Dier Periam 21 Eliz. 143	*AD*, fo. 820	110 Selden Soc. 373, pl. 458. *Annesley* v. *Johnson* (1579).
Dier Periam 22 Eliz. 143	*AD*, fo. 903	'subborn[ation]'; not identified in 110 Selden Soc. (1580).
M. 22 et 23 Eliz. Periam 146b	*Statuta*, fo. 168v	[partition]; not identified in 110 Selden Soc. (1580)
Hill. 23 Eliz. 150a, Periam	*Statuta*, fo. 144	[uses]; not identified in 110 Selden Soc. (1581)
23 Eliz. Dier Periam 152	*AD*, fo. 806v	110 Selden Soc. 391, pl. 507.
23 Eliz. 152a Periam	*C*, fo. 75	*Bishop of Worcester's Case* (1581)
23 Eliz. Periam 152b	*Statuta*, fo. 2v	110 Selden Soc. 392, pl. 509 *Ilderton's Case* (1581)
Dier Periam 23 Eliz. 155	*AB*, fo. 493v	110 Selden Soc. 387, pl. 503 *Mildmay* v. *Talbot* (1581)
Periam, lib. 1, 247[1]	*C*, fo. 119	'Sir James Croft';[2] not identified in 110 Selden Soc.

---

[1] I.e. the volume in secretary-hand.
[2] Cf. Sir James Croft's case, Pas. 29 Eliz., in Co. Litt. 2b. This was after Dyer's death.

CASES FROM
COKE'S COMMONPLACE BOOKS
AND MARGINALIA

CHRONOLOGICAL TABLE OF THE
NAMED CASES REPORTED IN VOLUME I

References are to the case numbers in this edition. The main entries, with notes of identification, are indicated with an asterisk.

1570	Bedingfield v. Pickering	. 242
1570	Bullock v. Burdett (dated 1573)	.198*, 199
1571 Trin.	Franklyn v. Davison	. 154
1571	Fitzwilliam v. Copley	. 307
1571–72	Copwood v. Clarke	. 107*, 177, 239
1572 Mich.	Cranmer's Case (Kyrke d. Cranmer v. Bales)	6, 106*, 123, 137, 217, 229, 235, 265
1572 Mich.	Vernon's Case (Vernon v. Stanley)	24, 78, 258*, 307
1572 Mich.	Winter's Case	52, 88*, 125, 150, 169, 205, 220, 221, 245, 311
1572	Apot's Case	. 304
1572 (circa)	Bishop of Norwich's Case	. 681
1573 Pas.	Copleston v. Stowell	. 20
1573 Pas.	Vernon v. Vernon	118*, 166, 233, 298, 310
1573 Mich.	Androwes v. Blunt	. 101*, 149, 192
1573	Lodge's Case	. 58
1573	Crane's Case	. 63
1573	Duke's Case (Ryngrose v. Prest)	. 105
1573	Jackson v. Darcy	23, 37, 109*
1573	Bracebridge's Case (Barewell v. Lucas)	117*, 182, 183, 186, 189
1573	Case of the Dean and Chapter of Gloucester	. 151
1573	Lord Audley's Case	. 213
1573	Ellis v. Vavasour	. 247
1573–74	Clache's Case (Glover v. Berry)	40, 41, 234, 269*
1574 Pas.	Sheldon v. Gilbert	. 122
1574 Trin.	Whoper v. Harewood	. 56
1574	Dimes' Case	. 59
1574	Delapré's Case	. 89*, 266
1574	Bettisford v. Foord	. 110
1574	Waring's Case	. 206
1575 Pas.	Humphreston's Case (Lane v. Cowper)	46, 75, 87*, 173, 206, 215, 216, 230, 249
1575 Mich.	Nichols v. Nichols	39, 90*, 155, 231, 236, 237, 250
1575 Mich.	Bradstock's Case	. 82
1575	Manser v. Annesley	30, 43
1575	Latton's Case (Eyston v. Studde)	51*, 64, 292, 297
1575	Brent's Case	15, 136, 191, 195, 207, 209*

Date	Case	Pages
1575	Toppe v. Eden	268
1575 (circa)	Wotton v. Cooke	46, 222, 230
1576 Pas.	Gyles v. Colshill	76, 113*, 241, 243, 280, 295, 324
1576 Pas.	Lord Parr's Case	272
1576 Pas.	Broadbridge's Case	172, 232
1576 Pas.	Eden v. Harris	140, 143
1576 Trin.	Haddon's Case (Manning v. Androwes)	38, 121, 197, 212*
1576 Trin.	Savage v. Chester	170
1576 Trin., 1577 Trin.	Onley v. Earl of Kent	34, 211, 218*, 223, 285, 286
1576 Mich.	Eccleston and Ireland v. Tuchett	13
1576 Mich.	Earl of Arundel v. Langar	71, 80, 82, 116*, 156, 271
1576 Mich., 1577 Mich.	Wyatt's Case (Multon v. Coveney)	94, 125, 147*, 157, 158, 160, 171, 252
1576	Tresham's Case	251
1576 (circa)	Countess of Lennox's Case	111
1577 Hil., Mich.	Buttell v. Wylford	17, 115*, 319, 320
1577 Pas.	Hill's Case	95
1577 Pas.	Grendon v. Dean of Worcester	119, 136*
1577 Pas.	Lancastell v. Aller	164*, 194
1577 Pas.	Countess of Essex's Case	187
1577 Pas.	Sir George Calverley's Case	271
1577 Pas.-Trin.	Dorrell v. Colyns	98, 163*
1577 Trin.	Earl of Lincoln's Case	97
1577 Trin.	Spell d. Cromwell v. Androwes	7
1577 Trin.	Appulton's Case	228
1577 Mich.	Earl of Rutland's Case	21
1577	Cromwell v. Androwes	2
1577	Chick's Case (Baker v. Raymond)	91, 277*
1577	Coventry's Case	294
1577-81	Lord Cromwell v. Dennye	55, 178*
1578 Hil.	Archer's Case	16*, 313
1578 Hil.	Eare v. Snowe	238
1578 Hil.	Hinde v. Lyons	276
1578 Pas.	Croft v. Howel (The Cooks' Case)	29
1578 Pas.	Barbour v. Long	302
1578 Pas.	Weltden v. Elkington	104*, 161, 278
1578 Trin.	Dr Julio's Case	139
1578 Mich.	West v. Stowell	35
1578	R. v. Trudgin	99
1578	Holcroft's Case	100, 318
1578	Hare v. Bickley	108

1578	Eare d. Trevelyan v. Snowe	238
1578	Att.-Gen. v. Sir John Constable	283, 284*
1579 Pas.	Francis Trugeon's Case	162
1579 Pas.	Spell d. Cromwell v. Nedeham	168
1579 Pas.	The Serjeants' Case	224*, 296, 307, 316
1579 Trin.	R. v. Wood	102
1579 Trin., 1580 Mich.	Kirkeby v. Thornborough	1, 300
1579 Mich.	Farrand d. Owen v. Ramsey	270
1579	Lovelace's Case	314
1579 (circa)	Markham's Case	10
1579 (circa)	Fox v. Collier	262
1581 Trin.	Dineley v. Assehton	109, 317*
1581 Mich.	Baker v. Smith	321
1582 Pas.	Drury v. Leventhorp	303, 322
1582	Paston v. Drewry	180
1584 Mich.	R. v. Edmund Paston	50
1584	Perrot's Case	207
1586	Calthorp's Case	323
1587 Mich.	Ognel v. Underhill and Appleton	314
Temp. Eliz.	Earl of Leicester's Case	8
Temp. Eliz.	Lord Compton v. Egerton	43
Temp. Eliz.	Radcliffe's Case	86
Temp. Eliz.	Case of the Broderers' Company	120
Temp. Eliz.	Hawles's Case	138
Temp. Eliz.	Wilshere's Case	181
Temp. Eliz.	Rolfe's Case	210
Temp. Eliz.	Denham v. Dorman	214
Temp. Eliz.	Payne's Case	315

CASES FROM THE COMMONPLACE BOOKS

[1]

AA, fo. 9 (magenta ink). *Ff*, fo. 170v. *Lb*, fo. 4 (extracts).

<Ejectione firme.>^s <[Trin. 21]¹ Eliz. ceux cases [fueront]² agre in common banke.>^s <Tr. 21 Eliz. [inter] Kirkeby³ et [Thorne]boroughe.⁴>^s

Nota quant home fait leas pur ans per fait a porter ejectione firme, si le fait port date devant le delivery, come si le fait port date 1 Maii et le fait est deliver 3 die Maii, sur le terre come oportet, la le pleintife doit dire per son fait portant date 1 Maii dimissa le 3 jour del May, car sil count dun demise 1 Maii et le fait ne fuit deliver devant le 3 jour le evidence ne mainteinera le count.

Auxi si home port ejectione firme dun mannour il covient prover attornment des tenauntes al ejecter ou autrement le pleintife ne recovera. Mes si le declaration soit dun mannour et 20 acres de terre, coment que nul attornment soit prove pur le mannour poet estre bone pur le 20 acres. Et le case del mannour avoit estre adjudge, come fuit dit.

Auxi si home port ejectione firme et count dun leas fait per J. S. a luy, et que J. N. ejecte luy, il covient prover in evidence que J. N. eject luy ou que ascun person ou persons per le commaundement del J. N. eject luy ou que les meniall servauntes de J. N. fist le ejectment, car si <J. S.>^d J. N. fuit le disseisor et <le d>^d avoit fait leasses pur ans, et le disseisie fist entrie et enseale un leas sur le terre et les lesses continue in possession apres ove lour cattell et paia lour rent al J. N., uncore J. N. nest le ejector mes les lessees (et uncore Serjaunt Fenner dit que fuit adjudge devant le Segnior Dier que il tiel case le paiment del rent al J. N. fait luy le ejectour, mes le contrarie est ore tenus).

Et la Serjaunt Fenner auxi dit que avoit estre adjudge que si home bargaine et vend son terre per fait indent et nul date est conteine deins les indentures, la les 6 moys serra accompt del delivery del fait, mes quant ascun date est deins le fait la les 6 moys serra accompt del date del fait et nemi del delivery. Et ceo semble destre auxi affirme.

Et la fuit auxi dit que si home fait leas del date del fait jesque al 21 ans, la le jour del date est prise inclusive. Mes quant le lease est fait del jour del date del leas, la le <leasse>^d jour del date est prise exclusive.

Vide le deane of Worcestres case, fol. 503b, que in ejectione firme monstre

---

[1] *Supplied from Ff.*
[2] *Supplied from Ff.*
[3] *Conjectural; appears to read* Kirleby.
[4] *First part of name missing; the full name is given below.*

CASES FROM THE COMMONPLACE-BOOKS

1. KIRKEBY v. THORNBOROUGH[1]

Common Pleas, Trin. 1579, Mich. 1580.

Ejectment. Trin. 21 Eliz., these cases were agreed in the Common Bench. Between Kirkeby and Thornborough.

Note that when someone makes a lease for years by deed, in order to bring ejectment, and the deed bears date before the delivery on the land (as it should) – for instance, if the deed bears date 1 May, and the deed is delivered on 3 May – the plaintiff ought to say 'by his deed, bearing date 1 May, he demised on 3 May', for if he counts on a demise on 1 May, and the deed was not delivered before 3 May, the evidence will not maintain the count.

Also if someone brings ejectment for a manor, he must prove an attornment by the tenants to the ejector, or else the plaintiff will not recover. If, however, the declaration is for a manor and 20 acres of land, even if no attornment is proved for the manor, it may be good for the 20 acres. It was said that the case of the manor had been adjudged.

Also if someone brings ejectment, and counts on a lease made to him by John Style, and that John Noke ejected him, he must prove in evidence that John Noke ejected him or that some person or persons by command of John Noke ejected him, or that John Noke's menial servants caused the ejectment; for if John Noke was a disseisor and had made leases for years, and the disseisee made an entry and sealed a lease upon the land, and the lessees continued in possession afterwards with their cattle and paid their rent to John Noke, John Noke is not then the ejector but the lessees are. *Serjeant Fenner* said it was adjudged before the lord Dyer that in such a case the payment of the rent to John Noke makes him the ejector; nevertheless, the contrary is now held.

Serjeant Fenner also said on this occasion that it had been adjudged that if someone bargains and sells his land by deed indented, and there is no date contained in the indentures, the six months[2] shall be reckoned from the delivery of the deed, but when there is any date in the deed the six months shall be reckoned from the date of the deed and not of the delivery.[3] This seemed also to be affirmed.

It was also said there that if someone makes a lease for twenty-one years from the date of the deed, the day of the date is to be understood inclusively. But when the lease is made from the day of the date of the lease, the day of the date is there understood exclusively.

See the dean of Worcester's case, fo. 503v,[4] that in ejectment it is usual to set out

---

[1] Cit. anonymously, as to enrolments, in *Clayton's Case* (1585) 5 Co. Rep. 1. Noted below, p. 157, no. 300 (anon.).
[2] This refers to the Statute of Enrolments, 27 Hen. VIII, c. 16.
[3] *Thomas* v. *Popham* (1562) Dyer 218; 4 Leon. 4; Moo. 40.
[4] *Grendon* v. *Bishop of Lincoln and the Dean and Chapter of Worcester* (1576) 2 Plowd. 493, at fo. 503v. Cf. below, p. 64, no. 114.

usualment le leasse fait per force de quel il fuit possesse, et ne monstre ascun entrie, et il est bone pur ceo que home ne poet estre possesse tanque il ad entre. Mes est dit, Pl. Com. 424b, que si home port ejectione firme et est trove que il ad title forsque al moite, le pleintife ne recovera pur ceo [que] il poet aver brefe ou bill de auter forme, scilicet del moite. Mes in ejectione firme dun acre, et ilz trovont que il fuit seise de demidio acre, ceo est assets bone. Nota differenciam inter dimidium et medietatem. Mes nota que fuit adjudge <mes fuit adjudge>[1] M. 22 Eliz. in banke le roy que si home port ejectione firme de 20 acres et le jurors trove que le pleintife ad droit forsque al moitie undivided, que uncore il recovera.

Et nota fuit tenus per le Segnior Dier in le dit case de Thorneborough que si disseisor fait leas pur ans rendant rent, ou a volunt rendant rent, et puis le disseisie enter, et le lesse pur ans ou a volunt reenter et paie le rent al disseisor, que il est le ejectour et est le novel disseisor.

Et issint fuit adjudge in auter case in mesme le terme.

[2]

AA, fo. 9v (magenta ink).

<Ejectione firme.>[s]

[Si un][2] home soit disseisie severalment de 2 acres et il fait lease deux et enter <et>[3] sur lun et deliver le fait sur le terre et [enter][4] sur lauter et deliver sur le terre. Fuit move in cest case in banke le roy in ejectione firme enter Dominum Crumwell et Androwes si cest leasse serra bone pur le 2 acres pur ceo que le fait prist effect come fait per le primer delivery.

[3]

AA, fo. 9v (magenta ink).

<Ejectione firme.>[s]

Nota fuit adjudge in 2 cases, P. 22 Eliz., que si home port ejectione firme de [3] acres et le jury trove le defendant culpable del moite del 3 acres que le pleintife avera judgment sur ceo. Et issint fuit adjudge 2 ou 3 termes devant per mesmes les justices in banke le roy.

---

[1] *Sic, but otiose.*
[2] *Words lost in top outer corner.*
[3] *Sic, but otiose.*
[4] *Word mostly missing.*

the making of the lease, 'by virtue whereof he was possessed', and not to show any entry; and this is good enough, because one cannot be possessed until he has entered. But it is said in Plowd. 424v[1] that if someone brings ejectment and it is found that he has title only to a moiety, the plaintiff shall not recover, because he could have a writ or bill in another form, namely for the moiety. If, however, in ejectment for one acre they find that he was seised of half an acre (*de dimidio acrae*), that is perfectly good. Note the difference between a half (*dimidium*) and a moiety (*medietas*). Note, however, that it was adjudged in Michaelmas term 22 Eliz. [1580], in the King's Bench, that if someone brings ejectment for 20 acres, and the jurors find that the plaintiff has right only to an undivided moiety, he shall nevertheless recover.[2]

And note that it was held by the lord DYER in the said case of Thornborough that if a disseisor makes a lease for years rendering rent, or a lease at will rendering rent, and then the disseisee enters, and the lessee for years or at will re-enters and pays the rent to the disseisor, he is the ejector and is the novel disseisor.

So it was adjudged in another case the same term.

2. LORD CROMWELL v. ANDROWES[3]

King's Bench, 1577.

Ejectment.

A man was disseised of two acres separately, and he made a lease of them both, and entered upon one of them and delivered the deed upon the land, and [then] entered upon the other and delivered upon the land. It was moved in this case in the King's Bench, in an ejectment between Lord Cromwell and Androwes, whether this lease was good for the two acres, inasmuch as the deed took effect as a deed by the first delivery.

3. ANON.

King's Bench, Pas. 1580.

Ejectment.

Note that it was adjudged in two cases in Easter term 22 Eliz. that if someone brings ejectment for three acres, and the jury find the defendant guilty with respect to a moiety of the three acres, the plaintiff shall have judgment on this. And it was so adjudged two or three terms earlier by the same justices in the King's Bench.

---

[1] Plowden's note to *Bracebridge* v. *Cooke* (1572) Plowd. 416, at fo. 424v.
[2] See below, no. 3 (Pas. 1580).
[3] Cf. two ejectments in the Common Pleas: (1) *Spell* d. *Lord Cromwell* v. *Androwes* (Trin. 1577) below, p. 99, no. 168; (2) *Spell* d. *Lord Cromwell* v. *Nedeham* (Pas., Mich. 1579), below, p. 6, no. 7. It seems that there was another ejectment even before these: below, p. 82, no. 130 (Common Pleas). The second case went to the King's Bench on a writ of error in Oct. 1579, so it seems that this cannot be the case reported here. For other proceedings in the very lengthy dispute see *Androwes* v. *Blunt* (1573) below, p. 52, no. 101; *Lord Cromwell* v. *Androwes* (1581) vol. ii, p. 180, and the notes on both pages.

[4]

AA, fo. 9v (magenta ink).

<Ejectione firme.>[s]

Nota, si ejectione firme soit port dun moitie dun messuage, la si le defendant clayme enterest in lauter moitie le pleintife covient a prover un expresse ouster, car coment que un tenant in common enter et dwelle in le meason ceo nest ouster car est loiall, et pur ceo un expresse expulsion covient estre prove. Mes si le defendant ne clayme interest desouth cesti que ad lauter moitie, la ne besoigne de prove un expresse expulsion mes un entre ou occupation suffist. Et ceo fuit issint tenus a Croydon a les assises devant Southcote et Gawdy, justices dassise.

[5]

AA, fo. 9v (magenta ink).

<Ejectione firme.>[s]

Nota, fuit tenus Mich. 22 et 23 Eliz. in banke le roy que ejectione firme port de una pecia terre continente per estimationem 10 acras sive pluis sive minus que cest declaration est insufficient, mes la fuit dun cotage auxi et pur ceo est bone pur le cotage. Et la semble auxi que ejectione firme gist bien dun lieu conus sauns expresse les acres.

[6]

AA, fo. [8]v[1] (25v).

<Withernam.>[s]

Nota fuit agree in le common banke anno 18 Eliz. que si le pleintife in repl. count sur un uncore detient et monstre le value des avers in son count come oportet et le defendant plead non cepit et trove vers luy al damages de 3 li., la le pleintife avera brefe al vicount pur faire deliverauns, et si deliverauns ne poet estre fait le pleintife avera brefe daver le value del avers et nemi les damages queux le <def>[d] jurors taxe. Et le court dit que le defendant in cest case gagera deliverauns. Quere car il nad jour en court.

---

[1] *In the new numbering which begins on fo. 17 (magenta ink).*

4. ANON.

Croydon Assizes, Lent or Summer 1580.

Ejectment.

Note that if ejectment is brought for a moiety of a messuage, and the defendant claims an interest in the other moiety, the plaintiff must prove an express ouster; for if one tenant in common enters and lives in the house, it is not an ouster [of the other], inasmuch as it is lawful, and therefore an express expulsion must be proved. If, however, the defendant does not claim an interest beneath the person who has the other moiety, there is then no need to prove an express expulsion, but an entry or occupation is sufficient. This was held at Croydon Assizes before SOUTHCOTE and GAWDY, justices of assize.

5. ANON.

King's Bench, Mich. 1580.

Ejectment.

Nota that it was held in Michaelmas term 22 & 23 Eliz., in the King's Bench, that if an ejectment is brought for 'a piece of land containing by estimation 10 acres, more or less', this declaration is insufficient; but there it was for a cottage also, and therefore it is good for the cottage. It also seemed in that case that ejectment lies well enough for a known place without expressing the number of acres.[1]

6. ANON.

Common Pleas, 1576.

Withernam.

Note that it was agreed in the Common Bench in the year 18 Eliz. that if the plaintiff in replevin counts upon an 'uncore detient' and sets out the value of the beasts in his count (as he ought), and the defendant pleads *Non cepit* and it is found against him with damages of £3, the plaintiff shall have a writ to the sheriff to make deliverance, and if deliverance cannot be made the plaintiff shall have a writ to have the value of the beasts and not the damages which the jurors taxed. And the court said that the defendant in this case may wage deliverance. (Query, for he has no day in court.)

---

[1] Cf. *Turner's Case* (1585) vol. ii, p. 272, and the note there.

[7]

AA, fo. 12v (29v).

<Travers.>[s]

Termino Pasche 21 Eliz. rott. mcccl° in ejectione firme port per Anthonie Nedhame del demise de Segnior Crumwell de certain terre in Leic. envers divers defendants, les defendants pledont que devant le Segnior Crumwell riens avoit un J. Blunt fuit seisie in fe et enfeffe Anthonie Andrews, que morust seisie, et ceo discende a Edward Andrewes, que lessa les terres a les defendants, et issint fueront ilz possesse tanque le dit J. Blunt entra sur eux et eux expulse et dissese le dit Edward Andrewes et issint seisi per disseisin enfeffe le dit Segnior Crumwell, que lessa al pleintife come in le count fuit alledge etc. <7 E. 4, 19.> <19 H. 6, 22, done in taile et morant disseisie, auterment fe.>[i] Le pleintife dit que longe temps devant le ejectment le dit J. Blunt fuit seisie in fe et issint seisie <morust seisie>[d] de ceo infeffe le dit Segnior Crumwell devant le <temps etc.>[d] ejectment, et mainteine le leasse in le count, absque hoc quod Johannes Blunt disseisivit predictum Edwardum Andrews. <9 H. 6, 9, 10, taile.>[i] <9 H. 6, 30, disseisin.>[i] <18 E. 4, 26b, disseisin.>[i] Et sur cest replication <de>[d] les defendants demurront in ley, car per lour pretence le feffment de J. Blunt serra travers et nemi le leasse, car le disseisin come cest case est ne fuit forsque conveiaunce. Et auxi le pleintife covient daver monstre coment Blunt apres son feffment demesne vient arere al un estate etc. Uncore fuit adjudge que le travers fuit bone. Et nota que Serjaunt Anderson arguendo prist mesme le ground prise devant, et le Segnior Dier monstre le reason breifment, car il dit lour clere opinion fuit que le disseisin in cest case fuit traversable. Et auxi il dit que le feffment et le discent auxi sont traversable come cest case est, mes clerement le disseisin. <9 H. 6>[d] Et il cite 9 H. 6, 35,[1] et eodem anno fol. 19 et 31, que est come un maxime come il dit in la ley que un disseisin alledge per matter in fait per voy de barre, replication, etc., serra unques traverses. Et il dit que in le case de 5 E. 4, 9, semble a luy que le feffment fuit traversable ou que le tenant fuit de plein age, mes il dit que in tiel case le seisin ne fuit traversable, car il ne puit enfeffe sinon que il fuit seisie. Et il cite L. 5 E. 4, fol. 136, tit. [Tra]verse, B. 201, valde bone case.

---

[1] *Altered from or to* 32.

[3] YB Trin. 19 Hen. VI, fo. 22, pl. 17.
[4] YB Mich. 7 Edw. IV, fo. 19, pl. 17.
[5] YB Pas. 9 Hen. VI, fos. 9–10, pl. 26.
[6] YB Trin. 9 Hen. VI, fo. 30, pl. 35.
[7] YB Hil. 18 Edw. IV, fo. 26, pl. 20.
[8] I.e. an introductory recital.
[9] YB Trin. 9 Hen. VI, fo. 19, pl. 12; Mich. 9 Hen. VI, fo. 32, pl. 2.
[10] YB Pas. 5 Edw. IV, *Long Quinto*, fo. 9.
[11] Bro. Abr., *Travers per sans ceo*, pl. 201, from YB Mich. 5 Edw. IV, *Long Quinto*, fo. 136.

7. SPELL d. CROMWELL v. NEDEHAM

Common Pleas, Pas. 1579.

Traverse.

In Pas. 21 Eliz., roll 1350,[1] in *ejectione firmae* brought [against] Anthony Nedeham, on the demise of Lord Cromwell, for certain land in Leicestershire, against various defendants, the defendants pleaded that before the Lord Cromwell had anything one John Blunt was seised in fee and enfeoffed Anthony Androwes, who died seised; and it descended to Edward Androwes,[2] who leased the lands to the defendants; and they were so possessed until the said John Blunt entered upon them and expelled them and disseised the said Edward Androwes; and, being thus seised by disseisin, they enfeoffed the said Lord Cromwell, who leased to the plaintiff (as alleged in the count). {19 Hen. VI, fo. 22,[3] gift in tail [without answering the] dying seised; otherwise of a feoffment in fee.} The plaintiff said that long before the ejectment the said John Blunt was seised in fee and (being so seised) enfeoffed the said Lord Cromwell thereof before the ejectment; and he maintained the lease in the count, 'without this, that John Blount disseised the aforesaid Edward Androwes'. {7 Edw. IV, fo. 19.[4] 9 Hen. VI, fos. 9, 10,[5] tail. 9 Hen. VI, fo. 30,[6] disseisin. 18 Edw. IV, fo. 26v,[7] disseisin.} Upon this replication the defendants demurred in law; for on their view it was the feoffment by John Blunt which should have been traversed, and not the [disseisin], for (as this case is) the disseisin is merely conveyance.[8] Moreover, the plaintiff ought to have shown how Blunt came to have an estate again after his own feoffment. Nevertheless, it was adjudged that the traverse was good. Note that *Serjeant Anderson* in his argument took the same ground that was taken before; and the lord DYER showed the reason briefly, for he said their clear opinion was that the disseisin in this case was traversable. He also said that the feoffment and the descent are traversable as well (as this case is); but clearly the disseisin [may be traversed]. And he cited 9 Hen. VI, fo. 35, and fos. 19 and 31 in the same year,[9] that it is, as it were, a maxim in the law (as he said) that a disseisin alleged by matter in fact, by way of bar, replication, and so forth, may always be traversed. He said that in the case of 5 Edw. IV, fo. 9,[10] the feoffment was traversable (as it seemed to him), or that the tenant was of full age; but he said that in such a case the seisin was not traversable, for he cannot enfeoff unless he was seised. He cited the Long 5 Edw. IV, fo. 136, Brooke, tit. *Traverse*, 201,[11] a very good case.

---

[1] CP 40/1366, m. 1350: Richard Spell v. Anthony, Ambrose, John, Francis, Richard and Robert Nedeham, and four others; ejectment for six messuages and land at Allexton, Leics., on the demise of Lord Cromwell; demurrer to the replication; c.a.v. to Mich. 1579; judgment for the plaintiff; note of a writ of error dated 30 Oct. 1579; KB 27/1272, m. 450: proceedings in error; c.a.v. to Hil. 1583; no judgment entered. Cf. what seems to be a different ejectment action in the same court, below, p. 99, no. 168. Note also *Androwes* v. *Lord Cromwell* (Mich. 1579) IT MS. Petyt 511.12, fo. 309. For a concurrent ejectment action in the King's Bench on behalf of Lord Cromwell see above, p. 4, no. 2. In 1598 Androwes brought three actions against Ambrose Nedeham in respect of a lease of the mansion house of Allexton allegedly granted in 1571: (1) KB 27/1352, m. 252: debt for rent; nonsuited, with £5 costs awarded to Nedeham, Mich. 1598; (2) ibid., m. 252d: trespass to the mansion house; pleads Not Guilty; verdict and judgment for the plaintiff, with £10 damages and £16 costs, Mich. 1599; affirmed in Exch. Ch., 8 Oct. 1600; (3) ibid., m. 253: covenant on the indenture of lease; demurrer to the plea in bar; no judgment entered.

[2] Admitted to Gray's Inn 1563. As of Gray's Inn, he granted a rent charged on the manor of Allexton to Sir John Arundell of Lanhearne in 1574: Cornwall Record Office, AR 1/707.

[8]

AA, fo. 28 (61).

<Disseisin.>^s

Nota que jeo ay oye que ou le roygne fuit seisie de certaine terres, un estrange intruda sur sa possession et prist les profitz, et puis le roigne grant ouster mesmes les terres a le countie de Leic. et lestrange continue in possession in pernant des profites. Et fuit tenus (come fuit dit) que il ne fuit disseisor, pur ceo que per son primer entre il ne puit gainer ascun franktenement vers le roy, et donques son continuauns puis le grant le roigne ne puit faire luy disseisor.

[9]

AA, fo. 39 (73) (text lightly struck through).

<Patentes.>^s

Nota fuit adjudge anno [*blank*] Eliz. in [*blank*] que si le roigne grant son manour de D. et toutz terres, tenementes et hereditamentes part, parcell ou member de mesme le manour ou repute come part, parcell ou member de mesme le manour, et 3 acres de terre que in veritie ne sont parcell come sever per grant et puis purchase et use et occupie temps dont come parcell, uncore ceo ne passera in le case del roy. Car cest paroll reputed est un paroll de graund uncertaintie, car ascun homes repute un chose et ascun auter chose, et le temps de reputation est auxi uncertaine. Et pur ceo fuit adjudge que riens passera forsque ceo que est parcell in droit.

[10]

AA, fo. 40 (74) (text lightly struck through).

<Patents.>^s

Nota fuit agree per Bromley, segnior chauncellor, Gerrard, attorney general, et Popham sollicitor, in le case inter le counte de Rutland et Markham que lou le roigne que ore est grant al Markham officium unius forestariorum de Shirewood vocatum officium custodis sive parcorum sive boscorum de Billowe et Birkelande in predicta foresta etc. que officia Henricus comes Rutland nuper habuit etc., et in veritie le counte de Rutland ne unques avoit les ditz offices, et uncore tenus que intant que les

---

[6] Cit. in *AA*, fo. 88v ('Nota in le case inter le counte de Rutland et Markham'); 10 Co. Rep. 113. See also *CSPD Suppl.* 22, an opinion by Wray C.J., Dyer C.J., Manwood C.B., Gawdy and Mead JJ. on a case between the earl of Rutland and Thomas Markham concerning his forestership in Sherwood, 1580; HEHL MS. EL 482, fo. 219. The case was still unresolved in 1599, when the queen asked Cecil to find a solution: *Cecil Papers*, ix. 359.

[7] Thomas Markham, standard-bearer of the gentlemen pensioners.

[8] Henry Manners (1527–63), second earl of Rutland; he was succeeded by his son Edward, the plaintiff.

[9] The original patent, dated 23 Oct. 1564, is in Sheffield City Archives, Arundel Castle MSS, ACM/WD/972. The grant was during the minority of Edward, earl of Rutland.

8. EARL OF LEICESTER'S CASE[1]

Temp. Eliz. (before 1588).

Disseisin.

Note that I have heard that where the queen was seised of certain lands, a stranger intruded upon her possession and took the profits, and then the queen granted over the same lands to the earl of Leicester;[2] but the stranger continued in possession, taking the profits. And it was held (as it was said) that he was not a disseisor, because he could not by his first entry gain any freehold against the king,[3] and therefore his continuing in possession after the queen's[3] grant could not make him a disseisor.

9. ANON.[4]

Temp. Eliz.

Patents.

Note that it was adjudged in the [*blank*] year of Elizabeth that if the queen grants her manor of Dale, 'and all lands, tenements and hereditaments which are part, parcel or member of the same manor, or reputed as part, parcel or member of the same manor', three acres of land which in truth are not parcel, [having been] severed by grant and then purchased, but have been used and occupied time out of mind as parcel, shall nevertheless not pass in the case of the king. This word 'reputed' is a word of great uncertainty, for some men repute one thing and others another; and the time of reputation is also uncertain.[5] Therefore it was adjudged that nothing should pass except that which is rightfully parcel.

10. EARL OF RUTLAND v. MARKHAM[6]

Reference from the Privy Council, *c.* 1579.

Patents.

Note that it was agreed by BROMLEY, lord chancellor, *Gerrard*, attorney-general, and *Popham*, solicitor-general, in the case between the earl of Rutland and Markham, that where the present queen granted to Markham[7] 'the office of one of the foresters of Sherwood called the office of keeper of the parks or woods of Bilhaugh and Birklands in the aforesaid forest ... which offices Henry, earl of Rutland,[8] lately had ...',[9] and in truth the earl of Rutland never had the said offices, it was nevertheless

---

[1] Cf. the next case, below, n. 4.
[2] Robert Dudley (1532–88), created earl of Leicester in 1564.
[3] Coke used 'roy' for the monarch generally, but 'roigne' for Queen Elizabeth in particular.
[4] Perhaps *Earl of Leicester's Case* (1578–79) Dyer 362; cit. in 6 Co. Rep. 66. There is nothing in the report to identify this with the previous case above.
[5] I.e. it might be a recent error, whereas reputation time out of mind would be indistinguishable from fact.

offices fueront grant per certaine nosme le grant fuit assetz bone al Markham. Et la fuit auxi dit que fuit adjudged que ou le roigne grant certaine terres per speciall nosme queux fueront conceale a luy et in veritie ilz ne fueront concealez uncore fuit adjudge que le grant fuit bone.

[11]

AA, fo. 40v (74v).

<Patents.>ˢ

Nota le solicitour le roigne dit que fuit adjudge que ou le roigne avoit grant terres a un et a les heires de son corps durante bene placito, que ceo [est] estate taile determinable sur le volunt le roigne. Vide le [mesme]¹ case Dier.

[12]

AA, fo. 48 (85).

<Prerogative.>ˢ

14 Eliz. in banke le roy, per Catlyn, leasse per le roigne south leschequer seale nest come leasse de recorde mes come auter l[ea]sse in escript: quod nullus negavit.

[13]

AA, fo. 50v (87v).

<Fines.>ˢ

Nota per Plowden in le argument de Irlands case in leschequer chamber que in chescun case fine loialment levie covient estre in brefe originall, come brefe de covenant etc., et donques le concorde que est le foundation del fine, que commence, Et est concordia talis quod predictus J. recognoscit predicta maneria cum pertinenciis etc., et sur ceo est le silver le roy enter. Et nota que ceo est le substance del fine, car le pee del fine et le note fuit forsque abstractes hors del fine. Donques est le pee del fine, et ceo add le jour et monstre devant queux justices, et ceo commence, Hec est finalis concordia facta in curia domini regis apud Westm. in die Pasche in xv dies anno regni etc. coram etc. inter etc. Et donques est le note del fine. Et nota que le note nest forsque un abstracte hors

---

¹ *Unclear; resembles* il.

⁴ KB 27/1230, m. 237 (Pas. 1569, three rolls; printed in Co. Ent. 231): George Ireland esq. and his wife Elizabeth, and Henry Eccleston esq. and his wife Margery v. Thomas Tuchett; error from Chester upon a *scire facias* to reverse a final concord of 1543 concerning the manor of Cronton, Lancs. (on the border of Ches.); fine affirmed, Hil. 1577. This was heard in the Exch. Ch. on 19 Nov. 1576: CUL MS. Ff.5.4, fos. 91–104; cf. Dyer 320 (Hil. 1573).

⁵ The learning under this heading may have inspired Coke's reading on fines, which he gave in Lyons Inn in 1579–80: above, p. lxxviii.

held that since the offices were granted by a certain name, the grant to Markham was good enough. It was also said on this occasion that it had been adjudged where the queen granted certain lands by particular names as lands which were concealed from her, and in truth they were not concealed, it was nevertheless adjudged that the grant was good.

11. ANON.

Temp. Eliz.

Patents.

Note that the queen's solicitor-general said it was adjudged that where the queen had granted lands to someone and the heirs of his body during the queen's pleasure (*durante bene placito*), this is an estate tail determinable at the queen's will. For which case see Dyer.[1]

12. ANON.[2]

King's Bench, 1572.

Prerogative.

14 Eliz., in the King's Bench, by CATLYN [C.J.], a lease by the queen under the Exchequer seal is not like a lease of record,[3] but is like any other lease in writing: which no one denied.

13. ECCLESTON and IRELAND v. TUCHETT[4]

Exch. Ch., 19 Nov. 1576.

Fines.[5]

Note, by *Plowden*, in the argument of Ireland's case in the Exchequer Chamber, that a fine lawfully levied must in every case be upon an original writ, such as a writ of covenant, and then the concord (which is the foundation of the fine) begins, 'And the concord is this, that the aforesaid J. acknowledges the aforesaid manors with the appurtenances ...', and thereupon the king's silver is entered. And note that this is the substance of the fine; for the foot of the fine, and the note, are but extracts of the fine. Then comes the foot of the fine, and this adds the day and shows before what justices; and this begins, 'This is the final concord made in the lord king's court at Westminster in the quindene of Easter in the ... year of the reign of ... before ... between ...'. Then there is the note of the fine. And note that the note is only extracted from the original

---

[1] Presumably *Lady Cromwell's Case* (1553) Dyer 94.
[2] I.e. by letters patent under the great seal.
[3] Cf. *Smith* v. *Lane* (1586) 2 Co. Rep. 16.

del originall brefe et hors del concorde, et commence, Inter J. M. querentem et T. C. deforciantem de manerio de T. cum pertinenciis in S. un[de] placitum conventionis summonitum fuit inter eos etc. scilicet quod predictus T. C. recognovit etc. Et nota que le pee del fine ou le note poet estre enter 3 ou 4 ans apres. Vide F.N.B. 147. Un fine dicitur destre ingrosse quant le cyrographer fait les indentures del fine et deliver eux al partie a que le conusans est fait. Vide 22 H. 6, 51, si fine soit levie et nient ingrosse, uncore ceo est un perfect record et poet estre executed devant que ceo soit ingrosse. Et devant le fine ingrosse le conusee avera quid juris clamat, et apres il navera. Nota bene fuit Carrels case que fem levie fine et apres concord fait et le silver le reigne enter le fem morust, et ceo adjudge bone fine. Vide 17 E. 3, 29, per Poole, fine tantoft[1] que ceo fuit ingrosse ceo serra maunde in le treasury: quod non negatur. Et nota que le custos brevium nad riens a medler <forsque>[d] ove les notes del fine tanque lestatut de 5 H. 4, cap. 14. Et nota que fine ne poet estre levie in banke le roy pur ceo que la nest ascun cyrographer. Vide 13 E. 3, tit. Estoppell, 231, partie conusor morust devant le <record>[d] fine record ou engrosse, et le venire facias fuit agard envers le heire le conusor, et donques le fine fuit record. 12 H. 4, 16. Et note est pledable devant ceo soit ingrosse. Vide 19 E. 1, Agard, 53, le institution et force dun fine.

[14]

AA, fo. 50v (87v).

<Fines.>[s]

H. 20 Eliz. fuit agre in le common banke que si tenant in taile levie un fine, lissue [pur][2] avoidance de cest fine poet dire quod partes finis nihil habuerunt tempore levatione finis. Mes tenant in fe simple ne dirra issint sil clayme per my cely que leva le fine. Et nota si fine soit plede in un formedon, le demandant poet dire generalment quod partes finis nihil habuerunt, sauns dire que donques un tiel fuit seisie etc., car sil contrediera que estate il abatera son brefe demesne. Mes quant le tenant pledra un fine il pledra issint.

[15]

AA, fo. 51 (88).

<Fines.>[s]

Nota quant un droit est in abeiauns et consideration del ley un fine ne barrera ceo

---

[1] *Sic, for* tantost.
[2] p[er].

---

[5] Mich. 13 Edw. III, Fitz. Abr., *Estoppell*, pl. 231; Mich. 13 Edw. III (RS), p. 109, pl. 57.
[6] YB Hil. 12 Hen. IV, fo. 16, pl. 11.
[7] Arthur Agard's MS. collection of records, of which Coke had a copy: above, p. cxxii.
[8] See below, p. 115, no. 209, and the note there. The present entry seems to be a commentary on the case rather than a report.

writ and the concord, and it begins, 'Between J. M., querent, and T. C., deforciant, for the manor of T. with the appurtenances in S., whereof a plea of covenant was summoned between them ... namely that the aforesaid T. C. has acknowledged ...'. And note that the foot of the fine, or the note, may be entered three or four years later. See Fitz. N.B. 147: a fine is said to be engrossed when the chirographer makes the indentures of the fine and delivers them to the party to whom the acknowledgment is made.[1] See 22 Hen. VI, fo. 51,[2] if a fine is levied and not engrossed, it is nevertheless a perfect record and may be executed before it is engrossed. Before the fine is engrossed the cognisee may have *quid juris clamat*, but afterwards he shall not. Note well Carell's case,[3] which was that a woman levied a fine, and after the concord made and the queen's silver entered the woman died, and this was adjudged a good fine. See 17 Edw. III, fo. 29,[4] by Pole, a fine shall be sent into the treasury [of the Bench] as soon as it is engrossed: which was not denied. And note that the custos brevium had nothing to do with the notes of fines until the statute of 5 Hen. IV, c. 14. Note that a fine may not be levied in the King's Bench, because there is no chirographer there. See 13 Edw. III, tit. *Estoppell*, 231,[5] a cognisor died before the fine was recorded or engrossed, and a *venire facias* was awarded against the heir of the cognisor, and then the fine was recorded. 12 Hen. IV, fo. 16.[6] Note that the fine is pleadable before it is engrossed. See 19 Edw. I, Agard, fo. 53,[7] as to the institution and force of a fine.

14. ANON.

Common Pleas, Hil. 1578.

Fines.

In Hilary term 20 Eliz., in the Common Bench, it was agreed that if tenant in tail levies a fine, the issue may, to avoid this fine, say that the parties to the fine had nothing at the time when the fine was levied. But a tenant in fee simple may not say that, if he claims through the person who levied the fine. Note that if a fine is pleaded in a formedon, the demandant may say generally that the parties to the fine had nothing, without saying that there was someone who was then seised, for if he gainsays the *que estate* he will abate his own writ. But when the tenant has to plead a fine, he must plead in that way.

15. BRENT'S CASE[8]

Common Pleas, 1575.

Fines.

Note that when a right is in abeyance and in consideration of the law, a fine will not bar

---

[1] Fitz. N.B. 147A.
[2] Clearly so written, but seemingly incorrect. Cf. *Bermingham's Case* (1443) YB Mich. 22 Hen. VI, fo. 13, pl. 17.
[3] *Warnecombe* v. *Carell* (1564) Dyer 220; Dal. 56; 12 Co. Rep. 124.
[4] *Coleworth* v. *Waltham* (1343) YB Pas. 17 Edw. III, fo. 29, pl. 28 (RS, p. 403), *per* Pole serjeant.

coment que les 5 ans passe, come fuit tenus in Brentz case. Et pur ceo si parson fait leas pur vie ove le consent del patron et ordinarie et morust et le lesse in temps de vacation levie fine et 5 ans passe, uncore le successour avoidra ceo. Issint si devant lestatut de 27 H. 8 tenant in taile in use fait feffment in fee et puis levie fine et 5 ans passe, uncore apres les 5 ans les feffees poient enter et revive luse in taile, car lestate taile fuit in suspens et consideration del ley. Quere si errionious recoverie soit ewe envers un home et puis cesti vers que le recoverie fuit ewe soit attaint de haut treason et puis le recoveror levie fine et les 5 ans passe, ore cest title de error est ale, et puis leire le person attaint est restore sicome nul atteindre ust estre, quere si cest fine barrera lheire, <car son brefe de error>¹ car al temps del fine levie le droit daction fuit ale. Mes ore quere si le restitution avera relation. Vies in le title de discontinuauns ou choses que sont in le consideration del ley ne poient estre discontinue.

[16]

AA, fo. 51 (88). Abridged in *V*, fo. 34.

<Fines.>ˢ

Nota est purveu per lestatut de 32 H. 8 that all and singuler fines aswell hertofore levied as hereafter etc. of anie manors etc. before the tyme of the same fine levied in anie wise intailed to the person or persons so levieng the same fine or to anie of his auncestors etc. 20 Eliz. le case fuit: terres fueront dones al baron et fem in special taile, le baron morust, lissue in taile enter sur sa mere et levie fine. Primerment fuit move si apres le mort le mier et lissue que levie le fine si lissue del issue poet avoider ceo. Et le Segnior Dier dit que lissue del issue serra barre, car les parolx sont 'to him that levie[s] the fine or to anie of his auncestors'. Et ceo semble as auters reasonable opinion per le suertie des purchasers. Donques a auter jour fuit move ouster que la fem enter sur le conuse del fine et defete son estate, et puis morust, et puis cesti que levie le fine morust: si lissue cesti que levie le fine serra barre? Et Manwood semble que non, car coment que lestatut dit 'all and singuler fines', uncore il dit que un fine avoided nest ascun fine deins le meaning del estatut. Come si tenant in taile levie fine, et ceo est revers per error, ceo ne liera car cest fine avoided. Et pur ceo tiel fine que liera lissue covient estre tiel fine que continuera bone fine. Et auxi il dit si lissue in taile levie fine in vie son pier <et>² cest fine ne liera lissue, car si les parties nont riens ceo nest fine que liera, car nest fine in ley mes in parolx solement.

---

¹ *Sic, but perhaps meant to be deleted.*
² *Sic, but otiose.*

it, even though the five years have passed: as was held in Brent's case. Therefore if a parson makes a lease for life with the consent of the patron and ordinary, and dies, and the lessee during a vacancy levies a fine, and five years pass, the successor may still avoid it. Likewise if, before the statute of 27 Hen. VIII,[1] a tenant in tail in use made a feoffment in fee and then levied a fine, and five years passed, nevertheless after the five years the feoffees could enter and revive the use in tail, for the estate tail was in suspense and in consideration of the law. But if an erroneous recovery is had against someone, and then the person against whom the recovery was had is attainted of high treason, and then the recoveror levies a fine and the five years pass, so that now his title of error is gone, and then the heir of the person attainted is restored as if no attainder had been, query whether this fine will bar the heir, for at the time of the fine levied the right of action by writ of error was gone: but now query whether the restitution will have relation back. See in the title of discontinuance, as to where things which lie in the consideration of the law cannot be discontinued.

16. ARCHER'S CASE[2]

Common Pleas, 1578.

Fines.

Note that it is provided by the statute of 32 Hen. VIII[3] that 'all and singular fines as well heretofore levied as hereafter to be levied of any manors, [lands, tenements or hereditaments] ... before the time of the same fine levied in any wise entailed to the person or persons so levying the same fine or to any of his ancestors ...' [shall be effective to bar the entail]. In 20 Eliz. the case was this: lands were given to a husband and wife in special tail; the husband died, and the issue in tail entered upon his mother and levied a fine. Firstly it was moved whether, after the death of the mother, and of the issue who levied the fine, the issue of the issue could avoid it. And the lord DYER said that the issue of the issue should be barred, for the words are 'to him that levies the fine or to any of his ancestors'. And this seemed to the others a reasonable opinion, for the security of purchasers. It was then further moved, on another day, that the wife entered upon the cognisee of the fine and defeated his estate, and then died, and then the person who levied the fine died: shall the issue of the person who levied the fine be barred? MANWOOD thought not, for although the statute says 'all and singular fines', nevertheless (as he said) a fine which has been avoided is not a fine within the meaning of the statute. Similarly if tenant in tail levies a fine, and it is reversed by writ of error, this will not bind, for it is a void fine. Therefore, in order to bind the issue, a fine must be such a fine as continues to be a good fine. He said also that if the issue in tail levies a fine in his father's lifetime, this fine will not bind the issue; for if the parties have nothing, it is not a fine which will bind, since it is not a fine in law but only in words.

---

[1] Statute of Uses, 27 Hen. VIII, c. 10.
[2] Cit. by this name below, p. 161, no. 313; and in 3 Co. Rep. 90; 9 Co. Rep. 141. Coke says in 3 Co. Rep. it was resolved by Dyer C.J., Manwood, Mounson and Mead JJ.
[3] 32 Hen. VIII, c. 36.

[17]

AA, fo. 54 (91).

<Extinguishment.>^{s 1}

Nota il fuit adjudge in le dean de Powles case, H. 19 Eliz., que si home face leas pur ans rendant rent sur condition, et puis enter sur le lesse pur ans et fait feffment in fe, et le lesse reentre, que ore le feffe ad le revercion et avera le rent et entra pur le condition infreint pur ceo que le rent est incident al revercion. Mes auterment fuit dun segniorie in grosse. Et issint est le livre in 9 H. 6, 16. F. abbridge ceo pluis plein que le livre alarge est. Loppinion de Loddington, 5 H. 5, 12b, contra, que le rent est extincte. Vide rent revive <apres>^d devant, 50. Vide 4 H. 7, 25. 50 E. 3, 9. Nota bone reason, car le lessour per son entre sur son lesse nad gaine ascun novell revercion.

[18]

AA, fo. 59 (96).

<Distres.>^s

Nota P. 17 Eliz. fuit agre per totam curiam in communi banco que si le segnior distreine les bestes son tenant, si le tenant tender les arrerages devant le distres prise, ou sur le distres, ceo est bone sauns tender des damages. <Fleta, lib. 2, cap. 40.>ⁱ <45 E. 3, 9. 27 E. 3, 5b.>ⁱ Mes sil ad un foitz distreine, la le tenant covient tender les arrerages ove damages. <22 H. 6, 57.>ⁱ Mes Manwood dit que si les averes soient un foitz impound, la tender des damages ove les arrerages est voide, si le segnior voet, car donques le defendant ad mitte ceo al triall del ley. <F.N.B. 69b. Dier Periam 11 Eliz. 57, irreplevisable, prender² lamendes. 13 H. 4, 17, accordant, nul tender apres imparkment.>ⁱ <Ceo nest ley come moy semble. Vide registrum judiciale, 37.>ⁱ 21 H.7, 30, in trespas de close debruse tender de sufficient amendes nest plea. Vies 2 H. 6, tit. Avowrie, F. 1, fol. 1, Bassets, si al temps del distres il tender a luy <il tender a luy>^d les arrerages, et le segnior refuse, le segnior ne unques avera retorne.

[19]

AA, fo. 64v (103v).

<Jurores.>^s

T. 19 Eliz., sur un postea, le case fuit tiel. Action de det fuit port sur un obligation

---

¹ *Title on fo. 53.*   ² *Unclear.*

⁷ *Sic*, but incorrect.   ⁸ YB Pas. 45 Edw. III, fo. 9, pl. 13.   ⁹ YB Trin. 27 Edw. III, fo. 5, pl. 19.
¹⁰ YB Trin. 22 Hen. VI, fo. 57, pl. 7.   ¹¹ Unidentified: cf. introduction, above, p. ccxxxv.
¹² YB Hil. 13 Hen. IV, fo. 17, pl. 14.   ¹³ YB Mich. 21 Hen. VII, fo. 30, pl. 9.
¹⁴ *Basset* v. *Prior of St John's* (1423) YB Mich. 2 Hen. VI, fo. 1, pl. 9; Fitz. Abr., *Avowrie*, pl. 1.

CASES FROM THE COMMONPLACE BOOKS   11

17. BUTTELL v. WYLFORD[1]

King's Bench, Hil. 1577.

Extinguishment.

Note that it was adjudged in the dean of St Paul's case, in Hilary term 19 Eliz., that if someone makes a lease for years, rendering rent upon condition [of re-entry for non-payment], and then enters upon the lessee for years and makes a feoffment in fee, and the lessee re-enters, the feoffee now has the reversion and shall have the rent, and may enter for breach of the condition, because the rent is incident to the reversion. But it is otherwise of a seigniory in gross. So is the book in 9 Hen. VI, fo. 16.[2] Fitzherbert abridges this more plainly than the book at large.[3] Against this is the opinion of Loddington in 5 Hen. V, fo. 12v,[4] that the rent is extinguished. See 'Rent revived' above, fo. 50.[5] See 4 Hen. VII, fo. 25;[6] 50 Edw. III, fo. 9.[7] Note that it makes good sense, for the lessor has not gained any new reversion by his entry upon his lessee.

18. ANON.

Common Pleas, Pas. 1575.

Distress.

Note that it was agreed in Easter term 17 Eliz., by the whole court in the Common Bench, that if the lord distrains his tenant's beasts, and the tenant tenders the arrears before the distress is taken, or upon the distress, this is good without a tender of the damages. {Fleta, lib. ii, cap. 40. 45 Edw. III, fo. 9;[8] 27 Edw. III, fo. 5v.[9]} Once the lord has distrained, however, the tenant must tender the arrears with damages. {22 Hen. VI, fo. 57.[10]} But MANWOOD said that once the beasts have been impounded, a tender of the damages with the arrears is void, if the lord so wishes, for then the defendant has submitted it to the trial of the law. {Fitz. N.B. 69B. Dyer-Peryam, 11 Eliz. 57,[11] irreplevisable, taking amends. 13 Hen. IV, fo. 17,[12] agrees with this: no tender after impounding.} {This is not law, as it seems to me. See the *Registrum Judiciale*, fo. 37.} 21 Hen.VII, fo. 30,[13] in trespass *quare clausum fregit* a tender of sufficient amends is no plea. See 2 Hen. VI, Fitz., tit. *Avowrie*, 1, fo. 1, Basset's [case],[14] if at the time of the distress he tenders him the arrears and the lord refuses, the lord shall have never have return.

19. ANON.

Trin. 1577.

Jurors.

In Trinity term 19 Eliz., upon a *postea*, the case was as follows. An action of debt

---

[1] See below, p. 68, no. 115, and the note there.   [2] *Sic*, but cf. YB Pas. 7 Hen. VI, fo. 26, pl. 14.
[3] Fitz. Abr., *Count*, pl. 11; *Double plee*, pl. 38.   [4] YB Hil. 5 Hen. V, fo. 12, pl. 30.
[5] *AA*, fo. 50 (87) (under the heading 'Rent revive').
[6] *Sic*, but there is no such folio in the vulgate. Cf. YB Trin. 11 Hen. VII, fo. 25, pl. 5.

pur le deliverie [de] certain quarters de wheate, et nul lieu expresse ou etc. Le defendant dit que le pleintife luy appointe a deliver a tiel lieu, et tender la, et le pleintife refusa. Le pleintife prist issue sur le tender etc., et apres lour charge et lour departure del barre le pleintife done <a luy>[d] a les jurors le dit obligation, que ne fuit devant monstre a eux. Mes uncore, pur ceo que le dit obligation fuit devant confesse del ambideux partes, ideo ceo fuit finable et ne avoide my le verdit. Et issint fuit rule. Mes auterment serroit sil avoit done ascun novel matter etc. <11 H. 4, 17, evidence privement done al jurors hors de court avoidra le verdit. 35 H. 6, tit. Examination, 17.>[1]

[20]

AA, fo. 68 (115).

<Corone.>[s]

P. 15 Eliz. inter Copston et Stowel. Fuit long et inveterate[2] mallice et puis Copston al Ludgate meet ove Stowel et dit que il voet pugner ove luy, quel Copston refuse, sur ceo Copston [fua][3] et Stowel senfua al mure et donques tua luy. Coment que <c>[d] la fuit mallice devant, ceo nest que se defendendo, car Stowel ne poet faire plus daver avoide luy. Et unquore quisque ob tutelam etc. <Et issint fuit resolve al Newgate.>[a] <3 E. 3, Corone, 226. Et Stanf. 15, non refiert que commence.>[a]

[21]

AA, fo. 74 (121).

<Fines.>[s]

Nota, est purveu per lestatut de 4 H. 7, cap. 24, come ensuist … Et nota que fuit adjudge M. 19 Eliz. que coment que les parolx sont generalles, et exception va solement a tiels enfantz que ne sont my parties al fines, uncore si enfaunt levie un fine il reversera ceo durant son nonage per brefe de error, car les generall parols ne sont intends de fines in queux est error mes de loiall et perfecte fines. Et pur ceo fuit

---

[1] *Written immediately before the report of 19 Eliz.*
[2] *Only* [...]*veter*[...] *remains*.
[3] *Conjectural; word lost in margin.*

pardon added); Moo. 86; R. Crompton, *Loffice et Auctorite de Justices de Peace* (1617 ed.), fos. 22v, 23, 27v (printed in 110 Selden Soc. 268).
[4] This is the date of the trial as given in the record. Coke's date, if correct, must refer to a pre-trial conference.
[5] 'What someone does in defence of his body is deemed to have been done lawfully.' D. 1.1.1.pr., from Florentinus.
[6] Coke seems to conflate two relevant cases: Mich. 3 Edw. III, Fitz. Abr., *Corone*, pl. 284; 42 Edw. III, ibid., pl. 226 (also in 42 Edw. III, Lib. Ass., pl. 31).
[7] Sta. P.C. 15, cit. same cases. In a much later (unrelated) note below the case, Coke reports a rape case at Bedford assizes in Lent 1611.

was brought upon a bond for the delivery of certain quarters of wheat, and no place was expressed where [it should be delivered]. The defendant said that the plaintiff appointed him to deliver at such and such a place, and he tendered the wheat there, and the plaintiff refused [to accept it]. The plaintiff took issue upon the tender, and after their charge and their departure from the bar the plaintiff gave the jurors the said bond, which had not been shown to them before. Nevertheless, since the said bond had already been confessed by both parties, this was finable but did not avoid the verdict. And so it was ruled. But it would have been otherwise if he had given them any new material. {11 Hen. IV, fo. 17:[1] evidence given privately to the jurors out of court will avoid the verdict. 35 Hen. VI, tit. *Examination*, 17.[2]}

20. COPLESTON v. STOWELL[3]

King's Bench, 12 Nov. 1573.[4]

Crown.

Easter term 15 Eliz., between Copleston and Stowell. There was long-standing and inveterate malice [between the parties]; then Copleston met Stowell at Ludgate and said he wished to fight with him, which Stowell refused, whereupon Copleston gave chase, and Stowell fled to a wall and then slew him. Even though there was previous malice, this was only self-defence (*se defendendo*), for Stowell could not have done any more to evade him. And 'quisque ob tutelam [corporis sui fecerit, jure fecisse existimetur].'[5] {So it was resolved at Newgate, 3 Edw. III, *Corone*, 226.[6] According to Stanford, fo. 15, it does not matter who began it.[7]}

21. EARL OF RUTLAND'S CASE

Probably King's Bench, Mich. 1577.

Fines.

Note that it is provided by the statute of 4 Hen. VII, c. 24, [that a fine with proclamations should bind strangers to the fine, except married women, persons under 21 years of age, persons in prison or abroad, and insane persons, not being parties to the fine]. And note that it was adjudged in Michaelmas term 19 Eliz. that even though these words are general, and the exception extends only to such infants as are not parties to the fine, yet if an infant levies a fine he may reverse it during his infancy,

---

[1] YB Mich. 11 Hen. IV, fo. 17, pl. 41.
[2] YB Mich. 19 Hen. VI, fo. 35, pl. 76; Bro. Abr., *Examination*, pl. 17.
[3] KB 27/1245, m. 206: Jane, widow of Hugh Copleston gent. v. John Stawell *alias* Stowell of Cothelstone, Som., and Westminster, esq.; appeal of death, naming six other principals who did not appear, for killing the deceased with a sword in St Bride's parish, London, on 7 Feb. 1573; pleads Not Guilty; special verdict at the Guildhall, 12 Nov. 1573, before Catlyn C.J., Whiddon and Southcote JJ., that the deceased of his malice aforethought assaulted and made affray upon the appellee with a sword in the high street, and that the appellee fled as far as he could towards Ludgate, pursued by the deceased, but when the crowd became too dense for him to go any further he slew the deceased in self-defence; judgment for the appellee. Differently reported in Dyer's notebook, 110 Selden Soc. 267, pl. 362 (with the text of his

auxi adjudge in le case de countie de Rutlande que lou fine fuit levie et le dedimus potestatem port date devant le brefe de covenant et les proclamations fueront passes, et uncore le fine fuit revers per brefe de error per leire. Et issint nota in le case de Greene supra, il avoide le fine pur ceo que il fuit deins age, per brefe derror, et uncore les proclamations fueront faitz.

[22]

AA, fo. 75v (124v).

<Fines.>ˢ

Nota per Wray chief justice anno 18 Eliz. in banke le roy que lestatute parle de toutz fines levied des terres tailez etc. et ne dit toutz fines levies per tenant in taile, et pur ceo si tenant in taile graunt totum statum et puis levie fine est barre etc.

[23]

AA, fo. 76 (125).

<Fines.>ˢ

Nota per Manwood justice et nient denie in 17 Eliz. in un demurrer sur evidence in partitione facienda que si <ten>ᵈ un common <person>ⁱ fait <leas>ᵈ done in taile, le remainder al roigne, que fine levie per tiel tenant in tail liera son issue car le primer parols del statute de 32 H. 8 sont generall que fine levie per ascun tenant in taile ove proclamations serra barre al issue in taile, et la est un proviso et savant tielz tenantes in tailes que sont per les lettres patentz ou per acte de parliament, le revercion esteant al roy, ou autrement il nest deins le proviso et donques lissue serra lye per les general parolx del estatute. Mes il semble que si un subjecte fait <leas>ᵈ done in taile et suffer recovery, le remainder esteant al roy, cest deins lestatute de 34 H. 8 car la ceux parolx remainder ou revercion sont.

[24]

AA, fo. 79 (130).

<Counterplea de voucher.>ˢ

P. 17 Eliz. fuit demurre in judgment in Vernons case si tenant in un formedon vouche

---

[6] 34 & 35 Hen. VIII, c. 20.

[7] See below, p. 141, no. 258, and the note there. Coke's other notes of the case are dated 14 Eliz., but some of the parallel reports are from 1575.

by writ of error, for the general words are not intended of fines in which there is error, but only of lawful and perfect fines. For this reason it was also adjudged, in the earl of Rutland's case, that where a fine was levied, and the *dedimus potestatem* bore date before the writ of covenant and [before] the proclamations were passed, the fine was reversible by the heir, by writ of error. Likewise, note that in Greene's case, above,[1] he avoided the fine by writ of error because he was under age, even though the proclamations had been made.

22. ANON.

King's Bench, 1576.

Fines.

Note by WRAY C.J. in the year 18 Eliz. in the King's Bench, that the statute speaks of all fines levied of entailed lands,[2] and does not say 'all fines levied by tenant in tail', and therefore if tenant in tail grants his whole estate and then levies a fine, it is a bar.

23. JACKSON v. DARCY[3]

Common Pleas, 1575.

Note by MANWOOD J. and not denied, in 17 Eliz. in a demurrer to the evidence in *partitione facienda*, that if common person makes a gift in tail, the remainder to the queen, a fine levied by such tenant in tail will bind his issue; for the first words of the statute of 32 Hen. VIII[4] are general, that a fine levied by any tenant in tail with proclamations shall be a bar to the issue in tail. There is a proviso and saving for such tenants in tail who are by letters patent or by act of Parliament, the reversion being to the king; but otherwise he is not within the proviso and therefore the issue shall be bound by the general words of the statute.[5] But it seems that if a subject makes a gift in tail and suffers a recovery, the remainder being to the king, this is within the statute of 34 Hen. VIII,[6] for the words there are 'remainder or reversion'.

24. VERNON'S CASE[7]

Common Pleas, Pas. 1575.

Counterplea of voucher.

In Easter term 17 Eliz. it was demurred in judgment in Vernon's case whether or not,

---

[1] Perhaps 37 Edw. III, Lib. Ass., pl. 5 (before Greene C.J.).
[2] 32 Hen. VIII, c. 36 ('All and singular fines ... levied ... of any ... lands ... entailed to the person or persons so levying the said fine'). Cf. below, p. 161, no. 312.
[3] See below, p. 21, no. 37; and p. 61, no. 109, where the record is cited.
[4] 32 Hen. VIII, c. 36.
[5] Other reports make the point more clearly that the proviso referred only to reversions in the king and therefore did not extend to remainders.

si le demandant poet counterplede que le vouche navoit riens forsque jointment ove J. S. que est in vie ou nemi. Auxi le case la fuit que baron et fem fueront implede et le baron fist defaut apres defaut et le feme fuit resceive et vouche et le demandant counterplede pur ceo que le baron et fem fueront jointenantes. Et auxi pur auter parte il counterplede que le tenant ad alien cest parte per fine pendant le brefe issint que il ne poet voucher en part que il ne poet recover in value. <Adjudge nul counterplea.>ⁱ
<Vide Mich 13 et 14 Eliz. rott. mmlxxxv.>^a

[25]

AA, fo. 85v (136v).

<Ou home confessera et avoidera estoppell.>^s

Nota, il fuit tenus per le meliour opinion del justices de common banke in temps cesti roigne que si disseisor fait feffment in fe sur condition, et le feffee levie fine, et 5 ans passe, ore le disseisee est conclude. Mes si le disseisor entra pur le condition infreint, ore le conclusion est remove. Vies 16 E. 3, tit. Continual claime, 10, si home ad droit en action a tenementes et fine est levie de mesme les tenementes et il myst son clayme deins lan et puis lan passe et un auter ad un droit paramont que ne fist ascun clayme, et puis cesti que fyst clayme recovera, ore cesti que ad droit paramount ne sera barre car le fine est defete.

[26]

AA, fo. 87 (140).

<Baron et fem.>^s

H. 17 le roigne Eliz. cest case fuit move as justices del banke le roy. Lease fuit fait al baron et fem et diutius viventi, le remaindre a les executores ou assignes del survivour de eux, et puis le baron et fem assigne <ceo al un et p>^d le terme al un et puis <devie>^d le baron devie, et le fem ceo assigne al auter. Et semble al Wray, chief justice, et Southcot que le grant le baron fuit voide, car cest terme ne fuit interest in eux mes possibilitie dun interest, le quel possibilitie ilz ne puissont graunter ouster. Et pur ceo ilz resemble cel a cest case: si leas pur vie soit fait a J. S., le remainder a ses droit heires, J. N. le droit heire de J. S. ne poet ceo grant ouster car il nad forsque possibilitie dun estate et nul estate in fait.

when a tenant in formedon vouches, the demandant may counterplead that the vouchee had nothing except jointly with John Style, who is living. Furthermore, the case there was that a husband and wife were impleaded, the husband made default after default, and the wife was received and vouched; and the demandant counterpleaded because the husband and wife were joint tenants. Also, as to another part, he counterpleaded that the tenant had aliened that part by fine while the writ was pending, so that he could not vouch in a part which he could not recover in value. (It was adjudged no counterplea.) See Mich. 13 & 14 Eliz., roll 1085.[1]

25. ANON.[2]

Common Pleas, *c.* 1565.

Where a man may confess and avoid an estoppel.

Note that it was held by the better opinion of the justices of the Common Bench, in the time of the present queen, that if a disseisor makes a feoffment in fee upon condition, and the feoffee levies a fine, and five years pass, the disseisee is estopped (*conclude*). If, however, the disseisor enters for breach of the condition, the estoppel is removed. See 16 Edw. III, tit. *Continuall claime*, 10:[3] if someone has a right in action to tenements, and a fine is levied of the same tenements, and he puts in his claim within the year, and then the year passes and someone who has a paramount right makes no claim, and then the person who made the claim recovers, the person with right paramount shall not be barred, for the fine is defeated.

26. ANON.[4]

King's Bench, Hil. 1575.

Husband and wife.

In Hilary term 17 Eliz. this case was moved to the justices of the King's Bench. A lease was made to a husband and wife and the longest liver of them, the remainder to the executors or assigns of the survivor; the husband and wife assigned the term to someone; the husband died; and the wife then assigned it to someone else. And it seemed to WRAY C.J. and SOUTHCOTE that the husband's grant was void, for in them this term was not an interest, but only a possibility of an interest, which possibility they may not grant over. And they likened it to this case: if a lease for life is made to John Style, remainder to his right heirs, John Noke (the right heir of John Style) cannot grant it over, for he has only a possibility of an estate and no estate in fact.

---

[1] *Recte* 2085: below, p. 141, n. 1.
[2] This may derive from the dictum in *Stowell* v. *Lord Zouche* (*c.* 1565) Plowd. 353, at fo. 358, *per* Dyer C.J., where the case of 16 Edw. III is cited (but misprinted as '16 E. 2').
[3] Hil. 16 Edw. III, Fitz. Abr., *Continuall claime*, pl. 10.
[4] Cit. in *AD*, fo. 822 in magenta ink ('Vide 17 Eliz. mes notes demesne, fol. 87 in principio'); Co. Litt. 46b ('Hil. 17 El. in the Kings Bench').

[27]

AA, fo. 94v (147v).

<Riotz.>ˢ

Nota que fuit adjudge circa annum 18 Eliz. in banke le roy in un [*blank*] case que le lesse pur ans sauns cesti in le revercion ne poet mainteiner un enditement sur lestatut de 8 H. 6, car ceux parolx expulit et disseisivit sont auxibien in lenditement come in laction sur lestatut de 8 H. 6.

[28]

AA, fo. 98 (151).

<Corporations.>ˢ

Mich. 19 Eliz. fuit dit per Manwood in le comon banke que fuit adjudge que si un deane que ad custodie dun kye et les prebendaries dun auter, et le deane ale al universitie ou ailours et[1] committe le kye a un des ses amyes et luy commaunde a mitter le[2] <seale>ᵈ common seale a toutz tielz grantes a queux les greindre part des prebendaries assentera: et ceo tenus bone agrement, et les faitz enseale in tiel mannour bone et effectuell in ley.

[29]

AA, fo. 98 (151).

<Corporations.>ˢ <Pl. Com. 537.>ˢ

P. 20 Eliz. trove fuit per especial verdit in banke le roy in un ejectione firme que le corporation des Cookes in London fuit incorporate per E. 4 lan 22 de son raigne per cest nosme, magistri sive gubernatores et communitas misterii cocorum de London. Et ils trovont ouster que lou [*blank*] H. 8 le dit <master>ᵈ corporation del cookes bargaine et vende per fait certein terres a un Dormer in fe etc., et cest fuit per nosme de magister et custodes et communitas misterii cocorum de London, et puis Dormer levie un fine in fe. <18 H. 6, 12, 16. 11[3] H. 6, 32. 8 E. 3, 20, labbe de Fount St Evraud: nota. 3 H. 6,

---

[1] *Written twice.*
[2] les.
[3] *Written over* 10.

---

537 in *AB*, fo. 304v. In CUL MS. Dd.11.64, fo. 164v (1588), Coke cites the case from Plowd. The report here may have been written before the publication of the second part of Plowd. in June 1579.

[5] Robert Dormer, esquire.
[6] The deed of 30 Nov. 1529, set out verbatim in the record, was in English and said 'Master and Wardens of the Craft and Mystery'. The recital in the record translated this as 'Magister et Gardiani Misteriae'.
[7] *Case of the Dean and Canons of Windsor* (1440) YB Trin. 18 Hen. VI, fo. 16, pl. 4. The reference to fo. 12 may be to *Prior of Merton* v. *Mayor of New Windsor*, ibid., fo. 12, pl. 1, though that was not a case of corporate misnomer.
[8] *Case of the Prior of St John's* (1433) YB Pas. 11 Hen. VI, fo. 32, pl. 19.
[9] *Case of the Abbot of Fontevraud* (1334) YB Pas. 8 Edw. III, fo. 20, pl. 8.

27. ANON.

King's Bench, *c.* 1576.

Riots.

Note that it was adjudged around the year 18 Eliz., in a case in the King's Bench, that the lessee for years, without the reversioner,[1] may maintain an indictment upon the statute of 8 Hen. VI,[2] for the words 'expelled and disseised' (*expulit et disseisivit*) are used in indictments as well as in actions on the statute of 8 Hen. VI.

28. ANON.

Common Pleas, Mich. 1577.

Corporations.

In Michaelmas term 19 Eliz. it was said by MANWOOD in the Common Bench to have been adjudged that if a dean has custody of one key [to the common seal] and the prebendaries another, and the dean goes off to the university or elsewhere and commits the key to one of his friends, and tells him to put the common seal to all grants to which the greater part of the prebendaries should assent, this is a good agreement. And the deeds sealed in this way were good and effectual in law.[3]

29. CROFT v. HOWELL: THE COOKS' CASE[4]

King's Bench, Pas. 1578.

Corporations. {Plowd. Comm. 537.}

In Easter term 20 Eliz. it was found by special verdict in the King's Bench, in an *ejectione firmae*, that the corporation of the Cooks in London was incorporated by Edward IV in the twenty-second year of his reign by this name, 'Masters or Governors (*magistri sive gubernatores*) and Commonalty of the Mystery of the Cooks of London'. And they further found that whereas, in the time of Henry VIII, the said corporation of the Cooks by deed bargained and sold certain lands to one Dormer[5] in fee, this was by the name of the 'Master and Wardens (*custodes*[6]) and Commonalty of the Mystery of the Cooks of London'; and then Dormer levied a fine in fee. {18 Hen. VI, fos. 12, 16;[7] 11 Hen. VI, fo. 32;[8] 8 Edw. III, fo. 20,[9] the abbey of Font St Evraud (note); 3 Hen. VI,

---

[1] The expulsion of a lessee was a disseisin of the reversioner. The question continued to be controversial until 1623: 21 Jac. I, c. 15.

[2] Statute of Forcible Entry, 8 Hen. VI, c. 9.

[3] A partly illegible two-line addition at the end refers to a case concerning Totnes corporation 'in temps Eliz. quant Popham fuit attorney' (1581/92). This may be the case referred to in vol. iii, p. 556. Cf. also *AA*, fo. 97v (150v): 'In temps Eliz. Totnes fuit incorporate et subvert quia major pars inhabitantium contra.'

[4] KB 27/1260, m. 671d (two rolls; printed in Plowd. 530, where it is misdated Pas. 19 Eliz., omitting the roll number): Edmund Croft v. Henry Howell; ejectment for a messuage in Marsh, Bucks., on the demise of the Masters or Governors of the Mystery of Cooks of London; pleads Not Guilty; special verdict at Aylesbury assizes, Lent 1578; c.a.v. to Mich. 1579; judgment for the defendant. Abridged from Plowd.

28. Vide tit. Variance.>[i] Et trovont ouster que le conuse demurt in possession 5 ans sans claime fait per le dit corporation. Et si sur cest matter le corporation del Cookes serra barre ou nemi del droit del terre, ceo fuit le question. <11 H. 6, 51b, optime.>[i] Et in ceo fuit 4 matters move per le recorder de London. Le primer fuit si cest misnomer del corporation ferra lour vend voide. Et <quant>[1] il argue que le vende fuit voide. Et quant a ceo il dit que chescun corps que ad capacitie a prender aut est naturell corps aut artificiall corps, et chescun artificiall corps aut est create et incorporate per parliament ou per les lettres patentes le roy ou per prescription. Nostre artificiall corps icy fuit create per les lettres patentes le roy. Et il dit que fuit un maxime in nostre ley que un corporation ou artificiall corps ne poet prender ascun franktenement ou devester ascun franktenement sauns escript. Et auxi auter maxime que chescun corporation covient pursuer lour verie nosme de lour corporate capacitie in toutz grantes etc. 19 H. 6, 64, et 12 E. 4, 2, silz grant per lour singuler nosmes riens del lour interest que ilz ad in lour corporate capacite passera. Et il dit que surplusage ascun foitz in le nosme del corporation ne ferra le grant voide. Mes ceo est quant le surplusage ne alter ou confounde le sence del text. Come in 20 E. 4, 12, per Choke. Mes quant le surplusage alter ou confounde le sence, donques le surplusage ferra le grant voide. Et pur ceo vide le registre, fol. 178. Auxi il dit que sicome nul poet create corporation sinon le roy solement, nient plus poet ascun change un corporation sinon le roy solement. Et sur ceo il cite loppinion de Cavendishe in 49 Ass., p. 8. Et uncore il dit, si auncient corporation que fuit foundue devant temps de memorie per un certein nosme, et ilz temps dont etc. ont use a faire grantes per auter nosme variange de lour verie nosme de corporation, ceo est assetz bone, car consuetudo est altera lex. 2 R. 3, 7: maior et com[munitas] de Southampton fueront, et le maior sole avoit use temps dont a faire acquittances, et pur ceo pur le usage les justices teignont ceo bone. Et issint 9 E. 4, 19. Vide la, et nota le pleding. 8 Ass., p. 24. 20 H. 6, 27, et 21 H. 6, 4, in toutz real actions corporations serra nosme per lour verie nosme, mes autermens est <per>[d] in personall actions suffist per nosme conus. 22 E. 4, 34. 12 H. 7, 14. 14 H. 8, [blank], Heckers case. Vide 14 H. 7, 1, Mes il dit que de corporations foundus novelment et deins temps de memorie, silz sont misnosme in lour grauntes le grant est tout oustrement void. 21 E. 4, 55, 56. 15 E. 4, 1. 38 E. 3, 14 et 28. Vide les auters pointes. <Vide 7 H. 6, 13. 8 E. 4, 18b. 1º Mar. 98, supremum caput nest que addition.>[a]

---

[1] *Sic, but otiose.*

[12] YB Pas. 20 Hen. VI, fo. 27, pl. 17.
[13] *Abbot of Colchester's Case* (1442) YB Mich. 21 Hen. VI, fo. 4, pl. 8.
[14] *Master and Brethren of the Fraternity of the Nine Orders of Angels, Brentford* v. *Pokit* (1482) YB Mich. 22 Edw. IV, fo. 34, pl. 13.
[15] Presumably the *Case of Oxford Corporation* (1498) YB Hil. 13 Hen. VII, fo. 14, pl. 6.
[16] *King's College, Cambridge* v. *Hekker* (1522) YB Mich. 14 Hen. VIII, fo. 2, pl. 2; 119 Selden Soc. 98.
[17] YB Mich. 14 Hen. VII, fo. 1, pl. 2.
[18] *Case of Norwich Corporation* (1481) YB Mich. 21 Edw. IV, fo. 55, pl. 28.
[19] *Kedwelly's Case* (1475) YB Mich. 15 Edw. IV, fo. 1, pl. 2.
[20] R. v. *Provost of the House of C.* (1364) YB Trin. 38 Edw. III, fo. 14; *Case of the Prioress of Dorchester* (1364) YB Mich. 38 Edw. III, fo. 28.
[21] *Case of Pontefract College* (1428) YB Mich. 7 Hen. VI, fo. 13, pl. 18.
[22] *Chamberlain of London's Case* (1468) YB Mich. 8 Edw. IV, fo. 18, pl. 29.
[23] Pas. 1 Mar., Dyer 98, para. 50. Cf. Dalison's report, 124 Selden Soc. 62–63.
[24] I.e. Supreme Head of the Church, a title which Mary I eschewed.

fo. 28.[1] See tit. *Variance*.} They further found that the cognisee remained in possession for five years without a claim made by the said corporation. And the question was, whether upon this matter the corporation of the Cooks should be barred from the right to the land, or not. {11 Hen. VI, fo. 51v,[2] is the best.} Thereupon four matters were moved by the recorder of London.[3] The first was whether this misnomer of the corporation should make their sale void. And he argued that the sale was void. As to this, he said that every body which has a capacity to take [by grant] is either a natural body or an artificial body, and every artificial body is created and incorporated either by Parliament or by the king's letters patent, or by prescription. Our artificial body here was created by the king's letters patent. And he said it was a maxim in our law that a corporation or artificial body cannot take any freehold or devest any freehold without writing. There is also another maxim, that every corporation must pursue their true name of their corporate capacity in all grants. 19 Hen. VI, fo. 64,[4] and 12 Edw. IV, fo. 2:[5] if they grant by their individual names, none of their interest which they have in their corporate capacity will pass. But he said that sometimes surplusage in the name of the corporation will not make a grant void. That, however, is when the surplusage does not alter or confound the sense of the text: as in 20 Edw. IV, fo. 12,[6] by Choke. When the surplusage alters or confounds the sense, then the surplusage will make the grant void. For this see the Register, fo. 178. He also said that, just as no one other than the king may create a corporation, no more may any change be made in a corporation except by the king alone. Thereupon he cited the opinion of Cavendish in 49 Ass., pl. 8.[7] Nevertheless, he said, if there is an ancient corporation which was founded before time of memory by a certain name, and from time immemorial they have used to make grants by another name, varying from their true name of incorporation, this is good enough, for *consuetudo est altera lex*.[8] 2 Ric. III, fo. 7:[9] there was a mayor and commonalty of Southampton, but the mayor alone had used from time immemorial to make acquittances, and therefore on account of the usage the justices held it good. Likewise, 9 Edw. IV, fo. 19.[10] See there, and note the pleading. 8 Ass., pl. 24;[11] 20 Hen. VI, fo. 27;[12] and 21 Hen. VI, fo. 4:[13] in all real actions corporations must be named by their true name, but it is otherwise in personal actions, where it is sufficient to use a known name. 22 Edw. IV, fo. 34;[14] 12 Hen. VII, fo. 14;[15] 14 Hen. VIII, [*blank*], Hekker's case.[16] See 14 Hen. VII, fo. 1.[17] But he said that if corporations newly founded within time of memory are misnamed in their [grants], the grant is utterly void. 21 Edw. IV, fos. 55, 56;[18] 15 Edw. IV, fo. 1;[19] 38 Edw. III, fos. 14 and 28.[20] See the other points. {See 7 Hen. VI, fo. 13;[21] 8 Edw. IV, fo. 18v.[22] 1 Mar. 98:[23] *supremum caput*[24] is only an addition.}

[1] YB Hil. 3 Hen. VI, fo. 28, pl. 10.
[2] *Case of the Prior of St John's* (1433) YB Trin. 11 Hen. VI, fo. 51, pl. 13.
[3] William Fleetwood of the Middle Temple, who held the office from 1571 until 1591; Coke succeeded him in 1592.
[4] *Rector of Edington's Case* (1441) YB Pas. 19 Hen. VI, fo. 62, pl. 1, at fo. 64, *per* Markham serjeant.
[5] 12 is clearly so written, but the intended reference is probably *Kedwelly's Case* (1475) YB Mich. 15 Edw. IV, fos. 1–2, pl. 2; n. 19, opposite.   [6] YB Mich. 20 Edw. IV, fo. 12, pl. 15.
[7] *Case of the Guild of the White-Tawyers* (1375) 49 Edw. III, Lib. Ass., pl. 8, *per* Cavendish C.J.
[8] Cf. below, p. 32, n. 69.
[9] *Case of Southampton Corporation* (1484) YB Mich. 2 Ric. III, fo. 7, pl. 13.
[10] *Master of Burton Lazars* v. *Prior of Sempringham* (1469) YB Trin. 19 Edw. IV, fo. 11, pl. 19.
[11] *Abbot of St Mary's, York* v. *Abbot of Selby* (1334) 8 Edw. III, Lib. Ass., pl. 24.

[30]

AA, fo. 108r-v (160r-v).

<Eschape.>[s] <Tr. 16 Eliz. rott. Dccc43. Mcccxliij rott. Vide 3 Eliz. 137. Vide 12[1] Eliz. Dier. 296. Vide 17 Eliz. 112 Periam.>[a]

17 Eliz. cest case fuit argue in le common banke. Un Maunsuer port bill de det vers garden del Flete, et le case fuit que le dit Mansuer port brefe de det envers un Dracot et ad judgment vers luy, et puis il ad capias ad satisfaciendum, et le viconte port eins son corps in le common banke et fuit commise al Fleet in execution, et per le plea le garden il appiert que mesme le jour que il fuit commise al Flete pur le det que il owe al Mansuer, a mesme le jour il fuit commise al Flete pur le det le roigne <per les barons del eschequer>[i] issint que il fuit in execution pur ambideux les sommes. <29 E. 3, 13b.>[i] Et puis le garden pleade que in anno 15 le roigne que ore est, 15 die Februarii, que est toutz foitz hors del terme, les barons del eschequer commande al gardein del Fleet que le dit Dracot alera per baston in Darbyshire et la a colliger et levie son dett que fuit due al roigne, per force de quel commaundement il licence le prisoner daler in D. ove baston, et puis il revient, le quel est mesme le evasion et eschape. Et sur cest matter le pleintife demurre. Et la fuit adjudge et agre per toutz les justices del common banke que ceo fuit un eschape et que le pleintife recovera. Et ils agre que al common ley le partie navoit nul remedie al common ley forsque action sur le case. <Plattes case, 36. 7 H. 6, 5b. 14 E. 4, 3.>[i] Et donques vient lestatut de W. 2, cap. 11, de servientibus, balivis etc., et ceo dona brefe de det envers baliffes etc. Et la per le voy il fuit agre que bill de det gist si[2] gardein soit un officer del court, contrarie al livre in 42 Ass., p. 11. Et ilz cite 7 H. 6, 5,[3] et Platz case, 4 E. 6, in Pl. Com., que billes de det fuit port un autiel case. Et puis pur ceo que les gardeins suffer lour prisoners per baille ou mainprise et ascun foitz sauns baile ou mainprise ove baston noctes et joures issint que les parties fueront longement delayes de lour droit, il fuit enacte 1° R. 2, cap. 12, que null gardein suffera ascun prisoner daler hors per baille per mainprise ne per baston sauns gre fait as parties sil ne soit par brefe ou auter maundement le roy, sur pein de forfeiter lour office etc. <Vide 7 H. 6, 5, accord. 8 Eliz., Dier 249. 24 H. 8.>[a]

---

[1] *Altered from* 17.
[2] *Followed by an unclear word which has been deleted.*
[3] *Altered from* 47.

[5] *Nevile* v. *De la Pole* (1355) YB Hil. 29 Edw. III, fo. 13.
[6] *Plat* v. *Sheriffs of London* (1550) Plowd. 35.
[7] YB Mich. 7 Hen. VI, fo. 5, pl. 9.
[8] YB Pas. 14 Edw. IV, fo. 3, pl. 1.
[9] 42 Edw. III, Lib. Ass., pl. 11. Cf. JRL MS., *per* Mounson J.: 'Et il dit que le livre in 42 Ass. ne fuit cy graunde authoritie mes il dit que il fuit misreporte …'.
[10] YB Mich. 7 Hen. VI, fo. 5, pl. 9.
[11] *Plat* v. *Sheriffs of London* (1550) Plowd. 35.
[12] YB Mich. 7 Hen. VI, fo. 5, pl. 9.
[13] *Worlay* v. *Harrison* (1566) Dyer 249, identifiable as *Wyrley* v. *Harryson*, i.e. *R.* v. *Sheriffs of London*, ex parte *Harryson*, CP 40/1243, m. 109 (*habeas corpus*).
[14] This refers to the Star Ch. decree of 1532, cited in Dyer 249, that prisoners in execution should be kept in strict custody.

30. MANSER v. ANNESLEY[1]

Common Pleas, 1575.

Escape. Trin. 16 Eliz., roll 1343. See 3 Eliz., fo. 137.[2] See 12 Eliz., Dyer, fo. 296;[3] 17 Eliz., Peryam, fo. 112.[4]

In 17 Eliz. this case was argued in the Common Bench. One Manser brought a bill of debt against the warden of the Fleet, and the case was that the said Manser had brought a writ of debt against one Dracot, and had judgment against him, and then he had a *capias ad satisfaciendum*, and the sheriff brought in his body into the Common Bench and he was committed to the Fleet in execution. By the warden's plea it appeared that, on the same day that he was committed to the Fleet for the debt which he owed Manser, he was that same day committed to the Fleet for the queen's debt by the barons of the Exchequer, so that he was in execution for both the sums. (29 Edw. III, fo. 13v.[5]) Then the warden pleaded that in the fifteenth year of the present queen, on 15 February (which is always outside term), the barons of the Exchequer commanded the warden of the Fleet that the said Dracot should go by baston into Derbyshire, and there collect and levy his debt which was owed to the queen, by force of which command he licensed the prisoner to go into Derbyshire with a tipstaff (*baston*), and then he returned, which is the same evasion and escape. Upon this matter the plaintiff demurred. And it was there adjudged and agreed by all the justices of the Common Bench that this was an escape, and that the plaintiff should recover. They agreed that at common law the party had no remedy other than an action on the case. {Plat's case, fo. 36;[6] 7 Hen. VI, fo. 5v;[7] 14 Edw. IV, fo. 3.[8]} Then came the statute of Westminster II, c. 11, *De servientibus, ballivis etc.*, and that gave a writ of debt against bailiffs and the like. And there, by the way, it was agreed that a bill of debt lies, if the warden is an officer of the court, contrary to the book in 42 Ass., pl. 11.[9] And they cited 7 Hen. VI, fo. 5,[10] and Plat's case, 4 Edw. VI, in Plowd. Comm.,[11] where a bill of debt was brought in such a case. Then, because wardens suffered their prisoners to go by night and day by bail or mainprise, and sometimes without bail or mainprise but with a tipstaff, so that parties were long delayed of their right, it was enacted in 1 Ric. II, c. 12, that no warden should suffer any prisoner to go out by bail, mainprise or baston without the agreement of the parties, unless it be by writ or other command from the king, upon pain of forfeiting their office. {See 7 Hen. VI, fo. 5,[12] accord. 8 Eliz., Dyer 249.[13] 24 Hen. VIII.[14] See the statute of 7 Hen. IV, c. 4.} And the justices in this case agreed that since the judgment was that the

---

[1] CP 40/1323, m. 1343 (printed in Benl. 238; summarised in 110 Selden Soc. 351): William Manser of Kirby Lonsdale, Westmd, gent. v. Brian Annesley esq., warden of the Fleet; bill of privilege; demurrer to the plea in bar; judgment for the plaintiff. Also noted below, p. 25, no. 49; cit. in Coke's Dyer (Holkham 8014), fo. 296v ('Vide 17 Eliz. in mes notes tit. Eschape. Tr. 16 Eliz. rott. 1343'); ibid., fo. 297 ('Vide in mes reportes tit. Eschape, 108, adjudge'). Differently reported in JRL MS. Fr. 118, fo. 26; Benl. 238; Dyer's notebook, 110 Selden Soc. 349 (and the MS. reports cited there); BL MS. Harg. 373, fos. 157v–163v; MS. Lansd. 1057, fos. 231v–237v. The judgment was affirmed on a writ of error in Trin. 1576: KB 27/1256, m. 437 (four rolls). See also Baker, *Magna Carta*, pp. 179–181.

[2] *Lord Dacres* v. *Lassells* (1561) Dyer 197.

[3] *Pledall* v. *Annesley* (1570) Dyer 296.

[4] This refers to Dyer's unpublished report of the case, from fo. 112 of the transcript in secretary-hand which Coke acquired; printed in 110 Selden Soc. 349–351. For the association with Peryam see above, p. lxxxii.

<Vide lestatut de 7 H. 4, cap. 4.>[a] Et la les justices agre que entant que le judgment fuit que le defendant alera al Fleet et ibidem moraturus quousque satisfecerit le partie, si le gardein suffer luy daler hors del Fleet per baston ou autermont, et coment que il ne soit in auter countie carie,[1] donques il ne demurre ibidem quousque. Et Manwood dit, et issint tout agre, que il covient remainer in salvo et arcta custodia. Et le Segnior Dier dit que les parolz del estatut de W. 2, cap. 11, sont et liberentur proxime gaole domini regis etc. et carceri manucipentur in ferris et sub bona custodia. Et il dit que carceri manucipentur est taunt adire come destre captive subjecte et [...][2] a le prison. Mes il dit que per cest estatut chescun gaoler poet mitter lour prisoner in fetters et irons, mes il dit que le gaoler poet licence les prisoners daler in le garden et la de ambuler pur lour recreation issint que il soit toutz foitz deins les walles del prison. <Mes vide Plates case 37b, les vicontes de Londres suffrent un daler ove baston deins le citie, ceo nest eschape pur ceo que ilz ont use de faire issint, et lour usages sont confirme per parliament.>[a] [fo. 108v] Et la fuit agre per eux toutz que lexecution le partie ne serra suspend tanque le roy soit satisfie, et que le barons del eschequer ne poient discharge le prisoner hors de execution quant al partie, mes quant al roy ilz poient sedente curia in temps de le terme et nemi hors del terme. <Vide 3 Eliz. 197.>[i] Et la le Segnior Dier dit que mesmes les justices queux donont judgment in le cause poient mitter pur le prisoner a vener al barre a eux etc. mes auters justices dun auter court ne poient. Et le Segnior Dier cite un president in temps le Roigne Marie que, ou home fuit in execution in le Fleete, lattorney le roye demanda de toutz les justices si ilz poient per brefe le roy amitter luy alarge daler a Berwicke pur le savegarde del roialme, et eux toutz responde que ilz ne poient sinon que le partie voille a ceo agreer. Et Mounson construe ceux parolx 'per brefe ou auter maundement le roy' in tiel forme, scilicet per brefe, come per habeas corpus ou supersedeas et similia, et maundement le roy il dit fuit per son privie seale solonque loppinion de Prisot, 30 H. 6, 6b. Et Manwood dit que maundement le roy fuit le commandement des justices de mesme le court in que le cause depend, et donques les justices seant poient maunder pur le prisoner et ceo est nul eschape. <Dyer, 5 Mar. 165.>[i] Mes si justices hors del terme voille maunder pur luy autermont est. Et le Segnior Dier construe maundement le roy destre un especial comaundement fait per le roy mesme, ou per son bouche demesne a son serjant darmes etc. ou per son privie seale. Et luy semble que les justices de mesme le court in que le cause fuit adjudge poient mitter pur le prisoner coment que lestatut parle per maundement le roy. Et la Justice Mounson cite un president in 10 H. 4, [blank], que in bill de dett vers gailour il dit que <et>[d] Sir William Gascoine, chief justice in banke le roy, maunde pur luy, seant le court, que il commaunde que le

---

[1] *Unclear.*   [2] *Unclear word; resembles* amortise.

[4] YB Trin. 30 Hen. VI, fo. 6, pl. 5, *per* Prisot C.J. This is not in Mounson J.'s argument in JRL MS.

[5] *R. v. Foxe* (1558) Dyer 164v. This is dated Mich. 5 & 6 Ph. & Mar. in the old editions, but Trin. 4 & 5 Ph. & Mar. in the 1794 edition. It is not exactly in point.

[6] Perhaps the undated case cited in Dyer 275, pl. 47. Cf. YB Mich. 7 Hen. IV, fo. 4, pl. 26, cited by Mounson J. in the JRL MS.

defendant should go to the Fleet, 'there to remain until he should satisfy the party', if the warden then allows him to go out, whether by baston or otherwise, even if it is not into another county, he does not 'remain there until …'.

MANWOOD said, and all agreed, that he must remain in safe and strict custody (*in salvo et arcta custodia*).

And the lord DYER said that the words of the statute of Westminster II, c. 11, are 'and let them be delivered to the next gaol of the lord king … and kept in prison in irons and in good custody' ('et liberentur proximae gaolae domini regis … et carceri manucipientur in ferris et sub bona custodia'). And he said that *carceri manucipientur* ('kept in prison') is as much as to say, kept as a captive subject and confined to the prison. And he said that by this statute every gaoler may put their prisoners in fetters and irons;[1] but he said that a gaoler may license the prisoners to go into the garden and walk there for their recreation, so long as they are at all times within the walls of the prison. {But see Plat's case, fo. 37v,[2] where the sheriffs of London allowed someone to go with a tipstaff within the city, and this was not an escape because they were accustomed to do it, and their usages are confirmed by Parliament.} And it was there agreed by them all that the party's execution should not be suspended until the king is satisfied, and that the barons of the Exchequer may not discharge the prisoner out of execution with respect to the party, though with respect to the king they may do so while the court is sitting (*sedente curia*) in term-time, but not out of term. {See 3 Eliz., fo. 137.[3]} The lord DYER said that the same justices who give judgment in the cause may send for the prisoner to come before them at the bar, but other justices from another court may not. And the lord DYER cited a precedent in the time of Queen Mary, where a man was in execution in the Fleet, and the king's attorney asked all the justices whether they could by the king's writ release him at large to go to Berwick for the defence of the realm; and they all answered that they could not, unless the other party would agree to it.

MOUNSON construed the words 'by writ or other command from the king' in this manner: 'by writ' means by *habeas corpus* or *supersedeas*, or such like, and 'command from the king' means by his privy seal. This is according to the opinion of Prisot, 30 Hen. VI, fo. 6v.[4]

MANWOOD said that 'command from the king' means a command from the justices of the same court in which the cause depends; and then the justices sitting in court may send for the prisoner, and that is not an escape. {Dyer, 5 Mar., fo. 165.[5]} But if justices send for him out of term, it is otherwise.

The lord DYER construed 'command from the king' to be a special command made by the king himself, either by his own mouth to his serjeant at arms, or such like, or by his privy seal. But it seemed to him that the justices of the same court in which the cause was adjudged may send for the prisoner, even though the statute speaks only of a command from the king.

MOUNSON J. cited a precedent in 10 Hen. IV,[6] where (as he said) in a bill of debt against a gaoler, Sir William Gascoigne, chief justice in the King's Bench, sent for

---

[1] Cf. 3 Co. Rep. 44.
[2] *Plat v. Sheriffs of London* (1550) Plowd. 35, at fo. 37v.
[3] *Lord Dacres v. Lassells* (1561) Dyer 197.

prisoner alera per baston, per force de quel il ala, a que le pleintife soy agrea, sur quel agrement issue fuit prise: issint la les justices teigne que le commaundement les justices seant en court sauns lagrement le partie ne poet <discharge>ᵈ licence luy daler per baston. <Nota bene cest lettre '[brefe] le roy ou auter maundement le roy' doit estre construe a un court, ou devant un judge etc.>¹ <Vide 29 E. 3, 13, tit. Audita querela, pl. 13. 29 E. 3, 13b, accordant. 13 Eliz. Dier 296, execution del partie est suspend.>ˢ ²

[31]

AA, fo. 109 (161).

<Eschape.>³

17 Eliz. per Wray, chief justice, si home soit en execution et puis il luy mesme eschape, et puis le gaoler reprise luy, il navera audita querela. Et ceo prove le livre in 14 H. 7, que in tiel case le gailor poet deteiner luy. Mes sil eschape per le sufferauns del gailour donques audita querela gist.

[32]

AA, fo. 112 (164).

<Faux imprisonment.>ᵃ

T. 18 Eliz. cest diversitie fuit agre in le common banke, que common fame et voice ut supra est bone justification in faux imprisonment. Mes autrement est in action sur le case pur appelle un thiefe ou traitour: quod nota diversitatem.

[33]

AA, fo. 116 (181).

<Chemyn.>ᵃ

Nota que fuit agre in banco regis M. 22 et 23 Eliz. que le meliour [con]usaunce⁴ a scaver a que le franktenement est est a intelliger que avoit prise les arbres ou les profitz in le haut chemyn. Mes <semble>ᵈ si nul avoit prise les profitz, donques semble <a eux>ⁱ que serra cesti que ad le terre adjoinaunt.

---

¹ *Written sideways in the outer margin.*
² *At the top of fo. 108v.*
³ *Title on fo. 108.*
⁴ *Conjectural; beginning of word obscured by blot.*

the gaoler while the court was sitting and commanded that the prisoner should go by baston, by virtue whereof he went, and the plaintiff agreed to this, and issue was taken upon the agreement: so the justices there held that a command from the justices sitting in court cannot permit the party to go by baston without the other party's agreement. {Note well that the words 'king's writ or other command from the king' ought to be construed as meaning in a court, or before a judge.} {See 29 Edw. III, tit. *Audita querela*, 13; 29 Edw. III, fo. 13v,[1] accord. 13 Eliz., Dyer 296:[2] the party's execution is suspended.}

31. ANON.

King's Bench, 1575.

Escape.

17 Eliz., *per* WRAY C.J.: if someone is in execution, and then escapes, and then the gaoler retakes him, he shall not have *audita querela*. This is proved by the book in 14 Hen. VII,[3] which says that in such a case the gaoler may detain him. If, however, he escapes through the sufferance of the gaoler, an *audita querela* lies.[4]

32. ANON.[5]

Common Pleas, Trin. 1576.

False imprisonment.

In Trinity term 18 Eliz. this distinction was agreed in the Common Bench: 'common reputation and talk (*fame et voice*)' is a good justification in false imprisonment,[6] but it is otherwise in an action on the case for calling someone a thief or traitor. Note the difference.

33. ANON.

King's Bench, Mich. 1580.

Highway.

Note that it was agreed in the King's Bench, in Michaelmas term 22 & 23 Eliz., that the best way to know to whom the freehold [in a highway] belongs is to find out who has taken the trees or the profits in the highway. If no one has taken the profits, however, then it seemed to them it should be the person who has the adjoining land.

---

[1] *Nevile* v. *De la Pole* (1355) YB Hil. 29 Edw. III, fo. 13; Fitz. Abr., *Audita querela*, pl. 37 (not 13).
[2] *Pledall* v. *Annesley* (1570) Dyer 296.   [3] YB Mich. 14 Hen. VII, fo. 1, pl. 1.
[4] Cf. JRL MS. Fr. 118, fo. 47 (Common Pleas, Pas. 18 Eliz.): '… Et nota que la fuit dit, si home soit in execution et puis ala alarge, soit ceo per assent del partie ou per le negligens del gailour ou auterment, il poet aver audita querela et estre relesse hors del prison: quod nota.'
[5] Cf. 1 Rolle Abr. 392, lines 13–15 ('Generallment le owner del soile d'ambideux sides le chimin avera les arbres crescent sur le chimin. 18 El. B.R. per curiam cite, P. 11 Jac. B.').
[6] I.e. where an arrest is made on suspicion arising from the *communis vox et fama*.

[34]

AA, fo. 117 (182).

<Contracts.>[a]

Nota bene que semble que un consideration passe, si le consideration continue, est bone consideration en un contracte. Mes si le consideration soit determine, donques assumpsit fait apres ne liera. Nota le erle de Kentz case T. 19 Eliz. La le countes de Kent dum sola fuit require Edward Onley esquier a travailer circa negotia, sectas et querelas sua dependentia etc. et puis el assume a paier tout ceo que il avoit expend: et bone, car le consideration continue. Issint est 4 E. 3, [*blank*], done in frankmariage apres espousels, car le mariage continue. Mes si jeo die, in consideration que vous <fait>[d] fesoitz a moy un leas pur ans al feast de Saint Michael darren passe, finete et compleate, jeo promise a vous xx li. ceo semble destre nul consideration. Vide devant 67a. Vide 21 E. 4, 53.

[35]

AA, fo. 117 (182).

<Contracts.>[s]

M. 20 Eliz. 2 homes sagitta al prickes et 2 auters que fueront bye bettours layd x li. of the matche et puis cesti que pard port action sur le case. Et le consideration fuit in consideration que le pleintife promisa al defendant x li. si J. S. vincera, le defendant promise a luy x li. si J. S. perdra.

Et Baber, novel serjaunt, mova que ceo ne fuit bon consideration, car le consideration est que le pleintife promisa le defendant et la est nul consideration de ceo et donques nudum pactum, et per consequens nul consideration.

Et Mounson semble que lour reciprocall adventure fuit bone consideration, car le consideration del promise del un fuit le promise del auter, et econtra.

Mes Manwood doubt de ceo, car il dit que tielz mattches reste principalment sur le foy des parties que suretie del ley. Et il dit que ilz del banke le roy ne voillont doner judgment sur tielz considerations.

Et Mounson dit, si un winne mes deniers ou chattellz al dise, cest bon et chaungera le propertie. Et Manwood dit que le reason de ceo fuit pur ceo que fuit un done in ley. Pacta conventa que contra [leges] non insunt non formant actionem.

---

of Effingham; count and imparlance only. Differently reported in 2 Leon. 154; CUL MS. Ll.3.14, fo. 249v; Exeter College, Oxford, MS. 119, fo. 66v; B. & M. 529.

[6] I.e. not betting on their own performance.

[7] Coke wrote 'perd' (lost), but this must be the meaning.

[8] Created on 19 Nov. 1577.

[9] Cf. Leon. (tr.): 'Manwood. At dice the parties set down their moneys and speak words which amount to a conditional gift ....'

[10] Adapted from the maxim in the Code, that agreements which are not against the law ought to be observed. The double negative here upsets the grammar, but the meaning is presumably something like: 'Agreements which are against the law do not give rise to an action.'

34. ONLEY v. EARL OF KENT[1]

Trin. 1577.

Contracts.

Note this well: it seems that a past consideration in a contract is a good consideration so long as the consideration continues; but, once the consideration is ended, an *assumpsit* made afterwards will not bind. Note the earl of Kent's case, Trinity term 19 Eliz., where the countess of Kent while she was single requested Edward Onley, esquire, to travel about her pending business, suits and complaints ('circa negotia, sectas et querelas sua dependentia'), and later she undertook to pay back all that which he had spent: and it was good, for the consideration continued. So is 4 Edw. III:[2] a gift in frankmarriage made after espousals [is good], for the marriage continues. But if I say, 'in consideration that you made me a lease for years at the feast of Michaelmas last past, finished and completed, I promise you £20', this seems to be no consideration. (See above, fo. 67.[3] See 21 Edw. IV, fo. 53.[4])

35. WEST v. STOWELL[5]

Common Pleas, Mich. 1577.

Contracts.

Michaelmas term 20 Eliz. Two men were shooting arrows at the pricks; two others, who were bye-betters,[6] laid £10 on the match, and afterwards the one who [won the bet][7] brought an action on the case. The consideration was, 'in consideration that the plaintiff promised the defendant £19 if John Style won, the defendant promised him £10 if John Style lost'.

Baber, one of the new serjeants,[8] moved that this was not a good consideration, for the consideration is that the plaintiff promised the defendant, and there is no consideration for [the plaintiff's promise]; therefore it is *nudum pactum*, and in consequence no consideration.

MOUNSON thought that their reciprocal hazard (*adventure*) was a good consideration, inasmuch as the consideration for the promise of the one was the promise of the other, and vice versa.

But MANWOOD doubted that, for he said that such matches rest principally on the good faith of the parties rather than the protection (*suretie*) of the law. And he said that in the King's Bench they would not give judgment upon such considerations.

MOUNSON said that if someone wins my money or chattels at dice, that is good and will change the property. But MANWOOD said the reason for that was because it was a gift in law.[9] *Pacta conventa quae contra [leges] non insunt non formant actionem.*[10]

---

[1] See below, p. 124, no. 218, and the note there.
[2] YB Hil. 4 Edw. III, fo. 8, pl. 14.
[3] *AA*, fo. 67 (106), under the heading 'Contracte'.
[4] YB Mich. 21 Edw. IV, fo. 53, pl. 20.
[5] CP 40/1346, m. 719: Thomas West esq. v. Sir John Stowell; trespass on the case upon mutual promises, setting out a wager on an archery contest at Salisbury, Wilts., between the defendant and Lord Howard

[36]

AA, fo. 1v[1] (189v).

<Estates.>[s]

Nota le case de Cranmer anno 14 Eliz. que fuit que Cranmer larchevesque fist feffment in fe al use de luy mesme pur terme de son vie sauns impechement de wast, et puis al use de ces executores pur xxj ans et apres les xxj ans ended al use de son fitz in taile et puis al use de luy et ses droit heires, et puis Cranmer fuit attaint de heresie et treason et combust, et le doubt fuit si cest terme fuit in Cranmer ou nemi issint que il puit ceo forfeit al roy. Et fuit adjudge que il ne fuit in Cranmer mes que les executors prendra ceo come purchasors. Et le prinicpall reason fuit pur ceo que cest limitation fuit a les executores in use et lestatut <limitt>[d] execute le possession in mesme le plite, qualite, condition et degre etc. Car Manwood tient fortement que in les cases supra al common ley devant lestatute de uses le terme fuit in le tenant pur vie pur doner ou forfeiter. Mes pur ceo que le principal case fuit in use, ceo fesoit le diversitie.

[37]

AA, fo. 2 (190).

<Estates.>[s]

18 Eliz. fuit dit si tenant in taile, le revercion al roy, fait feffment in fe, le done ad fe simple determinable sur le vie le tenant in taile per operation del ley.

[38]

AA, fo. 2v (190v).

<Estates.>[s]

Nota fuit dit per Wray, chief justice, pur clere ley in Sir Richard Haddons case, 18 Eliz., que si home devise terres a un et a son heire in le singuler nomber il nad que estate pur terme de vie. Issint il dit si un remainder soit limitte al doit heire J. S., il nad que estate pur vie. Mes si le droit heire averoit fe simple il doit aver heires in le plurall nomber. Et il cite le livre in 4 H. 5 que terres fueront dones a un home et a son heire (in le singuler nomber) del corps sa fem, et tenus come il dit que il fuit forsque estate pur terme de vie. Et la le principal case fuit que Sir Richard Haddon fist feffment al use de Katherin sa fem pur sa vie, et puis al use William son fitz pur son vie, et puis le <mort>[i] de luy et Jone sa fem al use de son

---

[1] *Coke's numbering begins again on the preceding folio.*

[4] See below, p. 118, no. 212, and the note there.
[5] *Sic*, but this year is not in print. Cf. 39 Edw. III, Lib. Ass., pl. 20; Co. Litt. 8b.

36. CRANMER'S CASE[1]

Common Pleas, 1572.

Estates.

Note the case of Cranmer in the year 14 Eliz., which was that Archbishop Cranmer made a feoffment in fee to the use of himself for term of his life without impeachment of waste, and then to the use of his executors for twenty-one years, and after the twenty-one years ended to the use of his son in tail, and then to the use of himself and his right heirs; then Cranmer was attainted of heresy and treason, and burned. The doubt was whether this term was in Cranmer, so that it could be forfeited to the king, or not. And it was adjudged that it was not in Cranmer, but that the executors should take it as purchasers. The principal reason was that this limitation was to the executors in use, and the statute[2] executed the possession 'in the same plight, quality, condition and degree …'. For MANWOOD held strongly that, in the cases above, at common law before the Statute of Uses the term was in the tenant for life to give away or forfeit; but because the principal case was in use, that made the difference.

37. JACKSON v. DARCY[3]

Common Pleas, 1576.

Estates.

In 18 Eliz. it was said that if tenant in tail, the reversion to the king, makes a feoffment in fee, the donee has a fee simple determinable upon the life of the tenant in tail, by operation of the law.

38. HADDON'S CASE[4]

King's Bench, 1576.

Estates.

Note that it was stated as clear law by WRAY C.J. in Sir Richard Haddon's case, 18 Eliz., that if a man devises lands to someone and his 'heir', in the singular number, the devisee has only an estate for term of life. Likewise (he said), if a remainder is limited to the right heir of John Style, he has but an estate for life. But if the right heir is to have fee simple there must be 'heirs' in the plural number. And he cited the book in 4 Hen. V,[5] where lands were given to a man and his 'heir' (in the singular number) begotten on the body of his wife, and it was held (as he said) that it was only an estate for term of life. The principal case here was that Sir Richard Haddon made a feoffment to the use of Katherine his wife for her life, and then to the use of William his son for his life, and after the deaths of him and his wife Joan to the use

---

[1] See below, p. 58, no. 106, and the note there.
[2] Statute of Uses, 27 Hen. VIII, c. 10.
[3] Conjectural identification: cf. above, p. 13, no. 23; below, p. 61, no. 109.

droit heire pur son vie, et puis al use del droit heire de cel droit heire. Et adjudge que toutz ceux navoient que estate pur terme de lour vies pur ceo que fueront in le singuler nomber.

[39]

AA, fo. 2v (190v).

\<Estates.\>ˢ

Nota per Manwood in Nichols case, si terres sont dones a J. S. per parliament le franktenement est in luy maintenant. Semble autrement des lettres patentz le roy.

[40]

AA, fo. 7 (203).

\<Taile. Queux parolles ferront un estate taile.\>ˢ

… Et Segnior Dier anno 16 le roigne in Claches case de devise dit que le case esteant que Clatch devise terres a sa file et a ses heires, et sil morust sans child que donques il remainera etc.: et luy semble que el ad estate in fe conditionel et nul estate taile, mes les auters trois justices fueront encounter luy …

Nota que Justice Manwood dit clerement in Claches case que si home done terres a un et semine suo, ou exitibus, ou prolibus, ou liberis ou filiis, in grantes il nest que estate pur vie, autrement in voluntes, car ceux parols heires fault.

[41]

AA, fo. 7v (203v).

\<Tenant per le curtesie.\>ˢ

Nota que le Segnior Dier dit arguendo in le case de Clache anno 16 le roigne que ore est que il fuit tenus in le chauncerie quant il fuit sergeaunt et accounsell ove le case et fuit tiel. Un Reps de Norff. prist fem seisie de certein terres, sa fem fuit grossment enseint per luy, et in sa travaile le fem morust, et lissue fuit rippe[1] hors de sa venter en vie, et pur ceo que le mere fuit mort devant le nester del issue ideo fuit tenus que le baron ne serra tenant per le curtesie.

---

[1] *Reads so in 8 Co. Rep. 35. In MS. resembles* crippe.

of his right 'heir' for his life, and then to the use of the right heir of that right heir. And it was adjudged that all of them had but an estate for term of life, inasmuch as they were in the singular number.

39. NICHOLS v. NICHOLS[1]

Common Pleas, 1574.

Estates.

Note by MANWOOD in Nichols's case that if lands are given to John Style by Parliament, the freehold is in him at once. It seems to be otherwise in the case of the king's letters patent.

40. GLOVER v. BERYE[2]

Common Pleas, 1574.

Tail. What words will make an estate tail.

… And the lord DYER, in the sixteenth year of the queen, in Clache's case concerning a devise, said the case was that Clache devised lands to his daughter and her heirs, and should she die without a child then it should remain over: and it seemed to him that she had an estate in fee conditional and not an estate tail, but the other three justices were against him …

Note that MANWOOD J. said clearly in Clache's case that if a man gives land to someone 'and his seed' (*semine suo*), 'issue' (*exitibus*), 'offspring' (*prolibus*), 'children' (*liberis*) or 'sons' (*filiis*), this is only an estate for life in the case of a grant – though it is otherwise in a will – for want of the word 'heirs'.

41. GLOVER v. BERYE, continued[3]

Common Pleas, 1574.

Tenant by the curtesy.

Note that the lord DYER said in argument in Clache's case, in the sixteenth year of the present queen, that it was held in the Chancery when he was a serjeant,[4] and of counsel in the case, that one Repps of Norfolk married a woman who was seised of certain lands; his wife was great with child by him, but died in labour, and the issue was ripped out of her womb alive;[5] and, because the mother was dead before the birth of the issue, it was held that the husband should not be tenant by the curtesy.

---

[1] See below, p. 45, no. 90, and the note there. The point noted here is also in that report, at p. 47.
[2] See below, p. 145, no. 269, and the note there.
[3] See the previous case. The present text was incorporated in *Paine's Case* (1587) 8 Co. Rep. 34, at fo. 35.
[4] I.e. between 1552 and 1557.
[5] I.e. by Caesarian section. Cit. in 8 Co. Rep. 35; Co. Litt. 39b.

[42]

AA, fo. 9 (205).

<Deliveries des faits.>[s]

Nota que fuit agre in le common banke P. 18 Eliz. regine <in ba>[d] que si home fait un obligation et deliver ceo al obligee a lyer, et ne dit come son fait, <ceo>[d] uncore ceo est bone deliverie del fait al obligee mesme.

[43][1]

AA, fo. 11v (207v).

<Conscience.>[a]

Temps Eliz. fuit tenus in le chauncery in un case inter le segnior Cumpton et un Egerton que lou fine fuit levie al Egerton dun segnorie et le fine fuit ingrosse devant que le conusee sua son quid juris clamat, et pur ceo que apres le ingrossing del fine il nad remedy il sua per sub pena in le chauncerie et fuit la tenus que intaunt que il puissoit aver ewe remedy per le common ley et ad surcesse ceo per son negligens que ilz ne voillont reliever luy.

[44]

AA, fo. 12 (208).

<Conscience.>[a]

Hill. 22 Eliz. in le chauncery fuit tenus per le master del rolls que si home soit mys in trust a purchaser terres ove les deniers del auter et il purchase le terre a son opes demesne et morust que in cest case <que>[d] le partie que fuit issint defraude avera remedie in le chancery vers le heire.

[45]

AA, fo. 13 (209).

<Statute marchaunt.>[s]

Nota Manwood dit veniendo de Westm. P. 19 Eliz. si home ad statute <merchant>[d] staple de 3c li. et ad terres in 3 severall counties, la le conuse poet vener in le

---

[1] *There are some heavy interlineations, but they seem to relate to the history of the Chancery in general rather than to this case, e.g.* 14 E. 3, Parning chancelour … Knivet, 46 E. 3. Nul decre contra common ley tanque le cardinall.

42. ANON.

Common Pleas, Pas. 1576.

Delivery of deeds.

Note that it was agreed in the Common Bench, in Easter term 18 Eliz., that if someone makes a bond and delivers it to the obligee to read, without saying 'as his deed', this is nevertheless a good delivery of the deed to the obligee himself.

43. LORD COMPTON v. EGERTON[1]

Chancery.

Conscience.

In the time of Elizabeth there was a case in the Chancery between the Lord Compton and one Egerton, where a fine was levied to Egerton of a lordship, and the fine was engrossed before the cognisee sued his *quid juris clamat*; and because he had no remedy after the engrossing of the fine, he sued by subpoena in the Chancery: and it was held there that since he could have had a remedy by the common law but had let it slip past by his negligence, they would not relieve him.

44. ANON.

Chancery, Hil. 1580.

Conscience.

In Hilary term 22 Eliz. in the Chancery it was held by the master of the rolls[2] that if someone is put in trust to purchase lands with the other's money, and he purchases the land to his own use, and dies, that in this case the party who was thus defrauded shall have his remedy in the Chancery against the heir.

45. STATUTE STAPLE

Between Westminster and the Temple, Pas. 1577.

Statute merchant.

Note that MANWOOD said, coming from Westminster[3] in Easter term 19 Eliz., that if someone has a statute staple for £300, and has lands in three separate counties, the

---

[1] Cf. C 2/Eliz./E5/45: William Egerton v. Henry, Lord Compton; pleadings in a Chancery suit for a rent-charge issuing out of the manors of Chaddenwick and Enford, Wilts.
[2] Sir William Cordell. [3] See the introduction, p. lxxx.

chauncerie et la ceux del chauncery usont de apportion le somme et de faire severall extentz in chescun countie pur chescun parte etc. Nota.

[46]

AA, fo. 17 (213).

<Faitz.>ˢ

Nota cest case fuit adjudge in le common banke come Wraye, chief justice, dit arguendo in le case de seniori puero que si 3 persones oblige eux mesmes et utrumque eorum, coment que properment utrumque est referre al 2, uncore le meaning del parties serra observe, et pur ceo fuit adjudge que ceo fuit un severall obligation et serra in ley cy bone come quemlibet. <Mesme le case, Dier, 14 Eliz. 310b.>ⁱ ¹

[47]

AA, fo. 21 (217).

[Execution.]

Nota fuit agre tempore Eliz. que si devant execution agard le lesse vende son terme bona fide le viconte ne poet extend ceo in les maynes le vendee.

[48]

AA, fo. 21v (217v).

<Execution sur statut et recognisauns.>ˢ

Nota bene que fuit tenus in M. 18 Eliz. que si home conust un statute et puis fait feffment, apres le jour incurre le conusee avera execution sauns scire facias ad satisfaciendum² et ceo per les parolx del statute in anno 13 E. 1, que fuit fait puis lestatut de Acton Burnel, car la est provide que le vicount luy livera seisin de toutz terres queux fueront in les maynes le feffour jour del recognisauns fait in quecunque mayns etc. Issint vide divers presidentz in le livre de entrees fol. 542 et 543 <et brefe de extent issue de extender toutz les terres que fuit al conisor die recognitionis facte>ᵃ.

---

¹ *Between the first and second lines.*
² ssf.

cognisee may come into the Chancery, where they of the Chancery are accustomed to apportion the sum and to make separate extents in each county for each part. Note that.

46. WOTTON v. COOKE[1]

Common Pleas (cited in the King's Bench, 1575).

Deeds.

Note that this case was adjudged in the Common Bench, as WRAY C.J. said in argument in the case of *seniori puero*:[2] if three persons bind themselves and 'either of them' (*utrumque eorum*), even though 'either' (*uterque*) properly refers only to two, nevertheless the meaning of the parties shall be respected; therefore it was adjudged that this was a several bond, and as good in law as if it had said 'any one of them' (*quemlibet eorum*). {The same case is in Dyer, 14 Eliz. 310v.[3]}

47. ANON.

Temp. Eliz.

Execution.

Note that it was agreed in the time of Queen Elizabeth that if, before execution awarded, a lessee sells his term *bona fide*, the sheriff may not extend it in the hands of the vendee.

48. ANON.

Mich. 1576.

Execution upon a statute and recognizance.

Note well that it was held in Michaelmas term 18 Eliz. that if someone acknowledges a statute and then makes a feoffment, after the day [of payment] incurred the cognisee shall have execution without a *scire facias ad satisfaciendum*. That is by the wording of the statute in the year 13 Edw. I,[4] which was passed after the statute of Acton Burnel;[5] for there it is provided that the sheriff shall deliver seisin to him of all lands which were in the hands of the feoffor on the day the recognizance was made, in whosesoever hands they should come. For this see various precedents in the book of entries, fos. 542 and 543.[6] {And the writ of extent issues to value all the lands which belonged to the cognisor on the day of making the recognizance.}

---

[1] See the note below, p. 127, no. 222.
[2] *Humphreston's Case* (1575) below, p. 40, no. 87, and the note there. The same point is noted below, p. 129, no. 230.
[3] *Anon.* (1572) Dyer 310, pl. 80.   [4] Statute *De Mercatoribus*, 13 Edw. I, stat. 3.
[5] 11 Edw. I, stat. 1.
[6] W. Rastell, *A Colleccion of Entrees* (1566), fos. 542–543.

[49]

AA, fo. 23v (219v).

<Executions.>[s]

Nota que Segnior Dier dit in largument del Mansuers case que si cesti que est in execution morust le partie pleintife nad remedie car qui non habet in aere luet in corpore. Et uncore si jeo distreine et le distres morust in le pounde nest satisfaction. Mes nota le reason fuit pur ceo [que] quant home ad election daver execution del corps ou des biens per fieri facias ou del moitie per elegit car il navera election de toutz per common ley.

[50]

AA, fo. 25 (221).

M. 26 et 27 Eliz. un information in Anglois fuit prefer in leschequer chamber vers Edmund Paston et auters pur intruding in le grand wast de Moushold in Norff. queux les defendants clayme come parcels del mannour de Blofield etc. Et Walmesly, serjaunt, accouncell ove les defendants, mova fortment que leschequer in course ne doit aver conusans de cest case, esteant inheritaunce, mes doit estre trie per le common ley. Et sic remanet.

[51]

AA, fo. 25 (221).

Nota le case de Latton anno 17 Eliz. Le case fuit que home seisie des terres in especial taile in droit sa fem et puis ilz ambideux levie un fine in le droit, le conuse grant et render mesme le terre arrere al baron et fem in taile, le remainder al fem in fe, et puis le baron devie, et el prist auter baron et levie fine in fe. Et adjudge que ceo ne fuit deins lestatut, car le consideration del grant et render vient del fem et nemi fuit ascun advancement al fem del purchase et inheritance le baron.

Mes la in mesme le terme un auter case fuit adjudge. Delaware anno 7 H. 7 grant terres per copie al baron et fem in fe, et puis 12 H. 8 pur xl s. paie per le baron le segnior fist done in taile al baron et fem, et puis le baron morust, et le fem suffer recoverie, et adjudge que ceo ne fuit deins lestatut car le terre vient del fem.[1]

---

[1] *Cf. JRL MS. Fr. 118, fo. 35v, at the end of Latton's Case:* Et a mesme le jour un auter case fuit adjudge sur mesme lestatute de 11 H. 7. Et le case fuit tiel. Anno 20 H. 7 le Segnior Delaware per copie de court [roll] graunt certaine customarie terre al baron et fem et a lour heires, et puis anno 7 H. 8 le baron pur xl s. paye obteine estate destre fait a luy et sa feme in taile solonque le course del common ley. Et puis le baron morust et el suffer un recoverie vers luy et leire le baron enter etc. Et fuit adjudge que ceo fuit deins lestatute de 11 H. 7, car fuit agre que si tenant in fe solonque le custome accept un estate taile, pur vie ou pur ans que le copyhold est extincte et ale. Et donques in le darren case ceo fuit clerement le purchase dell baron. Et issint 2 judgments done a un mesme jour, dont lun fuit deins lestatut de 11 H. 7 et lauter dehors. (*Translated on p. 26, n. 1.*)

49. MANSER v. ANNESLEY[1]

Common Pleas, 1575.

Executions.

Note that the lord DYER said in the argument of Manser's case that if someone who is in execution dies, the party plaintiff has no remedy, for *Qui non habet in aere luet in corpore*.[2] And yet if I distrain, and the distress dies in the pound, it is not satisfaction. But note the reason was that one has an election to have execution of the body, or of the goods by *fieri facias*, or of the moiety of lands by *elegit*; for he shall not have an election in respect of them all at common law.

50. R. v. EDMUND PASTON

Exchequer, Mich. 1584.

In Michaelmas term 26 & 27 Eliz. an English information was preferred in the Exchequer Chamber against Edmund Paston and others for intruding in the great waste of Mousehold in Norfolk, which the defendants claimed as parcel of the manor of Blofield. And *Walmsley*, serjeant, of counsel with the defendants, moved forcibly that in the ordinary course the Exchequer ought not to have cognizance of this case, being an inheritance, but it should be tried by the common law. And so it was left undecided.

51. EYSTON d. LATTON v. STUDDE[3]

Common Pleas, 1575.

Note Latton's case, in the year 17 Eliz. The case was that a man was seised of lands in special tail in right of his wife; then they both levied a fine in the right, and the cognisee granted and rendered the same land back to the husband and wife in tail, remainder to the wife in fee; then the husband died, and she married another husband and levied a fine in fee. And it was adjudged that this was not within the statute,[4] for the consideration of the grant and render came from the wife, and it was not an advancement of the wife from the purchase and inheritance of the husband.

In the same term another case was adjudged there: Delaware, in the year 7 Hen. VII, had granted lands by copy to a husband and wife in fee, and then in 12 Hen. VIII, for 40s. paid by the husband, the lord made a gift in tail to the husband and

---

[1] See above, p. 17, no. 30, and the note there.
[2] 'He who has nothing in his purse must suffer in person.' Cf. 12 Co. Rep. 126; 2 Co. Inst. 173.
[3] CP 40/1316, m. 106: Thomas Eyston v. Richard Studde of Ipswich, Suff., cooper; ejectment for a messuage in Ipswich on the demise of John Latton; pleads Not Guilty; continued in CP 40/1322, m. 1011 (unfit for production; printed in Plowd. 459): special verdict at bar; judgment for the defendant. Also below, p. 30, no. 64; p. 155, no. 291; p. 157, no. 297. Cited in Co. Litt. 365b–366 ('Pasch. 27 Eliz. in Com. Banco Lattons Case, which I my selfe heard and observed'). Differently reported in JRL MS. Fr. 118, fo. 35; Plowd. 462; Dyer's notebook, 110 Selden Soc. 332, and the MS. reports cited there; Benl. 238. This seems to be the case cited by Dyer in 110 Selden Soc. 255 ('termino Pasche 16 regine nunc, ad mensam in hospicio nostro', i.e. Serjeants' Inn, Fleet Street).   [4] 11 Hen. VII, c. 20.

[52]

AA, fo. 25v (221v).

[1]4[1] Eliz. in le case de Winter, Dier dit precisement que si home fait done in taile sur condition, <le rev>[d] et puis grant le revercion, ceo est hors del parolx del dit estatut car lestatut estre a [int]end de leasses pur vie ou ans. Et nota per luy que le leas [...][2] per fait indent solonque les parols del estatute.

[53]

AA, fo. 26 (222).

Leasses per corporations.

Quere si un evesque graunt un fostershipp ove un fee et puis graunt mesme loffice in revercion, si ceo soit bone ou nemi, ove le confirmation le deane et chapiter? Car cest fostershipp nest ascun tenement ne hereditament in luy. Et ad estre dit que si un evesque create novelment un rent hors de ses terres et le deane et chapiter ceo confirme, ceo est hors de lestatut. Et Anderson agrea le darren case. Mes il dit in le primer case que le 2 graunt fuit void, car le fostershipp fuit un hereditament in luy. Come graunt de cognitione placitorum ou tenere placita sont inheritaunces in le corone etc. Auxi il dit si evesque fait leas pur xxj ans et puis fait auter leas in revercion a commencer apres le primer ans determine, que cest deins le compas del statute. Uncore les parolx sont 'from the tyme as such leas shalbe made'. Mes nota, si un evesque a cest jour fait leas pur 3 vies, et le lesse fait leas pur mille ans, et levesque ove le deane et chapiter confirme ceo, ceo serra bon in perpetuitie, car ceo nest leas, graunte, feffment, conveians ne estate fait per levesque etc.

---

[1] *Numeral lost at edge of page.*
[2] *Word lost in corner of page.*

---

[3] 32 Hen. VIII, c. 34 (cited above it).
[4] Anderson is not accorded a title, which suggests this is before he became a serjeant. He may have been speaking as a bencher of the Inner Temple.
[5] 13 Eliz., c. 10, s. 3.

wife; then the husband died, and the wife suffered a recovery; and it was adjudged that this was not within the statute, for the land came from the wife.[1]

52. WINTER'S CASE[2]

Common Pleas, 1572.

In [14] Eliz., in Winter's case, DYER said specifically that if someone makes a gift in tail upon condition, and afterwards grants the reversion, this is outside the words of the said statute;[3] for the statute is to be understood of leases for life or years. And note, according to him, that the lease must be by deed indented according to the words of the statute.

53. ANON.

Before 1577.[4]

Leases by corporations.

If a bishop grants a forestership with a fee, and afterwards grants the same office in reversion, with the confirmation of the dean and chapter, is this good, or not? For this forestership is no 'tenement or hereditament' in him. And it has been said that if a bishop creates a new rent out of his lands, and the dean and chapter confirm it, this is outside the statute.[5] *Anderson* agreed the last case. But he said that in the first case the second grant was void, for the forestership was a hereditament in him. Likewise, a grant of cognizance of pleas, or to hold pleas, for they are inheritances in the crown. He also said that if a bishop makes a lease for twenty-one years, and afterwards make another lease in reversion to commence after the first years are determined, this is within the compass of the statute; and yet the words are, 'from the time as such lease shall be made' [*sic*]. But note that if a bishop at the present day makes a lease for three lives, and the lessee makes a lease for a thousand years, and the bishop (with the dean and chapter) confirms it, this shall be good in perpetuity, for it is not a lease, grant, feoffment, conveyance or estate made by the bishop.

---

[1] Cf. JRL MS. Fr. 118, fo. 35v (text on p. 25): '(tr.) And on the same day another case was adjudged upon the same statute of 11 Hen. VII. And the case was this. In the year 20 Hen. VII the Lord Delaware by copy of court roll granted certain customary land to a husband and wife and their heirs, and then in the year 7 Hen. VIII the husband, for 40s. paid, obtained an estate to be made to him and his wife in tail according to the course of the common law. Then the husband died, and she suffered a recovery against her, and the husband's heir entered. And it was adjudged that this was within the statute of 11 Hen. VII; for it was agreed that if a tenant in fee according to the custom accepts an estate tail, or an estate for life or for years, the copyhold is extinguished and gone. Therefore in the latter case this was clearly the purchase of the husband. Thus two judgments were given on one day, whereof one was within the statute of 11 Hen. VII and the other outside it.' In the margin Coke has written 'Stocbridges case'. (For *Stockbridge's Case*, Pas. 1575, see above, Appendix I, p. cxcix.)

[2] See below, p. 43, no. 88, and the note there.

[54]

AA, fo. 31v (227v).

<Vivarie.>ᵃ

Nota 18 Eliz. fuit dit per le Segnior Dier que cest parol vivarie signifie un lieu priviledge ou ascun mannour de vive chose est conserve et norishe.

[55]

AA, fo. 33v (229v).

<Evidence.>ᵃ

T. 19 Eliz. fuit dit per ascuns in le bank le roy si home port trespas et suppose le trespas 3 Maii, et il plede rien culpable, le pleintife poet doner in evidence ascun trespas fait <puis>ᵈ <devant>ⁱ le 3 jour, mes il ne poet doner en evidence ascun trespas fait <devant>ᵈ apres le 3 jour, car si le trespas fuit fait apres il nad cause daction adonques. Mes 5 E. 4, 5, semble contrarie. Vide Litt. 114.

[56]

AA, fo. 38 (234).

<Conusauns.>ˢ ¹

Tr. 16 Eliz. rott. mcccvij, in un bill vers un attorney del common banke, conusans de plea fuit grant al evesque de Welles in bille de trespas de assault, batterie et manasse del servant le pleintife apud Wells etc.

[57]

AA, fo. 40 (236).

<Priviledge.>ˢ

18 Eliz. fuit tenus in le common banke que si clarke del common banke fuit implede in Londres sur un concessit solvere il navera priviledge, car tiel customarie action ne gist al common ley. Mesme la ley de toutz auters customarie actions. Vies 38 H. 6,

---

¹ *Heading on fo. 35.*

⁶ CP 40/1323 is unfit for production.
⁷ Perhaps the case cited overleaf (in *AA*, fo. 236v) as 'P. 18 Eliz. in mon reportes'.
⁸ *The Lombard's Case* (1460) YB Pas. 38 Hen. VI, fo. 29, pl. 12.

54. ANON.

Common Pleas, 1576.

Vivary.

Note that it was said in 18 Eliz. by the lord Dyer that this word 'vivary' signifies a privileged place where any kind of living thing is conserved and nourished.[1]

55. LORD CROMWELL v. DENNYE[2]

King's Bench, Trin. 19 Eliz.

Evidence.

In Trinity term 19 Eliz. it was said by some, in the King's Bench, that if someone brings trespass and supposes the trespass on 3 May, and the defendant pleads Not Guilty, the plaintiff may give in evidence any trespass done before 3 May. But he may not give in evidence any trespass done after 3 May: for if the trespass was done afterwards, he had no cause of action then. But 5 Edw. IV, fo. 5,[3] seems contrary. See Litt. 114.[4]

56. WHOPER v. HAREWOOD[5]

Common Pleas, Trin. 1574.

Cognizance of pleas.

In Trin. 16 Eliz., roll 1307,[6] in a bill against an attorney of the Common Bench, cognizance of the plea was granted to the bishop of Wells in a bill of trespass for assault, battery and menacing of the plaintiff's servant at Wells.

57. ANON.[7]

Common Pleas, 1576.

Privilege.

In 18 Eliz. it was held in the Common Bench that if a clerk of the Common Bench is impleaded in London upon a *concessit solvere*, he should not have privilege, for such a customary action does not lie at common law. The law is the same of all other customary actions. See 38 Hen. VI, fo. 29.[8] Therefore, in those cases, if a writ of

---

[1] Cf. 2 Co. Inst. 100, glossing Merton c. 11, *De malefactoribus in parcis*.
[2] See below, p. 103, no. 178.
[3] YB Trin. 5 Edw. IV, fo. 5, pl. 18.
[4] I.e. the report, below, p. 103 (at Litt., fo. 114).
[5] CP 40/1325, m. 1707 (Mich. 1574; unfit for production; printed in Benl. 233): William Whoper v. John Harewood, attorney of the Bench; trespass, for assaulting, mistreating and threatening the plaintiff's servant Anne Wilmot at Wells. Differently reported in Dyer's notebook, 110 Selden Soc. 306, and the MSS. noted there.

29. Et pur ceo in tielz cases ou priviledg est agard procedendo serra allowe, mes auterment est ou le [*sic*] poet aver action al common ley et ad un special custome a aider luy en pleder, la procedendo ne serra graunte car il poet pleder ceo in le common banke. 1 E. 4, 6, mesme le diversite.

[58]

AA, fo. 40 (236).[1]

<Priviledge.>[s]

15 Eliz. in case dun Lodge, un del attorney[s] del common banke, certein somme dargent fuit <reteine>[d] attache in ses mayns in Londres per le custome, et ceo nient obstant il ad son priviledge, car nient obstant [que] il ne poet aver advauntage de cest custom icy uncore il nest pas a mischiefe car il poet aver son dette envers son proper dettour.

[59]

AA, fo. [41v] (237v).

<Cessante causa cessat lex.>[s]

Vies 9 E. 4, 20, si lannuitie soit grant pro decimis ou pro consilio in cest case sil denie counsaile ou deteina les dismes ceo determine lannuitie pur ceo que il nad auter remedie pur le counsaile ou pur les dismes. Mes si lannuitie soit grant pro decimis et le grauntee del annuitie graunta les dismes a lauter per fait indente com le case la fuit, la coment que les choses sont executorie, uncore coment que lun de eux estoppe lun, uncore lauter ne poet estopper lauter. Et issint fuit agree in le common banke anno 16 Eliz. in le common banke in le case dun Dimes.

[60]

AA, fo. 47 (243).

<Evidence.>[s]

Tr. 20 Eliz. fuit dit in common banke, si home soit oblige a J. S. in xx li. sur condition a payer a luy 10 li. a tiel jour, et puis al jour le obligor dona a luy un chivall in satisfaction del deniers, quel il accept, in cest case in action de det sur obligation il ne poet pleder que il ad paie les deniers etc., car coment que ceo est paiment in ley uncore ceo ne covient estre plede. Vide 34 Ass. [*blank*] et 33 E. 3, tit. Verdit. <Vide

---

[1] *Written after the note dated 18 Eliz.*

privilege has been awarded, a *procedendo* shall be allowed; but it is otherwise where he could have an action at common law and has a special custom to help him in pleading: there a *procedendo* shall not be granted, for he may plead the custom in the Common Bench. 1 Edw. IV, fo. 6:[1] the same distinction.

58. LODGE'S CASE[2]

Common Pleas, 1573.

Privilege.

In 15 Eliz., in the case of one Lodge, one of the attorneys of the Common Bench, a certain sum of money was attached in his hands in London by the custom [of foreign attachment], and still he had his privilege; for although he could not have the advantage of that custom here,[3] nevertheless he is not at mischief, for he could [recover] his debt against his own debtor.

59. DIMES' CASE

Common Pleas, 1574.

Cessante causa cessat lex.

See 9 Edw. IV, fo. 20,[4] if an annuity is granted for tithes or for counsel, and in this case he denies counsel, or withholds the tithes, this determines the annuity because he has no other remedy for the counsel or for the tithes. But if the annuity is granted for tithes, and the grantee of the annuity grants the tithes to the other by deed indented, as the case was there, then although the things are executory, and although one of the things estops one of them, nevertheless the other cannot estop the other. So it was agreed in the Common Bench in the year 16 Eliz. in the case of one Dimes.

60. ANON.[5]

Common Pleas, Trin. 1578.

Evidence.

In Trinity term 20 Eliz. it was said in the Common Bench that if someone is bound to John Style in £20 upon condition of paying him £10 at a certain day, and then at the day the obligor gives him a horse in satisfaction of the money, which he accepts, in this case in an action of debt on the bond he may not plead that he has paid the money, for even though it is a payment in law it must not be so pleaded. See 34 Ass.

---

[1] YB Mich. 1 Edw. IV, fos. 5–6, pl. 13.
[2] Differently reported in 2 Leon. 156 (misdated 20 Eliz.); the date cannot have been 20 Eliz., because Harper J. died on 29 Jan. 1577.
[3] I.e. at Westminster.
[4] YB Trin. 20 Edw. IV, fo. 19, pl. 22, at fo. 20.   [5] Cf. Co. Litt. 212b.

apres, fol. 76b en mes notes demesne, Claydon et Spencers case, H. 10 H. 8, bone case.>[a]

[61]

AA, fo. 46 (243).

<Evidence.>[s]

Nota M. 22 et 23 Eliz. fuit tenus per le Segnior Wray et totam curiam en banke le roy que si un home oblige luy mesme in un obligation et le condition fuit que il estoiera al agard de J. S. et si J. S. ne fist ascun agard [donques][1] al umpirage de [*blank*], et la fuit un blanke, et puis le delivery del fait le obligee escria un nosme in le condition. Et in det sur cest obligation le defendant pleada non est factum et dona in evidence le dit matter. Et fuit tenus clerement que coment que le obligation fuit un foitz son fait, uncore entaunt que lobligee avoit alter le fait puis le sealer et delivery de ceo pur ceo le fait fuit voide.

Et le segnior chiefe justice et Gawdy disoient que entant que home poet pleader lespecial matter et concluder et issint nient son fait, <ilz disoient que>[2] per ceo appiert que le matter est forsque evidence et solement enter pur doubte des layes gentes, car la lissue est non est factum.

Et le segnior chiefe justice dit que un fait <bone>[d] poet estre bone in part et voide in part.

[62]

AB, fo. 47v (246v).

<Dower.>[s]

17 Eliz. fuit agree per Dier et Manwood que in brefe de dower le 3 part covient estre [assigne],[3] et sil assigne le 3 part del capitall messuage lheire nad remedy.

[63]

AB, fo. 50 (249).

<Dower.>[s]

15 Eliz. in le case dun Crane le Segnior Dier dit si home seisie des terres in fe prist fem et levie un fine et morust, si la fem ne fist sa claime deins les 5 ans el serra barre

---

[1] *Unclear word, presumably to this effect.*   [2] *Conjectural.*   [3] *Apparently written as* ass[e]s.

[5] Differently reported in Dyer's notebook, 110 Selden Soc. 383, pl. 494 (Mich. 1580); CUL MS. Gg.3.26, fo. 113.   [6] Dr Squire, according to Dyer.   [7] I.e. the jurors.
[8] Cit. in Co. Litt. 31b ('Trin. 17 El. in the Court of Common Pleas, which I heard and observed').
[9] Reported more fully in JRL MS. Fr. 118, fo. 15, pl. 20 (copy in *Ff*, fos. 187v–188) as *Crane* v. *Broxhole*, with arguments by Manwood, Mead and Bendlowes; IT MS. Petyt 511.12, fo. 196v, sub nom. *Anon.* v. *Broxhorne*.

[*blank*],[1] and 33 Edw. III, tit. *Verdit*.[2] {See below, fo. 76v in my own notes:[3] Claydon and Spencer's case, Hil. 10 Hen. VIII,[4] a good case.}

61. ANON.[5]

King's Bench, Mich. 1580.

Evidence.

Note that in Michaelmas term 22 & 23 Eliz. it was held by the lord WRAY and the whole court in the King's Bench [as follows]. Someone bound himself in a bond, and the condition was that he should abide by the award of John Style, and if John Style should not make any award, then by the umpirage of '...'; here there was a blank, but after the delivery of the deed the obligee wrote a name[6] into the condition. And in debt upon this bond the defendant pleaded *Non est factum*, and gave the said matter in evidence: and it was held clearly that although the bond was once a deed, yet because the obligee had altered the deed after the sealing and delivery thereof, the deed was for that reason void.

And the lord chief justice [WRAY] and GAWDY said that since one could plead the special facts and conclude 'and so not his deed', it appears from this that the matter is only evidence and is entered solely for doubt of the lay folk;[7] for the issue here is *Non est factum*.

And the lord chief justice said that a deed may be good in part and void in part.

62. ANON.[8]

Common Pleas, 1575.

Dower.

In 17 Eliz. it was agreed by DYER [C.J.] and MANWOOD that in a writ of dower the third part must be assigned, and if [the sheriff] assigns a third of the capital messuage the heir has no remedy.

63. CRANE v. BROXHOLE[00]

Common Pleas, 1572/73.

Dower.

In 15 Eliz., in the case of one Crane, the lord DYER said that if someone seised of lands in fee marries a wife, levies a fine and dies, and the wife does not make her

---

[1] Probably 34 Edw. III, Lib. Ass., pl. 1.   [2] Hil. 33 Edw. III, Fitz. Abr., *Verdit*, pl. 47.
[3] It is actually on fo. 77v of *AB*, where the record is cited correctly from a MS. text of Bendlowes.
[4] CP 40/1023, m. 322: Leonard Spencer (executor of John Jullys, clerk) v. John Cleydon, clerk, and Henry Stannard gent., executors of Sir James Hobart (sometime attorney-general); detinue; plea that they had executed the will with their own money and retained the goods as their own. Cf. Benl. 11, cit. record imperfectly as 10 Hen. VIII, roll 422.

de sa dower per lestatute de 4 H. 7. Et il dit que in 4 H. 8 il fuit adjudge et allowe bon barre de sa dower. Et uncore fuit dit per ascuns que le fine ne serra barre a luy pur ceo que el navoit ascun title al temps del fine levie, car sa title de dower accrue per le mort sa baron et nemy devant.

[64]

AB, fo. 52 (253).

<Dower.>

Nota per Manwood in Lattons case que si fine soit levie a J. S. et J. S. grant et render arere al conusor pur vie et le remainder ouster in fe, que le feme le conusee ne unques avera dower, car fuit impossible que sa fitz inheritera. Mes luy semble que il serra charge per reason dun statut. Mesme la ley de feffment a J. S. al use J. D., la fem le feffe ne serra indowe. Mes le terre serra extend. 27 H. 8, 23. Cestui que use enter et fait feffment, sa fem ne serra indowe.

[65]

AB, fo. 54 (259).

<Copiholde.>

14 Eliz. Nota per le Segnior Dier in camera stellata si copiholder surrender al auter hors del court, ore si cestui que fist le surrender morust avant que le surrender soit [present] al prochein court, uncore sil soit present al prochein court ceo est bone, car lenterest et droit passa per le surrender conditionalement, que soit present al prochein court. Et auxi il dit que copiholder poet surrender al steward hors del court sil soit present al prochein court. Et auxi il dit que si le copiholder fist surrender al steward hors del court, et puis al prochein court mesme le copiholder soy mesme et fait surrender, la est bon countermaunde, come in le case de garrante dattorney.

[66]

AB, fo. 54 (259).

<Copiholde.>

14 Eliz. fuit tenus per Dier et Manwood que si copiholder fait leasse pur 3 ans per le custom cel lesse ne poet aver ejectione firme car est garrante solement per le

---

[1] *Conjectural; Coke seems to have omitted a word.*   [2] p[er].

[3] See above, p. 25, no. 51.   [4] YB Mich. 27 Hen. VIII, fo. 23, pl. 1.
[5] Cf. *Anon.* (1573) B. & M. 225, where it is said that the King's Bench judges were in favour of allowing the copyholder to bring ejectment, whereas the Common Pleas were against it on the different ground that he could not be put in possession by *habere facias possessionem*.
[6] I.e. a custom of the manor allowing tenants to make leases.

claim within the five years, she shall be barred from her dower by the statute of 4 Hen. VII.[1] And he said that in 4 Hen. VIII[2] it was adjudged and allowed to be a good bar of her dower. Nevertheless, it was said by some that the fine should not bar her, because she had no title at the time of the fine levied, in that her title to dower accrued on the death of her husband and not before.

64. EYSTON d. LATTON v. STUDDE[3]

Common Pleas, 1575.

Dower.

Note by MANWOOD in Latton's case that if a fine is levied to John Style, and John Style grants and renders back to the cognisor for life, remainder over in fee, the cognisee's wife shall never have dower, for it was impossible that her son could inherit. But it seemed to him that [the heir] would be charged by reason of a statute merchant. The law is the same of a feoffment to John Style to the use of John Dale: the feoffee's wife shall not be endowed, but the land may be extended. 27 Hen. VIII, fo. 23:[4] cestui que use enters and makes a feoffment, his wife shall not be endowed.

65. ANON.

Star Chamber, 1572.

Copyhold.

14 Eliz. Note by the lord DYER, in the Star Chamber: if a copyholder surrenders to another out of court, and the person who made the surrender dies before the surrender is [presented] at the next court, nevertheless if it is presented at the next court it is good; for the interest and right passed by the surrender, subject to the condition that it be presented at the next court. He also said that a copyholder may surrender to the steward out of court, if it is presented at the next court. And he also said that if a copyholder makes a surrender to the steward out of court, and then at the next court the same copyholder [appears] himself and makes the surrender, that is a good countermand, as in the case of a warrant of attorney.

66. ANON.[5]

Common Pleas, 1572.

Copyhold.

In 14 Eliz. it was held by DYER [C.J.] and MANWOOD that if a copyholder makes a lease for three years by the custom,[6] this lessee may not have *ejectione firmae*, for

---

[1] 4 Hen. VII, c. 24.

[2] A few cases from this year (which is not in the year books) occur at the beginning of Dyer as printed, but this is not one of them. Cf. *Ff*: 'pur ceo il vouche un cas 4 H. 8 que fuit rule et allow que tiel fine fuit un bon barre del dower sa feme'.

custome, car al common [ley] si lesse <pur ans fa>ᵈ a volunt fait lesse pur ans, le lesse pur ans, sil enter, est disseisour.

[67]

AB, fo. 54 (259).

<Copiholde.>ˢ

20 Eliz. in le common banke cest case fuit move. Fem tenant in taile generall dun copihold, le remainder in fe, prist baron et ad issue fitz, le baron morust, et el prist auter baron et ad issue auter fitz, et puis le baron et fem (le fem esteant examine come in un [fine]¹) surrender al opes de eux mesmes pur terme de lour vies, et puis al opes de lour eigne fitz in fe, barron et fem morueront, leigne fitz fuit admitt come tenant in fe simple et morust sans issue. Ore le question fuit quel de eux serra admitte, scilicet le quel le frere de demi sanke come heire in taile ou le collaterall cosin del entier sanke come heire al fem. Et primerment le Segnior Dier dit que le dit surrender ne docke lestate taile mes que lissue in taile poet aver pleint en nature de son formedon, mes il dit que ceo fuit un discontinuans. Et il dit si tenant in taile voille docker le taile covient a luy a faire un forfeiture et donques le segnior a seisier ceo et de faire novel grant. Et Manwood dit que coment que copihold ne poet estre tayle deins lestatut De donis conditionalibus, uncore per le custome del manour la poet estre estate taile dun copiholde. Et donques il agrea que le surrender ne docke lestate taile. Et auxi que leigne fitz, quant le remainder fuit ject sur luy, il fuit remitte, et donques coment que le segnior done seisin et admitte luy in fe ceo nest materiall, et donques le puisne fitz covient estre admitte.

[68]

AB, fo. 54 (259).

<Copiholde.>ˢ

M. 20 Eliz. cest case fuit move. Un copiholder surrender son estate al use dun pur vie, et puis al use de ses droit heires, si ceo serra revercion ou remainder in luy? Et semble que ceo fuit revercion in luy, car ne poet estre un use dun copihold mes le limitation del use nest forsque a directer le segnior a que il ferra le grant ouster. Et Mounson dit si la copiholder surrender son terre al opes del un pur vie que le revercion demurt in luy. Mes Manwood doubta pur [ceo que] in tiel case le segnior ceo avera. Et la ils agreont que maintenant per le surrender lestate del copiholder est surrender in le possession del segnior.

---

¹ *Conjectural: word omitted by Coke.*

his lease is warranted solely by the custom; for at common law if a lessee at will makes a lease for years, the lessee for years (if he enters) is a disseisor [of the reversioner].

67. ANON.

Common Pleas, 1578.

Copyhold.

In 20 Eliz. in the Common Bench this case was moved. A woman tenant in tail general of a copyhold, the remainder in fee, married a husband and had issue a son; the husband died; she married another husband, and had issue another son; then the husband and wife (the wife being examined, as in a fine) surrendered to the use of themselves for their lives, and then to the use of their elder son in fee; the husband and wife died; the elder son was admitted as tenant in fee simple, and died without issue. The question now was who should be admitted: should it be the brother of the half-blood as heir in tail, or the collateral kinsman of the whole blood as heir to the woman? Firstly, the lord DYER said that the surrender did not dock the estate tail, but that the issue in tail could have a plaint in the nature of formedon; but he said that it was a discontinuance. And he said that if tenant in tail [of a copyhold] wishes to dock the tail, he must make a forfeiture, and then the lord must seize it and make a new grant. MANWOOD said that although copyhold cannot be entailed under the statute *De Donis Conditionalibus*,[1] yet by the custom of the manor there may be an estate tail of a copyhold. Then he agreed that the surrender did not dock the estate tail, and also that when the remainder was cast upon the elder son he was remitted, and then it is immaterial that the lord has given seisin and admitted him in fee; therefore the younger son ought to be admitted.

68. ANON.

Common Pleas, Mich. 1577.

Copyhold.

In Michaelmas term 20 Eliz. this case was moved. A copyholder surrendered his estate to the use of someone for life, and then to the use of his right heirs: shall this be [considered] a reversion in him, or a remainder? It seemed that it was a reversion in him, for there cannot be a use of a copyhold, but the limitation of the use is only to direct the lord to whom he should make the grant over. MOUNSON said that if a copyholder surrenders his land to the use of someone for life, the reversion stays in him. But MANWOOD doubted this, because in such a case the lord shall have it. And they agreed there that by the surrender the copyholder's estate was forthwith surrendered into the lord's possession.

---

[1] Westminster II, c. 1.

[69]

AB, fo. 54 (259). *Ff*, fo. 56v.

<Copiholde.>ˢ

Nota T. 20 Eliz. fuit demande del Segnior Dier si un recoverie ewe in un base court sur pleint la dockera un estate taile per copie de court rolle. Et le Segnior Dier responde que fuit bone question a demander del steward del court, car la lour custome et usage estoit pur ley, et consuetudo altera lex.

[70]

AB, fo. 54 (259). *Ff*, fo. 56v.

<Copiholde.>ˢ

Nota fuit tenus tempore Eliz. devant Saunders et Loveles in lour circuite que si un copiholder <committe>ᵈ suffer wast, ceo nest forfeiture de son copiholde per le common ley sinon que ceo soit forfeiture per le custome del manour.

[71]

AB, fo. 262v (magenta ink) (Litt., fo. 16v).

Nota fuit dit in Leschequer Chamber in le countie de Arundels case que si surrender soit fait in les mayns le lessor al lauter opes et puis les ans expire que cestui in le revercion serra compell a graunter ceo.

[72]

AB, fo. 263v (magenta ink) (Litt., fo. 17v).

Hillarii 18 Eliz. fuit tenus per toutz les justices del common banke que <si>ᵈ si un copiholder <devient>ᵈ morust, son heire devant admission poet surrender ceo a ascun auter, car ilz disoient que il est tenant devant admission envers chescun forsque envers son segnior, car il serra de tiel possession possessio fratris come <est ore>¹ adjudge in le Chauncerie. Et auxi ilz disoient que quant le segnior [accept]² le surrender del heire al auter opes ceo amount a un admittauns in ley. Vide loppinion de Manwood in Hares case fol. 529b. Mes 15 H. 7, 10, que si evesque grant terres per copie et est translate, le grant est void. Vies 21 H. 6, 37.

¹ *Unclear; resembles* adcept.
² *Seemingly altered from* ad committe *Ff*.

69. ANON.

Common Pleas, Trin. 1578.

Copyhold.

Note that in Trinity term 20 Eliz. the lord DYER was asked if a recovery had in an inferior court, upon a plaint there, would dock an estate tail by copy of court roll. And the lord DYER answered that it was a good question to ask the steward of the court, for their custom and usage stands as law there, *et consuetudo altera lex*.[1]

70. ANON.

Oxford circuit, 1572/76.

Copyhold.

Note that it was held in the time of Elizabeth, before Saunders [C.B.] and [Serjeant] Lovelace in their circuit, that if a copyholder suffers waste, this is not a forfeiture of his copyhold by the common law unless it is a forfeiture by the custom of the manor.

71. EARL OF ARUNDEL v. LANGAR[2]

Exch. Ch., Mich. 1576.

Copyhold.

Note that it was said in the Exchequer Chamber, in the earl of Arundel's case, that if a surrender is made into the hand of the lessor to the use of another, and then the years expire, the reversioner shall be compelled to grant it.

72. ANON.

Hil. 1576.

Copyhold.

In Hilary term 18 Eliz. it was held by all the justices of the Common Bench that if a copyholder dies, his heir may surrender it to someone else before admission; for they said that before admission he is tenant as against everyone except his lord, and he shall have *possessio fratris* in respect of such possession: as was recently adjudged in the Chancery.[3] They also said that when the lord accepts the heir's surrender to the use of another, this amounts to an admittance in law. {See the opinion of MANWOOD in Hare's case, fo. 529v.[4]} But in 15 Hen. VII, fo. 10,[5] [it appears] that if a bishop grants lands by copy, and is translated, the grant is void. See 21 Hen. VI, fo. 37.[6]

---

[1] 'Custom is another law (i.e. an alternative kind of law).' The point is that the judges at Westminster had no knowledge of manorial customs unless pleaded.   [2] See below, p. 70, no. 116, and the note there.
[3] See below, p. 35, no. 74; vol. ii, p. 176.   [4] *Hare* v. *Bickley* (1578) Plowd. 526 at fo. 529.
[5] YB Trin. 15 Hen. VII, fo. 10, pl. 13.   [6] YB Pas. 21 Hen. VI, fo. 36, pl. 4, at fo. 37.

Et P. 18 Eliz. fuit tenus per les justices in le Common Banke que si divers remainders sont conveie in un copie, que si le primer particuler tenant soit admitte cest admission [se]rvera a toutz ceux in le remainder et ne besoigne a eux daver auter admission.

[73]

AB, fo. 57 (264).

<Copiholde.>ˢ

M. 14 Eliz. Lovelace mova al justices del common banke cest case. Le roigne esteant seisie dun manour a quel certain copiholders yssont un copiholder forfeit son terre, et puis le roigne south Leschequer seale lessa ceo pur xxj ans, per force de quel le lesse continue in possession per le space de 10 ans, et apres surrender son terme et prist ceo per copy de court roll per le mayns <per les mains>ᵈ del stuard accordant al custome. Le quel ceo soit ore copihold arere ou nemi, ceo fuit le questione.

Harper semble que ceo ne fuit copihold etc. Et son reason fuit pur ceo que copiholde covient estre customarie terre tenus de tiel mannour et demise ou demisable temps dont per copie de court <de>ᵈ roll, mes in le case al barre durant le leas pur ans il fuit nesque[1] demised neque demisable per copie de court roll. Mes il dit que coment que le segnior tient ceo in ces mayns per le space de xx ans nient que durant cest temps il ne fuit demised, uncore per tout cel temps il fuit demisable: quod Manwood et Dier concesserunt en tout. Et la fuit agree per le court que si un copihold eschet et le segnior fait feffment in fe sur condition, et puis enter pur le condition enfreint, uncore il ne unques inapres poet ceo graunter arere per copye. Mes la Dier <dit>ⁱ si segnior et tenant ysont per homage auncestrel et le tenant fait feffment in fe sur condition et puis enter pur le condition enfreint, le garrante et lacquitall est revive. Et uncore fuit agre per curiam que si tenant pur vie fait feffment in fe sur condition et puis enter pur le condition infreint que ceo est un forfeiture. <Et issint fuit adjudge in banke le roy M. 18 Eliz. que si le copihold soit un foitz leasse [per][2] indenture le prescription est enfreint.>ᵃ [3]

Report in the Rylands Manuscript

JRL MS. Fr. 118, fo. 1.[4]

Le roygne est seisie dun mannour, a quel mannour certaine copiholders ysont, et lun co[piholder] forfeit son terre, et puis le roigne south leschequer seale lease mesme la terre que est [issint] forfeit a J. S. pur terme de xxj ans, per force de quell le lesse continue possession

---

[1] *Sic.*
[2] p[ur].
[3] *Sideways in outer margin.*
[4] *This leaf is very rubbed, and part of the top outer corner is missing, with loss of text.*

And in Easter term 18 Eliz. it was held by the justices in the Common Bench that if various remainders are conveyed in one copy, and the first particular tenant is admitted, this admission shall serve for all the remainderman, and it is not necessary for them to have another admission.

73. ANON.[1]

Mich. 1572, with an addition of Mich. 1576.

Copyhold.

In Michaelmas term 14 Eliz. *Lovelace* moved this case to the justices of the Common Bench. The queen being seised of a manor to which certain copyholders belong, one copyholder forfeited his land, and then the queen leased it for twenty-one years under the Exchequer seal, by virtue whereof the lessee continued in possession for the space of ten years, and then he surrendered his term and took it by copy of court roll through the hands of the steward, according to the custom. The question was, whether this is now copyhold again, or not.

HARPER[2] thought it was not copyhold. His reason was that a copyhold must be customary land held of such and such a manor, demised or demisable time out of mind by copy of court roll, whereas in the case at bar it was neither demised nor demisable by copy of court roll during the lease for years. But he said that even if the lord retained it in his hands for the space of twenty years, during which it was not demised, it was still throughout that time demisable: which MANWOOD and DYER [C.J.] agreed *in toto*. And it was there agreed by the court that if a copyhold escheats, and the lord makes a feoffment in fee upon condition, and later enters for breach of the condition, he may never afterwards grant it again by copy. But DYER there said that if there are a lord and tenant by homage ancestral, and the tenant makes a feoffment in fee upon condition, and later enters for breach of the condition, the warranty and acquittal are revived. Nevertheless it was agreed by the court that if a tenant for life makes a feoffment in fee upon condition, and later enters for breach of the condition, that is a forfeiture. {And so it was adjudged in the Kings Bench, Mich. 18 Eliz., that if a copyhold is once leased by indenture the prescription is broken.}

Report in the Rylands Manuscript

JRL MS. Fr. 118, fo. 15, pl. 1, and fo. 15v, pl. 4.

The queen is seised of a manor, to which manor certain copyholders belong, and one of the copyholders forfeits his land; then the queen, under the Exchequer seal, leases the same land which was so forfeited to John Style for term of twenty-one years, by virtue whereof the lessee

---

[1] Differently reported in JRL MS. Fr. 118, fo. 15, pl. 1, and fo. 15v, pl. 4 (both printed below); *Gg*, fo. 103.

[2] Coke's spelling is used in this edition. It is the spelling used in his patent as a judge. On the judge's monument at Swarkestone, Derbs., the name is spelt Harpur. In his will he is Harpur *alias* Harper.

per le [space] de 10 ans et apres surrender son terme et puis prist ceo per copie de courte rolle [per] les maines del stuerd accordant al custome. Le quel ceo [soit][1] ore copyhold ou nemy, ceo [fuit] le question. Et cest case fuit move per Lovelace. Harper dit (Dier adonques in [le] starre chamber) que ceo ore ne fuit copihold pur ceo que copihold covient estre customarie [terre] tenus de tiel mannour, demised et demisable de temps dont memory etc. per copy de [court] roll, et ceo est le common prescription. Ore, quant le roygne lesse ceo per fait […] pur xxj ans ore lun article del prescription fault pur ceo que duraunt le temps que le [lesse] ceo avoit ceo ne fuit dimisible per copie de court roll. Mes coment que le segnior tient ceo en ces mains per le space de xx ans, uncore nient <obstant>ⁱ que il nest demised, pur ceo que il [fuit] dimisible a chescun temps quant il voet, il dit que ceo accord bien ove le prescription. [Mes] en le cas al barre neque fuit demised per copie etc. neque dimisible, per que etc.: <Man>^d quod Manwood concessit. Benloes dit que luy semble que le lease pur xxj ans fuit v[oide] entaunt que le leas ne fuit fait a launcient tenaunt, car il dit que il ad vew devaunt ces heures que ou un copiholder ad forfeit son copihold et le segnior de que ceo fuit tenus lesse ceo a un auter, et launcient tenant ad luy ouste, et le lesse sauns remedie. Harper et Manwood, adonques ceo fuit solonque le custome de tiel lieu, autermen nemi clerement. Manwood dit, si un lesse son segniorie pur ans ou a volunt, et un copyholder que tient de ceo fait un acte per que son copihold est forfeit, et le lesse a volunt ou pur terme dans lesse ceo per indenture, quere si le segnior ne poet dimitte ceo per copy de court rolle quant il vient en ses maines arere. Et Harper et Manwood disoient que ceo fuit un common usage quant <les>^d ascun copihold vient en les maines le segnior de lesser ceo per indenture et donques est le tenure chaunge. Residuum de cest case pagina sequente.

… [fo. 15v] Le case de copihold fuit ore reherce al Dier. Et luy semble que apres le surrender cest terre poet estre prise arere per copie de court rolle. Car il dit que coment apres le forfeiture le segnior tient ceo en ces mayns per le space de x ans, uncore il poet doner ceo assetz bien per copie. Harper et Manwood disoient (come lauter jour devant) que si le segnior reteigne ceo en ses mayns uncore il est dimisible per copie de court rolle coment que il ne soit demised, mes quant il ad lesse ceo per indenture pur xxj ans il ne fuit dimitted ne a cest temps dimisible per copy. Dier, le prescription des terres en gavelkinde sont que sont partite et partibiles solonque le custome, donques mittomus si un tenant en gavelkind ad issue forsque un fitz et morust, et le fitz vive 50 ou 60 ans, ore le terre nest partita nec partibilis, et uncore sil ad 4 issues il est clere que toutz ses fitz averont ceo solonque le custome et uncore le prescription fault. Et il dit que cest parol partible est un paroll de droit, et partitum un paroll de possession, sicome debet et solet sont. Harper, partibilis nihil aliud est <but>^d mes il est destre parted quant il covient estre parted, issint que coment que tiel tenant en gavelkind ad issue forsque un fitz uncore la terre est partible pur ceo que quant cest fitz ad issue plurores fitz adonques il est destre parted. Issint icy in nostre case, dimisible est destre demised quant il covient estre demised per copy de court roll. Et pur ceo quant il vient en maines le segnior, ore est destre dimisible per copy. <ore>^d Et pur ceo que a cest temps les terres sont en ses maynes il ad lesse eux per fait indent il ad enfreint le prescriptione. Lovelace, si le segnior ust fait feffment in fe sur condition et ad entre pur le condition enfreint, poet le segnior ore lesse ceo per copye? Et tota curia dit que non. Dier, si soit segnior et tenant per homage auncestrell, et le tenant fist feffment in fe sur condition, ore le feffe ne poet aver le voucher etc. mes <si>ⁱ launcient tenant entre pur le condition enfreint, nest le garrante ore revive? Verament il serroit. Lovelace, si lesse pur terme de vie fist feffment in fe sur condition et puis entre pur le condition enfreint, uncore ceo est un forfeiture: quod curia concessit.

---

[1] *Word om.*

continues in possession for a period of ten years, and afterwards surrenders his term and then takes it by copy of court roll through the hands of the steward, according to the custom. The question was, whether this is now copyhold, or not. And this case was moved by *Lovelace*. HARPER said (DYER being then in the Star Chamber) that it was no longer copyhold, because copyhold must be customary land held of such and such a manor, demised and demisable from time immemorial by copy of court roll; that is the common [mode of] prescription. Now, when the queen leased it by deed for twenty-one years, one of the articles of the prescription failed, because during the time when the lessee had it it was not demisable by copy of court roll. However, if the lord kept it in in his hands for a period of twenty years, although it was not demised, it was nevertheless demisable at any time he wished, and therefore (he said) that agreed well with the prescription. But in the case at bar it was neither demised by copy of court roll nor demisable, and so etc.: which MANWOOD granted. *Bendlowes* said he thought that the lease for twenty-one years was void, inasmuch as the lease was not made to the old tenant; for he said that he had seen in the past that where a copyholder forfeited his copyhold, and the lord from whom it was held leased it to someone else, and the old tenant ousted him, the lessee was without remedy. HARPER and MANWOOD: if so, it was according to the custom of that place, for otherwise it is clearly not so. MANWOOD said that if someone leases his seigniory for years, or at will, and a copyholder who holds of it does an act whereby his copyhold is forfeited, and the lessee at will or for term of years leases it by indenture, it is a question whether the lord may demise it by copy of court roll when it comes back into his hands. HARPER et MANWOOD said that it was a common usage when any copyhold comes into the lord's hands to lease it by indenture, and then the tenure is changed. (The rest of this case is on the following page.)

… The copyhold case was now stated to DYER. And he thought that after the surrender this land may be taken back by copy of court roll. For he said that even if the lord keeps it in his hands after the forfeiture for a period of ten years, he may still give it by copy perfectly well. HARPER and MANWOOD said (as they did the other day) that if the lord retains it in his hands it is still demisable by copy of court roll, albeit it was not demised; but when he leases it by indenture for twenty-one years it is neither demised nor (at that time) demisable by copy. DYER: the prescription for lands in gavelkind is that they are 'parted and partible' (*partitae et partibiles*) according to the custom; but suppose a tenant in gavelkind has issue only one son, and dies, and the son lives for fifty or sixty years, the land is not now *partita* or *partibilis*, and yet if [the son] has four children (*issues*) it is clear that all his sons shall have it according to the custom, even though the prescription failed. He said that this word *partibilis* is a word of right, and *partitum* a word of possession, just as *debet* and *solet* are. HARPER: *partibilis* is nothing other than that it is to be parted when it must be parted, and so even if such a tenant in gavelkind has issue only one son, the land is still partible, because when that son has issue several sons it is then to be parted. Likewise, here in our case, demisable means that it is to be demised when it must be demised by copy of court roll. Therefore, when it comes into the lord's hands, it is now demisable by copy. And because, while the lands are in his hands, he leased them by deed indented, he has broken the prescription. *Lovelace*: if the lord had made a feoffment in fee upon condition, and entered for breach of the condition, could the lord now lease it by copy? The whole court said, no. DYER: if there are a lord and tenant by homage ancestral, and the tenant makes a feoffment in fee upon condition, the feoffee cannot now have the voucher; but if the old tenant entered for breach of the condition, is not the warranty now revived? Truly, it ought to be. *Lovelace*: if a lessee for term of life makes a feoffment in fee upon condition, and then enters for breach of the condition, that is a forfeiture: which the court granted.

[74]

AB, fo. 57v (264v).

<Copiholde.>s

Nota il fuit agre per le court anno 17 Regine Eliz. que si copiholder dun estate de inheritauns accept un leas pur vie ou pur ans del segnior del mannour, ceo est un extinguishment de son copiholde a toutz joures. Mesme la ley est sil prist leas de tout le mannour ...

<Nota que il fuit adjudge in le chauncerie in temps cesti roigne que un copiholder avoit issue fitz et file per un venter et fitz per auter venter et morust seisie, et puis leigne fitz enter et prist les profites et devant admittauns morust, uncore fuit adjudge que il serroit possessio fratris, et le file inheritera come heire a luy. Quere sil poet surrender devant admittauns, semble que non.>a

<Nota quod dicitur que si parcels del mannour soient grant ouster per un copye [et le]1 copiholder fait wast in parcell que il forfeitera tout etc. Vies 22 Ass. [*blank*] [le] roy grant divers fraunchises a un in un mesme patent, et le grantee [mis]use et issint forfeit un, uncore il avera lauters. {Et ceo fuit le case dun Horewoode et Ann Skegnes.}>a

[75]

AB, fo. 268 (magenta ink) (Litt., fo. 21).

Issint fuit tenus in le case de seniori puero anno 17 Eliz. in banke le roy, ou estate fuit conveie al pier pur vie, le remainder seniori puero, <sil>d (si le case nust estre auter) que si le pier puis avoit issue file eigne et fitz puisne uncore le fitz inheritera car le fitz est pluis digne, car la ilz agreeont que cest parol puer poit server pur ambideux sexes, mes uncore la pur auters causes judgment fuit done envers le fitz.

[76]

AB, fo. 271 (magenta ink) (Litt., fo. 23).

Mes nota per Babb. 7 H. 6, 11b, si enfaunt sout marie in le vie son auncestor infra annos nubiles, et le fem devie, leire esteant impubes, le segnior avera le mariage de luy. Et uncore la ne fuit ascun disagrement. Mes fuit agre in Giles case anno 18

---

[1] *Words rubbed away in outer corner.*

[3] Cit. in J. Kitchin, *Jurisdictions* (1656 ed.), p. 160, as Horewood and 'Stegnes'. This refers to Chancery case.
[4] See below, p. 40, no. 87, and the note there.
[5] See below, p. 63, no. 113, and the note there.
[6] YB Mich. 7 Hen. VI, fo. 10, pl. 36, at fo. 11, *per* Babington Att.-Gen.

74. ANON.

1575.

Copyhold.

Note that it was agreed by the court in the year 17 Eliz. that if a copyholder of an estate of inheritance accepts a lease for life, or for years, from the lord of the manor, that is an extinguishment of his copyhold for ever. The law is the same if he takes a lease of the whole manor ...

{Note that it was adjudged in the Chancery in the time of the present queen that where a copyholder had issue a son and a daughter by one wife and a son by another wife, and died seised, and then the elder son entered and took the profits but died before admittance, there will be *possessio fratris*[1] and the daughter will inherit as his heir. Query whether he may surrender before admittance: it seems not.

Note that it is said that if several parcels of a manor are granted over by one copy, and the copyholder commits waste in one parcel, he shall forfeit all of them. (See 22 Ass.:[2] the king grants various franchises to someone in one same patent, and the grantee misuses and therefore forfeits one of them, he shall still have the others.) This was the case of one Horewoode and Ann Skegnes.[3]}

75. HUMPHRESTON'S CASE[4]

King's Bench. 1575.

So it was held in the case of *seniori puero* in the year 17 Eliz. in the King's Bench, where an estate was conveyed to a father for life, remainder to his elder child (*seniori puero*), that (had the case not been otherwise) if the father had issue a firstborn daughter and a later son, the son would still inherit, for the son is worthier. For they agreed there that this word *puer* may serve for both sexes. Nevertheless, for other causes, judgment was there given against the son.

76. GYLES v. COLSHILL[5]

Common Pleas, 1576.

Litt., tit. 'Fee taile'.

Note by Babington, in 7 Hen. VI, fo. 11v,[6] that if an infant is married *infra annos nubiles* in the lifetime of his ancestor, and the wife dies, the heir being still under marriageable age (*impubes*), the lord shall have his marriage, even though there was no disagreement [to the marriage]. But it was agreed in Gyles's case, in the year 18

---

[1] I.e. *possessio fratris in feodo simplici facit sororem esse heredem* ('a brother's possession in fee simple will cause a sister to be heir', rather than a brother of the half blood): Litt., s. 8. Cf. *Anon.* (1574) Dal. 110. The same point was decided by the Common Pleas in *Brown's Case* (1581) 4 Co. Rep. 22, identifiable as *Holme* v. *Taylor* (1581) vol. ii, p. 176.

[2] 22 Edw. III, Lib. Ass., pl. 34.

36   REPORTS FROM COKE'S NOTEBOOKS

Eliz. que si le garden luy marie infra annos nubiles et le fem morust devant lage de consent <dubitabatur>^d le segnior navera le mariage arere. Mes dubitavit in case le roy.

[77]

AB, fo. 55v (272v).

<Garde.>^s

20[1] Eliz. fuit agre in le common banke per tout le court que si home face feffment in fe al use de son fem durante viduitate sua, et puis al use de ses droit heires, que si in cest case le baron morust son issue <ne>^d serra in gard, car il nad[2] ceo come un remainder <et nemy>^d <mes>ⁱ come un revercion. Mes si cestui que use in fe soit et puis ses feffes sauns son request font feffment in fe al auters al use del cestui que use et sa fem pur vie et puis al use de ces heires, in cest case si le baron morust son issue serra in gard. Le reason de cest diversite est quant home est seisie des terres in fe simple in [qu]e[3] il nad ascun use, come la fuit agre, donques [qu]ant in le primer case il fait feffment al use dun auter pur vie [et p]uis al use de ses droit heires, cest un novell use … H. 27 H. 8. rott. 420.

[78]

AB, fo. 65 (280).

<Vernons case anno 14 Eliz.>^a

Un formedone fuit port per Vernon envers Sir H. Stanley, R. Manvers esquier et auters, et lour femes, al petit cape lour barons fesoient defaut, lour femes prieront destre resceive, le demandant counterplead ceo que les barons et lour fems <ont>^d avoient levie un fine de mesmes les terres pendant le brefe, sur quel les tenants demurreront in ley. Et fuit dit pur le demandant que nul resceit fuit per le common ley, mes lestatute de W. 2, cap. 3, provide in tiel manner, quod si vir absentaverit se et noluerit jus uxoris sue defendere etc. admittat uxor. Et sur ceo fuit dit que intant que per le fine tout le droit que les fems avoient fuit done hors de eux et nul droit remaine in luy, ideo le fem ne poet estre resceive per lestatut ad defendendum jus suum. Et sur ceo fuit le livre in 22 Ass. 13 cite, que si le baron et fem alien pendant le bref que la fem ne serra resceive. Mes 12 Ass. 41 et 34 E. 3 [*blank*] sont enconter ceo, pur ceo que la un droit remaine en la fem que el poit defender per lestatute. Et issint est le livre in 19 E. 3. <Dier fol. 315b.>^a <Dier 17 Eliz. 341.>^{a 4}

---

[1] *Unclear; perhaps altered from or to* 19.   [2] *Altered from* ad.
[3] *From here to the end some letters and words missing at foot of page.*
[4] *Added in the top margin.*

---

[6] 22 Edw. III, Lib. Ass., pl. 13.   [7] 12 Edw. III, Lib. Ass., pl. 41; 34 Edw. III, Lib. Ass., pl. 7.
[8] Hil. 19 Edw. III, Fitz. Abr., *Resceit*, pl. 113.   [9] Dyer's reports of the same case.

Eliz., that if the guardian marries him off *infra annos nubiles*, and the wife dies before reaching the age of consent, the lord shall not have the marriage again. But this was doubted in the case of the king.

77. ANON.

Common Pleas, 1577/78.

Wardship.

In 20[1] Eliz. it was agreed in the Common Bench by the whole court that if someone makes a feoffment in fee to the use of his wife during her widowhood, and then to the use of his right heirs, and the husband dies, his issue shall[2] be in ward, for he has it [not] as a remainder [but][3] as a reversion. But if there is a cestui que use in fee, and then (without his request) his feoffees make a feoffment in fee to others, to the use of the cestui que use and his wife for life, and to the use of his heirs, in this case if the husband dies his issue shall be in ward. The reason for this distinction, as was there agreed, is that when someone is seised of lands in fee simple in which he has no use, and he makes a feoffment to the use of another for life, and then to the use of his right heirs, this is a new use ... Hil. 27 Hen. VIII, roll 420.[4]

78. VERNON'S CASE[5]

Common Pleas, 1572.

Vernon's case, anno 14 Eliz.

A formedon was brought by Vernon against Sir Henry Stanley, [John Manners], esquire, and others, and their wives; at the petit *cape* their husbands made default and their wives prayed to be received; the demandant counterpleaded this, because the husbands and their wives had levied a fine of the same lands while the writ was pending; and thereupon the tenants demurred in law. For the demandant, it was said that receipt was by the common law, but the statute of Westminster II, c. 3, provided for it in this way: if the husband should absent himself and not defend his wife's right, the wife shall be admitted ('si vir absentaverit se et noluerit jus uxoris suae defendere ... admittat uxor'). Thereupon it was said that since by the fine all the right which the wives had was given away by them, and no right remained in them, a wife cannot be received under the statute 'to defend her right'. For this the book in 22 Ass. 13 was cited,[6] that if the husband and wife alienate pending the writ, the wife shall not be received. But 12 Ass. 41 and 34 Edw. III[7] are against this, because in that case a right remains in the wife which she may defend under the statute. And so is the book in 19 Edw. III.[8] {Dyer, fo. 315v; Dyer, 17 Eliz., fo. 341.[9]}

---

[1] Reading unclear; perhaps 19.   [2] Coke altered a negative in this sentence.
[3] Altered from 'and not'.   [4] *Abbot of Bury* v. *Bokenham* (1536) CP 40/1088, m. 420; Dyer 76; Benl. 16.
[5] See p. 141, below, no. 258, and the note there. On the following page of the MS. is a full summary of *Chapman's Case*, evidently based on *Chapman* v. *Dalton* (1564) Plowd. 284. This is the case referred to in *AA*, fo. 78 (127) ('Vide Chapmans case in mes notes ...').

[79]

AB, fo. 66v (281v). *Ff*, fo. 165v. *Gg*, fo. 22v.

Treis jointenants font done in taile, le remainder in taile al un des donours. Meade semble le remainder voide.

Manwood et Harper, justices. Si 2 jointenantes sont et lun fait leas pur vie et graunt le revercion a son compaignon, ceo fuit bone: quod fuit concessum.

Manwood. Si 2 jointenantes sont dun terme et lun grant son part a son compaignon per fait, cest bone sauns question, mes per parol poet estre question.

Et nota que le case fuit que le primer done in taile fuit done in especial taile al baron et fem et un des donees morust sauns issue, celuy que survesquist esteant tenant in taile apres possibilitie de issue extinct fist feffment in fe, un estraunge port brefe dentre in le post envers le feffe, que vouche le tenant in taile apres possibilitie, que vouch le comon crier, et cest recoverie fuit anno 34 H. 8. Et si cest recoverie fuit holpen per lestatute de 32 H. 8?

Dier et Manwood disoient que recoverie vers tenant pur vie come tenant in le precipe, ceo esteant un barre del remainder al comen ley, fuit remedie per lestatute de 32 H. 8. Mes recoverie vers tenant pur vie come vouchee fuit barre al remainder tanque lestatute de 14 Eliz.

Nota fuit agre que si un evesque devant lestatute de 13 fist leas pur 2 ans, et puis lestatute il fist leas pur xxj ans a commencer maintenant, cest bone leas coment que lauter continue.

Si 2 jointenantes sont dun office et lun fuit utlage de felonie, rien serra forfeit, mes si lun fait misfesauns doffice tout loffice est forfeit.

[80]

AB, fo. 67v (282v). Abridged in *Ff*, fo. 166; *Gg*, fo. 23v. *Lb*, fo. 5v.

Nota cest case fuit adjudge in temps mesme cesti roigne que <Beacher>[i] labbe de <Rochester>[d] Colchestre fuist seisie de certaine terres in fe et commit treason et puis fist leas pur 80 ans et puis in le Chauncerie surrender le abbathie et toutz ses possessions al roy et puis fuit attaint de haut treason et execute, et trove fuit per office que il fesoit le dit leas puis le treason perpetrate. Et uncore fuit adjudge que le leas fuit bone et ne serra avoide, car le roy fuit eins del estate accept per le surrender et issint desouth le leas, et ideo lattaindre ne puit aver relation. Et cest case fuit cite per Fettiplace, M. anno 18 Eliz. in Leschequer Chamber arguendo in le counte de Arundels case. Et nota que Anderson dit que le case fuit come jeo ay icy note et que il fuit accouncell ove le case.

---

[4] Seemingly unrelated to the foregoing. [5] 13 Eliz., c. 10, s. 3.
[6] This is followed on fos. 281v–282 by some cases of 10 and 11 Eliz.
[7] See below, p. 70, no. 116 (1577), and the note there.
[8] Cit. without date in Co. Uses, fo. 148v ('Vide le abbe de Colchesters case'). Cit. in 4 Leon. 141 and Moo. 319 as 13 Eliz., and in Lane 33 (1608) as 9 Eliz.
[9] John Beche or Beach, *alias* Marshall, D.D. (Oxon.), executed in 1539.
[10] Edmund Anderson was still a bencher of the Inner Temple; created serjeant in 1577.

79. ANON.[1]

Common Pleas, 1575.

Three joint tenants make a gift in tail, the remainder in tail to one of the donors. *Mead* thought the remainder void.

MANWOOD and HARPER JJ. If there are two joint tenants, and one of them makes a lease for life and grants the reversion to his companion, this is good: which was conceded.

MANWOOD. If there are two joint tenants of a term, and one of them grants his share to his companion by deed, this is good without question; but if the grant is by parol it is questionable.

Note that the case was that the first gift in tail was given in special tail to a husband and wife, and one of the donees died without issue; the one who survived, being tenant in tail after possibility of issue extinct, made a feoffment in fee; a stranger brought a writ of entry in the *post* against the feoffee, who vouched the tenant in tail after possibility, who vouched the common crier; and this recovery was in the year 34 Hen. VIII. Is this recovery helped by the statute of 32 Hen. VIII?[2]

DYER [C.J.] and MANWOOD said that a recovery against a tenant for life (as tenant to the *praecipe*) being a bar to the remainder at common law was remedied by the statute of 32 Hen. VIII. But a recovery against a tenant for life as vouchee barred the remainder until the statute of 14 Eliz.[3]

([4]Note that it was agreed that if a bishop, before the statute of 13 Eliz.,[5] made a lease for two years, and after the statute made a lease for twenty-one years to begin at once, this is a good lease even though the other continues.)

If there are two joint tenants of an office, and one of them is outlawed for felony, nothing shall be forfeited; but if one of them commits misfeasance in the office, the whole office is forfeited.[6]

80. EARL OF ARUNDEL v. LANGAR[7]

Exch. Ch., Mich. 1576, referring to an earlier anonymous case.

Note that this case was adjudged in the time of this same queen:[8] Beche, the abbot of Colchester,[9] was seised of certain lands in fee, and committed treason, and then he made a lease for eighty years; afterwards in the Chancery he surrendered the abbey and all its possessions to the king; then he was attainted of high treason and executed; and it was found by office that he made the said lease after the treason was perpetrated. It was nevertheless adjudged that the lease was good and may not be avoided, for the king was in of the estate accepted by the surrender, and therefore beneath the lease, and therefore the attainder cannot have relation. This case was cited by *Fetiplace* in Michaelmas term 18 Eliz., in the Exchequer Chamber, while arguing in the earl of Arundel's case. And note that *Anderson*[10] said the case was as I have here noted it, and that he was of counsel in the case.

---

[1] Probably the case reported in Dyer's notebook, 110 Selden Soc. 322, pl. 411 (Hil. 1575).
[2] 32 Hen. VIII, c. 31.   [3] 13 Eliz., c. 10; above, p. 26.

Citation by Coke in 1584

BL MS. Harley 4562, fo. 21

... *Cooke* de Inner Temple ... dit que fuit adjudge 26 H. 8 que abby de Colchester comitt treason et puis fist lease pur 20 ans, et puis surrender le abby terres al roye, et apres fuit attaint de treason, et coment per lattainder le title accrewe al roye del temps le treason comitte issint que le lease serroit voide, uncore fuit adjudge que per reason que roy ad fait acceptance del surrender le dit abbott que ceo ne defeate le lease nec lattainder navera relation mes que roy serra eins semper per le surrender. Et dit apres que fuit un Andrewes case 22 Eliz.

[81]

AB, fo. 67v (282v). *Lb*, fo. 5v.

Nota auxi cest case fuit agre pur ley in temps mesme cesti roigne circa 14 Eliz. come Benlos report in largument del case del appropriation 18 Eliz. que, levesque de Norwich esteant patron dun eglise, le eglise devient voide, et le roygne present un clark a ceo et levesque nient conusant son droit luy admitte et institute etc. Et fuit agre que il ad conclude luy mesme, et fuit sauns remedie. Come si un abbot admitte un ad un corody il lye le meason a toutz joures. 2 H. 4, 8, et 3 H. 4, 15, et 24 E. 3, 33 et 72.

[82]

AB, fo. 68 (283). Also in *Ff*, fo. 166; *Gg*, fos. 23v–24.

Bradstockes case fuit move, come Popham arguendo in le counte de Arundels [case] disoit, que home fist leas pur ans sur condition que si le lesse ferra tiel acte per que le terme serra forfeit que donques le terme cessera. Et puis Bradstocke committe felonie, et devant ascun inditement etc. il avoit son pardon. Et fuit tenus que le condition fuit infreint, car Bradstocke avoit fait tiel act que purroit estre cause del forfeture, et coment que il ne fuit de ceo convicte ne attainte uncore entant que ceo fuit forsque le proceding del ley et il ad fait le tort et committe le cause et riens remain al execution forsque acte in ley etc.

[83]

AB, fo. 68 (283). *Ff*, fo. 166. *Gg*, fo. 24. *Lb*, fo. 5v.

Nota que cest case fuit agree pur ley in le common banke circa annum 15 Eliz. que home fist sa fem son executrix et devise a luy divers biens et morust, le fem esteant

---

[4] Perhaps YB Pas. 3 Hen. IV, fo. 15, pl. 8.
[5] *R. v. Abbot of St Oswald's* (1350) YB Mich. 24 Edw. III, fo. 33, pl. 29, and fo. 72, pl. 84.
[6] Differently reported in 3 Leo. 86 as the *Earl of Arundel and Bradstocks Case* (Mich. 1575), perhaps confusing the two cases.
[7] See above, p. 37, no. 80; p. 70, no. 116.

Citation by Coke in 1584

Morris v. *Francklen* (Trin. 26 Eliz.)

... *Coke* of the Inner Temple said it was adjudged in 26 Hen. VIII,[1] where the abbot of Colchester committed treason, and afterwards made a lease for twenty years, and then surrendered the abbey lands to the king, and afterwards was attainted of treason, that although by the attainder the title accrued to the king from the time of the treason committed, so that the lease should have been void, nevertheless because the king accepted the surrender from the said abbot it did not defeat the lease, and the attainder shall not have relation, but the king shall be in always through the surrender. And he said afterwards that this was one Andrewes' case in 22 Eliz.

81. BISHOP OF NORWICH'S CASE (*c.* 1572)

Common Pleas, *c.* 1572 (cited in the Common Pleas, 1576).

Note also that this case was agreed as law in the time of this same queen, around 14 Eliz., as *Bendlowes* reported in arguing the case in 18 Eliz. concerning the appropriation:[2] the bishop of Norwich being patron of a church, the church became vacant, the queen presented a clerk to it, and the bishop (being unaware of his right) admitted and instituted him. And it was agreed that he had estopped himself, and was without remedy. Likewise, if an abbot admits someone to have a corrody, he binds the house for ever. 2 Hen. IV, fo. 8;[3] 3 Hen. IV, fo. 15;[4] and 24 Edw. III, fos. 33 and 72.[5]

82. BRADSTOCK'S CASE[6]

King's Bench, Mich. 1575 (cited in the *Earl of Arundel's Case*, 1576).

Bradstock's case was moved, as *Popham* said in argument in the earl of Arundel's case,[7] as follows: someone made a lease for years upon condition that if the lessee did such an act whereby the term would be forfeited, the term should thereupon cease; then Bradstock committed a felony, but before any indictment [or appeal] he had his pardon. And it was held that the condition was broken, for Bradstock had done such an act as could be a cause of forfeiture; and although he was not convicted or attainted of it, nevertheless that was only a legal proceeding, whereas he had done the wrong and committed the cause, and nothing remained to the execution except an act in law.

83. ANON.

Common Pleas, *c.* 1573.

Note that this case was agreed to be law in the Common Bench around the year 15 Eliz.: a man made his wife his executrix, devised to her various goods, and died; the

---

[1] Clearly an error.
[2] Probably the case of the impropriated rectory of Bedwyn, Wilts. (1576) Dyer 350.
[3] YB Mich. 2 Hen. IV, fo. 8, pl. 38.

possesse des biens prist baron, et le baron morust, les executors le baron prist les biens, et le fem port brefe de detinue. Et fuit agre (come jeo oye) que la fem recovera les biens, car tanque el ad fait son election el ad les biens come executrix et nemi come devisee.

[84]

AB, fo. 68 (283).

Putnammes case in temps mesme cesti roigne fuit tiel in effecte. Home fist feffment in fe fearme sur condition que si le rent fuit arrere que donques le feffor reentra, et un indenture de bargaine et sale fuit al primes fait inter le feffour et feffee in que fuit covenant que le dit feffement ove le reservation et condition serroit fait ut supra, et in mesme lendenture la fuit un generall covenant, scilicet que toutz assurraunces quecumque enapres destre faitz serroient al uses et intentz comprises in <mesmes>[d] lendentures. Et puis le feffor levie un fine al feffe sur conusans de droit etc. Et fuit adjudge (come fuit dit per les justices in Andrewes case) que neque le rent neque le condition fuit extincte per le fine, per le reason del generall covenant que toutz assurraunces serroient a mesmes les uses. Mes si le feffour ust levie fine generalment, le rent et le condition avoient estre extincte.

[85]

AB, fo. 68 (283). *Ff*, fo. 166. *Gg*, fo. 24.

Nota fuit adjudge, come Anderson dit, que ou tenant in taile morust son issue esteant del age de un an, et le segnior seisist le gard et lessa ceo pur xx ans rendant rent, et puis <vient>[d] leire vient al pleine age et fist leasse pur xxj ans rendant autiel rent, et cest terre ne avoiet estre use destre demise mes toutz foitz remaine in le possession launcestre leire forsque solement durant le garde. Et fuit adjudge, come il dit, que le leasse pur xxj ans ne fuit deins le compasse del estatute de 32 H. 8, car le generall parolls (scilicet, most commonly letten to fearme) serra intend des lesses faitz per le tenant in taile ou per ascun de les auncestres et nemi per gardens <est>[d] et similia: quod nota bene.

[86]

AB, fo. 68v (283v).

<Radcliffes case.>[s]

Le roy H. 8 fist done al counte de Sussex et Mary sa fem et a les heires males del

---

[2] Probably either *Androwes* v. *Blunt* (1573) below, p. 52, no. 101; or *Lord Cromwell* v. *Androwes* (1577) above, p. 4, no. 2.
[3] 32 Hen. VIII, c. 28. [4] Cf. Co. Litt. 44b.
[5] Robert Radcliffe (d. 1542), earl of Sussex, and his third wife Mary (d. 1557), daughter of Sir John Arundell of Lanherne, whom he married in 1537. Their son John was the earl's youngest son.

woman, being possessed of the goods, remarried; the [second] husband died, and the husband's executors took the goods; and the woman brought a writ of detinue. And it was agreed (as I heard) that the woman recovered the goods, for until she has made her election she has the goods as executrix and not as devisee.

84. PUTTENHAM v. DUNCOMBE[1]

Court of Wards, Hil. 1558 (cited in the 1570s).

Puttenham's case, in the time of this same queen, was in effect as follows. Someone made a feoffment in fee-farm upon condition that if the rent was in arrear, the feoffor could re-enter; an indenture of bargain and sale had already been made between the feoffor and feoffee, in which it was covenanted that the said feoffment should be made with the reservation and condition as above, and in the same indenture there was a general covenant, namely that all assurances whatsoever to be made thereafter should be to the uses and intents comprised in the indentures. Afterwards the feoffor levied a fine to the feoffee *sur conusans de droit etc.* And it was adjudged (as was said by the justices in Androwes's case[2]) that neither the rent nor the condition was extinguished by the fine, by reason of the general covenant that all assurances should be to the same uses. If, however, the feoffor had levied a fine generally, the rent and the condition would have been extinguished.

85. ANON.

Common Pleas, temp. Eliz.

Note that it was adjudged, as *Anderson* said, that where a tenant in tail dies, his issue being one year old, and the lord seizes the wardship and leases it for twenty years rendering rent, and then the heir reaches full age and makes a lease for twenty-one years rendering the like rent, and this land had not been accustomed to be demised but had always remained in the possession of the heir's ancestor except during the wardship: it was adjudged (as he said) that the lease for twenty-one years was not within the compass of the statute of 32 Hen. VIII,[3] for the general words 'most commonly letten to farm' are to be understood of leases made by the tenant in tail, or by any of his ancestors, and not by guardians and the like.[4] Note that well.

86. RADCLIFFE'S CASE

Court of Wards, temp. Eliz.

Radcliffe's case.

King Henry VIII made a gift to the earl of Sussex and Mary his wife,[5] and to the heirs

---

[1] Differently reported in Dyer 157 (Hil. 1558); 1 And. 18 (dated 1556); cit. from Dyer in 2 Co. Rep. 73.

corps del counte, le counte morust, et puis le countes morust ayant issue enter eux Sir John Radcliffe, chivaler, que fuit fait chivaler in le vie son pier, et tout cest matter trove per office, et que le dit Sir John Radcliffe, chivaler, fuit del age de 18 ans. Et quant le dit Sir John Radcliffe vient al plein age il pria son livery, et le court de gardes require de luy pur le roygne le value de son mariage. Et il per son councell dit que devant le title del gardshipp accrue, scilicet in temps le roy E. 6 (et nota que le dit countes morust in temps le roigne Marye) il fuit fait chivaler. Et sur ceo, sur graunde deliberation, il fuit discharge. Et nota les parols del statut de Magna Carta cap. 4 etc. Mes vide Brooke, tit. Gard, 72, sur le case in 15 E. 4, 10, car la un heire fuit un chivaler et uncore fuit in gard, et la Brooke prist difference que sil soit fait chivaler in le vie launcestre il serra in gard, mes auterment sil soit fait chivaler puis que il soit in gard. Et sic accidit, come Brooke dit, in le case de Sir Anthonie Browne, que fuit fait chivaler in le vie son pere in temps E. 6. <Vide Sir Drue Druryes case in mes reportes.>[a]

[87]

AB, fo. 69r-v (284r-v). *Ff*, fos. 166v–167v. *Gg*, fos. 24v–26. *V*, fos. 25–26.

<Le case del seniori puero. Salopia.>[s]

17 Eliz. in termino Pasche in banke le roy cest case fuit argue per les justices. William Humfreson esteant seisie del manour de Humfreson in fe et issint seisie anno 28 H. 8 J. S. et J. N. recoveront vers luy le dit mannour per brefe dentre in le post, et seisin ewe accordant, et cest recoverie fuit al entent que les recoverores ferront estate al W. H. et E. sa fem pur lour vies, le remainder seniori puero le dit W. H. in taile, le remainder al dit W. H. in taile, le remainder ouster al S. in taile, et puis les recoverors in mesme lan fesoient lestates accordant al entent avandit, et puis 2 E. 6 fuit agre parenter le dit Humfreson et Kindersly per indentures que estate serra fait al use de Humfreson et sa feme pur lour vies, le remainder senioris prolis le dit H., vocati in Englishe a childe, le remainder in taile a le dit K. etc., et monstre coment per advisement de K. fine fuit levie per le dit H. al uses avandit, per force de quel ilz fueront seisie etc. et puis E. sa fem morust, et puis [il][1] prist auter fem et ad issue Frances Humfreson sa primogenite file et William Humfreson son primogenite fitz,

[1] el.

Coke's Dyer (Holkham 8014), at fo. 308 ('Vide in case de seniori puero in mes reportes fol. 69. Pasch. 17 Eliz.'); Co. Uses, fos. 152v ('17 Eliz. Humfreson case'), 153 ('Le case de seniori puero'); cit. by Coke in *Gibbons* v. *Warner* (1595) below, p. 43. Differently reported in Dyer 337 (Trin. 1574, Pas. 1575); Moo. 103, cit. record as Pas. 17 Eliz.; 1 And. 40 (dated Mich. 1570); 2 Leon. 216 (Pas. 1574); Owen 64, sub nom. *Lane* v. *Coups*; Moo. 103; Benl. 195; *Gg*, fo. 24v (Mich. 17 Eliz.); BL MS. Harley 1699, fos. 112–117, sub nom. *Lund* v. *Cooper* (1583); MS. Harley 6811, fos. 178–182; MS. Harg. 4, fos. 63v–70; MS. Lansd. 1062, fos. 65v–71; MS. Lansd. 1104, fos. 61–65v; MS. Add. 35941, fos. 219v–220v; IT MS. Petyt 511.12, fos. 233–239v (Hil. 1575); HLS MS. 200.1 (1180.1), fos. 63v, 343–344v. Cf. KB 27/1244, m. 439d (Hil. 1573): Thomas Cowper v. John Lane; trespass *quare clausum fregit* at Stocking and Newlands in Humphreston, Salop.; *nihil dicit*; judgment by default; writ of inquiry; KB 27/1254, m. 295d (Trin. 1575): Thomas Lane esq. v. John Cowper and Ralph Goodhead (note the reversed forenames); replevin; the sheriff returns the cattle eloigned; no more is entered.

[6] In Donington, Salop.

male of the body of the earl; the earl died, and then the countess died, having issue between them Sir John Radcliffe, knight, who was knighted in his father's lifetime; and all this matter was found by office, and that the said Sir John Radcliffe, knight, was aged eighteen years. When the said Sir John Radcliffe came to full age he prayed his livery, and the Court of Wards required from him the value of his marriage for the queen. But he said, through his counsel, that he was knighted before the title to the wardship accrued, namely in the time of King Edward VI. And note that the said countess died in the time of Queen Mary. Thereupon, after great deliberation, he was discharged. Note the words of the statute of Magna Carta, c. [3].[1] But see Brooke, tit. *Garde*, 72, upon the case in 15 Edw. IV, fo. 10,[2] for there an heir was a knight and was nevertheless in ward, and Brooke there made the distinction that if he is knighted in the lifetime of his ancestor he shall be in ward, but it is otherwise if he is knighted after he is in ward. And so it happened, as Brooke said, in the case of Sir Anthony Browne, who was knighted in his father's lifetime in the time of Edward VI.[3] {See Sir Drew Drury's case in my reports.[4]}

87. LANE v. COWPER: HUMPHRESTON'S CASE[5]

King's Bench, Pas. 1575.

The case of *seniori puero*. Shropshire.

In Easter term 17 Eliz. in the King's Bench this case was argued by the justices. William Humphreston was seised of the manor of Humphreston[6] in fee, and in the year 28 Hen. VIII (he being so seised) John Style and John Noke recovered the said manor against him by writ of entry in the *post*, and seisin was had accordingly; and this recovery was to the intent that the recoverors should make an estate to William Humphreston and Eleanor his wife for their lives, remainder to the eldest child (*seniori puero*) of the said William Humphreston in tail, remainder to the said William Humphreston in tail, remainder over to S. in tail; then the recoverors in the same year made estates according to the aforesaid intent; and then, in 2 Edw. VI, it was agreed between the said Humphreston and one Kindersley, by indentures, that an estate should be made to the use of Humphreston and his wife for their lives, remainder to [the use of] the eldest child (*senioris prolis*) of the said Humphreston, called in English 'a child', remainder in tail to the said Kindersley, and so forth; and he showed how, by the advisement of Kindersley, a fine was levied by the said Humphreston to the aforesaid uses, by virtue whereof they were seised [to those uses]; then Eleanor his wife died, and he afterwards took another wife and had issue Frances Humphreston, his firstborn daughter, and William Humphreston, his firstborn son

---

[1] Magna Carta, c. 3 (tr.): '… if he is knighted while under age, the land shall nevertheless remain in the wardship of his lords until [the age of twenty-one].'
[2] *Skrene's Case* (1475) YB Mich. 15 Edw. IV, fo. 10, pl. 16; Bro. Abr., *Garde*, pl. 72.
[3] Anthony Browne (1528–92), afterwards Viscount Montagu, was created knight of the Bath at the coronation of Edward VI in 1547, a year before his father's death.
[4] 6 Co. Rep. 73 (Court of Wards, 1607).
[5] Noted above, p. 24, no. 46; p. 35, no. 75; below, p. 101, no. 173; p. 114, no. 206; p. 122, no. 215; p. 129, no. 230; p. 137, no. 249. Cit. in *AB*, fo. 451 ('17 El. Humphrestons case, seniori puero, grammarians');

esteant son 2 childe, et puis Humfreson le pier morust, Fraunces le file enter, le fitz deins age [enter][1] sur luy et fist leas envers T. Cooper sauns fait et sauns ascun rent reserve, et un per commaundement del file enter et le lesse port ejectione firme. Et le defendant plede non culpable, et tout cest matter fuit <port>[d] trove per le verdit.

Et fuit argue per Gawdy, le puisne justice, que le pleintife recovera, mes les auters 2, scilicet Southcote et Wraye, chiefe justice, fueront encounter luy.

Et in cest case divers matters fueront moves. Primerment, le recovery esteant al entent que les recoverors ferra estate arere al Humfreson, a quel use les recoverors serra seisies in le mesme temps? Et fuit agre per eux toutz que in le mesme temps les recoverors sera seisie[2] a lour use demesne, car silz serra seisie al use del H. donques ilz ne unques purront faire estate accordant al entent. Mes Southcote et Wray teignont que les recoverors covient de faire ceo in convenient temps ou auterment, come Wraye dit, un use serra raise al use del cesti vers que le recovery fuit ewe. <In fine vies 9, 10.>[i] Et la ilz agreont que cest parol intent est bon parol de create un use, mes nemi presentment come le case est icy. Et nota que ilz agreont que in cest case il fuit in convenient temps pur ceo que il fuit fait in mesme lan.

2 point, le quel remainder a un que ne fuit in esse fuit bone ou nemi. Et fuit agre que le remainder fuit bone. Et cest differens fuit agre pur ley, que quant un remainder est limitte per un generall nosme ceo est bone coment que il ne soit in esse, mes quant remainder est limit a certain person ou persons per lour proper nosmes ceo est voide silz ne sont in esse al temps, coment que apres ilz deveigne in esse. Et pur ceo si lease pur vie soit fait a J. S., le remainder al maior et cominalte de Islington, et puis tiel corporation est fait, ceo est voide, car il fuit per un certain nosme. Mes remainder primogenito filio est bon car ceo est un generalty et nemy certain. Issint de remainder as droit heires J. S. est bone. Mes sil ne soit ascun J. S. est voide, car il est nosme per son proper nosme. 10 E. 3. Leas pur vie, le remainder a W. son fitz, et al temps il nad fitz, et puis il ad fitz nosme William, et uncore agre que le remainder voide.

Auter matter fuit move que intant que le <fine>[d] 2 fine levie a les ditz uses fueront ove garrante quere si le garrante esteant collaterall barrera le fitz ou nemi? Et semble al Wray, chief justice, que le garrante fuit voide, et son reason fuit pur ceo que il ne attache in le po[ssession][3] [fo. 69v] le conusee in que possession il fuit fait, et pur ceo luy semble que cesti a que use ne unques prendra advantage de tiel garrante. Et resemble ceo al case in 22 Ass., p. 37, et 29 Ass., lou in le primer case le garrante fuit fait al villein et le segnior enter devant que le garrante fuit attache in le possession le villein etc.

Le 4 point fuit le quel un leas fait per un enfant pur ans sauns fait et sauns ascun render soit void ou voidable. Et Gawdy semble que le lease fuit que voidable, car

---

[1] *V.*
[2] *Written twice.*
[3] *V.*

[4] YB Mich. 10 Edw. III, fo. 45, pl. 8; cit. in *Cholmley's Case* (1597) 2 Co. Rep. 50, at fo. 51; below, p. 123, no. 215.
[5] 22 Edw. III, Lib. Ass., pl. 37; 29 Edw. III, Lib. Ass., pl. 34.

(being his second child); then Humphreston the father died, Frances the daughter entered, and the son (being under age) entered upon her and made a lease to T. Cooper without deed, and without any rent reserved; someone by command of the daughter entered, and the lessee brought ejectment. The defendant pleaded Not Guilty, and all this matter was found by the verdict.

It was argued by GAWDY, the puisne justice, that the plaintiff should recover; but the other two, namely SOUTHCOTE and WRAY C.J., were against him. And in this case various matters were moved.

First, the recovery being to the intent that the recoverors should make an estate back to Humphreston, to whose use were the recoverors seised in the meantime? It was agreed by them all that in the meantime the recoverors should be seised to their own use, for if they were seised to the use of Humphreston they could never make an estate according to the intent. But SOUTHCOTE and WRAY held that the recoverors must do this in a convenient time or else, as WRAY said, a use would be raised to the use of the person against whom the recovery was had. {See 9, 10, in 'Fine'.[1]} And they agreed there that this word 'intent' is a good word to create a use, but not presently (as the case is here).[2] And note that they agreed it was in this case done in a convenient time, because it was done in the same year.

The second point was whether a remainder to someone who was not *in esse* was good, or not.[3] And it was agreed that the remainder was good. And this distinction was agreed to be law: when a remainder is limited to someone by a generic name it is good, even if he is not *in esse*, but when a remainder is limited to a certain person or persons by their proper names it is void if they are not *in esse* at the time, even though they afterwards become *in esse*. Thus if a lease for life is made to John Style, remainder to the mayor and commonalty of Islington, and afterwards such a corporation is made, this is void, for it was limited by a certain name. But a remainder to a firstborn son (*primogenito filio*) is good, for this is a generality and uncertain. Likewise, a remainder to the right heirs of John Style is good – though if there is no John Style it is void – for he is named by his proper name. 10 Edw. III:[4] lease for life, remainder to his son William, and at the time he had no son, though afterwards he had a son named William, and yet it was agreed that the remainder was void.

Another matter was moved: since the second fine levied to the said uses was with warranty, should the warranty (being collateral) bar the son, or not? It seemed to WRAY C.J. that the warranty was void; and his reason was because it did not attach in the possession of the cognisee in whose possession it was made, and therefore it seemed to him that cestui que use could never take advantage of such a warranty. And he likened it to the case in 22 Ass. 37, and 29 Ass.,[5] where in the first case the warranty was made to a villein, and the lord entered before the warranty was attached in the villein's possession.

The fourth point was whether a lease for years made by an infant, without a deed, and without any rent, is void or voidable. GAWDY thought the lease was voidable, for

---

[1] Or 'in the end'. This does not refer to anything in MS. *A*.
[2] See below, p. 114, no. 206, where this is explained.
[3] Cf. below, p. 122, for another version of these arguments.

il dit que cest leas fuit pur son benefitte entant que il fuit a trier son title in cest ejectione firme. Auxi il dit que ascun livres sont agre que enfaunt ad port dum fuit infra etatem dun rent. Et il dit que enfaunt ferra toutz actes queux sont necessarie pur luy, come contracte ou obligation pur manger et boier etc. Et auxi il dit, si leas pur ans soit fait per enfaunt et livery fait in suertie de son terme que ceo nest que voidable, mes les auters 2 fueront enconter luy, car Wraye dit que enfaunt poet faire 2 mannores de actes queux concludra luy et ceux ou tielz a queux il est compellable de faire per la ley ou queux sont pur son benefit et availe, et pur ceo il dit leas pur ans reservant rent est voidable. 12 H. 4. Mesme la ley dun eschaunge. Issint assignement de dower et partition obligeront luy sil soit egall, car il est compellable per la ley.

Le 5 point, le quel le remainder esteant in consideration del ley soit destroy per cest fine levie ou nemi? Et fuit tenus clerement per eux toutz que il ne fuit, car Gawdye dit quant un chose est in le consideration del ley, pur ceo que est nul person in esse de aver cure de ceo mes le ley voet preserve et custodire ceo, come discent in temps del vacation ne noiera le successor pur ceo que le franktenement fuit in consideration del ley, issint discent ne tollera le discent dun enfant ne de fem covert ne de home in prison ne de home ouster le mere, car le ley priviledge lour persones. Et Southcote et Wray concessit. Et Wray dit que dissent durant le possession <le roy>[i] ne noiera leire, car le possession del terre est in consideration del ley. Et auxi il dit, si parson fait leas pur vie et morust, ore le fe est in suspense, [et] si durant le vacation le tenant fait feffment, quant le successor est inducte il poet enter coment que il ne fuit a son disinheritauns al temps, mes le inheritauns fuit in consideration del ley.

Le[1] 6 point fuit le quel puer poet estre entende cibien pur male come pur le female. Et fuit agre per eux toutz que poet estre prise pur lun sexe et lauter, et pur ceo que le 2 fine al use del senioris prolis vocati a child ideo Southcote et Wray prise cest darren clause come exposition del primer. Et pur ceo Wray et Southcote pense que le pleintife serra barre et Gawdy tient que le pleintife recovera. <Vide lour reasons in mon report alarge.>[a] <Vide Dier 16 [Eliz.] 337, dignitie del sex. Nota masculin[us] genus continetur femininus [sed] non econtra. Vide Larners[2] case, Pl. Com., nul preheminence de male. Nota in discentes dignitie del person serra preferre nemi[3] preheminence.>[a] [4]

---

[1] *Written twice.*
[2] *Unclear.*
[3] *Unclear.*
[4] *Added in top margin.*

he said that this lease was made for his benefit, inasmuch as it was to try his title in this ejectment. He also said that some books agree that an infant had brought *dum fuit infra aetatem* for a rent. And he said that an infant may do all acts which are necessary for him, such as a contract or bond for food and drink, and such like. He said also that if a lease for years is made by an infant, and livery made in security of his term, this is [not void] but voidable; but the other two were against him, for WRAY said that an infant may only perform two kinds of act which will estop him, namely those acts which he is compellable to do by the law and those which are for his benefit and advantage. Therefore (as he said) a lease for years reserving rent is [only] voidable. 12 Hen. IV:[1] the law is the same of an exchange. Likewise, an assignment of dower, or a partition, will bind him if they are fair (*egall*), for he is compellable [to do such things] by law.

The fifth point: was the remainder, being in consideration of the law, destroyed by this fine levied, or not? And it was held clearly by them all that it was not; for GAWDY said that when something is in the consideration of the law, the law will preserve and keep it, because there is no person *in esse* to take care of it: for example, a descent in time of a vacancy will not harm the successor, because the freehold is in consideration of the law. Likewise, a descent will not toll the [entry] of an infant, a married woman, a man in prison, or a man overseas, for the law privileges their persons. SOUTHCOTE and WRAY granted that. And WRAY said that a descent during the king's possession shall not harm the heir, for the possession of the land is in consideration of the law. He also said that if a parson makes a lease for life and dies, the fee is in suspense, and if during the vacancy the tenant makes a feoffment, the successor (when he is inducted) may enter, even though it was not to his disinheritance at the time, but the inheritance was in consideration of the law.

The sixth point was whether *puer* could be understood both for male and for female. And it was agreed by them all that it may be taken for either sex; and because the second fine was to the use of '*senioris prolis*, called a child', SOUTHCOTE and WRAY took this later clause as an exposition of the former.[2] Therefore WRAY and SOUTHCOTE thought that the plaintiff should be barred, and GAWDY held that the plaintiff should recover. {See their reasons in my report at large.[3] See Dyer, 16 Eliz. 337, as to distinction of sex.[4] *Nota quod masculinus genus continetur fœmininus, sed non econtra*.[5] See [Baynton's][6] case, Plowd. Comm., on the pre-eminence of males. Note that in descents the dignity of the person shall be preferred, not pre-eminence.}

---

[1] *Prior of St Bartholomew's, London* v. *Prior of Blythburgh* (1411) YB Hil. 12 Hen. IV, fo. 12, pl. 1.
[2] Cf. Gawdy J. in 2 Leon. 217: 'Divers authors of grammar have been produced to prove that *puer* may be taken both ways, *tam puer quam puella*, [as] Desporterius, Calapine, Melancthon, and the Grammar allowed; but I conceive that *puer* is a word proper for a boy and *puella* for a maid ...'.
[3] It is not clear to what this refers.
[4] Dyer 337, pl. 36 (reporting this case): 'ceo fuit lentention del auncestour come ils semble, coment que *puero* in Latin est intendable potius al male sex que al female, et uncore mults authors et scribes in le ley ont pris le parol indifferent *ad utrumque genus*'.
[5] 'Note that the masculine gender contains the feminine, though not vice versa.'
[6] This is not the name Coke wrote, but there is no case with a similar name in Plowd. It is most likely *Sharington* v. *Strotton* (*Baynton's Case*) (1565) Plowd. 298; B. & M. 526. Plowden there discussed the supposed inferiority of women, and cited Aristotle's *Politics* ('Mas est praestantior, deterior fœmina').

Coke's citation of a point in the case in 1595

BL MS. Harley 6745, fo. 143v; MS. Harg. 50, ff. 149v–150.

Coke en largument del Sir Edward Cleres case cite un case que fuit agre en largument del case de seniori puero in 16 Eliz., que fuit tile: home esteant seisi del terre suffer un recoverye de ceo, et ceo fuit sur trust et confidence, et les recovere[r]s[1] voylent executer arere un estate en taile, le remainder al son fites en fee, la ne fuit ascun condition expresse en le fait neque ascun covenant per que les recoverers poient estre compell de redoner le terre come il ad appoint mes solement un trust et confidence, et pur ceo en cest case fuit tenus per curiam que le ley suppliera cest want et rayser[a] les uses accordant, pur ceo que il nad ascun meanes pur compeller les recoverre[r]s pur executer les estates per le common ley, issint serroit en cest per reason de ceux parolles de trust et confidence quant les devises nont meanes pur compeller les executors pur executer les estates le ley supplyer[a] cest wante et vestera le possession. Et sur[2] ceo point il bien allowe lour opinions et auxi il tient si les executors ou le heire del survivor deux ne voet faire le partition limitted et appointed per le devisor, ils poient bien faire [*fo. 150*] ceo inter eux per brefe de partitione facienda.

[88]

AB, fo. 70r-v (285r-v).

<Winters case.>[s] <Enter 14 Eliz. rottulo 1015. Mannors. Dier, 14 Eliz.>[a]

Winters case in effect fuit que home seisie de 3 acres de terre, scilicet de A., B et C, fist leas de eux per fait indent reddendo inde pur A x li., reddendo pur B vj li., reddendo pur C iiij li., destre paie in un lieu hors del dit terre, proviso que si le rent <ou ascun parcell de ceo>[i] serroit arere que donques bien lierroit a le lessor de reentre, et puis le lessor bargaine et vende le revercion dun meese et 40 acres de terre parcel del mannor de A per fait indent et inroll et puis <le rent est arere et le bargaine demande le rent et enter>[d] il bargaine et vende tout le residue del revercion a un auter estraunge in fe per fait indent et inroll. Et si cest bargaine prendra advantage del condition, le rent esteant arere, ou nemi, ceo fuit le question. Et in cest case 3 questiones fureront moves.

Lun, si ceux severall reservations ferra severall lessees ou nemi? Et Mounson semble que cest reservation ferra eux severall lesses, et issint le revercion severall auxi. Et Manwood auxi semble que ilz fueront severall lessees pur ceo que les rentz et les mannores hors de quel le rent issue fueront severalles, et donques si severall rent severall revercions auxi. Harper al contrarie, que il fuit que un intier demise, car il dit que un reservation nest del substauns del leas et pur ceo ceo ne ferra un joint

---

[1] recoverors *Harg.*   [2] *Unclear.*

fos. 23–47 (a very full report), sub nom. *Appowell* v. *Monax*; MS. Lansd. 1060, fos. 101–115 (sim.), cit. record; MS. Harg. 15, fos. 30–37 (Mich. 1572); MS. Lansd. 1072, fos. 69–88v, sub nom. *Appowell* v. *Monnaux*; MS. Add. 35953, fos. 3–5v; CUL MS. Gg.5.2, fos. 92v–100v; MS. Hh.3.14, fos. 193v–196v (Mich. 1573); IT MS. Barrington 76(B), fos. 1–5v, sub nom. *Sir Nicholas Arnold* v. *Sir William Wynter* (14 & 15 Eliz.); HLS MS. 200.1 (1180.1), fos. 335–338 ('Le report de Winters case … cest byen at alarge in Ned Carpenters reportes').

[3] According to BL MS. Harg. 15, fo. 33, this was the first demurrer which Mounson J. argued after he was appointed J.C.P. He was appointed on 31 Oct. 1572, two weeks after Manwood J. According to Dyer 310, he was appointed after the judges argued but before judgment was given in *Cranmer's Case*.

Coke's citation of a point in the case in 1595

Sir Edward Clere's Case, probably *Gibbons* v. *Warner*[1] (Trin. 1595).

Coke, in the argument of Sir Edward Clere's case, cited a case which was agreed in the argument of the case of *seniori puero* in 16 Eliz., which was this: a man being seised of land suffered a recovery thereof, upon trust and confidence that the recoverors would execute back an estate in tail, remainder to his son in fee, but there was no condition expressed in the deed, nor any covenant, whereby the recoverors could be compelled to give the land back as he had appointed, but only a trust and confidence; and therefore it was held by the court that in this case the law would supply this want and raise the uses accordingly, because there are no means to compel the recoverors to execute the estates by the common law, and so by reason of these words of trust and confidence the law would in this case supply this want and vest the possession. And on this point he well allowed their opinions, and also held that if the executors or the heir of the survivor of them would not make the partition limited and appointed by the devisor, they could well make it between themselves by the writ *de partitione facienda*.

88. POWELL v. MONOUX: WINTER'S CASE[2]

Common Pleas, Mich. 1572.

Winter's case, entered 14 Eliz., roll 1015. Manors. Dyer, 14 Eliz.

Winter's case, in effect, was that someone seised of three acres of land, namely of A, B and C, made a lease of them by deed indented, rendering (*reddendo inde*) £10 for A, *reddendo* £6 for B, and *reddendo* £4 for C, to be paid in a place outside the said land, provided that if the rent or any parcel thereof should be in arrear, then it should be fully lawful for the lessor to re-enter; then the lessor bargained and sold the reversion of a house and 40 acres of land, parcel of the manor of A, by deed indented and enrolled; the rent was in arrear; and he bargained and sold all the residue of the reversion to another stranger in fee, by deed indented and enrolled. The question was, whether this bargainee could take advantage of the condition, the rent being in arrear, or not. And in this case three questions were moved.

1. Do these separate reservations of rent make separate leases, or not? MOUNSON[3] thought that this reservation makes them separate leases, and therefore the reversion is separate as well. MANWOOD also thought that they were separate leases, because the rents (and the manors out of which the rents issue) were separate, and if the rents are separate, then so also are the reversions. HARPER to the contrary, that it was but one entire demise; for he said that a reservation is not of the substance of the lease, and therefore it does not make a joint lease several; but he said that they were separate

---

[1] See vol. iii, p. 492, n. 1.
[2] Probably CP 40/1302, m. 1015 (unfit for production). Noted above p. 26, no. 52; below, p. 81, no. 128; p. 91, no. 150; p. 99, no. 169; p. 114, no. 205; p. 125, nos. 220, 221; p. 136, no. 245; p. 160, no. 311. Incorporated in a revised form in *Dumpor's Case* (1603) 4 Co. Rep. 119, at fo. 120 (anon.), cit. record as in MS. Differently reported in JRL MS. Fr. 118, fos. 18–19v, sub nom. *Powell* v. *Moneux* (Mich. 14 Eliz.); Dyer 308 (Pas. 1572), identified in Coke's Dyer (Holkham 8014), fo. 308, as *Winter's Case*; cit. from Dyer in 5 Co. Rep. 55; BL MS. Harley 6707, fos. 13v–14; MS. Harg. 5, fos. 104–105v (identified by Edward Umfreville as Harper's report), but naming the parties as *Powell* v. *Monnoux*, and cit. different record; MS. Harg. 6, fos. 54–55; MS. Harg. 8, fos. 180–183; MS. Harg. 20, fos. 26–38; MS. Harg. 373,

leas severall, mes il dit que ilz fueront severall rentz issaunt hors de chescun parcell solonque le limitation et severall avowries covient estre fait pur eux. Dier semble que il fuit que un joint demise. Et luy semble auxi que les rentz ne fueront severall mes que il poet distren pur tout le rent in ascun parcell del terre. Mes il dit que auterment fuit sil ust dit reddendo inde pur le mannour de A etc.

Le 2 point fuit le quell le condition poet estre devide et severe. <Vide Dier 45b.>[1] Et quant a ceo ilz toutz agreont que le condition fuit ale, car un condition ne poet estre devide per acte del partie mes per acte in ley il poet in plusores cases.

Le 3 point fuit si cest bargaine fuit deins le compas del statut de 32 H. 8 des grantes del revercion? Et fuit agre per eux toutz que il fuit un sufficient assignee car per le bargaine et sale luse del revercion passe hors del bargainour al bargainie issint que il fuit quant al use in le per per le bargaine, et donques lestatut execute le possession in mesme le mannour, qualite et condition come le use fuit limitte. Mes ilz agreont que toutz ceux queux veignont in le post sont hors de lestatut, come segnior per eschet, segnior del villeine, tenant in dower, tenant per le curtesie. Issint le conuse del estatut merchaunt, segnior per mortmaine, et toutz ceux queux teignont in le post sont dehors del compas de lestatute. [fo. 70v]

Et la le Segnior Dier dit que done in taile sur condition fuit hors del purveu del estatute, et le graunte del reversion sur tiel estate ne prendra advantage del condition. Auxi per luy le condition covient de trencher in benefitte del estate, come que le lesse ne ferra wast ou que il ne alienera in fe, et similia, et ne sur un somme in grosse et similia.

[89]

AB, fo. 71 (286). *Ff*, fo. 167v. *Gg*, fo. 26. *V*, fo. 26.

Delapres case, come <jeo ay>[1] oy, fuit que ou un tenant per le curtesie graunta ouster tout son estate et le graunte devise ceo a un auter, et cest devise fuit adjudge voide pur ceo que ne fuit deins lestatut de 32 H. 8 pur ceo que ne fuit inheritauns. Et auxi fuit tenus, come fuit dit per le recorder de Londres, que coment que le devise fuit le primer que enter uncore <un>[d] nul occupans puit estre dun estate del tenant per le curtesy, ne del tenant in dower.

[1] C[oke] *Ff, Gg*.

rents issuing out of each parcel according to the limitation, and separate avowries must be made for them. DYER [C.J.] thought it was but one joint demise. It also seemed to him that the rents were not separate, but that he could distrain for all the rent in one parcel of the land. But he said it would be otherwise if he had said '*reddendo inde* for the manor of A ...'.

The second point was whether the condition could be divided and severed. {See Dyer 45v.[1]} As to this, they all agreed that the condition was gone, for a condition cannot be divided by act of the party, though it may by an act in law in various cases.

The third point was this: was this bargain within the compass of the statute of 32 Hen. VIII,[2] concerning grantees of the reversion? And it was agreed by them all that [the bargainee] was a sufficient assignee, for by the bargain and sale the use of the reversion passed out of the bargainor to the bargainee, so that (as to the use) he was in in the *per* through the bargain, and therefore the statute executed the possession in the same manner, quality and condition as the use was limited. But they agreed that all those who come in in the *post* are outside the statute: for instance, the lord by escheat, the lord of a villein, tenant in dower, tenant by the curtesy. Likewise, the cognisee of a statute merchant, a lord [after forfeiture for] mortmain, and all those who hold in the *post*, are outside the compass of the statute.

And the lord DYER said on that occasion that a gift in tail upon condition was outside the purview of the statute, and that the grantee of the reversion upon such an estate may not take advantage of the condition. Also, according to him, the condition must trench in benefit of the estate, for instance that the lessee shall do no waste, or shall not alien in fee, and such like, but not [to pay] a sum in gross, and such like.

89. DELAPRÉ'S CASE[3]

1575.

Delapré's case, as I have heard, was that where a tenant by the curtesy granted over all his estate, and the grantee devised it to another, this devise was adjudged void because it was not within the statute of 32 Hen. VIII,[4] since it was not an inheritance. It was also held, as was said by the recorder of London,[5] that even if the devisee was the first to enter, still there can be no occupancy of an estate of a tenant by the curtesy, nor of a tenant in dower.

---

[1] *Minors' Case* (1539) Dyer 45.
[2] 32 Hen. VIII, c. 34.
[3] Also noted below, p. 144, no. 266. Cf. a paraphrase of this report in Cro. Eliz. 58 (Pas. 1587) as 'Delaper's Case, 17 Eliz. ... there shall be no occupant of an estate of tenant by courtesie, or tenant in dower, which are estates created by law. Ex relatione Edward[i] Coke'. There is another text in LI MS. Misc. 361, fo. 80v. It is preceded in Coke's notebook by *Carell's Case*, which is too early to be of Coke's own taking and is evidently abridged from Plowd. 295, where it is dated 1565. It is followed by a report of *Newdegate's Case* (1566), which is not dated here but is continued on fo. 72v (287v) with the date 8 Eliz.; a date before 1567 is confirmed by the fact that Browne J. is reported as speaking.
[4] Statute of Wills, 32 Hen. VIII, c. 1.
[5] William Fleetwood: cf. above, p. 16, n. 3.

[90]

AB, fo. 71v–72 (286v–287).

<Nicols case. M. 17 Eliz.>ˢ

Frauncis, Segnior Lovell, esteant seisie del fearme vocat. Bowells in fe anno 18 E. 4 per fait indent ceo lessa a un Thomas Wright pur vie, et si contigerit predictus Franciscus obire sine heredibus de corpore suo legittime procreatis tunc predictus Franciscus ulterius vult et concedit predictam firmam prefato Thome et heredibus suis. Et puis le Segnior Lovell fuit attaint anno 1 H. 7 de haut treason per acte de parliament, et ouster fuit ordein per mesme lacte que il forfeitra tout ses terres et tenementes etc. savaunt a toutz estraunges auters etc. all such right, title, action and interest as they should have had if the said acte had not beene made. Et puis anno 2 H. 7 il fuit mys a mort sauns heire de son corps. Et puis anno 11 le roigne que ore est trove fuit per force dun commission direct a certain persons que pretextu et ratione attincture et convictionis predictarum le roy H. 7 fuit seisie del revercion et que ceo discend al roy H. 8, car le dit T. Wright survive le dit H. 7, et issint per mesne conveiauns conveie ceo al roigne que ore est, que graunt ceo per ces lettres patentz grant ceo al Humfrey Nicols, pleintife, et J. Nicols conveie ceo per mesne conveiauns al J. Nicols. In cest case 3 questions fueront moves. 1, coment cest future estate limitte in fe sur le condition avandit al Thomas Wright inurera? Le 2, le quel per les avanditz parolx in le acte de parliament toutz les terres le Segnior Lovell fueront in le roy sauns office? Et auxi in le argument de cest point ilz parleront a le validitie del office trove in le temps cesti roygne. Le 3 scruple surde sur les parolx in le savaunt.

Quant al primer point Mounson, Harper et Dier teignont que per le mort del Segnior Lovel esteant attaint issint que il navoit heire de son corps, le fe simple serra ore adjudge in Wright ab initio, et ceo growe hors del primer livery. Et Mounson et Harper disoient que ceo enurera al Wright in nature dun remainder etc. Mes Manwood teigne le contrarie, car come grant del revercion il dit ceo ne poet passer car donques il reservera a luy meinder estate, [et] come remainder ceo ne poet passer pur ceo que ceo est limit immediatement a le lesse pur vie. Mes il dit si ceo passe ceo covient a passer come grant executorie, et ceo ne poet pur ceo que le grauntor est mort devant le grant prist son effecte. Mes nota la Manwood dit que Plowden, que fuit del auter side,¹ agre que si le lesse pur vie ust devie devant le Segnior Lovel que donques cest limitation ust estre voide. Issint <si>ᵈ il dit si le lesse ad fait feffment et le Segnior Lovel ust enter ou recover in wast, en ceux cases Manwood dit que cest limitation avoit estre destroy. Et fuit agre clerement que coment que le Segnior Lovel fuit attaint de haut treason devant le condition perimplie, issint que un title accrue al roy, uncore

---

¹ *Unclear; resembles* said. *Coke uses the English word* side *below, p. 66.*

AD, fo. 782, from Plowd. 486. Differently reported in Plowd. 481; Benl. 251; JRL MS. Fr. 118, fos. 38–42; IT MS. Petyt 511.12, fos. 243v–246 (Hil. 1575). Cf. an earlier related case in Dyer's notebook, 110 Selden Soc. 258 (Pas. 1572).

² 1 Hen. VII, c. iii (private).

³ Patent of 4 Feb. 1570. The patentees, Humphrey Councel and Robert Pistor, enfeoffed the plaintiff.

90. NICHOLS v. NICHOLS[1]

Common Pleas, Mich. 1575.

Nichols' case. Mich. 17 Eliz.

Francis, Lord Lovell, being seised in fee of a farm called Bowells, in the year 18 Edw. IV by deed indented leased it to one Thomas Wright for life, 'and if the aforesaid Francis should happen to die without heirs of his body lawfully begotten, then the aforesaid Francis further wills and grants the aforesaid farm to the said Thomas and his heirs'; then the Lord Lovell was attainted of high treason by act of Parliament in the year 1 Hen. VII,[2] and it was further ordained by the same Act that he should forfeit all his lands and tenements, saving to all others, strangers etc., 'all such right, title, action and interest as they should have had if the said Act had not been made'; then in 2 Hen. VII he was put to death, without heir of his body; then, in the eleventh year of the present queen (1569), it was found by force of a commission directed to certain persons that 'by virtue and by reason of the aforesaid attainder and conviction' King Henry VII was seised of the reversion, and that it descended to King Henry VIII (for the said Thomas Wright survived the said Henry VII), and thus [the plaintiff] traced it by mesne conveyance (indirectly) to the queen who now is, who granted it by her letters patent to Humphrey Nichols, the plaintiff;[3] and John Nichols [the defendant] traced it by mesne conveyance to John Nichols. In this case three questions were moved. (1) How shall this future estate limited in fee to Thomas Wright, upon the condition aforesaid, enure? (2) Were all the lands of the Lord Lovell in the king without office, by virtue of the aforesaid words in the act of Parliament? (In arguing this point they also spoke to the validity of the office found in the time of the present queen.) [3] The third scruple arose upon the words in the saving clause.

As to the first point, MOUNSON, HARPER and DYER [C.J.] held that by the death of the Lord Lovell, being attainted so that he had no heir of his body, the fee simple should now be adjudged in Wright *ab initio*, so that it grows out of the first livery. MOUNSON and HARPER said that it should enure to Wright in the nature of a remainder. But MANWOOD held the contrary, for it cannot pass (he said) as a grant of the reversion, for then he would reserve a lesser estate to himself, and it cannot pass as a remainder inasmuch as it is limited immediately to the lessee for life. He said that if it passes, it must pass as an executory grant; yet that cannot be, because the grantor was dead before the grant took effect. But note that MANWOOD said that *Plowden*, who was on the other side, agreed that if the lessee for life had died before the Lord Lovell, this limitation would have been void. Likewise (he said) if the lessee had made a feoffment and the Lord Lovell had entered, or if he had recovered in waste, in these cases (as MANWOOD said) this limitation would have been destroyed. And it was clearly agreed that although the Lord Lovell was attainted of high treason before the condition was fulfilled, so that a title accrued to the king, nevertheless when he died without issue the

---

[1] Probably CP 40/1322, m. 349 (unfit for production; printed in Plowd. 477 and Benl. 245): Humphrey Nichols v. John Nichols of Beirdley, Salop, yeoman; trespass *quare clausum fregit* at Alveley, Salop.; demurrer to the rejoinder; judgment for the defendant. Noted above, p. 22, no. 39; below, p. 94, no. 155; p. 130, no. 231; p. 132, nos. 236–237; p. 138, no. 250. Cit. in Co. Uses, fo. 154 ('Nichols case'); cit. in

quant il morust sauns issue le lesse avera fe ab initio, et cest relation defetera le title le roy. Et auxi coment que le lessour covient estre mort devant le perimplishment del condition, uncore ceo est assetz bone per voy de relation. Et sur ceo le Segnior Dier myst ceux 2 cases hors del Frowickes reading. Si alien soit et leasse est fait a luy sur condition que si le alien paye x li. a luy que donques il avera fe, et puis le roy fait luy denizen, et puis il performe le condition, uncore le roy avera le terme car ceo (come il dit) avera relation backward. Issint si home de non sane memorie face leas pur ans sur condition que si le lesse face tiel act que donques il avera fe, et puis il deveigne de sane memorie, et puis il performe le condition, uncore le lessor avoidra ceo. Et la le Segnior Dier dit que ne fuit [ab]surd[1] a dire que fe simple serra in abeiauns tanque le condition soit performe. Et il dit que <il>[d] fuit loppinion de Justice Shelley que toutz lez judges in construction de faitz averont grand regard et respect [al] meaninge del parties. Et le Segnior Dier dit que ceo ne poet [fo. 72] properment passe come remainder pur ceo que est limitte a mesme le lesse. Et auxi chescun remainder covient a passer hors del lessor maintenaunt (quel ne poet si le fe ne soit in abeiaunce). Mes il dit que ceo fuit un present gift del franktenement et un future gift del fe sur contingit et un ambiguite et condition, quel condition esteant performe le ley construera que il avera fe ab initio. Et il agre ove Mountague in Bewshins case que si home dona terres al maried home et maried fem ilz nont estate taile maintenaunt mes estates pur vie et severall moities maintenaunt et estate taile in suspence, contrarie al livre in 15 H. 7, 10. Et il dit que admitte que le revercion remayne in le lessour, uncore le lessee ayaunt possibilitie daver le fe sil fait wast le lessor ne punishera luy in wast ne il ne serra chase dattorner. Et Manwood et Harper teignont que per le dit acte et per le savant in ceo si Wright navoit auter matter le possibilitie que Wright avoit per cest condition ne fuit save pur ceo que il nad droit. Car Manwood dit que properment home est dit daver droit quant ascun auter fait a luy tort. Et Harper dit que il nad in re pur ceo que il ne poet aver action ne title ad rem. Title il navoit car cesti que ad title dentre ou autermont covient daver ceo per un condition, et condition nul poet aver forsque le feffor. Et auxi il dit, sil ad title il poet relesse ceo per relesse de conditions. Interest il nad pur ceo que un interest est grantable ouster: quod Harper concessit, car il dit que il nad interest tanque condition performe. Mes le segnior [Dier] teigne que il ad interest, car il dit que le fitz et heire apparaunt poet maintene son pier pur lenterest que il ad in le terre, et leigne fitz poet endower sa fem ex assensu patris pur lenterest que il ad. Et il dit que chescun subject in le realme ad un interest in le roigne pur luy protecter et defender.

[2.] Et Mounson, Harper et le Segnior Dier teignont que coment que lacte de parliament in que le Segnior Lovel fuit attaint done al roy toutz ses terres et tenementes, scilicet que il forfeitra eux al roy, ilz agreont que riens serra in le roy devant office, car ceo fuit devant lestatut de 33 H. 8. <Vide Dier, 15 Eliz. 325.>[i] Et

---

[1] *Unclear.*

[2] *Colthirst* v. *Bejushin* (1550) Plowd. 21; B. & M. 89, at p. 94.
[3] YB Trin. 15 Hen. VII, fo. 10, pl. 16, *per* Fyneux C.J.
[4] *Sic, presumably meaning Manwood.*

lessee had fee *ab initio*, and that relation back will defeat the king's title. Also, although the lessor must be dead before the fulfilment of the condition, nevertheless it is perfectly good by way of relation. On this the lord DYER put these two cases out of Frowyk's reading.[1] If there is an alien, and a lease is made to him upon condition that if the alien paid him £10 he should have fee, and afterwards the king makes him a denizen, and then he performs the condition, the king shall still have the term, for this (as he said) shall have relation retrospectively. Likewise, if a man of unsound mind makes a lease for years upon condition that if the lessee does a certain act he should then have fee, and then he becomes of sound mind, and afterwards the lessee performs the condition, the lessor may still avoid it. And the lord DYER said in this case that it was not absurd to say that the fee simple should be in abeyance until the condition is performed. He said it was the opinion of Shelley J. that in construing deeds all judges should have great regard and respect to the meaning of the parties. And the lord DYER said that this cannot properly pass as a remainder, because it is limited to the same lessee. Also every remainder must pass out of the lessor at once, and this cannot be so if the fee is not in abeyance. But he said that it was a present gift of the freehold, and a future gift of the fee upon a contingency, and an ambiguity and a condition, which condition being performed the law will construe it that he had the fee *ab initio*. And he agreed with Mountague in Bewshin's case,[2] that if a man gives lands to a married man and a married woman, they do not have an estate tail at once, but estates for life and separate moieties at once, and an estate tail in suspense, contrary to the book in 15 Hen. VII, fo. 10.[3] And he said, admit that the reversion remains in the lessor, nevertheless if the lessee (having a possibility of having the fee) commits waste, the lessor may not punish him in waste, nor shall he be driven to attorn. MANWOOD and HARPER held that if Wright had no other matter, the possibility which Wright had by reason of this condition was not saved by the said Act, and by the saving therein, because he had no right. For MANWOOD said that, properly speaking, a man is said to have right when someone else does him wrong. HARPER said that he did not have anything *in re* because he could not have an action or title *ad rem*. Title he did not have, for he who has a title to enter or otherwise must have it through a condition, and no one may have a condition except the feoffor. He said also that if he had title, he could release it by releasing the condition. Interest he did not have, because an interest is grantable over: which HARPER[4] conceded, for he said that he had no interest until the condition was performed. But the lord DYER said he had an interest, for he said that a son and heir apparent may maintain his father on account of the interest which he has in the land, and the eldest son may endow his wife *ex assensu patris* because of the interest which he has. And he said that every subject in the realm has an interest in the queen, to protect and defend her.

2. MOUNSON, HARPER and the lord DYER held that although the act of Parliament whereby the Lord Lovell was attainted gave the king all his lands and tenements – in providing that he should forfeit them to the king – they agreed that nothing could have been in the king before an office [was found], for this was before the statute of

---

[1] Thomas Frowyk read in the Inner Temple in 1495 on *Prerogativa Regis*. The same passage is cited below, p. 132, no. 236. Coke cited the reading in 1587 in 2 Leon. 127, 3 Leon. 192. There are numerous references to it in Bro. Abr. Cf. Plowd. 482v; 1 Leon. 8.

les parols ne donont plus que le common ley voille aver done, et lacte de parliament in cest case est in nature dun judgment et pur ceo devant execution per office. <Dier 325 accord. 13 H. 4, 7, in fresh force, contra.>[i] Et Mounson doubta si le <roy>[d] terres sont dones a J. S. per parliament si le franktenement serra in luy devant son entrie. Mes Manwood dit que le franktenement fuit in luy devant son entrie mes nemi daver trespas ne assise, car la lacte de parliament est in nature dun conveiaunce. Et Manwood tient que per le dit act de parliament les terres fueront in le roy per les parols avanditz, et son reason fuit pur ceo que est purveu per le dit acte que il forfeitra tout ses terres in fe simple, in taile, in possession ou in use, et pur ceo que les parolx donont pluis al roy que le comon ley voille aver done a luy per le dit attaindre, car a tiel temps terres in taile et in use ne fueront forfeitable pur treason, pur ceo cest acte enurera come un done al roy. Et nota la per Mounson clerement, et admitte per toutz, que si jeo face feffment in fe, le feffe fait treason, puis le condition est infreint, et puis office est trove que le feffe al temps de treason fuit seisie, ore loffice avera relation et defetera lestate que fuit loialment vest in le feffour. Mesme la ley si le disseisor fait treason et le disseisie entre, et puis office est trove etc. Et ceux cases sont intende devant lestatut de 33 H. 8. <Vide 13 H. 4, 7, in fresh force, adjudge contra: nota hunc librum que ne fuit cite in le dit case de Nichols.>[a]

[91]

AB, fo. 72v (287v). *Ff*, fo. 167v. *Gg*, fo. 26. *Lb*, fo. 4 (last two cases).

Nota fuit tenus in le common banke anno 19 Eliz., home devise son terre a sa fem in fe simple, et puis son mort a J. S. <son fitz>,[i] et fuit agre clerement que construction serra fait solonque lentent le testator, et ceo fuit que la fem avera estate pur vie, le remainder a J. S. pur vie, le remainder al droit heires le fem. <Vide Dier.>[a]

Auxi un auter case fuit la agre, que home devisa terre a un fem covert pur terme de sa vie sur condition que le <devise>[d] baron paiera a ses executors 20 li. per tiel jour, et sil faila de paier que donques le terre remainera a un auter in taile sur autiel condition, et <puis>[d] fist son heire et divers auters ses executors et morust, leire esteant executor ove les auters execute releasse al baron devant le jour, et puis apres le jour voille aver enter pur le condition enfreint, et pur ceo que il mesme fuit partie a le discharge des deniers pur ceo il ne prendra avantage de ceo. Mes la fuit dit, si un auter des executors ust release uncore leire esteant un 3 person puit aver enter pur le condition enfreint. Vies 12 E. 3, tit. Condition, 8.

---

[5] *Friske* v. *Peche* (1411) YB Mich. 13 Hen. IV, fo. 6, pl. 13.
[6] See below, p. 149, no. 277, and the note there.
[7] Dyer 357, sub nom. *Chycke's Case*.
[8] Hil. 12 Edw. III, Fitz. Abr., *Condicion*, pl. 8.

33 Hen. VIII.[1] {See Dyer, 15 Eliz. 325.[2]} And the words do not give more than the common law would have given, and the act of Parliament in this case is in the nature of a judgment, and therefore [nothing was in the king] before execution by office. {Dyer 325, agrees. 13 Hen. IV, fo. 7,[3] in fresh force, contrary.} MOUNSON doubted whether, if lands are given to John Style by Parliament, the freehold shall be in him before his entry.[4] But MANWOOD said that the freehold was in him before his entry, albeit not for the purpose of having trespass or an assize, for the act of Parliament is in the nature of a conveyance. And MANWOOD held that by the said act of Parliament the lands were in the king, by reason of the words aforesaid, and his reason was because it is provided by the said Act that he should forfeit all his lands in fee simple, in tail, in possession or in use, and because the words gave more to the king than the common law would have given him by the said attainder (for at that time lands in tail and in use were not forfeitable for treason), this Act shall enure as a gift to the king. And note that it was there held by MOUNSON clearly, and accepted by them all, that if I make a feoffment in fee, the feoffee commits treason, and then the condition is broken, and then an office is found that the feoffee was seised at the time of the treason, now the office shall have relation back and defeat the estate which was once lawfully vested in the feoffor. The law is the same if a disseisor commits treason and the disseisee enters, and then an office is found. These cases are to be understood before the statute of 33 Hen. VIII. {See 13 Hen. IV, fo. 7,[5] in fresh force, adjudged the contrary: note that book, which was not cited in the said case of Nichols.}

91. BAKER v. RAYMOND; and BURRES' CASE[6]

Common Pleas, 1577.

Note that it was held in the Common Bench in the year 19 Eliz., where a man devised his land to [a woman] in fee simple, and after her death to John Style her son, that (as was clearly agreed) a construction should be made according to the testator's intention: which was that the woman should have an estate for life, remainder to John Style for life, remainder to the right heirs of the woman. {See Dyer.[7]}

Another case was there agreed: a man devised his land to a married woman for term of her life, upon condition that her husband should pay £20 to his executors by a certain day, and should he then fail to pay the land should remain to another in tail upon the like condition; and he made his heir and various others his executors, and died; the heir, being an executor with the others, executed a release to the husband before the day; then, after the day, he would have entered for breach of the condition; and because he was himself party to the discharge of the money, he could not take advantage of it. But it was there said that if one of the other executors had released, the heir (being a third person) could nevertheless have entered for breach of the condition. See 12 Edw. III, tit. *Condicion*, 8.[8]

---

[1] 33 Hen. VIII, c. 20, s. 2.
[2] *Say's Case* (1573) Dyer 325, concerning the title of Anne, late marchioness of Northampton.
[3] *Friske* v. *Peche* (1411) YB Mich. 13 Hen. IV, fo. 6, pl. 13.
[4] This point is also noted above, p. 22.

Auxi fuit agre in mesme le terme que si home fait leasse sur condition que le lessee ne devisera ne alienera ouster son estate, et puis il devise le terme et le devisee disagree a ceo, uncore le Segnior Dier tient que le condition fuit infreint car le Segnior Dier dit si feffee grant un rent charge est infrinder del condition maintenant, uncore poet estre que le grantee voet porter brefe dannuitie. Burres case.

[92]

AB, fo. 72v (287v).

Nota que Serjaunt Anderson dit a moy que fuit adjudge que discent dun disseisor sans force tollera lentry deins lestatut de 32 H. 8.

[93]

AB, fo. 72v (287v).

<Mich. 19 Eliz.>[a]

Gerrard, attorney, dit in banke le roy que ad estre resolve per les justices sur lestatut de 1 H. 7, cap. 7, que si home hunt in le nuite in forestes, chases ou warrens ou ove painted faces etc. et si examine devant un del councel ou justice de peace et ceo conceale, ceo nest pas felony, mes les judges ount expounde lestatut que le clause del concealment serra couple ove le darrein clause, scilicet que si ascun person be convict of such hunting with visors etc. or in the night et <sur>[i] pleade<r de>[i] rien culpable (car issint sont [les] parolx conceale expound) donques ceo est felony, que est destre intend dun judiciall concealment ou denier, car ne unques fuit lentent del act a faire concealment ou denier devant justice de peace ou consimiles felonie, car ceo girra in averment le quel il conceal ceo ou nemi et peraventure al primes il poet ceo <confess>[d] denier ou conceale et apres confesse. Auxi si le hunting mesme in tiel mannour serra felony al primes, donques serra in le power del accuser daler ove ly al justice ou consailour et sil ceo confesse nest forsque trespas <et si>[d] ou sil voille luy immediatement indite et donques serra felony. Auxi lestatut [dit] after such conviction, scilicet sur concealment ou denier, il serra puny come felon, issint que conviction et denier ou concealment doit precede. Auxi lestatut fuit fait pur le meliour execution de primer[i] statut et carta de foresta, quod nullus amittat vitam vel membrum propter venationem. Auxi le preamble parle de rebellions, riottes etc.

---

[i] *Unclear.*

---

[3] Paraphrased in 3 Co. Inst. 77 ('Gerard, the queens attorney (who was a grave and reverend man), said openly in the King's Bench ... Mich. 19 & 20 Eliz. in the King's Bench, a report of the resolution of the justices upon this branch').
[4] These words are not in the statute, and so the point is difficult to understand.
[5] Carta de Foresta 1225, c. 10.

It was also agreed in the same term that if someone makes a lease upon condition that the lessee should not devise or alien over his estate, and then he devises the term, and the devisee disagrees to it, the lord DYER nevertheless held that the condition was broken; for the lord DYER said that if a feoffee grants a rent-charge, it is a breach of the condition at once, and yet it may be that the grantee will bring a writ of annuity. Burre's case.[1]

92. ENTRY TOLLED BY DESCENT

Conversation in 1577/82.

Note that Serjeant Anderson told me it was adjudged that a descent from a disseisor, without force, will toll the entry within the statute of 32 Hen. VIII.[2]

93. THE STATUTE OF HUNTING[3]

King's Bench, Mich. 1577.

Mich. 19 Eliz.

Gerrard, attorney-general, said in the King's Bench that it had been resolved by the justices upon the statute of 1 Hen. VII, c. 7, that if someone hunts in forests, chases or warrens in the night, or with painted faces [or visors], and on being examined before a member of the Council or a justice of peace he conceals it, this is not felony; for the judges have expounded the statute to mean that the clause concerning concealment should be coupled with the previous clause, namely 'if any person be convict of such hunting with visors … or in the night', then upon pleading Not Guilty (for so are the words 'conceal' expounded) it is felony, and it is to be understood of a judicial concealment or denial. It was never the intention of the Act to make a concealment or denial before a justice of peace, or such like, felony; for it will lie in averment whether he concealed it or not, and perhaps at first he will deny or conceal it but afterwards confess. Also, if the hunting in such a manner should itself be felony at the outset, then it would be in the power of the accuser to go with him to a justice or councillor, and if he confessed it would only be a trespass, whereas if he immediately indicted him it would be a felony. Also the statute says 'after such conviction',[4] upon a concealment or denial, he shall be punished as a felon, so that a conviction ought to precede the denial or concealment. Also the statute was made for the better execution of a former statute, and of the Carta de Foresta,[5] that no one should lose life or limbs for hunting ('quod nullus amittat vitam vel membra propter venationem'). Also the preamble speaks of rebellions, riots etc.

---

[1] Cit. in *C*, fo. 15 (vol. iii, p. 439) as 'Burres case que jeo oye in le common banke anno 19 Eliz.' For Dyer's case of the rent-charge see the citation in *Butler* v. *Baker* (1591) ibid.; Co. Litt. 222.
[2] 32 Hen. VIII, c. 33.

[94]

AB, fo. 73 (288).

Nota, fuit dit per le Segnior Dier in le argument de Sir Thomas Wiatz case que in aunciente temps les progenitors le roy avoient grant al evesque de Durham <daver>[d] [et] a ses successors daver jura regalia deins levesquerie, et ore <tard>[i] in le darrein rebellion in le north divers persons queux fueront seisie in taile fueront attaint de haut treason, per reason de quel attaindre et per force del estatutz de 26 H. 8 et 33 H. 8 lour terres tailes fueront forfeite, et fuit agre sur graund advice per toutz les justices que levesque de Durham, coment que il ad jura regalia etc., navera ceux forfeitures car al temps del lettres patentz faitz ceo fuit nul forfeiture des terres tailes.

[95]

AB, fo. 73 (288).

P. 19 Eliz. Nota un graund parrish in le west pays appell Ponteland[1] conteine in ceo divers villes <et tout>[d] scilicet A, B, C, D et E, et puis un common recoverie de certain terres (que gisoient in A) fuit ewe, et le brefe suppose que ceux gisoient in Pontelonde. Et la le court dit que si un parrishe conteine divers villes et peradventure ascun des villes soit ville mercatorie come Burntwoode et Brainforde, que uncore le precipe ne poet estre port in tielz [villes][2] car precipe ne poet giser in un hamlet, come la fuit agree. Car le Segnior Dier dit que tiel ville in que precipe girra covient daver un eglise. Et la fuit agre que loriginall covient estre port in le cheife parrish: quod nota. Mes la fuit agre que fine poet estre levie in un hamelet.

[96]

AB, fo. 73 (288).

M. 14 Eliz. fuit tenus in le common banke que lou home fist leasse pur ans [reservant][3] rent per fait indent, in mesme le fait le lessor covenant que le lessee avera fuel de toutz ses arbres purveu toutz foitz et le lesse covenant que il ne succidera ascun timber, et le question fuit si cest proviso ferra le leasse conditionel ou le covenant conditionel. Et tenus [per] Dier, Harper et Manwood que le covenant fuit conditionel. Et Manwood prist cest diversitie, si nul sentence soit perenter le covenant et le proviso donques le proviso trenchera solement al covenant, coment que le motes sont in severall sentences, mes si un sentence soit enterlace donques est tout auterment.

---

[1] *Sic, but in error for* Poleland.   [2] viells.   [3] *Unclear; smudged and worn.*

[5] Now Brentford, Midd. Likewise, it had a market and chapel but no church; it was in the parish of Hanwell. The substantial chapel (originally belonging to St Leonard's Hospital) became a church when the parish of New Brentford was created in the eighteenth century. William Noy, attorney-general to Charles I, was buried there in 1634.

[6] Cit. by that name below, p. 53. The text here is evidently derived from JRL MS. Fr. 118, fo. 15v, no. 56 (Mich. 14 Eliz.) (printed below). Differently reported in *Ff*, fo. 186v; BL MS. Harg. 8, fo. 155v.

94. MULTON v. COVENEY[1]

Common Pleas. 1576.

Note that it was said by the lord DYER, in the argument of Sir Thomas Wyatt's case, that in olden times the king's forebears granted to the bishop of Durham and his successors to have *jura regalia* within the bishopric, and now recently in the late rebellion in the North various persons who were seised in tail were attainted of high treason, by reason of which attainder, and by force of the statutes of 26 Hen. VIII and 33 Hen. VIII,[2] their entailed lands were forfeited; and it was agreed upon great advisement by all the justices that the bishop of Durham, even though he has *jura regalia*, should not have these forfeitures, for at the time when the letters patent were made there was no forfeiture of entailed lands.

95. HILL'S CASE

Common Pleas, Pas. 1577.

Easter term 19 Eliz. Note that a large parish in the West Country called Portland[3] contains in itself several vills, namely A, B, C, D and E. A common recovery was had of certain lands which lie in A, and the writ supposed that they lay in Portland. And the court said there that if a parish contains several vills, and perhaps some of the vills are even market towns (*villae mercatoriae*) like Burntwood[4] and Brainford,[5] nevertheless the *praecipe* cannot be brought in such vills, for a *praecipe* cannot lie in a hamlet, as was there agreed. For the lord DYER said that the vill in which a *praecipe* may lie must have a church. And it was there agreed that the original writ must be brought in the chief parish: note that. But it was there agreed that a fine may be levied in a hamlet.

96. PECKSALL'S CASE[6]

Common Pleas, 14 October 1572.

Michaelmas term 14 Eliz. in the Common Bench. Someone made a lease for years and reserved a rent by deed indented, and in the same deed the lessor covenanted that the lessee should have fuel from all his trees, provided always (and the lessee covenanted) that he should not fell any timber, and the question was whether this proviso made the lease conditional, or the covenant conditional: and it was held by DYER [C.J.], HARPER and MANWOOD that it made the covenant conditional. And MANWOOD drew this distinction: if there is no sentence between the covenant and the proviso, then the proviso will trench only to the covenant, even though the words are in separate sentences, whereas if a sentence is interposed (*interlace*) it is quite otherwise.

---

[1] See below, p. 89, no. 147, and the note there. [2] 26 Hen. VIII, c. 13; 33 Hen. VIII, c. 20.
[3] An island in Dorset containing several vills.
[4] Brentwood, Essex, had a flourishing market and a chapel but no church; it was in the parish of South Weald.

Version in the Rylands Manuscript

JRL MS. Fr. 118, fo. 15v; collated with Holkham Hall, BN 7938, fo. i (verso) (*H*), for which see also Appendix I, above, p. clxxx. Also in *Gg*, fo. 53.

Conditions.

Home seisie des terres en fe fist leas pur ans reservant <rent per fait indent>,[1] et le lessour covenant <in mesme le fait>[2] que le lesse avera sufficient fuell <pur>[d] de toutz ces arbres, purveu toutz foitz et le lessee covenant que il ne <succidera ascun>[3] timber etc. Et apres le lesse succide certain grosse[4] arbres, esteant timbre. Le question fuit le quel cest proviso ferra tantsolement[5] le covenant precedent conditionell ou que tout le leas serra conditionel et issint lentre le [lessor][6] congeable en tout pur le condition enfreint. Dier dit que le lesse al common ley avera trois bootes, houseboot, heybot et plowghboot, coment que le leas soit per paroll, come est agre 21 H. 6. Et le lessour icy nad done ascun chose per cest covenant al lesse mes ceo [que le][7] ley [sans ascun covenaunt][8] voille aver done a luy. Et luy semble que cest proviso ferra le covenant conditionell et serra come un limitation queux arbres il ne prendra pur son fuell. Manwood justice[9] prist cest diversitie, si nul sentence soit parenter le covenant et le proviso donques le proviso trenchera solement al covenant, <coment que le covenant et le proviso soient in divers sentences>,[10] mes si un[11] sentence fuit enterlace donques est tout ousterment: quod Harper concessit.

[97]

AB, fo. 73v (288v). Longleat MS. 240, unfol. Cf. JRL MS. Fr. 118, fo. 81v (below).[12]

<T. 19 Eliz.>[s]

Nota, Justice Gawdy dit a moy veniendo de Westm. que fuit adjudge in le case del segnior admirall que si home exhibit un bill de complaynt al roigne <ou>[13] in le starr chamber devers ascun de nobilitie de cest realme, et in le dit bill divers slaunderous et faux parolx sont, uncore nul action de scandalis magnatum gist. Mes la fuit agre si les matters in le bill de complaynt concerne auters que le compleynant, come sil conteine que le defendant ad oppresse et per son continuall vexation ad impoverish non solement le complaynant <se>[d] mes auxi toutz ses tenauntes ou inhabitauntz, la si ceo ne soit voier action sur le case ou action de scandalis magnatum gist. Et accordant a ceo fuit judgment done. Et lour reason fuit pur ceo que un bill de [compleint][14] est in lieu et nature dun sute et action in ley etc. Et pur ceo que in action port per le dit segnior les jurors taxe damages cybien pur les parolx queux concerne auters come pur ceux que concerne luy mesme entierment, ideo le dit segnior ne poet aver judgment. Mes il dit que un contrarie judgment de ceo fuit done devant Catelyn sur argument que action de scandalis magnatum gist coment que les parolx concern luy mesme.

---

[1] un rent en le leas *H*.   [2] *Om. H.*   [3] prendera *H*   [4] *Om. H.*   [5] *Om. H.*
[6] *H.* lesse JRL MS.   [7] *H.* quel JRL MS.   [8] *H.*   [9] en mesme le jour fait *H*.
[10] <mes>[d] car[i] si nul sentence soit enterlace coment que ne soit in mesme sentences mes in divers, uncore ex necessitate serra prise un limitation del covenant precedent *H*.
[11] ascun *H*.   [12] Both texts are illustrated in plate 5.
[13] *Altered to* or *from* in. *Word deleted in JRL MS.*   [14] *Appears to read* compelleunt.

---

[6] Cf. above, p. 23, no. 45.
[7] Edward Clinton, first earl of Lincoln, lord high admiral 1550–54, 1558–85.   [8] C.J.K.B. 1559–74.

Version in the Rylands Manuscript

See opposite.

Conditions.

Someone seised of lands in fee made a lease for years, reserving rent, by deed indented, and the lessor covenanted in the same deed that the lessee should have sufficient fuel from all his trees, provided always (and the lessee covenanted) that he should not fell any timber. Afterwards the lessee felled certain large trees, being timber. The question was whether this proviso makes only the preceding covenant conditional, or whether it makes the whole lease conditional, so that the lessor's entry for breach of the condition is permissible in the whole. DYER said that the lessee at common law should have three kinds of bote, housebote, haybote and ploughbote, even if the lease is by parol, as is agreed in 21 Hen. VI.[1] Here the lessor has given nothing to the lessee by this covenant but that which the law would have given him [without any covenant];[2] and it seemed to him that this proviso makes the covenant conditional, as a limitation on which trees he should take for his fuel. MANWOOD J., [appointed a justice the same day],[3] drew this distinction: if there is no sentence between the covenant and the proviso, then the proviso will trench solely to the covenant, even though the covenant and the proviso are in different sentences, whereas if a sentence is interposed (*enterlace*) it is quite otherwise:[4] which HARPER granted.

97. EARL OF LINCOLN'S CASE[5]

Conversation between Westminster and the Temple, Trin. 1577.

Trinity term 19 Eliz.

Note that Justice GAWDY told me, coming from Westminster,[6] that it was adjudged in the case of the lord admiral[7] that if someone exhibits a bill of complaint to the queen in the Star Chamber against any of the nobility of this realm, and in the said bill there are various slanderous and false words, still no action *de scandalis magnatum* lies. But it was there agreed that if the matters in the bill of complaint concern persons other than the complainant, for instance if it contains an allegation that the defendant has oppressed and by his continual vexation impoverished not only the complainant but also all his tenants or inhabitants, there, if it is not true, an action on the case or an action *de scandalis magnatum* lies. Judgment was given accordingly. Their reason was because a bill of complaint is in lieu of, and in the nature of, a suit and action in law. And in an action brought by the said lord, because the jurors taxed damages entirely, both for the words which concerned others and for those which concerned himself, the said lord could not have judgment. But he said that a judgment contrary to this was given before Catlyn,[8] upon argument, that an action of *scandalum magnatum* lies even though the words only concern himself.

---

[1] YB Pas. 21 Hen. VI, fo. 46, pl. 23.   [2] Holkham MS.
[3] Holkham MS.: see above, p. clxxxi. He was appointed on 14 Oct. 1572.
[4] Cf. a longer version of this sentence in the Holkham MS.
[5] Cit. in *Bedell* v. *Moore* (1588) vol. ii, p. 396, as 'reported by me'; and in *C*, fo. 21v (vol. iii, p. 455): 'quod habui ex relatione Thome Gawdy militis unius justiciariorum banci regii, et vide in mes reportes fol. [*blank*]'. There is a similar text in JRL MS. Fr. 118, fo. 81v, printed overleaf. See the introduction, p. lxxxvi. Differently reported in IT MS. Petyt 511.12, fo. 240v, where it is said that Wray C.J. dissented; it is also stated that the earl brought a new action for the words concerning himself alone.

Version in the Rylands MS.

JRL MS. Fr. 118, fo. 81v.

<T. 19 Eliz. Action sur le case.>[s]

Nota, Justice Gawdy dit a moy veniendo de Westm. que fuit adjudge ore tard in le case del segnior admirall que si home exhibite un bill de complain[t]e al roigne ou[1] in le starre chamber et in son bill de complainte divers slaunderous parols sont conteine queux sont fauxe, uncore nul action sur le case ne action de scandalis magnatum gist. Mes auterment est si les matters in le bill de complaint concerne auters que le complainant, si telz parolx sont faux, donques action gist de ceo. Et accordant a ceo judgment fuit done, come il dit. Car in le bill de complaint esteant exhibite encounter le segnior admiral divers slaunderous parolx fueront encounter le dit segnior et ascuns de eux touch le complainant mesme et ascuns estrangers, et pur ceo que in action port per le dit [segnior][2] les jurors taxe damages cybien pur lun parols come pur lauters, ideo le segnior ne poit aver judgment, per opinionem totius curie (savant le chiefe justice <Wraye>[i]). Mes il dit que un contrarie judgment a ceo fuit done devant le segnior Catelyn in temps mesme cesti roigne, scilicet que coment que les parolx concerne le complainant mesme que ceo nient obstant si les parolx sont faux action de scandalis magnatum gist.

[98]

AB, fo. 73v (288v). *Ff*, fo. 168.

P. et T. 19 Eliz. in bank le roy le case fuit que le master de colledge de Lyngfield ove le consent de ses confreres fist leasse pur ans de tout lour terres et tenementes in Hamburst <except lour manour howse>[i] (part de quel ville extende in Kent et part in le countie de Surrey) et in trespas port de trespas fait in parte de ville avandit in le countie de Kent les jurors trove cest especial verdit, videlicet que le master del colledge de Lyngfield <ha>[3] navoit ascun auter terre neque in le part del ville que extend in Kent neque in lauter parte que extende in Surrey. Et fuit adjudge T. 19 Eliz. primerment que coment que le graunt fuit per general parolx uncore intaunt que lespecial exception que veigne in un auter sentence controll le force del grant, lexception fuit voide. <Vide cest case pleno 204 in mes notes demesne.>[a] <Vide devant, 71a. Et ceo fuit mon case demesne pur le manour de Stoke etc. in leschequer 17 Jac.>[a]

[99]

AB, fo. 73v (288v). *Ff*, fo. 168.

Trudgins case de Devonshyre anno 20 Eliz. fuit que le dit Trudgin fuit indite sur lestatut de 13 Eliz. cap. 2 pur ceo que un Mayne avoit obteine un bull del bishoppe

---

[1] *Unclear; resembles* ho[r]. [2] *Seemingly deleted.* [3] *Unclear, perhaps deleted.*

[s] Actually of Golden-in-Probus, Corn. (record). The defendant's name is here spelt Trudgin, though in the record it is Trugeon, and the more common spelling is Tregeon or Tregian. He remained in prison for 28 years, and was eventually exiled to Spain, where he died in 1608: *ODNB*, sub nom. Tregian.

Version in the Rylands MS.

See opposite.

Trin. 19 Eliz. Action on the case.

Note that Justice GAWDY told me, coming from Westminster, that it was adjudged recently in the case of the lord admiral that if someone exhibits a bill of complaint to the queen, or in the Star Chamber, and in his bill of complaint are contained various slanderous words which are false, still no action on the case or action *de scandalis magnatum* lies. It is otherwise, however, if the matters in the bill of complaint concern persons other than the complainant: if such words are false, an action lies for it. And judgment was given accordingly, as he said. For in the bill of complaint which was exhibited against the lord admiral there were various slanderous words against the said lord, some of which touched the complainant himself and some which touched strangers, and in an action brought by the said lord the jurors taxed damages both for the former words and for the others, and therefore the lord could not have judgment: by the opinion of the whole court (saving WRAY C.J.). But he said that a judgment contrary to this was given before the lord Catlyn in the time of the present queen, namely, that even if the words concern the complainant himself, nevertheless if the words are false an action *de scandalis magnatum* lies.

98. DORRELL v. COLYNS[1]

King's Bench, Pas.-Trin. 1577.

In Easter and Trinity terms 19 Eliz., in the King's Bench, the case was that the master of Lingfield College, with the consent of his brethren, made a lease for years of all their lands and tenements (excepting their manor house) in Lamberhurst, part of which vill lies in Kent and part in the county of Surrey, and in trespass brought for a trespass committed in part of the aforesaid vill in the county of Kent the jurors found this special verdict: that the master of Lingfield College had no land either in the part of the vill which lay in Kent or in the other part which lay in Surrey. And it was adjudged in Trinity term 19 Eliz., firstly, that although the grant was by general words, nevertheless inasmuch as the special exception (which comes in another sentence) controls the force of the grant, the exception was void. {See this case fully at fo. 204 in my own notes.[2] See above, fo. 71. And this was my own case for the manor of Stoke[3] etc. in the Exchequer, 17 Jac.}

99. R. v. TRUGEON[4]

King's Bench, Trin.-Mich. 1578.

Trugeon's case, of Devonshire,[5] in the year 20 Eliz., was that the said Trugeon was indicted upon the statute of 13 Eliz., c. 2, because one Mayne had obtained a bull

---

[1] See below, p. 97, no. 163.   [2] *AC*, fo. 204 (i.e. below, p. 97).

[3] Stoke Poges, Bucks., which Coke acquired while he was attorney-general. It had belonged to the earl of Huntingdon.

[4] KB 27/1277, Rex, m. 5: R. v. Francis Trugeon; indictment for receiving Cuthbert Mayne; pleads a pardon. Differently reported in Dyer 363 (anon.), identified in Coke's Dyer (Holkham 8014), fo. 363 ('Ceo fuit Trudgins case'); 110 Selden Soc. 368. Cit. in 3 Co. Inst. 126, from 'Dier manuscript', sub nom. *Trudgyn's Case*.

de Rome et avoit ceo mys in ure, et tout le purveu del estatut monstre certainement. Et le dit Trudgin fuit endite sur auter braunch del estatut pur ceo que il fuit aydant et maintenaunt le dit Mayne contra formam statuti, et ne dit ea intentione to set forth, uphold or allowe the doing or execution of the said usurped power. Et fuit adjudge que lenditement fuit insufficient pur ceo que les parolx del estatut ne fueront pursue. <Dier 20 Eliz. 363.>ᵃ <Et puis fuit indit de premunire et attaint [et] adjudge que il ne forfetera taile.>ᵃ

[100]

AB, fo. 73v (288v). *Ff*, fo. 168. *Gg*, fo. 27.

Anderson serjaunt dit arguendo in Holecroftes case que ou un enformation fuit exhibite in leschequer sur lestatut de usurie et ne dit per corruptam usuriam et pur ceo que le letter del statut ne fuit pursue le judgment done sur le dit information fuit adjudge voide. <et puis fuit>ᵈ <20 Eliz. Dier Periam 136, per corrupt usur[ie].>ⁱ <Vide 11 H. 6, 2b, mesme le rule, forgery.>ᵃ

Auxi il dit que ad estre adjudge que ou home fuit indite de murdre per cest parol murdravit (sans ceux parolx ex malicia sua precogitata, come bien poet estre) il avera son clergie, car lestatut de 5 E. 6, cap. 9, parle solement of any willful murdre of mallice prepenced. Et uncore ceux parolz sont imply deins cest parol murdravit. <Stanford, fol. 130a. Dier, 3 Mar. 131, inquirie de abbettours [des] appeales sauns dire per maliciam.>ᵃ <Vide 2 Eliz. 183, Dier.>ᵃ

[101]

AB, fo. 74v–75 (289v–290). JRL MS. Fr. 118, fo. 45 (statement of case only).

<M. 15 et 16 Eliz.>ˢ

J. Blunt seisie de mannour de Alaxton in Lec. a que lavouson de mesme le ville est appendant in special taile, le remainder al droit heires de Segnior Mountjoie anno domini 1552 per fait indent en nient inrolle bargaine et vende mesme le mannour et

---

[10] CP 40/1297, m. 1658 (six rolls; printed in Co. Ent. 499–503v): Edward Androwes gent. v. Bishop of Lincoln, John Blunt and Ralph Bradley, clerk; *quare impedit* for the advowson of Allexton, Leics.; demurrer to the plea in bar; c.a.v. to Mich. 1573; judgment for the defendant. Noted below, p. 90, no. 149 (where many of the present arguments are repeated); p. 108, no. 192. Cit. by Coke in *Scott* v. *Scott* (1587) CUL MS. Dd.11.64, fo. 41v, sub nom. *Androes* v. *Cromewell*; 11 Co. Rep. 48 ('which I myself heard'); Co. Litt. 222b ('which I heard and observed'). The statement of the case in the first paragraph is the same as JRL MS. Fr. 118, fo. 45, apart from the ending (printed below). Differently reported in Dyer 311 (Pas. 1572, Mich. 1573, cit. roll 1443), whence Co. Uses, fo. 143v ('14 Eliz. Androwes case p. 311'); Benl. 201; Moo. 105; 1 And. 17; BL MS. Harley 1699, fo. 118 (1580); MS. Harg. 373, fos. 123v–128 (Mich. 1583); CUL MS. Gg.5.2, fos. 113v–118; IT MS. Petyt 511.12, fos. 193–195v (Trin. 1573). For the prolonged litigation between Lord Cromwell and Edward Androwes concerning Allexton see above, p. 6, n. 1, vol. ii, p. 180; 110 Selden Soc. 370, n. 3.

from the bishop of Rome and had put it in ure[1] – and all the provisions of the statute were set out with certainty – and the said Trugeon was indicted upon another branch of the statute for aiding and maintaining the said Mayne 'against the form of the statute'; but it did not say 'with the intention to set forth, uphold or allow the doing or execution of the said usurped power'. And it was adjudged that the indictment was insufficient, because the words of the statute were not pursued. {Dyer, 20 Eliz. 363. Afterwards he was indicted of *praemunire* and attainted, but it was adjudged that he should not forfeit an entail.[2]}

100. BURGH v. HOLCROFT[3]

King's Bench, 1578.

Anderson, serjeant, said in argument in Holcroft's case that where an information was exhibited in the Exchequer upon the Statute of Usury,[4] and it did not say 'by corrupt usury' (*per corruptam usuriam*), the judgment given upon the said information was adjudged void because the letter of the statute was not pursued. {20 Eliz., Dyer-Peryam 136: 'by corrupt usury'.[5] See 11 Hen. VI, fo. 2:[6] the same rule with respect to forgery.}

He also said it had been adjudged that where someone was indicted of murder by this word *murdravit*, without the words 'of malice aforethought' (*ex malicia sua praecogitata*), as it may well be, he shall have his clergy, for the statute of 5 Edw. VI, c. [10], speaks only of 'any wilful murder of malice prepensed'. Nevertheless those words are implied within the word *murdravit*. {Stanford, fo. 130.[7] Dyer, 3 Mar. 131:[8] an inquiry concerning abettors of appeals without saying *per maliciam*. See 2 Eliz. 183, Dyer.[9]}

101. ANDROWES v. BLUNT[10]

Common Pleas, Mich. 1573.

Mich. 15 & 16 Eliz.

John Blunt, being seised in special tail of the manor of Allexton in Leicestershire, to which the advowson of the same vill is appendant, remainder to the right heirs of Lord Mountjoy, in the year of our Lord 1552 by deed indented (but not enrolled)

---

[1] I.e. put it into effect.
[2] *Francis Trugeon's Case* (1579) below, p. 96, no. 162.
[3] Noted below, p. 162, no. 318, where it is said that the Exch. case was cited in Holcroft's appeal in the King's Bench. *Ff* and *Gg* both supply the other party's name as Burroughs, though that is not here in the notebook: cf. below, p. 162, n. 4.
[4] 13 Eliz., c. 8.
[5] Not found in what remains of Dyer's notebooks under this date (which is clearly written here as 20 Eliz.). Cf. *Weekes' Case* (1580) 110 Selden Soc. 380, which is in point but dates from 22 Eliz. Folio 136 of Peryam's MS. of Dyer did belong to the year 20 Eliz.: see the table, above, p. ccxxxvii.
[6] YB Mich. 11 Hen. VI, fo. 2, pl. 5.   [7] Sta. P.C. 130B.
[8] *Reade* v. *Rochforth* (1556) Dyer 131.
[9] *Anon.* (Pas. 1560) Dyer 183, pl. 59.

ladvouson a un Anthony Androwes pur iij C. xiij li. vj s. viij d. per ceux parolx, scilicet, The said J. Blunt doth covenaunt, grant, bargaine and sell the mannour of Alaxton with thadvowson to Anthonie Androws and his heires in such mannour as hereafter foloweth, the said J. Blunt doth covenaunt to suffer a recoverie before [blank] the day of [blank][1] of the said mannour with the advouson to thuse of the said Anthonie Androwes and his heires, yelding and paieng yearly to the said J. Blunt and his heires 42 li. of rent, with clause of distres and a nomine pene, and further the said John Blunt doth covenaunt and graunt for the further assurauns of the said rent to him selfe as of the said mannour with the advouson to Androwes to levie a fine sur conusauns de droit tantum before the feast of St John B. next comming unto Androwes with a render of a rent of 42 li. unto Blunt, provided that the said Androwes shall graunt the advouson backe againe to Blunt during his life, and that if he die before any presentment by him had then the said Androwes to grant the next avoidaunce to his executors so that they may have one presentment, and further it is covenaunted that all assurances herafter to be had or made to be to such uses and intentz as are comprised within these indentures and to no other uses and intentz. Et puis le dit Blunt suffer un recoverie accordant et apres le feast de St John Baptist, videlicet al octabis de Saint Michael, Blunt et Androwes joine in une fine al R[ichard][2] Perkins sur conusauns de droit come ceo que il ad de <son>ᵈ lour done ove render del rent al Blunt in taile, le remainder al James Blunt, Segnior Mountjoy, in fe, et puis devaunt ascun request Androwes morust anno 4 Marie, nul graunt de advouson esteant fait al Blunt in son vie etc., <et puis pur le condition nient perfourme Blunt enter in le mannour, leglise devient voide, Blunt present Bradley. Androwes port quare impedit vers Bradley, levesque de Lincolne et Blunt etc.>[3] In cest case 3 questions fueront move.

[1.] Si cest proviso esteant placed enter divers covenauntes serra condition ou un conditionel covenaunt. Et quant a ceo fuit tenus per totam curiam que ceo fuit un condition et nemi un covenaunt, car ilz agreont que le lieu et placinge dun condition nest materiall deins un fait issint que ceo nest referre al ascun covenaunt ou auter sentence, mes ceo stat substantive per soy mesme et est le commencement de un sentence [et] nest materiall ou ceo est placed: come fuit agree in le case dun Pecksall que home fist leasse pur ans et <le>ⁱ lessor graunt al lesse de succider toutz arbres proviso que il ne succider arbres de certain age et quantite, et ceo fuit tenus nul condition mes conditionel covenaunt, causa qua supra. Mes quant le proviso stat absolutement in quecunque lieu que il soit escrie ceo est condition.

Le 2 point fuit, si cest fine levie extincte [ou] destroyera le condition ou nemi? Et fuit argue al barre que le condition fuit destroye, car per le covenaunt le fine duit aver

---

[1] *Also blank in JRL MS.*
[2] *JRL MS.*
[3] *JRL MS ends differently:* et puis le roigne present un Hayes, et puis anno 8 Eliz. le dit Edward Androwes sua livery et puis John Blunt morust et pur ceo que Anthony Androwes nad regrant ladvowson William Blunt come fitz et heire de J. Blunt enter in le mannour, et donques lesglise devient voide, William Blunt present un Bradley, ore incumbent, et Androwes port quare impedit vers Bradley, levesque de Linc. et William Blunt.

bargained and sold the same manor and the advowson to one Anthony Androwes for £313. 6s. 8d., by these words: 'The said John Blunt doth covenant, grant, bargain and sell the manor of Allexton, with the advowson, to Anthony Androwes and his heirs in such manner as hereafter followeth. The said John Blunt doth covenant to suffer a recovery of the said manor with the advowson, before a certain day, to the use of the said Anthony Androwes and his heirs, yielding and paying yearly to the said John Blunt and his heirs £42 rent, with clause of distress and a *nomine poenae*,[1] and further the said John Blunt doth covenant and grant for the further assurance of the said rent to himself, as of the said manor with the advowson to Androwes, to levy a fine to Androwes *sur conusance de droit tantum* before the feast of St John Baptist next coming, rendering a rent of £42 to Blunt, provided that the said Androwes shall grant the advowson back again to Blunt during his life, and that if he should die before any presentation made by him then the said Androwes [is] to grant the next avoidance to his executors, so that they may have one presentation; and further it is covenanted that all assurances hereafter to be had or made should be to such uses and intents as are comprised within these indentures, and to no other uses and intents'. Then the said Blunt suffered a recovery accordingly, and after the feast of St John Baptist, namely at the octaves of St Michael, Blunt and Androwes joined in a fine to Richard Perkins *sur conusance de droit come ceo que il ad de lour done*, with render of the rent to Blunt in tail, remainder to James Blount, Lord Mountjoy, in fee; and afterwards, before any request, Androwes died in the fourth year of Mary, no grant of the advowson having been made to Blunt in his lifetime; <then Blunt entered in the manor for non-performance of the condition, the church became vacant, and Blunt presented Bradley. Androwes brought *quare impedit* against Bradley, the bishop of Lincoln and Blunt.>[2] In this case three questions were moved.

1. Is this proviso, being placed among various covenants, a condition or a conditional covenant? As to this, it was held by the whole court that it was a condition and not a covenant; for they agreed that the location and placing of a condition within a deed is not material, so long as it does not refer to any covenant or other sentence, but stands substantively by itself and is the commencement of a sentence.[3] And it is not material where it is placed: as was agreed in the case of one Pecksall,[4] where someone made a lease for years, and the lessor granted to the lessee that he could fell all trees, provided that he did not fell trees of a certain age and size, and this was held not to be a condition but a conditional covenant, for the above reason. However, when the proviso stands absolutely, in whatsoever place it is written, it is a condition.

The second point was whether the levying of this fine extinguished or destroyed the condition, or not. And it was argued at the bar that the condition was destroyed,

---

[1] A monetary penalty for non-payment of rent.
[2] The JRL MS ends differently (tr.; text opposite): 'then the queen presented one Hayes, and then in 8 Eliz. the said Edward Androwes sued livery; then John Blunt died, and because Anthony Androwes had not regranted the advowson, William Blunt (as son and heir of John Blunt) entered in the manor; then the church became vacant, William Blunt presented one Bradley, the present incumbent, and Androwes brought *quare impedit* against Bradley, the bishop of Lincoln, and William Blunt.' The presentation and resignation of Philip Hayes is mentioned in the record, but the defendant's name was John Blunt (son and heir of James).
[3] Cf. below, p. 90, no. 149 (in the same case).   [4] Cf. above, p. 49, no. 96 (1572).

estre levie al [And]rowes et nemy Blunt, et Androwes joine in une fine al Perkins que [fuit] estraunge et auxi le covenaunt fuit que le fine serra levie sur [conusans] de droit tantum et cest darren fine fuit levie sur conusauns [*fo. 75*] de droit come ceo que il ad de son done. Auxi fuit dit que in le darren fine la fuit un graunt et render dun rent, le quel est toutz foitz al use del conusees, et pur ceo ne poet estre al primer uses. Et ceo nient obstant fuit tenus per totam curiam que cest fine ne extinctera le condition, nient obstant ascun chose que ad estre dit, car ilz disoient que <ces>^d si cest darren covenant (scilicet que toutz assurauncs en apres destre fait serra al uses et intentz conteine in mesme les indentures) ust estre omyse in lendenture que donques le dit fine issint levie extinctera et destroiera le condition, car la fuit agre[1] clerement si home fait feffment in fe sur condition ou rendant rent, si puis le feffor levie un fine generalment al feffee son rent et condition sont ale et destroye. Mes fuit dit que cest generall covenant fait le condition executorie sur toutz assurauncs faitz, car apres recoverie ewe lestate create per le recoverie est subject a cest condition, et apres si fine soit levie le fine est deins mesme le predicament. Et issint quant a ceo ilz agreont que per reason de cest darrein generall covenant que ne fuit restraine a ascun particuler assurauns ne al ascun speciall person le fine ne ad destroye le condition. Et quant a ceo que fuit dit que pur ceo que fuit un graunt et render in le fine que pur ceo ceo serra al opes del conusees, fuit respondue que quant un graunt et render est fait in une fine icy est un use imply per la ley al conusees, et un nude averment dun auter opes ne poet estre averre encounter ceo, uncore quant un use est expresse ceo controlle le use implye, et pur ceo que les uses fueront expresses in les indentures coment que le fine fuit sur graunt et render uncore cest expresse use controllera le implied use. Mes Manwood dit que les parties poient alter et chaunge le use per auter indenture ou per auters uses expresses, mes serra prise contrarie tanque tiel especiall matter soit monstre.

Le 3 point fuit, si Blunt entra pur le condition enfreint entaunt que nul request fuit fait al Androwes in son vie? Et la Manwood prist le diversitie quant le request est parcell del condition et quant nemi. Car il dit si jeo enfeffe un sur condition que il reenfeffera un quant jeo luy requirera, la sil morust devant request jeo ne unques entera pur le condition enfreint, mes in nostre case le request nest parcell del condition, mes il dit que le feffe ad temps durant son vie si le feffor ne hasten ceo per request: quod Mounson et Harper concesserunt. Mez ilz disoient clerement que si le feffe ne graunt le advouson al feffor devant avoidaunce eschue donques est le feffee disable a faire le graunt, car ore ceo est in auter plite. Mes le Segnior Dier tient que in le principall case le condition fuit enfreint in le vie de Androwes, car il tient que le feffee covient daver regraunt ladvouson in convenient temps, car autermment peraventure le eglise puissoit devenir voide et issint disabilitie. Et Harper et le Segnior Dier teignont que si home face feffment in fe sur condition que le feffee regrantera ceo a luy un rent hors de mesme la terre durant son vie, in cest case le feffee est tenus de regranter a luy rent in le primer anne, car autermment il navera le rent annuelment durant son vie. Et issint il tient in cest case que le condition fuit infreint devant le

---

[1] *Written twice.*

for by the covenant the fine was to have been levied to Androwes, not Blunt, and Androwes joined in a fine to Perkins, who was a stranger; also the covenant was that the fine should be levied *sur conusance de droit tantum*, and this latter fine was levied *sur conusance de droit come ceo que il ad de son done*. Also it was said that in the latter fine there was a grant and render of a rent, which is always to the use of the cognisees, and therefore cannot be to the first uses. Notwithstanding this, it was held by the whole court that this fine did not extinguish the condition, whatever has been said. They said that if the last covenant (that 'all assurances to be made thereafter should be to the uses and intents contained in the same indentures') had been omitted in the indenture, then the said fine so levied would have extinguished and destroyed the condition; for it was clearly agreed there that if someone makes a feoffment in fee upon condition, or rendering rent, and afterwards the feoffor levies a fine generally to the feoffee, his rent and condition are gone and destroyed. But it was said that this general covenant made the condition executory upon all assurances made; for after a recovery had, the estate created by the recovery is subject to this condition, and if afterwards a fine is levied the fine is within the same predicament. Therefore, as to this point, they agreed that by reason of this last general covenant, which was not restricted to any particular assurance or any special person, the fine had not destroyed the condition. As to what had been said that, because there was a grant and render in the fine, therefore it shall be to the use of the cognisees, it was answered that when a grant and render is made in a fine there is a use implied by the law to the cognisees, and a bare averment of another use cannot be made against that, though when a use is expressed it controls the implied use; and because the uses were expressed in the indentures, even though the fine was upon a grant and render, this express use shall control the implied use. MANWOOD said that the parties could alter and change the use by another indenture, or by other express uses; but the contrary shall be assumed until such special matter is shown.

The third point was: may Blunt enter for breach of the condition, inasmuch as no request was made to Androwes in his lifetime? Here MANWOOD made a distinction between when the request is parcel of the condition and when not. For he said that if I enfeoff someone upon condition that he should re-enfeoff someone when I request him, and then he dies before a request, I may never enter for breach of the condition; but in our case the request is not parcel of the condition, but he said that the feoffee had time throughout his life [to make the regrant], if the feoffor did not hasten it by request: which MOUNSON and HARPER granted. But they said clearly that if the feoffee does not grant the advowson to the feoffor before an avoidance falls in, then the feoffee is disabled to make the grant, for it is now in another plight. But the lord DYER held that in the principal case the condition was broken in the life of Androwes, for he held that the feoffee had to regrant the advowson in a convenient time, for otherwise perhaps the church might become void and thus there would be a disablement. And HARPER, and the lord DYER, held that if someone makes a feoffment in fee upon condition that the feoffee should regrant to him a rent out of the same land during his life, in this case the feoffee is bound to regrant a rent to him in the first year, for otherwise he would not have the rent annually during his life. Therefore he held in this case that the condition was broken before the fine levied, because it was two years before the bargain and sale

fine levie pur ceo que fuit 2 ans devant le <feff>ᵈ bargaine et vend et le fine levie, et donques le advouson fuit arere in luy sauns clayme, come ilz tient, et donques quant il levie le fine il done ladvouson absolutement. Et nota, il tient auxi que quant <Androwes>ᵈ Blunt bargaine et vende, done et graunt le mannour et ladvouson etc. coment que le <feff>ᵈ bargain et vende ne fuit unques inrolle uncore ladvouson que puit loialment passer per graunt passera sauns inrollement. Mes uncore, ceo nient obstant, al darrein judgment fuit done pur <ple>ᵈ les defendants enconter Androwes, et le Segnior Anderson puis accorda a les auters justices.

Et la fuit dit que Putnams case in le court de gardes fuit que Putnam fist feffment in fe al A, B et C al Drinkston rendant rent et puis covenant de levier fine des dit terres ove graunt et render del rent et un generall covenant fuit auxi, come supra, et puis Putnam levie fine des terres a A et B tantum et uncore fuit [tenus] que in respect del generall covenant le fine ceo nient obstant fuit al [use de] mesme lendentures.

[102]

AB, fo. 75v (290v). *Ff*, fo. 168v. *Gg*, fo. 27.

<Woods case anno 21 Eliz. in leschequer termino Tr.>ˢ

Le roigne fist leasse pur ans desouth leschequer seale sur condition que si le rent soit arere que donques le leasse serra void, et puis le rent fuit arere et puis information fuit conceive vers le lesse sur intrusion, et puis lenformation office fuit trove que le rent fuit arere. Et fuit tenus per Manwood, chief baron, Baron Shute et totam curiam que coment que tout cest matter fuit trove per verdit sur lenformation que le roigne navera judgment sur cest verdit pur ceo que devant office le roigne ne fuit entitle et issint nul intrusion, coment que fuit diversitie quant le condition reserve un reentre et quant pur le non perfourmauns del condition le leasse serra void. Mes tout fuit tenus un quant a cest purpose. Et nota le relation del office ne puit faire lentrusion etc. pur maintener lenformation. <Nota bene si le roigne fist leasse rendant rent destre pay al maynes de ses baillies in cest case pur ceo que le rent nest paiable sur le terre <mes>ᵈ car le roigne nest tenus a demaunder ceo poet estre trove in ascun countie en Engliterre. Mes si le rent soit a paier al receit del Exchequer auterment.>ᵃ ¹

[103]

AB, fo. 75v (290v). *Ff*, fo. 168. *Gg*, fo. 26. *Lb*, fo. 4.

Nota que Serjaunt Fenner dit a moy² que fuit adjudge que ou A covenaunt ove B que si B ferra tiel act que donques il estoiera seisie al use to B et ses heires, et puis

---

¹ *Written above the report.*
² Ed. C[oke] *Ff.* E. C. *Gg.*

and the fine levied, and then the advowson was back in him without claim (as they held), and then when he levied the fine he gave the advowson absolutely. Note that he also held that when Blunt bargained and sold, gave and granted the manor and the advowson, even though the bargain and sale was never enrolled, still the advowson (which may lawfully pass by grant) passed without enrolment. Nevertheless, notwithstanding this, judgment was in the end given for the defendants against Androwes, and the lord ANDERSON afterwards agreed with the other justices.

And it was there said that Puttenham's case, in the Court of Wards,[1] was that Puttenham made a feoffment in fee to A, B and C at Drinkstone,[2] rendering rent, and afterwards covenanted to levy a fine of the said lands with grant and render of the rent, and there was also a general covenant, as above; and afterwards Puttenham levied a fine of the lands to A and B only; and yet it was held that, in respect of the general covenant, the fine was (notwithstanding this) to the use of the same indentures.

102. R. v. WOOD

Exchequer, Trin. 1579.

Wood's case, Trin. 21 Eliz., in the Exchequer.

The queen made a lease for years under the Exchequer seal, upon condition that if the rent should be in arrear the lease should then be void; afterwards the rent was in arrear; then an information *sur intrusion* was conceived against the lessee; and, after the information, an office was found that the rent was in arrear. And it was held by MANWOOD C.B., SHUTE B. and the whole court that although all this matter was found by verdict upon the information, the queen should not have judgment upon this verdict, because the queen was not entitled before office and therefore there was no intrusion. Although there was a distinction, when the condition reserves a re-entry and when for the non-performance of the condition the lease is to be void, it was held to be all one as to this purpose.[3] Note that the relation back of the office could not make an intrusion so as to maintain the information. {Note well that if the queen makes a lease rendering rent to be paid into the hands of her bailiffs, in this case inasmuch as the rent is not payable on the land – for the queen is not bound to demand it – it may be found in any county in England; but if the rent is to be paid at the Receipt of the Exchequer, it is otherwise.}

103. USES

Conversation, *c.* 1577/80.

Note that *Serjeant Fenner* told me it was adjudged that where A covenanted with B that if B performed a certain act he should then stand seised to the use of B and his

---

[1] Reported as *Puttenham* v. *Duncombe* (1558) Dyer 157; 1 And. 18; and see above, p. 39, no. 84.
[2] In Suffolk.
[3] The same question was litigated at length in the Exch. and Exch. Ch. in *Finch* v. *Throckmorton* (1589–94): see Baker, *Magna Carta*, p. 285, and the references there.

et devant le condition perfourme B disseisist A, et puis perfourme le condition, et il dit que nient obstant son feffment et enconter ceo le use serra vestue in B et ses heires.

[104]

AB, fo. 76 (291).

<Weldens Case.>[s]

P. 20 Eliz. Home ayant terme pur 60 ans per son testament devise in tiel forme, I will that Johan Davies my wife shall have and occupie my landes which are conteined in a leasse which I have etc. for so manie yeares as Johan shall fortune to live and after her deceasse the residue of the said yeares so unexpired <unto Frauces my>[d] I give and bequeath to Frauces my sonne and his assignes. Et puis fist le dit Johan son fem son sole executrix et puis morust. Johan prova le testament et enter in le terme enclaymant ceo come devise, le remainder ouster a son fitz Frauces. Et puis le dit fem prist baron et le baron et fem venda lentier terme et tout lour droit et interest al estraunge. Et puis le fem morust. Si ore lentre del Frauces ou de son administrator fuit congeable ou nemi, ceo fuit le question. Et fuit adjudge que cest vendition del baron et fem ne distroy le remainder al Frauces.

Et le reason de Meade fuit pur ceo que lentier interest ne fuit devise a fem, mes el ad forsque speciall interest et Frauces ad le generall interest, et le vend del cesti que [ad] forsque speciall interest ne barrera celuy in le remainder que ad le generall interest. Et il resemble ceo al case de 27 H. 8 [*blank*] inter Giles et John etc., et le case del garde que tient le terre pur le value, car en tielz cases ilz ont speciall interestes determinable sur un incertaintie. Mes il dit que sil ust devise le terme ou son interest pur un heure il ne unques puit limitter le remainder ouster.

Mounson argue a mesme lentent mes pur un auter reason. Et il dit que lentier terme fuit in le fem mes in un special mannour, scilicet subject a cest limitation que si el morust devant le terme que donques Frauces ceo avera. Et le volunt serra construe en cest forme come sil ust devise son terme a son fem cy longe come el vive et sil morust durant le terme que Frauces avera ceo. In cest case il dit clerement coment que le fem venda ceo uncore apres son mort Frauces poet enter per force del limitation. Et il dit que in voluntes le darren parolx serront construes in lieu del primers pur satisfier lentent et meaning del devisor. Et il dit si le done in taile que avoit fe simple conditionel devant lestatut et rien remaine in le donor forsque possibilitie de reverter, si le done devant lestatut et devant issue ust alien et morust sans issue uncore le donor avera le terre arere. Et cest feffment ne destroiera cest

---

commen place destre que le remainder est execute per admission de tenant pur vie copiholder': BL MS. Harley 1331, fo. 52. At the bottom of *AC*, fo. 223v (573v) there is a very defaced version of a dictum of Manwood J. in this case, cit. 'le case de Monninges in Templo' concerning exceptions in grants. Differently reported in Plowd. 516 (where Plowden says he did not hear the argument of Mead J.); Dyer 358; LI MS. Maynard 77, p. 187; B. & M. 208; BL MS. Harley 443, fos. 28v–30v.

[2] YB Pas. 27 Hen. VIII, fo. 5, pl. 15.

[3] Westminster II, c. 1, *De Donis Conditionalibus*.

heirs, and then (before the condition was performed) B disseised A, and afterwards performed the condition, then notwithstanding his feoffment – and against it (as he said) – the use would be vested in B and his heirs.

104. WELTDEN v. ELKINGTON[1]

Common Pleas, Pas. 1578.

Weltden's Case.

Easter term 20 Eliz. A man having a term for sixty years devised by his testament in this manner: 'I will that Joan Davies, my wife, shall have and occupy my lands which are contained in a lease which I have ... for as many years as Joan shall fortune to live, and after her decease the residue of the said years so unexpired I give and bequeath to Francis, my son, and his assigns'. Then he made the said Joan (his wife) his sole executrix, and afterwards died. Joan proved the testament and entered in the term, claiming it as devised, the remainder over to her son Francis. Then the said woman married another husband, and the husband and wife sold the whole term, and all their right and interest, to a stranger. Then the woman died. The question was, whether the entry of Francis, or of her administrator, was lawful, or not. And it was adjudged that this sale by the husband and wife did not destroy the remainder to Francis.

The reason given by MEAD was because the whole interest was not devised to the wife, but she had only a special interest and Francis had the general interest; and a sale by someone who has only a special interest will not bar the remainderman who has the general interest. He likened it to the case of 27 Hen. VIII between Giles and John,[2] and the case of the guardian who holds the land for the value, for in such cases they are special interests determinable upon an uncertainty. But he said that if he had devised the term or his interest for an hour, he could never have limited the remainder over.

MOUNSON argued to the same effect, but for another reason. He said that the whole term was in the wife, but in a special manner, namely subject to the limitation that if she died before the term Francis should have it. And the will should be construed in the same way as if he had devised his term to his wife so long as she lived, and if she died during the term then Francis should have it. In this case he said clearly that although the wife sold it, nevertheless after her death Francis could enter by virtue of the limitation. And he said that in wills the later words should be construed in place of the former words in order to satisfy the intent and meaning of the devisor. The donee in tail had a fee simple conditional before the statute,[3] and nothing remained in the donor except a possibility of reverter; and he said that if, before the statute (and before issue), he had aliened and died without issue, the donor would still have had the land back. And this feoffment will not destroy this possibility. Therefore he said

---

[1] CP 40/1344, m. 1226 (printed in Plowd. 516 and Benl. 308; summarised in B. & M. 208): William Weltden v. Thomas Elkington of Minchinhampton, Glos., clothier; trespass *quare causum fregit* at Minchinhampton; special verdict at bar; c.a.v. to Pas. 1578; judgment for the plaintiff, with £8 damages and £68 costs (an extraordinarily large sum). Noted below, p. 96, no. 161; p. 150, no. 278. In 1588 Coke said he had 'le very case escry southe Bendlose maine, que report lopinion de toutes les justices de

possibilitie. Et issint il dit in cest case que quant le fem est mort ore Fraunces puit enter per reason de cest executorie devise.

Manwood a mesme lentent mes put auter reason. Car il dit que le fem nad que speciall propertie, come si home pledge un chose pur deniers le pledgee ad un special interest. 5 H. 7, 1. Ou come sicome lesse pur xx ans graunt son estate rendant rent, et si le rent soit arere que il reentra et detenera quousque, in cest case il ad speciall interest. 29 E. 3. Issint si lesse pur ans soit extend pur meindre terme, le conusee ad speciall interest. Et issint est si lesse pur xx ans graunt rent charge hors de ceo a un pur vie, il ad estate pur xx ans in le rent sil vive cy longe. Et il agrea que si le devise ust estre de lentier terme al fem ut supra le vendition de luy ust barre le remainder.

Dier a mesme lentent mes pur auter reason. Car il dit que la fem nad forsque jus possessionis durant sa vie, et le fitz ad jus proprietatis, et prist di[versite] quant le terme fuit devise et quant le use fuit devise. Et ilz agreont que le vendition del fem come devise ve[s]tera le remainder in Fraunces issint que le vend de luy come executor ne puit barrer cesti en remainder <coment que el navoit que use et nul ter[me]>^a.

[105]

AB, fo. 76 (291). *Ff*, fo. 168v. *Gg*, fo. 27v.

<Dukes Case>⁵ <sur lestatut de 32 H. 8>^a.

<20 Eliz.>¹ Nota, Dukes case fuit in un ejectione firme parenter Ringrose et Priest que Richard Duke fuit seisie etc. et fist leas pur ans reservant rent sur condition, et apres levie un fine al Eden et auters al use luy et ces heires, et morust, et le revercion discend a Roger, que levie fine a Leson, que demande le rent et ne fuit pay, il enter et lessa a Ring[rose] que port laction de ejectione firme. Et fuit barre per judicium, et le reason de le judgment fuit pur ceo que ne fuit attornment, ergo nul loiall demande, et si nul loiall demaund nul benefit del condition. Et vide les parolx de lestatut de 32 H. 8 sont, that al manner of assignees shall and maye have and enjoy like advauntages against the lessees by entrie for non paiment of rent etc. as the said lessors or grauntors themselves or theire heires etc. ought, shoulde or might have enjoied at anie tyme or tymes in like manner and forme as if the revercion had not been graunted.

---

¹ *Ff, Gg, Lb, but not in AB.*

^a The present report is printed in the endnote in 110 Selden 273, but the word 'condition' at the end of the third line there is a misreading of 'reversion'; the reference given there (fo. 48r) is to the pencil number at the foot of the page.

⁴ The date 20 Eliz. is in three near-contemporary copies of Coke's report, but not in the autograph. The record has no continuances beyond Pas. 1573.

⁵ 32 Hen. VIII, c. 28.

that in this case, when the woman was dead, Francis could enter by reason of this executory devise.

MANWOOD to the same effect, but for another reason. For he said that the wife had but a special property, just as if someone pledges something for money, the pledgee has a special interest: 5 Hen. VII, fo. 1.[1] Or if a lessee for twenty years grants over his estate rendering rent, [on condition that] if the rent is in arrear he might re-enter and detain until [he is paid], in this case he has a special interest: 29 Edw. III.[2] Likewise if a lessee for years is extended for a lesser term, the cognisee has a special interest. So it is if a lessee for twenty years grants a rent-charge out of it to someone for life, he has an estate for twenty years in the rent if he lives so long. And he agreed that if the devise to the wife had been of the whole term as above, the sale by her would have barred the remainder.

DYER [C.J.] to the same effect, but for another reason. For he said that the wife had only *jus possessionis* during her life, and the son had *jus proprietatis*; and he drew a distinction between a devise of the term and a devise of the use. And they agreed that the sale by the wife as devisee vested the remainder in Francis, so that the sale by him as executor could not bar the remainderman, even though she only had a use and no term.

105. RYNGROSE d. LESON v. PREST: DUKE'S CASE[3]

Common Pleas, 1573.[4]

Duke's Case, upon the statute of 32 Hen. VIII.

Note that Duke's case, in an ejectment between Ryngrose and Prest, was that Richard Duke was seised of the land in question, and made a lease for years reserving rent upon condition, and afterwards levied a fine to Eden and others to the use of himself and his heirs, and died; the reversion descended to Roger, who levied a fine to Leson, who demanded the rent and was not paid; Leson entered and leased to Ryngrose, who brought the action of ejectment. And he was barred by judgment; and the reason of the judgment was because there was no attornment, and therefore no lawful demand; and if no lawful demand, no benefit of the condition. See the words of the statute of 32 Hen. VIII, that 'all manner of assignees shall and may have and enjoy like advantages against the lessees by entry for non-payment of rent ... as the said lessors or grantors themselves or their heirs ... ought, should or might have enjoyed at any time or times, in like manner and form as if the reversion had not been granted'.[5]

---

[1] *Lord Powes's Case* (1489) YB Mich. 5 Hen. VII, fo. 1, pl. 1; CP 40/910, m. 340d.
[2] YB Trin. 29 Edw. III, fo. 40, pl. [24].
[3] CP 40/1295, m. 311; CP 40/1302, m. 818 (abstracted in 110 Selden Soc. 264): Thomas Ryngrose v. Nicholas Prest of Frankton, Warw., yeoman; ejectment for lands in Frankton, on the demise of Anthony Leson or Leyson; pleads Not Guilty; demurrer to the evidence at Warwick assizes, March 1572; no judgment entered. Cit. in *AD*, fo. 806v ('Vide Dukes case devant fol. 76 in mes notes'). Differently reported in Dyer's notebook, 110 Selden Soc. 263, 273; LI MS. Hale 134, fo. 274, sub nom. *Ducke's Case* (dated 20 Eliz.) (giving the plaintiff's name as Ringer, as does *Ff*); LI MS. Misc. 361, fo. 80 (sim.).

58 REPORTS FROM COKE'S NOTEBOOKS

[106]

AB, fo. 76v (291v).

<Cranmers Case M. 14 Eliz.>ˢ

[C]ranmer larchevesque fist feffment in fe pur terme de son vie sauns impechment de wast, et puis son decesse al use de ces executors pur xxj ans, et apres le xxj ans finite al use de son fitz en taile, et pur defaut de tiel issue al use de luy et de ces droit heires, et puis in temps le roygne Marye le dit Cranmer fuit attaint de haut treason et combust pur heresie, et puis le roygne graunt ouster cest terme a un B, que enter, sur que cesti in le remainder enter et fist leas, quel esteant oust per le patente port ejectione firme. Et le principal et sole point in cest case fuit le quel cest terme fuit in le lesse pur vie ou nemi, ou si les executores averont ceo come purchasores et rien de ceo vest in le lesse pur vie. Et la un grounde fuit prise que auncestres et heires, testatour et executor, sont correlativa et in toutz cases quant le auncestre est nosme in le fait et prist ascun particuler interest et puis un estate est lymitte a ses droit heires que les heires prendra per discent et nemi per purchase. <18 E. 2, Feffmentes, 109.>ⁱ Mes auterment est quant launcestre ou le testatour nest pas nosme. Et al darrein fuit adjudge que le terme ne fuit in Cranmer, issint que il ne poet ceo forfeit al roy. Et lour principal reason fuit per lestatut de uses. Mes le Segnior Dier et Harper prist le common ley issint que per lordre de common ley le terme ne fuit in le testatour mes un libertie solement in luy pur nosmer et appointer ses executores. Et pristeront dyversite quant leas est fait al un pur vie, le remainder al luy et a ses executours pur ans, et quant ceo est limitte solement a ces executors. Mes Manwood, justice, tient le ley contrarie a ceo, mes postea mutavit opinionem sua[m] sur lestatut de uses. Vies in le title del estates quant le terme serra in le lesse pur vie et quant nemi.

[107]

AB, fo. 76v (291v). *Ff*, fo. 168v. *Gg*, fo 27v.

<Copwoods case 14 Eliz.>ˢ

Copwood pier et fitz, le pier fist leas pur vie al fitz, le remainder <al George¹ le fitz del fitz in tail, et pur defaut de tiel issue le remainder in fe al fitz etc., et al temps

---

¹ *Unclear.*

of Potter Newton, Yorks., esq. v. Thomas Cranmer of Kirkstall, Yorks., esq.; debt on a bond for £40; pleads infancy; found of full age; judgment for the plaintiff; KB 27/1245, m. 336 (Pas. 1573, continued from Hil 1570): Thomas Cranmer esq. v. Brian Bayles gent.; trespass *quare clausum fregit* in several places in Yorks.; pleads Not Guilty; *venire facias*.
² Cf. Co. Litt. 54b. ³ Cf. *Shelley's Case* (1581) 1 Co. Rep. 88; B. & M. 163.
⁴ Mich. 18 Edw. II, Fitz. Abr., *Feffements et faits*, pl. 109. ⁵ 27 Hen. VIII, c. 10.
⁶ Perhaps the previous note of this case, above, p. 21, no. 36; or *Haddon's Case* (1576) ibid., no. 38.
⁷ Noted below, p. 103, no. 177 (13 Eliz.); p. 133, no. 239. Cit. in *C*, fo. 205 ('come fuit adjudge in Copwoodes case'); 6 Co. Rep. 42 ('resolved by all the justices of the Common Pleas'). There is a similar text in LI MS. Misc. 361, fo. 80v. Differently reported in Dyer's notebook, 110 Selden Soc. 291 (Hil. 1574); LI MS. Hale 134, fo. 274 (12 Eliz., 'report per Glanvill'); BL MS. Add. 24845, fo. 102 (Pas. 1573).

106. KYRKE d. CRANMER v. BALES: CRANMER'S CASE[1]

Common Pleas, Mich. 1572.

Cranmer's Case, Mich. 14 Eliz.

Cranmer, the archbishop, made a feoffment in fee for term of his life, without impeachment of waste, and after his decease to the use of his executors for twenty-one years, and after the twenty-one years ended to the use of his son in tail, and for want of such issue to the use of him and of his right heirs; then, in the time of Queen Mary, the said Cranmer was attainted of high treason and burned for heresy; afterwards the queen granted over this term to one B., who entered, whereupon the remainderman entered and made a lease, and the lessee (being ousted by the patentee) brought ejectment. The principal and sole point in this case was whether this term was in the lessee for life or not, or whether the executors had it as purchasers and none of it vested in the lessee for life. And it was there taken to be a principle (*grounde*) that ancestors and heirs, or testators and executors, are correlative,[2] and in all cases when the ancestor is named in the deed and takes any particular interest, and afterwards an estate is limited to his right heirs, the heirs shall take by descent and not by purchase.[3] {18 Edw. II, *Feffements*, 109.[4]} But it is otherwise when the ancestor or the testator is not named. In the end it was adjudged that the term was not in Cranmer, and so he could not forfeit it to the king. Their principal reason was by virtue of the Statute of Uses.[5] But the lord DYER and HARPER took the common law to be that by the order of the common law the term was not in the testator, but only a liberty in him to name and appoint his executors. And they drew a distinction between when a lease is made to someone for life, remainder to him and to his executors for years, and when it is limited solely to his executors. MANWOOD J., however, held the law to be contrary to this; but he afterwards changed his opinion upon the Statute of Uses. See in the title of Estates,[6] when the term shall be in the lessee for life and when not.

107. COPWOOD v. CLARKE[7]

Common Pleas, 1572.

Copwood's case, 14 Eliz.

Copwood, father and son; the father makes a lease for life to the son, remainder to his heir male in tail; the son, having no issue, suffers a recovery with voucher;

---

[1] CP 40/1300, m. 938 (eight rolls; summarised in Benl. 207, pl. 245): Gilbert Kyrke v. Brian Bales of Potter Newton, Yorks., esq., John Wardman of Ardington, Yorks., yeoman, John Hunter of Cowrigg, Yorks., yeoman, and Jane Warde of Cowrigg, widow; ejectment for a large quantity of land in Leeds, Guiseley and Adel, Yorks., on the demise of Thomas Cranmer; demurrer to the several pleas in bar; c.a.v. to Mich. 1572; judgment for the plaintiff, with 5s. damages and £19. 15s. costs. Noted above, p. 21, no. 36; below, p. 78, no. 123; p. 85, no. 137; p. 123, no. 217; p. 129, no. 229; p. 131, no. 235; p. 144, no. 265. The text here is evidently based on the longer report which is partly printed in Appendix I. Differently reported in Dyer 309 (anon., Pas. 1572), identified in Coke's Dyer (Holkham 8014), fo. 309, as *Cranmer's Case*; Dyer's notebook, 110 Selden Soc. 260 (and see the headnote there for numerous other MS. reports); 1 And. 19, cit. record; BL MS. Harg. 373, fos. 48–50; IT MS. Petyt 511.12, fos. 203v–204v, sub nom. *Kirke* v. *Dale* (Mich. 1573). Cf. KB 27/1243, m. 431 (Mich. 1572): Brian Baylles

Copwood>d <a son heire male in taile>,[i] le fitz nad ascun issue et <puis Copwood le fitz>d suffer un recoverie ove voucher fait, et puis ad issue fitz et morust. Et tenus que le issue del fitz bien[1] puit aver formedone, car le recoverie ne puit barrer cesti [in] remainder in contingencie ou suspens pur ceo que le recompence que le ley intend ne puit aler a cesti que nest in esse.

Un parson fist un leas pur xxj ans a commencer apres son mort, et le patron et ordinarie confermont, et uncore tenus voide, car [quand] parson est mort son estate fuit determine.

Nota il fuit tenus in 8 Eliz. come Plowden et Segnior Wraye dit que si home fait leas pur ans a commencer a Michaelmas et a Michaelmas le lessor continue in possession per tout lan, le lessor navera action de dett, mes sil waive le possession et nul occupie ceo, ou si estraunge enter sur luy, le lessor avera action de det.

[108]

AB, fo. 8r-v[2] (300r-v).

<Hare & Bickleys case. Hill. 20 Eliz. rott. Dcxliiij.>[3] <Dier, 5 Eliz. 221. Vide 11 H. 4, 17.>[a]

Levesque de Lichfeld esteant patron dun prebend in le cathedrall eglise de Lichefeld collate un Albane Langdale a le dit prebend le 1 jour de Februarie anno 1 Eliz., le quel Albane Langdale apres institution et devant installation graunt un annuitie pur luy et ses successors hors de son prebend de 5 li. anuelment a un Edmund Hare, et levesque de Lichefeld ceo confirme, et puis Langdale fuit installe, et puis le deane et chapter confirme le dit graunt, et puis le dit Langdale fuit deprive, et puis levesque de Lichfield collate un Thomas Bickley a le dit prebend, le quel fuit admitt, institute et installe, vers que le dit Edmunde Hare port brefe dannuitie. Et fuit argue per les serjauntes et les justices, et toutz les justices argueront encounter le pleintife, scilicet que le dit graunt fait per le dit Langdale devant installation fuit tout ousterment voide a charger son successor.

Car Mead dit que il ne poet faire ascun temporell acte devant installation ne avera ascun temporell action ne distreiner pur ascun rent etc. Et il dit, si cesti que ad parsonage impropriate present a ceo, per le admission et institution leglise nest disapropriat tanque induction. Et il dit que larchdeacon poet refuser luy pur certain causes, quel prove que il nest parson devant.

Mounson a mesme lentent. Et il argue que il fuit un perfecte [*sic*] devant induction ou installation, car il ad le perfect spirituall function dun prebent per lenstitution, et lenstallation ne fait luy prebende car ceo nest que temporell acte. Mes coment que il

---

[1] *Apparently corrected from* biens.
[2] *In the new numbering of the portion which contains the reports printed below as Notebook 1.*

[3] *Archdale v. Beston* (1409) YB Mich. 11 Hen. IV, fo. 17, pl. 40.
[4] The prebend of Alrewas: record ('Alderwas').
[5] A younger brother of Nicholas Hare, bencher of the Inner Temple, he was admitted to that inn in 1558.
[6] Alban Langdale (d. 1580), a former fellow of St John's College, Cambridge, and sometime proctor of the University; a papist, he was deprived in 1559 for refusing to take the oath of supremacy: *ODNB*.

afterwards he has issue a son, and dies. And it was held that the issue of the son may well have formedon, for the recovery cannot bar the remainderman in contingency or suspense inasmuch as the recompense which the law presumes cannot go to someone who is not *in esse*.

[1]A parson made a lease for twenty-one years to commence after his death, and the patron and ordinary confirmed it, and yet it was held void; for when the parson was dead his estate was determined.

Note that it was held in 8 Eliz., as *Plowden* and the lord WRAY said, that if someone makes a lease to commence at Michaelmas, and at Michaelmas the [lessee] continues in possession for the whole year, the lessor shall not have an action of debt, but if he waives the possession and no one occupies it, or if a stranger enters upon him, the lessor shall have an action of debt.

108. HARE v. BYCKLEY[2]

Common Pleas, 1578.

{Hare and Byckley's case. Hil. 20 Eliz., roll 644. Dyer, 5 Eliz. 221. See 11 Hen. IV, fo. 17.[3]}

The bishop of Lichfeld, being patron of a prebend[4] in the cathedral church of Lichfield, collated one Alban Langdale to the said prebend on 1 February 1 Eliz. [1559], which Alban Langdale, after institution and before installation, granted for him and his successors an annuity of £5 out of his prebend [to be paid] annually to one Edmund Hare,[5] and the bishop of Lichfield confirmed this; then Langdale was installed, and afterwards the dean and chapter confirmed the said grant; afterwards the said Langdale was deprived,[6] and then the bishop of Lichfield collated one Thomas Byckley to the said prebend, who was admitted, instituted and installed; and the said Edmund Hare brought a writ of annuity against him. It was argued by the serjeants and the justices; and all the justices argued against the plaintiff, namely that the said grant made by the said Langdale before installation was utterly void to charge his successor.

MEAD said that he could not perform any temporal act before installation, or have any temporal action, or distrain for any rent etc. And he said that if someone who has an impropriated parsonage presents to it, the church is not disappropriated by the admission and institution until induction. And he said that the archdeacon might refuse [to induct] him for certain causes, which proves that he is not parson before induction.

MOUNSON to the same purpose. He argued that he was a perfect [prebendary] before induction or installation, for he had the perfect spiritual function of a prebendary by the institution, and the installation does not make him a prebendary, for it is only a

---

[1] The following two notes are probably separate. The reference to Wray C.J. must be later than 8 Nov. 1574, when he was appointed, and obviously he was not speaking in the Common Pleas.

[2] CP 40/1353, m. 644 (printed in Plowd. 526): Edmund Hare, scholar of Peterhouse, Cambridge v. Thomas Byckley, clerk, prebendary of Lichfield; writ of annuity for £80. 10s. arrears of an annuity of 100s. granted by the defendant's predecessor; demurrer to the plea in bar; c.a.v. to Trin. 1578; judgment for the defendant. Differently reported in Plowd. 528 (who says he did not hear Mead J. argue). The suit began fifteen years earlier: CP 40/1203, m. 860; Dyer 221.

soit prebend uncore devant installation il nad riens neque in fait neque in ley in les temporalties et pur ceo il ne poet charger devant installation intant que il nad riens in les temporalties, scilicet in le prebende, car nul parson ou prebend poet estre charge come parson ou prebend mes in respect dun parsonage ou dun prebende. Et il dit que un prebend consist de spirituelties et temporalties [et] per lenstitution il ad tout le espirituell jurisdiction, mes tanque installation il ad riens in les temporalties. Mes luy semble que il poet aver sute in le spirituel court pur subtraction de dismes, mes nemi silz sont severes del ix partes: quod Dier et Manwood negaverunt.

Manwood a mesme lentent. Et il dit que devant que le franktenement que est in suspence poet estre reduce a un parson, le patron que fuit le primer agent in le foundation covient faire le primer act, scilicet le presentment, lordinarie le 2 acte, et le archdeacon ou auter person que ad power de installe le 3 acte. Et il dit que le archdeacon fuit come un spirituel vicont. Et il dit que le institution est un judiciall acte, et le installation come execution de cest judgment. Et sicome un recoveror nad riens devant execution sue, issint nad le parson devant induction. Et uncore il agrea que apres admission et institution et devant induction le parson poet <charger>ᵈ purchase a luy et a ses successors. Mes il dit que le re[ason] [*fo. 8v*] que il ne puit charge fuit pur ceo <que>ⁱ quant un parson est destre charge ove un annuite come parson il covient estre charge in respect de son parsonage, et devant induction il nad le parsonage, et pur ceo il ne poet estre charge ove un annuite. Et a cest purpose vide 20 E. 3, tit. Annuitie, 34, in le case del prior alien. Et in mesme le case brefe de annuitie ne fuit maintenable daver judgment sur ceo et cessabit execution. <13 E. 3, Brefe, 264.>ⁱ Mes pur ceo que le roy ad seisie les temporaltes, ideo tanque restitution brefe dannuitie ne gist. 21 E. 4, 8, 9, 10, bone case. 1 H. 5, 1b. 45 E. 3, tit. Eschange.

Et le Segnior Dier argue a mesme lentent, mes Manwood semble que devant induction le parson poet prender les profitz, come 33 H. 6, 24, et 38 E. 3, 4, fuit. <Dier, 4 H. 8, 1b.>ⁱ Mes le Segnior Dier ceo denia etc. Et le Segnior Dier dit que parson ou nient parson serra trie per paiis, et issint serra induction. Et il dit que parson navera juris utrum devant induction. Et il dit, si issue fuit prise prebend ou nient prebend, sil ne soit install le <perso>ᵈ jurors troveront luy nient prebend.

Et issint judgment fuit done que le pleintife prist riens per son brefe. Vide 38 H. 6, 15, per Markham, 38 E. 3, 4. 22 H. 6, 27. 12 H. 4, 11. Mes la ilz toutz agreont que le parson de Byckley fuit charge come un private person et que le pleintife poet aver brefe dannuite envers luy, mes ne chargera son successor. <Vide Bracton, fol. 226b, cum successor fuerit institutus et statim nomine ecclesie est quasi in possessione. Bracton 225. Dier, 5 Eliz. 221.>ᵃ

---

[7] YB Hil. 28 Edw. III, fo. 3.   [8] *Bataille* v. *Cooke* (1512) Dyer 1; CP 40/990, m. 514.

[9] *Sir Thomas Dynham's Case* (1459) YB Mich. 38 Hen. VI, fo. 14, pl. [32] ('14'), at fo. 15, *per* Markham C.J.

[10] YB Hil. 38 Edw. III, fo. 4.

[11] *Sir John Dynham's Case* (1443) YB Mich. 22 Hen. VI, fo. 25, pl. 46, at fo. 27.

[12] YB Mich. 12 Hen. IV, fo. 11, pl. 21.

[13] *Bracton*, iii. 177: '(tr.) When his successor has been instituted, he is at once *quasi* in possession in the name of the church'.

[14] Dyer's report of the present case.

temporal act. However, even though he is a prebendary, nevertheless before installation he has nothing in the temporalities, either in fact or in law; therefore he may not charge them before installation, inasmuch as he has nothing in the temporalities, namely in the prebend: for no parson or prebendary may be charged as parson or prebendary save in respect of a parsonage or of a prebend. And he said that a prebend consisted of spiritualities and temporalities, and by the institution he has all the spiritual jurisdiction, but until installation he has nothing in the temporalities. It seemed to him, however, that he could have a suit in the spiritual court for subtraction of tithes, though not when they are separated from the nine parts: which DYER [C.J.] and MANWOOD denied.

MANWOOD to the same purpose. He said that before the freehold (which is in suspense) can be brought back to a parson, the patron (who was the first agent in the foundation) must perform the first act, namely the presentation, the ordinary the second act, and the archdeacon (or other person who has power to install) the third act. And he said that the archdeacon was like a spiritual sheriff, and that the institution was a judicial act, and the installation like an execution of that judgment. And, just as a recoveror has nothing before execution is sued, so, likewise, the parson has nothing before induction. Nevertheless, he agreed that after admission and institution, and before induction, the parson could purchase unto himself and his successors. But he said that the reason why he could not charge was because, when a parson is to be charged with an annuity as parson, he must be charged in respect of his parsonage, and before induction he does not have the parsonage, and therefore it may not be charged with an annuity. To this purpose see 20 Edw. III, tit. *Annuitie*, 34, in the case of the alien prior.[1] In the same case a writ of annuity was not maintainable, so as to have judgment thereon, and execution would be stayed. {13 Edw. III, *Briefe*, 264.[2]} But because the king had seized the temporalities, a writ of annuity did not lie until restitution. 21 Edw. IV, fos. 8, 9, 10, is a good case.[3] 1 Hen. V, fo. 1v.[4] 45 Edw. III, tit. *Exchaunge*.[5]

The lord DYER argued to the same purpose. MANWOOD, however, thought that before induction the parson could take the profits, as was said in 33 Hen. VI, fo. 24,[6] and 38 Edw. III, fo. 4.[7] {Dyer, 4 Hen. VIII, fo. 1v.[8]} But the lord DYER denied that. And the lord DYER said that 'parson or no parson' shall be tried by the country, as shall induction. He said that a parson shall not have *juris utrum* before induction. And he said that if issue is taken as to 'prebendary or no prebendary', and he is not installed, the jurors will find him not to be a prebendary.

Therefore judgment was given that the plaintiff take nothing by his writ. {See 38 Hen. VI, fo. 15, *per* Markham;[9] 38 Edw. III, fo. 4;[10] 22 Hen. VI, fo. 27;[11] 12 Hen. IV, fo. 11.[12] But they all agreed on this occasion that Byckley's person was charged as a private person, and that the plaintiff could have a writ of annuity against him, but it would not charge his successor. See Bracton, fo. 226v: 'cum successor fuerit institutus et statim nomine ecclesiae est quasi in possessione.'[13] Dyer, 5 Eliz. 221.[14]}

---

[1] Mich. 20 Edw. III, Fitz. Abr., *Annuitie*, pl. 34. See also below, p. 112, no. 201 (1576).
[2] Trin. 13 Edw. III, Fitz. Abr., *Briefe*, pl. 264.   [3] YB Pas. 21 Edw. IV, fos. 7–10, pl. 22.
[4] *Abbot of Leicester's Case* (1414) YB Hil. 1 Hen. V, fo. 1, pl. 2.
[5] Mich. 45 Edw. III, Fitz. Abr., *Exchaunge*, pl. 1.
[6] *Odingsells* v. *Prior of Maxstoke* (1455) YB Trin. 33 Hen. VI, fo. 24, pl. 3.

[109]

AB, fo. 8v (300v).

<M. 15 et 16 Eliz. rott. Mdccxlviij inter Jacson et Drurie[1] in partitione facienda.>[s]
<Fines. Tenant in taile, le remaindre al roy, levie fine.>[a] [2]

Tenant in taile, le remaindre al roy, apres 30 H. 8 levie un fine. Fuit adjudge que cest fine liera les issues, car le savant in le dit statut ne fait ascun mention del remaindre in le roy mes solement del revercion. Vide lestatut de 34 H. 8, cap. 20, de recoveries. Et vide le proviso in le dit statute que ad certain generall parolx que nul acte per tenant in taile prejudicera son issue. <Mesme la ley dun common recovery ewe vers le tenant in taile ou le revercion <ne>[d] fuit in le roy per discent del duke de Lancaster, Trin. 23 Eliz. inter Dinely et Asheton.>[a]

[110]

AB, fo. 8v (300v).

<P. 16 Eliz. rott. Mdxi. Confirmation.>[3]

Un A., prebend dun prebend in le eglise de Sarum, per fait indent in anno 32 H. 8 dimitta un rectorie, parcell de son prebende, pur lxx ans a un J. C., et apres levesque de Sarum confirma le dit leasse quant a 51 ans et nemy ouster, et issint le deane et chapter ceo confirma auxi pur lj ans et nemi ouster. Et fuit adjudge que ceux fueront bone confirmations pur lj ans al meyns et nemi voide. Et la semble que levesque, deane et chapter poent issint confirme especialment. Mes agre que home ne poet attorne pur parcell.

---

[1] *Sic.*
[2] *In outer margin.*
[3] *In outer margin.*

109. JACKSON and CLESBIE v. DARCY and CONYERS[1]

Common Pleas, 1574/75.

Mich. 15 & 16 Eliz., roll 1748, between Jackson and [Darcy] in *partitione facienda*. Fines. Tenant in tail, remainder to the king, levies a fine.

Tenant in tail, the remainder to the king, after [the statute of] Hen. VIII,[2] levied a fine. It was adjudged that this fine would bind the issue, for the saving in the said statute makes no mention of a remainder in the king, but only of the reversion. See the statute of 34 & 35 Hen. VIII, c. 20, concerning recoveries. And see the proviso in the said statute which has certain general words that no act by tenant in tail shall prejudice his issue. {The law is the same of a common recovery had against the tenant in tail where the reversion was in the king by descent from the duke of Lancaster: Trinity term 23 Eliz. between Dineley and Assheton.[3]}

110. BETTISFORD v. FORD[4]

Common Pleas, 1574.

Pas. 16 Eliz., roll 1511. Confirmation.

One A., prebendary of a prebend[5] in the [cathedral] church of Salisbury, by deed indented, in the year 32 Hen. VIII demised a rectory, parcel of his prebend, for seventy years to one J. C., and afterwards the bishop of Salisbury confirmed the said lease as to fifty-one years and no more, and, likewise, the dean and chapter confirmed it also for fifty-one years and no more. And it was adjudged that these were good confirmations for fifty-one years at least, and not void. And it seemed there that a bishop, dean and chapter may confirm specially in that way. But it was agreed that a man cannot attorn for parcel.

---

[1] CP 40/1325, m. 1748 (printed in Co. Ent. 414; summarised in 110 Selden Soc. 321): John Jackson and Askulph Clesbie v. Thomas Darcy esq. and Katherine Conyers; partition as to numerous manors in Yorks.; plea that they did not hold the tenements *pro indiviso*; special verdict at York assizes, Lent 1574; c.a.v. to Hil. 1575; judgment for the plaintiff. Also noted above, p. 13, no. 23 (anon.); p. 21, no. 37 (anon.). Cit. in *C*, fo. 202v (vol. iv, p. 762); 2 Co. Rep. 52. Differently reported in 3 Leon. 57 (Mich. 1574); 4 Leon. 40; Moo. 115 (dated Pas. 1578); 1 And. 46 (anon.), cit. record; Benl. 223 (sim.); Dyer's notebook, 110 Selden Soc. 320; LI MS. Maynard 87, fos. 200v–202v.

[2] 32 Hen. VIII, c. 36.

[3] Briefly reported below, p. 162, no. 317; in vol. ii, p. 192, and more fully in vol. iv, p. 895. The same case was cited by Dyer in his report of *Jackson* v. *Darcy*.

[4] Probably CP 40/1322, m. 1511 (unfit for production). Cf. the replevin action of this name (1596) in *C*, fo. 144; vol. iv, p. 678; 5 Co. Rep. 81, sub nom. *Foord's Case* (Pas. 1595). Differently reported in Dyer 338, pl. 43 (anon.), cit. record as above; Benl. 238, pl. 265, cit. record (m. '511'). The record is also cit. in 1 And. 47, following a report of the 1596 case.

[5] The prebend of King's Lyme (Lyme Regis) or Lyme-cum-Halstock, Dorset: vol. iv, p. 678. In the later editions of 5 Co. Rep. this is rendered as Kingston, modernising 'Kingstune' in the first edition; but Kingstune is a misreading of Kingslime. The prebendary in 1574 was David Yale. In 1575 he submitted to an arbitration concerning the lease of the prebend which William Elesdon claimed to have for many years yet to come: Salisbury Cathedral Archives, PR/LH/9.

[111]

AB, fo. 9 (301). *Ff*, fo. 178. *Gg*, fos. 33v–34. *Abridged in La*, fo. 130v;[1] *BL MS. Harley 1693*, fo. 101v.[2]

Countes de Lennox case. <[19 R. 2], tit. Estoppell, 28[1], que son heire ne fuit estoppe a dire que el fuit covert al temps et issint avoide.>[a]

Le counte de Lennox et la countes son fem consusteront un estatut [etc.][3] et puis le counte morust, et fuit adjudge que cest statut ne liera la fem car fem covert ne serra lye per statut conus ne per fait enrolle. Mes autermentest dun enfaunt, car ceux liera luy a toutz jours silz ne soient avoides durant son minoritie. Et le reason del difference enter fem covert et enfant est pur ceo que le judge poet aver prise conusauns le quel lenfaunt fuit deins age ou de plein age, et pur ceo ceo fuit error in le judge, et pur ceo tiel conusauns nest voide mes voidable, mes si le feme covert conus[t] un fait le judge per inspection ne per ascun auter voy judicialiter poet prender conusauns si el soit covert ou nemi, car examination ne gist in le case. 29 H. 8, tit. Faitz inrolle, 14, B. 7 E. 4, 5, accordant, et prist difference enter un fem covert et un enfant. 14 E. 3, tit. Execution, 73, la semble que fem covert serra ly per un estatute merchaunt conus, mes F. fait un quere de ceo. Vide 43 E. 3, tit. Audita querela, 16. 18 E. 3, 29,[4] enfaunt avoidra un statute. <Vide 31 E. 3, tit. Saver de defaut, 37, si ideot soit impled et fait defaut puis defaut al petit [cape][5] il ne savera son defaut pur ideoci car ne poet appere al justices. Issint si home de non sane memory fait recognisauns il navoidera ceo.>[a]

[112]

AB, fo. 9 (301). *Ff*, fo. 178.

<Dier, 22 Eliz. 368.>[a]

H. 21 Eliz. cest cas fuit move in le common banke <per Anderson>.[i] Home ad issue 2 fitz et oblige luy et ses <heires>[i] in un obligation et devie seisie de certaine terres issint que assetz discend a son heire, per que leigne fitz enter et morust seisie sans issue, per que le puisne fitz enter. Ore fuit move coment le brefe serra port vers le puisne fitz. Et la fuit tenus que le oblige avera generall brefe et special declaration, car fuit dit que si le defendant plede riens per discent de son pier, ceo serra trove

---

[1] *Ends:* ex libro Cooke reportes come jeo escrye ex libro Crewe.
[2] 22 et 23 Eliz. Le countess de Lynox case … Ex libro Coke.
[3] *Supplied from Ff*.
[4] 28 *Ff*.
[5] *Ff*.

[6] YB Pas. 7 Edw. IV, fo. 5, pl. 13.
[7] Trin. 14 Edw. III, Fitz. Abr., *Execucion*, pl. 73.
[8] Fitz. Abr., *Audita querela*, pl. 16, abridging *Savage's Case* (1369) YB Mich. 43 Edw. III, fo. 27, pl. 11.
[9] YB Trin. 18 Edw. III, fo. 29, pl. 38.
[10] Mich. 31 Edw. III, Fitz. Abr., *Saver de defaut*, pl. 37.
[11] Noted in Coke's Dyer (Holkham 8014), fo. 368 ('Vide in mes reportes in medio fol. 9'). Differently reported in Dyer 368, para. 46 (anon., Pas. 1580).

111. COUNTESS OF LENNOX'S CASE[1]

Chancery, *c*. 1576.[2]

Countess of Lennox's case. See 19 Ric. II, tit. *Estoppell*, 281,[3] where a woman's heir was not estopped from saying that she was covert at the time, so as to avoid a deed.

The earl of Lennox and the countess, his wife,[4] acknowledged a statute; then the earl died, and it was adjudged that this statute would not bind the wife, for a married woman shall not be bound by a statute acknowledged or by a deed enrolled. It is otherwise of an infant, for those things bind him for ever if they are not avoided during his minority. The reason for the difference between a married woman and an infant is that the judge could have taken cognizance whether the infant was under age or of full age, and so it was error in the judge, and therefore such an acknowledgment is not void but voidable, whereas if a married woman acknowledges a deed the judge cannot by inspection, or in any other way, judicially take cognizance whether she is married or not, for examination is to no avail in such a case. 29 Hen. VIII, Brooke, tit. *Faits enrol*, 14.[5] 7 Edw. IV, fo. 5,[6] agrees with this, and makes the same distinction between a married woman and an infant. 14 Edw. III, tit. *Execucion*, 73:[7] there it seems that a married woman shall be bound by a statute merchant acknowledged. But Fitzherbert makes a query of it: see 43 Edw. III, tit. *Audita querela*, 16.[8] 18 Edw. III, fo. 29,[9] an infant may avoid a statute. {See 31 Edw. III, tit. *Saver de defaut*, 37:[10] if an idiot is impleaded and makes default after default at the petit *cape*, he shall not save his default by reason of idiocy, for it cannot appear to the justices. Likewise if a man of unsound mind makes a recognizance, he shall not avoid it.}

112. ANON.[11]

Common Pleas, Hil. 1579.

Dyer, 22 Eliz. 368.

In Hilary term 21 Eliz. this case was moved in the Common Bench by *Anderson*. A man had issue two sons, and bound himself and his heirs in a bond; he died seised of certain lands, so that assets descended to his heir; the elder son entered and died seised without issue, and so the younger son entered. It was now moved how the writ should be brought against the younger son. And it was held that that the obligee should have a general writ and a special declaration, for it was said that if the defendant pleaded

---

[1] Differently reported in BL MS. Harg. 373, fo. 172; HLS MS. 197 (2071), fo. 71v.
[2] In MS. Harg. 373 it is said that the case was vouched in 15 Eliz. by Dyer C.J. and Lennard, the custos brevium, but this cannot be correct. In BL MS. Harley 1693 (n. 2, opposite) it is dated Mich. 1580, which seems too late. In the HLS MS. it is among cases of *c*. 1573–76. It must have been soon after the earl's death in 1576.   [3] Trin. 19 Ric. II, Fitz. Abr., *Estoppell*, pl. 281.
[4] Elizabeth (née Cavendish), widow of Charles Stuart, earl of Lennox. The earl died of consumption in 1576, aged around 21, and was buried in Westminster Abbey. The countess died in 1582, aged 26. Their daughter Arbella Stuart (1575–1615) was a claimant to the throne.
[5] 29 Hen. VIII, Bro. Abr., *Faits enrol*, pl. 14 ('Nota que fait del baron et feme ne sera enrol in communi banco nisi pur le baron tantum, et non pur le feme, racione del coverture …').

envers le pleintife. (Mes quere, car moy semble que ceo viendra eins per voy de replication, car nest use in tiel count daverrer ascun assetz discend mes generalment etc.) Et nota que fuit agre clerement que le heire serra charge. Et issint semble per le livre in 10 E. 4, 10. 49 E. 3, 5b, F.N.B.152, ou est dit que un heire ne serra charge ove un annuitie per prescription, car ne poet estre conus sil aver[1] per discent de mesme le annuitie ou nemi: ex quo sequitur que sil ad per discent de mesme le auncester que graunt, coment que il fuit de longe degree de luy, uncore il serra charge. Vide Pl. Com. in Pepys case, fol. 441, semble que leire mediate ne serra charge arere.[2] <Vide 32 E. 3, tit. Voucher, 94, si home ad issue fitz et file per un venter et fitz per auter venter et fait feffment de parcell de ces terres ove garrante et morust seisie del residue, leigne fitz enter et morust, la est agre que le puisne fitz come heire et le soer per reason de sa possession serra vouche et uncore le soer ne clayme immediatement de cesti que fist le garranty. Vide Dier 368.>[a]

[113]

AB, fo. 78v (341v).

<Giles case anno 18 Eliz. termino Pasche.>[s] <Dier 18 Eliz. 348.>[a]

In Giles quare impedit 3 questiones fueront. Un, si le roy ad title a presenter per laps et il present per ses lettres patentez et apres admission et institution le presentee morust devant induction, si ore le roy presentera arere? Et Mounson et le Segnior Dier teignont que le roy presentera arere, car devant induction leglise nest pleine. <38 H. 6, 15.>[i] Vies liv[ers] come dicitur 14 H. 6. <25 H. 6, 6b. 38 H. 6, 15.>[i] 22 H. 6, <27>.[i] 33 H. 6, 14. 38 E. 3, <3>.[i] 44 E. 3. Et toutz foitz le roy covient daver leffecte de son presentment. <38 H. 6. Vide Brooke, tit. Presentement, 46, tit. Quare impedit, 83.>[i] <3 E. 6, 67, Stringfellows case [...de execute ...].[3]>[i] Auxi ilz disoient si le roy marie son gard infra annos nubiles, et le fem morust devant que leire vient

---

[1] *Sic.* ad *Ff.*
[2] *Unclear; perhaps* quere.
[3] *Interlineation partly illegible.*

---

[7] *Sir Thomas Dynham's Case* (1459) YB Mich. 38 Hen. VI, fo. 14, pl. 14, at fo. 15.
[8] Possibly YB Pas. 14 Hen. VII, fo. 21, pl. 4.
[9] *Sic*, but there is no such year in print.
[10] Above, n. 7.
[11] *Sir John Dynham* v. *Bishop of Exeter* (1443) YB Mich. 22 Hen. VI, fo. 25, pl. 46, at fo. 27. This was a *quare impedit* for Hartland Abbey, Devon, dedicated to St Nectan ('Need' in the vulgate YB).
[12] *Bonham* v. *Broughton* (1455) YB Pas. 33 Hen. VI, fos. 12–14, pl. 3.
[13] YB Hil. 38 Edw. III, fo. 3.
[14] YB Hil. 44 Edw. III, fo. 3, pl. 14.
[15] R. v. *Abbess of Syon* (1460) YB Trin. 38 Hen. VI, fo. 33, pl. 2.
[16] Bro. Abr., *Presentement al esglise*, pl. 46, abridging Westminster II, c. 5.
[17] Bro. Abr., *Quare impedit*, pl. 83, abridging *Sir John Dynham* v. *Bishop of Exeter* (1443) YB Mich. 22 Hen. VI, fo. 25, pl. 46, which is cited above.
[18] *Stringfellow* v. *Brownesoppe* (1549) Dyer 67.

'Nothing by descent from his father', this would be found against the plaintiff. (Query, however, for it seems to me that this should come in by way of replication; for it is not used, in such a count, to aver any assets descended, but generally [that he was heir].) Note that it was agreed clearly that the heir shall be charged. So it seems by the books in 10 Edw. IV, fo. 10,[1] 49 Edw. III, fo. 5v,[2] and Fitz. N.B.152, where it is said that an heir shall not be charged with an annuity by prescription, for it cannot be known whether he has the same annuity by descent or not: from whence it follows that if he has it by descent from the same ancestor who granted, even though he was a long degree from him, he shall nevertheless be charged. See Plowd. Com. in Pepys's case, fo. 441,[3] [where] it seems that the heir mediate shall not be charged. {See 32 Edw. III, tit. *Voucher*, 94:[4] if a man has issue a son and a daughter by one wife, and a son by another wife, makes a feoffment of parcel of his lands with warranty, and dies seised of the residue, and the elder son enters and dies, it is agreed there that the younger son (as heir) and the sister (by reason of her possession) may be vouched, and yet the sister does not claim immediately from the person who made the warranty. See Dyer 368.[5]}

113. GYLES v. COLSHILL[6]

Common Pleas, Pas. 1576.

Gyles's case in Easter term 18 Eliz. Dyer, 18 Eliz. 348.

In Gyles's *quare impedit* there were three questions. One, if the king has title to present by lapse, and he presents by his letters patent, and after admission and institution the presentee dies before induction, may the king now present again? MOUNSON and the lord DYER held that the king may present again, for before induction the church is not full. {38 Hen. VI, fo. 15.}[7] See [these] books, as it is said: 14 Hen. VI;[8] {25 Hen. VI, fo. 6v;[9] 38 Hen. VI, fo. 15;[10] 22 Hen. VI, fo. 27;[11]} 33 Hen. VI, fo. 14;[12] 38 Edw. III, fo. 3;[13] 44 Edw. III.[14] And the king must always have the effect of his presentation. {38 Hen. VI.[15] See Brooke, tit. *Presentement*, 46;[16] tit. *Quare impedit*, 83.[17] 3 Edw. VI, fo. 67, Stringfellow's case: [execution stayed in Chancery until the king's debt was paid].[18]} They also said that if the king marries

---

[1] YB Trin. 10 Edw. IV, fo. 10, pl. 1, *per* Danby C.J.
[2] *Prioress of Markyate's Case* (1375) YB Hil. 49 Edw. III, fo. 5, pl. 8.
[3] *Davye* v. *Pepys* (1573) Plowd. 438 at fo. 440.
[4] Pas. 32 Edw. III, Fitz. Abr., *Voucher*, pl. 94.   [5] Dyer's report of the present case.
[6] Record recited in a writ to the high commissioners, transcribed for Coke, YLS MS. G.R24.1, fo. 100A: Richard Gyles v. William [Bradbridge], bishop of Exeter, and John Colshill; *quare impedit* for the church of Ashprington, Devon. Noted above, p. 35, no. 76; below, p. 134, no. 241; p. 135, no. 243; p. 150, no. 281; p. 156, no. 295; p. 164, no. 324. Cit. in Coke's Dyer (Holkham 8014), fo. 369v ('Vide 18 Eliz. mes reportes, Giles case, 78'); C, fo. 314 ('Issint fuit tenus per divers justices in Giles case anno 18 Eliz. in communi banco'). Probably the case referred to in Co. Litt. 249 (Hil. 1576, 'which I myselfe heard and observed'). Differently reported in Dyer 360 (Mich. 1577); Benl. 312 (Mich. 1577); JRL MS. Fr. 118, fos. 55v–59 (Collsile, Pas. 1576); BL MS. Harg. 5, fo. 63v; MS. Harg. 9, fos. 123v–129, 195, 205v; MS. Harg. 37, fos. 71–75v (Hil. 1576); MS. Harg. 373, fos. 135–141v; MS. Lansd. 1057, fos. 88v–92, 201–211; MS. Lansd. 1072, fos. 168–170v; MS. Lansd. 1145, fos. 101v–103; IT MS. Petyt 511.12, fos. 269–274; HLS MS 200.1 (1180.1), fos. 344v–345. Coke identified the case as *Weston's Case* (Hil. 1576) in Dyer 347, Weston being the name of the deceased incumbent: Coke's Dyer (Holkham 8014), fo. 347 ('Vide in mon report de cest case que jeo mesme oia').

ad annos nubiles, le roy avera le mariage arere, car le mariage ne fuit consummate. <Vide 6 E. 3, 56. 45 Ass., pl. 6. 18 E. 3, 57.>ⁱ Mes Harper et Manwood tient le contrarie pur ceo que il fuit parson tanque le roy countermaund ceo. Et le Segnior Dier cite le livre in 1 H. 5, 1, si un usurpe sur tenant in tail et son clarke est admitte et institute, et un collaterall auncestre del tenant in taile releas al usurpour, et devant induction le garrante ne liera le taile pur ceo que nul previty fuit gaine, come semble per le livre, devant induction. Et il cite auxi le livre in 45 E. 3, [*blank*], in title deschaunge.

Un auter question fuit, si lencumbent dun common person resigne et 6 moys passe sauns notice, et puis auters 6 moys passe, issint que si notice ust estre done le temps ust estre devolute al roigne, si ore le roigne presentera sauns notice? <Dier, 22 Eliz. 369.>ⁱ Et Mounson, Harper et Manwood tiendront que le roygne ne presentera sauns notice primerment done per le ordinarie, car les 6 moys covient estre accomptes del notice, ergo etc. Mes le Segnior Dier fuit encounter eux pur le prerogative le roigne.

Un auter point fuit quant le roygne est seisie dun advouson et leglise devient voide, et le roigne graunt ouster lavouson in fe sauns faire ascun mention de cest avoidauns, si cest avoidauns passe ou nemy? Et fuit agre per eux toutz que lavoidauns ne passera, car come Manwood dit fuit come un flowre fallen del stocke, et fuit chattell se[vere] del inheritauns. Et la fuit auxi agre que quant le roigne ad title de presenter per laps et puis fe simple del avouson est done al roigne per acte de parliament, uncore el presentera per reason del laps. <18 Eliz. 348.>^a <Vide hic devant in mes notes, 8, Hares case. Vide Pl. Com. 528 in Hares case.>^{a 1}

[114]

AB, fos. 79–80 (342–343).

<Deane de Worcestres case.>^s <Appropriation.>^{s 2}

M. 19 Eliz. in un quare impedit port per leire de patentee le roigne vers le deane et chapter de <Welles>^d <Worcestre>ⁱ le case fuit tiell. Le roy E. 6 fuit seisie del avouson del eglise de Dean en fe et per ses lettres patentz graunt mesme lavouson a le dit deane et chapter et a lour successors et que le dit deane et chapter et lour successors

---

^{oo} *Added above the report.*
^{oo} *Heading on fo. 80.*

¹⁰ Above, p. 59, no. 108.
¹¹ CP 40/1327, m. 952 (printed in Plowd. 493; Benl. 293): Roger Grendon gent. v. Thomas, bishop of Lincoln, and the dean and chapter of Worcester; *quare impedit* for the church of Dean, Beds.; demurrer to the plea by the dean and chapter; c.a.v. to Pas. 1577; judgment for the defendant. Differently reported in Plowd. 495 (Mich 1576); Dyer's notebook, 110 Selden Soc. 318 (Hil. 1575, Mich. 1576). Although there is an interlineation citing Plowden's report (published in 1579), Coke's report is clearly not derived from it and was doubtless written in 1576 or 1577. Also noted below, p. 77, no. 119. Cf. above, p. 3, where the same case is cited from Plowd. There is also a passage in *AA*, fo. 39v (73v), which is clearly derived from the report at Plowd. 502, though there is no citation to it; this must have been written much later, since there is an interlined reference to 8 Co. Rep. in the same hand.

off his ward under the age of marriage (*infra annos nubiles*), and the wife dies before the heir comes to the age of marriage, the king will have the marriage again, for the marriage was not consummated.[1] {See 6 Edw. III, fo. 56;[2] 45 Ass., pl. 6;[3] 18 Edw. III, fo. 57.[4]}[5] But HARPER and MANWOOD held the contrary, because he was parson until the king countermanded it. And the lord DYER cited the book in 1 Hen. V, fo. 1:[6] if someone usurps upon tenant in tail, and his clerk is admitted and instituted, and a collateral ancestor of the tenant in tail releases to the usurper, before induction the warranty will not bind the tail because (as it seems from the book) no privity was gained before induction. He also cited the book in 45 Edw. III, in the title *Exchaunge*.[7]

Another question was, if the incumbent of a common [patron] resigns, and six months pass without notice, and then another six months pass, so that if notice had been given the time would have devolved to the queen, may the queen present without notice? {Dyer, 22 Eliz. 369.[8]} MOUNSON, HARPER and MANWOOD held that the queen could not present without notice first given by the ordinary, for the six months must be reckoned from the notice, ergo etc. But the lord DYER was against them, in the interest of the queen's prerogative.

Another point was: when the queen is seised of an advowson, and the church becomes vacant, and the queen grants over the advowson in fee without making any mention of this avoidance, does this avoidance pass or not? And it was agreed by all of them that the avoidance will not pass, for (as MANWOOD said) it was like a flower fallen from the stock, and was a chattel severed from the inheritance. It was also there agreed that when the queen has title to present by lapse, and then the fee simple of the advowson is given to the queen by act of Parliament, she may still present by reason of the lapse. {18 Eliz. 348.[9] See this before in my notes, fo. 8, Hare's case.[10] See Plowd. Com. 528 in Hare's case.}

114. GRENDON v. DEAN OF WORCESTER[11]

Common Pleas, Mich. 1576, Trin. 1577.

Dean of Worcester's case. Appropriation.

In Michaelmas term 19 Eliz. in a *quare impedit* brought by the heir of the queen's patentee against the dean and chapter of Worcester, the case was this. King Edward VI was seised of the advowson of the church of Dean in fee, and by his letters patent granted the same advowson to the said dean and chapter and their successors, and that

---

[1] Cf. *Mynne* v. *Grey* (1572) above, p. clxxvii, no. 3.
[2] *Earl of Cornwall* v. *Bishop of Rochester* (1332) YB Mich. 6 Edw. III, fo. 56, pl. 65.
[3] *Margaret Chiseldon's Case* (1371) 45 Edw. III, Lib. Ass., pl. 6.
[4] Probably *R.* v. *Abbot of Bec Hellouin, Normandy* (1344) YB Mich. 18 Edw. III, fo. 57, pl. 87; Mich. 18 Edw. III (RS), pp. 349–353, pl. 87.
[5] These three cases concerned a different prerogative, but the first two are identifiable as those cited in the present context in *Holt's Case* (1611) 9 Co. Rep. 132.
[6] *Abbot of Leicester's Case* (1414) YB Hil. 1 Hen. V, fo. 1, pl. 2.
[7] Mich. 45 Edw. III, Fitz. Abr., *Exchaunge*, pl. 1.
[8] *Walpole* v. *Corbett* (1580) Dyer 369; Dyer's notebook, 110 Selden Soc. 380.
[9] Dyer's report of this case, sub nom. *Weston's Case*.

teignera le dit avouson in prop[r]ios usus apres le mort dun Haltman adonques esteant incumbent, <esteant pleine>^d et leglise adonques esteant pleyn etc., ove large parols de univimus, consolidavimus, aneximus etc. et ouster ex uberiori gracia, certa sciencia et mero motu graunta les terres appertanauntz a le dit eglise de Deane a le dit deane et chapter et a lour successors. Et puis lencumbent, scilicet Haltman, morust, apres que mort et devant ascun entre fait per le dit deane et chapter in les terres del dit eglise de Deane le roy E. 6 usurpe et graunt lavouson ctc., et le pleintife claym per mesne conveiauns <vers>^d desouth les lettres patentz. Et in cest case 3 maters fueront debate alarge per toutz les justices del common banke. Primerment, si le confirmation del immediate ordinarie fuit requisite al appropriation ou nemi. Le 2, si appropriation poet estre fait quant leglise fuit pleine. 3, si le usurpation le roy fait ceo disappropriate arrere.

 Quant al primer point, toutz les justices del common banke agreont in un que le licence ou confirmation del immediate <ordinarie>ⁱ ne fuit my requisite, <car>^d et lour reason fuit pur ceo que le roy fuit supreme teste de tout le spiritualtie cibien come del layte (et nota que les lettres patentz fait al dit deane et chapter etc. conteine que le roy graunt suprema nostra authoritate qua nunc fungimur). Et la fuit dit que les civilians teigne que le pope cy longe come son usurped authoritie fuit permisse et tollerate puit aver appropriate un benefice sauns lassent del immediate ordinarie pur ceo que il avoit plenitudinem potestatis, et il fuit accompt ordinarius ordinariorum, car le clargy de cest realme fuit parcell del clargy del Europe, et le pope usurpant sur luy le supremacy de tort avoit power come ilz disoient dappropriate ascun personage que fuit avouson dascun spirituel home (car il ne unques puit intermeddle ove les patronages des lay gentz) et ceo sauns lassent del immediate ordinarie. Et Mounson dit que il ad vieu divers presidentz de appropriations faitz per le <roy solem>^d pope solement. Et le reason fuit pur ceo que il fuit intende destre supreme teste. Mes ilz toutz agreont in un que les roys de cest realme[1] ont estre toutz temps in droit supreme teste deins lour realme demesne et que le supremacy que le pope avoit fuit forsque usurpation, come appiert per lestatut de 26 H. 8, cap. 1. Et nota [*fo. 79v*] que Manwood dit que Dieu come appiert in le veiel testament dona al Moyses ambideux les tables cybien le table que concerne relligion envers Dieu come lauter table que concerne civill governement, et il fuit immediate desouth Dieu, et Aaron fuit appoint et place per luy. Issint il dit que per le ley de Dieu le roy deins son realme demesne est supreme teste cybien des causes ecclesiasticall come civil et immediate governour desouth Dieu. Et auxi il cite le disant del Elutherius, pope del <roy>^d Roame que il escrie al Lucius, roy de cest terre, scilicet Quia vos estis vicarius Dei in regno vestro. Et auxi le[s] roys de cest realme ont aver toutz joures le collation del evesques a lour evesqueries quant ilz deveint voide, et le pape ne unques ceo avoit. Et ore auxi per lestatut de 26 H. 8, cap. 1, ceo est fait clere, et le supremacie et toutz auters ecclesiasticall jurisdictions dones al roy. Et sur ceo fuit agree que le roy esteant supreme teste que

---

[1] realmes.

the said dean and chapter and their successors should hold the said advowson to their own uses (*in proprios usus*) after the death of [Edmund] Haltman, being then incumbent and the church then being full, with broad words of 'we have united, consolidated, annexed ...', and furthermore 'of our more abundant grace, certain knowledge and mere motion' (*ex uberiori gracia, certa sciencia et mero motu*) granted the lands belonging to the said church of Dean to the said dean and chapter and their successors. Then the incumbent, namely Haltman, died; and after his death, but before any entry made by the said dean and chapter in the lands of the said church of Dean, King Edward VI usurped and granted the advowson etc., and the plaintiff claimed through an intermediate conveyance beneath the letters patent. In this case three matters were debated at large by all the justices of the Common Bench. Firstly, whether the confirmation of the immediate ordinary was requisite to the appropriation, or not. Secondly, whether an appropriation could be made when the church was full. Thirdly, whether the usurpation by the king caused it to be disappropriated again.

As to the first point, all the justices of the Common Bench agreed as one that the licence or confirmation of the immediate ordinary was not requisite; and their reason was that the king was supreme head of all the spiritualty as well as of the laity (and note that the letters patent made to the said dean and chapter said that the king granted by his supreme authority (*suprema nostra authoritate qua nunc fungimur*)). And it was there said that the Civilians hold that the pope, while his usurped authority was permitted and tolerated, could have appropriated a benefice without the assent of the immediate ordinary, because he had plenitude of power (*plenitudinem potestatis*) and was accounted the ordinary of ordinaries (*ordinarius ordinariorum*). For the clergy of this realm was part of the clergy of Europe; and the pope, wrongfully usurping to himself the supremacy, had power (as they said) to appropriate any parsonage which was an advowson of any spiritual man (though he could never meddle with the patronages of laymen), and that without the assent of the immediate ordinary. MOUNSON said he had seen various precedents of appropriations made by the pope alone; and the reason was that he was thought to be supreme head. But they all agreed as one that the kings of this realm have always in right been supreme head within their realm, and that the supremacy which the pope had was only a usurpation, as appears by the statute of 26 Hen. VIII, c. 1. And note that MANWOOD said that, as it appears in the Old Testament, God gave Moses both the tables, not only the table which concerned religion vis-à-vis God but also the other table which concerned civil government; and he was immediate under God, and Aaron[1] was appointed and put in place by him. Thus, as he said, by the law of God the king is supreme head within his own realm, both for ecclesiastical and civil causes, and is immediate governor under God. He also cited the saying of Eleutherius, pope of Rome, which he wrote to Lucius, king of this land,[2] namely, *Quia vos estis vicarius Dei in regno vestro*.[3] Moreover the kings of this realm have always had the collation of bishops to their bishoprics when they become void, and the pope never had this. Now also by the statute of 26 Hen. VIII, c. 1, this is made clear, and the supremacy and all other ecclesiastical jurisdictions given to the king. Thereupon it was agreed that, since the

---

[1] The chief priest.   [2] See the introduction, above, p. cxxv.
[3] 'Because you are the vicar of God in your realm.'

il <per le licence>^d ove le patron del eglise (si le patronage soit al common person) poet faire appropriation sauns lassent del immediate ordinarie. Car in presencia majoris cessat potestas minoris. Mes Manwood dit que uncore ascun foitz le confirmation del ordinarie est requisite et ascun foitz nemi. Car il dit quant le roy licence un de tener et appropriater un eglise etc. et daver ceo in proprios usus, la le confirmation del ordinarie est requisite, car la le roy mesme ne usa son authoritie, et issint sont les livres in 46 Ass., p. [blank], 14 H. 4, [blank]. Et issint in le livre dentres in le title de appropriation. Mes quant le roy mesme graunta ceo et prise le authoritie sur luy et dit appropriavimus, univimus, consolidavimus etc. donques il poet faire ceo saunz lordinarie. Et a ceo purpose il cite deux presidentes hors del livre dentries. Mes ilz agreont que in le principall case al barre le case fuit tout clere, car cest eglise fuit del patronage le roy et in tielz eglises lordinarie nad my ascun tiel interest come il ad in le case dun common person, car il ne presentera per laps, mes il sequestra etc. de veier le curc scrvc. Et in 7 E. 3, tit. Quare impedit 19, est admitte que William le Conquerour appropriate un advouson etc. sauns le pope et lordinarie.[1] Et nota que Manwood dit que il fuit provide per lestatutes de 15 R. 2, cap. 6, et 4 H. 4, cap. 12, que si ascun eglise soit appropriate sur quel un annuitie covenable nest graunt al povers homes del payse et un vicar covenablement in[dowe][2] cest appropriation fuit voide. Mes il dit si ascun tiel matter ust estre il viendra del auter side etc. <Vide Lindwoodes table, Appropriation. Bracton, lib. 2°, fol. 53.>^a Et nota [il] dit que les avaunditz statutes parle solement del licence le roy et nemi des grauntz le roy, come nostre case est. <9 H. 6, 16, le roy poet licence un a founder chantrie sauns le ordinarie. 4 H. 4, nu. 74, encounter impropriations.>^{a 3} <Vide 17 E. 3, 76, moitie dun eglise appropriate. Nota ex hoc que alternis vicibus advouson poet estre appropriate et presentable.>^{a 4} [fo. 80] <40 E. 3, 28, per Finch., si 2 eglises sont feble le ordinarie per assent de patrons poient faire consolidation. Vide Lindwood, table.>^{a 5} <18 E. 1, pet. parliam., fol. 4, prior de Gisborne.>ⁱ

Quant al 2 matter, ilz toutes auxi agreont que un appropriation poet estre fait quant leglise est pleine, et maxime per speciall parolx a prender effecte apres le mort del incumbent. Et ilz citont le livre in 50 E. 3, 26. Et ilz construont le livre in 6 H. 7, 14, ou est parle que un union est void esteant fait quant leglise est plein, destre intende destre voide solement quant al incumbent. Et Mounson dit que il ad vieu multz presidentz del appropriations fait al evesquerie de Caunterbury quant leglises

---

[1] *Unclear.* [2] *Word partly obscured in binding.*
[3] *In top margin.* [4] *Written sideways in outer margin.*
[5] *In top margin.*

---

[9] Rot. Parl., iii. 505 (Act to restrain attempts to revoke the annulment of a bull for the appropriation of several vicarages to Launceston priory).
[10] *R. v. Abbot of Rufford* (1343) YB Hil. 17 Edw. III, fo. 75, pl. 112, at fo. 76.
[11] YB Trin. 40 Edw. III, fo. 27, pl. 5, at fo. 28, *per* Finchden C.J.
[12] Rot. Parl., i. 54b, no. 128 ('Gisseburne'). The king granted the priory 'quantum in ipso est' authority to appropriate three churches of their own advowson.
[13] YB Mich. 50 Edw. III, fo. 26, pl. 8.
[14] *Case of Magdalen College, Oxford* (1491) YB Hil. 6 Hen. VII, fo. 13, pl. 2, at fo. 14; identifiable as *Purre v. Grene*, CP 40/911, m. 378; below, p. 68, n. 5.

king was supreme head, he could together with the patron of the church (if the patronage belonged to a common person) make an appropriation without the assent of the immediate ordinary. For *in presencia majoris cessat potestas minoris*.[1] But MANWOOD said nevertheless that sometimes confirmation by the ordinary is requisite and sometimes not. For he said that when the king licenses someone to hold and appropriate a church, and to have it *in proprios usus*, the confirmation of the ordinary is there requisite, for the king himself does not use his authority. Thus are the books in 46 Ass.,[2] 14 Hen. IV,[3] and likewise in the book of entries in the title of Appropriation.[4] But when the king himself grants it, and takes the authority upon himself and says 'we have appropriated, united and consolidated ...', then he may do it without the ordinary. To this purpose he cited two precedents out of the book of entries. But they agreed that in the principal case at the bar the case was wholly clear, for this church was of the king's patronage and in such churches the ordinary has no such interest as he has in the case of a common person; for he may not present on a lapse, though he may sequester etc. in order to see the cure served. In 7 Edw. III, tit. *Quare impedit*, 19, it is admitted that William the Conqueror appropriated an advowson without the pope and the ordinary.[5] And note that MANWOOD said it was provided by the statutes of 15 Ric. II, c. 6, and 4 Hen. IV, c. 12, that if any church is appropriated whereupon a suitable annuity is not granted to the poor people of the region and a vicar suitably endowed, this appropriation should be void. But he said that if any such matter had been, it should come in from the other side etc.[6] (See Lyndwood's table, s.v. Appropriation; Bracton, book ii, fo. 53.[7]) And note that he said the aforesaid statutes spoke only of the king's licence and not of the king's grants, as our case is. (9 Hen. VI, fo. 16:[8] the king may license someone to found a chantry without the ordinary. 4 Hen. IV, no. 74, against impropriations.[9] See 17 Edw. III, fo. 76,[10] a moiety of a church appropriated: from which note that an advowson by turns may be appropriated and presentable. 40 Edw. III, fo. 28,[11] *per* Finchden: if two churches are underendowed (*feble*), the ordinary by assent of the patrons may make a consolidation. See Lyndwood's table. 18 Edw. I, Petitions in Parliament, fo. 4:[12] the prior of Guisborough.)

As to the second matter, they also all agreed that an appropriation may be made when the church is full, and especially when it is by special words to take effect after the death of the present incumbent. They cited the book in 50 Edw. III, fo. 26.[13] And they construed the book in 6 Hen. VII, fo. 14,[14] where it is said that a union is void if made when the church is full, to mean that it is void with respect to the incumbent. MOUNSON said he had seen many precedents of appropriations made to the bishopric

---

[1] 'In the presence of the greater, the power of the lesser ceases.' Cf. below, p. 77, no. 119, and Plowd. 498.
[2] 46 Edw. III, Lib. Ass., pl. 4.
[3] Cf. YB Hil. 14 Hen. IV, fo. 17, pl. 20.
[4] W. Rastell, *A Colleccion of Entrees* (1566), fo. 456 (Quare impedit de advowson appropriate).
[5] Hil. 7 Edw. III, Fitz. Abr., *Quare impedit*, pl. 19.
[6] I.e. it was for those who impugned an appropriation on that ground to plead and prove it.
[7] W. Lyndwood, *Provinciale*, lib. iii, tit. 9, De Locato et Conducto, gl. Asserunt non ligari; Appropriationum (1679 ed., pp. 157–160); *Bracton*, ii. 160.
[8] YB Trin. 9 Hen. VI, fo. 16, pl. 8.

fueront pleine. <18 E. 1, nu. 53.>[i] Et Mounson auxi dit si patron et ordinarie graunt un rent charge duraunt le temps que leglise fuit pleine, ceo est bone a charger le successour. Et divers presidentes hors del livre dentrees fueront vouche, queux vide la.

Quant al 3 point, toutz les justices (except le chiefe justice) agre que le usurpation le roy ne fist ascun disappropriation pur ceo que le leglise fuit pleine et donques usurpation sur un plenartie est voide. Et quant a ceo ilz citont le case in 38 H. 6, 20, que usurpation sur parson imparsone est voide. <11 H. 6, 19, eglise appropriate al vicarage.>[i]

Mes le Segnior Dier fuit incounter le deane de Worcester, car il dit[1] pur auter causes que ne fueront moves lappropriation ne fuit bone. < 22 E. 3, 2, coment appropriate. 11 H. 7, 8, 9.>[i] Le primer fuit pur ceo que le roy ne graunt a eux destre parsons in parsones et donques a tener in proprios usus, car il covient daver fait eux parsons primes. Et pur ceo il dit que le common de[2] pleding quant un parson in parsone plede etc. il dirra que fuit seisie in jure ecclesie de D. <2 H. 4, 10, abbey appropriate al Winsor.>[i] <20 E. 4, 6b, lunion del vicarage.>[i] Et ouster il dit que le patent le roy fuit voide, car le roy graunta al deane et chapter de Worcester lavouson del eglise de Deane et ne dit nient obstante lestatut de mortmain, et donques le patent est void come est dit pur ceo que le patent le roy ne inurera a [deux][3] intentes. <21 E. 4, 37, appropriation.>[i] <34 H. 6, 15, appropriate a master et scollers.>[i] Et in prove de ceo il cite le case in 19 E. 3, tit. Graunt 58. Mes nota 41 Ass., pl. 19, est adjudge encounter son opinion. 22 E. 3, 2. <17 E. 3, 76, si lappropriation fuit defeate le vicarage est esteint.[4]>[i] <17 E. 3, 51, 76. 21 E. 4, 65, convent appropriate.>[i] Et auxi il dit que entant que le roy ad usurpe mesne parenter le mort del incumbent et <parson>[d] lentrie del deane et chapter leglise per ceo serra disappropriate pur ceo que le deane et chapter ne fueront parson[s] in parsones devant le entrie et seisin ewe. <2 E. 3, 25, nota.>[i] <Pl. Com. 497 appropriation al prebendary.>[i] Nota puis in Easter terme prochein insuaunt fuit adjudge solonque loppinion des 3 justices et Segnior Dier in manner agre al eux.<22 E. 3, 13, le pape solement ne poet faire appropriation. Vide tit. Present[ment] 84. 19 E. 3, Judgment 124.>[i]

---

[1] *Unclear.*
[2] *Sic, but otiose.*
[3] *Written as a dash, as for* in.
[4] *Unclear.*

---

[10] YB Mich. 34 Hen. VI, fo. 14, pl. 27, at fo. 15 (Pembroke Hall, Cambridge).
[11] Pas. 19 Edw. III, Fitz. Abr., *Graunt*, pl. 58.
[12] 41 Edw. III, Lib. Ass, pl. 19.
[13] YB Hil. 22 Edw. III, fo. 2, pl. 11.
[14] *R. v. Abbot of Clervaux* (1343) YB Mich. 17 Edw. III, fo. 51, pl. 25; *R. v. Abbot of Rufford* (1343) Hil. 17 Edw. III, fo. 75, pl. 112, at fo. 76.
[15] Unidentified.
[16] Unidentified.
[17] A report of the present case.
[18] YB Mich. 29 Edw. III, fo. 13, pl. 31.
[19] There are only 17 cases in this title in Fitz. Abr.
[20] YB Hil. 19 Edw. III, Fitz. Abr., *Judgement*, pl 124.

of Canterbury when the churches were full. (18 Edw. I, no. 53.[1]) MOUNSON also said that if a patron and ordinary grant a rent-charge while the church is full, this is good to charge the successor. And various precedents were vouched out of the book of entries: which see there.

As to the third point, all the justices (except the chief justice) agreed that the usurpation by the king did not cause any disappropriation because the church was full, and then a usurpation upon a plenarty is void. As to this they cited the case in 38 Hen. VI, fo. 20,[2] that a usurpation upon a parson imparsonate is void. (11 Hen. VI, fo.19,[3] a church appropriated to the vicarage.)

But the lord DYER was against the dean of Worcester, for he thought the appropriation was not good for other reasons which were not moved.[4] (22 Edw. III, fo. 2, how appropriated; 11 Hen VII, fos. 8–9.[5]) The first was that the king did not grant them to be parsons imparsonate and then to hold *in proprios usus*; for he ought to have made them parsons first. Therefore, he said, when a parson imparsonate pleads, the common pleading is for him to say that he was seised in right of the church (*in jure ecclesiae*) of Dale. (2 Hen. IV, fo. 10:[6] an abbey appropriated to Windsor. 20 Edw. IV, fo. 6v:[7] the union of the vicarage.) He further said that the king's patent was void, for the king granted to the dean and chapter of Worcester the advowson of the church of Dean and did not say 'notwithstanding the statute of mortmain', and therefore the patent is void because (as it is said) the king's patent cannot enure for two purposes.[8] (21 Edw. IV, fo. 37:[9] appropriation. 34 Hen. VI, fo. 15:[10] appropriation to a master and scholars.) In proof of this he cited the case in 19 Edw. III, tit. *Graunt*, 58.[11] Note, however, that 41 Ass., pl. 19,[12] is adjudged contrary to his opinion. 22 Edw. III, fo. 2.[13] (17 Edw. III, fo. 76: if the appropriation is defeated the vicarage is extinguished. 17 Edw. III, fos. 51, 76.[14] 21 Edw. IV, fo. 65:[15] a convent appropriated.) He also said that since the king has usurped between the death of the incumbent and the entry of the dean and chapter, the church shall be thereby disappropriated, because the dean and chapter were not parsons imparsonate before the entry and seisin had. (2 Edw. III, fo. 25:[16] note.) {Plowd. Com. 497:[17] appropriation to a prebendary.} Note that afterwards, in Easter term next following, it was adjudged according to the opinion of the three justices, and the lord DYER in effect agreed with them. (22 Edw. III, fo. 13:[18] the pope alone cannot make an appropriation. See tit. Present[ment], 84.[19] 19 Edw. III, *Judgement*, 124.[20])

---

[1] Cf. Rot. Parl., i. 39–40, Placita ad Parliamenta 18 Edw. I, no. 53, which concerned the claim of the bishop of Winchester to the advowson of St Julian's Hospital, Southampton. Rot. Parl., i. 49, Petitiones 18 Edw. I, no. 53, seems even less relevant.

[2] YB Hil. 38 Hen. VI, fo. 19, pl. 1, at fo. 20.

[3] YB Hil. 11 Hen. VI, fo. 18, pl. 11, at fo. 19.

[4] According to Plowden, because Dyer C.J. spoke last and raised various points which had not been addressed before, one of the defendants' counsel (probably Plowden himself) subsequently delivered to him a written answer to his objections, which the other justices saw.

[5] YB Hil. 22 Edw. III, fo. 2, pl. 11; *Case of Magdalen College, Oxford* (1490) YB Mich. 11 Hen. VII, fo. 8, pl. 30; identifiable as *Purre v. Grene*, CP 40/911, m. 378; above, p. 66, n. 14.

[6] YB Mich. 2 Hen. IV, fo. 10, pl. 47 (abbey of Saltash appropriated to St George's chapel, Windsor).

[7] YB Trin. 20 Edw. IV, fo. 6, pl. 7.

[8] This was refuted by Plowden: *AA*, fo. 39v (73v), derived from Plowd. 502.

[9] YB Trin. 21 Edw. IV, fo. 37, pl. 3.

<[No]ta per Plowden arguendo in banke le roy T. 19 Eliz. al primes parsonage ne puit estre appropriate [forsque] a cesti que ad cure, et puis quant il fuit appropriate al deane et chapter donques [le] vicarage [...] deane, mes toutz foitz covient destre appropriate al spirituel corporation. 16 E. 3, et 17 E. 3 [...][1] abbot ad advowson appropriat et fist feffment, ore ceo est disappropriat, car le feffe navoit [inte]rest aver parsonage appropriate quia merus laicus. <22 E. 3, 2.> 3 E. 3, 11b, Huntingfields case, per Herle, les templers apres appropriation a eux fait dun eglise ne poient graunt lour estate del appropriation al auter. Et la semble que quant les templers fueront dissolve leglise fuit disappropriate, car spirituel person fault. F.N.B. 33 in accord a ceo (et uncore vide 21 H. 7, 3, [ou est] dit que duos layes homes avoient personage impropriate). 21 H. 7, 5a, appropriation ne poet estre graunt ouster car il ne fuit lentent de ceux que eux appropriate, per Frowicke. Et pur [...][2] Plowden que ceo fuit un des causes del feasans del darren branche del [...] pur faire le patentees le roy et auters layes homes capable des appropriations. 16 E. 3, Graunt 56, appropriation.>[a 3]

[115]

AB, fo. 80v (343v).

<Deane de Poules case enter Burton, pleintife, et Willford, defendant. M. 19 Eliz.>[s]

Nota in mesme le case fuit tenus per Wray, chiefe justice, Gawdy et Southcote que un chauntrey reputative <et nemy>[d] <fuit deins lestatut>,[i] que nest pas incorpore per les lettres patentz le roy neque corporation per prescription mes in auncient temps terres fueront dones a trover un chauntrie priest et issint ad estre continue et use et repute come un chauntrie. Et issint le segnior Wraye dit que fuit adjudge in leschequer in le case del colledge de Landebrevie que le dit colledge de Landebrevie, coment que <ceo>[d] ne fuit un perfecte college incorpore per le ley, uncore intaunt

---

[1] *Unclear alteration.*
[2] *Corner of page worn away.*
[3] *Added at the foot of the page beneath a rule.*

in le deane de Poules case'); Coke's Dyer (Holkham 8014), fo. 368 ('Vide in mes reportes fol. 80b, M. 19 Eliz., inter Burton et Wilford, ceo fuit le deane de Powles case'). Differently reported in JRL MS. Fr. 118, fos. 61–64 (anon., Pas. 1576); Dal. 113; 4 Leon. 156, sub nom. *Sir Henry Gilford's Case*; BL MS. Harley 4717, fos. 143–149v, 158–159v, 162v–166 (heads of argument, probably by William Fleetwood); MS. Harg. 322, fos. 29v, 99 (Christopher Yelverton's notebook), sub nom. *Thornell* v. *Wilford*; IT MS. Petyt 511.12, fos. 263–264v (Hil. 1576); LI MS. Maynard 87, fo. 224 (1577); MS. Misc. 361, fo. 36; CUL MS. Ee.4.1, fos. 132–134 (Wray C.J.'s argument, undated); HLS MS. 204 (5048), fos. 51v–56v. Cf. *Thornhill* v. *Wilford* (Exch., Hil. 1580), reported anonymously in Dyer 368, pl. 47, but identified in Dyer's notebook, 110 Selden Soc. 379, as 'Inter le dean de Powles et Thornehil in Lescheker'; BL MS. Harley 4717, fos. 158–159v.

[9] Coke spelt the plaintiff lessee's name thus, but in the record it is Buttell.
[10] 1 Edw. VI, c. 14.
[11] Now in Dyfed.

Note by *Plowden*, arguing in the King's Bench in Trinity term 19 Eliz. [1577], that at first a parsonage could not be appropriated except to someone who had the cure, and then when it was appropriated to the dean and chapter [the] vicarage [came to the] dean, but it must always be appropriated to a spiritual corporation. 16 Edw. III, and 17 Edw. III,[1] [an] abbot had an advowson appropriate and made a feoffment: this is now disappropriated, for the feoffee had no interest to have a parsonage appropriate, being a layman (*merus laicus*). (22 Edw. III, fo. 2.[2]) 3 Edw. III, fo. 11v,[3] Huntingfield's case, *per* Herle: the Templars could not, after an appropriation made to them of a church, grant their estate in the appropriation to another. And it seems there that when the Templars were dissolved the church was disappropriated, for lack of a spiritual parson. Fitz. N.B. 33 agrees with this (and yet see 21 Hen. VII, fo. 3,[4] where it is said that two laymen had a parsonage impropriate). 21 Hen. VII, fo. 5:[5] an appropriation may not be granted over, for it was not the intention of those who appropriated it, *per* Frowyk. And *Plowden* said that this was one of the causes of the making of the last branch of the [statute] for making the king's patentees and other laymen capable of appropriations.[6] 16 Edw. III, *Graunt*, 56,[7] appropriation.

115. BUTTELL d. THORNHYLL v. WYLFORD[8]

King's Bench, Mich. 1577.

Dean of St Paul's case, between Burton,[9] plaintiff, and Wilford, defendant. Mich. 19 Eliz.

Note that it was held in the same case by WRAY C.J., GAWDY and SOUTHCOTE that a reputed chantry, which is not incorporated by the king's letters patent or a corporation by prescription, but in olden time lands were given to find a chantry priest and it has been thus continued and used, and reputed as a chantry, was within the statute.[10] And the lord WRAY said it was so adjudged in the Exchequer, in the case of the college of Llandewi Brefi,[11] that the said college of Llandewi Brefi, though not a perfect college incorporated by the law, was nevertheless within the

---

[1] Unidentified.
[2] YB Hil. 22 Edw. III, fo. 2, pl. 11; also cited above, p. 67, n. 5 and n. 13.
[3] *Roger de Huntingfield's Case* (1329) YB Pas. 3 Edw, III, fo. 7, pl. 1.
[4] *Prior of Castleacre* v. *Dean of St Stephen's* [1503] YB Hil. 21 Hen. VII, fo. 1, pl. 1, at fo. 3 (misdated).
[5] Ibid., fo. 5, *per* Frowyk C.J.
[6] Presumably 31 Hen. VIII, c. 13, s. 21.
[7] Pas. 16 Edw. III, Fitz. Abr., *Graunt*, pl. 56.
[8] KB 27/1245, m. 114 (five rolls; continued from Hil. 1570): William Buttell gent. v. Thomas Wylford; ejectment for a capital mansion house in St George's parish, Billingsgate, London, on the demise of Richard Thornhyll; pleads Not Guilty; special verdict at the Guildhall, 28 June 1574, setting out the will of Henry de Guylford (d. 1313), the conveyance by his executors to the dean and chapter of St Paul's in 1314, the conditions of the chantry as then settled, the demise in 1544 by John Incent, as dean, to Nicholas Wylford for 50 years, the bequest by Wylford to his wife Elizabeth, who bequeathed it to the defendant, the certificate of the chantry commissioners under the statute of 1549, and a title traced from Edward VI to Thornhyll, who entered for non-payment of rent and leased to the plaintiff; c.a.v. to 1577; judgment for the defendant. Noted above, p. 11, no. 17; below, p. 162, nos. 319–320. Cit. briefly in 4 Co. Rep. 108, where Coke conflates it with the Exch. case of 1580 reported by Dyer (opposite). Cit. by Coke in *AD*, fo. 881 ('Hill. 19 Eliz. in banke le roy in le deane de Powles case'); *C*, fo. 531 ('Issint fuit resolve 22 Eliz.

que ceo fuit repute et accepte come un colledge ceo fuit deins le compas del estatut coment que ceo avoit imperfecte commencement. Et nota que les parolx del estatut de 1 E. 6, that all mannour of colledges, fre chappels etc. having, being or in esse, queux parolx fueront mys eins al entent que tielz colledges et chaunteries queux fueront dones al roy per 37 H. 8 ne serra dones al roy per cest statut. Et auxi tiel colledges et chaunteries queux devant fuit dissolve et convert al bone use serront dones etc. si ceux parolx nussont estre etc. Et nota que Wray, chefe justice, dit que si home done terres <ou tenementes>[d] al value de x li. a trover dun chapleyn ou chaunterie priest a chanter etc. et que les feffees paiera v li. al priest, xl s. al reparations del chappel in que le priest chauntera, et le residue a cesti que visitera mesme le chaunterie, in cest case il dit que le roy avera tout le terre car les parols del estatut sont, wherwith or whereby anie chaunterie priest etc. was mainteined etc. Issint intaunt que les terres fueront dones a trover un priest coment que severall limitations de paimentes fueront faitz uncore intaunt que le reparation del chappell et le profittes assigne a cesti que visitera depend tout sur le chaunterie, et tout ceo est pur le supportation del chaunterie priest. Et il dit que <coment que cest>[d] si ascun de eux fueront imploy deins 5 ans que tout le terre serra forfeite, car lun depend sur lauter. Mes si lun chose soit collaterall del auter, come si home fait feffment in fe des terres sur confidens que les feffees paiera xx s. al un chaunterie priest et xx s. al use dun obite, si le chaunterie priest fuit trove et lobbite nemy le roy navera le terre <mes>[d]. Et il prist diversitie sur le parolx del acte quant terres fueront dones a trover un priest et que le priest avera un certain somme, la tout le terre serra al roy, mes si terres sont dones a un et a ses heires a doner et paier x markes al chaunterie priest, la pur ceo que le terre nest done a trover le chaunterie priest le roy navera forsque le x markes. Mes si terres sont dones a trover un chaunterie priest, coment que les feffees expend forsque parcell de profitz deins les 5 ans, uncore tout serra al roy. Et nota que le principall case la fuit forsque tiel, que terres fueront dones al deane et chapter a trover annuelment sustentation de x markes a un chaunterie priest et le residue des profites fueront graunt al deane et chapter a trover un annuel obite, except xx s. pur le perpetuel suertie del dit chaunterie, queux fueront graunt al maior et cominalte de Loundres ita quod ilz pres[enteront] al dit chaunterie quant ceo fuit voide. Et fuit dit per le segnior Wraye que intant que ne fuit trove per les jurores que le obite fuit use deins 5 ans etc. ideo le roy navera le terre, mes si le obite avoit estre trove[i] donques le terre serra al roy, mes pur ceo que ceo ne fuit trove et les terres [ne] fueront dones a trover chaunterie priest mes a trover et aver [...][1] pur un chaunterie priest, ideo le roy navera le terre per ceo [...]s.[2] Mes nota il dit, si terres sont done a trover un obite et [...][3] paiera le 3 parts de profitz a ceo, uncore <le roy>[i] avera tout.

---

[1] *Word lost in lower corner.*
[2] *Word or two lost in lower corner.*
[3] *A few words lost in lower corner.*

compass of the statute inasmuch as it was reputed and accepted as a college, even though it had an imperfect commencement. And note that the words of the statute of 1 Edw. VI,[1] namely 'all manner of colleges, free chapels ... having, being, or *in esse* [within five years next before the Act]', which words were put in with the intention that such colleges and chantries as were given to the king by 37 Hen. VIII[2] should not be given to the king by that statute. Also such colleges and chantries as were previously dissolved and converted to good use would have been given [to the king] if those words had not been added. And note that WRAY C.J. said that if someone gave lands to the value of £10 to find a chaplain or chantry priest to sing etc., and directed that the feoffees should pay £5 to the priest, 40s. towards the repairs of the chapel in which the priest is to sing, and the residue to the person who is to visit the same chantry, in this case (he said) the king shall have all the land, for the words of the statute are, 'wherewith or whereby any chantry priest ... was maintained ...'. Thus, inasmuch as the lands were given to find a priest, even though several limitations of payments were made, yet since the repair of the chapel, and the profits assigned to the person who should visit, all depended on the chantry, all of it is for the support of the chantry priest. And he said that if any of them were employed [in supporting a chantry priest] within five years, all the land would be forfeited, for the one depends on the other. If, however, one of the things is collateral to the other, for instance if a man makes a feoffment in fee of lands upon trust that the feoffees should pay 20s. to a chantry priest and 20s. to the use of an obit, and the chantry priest was found but not the obit, the king shall not have the land. And he took a distinction upon the wording of the Act: when lands are given to find a priest, and the priest is to have a certain sum, there all the land shall go to the king, but if lands are given to someone and his heirs to give and pay 10 marks to a chantry priest, there the king shall only have the 10 marks, because the land is not given to find the chantry priest. If, however, lands are given to find a chantry priest, then even if the feoffees spend only part of the profits within the five years, all shall nevertheless go to the king. And note that the principal case was simply this: lands were given to the dean and chapter to find 10 marks a year to maintain a chantry priest, and the residue of the profits were granted to the dean and chapter to find an annual obit, excepting 20s. for the perpetual security of the said chantry which were granted to the mayor and commonalty of London, so that they should present to the said chantry when it was void. And it was said by the lord WRAY that since it was not found by the jurors that the obit was used within five years [of the Act], the king should not have the land, whereas if the obit had been found, the land would have gone to the king; however, because this was not found, and the lands were [not] given to find a chantry priest but to find [10 marks][3] for a chantry priest, the king should not thereby have the land. But note that (as he said) if lands were given to find an obit and the donee was to pay over a third part of the profits towards this, the king would have the whole.

---

[1] 1 Edw. VI, c. 14, s. 2.
[2] 37 Hen. VIII, c. 4.
[3] Text unclear.

70   REPORTS FROM COKE'S NOTEBOOKS

[116]

AB, fo. 82r-v (345r-v). *Ff*, fos. 169–170. *Gg*, fos. 28–30. Abridged in LI MS. Misc. 791, fo. 111v.

<Le countie de Arundels case M. 19 Eliz.>[s] <Dier, 17 Eliz. 342.>[a] <Trin. 16 Eliz. rott. 1023.>[a]

Le countie de Arundel port trespas de son close debruse envers David Langor et assigne le trespas in un lieu, parcell del manour de Haselber Brian, et sur rien culpable plede les jurores done cest especial verdit. Ilz troveront que le countee de Arundel fuit seisie del mannor de Haselber Brian in son demesne come de fe, deins quel mannour le custome fuit que les segniors del mannour purront graunt copyes cy bien in reversion come in possession, et trove que le dit counte de Arundel graunt le lieu in que a un estraunge pur terme de son vie, et auxi ilz troveront un auter custome del mannour que le feme de chescun copiholder pur vie avera le terre dont sa baron fuit issint seisie apres son mort pur terme de son vie sel vive sole, et ouster ilz disoient que le dit counte de Arundel <iss>[d] esteant seisie del dit mannour de H. ceo dona a le jades counte de Northumberland et a ses heires males de son corps, et pur defaut de tiel issue le remainder a Sir Henry Percey ore counte de Northumberland et a ses heires males de son corps loialment issuantz, sub hac tamen conditione, si predictus comes Northumbrie vel <haeredes masculi d>[d] Henricus Percey obierint sine heredibus masculis de corporibus eorum aut si predictus comes vel Henricus Percey vel haeredes etc. eorum aliquam rem vel aliquod factum vel aliqua facta fecerunt vel permiserunt vel fieri vel permitti causarent directe vel indirecte, arte vel ingenio, quo minus manerium predictum cum pertinenciis et singulam inde parcellam mihi prefato comiti Arundel vel heredibus meis sine impedimento et dilatione in possessione reverti debeant et possunt si predictus comes Northumbrie et Henricus Percey sine heredibus masculis de corporibus etc. obire contigerunt, quod tunc bene liceat mihi prefato comiti Arundel et heredibus meis reintrare, per force de quel le dit countie fuit seisie, et issint seisie prist un fem, et auxi per copy de court rolle solonque le custom etc. graunt le lieu in que le trespas est ore suppose a Langer a aver et tener a luy immediatement puis le mort le dit Meredith adonques esteant tenant pur vie solonque le custome. Et troveront ouster que le dit Meredith prist fem et morust, et le fem tient eins per le custom et morust etc. Et troveront ouster que le dit countie de Northumberland fuit utlage del haut treason et judgment done devant les coroners accordant. Et ilz troveront lestatut de 26 H. 8 et 33 H. 8, et troveront ouster coment que le dit Langor apres le mort

---

[1] Vide mon report de cest case inter mes reportes fol. 82') and 344 ('Vide in mes reportes cest case fol. 82, in fine, bone diversitye'). Differently reported in Dyer 342 (Trin. 1575); cit. from Dyer in 3 Co. Rep. 34, 6 Co. Rep. 41, and 10 Co. Rep. 37, 40; JRL MS. Fr. 118, fo. 73. Cf. KB 27/1258, m. 368 (1576; seven rolls); Benl. 290: Earl of Arundel v. Thomas Loder (alias Miller), Ralph Ingram and John Toppe; error upon an assize of novel disseisin for tenements in Haselbury Bryan, Dors.; discontinued, Hil. 1577.
[2] This bundle (CP 40/1323) now ends at m. 1018.
[3] In Dorset. For this manor see also *Wilmot* v. *Cottle* (1588) vol. ii, p. 362.
[4] 26 Hen. VIII, c. 13; 33 Hen. VIII, c. 20.

116. EARL OF ARUNDEL v. LANGAR[1]

Exch. Ch., referred from the Common Pleas, Mich. 1576.

The earl of Arundel's case, Mich. 19 Eliz. Dyer, 17 Eliz. 342. Trin. 16 Eliz., roll 1023.[2]

The earl of Arundel brought trespass for his close broken against David Langar, and assigned the trespass in a place which was parcel of the manor of Haselbury Bryan;[3] and, upon Not Guilty pleaded, the jurors found the following special verdict. They found that the earl of Arundel was seised of the manor of Haselbury Bryan in his demesne as of fee, within which manor it was the custom that the lords of the manor could grant copies in reversion as well as in possession; and they found that the said earl of Arundel granted the locus in quo to a stranger for term of his life; they also found another custom of the manor, that the wife of every copyholder for life should have the land whereof her husband was so seised, after his death, for term of her life, if she remained unmarried; and they further said that the said earl of Arundel, being seised of the said manor of Haselbury, gave it to the late earl of Northumberland and his heirs male of his body, and for want of such issue the remainder to Sir Henry Percy (now earl of Northumberland) and his heirs male of his body lawfully issuing, but nevertheless upon this condition, that 'if the aforesaid earl of Northumberland or Henry Percy should die without heirs male of their bodies, or if the aforesaid earl or Henry Percy or their heirs [of their bodies] should do or permit or cause to be done or permitted any thing or any deed or deeds, directly or indirectly, by craft or scheming (*arte vel ingenio*), whereby the aforesaid manor with the appurtenances and every single parcel thereof ought not or could not revert in possession to me the said earl of Arundel or my heirs, without hindrance and delay, or if the aforesaid earl of Northumberland and Henry Percy should happen to die without heirs male of their bodies, that then it should be lawful for me the said earl of Arundel and my heirs to re-enter', by force whereof the said earl [of Northumberland] was seised, and (being so seised) he married a wife; [the earl] also, by copy of court roll, in accordance with the custom first aforesaid, granted to Langar the place in which the trespass is now supposed, to have and to hold unto him immediately after the death of [one] Meredith (then being tenant for life), in accordance with the custom; and they further found that the said Meredith married and died, and his wife held in by the custom, and died; and they further found that the said earl of Northumberland was outlawed for high treason, and judgment was given before the coroners accordingly; and they found the statutes of 26 Hen. VIII and 33 Hen. VIII,[4] and found further that the said Langar entered after the death of

---

[1] Noted above, p. 32, no. 71; p. 37, no. 80; p. 38, no. 82; below, p. 80, in no. 125; p. 94, no. 156. Cit. in *AB*, fo. 263v ('Et nota le case del feffe sur condition fuit adjudge in the counte de Arundels case anno 19 Eliz. termino Michaelis'); *AC*, fo. 557v ('Vide counte de Arundels case in mes reports, 82, in fine, bone diversite et reason'); *C*, fo. 32 (vol. iii, p. 468) ('Vide countee de Arundels case in mes reportes in fine'); Co. Litt. 59b ('and so it was holden in 17 Eliz. in the earl of Arundel's case, which I my selfe heard'); ibid. 252b ('This hath beene adjudged Mich. 14 & 15 Eliz. Roll 1458 [*sic*] in the Earl of Arundell's Case'); Coke's Dyer (Holkham 8014), fos. 342v ('Vide cest case Trin. 16, rott. 1023, in communi banco.

del fem del Meredith enter, le countie de Arundel enter sur luy, le dit Langor reenter, sur quel entre le countie de Arundel port cest action de trespas. Et in cest case 3 principall matters fueront moves et argue in leschequer chamber devant toutz les justices.

Le primer, si per le prisel del fem le condition devant recite fuit infreint, car fuit dit que poet estre que le fem serra indowe et que ambideux les donees moreront sauns issue et donques le terre ne revertera immediatement in possession, car coment que il ad le title de entre per les parolx del condition uncore ceo ne revert in possession. Le 2 fuit, si le graunt per cesty in revercion in mannour et forme avaundit fait fuit infreinder del condition, car fuit dit que coment que le condition fuit enfreint uncore lestate del copiholder loialment fait ne serra defeate etc. Le 3 fuit si lattaindre del dit jades countie fuit infreinder del dit condition intant que maintenant per lattaindre le terres fueront in le roigne per lestatut de 33 H. 8.

Et quant al primer point toutz les justices sur secrete communication enter eux mesmes <agreont>[i] (come Justice Gawdy dit a moy) que le prisel del fem ne fuit infreinder del condition, quar quant done est fait a un et a les heires de son corps engendres serra absurd in reason et contrarie al nature del done a prohibite mariage, sine quo il ne poet unques aver issue de son corps solonque le forme et intent del done, et auxi pur ceo que ceo est un charge que le ley create etc., et auxi pur ceo que fuit enconter nature et repugnant al done precedent. [*fo. 82v*]

Quant al 2 point ilz agreont, et issint fuit adjudge, que le graunt del copie in revercion ne fuit infreinder del condition, car fuit un loiall acte et garrante per le custome, et nul estate repute et esteeme in nostre ley. Et auxi ilz agreont que coment que lestate de Langor ne puit commencer immediatement apres le mort del Meredith solonque les parolx del graunt pur ceo que le fem del Meredith fuit daver ceo puis son mort durant son widowes estate, uncore ils teignont clerement que le graunt fuit assetz bone, car le widowes estate fuit continuans del auncient estate, et auxi fuit estate create loialment per le custome. Et les justices agreont, et issint fuit adjudge, que coment que le condition fuit infreint per lattaindre, come serra dit apres, uncore lestate del copiholder loialment fait per le feffee del condition ne serra defete, coment que le feffour ad entre pur le condition enfreint, car coment que un condition defetera toutz mesne actes et charges per le common ley sinon chattelx executed come gardes, perquisites de villeins, presentmentes al avousons et similia, uncore lestate del copiholder ne serra per ceo defete pur ceo que le custom est que le segnior pro tempore grauntera et pur ceo que il fuit loiall dominus pro tempore nient obstant que son estate fuit puis defeet per condition uncore le copiholde remain bone. Et pur ceo fuit agre si lesses pur auns, pur vie, done in taile ou lesse a volunte graunt terres per copy queux ont estre dimised ou dimisible etc. que ceo est bone et liera cesti in le revercion coment que lour etates determine. Mes ilz toutz agreont que si leire le dissesor ou le feffe le dissesor ou ascum auter que ad un tortious title et defesible estate et subjecte al droit et title paramount que toutz tielz copies faitz per tielz segniors serra avoide per cesti que droit ad apres que il ad recontinue son droit et

Meredith's wife, the earl of Arundel entered upon him, and the said Langar re-entered, upon which entry the earl of Arundel brought this action of trespass. And in this case three principal matters were moved and argued in the Exchequer Chamber before all the justices.

First, whether by marrying the wife the condition recited above was broken; for it was said that the wife might be endowed, and both the donees might die without issue, and then the land would not revert immediately in possession, for although he had the title to enter by the words of the condition, nevertheless it did not revert in possession. The second was, whether the grant made by the reversioner in manner and form aforesaid was a breach of the condition; for it was said that although the condition was broken, nevertheless the copyholder's estate, once lawfully made, shall not be undone. The third was, whether the attainder of the said late earl was a breach of the said condition, inasmuch as by the attainder the lands were at once in the queen by the statute of 33 Hen. VIII.

As to the first point, all the justices agreed – upon private communication among themselves (as GAWDY J. told me) – that marrying the wife was not a breach of the condition, for when a gift is made to someone and the heirs of his body begotten it would be absurd in reason and contrary to the nature of the gift to prohibit marriage, without which he can never have issue of his body according to the form and intent of the gift, and also because it is a charge which the law creates, and also because it was against nature and repugnant to the preceding gift.

As to the second point, they agreed (and so it was adjudged) that the grant of the copy in reversion was not a breach of the condition, for it was a lawful act and warranted by the custom, albeit not an estate reputed and esteemed in our law. They also agreed that although Langar's estate could not begin immediately after Meredith's death, according to the words of the grant, because Meredith's wife was to have it after his death during her widow's estate, nevertheless they held clearly that the grant was perfectly good, for the widow's estate was a continuance of the old estate, and also it was an estate lawfully created by the custom. And the justices agreed (and so it was adjudged) that although the condition was broken by the attainder, as will be said below, nevertheless the copyholder's estate lawfully made by the feoffee upon condition shall not be defeated, even if the feoffor has entered for breach of the condition, for although a condition will defeat all intermediate acts and charges at common law – apart from chattels executed, such as wardships, purchases by villeins, presentations to advowsons, and such like – nevertheless the copyholder's estate shall not be thereby defeated, because the custom is that the lord for the time being may grant, and because he was the lawful lord for the time being, notwithstanding that his estate was afterwards defeated by a condition, the copyhold still remains good. Likewise, it was agreed that if a lessee for years or for life, a donee in tail, or a lessee at will, grants lands by copy which have been demised or demisable time out of mind, this is good and will bind the reversioner even though their estates are finite. But they all agreed that if the heir of a disseisor, or the feoffee of a disseisor, or anyone else who has a tortious title and a defeasible estate subject to the right and title paramount, [grants a copyhold], all such copies made by such lords shall be avoided by the person who has right, after he has recontinued his right and recovered

recover son possession. Mes ilz agreont auxi que toutz actes que le dissessor, son heire ou feffees etc. fait queux il est compellable de faire liera le disseise et cesti que droit ad co[…] et ne serra defete per luy. Come si surrender soit fait per un copiholder in ses maynes al use dun auter, et il fait graunt accordant, ceo ne serra defeate per le dissese pur ceo que il fuit arctable et compellable a ceo faire et nul prejudice al disseise, mes autrement est de voluntarie grauntz pur ceo que il nest a eux faire compellable et auxi sont in prejudice del disseisie. Et nota bene que fuit dit que lestate dun copiholder nest pas arbitrable al volunt le segnior, car lestate dun copiholder est create et mainten per custome, et consuetuo privat communem legem. Come per custom le puisne fitz inheritera, et issint chaungera le course de inheritaunce. Et 20 H. 6, per custom le chiefe justice ayant que estate in son office a volunte grantera offices pur vie. Et vide Littleton, 16b, divers authorities provant estate et interest dun copiholder queux fueront cite et remember in le argument de cest case. Et nota Slowlyes case anno 7 Eliz. et Steeres case anno 5 Eliz. queux jeo ay note in Littleton, fol. 15b.

Et quant al 3 point ilz toutz agreont que per lattiendre le condition fuit enfreint, car maintenant per lattaindre le terres fueront in le actuel possession le roigne per lestatute de 33 H. 8, et coment que in mesme lestatut il soit un savant a toutz estraunges lour entrees, uncore pur ceo que puit estre que les donees moreront sauns issue durant le possession le roygne, et donques coment que le <roig>^d countie de Arundel purroit enter uncore les terres ne reverteront immediatement in possession solonque les parolx del condition. Et nota que le melior opinion des justices fuit (come Justice Gawdy dit a moy) que lentre del countie de Arundell fuit <save>^d congeable sur le roy[gne] pur ceo que son entre est save per mesme lestatut que intitle le roygne, scilicet per lestatut de 33 H. 8. Mes si home soit attaint per un statut et ses terres dones al roy in possession, et puis un auter estatute repeale ceo, et provide que le partie entra <sur le roigne>^d uncore la il ne poet enter de monstre son droit, et issint est tenus in 4 H. 7, 7. Nota bene le diversite. <Et semble reasonable que lour opinions quant al entre serront loiall pur ceo que est nul matter de record que intitle le roy, mes si soit office trove autrement est.>^a

---

[3] These were citations by Popham: *AB*, fo. 258v (magenta ink): 'Slowlyes case anno 7 Eliz. ... et fuit adjudge, come Popham dit in le countie de Arundels case, que les copies fueront defeate. Steres case in anno 5 Eliz. fuit tenus (come Popham auxi la dit) ...'. It thus appears that these cases were commonplaced by Coke as a result of their citation in the *Earl of Arundel's Case*. They are copied in *F*, fo. 156, as from 'Reportes Cook'.

[4] *Lord Ormond's Case* (1489) YB Pas. 4 Hen. VII, fo. 7, pl. 6; 64 Selden Soc. 138.

his possession. However, they also agreed that all acts done by the disseisor, his heir, or his feoffees, which he is compellable to perform, shall bind the disseisee and the person who has right and shall not be defeated by him. For instance if a surrender is made by a copyholder into his hands to the use of another, and he makes a grant accordingly, this shall not be defeated by the disseisee, because he was constrainable and compellable to do it, and it is no prejudice to the disseisee; but it is otherwise of voluntary grants, because he is not compellable to make them and also because they prejudice the disseisee. And note well that it was said that the estate of a copyholder is not arbitrary, at the will of the lord, for the estate of a copyholder is created and maintained by custom, and custom takes away common law (*consuetudo privat communem legem*). For instance, by a custom the youngest son may inherit, and that will change the course of inheritance. And 20 Hen. VI:[1] by custom the chief justice (though having but an estate at will in his office) may grant offices for life. And see in [my] Littleton, fo. 16v:[2] various authorities proving the estate and interest of a copyholder, which were cited and remembered in the argument of this case. Note also Slowlye's case in the year 7 Eliz., and Steere's case in the year 5 Eliz., which I have noted in Littleton, fo. 15v.[3]

As to the third point, they all agreed that the condition was broken by the attainder, for by the attainder the lands were forthwith in the actual possession of the queen by the statute of 33 Hen. VIII, and although in the same statute there is a saving to all strangers of their entries, nevertheless, inasmuch as the donees might die without issue during the queen's possession, and then the earl of Arundel could enter, the lands would still not revert immediately in possession according to the words of the condition. And note that the better opinion of the justices (as GAWDY J. told me) was that the entry by the earl of Arundel upon the queen was lawful, because his entry is saved by the same statute which entitles the queen, namely by the statute of 33 Hen. VIII. However if someone is attainted by one statute, and his lands given to the king in possession, and then another statute repeals that and provides that the party may enter, nevertheless he may not there enter to show his right. So it is held in 4 Hen. VII, fo. 7.[4] Note well the distinction. {And it seems reasonable that their opinions as to the entry should be law, because there is no matter of record which entitles the king; but it would be otherwise if an office was found.}

---

[1] *Pilkington's Case* (1441) YB Mich. 20 Hen. VI, fo. 8, pl. 17, *per* Fortescue C.J. See also YB Hil. 20 Edw. IV, fo. 18, pl. 8, *per* Catesby J.; Caryll's reports, 116 Selden Soc. 410 (1502), *per* Frowyk C.J. Appointments in Coke's time were still made during the queen's pleasure.

[2] This refers to the notes headed 'Copyholde' in *AB*, fo. 259 (magenta ink), which are between fos. 15 and 16 of the printed Littleton.

[117]

AB, fo. 83r-v (346r-v).

<Brasbridges Case anno 15.>[s] <H. 14 Eliz. rott. Dviij.>[a] <Mich. 14 Eliz. 85, Periam.>[a]

Le case fuit tiel in effect. Thomas Brasbrich esteant seisie del mannour de Kingesbury in Warwickeshire fist leas del 10 acres parcell del mannour a un C pur xxj ans rendant nul rent, per force de quel [le] lesse fuit possesse, et puis il lessa mesmes les ditz 10 acres de terre a un M. pur [per][1] xxj ans a commencer apres le primer ans determine, rendant xix s. de rent, et puis Thomas Brasb. <fi>[d] 5 E. 6 fist feffment del entier mannour a un G. F. et auters et a lour heires sur condition que si les feffees ne paieront x[m] li. deins 15 jours que donques ilz estoieront seisies al use de luy et de sa fem durant lour vies, le remainder al use de sa fem in taile, ove divers et multes remainders ouster, les feffees ne paieront les deniers deins les 15 joures, et apres le 15 jours passe le primer lessee attorne al feffees, per force de quel Brasb. fuit seisie ove sa fem del mannour per terme de lour vies, le remainder ouster a lour fitz ove les remainders ouster, et puis Brasb. et sa fem moreront, le primer leas finie, le 2 lesse enter, Brasbrich le fitz distreine, et le lesse port replevin. Et in cest case 2 matters fueront principalment argue. Le primer fuit si le revercion de cest parcell que fuit in leas pur ans passera al feffees devant attornement. Le 2, admittant que attornement soit requisite, le quel attornement apres le 15 joures soit bone a les feffees.

Quant al primer point Mounson argue que il covient daver attornement ou auterment riens passe. Et vide les livres <que>[2] <l>[d] il et les auters justices cite pur cest point in Litt. 125a. Et la Mounson cite le case in 30 E. 3, 4, in brefe de droit de gard, la home fist feffment dun mannour et toutz les tenantes attorne, savant un que tient per iiij s., et devant attornement per luy fait le feffe fist done in taile etc., et tenus que les services et le rent de cest tenant que ne attornera ne passera. Quant al 2 point, il semble que lattornement apres les 15 joures al feffees est bone. Mes il dit, si home graunte un revercion sur condition que si le grauntee ne paia x li. que donques son estate serra voide, attornement apres nest bone car le condition est annexe al graunt et le condition destroy le graunt. Mes icy est[3] le[4] condition est annex al use et nemi a lestate, car si luse limitt a les feffees ne prist effecte donques les feffees estoiera seisies al auter uses. Et le condition nest annex a lestate car coment que le primer use soit voide uncore le 2 use poet prender effect. Mes si un clause de reentre ust estre

---

[1] *Sic, but otiose.*   [2] *Unclear alteration.*
[3] *Sic, but otiose.*   [4] *Altered from* un; *resembles* xx.

---

m. 28 (*venire facias*, Trin. 1580); BL MS. Harley 2036, fos. 77–81; MS. Harley 4988, fos. 50–53v; MS. Harg. 11, fos. 14–19. The Bracebridge deeds relating to Kingsbury are BL Add. Ch. 48208–48256.

[2] Robert Curteys: record.

[3] William Moore *alias* Bysshop: record. His widow married the plaintiff.

[4] Sir George Gryffyth: record.

[5] I.e. in Coke's annotated Litt. at *AC*, fo. 614 (magenta ink) and the accompanying notes on attornment at fos. 615–621v.

[6] *Bishop of Norwich's Case* (1356) YB Hil. 30 Edw. III, fo. 5.

117. BAREWELL v. LUCAS: BRACEBRIDGE'S CASE[1]

Common Pleas, 1572/73.

Bracebridge's case in 15 Eliz. Hil. 14 Eliz., roll 508. Mich. 14 Eliz. 85, Peryam.

The case was, in effect, as follows. Thomas Bracebridge, being seised of the manor of Kingsbury in Warwickshire, made a lease of 10 acres, parcel of the manor, to one C.[2] for twenty-one years, rendering no rent, by force whereof the lessee was possessed; and afterwards he leased the same 10 acres of land to one M.[3] for twenty-one years, to commence after the first years were determined, rendering 19s. rent; then Thomas Bracebridge, in 5 Edw. VI, made a feoffment of the entire manor to one G. G.[4] and others, and their heirs, upon condition that if the feoffees did not pay £10,000 within fifteen days they should stand seised to the use of him and his wife during their lives, remainder to the use of his wife in tail, with various and many remainders over; the feoffees did not pay the money within the fifteen days, and after the fifteen days were past the first lessee attorned to the feoffees, by force whereof Bracebridge and his wife were seised of the manor for term of their lives, remainder over to their son, with the remainders over; afterwards Bracebridge and his wife died; the first lease ended; the second lessee entered; Bracebridge the son distrained; and the lessee brought replevin. And in this case two matters were principally argued. The first was whether the reversion of that parcel which was leased for years could pass to the feoffees before attornment. The second, admitting attornment to be requisite, was whether attornment to the feoffees after the fifteen days was good.

As to the first point, MOUNSON argued that there must be attornment, or else nothing passes. See the books which he and the other justices cited for this point in [my] Littleton, fo. 125.[5] And MOUNSON there cited the case in 30 Edw. III, fo. 4,[6] in a writ of right of ward, where a man made a feoffment of a manor, and all the tenants attorned save one who held by 4s., and before attornment by him the feoffee made a gift in tail of the manor, and it was held that the services and the rent of this tenant who did not attorn did not pass. As to the second point, he thought that the attornment to the feoffees after the fifteen days was good. But he said that if someone grants a reversion upon condition that if the grantee does not pay £10 his estate shall be void, an attornment afterwards is not good, for the condition is annexed to the grant and the condition destroys the grant. Here, however, the condition is annexed to the use and not to the estate, for if the use limited to the feoffees does not take effect, the feoffees are to stand seised to other uses. And the condition is not annexed to the estate, for even if the first use is void, the second use may still take effect. However, if a clause of re-entry had been reserved to the feoffees, an attornment afterwards

---

[1] CP 40/1300, m. 508 (two rolls; summarised in Benl. 208): Thomas Barewell v. William Lucas *alias* Gryme; replevin for cattle taken at Hurley in the parish of Kingsbury, Warw.; avows as bailiff of Thomas Bracebridge, lord of the manor of Kingsbury, setting out the leases as in the report; demurrer to the avowry; c.a.v. to Pas. 1573; judgment for the defendant. Noted below, pp. 104–105, nos. 182–183; p. 106, no. 186; p. 107, no. 189. Differently reported in Moo. 99 (Harwell); 2 Leon. 221; Dyer's notebook, 110 Selden Soc. 261, and the MS. reports cited there; BL MS. Harley 6811, fos. 173v–174; MS. Lansd. 1060, fos. 40v–42; CUL MS. Hh.2.9, fos. 71–76, 121–123v; IT MS. Barrington 76, fos. 43–44v. This was one of several suits concerning the same estate: see also *Bracebridge* v. *Cooke* (1572) Plowd. 416 (ejectment concerning a different manor in Kingsbury); *Stoneley* v. *Bracebridge* (1580–86) KB 27/1275,

reserve al feffees donques attornement apres ust estre voide. Et luy semble que cest attornement avera relation a faire le revercion de passer come parcell del manour. Mesme la ley des services, ilz ne passera devant attornement, mes quant attornement est fait donques il passera a principio. Come si home face leas de terre in 3 counties reservant rent, si apres il fist livery in une countie et [*fo. 83v*] puis in les auters counties ilz ne sont severall lesses ne severall tenantz mes un joint et entier leas coment que lexecution de ceo fuit a severall temps. Et la il dit, et Manwood auxi agre a ceo, que si le revercion ust passe in droit al feffee donques il ne besoigne daver prove attornement, car si un revercion fuit graunt <per fine>[i] al auter use cesti que use distrenera sauns attornement pur ceo que il nad mesne a faire le tenant dattorner et le revercion est in luy in droit.

Manwood auxi agre que le revercion ne passera sauns attornment, coment que il puit passer sauns fait, car cest reason fuit urge del auter side. Al 2 point luy semble que lattornement <nest barre>[i] car il dit que coment que les grauntors et les grauntees sont in vie uncore auxi le substaunce de chose graunt covient estre unaltered. Ad estre dit que coment que attornement ne poet server pur launcient use, uncore il servera pur le novel use, mes ceo ne poet estre car debile fundamentum fallit opus. Et les uses covient surder hors dun estate et si le estate soit destroie les uses auxi serra destroye.

Harper agre que le revercion ne passera sauns attornement. Et al auter point luy semble que lattornement apres fuit bone car lestate nest pas defait mes luse solement a que le condition fuit annexe et un novel use raise. Et un use poet estre voide in parte et bone in parte. Come feffment al use dun monke pur vie et puis al use dun auter in fe.

Dier agre que le revercion ne passera sauns attornement. Et le Segnior Dier dit que le scite del mannour et les demesnes sont le principall parte del mannour, car lavouson est appendant a les demesnes, car si home enfeffe un del mannour sauns attornement de tenantes <lavouson passera>.[i] Al 2 point luy semble que lattornement apres les 15 joures fuit bone, car le qualitie de cest condition nest a defeter lestate. Mes cest condition ad 2 respectz. Le primer est si le condition soit performe donques al use le feffees, le 2 si le condition ne soit performe donques al use le feffor, et coment que le primer use soit voide uncore le 2 poet estre bone. Et coment que ilz ne voillent aver ceo a lour use demesne uncore ilz poient aver ceo al use le feoffour. Et il dit que coment que les feffees navoient riens al temps del attornement uncore ceo avera relation a faire le chose de passer ab initio, mes nemi a charger le tenant in waste ne ove les arrerages, come[1] feffment del mannour et les tenants attorne 7 ans apres.

---

[1] *Apparently written* com^t.

would have been void. And it seemed to him that this attornment relates back so as to cause the reversion to pass as parcel of the manor. The law is the same of the services: they do not pass before attornment, but when attornment is made they pass *a principio*.[1] Likewise if someone makes a lease of land in three counties, reserving rent, and afterwards makes livery in one county and then in the other counties, these are not separate leases or several tenants but one joint and entire lease, even though the execution thereof was at several times. And he said, and MANWOOD also agreed, that if the reversion had passed in right to the feoffee, he would not have needed to prove an attornment; for if a reversion is granted by fine to another's use, cestui que use can distrain without attornment, because he has no means to make the tenant attorn and the reversion is in him in right.

MANWOOD also agreed that the reversion cannot pass without attornment, even though it could pass without a deed (for that was a reason urged on the other side). As to the second point, he thought that the attornment is barred; for he said that even if the grantors and grantees are alive, still the substance of the thing granted must be unaltered. It has been said that although attornment cannot serve for the old use, still it may serve for the new use; but that cannot be, for if the foundation is weak the structure collapses (*Debile fundamentum fallit opus*). And the uses must arise out of an estate, and if the estate is destroyed the uses also shall be destroyed.

HARPER agreed that the reversion cannot pass without attornment. As to the other point, he thought that the attornment afterwards was good, for the estate is not defeated, but only the use to which the condition was annexed, and a new use is raised. A use may be void in part and good in part. For example, a feoffment to the use of a monk for life and then to the use of another in fee.[2]

DYER agreed that the reversion cannot pass without attornment. And the lord DYER said that the site of the manor and the demesnes are the principal part of the manor, and the advowson is appendant to the demesnes; for if a man enfeoffs someone of a manor without attornment of tenants, the advowson will [not] pass. As to the second point, he thought that the attornment after the fifteen days was good, for the quality of this condition is not to defeat the estate. But this condition has two respects. The first is, if the condition is performed, then to the use of the feoffees; and the second, if the condition is not performed, then to the use of the feoffor. And even if the first use is void, still the second may be good; for even if they are not to have it to their own use, they may still have it to the use of the feoffor. And he said that although the feoffees had nothing at the time of the attornment, nevertheless it shall relate back so as to cause the thing to pass *ab initio*, albeit not so as to charge the tenant in waste, or with the arrears, [as where] there is a feoffment of a manor and the tenants attorn seven years afterwards.[3]

---

[1] Cf. below, p. 105.
[2] *Farington* v. *Darell* (1431) YB Trin. 9 Hen. VI, fo. 23, pl. 19, at fo. 24, *per* Godred serjeant; B. & M. 80, at p. 83.
[3] Cf. below, p. 99, no. 168.

[118]

AB, fo. 84–85 (347–348).

<Vernons case anno 15 Eliz.>[s] <termino Pasche>[a]. <Darbishire.>[a] <Dier 317.>[a]

M. Vernon port brefe de dower del terce parte del mannour de Sudbury in Darb. vers J. Vernon etc. Le tenant plede que son baron fuit auxi seisie des auters terres dans mesme le countie et de ceux enfeffa Sir T[homas] Gifford, chivaler, al use de luy pur terme de sa vie sauns impechement de wast, et apres son deceasse al use de son fem, ore demandant, pur terme de sa vie, le <def>[d] remainder ouster as droit heires le baron, et averre que cest feffment fuit fait in consideration de sa dower, et monstre que apres le mort le baron el enter et ad agre a ceo. A que le demandant replie et confesse que le baron fuit seisie de mesmes les terres in fe et que il fist le feffment a le dit Sir T. Gifford al use de luy pur son vie, et apres sa decesse al use de sa fem, ore le demandant, sur condition que el performera son darrein volunt, et monstre tout le volunt in certaine, et demande judgment si il serra resceive dalleger que cest estate fuit conveie a luy in consideration del jointure del feme, sur quel matter le tenant demurre in ley. Et in cest cas 3 matters fueront argue. Le primer, le quel cest conditionel estate in remainder al fem soit deins le compas del estatut <ou nemi>[d] de 27 H. 8, cap. 10, que il serra un jointure deins le purvieu de le dit estatute. Le 2 point, le quel un estate conditionel soit deins mesme lestatute de 27 H. 8. Le 3 point, le quel il poet averrer que ceo fuit in consideration de son jointure entaunt que le condition fuit expresse deins le fait que el performera son darrein volunt.

Et quant al primer point Mounson semble que cest estate in remainder fuit deins lestatute de 27 H. 8, car coment que il ne soit nul de lestates que sont expres in le dit estatute uncore il serra prise per equite, car les estates que sont expresse la sont mys pur examples et nemi a excluder toutz auters estates sinon eux solement. Et pur ceo si estate pur vie ou in taile soit conveie devant coverture ceo est bone, et uncore hors de parolx. Et auxi fuit adjudge 8 Eliz. que ou terres fueront dones al duke de Suffolke et al duches sa feme et a les heires le baron engendre del corps le feme, et ceo fuit adjudge un bone jointure deins le dit estatut. <Mes si lestate ust estre limitte in remainder al fem et a un estraunge jointment, ceo nest un jointure deins lestatute>[d] Mes si feffment ust estre fait al use del baron et estraunge pur lour vies, le remainder

---

C.112, p. 452; LI MS. Misc. 361, fos. 29–31v; IT MS. Petyt 511.12, fos. 145–151 (Trin. 1572); JRL MS. Fr. 118, fos. 27–28v (Vernham); LI MS. Misc. 361, fos. 29–31v (sim.).

[2] Cf. KB 27/1238, m. 442 (Trin. 1571): Margaret Vernon, Richard Harpur J.C.P. and Sir Humphrey Bradburne, executors of Sir Henry Vernon v. John Vernon esq.; trespass to grain at Sudbury and Aston, Derbs.; pleads a licence to take as much as he needed for the provision of his household; verdict and judgment for the plaintiffs with £54 damages and £5. 10s. costs; KB 27/1241, m. 29 (Hil. 1572): same parties; trespass for taking a stock of animals and chattels at Sudbury; pleads Not Guilty; *venire facias*. Margaret Vernon also sued her mother and the other executors in Chancery for a legacy left by Sir Henry: *Vernon* v. *Vernon* (1572) BL MS. Harg. 8, fos. 153–154 (tr. in 117 Selden Soc. 98, no. 9).

[3] Identified from the record, and 4 Co. Rep. He was enfeoffed with Humphrey Swynerton, esq.

[4] I.e. in lieu of dower. It is later said to be in consideration of her jointure, meaning that it was to be a jointure in lieu of dower.

[5] Katherine Bertie (d. 1580), *suo jure* Baroness Willoughby d'Eresby, dowager duchess of Suffolk, was married to Charles Brandon (d. 1545), first duke of Suffolk, and later to Richard Bertie.

118. VERNON v. VERNON[1]

Common Pleas, Pas. 1573.

Vernon's case in Easter term 15 Eliz. Derbyshire. Dyer 317.

Margaret Vernon[2] brought a writ of dower against John Vernon for a third part of the manor of Sudbury in Derbyshire. The tenant pleaded that the husband was also seised of other lands in the same county, and thereof enfeoffed Sir Thomas[3] Gifford, knight, to the use of himself for term of his life, without impeachment of waste, and after his decease to the use of his wife (now demandant) for term of her life, the remainder over to the husband's right heirs; and he averred that this feoffment was made in consideration of her dower,[4] and showed that after the husband's death she entered and agreed to it. To this the demandant replied; and she confessed that the husband was seised of the same lands in fee, and that he made the feoffment to the said Sir Thomas Gifford to the use of himself for his life, and after his decease to the use of his wife (now the demandant), [but this was] upon condition that she perform his last will, and she set out the whole will in detail, and demanded judgment whether he should be received to allege that this estate was conveyed to her in consideration of his wife's jointure; and upon this matter the tenant demurred in law. And in this case three matters were argued. The first was whether this conditional estate in remainder to the wife was within the compass of the statute of 27 Hen. VIII, c. 10, so that it will be a jointure within the purview of the said statute. The second point was whether a conditional estate is within the same statute of 27 Hen. VIII. The third point was whether the tenant could aver that it was in consideration of her jointure, inasmuch as the condition was expressed in the deed to be that she perform his last will.

As to the first point, MOUNSON thought that this estate in remainder was within the statute of 27 Hen. VIII, for even though it is not one of the estates expressed in the said statute, it shall be so understood by equity; for the estates which are there expressed are put as examples, and not so as to exclude all other estates but them. If, therefore, an estate for life or in tail is conveyed before coverture, it is good, and yet it is outside the words. Also, it was adjudged in 8 Eliz. that where lands were given to the duke of Suffolk and the duchess his wife, and the heirs of the husband begotten on the body of the wife, this was a good jointure within the said statute.[5] If, however, a feoffment had been made to the use of the husband and a stranger for their lives, remainder to the wife

---

[1] CP 40/1304, m. 952 (Trin. 1572, two rolls; partly printed in Benl. 210): Margaret Vernon v. John Vernon esq.; dower for a third part of the manors of Sudbury and Aston as widow of Sir Henry Vernon (d. 1569); demurrer to the replication; c.a.v. to Mich. 1573; nonsuit. Noted below, p. 98, no. 166; p. 130, no. 233; p. 157, no. 298; p. 160, no. 310. Revised and enlarged in 4 Co. Rep. 1–5 (dated Mich. 1572). Cit. in *AD*, fo. 808 (magenta) ('Novel statutes prise per equitie ... Vernons case anno 15 sur lestatut de anno 27 H. 8 de jointures in mes notes demesne 84a et b'); Coke's Dyer (Holkham 8014), fo. 317 ('Vernons case. Vide in mes reportes fol. 84 cest case report'). Differently reported in Dyer 317, 341 (identified in Coke's Dyer as 'Vernons case ... Vide in mon report de cest case'); 3 Leon. 28 (Mich. 1573); BL MS. Harg. 373, fos. 74–87 (attributed by Umfreville to Harper); MS. Harley 1624, fos. 241–248; MS. Harley 6707, fos. 20–25v; MS. Harg. 8, fos. 153–154; MS. Harg. 10, fos. 47v–49v; MS. Harg. 373, fos. 74–87; MS. Lansd. 1067, fos. 3–8v; MS. Harley 6811, fo. 182v; MS. Lansd. 1060, fos. 79v–91v (Mich. 1572 and Pas. 1573); MS. Lansd. 1145, fos. 87–100; MS. Add. 35953, fo. 29 ('Le report de Justice Mounson come fuit escrye desouth sa mayne'); MS. Add. 25222, fos. 14v–15; MS. Add. 24845, fos. 106–110; CUL MS. Gg.2.5, fos. 155–162; MS. Gg.3.3, fos. 25–36; MS. Gg.5.2, fos. 110–113; Bodl. Lib. MS. Rawlinson

al fem pur sa vie, uncore ceo nest un jointure deins le dit estatut pur ceo que poet estre que le estraunge poet survive <lest>[d] le baron et donques la fem ne prendra ceo immediatement apres le mort le baron. Issint et pur mesme le cause si estate ust estre fait pur vie al baron, le remainder a un estraunge pur vie, le remainder al fem pur vie. Issint si rent ust estre graunt al fem a comencer apres le mort le baron, ceo ust estre bone. Mes dun rent a comencer apres le mort dun estraunge ceo ust estre void. Manwoode agre a ceo et il dit que devant lestatute de 27 H. 8 quant le greinder part des terres fueront in use, donques fuit communement use a faire jointures et quant lestatut transferre les uses in possession les fesores del estatute provide que fems naveront lour dowers et jointures auxi. Et coment que cest estate in remainder ex vi termini soit hors del estatute, uncore il est deins le meaning del estatut, car le meaning des homes fueront a doner a la feme un competent jointure apres le mort sa baron. Et il dit, si le jointure soit [*fo. 84v*] fait durant le coverture le fem apres poet waiver son jointure et prender son dower, autermient sil soit fait devant le coverture, car donques el ne puit waiver ceo. Et il dit, si lestate taile soit fait al baron et fem et a lour heires males ou females, ceo est hors de parols et uncore deins le meaning de lestatute. Et il agre le cases de Mounson ou le feme ne fuit a prender lestate immediatement apres le mort le baron, come si estate soit fait a J. S. pur vie, le remainder al fem, car poet estre que J. S. survivera sa baron. Et Mounson et Manwood agre que fe simple ne poet estre averre destre un jointure pur ceo que null revercion est in le donour etc. Et le Segnior Dier agre auxi a eux, car il dit que junctura est un competent living al fem durant sa naturall vie a comencer immediament apres le mort le baron. Et le Segnior Dier dit que un estate fuit fait al duke de Sommerset et al duches et as heires males del corps del duke, et le duches sua per petition daver sa dower del roigne, et fuit adjudge que cest estate fait a luy, coment que il fuit hors del parolx del estatut, uncore il fuit deins le meaning del estatut et issint el fuit barre de sa dower. Et le Segnior Dier dit que cest estatut serra prise come lestatute de W. 2 de donis conditionalibus, car la nust expresse forsque 3 plattes del tailes, mes Littleton dit que il fuit multz auters estates prise per lequitie. <Vide 11 E. 2, tit. Garrante, sur lestatut de Glocester.>[i] Issint que estates que sont la expres sont que patternes et examples. Issint et in mesme le mannour sont le 5 formes del estates limitte et expresse in cest estatute. Et il dit que jointure vient in lieu del dower. Et le dower ne commence tanque apres le mort [le] baron, et pur ceo luy semble que un remainder apres le mort le baron fuit un bon jointure coment que el ne prist jointment ove sa baron. 40 E. 3 [*blank*], home assigne dower al fem ad hostium ecclesie deins le vieu, et uncore riens passe maintenaunt. Et le Segnior Dier semble que un jointure del fe simple fuit deins le compas del estatute, et il dit que issint fuit adjudge in le Dame Denneys case que [fuit] la fem Sir Morris Dennys.

---

[5] Statute of Gloucester 1278, c. 3, the limb concerning writs of aiel, besaiel and cosinage.
[6] YB Mich. 40 Edw. III, fo. 42, pl. 26, at fo. 43. The reference to the view is unclear.
[7] *Lady Denys's Case* (1566) Dyer 248. In *AB*, fo. 249v, Coke cited the case 'come le segnior Dier report in le argument del case del Vernon'. The question arose from a settlement on the marriage between Sir Maurice Denys and Elizabeth Statham in 1544.

for her life, this would not be a jointure within the said statute, because it may be that the stranger will survive the husband and then the wife will not take it immediately after the husband's death. Likewise, and for the same reason, if an estate had been made for the husband's life, remainder to a stranger for life, remainder to the wife for life. Likewise if a rent had been granted to the wife to commence after the husband's death, that would have been good, whereas a rent to commence after the death of a stranger would have been void. MANWOOD agreed; and he said that before the statute of 27 Hen. VIII, when the greater part of the lands were in use, it was a common practice to make jointures, and when the statute transferred the uses into possession the makers of the statute provided that wives should not have their dowers and jointures as well. Although this estate in remainder is outside the statute in express terms (*ex vi termini*), nevertheless it is within the meaning of the statute, for the meaning was to give the wife a competent jointure after her husband's death. And he said that if a jointure is made during the coverture, the wife may afterwards waive her jointure and take her dower; but it is otherwise if it was made before the coverture, for then she may not waive it. And he said that if an estate tail is made to a husband and wife and their heirs male or female, this is outside the words, and yet it is within the meaning of the statute. And he agreed MOUNSON's cases, where the wife was not to take the estate immediately after the husband's death – as where an estate is made to John Style for life, remainder to the wife – for it may be that John Style will survive her husband. And MOUNSON and MANWOOD agreed that a fee simple cannot be averred to be a jointure, because there is no reversion in the donor [and his heirs]. The lord DYER agreed with them also, for he said that a jointure (*junctura*) is a competent living for the wife during her natural life, to begin immediately after the husband's death. And the lord DYER said that an estate was made to the duke of Somerset and the duchess, and to the heirs male of the duke's body, and the duchess sued by petition to have her dower from the queen, and it was adjudged that this estate made to her, though outside the wording of the statute, was nevertheless within the meaning of the statute, and so she was barred from her dower.[1] And the lord DYER said that this statute should be understood in the like manner as the Statute of Westminster II, *De Donis Conditionalibus*,[2] for there only three examples (*plattes*) of entails were expressed, but Littleton says that many other estates are understood to be within the equity.[3] {See 11 Edw. II, tit. *Garrantie*,[4] upon the Statute of Gloucester.[5]} So the estates which are there expressed are but patterns and examples. Likewise, and in the same manner, are the five forms of estates limited and expressed in this statute. He said that a jointure comes in place of dower, and dower does not commence until after the husband's death; therefore he thought that a remainder after the husband's death was a good jointure, even though she did not take it jointly with her husband. 40 Edw. III:[6] a man assigned dower to his wife *ad hostium ecclesiae* within sight [of the land], and yet nothing passed at once. And the lord DYER thought that a jointure of a fee simple was within the compass of the statute, and he said it was so adjudged in the Lady Denys's case, who was the wife of Sir Maurice Denys.[7]

---

[1] *R.* v. *Duchess of Somerset* (1554) Dyer 96, 97.
[2] Westminster II, c. 1.
[3] Litt. s. 21.
[4] Mich. 11 Edw. II, Fitz. Abr., *Garrantie*, pl. 83. Cf. 4 Co. Rep., where it is cited from Statham.

Quant al 2 point les 3 <joint>^d justices auxi agre que coment que lestate fuit conditinel, uncore il fuit deins lestatut. Et le Segnior Dier cite un livre in 3 E. 2, tit. Dower, [*blank*], que dower fuit assigne ex assensu patris ita quod si le pier devie in le vie le fitz que lendowement serra voide, et tenus per le livre que cest estate in dower poet estre conditionell. <Et nota que estate pur vie conditionel est estate pur vie deins les parolx.>^i Et Manwood agre a ceo.

Et quant al 3 point ilz auxi agreont que nient obstant cest condition le partie serra bien resceive a cest averment <Dier 169>^i car il estoit [b]ien ove le condition. Mes ilz agreont que home ne unques ferra averment enconter consideration expresse sinon que il fuit fait in defrauding dun estatute, especialment ou [*fo. 85*] lestatute done laverment, car autrement toutz estatutez que sont faitz pro bono publico serra defraudes, come lestatute de usurie, lestatut que prohibite feffmentes sur collusion a defrauder les segniors de lour gardes. <[…]¹ rent graunt pur egalitie de partition ne poet estre averre al contrarie.>^a ² <3 H. 6, 49, per Martin, lestatut de additions covient estre observe in veritie. Vide Dier 169.>^a ³

[119]

AB, fo. 355 (magenta ink).

<Presencia majoris cessat potestas minoris.>^s

Nota in 19 Eliz. fuit agre in le common banke in le deane de Worcestres case que si le roy graunt a un religious home a tener un eglise in proprios usus ne besoigne ascun confirmation del immediat ordinarie, car le roy esteant le supreme teste de tout le spiritualtie et ordinarus ordinariorum, quant il graunt et impreigne sur luy son supreme jurisdiction le authoritie del immediate ordinarie est ob[…]ate.

[120]

AB, fo. 371v (magenta ink) (Litt., fo. 36v).

Nota cest case fuit adjudge in temps mesme cesti roigne, que terres fueront devise a un pur vie, le remainder a les imbroderers del Londres, lou ne fuit ascun tiel corporation al temps, et puis ilz obteine un corporation per mesme le nosme in le devise, et uncore adjudge voide.

---

¹ *Word or two lost in corner of page.*
² *Added at the foot of fo. 84v.*
³ *Added in the upper margin of fo. 85.*

⁹ 'In the presence of the greater, the power of the lesser ceases.' Cf. above, p. 66, and Plowd. 498, *per* Manwood J.

¹⁰ The Company of Broderers received a charter of incorporation in 1561, but, like several other companies, they had been in existence since at least the fourteenth century, before the requirements for valid incorporation were established.

As to the second point, the justices also agreed that although the estate was conditional, it was nevertheless within the statute. And the lord DYER cited a book in 3 Edw. II, tit. *Dower*,[1] where dower was assigned *ex assensu patris*, so that if the father died in the son's lifetime the endowment would be void, and it was held by the book that this estate in dower may be conditional. And note that a conditional estate for life is an estate for life within the words. MANWOOD agreed with this.

As to the third point, they also agreed that, notwithstanding this condition, the party may properly be received to this averment; for it is perfectly consistent with the condition. {Dyer 169.[2]} But they agreed that a man shall never make averment against an express consideration, unless it was done in order to defraud a statute, especially where the statute gives the averment, for otherwise all statutes which are made for the public good (*pro bono publico*) would be defrauded, such as the Statute of Usury,[3] or the statute which prohibits feoffments upon collusion to defraud lords of their wardships.[4] {If a rent is granted to achieve equality in a partition, it cannot be averred to the contrary. 3 Hen. VI, fo. 49,[5] by Martin: the Statute of Additions[6] must be observed in truth. See Dyer 169.[7]}

119. GRENDON v. DEAN OF WORCESTER[8]

Common Pleas, 1576 or 1577

In presencia majoris cessat potentia minoris.[9]

Nota that in 19 Eliz. it was agreed in the Common Bench in the dean of Worcester's case that if the king grants to a religious man to hold a church to his own uses, no confirmation is needed from the immediate ordinary; for the king being the supreme head of all the spiritualty, and the ordinary of ordinaries (*ordinarius ordinariorum*), when he grants and assumes upon himself his supreme jurisdiction the authority of the immediate ordinary is unnecessary.

120. CASE OF THE BRODERERS' COMPANY

Temp. Eliz.

Note that this case was adjudged in the time of this same queen: lands were devised to someone for life, remainder to the Embroiderers of London, where there was no such corporation at the time, and afterwards they obtained a corporation by the same name as in the devise,[10] and yet it was adjudged void.

---

[1] Pas. 3 Edw. II, Fitz. Abr., *Dower*, pl. 126.
[2] *Wilkes* v. *Leuson* (1559) Dyer 169; cit. below, p. 130, no. 233, *per* Harper J.
[3] 13 Eliz., c. 8.
[4] Statute of Marlborough, c. 6.
[5] YB Trin. 3 Hen. VI, fo. 48, pl. 9, at fo. 49, *per* Martin J.
[6] 1 Hen. V, c. 5.
[7] *Wilkes* v. *Leuson* (1559) Dyer 169; above, n. 7.
[8] See above, p. 64, no. 114, and the note there.

[121]

AB, fo. 371v (magenta ink) (Litt., fo. 36v).

<Devises enconter ley.>ˢ

T. 18 Eliz. in banke le roy, Wray, chief justice, dit si home devise terres a un in taile, scilicet a luy [et] a les heires de son corps ingendres durant <son>ᵈ <le>ⁱ vie solement de luy et de chescun de ses heires apres sa mort de corps, intendant daver abbridge de eux de aliener, car il dit si home devise terre a son fitz pur vie, le remainder a son heire de son corps (in le singuler nomber) pur son vie, le remainder a son heire de son corps durant son vie, ceo sont bon estates pur vie pur ceo que ilz sont limitte in singularitie, mes quant terres sont devise a un et a ses heires (in le generaltie) de son corps, donques le limitation apres est voide.

Et nota in temps cesti roigne case case fuit ajudge, come Southcote la dit, que terres fueront devises a 3 homes sur condition que si ascun de eux mor[eront] que son part discendera, et fuit adjudge que ilz fueront tenantes in common. Issint si jeo devise terres a 2 equally devided enter eux, ilz sont tenantes in common. 30 H. 8, tit. Devise, B. 29: home devise terres a 2 et heredibus suorum, cest [tenance]¹ in common, per Audely.

[122]

AB, fo. 372v (magenta ink) (Litt., fo. 37v).

Inter Sheldon et Guilbert, [Pas.] 16 Eliz. rott. 1559 […]² un in ventre sa mere. […]³ 13 Eliz. 304, semble […]⁴ case fuit voide.

[123]

AB, fo. 374v (magenta ink).

<Devises.>ˢ

Nota que Lovelace dit in largument in Cranmers case que il fuit adjudge ore tarde in banke le roy que si home devise terres a un home pur terme de vie, le remainder a ses droit heires, que in cest case le fe est execute.

---

¹ *Conjectural; word lost.*
² *Word or two lost at edge.*
³ *Word or two lost at edge.*
⁴ *Word lost at edge.*

121. HADDON'S CASE[1]

King's Bench, Trin. 1576.

Devises contrary to law.

In Trinity term 18 Eliz., in the King's Bench, WRAY C.J. said that if a man devised lands to someone in tail, namely to him and to the heirs of his body begotten, but only during the life of himself and the life of each of his heirs of his body after his death, intending to prevent them from alienating, [this is void]; for he said that if a man devises land to his son for life, remainder to his heir of his body (in the singular number) for his life, remainder to his heir of the body during his life, these are good estates for life because they are limited in singularity, but when lands are devised to someone and his heirs of his body (in the generality) the limitation afterwards is void.

Note that in the time of this queen this case was adjudged (as SOUTHCOTE there said): lands were devised to three men upon condition that if any of them died, his part should descend, and it was adjudged that they were tenants in common.[2] Likewise if I devise lands to two, to be equally divided between them, they are tenants in common. 30 Hen. VIII, Brooke, tit. *Devise*, 29:[3] a man devised lands to two and their heirs, this is tenancy in common, according to Audley [C.]

122. SHELDON v. GILBERT[4]

Common Pleas, Pas. 1574.

Between Sheldon and Gilbert, [Pas.] 16 Eliz. roll 1559: [a devise to a child] *en ventre sa mère*. [See Dyer], 13 Eliz. 304,[5] [where the devise was held] void.

123. CRANMER'S CASE[6]

Common Pleas, 1572.

Note that *Lovelace* said in argument in Cranmer's case that it was adjudged recently in the King's Bench that if someone devises lands to a man for term of life, remainder to his right heirs, in this case the fee is executed.

---

[1] Conjectural identification: see below, p. 118, no. 212, and the note there.
[2] Probably *Chapman's Case* (1574) Dyer 29 (held to be an entail). Cf. *Webster's Case* (1572) Dal. 77, identified there with *Anon.* (1571) Dyer 303, pl. 49; but neither report mentions a perpetuity clause.
[3] 30 Hen. VIII, Bro. Abr., *Devise*, pl. 29, *per* Audley C.
[4] Probably CP 40/1322, m. 1559 (Pas. 1574, unfit for production; printed in Benl. 235): Robert Sheldon v. George Gilbert of Stratford-upon-Avon, Warw., dyer; trespass for taking grain at Snitterfield, Warw.; pleads Not Guilty; special verdict at Warwick assizes, Lent 1575, finding that Thomas Gilbert left the tithes of Snitterfield by will to his sons 'and to the child that my wife goeth with if it fortune to be a man-child', and that the child was a boy; the boy (William Gilbert) then died without issue. Cit. in Coke's Dyer (Holkham 8014), fo. 304 ('Vide Pasch. 16 in communi banco inter Guilbert et Sheldon, rott. 1559, adjudge que le devise est bone ... Vide 15 Eliz. [Dyer] 326, contra').
[5] *Anon.* (1571) Dyer 303 at fo. 304.
[6] See above, p. 58, no. 106, and the note there. Cf. below, p. 85, no. 137, noting the same point as made by Lovelace. Both are derived from the long report of the case: see Appendix I, above, at p. clxxxi.

[124]

AB, fo. 374v (magenta ink).

<Devises.>ˢ

Nota que jeo ay oye que il fuit adjudge in le common banke que home commaund un auter a escrier son volunt, in que il devise terres a un tiel etc., et devant le revener de cesti que escrie ceo le devisor morust, et fuit adjudge que cest volunt fuit <bon>ᵈ voide, car <fuit dit que>ⁱ il doiet estre un assent del testator apres pur le doubt del variauns.

[125]

AB, fo. 379 (magenta ink).

<Office.>ˢ <Nota ou home avera petition, monstrans de droit ou travers, ou il entra sur le roy, et ou sur son patente.>ˢ

... Et nota bene le case de Wiate argue in T. 18 Eliz. ou il fuit attaint per <acte de p>ᵈ attaindre al comon ley, et puis ceo fuit confirme per parliament et toutz ses terres, tenementes, droitz etc. done al roy destre in son actuel possession, savant a toutz estrangers lour droitz, rentres etc., et puis le roygne grant certaine terres que fueront parcell de possession Sir Thomas Wiate a un Sir R. Baker in fe, et tenus que cesti que droit ad poet enter sur le patente pur ceo que ambideux les matters del recorde ne serveront solement et absolutement pur le roy, car per le savaunt toutz estrangers droitz etc. fueront saves. Et Manwood la dit que le reason pur quoy le roygne esteant[1] entitle per double matter de recorde, et le title le partie nient mention ou declare in ascun de eux, que le partie serra mys a son petition, fuit pur ceo que come le roygne fuit intitle per double matter de record issint le partie covient a defeater ceo per double matter de recorde <come>ᵈ car quant home sua per petition primerment sur son petition il avera commission a trover son title et droit, quel est un matter de record, et donques il avera son monstrans de droit, quel est lauter matter de recorde etc. <11 H. 4, 52, accordant a ceo. Stanf. Prerogative, 72, 73.>ⁱ <3 Mar. 139.>ⁱ Et nota il dit que in toutz cases <le p>ᵈ ou le roy est in possession et le partie poet aver son travers ou monstrans de droit vers le roy, la si le roy grant ouster tout son estate <le>ᵈ cesti que droit ad poet enter sur son patente sauns question. Mes auterment est quant le roy grant ouster forsque estate pur ans, pur vie, ou in taile, pur le revercion que remaine in luy. <25 E. 3, 48.>ⁱ <Pl. Com. 553.>ⁱ <Vide Pasch. 28 Eliz. per report de Justice Wyndam, 28.>ᵃ ² ... [*fo. 379v*]

---

[1] *Appears to read* seant.   [2] *Sideways in outer margin.*

[4] See below, p. 89, no. 147, and the note there.
[5] 1 & 2 Phil. & Mar., c. iii (private), summarised in Plowd. 552v–553. See also *Austin* v. *Baker* (1561) vol. iv, p. 719.
[6] *Lord Camoys* v. *Regem* (1410) YB Hil. 11 Hen. IV, fo. 52, pl. 30.
[7] W. Stanford, *An Exposition of the Kings Prerogative* (1567), fos. 72–73, s.v. Monstraunce de droyt.
[8] *Duke of Norfolk's Case* (1557) Dyer 139.
[9] *Vele* v. *Darcy* (1351) YB Mich. 25 Edw. III (1567 ed.), fo. 48, pl. 1 (fo. 91 of the vulgate edition).
[10] *Walsingham's Case* (1573) Plowd. 552, at fo. 553. This was an information in the Exch. for intrusion, in which the principal point concerned the same act of Parliament following the attainder of Sir Thomas Wyatt.

124. BROWNE v. SAKEVYLE (c. 1560)[1]

Devises.

Note: I have heard that it was adjudged in the Common Bench that a man[2] commanded another to write out his will, in which he devised lands to such and such etc.., and before the person[3] who wrote it out came back the devisor died; and it was adjudged that this will was void, for it was said that there must be an assent by the testator afterwards, because of the risk of variance.

125. MULTON v. COVENEY[4]

Common Pleas, Trin. 1576, Mich. 1577.

> Office. Note where one shall have a petition, *monstrans de droit*, or traverse, where he shall enter upon the king, and where he shall enter upon his patentee.

... And note well the case of Wyatt, argued in Trinity term 18 Eliz., where he was attainted by an attainder at common law, and then it was confirmed by Parliament,[5] and all his lands, tenements, rights, etc., were given to the king so as to be [deemed] in the king's actual possession, saving to all strangers their rights, re-entries, etc.; and then the queen granted certain lands which were part of the possessions of Sir Thomas Wyatt to one Sir Richard Baker in fee: and it was held that the person with right could enter upon the patentee because both the matters of record would not serve solely and absolutely for the king, for by the saving all strangers' rights etc. were saved. And MANWOOD said on this occasion that the reason why a party should be driven to his petition when the queen was entitled by double matter of record, and the party's title was not mentioned or declared in either of them, was because, just as the queen was entitled by double matter of record, so the party must defeat it by double matter of record. For when someone sues by petition, he shall first of all upon his petition have a commission to find his title and right, which is one matter of record, and then he shall have his *monstrans de droit*, which is another matter of record. {11 Hen. IV, fo. 52,[6] is in agreement with this. Stanford, *Prerogative*, fos. 72, 73.[7] 3 Mar. 139.[8]} And note that he said that in all cases where the king is in possession and the party may have his traverse or *monstrans de droit* against the king, if the king grants over all his estate, the party who has right may without question enter upon his patentee. But it is otherwise when the king grants over only an estate for years, for life, or in tail, and that is because of the reversion which remains in him. {25 Edw. III, fo. 48.[9] Pl. Com. 553.[10] See Pas. 28 Eliz., in the report by Justice Wyndham, fo. 28.} ...

---

[1] CP 40/1182, m. 609 (Trin. 1559); CP 40/1190, m. 516 (Hil. 1561; printed in Co. Ent. 224): Thomas Browne esq. v. Eleanor Sakevyle, widow; writ of entry in the *quibus* for tenements in Dorking, Surrey; confessed as to part, and nonsuited at the Guildhall with respect to the remainder. Differently reported in Dyer 72 (who says it was first moved in a different action in 1552); 1 And. 34; Benl. 61. According to these reports the will was upheld.

[2] Henry Browne (d. 1545), the defendant's late husband.

[3] Not a mere amanuensis, but (according to Dyer's report) T. Atkyns, of counsel, who took brief notes of his oral instructions and was asked to put the will into legal form. This was presumably Thomas Atkyns, bencher of Lincoln's Inn, who died in Jan. 1552.

<2 H. 4, 19, semble que recovery vers tenant pur vie devestera le revercion le roy.>[a] [1] Nota bene Wiatz case anno 18 Eliz., car la le Segnior Dier dit si a cest jour home soit seisie des terres in que jeo ay droit dentrie, et puis il est attaint de haut treason, et nota que per lestatut de 33 H. 8 le roy est maintenant in actuell possession, et in mesme lestatut est un savant a toutz estrangers lour entries, le Segnior Dier dit in cest case que jeo ne puis enter sur le roy ne sur le patente pur le double matter de recorde, mes il[2] suera per petition.

Mes Manwood semble que il ne entra sur le roy mes avera son monstrans de droit, pur ceo que son entrie est save, mes clerement que il poet enter sur le patente.

Mes Mounson et Harper semble que jeo puis enter sur le roy mesme. Vies 3 E. 4, 24.

Et nota bene les argumentz in Sir Thomas Wiatz case, et nota cest point fuit argue auxi M. 19 Eliz. in leschequer chamber in le countie de Arundels case. Et ascuns arguont que cesti que droit ad puit enter sur le roy, et[3] ascuns al contrarie. Et ascuns teigne diversite quant le droit est save per mesme lestatut, la cesti que droit ad poet enter, mes quant il est restore per auter acte et le primer acte adnul, la il ne poet enter. Come in le case in 4 H. 7. Et nota bene que in le case in 4 E. 4, 21, la le Segnior de Hungerford fuit attaint de treason anno 1 E. 4 et toutz terres dones al roy savaunt entries etc. Mes nota la fuit office trove puis, quel fuit le cause la que il ne poet enter, <quar loffice fuit trove puis lacte, et pur ceo ceo ne fuit remedy per lacte, et ceo est le reason rendus in le livre>[a].

[126]

AB, fo. 85 (348v).

Nota in temps le roigne que ore est fuit adjudge que lou un jointure fuit fait al fem durant le coverture soulonque lestatute de 27 H. 8 eto puis durant le coverture el et sa baron levie un fine de cest terre issint assure a luy pur sa jointure, que apres le mort le baron le fem ne poet <agree>[d] disagreer a le jointure come el puissoit si el nad levie fine de ceo, mes ore per le fine el ad conclude luy mesme a disagreer a ceo.

---

[1] *Upper margin.*   [2] *Sic.*   [3] *Written twice.*

[8] Written below a report of *Hill* v. *Grange* (1556) Plowd. 168, but followed by a case 'circa annum 10 mesme le roigne', i.e. Eliz. However, it may be that the note dates from before Coke's own time.
[9] Statute of Uses, 27 Hen. VIII, c. 10.

{2 Hen. IV, fo. 19:[1] it seems that a recovery against a tenant for life will divest the king's reversion.} Note well Wyatt's case in the year 18 Eliz., for the lord DYER said there that if at the present day a man is seised of lands in which I have a right of entry, and afterwards he is attainted of high treason – and note that by the statute of 33 Hen. VIII[2] the king is forthwith in actual possession, and in the same statute there is a saving to all strangers of their entries – the lord DYER said in this case that I may not enter upon the king, or upon the patentee, because of the double matter of record, but must sue by petition.

But MANWOOD thought that although he[3] may not enter upon the king, he may have his *monstrans de droit*, because his entry is saved; and clearly he may enter upon the patentee.

MOUNSON and HARPER, however, thought I could enter upon the king himself. See 3 Edw. IV, fo. 24.[4]

Note well the argument in Sir Thomas Wyatt's case, and note that this point was also argued in Michaelmas term 19 Eliz. in the Exchequer Chamber, in the earl of Arundel's case.[5] Some argued that the person who has right may enter upon the king, and some the contrary. And some drew a distinction, that when the right is saved by the same statute, there the person who has right may enter, but when he is restored by another Act, and the first Act is annulled, he may not enter: as in the case in 4 Hen. VII.[6] And note well that in the case in 4 Edw. IV, fo. 21,[7] the Lord Hungerford was attainted of treason in the year 1 Edw. IV, and all his lands given to the king, saving entries; but note that there was an office found afterwards, and that was the cause why he could not enter there, for the office was found after the Act, and therefore it was not remedied by the Act, and that is the reason given in the book.

126. ANON.

Temp. Eliz.

Note that it was adjudged in the time of the present queen,[8] where a jointure was made to a wife during the coverture in accordance with the statute of 27 Hen. VIII,[9] and then during the coverture she and her husband levied a fine of this land which was so assured to her for her jointure, that after the husband's death the wife cannot disagree to the jointure, as she could have done if she had not levied a fine of it; but now by the fine she has estopped (*conclude*) herself from disagreeing to it.

---

[1] YB Pas. 2 Hen. IV, fo. 19, pl. 15.   [2] 33 Hen. VIII, c. 20.
[3] Changing from the first person, to which Mounson and Harper JJ. reverted.
[4] *Earl of Northumberland's Case* (1463) YB Mich. 3 Edw. IV, fo. 24, pl. 19.
[5] *Earl of Arundel* v. *Langar* (1576) above, p. 70, no. 116.
[6] Probably *Lord Ormond's Case* (1489), above, p. 72, n. 4.
[7] *Lady Hungerford's Case* (1464) YB Mich. 4 Edw. IV, fo. 21, pl. 1.

[127]

AB, fo. 397 (magenta ink) (Litt., fo. 38).

<Tenure in burgage.>[s]

Nota que formedon in discender remaine uncore al common ley come jeo <y>[d] ay oye destre adjudge ore tarde in le temps le roigne que ore est sur demurrer.

[128]

AB, fo. 436 (magenta ink).

<Apportionment.>[s]

14 Eliz. Nota il fuit adjudge in Winters case que si home face leas pur ans de 3 severall mannores rendant un rent ove condition de reentrie, si in cest case le lessor grant le revercion de lun mannour ou ascun parcell de ceo a un estraunge, tout le condition est ale. Mes ilz agreont que un condition poet estre devide per 2 voies. 1, per acte in ley, come si home soit seisie des terres <guildable>[d] <in borowghenglishe>[i] et des auters al common ley, et il fait leas pur ans de tout rendant rent et sur condition etc. et il morust, ore cest revercion est devide per acte in ley et issint le condition serra auxi devide. Mesme la ley si leas soit fait des terres in fe et des terres in fee taile a luy et a sa 2 fem etc. 10 H. 6, [*blank*]. Home seisie de terres in fe et des auters terres pur ans fist leas de ambideux sur condition, et morust, et la tenus que pur le condition enfreint les executors entront in le terme et leire in les terres in fe. 8 E. 3, [*blank*]. Home fist feffment in fe reservant rent sur condition et morust, et la fem fuit indowe del 3 parte sauns condition, et le condition remaine pur les auters 2 parties: Perkins, fol. 162. Et le 2 est per lentrie dun estrange que ad eigne title. Come si jeo face leas de 2 acres sur condition, dont jeo ay un per disseisin, et le disseisee enter sur le lesse, in cest case le condition serra devide. Et a cest purpose auxi le case de dower poet estre applye. Mes ilz toutz agreont que per lacte del partie le condition ne poet estre devide. Et pur ceo cest case fuit la cite destre adjudge. Sir Thomas <Throckmortons>[1] case: un seisie des terres lessa pur ans rendant rent sur condition, et puis parcell del revercion ove le rent fuit extend, et tenus que tout le condition est ale etc.

Et le Segnior Dier dit que le reason pur quoy le condition ne poet estre devide est pur ceo que le tenant donques serra subjecte a 2 conditions, et auxi quant home entra pur condition enfreint il covient daver mesme lestate come il avoit al temps del condition fait, et ceo ne poet il quant il ad departe ove parte etc.

Mes Manwood la tient que in ascun case un condition poet estre devide, et ceo est

---

[1] *Unclear interlineation.*

[2] YB Mich. 10 Hen. VI, fo. 24, pl. 83.
[3] Perk. s. 822.
[4] Probably Thomas Throckmorton (d. 1568) of Tortworth, Glos., knighted in 1553.

127. ANON.

Common Pleas, c. 1572.

Tenure in burgage.

Note that formedon in the descender remains still at common law: as I have heard it was adjudged recently in the time of the present queen, upon demurrer.

128. WINTER'S CASE[1]

Common Pleas, 1572.

Apportionment.

14 Eliz. Note that it was adjudged in Winter's case that if a man makes a lease for years of three several manors, rendering one rent, with a condition of re-entry, and in this case the lessor grants a stranger the reversion of one of the manors, or of some parcel thereof, the whole condition is gone. But they agreed that a condition may be divided, in two ways. One is by act in law, as where someone is seised of lands in borough English and of others at common law, and he makes a lease for years of all of them, rendering rent upon condition of re-entry, and dies, this reversion is divided by act in law and therefore the condition shall also be divided. The law is the same if a lease is made of lands in fee and of lands in fee tail, to him and to his second wife: 10 Hen. VI.[2] A man seised of lands in fee, and of other lands for years, made a lease of both upon condition, and died, and it was there held that for a breach of the condition the executors could enter in the term, and the heir [could enter] in the lands in fee. 8 Edw. III. A man made a feoffment in fee reserving rent upon condition, and died, and the wife was endowed of a third part without condition, and the condition remained for the other two thirds: Perkins, fo. 162.[3] The second way [of dividing a condition] is by the entry of a stranger who has an older title. For instance, if I make a lease of two acres upon condition, one of which I have through disseisin, and the disseisee enters upon the lessee, in this case the condition shall be divided. And to this purpose also the case of dower may be applied. But they all agreed that the condition cannot be divided by the act of the party. As to that, this case was cited to be adjudged: Sir Thomas Throckmorton's case[4] was that someone who was seised of lands leased them for years, rendering rent upon condition, and then parcel of the reversion with the rent was extended, and it was held that the whole condition was gone.

And the lord DYER said that the reason why the condition cannot be divided is because the tenant would then be subjected to two conditions; moreover, when someone enters for breach of condition, he must have the same estate as he had at the time when the condition was made, and that he cannot have when he has parted with part of it.

But MANWOOD held that in some cases a condition may be divided, and that is

---

[1] There is also a brief mention of the case on fo. 436v ('Et nota bene que in Winters case le rent fuit reserve destre paye hors del terre a un auter lieu'), and another reference, largely worn away, in the lower corner of Litt., fo. 49 (fo. 195 in pencil). See further above, p. 43, no. 88, and the note there. This may be the discussion of apportionment of rent referred to in Co. Litt. 148 ('Hill. 14 Eliz. which I myselfe heard and observed'), though it is not the same point.

quant parcell del estate in leas est defeate per lacte et tort del lessee, come si lessee fait wast in parcell et le lessor recover in wast, ou sil fait feffment de parcel et il entra pur le <condition enfreint>ᵈ forfeiture, in ceux cases il dit que le condition serra apportion etc. Issint il dit que si le feffor confirme lestate del feffe a tener parcell sauns condition, et cite pur ceo 7 H. 6, in trespas, pur ceo que vaera al advantage del feffee. Et ceux cases estoient bien ove le reasons del Segnior Dier.

[129]

AB, fo. 143 (439).

<Ou un chose esteant joine ove auter chose passera.>ˢ

Nota que il fuit adjudge ore tarde in le common banke in temps le roigne Eliz. que si lesse pur vie, le remainder pur vie, soit, in cest case si lesse pur vie fait feffment in fe ore cesti in le remainder pur vie ne poet enter, et pur ceo sil confirme lestate le feffee cesti in le revercion in fe ne poet enter durant le vie cesti in le remainder. Mes il fuit adjuge que si tenant pur vie et cesti in le remainder pur vie joine in un feffment in fe, cesti in le [revercion]¹ in fe poet enter presentment, uncore ceo est le feffment le lesse pur vie et le confirmation cesti in le remainder pur vie, mes pur ceo que il fuit partie al forfeiture et joine in ceo ideo ambideux ont forfeit lour estates. <Vide pur [ceo] Saveryes case, Dier, 17 Eliz. 339, inter Blackaller et Martyn.>ᵃ ²

[130]

AB, fo. 148 (448).

<Ou recoverie in un action serra barre in auter action.>ˢ

Nota il fuit agree anno 18 Eliz. regine in le common banke in ejectione firme <inter>ᵈ parenter le Segnior Cromwell et Andrewes de Greys Inn que lou le <lesse de>ⁱ Segnior Cromwell port auterfoitz un ejectione firme envers Andrewes et trove fuit ove Andrewes, et puis le Segnior Cromwell fesoit auter leas al auter partie et il port un auter ejectione firme et admittebatur clare que gist bene.

[131]

AB, fo. 148v (448v).

<Barres in trespas.>ˢ

In trespas et brefe dentre sur lestatut il est bone plea adire que le defendant fuit seisie

---

¹ rem.   ² *Written above the report.*

point was confirmed in the Common Pleas in *Lennard's Case* (Trin. 1586) CUL MS. Hh.2.9, fo. 331 ('Leonard' of Lincoln's Inn), which says that on giving judgment the court smiled at Lennard as if to say that he had profited well by his action.   ³ See above, p. 4, no. 2; p. 6, no. 7; and the notes there.

when part of the estate in lease is defeated by the act and wrong of the lessee; for instance if the lessee commits waste in part, and the lessor recovers in waste, or if the lessee makes a feoffment of part and the lessor enters for the forfeiture, in these cases (he said) the condition shall be apportioned. Likwise, as he said, if the feoffor confirms the estate of the feoffee so as to hold part of it without condition – and for that he cited 7 Hen. VI,[1] in trespass – because it goes to the advantage of the feoffee. These cases are consistent with the reasoning of the lord DYER.

129. BLACKALLER v. MARTIN: SAVERY'S CASE[2]

Common Pleas, Mich. 1574.

Where one thing, being joined with another thing, shall pass.

Note that it was recently adjudged in the Common Bench (in the time of Queen Elizabeth) that if there is a lease for life, remainder for life, in this case if the lessee for life makes a feoffment in fee, the remainderman for life may not enter, and therefore if he confirms the feoffee's estate the reversioner in fee may not enter during the life of the remainderman. But it was adjudged that if the tenant for life and the remainderman for life join in a feoffment in fee, the reversioner in fee may enter presently, although it is the feoffment of the lessee for life and only a confirmation by the remainderman for life; for since he was party to the forfeiture and joined in it, both of them have forfeited their estates. {See for this Savery's case, Dyer, 17 Eliz. 339, between Blackaller and Martin.}

130. LORD CROMWELL v. ANDROWES[3]

Common Pleas, 1576.

Where recovery in one action shall be a bar in another action.

Note, it was agreed in the year 18 Eliz. in the Common Bench in *ejectione firmae* between the Lord Cromwell and Androwes of Gray's Inn that where Lord Cromwell's lessee previously brought an *ejectione firmae* against Androwes, and it was found for Andrewes, and then the Lord Cromwell made another lease to the other party and he brought another *ejectione firmae*, it was accepted clearly that it well lay.

131. ANON.

Common Pleas, Hil. 1577.

Bars in trespass.

In trespass and a writ of entry upon the statute it is a good plea to say that the

---

[1] YB Mich. 7 Hen. VI, fo. 7, pl. 10.
[2] Although Coke's addendum implies it is a different case, it would seem to be the same. Dyer cites the record from a MS. of Bendlowes as Pas. 15 Eliz., roll 214 (incorrect). Differently reported in Dyer 339; 1 And. 45 ('enter Martin, Martin et Savery'); 1 Leon. 262 (anon., dated 20 Eliz.); Benl. 222, pl. 253, cit. Pas. 15 Eliz., Whetley; New Benl. 32; cit. from Dyer in 1 Co. Rep. 76v; Co. Litt. 251b, 302b. The same

tanque le pleintife luy disseise sur que il enter et [fuit] possesse tanque le pleintife prist ceo etc, H. 19 Eliz. fuit touche in le common banke que autiel plea nest bone plea in ejectione firme.

[132]

AB, fo. 152 (452).

\<Chattelx.\>ˢ

T. 18 Eliz. fuit tenus in le common banke que si lesse pur ans fixe ascun chose come wainscotte ou furneis ou similia al wall ou timber del meason ou al floure del meason issint que si mesme le chose soit tolle le inheritauns soit impare, come si wainscott soit fixed ove graunde nailes issint que le timber in le mure serra per ceo impaire ou enfeble, ou si furneis soit fixe al terre issint que le terre covient estre digge etc., que in ceux cases le termour ne poet remove eux. Autrement est si eux sont fixe forsque ove petit nailes etc. le remover de quel ne serra ascun impairement al inheritauns.

[133]

AB, fo. 155v (455v).

\<Infantz.\>ˢ

… Et nota que in P. 18 Eliz. regina cest cas fuit agre que un formedon fuit port vers un infaunt que appiert et confesse laction sur que judgment fuit done, et puis lenfaunt vient a pleine age et voille aver sue un brefe de error, et non potuit, et le reason fuit pur ceo que il covient estre trie per inspection, quel ne poet estre quant le infant est de pleine age, car ceo ne serra trie per proves ne per paijs \<enta\>ᵈ encounter le recorde.

[134]

AB, fo. 461 (magenta ink).[1]

\<Feffmentz.\>ˢ

14 Elyz. Home fist feffment a J. S. apres le mort dun tiel que fuit son copiholder, habendum a luy pur terme de son vie apres le mort le dit copiholder etc. Et la fuit agre que si le habendum soit contrary al premisses le habendum serra bone et le premisses voide, mes lou le parolx repugnantes sont in le done devant le habendum la tout est void, car riens operatur per le livery car ceo fuit fait secundum formam carte.

---

[1] *There seems to be a chasm of one folio in Coke's original numbering, which is no longer legible on fos. 461–463. Fo. 458 (magenta) was his fo. 158, then fos. 459–460 are from Littleton, but fo. 464 (magenta) was his fo. 160.*

defendant was seised until the plaintiff disseised him, upon whom he entered and was possessed until the plaintiff took it. But in Hil. 19 Eliz. it was said by the way in the Common Bench that such a plea is not a good plea in *ejectione firmae*.

132. ANON.

Common Pleas, Trin. 1576.

Chattels.

In Trinity term 18 Eliz. it was held in the Common Bench that if a lessee for years fixes something, such as wainscot, or an oven, or such like, to the wall or timber of the house, or to the floor of the house, in such a way that if the same thing is taken away the inheritance would be impaired – as where wainscot is fixed with large nails, so that the timber in the wall would be thereby impaired or weakened, or if an oven is fixed into the land so that the land would have to be dug up – in these cases the termor may not remove them.[1] It is otherwise if they are only fixed with little nails or the like, the removal of which would not be any impairment to the inheritance.

133. ANON.

Common Pleas, Pas. 1576.

Infants.

And note that in Easter term 18 Eliz. this case was agreed. A formedon was brought against an infant, who appeared and confessed the action, whereupon judgment was given. Then the infant came of age and wanted to sue a writ of error, and he could not. The reason was that the infancy must be tried by inspection, which cannot be once the infant is of full age; for it cannot be tried by proofs, or by the country, contrary to the record.

134. ANON.[2]

Common Pleas, 1572.

Feoffments.

14 Eliz. A man made a feoffment to John Style after the death of someone who was his copyholder, *habendum* unto him for term of his life after the death of the said copyholder. And it was there agreed that if the *habendum* is contrary to the premises, the *habendum* shall be good and the premises void; but where the repugnant words are in the gift before the *habendum*, everything is void, for nothing enures by the livery inasmuch as it was made according to the form of the charter (*secundum formam cartae*).

[1] Cf. Co. Litt. 53.
[2] The same case seems to be cited below, p. 102, no. 174 (in 1576). Cf. JRL MS. Fr. 118, fo. 15v.

Et la le Segnior Dier cite le case in 8 E. 3 que si terres soient dones a 2, habendum a lun pur vie et le remainder a lauter, que ceo est bone, et uncore semble destre repugnant. Et la Harper cite le case in 8 H. 7, 1, et 38 H. 6, 34. Et le diversite perenter rent in esse et rent que est novelment create.

Et la le Segnior Dier dit que il fuit adjudge in le common banke ore tard que un fuit possesse dun terme pur 3 cent ans et grant ceo le dit terre a J. S. <habendum>[i] apres son mort, ceo fuit void habendum et le premisses estoieront.

Report from the Rylands Manuscript

JRL MS. Fr. 118, fo. 15*bis*, pl. 9. Also *Ff*, fo. 186.

Home fist feffment a J. S. apres le mort dun tiel que fuit son copyholder habendum a luy pur terme de son vie, et fist letter datturney a faire livery accordant al fait, et il fist ceo accordant. Le quel ceo fuit bon feffment ou nemy, ceo fuit le question. Harper, si je enfeffe un, habendum a luy et a ces heires apres le feast de Saint Michaell et face livery accordant, pur ceo que le livery covient execute <lestat>[i] les parols apres le feast de Saint Michaell [sont][i] void. Manwood, si un habendum soit repugnant as premises le habendum serra voide et les premises estoieront. Et pur ceo si jeo enfeffe un, habendum a deux, il est <voide>[i] al auter pur ceo que est repugnant. Issint si jeo enfeffe 2, habendum a luy et a ses heirs, uncore ilz serroient jointenantes, lun pur vie lauter in fe. Et pur ceo que le grant de chescun serra prise pluis fort encounter le grauntor, pur ceo ceux repugnant parols serra[2] voide et le feffment bon. Lovelace, les parols repugnaunt sont en le done, devant le habendum. Dier, jeo bien agre al opinion de Manwood car ceo semble reasonable, mes icy le case est auterment, car les parols repugnantes sont en le done devaunt le habendum, car il done les terres apres le mort etc. habendum a luy pur terme de son vie. Harper cite le case de 8 H. 7 que si jeo ay rent in esse et graunt ceo a un auter apres mon mort en fe, ceo est voide. Auterment est lou le rent ne fuit in esse al temps. Dier, cest case fuit ore tarde adjudge devant nous: si jeo soy possesse dun terme pur trois cent annes et jeo voill graunt cest terme habendum apres mon decesse, ceo est voide habendum et le grauntee avera lentier terme maintenant, uncore le habendum est apres le mort. 8 E. 3. La terres fueront dones a 2 per le premises, habendum lintier a lun deux, le remainder al auter, et cest habendum fuit tenus bon, et uncore semble repugnant et contrarie al premises. Lovelace, sir, nostre case est per liverie. Dier, le liverie est secundum formam cartam et le done in luy mesme voide ab initio, et nemy le habendum solement.

[135]

AB, fo. 462 (magenta ink).

<Feffements.>[s]

P. 19 Eliz. Fuit agre in le common banke in un Devonshire case inter Lancastel, pleintife, et Aller, defendant, in ejectione firme que lou pier et fitz fueront et le pier enfeffe le fitz al use de luy mesme pur terme de sa vie et puis al use de son fitz et ses

---

[1] soit.   [2] *Sic.*

[5] Probably CP 40/1329, m. 304 (unfit for production; the *postea* printed in Benl.): Thomas Lancastell v. John Aller; ejectment for land in Devon; special verdict. Noted below, p. 109, no. 194 (where there is an incorrect roll reference). Differently reported in Dyer 358, cit. record (roll '30'); 1 And. 51, cit. record; Benl. 288 (Langastell), cit. record. Bendlowes says the judges gave their opinion against the defendant, whereupon the parties settled.

And the lord DYER there cited the case in 8 Edw. III,[1] that if lands are given to two, *habendum* to one of them for life and remainder to the other, this is good: and yet it seems to be repugnant. And HARPER there cited the case in 8 Hen. VII, fo. 1,[2] and 38 Hen. VI, fo. 34;[3] and drew a distinction between a rent *in esse* and a rent which is newly created.

And the lord DYER there said that it was adjudged in the Common Bench recently,[4] where someone was possessed of a term for 300 years and granted the said land to John Style, *habendum* after his death, that this was a void *habendum* and the premises should prevail.

Report from the Rylands Manuscript

See opposite.

A man made a feoffment to John Style after the death of one who was his copyholder, *habendum* unto him for term of his life, and made a letter of attorney to make livery in accordance with the deed, and he did this accordingly. The question was, whether this was a good feoffment or not. HARPER. If I enfeoff someone, *habendum* unto him and his heirs after the feast of St Michael, and make livery accordingly, the words 'after the feast of St Michael' are void because the livery must execute the estate. MANWOOD. If a *habendum* is repugnant to the premises, the *habendum* shall be void and the premises shall stand. Therefore, if I enfeoff one, *habendum* to two, it is void as to the other, because it is repugnant. Likewise, if I enfeoff two, *habendum* to him and his heirs, they shall nevertheless be joint tenants, one for life and the other in fee. Thus everyone's grant shall be understood more strongly against the grantor, so that these repugnant words shall be void and the feoffment good. *Lovelace*. The repugnant words are in the gift, before the *habendum*. DYER. I entirely agree with Manwood's opinion, for that seems reasonable. But here the case is different: the repugnant words are in the gift before the *habendum*, for he gave the land after the death etc. *habendum* to him for term of his life. HARPER cited the case of 8 Hen. VII, that if I have a rent *in esse* and grant it to another after my death in fee, this is void; it is otherwise where the rent was not *in esse* at the time. DYER. This case was recently adjudged before us: if I am possessed of a term for 300 years and I grant this term, *habendum* after my decease, this is a void *habendum* and the grantee shall have the whole term forthwith, although the *habendum* is after the death. In 8 Edw. III lands were given to two by the premises, *habendum* the whole to one of them, the remainder to the other, and this *habendum* was held good even though it seems repugnant and contrary to the premises. *Lovelace*. Sir, our case is by livery. DYER. The livery is 'according to the form of the charter' and the gift in itself is void *ab initio*, and not merely the *habendum*.

135. LANCASTELL v. ALLER[5]

Common Pleas, Pas. 1577.

Feoffments.

In Easter term 19 Eliz. it was agreed in the Common Bench, in a Devonshire case between Lancastell, plaintiff, and Aller, defendant, in ejectment, that where there were a father and son, and the father enfeoffed the son to the use of himself for term

---

[1] YB Mich. 8 Edw. III, fo. 59, pl. 16; Co. Litt. 183b.
[2] *Abbot of Tewkesbury's Case* (1493) YB Trin. 8 Hen. VII, fo. 1, pl. 1.
[3] *R. v. Abbess of Syon* (1460) YB Trin. 38 Hen. VI, fo. 33, pl. 2, at fo. 34.
[4] Probably *Lilley v. Whitney* (1568) Dyer 272, though in the printed report it is said to have been 'in B. R.'

heires <et puis>ᵈ et puis le pier et le fitz vient sur le terre et ea intentione quod pater suus habilis esset facere et facere potuisset quandam dimissionem de tenementis predictis pro termino sexaginta annorum filius predictus sine scripto feoffavit patrem suum. Et tenebatur per le Segnior Dier, Manwood et Mounson que cest bon feffment et que ceo serra surrender del pier.

Mes la fuit tacite agre que si le lesse pur vie agrea, esteant sur le terre, que le lessour ferra livery cest voide si ne soit per fait. Mes auterment est del lesse pur ans.

Et la Manwood dit si 2 jointenantes sont, lun pur vie, lauter in fe, et ilz ambideux joine in feffment per parol que le fe del ambideux acres passera, et uncore chescun done forsque le moitie per son livery, et donques coment passera le revercion que est expectant sur lestate lauter jointenant pur vie?

Et le Segnior Dier semble dagreer que le feffment fuit bon per parol et que lentier fe simple passera. Et la Mounson dit si lessor et lesse pur vie font feffment per parol que ceo serra le feffment le lessor et surrender del lesse pur vie, car issint le interest de chescun de eux passera. Mes le Segnior Dier dit expressement si lesse pur vie, le remainder in taile, fait feffment, ceo nest discontinuans.

[136]

AB, fo. 470*bis* (Litt. fo. 63).

Vies Brentes case anno 17 Eliz.: feffment in fe al use de D. sa fem et puis sa decesse al use de luy et sa fem que serra etc. Quere de auters persons si jeo disseise un al use de 2 et lun agre, et puis lauter agre: ilz sont jointenantes, et uncore ilz veigne a ceo a several temps.

[137]

AB, fo. 164 (471).

<Quant un fe simple veignant al particuler estate serra execute.>ˢ

14 Elyz. Lovelace in le argument del Cranmers case rehers cest case: si home devise terres a un pur vie, le remainder a ces droit heires, que in cest case le fe fuit execute, et cest (il dit) fuit adjudge in banke le roy. Et in mesme le case fuit dit per Harper, que si home fist feffment al use dun pur vie, et apres son decesse a remaine a ces droit heires, in cest case per reason de lestatut le fe nest pas execute: quod non est lex.

of his life, and then to the use of his son and his heirs, and then the father and son came onto the land, 'and with the intention that his father should be enabled and be able to make a certain demise of the aforesaid tenements for the term of sixty years, the aforesaid son without writing enfeoffed his father', it was held by the lord DYER, MANWOOD and MOUNSON that it was a good feoffment and was a surrender from the father.

But it was there tacitly agreed that if a lessee for life agrees, being on the land, that the lessor may make livery, this is void unless it is by deed. It is otherwise, however, of a lessee for years.

MANWOOD there said that if there are two joint tenants, one for life, and the other in fee, and they both join in a feoffment by parol, the fee of both acres will pass. Yet each of them gives only a moiety by his livery, so how can the reversion pass which is expectant on the estate of the other joint tenant for life?

The lord DYER seemed to agree that the feoffment was good by parol, and that the whole fee simple passed. And MOUNSON there said that if a lessor and a lessee for life make a feoffment by parol, this shall be the feoffment of the lessor and a surrender by the lessee for life, for in that way the interest of each of them may pass. But the lord DYER said expressly that if a lessee for life, the remainder in tail, makes a feoffment, that is a discontinuance.

136. BRENT'S CASE[1]

Common Pleas, 1574/75.

See Brent's case, in the year 17 Eliz.: a feoffment in fee to the use of Dorothy, his wife, and after her decease to the use of himself and his future wife. Inquire of others. If I disseise someone to the use of two, and one of them agrees, and afterwards the other agrees, they are joint tenants: and yet they came to it at separate times.

137. CRANMER'S CASE[2]

Common Pleas, 1572.

When a fee simple, coming to the particular estate, shall be executed.

14 Eliz. *Lovelace*, in the argument of Cranmer's case, related this case: if a man devises lands to someone for life, the remainder to his right heirs, in this case the fee is executed; and that (he said) was adjudged in the King's Bench. And in the same case it was said by HARPER that if a man makes a feoffment to the use of someone for life, and after his decease to remain to his right heirs, in this case the fee is not executed by reason of the statute:[3] but that is not law (*quod non est lex*).

---

[1] See below, p. 115, no. 209, and the note there.
[2] For the case see above, p. 58, no. 106, and the note there. The point attributed to Lovelace is also noted above, p. 78, no. 123.
[3] Statute of Uses, 27 Hen. VIII, c. 10.

[138]

AB, fo. 164v (471v).

Nota que fuit tenus et adjudge in temps le roigne Eliz. in le case dun Hawles que le pier come le case la fuit fait leas a son fitz pur terme dans et puis le fitz est ejecte et port ejectione firme, et puis le pier morust, que per cest discent del droit del revercion sur luy le brefe abatera. Et nota auxi in mesme le case si le fitz esteant lesse soit ouste et le pier disseisie, et puis le disseisor morust, ore nest question mes que le fitz poet enter. Mes si le pier morust issint que le droit del fe discende sur cest droit al particuler estate, ore le droit del fe est execute et il ne poet enter.

[139]

AB, fo. 472 (magenta ink) (Litt., fo. 64).

Trin. 20 Eliz. Julio, doctour de phisicke, et sa fem port bref de det in droit le fem come executrix, et coment que le dit Julio fuit un alien nee uncore il ne puit aver triall per medietatem.

[140]

AB, fo. 473 (magenta ink) (Litt., fo. 65).

Mich. 16 & 17 Eliz. inter Harrys et Eden cest case fuit adjudge, come appiert rott. mcccxl. Home aiant issue 2 files devise ses terres a eux et a ses heires de lour 2 corps ingendres, ilz pristeront barons et fesoient partition. Et le partition per paroll adjudge voide … Pas. 18 Eliz. fuit agre per les justices in le common banke que partition enter jointenantes fuit voide sans fait a cest jour. <18 Eliz. Dier 350b.>[a,1]

Nota que jeo oy in le common banke Weston in 13 Eliz. adire que il fuit adjudge que partition est voide inter eux sans fayt.

[141]

AB, fo. 165v (474v).

<Trust et authoritie survive.>[s]

Nota fuit agre per Serjaunt Anderson, Popham et Windham sur secret conference que si jeo covenant ove J. S., J. D. et J. F. sur request destre fait per J. S., J. D. et J. F. que il[1] inffera J. S. et J. D. del mannour de D., si J. F. devie devant request cest request

[1] *Sic.*

---

trespass *quare clausum fregit* at Oby; special verdict at Norwich assizes, setting out the will of Thomas Clipsby esq., whose daughter Cicely married the plaintiff; the defendant claimed through the other daughter, Hester, who married Clement Hill; judgment for the plaintiff. Differently reported in Dyer 350; 1 And. 50; Benl. 258.

138. HAWLES'S CASE

Temp. Eliz.

Note that in the case of one Hawles, where a father (as the case was there) made a lease to his son for term of years, and then the son was ejected and brought ejectment, and then the father died, it was held and adjudged in the time of Queen Elizabeth that by this descent upon him of the right of the reversion the writ should abate. Note also in the same case that if the son, being lessee, is ousted and the father disseised, and afterwards the disseisor dies, there is now no question but that the son may enter. But if the father dies, so that the right of the fee descends upon this right to the particular estate, now the right of the fee is executed and he may not enter.

139. DR JULIO'S CASE[1]

Common Pleas, Trin. 1578.

In Trinity term 20 Eliz. Julio, doctor of physic, and his wife brought a writ of debt in the wife's right as executrix, and although the said Julio was an alien nee he nevertheless could not have a trial *per medietatem linguae*.

140. EDEN v. HARRIS[2]

Common Pleas, Pas. 1576.

In Michaelmas term 16 & 17 Eliz. between Harris and Eden this case was adjudged, as appears in roll 1340. A man having issue two daughters devised his lands to them and their heirs of their two bodies begotten, they married, and made partition. And the partition by parol was adjudged void. ... In Easter term 18 Eliz. it was agreed by the justices in the Common Bench that a partition between joint tenants was void at the present day without a deed. {18 Eliz., Dier 350v.}

Note that I heard Weston say in the Common Bench in 13 Eliz. that it was adjudged that a partition between joint tenants is void without a deed.

141. SURVIVORSHIP

Conference, *c.* 1577/79.

When a trust and authority survive.

Note that it was agreed by *Serjeants Anderson*, *Popham* and *Wyndham*, upon private conference, that if I covenant with J. S., J. D. and J. F. that, upon request to be made by J. S., J. D. and J. F., I will enfeoff J. S. and J. D. of the manor of Dale, and J. F.

---

[1] Cit. in Cro. Eliz. 275 (dated 23 Eliz.). Dr Giulio Borgarucci, the queen's physician, was involved in a notorious divorce case around this time: J. Baker, 'Some Elizabethan Marriage Cases', in *Studies in Canon Law and Common Law in Honor of R. H. Helmholz*, ed. T. L. Harris (2015), at p. 186.

[2] CP 40/1325, m. 1340 (printed in Benl. 257): Leonard Eden v. Robert Harris of Oby, Norf., husbandman;

ne survivera, car J. F. ne fuit daver ascun interest. Mes si feffment serroit a eux 3, la coment que lun devie uncore lauter poet faire request.

[142]

AB, fo. 165v (474v).

<Ou un nude authoritie sauns ascun interest survivera.>^s

19 Eliz. Home fuit tenus a estoier al agard de J. S. destre fait enter luy et J. D., J. S. agard que neque lobligor neque J. D. durant lour naturall vies enclosera del common queux ilz avoient jointment, et puis lun devie: si ore le survivour inclosera? Et fuit tenus per le Segnior Dier et Mounson clerement que le survivour ne inclosera car ceo fuit lentent des parties. Et la Manwood [dit] que si leasse soit fait a J. S. et J. N. durant lour vies, la le survivour tiendra lieu pur ceo que interest passa, mes si leasse soit fait a un durant le vie J. N. et de J. D., la si lun morust le lease est determine. Issint il dit si home fait leas a 2 pur lour vies et ilz covenant que ilz durant lour vies voillont repairer les measons etc., la si lun morust uncore le survivour est ly a performer cest covenant car cest covenant fuit foundue sur un interest. Mes si 2 covenant durant lour vies a faire tiel chose, la si lun morust lauter nest tenus a performer ceo.

[143]

AB, fo. 476v (magenta ink) (Litt., fo. 67v).

18 Eliz. cest cas fuit move a les justices del common banke, scilicet, 2 joint lessees pur terme de 50 ans et lun fist leas de tout pur 40 ans et puis lauter lesse que ne lessa pas morust. Et semble que quant le lun lesse fist leas de tout que ceo fuit un severans del jointure, et que lexecutors lauter recovera arere le terme que affiert a lour testatour. Et la ilz disoient que si 2 joint lessees pur xx ans sont et lun fist leas de son parte pur un an, que ceo est un absolute severans del jointure a toutz jours ambideux devant come apres lans determine, et nient semble al case del baron et fem, car si le baron ad leas in droit sa fem et grant parcell uncore le revercion demurt in droit la fem. 7 H. 6, 2, accord., per Godred et alios. Pasch. 18 Eliz.

dies before request, this request will not survive, for J. F. was not to have any interest. But if there is a feoffment to three, then even if one of them dies the other may still make request.

142. ANON.

Common Pleas, 1577.

Where a bare authority without any interest will survive.

19 Eliz. A man was bound to stand to the award of John Style, to be made between him and John Dale; John Style awarded that neither the obligor nor John Dale during their natural lives should enclose the common which they had jointly; then one of them died: may the survivor now enclose? It was clearly held by the lord DYER and MOUNSON that the survivor may not enclose, for that was the intention of the parties. And MANWOOD there said that if a lease is made to John Style and John Noke during their lives, survivorship will operate because an interest passes; but if a lease is made to someone during the lives of John Noke and John Dale, there if one of them dies the lease is determined. Similarly (he said) if a man makes a lease to two for their lives, and they covenant that during their lives they will repair the houses, and one of them dies, the survivor is still bound to perform this covenant, for the covenant was founded upon an interest. But if two covenant to do something during their lives, and one of them dies, the other is not bound to perform it.

143. EDEN v. HARRIS[1]

Common Pleas, Pas. 1576.

In 18 Eliz. this case was moved to the justices of the Common Bench: there were two joint lessees for a term of fifty years, and one of them made a lease of the whole for forty years, and then the other lessee (who did not lease) died. And it seemed that when the one who leased made a lease of the whole, that was a severance of the jointure, and that the executors of the other may recover back the term which belonged to their testator. And they said there that if there are two joint lessees for twenty years and one of them makes a lease of his part for one year, this is an absolute severance of the jointure for ever, both before and after the years determined. It is not like the case of the husband and wife; for if the husband has a lease in his wife's right and grants part of it, the reversion still remains in the wife's right. 7 Hen. VI, fo. 2,[2] accord., *per* Godred and others. (Easter term, 18 Eliz.)

---

[1] Conjectural: see above, p. 86, no. 140. One of the husbands in that case had made a lease following the void partition.
[2] YB Mich. 7 Hen. VI, fo. 1, pl. 6, at fo. 2.

[144]

AB, fo. 167 (478).

<Action sur lestatut.>

H. 14 Eliz., rott. Dviij. In action sur lestatut de Winchester avandit les inhabitantes plead quod predictus le pleintife immediate post feloniam et spoliationem predictam superius fieri suppositam apud D. predictam non fecit hutesium et clamorem de roberia predicta secundum formam statuti predicti prout ipse superius narravit. Et ceo fuit adjudge bone plea. Vide [H.] 4 H. 8, rott. Dxxv, et Pasche sequenti rott. cccv, M. 6 H. 8, rott. 1, et P. 12 et 13 H. 8, rott. Dviij.

Vide 39 E. 3, 20, in trespas pur distres in haut chemyn contra statutum de Marlebr. cap. 12 et eux detient tanque le pleintife fist fine a xls. Et nota 2 choses joine in un action, dont lun est al common ley et lauter per lestatut, et la severall issues prise.

Action de scandalis magnatum M. 1 Mar., rott. Dccxvij, in communi banco, one Chaffyn said that the Lord Sturton had burnt his barne. T. 2 H. 8, rott. 36, in bank le roy, 'My lord of Winchester toke me and caused me to be imprisoned wrongfully and there kept me untill such tyme that I was fayne to make and s[e]ale an obligation of x li. <with> to thuse of the king without ground or cause. Hillarii 19 Eliz., ccclxxxvij, in banke le roy, Sir Walter Waller said that my Lord of Bargavenie sendeth for men to come before him and when they come he doth so straightlie deale with them that men be afrayd to come before him, for some he putteth into the colehouse and some into the stockes and some into a place of his howse called little ease and put both there legges [in] the stockes.

[145]

AB, fo. 172 (489).

<Joindre in action.>

T. 19 Eliz. fuit demande del court si 3 coparceners font leas pur ans, et puis lun prist baron et ad issue, et le fem morust: et fuit agree que le tenant per le curtesie et son issue et lauters 2 coparceners joindra in wast et countera ad exheredationem del issue et del auters 2. Et uncore la est agre si fem fait leas pur ans et puis prist baron et ad issue, fem morust, lissue navera action de wast. Vies 22 H. 6, 24. Et nota in le primer case toutz recoveront le lieu wast in common et damages solvenda a ceux in revercion del fe etc.

---

[4] *Gaunte qui tam etc.* v. *Hundred of Cheveley* (1513) CP 40/998, m. 525; CP 40/1008, m. 1d (respite of the jury in the same case, Mich. 1514); *Coveney qui tam etc.* v. *Inhabitants of Denton-juxta-Gravesend* (1521) CP 40/1032A, m. 508.
[5] YB Mich. 39 Edw. III, fo. 20, pl. [2].   [6] On the statute 2 Ric. II, stat. 1, c. 5.
[7] *Lord Stourton* v. *Thomas Chaffyn* (1553) CP 40/1156, m. 717; pleads that he only spoke of suspicion of the plaintiff's servants, who had sent him threats; verdict and judgment for the plaintiff, with £100 damages and £5 costs.
[8] *Bishop of Winchester* v. *Thomas Jonys* (1510) KB 27/996, m. 36; verdict and judgment for the plaintiff, with 20s. damages and 26s. 8d. costs.   [9] *Lord Abergavenny* v. *Sir Walter Waller* (1577) KB 27/1260, m. 497; issue on the words; verdict and judgment for the plaintiff, with £40 damages and 40s. costs.
[10] Record.   [11] YB Mich. 22 Hen. VI, fo. 24, pl. 45.

144. ACTIONS ON STATUTES

Records of Hil. 1572, Hil. 1577 and earlier.

Actions upon statutes.

(Hil.14 Eliz., roll 508.[1]) In an action on the Statute of Winchester aforesaid,[2] the inhabitants pleaded that 'the aforesaid plaintiff, immediately after the aforesaid felony and robbery (*spoliatio*) above supposed to have been committed at Dale aforesaid, did not make the hue and cry for the aforesaid robbery (*roberia*), according to the form of the statute aforesaid, as he has above declared'. And this was adjudged a good plea.[3] See 4 Hen. VIII, roll 525, and the Easter term following, roll 305; Mich. 6 Hen. VIII, roll 1; and Pas. 12 & 13 Hen. VIII, roll 508.[4]

See 39 Edw. III, fo. 20,[5] trespass for taking a distress in the highway contrary to the Statute of Marlborough, c. 12, and detaining it until the plaintiff made a fine of 40s.: note two matters joined in one action, one of which was at common law and the other by the statute, and several issues were taken there.

Actions *de scandalis magnatum*.[6] Mich. 1 Mar., roll 717, in the Common Bench:[7] one Chaffyn said that the Lord Stourton had burned his barn. Trin. 2 Hen. VIII, roll 36, in the King's Bench:[8] 'My lord of Winchester took me and caused me to be imprisoned wrongfully and there kept me until such time that I was fain to make and seal an obligation of £10 to the use of the king without ground or cause'. Hilary term 19 Eliz., roll 497, in the King's Bench:[9] Sir Walter Waller said that 'my Lord of Abergavenny sendeth for men to come before him, and when they come he doth so straitly deal with them that men be afraid to come before him, for some he putteth into the coal-house and some into the stocks and some into a place of his house called Little Ease, and puts both their legs in the stocks [at once, and a block under their backs].[10]

145. ANON.

Common Pleas, Trin. 1577.

Joinder in action.

In Trinity term 19 Eliz. the court was asked about this. Three coparceners make a lease for years; one of them takes a husband and has issue; and the wife dies. And it was agreed that the tenant by the curtesy and his issue, and the other two coparceners, may join in waste and count to the disinheritance of the issue and of the other two. Nevertheless, it was there agreed that if a woman makes a lease for years, and then marries a husband and has issue, and the wife dies, the issue shall not have an action of waste. See 22 Hen. VI, fo. 24.[11] And note that in the former case all of them recovered the place wasted in common, but the damages were to be paid to the reversioners of the fee.

---

[1] This is an error: it is the record of *Barewell* v. *Lucas*, above, p. 73, no. 117.
[2] 13 Edw. I, Statute of Winchester. The 'aforesaid' refers to a citation in the commonplace-book.
[3] Cf. *Benjamen* v. *Hundred of Buxton* (1564) Dyer's notebook, 109 Selden Soc. 104, where it seems to have been held that the plaintiff had to make fresh suit in all the vills within the hundred. Coke later said it was adjudged by the Common Pleas in 1585 that the hue and cry was not necessary: *Ashpole* v. *Hundred of Evingar* (1585) 6 Co. Rep. 6; CP 40/1445, m. 725. But the record shows that the plaintiff in that case counted on a hue and cry, and the defendants pleaded Not Guilty.

[146]

AB, fo. 172v (489v).

<Joindre in action.>[s]

P. 19 Eliz. fuit tenus per toutz les justices in le common banke, si lesse pur ans grant tout son estate ouster in part al un, et le residue al auter, le lessour covient daver severall actions de wast. Mes si le lesse grant son terme, habendum lun moitie a lun et lauter moitie a lauter, la covient daver que un brefe de wast, car le moitie dun arbre ne poet estre recover. 22 Ass., p. 52, accordant, que si lesse pur vie grant ouster son estate severalment, severall actions de wast serra port.

[147]

AC, fo. 499 (magenta ink) (Litt. fo. 74).

<Mich. 16 Eliz., rott. 816. Vies postea, 197.>[s]

Nota in Sir Thomas Wiatz case T. 18 Eliz. regine le case fuit que un Moulton infeffe Sir Thomas del mannour de Hunton sur condition que sil soit evicte dun manour quel il ad del feffment le dit Sir Thomas que donques il reentra in le mannour de Hunton, sinon que le dit Sir Thomas Wiat ou ses heires gardera le dit Moulton sauns damage de mesme le eviction deins un moys apres notice a luy ou ses heires fait, et puis Sir Thomas fuit attaint per parliament et execute pur haute treason issint que ore il navoit ascun heire, et durant cest temps Moulton fuit evicte del mannour (come la fuit admitte) <et puis>[d] <mes devant le eviction>[i] leire de Sir Thomas Wiat fuit restore per parliament (sicome null tiel <ust>[d] attainder ust estre) al sank solement, et puis le dit Moulton fist notice a luy, et pur ceo que il ne fuit gard sauns damage il reentra.

Et fuit tenus per le Segnior Dier et 2 des auters justices que coment que le condition fuit un foitz suspende, uncore per le restitution le condition esteant un hereditament serra revive, coment a un temps ne fuit ascun apparaunt possibilitie de ceo reviver. Et ilz disoient que si le restitution nust estre le condition fuit discharge, pur ceo que quant condition veigne imposible per lacte del ley ou lacte de dieu la lestate remaine absolute, mes quant le condition deveigne impossible per lacte et tort del partie auterment est. Mes icy lattaindre de le mort est part lact del ley et part lacte de dieu et issint le condition discharge tanquam etc. <Vide Pl. in Com. 562b. Vide 17 Eliz. 107, 108, Periam.>[a]

---

pleas in sir Thomas Wiat's case, which I heard and observed'); 2 Co. Inst. 502 ('Tr. 18 Eliz. in communi banco, in Wyats case. Per cur[iam] which I heard and observed'). Differently reported in Plowd. 562; Benl. 260; Dyer's notebook, 110 Selden Soc. 329, and the numerous MSS. cited there; BL MS. Harley 5030, fos. 11v, 16v ('... Et fuit fait un Eschequer Chamber case ou il uncore dependist'); MS. Lansd. 1060, fos. 115v–125v; MS. Harg. 373, fos. 145v–155v; MS. Lansd. 1057, fos. 188–200v, sub nom. *Sir Thomas Walsingham's Case* (evidently an error for Wyat); JRL MS. Fr. 118, fos. 49–50 (Pas. 1576), 67–70 (Trin. 1576).

[3] This refers to the note of the case printed below, p. 96, no. 160, which is in *AC*, fo. 197.

[4] This was granted by Mary I to the defendant's lessor's father, Sir John Baker (d. 1558), following the attainder of Sir Thomas Wyatt in 1554.

[5] The manor of East Peckham, Kent, which was granted to Wyatt's father by Henry VIII in 1538.

[6] *Att.-Gen.* v. *Walsingham* (1579) Plowd. 547 at fo. 562v.

[7] I.e. Dyer's report of the same case in his notebook, as in 110 Selden Soc. 329.

146. ANON.

Common Pleas, Pas. 1577.

Joinder in action.

In Easter term 19 Eliz. it was held by all the justices in the Common Bench that if a lessee for years grants all his estate over, part to one person and the rest to another, the lessor must have separate actions of waste. But if the lessee grants his term, *habendum* as to one moiety to one of them and as to the other moiety to the other, then there shall be but one writ of waste, for the moiety of a tree cannot be recovered. 22 Ass., pl. 52,[1] accord.: if lessee for life grants over his estate severally, several actions of waste must be brought.

147. MULTON v. COVENEY: WYATT'S CASE[2]

Common Pleas, Trin. 1576.

Mich. 16 [& 17] Eliz., roll 816. See below, fo. 197.[3]

Note that in Sir Thomas Wyatt's case, in Trinity term 18 Eliz., the case was this: one Multon enfeoffed Sir Thomas of the manor of Hunton,[4] upon condition that if he (Multon) was evicted from a manor[5] which he had by the feoffment of the said Sir Thomas, he could then re-enter in the manor of Hunton, unless the said Sir Thomas Wyatt or his heirs should keep the said Multon harmless in respect of the same eviction within one month after notice given to him or his heirs; afterwards Sir Thomas was attainted by Parliament and executed for high treason, so that now he had no heir; during this time Multon was evicted from the manor (as was there admitted), but before the eviction the heir of Sir Thomas Wyatt was restored by Parliament to the blood only, as if no such attainder had been; then the said Multon gave him notice [to save him harmless], and because he was not kept harmless he re-entered.

And it was held by the lord DYER and two of the other justices that although the condition was once suspended, nevertheless by the restitution the condition (being a hereditament) was revived, even though at one time there was no apparent possibility of its reviving. And they said that if there had been no restitution, the condition would have been discharged, because when a condition becomes impossible by the act of the law, or the act of God, the estate remains absolute, but when the condition becomes impossible by the act and wrong of the party it is otherwise. Here, however, the attainder of the deceased was partly the act of the law and partly the act of God, and therefore the condition was discharged *tanquam* etc. {See Plowden's *Comentaries*, fo. 562v.[6] See 17 Eliz. 107, 108, Peryam.[7]}

---

[1] 22 Edw. III, Lib. Ass., pl. 52.

[2] CP 40/1324, m. 816 (three rolls; summarised in Benl. 260): George Multon esq. v. Roger Coveney of Hunton, Kent, yeoman (lessee of Sir Richard Baker); trespass *quare clausum fregit* in part of the manor of Hunton; demurrer to the rejoinder; c.a.v. to Trin. 1576; judgment for the defendant. Noted above, p. 49, no. 94; p. 79, no. 125; below, pp. 94–95, no. 157–158; p. 96, no. 160; p. 101, no. 171; p. 139, no. 252. Cit. in Co. Litt. 77 ('Tr. 18 Eliz. in Com. Banco ... which my self heard and noted, in Sir Thomas Wyat's case); ibid., fo. 221b ('as it was resolved Trin. 18 Eliz. in Communi Banco in sir Thomas Wiat's Case, which I heard and observed'; ibid., fo. 269a ('and so it was resolved Trin. 18 Eliz. in the court of common

[148]

AC, fo. 500 (magenta ink) (Litt. fo. 75).

<Estate sur condition.>s

P. 18 Eliz. fuit agree in grantes et feffmentes ea intentione, ou ad propositum, ou ad effectum, ne sont conditions sinon que il soit in le case de roy ou un devise.

[149]

AC, fo. 502r-v (magenta ink).

<Conditions.>s

15 Eliz. fuit tenus per toutz les justices del common banke in le case de Blunt et Andrewes que un proviso fait toutz foitz un condition sil ne soit referre a ascun covenant pur abbridge ceo ou pur explicate ceo. Come si jeo bargaine a vous toutz mes terres in Kent proviso que vous naveres mon mansion house, in cest case nest que un qualification del generall covenant et nemy un condition. Issint, come le case est in 9 H. 6, 35, si home fait leas sauns impechement de wast proviso que il ne ferra voluntarie wast, pur ceo que il est referre a un especiall covenant. Mes quant le proviso nest referre a null auter mes estoit per soy mesme substantive et est le commencement dun sentence, la in quecumque lieu que il soit placed, soit ceo puis le habendum ou soit que il vient inter alias conventiones ou que il vient in le fine del fait, il est toutz foitz un condition. Et pur ceo le case de Blunt fuit que Blunt, esteant seisie de manor de A <ove lavouson appendant>i bargaine et vend ceo per fait et nient enro[lle] a Andrewe in fe, et puis le habendum etc. Blunt covenant de suffer un recoverie devant tiel jour et auxi un auter covenant fuit que un fine serra levie per le dit Blunt a Andrewes ove graunt et render de le rent a Blunt in fe, et apres ceux covenantes etc. proviso semper que le dit Andrewes graunt lavouson a Blunt arere durant sa vie, et apres divers covenants fueront in lendentures, et nient obstant que cest proviso vient enter alias conventiones uncore fuit adjudge que il fuit un condition et le placinge de ceo nest materiall.

Et [in] mesme le case fuit tenus per Mounson, Manwood et Harper que si feffment soit fait sur condition de reenfeffe le feffour que in cest case le fe[ffe][1] ad temps durant sa vie, mes ilz agre que le feffor poet ha[sten][2] ceo per son request, car sil request le feffe de luy reinfeffe et il refuse, coment nul temps soit limitte, uncore il bien poet enter pur le condition enfreint. <Mes Dier a ceo ne agree, car il dit>d Et ilz agreont que null request est necessarie de part le feffor, issint que sil ne request que il ne entra pur le condition enfreint, car si le feffe devie devant ascun request fait per le feffor ilz agreont clerement que uncore le feffor poet enter pur le condition enfreint.

[1] *Partly cut off.*
[2] *Partly cut off. For the word cf. above, p. 54.*

148. ANON.

Common Pleas (probably), Pas. 1576.

Estate upon condition.

In Easter term 18 Eliz. it was agreed that, in grants and feoffments, the words 'with the intention' (*ea intentione*), 'for the purpose' (*ad propositum*), or 'to the effect' (*ad effectum*) are not conditions unless it is in the case of the king or a devise.

149. ANDROWES v. BLUNT[1]

Common Pleas, 1572/73.

Conditions.

In 15 Eliz. it was held by all the justices of the Common Bench, in the case of Blunt and Androwes,[2] that a proviso always makes a condition, unless it refers to some covenant in order to abridge or explain it. For instance if I bargain to you all my lands in Kent, *proviso* that you shall not have my mansion house, in this case it is only a qualification of the general covenant and not a condition. Likewise, as the case is in 9 Hen. VI, fo. 35,[3] if someone makes a lease without impeachment of waste, *proviso* that he should not commit voluntary waste, because this refers to a specific covenant. But when the proviso does not refer to anything else, but stands by itself substantively, and is the commencement of a sentence, then wherever it is placed – whether it is after the *habendum*, or amongst other covenants, or coming at the end of the deed – it is always a condition.[4] And Blunt's case was that Blunt, being seised of the manor of Allexton with the advowson appendant, bargained and sold it by deed unenrolled to Androwes in fee, and after the *habendum* Blunt covenanted to suffer a recovery before a certain day, and there was also another covenant that a fine should be levied by the said Blunt to Androwes, with a grant and render of the rent to Blunt in fee; and after these covenants the deed said 'provided always' (*proviso semper*) that the said Androwes would grant the advowson back to Blunt during his life; and then there were various covenants in the indentures. Notwithstanding that this proviso came amongst other covenants, it was nevertheless adjudged that it was a condition and its position was immaterial.

In the same case it was held by MOUNSON, MANWOOD and HARPER that if a feoffment is made upon condition to re-enfeoff the feoffor, in this case the feoffee has time to do so during his life. But they agreed that the feoffor may hasten it by his request, for if he requests the feoffee to re-enfeoff, and he refuses, even though no time is limited, he may well enter for breach of the condition. And they agreed that no request is necessary on the part of the feoffor, so that if he does not request he may not enter for breach of the condition: [but] if the feoffee dies before any request made by the feoffor, they agreed clearly that the feoffor could nevertheless enter for breach of the condition.

---

[1] See above, p. 52, no. 101, and the note there. Many of the same arguments occur in that report.
[2] Androwes was the plaintiff. For his litigation concerning Allexton see above, p. 6, n. 1; below, p. 99, n. 1.
[3] YB Trin. 9 Hen. VI, fo. 35, pl. 6.   [4] Cf. above, p. 52, no. 101 (in the same case).

Mes Dier a ceo ne agree, car il dit que entaunt que le feffor et le feffe doient occurre ensemble, lun pur doner liverye et lauter pur prender ceo, ideo in congr[uitie]¹ [*fo. 502v*] de reason coment que le feffor nest compell de faire request uncore semble que il covient de faire un notification al feffe quaunt il voille aver le feffment fait a luy.

Et auxi les 3 justices avandit agreont clerement que in cest case Andrewes ad temps de graunter lavowson arere durant son vie sur 2 contingentez, lun si le feffour ne hasten et shorten ceo per son request, lauter si nul avoidauns eschue devant son graunt, car ilz agreont clerement que si ascun avoidauns eschue coment que il graunt lavouson apres al feffour uncore le condition est enfreint pur ceo que il ne recovera lavouson en tiel plite come il ad devant, car ilz agre que si leglise devient void et puis il graunt lavouson ouster en fe que le grante navera lavoidaunce que fuit eschue devant: quod Dier auxi concessit quant a ceo. Mes il tient que si home graunt un avouson sur condition que il graunt ceo a luy arere duraunt son vie que il doit faire ceo in convenient temps pur ceo que auterment leglise poet vener voide in le mesne temps et donques il serra disable a faire le graunt arere in tiel plite etc. come ad estre agre. <14 E. 3, tit. Dett, 138: rent covient estre graunt in convenient temps devant arere.>ⁱ Et pur ceo que in le principal case <pur ceo que>ⁱ Andrewes ne graunt lavouson a Blunt deins 2 ans il semble que le condition fuit enfreint. Et auxi il tient que le condition esteant enfreint lavouson fuit arere in Andrewes et sauns ascun clayme. Et quaunt request serra fait et quaunt nemy vide 44 E. 3, 8. <42 Ass. 6.>ⁱ 9 E. 4, 22b. 21 E. 4, 41b. <Vide apres 2 E. 4, 3 et 4, in mes notes demesne, 187b. Dier, 3 Mar. 138.>ᵃ

[150]

AC, fo. 503 (in magenta ink) (Litt. 76).

<Estate sur condition.>ˢ

Nota per le Segnior Dier 14 Elyz. in le argument de Winters case que un condition est un compulsive chose et va in defesauns del estates, et pur ceo est odious en ley, et serra prise toutz foitz stricte. Et pur ceo la fuit adjudge que un condition ne poet estre apportion per act des parties <de>ᵈ mes pluistost determine et extinct in tout, come la case la fuit adjudge.

---

¹ *Partly cut off.*

⁷ *Merton College, Oxford* v. *Wodelark* (1463) YB Trin. 3 Edw. IV, fos. 1–8, pl. 1, at fos. 3–4.
⁸ *AC*, fo. 187v (514v).
⁹ *Duke of Norfolk's Case* (1557) Dyer 138. This citation is followed by some closely written notes which seem to be a digression rather than part of a report of the case.
¹⁰ See above, p. 43, no. 88, and the note there.

But DYER did not agree with this, for he said that inasmuch as the feoffor and the feoffee must concur with each other, the one to give livery and the other to take it, therefore in congruity of reason, although the feoffor is not compelled to make request, it nevertheless seemed that he must give notice to the feoffee when he wants to have the feoffment made to him.

The three justices aforesaid also agreed clearly that in this case Androwes had time to grant back the advowson during his life upon two contingencies, the one if the feoffor did not hasten and shorten it by his request, the other if no avoidance fell in before his grant; for they agreed clearly that if any avoidance fell in, even though he granted the advowson afterwards to the feoffor, the condition would still be broken, because he could not recover the advowson in the same plight as he had it before. For they agreed that if the church became vacant, and afterwards he granted the advowson over in fee, the grantee would not have the avoidance which had fallen in before. DYER also conceded that, as to that point. But he held that if someone grants an advowson upon condition that he should grant it back to him during his life, he ought to do it within a convenient time, because otherwise the church may become vacant in the meantime and then he would be disabled from making the grant back in the same plight as before, as had been agreed. {14 Edw. III, tit. *Dett*, 138:[1] rent must be granted in a convenient time before it is in arrear.[2]} In the principal case, because Androwes did not grant the advowson to Blunt within two years, it seemed that the condition was broken. He also held that, the condition being broken, the advowson was back in Androwes without any claim. As to when a request shall be made, and when not, see 44 Edw. III, fo. 8;[3] {42 Ass. pl. 6;[4]} 9 Edw. IV, fo. 22v;[5] 21 Edw. IV, fo. 41v.[6] {See afterwards 2 Edw. IV, fos. 3 and 4,[7] in my own notes, fo. 187v.[8] Dyer, 3 Mar. 138.[9]}

150. WINTER'S CASE[10]

Common Pleas, 1572.

Estate upon condition.

Note, by the lord DYER in 14 Eliz., in the argument of Winter's case, that a condition is a compulsory thing and goes in defeasance of estates, and is therefore odious in law and shall always be taken strictly. Therefore it was adjudged in that case that a condition cannot be [apportioned] by act of the parties, but shall rather be determined and extinguished *in toto*, as the case there was adjudged.

---

[1] Pas. 14 Edw. III, Fitz. Abr., *Dett*, pl. 138.
[2] The point of the reported argument was that if there was a bond upon condition to enfeoff the obligee with a rent, without specifying a time-limit, it was at the obligor's pleasure when he would do it. But the obligor in the end pleaded that he had always been ready to make the feoffment and still was.
[3] *Abbot of York's Case* (1370) YB Pas. 44 Edw. III, fo. 8, pl. 10.
[4] 42 Edw. III, Lib. Ass., pl. 6.
[5] YB Trin. 9 Edw. IV, fo. 22, pl. 24.
[6] *Atwill* v. *Tailor* (1481) YB Mich. 21 Edw. IV, fo. 38, pl. 4, at fo. 41.

[151]

AC, fo. 505v (magenta ink).

<Conditions.>ˢ

Nota que fuit tenus anno 15 le roygne que ore est que si home lessa un boys reservant un rent et pur default de payment <de>ᵈ un reentre, que le lessor covient demande ceo in le pluis apiert lieu. Mes semble que si in le boys sont divers appert plotz que la il prendra son election a demander ou il luy voille, et si ne sont ascun tielz plottes donques il covient demander ceo a le port del boys car ceo est le pluis convenient lieu. <et en le principal case>ᵈ Et la fuit agre al darren que si tiel leas soit fait dun boys et le lessor alledge un demande a le dit boys, que suffist a le lesse a traverser le demande, car coment que il demande ceo al boys uncore sil ne demande ceo in le pluis convenient lieu donques il serra trove vers le defendant.

Et un case fuit la cite que fuit adjudge ore tard <in b>ᵈ, et le case fuit [in] Barckshire, que un vient a un backedore a demaund son rent et le tenant fuit prist a le foredore, et issue fuit prise que le lessor ne demande pas, car il fuit null demaund in ley. <Vies 49 Ass., p. 5, per Hanmer. Vide Dier, 15 Eliz. 329. Bendloes in mes notes, fol. 5b, optime.>ⁱ

[152]

AC, fo. 18[2] (509).

<Conditions.>ˢ

T. 19 Eliz fuit dit per le Segnior Dier si home fait leasse pur ans a un home et a ses assgnees sur condition que il ne assignera ceo ouster ceo est bone et nemi repugaunt, car assignes in primo loco sont voide.

[153]

AC, fo. 183 (510).

<Conditions.>ˢ

Nota bene fuit tenus in temps mesme cesti roigne que si home face leasse pur ans rendant [rent]¹ et un condition pur default de payment, le lessor covient a demander son rent sur le terre, car nest assetz pur luy a vener pres le² terre, scilicet a le meason, et la demander mes il covient vener sur le terre in leasse etc.

---

¹ rend.
² *Written twice.*

151. CASE OF THE DEAN AND CHAPTER OF GLOUCESTER[1]

Common Pleas, 1573.

Conditions.

Note that it was held in the fifteenth year of the present queen that if someone leases a wood, reserving a rent, and for default of payment a re-entry, the lessor must demand it in the most open place. And it seems that if there are various open plots in the wood, he may make his election to demand it where he will, but if there are no such plots he must demand it at the gate of the wood, for that is the most convenient place. And it was there agreed in the end that if such a lease is made of a wood, and the lessor alleges a demand at the said wood, it suffices for the lessee to traverse the demand, for even if he demanded it at the wood, nevertheless if he did not demand it in the most convenient place it shall be found against the [lessor].

And a case was cited there which was adjudged recently, and the case was in Berkshire, where someone came to a back door to demand his rent, and the tenant was ready at the front door ('foredore'), and issue was taken that the lessor did not make a demand, for it was no demand in law.

{See in 49 Ass. pl. 5,[2] by Hanmer. See Dyer, 15 Eliz. 329.[3] Bendlowes in my notes, fo. 5v: the best.[4]}

152. ANON.

Common Pleas, Trin. 1577.

Conditions.

In Trinity term 19 Eliz it was said by the lord DYER that if someone makes a lease for years to a man and his assigns upon condition that he should not assign it over, this is good and not repugnant, for the word 'assigns' in the first place is void.

153. ANON.

Temp. Eliz.

Conditions.

Note well that it was held in the time of this same queen that if someone makes a lease for years, rendering rent, with a condition for default of payment, the lessor must demand his rent upon the land. It is not enough for him to come near to the land, namely to the house, and demand it there, but he must come upon the land in lease.

---

[1] Differently reported in Dyer 329, whence Co. Litt. 202b.
[2] 49 Edw. III, Lib. Ass., pl. 5.   [3] Dyer's report of the present case.
[4] Perhaps *Elliott* v. *Nutcombe* (1559) CP 40/1174, m. 641; Benl. 59; 1 And. 27; 3 Leon. 4; cit. in Dyer 329. There land in Cornwall was leased by the bishop of Exeter, the rent to be paid in Exeter (not saying exactly where), and a tender was pleaded at the palace gate. See also Mich. 6 Edw. VI (1552) in *AB*, fo. 5v (297 in magenta ink); Cro. Eliz. 15, pl. 6 ('ex relatione Fountaine, incerti temporis').

[154]

AC, fo. 191 (518).

<Conditions.>[5]

T. 13 Eliz. in attaint le case fuit tiel. Un Davison fuit oblige in un obligation a un Franklyn sur condition que il performera lagard de J. S. et J. N. issint que larbitrement soit fait al ou avant le 33[1] jour del June, videlicet sealed et delivered etc. Et le veritie del case fuit que le agard fuit ingrosse 33 die Junii et J. S. inseale ceo in le afternoone circa horam 3, et lauter ceo inseale apres le coucher del sol circa horam 9, et ceo fuit deliver al parties mesme le nuite. Et le question fuit coment le jour serra accompt, car fuit agre que dies solaris est del rising del sol jesque al coucher de ceo, mes dies naturalis est jesque al midnight. Et la ilz pristont le differens que lou home est tenus de faire ascun acte a un auter et lauter est tenus a doner son attendauns, come sur tender de money a ascun certen lieu, ou fesaunt dun feffment, in ceux cases le tender et le feffment covient estre fait devant le coucher del sol pur ceo que les parties covient daver sufficient temps a resorter a lour lodgment. Mes quant le acte est destre solement fait per lun partie tantum in le absens de lauter partie, la sil fait ceo devant midnight ceo suffist. Come si jeo sue tenus a departer hors de Norff. by the 2 daye of June, si jeo departe hors de ceo apres le coucher del sol et devant midnighte ceo suffist. Nota bene. Issint est in le principall case: quod nota.

Nota quandocumque un chose est prohibite per condition <et>[6] que trench in defesauns dun estate, ou quandocumque un penall ley prohibite ascun chose, si home ne face directment enconter les parolx del condition ou del acte ceo est infreinder del condition etc. Come si home lessa terres pur vie sur condition que le lesse ne ferra wast, si estrange fait waste ceo nest infreinder del condition pur ceo que le lesse est tantsolement prohibite. Issint 5 H. 6, [*blank*], in estrepement, si estrange fait wast le tenant ne serra punie pur ceo que le tenant est solement restraine. Issint si le garden ne fait wast mes estrange, le garden ne serra punye. 44 E. 3. Et issint toutz foitz quant un voill prendre availe dun condition il covient de performer les parolx, come fuit tenus in Wiatz case T. 18 Eliz. regine. 21 E. 4, 52,[7] si le condition soit que si jeo recover 20 acres vers J. S. que vous avera le moitie, si jeo recover que 10 acres vous averes rien. Doctor et Student:[8] si leasse soit fait sur condition etc. que si le lesse fait wast que donques etc., in cest case si estrange wast les terres ceo nest infreinder del condition. 12 H. 4, 5,[9] in mesme le case si le meason eschuit per le vent ceo nest infreinder del condition: uncore les parolx fueront, si wast soit fait.

---

[1] *Sic, but obviously an error.*

[5] YB Mich. 44 Edw. III, fo. 27, pl. 4.
[6] *Multon* v. *Coveney* (1576), which is the next case, though not noted on this point.
[7] YB Mich. 21 Edw. IV, fo. 52, pl. 16.
[8] *St German's Doctor and Student*, ed. Plucknett and Barton, 91 Selden Soc. 184–187.
[9] *Abbot of Sherborne's Case* (1410) YB Mich. 12 Hen. IV, fo. 5, pl. 11.

154. FRANKLYN v. DAVISON

Trin. 1571.[1]

Conditions.

In Trinity term 13 Eliz., in an attaint, the case was this. One Davison was bound in a bond to one Franklyn upon condition that he should perform the award of John Style and John Noke, provided the arbitration was made on or before 3[2] June, namely sealed and delivered [to the parties]. The truth of the case was that the award was engrossed on 3 June, and John Style sealed it in the afternoon around 3 o'clock, and the other sealed it after sunset around 9 o'clock, and it was delivered to the parties the same night. The question was, how the day should be reckoned. For it was agreed that the solar day (*dies solaris*) is from sunrise until sunset, whereas the natural day (*dies naturalis*) is until midnight. And they drew the distinction that where someone is bound to do any act to another, and the other needs to give his attendance, as upon a tender of money at some certain place, or making a feoffment, in these cases the tender or the feoffment must be made before sunset, because the parties must have sufficient time to return home. But when the act is to be done solely by one party alone, in the absence of the other party, it is sufficient if he does it before midnight. Thus if I am bound to leave Norfolk by 2 June, it suffices if I leave after sunset but before midnight. Note this well. So it is in the principal case: note that.

[3]Note that whenever a thing is prohibited by a condition, and it works in defeasance of an estate, or whenever a penal law prohibits anything, it is [only] a breach of the condition [or Act] if someone acts directly against the words of the condition or the Act. For instance, if someone leases lands for life upon condition that the lessee should not commit waste, and a stranger commits waste, this is not a breach of the condition, because only the lessee is prohibited. Likewise, 3 Hen. VI,[4] in estrepement: if a stranger commits waste, the tenant shall not be punished for it, because only the tenant is restrained. Likewise if the guardian does not commit waste, but a stranger, the guardian shall not be punished: 44 Edw. III.[5] Likewise, [conversely], whenever anyone wishes to take advantage of a condition he must perform the words, as was held in Wyatt's case in Trinity term 18 Eliz.[6] 21 Edw. IV, fo. 52:[7] if the condition is that, should I recover 20 acres against John Style, you will have the moiety, and I only recover 10 acres, you shall have nothing. *Doctor and Student*:[8] if a lease is made upon condition that if the lessee commits waste [the lessor may re-enter], in this case if a stranger wastes the lands it is not a breach of the condition. 12 Hen. IV, fo. 5:[9] in the same case, if the house falls down through the wind, it is not a breach of the condition; and yet the words were, 'if waste be committed'.

---

[1] Coke was at this time a student Clifford's Inn, and his Littleton was purchased in 1572, so this may not be his own report; but there is no indication of another source. Cf. *Roofe v. Light* (1578) in Dyer's notebook, 110 Selden Soc. 359, which Coke later copied (*AC*, fo. 529).

[2] Coke clearly wrote 33, twice, but this was obviously an error.

[3] Although not the report of a case, this further note is included on account of the citation of *Wyatt's Case* (1576), which is often referred to elsewhere, including the next case.

[4] YB Mich. 3 Hen. VI, fos. 16–17, pl. 22.

[155]

AC, fo. 191v (518v).

<Conditions.>ˢ

Quere si home fait leas pur vie sur condition que si le lessor morust sauns issue de son corps que donques le lesse avera fe, le lessor morust ayaunt issue, et puis lissue morust, issint que ore sur le matter le lessor est mort sauns issue, quere in cest case si le lesse avera fe. Et semble per Manwoode in le argument de Nicols case que si le limitation fuit bone quel il denie (mes les auters justices affirme) que le lesse avera fe.

[156]

AC, fo. 524v (magenta ink) (Litt. fo. 84).

<Estate sur condicion.>ˢ

Fuit un doubt in le countie de Arundels case que si home fait done in taile sur condition que si le done morust sauns issue que le donour reentra, si cest condition soit bone. Ascuns disoient que ceo fuit void pur ceo que le nature dun condition est a defeater estate, et in cest case lestate serra determine devant per le limitation de ceo. Et auters disoient que le condition fuit bone, car poet estre que le done voille faire discontinuauns et donques lentre del donour serra congeable. Quere si ceo avoidra dower.

[157]

AC, fo. 194 (527).

[1] ... issint nota, come moy semble, per ceux 2 estatutz si tenant in taile soit disseisie et fait treason, semble que cest droit ne serra forfeit, car al common ley attaindre de treason ne forfeitra terres taile, et lestatut de 26 H. 8 done toutz terres, tenementes et hereditamentz in use ou in possession, et cest statut de 33 H. 8 done toutz [sic] droit que le person attainted poet loialment forfeit, et tenant <in taile>[2] per ordre del ley ne poet doner ne forfeiter son droit forsque solement durant son vie. Et vies lestatut de 5 E. [6], c. 11, et vies Stanford in Pleas del corone, fol. 18. <Mes ceo nest pas ley.>ⁱ Et nota bene le construction del estatut de anno 1 Mar., car ove mesme le construction agre le Segnior Dier in le argument de Wiatz case anno 18 Eliz. Et dit que issint fuit rule in temps le Roigne Marie per toutz les justices que le dit estatut ne repeale le forfeiture le terre taile pur treason per lestatutz de 26 H. 8, 33 H. 8 et 5 E. 6. Et vide bene Wiatz case anno 18 Eliz.

---

[1] *Begins with a summary of two statutes, part of which has been torn away.*
[2] *Written twice.*

---

[7] *Austin* v. *Baker* (1554) cit. in Plowd. 560; 7 Co. Rep. 8; vol. iv, p. 719 (1561). Cf., concerning other aspects of the repeal, Dyer 131; Dalison's reports, 124 Selden Soc. 26.
[8] This aspect is discussed in Dyer's report, omitted from the old edition, in 110 Selden Soc. at pp. 330–331.

155. NICHOLS'S CASE[1]

Common Pleas, Mich. 1575.

Conditions.

If someone makes a lease for life upon condition that if the lessor dies without issue of his body the lessee should have fee, the lessor dies having issue, and then the issue dies, so that now upon the facts the lessor is dead without issue, shall the lessee in this case have fee? It seemed to MANWOOD in the argument of Nichols's case that, if the limitation was good (which he denied, though the other justices affirmed it), the lessee should have fee.

156. EARL OF ARUNDEL'S CASE[2]

Common Pleas, 1576.

Estate upon condition.

It was a doubt in the earl of Arundel's case, if someone makes a gift in tail upon condition that if the donee dies without issue the donor should re-enter, whether this condition is good. Some said it was void because the nature of a condition is to defeat an estate, and in this case the estate will be determined before by the limitation thereof. Others said that the condition was good, for it may be that the donee will make a discontinuance and then the entry of the donor would be permissible. Query whether it will avoid dower.

157. MULTON v. COVENEY[3]

Common Pleas, 1576.

Note that, as it seems to me, by these two statutes,[4] if a tenant in tail is disseised and commits treason, the right shall not be forfeited; for at common law an attainder of treason does not cause a forfeiture of entailed lands, and the statute of 26 Hen. VIII gives all lands, tenements and hereditaments in use or in possession; and the statute of 33 Hen. VIII gives all right which the person attainted may lawfully forfeit: and by the order of the law tenant in tail cannot give or forfeit his right except during his lifetime. See the statute of 5 Edw. VI, c. 11.[5] And see Stanford, *Plees del Corone*, fo. 18. {But that is not law.} And note well the construction of the statute of 1 Mar.,[6] for the lord DYER agreed with the same construction in the argument of Wyatt's case in the year 18 Eliz. And he said that it was ruled in the time of Queen Mary, by all the justices, that the said statute did not repeal the forfeiture of entailed land for treason by the statutes of 26 Hen. VIII, 33 Hen. VIII and 5 Edw. VI.[7] Take a good look at Wyatt's case, in the year 18 Eliz.[8]

---

[1] See above, p. 45, no. 90, and the note there.   [2] See above, p. 70, no. 116, and the note there.
[3] See above, p. 89, no. 147, and the note there.
[4] 26 Hen. VIII, c. 13, s. 4; 33 Hen. VIII, c. 20, s. 2. On these statutes see also 3 Co. Inst. 19.
[5] 5 & 6 Edw. VI, c. 11, s. 6.   [6] 1 Mar., sess. 1, c. 1 (repealing certain statutes concerning treasons).

[158]

AC, fo. 194r-v (527r-v).

<Forfeiture.>[s 1] <Mich. 16 et 17 Eliz. rott. 816, Moulton versus Coveney. 18 Eliz.>[s]

Nota fuit tenus per toutz les justices in le common banke <an>[d] Trin. 18 Eliz. que ou le roy H. 8 dona un mannour a Sir Thomas Wiate in taile, et le dit Sir Thomas esteant de ceo seisie, le revercion esteant al roy, de ceo inffa un Moulton in fe, et puis fuit attaint de haut treason in anno 1 Mar. et le quel attaindre fuit confirm in anno 2 & 3 Ph. et Mar. per parliament, et toutz ses terres, tenementes, droitz, titlez etc. done al roigne. Et fuit adjudge que per le feffment Sir Thomas W., coment le revercion esteant al roy ne fuit discontinue, uncore quant a luy tout son droit fuit ale hors del luy et le droit destate taile fuit in abeiauns. Et fuit relye grandment sur les cases in Litt. fol. 145a. Et auxi pur ceo que al common ley tenant in taile puit aver alien devant issue a barrer les issues mes nemi cesti in revercion, et lestatute de donis conditionalibus fuit fait solement a benefite del issues del tenant in taile et nemi del tenant in taile mesme. Et la fuit agre que estate[2] taile apres lestatute de donis conditionalibus et devant lestatute de 26 H. 8 ne forfeitra[3] son terre pur haut treason, come 7 H. 4, 32, fuit agre.

Et la le Segnior Dier prist cest ground, que un droit escheatera et serra forfeit in toutz cases quaunt cesti que droit ad in son vie puit loialment [enter][4] et ne fuit mys a son action. Et le segnior ne fuit chace de alter son avowre sinon in especial cases, sicome si enfaunt fait feffment ou non compos mentis et puis morust sans heire, ceux droitz ne eschetera. Mes si mon done soit disseisie et puis morust sauns heire, ou soit attaint, cest droit eschetera. Autermet si le disseisour ust morust seisie issint que le attendance del segnior fuit alter. Et il [...][5] que droitz al chattelx sera forfeit, come in le case [...][6] [*fo. 527v*]

<5 E. 4, tit. Petition, B. 26 [...] case [...][7]>[i] Nota per le Segnior Dier arguendo in W[iatz case dit que][8] in long 5 E. 4 le case fuist que Sir Simon Moundeford fuit founder del abbathie de Leicestre et avoit corodie in ceo de common droit, et puis le dit Sir Simond fuit attaint de haut treason, et tenus per cest livre, come il collecte, que cest foundershippe ne serra forfeit al roy pur ceo que ceo fuit un inheritauns knitte et annexe al person del dit Sir Simond et ne serra forfeite. Et Brooke, tit. Corrody, 5, que puis le augmentation court fuit tenus in temps H. 8 que un foundershippe ne serra forfeit al roy pur ceo que il est annexe al sanke et ne poet estre devide. Et issint nota in ascun cases home poet graunt ouster chose que il ne poet forfeit. Nota bene. <Pl. Com. 381.>[a]

---

[1] *Heading on fos. 526, 528.*
[2] *Sic, presumably a slip for* tenant.
[3] forfeitrat.   [4] entier.
[5] *Words lost in corner.*
[6] *Words lost in corner.*
[7] *Words lost at top edge.*
[8] *Conjectural; piece missing at top.*

---

[10] Temp. Hen. VIII, Bro. Abr., *Corodies*, pl. 5 ('... et dicitur alibi ... tempore H. 8 quod nota').
[11] *Sir Henry Nevill's Case* (1570) Plowd. 377 at fo. 381.

158. MULTON v. COVENEY, continued[1]

Common Pleas, Trin. 1576.

Forfeiture. Mich. 16 & 17 Eliz., roll 816, Multon against Coveney. 18 Eliz.

Note that it was held by all the justices in the Common Bench in Trinity term 18 Eliz. that where King Henry VIII gave a manor to Sir Thomas Wyatt in tail, and the said Sir Thomas (being so seised thereof, the reversion being to the king) thereof enfeoffed one Multon in fee, and was afterwards attainted of high treason in the first year of Mary, which attainder was confirmed in the year 2 & 3 Phil. & Mar. by Parliament,[2] and all his lands, tenements, rights, titles etc. given to the queen, it was adjudged that by the feoffment of Sir Thomas Wyatt, although the reversion (being to the king) was not discontinued, nevertheless as to him all his right was gone out of him and the right of the estate tail was in abeyance. And there was great reliance on the cases in [my] Littleton, fo. 145.[3] [Another reason was] that at common law a tenant in tail could have aliened before having issue, so as to bar the issue but not the reversioner, and the statute *De Donis Conditionalibus*[4] was made solely for the benefit of the issue of the tenant in tail, and not for the tenant in tail himself. And it was there agreed that a tenant in tail after the statute *De Donis Conditionalibus*, and before the statute of 26 Hen. VIII,[5] could not forfeit his land for high treason, as 7 Hen. IV, fo. 32,[6] was agreed.

And the lord DYER there took it to be a principle (*ground*) that a right will escheat and be forfeited in all cases when the person who has right in his lifetime may lawfully enter and is not driven to his action. And the lord was not driven to alter his avowry except in special cases, as where an infant (or someone of unsound mind) makes a feoffment and then dies without heir, for those rights do not escheat. But if my donee is disseised and then dies without heir, or is attainted, this right will escheat. It is otherwise if a disseisor had died seised, so that the attendancy of the lord was altered. And he said that rights to chattels shall be forfeited, as in the case [*blank*].

{5 Edw. IV, Brooke, tit. *Petition*, 26.[7]} Note by the lord DYER, arguing in Wyatt's case,[8] that in the *Long Quinto* of Edw. IV the case was that Sir Simon de Montfort was founder of Leicester Abbey, and had a corrody therein of common right, and afterwards the said Sir Simon was attainted of high treason, and it was held by this book (as he recollected) that the foundership should not be forfeited to the king, because it was an inheritance knitted and annexed to the person of the said Sir Simon and should not be forfeited.[9] Brooke, tit. *Corodies*, 5,[10] says that after the Augmentation Court was erected in the time of Henry VIII a foundership shall not be forfeited to the king, because it is annexed to the blood and cannot be divided. Thus note that in some cases a man may grant over something which he cannot forfeit. Note that well. {Plowd. Com. 381.[11]}

---

[1] See above, p. 89, no. 147, and the note there. [2] 2 & 3 Phil. & Mar., c. iii (private).
[3] I.e. Coke's annotations to Litt. in *AC*, fo. 659. [4] Westminster II, c. 1.
[5] 26 Hen. VIII, c. 13. [6] *Earl of Kent's Case* (1405) YB Mich. 7 Hen. IV, fo. 32, pl. 19.
[7] 5 Edw. IV, Bro. Abr., *Petition*, pl. 26, which is the case in the *Long Quinto*, below.
[8] *Multon* v. *Coveney* (1576) above, p. 89, no. 147.
[9] *Abbot of Leicester's Case* (1465) YB Mich. 5 Edw. IV, *Long Quinto*, fo. 118. The report says the founder was Robert 'Mylain' (Meulen) and that the patronage descended to Sir Simon.

[159]

AC, fo. 196 (529).

<Jour.>[s]

Nota Manwood dit P. 19 Eliz. que si home fait lease pur ans rendant rent a Michaelmas sur condition que si le rent soit arere per un moys etc., que in cest case le jour del Michaelmas serra prise exclusive, car nest arere tanque al darren instant del jour, ne le lessor ne poet ceo demander nemy per action ne distrenera pur ceo.

[160]

AC, fo. 197 (530).

<17 Eliz. 108, Periam.>[a][1]

Nota Wiatz case anno 18 Eliz., escrie icy in Litt. fo. 74°. Et nota la Manwood dit si jeo face lease pur tant des ans come J. S. ou ses heires nosmera, J. S. est attaint de felonie et morust, ore son heire fault <et>[i] est disabled. Mes si apres leire soit restore, donques il est fait able arere. Issint si jeo voille que si mes dettz[2] ne sont sufficient a paier mes dettz que J. S. ou ses heires vendera mon terre, J. S. est attaint et morust, les biens ne suffice, son heire puis est restore: il poet vender.

[161]

AC, fo. 201 (534).

<Quant un possibilitie serra destroy per lact dun auter person.>[s]

Weldens case P. 20 Eliz.: si home devise son terme a sa fem durant son vie, et si el devia durant le terme que le remnaunt de ceo remainera al estrange, si sa fem morust lestrange avera le residue, mes si la fem ust alien ceo donques le possibilitie que le fem avoit est destroye. <33 H. 8, tit. Chattelx, B. 23.>[a]

[162]

AC, fo. 203v (539v).

Dier 21 Eliz. 143 Periam: fuit resolve per toutes les justices que lestatut de 16 R. 2 de premunire, que done forfeiture de les terres et biens del offender al roy, que tenant

---

[1] *Inner margin.*   [2] *Sic, presumably a slip for* bienz.

of Trugeon's lands, and referred by the Council to the judges: 110 Selden Soc. 369 (where Dyer's text is dated Hil. 1580). Cf. *Acts of the Privy Council*, xi. 231, 277.

[5] The present text was evidently abridged by Coke from Dyer's unpublished reports. Cf. the abridged text in 110 Selden Soc. 368, which shows that it was on fo. 143 of the transcript in secretary hand (ibid., fo. 369). This shows that 'Dyer Peryam' in Coke's notes is the transcript in secretary-hand from Dyer's later notebooks. Cited in *AC*, fo. 573v ('Vide bone case P. 19 Eliz. devant fol. 204 ...').   [6] 16 Ric. II, c. 5.

159. ANON.

Common Pleas, Pas. 1577.

Day.

Note that MANWOOD said in Easter term 19 Eliz. that if someone makes a lease for years, rendering rent at Michaelmas, upon condition that if the rent is behind for a month [he may re-enter], in this case Michaelmas day shall be understood exclusively, for the rent is not behind, nor may the lessor demand it, or bring an action, or distrain for it, until the last instant of the day.

160. MULTON v. COVENEY[1]

Common Pleas, 1576.

17 Eliz. 108, Peryam.

Note Wyatt's case in the year 18 Eliz., written here at Litt. fo. 74.[2] Note that MANWOOD said there that if I make a lease for so many years as John Style or his heirs should name, and John Style is attainted of felony and dies, his heir now fails and is disabled. But if the heir is afterwards restored, he is made able again. Likewise, if I will that, should my goods be insufficient to pay my debts, John Style or his heirs should sell my land, and John Style is attainted and dies, and the goods do not suffice, and his heir is afterwards restored, he may sell [the land].

161. WELTDEN v. ELKINGTON[3]

Common Pleas, Pas. 1578.

When a possibility shall be destroyed by the act of another person.

Weltden's case, in Easter term 20 Eliz.: if a man devises his term to his wife during her life, and, should she die during the term, the rest of it to remain to a stranger, and the wife dies, the stranger shall have the residue; but if the wife alienates it, then the possibility which the wife had is destroyed. {33 Hen. VIII, Bro. Abr., tit. *Chattels*, 23.}

162. TRUGEON'S CASE[4]

Privy Council, Pas. 1579 or Hil. 1580.

Dyer 21 Eliz. 143, Peryam:[5] it was resolved by all the justices that the Statute of Praemunire of 16 Ric. II,[6] which gives a forfeiture to the king of the lands and goods

---

[1] See above, p. 89, no. 147, and the note there.　　[2] *AC*, fo. 499; i.e. above, p. 89.
[3] See above, p. 56, no. 104, and the note there.
[4] Or Tregeon: see above, p. 51, no. 99. Cit. in Co. Litt. 130 ('Hil. 12 Eliz. Trugins case resolve per les Justices'); 3 Co. Inst. 126 ('Pas. 21 El. resolution of the judges in Trudgyns case, Dier manuscript'); Coke's Sta. P.C. (Holkham 7171), fo. 186v ('Vide pur forfeiture in premunire in mes reportes Trudgins case'). The case was moved in the Privy Council by Sir George Cary, who had been granted the forfeiture

in taile ne <forsque>[d] forfetra forsque pur terme de son vie, car lestatut est destre intend de ceo que il poet loialment <forsque>[d] forfeiter[1] et ne extendra per generall parolx a toller lexpres et particuler purveu de donis conditionalibus. Mes lestatut de 26 H. 8. cap. 13 ad plus precise et speciall paroles. Et ceo fuit le case de Trodgeon.

[163]

AC, fo. 204 (540).

<Spilman, 11 H. 8, fol. 11°, semble adjudge in rent charge.>[s]

P. et T. 19 Eliz. fuit adjudge in le banke le roy in le case dun Colyns et le case fuit tiel. Le master del colledge de Lingfield in Surrey with the consent etc. made a lesse for yeares de toutz ses terres et tenementz in Lamburst (part de quelle ville extend in Surrey et part in Kent) except[ant] et reservant hors de mesme le demise lour mannour de L[2] Horpley in le ville avantdit et in [*blank*]. Et sur rien culpable in Kent fuit trove que le master del colledge de Lingfield nad ascun auters terres ne tenementz en Lamburst forsque le dit mannour de H. neque in tiel parte del ville que extende in <Lambhurst>[d] le countie de Kent neque in le parte que extende in Surrey.

Et fuit adjudge que coment que les parolx in le demise fueront generall, uncore pur ceo que lexception vient in auter sentence et restrayne lentier force del graunt que lexception fuit voide. Mes ilz agreont clerement que si home graunt toutz ses terres in D. queux il ad per discent de son pier, et in veritie in ad nul terres forsque ceux que discende de sa mier, uncore pur ceo que les parolz veigne tout a un sentence et sont parcell de graunt et qualefie et limitte le graunt[3] et pur ceo si home graunt rent charge hors de son manour de D., sil nad manour uncore cest bone, come Babb. dit in 9 H. 6, 53. <Adjudge 11 H. 8, Spilman 11.>[i] Et pur ceo semble sil annex un proviso a tiel graunt que il ne chargera son person, cest voide, et uncore nul repugnancie appiert in le fait. Et fuit adjudge auxi que les jurors poient trover ut supra que le dit master nad auters terres in lauter parte de ville que extende in auter countie, car cibien come ilz puissoient aver done lour verdit tacite et generallment culpable ou nient culpable, cibien poient ilz ceo doner specialment.

[164]

AC, fo. 545v (in magenta ink) (Litt., fo. 90v).

<Estate sur condicion.>[a]

Nota per Manwood, P. 20 Eliz., que si home devisa son terre a ses executours a vender et les deniers a distributer etc. in cest case il dit que les mesne profitz que ilz pristeront

---

[1] *Reads* forfeitur.   [2] *Sic.*   [3] *Sic; unfinished sentence.*

been a reputed manor in the eastern part of Lamberhurst parish, granted after the dissolution to Thomas Hawarden.   [5] I.e. by a jury of Kent, presumably at the assizes.

[6] *Queen Joan's Case* (1430) YB Mich. 9 Hen. VI, fo. 53, pl. 36, *per* Babington C.J.

[7] Also cit. in Co. Litt. 146. This was unidentified in 93 Selden Soc., introduction, p. xix; but it might refer to *The Duke of Norfolk's Case* (1518/19) ibid. 149. See Appendix VII, above, at p. ccxxxi.

of the offender, does not mean that tenant in tail should forfeit except for term of his life, for the statute is to be understood of that which he may lawfully forfeit, and it shall not stretch (by general words) to take away the express and specific provision of *De Donis Conditionalibus*. But the statute of 26 Hen. VIII, c. 13, has more precise and specific words. This was the case of Trugeon.[1]

163. DORRELL v. COLYNS[2]

King's Bench, Pas., Trin. 1577.

Spelman, 11 Hen. VIII, fo. 11, similarly adjudged as to a rent-charge.[3]

In Easter and Trinity terms 19 Eliz. it was adjudged in the King's Bench, in the case of one Colyns, as follows. The master of Lingfield College in Surrey, with the consent [of the chaplains], made a lease for years of all his lands and tenements in Lamberhurst (part of which vill lay in Surrey and part in Kent), excepting and reserving out of the same demise their manor of [Hodleigh][4] in the aforesaid vill. And, upon Not Guilty, it was found in Kent[5] that the master of Lingfield College had no other lands or tenements in Lamberhurst other than the said manor of Hodleigh, either in that part of the vill which lies in the county of Kent or in the part which lies in Surrey.

And it was adjudged that although the words in the demise were general, nevertheless because the exception comes in another sentence, and restrains the whole force of the grant, the exception was void. They clearly agreed, however, that if someone grants all his lands in Dale which he has by descent from his father, and in truth he has no lands other than those which descended from his mother, nevertheless because the words come all in one sentence [they] are parcel of the grant and qualify and limit the grant. Therefore if someone grants a rent-charge out of his manor of Dale, and he has no manor, it is still good: as Babington says in 9 Hen. VI, fo. 53.[6] {This is adjudged in 11 Hen. VIII, in Spelman, fo. 11.[7]} Therefore it seems that if he annexes a proviso to such a grant that he shall not charge his person, this is void, and yet no repugnancy appears in the deed. It was also adjudged that the jurors may properly find, as above, that the said master had no other lands in the other part of the vill which lay in the other county, for just as they could have given their verdict tacitly and generally, as Guilty or Not Guilty, so may they give it specially.

164. ANON.

Common Pleas, Pas. 1578.

Note by MANWOOD, in Easter term 20 Eliz., that if someone devises his land to his executors to sell and to distribute the money [for the good of his soul], in this case

---

[1] For his indictment see *R.* v. *Trugeon* (1578) above, p. 51, no. 99.
[2] Noted above, p. 51, no. 98; cit. in *AC*, fo. 223v (573v) ('Vide bon case P. 19 Eliz. devant fol. 204 ...'). Differently reported as *Dorrell* v. *Collins* (under Trin. 1582) Cro. Eliz. 6.
[3] See n. 7, opposite.
[4] See E. Hasted, *History of the County of Kent*, vol. 5 (Canterbury, 1798), p. 301, where it is said to have

in le mesne temps devant le vend ne serra assetz, et pur ceo serra bon pur le testatour que le mesne profitz prises devant le vende serra distributez auxi pur son alme.

[165]

AC, fo. 545v (in magenta ink) (Litt., fo. 90v).

Nota il fuit dit per ascuns serjauntes in le common banke anno 18 Eliz. que quant home devise ses terres a paier legacies ou a vender pur paier ses dettes ou a faire ascun auter chose, le ley implie un condition que sil ne face mesme lacte le droit heire le devisour poet enter, car nul peine est limitte al devise sil ne face ceo ne nul remedie pur compeller luy de ceo faire.

[166]

AC, fo. 207 (547).

<Discentz.>ˢ

Nota que est purveu per lestatute anno 32 H. 8, cap. 33, que cesti que disseise un ove force et sauns title et morust seisie, tiel moraunt seisie ne tollera lentre del disseisie sinon que tiel disseisour ust ad le pesible possession des tielx terres dont il morust seisie per le space de 5 ans prochein ensuaunt le disseisine. Quere si un disseise un sauns force et morust seisie deins 5 ans, si tiel disseisour soit deins le purveu del estatute, car il est hors del parolx.

Harper dit in le argument de Vernons case, anno 15 Eliz., que[1] si un abatour devie seisie ceo nest deins le compas del estatute.

[167]

AC, fo. 210v (550v).

<Entre.>ˢ

18 Eliz. cest case fuit tenus clerement que si disseisie fait releas al disseisour et enter sur le terre al intent a deliver le releas, le releas est bone et ne serra dit un entre.

---

[1] *Written twice.*

(he said) the mesne profits which he takes in the meantime before the sale shall not be assets, and therefore it is good for the testator that the mesne profits taken before the sale should also be distributed for his soul.

165. ANON.

Common Pleas, 1576.

Note that it was said by some serjeants in the Common Bench in the year 18 Eliz. that when a man devises his lands to pay legacies, or to be sold in order to pay his debts or to do some other thing, the law implies a condition that if he does not perform the same act the right heir of the devisor may enter, for no penalty is appointed for the devisee if he does not do it, and there is no other remedy to compel him to do it.

166. VERNON v. VERNON[1]

Common Pleas, 1572/73.

Descents.

Note that it is provided by the statute of the year 32 Hen. VIII, c. 33, that when someone disseises another with force and without title, and dies seised, such dying seised shall not toll the entry of the disseisee unless such disseisor had had peaceable possession of such lands whereof he died seised for a period of five years next following the disseisin. Query, if someone disseises another without force, and dies seised within five years, whether such disseisor is within the purview of the statute, for he is outside the words.

HARPER said in the argument of Vernon's case, in the year 15 Eliz., that if an abator dies seised it is not within the compass of the statute.

167. ANON.

Common Pleas (probably), 1576.

Entry.

In 18 Eliz. this case was held clearly: if a disseisee makes a release to the disseisor and enters on the land in order to deliver the release, the release is good and it shall not be called an entry.

---

[1] See above, p. 75, no. 118, and the note there. Perhaps the first paragraph here is not related to the case.

[168]

AC, fo. 222 (572).

T. 19 Eliz. in ejectione firme parenter le Segnior Crumwells lesse et Andrewes fuit dit per le Segnior Dier que si home soit seisie dun mannour a que advouson soit appendant, et il bargaine et vende, done et graunt mesme le mannour et lavouson, et le fait est ne unques inrolle, uncore ladvouson passera, car ceo poet passer per graunt et le graunt de chescun home serra prise pluis forcible vers luy: quod Manwood concessit. Et il dit si lenrollment apres vient ladvouson serra appendant arere per relation. Come si home fait feffment del mannour, ore les demesne passe maintenaunt, et ore nest mannour, mes si les tenants apres attorne cest attornement a tiel purpose avera relation de faire ceo mannour. Et fuit objecte que si home bargaine et vende son mannor de D. et toutz [boys][1] et underwoodes etc. que si le fait ne fuit inrolle les boys ne passera, quod Manwood concessit, pur ceo que la les boys fueront parcell etc. Et Manwood agrea le case supra del garrante,[2] car la si le garrante ne expecte le garrante serra voide, que le ley ne voet suffer.

[169]

AC, fo. 223v (573v).

<Reservation.>[5]

Nota Winters case anno 15 Eliz. fuit tiel in effecte. Home seisie de 3 acres de terre, A, B et C, demisa eux a J. S., habendum les ditz 3 acres a luy pur certain ans reddendo et solvendo pro A 3s., reddendo et solvendo pur B 4s., et reddendo et solvendo pur C 5s. Et le question fuit si cest severall reservation ferra le leasses severall, ou nemi.

Et Mounson et Manwoode semble que le <leasses>[d] <rentes>[i] per ceo fueront severall. Et le reason de Manwood fuit pur ceo que les choses hors de que le rent fuit issuant fueront severall, et pur ceo il cite le case in 31 E. 3, [*blank*]: un devant lestatut de quia emptores terrarum, ou a cest jour per licence, enfeffe un de 2 acres de terre tenendum lun acre de luy per xij d. et lauter acre de luy per ij d., in cest case le severall

---

[1] *Conjectural; word omitted at end of line.*
[2] *Presumably the case on the same page*: Si home fait feffment in fe ove garrante et deliver le fait al feffe, et puis deliver seisin al feffe secundum formam carte, le garrante est bone, et uncore chescun garrante doit enure sur un estate etc.

---

a counsel's opinion (for which he was fined £10): BL MS. Harley 2143, fo. 34 (abridged from the lost register, fo. 99). In 1580 he brought an assize: see vol. ii, p. 180 (1581), where subsequent proceedings are noted. He also brought an attaint: Cro. Eliz.15 (Pas. 1583); BL MS. Harg. 15, fo. 127 (attaint tried, Pas. 1583).
[2] Edward Androwes of Gray's Inn.
[3] Presumably the case on the same page (text n. 2, above): '(tr.) If someone makes a feoffment in fee with warranty, and delivers the deed to the feoffee, and then delivers seisin to the feoffee according to the form of the charter (*secundum formam cartae*), the warranty is good, and yet every warranty ought to operate upon an estate.'
[4] See above, p. 43, no. 88, and the note there.
[5] Perhaps Hil. 31 Edw. III, Fitz. Abr., *Briefe*, pl. 331 (*scire facias* for 20s. of rent against a tenant who owed 10s. as rent-charge for one acre and 10s. as rent-service for another). This year is not in print except in Fitz. Abr.

168. SPELL d. CROMWELL v. ANDROWES[1]

Common Pleas, Trin. 1577.

In Trinity term 19 Eliz., in ejectment between the Lord Cromwell's lessee and Androwes,[2] it was said by the lord DYER that if a man is seised of a manor to which an advowson is appendant, and he bargains and sells, gives and grants the same manor and the advowson, and the deed is never enrolled, the advowson will still pass, for it may pass by grant, and every man's grant shall be taken more forcibly against him: which MANWOOD conceded. And he said that if an enrolment comes afterwards, the advowson will be appendant again, by relation. Likewise if a man makes a feoffment of a manor, the demesnes pass forthwith, but still it is not a manor; if, however, the tenants afterwards attorn, this attornment shall relate back for this purpose to make it a manor. And it was objected that if someone bargains and sells his manor of Dale, and all woods and underwoods [appendant to the manor], the woods do not pass unless the deed is enrolled: which MANWOOD conceded, because there the woods were parcel of the manor. And MANWOOD agreed the case above, of the warranty,[3] for there if the warranty is not prospective it will be void, which the law will not allow.

169. WINTER'S CASE[4]

Common Pleas, 1572/73.

Reservation.

Note that Winter's case, in the year 15 Eliz., was as follows, in effect. A man seised of three acres of land, A, B and C, demised them to John Style, *habendum* the said three acres unto him for certain years, yielding and paying (*reddendo et solvendo*) 3s. for A, *reddendo et solvendo* 4s. for B, and *reddendo et solvendo* 5s. for C. And the question was, whether this several reservation will make the leases several, or not.

MOUNSON and MANWOOD thought that the rents were thereby several. And MANWOOD's reason was that the things out of which the rent was issuing were several. For this he cited the case in 31 Edw. III:[5] someone before the statute of *Quia Emptores Terrarum* (or at the present day by licence) enfeoffs another of two acres of land, to hold one of the acres of him by 12d. and the other acres of him by 2d., in this case the several tenendums make the tenures and the rents several. But he said it was

---

[1] CP 40/1334, m. 157d (imparlance, Pas. 1576); CP 40/1336, m. 955 (roll unfit for production; but it is recited in the King's Bench record): Richard Spell v. Edward Androwes of Harringworth, Northants., gent., Anthony Nedeham of Allexton, Leics., yeoman, and five others; ejectment for tenements in Allexton, on the demise of Henry, Lord Cromwell; verdict at bar and judgment for the plaintiff, Hil. 1578; KB 27/1266, m. 948 (two rolls): writ of error commenced by Androwes, Trin. 1578; c.a.v. to Hil. 1584; no judgment entered. Differently reported in Dyer 355 (seemingly Exch. Ch., Hil. 1577); 110 Selden Soc. 370 (1578); BL MS. Harg. 6, fo. 55; MS. Harg. 8, fos. 184–185v (dated Mich. 15 Eliz.); CUL MS. Hh.3.14, fos. 197v–198v (dated Mich. 1573). Cf. other ejectments in the King's Bench: Dyer 365 (against Androwes's lessee, Mich. 1579); above, p. 4, no. 2; p. 6, no. 7. The litigation over the manor and advowson of Allexton, Leics., began with a *quare impedit* in 1571 and continued until at least 1605: see the references in 110 Selden Soc. 370, n. 3; vol. ii, p. 180. For the *quare impedit* action see above, p. 52, no. 101, and the note there. In 1578 Cromwell sued Androwes in the Star Ch. 'for practices about the counterfeiting of a grant' of the advowson of Allexton (which were pardoned), and for forging

tenendum fait le tenures et les rentz severall. Mes il dit que auterment fuit quant le rent issuit hors dun mesme chose, quar la coment que ceo soit severalment limitte uncore il est forsque un rent: come 5 Ass. 6. 15 Ass. 11. 7 Ass. p. 1: un grant rent charge hors de son mannour de D. a prender x s. per le mayns un tiel tenant del mannour et v s. per les maynes dun auter etc., uncore ceo nest forsque un entier rent et nemi severall, car issuit hors dun mesme chose. 5 E. 4, 2. 7 E. 3. 15 E. 3, tit. Execut[ion], 63. Leas pur ans ou vie, rendant le primer an un rose, le 2 an un d. etc. Et issint 17 E. 4, [blank], si home vende 2 chivalles solvendum pur lun iij li. et pur lauter 6 li., ceux sont severall contractes. 17 E. 3, 52 <17 E. 3, 55>¹ et 17 Ass.: un home lessa c acres de terre et¹ 15 acres de bois, rendant xx s., scilicet x s. del terre et x s. del boys, per lassise trove fuit la disseisin in le bois, per que agard fuit que il recovera solement les x s., car cest severall reservation fesoit les rentes severall. Vies 29 E. 3, tit. Grantz, 101.

Harper semble que il fuit un joint leas et un joint reservation mes severall rentz, car il dit que 4 choses sont incidentz et necessarie a chescun leas, scilicet lessor, lesse, chose que gist en leas, et certaine commencement et certaine fine. Mes un reservation ne ferra joint leas severall. Mes il dit que auterment fuit in contractes, come le livre fuit in 17 E. 4, [blank], car la le price est del substauns del contracte, car la covient destre quid pro quo. Et il agre le case in 31 E. 3 devant mys.

Et Dier, chief justice, semble que il fuit forsque un demise et forsque un rent, car il dit que les parolx [sont] 'yelding and paieng for the mannour of Newelm etc.' et ne dit 'yelding and paieng out of the mannour of Newelm'. Et auxi il dit que le revercion fuit le principall et le rent forsque accessorie a ceo, et pur ceo entant que le revercion est joint et entier, le rent que est incident a ceo ne poet estre severall. Mes il agree le case in 31 E. 3, pur ceo que la nul revercion remaine in le feffour.

[170]

AC, fo. 226 (578).

<Reservation.>⁸

P. 5 Eliz. rott. 1029 in quare [impedit] per Beawpre envers levesque de Norwich le case fuit tiel ... Quere de leasses future sur que laccustomed rent fuit reserve. Similis casus Trin. 18 Eliz. inter Savage et Chester, rott. 1035, mes pur default de pledre le matter in ley ne veigne al judgment.

---

¹ *Written twice.*

⁷ *Prior of Holy Trinity, London* v. *Abbess of Stratford ['Stafford']* (1355) Trin. 29 Edw. III, Fitz. Abr., *Grauntes*, pl. 101, abridging YB Trin. 29 Edw. III, fo. 39.
⁸ This dictum is also noted below, p. 136, no. 245.
⁹ Perhaps Ewelme, Oxon.
¹⁰ CP 40/1211, m. 1029 (four rolls): Edmund Beaupé esq. v. Bishop of Norwich, Edward Leedes and Richard Bartonne, clerk; *quare impedit* for the advowson of Upwell, Norf.; demurrer to the rejoinder; c.a.v. to Trin. 1564; judgment for the plaintiff; writ of error received, 26 Jan. 1565. This case is also noted at the foot of *AC*, fo. 222v (572v), with the same roll reference.
¹¹ CP 40/1337 is unfit for production.

otherwise when the rent issues out of one same thing, for there, even if it is separately limited, it is still but one rent: as 5 Ass., pl. 6; 15 Ass., pl. 11; 7 Ass., pl. 1.[1] Someone granted a rent-charge out of his manor of Dale, 10s. to be taken by the hands of such and such a tenant of the manor, and 5s. by the hands of another, this is nevertheless but one entire rent and not several, for it issues out of one same thing. 5 Edw. IV, fo. 2.[2] 7 Edw. III.[3] 15 E. III, tit. *Execution*, 63.[4] A lease for years or for life, yielding in the first year a rose, the second year a penny etc. Likewise, 17 Edw. IV,[5] if a man sells two horses, £3 to be paid for one and £6 for the other, these are several contracts. 17 Edw. III, fo. 52, and 17 Ass.:[6] someone leased 100 acres of land and 15 acres of wood, yielding 20s., namely 10s. from the land and 10s. from the wood; the assize found a disseisin in the wood, and so it was awarded that he should recover only the 10s., for this several reservation made the rents several. See 29 Edw. III, tit. *Graunte*, 101.[7]

HARPER thought it was a joint lease and a joint reservation, but several rents; for he said that four things are incident and necessary to every lease, namely a lessor, a lessee, a thing which lies in lease, and a certain commencement and certain end.[8] A reservation cannot make a joint lease several. But he said that it was otherwise in contracts, as the book was in 17 Edw. IV, for there the price is of the substance of the contract, for there must be *quid pro quo*. And he agreed the case in 31 Edw. III, put before.

DYER C.J. thought that it was but one demise and one rent, for he said that the words were 'yielding and paying for the manor of Newelm[9]' and not 'yielding and paying out of the manor of Newelm'. Also, he said that the reversion was the principal thing and the rent only accessory thereto, and therefore, since the reversion is joint and entire, the rent which is incident thereto cannot be several. But he agreed the case in 31 Edw. III, because there no reversion remained in the feoffor.

170. SAVAGE v. CHESTER

Common Pleas, Trin. 1576.

Reservation.

Pas. 5 Eliz., roll 1029, in *quare impedit* by Beaupré against the bishop of Norwich, the case was as follows ....[10] Query concerning future leases upon which the accustomed rent was reserved. There was a similar case in Trinity term 18 Eliz. between Savage and Chester, roll 1035,[11] but because of a default in pleading the matter in law did not come to judgment.

---

[1] 5 Edw. III, Lib. Ass., pl. 6, continued in 7 Edw. III, Lib. Ass., pl. 1, and perhaps (similar facts) in 15 Edw. III, Lib. Ass., pl. 11.
[2] YB Pas. 5 Edw. IV, fo. 2, pl. 10.
[3] YB Hil. 9 Edw. III, fo. 9, pl. 20; abridged as Mich. 7 Edw. III, Fitz. Abr., *Assise*, pl. 132. This is a fuller report of the case in 7 Edw. III, Lib. Ass., pl. 1.
[4] Mich. 15 Edw. III, Fitz. Abr., *Execution*, pl. 63; Mich. 15 Edw. III (RS), p. 327, pl. 20.
[5] There is a discussion of horse sales in YB Pas. 17 Edw. IV, fo. 1, pl. 2, but not this point.
[6] YB Mich. 17 Edw. III, fo. 52, pl. 29 (RS, p. 149); 17 Edw. III, Lib. Ass., pl. 10.

[171]

AC, fo. 583v (Litt., fo. 106v).

T. 18 Eliz. Nota il fuit in mannour agre in Sir Thomas Wiatz case que si le done fist feffment in fe, le donour ne serra chase davower sur le feffe, car donques il covient de monstre le feffment et donques il confessera le revercion destre hors de luy, et per consequens il ne poet avower pur le rent que est incident al revercion. 10 E. 3, tit. Avowrie, 159: si le discontinue endowe la fem le tenant in taile el ne serra attendant a luy, car el nest chargeable al donour, mes le discontinue tient del segnior paramont, come la fuit agree, et la fem ne serra attendant a luy in respect del segnior paramount. <1 H. 7, 13. 9 H. 7, 26. 13 R. 2. M. 21 E. 4, 60, p. 10.>[a]

[172]

AC, fo. 228 (586).

<Releasses.>[s]

Mes nota fuit tenus P. 18 Eliz. per Wraye chiefe justice et Gawdy que si executors dona[1] omnia bona sua que les biens queux ilz avoient come executors passera. Issint si baron ad terme in droit sa fem et dona omnia bona sua que le terme que il ad in droit sa fem passera, et uncore il avoit ceo in droit sa fem. Et ceo fuit le principal case come jeo oyse.

[173]

AC, fo. 589 (magenta ink (Litt., fo. 108).

Et nota bene loppinion del Wray in le case de seniori puero fuit que si home <recover>[d] suffer recoverie al intent que les recoverors ferra estate a luy, icy in le mesne temps le recoverors serront seisies a lour opes demesne, mes silz ne font[2] ceo in convenient temps donques un use serra create in ley al feffour.

12 Eliz. per Brown si home fait feffment in fe sur condition de refeffer luy a tiel jour, ou sauns ascun jour limitte, et le feffour luy require et il refuse, ore le feffe estoiera seisie al opes le feffour, mes tanque request le feffee serra seisie a son opes car autrement ne puit faire lestate.

---

[1] *Sic, for* donont.   [2] *Reads* sont.

[5] Mich. 13 Ric. II, Fitz. Abr., *Avowrie*, pl. 89; identifiable as *Sengedon v. Lancastell* (1389) YB Mich. 13 Ric. II (Ames Fdn), p. 47, pl. 9.
[6] YB Mich. 21 Edw. IV, fo. 50, pl. 10. This is on fo. 60 of the earlier editions.
[7] See below, p. 130, no. 232, and the note there.
[8] See above, p. 40, no. 87, and the note there.
[9] *Sic*, but Browne J. died in 1567.

171. MULTON v. COVENEY[1]

Common Pleas, Trin. 1576.

Trinity term 18 Eliz. Note that it was in effect agreed in Sir Thomas Wyatt's case that if the donee makes a feoffment in fee, the donor shall not be driven to avow upon the feoffee, for then he would have to show the feoffment, and then he would confess the reversion to be out of him, and in consequence he could not avow for the rent which is incident to the reversion. 10 Edw. III, tit. *Avowrie*, 159:[2] if the discontinuee endows the wife of the tenant in tail, she shall not be attendant to him, for she is not chargeable to the donor, but the discontinuee holds of the lord paramount (as was there agreed) and the wife shall not be attendant to him in respect of the lord paramount. {1 Hen. VII, fo. 13;[3] 9 Hen. VII, fo. 26;[4] 13 Ric. II;[5] Mich. 21 Edw. IV, fo. 60, pl. 10.[6]}

172. BROADBRIDGE'S CASE[7].

King's Bench, Pas. 1576.

Releases.

Note that it was held in Easter term 18 Eliz. by WRAY C.J. and GAWDY that if executors give 'all their goods' (*omnia bona sua*), all the goods which they have as executors will pass. Likewise if a husband has a term in his wife's right and gives *omnia bona sua*, the term which he in his wife's right will pass, and yet he only had it in right of his wife: and that was the principal case, as I heard.

173. HUMPHRESTON'S CASE[8]

King's Bench, 1575.

Note well the opinion of WRAY [C.J.], in the case of *seniori puero*, that if someone suffers a recovery to the intent that the recoverors should make an estate to him, in this case in the meantime the recoverors shall be seised to their own use; but if they do not do it within a convenient time a use will be created in law to the feoffor.

In 12 Eliz., *per* Browne:[9] if someone makes a feoffment in fee upon condition to refeoff him by a certain day, or without any day appointed, and the feoffor requests him to do so and he refuses, the feoffee will now stand seised to the use of the feoffor; but until request the feoffee shall be seised to his use, for otherwise he could not make the estate.

---

[1] Above, p. 89, no. 147, and the note there.
[2] YB Pas. 10 Edw. III, fo. 26, pl. 52; Fitz. Abr., *Avowrie*, pl. 159.
[3] Probably YB Pas. 1 Hen. VII, fo. 17, pl. 3. This is on fo. 3v of the earlier editions of 1–8 Hen. VII, though the numeral is clearly written as 13.
[4] YB Pas. 9 Hen. VII, fos. 25–26, pl. 12.

[174]

AC, fo. 232 (594).

<Habendum.>ˢ

Nota per Dier que ascun foitz un habendum donera un estate ou rien fuit done devant [le] habendum, ascun foitz a un person que ne fuit nosme devant le habendum, et ascun foitz [le] habendum altera lestate in le premisses …

Nota quod H. 18 Eliz. fuit tenus per toutz les justices del banke le roy que si lesse pur ans soit de certain terre et il lessa et grant mesme le terre habendum tant des ans come serra a vener al temps de son mort, que cest graunt est tout ousterment voide. Mes ilz disoient que il fuit adjudge ore tarde que si lesse pur ans graunta tout son <terme>,¹ estate, droit, interest, demise ou leas que il ad in le terre habendum apres son decesse, que icy le habendum est tout ousterment voide pur ceo que per le premisses tout son droit in le terre fuit done et issint le habendum voide. Mes quant lesse pur ans demise, lesse ou graunta le terre, icy sauns pluis dire le graunte nad forsque un estate a volunt.

[175]

AC, fo. 232 (594).

<Habendum.>ˢ

Nota Anderson dit clerement, si home fait feffment in fe del mannour de Dale habendum a J. S. et a ses heires, est bon feffment non obstant que J. S. ne soit nosme in le premisses. Et issint econtra, si home done terres a J. S. et a ses heires sans ascun habendum.

[176]

AC, fo. 232v (594v).

<Habendum.>ˢ

M. 2 et 3 Ph. et Marie fuit tenus clerement si leas soit fait a 2, habendum a lun pur vie, remainder a lauter, que ceo est void et ils sont jointenantes, car le habendum ne poet toller de luy ceo que fuit done a luy devant. Issint si 2 acres sont dones a 2 homes habendum lun acre a lun et lauter acre a lauter, ceo est void, car per le premisses il ad un moitie en chescun acre, mes habendum lun moitie al un et lauter moitie al auter est bone, car il ad moitie en chescun acre etc. Mes nota M. 18 Eliz. loppinion del Segnior Dier et Manwood fuit clerement que in tiel cases le remainder fuit bone, car

174. ANON.

Common Pleas, undated; King's Bench, Hil. 1576.

Habendum.

Note, by DYER, that sometimes a *habendum* will give an estate where nothing was given before the *habendum*, sometimes to a person who was not named before the *habendum*, and sometimes the *habendum* will alter the estate in the premises …

Note that in Hilary term 18 Eliz. it was held by all the justices of the King's Bench that if there is a lessee for years of certain land, and he leases and grants the same land, *habendum* for as many years as shall be to come at the time of his death, this grant is utterly void. And they said that it was recently adjudged that if a lessee for years grants all his term, estate, right, interest, demise or lease that he has in the land, *habendum* after his decease, here the *habendum* is utterly void because by the premises all his right in the land was given, and therefore the *habendum* is void.[1] But when a lessee for years demises, leases or grants the land, without saying more, the grantee has an estate at will.

175. ANON.

Temp. Eliz., before 1582.

Habendum.

Note that *Anderson*[2] said clearly that if someone makes a feoffment in fee of the manor of Dale, *habendum* to John Style and his heirs, it is a good feoffment even though John Style is not named in the premises. Likewise, in reverse, if a man gives lands to John Style and his heirs without any *habendum*.

176. ANON.[3]

Common Pleas, Mich. 1576.

Habendum.

In Michaelmas term 2 & 3 Phil. & Mar. [1555] it was clearly held that if a lease is made to two, *habendum* to one of them for life, remainder to the other, this is void and they are joint tenants, for the *habendum* cannot take from him that which was given to him before. Likewise if two acres are given to two men, *habendum* one acre to one of them and the other acre to the other, this is void, for by the premises [each] has a moiety in each acre.[4] But *habendum* one moiety to one of them and the other moiety to the other is good, for [each] has a moiety in each acre. Note, however, that in Michaelmas term 18 Eliz. the opinion of the lord DYER and MANWOOD was clearly

---

[1] See *Anon.* (1572) above, p. 83, no. 134.
[2] Perhaps as a bencher of the Inner Temple.
[3] The judgment of Manwood J. is cit. in *C*, fo. 2 (vol. iii, p. 411) ('in mes notes tit. Habendum, 232b').
[4] *Throckmorton* v. *Tracy* (1555) Plowd. 145, at fo. 153.

Manwood dit quant leas est fait a 2, in le premisses ore est un jointenancie implie, et il [est] forsque un implication, car nest dit expressement conjunctim, et pur ceo le expres habendum controllera le implied premisses, et nest repugnant mes bene estoit ove le premisses. Et ilz citont le livre in 8 E. 3, 42. Et nota auxi le Segnior Dier dit que per le premisses il passa forsque estate a volunte, <quel>^d issint que le habendum enlarge ceo, et issint nest repugnant. <8 E. 3, 42, loppinion de Herle et Shard. econtra. Vide M. 28 et 29 in mes reportes 17. 20 Eliz. D. 361. Vide le case inter Dowce et Sutton in mes reportes.>^a

[177]

AC, fo. 595 (Litt. s. 113).

<Relesses.>^s

Nota que ore est provide per lestatut de 32 H. 8, cap. 3, que un recovery ewe vers le lessee pur vie per covin serra voide a eux in le[1] revercion ou remainder sinon que ilz assent[2] a le recoverie per matter de record. Et uncore fuit tenus in le case dun Copwood 13 Eliz. que la Copwood le pier fist feffment al use de luy pur son vie et puis al use [de] son droit heire male in taile et puis Copwood le pier suffer recoverie et adjudge que cest liera son heire male apres son mort car il nad riens[3] in esse son[4] temps mes possibilitie.

[178]

AC, fo. 598 (magenta ink) (Litt., fo. 114).

<Relesses.>^s

Nota fuit tenus in banco regis anno 19 Eliz. in action de scandalum magnatum port per le Segnior Crumwell que si home port action sur le case et suppose les parolx destre parle anno 17 Eliz. ou in veritie fueront parle anno 19 Eliz. le partie poet savement parler Non culpable, car il nad cause daction anno 17. Mes si les parolx fueront parles anno 17 il poet suppose que ilz fueront parles anno 19, car donques a mesme le temps il ad cause daction. Vide 19 H. 6, 47a, semble al contrarie, per Newton. Vide 5 E. 4, 5. Vide 21 E. 4, 66a.

---

[1] *Reads* les.   [2] *Reads* assents.   [3] *Appears to read* reins.   [4] *Unclear.*

[7] KB 27/1266, m. 28 (Trin. 1578): Henry, Lord 'Crumwell' v. Edmund Dennye, clerk; action on the statute 2 Ric. II, stat. 1, c. 5; the damages were laid as £1,000; demurrer to the plea in bar; c.a.v. to Mich. 1578; no judgment entered. Probably the case noted above, p. 27, no. 55. More fully reported at a later stage in vol. ii, p. 191 (where the words are set out); 4 Co. Rep. 12. Coke said this was the first case he moved in the King's Bench.
[8] The entry is in Trin. 20 Eliz., but the case was continued by imparlance from Pas. 19 Eliz.
[9] The words were alleged to have been spoken on 23 Dec. 1574 (17 Eliz.) in the parish of St Mary Woolnoth, London.
[10] YB Mich. 19 Hen. VI, fo. 47, pl. 101.   [11] YB Trin. 5 Edw. IV, fo. 5, pl. 18; above, p. 27, n. 3.
[12] Probably YB Mich. 21 Edw. IV, fo. 66, pl. 46.

that in such cases the remainder was good, for (as MANWOOD said) when a lease is made to two, there is now an implied joint tenancy in the premises; but it is only an implication, for it does not expressly say 'jointly' (*conjunctim*), and therefore the express *habendum* will control the implied premises; and it is not repugnant, but can well stand with the premises. And they cited the book in 8 Edw. III, fo. 42.[1] Note also that the lord DYER said that all that passed by the premises was an estate at will, and therefore the *habendum* enlarges it, and so it is not repugnant. {In 8 Edw. III, fo. 42, the opinion of Herle and Shardlow is to the contrary.[2] See Mich. 28 & 29 Eliz. in my reports, fo. 17.[3] 20 Eliz., Dyer 361.[4] See the case between Dowce and Sutton, in my reports.[5]}

177. COPWOOD'S CASE[6]

Common Pleas, 1571.

Releases.

Note that it is now provided by the statute of 32 Hen. VIII, c. [31], that a recovery had against the lessee for life by covin shall be void against those in the reversion or remainder unless they assent to the recovery by matter of record. And yet it was held in the case of one Copwood in 13 Eliz., where Copwood the father made a feoffment to the use of himself for his life and then to the use of his right heir male in tail, and then Copwood the father suffered a recovery, and it was adjudged that this will bind his heir male after his death, for he had nothing *in esse* at the time but only a possibility.

178. LORD CROMWELL v. DENNYE[7]

King's Bench, 1578.

Releases.

Note that it was held in the King's Bench in 19 Eliz.,[8] in an action of *scandalum magnatum* brought by the Lord Cromwell, that if someone brings an action on the case and alleges that the words were spoken in the year 17 Eliz.,[9] whereas in truth they were spoken in the year 19 Eliz., the party may safely plead Not Guilty, for he has no cause of action in the seventeenth year. But if the words were spoken in the seventeenth year he may allege that they were spoken in the nineteenth year, for then he has a cause of action at that time. See 19 Hen. VI, fo. 47,[10] *per* Newton, seemingly to the contrary. See 5 Edw. IV, fo. 5;[11] 21 Edw. IV, fo. 66.[12]

---

[1] *Sic*, and repeated thus below, but the case intended seems to be YB Mich. 8 Edw. III, fo. 59, pl. 16; cit. in Dyer 160.
[2] See the previous note.
[3] Presumably *Wynsmore* v. *Hulbert* (1586) vol. ii, p. 314, though it is on fo. 18v of *AD*.
[4] *Anon.* (1578) Dyer 361, §8.
[5] *Dowce* v. *Sutton* (1583) in *AB*, fo. 38v (330v); vol. ii, p. 244.
[6] See above, p. 58, no. 107 (14 Eliz.), and the note there.

[179]

AC, fo. 601v (Litt. s. 117v).

<Relesses.>^s

Il¹ ne poet releas toutz actions devant le jour incurre. Mes sil receive le rent devant le jour et acquite et discharge le lesse per son fait ceo dischargera le lesse de mesme le rent coment que lacquittauns soit fait devant le jour et le paiment auxi, per Harper, Munson et Manwood justices 14 Elyz. Mes quere sil fuit bon barre envers leire si cesti que fist ceo morust devant le jour.

[180]

AC, fo. 234v (602v).

<Estovers.>^s

24 Eliz. in le case perenter Clement Paston, esquier, et Drury fuit <tenus>^d <move pur un question>ⁱ per le Segnior Dier et curiam que si home ad common appendant a son mannour de D. que sil alien un part del mannour a que <si>ⁱ le common <nest>^d <soit>ⁱ extincte? <Et semble que non.>ⁱ Et uncore nota la que fuit common pur barbites non exceding le nomber de 600. Et jeo fuit accouncell in le case.

[181]

AC, fo. 235v (605v).

<Confirmation.>^s

Nota que il fuit un case adjudge in temps cesti roigne in le case dun Wilshire que le evesque de D., seisie dun mannour, lessa ceo pur terme dans et puis, devant ascun confirmation fait per le deane et chapter, levesque enfeffa un auter de mesne le mannour et le deane et chapter confirme ceo, et puis ils confirme lestate le lessee: et fuit adjudge que le lesse pur ans tiendra son terme per cest confirmation envers le feffee pur ceo que le confirmation confirme lestate come il est et ne alter ceo.

[182]

AC, fo. 614 (Litt., fo. 125).

Toutes les justices del common banke anno 15 Ely. agreont que per le feffment del

---

¹ *This refers to the lessor in Litt., s. 513:* si home lessa terre a un auter pur terme de un an, rendant a luy al feast de S. Mich prochein ensuant xl s. et puis devant mesme le feast il relessa al lessee touts actions, uncore apres mesme le feast il avera action de det pur non paiment de lez xl s. nient obstant le dit releas.

179. ANON.

Common Pleas, 1572.

Releases.

[The lessor] may not release all actions before the day arrives. But if he receives the rent before the day and acquits and discharges the lessee by his deed, this will discharge the lessee from the same rent even though the acquittance was made before the day, and the payment also: *per* HARPER, MOUNSON and MANWOOD JJ. in 14 Eliz. Query, however, whether it would be a good bar against the heir if the person who did it died before the day.

180. PASTON v. DRURY[1]

Common Pleas, 1582.

Estovers.

In 24 Eliz., in the case between Clement Paston, esquire, and Drury, this was moved as a question by the lord DYER and the court: if someone has common appendant to his manor of Dale, and he alienates a part of the manor, is the common extinguished? It seems not. Nevertheless, note that in that case it was a common for sheep not exceeding the number of 600. I was of counsel in the case.[2]

181. WILSHIRE'S CASE

Temp. Eliz.

Confirmation.

Note that there was a case adjudged in the time of this queen, being the case of one Wilshire: the bishop of D., seised of a manor, leased it for a term of years and then, before any confirmation made by the dean and chapter, the bishop enfeoffed another of the same manor, and the dean and chapter confirmed it, and then they confirmed the lessee's estate: and it was adjudged that the lessee for years should hold his term by virtue of this confirmation against the feoffee, because the confirmation confirms the estate as it is and does not alter it.

182. BRACEBRIDGE'S CASE[3]

Common Pleas, 1572/73.

All the justices of the Common Bench in the year 15 Eliz. agreed in the case of

---

[1] Reported in vol. ii, p. 190. The manor was that of Caister, Norf. In Aug. 1582 Coke married Bridget, the plaintiff's niece.
[2] Coke was of counsel with Drury: vol. ii, p. 190. But this does not mean that he argued the case in court. He had no right of audience in the Common Pleas.   [3] See above, p. 73, no. 117, and the note there.

mannour les services ne passeront devant attturnement, in le case de Brasbriche et Barwell …

Nota que en le case de Brasbriche anno 15 Ely. Dyer dit que ascun foitz un attornement avera relation. Come feffment soit fait dun mannour et les tenantes attorne 7 ans apres, ceo avera relation ab initio, car sil naveroit relation forsque al temps del attornement donques il ne poet passer per le livery del mannour et issint covient daver un fait. Issint attorneigne avera relation a faire ceo a passer hors del feffor ab initio, mes il navera relation a charger le tenant pur les arrerages mesnes ou pur wast devant attornement ou pur ascun chose que poet charger le tenant.

[183]

AC, fo. 239v (615v).

<Atturnement.>[1]

Nota que fuit tenus per Mounson et Dier in le case de Brasbriche anno 15 Elyz. que si home soit seisie del rent in fe et graunt ceo a un auter pur terme de vie, et apres graunt le revercion del rent in fe, in cest case suffiste que le graunte pur vie attorne et nemi le tenant del terre.

[184]

AC, fo. 619v (Litt., fo. 128v).

<Attornement.>[a]

Dier 15 Ely. in le case de Brasbrishe, note cest parol 'suffist' car il dit que lentent de Littleton ne fuit que covient que le tenant del franktenement attornera, car il dit si le lesse pur ans attorne ceo est assetz bon in cest cas.

[185]

AC, fo. 621v (magenta ink).

<Attornement.>[a]

Nota si home soit seisie dun mannour et il levie un fine de ceo al estrange et reprist estate a luy in fe arrere et le tenant paia le rent nient sachaunt de ceux fines ceo nest pas[2] attornement, car chescun attornement est un assent et home ne poet assent a cest chose dont <ne>[d] il ne sache riens. Et pur ceo jeo ay oye que ceo fuit adjudge in temps le roigne que ore est que home ad issue 2 fitz dun mesme nosme, scilicet John, et il morust <seisi dun mannour>[i] et puis leigne fitz enter in le dit mannour et puis

---

[1] *Heading on recto.*
[2] *Reads* past.

Bracebridge and Barewell that by a feoffment of the manor the services will not pass before atttornment …

Note that in Bracebridge's case, in the year 15 Eliz., DYER said that sometimes an attornment may have relation. For instance, a feoffment is made of a manor, and the tenants attorn seven years afterwards: this shall relate back *ab initio*, for if it were to relate only to the time of the attornment it could not pass by the livery of the manor and therefore it would be necessary to have a deed. Thus, attornment shall have relation to make it pass out of the feoffor *ab initio*; but it shall not relate back so as to charge the tenant for the intermediate arrears, or for waste committed before before attornment, or for anything which could charge the tenant.

183. BRACEBRIDGE'S CASE, continued

Common Pleas, Pas. 1573.

Attornment.

Note that it was held by MOUNSON and DYER in Bracebridge's case, in the year 15 Eliz., that if someone is seised of a rent in fee and grants it to another for term of life, and then grants the reversion of the rent in fee, in this case it suffices for the grantee for life to attorn and not the terre-tenant.

184. BRACEBRIDGE'S CASE, continued

Common Pleas, Pas. 1573.

Attornment.

Note this word 'suffist',[1] for DYER said in 15 Eliz. in Bracebridge's case that Littleton's meaning was not that the freehold tenant must attorn, for he said that it is perfectly good if the lessee for years attorns in this case.

185. ANON.

Temp. Eliz.

Attornment.

Note that if someone is seised of a manor and levies a fine thereof to a stranger and takes back an estate to himself in fee, and a tenant pays the rent not knowing of these fines, this is not an attornment; for every attornment is an assent, and one cannot assent to something of which he knows nothing. For this reason, as I have heard, this case was adjudged in the time of the present queen. Someone had issue two sons with the same name (John) and died seised of a manor; the elder son entered in the said

---

[1] In Litt., s. 571: '… lou le revercion est dependent sur lestate del franktenement, suffist qui le tenaunt del franktenement atturna sur tiel grant del reversion'. See further p. 106, below, n. 2.

ala ouster le mere, le puisne fitz enter in le mannour et teignoit les courtes in le nosme Johannis S. que fuit le nosme dambideux, et les tenantes del mannour attorne. Et puis leigne fitz revient et releas tout le droit al puisne fitz. Et tenus que riens des services passe per cest releas car les tenantes ne sache si cest court fuit tenus in le nosme del eigne ou del puisne. Car nota que si home abate in un mannour il covient daver attornement des tenantes. Vies 2 R. 2, tit. Attornement, 8.

[186]

AC, fo. 622 (Litt., fo. 130).

Segnior Dier 15 Eliz. en le case de Brasbriche dit que un es[...][1] del lesse countervailera un atturnement. Et il dit que 2 H. 5 diversite est parenter leas pur ans et leas pur vie, car si lessor dissese son lesse pur vie et fist feffment, coment [que] le lesse pur vie reentre uncore le livre dit que ceo nest pas atturnement et que le lesse navera action de wast.

[187]

AC, fo. 244 (626).

P.[2] 19 Eliz. un issue fuit joine in le common banke in quare impedit le quel le countes de Essex present <J. S.>[i] a un eglise ove le consent de Sir W. Walgrave. Et fuit done in evidence que le Roygne Marie in consideration de bon favor que le dit countes ad a luy fait avoit lesse mesme le mannour a que lavouson del eglise fuit appendant al dit Sir W. Walgrave pur ans sur trust et confidence etc. et le dit Sir W. Walgrave obtein le dit leas south le graund seale et deliver [le][3] patent a la dit countes et dit a luy que le dit <lease fuit>[d] que le dit countes ferra toutz choses et toutz actz sicome le dit leasse avoit estre fait a luy mesme. Et fuit teigne que cest assent fuit precedent et devant lavoidance est fait, et auxi lassent ne fuit que J. S. serra present, et uncore tenus per Mounson et Manwood que le generalitie del assent include chescun particularitie. Mes le Segnior Dier doubta de ceo.
    <F.N.B. 189. 8 H. 5, 1. 26 E. 3, 57, singuler pur plurell. 4 H. 6, 25, devant un auditor. 9 H. 6, 25, distinct propertie, per Paston. Lib. 4, 49, Ognels case, conjunctive.>[i]

---

[1] *Part of top line missing, probably four or five words.*
[2] *Apparently altered to* M.   [3] les.

---

[4] Seemingly altered to Michaelmas.
[5] Presumably Mary (née Blount), widow of Henry Bourchier, earl of Essex; she died in 1555.
[6] Of Bures and Sudbury, Suff.; knighted 1533; M.P. Suff. in 1545, sheriff of Norf. and Suff. 1550–51; died 1554: *Men of Court*, ii. 1608.
[7] YB Hil. 8 Hen. V, fo. 1, pl. 1 ('per primos juratores' includes a single juror from the first jury).
[8] YB Hil. 26 Edw. III (1567 ed.), fo. 56, pl. 10, at fo. 57 (fo. 3 of the vulgate edition).
[9] YB Trin. 4 Hen. VI, fo. 25, pl. 3 ('before auditors' does not include a single auditor).
[10] *Case of the Abbot of Fountains* (1431) YB Trin. 9 Hen. VI, fo. 25, pl. 21, *per* Paston J. (personal property belonging to an abbot and simultaneously to his house).
[11] *Ognel* v. *Underhill* (1587) 4 Co. Rep. 48 at fo. 50.

manor and then went abroad; the younger son entered in the manor and held the courts in the name of John S., which was the name of them both, and the tenants of the manor attorned. Then the elder son returned and released all the right to the younger son. And it was held that nothing of the services passed by this release, for the tenants did not know whether the court was held in the name of the elder or the younger. Note that if someone abates in a manor it is necessary to have an attornment of the tenants. See 2 Ric. II, tit. Attournement, 8.[1]

186. BRACEBRIDGE'S CASE, continued

Common Pleas, Pas. 1573.

The lord DYER said in 15 Eliz., in Bracebridge's case, that [entry by][2] the lessee is equivalent to an attornment. And he said that in 2 Hen. V[3] a distinction is drawn between a lease for years and a lease for life, for if the lessor disseises his lessee for life and makes a feoffment, and the lessee for life re-enters, the book nevertheless says that this is not an attornment and that the lessee shall not have an action of waste.

187. COUNTESS OF ESSEX'S CASE

Common Pleas, Pas. or Mich. 1577.

In Easter[4] term 19 Eliz. an issue was joined in the Common Bench in *quare impedit*, whether the countess of Essex[5] had presented John Style to a church with the consent of Sir William Waldegrave;[6] and it was given in evidence that Queen Mary, in consideration of the good favour which the said countess had done her, had leased the same manor to which the advowson of the church was appendant to the said Sir William Waldegrave for years, upon trust and confidence [for the countess], and the said Sir William Waldegrave obtained the said lease under the great seal, and delivered the patent to the said countess, and said to her that the said countess should do all things and perform all acts as if the said lease had been made to herself. Although this assent was precedent and before the avoidance occurred, and also the assent was not that John Style should be presented, nevertheless it was held by MOUNSON and MANWOOD that the generality of the assent included every particularity. But the lord DYER doubted this.

{Fitz. N.B. 189. 8 Hen. V, fo. 1;[7] 26 Edw. III, fo. 57:[8] singular for plural. 4 Hen. VI, fo. 25:[9] before one auditor. 9 Hen. VI, fo. 25:[10] as to distinct property, *per* Paston. Lib. 4, 49, Ognel's case: conjunctive.[11]}

---

[1] Trin. 2 Ric. II, Fitz. Abr., *Attournement*, pl. 8.
[2] Conjectural: word or words lost. Cf. Co. Litt. 316b–317: 'Note that Littleton saith not here that the tenant of the franktenement ought in this case to attorn, but that it sufficeth that he doth attorn. And I heard Sir James Dyer, chief justice of the Common Pleas, hold that in this case if the tenant for years did attorn it would vest the reversion, for seeing the estate for years is able to support the estate for life, he shall bind him in the remainder by his attornment in respect of his estate and privity. Pasch. 15 Eliz. in Brasbritches case in Communi Banco.' The discussion of attornment in this case above, p. 73, no. 117, does not touch on the present point.   [3] YB Pas. 2 Hen. V, fo. 4, pl. 19; Hil. 5 Hen. V, fo. 12, pl. 30.

[188]

AC, fo. 246 (630).

<Hariot.>[5]

H. 20 Eliz. fuist tenus que le segnior ne poet seisier hariot service sans prescription, nient pluis que si le tenure soit per chival service il ne poet seisier.

Nota que fuit agre per toutz les justices in Woodlans case envers Mantell et resolve que le segnior poet cy bien seisier heriot service come distrener pur ceo. <Fleta, lib. 2, cap. 50.>[6] Mes la est admitte que pur heriot custome home ne poet distrener mes solement seisier.

[189]

AC, fo. 631v (magenta ink) (Litt., fo. 134v).

Si leas soit fait de parcel del mannour pur vie ou pur ans en droit le revercion est parcell del mannour: et ceo fuit agre per toutz les justices del common banke 15 Ely. in le case de Brasbriche.[7]

[190]

AC, fo. 247v (632v).

<Discontinuauns.>[5]

Nota que un chose que est in consideration del ley ne poet estre discontinue. Come le fe simple dun eglise est in abeiauns et pur ceo si un parson face feffment in fe ceo nest discontinuauns pur ceo que <nest>[d] est in abeiauns. Et issint et pur cest cause tient Mounson, justice, anno 17 Elyz. in le case Sir Thomas Pawlet. Et auxi le case in Brook fuit cite, tit. Feffmentes al uses, 50, 30 H. 8,[8] que un use in esse poet estre discontinue per feffment fait sur consideration ou sauns consideration a eux que nont notice del primer use. Mes un use que est in abeiauns ne poet estre discontinue. Come si home covenant que quant B infeffe luy de 3 acres que il et toutz auters seisies de son mannour de Dale serra seisies al use B et ses heires, et puis il fait feffment de ceux terres a un que ad notice del primer use, et puis B infeffe luy de les ditz 3 acres, ore les feffees serra seisies al use B. Auterment dun use in possession. Mes nota que in mesme le terme Plowden in largument del case de seniori puero dit que si parson

---

[4] See above, p. 73, no. 117, and the note there.
[5] Conjectural: see below, p. 115, no. 209, and the note there.
[6] Cf. *Humphreston's Case* (1575), above, p. 40, no. 87.
[7] I.e. *Brent's Case*: see below, p. 115, no. 207.
[8] 30 Hen. VIII, Bro. Abr., *Feffements al uses*, pl. 50.

188. ANON.[1]

Hil. 1578.

Heriot.

In Hilary term 20 Eliz. it was held that the lord may not seize heriot-service without prescription,[2] any more than where the tenure is by knight-service (when he may not seize it).

Note that it was agreed by all the justices and resolved, in Woodland's case against Mantell,[3] that the lord may seize heriot-service as well as distrain for it. {Fleta, lib. 2, c. 50.} But it is admitted there that for heriot-custom one may not distrain, but only seize.

189. BRACEBRIDGE'S CASE[4]

Common Pleas, 1573.

If a lease is made of parcel of a manor for life, or for years, in right the reversion is parcel of the manor: and this was agreed by all the justices of the Common Bench in 15 Eliz., in Bracebridge's case.

190. BRENT'S CASE[5]

Common Pleas, 1575.

Discontinuance.

Note that something which is in consideration of the law cannot be discontinued.[6] For example, the fee simple of a church is [always] in abeyance, and therefore if a parson makes a feoffment in fee it is not a discontinuance, because it is in abeyance. So held MOUNSON J., and for this reason, in the year 17 Eliz. in the case of Sir Thomas Pawlet.[7] The case in Brooke was also cited, tit. *Feffements al uses*, 50,[8] 30 Hen. VIII, that a use *in esse* may be discontinued by a feoffment made upon consideration (or without consideration) to persons who have no notice of the first use. But a use which is in abeyance cannot be discontinued. Thus if someone covenants that when B enfeoffs him of three acres he and all others who are seised of his manor of Dale shall be seised to the use of B and his heirs, and then he makes a feoffment of these lands to someone who has notice of the first use, and then B enfeoffs him of the said three acres, now the feoffees shall be seised to the use of B. It is otherwise of a use in possession. But note that, in the same term, *Plowden* said in arguing the case of *seniori*

---

[1] Perhaps the anonymous case reported in BL MS. Harg. 6, fo. 68 (dated 18 Eliz.). See also vol. ii, p. 231.
[2] I.e. a custom.
[3] Plowd. 94. The record is KB 27/1161, m. 38: Richard Woodland v. Walter Mantell gent. and William Redsole; replevin on a taking at Horton, Kent; issue on the custom; verdict at bar for the plaintiff, Trin. 1553; c.a.v. to Mich. 1553; judgment for the plaintiff, with 16d. damages and £6. 8s. 8d. costs; reported in Plowd. 94. Cf., to the same effect, *Peter v. Knoll* (1584) Cro. Eliz. 32.

per consent del patron et ordinarie fait leas pur vie et morust, et in temps del vacation le lesse fist feffment in fe, et puis un auter parson est inducte, ore il poet enter pur le forfeiture, quel prove que le fe simple fuit done per le feffment car auterment ne serroit un forfeiture. Et sur mesme le reason fuit le case de seniori puero adjudge quant a cest purpose.

Et nota le case de Sir Thomas Wiate que chose in abeiaunce ne poet estre forfeit. Et nota le case de Copwood que tenancie in abeiauns ne puit estre barre.

[191]

AC, fo. 634v (Litt., fo. 139v).

Nota [que][1] 16 Eliz. fuit dit per aliquos in leschequer que si tenant in taile soit dun mannour, parte de quel est in leas pur ans, et puis tenant in taile fist feffment del mannour et fist liverie in auters terres que fuit in leas, et le lesse attorne, que ceo nest discontinuans del terre que est in leas car ceo ne passa my per le livery eins per le attornement del lessee, car si soit sauns fait ceo est voide. Vide 23 Ass., p. 8.

[192]

AC, fo. 248 (635).

<Discontinuauns.>[s]

Nota per le Segnior Dier in Bluntes case que si home bargaine et vende per fait indent le mannour de D. et lavouson appendant, coment que le fait ne soit unques enrolle uncore lavouson passera.

[193]

AC, fo. 248v (635v).

<Discontinuauns.>[2]

Nota per le Segnior Dier clerement H. 19 Eliz. que si tenant in taile fait leasse pur vie solonque lestatut de 32 H. 8 que ceo nest discontinuaunce del revercion car un acte de parliament ne voet faire tort a ascun home. Come lestatut de 1 R. 3 dit que toutz feffmentes etc. fait per cesti que use etc., uncore si cesti que use in taile fait feffment ceo nest discontinuaunce del use mes forsque graunt pur terme de son vie et lestate determine maintenaunt per son mort. 27 H. 8, 20. Vies 30 H. 8, tit. Feffmentes al use, 48.

---

[1] p[er], *possibly a slip for* P.   [2] *Heading on recto.*

[5] See above, p. 52, no. 101.   [6] Cf. Co. Litt. 333.
[7] 32 Hen. VIII, c. 28.   [8] 1 Ric. III, c. 1.
[9] YB Trin. 27 Hen. VIII, fo. 20, pl. 9.   [10] 30 Hen. VIII, Bro. Abr., *Feffements al uses*, pl. 48.

puero[1] that if a parson, by consent of the patron and ordinary, makes a lease for life and dies, and in time of vacancy the lessee makes a feoffment in fee, and then another parson is inducted, he may now enter for the forfeiture: and this proves that the fee simple was given by the feoffment, for otherwise it would not be a forfeiture. And upon the same reasoning was the case of *seniori puero* adjudged, as to this purpose.

Note Sir Thomas Wyatt's case,[2] that a thing in abeyance cannot be forfeited. And note Copwood's case,[3] that a tenancy in abeyance cannot be barred.

191. ANON.

Exchequer, 1574.

Note that in 16 Eliz. it was said by some in the Exchequer that if there is a tenant in tail of a manor, part of which is in lease for years, and then the tenant in tail makes a feoffment of the manor, and makes livery in lands other than those which are in lease, and the lessee attorns, this is not a discontinuance of the land which is in lease, for it does not pass by the livery but by the attornment of the lessee; for if it is without deed it is void. See 23 Ass., pl. 8.[4]

192. ANDROWES v. BLUNT[5]

Common Pleas, 1573.

Discontinuance.

Note by the lord DYER, in Blunt's case, that if someone bargains and sells by deed indented the manor of Dale, and the advowson appendant, even though the deed is never enrolled, the advowson will nevertheless pass.

193. ANON.[6]

Common Pleas, Hil. 1577.

Discontinuance.

Note by the lord DYER, clearly, in Hilary term 19 Eliz. that if tenant in tail makes a lease for life in accordance with the statute of 32 Hen. VIII,[7] this is not a discontinuance of the reversion, for an act of Parliament will not do wrong to anyone. Thus the statute of 1 Ric. III[8] says 'all feoffments ... made by cestui que use ...', and yet, if cestui que use in tail makes a feoffment it is not a discontinuance of the use but only a grant for term of his life, and the estate ends immediately on his death. 27 Hen. VIII, fo. 20.[9] See 30 Hen. VIII, tit. *Feffements al uses*, 48.[10]

---

[1] *Humphreston's Case* (1575) above, p. 40, no. 87.
[2] *Multon v. Coveney* (1576) above, p. 89, no. 147.
[3] *Copwood's Case* (1572) above, p. 58, no. 107.
[4] *Sic*, but probably 23 Edw. III, Lib. Ass., pl. 18.

[194]

AC, fo. 250v (639v).

<Surrender.>[s] <Crewtes case in Devonshire sur un postea, M. 18 Eliz. rott. cccvj°.>[a] <Dier 19 Eliz. 358.>[1]

P. 19 Eliz. fuit tenus per Dier, Manwood et Mounson in le common banke que lou pier et fitz fueront et <puis>[d] le pier fist feffment in fe al use de luy mesme pur terme de son vie et puis al use [de] son fitz in fe, et puis al entent que le pier serr[oit] able a faire leas pur lxxx ans le pier et fitz veignont sur le terre et la le fitz infeffe le pier per parol et le pier accept le livery, et ceo est surrender de son estate.

Et la Mounson dit, si lessour et lesse pur vie joine in feffment in fe per parol ceo serra le feffment le lessour et le surrender del lesse. Auterment sil soit per fait, quar la le Segnior Dier dit expressement que home puit surrender in un forrein counte mes le franktenement ne serra in luy tanque il entre. Et il dit que Fitz. fuit del opinion que si lesse pur ans agree que son lessour ferra livery, ceo nest surrender de son leasse, mes si lesse pur vie agrea que le lessour ferra [liver]y ceo est voide, come les 3 justices teignont, car la [… a diss…][2] le tenant pur vie etc. Inter Lancastell [et] Aller.

[195]

AC, fo. 251 (640).

Nota per le Segnior Dier in largument de Brents case que si home fait leas pur vie et puis fait chartre de feffment et fait lettre dattorney de faire liverie et lattorney fait liverie et disseise le lesse pur vie in cest case le lessor mesme est un disseisor et le fe simple passera de luy pur ceo que il ad colour per reason del revercion. Auterment semble sil nad ascun colour.

[196]

AC, fo. 253v (642v).

<Assuraunces.>[s]

Nota per Wray, chiefe justice, in bank le roy P. 18 Eliz. que si <hom>[d] fem fait leas pur ans et puis intermarie ove le lesse le terme est ale. Mes le case la fuit que son estate fuit fait <pur vie>[i] al baron et fem et a les heires le baron, le baron fist leas pur xxj ans et morust, le fem enter et ouste le lesse, et puis le lesse entermarie ove le fem, et puis le fem morust. In cest case il dit que le terme remaine pur ceo que <le>[i] lesse

---

[1] *Margin.*
[2] *Words lost in last line.*

194. LANCASTELL v. ALLER[1]

Common Pleas, Pas. 1577.

Surrender. Crewte's case in Devonshire upon a *postea*, Mich. 18 Eliz., roll 206.[2] Dyer, 19 Eliz. 358.

In Easter term 19 Eliz. it was held by DYER, MANWOOD and MOUNSON in the Common Bench that where there are a father and son, and the father makes a feoffment in fee to the use of himself for term of his life, and then to the use of his son in fee, and afterwards (to the intent that the father should be able to make a lease for eighty years) the father and son come onto the land, and the son enfeoffs the father there, by parol, and the father accepts the livery, this is a surrender of his estate.

And MOUNSON there said that if a lessor and lessee for life join in a feoffment in fee by parol, this will be a feoffment by the lessor and a surrender by the lessee. It is otherwise if it is by deed, for the lord DYER there said expressly that a man may surrender in a different county, though the freehold will not be in him until he enters. And he said that Fitzherbert was of the opinion that if a lessee for years agrees that his lessor may make a livery, this not a surrender of his lease, whereas if a lessee for life agrees that the lessor may make a livery, it is void, as the three justices there held, for there [it would be a disseisin of][3] the tenant for life. Between Lancastell and Aller.

195. BRENT'S CASE[4]

Common Pleas, 1575

Note by the lord DYER, in the argument of Brent's case, that if someone makes a lease for life, and then makes a charter of feoffment and a letter of attorney to make livery, and the attorney makes livery and disseises the lessee for life: in this case the lessor himself is a disseisor and the fee simple will pass from him, because he has colour by reason of the reversion. It seems it would be otherwise if he had no colour.

196. ANON.

King's Bench, Pas. 1576.

Assurances.

Note by WRAY C.J. in the King's Bench, in Easter term 18 Eliz., that if a woman makes a lease for years and then marries the lessee, the term is gone. But the case there was that her estate was made for life to the husband and wife, and to the heirs of the husband; the husband made a lease for twenty-one years and died; the woman entered and ousted the lessee; then the lessee married the woman; and then the woman died. In this case, he said that the term remained, because the lessee had but a

---

[1] Above, p. 84, no. 135. [2] Incorrect reference.
[3] Conjectural.
[4] Conjectural: see below, p. 115, no. 209, and the note there.

navoit que un possibilitie, que ne poet estre surrender per le lessee: quod nota. Et nota Sir Fraunces Fleminges case circa anno 16 Eliz. Regine.

[197]

AC, fo. 644 (magenta ink) (Litt., fo. 142).

Nota per le common ley un <revercion poet>^d estate taile puit estre discontinue et uncore le revercion ne serra discontinue. Come Wraye, chief justice, mist le case arguendo in Haddons case anno 18 Eliz.: si tenant in taile, le remainder[1] al droit heires J. D., et tenant in taile fait feffment in fe et puis J. D. morust, et puis tenant in taile morust, ore le droit heire J. D. entra, car remainder[2] in abeiauns ne poet estre barre ne discontinue. Et pur ceo nota le case de seniori puero et Copwodes case.

[198]

AC, fo. 263v (656v).

<Election.>[s]

Bullockes case 15 et 16 Eliz. Evesque de Sarum seisie <de[l] mannour>[3] de S. in que fuit un meason, 3 boves de terre et 1000 acres de boys appel Levewoode, temps E. 2 infeffe un R. Bullocke <enfeffe le>^d per fait del dit meason, les dits 3 boves de terre, et de 17 acres de boys destre eslieu per le dit Bullock et ses heires, et liverie fuit fait in le dit meason in le nosme de toutz. Bullocke devant election morust, et si son heire puit faire election ou nemi, ceo fuit le question.

Et la Weston dit que in multz cases quant le chose est incertain ceo serra al election del grante. Come si jeo lessa le mannour de D. ou le mannour de S. Mesme la ley de graunt un des mes chivalles in mon stable. Et in ceux cases il dit que le propertie de chose ou le franktenement de ceo nest pas in le grantee devant election. Mesme la ley si je releasse a vous tout mon droit in le mannour de D. ou in le mannour de S. Issint icy nest ascun estate de inheritauns vestue in Bullocke devant son election. Et il dit, ou le chose est incertaine come in les cases devant myses le grantee in son vie covient a faire le election, car riens discend a son heire ou va a ces executores dont

---

[1] rem'.   [2] rem', *possibly* rev[ercion].   [3] *Written twice*.

John Inglefyld, esquire; demurrer to the replication, which also sets out the attainder of the duke of Somerset; c.a.v. to Pas. 1570; no judgment entered. Cit. in Co. Uses, fo. 153v ('Bullockes case'). Differently reported in Dyer 281; 1 And. 12; Benl. 148; Moo. 81, cit. record; BL MS. Harley 443, fos. 36v–38 (Pas. 1565), 91v–92 (Hil. 1565); MS. Harg. 15, fos. 20–21v; MS. Harg. 37, fos. 67–68v (Mich. 1568); MS. Harg. 373, fos. 98–101 (12 Eliz.); MS. Lansd. 1095, fos. 106–107v, cit. record; MS. Add. 35953, fos. 6–7 (12 Eliz.); LI MS. Misc. 361, fos. 25–27, cit. record; HLS MS. 200.1 (1180.1), fos. 63v–64.

[6] Coke's date must be wrong, since Weston J. died on 6 July 1572. Dyer says judgment was given in Pas. 1570. Croke copied a report of the case dated Pas. 1570 (*V*, fo. 38); and the report in BL MS. Harg. 373, fos. 98–101v, is dated 12 Eliz. Perhaps Coke heard it cited in Mich. 1573.

[7] In Berks.: record. Cf. BL MS. Lansd. 21(71, 73).

[8] 'Beare Wood' in Hurst, Berks.: record. The Victorian mansion called Bearwood House is now a school.

possibility, which cannot be surrendered by the lessee: note that. And note Sir Francis Fleming's case, around the year 16 Eliz.[1]

197. HADDON'S CASE[2]

King's Bench, 1576.

Note that by the common law an estate tail could be discontinued and yet the reversion would not be discontinued. WRAY C.J. put this case while arguing in Haddon's case in 18 Eliz.: if there is a tenant in tail, the remainder to the right heirs of John Dale, and the tenant in tail makes a feoffment in fee, and then John Dale dies, and then the tenant in tail dies, the right heir of John Dale shall now enter, for the remainder in abeyance cannot be barred or discontinued. For this, note also the case of *seniori puero*,[3] and Copwood's case.[4]

198. BULLOCK v. BURDETT (*c.* 1570)[5]

Common Pleas, dated Mich. 1573 but probably 1565/70.[6]

Election.

Bullock's case, 15 & 16 Eliz. The bishop of Salisbury, seised of the manor of Sonning,[7] in which there were a house, three bovates of land and 1,000 acres of wood called Bearwood,[8] in the time of Edward II enfeoffed one Richard Bullock by deed of the said house, the said three bovates of land, and 17 acres of wood to be chosen by the said Bullock and his heirs, and livery was made in the said house in the name of everything. Bullock died before making election, and the question was whether his heir could make election, or not.

WESTON there said that in many cases when a thing granted is uncertain it shall be at the election of the grantee. For instance, if I lease 'the manor of Dale or the manor of Sale'. The law is the same of a grant of one of my horses in my stable. In these cases (he said) the property of the thing, or the freehold thereof, is not in the grantee before election. The law is the same if I release to you all my right in 'the manor of Dale or in the manor of Sale'. Thus here, there is no estate of inheritance vested in Bullock before his election. And he said that where the thing is uncertain, as in the cases put above, the grantee must make the election in his lifetime, for nothing descends to his heir (or goes to his executors) in respect of which he may make an election. And he said that if

---

[1] *Turner* [d. *Fleming*] v. *Gray* (1574) Co. Litt. 338b, cit. Mich. 16 & 17 Eliz., roll 945 (incorrect); cit. in *C*, fo. 577v (Pas. 1603), with the same roll number; Dyer's notebook, 109 Selden Soc. 38, and the numerous MS. reports cited ibid., n. 6. This concerned St Katherine's hospital, London, of which Fleming (through whom the plaintiff claimed) had been master.
[2] See below, p. 118, no. 212, and the note there.
[3] *Humphreston's Case* (1575) above, p. 40, no. 87.
[4] *Copwood* v. *Clarke* (1572) above, p. 58, no. 107.
[5] CP 40/1231, m. 1008 (Pas. 1565; four rolls): Richard Bullocke v. Humphrey Burdett and William Irysshe; replevin for billets taken in Bearwood in the parish of Hurst; avowry and acknowledgment as servant of

il puit faire election. Et il dit, si un soit seisie del terre de parte son pier et de auter terre de parte sa mere, et fist feffment de tout sa terre de parte son pier ou de parte sa mere, et fist livery in terre de part sa mere, ore le feffe ne poet faire election daver le terre de parte le pier, et si lettre dattorney soit fait a faire livery secundum formam carte il poet faire livery in quel terre il voet. Si home face leasse de 40 acres et puis il graunt le revercion de x acres, le tenant poet attorner pur quel de eux il voille, et si in mesme le case le lessour levie fine de les x acres le conuse esliera quel 10 acres il voille. Et il dit que un livery ne poet passer chose in abeiaunce, et le franktenement covient destre in ascun person certain al temps del livery. Et auxi il dit que si leire esliera que il serra eins per purchase, car ceo ne unques fuit in le pier. Et il dit que si lannuitie soit graunt al pier et ses heires, le fitz ne poet faire ceo annuitie car donques la fem perdra dower.

Mes Dier ceo negavit et dit clerement que leire poet aver brefe de annuitie. Dier argue a mesme lentent, et il dit que lou chose uncertain est graunt pur vie ou auterment si mesme le chose gist in prender il est toutz foitz in election del grantee a prender quel de eux il voille, mes si le chose gist in render donques est in election del grantor a paier que de eux il voille. Et il dit que si un annuitie de x s. ou un robe soit graunt annuelment al feaste de Easter pur vie le grante, coment que le jour soit passe le grantee ne poet demaunde que de eux il voille mes covient demander lun ou lauter pur ceo que le chose eyt continuans. Mes si le graunt soit a paier x s. ou un robe a tiel jour, que nest que un payment, la apres le jour le grante poet demander quel de eux il voille. Et si home fait leasse pur vie, rendant annuelment al feste de M. un paire de spurres ou xij d., in avowre il covient avower pur lun ou lauter. Et il dit, si home enfeffe un auter de 2 acres, lun in fe et de lauter in taile, et le feffee fait feffment in fe de ambideux, son issue poet eslier quel de eux il portera son formedon. <Dier, 354.>ⁱ Et il dit que Bullocke nad riens devant election, et pur ceo riens poet discender al heir. <Dier, 354.>ⁱ Et auxi agre que un livery covient a doner estate presentment ou nunquam. Et auxi franktenement ne poet estre in abeiauns forsque in le case le parson. Et fuit agre in cest case que Bullocke ne puit estre tenant in common ove le feffour pur ceo que il ad certain nomber des acres et il ne poet occupie tout le boys in common ove le feffour come chescun tenant in common que tient pro indiviso serra. 29 Ass., p. 55, corodie grant apprender de septimana in septimana, ou de 15 jours in 15 jours, est in election del grantee.

[199]

AC, fo. 264v (657v).

<Election.>^s

Nota que fuit agre in Bullockes case in temps le roygne que ore est que quant ascun chose passa al bargainee la le election discendera al heire. Come si home face

someone is seised of land from his father's side, and of other land from his mother's side, and makes a feoffment of 'all his land from his father's side or his mother's side', and makes livery in land from his mother's side, the feoffee cannot now make election to have the land from the father's side; but if a letter of attorney is made to make livery according to the form of the charter (*secundum formam cartae*), [the attorney] may make livery in which land he wishes. If a man makes a lease of 40 acres, and then grants the reversion of 10 acres, the tenant may attorn for which of them he will; and if in the same case the lessor levies a fine of the 10 acres, the cognisee may choose which 10 acres he will. And he said that a livery cannot pass something in abeyance, and the freehold must be in some certain person at the time of the livery. He also said that if the heir made election, he would be in by purchase, for it was never in the father. And he said that if an annuity is granted to the father and his heirs, the son cannot have this annuity, for then the wife would lose dower.

But DYER denied this, and said clearly that the heir may have a writ of annuity. DYER argued to the same purpose [as Weston], and said that where an uncertain thing is granted for life or otherwise, if the same thing lies in prender (taking) it is always in the election of the grantee to take which of the choices he will, but if the thing lies in render then it is in the election of the grantor to pay which of them he will. And he said that if an annuity of 10s. or a robe annually at the feast of Easter is granted for the life of the grantee, once the day is past the grantee cannot demand whichever of them he will but must demand the one or the other because the thing has continuance. But if the grant is to pay 10s. or a robe at a certain day, which is but one payment, there after the day the grantee may demand which of them he will. If someone makes a lease for life, rendering annually at the feast of Michaelmas a pair of spurs or 12d., in an avowry he must avow for one or the other. And he said that if someone enfeoffs another of two acres, one of them in fee and the other in tail, and the feoffee makes a feoffment in fee of both, his issue may elect for which of them he shall bring his formedon. {Dyer 354.[1]} And he said that Bullock had nothing before election, and therefore nothing could descend to the heir. {Dyer 354.} He also agreed that a livery must give an estate presently, or never, and also that a freehold cannot be in abeyance except in the case of the parson. And it was agreed in this case that Bullock could not be a tenant in common with the feoffor, because he had a certain number of acres, and he cannot occupy the whole wood in common with the feoffor, as does every tenant in common who holds *pro indiviso*. 29 Ass., pl. 55:[2] a corrody granted to be taken from week to week, or from fortnight to fortnight, is in the election of the grantee.

199. BULLOCK v. BURDETT, continued

Common Pleas, dated Mich. 1573 in pl. 162, but probably 1565/70.

Election.

Note that it was agreed in Bullock's case, in the time of the present queen, that when anything passes to the bargainee the election will descend to the heir. For instance if a

---

[1] *Anon.* (1576) Dyer 354, pl. 33.   [2] *Gold* v. *Abbot of Abingdon* (1355) 29 Edw. III, Lib. Ass., pl. 55.

feffment de 2 acres, habendum lun pur vie et lauter in fe, la pur ceo que le terre passa le election discendera. Mes lou riens passe forsque nude election, sicome jeo bargaine a vous <mes mannours>[d] xx acres de boys a prender ou vous pleast, ceo ne discendera pur ceo que il est un nude election et riens passa.

[200]

AC, fo. 264v (657v).

<Election.>[s]

Nota fuit adjudge circa annum 14 Eliz. in bank le roy, si home face leas pur vie et puis fait leas pur ans a commencer apres le mort, surrender ou forfeiture del leas pur vie, que in cest case le lesse nad election a aver le terme a commencer a quel de temps luy pleyt, mes quel de eux primes happa donques ceo enjoiera. <Et issint fuit loppinion del Segnior Dier clerement 18 Eliz.>[a]

[201]

AC, fo. 659 (Litt., fo. 145).

Nota il fuit <adjudge>[d] <tenus>[i] in temps le roygne que ore est que si un parson apres institution et devant induction graunt un annuitie et le patron et ordinarie ceo confirme, ceo est voide. Vies 11 H. 4, [*blank*], que un confirmation devant induction est voide. 45 E. 3, tit. Eschange, 10, si 2 persons permute lour benefices et eux resigne in les mayns lordinarie a mesme lentent, et lun deux est admitted, instituted et inducted et lauter nest forsque admitted et instituted et devie devant induction, auter person ne resceivera le benefice in quel il fuit induct car lexchange nest perfitted pur ceo que il ne fuit executed. Vies 22 H. 6, 26.

Et nota un auter case fuit anno 18 Eliz. move in le common banke que parson devant induction et apres institution fist leas pur ans et ceo fuit conferme per le patron et ordinarie, et uncore fuit tenus la que […][1] avoidera cest leas pur ceo que il nest parson devant induction car […] que le parson ne poet estre charge a annuitie devant induction […]

[202]

AC, fo. 664v (magenta ink) (Litt., fo. 149v).

Nota fuit tenus P. 19 Eliz. que si baron et fem sont vouche et ilz vouche ouster, ceo liera le fem.

---

[1] *Words lost in lower corner.*

[4] Mich. 45 Edw. III, Fitz. Abr., *Exchaunge*, pl. 10.
[5] *Sir John Dynham's Case* (1443) YB Mich. 22 Hen. VI, fo. 25, pl. 46, at fo. 26.
[6] Reported in JRL MS Fr. 118, fo. 47. Cf. *Gyles* v. *Colshill* (1576) above, p. 63, no. 113; *Hare* v. *Byckley* (1578) above, p. 59, no. 108.

man makes a feoffment of two acres, *habendum* one of them for life and the other in fee, there, because the land passes, the election will descend. But where nothing passes except a bare election, as where I bargain to you 20 acres of wood to be taken where you please, this will not descend because it is a bare election and nothing passes.

200. ANON.[1]

King's Bench, *c.* 1572; Common Pleas, 1576.

Election.

Note that it was adjudged around the year 14 Eliz. in the King's Bench that if someone makes a lease for life, and then makes a lease for years to commence after the death, or the surrender or forfeiture of the lease for life, in this case the lessee does not have an election to have the term commence at which of the times he pleases, but he shall enjoy whichever happens first. {And so was the opinion of the lord Dyer, clearly, in 18 Eliz.}

201. ANON.[2]

Common Pleas, [?1578] and 1576.

Note that it was adjudged in the time of the present queen that if a parson after institution but before induction grants an annuity, and the patron and ordinary confirm it, this is void. See 11 Hen. IV,[3] that a confirmation before induction is void. 45 Edw. III, tit. *Exchaunge*, 10:[4] if two parsons exchange their benefices and resign them into the hands of the ordinary for the same purpose, and one of them is admitted, instituted and inducted, and the other is only admitted and instituted but dies before induction, the other parson may not receive the benefice into which he was inducted, for the exchange was not perfected inasmuch as it was not executed. See 22 Hen. VI, fo. 26.[5]

Note that there was another case in the year 18 Eliz.[6] moved in the Common Bench: a parson before induction and after institution made a lease for years, and this was confirmed by the patron and ordinary, and yet it was held there that [the successor] could avoid this lease, because he was not parson before induction, and the parson cannot charge the parsonage with an annuity before induction.

202. ANON.

Pas. 1577.

Note that it was held in Easter term 19 Eliz. that if a husband and wife are vouched, and they vouch over, this will bind the wife.

---

[1] Noted in almost the same words below, p. 136, no. 244.
[2] Perhaps *Hare* v. *Byckley* (1578) above, p. 59. Above on the same page is a note attributed to 'Manwood in son reding', but there is a piece torn out of the leaf at that point and about half of it is missing. Manwood read in the Inner Temple in 1565 and 1567, before Coke's admission.
[3] *Archdale* v. *Beston* (1409) YB Mich. 11 Hen. IV, fo. 17, pl. 40.

[203]

AC, fo. 277v (689v).

<Garranties.>ˢ

Nota que il fuit loppinion de Justice Manwood que si home fist feffment in fe ove garrante et fist lettre datturney de faire liverie, et puis liver le fait al feffee come son fait, et puis lattorney deliver liverie et seisin, cest garrante nest bon pur ceo que chescun garrante covient prender effect al temps del liverie et feffment fait, et pur ceo que le fait que comprent le garrante fuit deliver devant ideo le garrante est voide.

[204]

AC, fo. 279v (692v).

<Garranties.>ˢ <Vide devant 278b.>

14 Elyz. cest case fuit move al justices del common place. Home fist feffment in fe per ceux parolx dedi et concessi habendum a luy et a ces heires et assignes ove garrantie a le feffee et a ces heires a toutz <no>ᵈ joures, et apres le feffe fist feffment ouster, le quel le feffee vouchera le feffour come assigne per cest paroll dedi (car fuit agre per tout le court si home garrante terres a un et a ces heires, ses assignes ne voucheront silz ne sont nosmes).

Harper semble que il ne vouchera come assigne pur ceo que cest parol dedi covient de curger in privitie. Et il cite le livre in 3 E. 3, itin. North., si enfeffe un et ces heires per cest parol dedi et le feffe morust, le livre est que son heire rebuttera mes il ne vouchera.

Dier al contrarie. Mes il dit que ne fuit questione mes si home ad garrantie in fait et garrantie in ley <mes>¹ il poet eslier quel de eux il voet user. Et luy semble que lassigne prendra advantage de cest parol assigne, car il dit que durant le vie le feffour leire le feffee vouchera luy per cest paroll dedi. Et il mist le case de eschaunge que si home fait eschaunge ove auter ceo imply un garrantie in ley et pur ceo luy semble que si lun deschangers assigne son part ouster que lassigne prendra advantage de cest garrantie en ley: quod Harper et Lovelace negaverunt. Mes Dier retient son opinion et dit si segnior, mesne et tenant soient per owelty des services et le tenant fist feffment ouster in fe, le feffe avera brefe de mesne et avera acquitance et uncore ceo fuit forsque garrantie en ley. Et 9 E. 3, [blank], est que si le demandant in quod ei

---

¹ *Sic, but otiose.*

³ *Derebought* v. *Taillour* (1330) 98 Selden Soc. 680.
⁴ Perhaps YB Pas. 9 Edw. III, fo. 15, pl. 26. This is cited in the margin of Co. Litt. 384 against the reference to the present case.

203. ANON.

Common Pleas, probably 1572.[1]

Warranties.

Note that it was the opinion of MANWOOD J. that if someone makes a feoffment in fee with warranty, and makes a letter of attorney to make livery, and then delivers the deed to the feoffee as his deed, and then the attorney delivers livery and seisin, this warranty is not good, inasmuch as every warranty must take effect at the time of the livery and feoffment made; and since the deed containing the warranty was delivered before that, the warranty is void.

204. ANON.[2]

Common Pleas, 1572.

Warranties. See above, fo. 278v.

In 14 Eliz. this case was moved to the justices of the Common Place. Someone made a feoffment in fee by these words 'I have given and granted' (*dedi et concessi*), *habendum* to him and his heirs and assigns with warranty to the feoffee and his heirs for ever. Afterwards the feoffee made a feoffment over. May the feoffee vouch the feoffor as assign by virtue of this word *dedi*? (For it was agreed by the whole court that if a man warrants lands to someone and his heirs, his assigns may not vouch if they are not named).

HARPER thought he could not vouch as assign, because this word *dedi* must run in privity. And he cited the book in 3 Edw. III, the eyre of Northampton:[3] if someone and his heirs is enfeoffed by this word *dedi* and the feoffee dies, the book says that his heir may rebut but not vouch.

DYER to the contrary. But he said it was not questioned that if someone has a warranty in fact and a warranty in law he may choose which of them he will use. It seemed to him that the assign could take advantage of this word 'assign'; for he said that during the the feoffor's life the feoffee's heir may vouch him by virtue of this word *dedi*. And he put the case of an exchange: if someone makes exchange with another, this implies a warranty in law, and therefore it seemed to him that if one of the exchangers assigns his part over, the assignee may take advantage of this warranty in law: which HARPER and *Lovelace* denied. But DYER held to his opinion and said that if there are a lord, mesne and tenant by equality of services, and the tenant makes a feoffment over in fee, the feoffee may have a writ of mesne and have acquittance, and yet it was only a warranty in law. And 9 Edw. III[4] says that if the demandant in

---

[1] If the case is the same as the next, from which there is a cross-reference.
[2] Probably the case also noted below, p. 128, no. 225. Noted in *Nokes's Case* (1599) 4 Co. Rep. 80, at fo. 81 ('Et jeo oya le Segnior Dyer et tout le court del common Banke Hill. 14 Eliz. resolve ...'); Co. Litt. 384 ('Hil. 14 Eliz. ... which I myselfe heard and observed'). Differently reported in *Ff*, fo. 185v; JRL MS. Fr. 118, fo. 15, pl. 3 (Mich. 1572); BL MS. Add. 24845, fo. 92v (which gives the opinion of the court 'come Meade report a son client'); MS. Harg. 374, fo. 72 (same report); CUL MS. Gg.5.2, fo. 102v; Hh.2.9, fo. 77v; HLS MS. 197 (2071), fos. 35–36.

deforciat ad un garrantie in ley come per reason dun revercion il vouchera, et uncore lestatut dit si warrantia habeat […]¹ semble que lassigne ne prendra advantage dun garrantie in ley come in le case deschaunge. Mes luy semble que […] case ceo est un garrantie in fait car un garrantie in ley est […] le ley fait ceo sauns parolx del partie. Mes ore […] parol dedi soit in le fait etc.: quod Harper neg[avit].

[205]

AC, fo. 284 (704).

<Voucher.>ˢ

Nota que Barrham in largument de Winters case cite un judgment que fuit done ore tarde que si home face leas pur vie sur condition et apres le lessour graunt le revercion a un auter pur terme de vie, coment que il nad forsque particuler estate in revercion et nemi lentier revercion uncore il fuit adjudge que il entra pur le condition enfreint, et uncore lestatut dit del grante del revercion. Et le Segnior Dier dit, si home face leas pur vie et puis graunt le revercion a 2 et a les heires de lun de eux, et cesti que ad le fe morust, que lauter est sufficient grante de prender advantage del condition etc. Et la fuit agre que cesti que ad forsque estate pur vie in revercion serra resceve per lestatute de W. 2, cap. [*blank*], uncore lestatut dit, illi ad quos spectat revercio. Et Harper dit expressement in mesme cest case que un lesse pur vie ou done in taile ou tenant in dower ne prendra advantage dun garrante come assignee pur ceo que il nad lentier estate a que le garrante fuit annex.

[206]

AD, fo. 6 (761).

<Uses.>ˢ

P. 17 Regine Eliz. fuit agre in le case del seniori puero in banke <que>² le roy que si home suffer recoverie vers luy al entent que le recoveror ferra estate a luy, in cest case cest parol entent raisera un use, mes nemi presentment, mes le recoverors serr[ont] seisie a lour use demesne in le mesne temps, car auterment le recoverors ne poient faire estate accordant al entent. Mes Wray, chife justice, semble que silz ne font ceo in convenient temps donques un use serra raise al use de[l] feffour et ses heires. Et la Southcote dit que si home fait feffment in fe sur condition que le feffee ferra estate al estraunge, in le mesne temps le feffee serra seisie a son use demesne.

---

¹ *Words lost in lower outside corner.*
² *Sic, but otiose.*

quod ei deforciat has a warranty in law, for instance by reason of a reversion, he may vouch; and yet the statute says *si warrantum habeat*.[1] Yet it seems that an assign may not take advantage of a warranty in law, as in the case of an exchange. But it seemed to him that in this case it is a warranty in fact, for a warranty in law is only where the law makes it without any words from the party, whereas here the word *dedi* is in the deed. HARPER denied this.

205. WINTER'S CASE[2]

Common Pleas, 1572, citing a slightly earlier case.

Voucher.

Note that *Barham*, in the argument of Winter's case, cited a judgment which was given recently: if someone makes a lease for life upon condition, and afterwards the lessor grants the reversion to another for term of life, even though he has only a particular estate in reversion and not the whole reversion, it was nevertheless adjudged that he may enter for breach of the condition; and yet the statute[3] speaks of the grantee of the reversion. And the lord DYER said that if someone makes a lease for life and then grants the reversion to two and to the heirs of one of them, and the one who has the fee dies, the other is a sufficient grantee to take advantage of the condition. And it was there agreed that someone who has only an estate for life in reversion may be received under the Statute of Westminster II, c. [3]; and yet the statute says, 'those to whom the reversion belongs' (*illi ad quos spectat revercio*). And HARPER said expressly in this same case that a lessee for life, donee in tail or tenant in dower may not take advantage of a warranty as assignee, inasmuch as he does not have the whole estate to which the warranty was annexed.

206. HUMPHRESTON'S CASE[4]

King's Bench, Pas. 1575.

Uses.

In Easter term 17 Eliz. it was agreed in the case of *seniori puero* in the King's Bench that if someone suffers a recovery against himself 'to the intent that' the recoveror should make an estate to him, in this case the word 'intent' shall raise a use, albeit not presently, but the recoverors shall be seised to their own use in the meantime, for otherwise the recoverors could not make an estate according to the intent. But WRAY C.J. thought that if they did not do it within a convenient time, a use would be raised to the use of the feoffor and his heirs. And SOUTHCOTE there said that if someone makes a feoffment in fee upon condition that the feoffee make an estate to a stranger, in the meantime the feoffee shall be seised to his own use.

---

[1] Perhaps paraphrasing *De Bigamis*: below, p. 128.
[2] Above, p. 43, no. 88, and the note there.
[3] 32 Hen. VIII, c. 34.   [4] See above, p. 40, no. 87.

[207]

AD, fo. 6v (761v).

<Uses. Notice.> s

17 Elyz. in largument de Sir Thomas Pawletz case fuit dit per Harper arguendo que si feffees al use devant lestatut ussont fait feffment a un que ad notice del use, si ceo fuit sur consideration ou sur use expresse, uncore serra al primer. Le quel opinion le Segnior Dier in son argument denia, et dit que si le feffment soit sur consideration le notice nest materiall.

[208]

AD, fo. 6v (761v).

<Uses. Notice.> s

Cesti que use in taile devant lestatut fait feffment, ceo liera ses issues, mes les feffees <avoidera>.ⁱ Mes si les feffees enfeffe cesti que use et ses heires, la lestat taile est tout ousterment extinct, car la les feffees encounter lour feffment demesne ne poent enter: per Lovelace in Brentz case in leschequer chamber arguendo 17 Eliz . <30 H. 8, tit. Feffmentes al uses, 47. Vide 22 H. 7, 93.>ⁱ Et jeo aye oye sur mesme le reason que il fuit loppinion de Segnior Mountegue que si cesti que use fem prist baron et les feffees fait feffment al baron et fem in fe et le fem morust et le baron auxi que leire le baron reteignera.

[209]

AD, fo. 7r-v (762r-v).

<Uses.> s <Ejectione firme.> < Dier, 17 Eliz. 340. Mich. 15 et 16 Eliz. rott. 2189. >ᵃ <Bracton 220.>ᵃ

H. 17 Eliz. Nota que le case de Brent fuit tiel in effecte. J. Brent, seisie del mannour

---

Harg. 6, fos. 64–67v; MS. Harg. 8, fos. 215–227v; MS. Lansd. 1121, fos. 109v–110v, sub nom. *Lord Pawlet* v. *Brent*; MS. Add. 24845, fos. 101v–102 (Pas. 1573); CUL MS. Gg.3.3, fos. 7–16; MS. Hh.3.14, fos. 229–240v (dated 18 Eliz.); Bodl. Lib. MS. Rawlinson C.112, pp. 299–407, sub nom. *Sir Thomas Pawlet's Case* (Hil. 1575); IT MS. Petyt 511.12, fo. 243 (Hil. 1575). Cit. as *Brent* v. *Lord Pawlett* in Snagge's reading (Middle Temple, 1581) 132 Selden Soc. 258, *per* Peryam J. Lengthy opinions on the case were given by Plowden and Popham in Mich. 1584: BL MS. Harley 2036, fos. 115–121v; CUL MS. Gg.5.2, fos. 176–178; MS. Hh.2.9, fos. 286–295. Cf. an earlier King's Bench case on the same facts, *Brent* v. *Gylbert* (1572–73) Dal. 111; B. & M. 158, n. 4; BL MS. Add. 24845, fos. 111v–112 (Mich. 1573).

[8] This roll is now missing.
[9] Presumably *Bracton*, iii. 162, discussing usufruct. Cf. below, p. 118, n. 5.
[10] Coke used the initial J., but it was actually Richard: next note. The name is given correctly in several of the other reports.

207. BRENT'S CASE[1]

Common Pleas, 1575.

Uses.

In 17 Eliz., in the argument of Sir Thomas Pawlet's case, it was said in argument by HARPER that if feoffees to use before the statute[2] made a feoffment to someone who had notice of the use, even if it was upon consideration, or upon an express use, it would still have been to the former [use]. Which opinion the lord DYER denied in his argument, and he said that if the feoffment is upon consideration the notice is immaterial.

208. BRENT'S CASE[3]

Exch. Ch., 1575.

Uses. Notice.

If cestui que use in tail before the statute[4] made a feoffment, that would bind his issues, though the feoffees could avoid it. However, if the feoffees enfeoff cestui que use and his heirs, the estate tail is utterly extinct, for there the feoffees cannot enter against their own feoffment: according to *Lovelace*, arguing in Brent's case in the Exchequer Chamber in 17 Eliz. (30 Hen. VIII, tit. *Feffements al uses*, 47.[5]) {See 22 Hen. VII, fo. 93.[6]} I have heard that, upon the same reason, it was the opinion of the lord Mountague that if a woman cestui que use marries a husband, and the feoffees make a feoffment to the husband and wife in fee, and the wife dies, and the husband also, the husband's heir may retain it.

209. HODY d. BRENT v. GILBERT: BRENT'S CASE[7]

Common Pleas, Hil. 1575.

Uses. Ejectment. {Dyer, 17 Eliz. 340. Mich. 15 & 16 Eliz., roll 2189.[8] Bracton, fo. 220.[9]}

Hilary term 17 Eliz. Note that Brent's case was as follows, in effect: [Richard][10] Brent,

---

[1] See below, no. 209, and the note there (where Pawlet is identified).
[2] 27 Hen. VIII, c. 10.
[3] See n. 7, below.
[4] 27 Hen. VIII, c. 10.
[5] 30 Hen. VIII, Bro. Abr., *Feffements al uses*, pl. 47.
[6] Trin. 22 Hen. VII, Keil. 93, pl. 8; 116 Selden Soc. 562. This refers to the 1602 edition.
[7] An action of ejectment by Hody against Gilbert 'en droit Brent et le seignior Thomas Pawlett': BL MS. Harg. 9, fos. 233–247v; MS. Lansd. 1057, fos. 238–251; CUL MS. Gg.3.3, fos. 7–16. Cit. in Coke's Dyer (Holkham 8014), fo. 339v ('Vide in mes <reportes>ᵈ notes, tit. Uses, fol. 7, et ceo fuit Brentes case'); Co. Uses, fos. 145 ('17 Eliz. Seignior Pawletts case'), 153v, 155v, 157 ('17 Eliz. Bretts case'). Noted above, p. 85, no. 136; p. 107, no. 190; p. 109, no. 195; above, nos. 207–208. Differently reported in Dyer 340; 2 Leon. 14; B. & M. 157; JRL MS. Fr. 118, fos. 33, 44 (anon., partly missing); BL MS. Harley 443, fos. 44v–45; MS. Harley 6811, fos. 175v–178, 184–185, sub nom. *Hody d. Brent v. Paulet*; MS.

de Godwinsborough, covenant per fait indent ove un Broughton anno 6 E. 6 que il assignera le dit mannour al use de <luy et de>[d] Dorothe adonques sa fem pur terme de <sa vie>,[1] et puis al use le dit J. Brent sil survive le dit Dorothe et <a>[i] sa fem que serra et a les heires de lour 2 corps ingendres, le remainder al use dun file le dit J. Brent et a J. fitz le dit Broughton en taile, le remainder al droit heires le dit Broughton. <et puis faire fine levie al use de mesme lendentures>[d] <Agarde, 127, 34 E. 1, uses limitte.>[i] Et puis feffment fuit fait al Cuffe et Cuffe al use de mesme lendentures, et puis un fine fuit levie accordant, et puis le dit J. Brent levie un fine al Broughton al auter uses, et puis Browton, J. Brent, Cuffe et Cuffe que fueront les feffees joine in un feffment a un auter, et puis divers fines fueront levies a mesme lententz, et puis Dorothie morust et le dit J. Brent prist auter fem etc. Et le question fuit si lestate devant limite a le 2 fem le dit J. Brent fuit void al primes, et si ne fuit voide donques si per ascun matter ex post facto il fuit destroye. <Dier, 17 Eliz. 340b.>[i]

Et pur ceo Mounson, Manwood et Harper agreont que cest limitation al 2 fem fuit bon et que in le mesne temps le dit J. Brent avera estate forsque pur terme de vie et un remainder in expectancie et sur un contingit a luy et a sa 2 fem en taile. <Mes>[d] Mes ilz agreont le ley tout autrement in un grant in possession, car la ilz agreont que in toutz grantes in possession si ascun chose soit grant a <un>[d] 2 et lun poet ceo prender et lauter ne poet, donques cesti que poet ceo prender prendra tout. 1 Ass. 11, purchase a luy et a sa fem que serra est voide. 17 E. 3, terres dones a J. S. et primogenito filio, et nad fitz al temps. 38 E. 3, terres done a J. S. pur vie, le remainder a J. N. et as droit heires J. D., J. N. prist tout etc. Mes ilz disoient que in uses le ley est tout auter, car uses ne sont subject a les rules et maximes del common ley. Car in uses un fe poet depender sur auter fe per voy de remainder. Al common ley terres ne fueront devisable, mes un use fuit. Use ne puissoit estre forfeit. Le segnior del villein navera le gard tanque al 19 H. 7 quant lestatut fuit fait. Le segnior navera le gard tanque al 4 H. 7. Feffment al use dun abbot ne fuit mortmain devant lestatut de 15 R. 2, come appiert 8 H. 4. Mes ilz agreont que sicome uses sont create per les parolx les parties sur trust et confidence, issint ilz sont directe et rule per les parols les parties accordant a lour voluntes.

Mes le Segnior Dier fuit inconter eux, que le limitation del use a un que ne fuit in esse fuit tout ousterment voide pur ceo que il fuit un person de sufficient capacitie in esse[2] de prender tout, et auxi jointment ilz ne poent prender car donques ilz covient prender tout a un temps.

---

[1] *Altered from* lour vies. [2] *Unclear; resembles* in[e]sse.

436. On the other hand, Leon. says Dorothy's husband was Robert Brent. Neither is correct. In fact Dorothy's husband was John Brent's great-grandson Richard Brent (d. 1581), whose daughter Anne in 1564 married Thomas Paulet: VCH, *Hampshire*, iv. 495; *The Men of Court*, i. 358. Anne had originally been intended to marry a son of Thomas Broughton, presumably the 'J. Broughton' of the report.
[2] Coke's MS. of Arthur Agard's repertory of records: cf. above, p. 9.
[3] Dyer's report of the present case.   [4] 1 Edw. III, Lib. Ass. pl. 11.
[5] *Prior of Grimsby's Case* (1343) YB Pas. 17 Edw. III, fo. 29, pl. 30.
[6] Probably YB Mich. 38 Edw. III, fo. 26.
[7] 19 Hen. VII, c. 15.   [8] 4 Hen. VII, c. 17.   [9] 15 Ric. II, c. 5.
[10] YB Mich. 8 Hen. IV, fo. 15, pl. 17.

seised of the manor of Godwins Bower,[1] covenanted by deed indented with one [Thomas] Broughton in the year 6 Edw. VI that he would assign the said manor to the use of Dorothy, then his wife, for term of her life, and then to the use of the said [Richard] Brent (if he survived the said Dorothy) and [any] future wife, and the heirs of their two bodies begotten, remainder to the use of a daughter of the said [Richard] Brent and to J., son of the said Broughton, in tail, remainder to the right heirs of the said Broughton. {Agard, fo. 127, 34 Edw. I:[2] uses limited.} Then a feoffment was made to Cuffe and Cuffe, to the use of the same indentures, and a fine was levied accordingly; then the said [Richard] Brent levied a fine to Broughton to other uses; then Broughton, [Richard] Brent, Cuffe and Cuffe (who were the feoffees) joined in a feoffment to another, and various fines were levied to the same purposes; then Dorothy died, and the said [Richard] Brent married another wife. The question was, whether the estate previously limited to the second wife of the said [Richard] Brent was void at the outset, and if it was not void, whether it was destroyed by any matter *ex post facto*. {Dyer, 17 Eliz. 340v.[3]}

As to this, MOUNSON, MANWOOD and HARPER agreed that this limitation to the second wife was good, and that in the meantime the said [Richard] Brent had an estate only for term of life, and a remainder in expectancy and upon a contingency to him and his second wife in tail. But they agreed that the law would be quite otherwise with respect to a grant in possession, for they agreed that in all grants in possession where something is granted to two, and one of them can take it and the other cannot, the one who can take it shall take everything. 1 Ass., pl. 11:[4] a purchase unto him and his wife-to-be is void [as to her]. 17 Edw. III:[5] lands given to John Style and his firstborn son, and he has no son at the time. 38 Edw. III:[6] lands given to John Style for life, remainder to John Noke and to the right heirs of John Dale, and John Noke took everything. But they said that in uses the law is quite otherwise; for uses are not subject to the rules and maxims of the common law. For in uses a fee may depend on another fee by way of remainder. At common law lands were not devisable, but a use was. A use could not be forfeited. The lord of a villein could not have the wardship [of cestui que use] until 19 Hen. VII, when the statute was made.[7] The lord could not have the wardship [of cestui que use] until 4 Hen. VII.[8] A feoffment to the use of an abbot was not mortmain before the statute of 15 Ric. II,[9] as appears in 8 Hen. IV.[10] But they agreed that, just as uses are created by the words of the parties, upon trust and confidence, so they are directed and ruled by the words of the parties according to their wishes.

But the lord DYER was against them, that the limitation of the use to someone who was not in being was utterly void, because there was a person of sufficient capacity in being to take all; moreover, they cannot take jointly, for then they would have to take everything at once.

---

[1] In Dunwear, Som. The manor was purchased from the Godwin family by one Robert Brent in 1507. Robert's son John (d. 1524) of Cossington, Som., and the Middle Temple, had an eldest son William, who had two sons, William and Richard (d. 1571) of the Inner Temple. The younger William's eldest son, another Richard Brent, died in 1581 without male issue. Collinson says that Cossington and Godwins Bower were purchased by one John Brent, son of Stephen Brent, a lawyer of Dorchester, whom he stated to be a son of John (d. 1524): J. Collinson, *History and Antiquities of the County of Somerset* (1791), iii.

Mes quant al 2 point ilz ne agreont, car Mounson et Harper teignont que quant estate fuit fait al uses come est avandit que toutz lent[erest] et le authoritie del feffees fueront hors de eux per lestatut de 27 H. 8. Car ilz disoient que le meaninge del fesors del estatut ne sont <de>[d] que ascun interest remainera in les feffees, et issint pensont que neque intereste neque un power dentrie de raiser le use remaine in les feffees, mes que cesti que use bi[en] [*fo. 7v*] poet enter sauns ascun entre fait per les feffees. Et <il>[d] in le mesne temps ilz pensont que luse est in consideration del ley, et serra execute quant il veigne in esse per lestatut de 27 H. 8, car la est parle de toutz uses que sont ou que in apres serront. Et la Mounson dit que si home face feffment al use de son primer fitz que serra, que in le mesne temps les feffees serra seisie al use del feffor. Et issint ilz conclude que, intant que riens remaine in les feffees, et que luse est in abeiauns, que ceo ne poet estre discontinue etc.

Mes Manwood et Dier teignont le contrarie. Car ilz disoient que un estate remaine in les feffees pur server le use que ore est in abeiauns quant il deveignera in esse. Et lestatut de 27 H. 8 execute solement uses in possession et relinquishe un estate in les feffees pur les uses in abeiaunce pur ceo que ilz ne poient estre executed. Et donques, si un estate remaine in les feffees, si devant le essens del uses lestate soit discontinue, les uses que issue hors de mesme lestate sont discontinue auxi, car lestate les feffees est le roote hors de quel les use[s] tanquam braunches springe, et donques si le roote soit subverte les braunches auxi serra destroye. Et pur ceo Manwood semble que si feffment soit fait al use J. D. et puis al use droit heires J. S., J. S. adonques esteant in vie, que in cest case le use del fe simple remaine suspende, et que si J. D. fait feffment in fe que les feffees come a luy semble entra pur le forfeiture, car in le mesne temps ilz ne serra seisie al use del feffour mes al use dun use suspend issint que lestate et luse suspend remaine in eux.

Et auxi Geffreys, serjaunt, arguendo mist cest case, que si devant lestatut home ust fait feffment al use de un pur xx ans et puis al use de droit heires J. S., et donques vient lestatut de 27 H. 8, moy semble que ore le use del remainder in fe remaine in lestate les feffees suspend, car un franktenement ne poet estre suspend.

[210]

AD, fo. 7v (762v).

<Pl. Com. in Morgans case, 4b. Covenant in consideration de argent covient estre enrol.>[a,s]

Nota que il ad estre adjudge in le case de un Rolfe que si home in consideration que J. S. avoit releas a luy tout le droit que il avoit in le mannour de D. covenant ove le dit J. S. a estoier seisie al use le dit J. S. et a ses heires, et il fuit adjudge [que] cest

As to the second point they did not agree,[1] for MOUNSON and HARPER held that when an estate was made to the uses as aforesaid, all the interest and the authority of the feoffees were out of them by virtue of the statute of 27 Hen. VIII.[2] For they said that it was not the meaning of the makers of the statute that any interest should remain in the feoffees, and so they thought that neither an interest nor a power of entry to raise the use remained in the feoffees, but that cestui que use could well enter without any entry made by the feoffees. And they thought that in the meantime the use is in consideration of the law, and is to be executed (when it comes into being) by the statute of 27 Hen. VIII, for the statute speaks of all uses which are 'or which shall be hereafter'. And MOUNSON there said that if a man makes a feoffment to the use of his first son-to-be, in the meantime [before the birth] the feoffees shall be seised to the use of the feoffor. Thus they concluded that, inasmuch as nothing remained in the feoffees, and the use is in abeyance, it cannot be discontinued.

But MANWOOD and DYER held the contrary. For they said that an estate remained in the feoffees to serve the use, which is now in abeyance, when it comes into being. And the statute of 27 Hen. VIII only executed uses in possession, and left an estate in the feoffees with respect to the uses in abeyance because they could not be executed. If, then, an estate remains in the feoffees, and before the existence (*essens*) of the uses the estate is discontinued, the uses which issued out of the same estate are discontinued also; for the estate of the feoffees is the root out of which the uses spring like branches, and if the root is dug up the branches will be destroyed also. Therefore MANWOOD thought that if a feoffment is made to the use of John Dale, and then to the use of the right heirs of John Style (John Style being then alive), in that case the use of the fee simple remains in suspense; and if John Dale makes a feoffment in fee, the feoffees (as he thought) could enter for the forfeiture, for in the meantime they shall not be seised to the use of the feoffor but to the use of the suspended use, and so the estate and the suspended use remain in them.

Jeffrey, serjeant, also put this case in argument: if, before the statute, someone had made a feoffment to the use of someone for twenty years, and then to the use of the right heirs of John Style, and then the statute of 27 Hen. VIII came along, it seems to me that the use of the remainder in fee now remains suspended in the estate of the feoffees, for a freehold cannot be suspended.

210. ROLFE'S CASE

Probably temp. Eliz.

Plowd. Com. in Morgan's case, fo. 4v.[3] A covenant in consideration of money must be enrolled.

Note that it was adjudged in the case of one Rolfe that if, in consideration that John Style had released to him all the right which he had in the manor of Dale, someone covenanted with the said John Style to stand seised to the use of the said John Style

---

[1] I.e. were evenly divided.
[2] Statute of Uses, 27 Hen. VIII, c. 10.
[3] Not fo. 4v in *AB* or *AD*. Cf. 8 Co. Rep. 94; 2 Co. Inst. 672..

indenture <ne>^d besoigne destre enroll <car il fuit hors del estatute de 32>^d. Et la fuit auxi agre que ne gist in averment le quel cesti que releas avoit ascun droit ou nemi. <Vies 36 H. 8, tit. Feffmentes al uses, Br.>^a

[211]

AD, fo. 7v (762v).

Le Segnior Dier in 19 Eliz. in le countie de Kentz case dit si lesse pur ans ust fait leasse de son estate al auter opes, que il ne poet faire grant per lestatut de R. 3. Cestui que use dun obligation ne poet releasse.

[212]

AD, fos. 8–9 (763–764).

<Uses.>^s <Bracton 209 pur le antiquitie des uses.>^a

Nota Tr. 18 Eliz. autiel case come Brentz fuit, fuit argue in le banke le roy. Et in substans a cest purpose le case fuit tiel. Sir Richard Haddon devant lestatut de uses ayant[1] feffees a son use devise per son volunt anno 8 H. 8 que ses feffees estoieront seisies al use sa fem etc. et puis al use son fitz en[2] taile, proviso que si son fitz <a>[3] bargainera, alienera ou suffera recoverie ou[4] leviera fine que donques ses feffees estoieront seisie al auter uses etc. Et puis son fitz bargaine le dit terre et levie fine etc. Et le grand question fuit, le quel un estate puis lestatut de 27 H. 8 <fuit>^d remaine en les feffees ou in le feffor pur server les uses in contingency quant ilz deveignera in esse, ou si tout lestate soit hors de feffees et le terre lye ove luse issint que neque le feffour neque le feffee poet discontinue ou cutte of le dit use.

Et la Gawdy, justice, argue fortement que estate remaine in les feffees ou in le feffor a server le use quant ceo deveignera in esse, mes il dit que si les feffees ou le feffor vende le terre sur bon consideration a un que nad notice del use in contingencie il ne serra unques seisie al <primer>^d use in abeiauns quant ceo viendra in esse. Et il ground son opinion mult sur les parolx del estatut de 27 H. 8, car la

---

[1] aysaunt.
[2] et.
[3] *Sic, but otiose.*
[4] a.

---

[5] *Bracton*, iii. 162 ('… potest quis habere in libero tenemento jus et proprietatem et feodum, et alius liberum tenementum. Item, unus feodum et liberum tenementum, et alius jus merum. Item, unus haec omnia, et alius usufructum. Item, unus haec omnia et usum, et alius fructum …'). Cf. above, p. 115, n. 9.
[6] This date is also given in MS. Lansd. 1057, and is corroborated by the mention of Jeffreys J. as recently appointed. However, the record shows continuances only until Hil. 1576, when judgment was supposedly given.
[7] See above, p. 115, no. 209.
[8] PROB 11/18, fos. 226v–228v; extracted in B. & M. 156.
[9] Statute of Uses, 27 Hen. VIII, c. 10.

and his heirs, this indenture needs to be enrolled. And it was also then agreed that it does not lie in averment whether or not the person who released had any right. {See 36 Hen. VIII, tit. *Feffements al uses*, Brooke.[1]}

211. ONLEY v. EARL OF KENT[2]

Common Pleas, Trin. 1577.

The lord DYER said in 19 Eliz., in the earl of Kent's case, that if a lessee for years has made a lease of his estate to the use of someone else, he may not make a grant by the statute of Richard III.[3] Cestui que use of a bond may not release.

212. MANNYNG v. ANDROWES: HADDON'S CASE[4]

King's Bench, Trin. 1576.

Uses. {[See] Bracton, fo. 209, for the antiquity of uses.[5]}

Note that in Trinity term[6] 18 Eliz. a similar case to Brent's[7] was argued in the King's Bench. And in substance, as to this purpose, the case was as follows. Sir Richard Haddon, having feoffees to his use before the Statute of Uses, devised by his will in the year 8 Hen. VIII[8] that his feoffees should stand seised to the use of his wife, and then to the use of his son in tail, *proviso* that if his son should bargain, alien or suffer a recovery or levy a fine, his feoffees should then stand seised to other uses. Then his son bargained the said land and levied a fine. And the great question was whether an estate remained in the feoffees after the statute of 27 Hen. VIII,[9] or was in the feoffor, to serve the uses in contingency when they should come into being, or whether the whole estate was out of the feoffees and the land bound with the use, so that neither the feoffor nor the feoffee could discontinue or cut off the said use.

GAWDY J. argued forcefully that an estate remained in the feoffees, or in the feoffor, to serve the use when it came into being; but he said that if the feoffees or the feoffor sold the land upon good consideration to someone who had no notice of the use in contingency, the purchaser would never be seised to the use in abeyance when it came into being. And he based his opinion chiefly upon the words of the statute of 27 Hen. VIII; for it says there, 'when any person or persons stand and be seised, or at any time

---

[1] 36 Hen. VIII, Bro. Abr., *Feffements al uses*, pl. 54.
[2] See below, p. 124, no. 218, and the note there.   [3] 1 Ric. III, c. 1.
[4] KB 27/1243, m. 338 (three rolls; continued from Pas. 1572): John Mannyng gent. v. John Androwes; ejectment for the manor-house of Asthall, Oxon., on the demise of Percival Haddon; pleads Not Guilty; special verdict at the Guildhall, 17 June 1573, setting out the will of Sir Richard Haddon and a subsequent fine and recovery; c.a.v. to Hil. 1576 (*sic*); judgment for the defendant. Noted above, p. 21, no. 38; p. 78, no. 121; p. 110, no. 197. Cit. by Coke as *Haddon's Case*: Co. Uses, fo. 145 ('18 Eliz. in banke le roy in Haddons case'); Moo. 372, *per* Coke (1594). Differently reported in 1 Leon. 256; 4 Leon. 2; BL MS. Harley 2036, fos. 57–73 (Hil. 1576); MS. Harg. 9, fos. 206–225; MS. Harg. 11, fos. 66–86v; MS. Lansd. 1057, fos. 211v–231v (Hil. and Trin. 1576); MS. Lansd. 1106, fos. 74v–76v; CUL MS. Ll.3.8, fo. 263 (tr. in B. & M. 157). Cf. KB 27/1240, m. 258 (continued from Mich. 1571): Michael Haddon gent. v. John Androwes; ejectment for a messuage and land in Asthall on the demise of Percival Haddon; pleads Not Guilty; *venire facias*.

est dit, when anie person or persons stand and be seased or at any tyme herafter shallbe seased of anie landes to the use, confidence or trust etc. Ore il dit, si feffment soit fait al use de J. S. et ses heire[s] et quant J. N. paia C. livers a J. S. que donques les feffees serra seisies al use J. N. et ses heires, ore si in le mesne temps J. S. vend le terre sur bon consideration a un que nad notice del use, et puis J. N. paia les deniers, uncore il dit que lentre des feffees est requisite a reviver le use, car lestatut vest toutz uses in possession et pur ceo primerment covient daver use, et ceo ne poet estre sauns lentre del feffees. Auxi il dit que lestatut providera pur un mischief, et un inconvenience commencera, car donques le segnior serra deprive de son gard, le roygne et auters segniors barre et forclose de lour escheates, et serra un perillous chose pur purchasores queux emeront tielz terres sur bone consideration et nient conusaunt les ditz future uses. Et il dit que uses in abeiauns devant lestatut de 27 H. 8 poient estre discontinue, come si feffment ust estre fait devant lestatut al use J. S. pur vie et puis al use de droit heires J. S., ore si les feffees ussont estre disseise ou morust sauns heire ou ussont vend le terre sur bon consideration, cybien les uses in abeiauns come les <issues>^d uses in esse ussont estre destroy. Issint il dit a cest jour etc. Et il denia le case in Brooke, tit. Feffment[es] al uses, en 30 H. 8 etc.

Et Jeffreies, justice novelment fait, fuit de mesme loppinion, mes Southcote et Wraye fueront enconter eux.

Et le Segnior Wraye dit que le nature de uses fueront chaunge in auter nature que ilz fueront <al>^d devant lestatut de 27 H. 8, car devant le dit estatut il dit que un use ne fuit forsque un trust et confidence enter les parties, et pur ceo le trust et confidence in multes cases puit estre enfreint, le quel fuit le chiefe cause del fesaunt del estatut. Mes il dit que puis lestatut nul confidence ne trust est repose in les feffees mes ore le terre mesme est charge ove le use in quecunque mayns ceo veigne. Et, come il dit, ore le terre mesme est trust ove luse. Et il dit que a cest jour luse del terre ne fuit auter mes limitatio usus terre. [*fo. 8v*] Et il devide tout son argument quant a cest purpose en 5 partes.

Le primer fuit, coment et in quel mannour le use vestera a ceo jour. Et pur ceo il dit sur ceux parols del estatut, shalbe deemed in lawefull season, estate and possession etc., que si a cest jour feffment soit fait a J. S. al use J. D. que maintenant J. D. est in possession actuelment issint que il avera trespas maintenant devant ascun entre. Car il dit que un acte de parliament poet issint faire etc. Et auxi lestatut dit que cesti que use avera le terre in mesme le plite come il ad le use, et le use il ad in possession etc.

Le 2 matter fuit, si ascun <ch>^d estate remaine in les feffees. Et il semble que non, et ceo auxi sur les parolx et meaninge del estatute. Car le mischief fuit pur[1] [ceo que] le consciences del feffees fueront trope large et proud a defender cesti que use contrarie a le trust et confidence repose in eux, lestatut dit, to the entent that the kinges subjectes herafter shall not by anye meanes or inventions be deceaved,

---

[1] *Sic.*

hereafter shall be seised, of any lands to the use, confidence or trust [of another] …'. Now (he said) if a feoffment is made to the use of John Style and his heirs, and when John Noke should pay £100 to John Style then the feoffees should be seised to the use of John Noke and his heirs, and in the meantime John Style sells the land upon good consideration to someone who has no notice of the use, and then John Noke pays the money, still (as he said) the entry of the feoffees is requisite to revive the use, for the statute vests all uses in possession and therefore there must in the first place be a use, and that cannot be without the entry of the feoffees. He also said that the statute provided for a mischief, and yet an inconvenience would begin [if no one were seised], for then the lord would be deprived of his wardship, the queen and other lords would be barred and forclosed from their escheats, and it would be a perilous thing for purchasers who bought such lands upon good consideration not knowing about the said future uses. And he said that uses in abeyance could be discontinued before the statute of 27 Hen. VIII: for instance if a feoffment were made before the statute to the use of John Style for life, and then to the use of the right heirs of John Style, and the feoffees were disseised or died without heir, or sold the land upon good consideration, both the uses in abeyance and the uses *in esse* would have been destroyed. So it is (he said) at the present day. And he denied the case in Brooke, tit. *Feffements al uses*, in 30 Hen. VIII.[1]

JEFFREY, recently made a justice,[2] was of the same opinion; but SOUTHCOTE and WRAY [C.J.] were against them.

The lord WRAY said that the nature of uses had been changed into another nature than that which they had before the statute of 27 Hen. VIII. Before the said statute (as he said) a use was only a trust and confidence between the parties; and therefore the trust and confidence could in many cases be broken, which was the chief cause of the making of the statute. But he said that since the statute, no confidence or trust is reposed in the feoffees, but now the land itself is charged with the use, into whosesoever hands it comes. And (as he said) the land itself is now entrusted with the use. And he said that at this day the use of the land is nothing other than a limitation of the use of the land (*limitatio usus terrae*). And he divided his whole argument, as to this purpose, into five parts.

[1] The first was how and in what way the use will vest at the present day. As to this, he [explained] the words of the statute, 'shall be deemed in lawful seisin, estate and possession …', to mean that if at the present day a feoffment is made to John Style to the use of John Dale, John Dale is forthwith actually in possession, so that he may have trespass immediately, before any entry. For (as he said) an act of Parliament can do that. Moreover, the statute says that cestui que use shall have the land in the same plight as he had the use, and he had the use in possession.

[2] The second matter was whether any estate remains in the feoffees. He thought not, and that was also based on the words and meaning of the statute. For the mischief was that the consciences of feoffees were too large and proud to defend cestui que use, contrary to the trust and confidence reposed in them; and the statute says, 'to the intent that the king's subjects hereafter shall not by any means or inventions be deceived,

---

[1] 30 Hen. VIII, Bro. Abr., *Feffements al uses*, pl. 50.
[2] On 15 May 1576. The King's Bench had been short of a puisne since the promotion of Wray to be chief justice in 1574.

damaged or hurted etc. Mes il dit, si ascun estate remaineroit in les feffees mesme le mischief que fuit devant lestatut remain[eroit], cestasavoir daver les uses in abeiauns subjecte al volunt et pleasur de les feffees. Et auxi il dit que serra enconter les parolx del estatut, car les parols sont, and that the estate, title, right and possession which was in the feffees etc. be from thensforth clearely deemed and adjudged in him or them which herafter shall have such use etc. Et il dit, si jeo face feffment in fe al J. S. al use de luy et ses heire[s] tanque J. D. ad paye a luy xx li. et donques al use de luy et ses heires, in cest case J. S. ad un fe simple primerment, et sil averoit estate pur server lauter use in contingencie donques il covient daver 2 fe simples, quel ne poet estre. Et si jeo face feffment in fe al use de moy [mesme] pur terme de ma vie et <puis>[1] al use de ma fem que serra pur terme de sa vie et puis al use de mes droit heires, ore le franktenement et le fe simple covient estre execute accordant al estatute, et si ascun estate remainera in les feffees il serra forsque pur vie, et il dit que le ley ne voille suffer tiel apportionment del estates. Et il dit que les feffees a cest jour fueront semble al un organe pipe le quel serve solement a conveier le winde hors del organe. Et il dit que le fem del feffee a cest jour ne serra indowe.

3, coment ceux uses in contingencie prist lour commencement et unde. Et il dit que toutz les usses prist lour esse et commencement per le primer liverye, et toutz les uses surdont hors del terre come hors dun masse et lompe, come il parle. Et il dit que le terre carrie toutz les uses sicome le terre carie et conveie les springes et founteines del ewe. Et pur ceo il resemble ceo al case de Plesington in 6 R. 2, car la est agre, si leas pur vie soit fait sur condition que si le lessor morust deins le terme que donques le lesse avera fe, si le lessour morust deins le terme le lesse avera le fe per le primer livery. Issint in Colthirst et Bejushins case, Pl. Com., leas pur vie al baron et fem pur vies, le remainder a William lour fitz pur terme de son vie, et sil morust durant les vies le baron et fem que ceo remainera a lour fitz puisne, et puis le fits eigne morust durant lour vies, et le puisne fitz avoit le remainder per le primer livery.

4, si lentre des feffees soit congeable pur reviver le uses. Et il semble que non, car il dit que devant lestatut les feffees avoit le terre et cesti que use ad forsque trust, mes ore est quite contrarie, car ore lestatut devest tout lestate in cesti que use, et pur ceo si devant lestatut les feffees ont estre disseisie cesti que use ne puit enter pur reviver le use mes les feffees, car le tort fuit fait a eux et toutz foitz il entra a que le tort fuit fait, mes ore quant jeo face feffment in fe al use J. S. et ses [heires] tanque J. N. ad paie a luy C. s. et donques al use de luy et ses heires, ore si nul alteration de possession soit mes J. S. continuant in possession J. N. paia a luy les deniers, ore lentre de[s] feffees nest requisite mes cesti que use poet enter luy mesme. Et [fo. 9] il dit, si lentre des feffees fuit necessarie, donques lestatut nad pas sufficientment provide pur le mischeif, scilicet que cesti que use ne serra subjecte al hurt et damage del feffees.

---

[1] *Deleted unnecessarily.*

[1] *Colthirst* v. *Bejushin* (1550) Plowd. 21; B. & M. 89.

damaged or hurted ...'. However (as he said) if any estate were to remain in the feoffees, the same mischief which was before the statute would remain, namely having the uses in abeyance subject to the will and pleasure of the feoffees. He also said that it would be against the words of the statute, for the words are, 'and that the estate, title, right and possession which was in the feoffees ... be from thenceforth clearly deemed and adjudged in him or them which hereafter shall have such use ...'. And he said that if I make a feoffment in fee to John Style, to the use of him and his heirs until John Dale pays him £20, and then to the use of him and his heirs, in this case John Style has a fee simple at the outset, and if he were to have an estate to serve the other use in contingency, then he must have two fee simples, which cannot be. If I make a feoffment in fee to the use of myself for term of my life, and then to the use of my future wife for term of her life, and then to the use of my right heirs, the freehold and the fee simple must now be executed according to the statute, and if any estate were to remain in the feoffees it would only be for life; but he said that the law would not suffer such apportionment of estates. And he said that feoffees at the present day were like an organ pipe, which serves only to convey the wind out of the organ.[1] And he said that the feoffee's wife at the present day shall not be endowed.

3. How and whence these uses in contingency took their beginning. He said that all the uses took their being and commencement from the first livery, and all the uses arise out of the land as if out of a mass and lump (as he put it). He said that the land carries all the uses, just as the land carries and conveys the springs and fountains of water. Therefore he likened it to Plesington's case, in 6 Ric. II,[2] for it is agreed there that if a lease for life is made upon condition that if the lessor should die within the term the lessee would have fee, and the lessor dies within the term, the lessee would have the fee by the first livery. Likewise, in Colthirst and Bejushin's case, Plowd. Com.,[3] a lease for life to husband and wife for their lives, remainder to William their son for term of his life, and should he die during the lives of the husband and wife, remainder to their younger son; then the elder son died during their lives, and the younger son had the remainder by the first livery.

4. Whether an entry by the feoffees is permissible to revive the uses. He thought not, for he said that before the statute the feoffees had the land, and cestui que use had only a trust; but now it is quite contrary, for now the statute divests all the estate into cestui que use. If, before the statute, the feoffees had been disseised, cestui que use could not have entered to revive the use; but the feoffees could, for the wrong was done to them, and the person who enters must always be the person to whom the wrong was done. But now, when I make a feoffment in fee to the use of John Style and his heirs until John Noke has paid him 100s., and then to the use of him and his heirs, and there is no alteration of possession, but while John Style is continuing in possession John Noke pays him the money, an entry by the feoffees is no longer requisite but cestui que use may enter himself. And (as he said) if an entry by the feoffees was necessary, then the statute would not have sufficiently provided for the mischief, namely that cestui que use should not be subject to hurt and damage from the feoffees.

---

[1] Cf. 2 Leon. 260 ('the feoffees are not to any purpose but as a pipe to convey the lands to others').
[2] *Plesington's Case* (1382) Mich. 6 Ric. II, Fitz. Abr., *Quid juris clamat*, pl. 20; YB Mich. 6 Ric. II (Ames Fdn), p. 93, pl. 17.

Le 5 point que il fist fuit, le quel lentre del feffees fuit requisite a raiser le use in abeiauns quant ceo deveigne in esse quant le possession fuit alter devant le rising de ceo. Et il dit que lentre des feffees ne fuit la congeable neque. Et pur directe authoritie il note[1] 30 H. 8, 3 Mar., 5 E. 6, tit. Feffmentes al uses in Brooke, que le terre serra lye ove luse in futuro in quecunque maynes que le terre vient. Et il dit que le terre fuit tied ove ceo, et resemble ceo al condition, ou common, ou rent charge. Et auxi il dit que ceo que nest [pas][2] in esse ne poet estre discontinue per feffment, <oue>[3] auterment, come Litt. dit si <le>[4] lissue del tenant in taile disseisie son pier et fait feffment ceo ne poet discontinue lestate taile pur ceo que lestate ne unques fuit in luy et il ne fuit unques seisie per force del taile. Auxi si tenant in taile, le remainder as droit heires J. D., et tenant in taile fait feffment in fe, et puis J. D. morust, et puis tenant in taile morust sauns issue, ore le droit heire J. D. [ne][5] poet enter, car al temps del feffment fait il navoit ascun remainder mes son remainder fuit in abeiauns. Et il dit que in nostre case icy le terre est solement trust ove le use, et nul trust repose in les feffees puis lestatute. Et a cest purpose il cite le case in 50 E. 3, que si jeo devise que mes exeutors venderont mon terre, et jeo morust, et mon terre discend a mon heire, uncore ilz poient ceo vender. Et issint est le livre, coment que les <esch>[d] terres escheteront al roy, uncore les executors poient vender le terre esteant in les maynes le roy pur ceo que ilz ont[6] nul interest ne droit in le terre et pur ceo in quecunque maines ceo vient, sive in les maynes le <roy>[d] heire sive in les maynes le roy ou auters segniores per eschete, le terre est lye ove le power que fuit done as executores en le volunt. Et il mitte le common case que si home mor[g]age son terre sur condition que si le feffour paia C. livres a Mich. <de>[7] le morgage serra seisie al use de luy et ses heires, si ore devant Michaelmas le morgageour paia les deniers il avera sa terre arere coment que devant Michaelmas le feffee ad fait divers feffmentes ou suffer[8] recoveries etc. Et il dit que il voet estre demande coment luse serra vest in cesti a que use quant ceo viendra in esse, entant que lentre des feffees nest requisite. Et il dit que le franktenement et le fe serra vest maintenant in cesti que use per lestatut, et serra in son actuell et reall possession. Et il mist plusores cases ou un fe et franktenement lepera hors de lun in auter per le common ley, come in le case de Littleton. Et vide la plusores auters cases queux il remember. Et il dit, si lentre des feffees fuit requisite a raiser un use in abeiauns ou auterment, ceo ne vestera. Donques il mitt le case que il fist feffment in fe al use de luy mesme pur terme de sa vie et puis al use de sa fem que serra et puis al use de ses droit heires in fe, et puis il prist fem, ore <si>[9] lentre des feffees nest congeable pur ceo que jeo soy in possession, mes est clere que le estate vestera maintenant in le fem, et ceo sauns lentre des feffees.

<14 Eliz. 314, use transferre del un al auter sauns ascun acte.>[a]

---

[1] *Perhaps* cite, *though there is an extra letter after the first two minims which seems to resemble an* o.
[2] pais.
[3] *Amended and unclear, perhaps* car.
[4] *Sic, but otiose.*
[5] *Conjectural insertion.*
[6] sont.
[7] *Sic, but otiose.*
[8] suffers.
[9] *Sic, but otiose.*

[5] The fifth point he made was whether an entry by the feoffees was requisite to raise the use in abeyance when it came into being, when the possession had been altered before it arose. And he said that the entry of the feoffees was not permissible there. For direct authority he cited 30 Hen. VIII, 3 Mar., 5 Edw. VI, tit. *Feffements al uses* in Brooke,[1] that the land shall be tied with the use *in futuro*, into whosesoever hands the land comes. And he said that the land was tied with it, in the same way as a condition, common or rent-charge. Also he said that what is not *in esse* cannot be discontinued by feoffment or otherwise. Likewise, as Littleton says, if the issue of tenant in tail disseises his father and makes a feoffment, this cannot discontinue the estate tail, because the estate was never in him and he was never seised by force of the tail.[2] Then again, if there is a tenant in tail, remainder to the right heirs of John Dale, and the tenant in tail makes a feoffment in fee; then John Dale dies; and then the tenant in tail dies without issue: now the right heir of John Dale cannot enter, for at the time of the feoffment made he had no remainder, but his remainder was in abeyance. And he said that in our case here only the land is trusted with the use, and no trust is reposed in the feoffees since the statute. To this purpose, he cited the case in 50 Edw. III:[3] if I devise that my executors should sell my land, and I die, and my land descends to my heir, the executors may nevertheless sell it. So is the book. Even if lands escheat to the king, the executors may still sell land while it is in the king's hands, although they have no right in the land. Therefore, into whosesoever hands it comes, whether in the hands of the heir or in the hands of the king or other lords by escheat, the land is tied with the power which was given to the executors in the will. And he put the common case where someone mortgages his land upon condition that if the feoffor pays £100 at Michaelmas the mortgagee shall be seised to the use of him and his heirs, and before Michaelmas the mortgagor pays the money: he shall have his land back, even if before Michaelmas the feoffee has made various feoffments or suffered recoveries. He said it might well be asked how the use can be vested in cestui que use when it comes into being, given that an entry by the feoffees is not requisite. And he said that the freehold and the fee shall be vested forthwith in cestui que use by the statute, and shall be in his actual and real possession. And he put several cases where a fee and freehold shall leap out of one person into another by the common law: as in Littleton's case.[4] See there various other cases which he remembered. And (as he said) if the entry of the feoffees was requisite to raise a use, whether in abeyance or otherwise, it would not vest. Then he put the case that someone makes a feoffment in fee to the use of himself for term of his life, and then to the use of his future wife, and then to the use of his right heirs in fee; then he marries a wife: the entry of the feoffees is not permissible here, because [he is] in possession, but it is clear that the estate will vest forthwith in the woman without any entry by the feoffees.

{14 Eliz. 314:[5] a use transferred from one to another without any act.}

---

[1] Bro. Abr., *Feffements al uses*, pl. 50, 57, 59.
[2] Litt. s. 641.
[3] *Recte* YB Pas. 49 Edw. III, fo. 16, pl. 10.
[4] The words 'See there' in the next sentence may indicate that this refers to Coke's notes on Littleton.
[5] *Anon.* (1572) Dyer 314, §97.

[213]

AD, fo. 10 (764).

\<Uses.\>ˢ

Nota que sont 2 manner de uses, scilicet un Chancery use et un use execute per lestatute de 27 H. 8. Nota que Serjeant Anderson dit a moy que issint fuit adjudge in le Segnior Audleys case et difference prise enter voluntes et \<uses\>.[1]

[214]

AD, fo. 11 (765).

\<Uses.\>ˢ

\<Ou use serra create sur releas\>ˢ

Denham et Dormans case fuit tiel. Denham per fait indent morgage son terre al Dorman et puis Denham releas tout son droit al morgagee \<per fine\>ⁱ al use de mesme lendenture. Et adjudge que le condition fuit extincte car nul use poet estre raise sur tiel releas etc. Mes sur releas que create un estate, come le livre est in 15 H. 7, 13, home poet create un use. \<Vide 10 E. 4, 3, et Perkins 133, si le disseisie releas al disseisor rendant rent cest voide reservation pur ceo que il ne depart mes ove un nude droit.\>ᵃ

[215]

AD, fo. 19 (774).

\<Remainder.\>ˢ \<Nota quant un remainder serra bon a un person que nest in esse.\>ˢ

Wray, chiefe justice, dit in arguendo in le case de seniori puero que quant un remainder est limitte per un generall nosme ceo est bon coment [que] le partie ne soit in esse al temps. \<Fleta, lib. 2, cap. 4.\>ⁱ Come le remainder al droit heires J. S. ou le remainder seniori puero J. S., ceo est bon, come le case la fuit adjudge. \<P. 32 E. 3, 57b, al priores[2] in fe.\>ⁱ Mes quant le remainder est limitte a un person certaine per son proper nosme, come le remainder a le maior et cominalte de Islington, et al temps nest ascun tiel corporation, coment que il soit durant le particuler estate uncore ceo est voide. 9 H. 6, 24, accordant a ceo. Issint si le remainder soit limitt as droit heires J. S. si nul tiel J. S. soit al temps mes puis un est nee de mesme le nosme. Et issint

---

[1] *Unclear.*
[2] praores.

---

[6] Cf. above, p. 41, for another version of these arguments.

[7] *Sic*, but this year is not in print. Cf. 50 Edw. III, Lib. Ass., pl. 1 (remainder to the prioress of Dartford and her successors for ever).

[8] I.e. the corporation comes into being before the remainder falls in.

[9] *Farington* v. *Darell* (1431) YB Trin. 9 Hen. VI, fo. 23, pl. 19, at fo. 24, *per* Babington C.J.; B. & M. 80, at p. 83.

213. LORD AUDLEY'S CASE[1]

Common Pleas, 1573 (related in 1577/82).

Uses.

Note that there are two kinds of uses, namely a Chancery use and a use executed by the statute of 27 Hen. VIII.[2] Note that Serjeant Anderson told me it was so adjudged in Lord Audley's case, and a distinction drawn between wills and uses.

214. DENHAM v. DORMAN

Temp. Eliz.

Uses.

Where a use shall be created upon a release.

Denham and Dorman's case was as follows. Denham, by deed indented, mortgaged his land to Dorman, and later Denham released all his right to the mortgagee by fine, to the use of the same indenture. And it was adjudged that the condition was extinguished, for no use may be raised upon such a release. However, upon a release which creates an estate, as the book is in 15 Hen. VII, fo. 13,[3] one may create a use. See 10 Edw. IV, fo. 3,[4] and Perkins, fo. 133: if a disseisee releases to the disseisor, rendering rent, this is a void reservation because he only parts with a bare right.

215. HUMPHRESTON'S CASE[5]

King's Bench, 1575.

Remainder. Note when a remainder shall be good to a person who is not *in esse*.

WRAY C.J. said in argument in the case of *seniori puero* that when a remainder is limited by a general name it is good, even if the party is not *in esse* at the time.[6] {Fleta, lib. ii, c. 4.} For instance, a remainder to the right heirs of John Style, or a remainder to the older child (*seniori puero*) of John Style, is good, as the case there was adjudged. {Pas. 32 Edw. III, 57v:[7] to a prioress in fee.} But when the remainder is limited to a certain person by his proper name, such as a remainder to the mayor and commonalty of Islington, and at the time there is no such corporation, even though there is during the particular estate,[8] it is still void. 9 Hen. VI, fo. 24,[9] accord. Likewise if the remainder is limited to the right heirs of John Style, and there is no such John Style at the time, though one is born afterwards with the same name. So is

---

[1] Differently reported in Dyer 314, 324; 2 Leon. 159; 4 Leon. 166, 210 (three versions of the same report). Dyer said the case was first moved in 1559. It arose from the attainder of James Tuchet, Lord Audley, in 1497.
[2] Statute of Uses, 27 Hen. VIII, c. 10.
[3] *Vampage's Case* (temp. Edw. IV), cit. by Vavasour J. in YB Mich. 15 Hen. VII, fo. 13, pl. 2., where all the justices held void a release to a lessee before he had entered, because he had no possession.
[4] YB Pas. 10 Edw. IV, fo. 3, pl. 6.   [5] See above, p. 40, no. 87, and the note there.

est 1 H. 7, 10. Vies 10 E. 3, Resceit, 40, leas pur vie, le remainder a William son fitz, son fem esteant adonques enseint ove fitz, et puis le fits fuit nee et fuit baptise per le nosme de William, et uncore il prist riens. Vide 18 E. 3, [blank], et 17 E. 3, [blank]. 10 E. 3, tit. Resceit, 40. <Vies 2 H. 7, 13b, mesme le diversite per Keble.>[a] [1]

[216]

AD, fo. 19v (774v).

<Remaindre.>[s]

11 R. 2, tit. Detinue, 46. Tenant in taile, le remainder as droit heires J. S., tenant in taile fist feffment in fe, J. S. morust, le tenant in taile morust sauns issue, et fuit tenus bon remainder, car la lissue J. S. port brefe de detinue pur les chartres et fuit barr. Vide le case de seniori puero apres fol. 25. Mes nota que in le [dit][2] case de seniori puero si lesse pur vie, le remaindre al droit heires J. S., [fait][2] feffment in fe, et puis J. S. morust, il entra pur le forfeiture. <Mes [le][2] contrarie fuit adjudge Trin. 36 El. rott. 1676 in commini banco [in Ar]chers case. Et issint tenus per divers justices in Dill[on et] Freins case.>[a]

[217]

AD, fo. 20v (775v).

<Remaindre.>[s]

14 Eliz. in le case de Cranmer fuit agre per toutz les justices de common banke que cest remaindre fuit bone, scilicet, Cranmer fist feffment in fe al use de luy mesme pur terme de son vie et puis al use de ces executores pur xxj ans ove divers remainders ouster. In cest case fuit agre [per][3] toutz que cest terme ne fuit in Cranmer mesme <et>[d] mes que il serra bone a ces executors apres sa morant. Et ilz agreont que le remainder fuit bon. Loppinion de queux semble daccorder ove 7 H. 4, car sicom home nad un heire in sa vie issint il nad executors in son vie, issint que nest de necessitie que un remainder vestera durant le particuler estate. Et la le Segnior Dier mitt cest case: si jeo face leas pur vie al piere, le remainder a son droit heire pur ans, ceo est bone, et uncore il ne poet vest durant le particuler estate, car il ne poet aver heire en son vie, mes eo instante que le particuler estate determine <m[esme]>[d] in mesme lenstaunt le remainder prent effect. <Hil. 14 Eliz. rott. Dccccxxx8.>[a] [4]

---

[1] *Written sideways in inner margin.*   [2] *Words lost in bottom outer corner.*
[3] in.   [4] *Written sideways in margin.*

---

[6] See above, p. 40, no. 87, and the note there.
[7] Pas. 11 Ric. II, Fitz. Abr., *Detinue*, pl. 46; YB Pas. 11 Ric. II (Ames Fdn), p. 283, pl. 31.
[8] *Archer's Case*, i.e. *Baldwyn v. Smith* (1597) CP 40/1533, m. 1676d; vol. iv, p. 818; 1 Co. Rep. 63. This is not the Archer's case noted above p. 10, no. 16.
[9] *Chudleigh's Case* (1594) 1 Co. Rep. 113; above, p. clv.
[10] See above, p. 58, no. 106, and the note there.   [11] YB Hil. 7 Hen. IV, fo. 6, pl. 2.
[12] CP 40/1300, m. 938 (printed in Benl. 207); above, p. 58, n. 1.

1 Hen. VII, fo. 10.[1] See 10 Edw. III, tit. *Resceit*, 40:[2] a lease for life, remainder to William his son, his wife then being pregnant with a son, and then the son was born and was baptised by the name of William, and yet he took nothing. See 18 Edw. III and 17 Edw. III;[3] 10 Edw. III, tit. *Resceit*, 40.[4] {See 2 Hen. VII, fo. 13v:[5] the same distinction made by Kebell.}

216. HUMPHRESTON'S CASE, continued[6]

King's Bench, 1575.

Remainder.

11 Ric. II, tit. *Detinue*, 46.[7] Tenant in tail, remainder to the right heirs of John Style, the tenant in tail makes a feoffment in fee, John Style dies, the tenant in tail dies without issue, and it was held a good remainder: for there the issue of John Style brought a writ of detinue for the charters and was barred. See the case of *seniori puero*, below, fo. 25. But note that in the said case of *seniori puero*, if a lessee for life, remainder to the right heirs of John Style, makes a feoffment in fee, and then John Style dies, he may enter for the forfeiture. {But the contrary was adjudged in Trin. 36 Eliz., rot. 1676 in the Common Bench, in Archer's case.[8] And so it was held by several of the justices in Dillon and Freine's case.[9]}

217. CRANMER'S CASE[10]

Common Pleas, 1572.

Remainder.

In 14 Eliz., in Cranmer's case, it was agreed by all the justices of the Common Bench that this remainder was good: Cranmer made a feoffment in fee to the use of himself for term of his life, and then to the use of his executors for twenty-one years, with various remainders over. In this case it was agreed by them all that this term was not in Cranmer himself, but would be good for his executors after his death. And they agreed that the remainder was good. This opinion seems to accord with 7 Hen. IV,[11] for just as a man has no heir in his lifetime, so he has no executors in his lifetime, and so it is not of necessity that a remainder should vest during the particular estate. And in that case the lord DYER put this case: if I make a lease for life to a father, remainder to his right heir for years, this is good, and yet it cannot vest during the particular estate, for he cannot have an heir in his lifetime, but *eo instante* that the particular estate determines, in that same instant the remainder takes effect. {Hil. 14 Eliz., roll 938.[12]}

---

[1] Hil. 1 Hen. VII, Fitz. Abr., *Feffements et faits*, pl. 30 (Differently reported in YB Trin. 1 Hen. VII, fo. 28, pl. 6). It is not in the old edition of 1–8 Hen. VII at fo. 10.
[2] YB Mich. 10 Edw. III, fo. 45, pl. 8; Fitz. Abr., *Resceit*, pl. 40; above, p. 41, n. 4.
[3] *The Prior of Grimsby's Case* (1343–44) YB Pas. 17 Edw. III, fo. 29, pl. 30; continued in Mich. 18 Edw. III, fo. 59, pl. 91
[4] YB Mich. 10 Edw. III, fo. 45, pl. 8; Fitz. Abr., *Resceit*, pl. 40.
[5] YB Hil. 2 Hen. VII, fo. 13, pl. 16.

[218]

AD, fo. 26 (781).

<Discharge.>[s]

Trin. 18 Eliz. rott. 934, North., le case fuit tiel in effect. Leasse fuit fait al Onley pur certayn ans a commencer apres le mort le countes de Darbye, et sur lacceptauns del leas Onley promise a le dit countes que le dit Onley <a le dit count>[d] assignera ou conveiera mesme le terme a ascun person ou persons destre nosme ou appoint per le dit countes etc., et del auter parte le dit Onley avoit expend divers summes de deniers circa negotia le dit countes, queux sommes et chescun parcell de ceo le dit countes avoit promise a le dit Onley a paier, et puis le dit countes de Darby prist a baron le counte de Kent, et puis le counte de Kent et le dit Onley agrea ensemble que le dit Onley in consideration de ses expences avera le dit terme absque aliqua assuerencia etc. et promissione et que ceo serra in plein satisfaction del promise fait per le dit countes, issint que in effect lagrement fuit que chescun de eux serra quite vers auter de lour severall assumpsitz et promises.

Et Mounson semble que ceo fuit bone discharge de lour promises etc. Et il dit que accord poet cibien determine chose in action et cause de action come arbitrement fuit clere.

Mes Manwood prist diversitie inter arbitrement et accord, car arbitratours sont indifferent persons nient parties mes judges del cause, et per ceo come ilz poent create actions ilz poent extincter actions, mes les parties mesme sicome ilz ne poent create actions issint ilz ne poent extincter actions. Et il dit que cause de action ne poet estre releas ou discharge per parol solement sauns ascun satisfactyon, et donques icy si cause de action ne poet estre discharge per parol donques nul satisfaction. Et 16 E. 4, 8, est expressement in le point, que si cause de action soit reciprocal done inter 2 persons ilz ne poient accorder que chescun irra quite.

Et le Segnior Dier agrea a ceo, que chose in action ou cause de action ne poet estre discharge per parol.

Mes ilz disoient que arbitrators poent discharge actions et create actions pur ceo que ilz sont judges del cause. Vide […],[1] 6, 7. 14 H. 4, 27. 46 E. 3, 33. 12 H. 8, 1b. 12 R. 2, tit. Barre, 243.

---

[1] *Obscured by blot.*

[4] Cf. YB Hil. 14 Hen. IV, fo. 19, pl. 21.
[5] Cf. YB Trin. 46 Edw. III, fo. 17, pl. 14.
[6] Clearly so written, but seemingly incorrect.
[7] Trin. 12 Ric. II, Fitz. Abr., *Barre*, pl. 243; identifiable as *Bildistone* v. *Reyne* (1388) Trin. 12 Ric. II (Ames Fdn), p. 6, pl. 4.

218. ONLEY v. EARL OF KENT[1]

Common Pleas, Trin. 1576.

Discharge.

Trin.18 Eliz., roll 934, Northamptonshire, the case was as follows, in effect. A lease was made to [Edward] Onley for certain years, to commence after the death of the countess of Derby,[2] and upon the acceptance of the lease Onley promised the said countess that the said Onley would assign or convey the same term to any person or persons to be named or appointed by the said countess, and on the other side the said Onley had spent various sums of money about the affairs of the said countess, which sums, and every parcel thereof, the said countess had promised the said Onley to [re]pay; then the said countess of Derby married the earl of Kent; and then the earl of Kent and the said Onley agreed together that the said Onley, in consideration of his expenses, should have the said term without any assurance and promise, and that this should be in full satisfaction of the promise made by the said countess: so that the agreement, in effect, was that each of them should be quit against the other in respect of their several assumpsits and promises.

MOUNSON thought it was a good discharge of their promises. And he said that an accord may well determine a chose in action and a cause of action, as in the case of arbitration (which was clear).

But MANWOOD drew a distinction between an arbitration and an accord; for arbitrators are indifferent persons who are not parties but judges of the cause, and therefore just as they may create actions they may extinguish actions; but the parties themselves, just as they cannot create actions, so they cannot extinguish actions. And he said that a cause of action cannot be released or discharged by parol only, without any satisfaction; and so here, if a cause of action cannot be discharged by parol, then there is no satisfaction. 16 Edw. IV, fo. 8,[3] is expressly in the point, that if there are reciprocal causes of action between two persons they cannot make an accord that each of them shall go quit.

The lord DYER agreed with that, namely that a chose in action or a cause of action cannot be discharged by parol.

But they said that arbitrators may discharge actions and create actions, because they are judges of the cause. See 14 Hen. IV, fo. 27;[4] 46 Edw. III, fo. 33;[5] 12 Hen. VIII, fo. 1v;[6] 12 Ric. II, tit. *Barre*, 243.[7]

---

[1] Probably CP 40/1337, roll 934 (unfit for production; partly printed in Benl. 297): Edward Onley v. Henry, earl of Kent, and his wife Mary; *assumpsit*; demurrer to the lengthy plea in bar. Noted above, p. 20, no. 34; p. 118, no. 211; below, p. 152, nos. 285–286. Differently reported in JRL MS. Fr. 118, fos. 84–86 (see below, p. 153); *Ff*, fos. 189v–193v (with a transcript of the record); Dyer 355, cit. record; IT MS. Petyt 511.12, fos. 282 (Hil. 1577), 290 (Trin. 1577); LI MS. Maynard 87, fo. 236v; HLS MS. 1202 (2079), fo. 162. For subsequent litigation on different matters see *Onley* v. *Earl of Kent* (Chancery, 1579) 117 Selden Soc. 181, no. 60e; (Chancery, 1585) ibid. 179, no. 52; *Earl of Kent* v. *Onley* (Mich. 1586) CUL MS. Gg.3.26, fo. 133; *Onley* v. *Earl of Kent* (Mich. 1588) BL MS. Add. 35943, fos. 215v–216; MS. Lansd. 1073, fo. 92.

[2] Mary (née Cotton) (d. 1580), dowager countess of Derby since the earl's death in 1572; she later married Henry Grey (1541–1615), earl of Kent.

[3] YB Mich. 16 Edw. IV, fo. 8, pl. 5.

[219]

AD, fo. 41 (798).

<Accessarie.>[s]

Nota que fuit tenus clerement per les justices del banke le roy que home ne poet estre accessory coment que il receive cesti que ad ferue un mortallment, coment que le partie devie del plague deins lan puis, car nest felonie tanque le mort ensue.

[220]

AD, fo. 799v.

<Severauns que le ley fait.>[s]

14 Elyz. in le case de Winter ceux cases fueront myse per Barrham et agre puis per divers auters des justices. Si 2 homes voillont faire leas de lour several terres reservaunt rent etc., coment que les parolx sont joint uncore en ley ilz sont severall lesses. Issint si 2 tenants in common font leas pur ans, le ley construe ceo destre severall lesses. Et le <ley>[d] reason del ley in ceux cases est pur le severall interest des <partes>[d] <grauntors>.[i] Ascun foitz le ley fait severauns pur le capacite des grantees, come leas fait al abbe et a un seculer home. Ascun foitz[1] pur avoider inconveniens, come si terres soient dones a un frere et soer et a les heires de lour 2 corps ingendres, in cest case le ley fait un severauns, comes les livres sont, 7 H. 4, Litt., fo. 62, 17 E. 3, si terres fuerent dones a frere et soer etc. Issint le ley fait severauns ascun foitz in contractes, come le livre est in 17 E. 4, si jeo vende 2 chivalls solvendum pur lun x li. et pur lauter v li. <issint>[d] icy sont severall contractes.

Auxi a mesme le temps cest case fuit myse per Mounson, justice: cesti que use de certaine terres et des auters in possessione <il fist>[2] un leas dambideux reservant un rent, coment que les parolx sont joint uncore le ley fait un severauns, scilicet le reversion del terres in use al feffees et le revercion de terres in possession a cesti que [use][3]. Issint 20 H. 6, 3 coparceners font partition et lun pur egaltie de partition graunt a les auters 2 un annuell rent, cest rent, coment que il fuit joint grant, uncore il inurera severalment. Et issint est 15 H. 7, 14. 30 <E. 3>,[i] Lib. Ass., p. […][4] est tenus si home lessa son mannour ove le moulture de son molyn, reservaunt pur le moline ij d. et pur le mannour xij d., uncore la il ne sont severall lesses.

Et a mesme le temps Manwood, justice, prist cest diversite quant un reservation est hors de un mesme chose, coment que le reservation soit <joint>[d] severall uncore il est forsque un entier demise, mes quant les choses sont severall, coment que le

---

[1] *Written twice.*
[2] *Written twice.*
[3] *Word missing at edge.*
[4] *Numeral missing at edge.*

[6] Seemingly YB Mich. 21 Hen. VI, fo. 10, pl. 24.
[7] YB Mich. 15 Hen. VII, fo. 14, pl. 5.
[8] *Recte* 9 Edw. III, Lib. Ass., pl. 24; below, p. 126.

219. ANON.

King's Bench, temp. Eliz.

Accessory.

Note that it was clearly held by the justices of the King's Bench that if someone receives a person who struck another mortally, he cannot be an accessory, even though the party dies of the blow within a year after, for it is not felony until the death ensues.

220. WINTER'S CASE[1]

Common Pleas, Mich. 1572.

Severance made by the law.

In 14 Eliz., in Winter's case, these cases were put by *Barham* and afterwards agreed by several of the justices. If two men make a lease of their several lands, reserving rent, even though the words are joint, in law they are nevertheless separate leases. Likewise if two tenants in common make a lease for years, the law construes this as separate leases. And the reason of the law in these cases is because of the separate interests of the grantors. Sometimes the law makes severance because of the capacity of the grantees, as where a lease is made to an abbot and a secular man. And sometimes it does so to avoid inconvenience, as where lands are given to a brother and sister and the heirs of their two bodies begotten: in that case the law makes a severance, as the books are in 7 Hen. IV;[2] Litt., fo. 62;[3] 17 Edw. III,[4] of lands given to a brother and sister. Likewise, the law sometimes makes severance in contracts, as the book is in 17 Edw. IV:[5] if I sell two horses, *solvendum* for one of them £10 and for the other £5, they are separate contracts.

On the same occasion this case also was put by MOUNSON J.: cestui que use of certain lands, [being seised] of others in possession, made a lease of both, reserving one rent; here, although the words are joint, the law nevertheless makes a severance, namely the reversion of the lands in use to the feoffees, and the reversion of the lands in possession to cestui que use. Likewise, in 20 Hen. VI:[6] three coparceners make partition, and to make the partition equal one of them grants the other two an annual rent; this rent, though it was granted jointly, will enure severally. So it is in 15 Hen. VII, fo. 14.[7] In 30 Edw. III, Lib. Ass.,[8] it is held that if someone leases his manor with the multure of his mill, reserving for the mill 2d. and for the manor 12d., these are not several leases.

On the same occasion, MANWOOD J. made this distinction: when there is a reservation out of one same thing, even if the reservation is several, it is nevertheless but one entire demise; but when the things are several, even if the reservation is joint,

---

[1] Above, p. 43, no. 88, and the note there.
[2] YB Trin. 7 Hen. IV, fo. 16, pl. 9, *per* Thirning C.J.
[3] This refers to Coke's copy of Littleton, *AB*, fo. 470 (magenta ink).
[4] YB Mich. 17 Edw. III, fo. 51, pl. 24, and fo. 78, pl. 116; discussed in 8 Co. Rep. 87.
[5] Cf. above, p. 100.

reservation soit joint uncore sont severall leasses. Et pur ceo <si jeo lessa>ᵈ le livre est in [1]5 Lib. Ass., [*blank*], si jeo graunt rent hors de mon mannour de D., scilicet x li. de rent percipiendum [v]¹ li. per les maynes dun tiel et v li. per les maynes dun auter etc., il nest forsque un mesme rent pur ceo que il issuit hors dun mesme chose. <In 5 E. 4>ᵈ Issint 5 E. 4, 7 E. 3, si jeo lessa terres pur ans reservant le primer an un rose, le 2 anne un denier, ore le seisin de lun est seisin de toutz causa qua supra. Issint est le livre in 9 Lib. Ass., home lessa un mannour ove le moulture de son molyn, reddendum pur le mannour x s. et pur le moulture ij s., in cest case nest que un rent car sont issuant hors del mannour et riens hors del moulture. Mes auterment est quant le rent issuit hors de severall choses, come si jeo done a vous mon mannores de D. et S. en taile, reddendum pur S. x li. et pur D. v li., icy sont severall rentes. Issint est 8 E. 3, [*blank*], de leas de 2 acres de terre reddendo pur lun j d. et pur lauter ij d. etc., que ilz sont severall rentes pur ceo que ilz issuont hors de severall choses. Et la fuit agre que si home devant lestatut de quia emptores fist feffment de 2 acres de terre tenendum lun acre pur un ij d. et lauter acre per iiij d. que in cest case ilz sont severall tenures et le segnior covient daver severall brefes de <wast>ᵈ cessavit.

Et a mesme le temps Dier, chief justice,² cite le case 18 E. 3, si jeo graunt un rent hors des terres in 3 counties, icy nest que un rent, car jeo puis distreine in chescun counte pur tout le rent.

Et Harper, justice, tient fortment que un reservation ne unques ferra un joint leas, mes un chose accidentall, car nient obstant que il fault uncore le lease est assetz bon. Mes il dit que 4 choses sont del substauns del leas, scilicet grauntor, graunte, chose [...]³ et un certaine commencement et certaine fine.

[221]

AD, fo. 800.

<Severans que le ley fait.>ˢ

Quere si home fait leas de 2 acres habendum lun acre pur vie et lauter acre pur ans reservant un rent, si tout le rent issuera hors del acre que est leas pur vie pur ceo que ceo est un estate de franktenement et plus digne, ou que il issera hors del ambideux, ou si le rent serra severall? Et moy semble que le rent serra severall pur ceo que le revercion de ceux 2 acres est severall et auxi pur ceo que le lesses sont severall, scilicet lun pur ans et lauter pur vie. Et pur ceo si home soit seisie dun acre in use et dauter in possession et fist leas dambideux reservant un rent, coment que le reservation fuit joint uncore severall leasses et per consequens severall rentes. Issint si 2 tenantes in common joine in un leas rendant rent etc. Vies le principall case de

---

¹ x.
² *Written twice.*
³ *Word lost at foot of page.*

they are nevertheless several leases. The book is thus in 15 Lib. Ass.:[1] if I grant a rent of £10 out of my manor of Dale, £5 of which is to be received by the hands of one certain person and £5 by the hands of another, it is only one same rent, because it issues out of the same thing. So is 5 Edw. [III] and 7 Edw. III.[2] If I lease lands for years, reserving in the first year a rose and in the second year a penny, seisin of one of them is a seisin of all, for the above reason. So is the book in 9 Lib. Ass.:[3] a man leased a manor with the multure of his mill, *reddendum* for the manor 10s. and for the multure 2s., in this case it is but one rent, for the sums are issuing out of the manor and nothing issues out of the multure. But it is otherwise when the rent issues out of several things, as where I give you my manors of Dale and Sale in tail, *reddendum* for Sale £10 and for Dale £5: here the rents are several. So is 8 Edw. III, concerning a lease of two acres of land, *reddendo* for one of them 1d. and for the other 2d.: these are several rents, because they issue out of several things. And it was there agreed that if someone before the statute of *Quia Emptores* made a feoffment of two acres of land, to hold one of the acres by 2d. and the other by 4d., in this case they are several tenures and the lord must have separate writs of *cessavit*.[4]

On the same occasion DYER C.J. cited the case in 18 Edw. III:[5] if I grant a rent out of lands in three counties, there is only one rent, for I may distrain in each county for the whole rent.

HARPER J. held strenuously that a reservation shall never make a joint lease, but it is something incidental; for even if it fails, the lease is still perfectly good. But he said that there are four things which are of the substance of a lease, namely a grantor, a grantee, a thing [leased] and a certain commencement and certain end.[6]

221. WINTER'S CASE, continued[7]

Common Pleas, Mich. 1572.

Severance made by the law.

If someone makes a lease of two acres, *habendum* one of the acres for life and the other acre for years, reserving one rent, whether the whole rent shall issue out of the acre which is leased for life because it is an estate of freehold and worthier, or out of both, or whether the rent shall be several? It seems to me that the rent shall be several, because the reversion of these two acres is several, and also because the leases are several, namely one of them for years and the other for life. Therefore if someone is seised of one acre in use and another in possession, and makes a lease of both, reserving one rent, even though the reservation was joint they are still several leases, and in consequence several rents. Likewise if two tenants in common join in one

---

[1] 15 Edw. III, Lib. Ass., pl. 11.
[2] 5 Edw. III, Lib. Ass., pl. 6, continued in 7 Edw. III, Lib. Ass., pl. 1. Cf. above, p. 101.
[3] 9 Edw. III, Lib. Ass., pl. 24; abridged from YB Mich. 9 Edw. III, fo. 35, pl. 37.
[4] Cf. Co. Litt. 23.
[5] YB Mich. 18 Edw. III, fo. 32, pl. 7; discussed in 7 Co. Rep. 3.
[6] The same dictum is reported in different words below, p. 136, no. 245.
[7] Above, p. 43, no. 88, and the note there.

Winter etc. Et nota bene que la severall reservationes ne ferra le leas que fuit joint severall. Nec joint reservation ne poet faire severall lesses joint. Et nota bene toutz les cases devant etc. 10 H. 6, [*blank*], come fuit cite per Manwood in Winters case, si home soit seisie dun acre in fe et dun auter acre pur xl ans lessa ambideux pur xx ans rendant rent sur condition, le lessor morust, et le rent est arrere, ore les executors entront pur le condition enfreintt del parte et le heire del auter parte, quel prove que ceux sont ore severall etc.

[222]

AD, fo. 800v.

<Severans que le ley fait.>[s]

Nota, Anderson serjaunt dit que fuit adjudge in le case inter Sir Anthonie Cooke, chivaler, et Wootton, esquier, que si jeo covenant ove J. S., J. D. et J. N. et chescun de eux de faire feffment a J. S. del mannour de D., a J. D. del mannour de S., et a J. N. del mannour de W., sur reasonable request destre fait a luy per le dit J. S., J. D. et J. N., in cest case coment que le request est limitt destre fait jointment uncore intant que severall interests accrueront a eux chescun de eux poet faire severall requestes daver estate de estre <chescun>[d] fait [a] eux solonque le purport del covenant.

[223]

AD, fo. 46 (805).

<Ou un generall statute serra prise particularement et ou nemy.>[s]

Nota lestatut de 1 R. 3 est generall que chescun graunt etc. des ascuns terres ou tenementz etc. per cesti que use serra bon, uncore si cesti que use dun terme graunt ouster le terme ceo nest bone (vide 15 H. 7, [*blank*] cont[ra]) car coment que le primer parolx sont generall uncore apres est dit in mesme lestatut que tiel graunt serra bone envers cesti que use et ses heires et toutz auters inclaymant a lour use et lour heires, issint les parolx subsequentes expound le parolx generall etc. Et le Segnior Dier in Onlyes case dit que graunt fait per cesti que use dun terme fuit voide.

---

[3] Anderson was created serjeant 1577 and appointed C.J.C.P. 1582.
[4] See above, p. 124, no. 218, and the note there.
[5] 1 Ric. III, c. 1.
[6] Probably YB Mich. 15 Hen. VII, fo. 2, pl. 4, concerning a lease for life.

lease, yielding rent. See the principal case of Winter. And note well there that several reservations will not cause a lease which was joint to be several. Nor may a joint reservation cause several leases to be joint. And note well all the cases above. 10 Hen. VI, as it was cited by MANWOOD in Winter's case:[1] if someone seised of one acre in fee and of another acre for forty years leases both for twenty years, yielding rent, upon condition, the lessor dies, and the rent is behind, the executors may now enter for breach of the condition for part, and the heir for the other part, which proves that they are now several.

222. WOTTON v. COOKE[2]

Common Pleas, *c.* 1575, cited *c.* 1577/82.[3]

Severance made by the law.

Note that *Anderson*, serjeant, said it was adjudged in the case between Sir Anthony Cooke, knight, and Wootton, esquire, that if I covenant with John Style, John Dale and John Noke, and each of them, to make a feoffment to John Style of the manor of Dale, to John Dale of the manor of Sale, and to John Noke of the manor of Whiteacre, upon reasonable request to be made to him by the said John Style, John Dale and John Noke, in this case, although the request is directed to be made jointly, nevertheless, inasmuch as several interests will accrue to them, each of them may make a separate request to have an estate made to him according to the purport of the covenant.

223. ONLEY v. EARL OF KENT[4]

Common Pleas, 1576.

Where a general statute shall be taken particularly, and where not.

Note that the statute of 1 Ric. III[5] is general, that every grant etc. of any lands or tenements etc. by cestui que use shall be good; and yet if cestui que use of a term grants over the term, it is not good (see 15 Hen. VII,[6] to the contrary), for although the first words are general, nevertheless it says afterwards in the same statute that such grant shall be good as against cestui que use and his heirs and all others claiming to their use and the use of their heirs, and so the subsequent words expound the general words. And the lord DYER said in Onley's case that a grant made by cestui que use of a term was void.

---

[1] YB Mich. 10 Hen. VI, fo. 24, pl. 83; above, p. 81.
[2] Probably CP 40/1321, m. 925 (Hil. 1574; unfit for production; partly printed in Benl. 228): Thomas Wotton esq. v. Sir Anthony Cooke; covenant on an indenture of 1537 made with the plaintiff's father, Sir Edward Wotton; issue on performance; verdict and judgment for the plaintiff with £2,000 damages. Noted above, p. 24, no. 46; below, p. 129, no. 230. Differently reported in Dyer 337, cit. Hil. 26 Eliz., roll 925 (incorrect); Benl. 228; 1 And. 53. This was one of several suits between the same parties concerning (inter alia) the manor of Dassett, Warw.: see 110 Selden Soc. 202.

[224]

AD, fo. 47 (806).

<Nota coment cest parol 'suche' serra prise.>[5]

Nota per Fenner, serjaunt, arguendo in le serjauntes case, que si leas soit fait pur ans sauns fine ou incume ou si lease soit fait a commencer a Mich., ambideux ceux cases sont deins lestatut de 21 H. 8, et uncore le corps del act dit 'such', que refiert al preamble. <Vide 40 Eliz. 284.>[a]

[225]

AD, fo. 54v (811v).

<Statutes.>[s]

Nota, est purveu per lestatute de bigamis, cap. 2, in carta ubi continetur dedi et concessi tenendum de capitalibus etc. sine clausula warrantie ad huc donator in <vita sua>[1] debet warrant[izare]. Et uncore fuit agre anno 15 Eliz. que coment que il soit un expresse garrante deins le fait, uncore le feffee vouchera per cest parol dedi expressement enconter les parolx.

[226]

AD, fo. 55 (812).

<Estatutes.>[s]

Nota fuit dit in le common banke anno [...][2] que si fem deins age accept jointure devant le coverture que el ne d[...][2] ceo per lestatut de 27 H. 8. Mes la fuit agre que si le baron et fem fait les[se pur][2] xxj ans solonque lestatut de 32 H. 8 la fem covient estre de plein [age].[2]

---

[1] *Reads* vite sue.
[2] *Words lost in bottom outer corner.*

---

[5] *Dineley* v. *Assheton* (1581) as noted under Trin. 40 Eliz. in *C*, fos. 283–284v, at fo. 284 (vol. iv, p. 895); noted above, p. 61, no. 109; below, p. 162, no. 317; and in vol. ii, p. 192. This concerned the interpretation of the statute 34 & 35 Hen. VIII, c. 20, which (like 21 Hen. VIII, c. 15) gave protection against feigned recoveries.
[6] See above p 113, no. 204, and the note there.
[7] The text clearly reads *adhuc*, but this seems to be the sense. The statute is not here quoted verbatim.
[8] This seems from Coke's other citations to be a slip for 14 Eliz.
[9] This may be a dictum in *Vernon's Case* (1572) below, p. 141, no. 258.
[10] Statute of Uses, 27 Hen. VIII, c. 10.
[11] 32 Hen. VIII, c. 28.

224. THE SERJEANTS' CASE[1]

Common Pleas, Pas. 1579.

Note how the word 'such' shall be understood.

Note by *Fenner*, serjeant, arguing in the serjeants' case,[2] that if a lease is made for years without a fine or income,[3] or if a lease is made to commence at Michaelmas, both these cases are within the statute of 21 Hen. VIII,[4] and yet the body of the Act says 'such', which refers to the preamble. {See 40 Eliz. 284.[5]}

225. ANON.[6]

Common Pleas, Hil. 1572.

Statutes.

Note that it is provided by the Statute *De Bigamis*, c. [6], that in a charter which contains [the words] 'I have given and granted (*dedi et concessi*) ... to hold of the chief lords [and not of the donor]', without a clause of warranty, the donor during his lifetime ought still[7] to warrant. And yet it was agreed in 15 Eliz.[8] that even if there is an express warranty in the deed, the feoffee may nevertheless vouch by reason of the word *dedi*, expressly contrary to the words.

226. ANON.

Common Pleas, perhaps 1572.[9]

Statutes.

Note that it was said in the Common Bench that if a woman under age accepts a jointure before the coverture she shall not [be barred from dower] by the statute of 27 Hen. VIII.[10] But it was there agreed that if the husband and wife make a lease for twenty-one years in accordance with the statute of 32 Hen. VIII,[11] the wife must be of full age.

---

[1] Fully reported in 4 Co. Rep. 8–12, sub nom. *Bevil's Case*, cit. Mich. 17 & 18 Eliz., roll 1739 (unfit for production), and Hil. 20 Eliz., roll 1745 (no such roll). Noted below, p. 156, no. 296; p. 159, no. 307 (dated Pas. 1579); p. 162, no. 316. Cit. in *C*, fo. 520*bis* (with the same roll reference); and in Coke's *Statuta* (Holkham 7834), fo. 202v ('Vide le serjeauntes case anno 21 Eliz. report per moy ...'). Differently reported in 1 And. 83–86; BL MS. Harley 6682, fos. 2v–7 (Popham's argument); MS. Harg. 37, fos. 40v–44v; MS. Lansd. 1057, fos. 61–65; MS. Lansd. 1072, fos. 126–129; MS. Lansd. 1095, fo. 121; MS. Lansd. 1145, fos. 105–119v; MS. Add. 16169, fos. 102v–105v, cit. Hil. 21 Eliz., roll 1785. Coke said the case was still being argued after Dyer C.J.'s death (1582).

[2] The case argued by the new serjeants created in 1577, and also by Rodes and Popham (created in 1578). Noted on another point in 4 Co. Rep. 8, cit. Hil. 20 Eliz., roll 1745.

[3] I.e. entry payment or premium. The preamble of the statute mentioned fines for incomes: cf. below, p. 156, no. 296; p. 160, no. 309.

[4] Presumably 21 Hen. VIII, c. 15 (protection of lessees against common recoveries), though the 'such' there refers to the recoveries and the relevance of the point in the text is not obvious. Cf. c. 13, which does not have a preamble.

[227]

AD, fo. 55v (812v).

<Statutes.>ˢ

Vies le case de Segnior Parre in P. 18 Eliz. in mes notes demesne.

[228]

AD, fo. 58v (815v).

<Utlagarie.>ˢ

Nota, fuit tenus clerement in le common banke T. 19 Eliz. si home demurt in Essex et fait obligation et puis remove in Suff., et puis action de det sur le obligation est port in Midd. vers le obligor nuper de Essex, in cest case le proclamation ne besoigne ore de issuer a le viconte ou il est ore demurrant mes al viconte ou il fuit nuper etc. Et ceo per les expresse parolx del statut de 6 H. 8. Et ceo fuit le case de un Appulton.

[229]

AD, fo. 61v (818v).

<Queux serron[t] bone nosme[s] [de] purchase.>ˢ

14 Eliz. in le case de Cranmer fuit agree per toutes les justices et serjauntes que executores sont bone nosme de purchase car la le case fuist, Cranmer fist feffment al use de luy mesme pur vie et apres son decesse al use de ces executors pur xxj ans etc.

[230]

AD, fo. 62 (819).

<Entente.>ˢ

Note, Wraye, chiefe justice, in largument de seniori puero, dit que il fuit adjudge in temps le roygne que ore est que ou trois oblige eux et utrumque eorum, et coment que uterque est properment referred al 2, et uncore fuit adjudge que il fuit un severall obligation et fuit prise come pro quemlibet solonque lentent des parties et nemi solonque le grammaticall sense.

227. LORD PARR'S CASE

Pas. 1576.

Statutes.

See the case of Lord Parr in Easter term 18 Eliz., in my own notes.[1]

228. APPULTON'S CASE

Common Pleas, Trin. 1577.

Outlawry.

Note that it was held clearly in the Common Bench in Trinity term 19 Eliz. that if someone lives in Essex and makes a bond, and then moves to Suffolk, and then an action of debt on the bond is brought in Middlesex against the obligor as 'late of Essex', in this case the proclamation [of outlawry] does not need to issue to the sheriff where he is now living, but to the sheriff where he lately was (*nuper*). That is by the express words of the statute of 6 Hen. VIII.[2] This was the case of one Appulton.

229. CRANMER'S CASE[3]

Common Pleas, Mich. 1572.

What shall be good names of purchase.

In 14 Eliz. in Cranmer's case it was agreed by all the justices and serjeants that 'executors' is a good name of purchase; for the case was that Cranmer made a feoffment to the use of himself for life, and after his decease to the use of his executors for twenty-one years.

230. WOTTON v. COOKE[4]

Common Pleas, *c.* 1575, *c*ited in the King's Bench.

Intention.

Note that WRAY C.J. said in the argument of *seniori puero*,[5] that it had been adjudged in the time of the present queen that where three bind themselves 'and either of them' (*utrumque eorum*), although 'either' (*uterque*) properly refers to two, nevertheless it was a several bond; and it was understood to mean 'any one' (*quemlibet*), according to the intention of the parties, and not according to the grammatical sense.

---

[1] This has eluded discovery. William, Lord Parr, died in 1547 without male issue.
[2] 6 Hen. VIII, c. 4.
[3] See above, p. 58, no. 106, and the note there.
[4] See above, p. 24, no. 46, where the same point is noted. Also noted above, p. 127, no. 222.
[5] *Humphreston's Case* (1575): see above, p. 40, no. 87, and the note there.

[231]

AD, fo. 62v (819v).

<Intente.>[s]

Nota per Manwood in Nicols case M. 17 Eliz. que chescun graunt covient estre execute in le vie del grantor et del grantee, car si devant le execution del graunt ascun de eux sont mort donques est le graunt voide. Et sur cest ground il mist ceux case[s] ...

[232]

AD, fo. 65 (822).

<Possibilitie.>[s]

P. 18 Eliz. Si baron soit possesse dun terme in droit sa fem et dona omnia bona sua, le terme passera. Et issint fuit adjudge, come jeo oye. Et issint la fuit tenus si executors dona omnia bona sua que toutz lour biens queux ilz avoient come executors passeront.

[233]

AD, fo. 72 (829).[1]

<Uses.>[s] <Vide Dier, 169.>[a] <30 H. 6, un use averre sur un devise.>[a]

15 Eliz. fuit agree per toutz les justices in le common banke in Vernons case que un use expresse est de pluis haut nature que un use implye et pur ceo un use expresse toutz foitz controlle un use implye, mes un use implie ne unques controlle un use expresse. Et pur ceo si home face feffment in fe al use de J. D. il ne poet aver ceo destre al use de J. S. pur ceo que un use implie ne unques controlle use expresse. <Dier, 169.>[i] Mes si home face feffment in fe sauns pluis dire, ore icy est un use im[plie] que il serra al use le feffor, mes sil expresse un use sur ceo nest question mes que cest use expresse tollera luse implie.

Et la fuit cite per Harper que il fuit grandement debate in le chan[cerie] et in le court de gardes parenter Luson et Wilkes que lou Luson inteffe un auter in consideration de m li. et in verite le feffor nad riens del dit deniers, et uncore fuit tenus que il poet averre que ceo fuit a son use demesne encounter le expresse consideration. Et la fuit agre que si home done terres in taile, icy est un <imp>[d] use implie, scilicet al use del done et ses heires, mez ils disoient que si home done terres in taile al use dun a[uter] cest use expresse controllera luse implie. 24 H. 8. 5 E. 6,

---

[1] *There is some loss of words and letters on the outer edge of the page.*

[4] Trin. 30 Hen. VI, Statham Abr., *Devise* (Exch. Ch.), where Fortescue C.J. referred to a devise 'de trust'.
[5] See next note.
[6] *Wilkes* v. *Leuson* (1559) Dyer 169. This was not in print in the 1570s.

231. NICHOLS v. NICHOLS[1]

Common Pleas, Mich. 1575.

Intent.

Note by MANWOOD, in Nichols's case, in Michaelmas term 17 Eliz., that every grant must be executed in the lifetime of the grantor and the grantee, for if either of them dies before the execution of the grant, the grant is void. Upon this ground he put these cases ...

232. BROADBRIDGE'S CASE[2]

King's Bench, Pas. 1576.

Possibility.

Easter term 18 Eliz. If a husband is possessed of a term in right of his wife and makes a gift of all his goods (*omnia bona sua*), the term will pass. And so it was adjudged, as I hear. Likewise, it was there held that if executors give 'all their goods' (*omnia bona sua*), all their goods which they have as executors will pass.

233. VERNON v. VERNON[3]

Common Pleas, 1572/73.

Uses. See Dyer 169. 30 Hen. VI, a use averred upon a devise.[4]

In 15 Eliz. it was agreed by all the justices in the Common Bench in Vernon's case that an express use is of a higher nature than an implied use, and therefore an express use always controls an implied use, whereas an implied use never controls an express use. Thus if someone makes a feoffment in fee to the use of John Dale, he may not aver this to be to the use of John Style, because an implied use never controls an express use. {Dyer 169.[5]} If someone makes a feoffment in fee, without saying more, here there is an implied use that it shall be to the use of the feoffor; but if he expresses a use upon it, there is no question but that this express use will take away (*tollera*) the implied use.

And this case HARPER cited a great debate in the Chancery, and in the Court of Wards, between Leuson and Wilkes,[6] where Leuson enfeoffed another in consideration of £1,000, and in truth the feoffor received none of the said money: and it was held that he could aver that this was to his own use, contrary to the express consideration. And it was there agreed that if someone gives lands in tail, there is an implied use, namely to the use of the donee and his heirs; but they said that if a man gives lands in tail to the use of another, this express use will control the implied use.

---

[1] See above, p. 45, no. 90, and the note there.
[2] Cit. as such in 1 Leon. 263 (1577), where the opinion is attributed to Wray C.J. and Plowden. Cf. above, p. 101, no. 172, where the dictum about executors is attributed to Wray C.J. and Gawdy J.
[3] See above, p. 75, no. 118, and the note there.

27. 30 H. 8 est encounter lour opinion. Perkins, 103b. Contra Pl. Com. 555. <27 H. 8, 10, Mountague dit que fuit adjudge que un use ne poet estre limitte sur estate taile.>[1]

[234]

AD, fo. 72 (829).[2]

<Uses.>[s]

Nota que fuit adjudge in Clatches case que un implied d[evise] ne unques controllera un expresse devise. Et pur <ceo>[i] le c[as] la fuit que home <devise>[d] ayant 2 files devise certain terres al eigne <in fe>[i] et certain terres al puisne et a ses heires, et si <le>[3] leigne morust devant que el ad accomplishe lage de xxvj a[ns] que donques son parte rem[ainera] al puisne, et si le puisne devie sauns childe que donques sa part rem[ainera] al eigne, et si ambideux morust sauns childe que le terre rem[ainera] al droit heires Henry Clatche. Le question fuit, si lun de eux morust sans child si le droit heire de Clatche entra maintenant ou que il targera tanque lauter soit mort auxi, pur ceo que fuit dit que est un cross remainder implied in ceux parolx silz ambideux morust sauns issue que donques etc. Uncore fuit adjudge que [pur] ceo que il fuit un expresse devise fait a eux devant cest implied devise ne serra de effecte. Et pur ceo Manwood dit, et Dier accord, que si home soit seisie dun mannour et d[evise] le <mannour>[d] demesnes del mannour a sa fem pur terme de son vie et les services pur 7 ans, et apres son mort a remainer a [...]in cest case el navera les services forsque pur 7 ans pur ceo [que] un implied devise ne unques controllera un expresse limit[ation]. Issint per luy et le Segnior Dier fuit adjudge in le case de Frencham, le case de quel fuit que home devise terres a un et a ses heires males de son corps et sil morust sauns issue a remainer ouster en fee, il ad issue female et morust, et fuit adjudge que cesti female na[vera] le terre car limplied devise ne controllera lexpresse limitation. [Mes], per Manwood, si home devise terre a son fem durant sa vie, et sil [devie] durant 7 ans a remainer a J. D. pur vie, et apres le mort [...].[4]

[235]

AD, fo. 74v (831v).

<Uses.>[s]

Graund diversite parenter feffment al use et feffment in possession, car home poet

---

[1] *Written sideways in inner margin.*
[2] *Part of the outer edge of the page is missing, and also the bottom line.*   [3] *Sic, but otiose.*
[4] *The remainder, including the whole of the last line, is missing at the foot of the page.*

[6] *Re Lord Dacre of the South* (1535) YB Pas. 27 Hen. VIII, fo. 9, pl. 22, at fo. 10, *per* Mountague serjeant ('fuit ajuge ore tard per advis de touts les justices que tenant in tail ne peut estre seisi al auter use').
[7] See below, p. 145, no. 269, and the note there.
[8] *Tucke* v. *Frencham* (1558) CP 40/1174, m. 923; below, p. 148, Dyer 171 ('Turke'); Benl. 68; Moo. 13; 1 And. 8.   [9] End of text missing.   [10] See above, p. 58, no. 106, and the note there.

24 Hen. VIII;[1] 5 Edw. VI, fo. 27.[2] 30 Hen. VIII[3] is against their opinion. {Perkins, fo. 103v.[4] Contra, Plowd. Com. 555.[5]} {In 27 Hen. VIII, fo. 10,[6] Mountague said it was adjudged that a use may not be limited upon an estate tail.}

234. GLOVER v. BERYE: CLACHE'S CASE[7]

Common Pleas, 1574.

Uses.

Note that it was adjudged in Clache's case that an implied devise will never control an express devise. The case there was that a man having two daughters devised certain lands to the elder one in fee, and certain lands to the younger one and her heirs; and if the elder should die before she accomplished the age of 26 years, her part should remain to the younger; and if the younger should die without child, then her part should remain to the elder; and if both died without child, then the land should remain to the right heirs of Henry Clache. The question was, if one of them died without child, could the right heir of Clache enter at once, or must he wait until the other is also dead, because (as was said) there is an implied cross-remainder in the words 'if they should both die without issue, then …'. Nevertheless, it was adjudged that because there was an express devise made to them previously, this implied devise shall be of no effect. In support of this MANWOOD said, and DYER [C.J.] agreed, that if someone is seised of a manor and devises the demesnes of the manor to his wife for term of her life and the services for seven years, and after her death remainder to another, in this case she shall have the services only for seven years, because an implied devise will never control an express limitation. And so it was adjudged, according to him and the lord DYER, in Frencham's case,[8] the case there being that a man devised lands to someone and his heirs male of his body, and if he should die 'without issue' they were to remain over in fee; he had female issue, and died; and it was adjudged that this female should not have the land, for the implied devise will not control the express limitation. But, by MANWOOD, if someone devises land to his wife during her life, and if she should die within seven years remainder to John Dale for life, and after the death […].[9]

235. CRANMER'S CASE[10]

Common Pleas, Mich. 1572.

Uses.

There is a great difference between a feoffment to use and a feoffment in possession.

---

[1] 24 Hen. VIII, Bro. Abr., *Feffements al uses*, pl. 40; discussed in 2 Co. Rep. 78; Co. Litt. 19b.
[2] *Sic*, but perhaps *Rayner v. Rayner* (1552) Dyer 77.
[3] *Gresley's Case* (1538) 30 Hen. VIII, Bro. Abr., *Feffements al uses*, pl. 48.
[4] Perk. s. 537 says the express use prevails over the implied use.
[5] *Att.-Gen. v. Walsingham* (1573) Plowd. 547 at fo. 555 ('Mes nota (lecteur) que use ne puit estre limit sur estate taile, come pois voier ajudge in 24 H. 8 en le title de uses en les abridgments seignior Brooke, que sont ore in print').

faire feffment in fe al use de lun <p>ᵈ et de ses heires et que sil morust sauns heires que les feoffees estoieront seisie al use estrange. Auterment de feffment in possession. Issint home voet faire feffment al use de luy mesme et de vie tiel que serroit son fem, ceo est bon etc. Auterment in possession, come 1 E. 3, Lib. Ass., et 17 E. 3, [*blank*], agre. Et ceux case[s] fueront mise et agre in case de Cranmer anno 14 Elyz. Issint la fuit agre que si baron discontinue les terres son fem, et le feffe fist feffment al use del baron et fem, in cest case la fem nest pas remitte. Auterment si le feffe ust fist feffment in possession al baron et fem, la le fem serra remitt clerement. Et la fuit dit per Harper, justice, si home face feffment in fe al use de J. S. et puis al use de ses droit heires, in cest case le fe nest pas execute. Auterment de tiel estate in possession.

[236]

AD, fo. 78 (835).

<Relation.>ˢ

Nota que le Segnior Dier in le argument de Nicols case cite cest case ex lectura Frowicke. Home fist leas pur ans a un alien sur condition que si ferra tiel acte que donques il avera fe, et puis le roy per ses lettres patentz fait luy un denizen, et puis le alien performe le condition: le roy avera ceux terres, et uncore al temps del condition performe il <avoit forsque>ᵈ fuit denizen, mes le perimplishment del condition avoit relation al temps del leas fait.

[237]

AD, fo. 78v (835v).

<Relation.>ˢ

M. 17 Eliz. cest case fuit adjudge in le common banke. <Fraunces>,ⁱ Segnior Lovell, esteant seisie de certain terres in fe, fist leas pur vie a un Wright et si contigerit predictus le Segnior Lovell obire sine heredibus de corpore suo legittime procreatis tunc predictus Franciscus ulterius vult et concedit predictas terras prefato Thome Wright et heredibus suis imperpetuum. Et puis anno 1 H. 7 le Segnior Lovell fuit atteint de haut treason per acte de parliament, et ouster que il forfeitra tout ses terres et tenementes, savaunt a toutz estrangers all such right, title, action and interest etc.

---

[3] See above, p. 45, no. 90, and the note there.
[4] Cf. above, 45, where the same point is noted.
[5] 1 Hen. VII, c. iii (private).

For one may make a feoffment in fee to the use of someone and his heirs, and should he die without heirs the feoffees to stand seised to the use of a stranger; but it is otherwise of a feoffment in possession. Likewise, a man may make a feoffment to the use of himself and for the life of his future wife, and this is good; though it is otherwise of a feoffment in possession, as was agreed in 1 Edw. III, Lib. Ass.,[1] and 17 Edw. III.[2] These cases were put and agreed in Cranmer's case, in 14 Eliz. It was likewise agreed in that case that if a husband discontinues his wife's lands, and the feoffee makes a feoffment to the use of the husband and wife, in this case the wife is not remitted; but it would be otherwise if the feoffee had made a feoffment in possession to the husband and wife, for there the wife would clearly be remitted. And it was there said by HARPER J. that if someone makes a feoffment in fee to the use of John Style [for life], and then to the use of his right heirs, the fee is not in this case executed; but it would be otherwise of such an estate in possession.

236. NICHOLS v. NICHOLS[3]

Common Pleas, Mich. 1574.

Relation.

Note that the lord DYER, in the argument of Nichols's case, cited this case from Frowyk's reading.[4] A man made a lease for years to an alien upon condition that if he should perform such an act, he should have fee; and afterwards the king by his letters patent made him a denizen, and then the alien performed the condition: the king shall have these lands, and yet at the time when the condition was performed he was a denizen, but the fulfilment of the condition related back to the time when the lease was made.

237. NICHOLS v. NICHOLS, continued

Common Pleas, Mich. 1575.

Relation.

In Michaelmas term 17 Eliz. this case was adjudged in the Common Bench. Francis, Lord Lovell, being seised of certain lands in fee, made a lease for life to [Thomas] Wright, 'and if the aforesaid Lord Lovell should happen to die without heirs of his body lawfully begotten, then the aforesaid Francis further wills and grants the aforesaid lands to the said Thomas Wright and his heirs for ever'. Afterwards, in the year 1 Hen. VII, the Lord Lovell was attainted of high treason by act of Parliament,[5] and it was further enacted that he should forfeit all his lands and tenements, 'saving to all strangers all such right, title, action and interest …'. Afterwards in the same year the

---

[1] 1 Edw. III, Lib. Ass., pl. 11.
[2] The citation was probably to the case of the grant to a firstborn son, where there was no son at the time of the grant: *The Prior of Grimsby's Case* (1343–44) YB Pas. 17 Edw. III, fo. 29, pl. 30; continued in Mich. 18 Edw. III, fo. 59, pl. 91. Cf. the report of *Cranmer's Case* in Appendix I, at pp. cxci, cxciii.

Et puis mesme lan le Segnior Lovell fuit execute et morust sauns issue. Et fuit adjudge que Wright avera le fe simple nient obstant que il fuit limitt apres le mort le Segnior Lovell, issint que devant le perimplishment del condition le ley transfer ceo a un auter, uncore pur ceo que quant le Segnior Lovell morust sauns issue ceo avoit relation al temps del condition fait, issint que ore (come le Segnior Dier dit) il avoit fe ab initio. Et pur ceo le Segnior Dier dit, si home fait obligation et deliver ceo a un estrange come escrowe a deliver a J. S. quant il ad performe certain conditions, si lobligor morust et puis J. S. performe les conditions, et lestrange deliver a luy lobligation, ceo est bone et liera les executors lobligor. 27 H. 6, 7. Issint il dit si home de non compos mentis face leas pur vie sur condition que si le lesse ferra tiel acte que donques il avera fe, et devant le perimplishment del condition il deveigne de sane memorie, et puis le condition est performe, uncore il avoidera ceo per relation.

Nota le case devant superiori pag[ina] de lalien nee.

[238]

AD, fo. 80 (837).

<Recovery in value.>[5] <Pl. Com. 514. Vide 38 E. 3, 5. Vide Cuppledike case.>[a]

H. 20 Eliz. fuit adjudge in banke le roy que si tenant in taile generall prist fem et puis brefe dentre en le post est port envers le baron et fem (ou in verite le fem nad riens) et ilz vouch et le vouche entre in le garrante etc., cest bon barre al fem de son dower car cest intended recompence irra al feme per voy de conclusion. Mes si lissue in taile ousta la fem de cest recompence, come il poet (si ascun soit) car lissue in taile nest conclude, donques la fem avera dower. Quod nota.

[239]

AD, fo. 80 (837).

<Recovery in value.>[5]

14 Eliz. Copwoodes case. Pier et fitz, le pier fist feffment in fe al use de luy mesme et puis al use de son heire male in taile, et puis, devant lestatut de 14 Elizab. de recoveries ewes vers tenant pur vie, le pier suffer recoverie ove voucher et puis morust. Et fuit adjudge que cest recoverie ove le intended recompence ne concludera

---

[a] Differently reported in Plowd. 541. Cit. in *AB*, fo. 46 (245) ('Vide 20 Eliz. in mes notes demesne tit. Recoverie in value, 80, barre in brefe de dower per recoverie in value').
[5] *Sic*, but probably YB Pas. 38 Edw. III, fo. 9.
[6] *Cuppledyke's Case* (1602) C, fos. 486v–489; 3 Co. Rep. 5.
[7] See above, p. 58, no. 107, and the note there.
[8] 14 Eliz., c. 8.

Lord Lovell was executed, and he died without issue. And it was adjudged that Wright should have the fee simple, notwithstanding that it was limited after the death of the Lord Lovell, in that before the fulfilment of the condition the law had transferred it to another,[1] for when the Lord Lovell died without issue this related back to the time when the condition was made, so that now (as the lord DYER said) he had the fee *ab initio*. In support of this, the lord DYER said that if someone makes a bond and delivers it to a stranger as an escrow, to deliver to John Style when he has performed certain conditions, and the obligor dies, and then John Style performs the conditions, and a stranger delivers him the bond, this is good and will bind the obligor's executors. 27 Hen. VI, fo. 7.[2] Likewise, (he said) if someone of unsound mind makes a lease for life upon condition that if the lessee performed a certain act he should have fee, and before the fulfilment of the condition the lessor becomes of sound mind, and then the condition is performed, he may nevertheless avoid it by relation.

Note the case above, on the previous page, of the alien nee.[3]

238. EARE d. TREVELYAN v. SNOWE[4]

King's Bench. Hil. 1578.

Recovery in value. Plowd. Com. 514. See 38 Edw. III, fo. 5.[5] {See Cuppledike's case.[6]}

In Hilary term 20 Eliz. it was adjudged in the King's Bench that if tenant in tail general marries a wife, and then a writ of entry in the *post* is brought against the husband and wife (whereas in truth the wife has nothing), and they vouch, and the vouchee enters into the warranty [and loses by default], this is good to bar the wife of her dower, for the presumed recompense shall go to the woman by way of estoppel. If, however, the issue in tail ousts the wife of this recompense, as he may (if there be any), since the issue in tail is not estopped, the wife shall have dower. Note that.

239. COPWOOD v. CLARKE[7]

Common Pleas, 1572.

Recovery in value.

14 Eliz., Copwood's case. Father and son; the father makes a feoffment in fee to the use of himself, and then to the use of his heir male in tail; then, before the statute of 14 Eliz. concerning recoveries had against tenant for life,[8] the father suffers a recovery with voucher, and afterwards dies. And it was adjudged that this recovery with the

---

[1] I.e. the forfeiture took effect from the date of the attainder, which was before the execution.
[2] YB Hil. 27 Hen. VI, fo. 7, pl. 3.
[3] This refers to the previous case printed here, as is indicated in the MS. by a trefoil.
[4] KB 27/1258, m. 495 (four rolls; printed in Plowd. 504): Nicholas Eare v. Nicholas Snowe *alias* Jacobbe, Agnes Elsworthie, widow, and Thomas Elsworthie; ejectment four houses and lands in Luccombe, Minehead, Dunster and Timberscombe, Som., on the demise of Hugh Trevylyane; special verdict at bar, Pas. 1577; c.a.v. to Hil. 1578; judgment for the plaintiff with 10s. damages and £13. 6s. 8d. costs.

le fitz per lordre del common ley, car le intended recompence ne poet aler a cesti que donques ne fuit in esse, et sauns recompence il ne serra barre.

[240]

AD, fo. 82 (841).

<Presentation et quare impedit.>[s] <Vide Mich. 42 et 43 Eliz. 430.>[a]

H. 18 Eliz. cest case fuit move in le common banke, que si home grant 3 avoidances a J. S., et puis leglise devient voide et le grauntour usurpe, et loppinion de les justices del common banke fuit que ceo ne mittera le grantee hors de possession mes que al prochein avoidaunce il poet present. Et lour reason fuit pur le privitie parenter eux. <2 R. 3, tit. Quare impedit, 102, cesti que ad nomi[nation].>[i] <17 E. 3, 40. 11 E. 3, Quare impedit, 157.>[i] Et auxi il ne poet estre usurpour pur ceo que il averoit le fe et <avoyt tout le>[1] avouson devant droiturelment. <Vies 1 H. 5, 1, si jeo grant a vous que {vous nosmera}[2] un clarke etc. {…}.[3]>[a]

[241]

AD, fo. 82v (841v).

<Quare impedit.>[s]

Et nota que il fuit tenus in 18 Eliz. per le melior opinion des justices del common banke que le ordinarie covient a doner notice al person le patron et nemi al eglise.

[242]

AD, fo. 83 (842).

<Presentation et mariage voide.>[s]

Nota fuit agre in le common banke in 12 Eliz. regine in le case dun Pickeringe de Norff. que si un home que est mere laicus soit present, admitte et institute, que leglise nest my voide, mes tiel laye person est destre deprive per le ordinarie, et remaine parson quousque. Mes uncore per le ley comon un que est mere laicus nest

---

[1] *Unclear.*
[2] *Words rubbed at foot of page.*
[3] *Words lost in lower corner.*

---

the church of Eriswell, Suff.; demurrer to the plea in bar; c.a.v. to Hil. 1571; judgment for the plaintiff. Differently reported in Dyer 292; Benl. 195; 1 And. 16.

[8] The case is too early to be have been heard by Coke. The plaintiff was stepfather to Coke's first wife, Bridget, though he did not marry her until 1582. The same point arose in *Anon.* (1584) HLS MS. 1042 (1058), fos. 15v–16, but that is probably too late to account for the present citation.

[9] The canon law term for an absolute layman. Pickering received the tonsure while at Cambridge in 1550, but was not ordained: see J. and J. A. Venn, *Alumni Cantabrigienses to 1751*, iii. 360.

intended recompense shall not estop the son by the order of the common law, for the presumed recompense cannot go to someone who was not then *in esse*, and without recompense he shall not be barred.

240. ANON.

Common Pleas, Hil. 1576.

Presentation and *quare impedit*. {See Mich. 42 & 43 Eliz. 430.[1]}

In Hilary term 18 Eliz. this case was moved in the Common Bench: a man granted three avoidances to John Style, and then the church became vacant and the grantor usurped. And the opinion of the justices of the Common Bench was that this will not put the grantee out of possession, but he may present at the next avoidance. Their reason was because of the privity between them. {2 Ric. III, tit. *Quare impedit*, 102: someone who has the nomination of a clerk.[2] 17 Edw. III, fo. 40.[3] 11 Edw. III, *Quare impedit*, 157.[4]} Also, he cannot be a usurper, because he is to have the fee, and he had all the advowson before rightfully. {See 1 Hen. V, fo. 1,[5] where I grant you that you should name a clerk.}

241. GYLES v. COLSHILL[6]

Common Pleas, Pas. 1576.

Quare impedit.

Note that it was held in 18 Eliz., by the better opinion of the justices of the Common Bench, that the ordinary must give notice to the patron in person and not at the church.

242. BEDINGFIELD v. PICKERING[7]

Common Pleas, 1570.[8]

Presentation and marriage void.

Note that it was agreed in the Common Bench in 12 Eliz., in the case of one Pickering of Norfolk, that if a man who is *merus laicus*[9] is presented, admitted and instituted [to a benefice], the church is not vacant, but such lay person must be deprived by the ordinary and remains parson until then. Nevertheless, by the common law, someone

---

[1] *Rudde* v. *Topfield* (1600) in C, fos. 429v–430v; vol. v, p. 1108.
[2] Hil. 2 Ric. III, Fitz. Abr., *Quare impedit*, pl. 102.
[3] *R.* v. *Archbishop of York* (1343) YB Trin. 17 Edw. III, fo. 40, pl. 17.
[4] Trin. 11 Edw. III, Fitz. Abr., *Quare impedit*, pl. 157.
[5] *Abbot of Leicester's Case* (1414) YB Hil. 1 Hen. V, fo. 1, pl. 2.
[6] Conjectural identification. See above, p. 63, no. 113, and the note there.
[7] CP 40/1284, m. 930 (unfit for production; printed in Co. Ent. 507v–508v; partly but inaccurately printed in Benl. 195): Edmund Bedingfield ('Pedyngfeld') v. Marmaduke Pickering, clerk; *quare impedit* for

my capable dun benefice. <29 E. 3, 44.>[i] Mes uncore in nostre ley quant il ad toutz les solemnities performe que le spirituel ley require, nous adjudge luy parson tanque il soit deprive. Come est dit in civill ley, quod consensus non concubitus facit matrimonium, et pur ceo ilz diont que devant lage de consent le mariage est void, uncore in nostre ley si 2 sont maries infra annos nubiles ceo est bone tanque disagrement. <9 H. 6, 32, 33.>[i] Issint fuit agre que quant home est present a un benefice que per nul possibilitie in droit ne poet estre capable de ceo, coment que les droitz et solemnities de saint eglise sont performe, uncore leglise demurt void. Come si fem soit issint present etc. pur ceo que per nul possibilitie in droit el ne poet etc. <7 H. 6, 10, infant al age de 14 ans mariage in nostre ley.>[i] Mes auterment est dun mere laicus. Issint si frere et soer marie, cest voide. Issint de mere et fitz, pur ceo que per nul possibilitie in droit ilz ne poient marier. Mes auterment est des cosins deins les degrees. 11 H. 4, 76: home marie son cosin infra les degrees, et ad issue et morust, lissue nest bastard car lespouselx <ne>[i] fueront voides <et>[d] mes voidable.

[243]

AD, fo. 85 (844).

<Quare impedit.>[1]

18 Eliz. fuit tenus in le common banke que si un parson resigne et les 6 moys passe sauns ascun notice, et puis auter 6 moys passe, issint que le temps si notice ust estre done est devolute al <ordinarie>[d] metropolitane, et puis auter 6 moys passe, in cest case les justices teignont clerement que le roygne navera le presentment, car fuit dit que le metropolitane ne le roygne ne poet estre intitle sinon que le ordinarie fuit in le commencement intitle, et devant notice son title ne commence, et donques intaunt que lordinarie nunques avoit title, ceo esteant le primer stepp come fuit dit, le temps ne poet estre devolute a le roigne. Auxi fuit dit que un home ad un inheritauns in lavouson, et ceo serra assetz, et home ne unques perdra son inheritauns sauns defaut in luy, et quant le patron ad present un able person, et il resigne, le ordinarie covient a luy doner notice, et sauns notice nul defaut est in luy. Mes le Segnior Dier ceo denia, et dit que le roygne per sa prerogative avera le presentment coment que notice ne fuit done.

[1] *Heading on previous page.*

who is *merus laicus* is not capable of a benefice. {29 Edw. III, fo. 44.[1]} In our law, however, when all the solemnities have been performed which the spiritual law requires, we adjudge him a parson until he is deprived. Likewise, it is said in the Civil law that it is consent, rather than lying together, which constitutes matrimony (*consensus non concubitus facit matrimonium*), and therefore they say that, before the age of consent, a marriage is void; and yet in our law if two are married under age (*infra annos nubiles*) it is good until disagreement. {9 Hen. VI, fos. 32, 33.[2]} Nevertheless, it was agreed that when a person is presented to a benefice for which he may by no rightful possibility be capable, even if the rights and solemnities of Holy Church have been performed, the church still remains void: for instance, if a woman is presented to a benefice, because in right she cannot be capable by any possibility. {7 Hen. VI, fo. 10:[3] an infant at the age of 14 may marry in our law.} But it is otherwise of *merus laicus*. Likewise, if a brother and sister marry, it is void. Similarly mother and son, because by no rightful possibility may they marry. But it is otherwise of kinfolk within the degrees. 11 Hen. IV, fo. 76:[4] a man marries his kinswoman within the degrees, and has issue and dies, the issue is not a bastard, for the espousals were not void but voidable.

243. GYLES v. COLSHILL[5]

Common Pleas, Pas. 1576.

Quare impedit.

In 18 Eliz. it was held in the Common Bench that if a parson resigns, and the six months pass without any notice given, and then another six months pass, so that if notice had been given the time would have devolved to the metropolitan, and then another six months pass, in this case (as the justices held clearly) the queen should not have the presentation, for (as it was said) neither the metropolitan nor the queen can be entitled unless the ordinary was entitled in the first place, and his title does not begin before notice; therefore, inasmuch as the ordinary never had title – that being the first step (as was said) – the time cannot devolve to the queen. It was also said that if someone has an inheritance in the advowson, this may be assets, and a man will never lose his inheritance without some default in him, and when the patron has presented an able person, and he resigns, the ordinary must give him notice, for without notice there is no default in him. But the lord DYER denied this, and said that the queen by her prerogative should have the presentation even though notice was not given.

---

[1] YB Mich. 29 Edw. III, fo. 44, pl. [3].
[2] *Case of the Abbot of Fountains* (1407) YB Mich. 9 Hen. VI, fo. 32, pl. 3.
[3] YB Mich. 7 Hen. VI, fo. 10, pl. 36.
[4] *R.* v. *Bishop of Salisbury* (1410) YB Trin. 11 Hen. IV, fo. 76, pl. 18.
[5] See above, p. 63, no. 113, and the note there.

[244]

AD, fo. 87 (846).

<Leasses.>ˢ

Nota fuit tenus in banke le roy circa 14 Eliz. que si home face leas pur vie a J. S. et puis fait leas pur xl ans a commencer apres le mort, <deter>ᵈ surrender ou forfeiter del leas pur vie, que in cest case si J. S. surrender etc. le leas commencera maintenant et le lesse nad election a aver ceo commense a son pleasure a ascun de eux. M. 18 Eliz. per Dier.

[245]

AD, fo. 88 (847).

<Leasses.>ˢ

[1]4 Elyz. in le case de Winter, per Harper, 4 choses sont incident et necessarie a un leas. 1, covient <exprimer>¹ un sufficient lessour. 2, un capable lesse. 4, un chose que gist in leas. 5, un certaine commencement.

[246]

AD, fo. 89v (848v).

<Waste.>ˢ

M. 15 Elyz. Benlos serjaunt mova si home fait leas pur ans, le remainder in fe a un baron et fem et a les heires le baron, le baron morust, et apres la fem et leire in revercion graunt lour estate a un auter in fe, le lesse pur ans fist wast, et le lessour port brefe de wast. Et il mova si laction ne girra pur ceo que duraunt le vie la fem le graunte est eins de son estate et donques duraunt son vie le wast est dispunishable. Car il dit si leas pur vie soit fait, le remainder pur vie, si le lesse pur vie fait wast le wast est dispunishable: quod fuit concessum. Et fuit agre per totam curiam que laction de wast fuit bien maintenable, car le mesne estate que fuit lempediment pur que la action ne girroit est merge et drowne in le revercion in fe, et coment quant a ascun respectes le graunte serra eins destate del tenancie pur vie ou choses doient estre fait devant le joindre in graunt ou le surrender, mes in toutz choses apres le graunt ou surrender il est tout ousterment execute a toutz purposes.

Et le Segnior Dier dit que si le leas pur vie soit fait a un pur vie, le remainder a un

---

¹ *Unclear.*

244. ANON.[1]

King's Bench, *c.* 1572; Common Pleas, Mich. 1576.

Leases.

Note that it was held in the King's Bench around the year 14 Eliz. that if someone makes a lease for life to John Style, and then makes a lease for forty years to commence after the death, surrender or forfeiture of the lease for life, in this case if John Style surrenders [his estate for life], the lease will commence forthwith, and the lessee does not have an election to have it commence at any of the times at his pleasure. Michaelmas term 18 Eliz., by DYER.

245. WINTER'S CASE[2]

Common Pleas, 1572.

Leases.

14 Eliz., in Winter's case, by HARPER: four things are incident and necessary to a lease. It must express, 1, a sufficient lessor; 2, a capable lessee; [3], a thing which lies in lease; [4], a certain commencement.

246. ANON.[3]

Common Pleas, Mich. 1573.

Waste.

In Michaelmas term 15 Eliz. *Serjeant Bendlowes* moved this case: someone makes a lease for years, the remainder in fee to a husband and wife and the heirs of the husband; the husband dies; and afterwards the woman and the heir in reversion grant their estate to another in fee; the lessee for years commits waste, and the lessor brings a writ of waste. And he moved that the action should not lie, because during the woman's life the grantee is in of her estate and therefore during her life the waste is unpunishable. For he said that, if a lease is made for life, the remainder for life, and the lessee for life commits waste, the waste is unpunishable: which was accepted. And it was agreed by the whole court that the action of waste was well maintainable, for the mesne estate (which was the impediment for which the action would not lie) is merged and drowned in the reversion in fee; and although in some respects the grantee shall be in of the estate of the tenancy for life, where things are to be done before the joinder in grant or the surrender, in all things after the grant or surrender it is absolutely executed for all purposes.

The lord DYER said that if a lease is made to someone for life, remainder to another

---

[1] Cf. above, p. 112, no. 200, in almost the same words.
[2] See above, p. 43, no. 88, and the note there. The same dictum is noted above, p. 100, no. 169; p. 126, no. 220.
[3] Perhaps an argument in *Ellis* v. *Vavasour* (the same year): see no. 247. Cf. also no. 249.

auter pur vie, le 2 graunt lour estate a un et font livery accordant, in cest case le graunte ad estate pur terme de lour 2 vies, in cest case sil fait wast in [ceo],¹ entaunt que cesti que fist le tort ad auxi le mesne remainder, le wast est punishable.

Et Harper dit que 4 E. 3, 18, est tenus que si leas pur ans soit fait, le remainder pur ans, si le lesse pur vie fait wast le wast est pu[nishable] nient obstant le mesne remainder pur ans. Et la fuit auxi agre que si le[as] pur vie soit fait, le remainder a 2 et a les heires de lun, ilz 2 joindront in action de wast.

[247]

AD, fo. 90v (851v).

<Waste.>ˢ

15 Eliz. Nota per Manwood si lesse pur ans dun parke destroy le greinder parte des dames ceo est waste. Mesme la ley si termor dun columbarie tua le greinder parte del flight. Issint dun termour de boys de hasils et willowes sil succide le greinder part cest waste.

[248]

AD, fo. 91 (852).

<Wast.>ˢ

Nota le case devant 17 E. 3, <fol. 68>,ⁱ tit. Confirmation, 9. Et nota loppinion del Segnior Dier que coment que il soit un mesne estate uncore pur ceo que il est partie al tort il serra punie …

[249]

AD, fo. 91 (852).

<Wast.>ˢ

Ad estre dit si leas pur vie soit fait, le remainder pur vie, le revercion in fe, ore si le primer lesse pur vie fist <wast>,ⁱ ore est dispunishable pur ceo que il est mesne remainder pur vie. Mes si <le>ᵈ cesti in le remainder pur vie morust, ore il est dit que

---

⁰¹⁰ *Piece missing at edge of page.*

³ Mich. 17 Edw. III, Fitz. Abr., *Confirmation*, pl. 9; YB Mich. 17 Edw. III, fo. 68, pl. 92.
⁴ See above, p. 40, no. 87, and the note there. Although the case is here referred to, the bulk of the note may consist of Coke's own collections rather than a report of the case. Cf. also no. 246.

for life, and the two of them grant their estate to one and make livery accordingly, in which case the grantee has an estate for term of their two lives, and he commits waste, the waste is punishable, since the person who did the wrong also had the mesne remainder.

HARPER said that in 4 Edw. III, fo. 18,[1] it is held that if a lease is made for years, remainder for years, and the lessee for life commits waste, the waste is punishable notwithstanding the mesne remainder for years. And it was also there agreed that if a lease is made for life, remainder to two and the heirs of one of them, the two of them shall join in an action of waste.

247. ELLIS v. VAVASOUR[2]

Common Pleas, 1573.

Waste.

15 Eliz. Note, by MANWOOD, if the lessee for years of a park destroys the greater part of the deer, this is waste. The law is the same if the termor of a dovecote kills the greater part of the flight. Likewise of a termor of a wood of hazels and willows, if he cuts down the greater part, this is waste.

248. ANON.

Common Pleas, temp. Eliz.

Waste.

Note the case above of 17 Edw. III, fo. 68, tit. *Confirmation*, 9.[3] And note the opinion of the lord DYER that although there is a mesne estate, nevertheless because he is party to the wrong he shall be punished ...

249. HUMPHRESTON'S CASE[4]

King's Bench, 1575.

Waste.

It has been said that if a lease is made for life, remainder for life, the reversion in fee, and the first lessee for life commits waste, it is unpunishable, because there is a mesne remainder for life. But if the remainderman for life dies, now (as it is said) the

---

[1] YB Pas. 4 Edw. III, fo. 18, pl. 12.
[2] Differently reported, under this name, in 2 Leon. 222; 3 Leon. 53; Dal. 100 (three versions of the same report); Owen 36. Manwood J. was differing from the opinion of Dyer C.J. that it was only waste if all the deer were destroyed. In this case Ellis leased the manor of Woodhall to William Vavasour and his wife for the life of the wife, remainder to the husband's heirs, and the husband made a feoffment to the use of himself and his wife for lives, remainder to his heirs; the husband died; and the widow committed waste in a park, part of the manor.

<le>^d cesti in le reversion poet aver action de wast pur ceo que le mesne estate pur vie que fuit le impediment est remove. Et pur ceo il est agre in 41 E. 3, et 41 Ass. 9, que si tenant pur vie, le remainder in taile pur vie, le remainder al droit heires le lesse pur vie, si lesse pur vie enfeffe cesti in le primer remainder in taile et sa fem, que est estrange al estate taile, ore ceo est un forfeiture, mes pur ceo que cesti in remainder immediate in taile est partie ceo est dispunishable. <Vide M. 35 et 36 Eliz. fol. 74.>[i] Mes si cesti in le remainder in taile morust sauns issue, donques poet cesti in le 2 remainder enter pur forfeiture, et uncore al temps ceo fuit dispunishable. Issint il fuit pense per Plowden in largument del case de seniori puero, que si un parson fait leas pur vie, et le patron et lordinarie confirme ceo, et le parson morust, ore est le fe simple in abeiauns. Ore si in temps de vacation le lesse pur vie face feffment in fe il est nul que poet prender advauntage de cest forfeyture, mes si un parson soit apres eslieu il entra pur le forfeiture, et uncore al temps ceo fuit dispunishable. Issint si leas pur vie soit fait, le remainder al droit heires de J. S., ore si le lesse in le vie J. S. face feffment in fe, uncore null poet enter pur le forfeiture. Mes si J. S. morust […].[1]

[250]

AD, fo. 92 (853).

<Waste.>[s]

Nota quil fuit loppinion del Segnior Dier arguendo in <Clatches>^d Nicols case que si home face leas pur vie a J. S. sur condition que sil durant son vie paia x li. que donques il avera fe, in cest case son opinion fuit que [si] le lesse fait wast devant le perimplishment del condition uncore le lessor navera action de wast, car le lesse ad un possibilitie daver fe per un matter ex post facto, et quant le condition est performe le lesse avera fe ab initio. Vies 43 E. 3, 35, leas pur ans sur condition que si le lesse fait <wast>^d tiel chose a un jour avener que donques il avera fe, et devant le jour il fait wast, quere si le lessor punishera luy. Mes per loppinion del Segnior Dier il ne serra punyse (quod Plowden, esteant adonques in le court, tacite concessit).

[251]

AD, fo. 94v (855v).

<Issues et jeofailes et repleder.>[s]

Nota per Manwood 18 Eliz. in le case dun Tresham que un jeofaile ne unques serra forsque per un de ceux voics, scilicet lou un issue est joine sur 2 affirm[atives], come

---

[1] *Words lost at foot of page.*

[4] Above, p. 45, no. 90, and the note there.
[5] YB Mich. 43 Edw. III, fo. 35, pl. 52.
[6] Present as an observer, it seems, since he had no right of audience there.

reversioner may have an action of waste, because the mesne estate for life – which was the impediment – is removed. Therefore it is agreed in 41 Edw. III, and 41 Ass. [2],[1] that if there is a tenant for life, remainder in tail for life, remainder to the right heirs of the lessee for life, and the lessee for life enfeoffs the first remainderman in tail and his wife (who is a stranger to the estate tail), this is a forfeiture, but because the immediate remainderman in tail is party [to the feoffment] it is unpunishable. {See Mich. 35 & 36 Eliz., fo. 74.[2]} If, however, the remainderman in tail dies without issue, then the second remainderman may enter for the forfeiture, even though it was formerly unpunishable. Likewise, it was thought by *Plowden*, in the argument of the case of *seniori puero*,[3] that if a parson makes a lease for life, and the patron and the ordinary confirm it, and the parson dies, the fee simple is now in abeyance; if the lessee for life then makes a feoffment in fee, in time of vacancy, there is no one who can take advantage of this forfeiture; but if a parson is afterwards chosen, he may enter for the forfeiture, even though it was at the time unpunishable. Likewise, if a lease is made for life, remainder to the right heirs of John Style, and the lessee makes a feoffment in fee in the life of John Style, no one may enter for the forfeiture; but if John Style dies [the heir may enter].

250. NICHOLS v. NICHOLS[4]

Common Pleas, 1574.

Waste.

Note that it was the opinion of the lord DYER, arguing in Nichols's case, that if someone makes a lease for life to John Style upon condition that if he pays £10 during his life he should then have fee, and the lessee commits waste before the fulfilment of the condition, in this case the lessor may nevertheless not have an action of waste, for the lessee has a possibility to have fee by matter *ex post facto*, and when the condition is performed the lessee will have fee *ab initio*. See 43 Edw. III, fo. 35,[5] where a lease for years was made upon condition that if the lessee did a certain thing at a day to come he should have fee, and before the day he committed waste: query whether the lessor may punish him. By the opinion of the lord DYER, however, he shall not be punished: which *Plowden*,[6] being then in the court, tacitly conceded.

251. TRESHAM'S CASE

Common Pleas, 1576.

Issues, jeofails and repleader.

Note, by MANWOOD, in 18 Eliz. in the case of one Tresham, that there shall never be a jeofail except in one of the following ways. [1] Where an issue is joined upon two

---

[1] YB Mich. 41 Edw. III, fo. 21, pl. 7; Lib. Ass., pl. 2.
[2] *Clifton v. Southcote* (1593) C, fo. 74v; vol. iii, p. 561.
[3] I.e. *Humphreston's Case*.

vies 8 H. 6, 6, et 2 H. 6, 15, 6 H. 7,[1] 6, le case de mort et vie. Ou lou un chose est travers que ne fuit affirme ou plede devant. Viez 6 H. 7, 10, in trespas, le defendant plede in barre un concord, cestasavoier que il ferra certaine feenestres et paia certain deniers, et dit que il ad paie les deniers, et lauter plede null tiell concord, et ceo fuit agre destre un jeofaile per curiam car nul concorde in ley fuit devant alledge, car nest perfitt concord tanque tout soit performe, issint la il travers chose que devaunt ne fuit alledge. 3, ou lou un joine un issue sur un insufficient matter. Come 6 H. 7, 4a. Mes le il dit si lissue soit bien joine, scilicet sur un affirmative et negative, et sur auter sufficient matter, coment que le pleding devant soit vicious et faultie uncore ceo nest pas un jeofaile. <Vide 7 H. 7, 4a.>[a] <Vies 32 H. 6, 14a, issue prise sur tiel matter que est forsque nugation. Vide 26 E. 3, 55a.>[a]

[252]

AD, fo. 99v (860v).

<Tenures.>[s]

Nota, il fuit in mannour agre in Sir Thomas Wiatz case in T. 18 Eliz. que si le done in taile fait feffement in fe que le feffee tient del segnior paramont, car le donour ne unques avowera sur luy, car sil avowera sur luy il covient a luy a monstre <son>[d] <le>[i] feffment del tenant in taile, et donques il poet appierer que le revercion est hors de luy, et per consequens le rent etc. Et pur ceo le Segnior Dier, Harper et Manwood teignont que le feffe tiendra del segnior paramont et que il avera le gard del heire de luy, et leire le discontinue ne poet luy avoidre. Et issint semble que il avera 2 gardes, scilicet del heire del donour et del heire le discontinue. <Vide 31 E. 3, tit. Gard, 117 [...].[2]>[a]

[253]

AD, fo. 100v (861v).

<Arbitrement.>[s]

Et nota appiert in 19 E. 4, 1, in le residuum de cest case, que les parties fueront oblige in un obligation a estoier a cest agard et la le reason de Choke est pur ceo que ilz ne poient faire agard de tiel chose que nest commisse a eux. Et nota que le ley est tout un quant ilz ferront agard dun chose hors de submission come dun person hors de

---

[1] *Altered from 6.*
[2] *Numerous further cases are cited at the end.*

[6] YB Mich. 7 Hen. VII, fo. 4, pl. 3.
[7] YB Mich. 32 Hen. VI, fo. 14, pl. 21.
[8] YB Hil. 26 Edw. III (1567 ed.), fo. 55, pl. 1; this is on fo. 1 of the vulgate edition.
[9] See above, p. 89, no. 147, and the note there.
[10] Pas. 31 Edw. III, Fitz. Abr., *Garde*, pl. 116 (not 117).
[11] YB Mich. 19 Edw. IV, fo. 1, pl. 1.

affirmatives, as may be seen in 8 Hen. VI, fos. 6, 7,[1] 2 Hen. VI, fo. 15,[2] and 6 Hen. VII, fo. 6,[3] the case of death and life. Or [2] where something is traversed which was not affirmed or pleaded before. See 6 Hen. VII, fo. 10,[4] in trespass, where the defendant pleaded in bar an accord, namely that he should make certain windows and pay certain money, and he said that he had paid the money, and the other pleaded 'No such accord', and it was agreed by the court to be a jeofail, for no accord in law was previously alleged, as it is not a perfect accord until all has been performed, and so the traverse was to something which was not alleged before. (3) Or where someone joins issue upon an insufficient matter, as in 6 Hen. VII, fo. 4.[5] But he said that if the issue is well joined, namely upon an affirmative and negative, and upon other sufficient matter, then even if the previous pleading is vicious and faulty it is still not a jeofail. {See 7 Hen. VII, fo. 4.[6] See 32 Hen. VI, fo. 14,[7] issue taken upon matter which is merely nugatory. See 26 Edw. III, fo. 55.[8]}

252. MULTON v. COVENEY[9]

Common Pleas, Trin. 1576.

Tenures.

Note that it was in effect agreed in Sir Thomas Wyatt's case, in Trinity term 18 Eliz., that if the donee in tail makes a feoffment in fee, the feoffee holds of the lord paramount, because the donor shall never avow upon him; for if he were to avow upon him he would have to show the feoffment of the tenant in tail, and then it might appear that the reversion is out of him, and consequently the rent also. Therefore the lord DYER, HARPER and MANWOOD held that the feoffee should hold of the lord paramount, and that he should have the wardship of his heir, and the discontinuee's heir cannot avoid it. Thus it seems the lord shall have two wardships, namely of the donor's heir and of the discontinuee's heir. {See 31 Edw. III, tit. *Gard*, 117.[10]}

253. ANON.

King's Bench, Pas. 1576.

Arbitration.

Note that it appears in 19 Edw. IV, fo. 1,[11] in the residuum of that case, that the parties were bound in a bond to abide by the award; but the reason given there by Choke was that they could not make an award in respect of something which was not committed to them. Note that the law is all one whether they make an award in respect of a thing outside the submission or of a person outside the submission. Likewise it

---

[1] *Prior of Lewes's Case* (1406) YB Mich. 8 Hen. VI, fo. 6, pl. 15.
[2] YB Trin. 2 Hen. VI, fo. 15, pl 16.
[3] YB Mich. 6 Hen. VII, fo. 6, pl. 1.
[4] YB Mich. 6 Hen. VII, fo. 10, pl. 18.
[5] YB Trin. 6 Hen. VII, fo. 4, pl. 3; identifiable as *Wodeward* v. *Kyp* (1490) CP 40/916, m. 399.

submission. Et issint il fuit tenus in <18 El.>ᵈ P. 18 Eliz. regine in banke le roy in mesme le case que larbitrement fuit voide coment que les parties fueront obliges a ceo, car le condition del obligation fuit a estoier al agard de toutz choses inter eux 2, issint quant ilz arbitrate que estraunge serra oblige ove luy cest voide et hors de submission. Et uncore nota que in ascun cases un obligation ferra un voide arbitrement bone ...

[254]

AD, fo. 101 (862).

<Arbitrement.>ˢ

M. 18 Eliz. fuit dit in le common banke que si home soit oblige de <faire void>ᵈ <estoier al>ⁱ agard de J. S., si J. S. fait void agard, come a paier deniers a un estrange que nest partie al submission, la cest est voide. Mes auterment est quant lagard est de void chose, come lun partie enfeffera lauter de son parte demesne, ou si il inffera sa fem demesne, [ou]¹ ascun auter voide acte. Et cest diversitie semble destre agree. <Mes vide contrarie apres 21 E 4, 28, at Willes case.>ᵃ

[255]

AD, fo. 101v (862v).

<Arbitrement.>ˢ

Et nota jeo ay oy Justice Manwood in le common banke a prender cest difference, que quant <2>ⁱ homes <font>ᵈ soy mittront in lagard de J. S. de 3 special choses, come de droit del manour de D. et del delivery dun obligation et del propertie de certein chivalles, la il ne poet faire agard de lun solement, mes quant le submission est de toutz actions reall et personell [en]² generaltie la les arbitrators poent faire agard de actions [...]² solement. Et issint est per curiam 19 H. 6, 6b. <Dier, 7 Eliz. 242.>ⁱ

[256]

AD, fo. 102v (863v).

<Seisine.>ˢ

Nota, si il soit segnior et tenant per fealtie et certain quantitie de salte, et le tenant ad use temps dont memorie ne court etc. a paier al segnior ij s. annuatim pur le salte,

---

¹ *Unclear; resembles* apte *or* axte.
² *Words lost in lower corner.*

was held in Easter term 18 Eliz. in the King's Bench, in the same case, that an arbitration was void even though the parties were bound to it, for the condition of the bond was to abide by the award in respect of all matters between them both, and therefore when they arbitrate that a stranger should be bound with one of the parties this is outside the submission and void. Nevertheless, note that in some cases a bond may make a void arbitration good …

254. ANON.[1]

Common Pleas, Mich. 1576.

Arbitration.

In Michaelmas term 18 Eliz. it was said in the Common Bench that if someone is bound to stand to the award of John Style, and John Style makes a void award, such as to pay money to a stranger who is not party to the submission, this is void. But it is otherwise when the award is of something void, as where one party is to enfeoff the other of his own share, or to enfeoff his own wife, or some other void act. This distinction seems to be agreed. {But see below, to the contrary, in 21 Edw. IV, fo. 38, Atwill's case.[2]}

255. ANON.

Common Pleas, 1572/78.

Arbitration.

Note that I have heard MANWOOD J. in the Common Bench make this distinction: when two men submit themselves to the award of John Style for three specific things, such as the right of the manor of Dale, the delivery of a bond, and the property of certain horses, he may not make an award in respect of one only; but when the submission is in respect of 'all actions real and personal', in general terms, the arbitrators may make an award for [personal] actions only: so it is held by the court in 19 Hen. VI, fo. 6v.[3] {Dyer, 7 Eliz. 242.[4]}

256. ANON.

Common Pleas, Pas. 1576.

Seisin.

Note that if there are a lord and tenant by fealty and a certain quantity of salt, and the tenant had been accustomed since time immemorial to pay the lord 2s. annually for

---

[1] Cf. *Dudley* v. *Mallery* (King's Bench, Trin. 1576) 3 Leon. 62 (same point).
[2] Abridged further down the page as '21 E. 4, 39', i.e. *Atwill* v. *Tailor* (1481) YB Mich. 21 Edw. IV, fo. 38, pl. 4, at fo. 39.   [4] YB Mich. 19 Hen. VI, fo. 6, pl. 12, *ad finem*.
[5] *Anon.* (1565) Dyer 242, pl. 51, cit. Mich. 6 & 7 Eliz., roll 1887.

uncore le segnior poet distreiner quant luy pleist pur le salt, car lauter fuit paie in lieu de ceo: ut dicitur fuit P. 18 Eliz. regine in communi banco. Mez ilz disoient que auterment fuit si le rent use estre paye generalment, car donques serra intend que il fuit per compositione[m].

Et nota que Harper dit que ad estre adjudge, et il dit que il fuit son case demesne, que si parson dun ville ad use temps dont a prender chescun anne certainement pur chescun calfe ou porce xij d., la le parson ne poet waive le xij d. et prender son calfe ou porce, mes sil ad use temps dont a prender allowance pur le calfe ou porce, scilicet in ascun anne xij d. et ascun foitz viij d., solonque lour agrement, la il bien poet waiver le alowans et prender son tithe quant luy pleist. Ideo quere del primer case.

[257]

AD, fo. 102v (863v).

<Seisine.>[s]

[1]Mes nota que Justice Manwood dit in le common banke que si home soit seisie dun <de>[2] segniorie de fealte et rent et certain worke days per an, le seisin de rent[3] nest seisin de worke days pur ceo que ambideux sont annuell. Mes il agre que seisin de fealtie est seisin de rent pur faire avowrie, car nest anuell. Quere le diversite.

[258]

AD, fo. 105v (866v).

<Resceit.>[4]

M. 14 Eliz. Vernon port un formedon vers Sir H. Stanley et sa fem et Jo[h]n Manley et sa fem, al petit cape les baron[s] font defaut <apres defaut>[d] [et] lour femes priont estre resceives. Le demandant counterplede le resceit pur ceo que les barons et lour femes ont levie un fine de mesme les terres pendant le brefe. Et coment que lestatut de W. 2, cap. 3, done resceit al fem sur defaut son baron a defender son droit, et ore son droit est ale per le fine, uncore entant que les femes nient obstant lalienation remaine tenantes del demandant per estoppell, scilicet per le user del brefe, ideo fuit adjudge que les femes fueront resceives.

---

[1] *Following a discussion of several earlier cases.*
[2] *Sic, but otiose.*   [3] *Written twice.*   [4] *Heading on recto.*

Noted in Coke's Dyer (Holkham 8014), fo. 341 ('Vernons case … Vide in mon report de cest case'). Differently reported in JRL MS. Fr. 118, fos. 19v–21, sub nom. *Vernham* v. *Stanley*; Dyer 315, 319 (Mich. 1572), 341 (Pas. 1575); 1 And. 18; Dal. 107; Plowd. 425 (on another point); Benl. 198, 204, cit. record; BL MS. Harley 443, fo. 72v; MS. Harley 6707, fos. 20–25; MS. Harg. 10, fos. 38v, 52; MS. Harg. 15, fos. 96v–97; MS. Add. 25222, fo. 47 (Trin. 1573); MS. Add. 24845, fos. 96v–98v (Mich. 1572); CUL MS. Gg.5.2, fo. 101; IT MS. Barrington 76, fos. 40v–42. Cf. *Vernon* v. *Madder* (1570) Dyer 298; Hil. 12 Eliz., roll 1509 (roll now missing; printed in Co. Ent. 338v–340v): formedon for lands in Wirksworth, Derbs.

[2] Succeeded as earl of Derby on his father's death, 24 Oct. 1572.

the salt, the lord may nevertheless distrain for the salt when he pleases, for the money was paid in lieu of it: so it was said in Easter term 18 Eliz., in the Common Bench. But they said that it would be otherwise if the rent had been paid generally, for then it would be presumed that it was by a composition.

Note that HARPER said it had been adjudged – and he said it was his own case – that if the parson of a vill has been accustomed time out of mind to take 12d. every year with certainty for every calf or pig, the parson cannot waive the 12d. and take his calf or pig; but if he has been accustomed time out of mind to take an allowance for the calf or pig, namely 12d. in some years and sometimes 8d., according to their agreement, there he may well waive the allowance and take his tithe when he pleases. Query, therefore, concerning the former case.

257. ANON.

Common Pleas, 1572/78.

Seisin.

... Note that MANWOOD J. said in the Common Bench that if someone is seised of a lordship consisting of fealty and rent and certain work-days every year, the seisin of the rent is not seisin of the work-days, because both are annual. But he agreed that seisin of the fealty is seisin of the rent for the purpose of making avowry, for it is not annual. Query the distinction.

258. VERNON v. STANLEY and MANNERS[1]

Common Pleas, Mich. 1572.

Receipt.

In Michaelmas term 14 Eliz. Vernon brought a formedon against Sir Henry Stanley[2] and his wife and [John Manners] and his wife; at the petit *cape* the husbands made default, and their wives prayed to be received; and the demandant counterpleaded the receipt, because the husbands and their wives had levied a fine of the same lands while the writ was pending. And although the statute of Westminster II, c. 3, entitles the wife to be received upon her husband's default to defend her right, and her right is now gone by reason of the fine, nevertheless, inasmuch as the wives (notwithstanding the alienation) remain the demandant's tenants by estoppel, namely through his using the writ, it was therefore adjudged that the wives should be received.

---

[1] CP 40/1298, m. 2085 (Mich. 1571; printed in Co. Ent. 328v–338v): John Vernon esq. v. Sir Thomas Stanley and his wife Margaret, and John Manners esq. and his wife Dorothy; formedon for 160 messuages and other tenements in Blackwell, Ashbourne and Youlgreave, Derb.; Margaret and Dorothy pray to be received; the demandant counterpleads the receipt; judgment for them to be received; lengthy pleadings follow concerning different parcels; no judgment entered. Noted above, p. 13, no. 24; p. 36, no. 78; and below, p. 159, no. 307; there is also a brief unfinished note in *AB*, fo. 303v, abridged from Plowd. 425 ('Formedon per Vernon envers Madder que vouch Thomas Stanley chivaler et Margaret sa fem et Thomas Manners et Dorothe sa fem, que apperont et travers le point del brefe et fueront a issue et le jury appert').

[259]

AD, fo. 107v (868v).

<Relation.>ˢ

Nota, jeo oy Bromley, sollicitour, dire que fuit adjudge in leschequer chamber que ou executors port action et recover et ad le defendant in execution, et puis le testament est disprove et adnull, que ore le defendant avera audita querela. Et issint fuit adjudge 4 H. 7, 11, per Hawes, si un recover per erronious judgment manour a que villein est regardant, et le villein purchase terres, et le recoveror enter, ou sil seisist gardes et present al advousons, in ceux cases coment que le judgment soit revers et disaffirme uncore il avera ceux choses vestue. Et Brian denie ceux case[s] forsque le case del parson. <Vide 28 H. 8, 32b, Dier, reverser in brefe derrour navera relation pur costes.>ⁱ

[260]

AD, fo. 109 (870).

<Leasses.>ˢ

[*Blank*] Eliz. Home fist leas de 2 acres de terre pur 6 ans, et le lessour covenant et graunt que sil ou ses heires apres les ditz ans ne occupie ne manure les ditz 2 acres de terre, that then and from thensforth the lesse shall have the said 2 acres for 15 yeares. Manwood semble que cest fuit covenaunt executorie et nemi conditionel lesse pur ceo que les parolx sont in le future temps, videlicet, that then the lesse shall have.

[261]

AD, fo. 109 (870).

<Leasses.>ˢ

15 Eliz. Benloes mova, si evesque fist leas pur xxj ans et puis lestatut de 13 Eliz. il lessa le terre al un pur vie et fait lettre datturney a faire livery et seisin, et lattorney ousta le termour et fait livery, et le lesse reenter, le quel cest soit bon leasse (les parolz del estatut esteant all leasses made etc. other then for xxj yeres or three lives to beginne from the making of the same leasse to be voide etc.).

Manwood semble le leasse bone.

---

⁴ Dyer 32, pl. 5, identifiable as *Cokkys* v. *Playfote*, CP 40/1079, m. 455.
⁵ 13 Eliz., c. 10.

259. ANON.

Exch. Ch., before 1579.[1]

Relation.

Note that I heard *Bromley*, solicitor-general, say that it was adjudged in the Exchequer Chamber that where executors bring an action and recover, and have the defendant in execution, and then the testament is disproved and annulled, the defendant may now have *audita querela*.[2] It was thus adjudged in 4 Hen. VII, fo. 11,[3] by Haugh [J.]: if one recovers by erroneous judgment a manor to which a villein is regardant, and the villein purchases lands, and the recoveror enters, seizes wardships and presents to advowsons, in these cases, even though the judgment is reversed and disaffirmed, he shall still have these things vested. But Bryan [C.J.] denied those cases, except the case of the parson. {See 28 Hen. VIII, Dyer 32v,[4] that reversal in a writ of error shall not relate back for the purpose of costs.}

260. ANON.

Common Pleas, 1572/78.

Leases.

Someone made a lease of two acres of land for six years, and the lessor covenanted and granted that if after the said years he or his heirs did not occupy or work the said two acres of land, 'that then and from thenceforth the lessee shall have the said two acres for fifteen years'. MANWOOD thought this was a covenant executory and not a conditional lease, because the words are in the future tense, namely, 'that then the lessee shall have …'.

261. ANON.

Common Pleas, 1573.

Leases.

In 15 Eliz. *Bendlowes* moved this: if a bishop made a lease for twenty-one years, and after the statute of 13 Eliz.[5] leased the land to someone for life, and made a letter of attorney to make livery and seisin, and the attorney ousted the termor and made livery, and the lessee re-entered, is this a good lease? The words of the statute are, 'all leases made [by bishops], other than for twenty-one years or three lives to begin from the making of the same lease, to be void …'.

MANWOOD thought the lease good.

---

[1] Before 26 April 1579, when Thomas Bromley Sol.-Gen. became lord chancellor.
[2] This refers to *Mower* v. *Carvanell* (1543) KB 27/1061, m. 74; Dyer 203; cit. 8 Co. Rep. 144; Differently reported in 102 Selden Soc. 74; 121 Selden Soc. 425–430.
[3] YB Trin. 4 Hen. VII, fo. 10, pl. 6, at fo. 11, *per* Haugh J. The report must be misdated, because Haugh J. died on 14 March 1489.

Mounson dit que il ad conus cest case in experience, scilicet evesque fist leas pur x ans et puis il lessa mesme le terre al auter pur xxj ans, puis le dit statut, a commencer imediatment, ceo est bon leasse. Et ceo fuit le case levesque de Yorke.

Manwood dit que si le catell le lessour in cest case veigne sur le terre, le 2 lessee poet eux prender damage fesaunt.

[262]

AD, fo. 109 (870).

<Leasses.>[s]

Nota, fuit adjudge circa annum 21 Eliz. in banke le roy que si evesque fait leasse pur 21 ans et puis fait leasse pur xxj ans a commencer apres le primer xxj ans, que le 2d leasse est voide per lestatut de anno primo. Et ceo jeo ay del Bullockes report.

[263]

AC, fo. 110v (871v).

<Relation.>[s]

Appiert per un proclamation fait le 10 jour de March anno 23 Eliz. que lou le act de 13 Eliz. encounter usurie, quel act fuit fait a continuer pur 5 ans puis le fine del dit parliament, et a le fine des ditz 5 ans to the end of the first cession of the parliament then next ensuinge, les 5 ans expire anno 18 during le temps del second cession del parliament. Et fuit adjudge per toutz les justices que next ensuing avera relation al parliament etc. <Vide Dier, 23 Eliz. 376. Vide Dier, 6 Eliz. 226.>[a1]

[264]

AD, fo. 111v (872v).

<Countermaund.>[s]

M. 15 Eliz. fuit tenus per tout le court que si le roigne present un per ses letttres patentz que el poet countermaund et repeale ceo, et pur ceo sil present un auter per ses lettres patentz ceo est countermaund del primer <si le primer soit recite, auterment

---

[1] *Added above the case.*

[5] Differently reported in Dyer 376 (Pas. 1581). The proclamation was the outcome of the judicial opinion.
[6] 13 Eliz., c. 8.
[7] According to Dyer, it was a majority.
[8] I.e. the statute continued in force until the end of the first session of the next parliament (1581).
[9] Dyer 226, pl. 36 (1573), an opinion by all the justices on an adjournment of the term by proclamation from the 'quindene next to come' (*proxime futura*).

MOUNSON said he had known this case in experience: a bishop made a lease for ten years, and afterwards leased the same land to another for twenty-one years, after the said statute, to commence immediately; and that was a good lease. It was the archbishop of York's case.[1]

MANWOOD said that if in this case the lessor's cattle come upon the land, the second lessee may take them damage feasant.

262. FOX v. COLLIER[2]

King's Bench, *c.* 1579.

Lease.

Note that it was adjudged around the year 21 Eliz., in the King's Bench, that if a bishop makes a lease for twenty-one years, and then makes a lease for twenty-one years to commence after the first twenty-one years, the second lease is void by the statute of the first year.[3] This I have from Bullock's report.[4]

263. QUESTION CONCERNING A PROCLAMATION[5]

Reference from the Privy Council, March 1581.

Relation.

It appears by a proclamation made on 10 March 23 Eliz. that, whereas the Act of 13 Eliz. against usury[6] was made to continue for five years after the end of the said parliament, and at the end of the said five years 'unto the end of the first session of the parliament then next ensuing', the five years expired in the eighteenth year [1576], during the time of the second session of the parliament. And it was adjudged by all[7] the justices that 'next ensuing' refers to the parliament [and not the session].[8] {See Dyer, 23 Eliz. 376. See Dyer, 6 Eliz. 226.[9]}

264. ANON.

Common Pleas, Mich. 1573.

Countermand.

In Michaelmas term 15 Eliz. it was held by the whole court that if the queen presents someone by her letters patent she may countermand and repeal this; and therefore if she presents someone else by letters patent this is a countermand of the first (if the first

---

[1] Probably no. 262, below, which concerned the archbishop of York.
[2] The other reports of this case are dated from 1581 to 1583, and the judgment was in 1583, but it was entered in Trin. 21 Eliz.: Moo. 107; vol. ii, p. 342 (see n. 6 there). The lease in question was made by Edmund Grindal as archbishop of York in 1576.
[3] 1 Eliz., c. 19.
[4] Probably John Bullock, who became a bencher of the Inner Temple in 1574.

nemy>.[i] Mes la fuit agre que si le roy present un et apres present auter et devant que levesque ad notice del 2 presentment il admitte etc. le primer, la le primer presentee ceo avera: per curiam.

[265]

AD, fo. 111v (872v).

14 Eliz. in le case de Cranmer, Cranmer larchevesque fist feffment al use de luy pur sa vie, le remainder a ces executors pur xxj ans, et apres les xxj ans explete et ended a remainder a son fitz in taile, Cranmer fuit attaint et issint le terme voide per judgment del court. Et fuit move si occupanti concederetur durant les xxj ans, pur ceo que les parols fueront, et apres les xxj ans ended a remainder ouster etc. Et loppinion del court fuit que serra null occupans en le case.

[266]

AD, fo. 112 (873).

<Occupans.>[s]

Vide Litt. 167b. 27 Ass., p. 31, ou un occupauns poet estre dun estate de tenant per le curtesie. Mes jeo oy le recorder de Londres dire que il ad vieu le recorde in 31 E. 3 enter les recordes de Londres in le Tower, in le iter de Londres, que un tenant per le curtesie graunta son estate a un fem que apres fuit professe in le nunrie de Barkinge et la fuit adjudge come il dit que coment que le tenant per le curtesie fuit in vie et un auter avoit primerment enter uncore del estate de tenant per le curtesie ne puissoit estre un occupans. Mesme la ley dun tenant in dower. Quere de ceo.

[267]

AD, fo. 112 (873).

<Occupans.>[s]

Chescun que vient al terre soit ceo per tort ou per droit rebuttera le pleintife per son garrante. Mesme la ley in le case de occupans, per son livery. Et nota le Segnior Dier tient in le starre chamber que coment que le lessour primerment enter uncore il ne serra dit occupauns car auter poet enter sur luy durant <son>[d] le vie cesti que vie.

---

[3] This refers to Coke's gloss, *AC*, fo. 699v, cit. 27 Edw. III, Lib. Ass., pl. 31. In later life, Coke was clear that there could not be an occupant of estates created by law, such as curtesy and dower: Co. Litt. 41b.

[4] 27 Edw. III, Lib. Ass., pl. 31.

[5] William Fleetwood, recorder of London 1571–91.

[6] The last eyre of London was in 14 Edw. II, and the case does not appear in the reports of that eyre.

patent is recited, otherwise not). But it was there agreed that if the king presents one and afterwards presents another, and before the bishop has notice of the second presentation he admits and institutes the first, there the first presentee shall have it: *per curiam*.

265. CRANMER'S CASE[1]

Common Pleas, Mich. 1572.

14 Eliz., in Cranmer's case: Cranmer, the archbishop, made a feoffment to the use of himself for his life, remainder to his executors for twenty-one years, and after the twenty-one years expired and ended remainder to his son in tail; Cranmer was attainted, and the term was therefore declared void by judgment of the court. And it was moved whether it should be allowed to the occupant (*occupanti concederetur*) during the twenty-one years, because the words were, 'and after the twenty-one years to remain over …'. And the opinion of the court was that the occupancy principle should not apply in this case.

266. DELAPRÉ'S CASE[2]

Citation by Serjeant Fleetwood, 1575.

Occupant.

See Litt. 167v,[3] 27 Ass., pl. 31,[4] as to where there may be an occupant of an estate of tenant by the curtesy. But I heard the recorder of London[5] say that he had seen the record in 31 Edw. III among the London records in the Tower, in the eyre of London,[6] that a tenant by the curtesy granted his estate to a woman who was afterwards professed in the nunnery of Barking, and it was there adjudged (as he said) that although the tenant by the curtesy was alive and someone else had already entered, nevertheless there could not be an occupant of the estate of tenant by the curtesy. The law is the same of a tenant in dower. Query as to this.

267. ANON.

Star Chamber, temp. Eliz.

Occupant.

Everyone who comes to land, whether by wrong or by right, may rebut the plaintiff by his warranty. The law is the same in the case of an occupant, by his livery. And note that the lord DYER held in the Star Chamber that even if the lessor enters first, he shall still not be called *occupans* because another might enter upon him the life of cestui que vie.

---

[1] See above, p. 58, no. 106, and the note there.
[2] See above, p. 44, no. 89, where the case is identified.

[268]

AD, fo. 113v (874v).

<Arbitrement.>ˢ

Nota un difference parenter un arbitrement et un ordinaunce, ordre ou rule, car les arbitratours ne poent faire arbitrement dun chose que est future mes des choses et trespasses passe et preterit. Mes ilz poient faire un ordre ou rule ou un ordinaunce dun chose in future. Et issint fuit adjudge in Toppe et Edens case anno 17 Eliz. in bank le roy.

[269]

AD, fo. 119r-v (880r-v).

<Devise.>ˢ

15 Elizab. Clatches case in effect fuit, Clatch seisie des terres in fe ad issue 2 files, scilicet Tomasin et Alice, et devise certain terres al Thomasin et ses heires et certain terre al A. et a ses heires, et si T. devie devant que el ad accomplishe lage de 16 ans sa file A. vivant A. avera in fe, et si A. devie sauns child vivaunt T. que donques sa part remainera al T. et a ses heires, et si ambideux devie sauns issue que il remanera al droit heires Henrie Clatche.

Et fuit argue per les serjauntz que in cest case il serra un crosse remainder et que le terre ne remaindera as droit heires Henrie Clatche tanque ambideux sont mortes entaunt que il dit, Et si ilz ambideux devie sauns issue a remainer a droit heires Henrie Clatche. Mes fuit agre et adjudge que pur ceo que un expresse estate fuit devise a eux devaunt, le quel ne poet estre controll per un implicative meaninge, pur cest cause si lun de eux morust sauns issue le droit heire H. Clatche poet enter maintenant. Vide mult cases ou un expresse devise ne serra controll per un implicative [meaninge] in le title de Uses in le fol. devant 16. [*fo. 119v*] <Vies devises encounter ley, Litt. 37b.>ᵃ

Nota per Mounson in le argument de Clatches case anno 15 Elyz. que il est un grand differens parenter grantes execute in vie et voluntes, queux pur le greinder part sont faitz in extremitie etc. Car grantz executes in vie sont expound solonque les parolx des parties, mes in voluntes le meaning et intention del testatour est graundment destre consider. Et pur ceo in grantes ceux parolx heires font tantsolement estate de inheritaunce, in voluntes a toutz joures, imperpetuum etc. Ou sil devise

---

Catesby (1596) BL MS. Add. 35947, fo. 13 (both dated 16 Eliz.). Differently reported in Dyer 330 (Mich. 1573, argued Hil. 1574), sub nom. *Clache's Case*, cit. record; Dyer's notebook, 110 Selden Soc. 288; BL MS. Harg. 9, fos. 248–253v, 268–271; MS. Harg. 373, fos. 129–134; MS. Lansd. 1057, fos. 272v–276v, 252–257; CUL MS. Gg.5.2, fos. 119v–121v, sub nom. *Clache's Case*; HLS MS. 197 (2071), fos. 53v–56 (Hil. 1574). No report has been found of any argument on the writ of error.

[2] This must refer to *AD*, fo. 829, though that was fo. 72 in Coke's numbering. Cf. the table on *AC*, fo. 76*v ('Feffmentz al uses, 16').

[3] This refers to Coke's notes in *AB*, fo. 372v (magenta), referring to wills of burgage tenements.

268. TOPPE v. EDEN

King's Bench, 1575.

Arbitration.

Note a difference between an arbitration and an ordinance, order or rule: arbitrators cannot make an arbitration in respect of something in the future, but only of things and trespasses past and preterite; but they may make an order or rule, or an ordinance, concerning a future thing. So it was adjudged in Toppe and Eden's case, in the year 17 Eliz., in the King's Bench.

269. GLOVER v. BERYE: CLACHE'S CASE[1]

Common Pleas, 1573.

Devises.

In 15 Eliz. Clache's case was in effect this: Clache, being seised of lands in fee, had issue two daughters, Thomasine and Alice, and devised certain lands to Thomasine and her heirs and certain land to Alice and her heirs, and if Thomasine should die before she accomplished the age of 16, his daughter Alice then living, Alice should have it in fee, and if Alice should die without a child while Thomasine was living, then her part should remain to Thomasine and her heirs, and if both should die without issue it should remain to the right heirs of Henry Clache.

It was argued by the serjeants that in this case it should be considered as a cross-remainder and that the land should not remain to the right heirs of Henry Clache until both were dead, since he said, 'And if both die without issue, remainder to the right heirs of Henry Clache'. But it was agreed and adjudged that because an express estate was devised to them previously, which could not be controlled by an implicative meaning, for that reason if one of them dies without issue the right heir of Henry Clache may enter forthwith. See many cases where an express devise shall not be controlled by an implication in the title 'Uses' in folio 16, above.[2] <See devises against law, Litt., fo. 376v.>[3]

Note by MOUNSON, in the argument of Clache's case in the year 15 Eliz., that there is a great difference between grants executed *inter vivos* and wills, which for the most part are made in extremity. For grants executed *inter vivos* are expounded according to the words of the parties, whereas in wills the meaning and intention of the testator is greatly to be considered. Therefore, in grants, only the word 'heirs' can make an estate of inheritance, whereas in wills 'for ever', *imperpetuum* and so forth [will have the same effect]. Or if someone devises lands to someone to pay his debts: the devisee

---

[1] CP 40/1302, m. 340 (Pas. 1572; copied in KB 27/1251, m. 64; printed in Benl. 212): Edmund Glover and his wife Alice v. John Berye of Lydd, Kent, yeoman, and his wife Katherine; trespass *quare clausum fregit* at Old Romney, Kent; demurrer to the plea setting out the will of Edward Clache; c.a.v. to Trin. 1574; judgment for the defendant; writ of error received, 6 June 1574; KB 27/1251, m. 64; writ of error dated 17 May 1574; discontinued, Hil. 1577. Noted above, p. 22, nos. 40–41; p. 131, no. 234. Cit. by Coke in *Shelley's Case* (1581) 1 Co. Rep. 93, at fo. 103, sub nom. *Clatch's Case*; and in *Downall* v.

terres a un pur paier ses dettz, le devise ad fe simple. 29 H. 8, Broke, si home devise terre paiant pur ceo xx li. le devise ad le fe simple. 7 E. 6, ibidem, home devise terres pur doner ou vender ou faire son pleasur etc. Un remainder in un volunt poet depender sur condition, come Fitzherbert dit in brefe de ex gravi querela, mes le ley est tout auter in grantes. <9 H. 6>[d] <11 H. 6, 13>[i][1]: home poet devise a une in ventre sa mere, auterment del grant. Et le reason de ceux diversites est pur ceo que quant <homes>[i] face un grant in plein vie et de bone memorie ilz poient traveiller a counseyle, et pur ceo le ley require sufficient et prescript parols in grantes. Mes en voluntz pur ceo que le ley intend que le testatour fault soundnes del memory et pur ceo que le infirmite de son corps est tiel, et le temps de son vie est cy brefe et cy uncertain, issint que il ne poet travell a counseyle, pur ceo le ley voille construe son meaning et intention coment que parolx requisite in ley fault.

Et la, per Manwoode, in voluntz come ad estre dit lentent serra prise sil accord ove ley, mes coment que un intent appert uncore si ceo soit enconter ley ceo est tout ousterment voide. Come si home voille que ses terres serront vende, icy appert un meaninge et uncore ceo est voide pur ceo que il naccord ove le ley. Mes sil dit pur paier ses dettes auterment est, car un meaning et intention nest destre construe hors del maimed parolx et blind sentences, come il dit.

Harper accord, et dit que coment que le intent del testator serra prise uncore il covient daver parolx que <irre>[d][1] port ascun <in asc>[d] meaning. Mes coment que les parolx sont imperfect le ley supplie cest defecte. Et pur ceo il <dit>[d] cite le case in 22 Lib. Ass., si tenant en taile voille faire devise, le devise est tout ousterment voide pur ceo que la il fault un able et sufficient testatour. Issint si al common ley un voiloit aver devise terres queux ne sont devisable, ceo est void pur ceo que le chose devised nest devisable. Issint 49 E. 3, un devise fuit fait a le fraternitie del Whitawers ou fueront null tiel, et voide pur le insufficiencie del devisee. Issint per luy in toutz devises il covient estre un sufficient devisor, un chose devisable et un devisee que ad sufficient capacitie a prender. Et il cite loppinion de Reede, 15 H. 7, et del F. et Norwich in 19 H. 8, que in voluntz lentent del testatour est destre prise sil accorde ove le ley. Et mist le case 37 H. 6, si home devise terres a un monke, le remainder ouster in fe, ceo est bone. <9 H. 6, 24, per Godred.>[i] Auterment est in grantes. Et la le Segnior Dier dit que index animi sermo, et pur ceo il dit que per les parolx le meaning et entent est destre prise. Et il agre que in [un] volunt obscure et imperfecte parolx serra expound solonque [le][2] intent del devisor. <37 H. 6, 30, devise de biens al parochiens etc.>[a] <[21] R. 2, tit. Devise, 27, devise pur vie, le remainder ecclesie Sancte [And]ree in Holborne, et le parson port ex gravi querela.>[a]

---

[1] *Unclear deletion; resembles* i'en.   [2] *Several words lost in the outer corner.*

[7] YB Trin. 15 Hen. VII, fo. 11, pl. 22, *per* Rede J. Cf. YB Hil. 13 Hen. VII, fo. 17, pl. 22, *per* Fyneux C.J.
[8] YB Trin. 19 Hen. VIII, fo. 9, pl. 4.   [9] YB Trin. 37 Hen. VI, fo. 30, pl. 11; n. 12, below.
[10] *Farington* v. *Darell* (1431) YB Trin. 9 Hen. VI, fo. 23, pl. 19, at fo. 24, *per* Godred serjeant; B. & M. 80 at 83.
[11] 'A spoken utterance is an indication of the mind.'
[12] *Glover and Brown* v. *Forden* (1459) YB Trin. 37 Hen. VI, fo. 30, pl. 11; CP 40/794, m. 291 (bequest of a grail).
[13] Pas. 21 Ric. II, Fitz. Abr., *Devise*, pl. 27.

has fee simple. 29 Hen. VIII, Brooke:[1] if a man devises land, the devisee paying £20 for it, the devisee has the fee simple. 7 Edw. VI, *ibidem*:[2] a man devised lands to give or sell or do his pleasure. A remainder in a will may depend upon a condition, as Fitzherbert says in the writ of *ex gravi querela*,[3] but the law is quite otherwise in grants. 11 Hen. VI, fo. 13:[4] a man may devise to someone in his mother's womb; otherwise of a grant. And the reason for these differences is that when men make grants in their lifetimes, when they are of good memory, they may travel to counsel, and therefore the law requires sufficient and prescribed words in grants. But in wills, because the law presumes that the testator lacks soundness of memory, and because the infirmity of his body is such, and the time of his life is so short and so uncertain, that he cannot travel to counsel, the law will construe his meaning and intention even if the words requisite in law are lacking.

According to MANWOOD in the same case, in wills (as has been said) the intention shall be followed, if it accords with law; but even when an intention appears, if it is against law it is utterly void. For instance, if someone wills that his lands should be sold [without more], here a meaning appears, and yet it is void because it does not accord with the law, whereas if he says 'to pay his debts' it is otherwise. For a meaning and intention is not to be construed out of maimed words and blind sentences (as he said).

HARPER agreed and said that although the testator's intention shall be followed, nevertheless there must be words which bear some meaning. If, however, the words are imperfect the law supplies this defect. For this he cited the case in 22 Lib. Ass.:[5] if a tenant in tail purports to make a devise, the devise is utterly void because there lacks an able and sufficient testator. Likewise, if at common law someone purported to devise lands which were not devisable, that was void, because the thing devised was not devisable. Likewise, 49 Edw. III:[6] a devise was made to the fraternity of the White-Tawyers, where there was no such fraternity, and it was void for the insufficiency of the devisee. Thus, according to him, there must in all devises be a sufficient devisor, a thing devisable and a devisee who has sufficient capacity to take. And he cited the opinion of Rede in 15 Hen. VII,[7] and of Fitzherbert and Norwich in 19 Hen. VIII,[8] that in wills the intent of the testator is to be followed, if it accords with the law. And he put the case in 37 Hen. VI.[9] If someone devises lands to a monk, the remainder over in fee, this is good: 9 Hen. VI, fo. 24, *per* Godred.[10] It is otherwise in grants. The lord DYER there said that *index animi sermo*,[11] and therefore (he said) the meaning and intention is to be taken from the words. And he agreed that obscure and imperfect words in a will should be expounded according to the meaning of the devisor. {37 Hen. VI, fo. 30:[12] a devise of goods to parishioners [in remainder]. [Pas. 21] Ric. II, tit. *Devise*, 27:[13] a devise for life, remainder to the church of St Andrew in Holborn, and the parson brought *ex gravi querela*.}

---

[1] 29 Hen. VIII, Bro. Abr., *Testament et volunt*, pl. 18.
[2] 7 Edw. VI, Bro. Abr., *Devise*, pl. 39. See also Mich. 4 Edw. VI, Bro. Abr., *Estates*, pl. 78.
[3] Fitz. N.B. 201C.
[4] *Farington v. Darell* (1432) YB Mich. 11 Hen. VI, fo. 12, pl. 28, at fo. 13, *per* Babington C.J.; n. 10, opposite. [5] *Sic*, but perhaps 27 Edw. III, Lib. Ass., pl. 60.
[6] *Jordan's Case* (1375) YB Hil. 49 Edw. III, fo. 3, pl. 7. There was a guild of white-tawyers de facto, and it made ordinances, but it was not incorporated by charter; it was later absorbed into the Leathersellers Company.

[270]

AD, fo. 120 (881).

<Devises per implication.>

M. 21 Eliz. fuit agre per le Segnior Dier et Mounson arguendo in Ramseys case que si home fait feffment in fe sur condition que si le feffe refuse de enfeffer estranger etc. que in cest case le estranger covient a faire request. 16 H. 7, 13.

[271]

AD, fo. 120v (881v).

<Willes et devises des terres.>

[2] E. 6, tit. Testament, 24, per les justices, si le tenant que tiendra in capite done tout son terre al estranger per acte executed in son vie, et devie, uncore le roy avera le 3 parte in gard, et avera le heire auxi sil soit deins age, et <per>[1] ceo per le savant in lestatut de 32 H. 8. Et cest case fuit denie oustrement per Plowden en P. 19 Eliz. arguendo en Sir George Calvarleys case in le court de gardes <ousterment denia>.[2] Mes Popham dit que loppinion dun Gilbert, reader sur le dit statut, fuit que quant home conveie son terre de son mere liberalitie et nemi per bargaine et sale, la <il>[d] le roy avera le 3 parte, come sil done a son frere etc. Et <son>[3] le reason de son opinion fuit per cause de cest parol 'otherwise' in lestatute. Mes il tient le ley contrarie a son opinion, car donques les parolx in lestatut de 32 H. 8, 'to the advancement of his wife, preferment of his childerne and payment of his detz' serroient voides. <Sir George Calverlyes case, Dier 354.>[i]

Arundels case (come Plowden la dit), Mich. 18 Eliz., fuit que fem seisie de certaine terres ad issue bastard file [et] conveie tout sa terre a sa bastard file puis sa mort, et adjudge que le roygne avera riens, car bastard nest pas tiel child que est intende deins lestatut. <Dier, 18 Eliz. 345, mesme le case.>[i] Et uncore il dit que fem poet doner terres in frankmariage ove sa file bastard, car est certain que el ad mere, et serra appell filia matris sue, come 41 E. 3, 19 etc. Mes nota in le preamble le dit statut un des causes del fesauns del estatut fuit a provide pur loialles generations. <Dier 313 pur bastard fitz, Mich. 22 Eliz., Mathew Drapers case.>[a]

---

[1] *Sic, but otiose.*   [2] *Sic, but otiose.*   [3] *Sic, but otiose.*

MS. Lansd. 1060, fos. 23–25v; MS. Add. 24845, fos. 105–106 (Trin. 1573, argued by Plowden and Popham), 253v–255 (argued on the last day of Pas. 1577 after dinner).

[4] 2 Edw. VI, Bro. Abr., *Testament*, pl. 24 ('per cancellarium Anglie et justiciarios').
[5] Statute of Wills, 32 Hen. VIII, c. 1.
[6] Cf. JRL MS.: 'Plowden ... dit que le case [fuit] insert in labbridgement del Brooke, car intend que ne fuit unques escrie per Brooke mesme, il esteant un judge de graund erudition et science ... mes il dit que cest opinion fuit fauxement insert per ascuns et le case graundment absurd.'
[7] Ambrose Gilbert read on the Statute of Wills in Lincoln's Inn, Lent 1556: *Readers and Readings*, p. 124.
[8] *Sir George Calverley's Case* (Mich. 1576) Dyer 354.   [9] Cf. above, p. 70.
[10] *Thornton's Case* (Mich. 1575) Dyer 345.   [11] YB Mich. 41 Edw. III, fo. 17, pl. 2, at fo. 19.
[12] *Gray's Case* (1572) Dyer 313.   [13] In the Court of Wards: 6 Co. Rep. 77.

270. FARRAND d. OWEN v. RAMSEY[1]

Common Pleas, Mich. 1579.

Devises by implication.

In Michaelmas term 21 Eliz. it was agreed by the lord DYER and MOUNSON, arguing in Ramsey's case, that if someone makes a feoffment in fee upon condition that if the feoffee refuses to enfeoff a stranger [the feoffor may re-enter], in this case the stranger must make a request. 16 Hen. VII, fo. 13.[2]

271. SIR GEORGE CALVERLEY'S CASE[3]

Court of Wards, Pas. 1577.

Wills and devises of lands.

2 Edw. VI, tit. *Testament*, 24,[4] by the justices: if a tenant who holds in chief gives all his land to a stranger, by act executed in his lifetime, and dies, the king shall still have the third part in ward, and shall have the heir also if he is under age. This is by reason of the saving in the statute of 32 Hen. VIII.[5] But this case was utterly denied by *Plowden* in Easter term 19 Eliz., during the argument in Sir George Calverley's case in the Court of Wards.[6] However, *Popham* said it was the opinion of one Gilbert, reader on the said statute,[7] that even when someone conveyed his land of his pure liberality, and not by way of bargain and sale – for instance, where he gave it to his brother – the king shall have the third part. And the reason of his opinion was because of the word 'otherwise' in the statute. But he held the law to be the contrary of his opinion, for then the words in the statute of 32 Hen. VIII, 'to the advancement of his wife, preferment of his children and payment of his debts' would be ineffective (*voides*). {Sir George Calverley's case, Dyer 354.[8]}

Arundel's case (as *Plowden* said in that case), in Michaelmas term 18 Eliz.,[9] was that a woman seised of certain lands had issue a bastard daughter, and conveyed all her land to her bastard daughter, and after her death it was adjudged that the queen should have nothing, for a bastard is not such a 'child' as is meant in the statute. {The same case is in Dyer, 18 Eliz. 345.[10]} Nevertheless, he said that a woman may give lands in frankmarriage with her bastard daughter, for it is certain that she has a mother, and she shall be called her mother's daughter (*filia matris suae*), as in 41 Edw. III, fo. 19.[11] Note, however, in the preamble of the said statute, one of the causes for making the statute was to provide for lawful generation. {As to a bastard son, see Dyer 313.[12] Mich. 22 Eliz., Matthew Draper's case.[13]}

---

[1] CP 40/1342, m. 748 (printed in Benl. 313): Edmund Farrand v. William Ramsey of London, grocer; ejectment for a messuage in St Christopher's parish, Cornhill, on the demise of Israel Owen; demurrer to the evidence at the Guildhall, Lent 1577; c.a.v. to Mich. 1579; judgment for the plaintiff. Cf. *AC*, fo. 321v; *AD*, fo. 835v ('Dier Periam 21 El. 140 Ramseys case ...'); identifiable in 110 Selden Soc. 373. Differently reported ibid.; 1 Leo. 268 (Ferrand); BL MS. Harg. 9, fos. 42v–43; MS. Add. 25197, fo. 6.

[2] YB Trin. 16 Hen. VII, fo. 13, pl. 7, which is attributable to Caryll: 115 Selden Soc. 256.

[3] Partly incorporated in the printed version of *Sir George Curson's Case* (1607) 6 Co. Rep. 75, at fos. 76–77. Differently reported in Dyer 354; JRL MS. Fr. 118, fos. 78–79; BL MS. Harley 2036, fos. 96–97v;

Sir Rowland Hilles case (come Plowden auxi dit) fuit: si home convey son terre a sa collaterall cosin que est son heire apparaunt, le roy avera le 3 parte deins lestatut. Et la Plowden dit que ad estre adjudge que le childes child nest deins lestatut. Mes Popham dit que <pr>^d nepos, pronepos etc. est filius deins lestatut. <Vide Bracton, lib. 1, cap. 9. Calverleys case, Dier 354.>^a

Coppings case fuit tiel, come Popham dit: home seisie de 2 mannorz, lun de value de xx li. et lauter de value de x li., <et>^1 il fist feffment in fe del mannour de x li., que fuit value del 3 parte, al use de sa fem in consideration de sa dower, ove remainder ouster al estrangers, et fuit adjudge que la le roigne avera le 3 parte del mannour de <xx li.>^d x li. pur ceo que el ad accept ceo encounter common droit.

[272]

AD, fo. 120v (881v).

<Willes et devises des terres.>^s

14 Eliz. un home seisie des terres tenus in soccage devisa eux a un B et a ses heires de son corps, et voille ouster per mesme le volunt que si le dit B devie que les terres serront a un auter in fe, et fuit tenus per toutz les justices del common banke que uncore le devise ad estate taile et nemi estate pur vie per les darrein parolx. <Bendlowes, 9 H. 8.>^a

[273]

AD, fo. 121 (882*).

<Willes et devises.>^s

17 Eliz. per Dier, devise a un in ventre sa mere nest bone pur ceo que nest in esse a prender. Et il dit que ilz sont forsque 2 capacities, lun corps naturell, lauter corps politique, [et] cesti que est in ventre sa fem nest ascun de eux car precipe ne gist vers luy coment que il poet estre vouche. Quant chose est destre done de uno in alium, la besoigne destre un de ceo prender, mes un remainder ne poet estre in abeiauns.

Mes fuit adjudge apres que devise a tiel enfaunt fuit bone sur solemne argument per Mounson [et] Manwood.

---

[1] *Sic, but otiose.*

Sir Rowland Hill's case,[1] as *Plowden* also said, was this: if a man conveys his land to his collateral kinsman, who is his heir apparent, the king shall have the third part under the statute. And *Plowden* there said that it had been adjudged that a child's child is not within the statute.[2] But *Popham* said that a grandson (*nepos*), great-grandson (*pronepos*) or the like is a 'son' (*filius*) within the statute. {See Bracton, lib. I, c. 9.[3] Calverley's case, Dyer 354.}

Copping's case, as *Popham* said, was this: a man seised of two manors, one worth £20 and other worth £10, made a feoffment in fee of the manor worth £10, which was a third part of the value [of both], to the use of his wife in consideration of her dower, with remainder over to strangers; and it was adjudged that the queen should have the third part of the manor worth £10, because the woman had accepted it against common right.

272. ANON.[4]

Common Pleas, 1572.

Wills and devises of lands.

In 14 Eliz. a man seised of lands held in socage devised them to one B and his heirs of his body, and willed further by the same will that if the said B should die, the lands should be to another in fee: and it was held by all the justices of the Common Bench that the devisee nevertheless had an estate tail and not an estate for life as a result of the latter words. {Bendlowes, 9 Hen. VIII.[5]}

273. ANON.

Common Pleas, 1574/75.

Wills and devises.

17 Eliz., by DYER [C.J.], a devise to someone in his mother's womb is not good, because he is not *in esse* to take.[6] He said that there were only two capacities, the one a natural body, and the other a body politic, and someone who is in his mother's womb is neither of them, for a *praecipe* does not lie against him – although he can be vouched. When something is to be given from one person to another, there needs to be someone to take it, though a remainder may be in abeyance.

But afterwards, upon solemn argument, it was adjudged by MOUNSON and MANWOOD that a devise to such an infant was good.

---

[1] Also in the Court of Wards: ibid.
[2] Plowden says the same in vol. ii, p. 175 (1581).
[3] *Bracton*, ii. 189.
[4] Differently reported in 1 And. 33 (Hil. 1572).
[5] Presumably *Tucke* v. *Frencham* (1558) CP 40/1174, m. 923; Benl. 68 (whence Moo. 13); cit. by Dyer C.J. above, p. 131. Differently reported in Dyer 171; 1 And. 8. The reference to 9 (or possibly 19) Hen. VIII is obscure.
[6] Cf. above, p. 146, no. 269.

[274]

AD, fo. 121 (882*).

<Willes et devises.>[s]

12 Eliz. fuit adjudge si terres sont devised al un in fe, et <al aut>[i,d] in auter parte del testament ilz sont devised al auter in fe, ilz serront jointenantes.

[275]

AD, fo. 121 (882*).

<Willes et devises.>[s]

17 Eliz. fuit tenus que si home devise per fait que ses executors venderont son terres, et oblie de escrier executors, et puis per parol nominate executors et ilz vende, et tenus que lour vendition fuit bon per cest estatut car le substauns del devise est in escript.

[276]

AD, fo. 121 (882*).

<Willes et devises.>[s]

Hil. 20 Eliz. fuit tenus que si home devisa ses terres a son fitz et heire in fe, cest devise est voide, mes sil dit que sil survive lage de xiiij ans donques il avera mesme les terres a luy et a ses heires de son corps, in cest case in le mesne temps il avoit que fe simple determinable et sil survive lage de xiiij ans donques lestate in fe serra chaunge al estate in taile.

[277]

AD, fo. 121 (882*).

<Willes et devises.>[s]<Dier, 19 Eliz. 358.>[i]

Bakers case [in] temps cesti roigne, come Meade, justice, arguendo in Weldens case report, que home devisa terres a un fem in fe simple et que puis son mort que son fitz avera le terre pur terme de son vie, et fuit adjudge que le fem avera estate pur vie, le

---

Guildhall, 24 Nov. 1576, setting out the devise by William Chyck and tracing the title to Elizabeth Raymond as executrix of Richard Reyson, assignee of a lease from Alice Ludlam; c.a.v. to Pas. 1577; judgment for the plaintiff, with 12d. damages and £4 costs. Noted above, p. 47, no. 91. Differently reported in Dyer 358, sub nom. *Chycke's Case* (Pas. 1577); Benl. 300.

[4] See no. 278, immediately below.

[5] The words of the will as set out in the special verdict were 'to Alice Ludlam my cosin the fee simple of my bigger house in Soper Lane in London and after her decease to William her sonne'. Since they did not specify the son's estate, by presumption it was for life only.

274. ANON.

Probably Common Pleas, 1570.

Wills and devises.

In 12 Eliz. it was adjudged that if lands are devised to someone in fee, and in another part of the testament they are devised to another in fee, they shall be joint tenants.

275. ANON.

Probably Common Pleas, 1575.

Wills and devises.

In 17 Eliz. it was held that if someone devises by deed that his executors should sell his lands, and he forgets to write [the names of the] executors, and then by parol he nominates executors, and they sell, their sale is good by the statute,[1] for the substance of the devise is in writing.

276. HINDE v. LYONS[2]

Common Pleas, Hil. 1578.

Wills and devises.

In Hilary term 20 Eliz. it was held that if someone devises his lands to his son and heir in fee, this devise is void; but if he says that, should he survive the age of fourteen, he should have the same lands unto him and his heirs of his body, in this case in the meantime he has but a fee simple determinable, and if he survives the age of fourteen the estate in fee shall be changed into an estate in tail.

277. BAKER d. LUDLAM v. RAYMOND[3]

Common Pleas, Pas. 1577.

Wills and devises. Dyer, 19 Eliz. 358.

Baker's case, in the time of this queen, as MEAD J. reported during argument in Weltden's case,[4] was that someone devised his lands to a woman in fee simple, and that after her death her son should have the land for term of his life,[5] and it was

---

[1] The Statute of Wills, 32 Hen. VIII, c. 1, gave the testator power 'to give, dispose, will and devise [his lands], as well by his last will and testament in writing or otherwise by act or acts lawfully executed in his life …'.

[2] Identified from 2 Leon. 11 (Hil. 1578); 3 Leon. 64 (Mich. 1577), 70 (1578). In these reports the age in the condition is 24, not 14. The testator, 'Sir John Lyons', was probably Sir John Lyon (d. 1565), alderman of London.

[3] CP 40/1338, m. 306 (Mich 1576; partly printed in Benl. 300): Walter Baker, attorney of the Common Pleas v. Edward Raymond and Elizabeth his wife; ejectment for a messuage in the parish of St Pancras Soper Lane, London, on the demise of William Ludlam; pleads Not Guilty; special verdict at the

remainder pur vie al fitz, [le] remainder in fe al fem, issint que toutz les partes del volunt poient estoier.

[278]

AD, fo. 123 (884).

<Propartie.>ˢ

Nota per Segnior Dier in Weldens case que est jus possessionis et jus proprietatis.

[279]

AD, fo. 123 (884).

Nota que les justices agree in le case de Norwood envers Segnior Darcye que si le testatour soit indet al executor, si lexecutor ad tant de biens en ses maines come son det amount le properte de ceo serra change in luy mesme, scilicet il ad eux come ses biens propres et nemi come executor, et issint il est transmutation del propertie per acte in ley sans suit ou execution, pur ceo que il ne poet commencer action vers luy mesme. Et ceo semble a moy si tenant in taile vouche luy mesme pur saver le taile […]¹ in cest case il serra seisie in taile des auters terres recover in […]² sauns ascun proces ou suite in ley.

[280]

AD, fo. 127v (888v).

<Appendauntz.>ˢ

18 Eliz. termino Pasche fuit agre in le common banke que un vicarage poet estre appendant a un mannour. Et uncore fuit object que nul poet aver <vicar>ᵈ avouson del vicarage forsque spirituell home.

[281]

AD, fo. 128v (889v).

<Notice.>ˢ

Nota, fuit agre in Giles quare impedit T. 18 Eliz. que toutz foitz quant un eglise

¹ *One or two words lost at edge of page.*
² *Several words worn or lost in lower corner.*

³ Norwood in MS. The plaintiff's name seems to be confused with that of Richard Norwood in *Norwood* v. *Rede* (1557) Plowd. 180, which settled that *assumpsit* lay against executors.
⁴ See above, p. 63, no. 113, and the note there.

adjudged that the woman should have an estate for life, remainder for life to the son, remainder in fee to the woman, so that all the parts of the will may stand.

278. WELTDEN v. ELKINGTON[1]

Common Pleas, Pas. 1578.

Property.

Note by the lord DYER, in Weltden's case, that there is *jus possessionis* and *jus proprietatis*.

279. WOODWARD v. LORD DARCY (1558)[2]

Probably from Plowd.

Note that the justices agreed in the case of [Woodward][3] against Lord Darcy that if the testator is indebted to the executor, and the executor has goods in his hands to the amount of his debt, the property in them shall be changed in himself: that is, he has them as his own goods and not as executor. Thus, there is a transmutation of the property by act in law, without suit or execution, because he may not commence an action against himself. Likewise, (as it seems to me) if a tenant in tail vouches himself to save the tail, in this case he shall be seised in tail of the other lands recovered in [value], without any process or suit in law.

280. ANON.

Common Pleas, Pas. 1576.

Appendants.

In Easter term 18 Eliz it was agreed in the Common Bench that a vicarage may be appendant to a manor. And yet it was objected that no one may have the advowson of the vicarage except a spiritual man.

281. GYLES v. COLSHILL[4]

Common Pleas, Trin. 1576.

Notice.

Note that it was agreed in Gyles's *quare impedit*, in Trinity term 18 Eliz., that whenever

---

[1] See above, p. 56, no. 104, and the note there.
[2] Reported in Plowd. 184: Thomas Woodward v. Thomas, Lord Darcy of Chiche, Sir John Chichester and Humphrey Coles esq., executors of Thomas Windham, executor of Sir John Luttrell; debt on a bond for £140 made by Luttrell.

devient voide per acte de parliament, come per prisel dun auter benefice, ou per recusaunte a paier tentz in leschequer ne besoigne ascun notice done, mes les 6 moys serra accompt del avoidance. <Dier, 348.>ᵃ

[282]

AD, fo. 141v (902v).

<Avowries.>ˢ

20 Eliz. In avowrie pur rent nest plea pur le pleintife adire que il fuit al jour etc. prist de paier et la tender etc., car tender nest plea mes pur saver penaltie etc., et lavowant nest chase in cest case a demande ceo. Mes est bon plea que al temps del distres il tender etc.

[283]

AD, fo. 142 (903).

<Wrecke.>ᵃ

Nota que il fuit loppinion de Justice Gawdy que le difference parenter waive et wrecke est que si toutz fue hors del niefe issint que nul creature remaine in le niefe uncore si le partie poet prove que ilz fueront ses biens ceo ne serra dit wrecke, mes il dit si toutz alont hors del niefe etc. et fuont hors del viewe del niefe ceo est waive. Mes il dit si le parte continue deins le vieu del niefe ceo ne serra dit waive, car le fuer serra intende solement pur le save gard de son vie. Vide 22 E. 3, 16.

[284]

AD, fo. 918*.

<Wrecke.>ˢ

Nota, Plowden dit in largument de Sir John Constables case in quo w[arranto] que ceux del west country prescribe daver wreke de haut mere cy farre come ilz poient voier un humber barrell. <39 E. 3, 32b, prescribe daver roiall pissons prise in alto mare.>ᵃ

---

report of *Sir Henry Constable's Case* (1601) 5 Co. Rep. 106 (which concerned the same title): i.e. *Constable v. Gamble*, KB 27/1360, m. 858.

[7] Cf. C. Molloy, *De Jure Maritimo* (1676), p. 230. An account of the custom in Poole, Dorset, is given in J. Sydenham, *History of the Town and County of Poole* (Poole, 1839), pp. 371–372: 'The water bailiff, with several of the jurymen, went off to sea in a boat from North Haven point, and when they had found out certain old marks or bearings they put a humber barrel out of the boat and laid it floating on the water. This is supposed to be the extreme point at which it could be descried by the naked eye from an elevated sand bank at North Haven, on which others of the jury remained. The distance at which the floating barrel was thus seen is about three miles.' It is also mentioned as a custom in Devon in *Calmady v. Rowe* (1848) 6 C.B. 861, at p. 877. A humber barrel was large: *The Assembly Books of Southampton*, vol. i, ed. J. W. Horrocks (1917), p. 101 (42 gallons).

[8] YB Mich. 39 Edw. III, fo. 35, pl. [42].

a church becomes vacant through an act of Parliament, for instance by taking another benefice, or by refusing to pay tenths in the Exchequer, there is no need for any notice to be given, but the six months shall be reckoned from the avoidance. {Dyer 348.[1]}

282. ANON.

Probably Common Pleas, 1578.

Avowries.

20 Eliz. In an avowry for rent, it is no plea for the plaintiff to say that he was [in a certain place] at the day ready to pay, and there tendered [the rent], for a tender is no plea except to save a penalty [for non-payment], and the avowant is not driven in this case to demand it. But it is a good plea that he tendered at the time of the distress.

283. ATT.-GEN. v. CONSTABLE[2]

King's Bench, 1578.

Wreck.

Note that it was the opinion of GAWDY J.[3] that the difference between waif and wreck is as follows. If everyone flees from the ship, so that no creature remains in the ship, nevertheless if the party can prove that the goods were his, this shall not be called wreck; but (as he said) if everyone leaves the ship, and flees out of sight of the ship, [the property] is waived. But he said that if the party continues to be within sight of the ship it shall not be said to be waived, for the fleeing shall then be presumed solely to save his life. See 22 Edw. III, fo. 16.[4]

284. ATT.-GEN. v. CONSTABLE, continued[5]

King's Bench, 1578.

Wreck.[6]

Note that *Plowden* said, in the argument of Sir John Constable's case in a *quo warranto*, that those of the West Country prescribe to have wreck of the high sea so far as they can see a humber barrel.[7] {39 Edw. III, fo. 32v,[8] prescription to have royal fish caught in the high sea (*in alto mare*).}

---

[1] Dyer's report of the present case. [2] Conjectural: see the next case.
[3] Appointed J.K.B. in Mich. 1574.   [4] YB Mich. 22 Edw. III, fo. 16, pl. 63.
[5] KB 27/1294, Rex, m. 2: Att.-Gen. v. Sir John Constable; information in the nature of *quo warranto* for (inter alia) taking wreck between high and low watermark adjoining the manor and lordship of Holderness in Lincs. and Yorks.; traces title from the duke of Buckingham, and from King Henry VIII following the duke's attainder for treason, and disclaims any wreck below low watermark; judgment for the defendant. Differently reported in 1 And. 86–94; 3 Leon. 72; BL MS. Harg. 15, fos. 95v–96v (tr. in S. A. Moore, *History of the Foreshore* (3rd ed., 1888), pp. 225–232); IT MS. Barrington 76, fos. 36v–39; HLS MS. 200.1 (1180.1), fos. 401–403 (Pas. 1577); and the MSS. cited in 109 Selden Soc. liv, n. 67.
[6] The upper half of the page is taken up with an explanation of the distinction between wreck, flotsam, jetsam and lagan. This seems to have been written earlier, though it was incorporated in the printed

[285]

AD, fo. 918*v.

18 Eliz. in Onleys case fuit dit per le Segnior Dier que [in] action sur le case le brefe et le count sont tout un et ne sont include deins ascun certaine forme in le registre, car le diversite des cases fait les brefes divers et de severall formes, et pur ceo tiel prescript forme nest requisite in actions sur le case come sont in auters brefes. 7 H. 4, 4, si laction sur le case ad substauns le brefe nabatera. Vide 31 E. 3, Brefe, 335. <16 H. 6, Action sur le case, 44.>[i]

[286]

AD, fo. 919v (magenta ink).

<Action sur le case.>[s]

Nota bene quant home est a porter action sur le case sur un assumpsit il covient a luy a declare le consideration in mesme le mannour et forme come ceo est, et auxi il doit declarer le promise in mesme le mannour et fourme come ceo est, car si jeo in consideration dun chivall et de 2s. promise a vous etc., in cest case si vous port action etc. besoigne a vous a declarer sur ceux ambideux considerations ou auterment jeo pledra non assumpsit modo et forma etc. Mes nota bene quant le consideration est destre prove in evidence, et quant nemi, car quant le consideration est executorie, come jeo promise a vous que si vous aleres a L. ove moy jeo donera a vous 20 li., ore in action sur le case vous covient declarer in fait que vous ales etc. et cest aler a L. est traversable, et si in cest case jeo plead non assumpsit modo et forma vous ne besoigne de prover vostre aler in evidens car ceo puissoit aver estre travers. <3 H. 6, 33, tit. Count B. 5.>[i] Mes si le consideration soit executed, la le consideration nest traversable come in le case supra, et pur ceo le <pl>[d] partie pledra non assumpsit modo et forma et toutz les considerations covient estre proves. Vide Justice Manwoods argument in le case de Onlye et le countee de Kent etc. <27 H. 8, 24a, declare sur un assumpsit fait a luy mesme et done in evidence assumpsit fait a son fem a que il agrea.>[a]

[1]Nota bene per Manwood in Onlyes case anno 18 Eliz. T. que quant considerations sont traversable, la ilz covient estre plede certeinment. Et Manwood dit que quaunt lassumpsit est foundue sur un certein consideration, donques le consideration nest traversable, car la lassumpsit est le weight et substauns del action. Mes quant lassumpsit referre al incertein consideration, come la fuit a contenter et paier omnia onera et expensa qualia[2] Onley expendidit, icy le consideration est traversable car le

---

[1] *This paragraph appears to have been added.*
[2] *Written twice.*

an even fuller report of Mounson J.'s argument, with which Manwood J. disagreed, and which Coke evidently chose to ignore.

[7] YB Mich. 27 Hen. VIII, fo. 24, pl. 3; identifiable as *Holygrave* v. *Knightsbridge* (1535) KB 27/1094, m. 30d; 94 Selden Soc. 256; Spelman's reports, 93 Selden Soc. 7; B. & M. 454.

285. ONLEY v. EARL OF KENT[1]

Common Pleas, 1576.

In 18 Eliz., in Onley's case, it was said by the lord DYER that in an action on the case the writ and the count are all one, and they are not included within any certain form in the Register, for the diversity of the cases makes the writs various and of several forms, and therefore no such prescribed form is requisite in actions on the case as in other writs. 7 Hen. IV, fo. 4:[2] if an action on the case has substance, the writ will not abate. See 31 Edw. III, *Briefe*, 335;[3] 16 Hen. VI, *Accion sur le case*, 44.[4]

286. ONLEY v. EARL OF KENT, continued

Common Pleas, Trin. 1576.

Action on the case.

Note well that when someone is to bring an action on the case upon an *assumpsit* he must declare the consideration in the same manner and form as it is, and he ought also to declare the promise in the same manner and form as it is; for if I make a promise to you in consideration of a horse and of 2s., and you bring an action [on the promise], in this case you must declare upon both these considerations, or else I may plead that I did not undertake 'in the manner and form alleged' (*Non assumpsit modo et forma etc.*). But note well when the consideration is to be proved in evidence, and when not. When the consideration is executory – as where I promise you that if you go to London with me, I will give you £20 – now in an action on the case you must declare in fact that you went with me, and this going to London is traversable, and if in this case I plead *Non assumpsit modo et forma*, you need not prove your going in evidence, for it could have been traversed. {3 Hen. VI, fo. 33, B[rooke], tit. *Count*, 235.[5]} But if the consideration is executed, the consideration is not traversable, as in the case above, and therefore the party may plead *Non assumpsit modo et forma* and all the considerations must be proved. See Manwood J.'s argument in the case of Onley and the earl of Kent.[6] {27 Hen. VIII, fo. 24:[7] declares upon an *assumpsit* made to himself, and gives in evidence an *assumpsit* made to his wife, to which he agreed.}

Note well by MANWOOD, in Onley's case, in Trinity term 18 Eliz., that when considerations are traversable they must be pleaded with certainty. And MANWOOD said that when an *assumpsit* is based on a certain consideration, the consideration is not traversable, for there the *assumpsit* is the weight and substance of the action; but when the *assumpsit* refers to an uncertain consideration – as (in this case) to content and pay back all the charges and expenses which Onley laid out – the consideration is here

---

[1] See above, p. 124, no. 218, and the note there.
[2] *Abbot of Stratford's Case* (1406) YB Hil. 7 Hen. IV, fo. 8, pl. 10.
[3] Hil. 31 Edw. III, Fitz. Abr., *Briefe*, pl. 335.
[4] Mich. 16 Hen. VI, Fitz. Abr., *Accion sur le case*, pl. 44.
[5] YB Hil. 3 Hen. VI, fo. 33, pl. 26; Bro. Abr., *Count*, pl. 5.
[6] This is probably a reference to what is now Rylands MS. Fr. 118, fo. 85 (printed below), from which (it seems) an abridged version of Manwood J.'s argument there was inserted here. The Rylands MS. contains

substauns del action est le consideration, car sil ad expend mult il recovera mult etc. Et il dit clerement que le pleintife ne besoigne de prover in evidence toutz le considerations, car sil prove ascun deux ceo suffist. Et il et le Segnior Dier agreont que si ascun des considerations [sont][1] inconter ley, uncore si ascun des considerations sont sufficient laction bien [girr]a.

Manwood J.'s Argument in the Rylands MS.
JRL MS. Fr. 118, fo. 85.

... Manwood a mesme lentent. Et il dit que le barre fuit insufficient, et in ceo il fuit contrarie al Mounson, et que le counte fuit insufficient auxi. Quant al count il dit que il avoit estre objecte al barre que pur le generalte et pur le multiplicitie ne besoigne de monstre chescun busines et auter chose in <certaine>[d] particularite. Mes coment que ceo est voire, uncore est requisite que le counte soit certaine et sufficient, car come il dit fuit un mesne parenter starringe et starke blinde, car nient obstant que le particularitie de chescun chose nest requisite, uncore le certainte del chose est necessarie et principalment in countes. Et il agree ove Mounson que <cest>[d] ascun parte del cest consideration fuit apparaunt encounter ley pur ceo que la prosecution del sute et expending de ses deniers demesne fuit maintenance. Et il dit que un count ne serra my prise per intendment mes covient estre certaine et sufficient, et pur ceo que le pleintife ou est a recover le chose demande ou a devester un interest ou auter chose del defendant, le quel il ne ferra sauns sufficient et certaine title monstre al court. Mes auterment est in barres, car la melior est conditio possidentis et pur ceo la common intent servera. Et il dit que querela signifie un complaint et secta declare et signifie sute in ley, mes negotium il dit fuit generall parol et poet estre referre a chescun affaire et busines, et donques son count serra prise per intendement il poet intende loiall busines. Mes il dit que pur ceo que dependentia vient in fine et est knitt et referre a toutz, ceo <shutte cest>[d] limitte et qualifie le generaltie de cest parol negotium, et pur ceo que dependentia est referre et knitt a luy ceo ne poet estre intend mes les suites dependentia in lege. 9 E. 4, 43: 2 fueront oblige a estoier al arbitrement de J. S. de omnibus actionibus personalibus, sectis et querelis, et la le livre agre que cest parol personalibus referre a toutz les substantives et qualifiera lour generalitie, et que le authoritie del arbitrators in tiel case est solement a faire agarde de personal choses. Et auxi il dit que le livre in 18 H. 8, 5, in estrepement, fuit que un brefe nest pendent tanque ceo soit retorne. Et il cite le case in 20 E. 4, si home in quare impedit per voy de count fist title que J. S. fuit seisie et present et grant a luy le prochen avoidauns, et puis leglise devient voide etc., il covient daverrer que ceo fuit le primer avoidaunce. Et in cest case al barre il dit que le consideration fuit incertaine et pur ceo insufficient, car il covient daver monstre le lieu ou les busines fueront, et inter queux persons les busines, sutes, quarells etc. fueront, et queux choses ilz concerne, come biens ou charters etc. Come si home soit oblige a coiller tout sa grene waxe, et il plede que il ad coille tout son grene waxe, <cest>[d] ceo nest bone, mes covient dier tout le grene waxe <de tiel ma>[d] deins tiel mannour. Mes voet estre dit que considerations in action sur le case ne sont my traversable, et pur ceo ne besoigne de monstre le certaintie. Mes il dit que in ascun cases le consideration in action sur le case est traversable et in ascun case nemi. <il dit>[d] Car il dit si lassumpsit conteine certainte donques le consideration nest my traversable, mes si lassumpsit referre al consideration et est destre reduce al certaintie per le consideration donques le consideration est traversable, car la le consideration est le weight et substaunce del assumpsit. Et pur ceo si

---

[1] *Word rubbed out in bottom outer corner.*

traversable, inasmuch as the substance of the action is the consideration: for if he has spent much, he will recover much. And he said, clearly, that the plaintiff need not prove all the considerations in evidence, for if he proves any of them it suffices. He and the lord DYER agreed that if any of the considerations is against the law, nevertheless if any of the other considerations is sufficient the action will lie perfectly well.

Manwood J.'s Argument in the Rylands MS.
JRL MS. Fr. 118, fo. 85.

... MANWOOD to the same effect.[1] And he said that the bar was insufficient – and in this he was contrary to Mounson – and that the count was also insufficient. As to the count, he said that it had been objected at the bar that because of the generality and the multiplicity there was no need to set out every business and every other thing with particularity. But although that is true, it is still requisite that the count should be certain and sufficient, for (as he said) there is a middle way between staring and stark blind; for although the particularity of every item is not requisite, yet the certainty of the thing is necessary, and especially so in counts. He agreed with Mounson that part of this consideration was evidently against law, because prosecuting the suit and spending his own money [on it] was maintenance. And he said that a count shall not be understood by presumption, but must be certain and sufficient, because the plaintiff is either to recover the thing demanded or to divest an interest or something else from the defendant, and he cannot do that without a sufficient and certain title shown to the court. It is otherwise, however, in bars, for there *melior est conditio possidentis*[2] and therefore a common presumption will serve. He said that *querela* signifies a complaint and *secta* declares and signifies a suit in law, but *negotium* (he said) was a general word and could refer to all kinds of affairs and business, and therefore his count should be taken by presumption to intend lawful business. But he said that because *dependentia* comes at the end, and is knitted and referred to everything, this limits and qualifies the generality of this word *negotia*; and because *dependentia* is referred and knitted to it, it can only be understood of suits pending in law (*dependentia in lege*). 9 Edw. IV, fo. 43:[3] two were bound to stand to the arbitration of John Style with respect to all personal actions, suits and complaints (*de omnibus actionibus personalibus, sectis et querelis*), and there the book agrees that this word *personalibus* refers to all the substantives and qualifies their generality, and that the authority of the arbitrators in such case is only to make an award with respect to personal things. Also he said that the book in 18 Hen. VIII, fo. 5,[4] in estrepement, was that a writ is not 'pending' until it is returned. And he cited the case in 20 Edw. IV: if in *quare impedit* someone (by way of a count) makes title that John Style was seised and presented, and granted him the next avoidance, and then the church fell vacant, he must aver that this was the first avoidance. And in this case at bar he said that the consideration was uncertain, and therefore insufficient, for he ought to have shown the place where the business was done, and between what persons the business, suits, plaints and so forth were, and what things they concerned, such as goods or charters. Similarly, if someone is bound to collect all his green wax, and he pleads that he has collected all his green wax, this is not good, but he must say 'all the green wax within such and such a manor'. But it could be said that considerations in an action on the case are not traversable, and therefore there is no need to show the certainty. However, he said that in some cases the consideration in an action on the case is traversable and in some cases not. For (he said) if the *assumpsit* contains certainty the consideration is not traversable, but if the *assumpsit* refers to the consideration, and is to be reduced to certainty by the consideration, then the consideration is traversable, for there the consideration is the weight

---
[1] This refers to the argument of Mounson J., with which the report begins.
[2] 'The person in possession is in the better position.'
[3] YB Mich. 9 Edw. IV, fo. 43, pl. 30.   [4] YB Mich. 18 Hen. VIII, fo. 5, pl. 18.

jeo die a vous, in consideration que <jeo ay>^d vous aves fait service a moy et auxi done a moy 20 li. jeo promise a vous xxx li., in cest case le assumpsit est certaine et pur ceo le consideration nest traversable. Mes il dit clerement que ne besoigne de prover toutz le considerations, car il dit sil prove ascun de eux ceo suffist, et ceo est common experience in le banke le roy. [*fo. 85v*] Mes quant lassumpsit est referre al consideration et depend sur ceo, et laction est chose uncertaine, come in nostre case il est, la le consideration est traversable. Car icy lassumpsit est a recompencer omnia talia onera et expensa qualia le pleintife exposuissit circa negotia etc., issint que le weight del assumpsit gist tout sur le consideration, car sil ad expend mult il recovera accordant, et sil ad expend petit ou riens il recover auxi accordant. Et donques si le consideration soit traversable, donques covient estre pleade certainement, pur ceo que issue puissoit aver estre prise sur ceo et les jurors ne serra inveigle ove incertaintie. Et il dit si home ad 3 ou 4 files, et il maria un et done ove luy in mariage c li., et puis il marie un auter et done a luy cc li., et puis un auter est destre marie et il promise a cesti que serra sa baron tant quant il avoit done ove ascun de ses auters files, in det sur cest assumpsit il covient de monstre especialment ou il done, a que il done, et ove que il dona, et quant il dona.

Cases from Marginalia at Holkham Hall

[287]

Coke's *Statuta* (Holkham 7834), fo. 115v.

Pasch. 17 Eliz. Si un justice de peace sur complaint veigne a un mese, et il ne poet estre suffer a vener eins a veier nisi le huis serroit enfreint, et issint le justice depart sans rien de faire, uncore il poet record le force assetz bien. Et issint fuit adjudge in banco regis. Dier.

[288]

Coke's *Statuta* (Holkham 7834), fo. 117.

6 H. 8 in trespas sur cest statute si lattorney le defendant plede quod non est informatus, ou si nihil dicit soit enter envers le defendant, le pleintife recovera ses treble damages auxibien come si un judgment ust estre done pur luy sur un issue joine. Et autiel judgment fuit done in brefe de error anno 4 et 5 Ph. et Mar. ex libro Bendlowes in mes notes demesne, apres 76. Mesme la ley dun recoverie per defaut come fuit adjudge, come jeo oy le segnior Dier dire M. 14 Eliz.

and substance of the *assumpsit*. Therefore if I say to you, in consideration that you have done me service and also given me £20, I promise you £30, in this case the *assumpsit* is certain and therefore the consideration is not traversable. But he said clearly that there is no need to prove all the considerations, for he said that if he proves any of them it suffices, and that is the common experience in the King's Bench. But when the *assumpsit* is referred to the consideration and depends on it, and the action is something uncertain, as it is in our case, there the consideration is traversable. For here the *assumpsit* is to recompense 'all such charges and expenses as the plaintiff has laid out for the business ...', so that the weight of the *assumpsit* rests wholly upon the consideration; for if he has spent much he will recover accordingly, and if he has spent little or nothing he will also recover accordingly. Now, if the consideration is traversable, it must be pleaded certainly, because issue could have been taken on it and the jurors must not be inveigled with uncertainty. And he said that if someone has three or four daughters, and he marries off one and gives £100 with her in marriage, and then he marries off another and gives £200 with her, and then another is to be married and he promises the person who is to be her husband as much as he has given with any of his other daughters, in debt upon this *assumpsit* he must show specially where he gave, to whom he gave, with whom he gave, and how much he gave.[1]

Cases from Marginalia at Holkham Hall[2]

287. ANON.

King's Bench, Pas. 1575 (cited in the Common Pleas).

Easter term 17 Eliz. If a justice of the peace comes to a house following a complaint, and he will not allow him to come in and look without breaking the door, and so the justice leaves without doing anything, he may nevertheless record the force perfectly well. So it was adjudged in the King's Bench, according to DYER.

288. ANON.[3]

Common Pleas, Mich. 1572.

In 6 Hen. VIII in trespass upon this statute,[4] if the defendant's attorney pleads that he has not been informed (*non est informatus*), or if a *nihil dicit* is entered against the defendant, the plaintiff shall recover his treble damages just as well as if a judgment had been given against him upon an issue joined. A like judgment was given in a writ of error in the year 4 & 5 Phil. & Mar.: from Bendlowes' book in my own notes, following fo. 76.[5] The law is the same of a recovery by default: this has been adjudged, as I heard the lord DYER say in Michaelmas term 14 Eliz.

---

[1] Here the report ends, omitting the argument of Dyer C.J.
[2] For *Lord Cheyney's Case* (1582) on fo. 212v of Coke's *Statuta*, see vol. ii, p. 188. The text is printed there.
[3] Cit. in 11 Co. Rep. 60 ('Issint jeo mesme oye le Seignior Dyer Mich. 14 & 15 Eliz. a dire ...').
[4] Statute of Forcible Entry, 8 Hen. VI, c. 9.
[5] *AB*, fo. 296 (magenta). The passage cited refers to both the decision of 6 Hen. VIII and that of 4 & 5 Phil. & Mar. It is Benl. 11, pl. 6, in the printed edition of 1689.

[289]

Coke's *Statuta* (Holkham 7834), fo. 120.

Disseisor fait lease pur vie et puis levy fine etc., et 5 ans passe, le disseisor ne entra sur le lessee: adjudge come Serjant Popham report.

[290]

Coke's *Statuta* (Holkham 7834), fo. 120v.

[1][…] Plowden dit a moy que fuit adjudge in common banke […] le lessour avera 5 ans apres le mort le lesse […] de faire clayme deins 5 ans apres le fine levie.

[291]

Coke's *Statuta* (Holkham 7834), fo. 122.

Vide Lattons case P. 17 Eliz. Baron et fem seisie de certain terres come de droit la feme in taile leviont un fine in fe, le conuse graunt et render ceo al baron et fem in especial taile, le remainder al droit heires la fem, et ilz ont issue, le baron morust, la fem entermarye arere, et el et sa 2 baron levie fine in fe, et lissue que el ad per sa primer baron enter supposant son entre destre loiall sur cest statut, car in cest case coment que cest grant et render ad [relation a][2] lestate del terre, et le baron et fem fueront eins dun mesme estate per purchase, uncore pur ceo que le terre move del fem et ceo ne fuit ascun advauncement a luy, mes el per ceo advaunce sa baron, […][3] est […] done in frankmariage sont hors de cest statut, quar ceo que el […].[3]

[292]

Coke's *Statuta* (Holkham 7834), fo. 122v.

Nota cest practise fuit invent anno 18 Eliz. que fem tenant in tail del done sa baron deins cest estatute accept un fine dun estraunge sur conusauns de droit come ceo que el ad etc. et el graunt et render mesme le terre al conusor pur 2 hundred ans, et ceo per lour pretence ne fuit discontinuans ne alienation deins cest statut. Mes le segnior Dier ne voile suffer cest fine de passer car il dit que il fuit fait per covin. Mes a mesme le temps Manwood et Mounson teign[ont] que il serra deins cest parol alienation ou deins lequitie. <Vies 46 E. 3, tit. Forfeiture, 18, et nota lestatut de W. 2, cap. 41. Vide 4 Mar. 148.>[a]

---

[1] *Much of the text lost through wear at foot of page.*   [2] *Unclear.*
[3] *Some text lost through wear at foot of page.*

---

[3] So named in vol. ii, p. 232, where it is cited in 1583.   [4] See above, p. 25, no. 51.
[5] 11 Hen. VII, c. 20.   [6] Some words lost.
[7] Noted in *Sir George Browne's Case* (1594) 3 Co. Rep. 50, at fo. 51v ('et issint fuit tenus in communi banco Pasc. 18 Reg. Eliz. per Sir James Dyer, Manwood, et Mounson Justices, come jeo mesme oye').
[8] 11 Hen. VII, c. 20.   [9] Hil. 46 Edw. III, Fitz. Abr., *Forfeiture*, pl. 18.
[10] *Villers* v. *Beamont* (1557) Dyer 146, at fo. 148.

289. FINAL CONCORDS

Probably Common Pleas, 1578/79.[1]

If a disseisor makes a lease for life and then levies a fine, and five years pass,[2] the disseisor may not enter upon the lessee: this has been adjudged, as *Serjeant Popham* reported.

290. SOME'S CASE[3]

Common Pleas, before 1583.

Plowden told me it had been adjudged in the Common Bench that a lessor has five years after the death of the lessee to make claim within five years of the fine levied.

291. EYSTON d. LATTON v. STUDDE[4]

Common Pleas, Pas. 1575.

See Latton's case in Easter term 17 Eliz. Husband and wife, seised of certain lands in right of the wife in tail, levy a fine in fee; the cognisee grants and renders them to the husband and wife in special tail, remainder to the right heirs of the woman; they have issue; the husband dies; the woman marries again; she and her second husband levy a fine in fee; the issue which she has by her first husband enters, supposing his entry to be lawful under this statute,[5] for in this case even though this grant and render relates to the estate of the land, and the husband and wife were in of one same estate by purchase, nevertheless because the land moved from the woman and was no advancement for her, but rather she thereby advanced her husband, [it is within the statute].[6] But gifts in frankmarriage are outside the statute.

292. ANON.[7]

Common Pleas, Pas. 1576.

Note this devious scheme (*practise*) was invented in the year 18 Eliz.: a woman tenant in tail by the gift of her husband within this statute[8] accepted a fine from a stranger *sur conusauns de droit come ceo que el ad de son done*, and she granted and rendered the same land to the cognisor for 200 years, and this (by their pretence) was not a discontinuance or alienation within this statute. But the lord DYER would not allow this fine to pass, for he said it was made by covin. On the same occasion, however, MANWOOD and MOUNSON held that it fell within this word 'alienation', or within the equity. See 46 Edw. III, tit. *Forfeiture*, 18.[9] And note the statute of Westminster II, c. 41. {See 4 Mar. 148.}[10]

---

[1] Popham was created serjeant in 1578 but was dispensed from the coif on becoming solicitor-general in 1579.

[2] This refers to the statute 4 Hen. VII, c. 24.

[293]

Coke's *Statuta* (Holkham 7834), fo. 128v.

[Nota que][1] fuit dit in le duchie chamber T. 18 Eliz. que fuit adjudge anno 4 Eliz. que si apres le feast de Michael mention in cest acte un parson ou auter spirituell home prist ascun leas que ceo ne serra void per cest braunch del estatut car ceo frustrate solement tielx leasses que fueront devant le dit feste. Et la fuit dit auxi que un leas fuit fait a un parson et a un Underwood et adjudge le lease ne fuit voide, mes le parson sil occupie ceo incurgera le penaltie limitte in cest statute, scilicet chescun moys 10 livres. Et issint fuit tenus in Coventries case anno 19 Eliz. <Vide Dier 19 Eliz. 358 accordant.>[a]

[294]

Coke's *Statuta* (Holkham 7834), fo. 130.

Fuit tenus <anno>[d] H. 19 Eliz. per Harper et Manwood justices que si un parson al temps del fesauns de cest estatute avoit un lease pur ans pur le maintenance de hospitalitie, si cest leas soit save per cest proviso, car les primer parols font ceo voide etc. et icy les parols sont 'may take', et in cest case les terres sont taken. Et uncore ilz disoient clerement que ceo serra construe solonque lentent del fesoures et serra deins cest proviso, et in cest case 'may take' serra expound pur 'may holde'.

[295]

Coke's *Statuta* (Holkham 7834), fo. 130.

Nota fuit agree in le common banke P. 18 Eliz. que si un parson soit admitte et institute en un benifice et nemi inducte, et puis prist auter benifice etc. et a ceo soit inducte, le primer benifice est voide, car les parols del estatut font un expresse diversitie etc.

[296]

Coke's *Statuta* (Holkham 7834), fo. 137.

Nota nient obstant cest parol 'such' uncore si leas pur ans soit fait sauns fine ou incumme [*sic*], ou si leas soit fait a commencer a Mich., ceux sont remedie per cest statute come <Fenner serjant>[d] fuit dit arguendo in le serjauntes case.

---

[1] *Top line trimmed, with loss of the first words.*

[8] See above, p. 63, no. 113.   [9] 21 Hen. VIII, c. 13.   [10] See above, p. 128, no. 224.
[11] In the first branch of the statute 21 Hen. VIII, c. 15 ('that all such termors shall and may falsify …').
See also below, p. 160, no. 309.
[12] The preamble to the statute referred to fines for incomes, i.e. entry fines; but Coke is using the word income as a synonym for the entry fine.   [13] 'by Serjeant Fenner' deleted.

293. ANON.

(1) Duchy Chamber, Trin. 1576. (2) Common Pleas, 1577.

Note that it was said in the Duchy Chamber in Trinity term 18 Eliz. that it was adjudged in the year 4 Eliz. that if, after the feast of St Michael mentioned in this Act,[1] a parson or other spiritual man took any lease, it would not be avoided by this branch of the statute, for this frustrates only such leases as were made before the said feast. It was also said there that a lease was made to a parson and to one Underwood,[2] and it was adjudged that the lease was not void; but if the parson occupied it he would incur the penalty appointed in this statute, namely £10 for every month. And so it was held in Coventry's case in the year 19 Eliz.[3] {See Dyer 19 Eliz. 358, accord.}[4]

294. COVENTRY'S CASE[5]

Common Pleas, Hil. 1577.

It was [a question] in Hilary term 19 Eliz. by HARPER and MANWOOD JJ. that if a parson at the time of making this statute[6] had a lease for years for the maintenance of hospitality, whether this lease is saved by this proviso, for the first words make it void: and the words here are 'may take', whereas in this case the lands have been taken.[7] Nevertheless they said clearly that it should be construed according to the intention of the makers, and that it should be within this proviso; and in this case 'may take' should be expounded as 'may hold'.

295. GYLES v. COLSHILL[8]

Common Pleas, Pas. 1576.

Note that it was agreed in the Common Bench in Easter term 18 Eliz. that if a parson is admitted and instituted into a benefice but not inducted, and then takes another benefice and is inducted into that, the first benefice is void; for the words of the statute[9] make an express distinction etc.

296. THE SERJEANTS' CASE[10]

Common Pleas, 1579.

Note that notwithstanding this word 'such',[11] if a lease for years is made without fine or income,[12] or if a lease is made to commence at Michaelmas, these are remedied by this statute: as was said in argument in the serjeants' case.[13]

---

[1] 21 Hen. VIII, c. 13.   [2] *Underwood's Case*, cit. in 3 Leon. 122.   [3] See below, no. 294.
[4] *Anon.* (Pas. 1577) Dyer 358, cit. *Woodley* v. *James* (1570).
[5] Identified in the previous case. Differently reported anonymously in Dyer 358.
[6] 21 Hen. VIII, c. 13.
[7] This refers to the wording of the proviso, '… may take in farm other lands … for the only expenses in their households and hospitalities'.

[297]

Coke's *Statuta* (Holkham 7834), fo. 146.

Le Segnior Dier in Lattons case P. 17 dit que fuit adjudge que ou un Beamount fuit seisie de certain terres in droit sa fem il et sa fem leviont un fine in le mannour de Grace de Die[u] a eux in taile, et puis Beamont morust, et sa fem port brefe de dower et le heire averre que lestate taile fuit fait a luy in consideration de sa jointure, a que el dit que lestat taile fuit fait a luy in consideration del dit fine levie de sa terre demesne. Et fuit adjudge que el recovera dower.

[298]

Coke's *Statuta* (Holkham 7834), fo. 146v.

Mes nota fuit agre in Vernons case anno 15 Eliz. que si le jointure soit fait devant le coverture come bien poet estre, coment que soit hors del paroles del statut, que in cest case le fem ne poet waiver tiel jointure. Et issint fuit agre P. 18 Eliz. coment que la fem fuit deins age.

[299]

Coke's *Statuta* (Holkham 7834), fo. 149v.

Ad estre adjudge que covenant [est] destre inrolle in parchment deins 6 moys et nemi in paper, come fuit cite per Edmund Plowden in parliament anno 23 devant les segniors.

[300]

Coke's *Statuta* (Holkham 7834), fo. 149v.

Nota que Serjaunt Fenner dit in le common banke Tr. 21 Eliz. que fuit adjudge que si lendenture del bargaine et sale port mesme le date la le 6 moys serra accompt del delivery del fait, mes si ascun date soit in lendenture les 6 moys serra accompt del temps del date et nemi del delivery. <4 Eliz. Dal. 3, del temps del date et nemi del delivery. Et fait inrolle mesme le jour suffist.>[a]

---

[3] This aspect of the case is not touched on in Coke's later account of it. The heir was John's son Francis Beaumont (d. 1598), justice of the Common Pleas. The case continued to cause difficulties for over fifty years: see *Baker* v. *Willis* (1637) Cro. Car. 476; Wm Jones 393, sub nom. *Dixie* v. *Beaumont*.

[4] See above, p. 75, no. 118.

[5] As Speaker of the House of Commons.

[6] See above, p. 3, no. 1, where an almost identical passage occurs.

[7] This refers to the Statute of Enrolments, 27 Hen. VIII, c. 16.

[8] *Anon.* (1562) Dal. 41, pl. 18, in the 1689 edition. More fully reported as *Thomas* v. *Popham* (1562) Dyer 218; CP 40/1201, m. 811 (printed in Co. Ent. 595v).

297. BEAUMONT'S CASE

Cited in the Common Pleas, Pas. 1575.

The lord DYER said in Latton's case,[1] in Easter term 17 Eliz., that it was adjudged where one Beaumont[2] was seised of certain lands in right of his wife, he and his wife levied a fine of the manor of Grace-Dieu unto themselves in tail, and then Beaumont died, and his wife brought a writ of dower, and the heir averred that the estate tail was made to her in consideration of her jointure, to which she said that the estate tail was made to her in consideration of the said fine levied of her own land; and it was adjudged that she should recover dower.[3]

298. VERNON v. VERNON[4]

Common Pleas, Pas. 1573, and an anonymous case of Pas. 1576.

But note that it was agreed in Vernon's case in 15 Eliz. that if the jointure is made before the coverture – as it may well be – then although it is outside the words of the statute, the woman in this case may not waive such jointure. And it was so agreed in Easter term 18 Eliz., even if the woman was under age.

299. ENROLMENT

House of Lords, 1581.

It has been adjudged that a covenant must be enrolled in parchment within six months, and not in paper: this was cited by Edmund Plowden[5] in Parliament in 23 Eliz., before the Lords.

300. KIRKEBY v. THORNBOROUGH[6]

Common Pleas, Trin. 1579.

Note that *Serjeant Fenner* said in the Common Bench in Trinity term 21 Eliz. that it has been adjudged that if the indenture of bargain and sale bears the same date [as the delivery], the six months[7] shall be reckoned from the delivery of the deed, whereas if there is any date in the indenture the six months shall be reckoned from the time of the date and not of the delivery. {4 Eliz., Dal. 3:[8] from the time of the date and not of the delivery. And a deed enrolled on the same day suffices.}

---

[1] *Eyston* v. *Studde* (1575) above, p. 25, no. 51.

[2] John Beaumont (d. 1557), bencher of the Inner Temple, sometime master of the rolls (1550–52). The monastic site or manor of Grace-Dieu, Leics., was given to him and his wife Elizabeth in special tail by Sir Humphrey Foster. After he was dismissed from office in 1552, Beaumont was forced to convey it to the king by fine, and the king granted it to the earl of Huntingdon, but after Beaumont's death his wife entered on the earl, and this was held to be lawful by reason of the statute 32 Hen. VIII, c. 28: *R.* v. *Earl of Huntingdon* (1562) 2 Co. Inst. 681 (cit. Dyer's MS.: see 109 Selden Soc. 79); *Beaumont's Case* (1612) 9 Co. Rep. 138. Coke said this construction of the statute 'hath been commonly cited in arguments in Westminster Hall, and at moots etc., by the name of Beaumont's case': 2 Co. Inst. 681.

[301]

Coke's *Statuta* (Holkham 7834), fo. 165.

Nota, Justice Gawdy dit a moy que le meliour opinion de les justices fuit que coment que les terres et le parsonage etc. queux fueront ambideux in les maynes del abbot et issint discharge des dismes per unity de possession soient ore severe uncore les dismes ne serra payes mes serront discharge. Et uncore il dit que ilz usont in tiel case a granter prohibition si cesti que ad le parsonage sua pur eux in court christien. <Mes ore le case ad estre adjudge sovent foitz que dismes ne serront payd.>[a]

[302]

Coke's *Statuta* (Holkham 7834), fo. 168v.

P. 20 Eliz. inter Barbour et E. sa fem, pleintifes, et William Long, defendant, in partitione facienda, fuit tenus per les justices sur un especial verdit que si home soit seisie de certayne terres in Midd. et de divers meses in London, que toutz les meses in London passeront per devise nient obstant lestatut, car ceux fueront devisable devant lestatut, et lestatut ne provide forsque pur ceux terres que al temps del dit statute fait ne fueront devisable. <M. 22 et 23 Eliz. Periam 146b.>[a] <Periam 146b ... Vide 20 Eliz. Bendloes, pl. 29.>[a]

[303]

Coke's *Statuta* (Holkham 7834), fo. 170.

Vide in le court de gardes Pasch. 24 Eliz. inter Sir William Drury et Leventhorpe. Edward Leventhorp teigne le mannour de Shinglehall per service de chivaller per meane tenure del roy in capite et le mannour de Ousley in socage del roy devise le mannour tenus per service de chivaller et leva lauter in soccage que fuit pleine 3 part a discender, et resolve que le devise fuit voide pur 3 part del mannor de S. <Vide 21 Eliz. 366, Dier.>[a]

---

[9] Also known as Shingey, in Sawbridgeworth, Herts.
[10] Ousley in MS. This must be a slip for Ugley, the Essex manor which had belonged to the Leventhorpes for over a century and is so named in the will (next note).
[11] By his will dated 8 March 1566, and proved on 18 Dec. following, he left the manor of Ugley as the third part to descend to his heir and settled the other two-thirds (which are unspecified): PCC 33 Crymes (PROB 11/48). He died in Rome that year: brass inscription in Sawbridgeworth church.
[12] *Anon.* (Mich. 1579) Dyer 366, pl. 38.

301. ANON.[1]

King's Bench, Mich. 1575.

Note that GAWDY J.[2] told me that the better opinion of the justices was that even if the lands and the parsonage were both in the hands of an abbot (and therefore discharged of the tithes by unity of possession) and are now severed, the tithes shall still not be paid but shall be discharged. Nevertheless he said that they are accustomed in such cases to grant a prohibition if the person who has the parsonage sues for them in court Christian. {The case has now often been adjudged that the tithes shall not be paid.[3]}

302. BARBOUR v. LONG[4]

Common Pleas, Pas. 1578.

In Easter term 20 Eliz., between Barbour and E. his wife, plaintiffs, and William Long, defendant, in *partitione facienda*, it was held by the justices upon a special verdict that if someone is seised of certain lands in Middlesex and of various houses in London, all the houses in London will pass by a devise notwithstanding the statute,[5] for they were devisable before the statute, and the statute provides only for those lands which were not devisable at the time of the said statute. {Mich. 22 & 23 Eliz., Peryam 146b[6] ... See 20 Eliz., Bendlowes, pl. 29.[7]}

303. DRURY v. LEVENTHORPE[8]

Court of Wards, Pas. 1582.

See in the Court of Wards in Easter term 24 Eliz. between Sir William Drury and Leventhorpe: Edward Leventhorpe, who held the manor of Shinglehall[9] by knight-service by a mesne tenure of the king *in capite* and the manor of Ugley[10] of the king in socage, devised the manor held by knight-service and left the other in socage (which was a full third part) to descend;[11] and it was resolved that the devise was void as to a third part of the manor of Shinglehall. {See 21 Eliz. 366, Dyer.[12]}

---

[1] Probably the case reported anonymously in Godb. 1 (Mich. 1575). Cf. *Anon.* (1583) vol. ii, p. 208.
[2] Sir Thomas Gawdy (d. 1588), appointed J.K.B. on 16 Nov. 1574.
[3] See *Knightley* v. *Spencer* (1592) vol. iv, p. 690; *Grevill* v. *Trott* (1596) ibid. 692; *Grene* v. *Balser* and *Grene* v. *Buffkyn* (1596) ibid. 693.
[4] Differently reported in 1 And. 52, sub nom. *Barker* v. *Long*; Benl. 317. According to these reports, the Middlesex property (The Red Lion in East Smithfield) was held in chief by knight-service, and the London property was held in burgage, which was deemed to be a form of socage. The liberty of East Smithfield was a detached part of Middlesex, surrounded by the city of London; West Smithfield was in the city.
[5] Statute of Wills, 32 Hen. VIII, c. 1.
[6] Not in 110 Selden Soc.
[7] Bendl. 317, pl. 300, in the 1689 edition.
[8] Noted below, p. 163, no. 322.

[304]

Coke's *Statuta* (Holkham 7834), fo. 171v.[1]

[…] 14 Eliz. in libro decretorum in curia wardorum James Apot […] certeine <terres>[d] meses in Holborne tenus del roigne […] service de chivaller al Roger Apot son fitz et […]an sa fem et les heires de lour 2 corps […] remainder al droit heires Roger, que morust, son issue ne serront in garde.

[305]

Coke's *Statuta* (Holkham 7834), fo. 172.

25 Eliz. in court de gardes Wray dit que fuit resolve in le court de gardes que si le heire de cesti que ad fee soit de pleine age et il morust son heire deins age vivant tenant pur vie, que il ne serra in gard, car hors de cel statut.

[306]

Coke's *Statuta* (Holkham 7834), fo. 173.

Warings case 16 Eliz. in common banke, le avowant ne besoigne a monstre seison deins 50 ans mes viendra eins del auter parte.

[307]

Coke's *Statuta* (Holkham 7834), fo. 173v.

Fuit adjudge in Fitzw. et Copleys case, et auxi in Vernons case, que formedon in le discender ne fuit deins cest statute. Et issint Popham serjaunt cite ceo in largument de serjauntes case P. 21 Eliz. Et il dit que le reason de ceo fuit pur ceo que lestatut de donis conditionalibus ad provide especialment que les issues in taile ne serra prejudice, et cest statut esteant fait in generall parolx ne donera liberty al tenant in taile a faire tiel prejudice a son issue car donques tenant in taile poet discontinue et suffer 60 ans a passer et donques son issue ou lissue del issue serra barre, quel ne unques fuit lentention del fesors. Auxi nota que formedone gist dun rent secke, et brefe de droit ne gist de ceo, et pur ceo nest properment un brefe de droit. <Vide

---

[1] *Much of text missing where bottom corner worn away.*

[6] CP 40/1298, m. 1953 (printed in Co. Ent. 317): Hugh Fitzwilliam esq. v. Philip Copley esq.; formedon in the descender for the manor of Sprotborough, Yorks. Differently reported in Dyer 290; Dal. 75. The judgment for the plaintiff (as to part) was reversed in 1576: KB 27/1253, m. 24; report in BL MS. Add. 48196C, fos. 5–15. For the long saga of Hugh Fitzwilliam's litigation see J. Baker, 'Tudor Pedigree Rolls and their Uses' in *Heralds and Heraldry in Shakespeare's England*, ed. N. Ramsay (Donington, 2014), pp. 125–165, at pp. 149–163.
[7] See above, p. 141, no. 258 (Mich. 1572).   [8] 32 Hen. VIII, c. 2.
[9] For *The Serjeants' Case* (1579) see above, p. 128, no. 224, and the note there.
[10] Westminster II, c. 1.

304. APOT'S CASE

Court of Wards, 1572.

In 14 Eliz., in the decree-book of the Court of Wards, James Apot [devised[1]] certain houses in Holborn held of the queen by knight-service to Roger Apot, his son, and his wife, and the heirs of their two bodies begotten, remainder to Roger's right heirs; Roger died;[2] his issue shall not be in ward.

305. ANON.[3]

Court of Wards, 1583.

25 Eliz. in the Court of Wards: WRAY [C.J.] said it was resolved in the Court of Wards that if the heir of the person who has fee is of full age, and dies, his heir under age, while the tenant for life is living, he shall not be in ward, for it outside this statute.[4]

306. WARING'S CASE

Common Pleas, 1574.

Waring's case, 16 Eliz. in the Common Bench: an avowant need not show seisin within fifty years,[5] but it shall come in from the other side.

307. FITWILLIAM v. COPLEY;[6] VERNON v. STANLEY[7]

Common Pleas, 1571 and 1572; cited in *The Serjeants' Case* (1579).

It was adjudged in Fitzwilliam and Copley's case, and also in Vernon's case, that formedon in the descender was not within this statute.[8] So *Serjeant Popham* cited it in the argument of the serjeants' case, Easter term 21 Eliz.[9] And he said that the reason for that was because the statute *De Donis Conditionalibus*[10] has explicitly provided that the issues in tail shall not be prejudiced, and this [later] statute (being made in general words) does not give liberty to the tenant in tail to cause such a prejudice to his issue, for then tenant in tail could discontinue and allow sixty years to pass, and then his issue (or the issue of the issue) would be barred, which was never the intention of the makers. Note also that formedon lies for a rent seck, whereas a writ of right does not lie for it, and therefore it is not properly a writ of right. {See a better

---

[1] Conjectural. His will was dated 13 Jan. 1557 but not registered: J. C. C. Smith, *Index to Wills proved in the Prerogative Court of Canterbury 1383–1558* (1893), p. 16. He was a London grocer: C 1/1520/2.

[2] Roger's will, dated 8 July 1557, was proved on 24 Aug. 1561: PCC 27 Loftes (PROB 11/44/295). He left lands and houses in Holborn, and many others, to his wife for life, remainder in tail, with provisions for a school to be founded by the Grocers Company. In the coronation pardon of 1559 he was described as of Lyons Inn *alias* citizen and grocer of London: *CPR 1558–1560*, p. 181.

[3] Incorporated in *Floyer's Case* (1611) 9 Co. Rep. 126. Cf. *Tisur's Case* (1583) in Dyer (ed. Treby), fo. 190v, margin.   [4] Statute of Wills, 32 Hen. VIII, c. 1.

[5] For the purposes of the Statute of Limitations, 32 Hen. VIII, c. 2.

meliour reason Dier 298, scilicet que le season de done ne unques fuit traversable, et tenant in taile poet viver 60 ans apres discontinuans.>ᵃ

[308]

Coke's *Statuta* (Holkham 7834), fo. 185.

Mes nota nient obstant cest statut et lestatut auxi de 18 Eliz. coment que verdit soit done uncore si appiert al court que le pleintife nad cause daction ou sil nappiert que il ad cause daction la nul judgment serra done, come fuit adjudge in le case de Lovelace 21 Eliz.

[309]

Coke's *Statuta* (Holkham 7834), fo. 187v.

Trin. 19 Eliz. fuit tenus per le segnior Dier et curiam que si home diseisist auter sauns force que tiel disseisor est deins cest statute, car 'such disseisor' serra intend such in mischiefe et such yn inconvenience, mes come le preamble del statut de 21 H. 8, cap. 15, recite que divers lessees avoient paye divers graund incummes etc. be it enacted that al such termors etc. in quel case 'such' serra prise pur such in mischiefe etc.

[310]

Coke's *Statuta* (Holkham 7834), fo. 187v.

15 Eliz. in Vernons case fuit dit que abators, intruders et similia sont hors de cest estatute. Issint dit Saunders et Harryes in Wimbisshe case, le disseisin covient destre immediate, car si mon lesse pur vie soit disseise etc. et le disseisor morust seisie et puis le tenant pur vie morust, en cest case lentre de cesti in le revercion est tolle pur ceo que cesti in le revercion ne puit aver enter al temps del discent, mes si lessee pur vie ust morust primes auterment serroit, car donques cesti in le reversion puit aver enter al temps del discent.

[311]

Coke's *Statuta* (Holkham 7834), fo. 189.

Nota per Mounson in Winters case que un estate taile est deins lequitie de cest estatute et uncore lestatute parle des lessees. Mes le segnior Dier dit expressement.

---

[6] See above, p. 75, no. 118.   [7] Statute of Limitations, 32 Hen. VIII, c. 2.
[8] *Wimbish* v. *Tailbois* (1550) Plowd. 38 at fo. 47; CP 40/1133, m. 443.
[9] See above, p. 43, no. 88.   [10] 32 Hen. VIII, c. 28.

reason in Dyer 298,[1] namely that the donee's seisin was never traversable, and a tenant in tail may live for sixty years after a discontinuance.}

308. LOVELACE'S CASE

Common Pleas (probably), 1579.

But note that despite this statute,[2] and also that of 18 Eliz.,[3] even if a verdict is given, if it appears to the court that the plaintiff has no cause of action – or if it does not appear that he has a cause of action – no judgment shall be given: as was adjudged Lovelace's case, 21 Eliz.

309. ANON.

Common Pleas, Trin. 1577.

In Trinity term 19 Eliz. it was held by the lord DYER and the court that if someone disseises another without force, such a disseisor is within this statute,[4] for 'such disseisor' shall be understood as such in mischief and such in inconvenience. But where the preamble of the statute of 21 Hen. VIII, c. 15, recites that, whereas various lessees have paid various great incomes, 'be it enacted that all such termors …', in that case 'such' shall be understood as such in mischief.[5]

310. VERNON v. VERNON[6]

Common Pleas, 1573.

In Vernon's case in 15 Eliz. it was said that abators, intruders and the like are outside this statute.[7] Thus Saunders and Harris said in Wimbish's case[8] that the disseisin must be immediate, for if my lessee for life is disseised, and the disseisor dies seised, and then the tenant for life dies, in this case the entry of the reversioner is tolled because the reversioner could not have entered at the time of the descent; but if the lessee for life had died first, it would have been otherwise, for then the reversioner could have entered at the time of the descent.

311. WINTER'S CASE[9]

Common Pleas, Mich. 1572.

Note by MOUNSON, in Winter's case, that an estate tail is within the equity of this statute,[10] even though the statute speaks of lessees. But the lord DYER said it was [mentioned] expressly.

---

[1] *Vernon* v. *Madder* (1571) Dyer 298.   [2] Statute of Jeofails, 32 Hen. VIII, c. 30.
[3] 18 Eliz., c. 14.   [4] 32 Hen. VIII, c. 33.
[5] See above, p. 128, no. 224, and p. 156, no. 296 (where 'income' is explained).

[312]

Coke's *Statuta* (Holkham 7834), fo. 191.

Wray, T. 18 Eliz., dit si tenant in taile fait feffment et puis levie fine, cest fine liera ces heires, car coment que al temps del fine il nest tenant in taile uncore fine est levie des terres intailed.

[313]

Coke's *Statuta* (Holkham 7834), fo. 191.

Archers case, H. 20 Eliz. Terres fueront done al baron et fem in special taile, <le>[d] ilz avoient issue, le baron morust, lissue dissese sa mere et levie fine, le mere morust sauns ascun regres, et puis lissue que levie le fine morust: si son issue avoidra le fine? Et fuit tenus que il navoidra ceo, car cest terre fuit entaile al auncestor del issue que levie le fine. Et nota les parolx sont in le disjunctive. Mes si le mere <sa>[d] ad fait regresse donques le fine avoit estre tout ousterment defeate.

[314]

Coke's *Statuta* (Holkham 7834), fo. 193v.

Vide M. 29 et 30 Eliz. inter Ognel, pleintife, et Underhill et Appleton, defendants, le feffee del tenant et son tenant a volunt est deins cest statut, mes le feffee del feffee est hors de ceo, car il ne clayme 'only by or from the tenant'. <Vide lib. 5, 118, lib. 8, 64, 65.>[a]

[315]

Coke's *Statuta* (Holkham 7834), fo. 195v.

Nota, fuit tenus in Paynes case in temps mesme cesti roigne <Eliz.>[i] que si home soit seisie de un acre tenus del roy in chief et de 2 acres tenus dauter segnior et de 10 acres tenus in socage devisable per le <common ley>[d] custome, in cest case si le tenant devisa tout ses terres primerment ceo est bone pur tout le terre devisable per le common ley, et bon auxi pur 2 partes de lauters terres devisable, mes uncore nota que le roy avera le gard de […] de tout si le heire soit deins age, ou si le primer seisin […] de pleine age del 3 parte, et ceo ratione del savinge.

---

[5] 32 Hen. VIII, c. 37.
[6] *Edrich's Case* (1603) 5 Co. Rep. 118; *Sir William Foster's Case* (1608) 8 Co. Rep. 64; cf. Co. Litt. 162.
[7] I.e. custom.
[8] In the Statute of Explanation of the Statute of Wills, 34 & 35 Hen. VIII. c. 5.

312. ANON.[1]

King's Bench, Trin. 1576.

WRAY said in Trinity term 18 Eliz. that if tenant in tail makes a feoffment and then levies a fine, this fine will bind his heirs, for although at the time of the fine he is not tenant in tail, the fine is still levied of entailed lands.

313. ARCHER'S CASE[2]

Common Pleas, Hil. 1578.

Archer's case, in Hilary term 20 Eliz. Lands were given to a husband and wife in special tail; they had issue; the husband died; the issue disseised his mother and levied a fine; the mother died without any regress; and then the issue who levied the fine died. May his issue avoid the fine? It was held that he may not avoid it, for this land was entailed to the ancestor of the issue who levied the fine. Note that the words are in the disjunctive.[3] But if the mother had made regress, then the fine would have been utterly defeated.

314. OGNEL v. UNDERHILL and APPLETON[4]

Common Pleas, Mich. 1587.

See in Michaelmas term 29 & 30 Eliz. between Ognel, plaintiff, and Underhill and Appleton, defendants: the tenant's feoffee and his tenant at will are within this statute,[5] but the feoffee's feoffee is outside it, for he does not claim 'only by or from the tenant'. {See lib. 5, fo. 118; lib. 8, fos. 64, 65.[6]}

315. PAYNE'S CASE

Undated, temp. Eliz.

Note that it was held in Payne's case in the time of this Queen {Elizabeth} that if someone is seised of one acre held of the king in chief, and of two acres held of another lord, and of ten acres held in socage devisable by the custom, and the tenant in this case devises all his lands, this is good in the first place for all the land devisable by the common law,[7] and it is good also for two-thirds of the other devisable lands; but note that the king shall nevertheless have the wardship of [the body] for the whole if the heir is under age, or the primer seisin of the third part [if the heir is] of full age, and that by reason of the saving.[8]

---

[1] Also noted above, p. 13, no. 22.
[2] See above, p. 10, no. 16.
[3] This refers to the statute 32 Hen. VIII, c. 36.
[4] More fully reported in 4 Co. Rep. 48 (dated Hil. 1578), sub nom. *Andrew Ognel's Case*. Differently reported in 1 And. 178; 4 Leon. 115; HLS MS. 1041 (1057), fos. 155v–157 (Brocke's reports). This was a replevin concerning a rent-charge issuing out of a farm called Cryfield Grange in Stoneleigh, Warw.

[316]

Coke's *Statuta* (Holkham 7834), fo. 202v.

Vide le serjauntes case anno 21 Eliz. report per moy, ou lun poynt fuit si le roygne soit in remainder del done dun common person si <ceo>^d recovery ewe envers le tenant in tayle ledra ses issues ou nemy.

[317]

Coke's *Statuta* (Holkham 7834), fo. 202v.

Semble per les parolx devant subjects etc. et ceux parolx[1] que done in taile per progenitor le roy que ne fuit roy al temps del done nest deins cest act. <Tr. 23 Eliz. inter Dinely et Ashton in curia wardorum resolve que done in taile fait per duke de Lancaster (que fuit que subject) nest deins cest act pur les causes devant.>^a

[318]

Coke's *Statuta* (Holkham 7834), fo. 206.

Nota, fuit dit per Serjaunt Aunderson arguendo in Holecrofts appeale in banke le roy que fuit adjudge in leschequer [ou] information fuit conceive sur cest statut et lestatut ne dit per corruptam usuriam et judgment fuit ent done, et ceo fuit reverse per error pur ceo que lenformation covient pursuer le letter del ley. Et nota il mitte le case dun inditement de usurye.

[319]

Coke's *Statuta* (Holkham 7834), fo. 214.

18 Eliz. fuit adjudge que reputative chaunterie que ne fuit duement incorporate per les lettres patentz le roy mes solement repute et nosme un chaunterie fuit deins cest statute. In le deane de Powles case.

---

[1] *In the statute: see opposite.*

[5] See above, p. 52, no. 100, and the note there.
[6] Statute of Usury, 37 Hen. VIII, c. 9.
[7] See above, p. 68, no. 115, and the note there.
[8] 1 Edw. VI, c. 14.

316. THE SERJEANTS' CASE[1]

Common Pleas, Pas. 1579.

See the serjeants' case in the year 21 Eliz., reported by me, where one point was: if the queen is in remainder by the gift of a common person, and a recovery is had against the tenant in tail, shall this harm her issue, or not?

317. DINELEY v. ASSHETON[2]

Common Pleas, Trin. 1581.

It seems from the previous words 'subjects ...', and these words 'done to the kings of this realm',[3] that a gift in tail by a progenitor of the king who was not king at the time of the gift is not within this Act. In Trinity term 23 Eliz. between Dineley and Assheton, in the Court of Wards, it was resolved that a gift in tail made by the duke of Lancaster (who was but a subject) is not within this Act for the reasons aforesaid.

318. BURGH v. HOLCROFT[4]

King's Bench, 1579, referring to an Exchequer case of 1578.[5]

Note that it was said by *Serjeant Anderson* in arguing Holcroft's appeal in the King's Bench that it was adjudged in the Exchequer, where an information was conceived upon this statute[6] and the [information] did not say 'by corrupt usury' (*per corruptam usuriam*), but judgment was given thereon, and it was reversed by writ of error because the information must pursue the letter of the law. (Note that he put this case upon an indictment for usury.)

319. BUTTELL v. WYLFORD[7]

King's Bench, 1576.

In 18 Eliz., in the dean of St Paul's case, it was adjudged that a reputative chantry which was not duly incorporated by the king's letters patent, but merely reputed and called a chantry, was within this statute.[8]

---

[1] See above, p. 128, no. 224, and the note there.
[2] See above, p. 61, no. 109, at the end; vol. ii, p. 192; vol. iv, p. 895. This concerned the manor of Downham in Whalley, Lancs.
[3] Words underlined in the text of 34 & 35 Hen. VIII, c. 20, where this gloss is written.
[4] KB 27/1267, m. 47 (three rolls; printed in Co. Ent. 53–56): Thomas Burgh v. Thomas Holcroft esq.; appeal of death for killing his brother with a rapier at Hampton, Midd.; pleads he had confessed an indictment and claimed clergy, but no judgment was given; demurrer, Mich. 1578; c.a.v. to Mich. 1579. Cit. in *Wrote* v. *Wigges* (1591) *C*, fo. 5 (vol. iii, p. 418) ('le case de Burgh et Holcroft devant'); 4 Co. Rep. 45; 3 Co. Inst. 131. Differently reported in BL MS. Harley 4988, fos. 1–3, sub nom. *Holcroft* v. *Burroughes*; MS. Add. 35942, fos. 3–5; LI MS. Maynard 29, fo. 49; HLS MS. 200.1 (1180.1), fos. 51v–52; HEHL MS. EL 482, fos. 84–98v (Egerton's version of an argument).

[320]

Coke's *Statuta* (Holkham 7834), fo. 214v.[1]

Nota fuit dit in le deane de Powles case que fuit adjudge que ou 2 tenementz fueront, scilicet le Bull et le Swan icy in Londres, et le Swan fuit done a maintener [...] J. D., et le Bulle fuit conveie a maintener le chaunterye [...] et le chaunterie de J. S. fuit mainteine ove le Swane et [... chaun]terie de J. D. fuit mainteine ove le Bull, mere contrarie [...] et uncore fuit adjudge que le roy avera ambideux, car les parolx sont wherewith or whereby etc.

[321]

Coke's *Statuta* (Holkham 7834), fo. 239v.

Quere si covinous done soit fait in defrauding de divers creditors si toutz covient joindre in action sur cest statut, car cest exception fuit prise in 23 Eliz. in Bakers case. Inter Baker et Smith, M. 23 et 24 Eliz.

[322]

Coke's Dyer, fo. 366v, para. 38.

Decre Pasch. 24 Eliz. in court de gardes inter Drury et Leventhorpe. Car icy semble a les justices que si le devise serroit bone pur tout le capite le roy naveroit gard ne primer season, car le heire navera ascun terre in capite dont il poet suer livery, car solement le socage terre discend a luy. Mes ceo nest ascun reason car [*blank*].

[323]

Coke's Dyer, fo. 366v, para. 38 (immediately below the foregoing).

Vide Caltrops case, 28 Eliz. inter les decrees de court de gardes. La fuit del act execute et tout le capite terre convey et riens forsque socage discende, il suera livery pur acre de capite terre et tout le socage. Et 28 Eliz. in communi banco fuit adjudge que le devise fuit bone pur tout et uncore le roigne avera gard per le savant in mesme le mannour come ou le puisne fitz est infeff de tout. <Issint note diversitie enter sudden motion et argument fait.>[a]

---

[1] *Much of the text lost through tear in lower corner.*

[3] 13 Eliz., c. 5.
[4] Noted above, p. 158, no. 303.
[5] In the Statute of Wills, 32 Hen. VIII, c. 1.

320. BUTTELL v. WYLFORD, continued

King's Bench, 1576.

Note that it was said in the dean of St Paul's case to have been adjudged that where there were two tenements, namely The Bull and The Swan here in London,[1] and The Swan was given to maintain the chantry of John Dale, and The Bull was conveyed to maintain the chantry of John Style, and [in fact] the chantry of John Style was maintained with The Swan and the chantry of John Dale was maintained with The Bull, completely contrary to the gifts, it was nevertheless adjudged that the king should have both, for the words are 'wherewith or whereby …'.[2]

321. BAKER v. SMITH

Mich. 1581.

If a covinous gift is made in fraud of various creditors, query whether they must all join in an action upon this statute[3] – for that exception was taken in 23 Eliz. in Baker's case. Between Baker and Smith, Michaelmas term 23 & 24 Eliz.

322. DRURY v. LEVENTHORPE[4]

Court of Wards, Pas. 1582.

See the decree in Easter term 24 Eliz. in the Court of Wards between Drury and Leventhorpe. For it seemed there to the justices that if the devise should be good for all the land *in capite* the king would have wardship or primer seisin, for the heir would not have any land *in capite* whereof he could sue livery, for only the socage land descended to him. But that is no reason.

323. CALTHROP'S CASE

Court of Wards, and Common Pleas, 1586.

See Calthrop's case, 28 Eliz., among the decrees of the Court of Wards. There it was by an act executed [in his lifetime], and all the land *in capite* was conveyed and nothing except socage descended, and it was decreed that he should sue livery for an acre of land *in capite* and all the socage. But in 28 Eliz. it was adjudged in the Common Bench that the devise was good for the whole, and yet the queen would have wardship by reason of the saving,[5] in the same way as where a younger son is enfeoffed with the whole. {Thus note a difference between a sudden motion and an argument made.}

---

[1] The record mentions only a capital mansion house in St George's parish, Billingsgate, later known as St George, Botolph Lane. In the chantry certificate it is 'a messuage with certain shops'. The Swan was in Botolph Lane and The Bull was in Pudding Lane.

[2] 1 Edw. VI, c. 14.

[324]

Coke's Dyer, fo. 369v, para. 7.

Giles case. Jeo oye le argument de cest case, et in ceo 3 questions fueront move.

1, Si le roigne ayant title a presenter per laps, et el present, et son clarke est admitte et institut et morust devant induction, si le roigne presentera arere? Et semble que cy, per le meliour opinion. Et puis issint resolve. Le quel appert icy, car ilz resolve que serra intende.

2 question, in case quant notice est requisite, si nul notice soit done et temps divolve al roigne, si le roigne presentera sans notice? Et agree que non.

3, Si le roigne ad avouson et deveigne voide, et le roigne grant lavouson, le presentment ne passera. Econtra 9 E. 3, [blank] et F.N.B. Vide in mes reportes, 78b.

[325]

Holkham Hall, BN 7831(2), fo. 7.

Premunire pur sutes – in courtes nient allow per ley

Mich. 26 et 27 Eliz. coram regina inter John Perrot et Doctor Levans by bill in premunire, roygne grant court de equitie, que nest de force in ley, uncore silz teigne ple de chose que perteyne al common ley est premunire. <Issint de court de requestes.>[a]

BL MS. Lansd. 50, fos. 102v–103

To the right honorable the Lord Burghley, lorde high treasorer of Englande

In most lamentable wise shewethe unto your honour your dailie orator Leonarde Parrot that, whereas there hathe bine greate suyte of lawe in the Kings Benche and Common Place the space of ix yeares betweene youre said orator and the deane and chapter of Christechurche in Oxforde, for a lease for yeares of the lordshipp of Bindsey graunted in the xxxiiij[or] yeare of King Henry the eight by their predecessors, the deane and canons of King Henrie the eightes colledge in Oxforde, under theire common seale, which suyte hath growen by reason the said

---

[7] The son of Leonard Perrot (or Parrot), whose dispute with Christ Church about the manor of Bindsey, Oxon., was eventually referred to arbitration: Burghley papers, in BL MSS. Lansd. 50 and 55. A suit in the university court was brought in about 1583 for trespass to land at Hinksey, Berks., and the defendants were imprisoned in the Bocardo. Three writs of *habeas corpus* were stoutly resisted by the university in 1584, and the matter was referred to Gerrard M.R. and Thomas Egerton Sol.-Gen.: J. Ayliffe, *The Ancient and Present State of the University of Oxford* (1714), ii. 65–72, citing university records. Leonard Perrot's petition to Lord Burghley, which mentions the suit in the vice-chancellor's court against John Perrot, is printed below. The case is stated in a brief in the Burghley papers, BL MS. Lansd. 50, fos. 106v–107. Leonard Perrot died *c*. 1594: C 142/242/8.

[8] Probably William Lewyn LL.D.

[9] Cf. the undated autograph note by Coke (YLS MS. G.R24.1, fo. 190) on *Peddington* v. *Otteworth* (1406), where he noted that Oxford University was not liable in that case to a *praemunire* for exercising a jurisdiction according to the Civil law because it had done so by colour of a royal charter, albeit that the charter was void. For the 1406 case see Baker, *Magna Carta*, p. 385.

324. GYLES v. COLSHILL[1]

Common Pleas, Pas. 1576.

Gyles's case. I heard the argument of this case, and three questions were moved in it.

(1) If the queen has title to present by reason of lapse, and she presents, and her clerk is admitted and instituted but dies before induction, may the queen present again? And it seemed so, by the better opinion. Later it was so resolved. This appears here, for they resolved that it shall be presumed.

(2) The second question was, in a case where notice is requisite and no notice is given, and the time devolves to the queen, may the queen present without notice? It was agreed that she could not.

(3) If the queen has an advowson and it becomes vacant, and the queen grants the advowson, the [next] presentation will not pass. This is contrary to 9 Edw. III, [fo. 25],[2] and Fitz. N.B.[3] See in my reports, fo. 78v.[4]

325. PERROT'S CASE[5]

King's Bench, Mich. 1584.

Praemunire for suits – in courts not allowed by law.[6]

Michaelmas term 26 & 27 Eliz., *coram regina*, between John Perrot[7] and Dr Levans[8] by bill, in a *praemunire*: the queen granted a court of equity, which is of no force in law, and if they hold plea of something which belongs to the common law it is *praemunire*.[9] Likewise, of a court of requests.

Leonard Perrot's petition to Lord Burghley (1586)

[*contd from opposite page*]

deane and chapter wold wreste from your said orator and others the same lease, contrarie to all equitie and good conscience, uppon two cavelles. The first is, as they saie, that the same lease lacketh wordes of corporation, which if it did so it weare against reasone and good conscience in them to take advantage thereof, but rather to amende the same, being made by theire owne clarkes at theire owne appointement, and also for that the quenes majestie geveth to them theire livings of pietie and charitablenes. The seconde is that, whereas the said deane

---

[1] See above, p. 63, no. 113, and the note there.

[2] *R. v. Prior of St John's* (1335) YB Trin. 9 Edw. III, fo. 25, pl. 24: see *Stephens v. Wall* (1569) Dyer 283.

[3] Fitz. N.B. 34N.

[4] *AB*, fo. 78v; i.e. the text printed above, p. 63.

[5] This refers to the report originally in *AB*, in the portion now missing (see vol. ii, p. 266). It was a bill on the statute of 16 Ric. II c. 5, in the *qui tam* form, but the attorney-general entered a *nolle prosequi*, and it was decided that Perrot could not proceed in that way. Differently reported in 3 Leon. 139 (dated Mich. 1586); BL MS. Harley 4556, fos. 108–109 (Clench's reports), sub nom *Pary v. Dr Mathew*; MS. Harley 4562, fos. 38–39; MS. Harley 4779, fo. 216; MS. Add. 35941, fo. 67v; MS. Add. 35943, fo. 13 (all four the same, 1584); MS. Add. 48486, fo. 424, sub nom. *Parret's Case* (1583); CUL MS. Ii.5.38, fos. 164v–165 (Mich. 1584). Cf. the related and more decisive Chancery case of *Perrot v. Mathew* (1588) vol. ii, p. 372. Coke wrote the above note around 1616 and may have confused the two cases.

[6] This entry occurs in a diagram setting out the various applications of *praemunire*. On the same page are references to Cardinal Wolsey's case (1529) and to a case of 1615/16 in the lost MS. *F*, fo. 20.

and canons surrendered theire said colledge and landes to the king in the xxxxvij^{tie} yeare of King Henry the eight, which in truth was to be indued with more landes, for thereuppon his highnes made of that colledge a cathedrall churche of deane and chapter, as they be now, and gave them a mcc li. of yearelie revenues more then they had before, yet now by reasone of the same surrender, which was to theire greate profitte, they wolde bring the said King Henrie the eightes colledge within the compass of the statute made in the xxxj^{tie} yeare of King Henrie the eighte for the dissolution of monasteries and religious howses, to the entent not onlie to make voide your said orators lease but also all other leases graunted by the said deane and canons, whereuppon your said orator, in the defence and mayntenaunce of his said lease and title, was inforced to seeke the same deede of surrender, in which the said deane and chapter hath not onlie vexed and oppressed your said orator the space of ix yeares with contenewall suytes in lawe, to the greate ympoverishment of your said orator, his wiefe and childrene, but also have sought in all extreame manner contrarie to the lawes and statutes of this realme to defeate your said orator of his lawfull ynterest therein. And for declareation that the said deane and chapter hath done contrarie to the lawes and statutes of this realme, whereuppon the premunire dothe lye against the offenders therein, the case is this. After the same lease had depended in sewte v or vj yeares in the Kings Benche, the said deane and chapter, not contented with the queenes majesties lawes to trye theire title, arrested John Parrot, your orators sonne, and twoo of your orators servauntes, for commyng upon a parcell of the same groundes of Bindseie leased to your orator, and brought an action of trespas in landes vi et armis in the civill law courte[1]

---

[1] Clench (BL MS. Harley 4556, fo. 158) refers to it as 'lour court de cyvell ley'. The other manuscript reports call it a 'consistory'.

against those iij persones before Doctor Thornetone, one of the same chapter, and then vice-chauncellor of Oxforde, and so wold be judge in theire owne cawse, which deane and chapter pleaded by libell and then excommunicated them, and also pronounced sentence of condemnation against those iij persones according to the course of the civill lawe, and asessed damages to xx s. and for costes xxxv s. ix d., and uppon the same action deteined those iij persones in prysone the space of xvij weekes, without bayle or mainprise, albeit they offered unto them baile of a m li. to aunswere them according to the lawes of the realme, which deane and chapter, regarding not the lawes of the realme, disobeied iij of the queenes severall writtes of habeas <corpora>[i] directed out of the Kings Benche for the deliverie of those iij prisoners. Maye it therefore please your honour of your accustomed goodnes to helpe the oppressed, and to be a meane that your said orator maie quietlie enjoye his said lease and tearme of yeares without further sewte in lawe, and your said oratour wille not onlie be contented to loose all his costes and charges spent in the defence of his said lease, being the somme of ix c li., and to putt upp all the said injuries, but also wille dailie praye to God during his liefe longe to continew your honour in healthe and prosperitie. But if the said deane and chapter wille take advantage and toche your said orators lease, then your said orator trustethe that with your honors favor he maie aswell take advantages and enjoye the benefitte of the lawes of the realme <againste them>[i] for the redresse and recoverie of his wronges and damages susteined at theire handes.